New Perspectives Microsoft® 365® & Office®

First Edition

Introductory

Jennifer T. Campbell
Patrick Carey
Lisa Ruffolo
Ann Shaffer
Mark Shellman
Sasha Vodnik

Australia • Brazil • Canada • Mexico • Singapore • United Kingdom • United States

***New Perspectives Microsoft® 365® & Office® Introductory,* First Edition**

Jennifer T. Campbell, Patrick Carey, Lisa Ruffolo, Ann Shaffer, Mark Shellman, Sasha Vodnik

SVP, Product Management: Cheryl Costantini

VP, Product Management & Marketing: Thais Alencar

Senior Product Director, Portfolio Product Management: Mark Santee

Portfolio Product Director: Rita Lombard

Senior Portfolio Product Manager: Amy Savino

Senior Product Assistant: Ciara Boynton

Learning Designer: Zenya Molnar

Content Manager: Christina Nyren

Digital Project Manager: Jim Vaughey

Developmental Editor: Robin Romer, Lisa Ruffolo, Dan Seiter, Mary Pat Shaffer, Michael Sanford

Senior Director, Product Marketing: Danae April

Senior Product Marketing Manager: Mackenzie Paine

Portfolio Specialist: Matt Schiesl

Content Acquisition Analyst: Callum Panno

Production Service: Lumina Datamatics Ltd.

Senior Designer: Erin Griffin

Cover Image Sources: Marco Bottigelli/Moment/Getty Images, Denis Belitsky/Shutterstock.com

Mac Users: If you're working through this product using a Mac, some of the steps may vary. Additional information for Mac users is included with the Data files for this product.

Disclaimer: The material in this text was written using Microsoft Windows 11 and Office 365 Professional Plus and was Quality Assurance tested before the publication date. As Microsoft continually updates the Windows operating system and Office 365, your software experience may vary slightly from what is presented in the printed text.

Previous editions: © 2023, © 2020, © 2017

For product information and technology assistance, contact us at **Cengage Customer & Sales Support, 1-800-354-9706 or support.cengage.com.**

For permission to use material from this text or product, submit all requests online at **www.copyright.com.**

Library of Congress Control Number: 2024931368

Student Edition ISBN: 978-0-357-88208-5

Loose-leaf Edition ISBN: 978-0-357-88209-2

K12 Edition ISBN: 978-0-357-88210-8

Cengage
5191 Natorp Boulevard
Mason, OH 45040
USA

Cengage is a leading provider of customized learning solutions with employees residing in nearly 40 different countries and sales in more than 125 countries around the world. Find your local representative at **www.cengage.com.**

To learn more about Cengage platforms and services, register or access your online learning solution, or purchase materials for your course, visit **www.cengage.com.**

Notice to the Reader

Printed at CLDPC, USA, 04-24

Brief Contents

Contents

Module 3: Creating Tables and a Multipage Report

Module 4: Enhancing Page Layout and Design

Excel

Module 1: Getting Started with Excel

Module 2: Formatting a Workbook

Access

PowerPoint

Module 1: Creating a Presentation

Presenting Information About a Staffing Agency ..... PPT 1-1

Module 2: Adding Media and Special Effects

Using Media in a Presentation for a Parks and Recreation Department ..... PPT 2-1

Preface for New Perspectives Series Microsoft 365 and Office

About the Authors

Access: Dr. Mark Shellman is an instructor and chair of the Information Technology Department at Gaston College in Dallas, North Carolina. Dr. Mark, as his students call him, prides himself on being student-centered and loves learning himself. His favorite subjects in the information technology realm include databases and programming languages. Dr. Mark has been teaching for more than 30 years and has co-authored several texts in the New Perspective series on Microsoft® Office 365 & Access® along with a textbook on Structured Query Language.

Excel: A leading textbook author, lecturer, and instructor, Patrick Carey has authored or co-authored more than 40 popular educational and trade texts for the academic market. He has taught and written about a wide range of topics, including website design, JavaScript programming, Microsoft Office and Excel, statistics, data analysis, and mathematics. Mr. Carey received his M.S. in biostatistics from the University of Wisconsin, where he worked as a researcher designing and analyzing clinical studies. Today, he splits his time between Wisconsin and Colorado, and when he is not writing, he can be found hiking and cycling.

PowerPoint: Jennifer T. Campbell has written and co-authored several leading technology texts, including *New Perspectives on Microsoft® PowerPoint 365, Technology for Success*; *Discovering Computers: Digital Technology, Data, and Devices*; *Discovering the Internet*; *Web Design: Introductory*; and many others. For over 25 years, she has served integral roles in computer educational publishing as an editor, author, and marketing manager. She holds a B.A. in English from The College of William and Mary.

Word: Ann Shaffer is the author of *New Perspectives on Microsoft® Word 365* and has contributed to many other Cengage publications. She has more than 30 years of experience as a developmental editor and co-author of books, journal articles, and multimedia in a variety of fields, including computer science, mathematics, history, engineering, and social sciences. She holds a master's degree in English from the University of Wisconsin-Madison.

Preface for the Instructor

The New Perspectives series' unique in-depth, case-based approach helps students apply Microsoft Office skills to real-world business scenarios based on market insights while reinforcing critical thinking and problem solving abilities. Professional tips and insights are incorporated throughout, and ProSkills boxes help students strengthen their employability. Module learning objectives are mapped to Microsoft Office Specialist (MOS) certification objectives, preparing students to take the MOS exam, which they can leverage in their career. MindTap and updated SAM (Skills Assessment Manager) online resources are also available to guide additional study and ensure successful results.

New Perspectives is designed primarily for students at four-year schools. It can also be used at two-year schools and in continuing education programs. The New Perspectives series is comprised of three parts: introductory, intermediate, and advanced. The series offers a comprehensive title that includes the four main Microsoft applications (Word, Excel, PowerPoint, and Access) at the introductory level. The MindTap Collection includes additional module coverage, including Outlook, Operating Systems, and Teams.

Market research is conducted semi-annually with both current Cengage users and those who use other learning materials. The focus of our market research is to gain insights into the user experience and overall learner needs so we can continuously evolve our content to exceed user expectations. We survey hundreds of instructors to ensure we gather insights from a large and varied demographic.

New to This Edition

Access: New features in the Access Collection include updated, real-world scenarios from a variety of industries that illustrate the relevance of Access databases in today's businesses. Completely updated projects use gapped Start and Solution files to ensure students use new, authentic files for each project from one module to the next.

Excel: With the thoroughly updated coverage in the Excel Collection, students learn both long-standing Excel functions and tools as well as the most recent innovations. New Microsoft® Excel 365® features include dynamic arrays and dynamic array functions such as the FILTER, SORT, SORTBY, and UNIQUE functions. This edition also introduces LAMBDA and LET for generating custom functions and function variables, Excel data types, and the Analyze Data tool for spotting trends and gaining insight into data.

PowerPoint: The PowerPoint Collection introduces the new commenting experience, which lets users display comments in contextual view or in the Comments pane. The comment anchor helps reviewers identify specific slide elements with comments and place the comment bubble anywhere on the slide. With the revised search feature, users can enter a word or phrase in the Search box to find the definition. Microsoft Search also provides support articles to help perform tasks.

Word: New features in the Word Collection include the enhanced Accessibility Checker, which identifies potential accessibility issues and presents suggestions to make documents more inclusive. The Word Collection also introduces Focus mode, the updated collaboration experience, Microsoft's expanded search tool, and voice options. The Immersive Reader is covered, as is the ability to create a private document copy and use Word's screen reader.

Organization of the Text

New Perspectives Microsoft 365 & Office, First Edition is a comprehensive introduction to Microsoft applications—Word, Excel, PowerPoint, and Access—and is well-suited for business programs. Each application is divided into modules within the three levels—introductory, intermediate, and advanced. Each module introduces a topic through an engaging real-world case scenario and presents content that aligns directly with the learning objectives listed at the beginning of the module. Skills are taught progressively to encourage student learning and advancement to proficiency. After completing each part in the module, students verify their understanding by answering Quick Check questions. End-of-module activities range from applying skills to working independently as they explore new features and solutions. All the activities are based on real-life scenarios from the top industries for each application and provide students with opportunities to engage in higher-level thinking and increase their confidence in their abilities.

Features of the Text

The features of the text, which are found consistently throughout all modules, are designed to aid the student in a specific way.

The projects present authentic case scenarios, which are focused on employability and based on research and data.

The Visual Overview is a screenshot of the application and spans a two-page spread at the start of each part in the module. It serves as a preview of the part content and a study tool for later reference. Callouts in the image align to the learning objectives for the module.

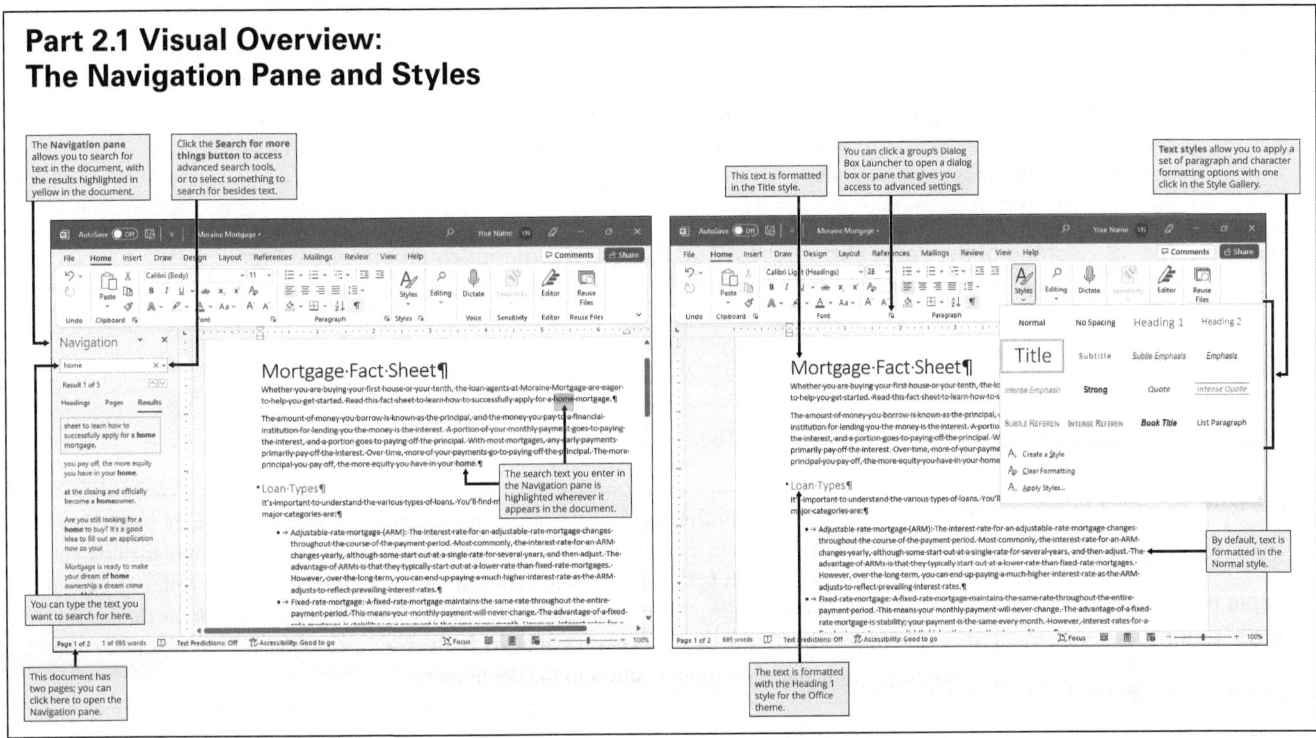

Heading levels organize topics within a module. Step-by-step task sequences provide numbered steps that guide students to complete the case project.

Step-by-step sequences include the following features:

Key Steps draw attention to a particular step that students must complete accurately to avoid real difficulty later on. The Key Step text reminds students how to perform the step correctly.

> **To center-align the text:**
>
> **1.** Make sure the Home tab is still selected, and press **CTRL+A** to select the entire document.
>
> > **Key Step** Use CTRL+A to select the entire document, instead of dragging the pointer. It's easy to miss part of the document when you drag the pointer.

Tips are additional pieces of information to enhance learning and provide further explanation about a specific topic or an alternative way of performing a task.

> **4.** In the Clipboard group, click the **Cut** button. The selected text is removed from the document and copied to the Clipboard. The space that originally appeared before the sentence remains, so you have to delete it.
>
> **Tip** You can also press CTRL+X to cut selected text. Press CTRL+V to paste the most recently copied item.

Trouble? elements refer to a particular step and provide troubleshooting advice or information about avoiding common errors.

> **7.** In the Clipboard group, click the **Paste** button. The sentence appears in the new location. Note that Word also inserts a space before the sentence. The Paste Options button appears near the newly inserted sentence.
>
> **Trouble?** If a menu opens below the Paste button, you clicked the Paste arrow instead of the Paste button. Press ESC to close the menu, and then repeat Step 7, taking care not to click the arrow below the Paste button.

Other in-text pedagogical elements include the following:

Key terms appear in blue and bold text. In MindTap, the key terms appear as clickable text linked to their definitions.

> The Navigation pane simplifies the process of moving through a document page by page. You can also use the Navigation pane to locate a particular word or phrase. You start by typing the text you're searching for—the **search text**—in the Search box at the top of the Navigation pane. As shown in the Part 2.1 Visual Overview, Word highlights every instance of the search text in the document. At the same time, a list of the **search results** appears in the Navigation pane. You can click a search result to go immediately to that location in the document.

InSight boxes give expert advice and best practices for using the software effectively and are included in explanatory paragraphs separate from the steps.

> ## Insight
>
> ### Searching for Formatting
>
> You can search for formatting just as you can search for text. For example, you might want to check a document to look for text formatted in bold and the Arial font. To search for formatting from within the Navigation pane, click the Search for more things button to display the menu, and then click Advanced Find. The Find and Replace dialog box opens with the Find tab displayed. Click the More button, if necessary, to display the Search Options section of the Find tab. Click the Format button at the bottom of the Search Options section, click the category of formatting you want to look for (such as Font or Paragraph), and then select the formatting you want to find.
>
> You can look for formatting that occurs only on specific text, or you can look for formatting that occurs anywhere in a document. If you're looking for text formatted in a certain way (such as all instances of "Moraine Mortgage" that are bold), enter the text in the Find what box, and then specify the formatting you're looking for. To find formatting on any text in a document, leave the Find what box empty, and then specify the formatting. Use the Find Next button to move through the document, from one instance of the specified formatting to another.
>
> You can follow the same basic steps on the Replace tab to replace one type of formatting with another. First, click the Find what box and select the desired formatting. Then click the Replace with box and select the desired formatting. If you want, type search text and replacement text in the appropriate boxes. Then proceed as with any Find and Replace operation.

ProSkills boxes provide information about using the app in the context of the following professional skills: Written Communication, Decision Making, Verbal Communication, Teamwork, and Problem Solving.

Proskills

Written Communication: Acknowledging Your Sources

A research paper is a means for you to explore the available information about a subject and then present this information, along with your own understanding of the subject, in an organized and interesting way. Acknowledging all the sources of the information presented in your research paper is essential. If you fail to do this, you might be subject to charges of plagiarism, or trying to pass off someone else's thoughts as your own. Plagiarism is an extremely serious accusation for which you could suffer academic consequences ranging from failing an assignment to being expelled from school.

To ensure that you don't forget to cite a source, you should be careful about creating citations in your document as you type. In this module, you will insert citations into completed paragraphs as practice, but in real life you should insert citations as you type your document. It's easy to forget to go back and cite all your sources correctly after you've finished typing a research paper. Failing to cite a source could lead to accusations of plagiarism and all the consequences that entails. If you don't have the complete information about a source available when you are typing your paper, you should at least insert a placeholder citation. But take care to go back later and substitute complete citations for any placeholders.

Reference boxes provide a bulleted summary of steps for performing a task, which students can use as a future reference.

Reference

Finding and Replacing Text

- Press CTRL+HOME to move the insertion point to the beginning of the document.
- In the Editing group on the Home tab, click the Replace button, or in the Navigation pane, click the Search for more things button, and then click Replace.
- In the Find and Replace dialog box, click the More button, if necessary, to display the Search Options section of the Replace tab.
- In the Find what box, type the search text.
- In the Replace with box, type the replacement text.
- Select the appropriate check boxes in the Search Options section of the dialog box to narrow your search.
- Click the Find Next button.
- Click the Replace button to substitute the found text with the replacement text and find the next occurrence.
- Click the Replace All button to substitute all occurrences of the found text with the replacement text without reviewing each occurrence. Use this option only if you are absolutely certain that the results will be what you expect.

SAM Upload and Download icons are for SAM users. A SAM download icon appears next to any step where students download a data file to begin a SAM Project.

1. sam↓ On the Windows taskbar, click the **Start** button. The Start menu opens.

A SAM upload icon appears next to any step where students submit a file to SAM for a completed SAM project.

4. Click anywhere in the document to deselect the numbered list.
5. sam↑ Save the document.

Course Solutions

Online Learning Platform: MindTap with SAM

The New Perspectives Series MindTap Collection, powered by SAM (Skills Assessment Manager), enables proficiency in Microsoft Office and computing concepts for your Introductory Computing courses. With a library of renowned course materials, including ready-to-assign, auto-graded learning modules, you can easily adapt your course to best prepare students for the evolving job market. In addition to an eReader that includes the full content of the printed book, the New Perspectives Collection, First Edition MindTap course includes the following:

- SAM Textbook Projects: Follow the steps and scenarios outlined in the textbook readings; enable students to complete projects based on a real-world scenario live in Microsoft Office applications and submit them in SAM for automatic grading and feedback.
- SAM Training and Exam: Trainings teach students to complete specific skills in a simulated Microsoft application environment while exams allow students to demonstrate their proficiency (also in a simulated environment).
- SAM Projects: Students complete projects based on real-world scenarios live in Microsoft applications and submit the projects in SAM for automatic grading and feedback. SAM offers several types of projects, each with a unique purpose: 1A and 1B, critical thinking, end of module, capstone, and integration.
- Microsoft Office Specialist (MOS) resources: Training and exams are based on the Microsoft Office 365 Objective Domains for the MOS Exam and exam simulation that replicates the test-taking environment of the MOS exam for Word, Excel, Access, PowerPoint, and Outlook.

To learn more, go to: https://www.cengage.com/mindtap-collections/

Ancillary Package

Additional instructor and student resources for this product are available online. Instructor assets include an Instructor Manual, an Educator Guide, PowerPoint® slides, a Guide to Teaching Online, Solution Files, a test bank powered by Cognero®, and a Transition Guide. Student assets include data files and a glossary. Sign up or sign in at **www.cengage.com** to search for and access this product and its online resources. The instructor and student companion sites contain ancillary material for the full New Perspectives Series Collection, along with instructions on how to find specific content within the companion site.

- Instructor Manual: This guide provides additional instructional material to assist in class preparation, including module objectives, module outlines, discussion questions, and additional activities and assignments. Each outline corresponds directly with the content in the module, and additional discussion questions and activities are aligned to headings in the book.
- Educator Guide: The MindTap Educator Guide contains a detailed outline of the corresponding MindTap course, including activity types and time on task. The SAM Educator Guide explains how to use SAM functionality to maximize your course.
- PowerPoint slides: The slides may be used to guide classroom presentations, to provide to students for module review, or to print as classroom handouts. The slides align closely with the book while activities and the self-assessment align with module learning objectives and supplement the content in the book.
- Guide to Teaching Online: This guide presents technological and pedagogical considerations and suggestions for teaching the Introductory Computing course when you can't be in the same room with students.

- Solution files: These files provide solutions to all textbook projects for instructors to use to grade student work.
    - Instructors using SAM do not need solution files since projects are auto-graded within SAM.
    - Solution files are provided on the instructor companion site for instructors *not* using SAM.
- Data files: These files are provided for students to complete the projects in each module.
    - Students using SAM to complete the projects download the required data files directly from SAM.
    - Students who are *not* using SAM to complete the projects can find data files on the student companion site and within MindTap.
- Test banks: A comprehensive test bank, offered in Cognero, Word, Blackboard, Moodle, Desire2Learn, Canvas, and SAM formats, contains questions aligned with each module's learning objectives and are written by subject matter experts. Powered by Cognero, Cengage Testing is a flexible, online system that allows you to author, edit, and manage test bank content from multiple Cengage solutions and to create multiple test versions that you can deliver from your LMS, your classroom, or wherever you want.
- Transition Guide: This guide highlights all the changes in the text and in the digital offerings from the previous edition to the current one so that instructors know what to expect.

Acknowledgments

Mark Shellman: I would first like to dedicate this text to the memory of my parents, Mickey and Shelba Shellman. No child has ever been more loved and supported in their life than I. I would also like to thank my wonderful wife Donna Sue, and my children, Taylor and Kimberly, for their support and patience during this project. All of you girls are my world! Last, but certainly not least, I would like to thank the entire development team of Amy Savino, Christina Nyren, and Lisa Ruffolo. Thank you all from the bottom of my heart for all of your support, caring, and patience during this project. It means more that you will ever know. You are truly the best!

Patrick Carey: I would like to thank the people who worked so hard to make this book possible. Special thanks to my developmental editor, Robin Romer, for her hard work, attention to detail, and valuable insights, and to Content Manager Christina Nyren, who has worked tirelessly in overseeing this project and made my task so much easier with enthusiasm and good humor. Other people at Cengage who deserve credit are Amy Savino, senior portfolio product manager; Amberlea Cogan, technical content program manager; Zenya Molnar, learning designer; Ciara Boynton, product assistant; Erin Griffin, senior designer; Seth Cohn, senior planner buyer; and Lumina Datamatics Ltd., compositor. This book is dedicated to my wife Joan who is my inspiration and role model for her good humor, dedication, and tireless support.

Jennifer T. Campbell: Many thanks to my editor, Mike Sanford, for his wisdom and hard work, as well as the team at Cengage, including Christina Nyren, Amy Savino, Zenya Molnar, and Ciara Boynton. As always, Mike, Emma, and Lucy were my biggest cheerleaders and inspiration.

Ann Shaffer: Thanks to the publishing professionals at Cengage Learning who are smart, fun to work with, and great at their jobs: Amy Savino, senior product manager; Zenya Molnar, learning designer; Christina Nyren, content manager; Ciara Boynton, senior product assistant. They made this revision a total pleasure. Many thanks to Neha Bhargava, project manager, and the team at Lumina Datamatics, who magically turned a pile of text and art manuscript files into the finished product. I will never understand how they can manage the 10 million details involved in publishing books like this, but somehow, they do it. I am grateful to Amit Tomar and the team at Qualitest for checking every step and exercise for errors. Their thoroughness made every module better. My biggest thank you goes to Mary Pat Shaffer, development editor extraordinaire, who pulled me along through the long process of this revision with endless patience, stunning attention to detail, an ability to remember everything that needed to be remembered, and a warm-hearted sense of humor that made me look forward to every morning's conversation as the highlight of my day. This book is dedicated to Mary Pat, whose fortitude and kindness always amazes me.

Getting to Know Microsoft Office Versions

Cengage is proud to bring you the next edition of Microsoft Office. This edition was designed to provide a robust learning experience that is not dependent upon a specific version of Office.

Microsoft supports several versions and editions of Office: (Refer to Table 1 below for more information)

- **Microsoft 365 (formerly known as Office 365):** A service that delivers the most up-to-date, feature-rich, modern Microsoft productivity applications direct to your device. There are several combinations of Microsoft 365 programs for business, educational, and personal use. Microsoft 365 is cloud-based, meaning it is stored, managed, and processed on a network of remote servers hosted on the Internet, rather than on local servers or personal computers. Microsoft 365 offers extra online storage and cloud-connected features, as well as updates with the latest features, fixes, and security updates. Microsoft 365 is purchased for a monthly subscription fee that keeps your software up to date with the latest features.
- **Office 2021:** The Microsoft "on-premises" version of the Office apps, available for both PCs and Macintosh computers, offered as a static, one-time purchase and outside of the subscription model. Unlike Microsoft 365, Office 2021 does not include online product updates with new features.
- **Microsoft 365 Online (formerly known as Office Online):** A free, simplified version of Microsoft web applications (Teams, Access, Word, Excel, PowerPoint, and OneNote) that lets users create and edit files collaboratively.
- **Office 365 Education:** A free subscription including Word, Excel, PowerPoint, OneNote, and now Microsoft Teams, plus additional classroom tools. Only available for students and educators at select institutions.

Table 1 Microsoft Office applications — uses and availability

Application	Use	Availability/Editions
Word	Create documents and improve your writing with intelligent assistance features.	Microsoft 365 Family, Home, Business, Office 2021, Office 365 Education
Excel	Simplify complex data into easy-to-read spreadsheets.	Microsoft 365 Personal, Home, Business, Office 2021, Office 365 Education
PowerPoint	Create presentations that stand out.	Home, Business, Office 2021, Office 365 Education
OneNote	A digital notebook for all your note-taking needs.	Home, Office 365 Education
OneDrive	Save and share your files and photos wherever you are.	Home, Business
Outlook	Manage your email, calendar, tasks, and contacts all in one place.	Home, Business
SharePoint	Create team sites to share information, files, and resources.	Business
Publisher	Create polished, professional layouts without the hassle.	Home, Business, Office 2021 (PC only)
Access	Create your own database apps easily in formats that serve your business best.	Home, Business, Office 2021 (PC only)
Teams	Bring everyone together in one place to meet, chat, call, and collaborate.	Business, Office 365 Education
Exchange	Business-class email and calendaring.	Business

Over time, the Microsoft 365 cloud interface will continuously update using its web connection, offering new application features and functions, while Office 2021 will remain static.

Because Microsoft 365 releases updates continuously, your onscreen experience may differ from what you see in this product. For example, the more advanced features and functionalities covered in this product may not be available in Microsoft 365 Online, may have updated from what you see in Office 2021, or may be from a post-publication update of Microsoft 365.

For up-to-date information on the differences between Microsoft 365, Office 2021, and Microsoft 365 Online, please visit the Microsoft Support website.

Cengage is committed to providing high-quality learning solutions for you to gain the knowledge and skills that will empower you throughout your educational and professional careers.

Thank you for using our product, and we look forward to exploring the future of Microsoft Office with you!

Using SAM Projects and Textbook Projects

SAM (Skills Assessment Manager) **Projects** allow you to actively apply the skills you learned in Microsoft Word, Excel, PowerPoint, or Access. You can also submit your work to SAM for online grading. You can use SAM Projects to become a more productive student and use these skills throughout your career.

To complete SAM Textbook Projects, please follow these steps:

SAM Textbook Projects allow you to complete a project as you follow along with the steps in the textbook. As you read the module, look for icons that indicate when you should download **sam**↓ your SAM Start file(s) and when to upload **sam**↑ your solution file to SAM for grading.

Everything you need to complete this project is provided within SAM. You can launch the eBook directly from SAM, which will allow you to take notes, highlight, and create a custom study guide, or you can use a print textbook or your mobile app. Download IOS or Download Android.

To get started, launch your SAM Project assignment from SAM, MindTap, or a link within your learning management system.

1. Step 1:
   Download Files
   - Click the "Download All" button or the individual links to download your **Start File** and **Support File(s)** (when available). You must use the SAM Start file.
   - Click the Instructions link to launch the eBook (or use the print textbook or mobile app).
   - Disregard any steps in the textbook that ask you to create a new file or to use a file from a location outside of SAM.
   - Look for the SAM Download icon **sam**↓ to begin working with your start file.
   - Follow the module's step-by-step instructions until you reach the SAM Upload icon **sam**↑.
   - Save and close the file.

2. Step 2:
   Save Work to SAM
   - Ensure you rename your project file to match the Expected File Name.
   - Upload your in-progress or completed file to SAM. You can download the file to continue working or submit it for grading in the next step.
3. Step 3:
   Submit for Grading
   - Upload your completed solution file to SAM for immediate feedback and to view the available Reports.
     - The **Graded Summary Report** provides a detailed list of project steps, your score, and feedback to aid you in revising and resubmitting the project.
     - The **Study Guide** provides your score for each project step and links to the associated training and textbook pages.
   - If additional attempts are allowed, use your reports to assist with revising and resubmitting your project.
   - To re-submit your project, download the file you saved in step 2.
   - Edit, save, and close the file, then re-upload and submit it again.

For all other SAM Projects, please follow these steps:

To get started, launch your SAM Project assignment from SAM, MindTap, or a link within your learning management system.

1. Step 1:
   Download Files
   - Click the "Download All" button or the individual links to download your **Instruction File**, **Start File**, and **Support File(s)** (when available). You must use the SAM Start file.
   - Open the Instruction file and follow the step-by-step instructions. Ensure you rename your project file to match the Expected File Name (change _1 to _2 at the end of the file name).

2. Step 2:
   Save Work to SAM
   - Upload your in-progress or completed file to SAM. You can download the file to continue working or submit it for grading in the next step.
3. Step 3:
   Submit for Grading
   - Upload the completed file to SAM for immediate feedback and to view available Reports.
     - The **Graded Summary Report** provides a detailed list of project steps, your score, and feedback to aid you in revising and resubmitting the project.
     - The **Study Guide** provides your score for each project step and links to the associated training and textbook pages.
   - If additional attempts are allowed, use your reports to assist with revising and resubmitting your project.
   - To re-submit the project, download the file saved in step 2.
   - Edit, save, and close the file, then re-upload and submit it again.

For additional tips to successfully complete your SAM Projects, please view our SAM Video Tutorials.

Creating and Editing a Document

Writing a Business Letter and Formatting a Flyer

Case: Department of Urban Development

Leonel Villalba is the communications director for the Department of Urban Development in Salem, Oregon. As part of his outreach efforts, he has produced a set of brochures promoting the city's transition to alternative energy sources such as solar power and heat pumps. Leonel has asked you to create a cover letter to accompany the brochures he is sending to the organizers of a national sustainability conference. He has also asked you to create an envelope for sending an energy conservation report to an environmental engineering publication. Next, he wants your help creating a flyer encouraging community members to join a citizen advisory panel. Finally, he would like to add bulleted and numbered lists to the minutes of a recent advisory panel meeting.

You will create the letter and flyer using **Microsoft Word 365** (or simply **Word**), a full-featured word processing app that lets you create professional-looking documents and revise them easily. You'll start by opening Word and saving a new document. Then you'll type the text of the cover letter and print it. In the process of entering the text, you'll learn several ways to correct typing errors and how to adjust paragraph and line spacing. When you create the envelope, you'll learn how to save it as part of a document for later use. As you work on the flyer, you will learn how to open an existing document, change the way text is laid out on the page, format text, add a page border, and insert and resize a photo. Finally, you'll add bulleted and numbered lists to a document, and then learn how to use Microsoft Word Help.

Starting Data Files: Word1

Module
NP_WD_1-1.docx
NP_WD_1-2.docx
Support_WD_1_Solar.jpg

Review
NP_WD_1-3.docx
NP_WD_1-4.docx
Support_WD_1_House.jpg

Case1
(none)

Case2
NP_WD_1-5.docx
Support_WD_1_Produce.jpg

Objectives

Part 1.1

- Create and save a document
- Enter text and correct errors as you type
- Use AutoComplete and AutoCorrect
- Select text and move the insertion point
- Undo and redo actions
- Adjust paragraph spacing, line spacing, and margins
- Preview and print a document
- Create an envelope

Part 1.2

- Open an existing document
- Proofread a document using the Editor pane
- Change page orientation, font, font color, and font size
- Apply text effects and align text
- Copy formatting with the Format Painter
- Insert a paragraph border and shading
- Delete, insert, and edit a photo
- Add a page border
- Create bulleted and numbered lists
- Look up information in Microsoft Word Help

Part 1.1 Visual Overview: The Word Window

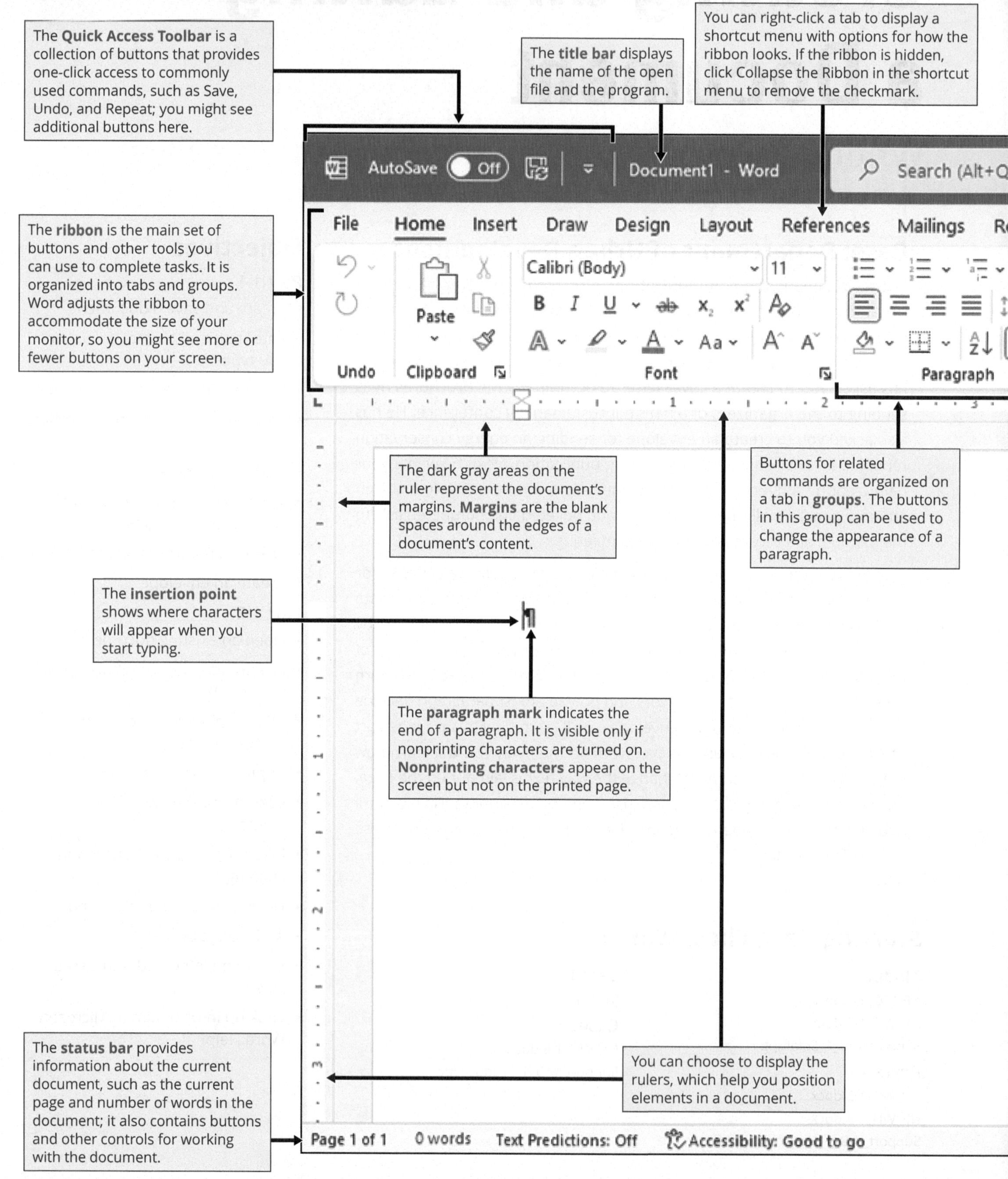

The **Quick Access Toolbar** is a collection of buttons that provides one-click access to commonly used commands, such as Save, Undo, and Repeat; you might see additional buttons here.
The **title bar** displays the name of the open file and the program.
You can right-click a tab to display a shortcut menu with options for how the ribbon looks. If the ribbon is hidden, click Collapse the Ribbon in the shortcut menu to remove the checkmark.
AutoSave
Off
Document1 - Word
Search (Alt+Q
File
Home
Insert
Draw
Design
Layout
References
Mailings
The **ribbon** is the main set of buttons and other tools you can use to complete tasks. It is organized into tabs and groups. Word adjusts the ribbon to accommodate the size of your monitor, so you might see more or fewer buttons on your screen.
Calibri (Body)
11
Paste
Undo
Clipboard
Font
Paragraph
The dark gray areas on the ruler represent the document's margins. **Margins** are the blank spaces around the edges of a document's content.
Buttons for related commands are organized on a tab in **groups**. The buttons in this group can be used to change the appearance of a paragraph.
The **insertion point** shows where characters will appear when you start typing.
The **paragraph mark** indicates the end of a paragraph. It is visible only if nonprinting characters are turned on. **Nonprinting characters** appear on the screen but not on the printed page.
The **status bar** provides information about the current document, such as the current page and number of words in the document; it also contains buttons and other controls for working with the document.
You can choose to display the rulers, which help you position elements in a document.
Page 1 of 1
0 words
Text Predictions: Off
Accessibility: Good to go

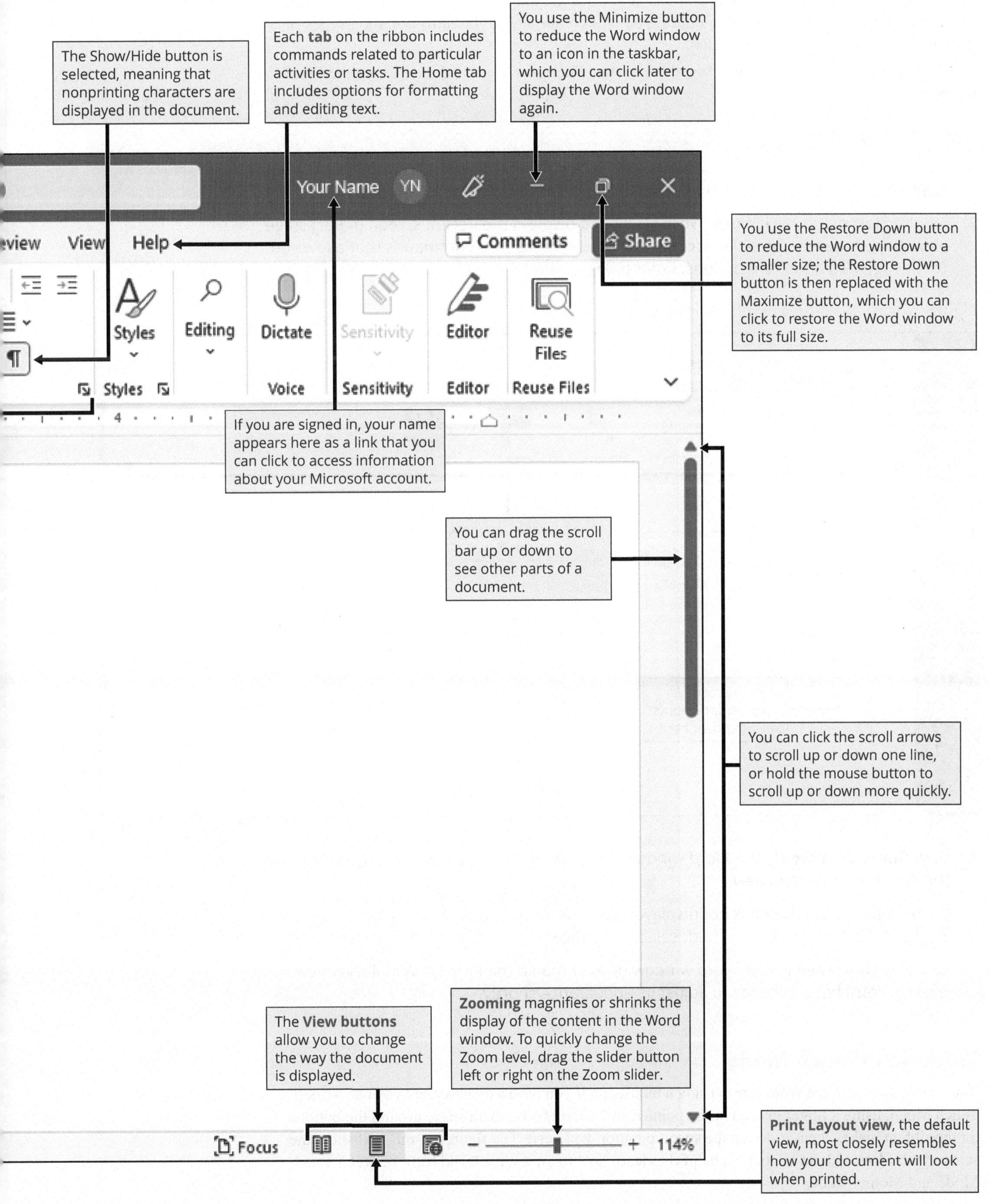

The Show/Hide button is selected, meaning that nonprinting characters are displayed in the document.
Each **tab** on the ribbon includes commands related to particular activities or tasks. The Home tab includes options for formatting and editing text.
You use the Minimize button to reduce the Word window to an icon in the taskbar, which you can click later to display the Word window again.
Your Name
YN
view
View
Help
Comments
Share
Styles
Editing
Dictate
Sensitivity
Editor
Reuse Files
Styles
Voice
Sensitivity
Editor
Reuse Files
You use the Restore Down button to reduce the Word window to a smaller size; the Restore Down button is then replaced with the Maximize button, which you can click to restore the Word window to its full size.
If you are signed in, your name appears here as a link that you can click to access information about your Microsoft account.
You can drag the scroll bar up or down to see other parts of a document.
You can click the scroll arrows to scroll up or down one line, or hold the mouse button to scroll up or down more quickly.
The **View buttons** allow you to change the way the document is displayed.
Zooming magnifies or shrinks the display of the content in the Word window. To quickly change the Zoom level, drag the slider button left or right on the Zoom slider.
Focus
114%
Print Layout view, the default view, most closely resembles how your document will look when printed.

Starting Word

With Word, you can quickly create polished, professional documents. You can type a document, adjust margins and spacing, create columns and tables, add graphics, and then easily make revisions and corrections. In Part 1.1 of this module, you will create one of the most common types of documents—a block-style business letter.

To begin creating the letter, you first need to start Microsoft Word and then set up the Word window.

To start Word:

1. On the Windows taskbar, click the **Start** button. The Start menu opens.
2. On the Start menu, click **Word**. Word starts and displays the Recent screen in Backstage view. Backstage view provides access to various screens with commands that allow you to manage files and Word options. Refer to Figure 1-1.

Figure 1-1 Recent screen in Backstage view

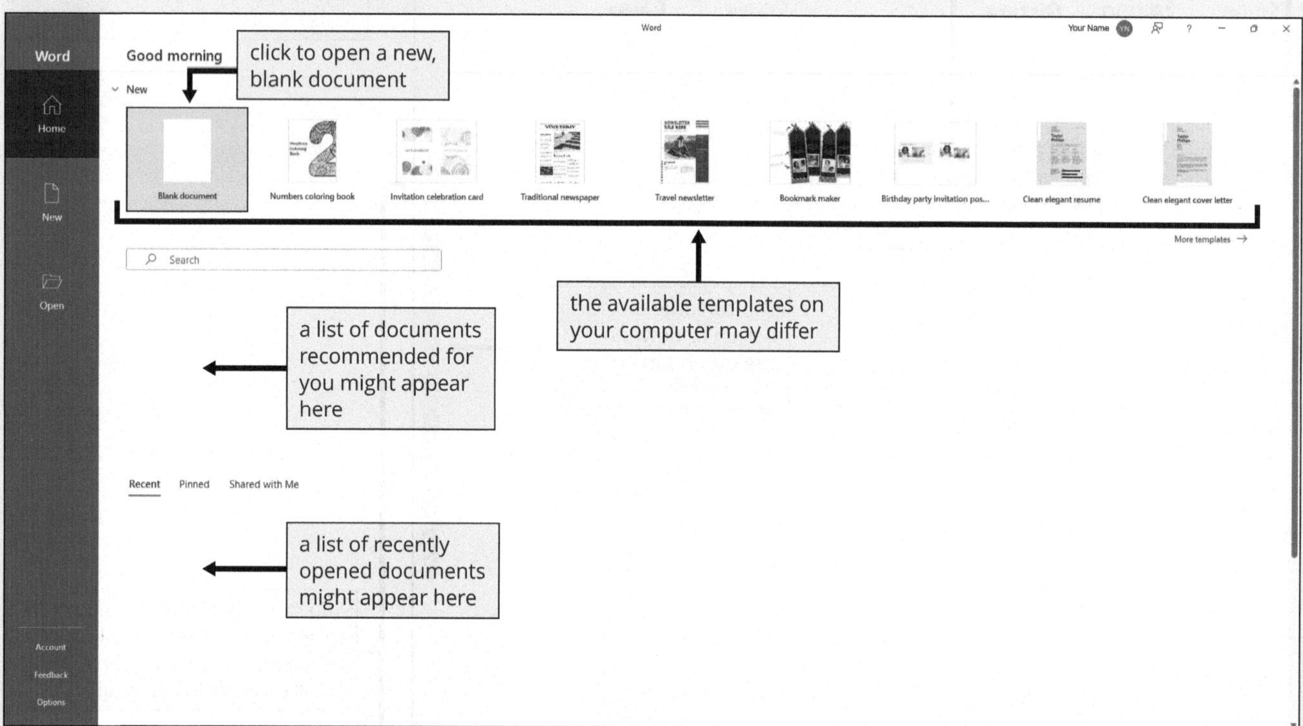

3. Click **Blank document**. The Word window opens, with the ribbon displayed, as shown in the Part 1.1 Visual Overview.

   Trouble? If the ribbon is not displayed on your screen, right-click any tab and then click Collapse Ribbon to deselect it, as shown in the Part 1.1 Visual Overview.

   Don't be concerned if your Word window doesn't match the Part 1.1 Visual Overview exactly. You'll have a chance to adjust its appearance shortly.

Working in Touch Mode

You can interact with the Word screen using a mouse, or, if you have a touchscreen, you can work in Touch Mode, using a finger instead of the pointer. In **Touch Mode**, extra space around the buttons on the ribbon makes it easier to tap the specific button you need. The figures in this text show the screen with Mouse Mode on, but it's helpful to learn how to switch back and forth between Touch Mode and Mouse Mode.

To switch between Touch and Mouse Mode:

1. On the Quick Access Toolbar, click the **Customize Quick Access Toolbar** button to open the menu. The Touch/Mouse Mode command near the bottom of the menu does not have a checkmark next to it, indicating that it is currently not selected.

   Trouble? The steps in this module assume that you are using a mouse. If you are instead using a touch device, read these steps but don't complete them so that you remain working in Touch Mode.

   Trouble? If the Touch/Mouse Mode command has a checkmark next to it, press ESC to close the menu, and then skip to Step 3.

2. On the menu, click **Touch/Mouse Mode**. The menu closes, and the Touch/Mouse Mode button appears on the Quick Access Toolbar.
3. On the Quick Access Toolbar, click the **Touch/Mouse Mode** button. A menu opens with two options—Mouse and Touch. The icon next to Mouse is shaded gray to indicate it is selected.

   Trouble? If the icon next to Touch is shaded gray, press ESC to close the menu and skip to Step 5.

4. On the menu, click **Touch**. The menu closes, and the ribbon increases in height so that there is more space around each button on the ribbon. Refer to Figure 1–2. Note that on small monitors, you might see fewer buttons than are visible in Figure 1–2. Word adapts the ribbon to accommodate the size of your monitor.

Figure 1–2 Word window in Touch Mode

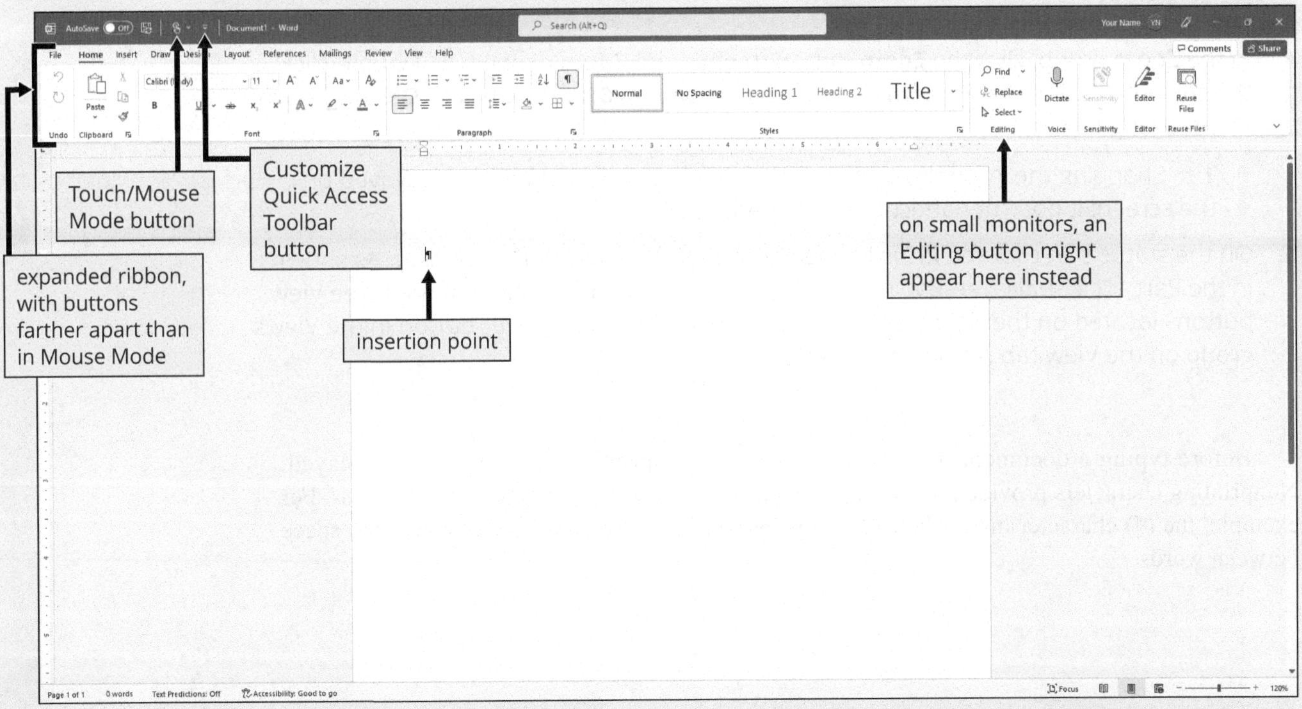

Touch/Mouse Mode button

Customize Quick Access Toolbar button

expanded ribbon, with buttons farther apart than in Mouse Mode

insertion point

on small monitors, an Editing button might appear here instead

5. On the Quick Access Toolbar, click the **Touch/Mouse Mode** button, and then click **Mouse**. The ribbon changes back to its Mouse Mode appearance, as shown in the Part 1.1 Visual Overview.
6. On the Quick Access Toolbar, click the **Customize Quick Access Toolbar** button, and then click **Touch/Mouse Mode** to deselect it. The Touch/Mouse Mode button is removed from the Quick Access Toolbar.

Setting Up the Word Window

Before you start using Word, you should make sure you can locate and identify the different elements of the Word window, as shown in the Part 1.1 Visual Overview. In the following steps, you'll make sure your screen matches the Visual Overview.

To set up your Word window to match the figures in this book:

1. If the Word window does not fill the entire screen, click the **Maximize** button in the upper-right corner of the Word window.
2. On the ribbon, click the **View** tab. The ribbon changes to show options for changing the appearance of the Word window.
3. In the Show group, click the **Ruler** check box to insert a checkmark, if necessary. If the rulers were not displayed, they are displayed now.

   The insertion point on your computer should be positioned about an inch from the top of the document, as shown in Figure 1–2, with the top margin visible.

   > **Trouble?** If the insertion point appears at the top of the document, with no white space above it, position the pointer between the top of the document and the horizontal ruler, until it changes to , double-click, and then scroll up to the top of the document.

   Next, you'll change the Zoom level to a setting that ensures that your Word window will match the figures in this book. To increase or decrease the screen's magnification, you could drag the slider button on the Zoom slider in the lower-right corner of the Word window. But to choose a specific Zoom level, it's easier to use the Zoom dialog box.
4. In the Zoom group, click the **Zoom** button to open the Zoom dialog box. Double-click the current value in the **Percent** box to select it, type **120**, and then click **OK** to close the Zoom dialog box.

   > **Tip** Changing the Zoom level affects only the way the document is displayed on the screen; it does not affect the document itself.
5. On the status bar, click the **Print Layout** button to select it, if necessary. As shown in the Part 1.1 Visual Overview, the Print Layout button is the middle of the three View buttons located on the right side of the status bar. The Print Layout button in the Views group on the View tab is also now selected.

Before typing a document, you should make sure nonprinting characters are displayed. Nonprinting characters provide a visual representation of details you might otherwise miss. For example, the (¶) character marks the end of a paragraph, and the (•) character marks the space between words.

To verify that nonprinting characters are displayed:

1. On the ribbon, click the **Home** tab.
2. In the blank Word document, look for the paragraph mark (¶) in the first line of the document, just to the right of the blinking insertion point.

   Trouble? If the paragraph mark is not displayed in your document, click the Show/Hide ¶ button ¶ in the Paragraph group.

   In the Paragraph group, the Show/Hide ¶ button should be highlighted in gray, indicating that it is selected, and the paragraph mark (¶) should appear in the first line of the document, just to the right of the insertion point.

Saving a Document

Before you begin working on a document, you should save it with a new name. When you click the File tab and then click Save to save a document for the first time, Word displays the Save As screen in Backstage view. On the Save As screen, you can select the location where you want to store your document. After that, you can click the Save button on the Quick Access Toolbar to save your document to the same location you specified earlier and with the same name.

Tip To save a document to OneDrive for the first time, you can click the Save button on the Quick Access Toolbar.

To save the document:

1. Click the **File** tab on the ribbon, and then click **Save**. Word switches to the Save As screen in Backstage view, as shown in Figure 1-3.

Figure 1-3 Save As screen in Backstage view

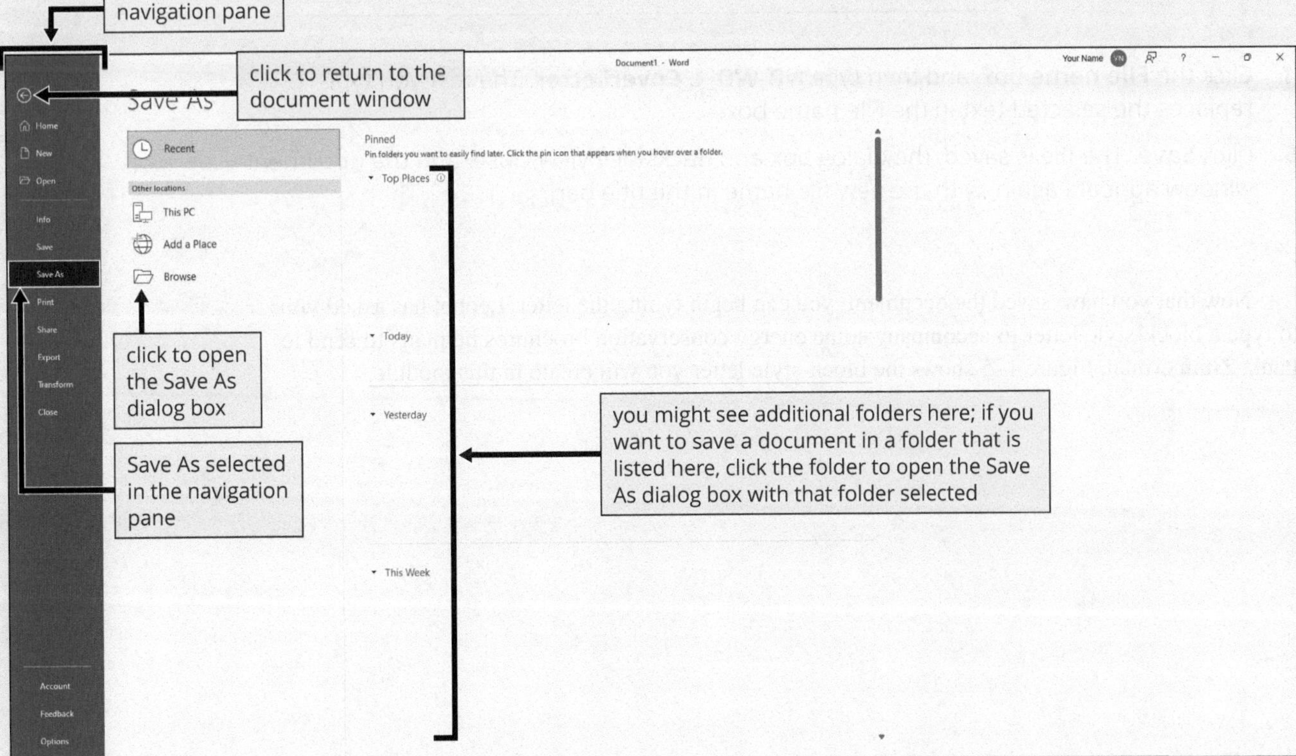

Because a document is now open, more commands are available in Backstage view than when you started Word. The **navigation pane** on the left contains commands for working with the open document and for changing settings that control how Word works.

2. Click the **Browse** button. The Save As dialog box opens.

> **Trouble?** If your instructor wants you to save your files to your OneDrive account, click OneDrive, and then log in to your account.

3. Navigate to the location specified by your instructor. The default file name, "Doc1," appears in the File name box. You will change that to something more descriptive. Refer to Figure 1–4.

Figure 1–4 Save As dialog box

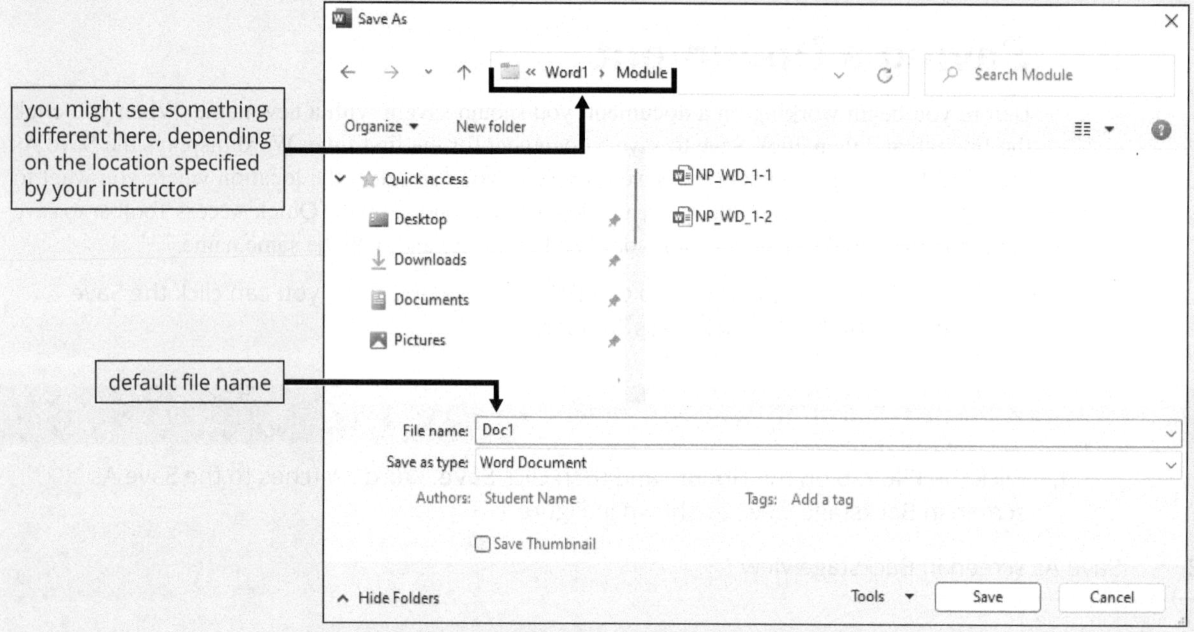

4. Click the **File name** box, and then type **NP_WD_1_CoverLetter**. The text you type replaces the selected text in the File name box.
5. Click **Save**. The file is saved, the dialog box and Backstage view close, and the document window appears again, with the new file name in the title bar.

Now that you have saved the document, you can begin typing the letter. Leonel has asked you to type a block-style letter to accompany some energy conservation brochures he plans to send to Paula Zimmerman. Figure 1–5 shows the block-style letter you will create in this module.

Figure 1–5 Completed block-style letter

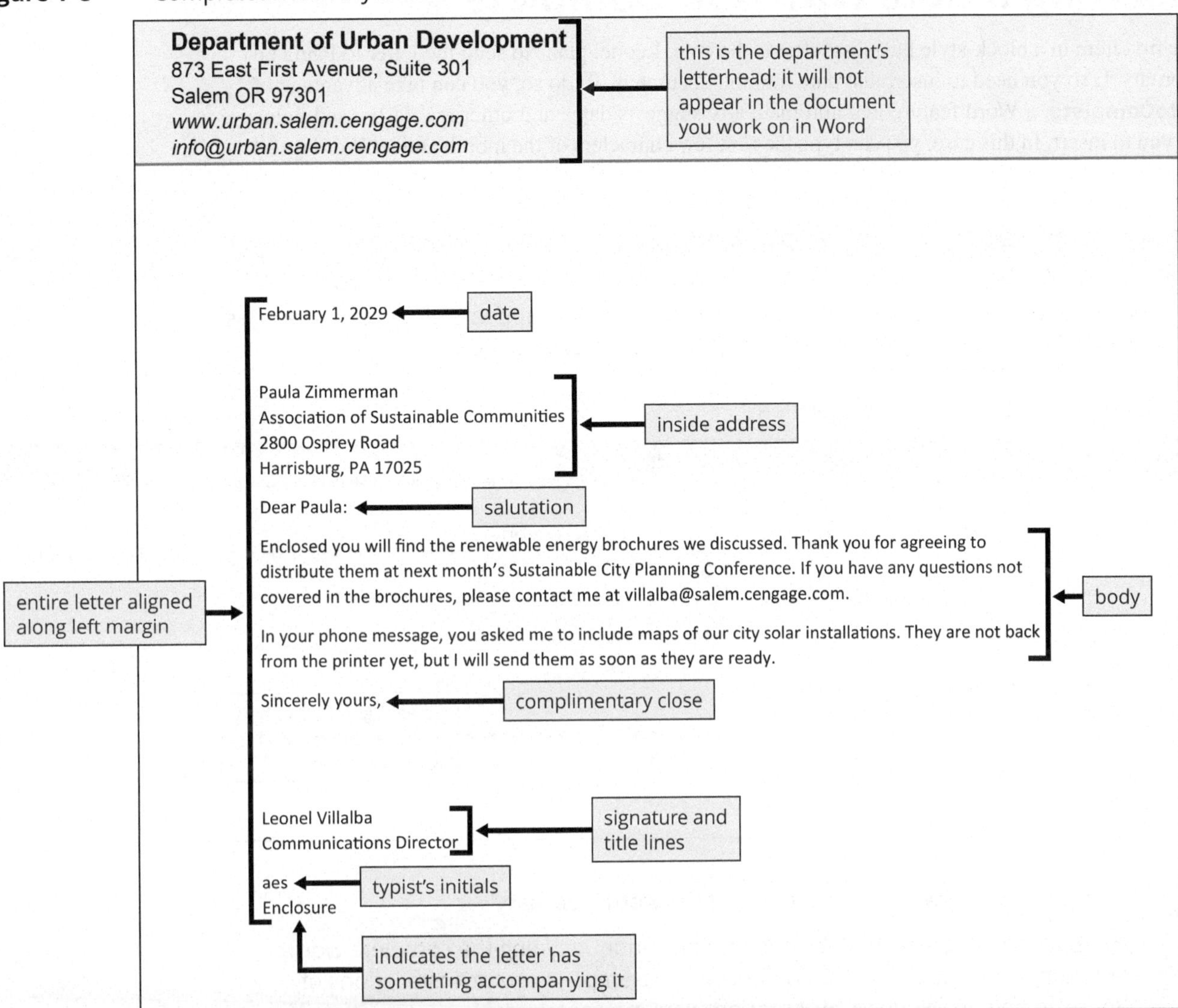
Department of Urban Development
873 East First Avenue, Suite 301
Salem OR 97301
www.urban.salem.cengage.com
info@urban.salem.cengage.com
this is the department's letterhead; it will not appear in the document you work on in Word
February 1, 2029
date
Paula Zimmerman
Association of Sustainable Communities
2800 Osprey Road
Harrisburg, PA 17025
inside address
Dear Paula:
salutation
Enclosed you will find the renewable energy brochures we discussed. Thank you for agreeing to distribute them at next month's Sustainable City Planning Conference. If you have any questions not covered in the brochures, please contact me at villalba@salem.cengage.com.
In your phone message, you asked me to include maps of our city solar installations. They are not back from the printer yet, but I will send them as soon as they are ready.
body
entire letter aligned along left margin
Sincerely yours,
complimentary close
Leonel Villalba
Communications Director
signature and title lines
aes
typist's initials
Enclosure
indicates the letter has something accompanying it

Proskills

Written Communication: Creating a Business Letter

Several styles are considered acceptable for business letters. The main differences among the styles have to do with how parts of the letter are indented from the left margin. In the block style, which you will use in this module, each line of text starts at the left margin. In other words, nothing is indented. Another style is to indent the first line of each paragraph. The choice of style is largely a matter of personal preference, or it can be determined by the standards used in a particular business or organization. To further enhance your skills in writing business correspondence, you should consult an authoritative book on business writing that provides guidelines for creating a variety of business documents, such as *Business Communication: Process & Product* by Mary Ellen Guffey and Dana Loewy.

Inserting a Date with AutoComplete

The first item in a block-style business letter is the date. Leonel plans to send the letter to Paula on February 1, so you need to insert that date into the document. To do so, you can take advantage of **AutoComplete**, a Word feature that automatically suggests dates and other regularly used items for you to insert. In this case, you can type the first few characters of the month and let Word insert the rest.

To insert the date:

1. Type **Febr** (the first four letters of "February"). A ScreenTip appears above the letters, as shown in Figure 1-6, suggesting "February" as the complete word.

Figure 1-6 AutoComplete suggestion

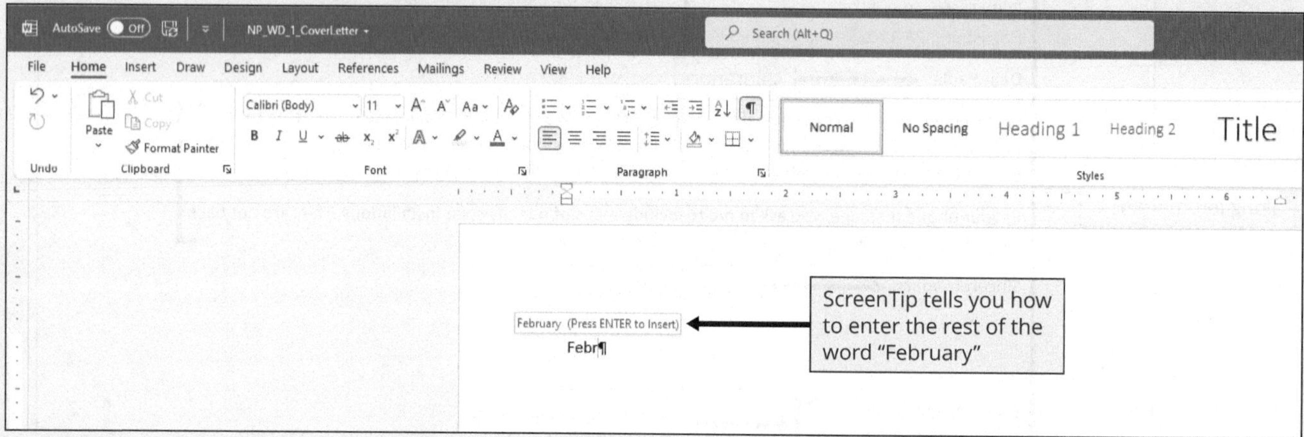

ScreenTip tells you how to enter the rest of the word "February"

> **Trouble?** If the ScreenTip does not appear, continue typing the complete word "February," and then read but do not complete Step 2. In some installations of Word running on Windows 11, AutoComplete may not work.

A **ScreenTip** is a label with descriptive text or an explanation about what to do next.

If you wanted to type something other than "February," you could continue typing to complete the word. In this case, you want to accept the AutoComplete suggestion.

2. Press **ENTER**. The rest of the word "February" is inserted in the document.
3. Press **SPACEBAR**, type **1, 2029** and then press **ENTER** twice, leaving a blank paragraph between the date and the line where you will begin typing the inside address, which contains the recipient's name and address. Notice the nonprinting character (•) after the word "February" and before the number "1," which indicates a space. Word inserts this nonprinting character every time you press SPACEBAR.

> **Trouble?** If February happens to be the current month, a second AutoComplete suggestion will display the current date after you press SPACEBAR. To ignore that AutoComplete suggestion, continue typing the rest of the date, as instructed in Step 3.

Note that you can also insert the current date (as well as the current time) by clicking the Insert Date and Time button in the Text group on the Insert tab. This opens the Date and Time dialog box, where you can select from a variety of date and time formats. If you want Word to update the date or time automatically each time you reopen the document, select the Update automatically check box. In that case, Word inserts the date and time as a special element called a field, which you'll learn more about as you become a more experienced Word user. However, for typical correspondence, it makes more sense to deselect the Update automatically check box so the date and time are inserted in the document as ordinary text.

Another Word feature, **text predictions**, is similar to AutoComplete, except that it displays suggestions directly in the document, in a fainter color than surrounding text, as shown in Figure 1–7. To accept the suggestion, press the Tab key. You can turn text predictions on or off using the "Show text predictions while typing" check box in the Editing options section of the Advanced tab in the Word Options dialog box. Note that text predictions are a relatively new feature in Word and will evolve over time to become more effective. If you find that text predictions interfere with your work on this or other modules, consider turning them off.

Figure 1–7 Working with text predictions

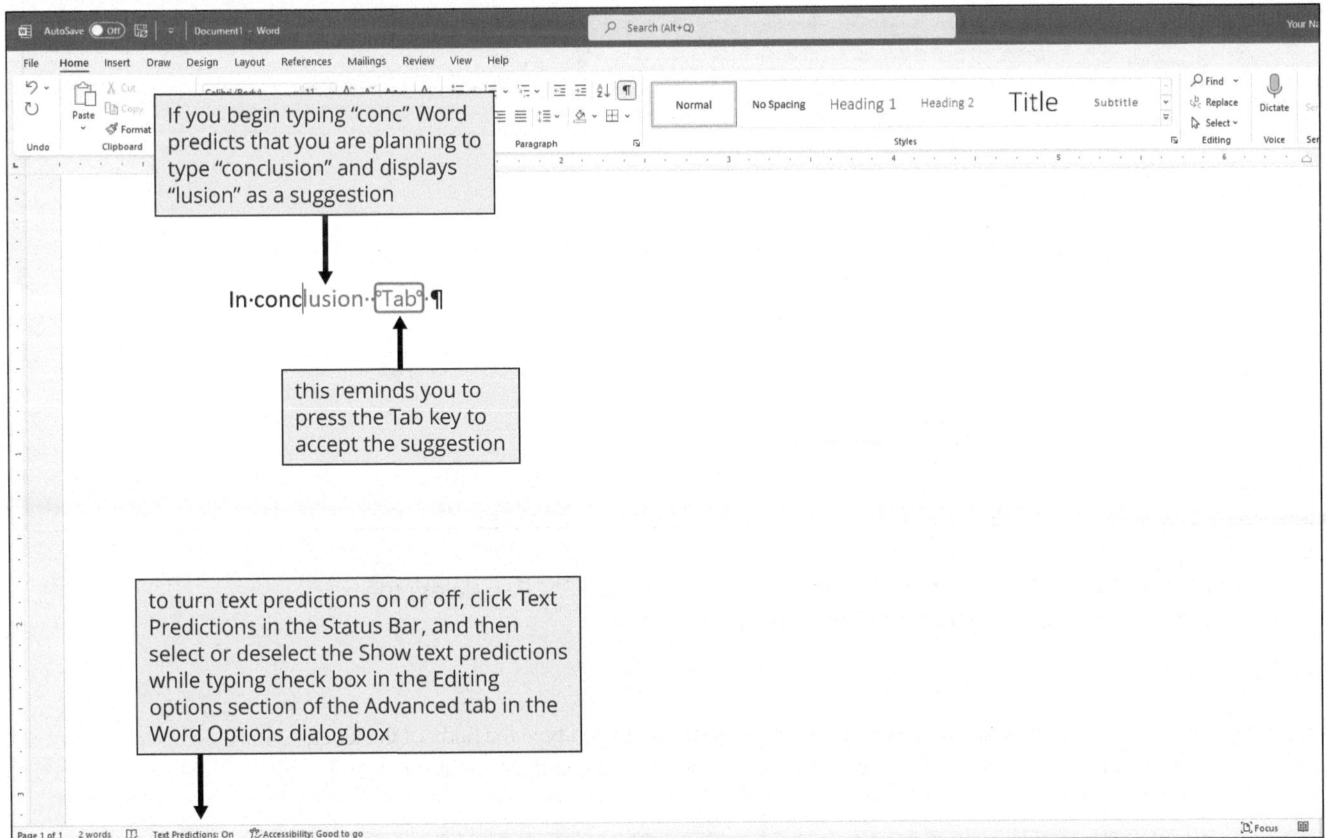

Typing a Block-Style Letter

In a block-style business letter, the inside address appears below the date, with one blank paragraph in between. Some style guides recommend including even more space between the date and the inside address. But in the short letter you are typing, more space would make the document look out of balance.

To insert the inside address:

1. Type the following information, pressing **ENTER** after each item:

   Paula Zimmerman

   Association of Sustainable Communities

   2800 Osprey Road

   Harrisburg, PA 17025

   Remember to press ENTER after you type the zip code. Your screen should look like Figure 1–8. Don't be concerned if the lines of the inside address seem too far apart. You'll use the default spacing for now, and then adjust it after you finish typing the letter.

Figure 1–8 Letter with inside address

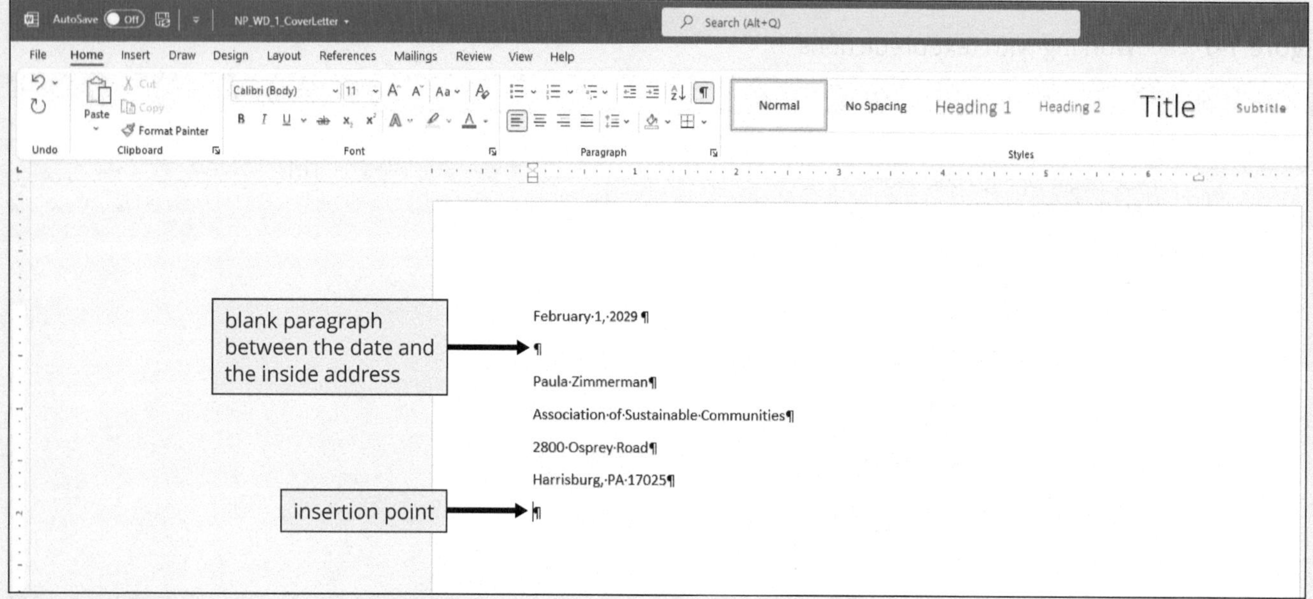

> **Trouble?** If you make a mistake while typing, press BACKSPACE to delete the incorrect character, and then type the correct character.

Now you can move on to the salutation and the body of the letter. As you type the body of the letter, notice that Word automatically moves the insertion point to a new line when the current line is full.

To type the salutation and the body of the letter:

1. Type **Dear Paula:** and then press **ENTER** to start a new paragraph for the body of the letter.
2. Type the following sentence, including the period: **Enclosed you will find the alternative energy brochures we discussed.**
3. Press **SPACEBAR**. Note that you should only include one space between sentences.

> **Tip** The obsolete practice of pressing SPACEBAR twice at the end of a sentence dates back to the age of typewriters, when the extra space made it easier to see where one sentence ended and another began.

4. Type the following sentence, including the period: **Thank you for agreeing to distribute them at next month's Sustainable City Planning Conference.**
5. On the Quick Access Toolbar, click the **Save** button . Word saves the document as **NP_WD_1_CoverLetter** to the same location you specified earlier.

The next sentence you need to type includes Leonel's email address.

Inserting a Hyperlink

When you type an email address and then press ENTER or SPACEBAR, Word converts it to a hyperlink, with blue font and an underline. A **hyperlink** is a specially formatted word, phrase, or graphic that, when clicked or tapped, lets you display a webpage on the Internet, another file, an email, or another location within the same file; it is sometimes called hypertext or a link. Hyperlinks are useful in documents that you plan to distribute via email. In printed documents, where blue font and underlines can be distracting, you'll usually want to convert a hyperlink back to regular text.

To add a sentence containing an email address:

1. Press **SPACEBAR**, and then type the following sentence, including the period: **If you have any questions not covered in the brochures, please contact me at villalba@salem.cengage.com.**
2. Press **ENTER**. Word converts the email address to a hyperlink, with blue font and an underline. The same thing would happen if you pressed SPACEBAR instead of ENTER.
3. Position the pointer over the hyperlink. A ScreenTip appears, indicating that you could press and hold CTRL and then click the link to follow it—that is, to open an email message addressed to the Leonel.
4. With the pointer positioned over the hyperlink, right-click—that is, press the right mouse button. A shortcut menu opens with commands related to working with hyperlinks.

   You can right-click many items in the Word window to display a **shortcut menu** with commands related to the item you right-clicked. The **Mini toolbar** also appears when you right-click or select text, giving you quick access to the buttons and settings most often used when formatting text. Refer to Figure 1–9.

Figure 1–9 Shortcut menu

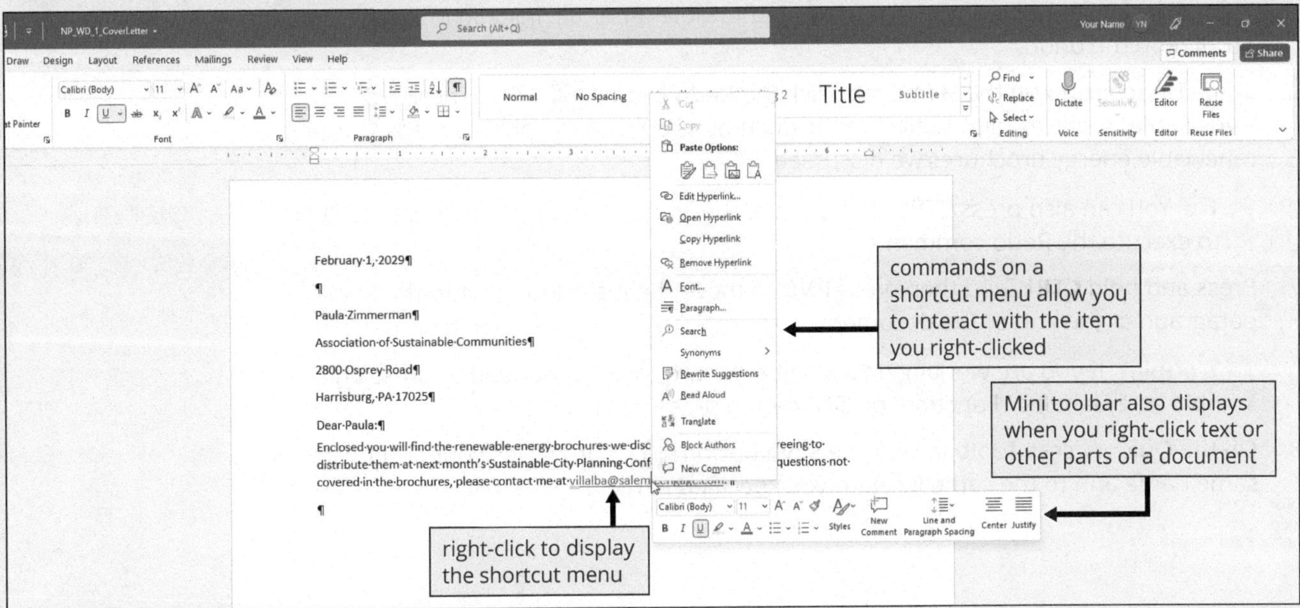

5. Click **Remove Hyperlink** in the shortcut menu. The shortcut menu and the Mini toolbar are no longer visible. The email address is now formatted in black, like the rest of the document text.
6. On the Quick Access Toolbar, click the **Save** button .

Using the Undo and Redo Buttons

When you first open Word, the Undo button and the Repeat button are displayed in the Undo group on the Home tab. To undo (or reverse) the last thing you did in a document, you can click the Undo button. Once you click the Undo button, the Repeat button is replaced with the Redo button. To restore your original change, click the Redo button, which reverses the action of the Undo button (or redoes the undo). To undo more than your last action, you can continue to click the Undo button, or you can click the Undo arrow on the Home tab to open a list of your most recent actions. When you click an action in the list, Word undoes every action in the list up to and including the action you clicked.

Leonel asks you to change "alternative" to "renewable" in the first sentence you typed. You'll make the change now. If Leonel decides he doesn't like it after all, you can always undo it. To delete a character, space, or blank paragraph to the right of the insertion point, you press DELETE, or to delete an entire word, you can press CTRL+DELETE. To delete a character, space, or blank paragraph to the left of the insertion point, you press BACKSPACE, or to delete an entire word, you can press CTRL+BACKSPACE.

To change the word "alternative":

1. Press the ↑ key twice and then press the ← key as necessary to move the insertion point to the left of the first "a" in the word "alternative."
2. Press and hold **CTRL**, and then press **DELETE** to delete the word "alternative."
3. Type **renewable** as a replacement, and then press **SPACEBAR**. After reviewing the sentence, Leonel decides he prefers the original wording, so you'll undo the change.
4. In the Undo group on the Home tab, click the **Undo** button . The word "renewable" is removed from the sentence.
5. Click the **Undo** button again to restore the word "alternative."

   Leonel decides that he does want to use "renewable" after all. Instead of retyping it, you'll redo the undo.
6. In the Undo group on the Home tab, click the **Redo** button twice. The word "renewable" replaces "alternative" in the document, so that the phrase reads "... the renewable energy brochures we discussed."

   Tip You can also press CTRL+Z to execute the Undo command, and press CTRL+Y to execute the Redo command.
7. Press and hold **CTRL**, and then press **END** to move the insertion point to the blank paragraph at the end of the document.

   Trouble? If you are working on a small keyboard, you might need to press and hold a key labeled "Function" or "FN" before pressing END.
8. On the Quick Access Toolbar, click the **Save** button . Word saves your letter with the same name and to the same location you specified earlier.

In the previous steps, you used the arrow keys and a key combination to move the insertion point to specific locations in the document. For your reference, Figure 1–10 summarizes the most common keystrokes for moving the insertion point in a document.

Figure 1–10 Keystrokes for moving the insertion point

To Move the Insertion Point	Press
Left or right one character at a time	← or →
Up or down one line at a time	↑ or ↓
Left or right one word at a time	CTRL+ ← or CTRL+ →
Up or down one paragraph at a time	CTRL+ ↑ or CTRL+ ↓
To the beginning or to the end of the current line	HOME or END
To the beginning or to the end of the document	CTRL+HOME or CTRL+END
To the previous screen or to the next screen	PAGE UP or PAGE DOWN
To the top or to the bottom of the document window	ALT+CTRL+PAGE UP or ALT+CTRL+PAGE DOWN

Correcting Errors as You Type

As you have seen, you can press BACKSPACE or DELETE to remove an error, and then type a correction. In many cases, however, the AutoCorrect feature will do the work for you. Among other things, **AutoCorrect** automatically detects and corrects common typing errors, such as typing "adn" instead of "and." For example, you might have noticed AutoCorrect at work if you forgot to capitalize the first letter in a sentence as you typed the letter. After you type this kind of error, AutoCorrect automatically corrects it when you press SPACEBAR, TAB, or ENTER.

Word draws your attention to other potential errors by marking them with underlines. If you type a word that doesn't match the correct spelling in the Word dictionary, or if a word is not in the dictionary at all, a wavy red line appears beneath it. A wavy red underline also appears if you mistakenly type the same word twice in a row. Misused words (for example, "you're" instead of "your") are underlined with a double blue line, as are problems with punctuation and potential grammar errors, such as a singular verb used with a plural subject. Possible wordiness is marked with a dotted purple underline, although keep in mind that this feature does not produce consistent results. Word might mark a phrase as wordy in one document, but then not mark the same phrase in a different document. This feature can be a helpful guide, but ultimately you'll need to make your own decisions about whether a phrase could be more concise.

You'll see how this works as you continue typing the letter and make some intentional typing errors.

To learn more about correcting errors as you type:

1. Type the following sentence, including the errors: **in you're phone mesage, you asked me me to include maps of our city solar installadions. They are not back from teh printer yet, but I will send them as soon as they are actually ready.**

   As you type, AutoCorrect changes the lowercase "i" at the beginning of the sentence to uppercase. It also changes "mesage" to "message" and "teh" to "the." Also, the incorrectly used word "you're" is marked with a double blue underline. The second "me" and the spelling error "installadions" are marked with wavy red underlines.

2. Press **ENTER**. One additional error is now visible—the phrase "actually ready" is marked with a dotted purple underline, indicating a lack of conciseness. Refer to Figure 1–11.

Figure 1–11 Errors marked in the document

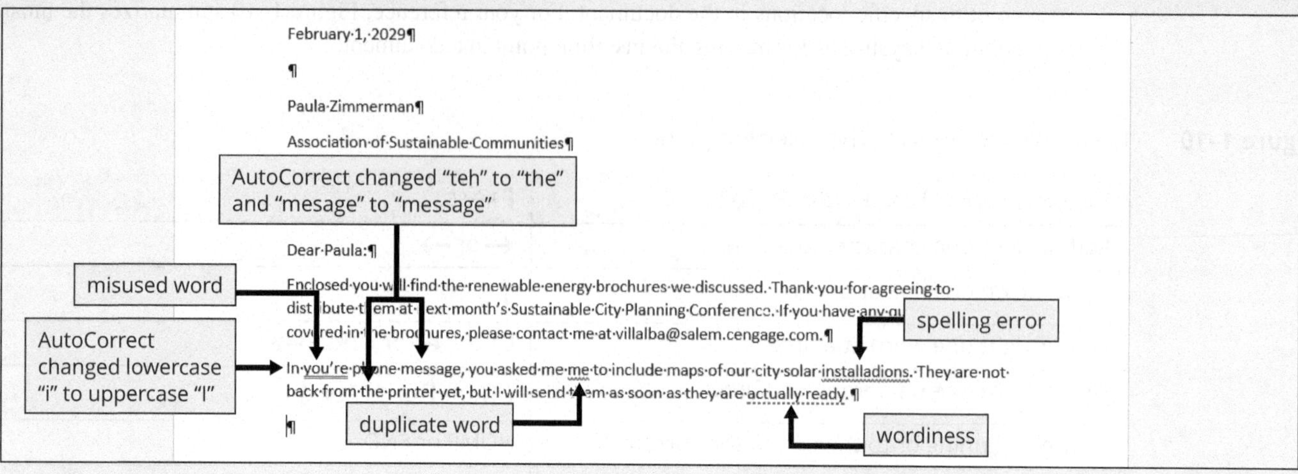
February·1,·2029¶
¶
Paula·Zimmerman¶
Association·of·Sustainable·Communities¶
AutoCorrect changed "teh" to "the" and "mesage" to "message"
Dear·Paula:¶
misused word
AutoCorrect changed lowercase "i" to uppercase "I"
spelling error
In·you're·phone·message,·you·asked·me·me·to·include·maps·of·our·city·solar·installadions.·They·are·not·
back·from·the·printer·yet,·but·I·will·send·them·as·soon·as·they·are·actually·ready.¶
duplicate word
wordiness

To correct an error marked with an underline, you can click the error and then click a replacement in the shortcut menu. If the shortcut menu does not contain the correct word, click anywhere in the document to close the menu, and then type the correction yourself. You can also bypass the shortcut menu entirely and simply delete the error and type a correction.

To correct the spelling, grammar, and wordiness errors:

1. Position the mouse pointer over the word **you're** to display a blue highlight.
2. Click **you're** to display a shortcut menu. The menu includes an explanation of the grammar problem and a suggested correction (the word "your"). Refer to Figure 1–12.

Figure 1–12 Shortcut menu with suggested spelling

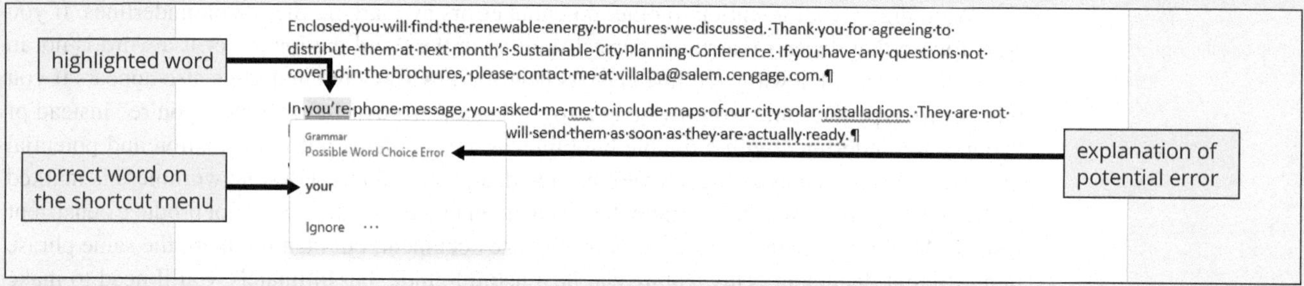
Enclosed·you·will·find·the·renewable·energy·brochures·we·discussed.·Thank·you·for·agreeing·to·
distribute·them·at·next·month's·Sustainable·City·Planning·Conference.·If·you·have·any·questions·not·
covered·in·the·brochures,·please·contact·me·at·villalba@salem.cengage.com.¶
In·you're·phone·message,·you·asked·me·me·to·include·maps·of·our·city·solar·installadions.·They·are·not·
will·send·them·as·soon·as·they·are·actually·ready.¶
highlighted word
Grammar
Possible Word Choice Error
correct word on the shortcut menu
your
Ignore
explanation of potential error

> **Tip** To hear the suggested correction read aloud or spelled out, make sure your computer's speakers are turned on, move the mouse pointer over the suggested correction to display an ellipsis (three dots), click the ellipsis, and then click Read Aloud or Spell out.

3. On the shortcut menu, click **your**. The correct word is inserted into the sentence, and the shortcut menu closes.
4. Use a shortcut menu to replace the spelling error "installadions" with the correct word "installations." Notice that this time the shortcut menu includes several potential corrections, so make sure to click "installations."

   You could use a shortcut menu to remove the second instance of "me," but in the next step you'll try a different method—selecting the word and deleting it.
5. Double-click anywhere in the underlined word **me**. The word and the space following it are highlighted in gray, indicating that they are selected. The Mini toolbar is also visible, but you can ignore it.

> **Tip** To deselect highlighted text, click anywhere in the document.

> **Trouble?** If the entire paragraph is selected, you triple-clicked the word by mistake. Click anywhere in the document to deselect it, and then repeat Step 4.

6. Press **DELETE**. The second instance of "me" and the space following it are deleted from the sentence. Finally, you need to correct the error related to concise language.
7. Click the phrase **actually ready** and use the shortcut menu to choose the more concise option, **ready**.
8. On the Quick Access Toolbar, click the **Save** button.

AutoCorrect and the multicolored underlines make quick work of correcting common typing errors, especially in a short document that you are typing yourself. If you are working on a longer document or a document typed by someone else, you'll also want to have Word check the entire document for errors. You'll learn how to do this in Part 1.2.

Next, you'll finish typing the letter.

To finish typing the letter:

1. Press **CTRL+END**. The insertion point moves to the end of the document.
2. Type **Sincerely yours,** (including the comma).
3. Press **ENTER** three times to leave space for the signature.
4. Type **Leonel Villalba** and then press **ENTER**. Because Leonel's last name is not in the Word dictionary, a wavy red line appears below it. You can ignore this for now.

   > **Trouble?** The wavy red line might not appear for a few seconds, or you might not see it on your computer at all.

5. Type your first, middle, and last initials in lowercase, and then press **ENTER**. AutoCorrect wrongly assumes your first initial is the first letter of a new sentence and changes it to uppercase. If your initials do not form a word, a red wavy underline appears beneath them. You can ignore this for now.

   > **Tip** You need to include your initials in a letter only if you are typing it for someone else.

6. In the Undo group on the Home tab, click the **Undo** button. Word reverses the change, replacing the uppercase initial with a lowercase one.
7. Type **Enclosure** so your screen looks like Figure 1–13.

Figure 1–13 Letter to Paula Zimmerman

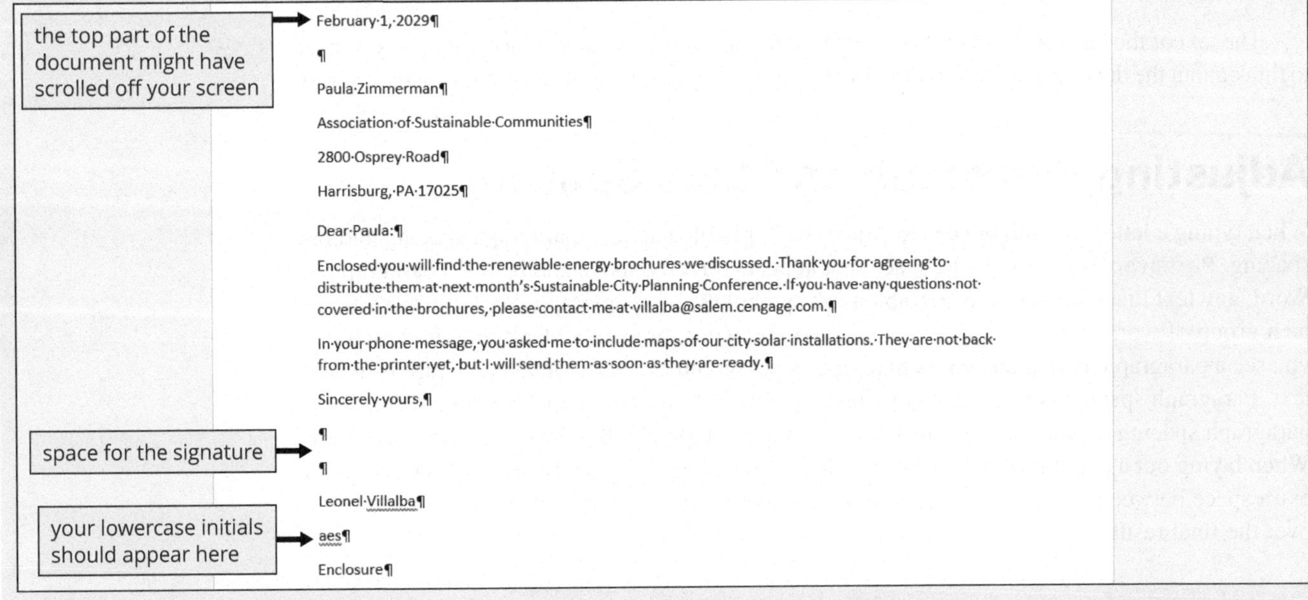
the top part of the document might have scrolled off your screen
February·1,·2029¶
¶
Paula·Zimmerman¶
Association·of·Sustainable·Communities¶
2800·Osprey·Road¶
Harrisburg,·PA·17025¶
Dear·Paula:¶
Enclosed·you·will·find·the·renewable·energy·brochures·we·discussed.·Thank·you·for·agreeing·to·distribute·them·at·next·month's·Sustainable·City·Planning·Conference.·If·you·have·any·questions·not·covered·in·the·brochures,·please·contact·me·at·villalba@salem.cengage.com.¶
In·your·phone·message,·you·asked·me·to·include·maps·of·our·city·solar·installations.·They·are·not·back·from·the·printer·yet,·but·I·will·send·them·as·soon·as·they·are·ready.¶
Sincerely·yours,¶
space for the signature
¶
¶
Leonel·Villalba¶
your lowercase initials should appear here
aes¶
Enclosure¶

Notice that as you continue to add lines to the letter, the top part of the letter scrolls off the screen. For example, depending on the size of your monitor, you may no longer see the date on your screen. Don't be concerned if more or less of the document has scrolled off the screen on your computer.

8. Save the document.

Now that you have finished typing the letter, you need to proofread it.

Proofreading a Document

After you finish typing a document, you need to proofread it carefully from start to finish. Part of proofreading a document in Word is removing all wavy underlines, either by correcting the text or by telling Word to ignore the underlined text because it isn't really an error. For example, Leonel's last name is marked as an error, when in fact it is spelled correctly. You need to tell Word to ignore "Villalba" wherever it occurs in the letter. You need to do the same for your initials.

To proofread and correct the remaining marked errors in the letter:

1. Click **Villalba**. A shortcut menu opens.

> **Trouble?** If "Villalba" does not have a wavy red underline on your screen, read steps 1 and 2 but do not attempt to perform them.

2. On the shortcut menu, click **Ignore All** to indicate that Word should ignore the word "Villalba" each time it occurs in this document. (The Ignore All option can be particularly helpful in a longer document.) The wavy red underline disappears from below Leonel's last name.

3. If you see a wavy red underline below your initials, click your initials. On the shortcut menu, click **Ignore All** to remove the red wavy underline. To choose to ignore something just once in a document, click the three-dot icon to display a popup menu, and then click Ignore.

4. Read the entire letter to proofread it for typing errors. Correct any errors using the techniques you have just learned.

5. Scroll up, if necessary, to display the complete inside address, which you'll work on next, and then save the document.

The text of the letter is finished. Now you need to think about its appearance—that is, you need to think about the document's **formatting**. First, you need to adjust the spacing in the inside address.

Adjusting Paragraph and Line Spacing

When typing a letter, you might need to adjust two types of spacing—paragraph spacing and line spacing. **Paragraph spacing** is the space that appears directly above and below a paragraph. In Word, any text that ends with a paragraph mark symbol (¶) is a paragraph. So, a **paragraph** can be a group of words that is many lines long, a single word, or even a blank line, in which case you see a paragraph mark alone on a single line. A paragraph can also contain a picture instead of text. Paragraph spacing is measured in points; a **point** is 1/72 of an inch. The default setting for paragraph spacing in Word is 0 points before each paragraph and 8 points after each paragraph. When laying out a complicated document, resist the temptation to simply press ENTER to insert extra space between paragraphs. Changing the paragraph spacing gives you much more control over the final result.

Line spacing is the space between lines of text within a paragraph. Word offers a number of preset line spacing options. The 1.0 setting, which is often called **single-spacing**, allows the least amount of space between lines. All other line spacing options are measured as multiples of 1.0 spacing. For example, 2.0 spacing (sometimes called **double-spacing**) allows for twice the space of single-spacing. The default line spacing setting is 1.08, which allows a little more space between lines than 1.0 spacing.

Now consider the line and paragraph spacing in the letter. The four lines of the inside address are too far apart. That's because each line of the inside address is actually a separate paragraph. Word inserted the default 8 points of paragraph spacing after each of these separate paragraphs. Refer to Figure 1–14.

Figure 1–14 Line and paragraph spacing in the letter to Paula Zimmerman

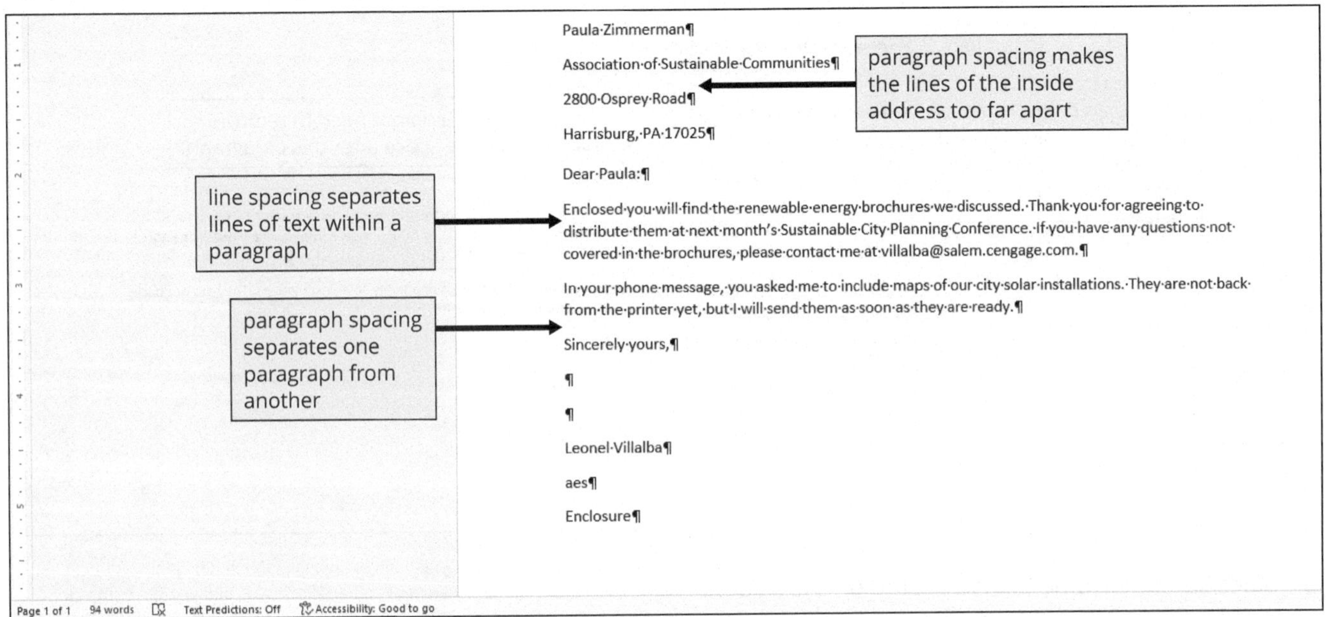
Paula·Zimmerman¶
Association·of·Sustainable·Communities¶
2800·Osprey·Road¶
Harrisburg,·PA·17025¶
Dear·Paula:¶
Enclosed·you·will·find·the·renewable·energy·brochures·we·discussed.·Thank·you·for·agreeing·to·distribute·them·at·next·month's·Sustainable·City·Planning·Conference.·If·you·have·any·questions·not·covered·in·the·brochures,·please·contact·me·at·villalba@salem.cengage.com.¶
In·your·phone·message,·you·asked·me·to·include·maps·of·our·city·solar·installations.·They·are·not·back·from·the·printer·yet,·but·I·will·send·them·as·soon·as·they·are·ready.¶
Sincerely·yours,¶
¶
¶
Leonel·Villalba¶
aes¶
Enclosure¶
paragraph spacing makes the lines of the inside address too far apart
line spacing separates lines of text within a paragraph
paragraph spacing separates one paragraph from another
Page 1 of 1
94 words
Text Predictions: Off
Accessibility: Good to go

To follow the conventions of a block-style business letter, the four paragraphs that make up the inside address should have the same spacing as the lines of text within a single paragraph—that is, they need to be closer together. You can accomplish this by removing the 8 points of paragraph spacing after the first two paragraphs in the inside address. To conform to the block-style business letter format, you also need to close up the spacing between your initials and the word "Enclosure" at the end of the letter.

To adjust paragraph and line spacing in Word, you use the Line and Paragraph Spacing button in the Paragraph group on the Home tab. Clicking this button displays a menu of preset line spacing options (1.0, 1.15, 2.0, and so on). The menu also includes two paragraph spacing options that allow you to add 12 points before a paragraph or remove the default 8 points of space after a paragraph.

Next you'll adjust the paragraph spacing in the inside address and after your initials. In the process, you'll also learn some techniques for selecting text in a document.

To adjust the paragraph spacing in the inside address and after your initials:

1. Move the pointer to the white space just to the left of "Paula Zimmerman" until it changes to a right-pointing arrow.
2. Click the mouse button. The entire name, including the paragraph symbol after it, is selected.

Trouble? If the Mini toolbar obscures your view of Paula's name, move the pointer away from the address to close the Mini toolbar.

Tip The white space in the left margin is sometimes referred to as the selection bar because you can click it to select text.

3. Press and hold the mouse button, drag the pointer down to select the next two paragraphs of the inside address as well, and then release the mouse button. If the Mini toolbar obscures your view of the selected text, move the mouse pointer to a blank part of the page.

   Paula's name, the name of her organization, and the street address are selected as well as the paragraph marks at the end of each paragraph. You did not select the paragraph containing the city, state, and zip code because you do not need to change its paragraph spacing. Refer to Figure 1–15.

Figure 1–15 Inside address selected

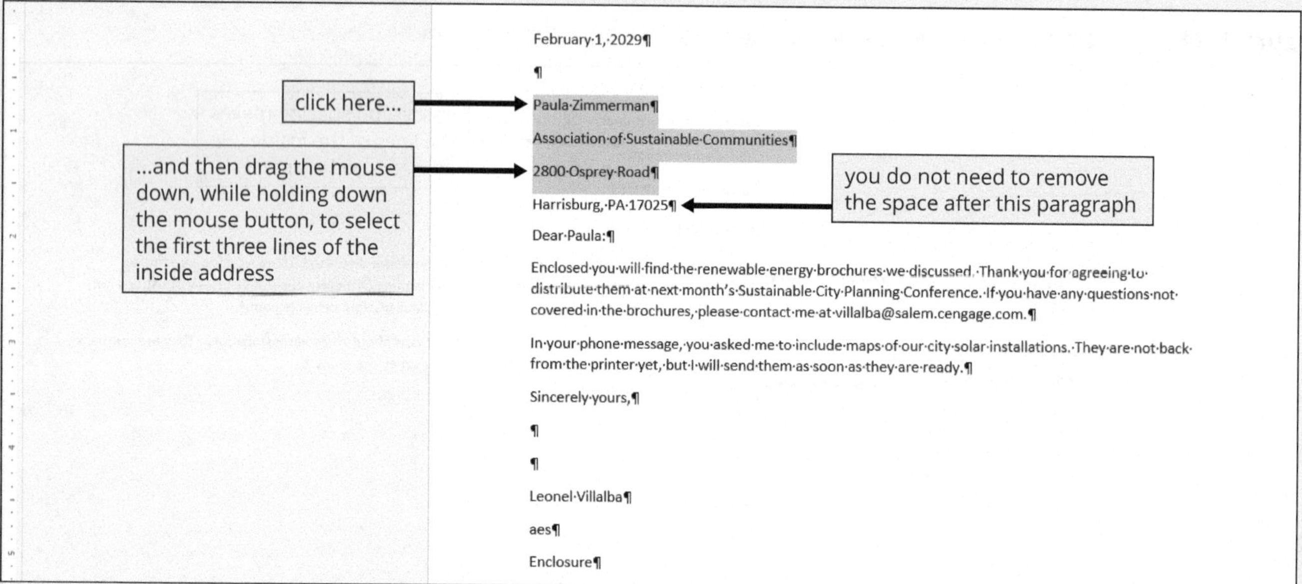
February·1,·2029¶
¶
click here...
Paula·Zimmerman¶
Association·of·Sustainable·Communities¶
...and then drag the mouse down, while holding down the mouse button, to select the first three lines of the inside address
2800·Osprey·Road¶
you do not need to remove the space after this paragraph
Harrisburg,·PA·17025¶
Dear·Paula:¶
Enclosed·you·will·find·the·renewable·energy·brochures·we·discussed.·Thank·you·for·agreeing·to·distribute·them·at·next·month's·Sustainable·City·Planning·Conference.·If·you·have·any·questions·not·covered·in·the·brochures,·please·contact·me·at·villalba@salem.cengage.com.¶
In·your·phone·message,·you·asked·me·to·include·maps·of·our·city·solar·installations.·They·are·not·back·from·the·printer·yet,·but·I·will·send·them·as·soon·as·they·are·ready.¶
Sincerely·yours,¶
¶
¶
Leonel·Villalba¶
aes¶
Enclosure¶

4. Make sure the Home tab is selected on the ribbon.
5. In the Paragraph group on the Home tab, click the **Line and Paragraph Spacing** button. A menu of line spacing options appears, with two paragraph spacing options at the bottom. Refer to Figure 1–16.

Figure 1–16 Line and paragraph spacing options

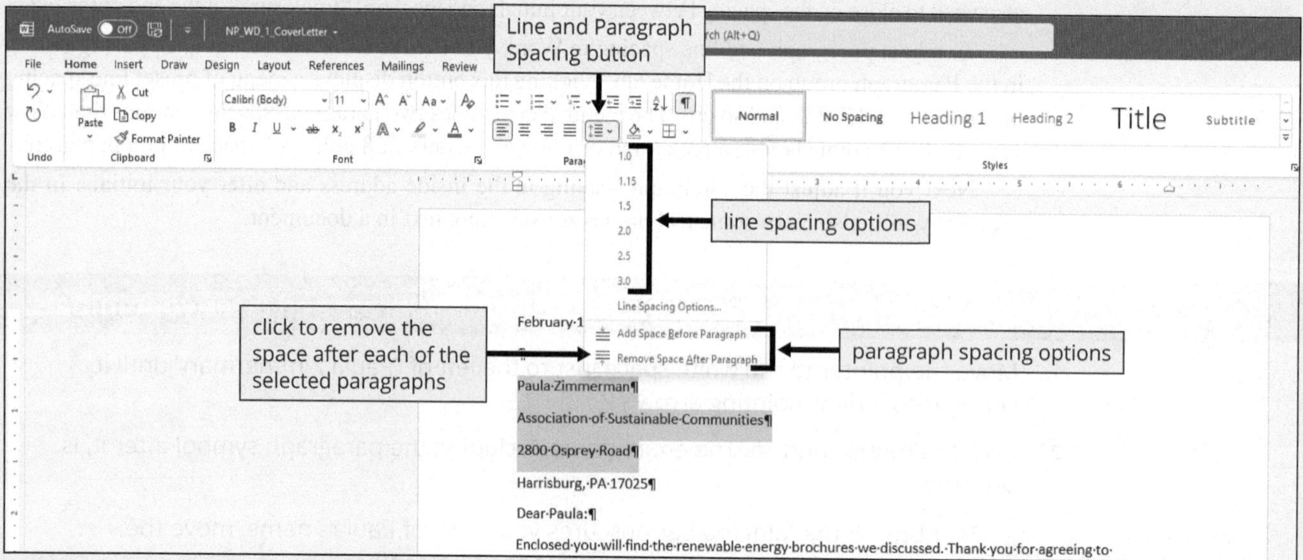
AutoSave Off
NP_WD_1_CoverLetter
Line and Paragraph Spacing button
File
Home
Insert
Draw
Design
Layout
References
Mailings
Review
Cut
Copy
Paste
Format Painter
Calibri (Body)
11
Normal
No Spacing
Heading 1
Heading 2
Title
Subtitle
Undo
Clipboard
Font
Styles
1.0
1.15
1.5
2.0
2.5
3.0
line spacing options
Line Spacing Options...
Add Space Before Paragraph
Remove Space After Paragraph
click to remove the space after each of the selected paragraphs
paragraph spacing options
Paula·Zimmerman¶
Association·of·Sustainable·Communities¶
2800·Osprey·Road¶
Harrisburg,·PA·17025¶
Dear·Paula:¶
Enclosed·you·will·find·the·renewable·energy·brochures·we·discussed.·Thank·you·for·agreeing·to·

At the moment, you are interested only in the paragraph spacing options. Your goal is to remove the default 8 points of space after the first two paragraphs in the inside address.

6. Click **Remove Space After Paragraph**. The menu closes, and the paragraphs are now closer together.
7. Double-click your initials to select them and the paragraph symbol after them.
8. In the Paragraph group, click the **Line and Paragraph Spacing** button, click **Remove Space After Paragraph**, and then click anywhere in the document to deselect your initials.

Another way to compress lines of text is to press SHIFT+ENTER at the end of a line. This inserts a **manual line break**, also called a **soft return**, which moves the insertion point to a new line without starting a new paragraph. You will use this technique now as you add Leonel's title below his name in the signature line.

To use a manual line break to move the insertion point to a new line without starting a new paragraph:

1. Click to the right of the second "a" in "Villalba."
2. Press **SHIFT+ENTER**. Word inserts a small arrow symbol, indicating a manual line break, and the insertion point moves to the line below Leonel's name.
3. Type **Communications Director**. Leonel's title now appears directly below his name with no intervening paragraph spacing, just like the lines of the inside address.
4. Save the document.

Insight

Understanding Spacing between Paragraphs

When discussing the correct format for letters, many business style guides talk about single-spacing and double-spacing between paragraphs. In these style guides, to single-space between paragraphs means to press ENTER once after each paragraph. Likewise, to double-space between paragraphs means to press ENTER twice after each paragraph. With the default paragraph spacing in Word, however, you need to press ENTER only once after a paragraph. The space Word adds after a paragraph is not quite the equivalent of double-spacing, but it is enough to make it clear where one paragraph ends and another begins. Keep this in mind if you're accustomed to pressing ENTER twice; otherwise, you could end up with more space than you want between paragraphs.

As you corrected line and paragraph spacing in the previous set of steps, you used the mouse to select text. Word provides multiple ways to select, or highlight, text as you work. Figure 1–17 summarizes these methods and explains when to use them most effectively. Note that there are multiple ways to select each element in a document. Three especially useful options are: (1) selecting an entire paragraph by triple-clicking it; (2) selecting nonadjacent text by pressing and holding CTRL, and then dragging the mouse pointer to select multiple blocks of text; and (3) selecting an entire document by pressing CTRL+A.

Figure 1–17 Methods for selecting text

To Select	Mouse	Keyboard	Mouse and Keyboard
A word	Double-click the word	Move the insertion point to the beginning of the word, press and hold CTRL+SHIFT, and then press →	
A line	Click in the white space to the left of the line	Move the insertion point to the beginning of the line, press and hold SHIFT, and then press ↓	
A sentence	Click at the beginning of the sentence, then drag the pointer until the sentence is selected		Press and hold CTRL, then click any location within the sentence
Multiple lines	Click and drag in the white space to the left of the lines	Move the insertion point to the beginning of the first line, press and hold SHIFT, and then press ↓ until all the lines are selected	
A paragraph	Double-click in the white space to the left of the paragraph, or triple-click at any location within the paragraph	Move the insertion point to the beginning of the paragraph, press and hold CTRL+SHIFT, and then press ↓	
Multiple paragraphs	Click in the white space to the left of the first paragraph you want to select, and then drag to select the remaining paragraphs	Move the insertion point to the beginning of the first paragraph, press and hold CTRL+SHIFT, and then press ↓ until all the paragraphs are selected	
An entire document	Triple-click in the white space to the left of the document text	Press CTRL+A	Press and hold CTRL, and click in the white space to the left of the document text
A block of text	Click at the beginning of the block, then drag the pointer until the entire block is selected		Click at the beginning of the block, press and hold SHIFT, and then click at the end of the block
Nonadjacent blocks of text			Press and hold CTRL, then drag the mouse pointer to select multiple blocks of nonadjacent text

Adjusting the Margins

Another important aspect of document formatting is the amount of margin space between the document text and the edge of the page. You can check the document's margins by changing the Zoom level to display the entire page.

To change the Zoom level to display the entire page:

1. On the ribbon, click the **View** tab.
2. In the Zoom group, click the **One Page** button. The entire document is now visible in the Word window. Refer to Figure 1–18.

Figure 1–18 Document zoomed to show entire page

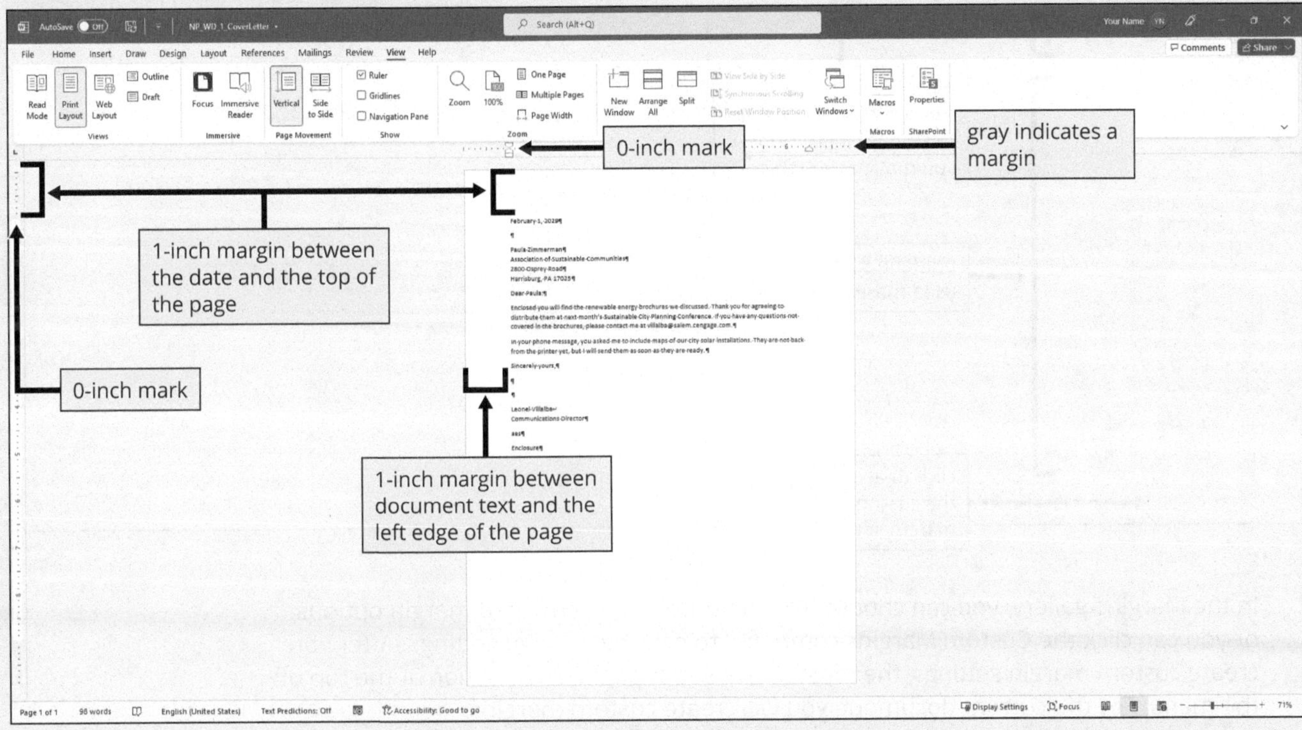

On the rulers, the margins appear gray. By default, Word documents include 1-inch margins on all sides of the document. By looking at the vertical ruler, you can see that the date in the letter, the first line in the document, is located 1 inch from the top of the page. Likewise, the horizontal ruler indicates the document text begins 1 inch from the left edge of the page.

Reading the measurements on the rulers can be tricky at first. On the horizontal ruler, the 0-inch mark is like the origin on a number line. You measure from the 0-inch mark to the left or to the right. On the vertical ruler, you measure up or down from the 0-inch mark.

Leonel plans to print the letter on the Department of Urban Development letterhead, which includes the department's address. To allow more blank space for the letterhead, and to move the text down so that it doesn't look so crowded at the top of the page, you need to increase the top margin. The settings for changing the page margins are located on the Layout tab on the ribbon.

To change the page margins:

1. On the ribbon, click the **Layout** tab. The Layout tab displays options for adjusting the layout of your document.
2. In the Page Setup group, click the **Margins** button. The Margins gallery opens, as shown in Figure 1–19.

Figure 1–19 Margins gallery

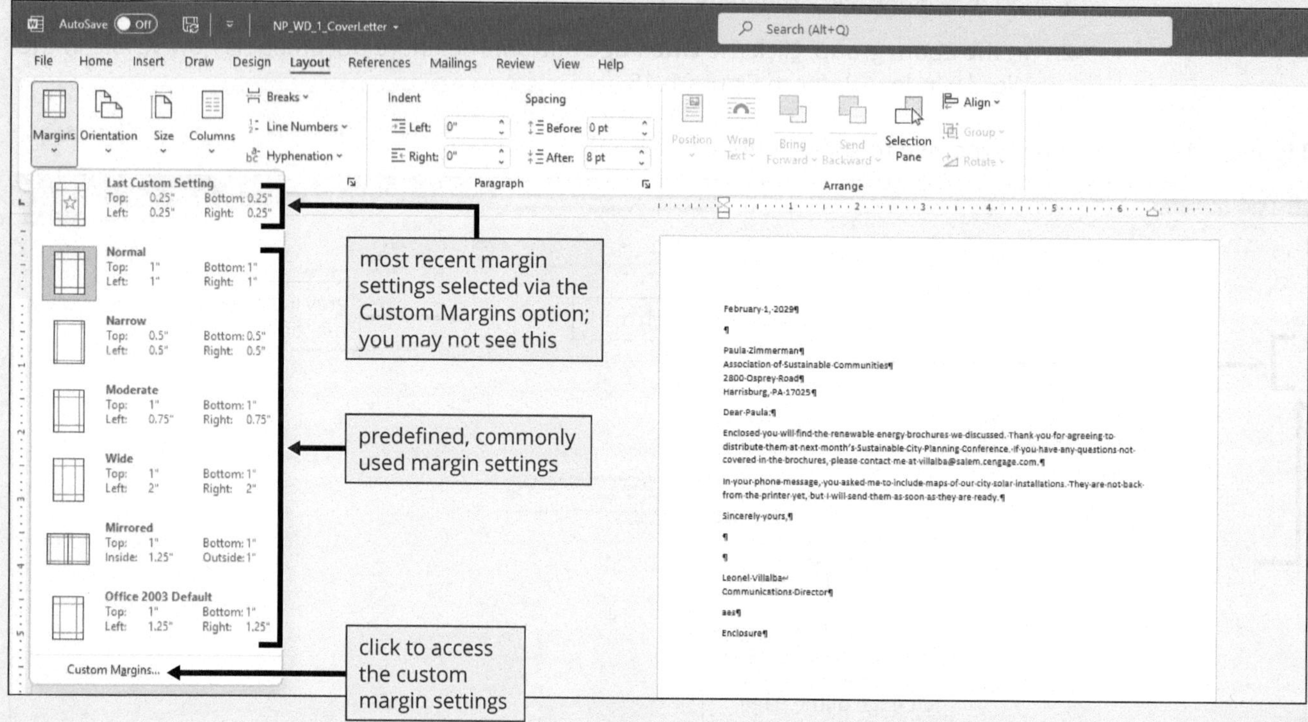

In the Margins gallery, you can choose from a number of predefined margin options, or you can click the Custom Margins command to select your own settings. After you create custom margin settings, the most recent set appears as an option at the top of the menu. For the current document, you will create custom margins.

3. Click **Custom Margins**. The Page Setup dialog box opens with the Margins tab displayed. The default margin settings are displayed in the boxes at the top of the Margins tab. The top margin of 1" is already selected, ready for you to type a new margin setting.
4. In the Top box in the Margins section, type **2.5**. You do not need to type an inch mark ("). Refer to Figure 1–20.

Figure 1–20 Creating custom margins in the Page Setup dialog box

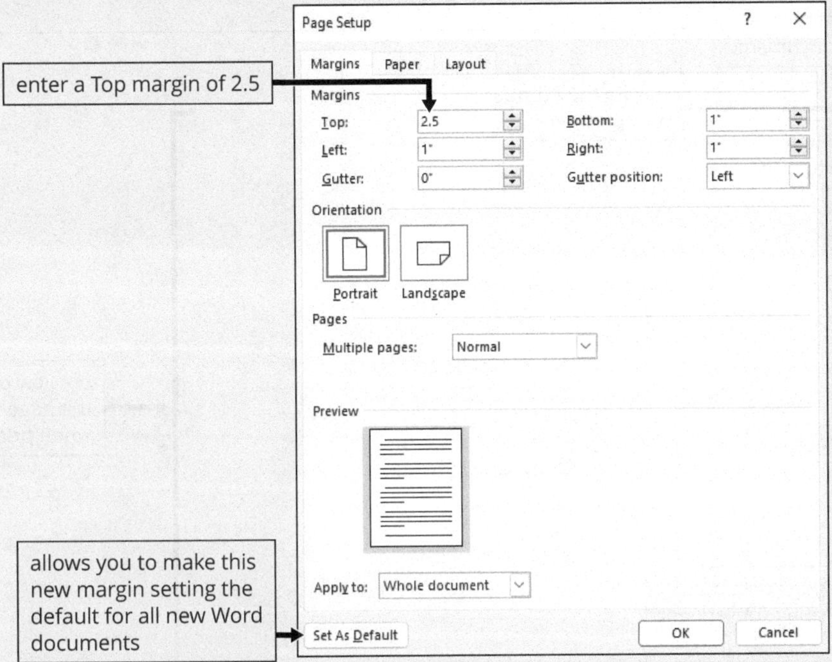

5. Click **OK**. The text of the letter is now lower on the page. The page looks less crowded, with room for the company's letterhead.
6. Save the document.

For most documents, the Word default of 1-inch margins is fine. In some professional settings, however, you might need to use a particular custom margin setting for all your documents. In that case, define the custom margins using the Margins tab in the Page Setup dialog box, and then click the Set As Default button to make your settings the default for all new documents. Keep in mind that most printers can't print to the edge of the page; if you select custom margins that are too narrow for your printer's specifications, Word alerts you to change your margin settings.

Previewing and Printing a Document

To make sure the document is ready to print, and to avoid wasting paper and time, you should first review it in Backstage view to make sure it will look right when printed. Like the One Page zoom setting you used earlier, the Print option in Backstage view displays a full-page preview of the document, allowing you to see how it will fit on the printed page. However, you cannot actually edit this preview. It simply provides one last opportunity to look at the document before printing.

To preview the document:

1. Increase the Zoom level to a setting that makes it easy for you to read the document, proofread it one last time, and correct any remaining errors.
2. Click the **File** tab to open Backstage view.
3. In the navigation pane, click **Print**.

   The Print screen displays a full-page version of your document, showing how the letter will fit on the printed page. The Print settings to the left of the preview allow you to control a variety of print options. For example, you can change the number of copies from the default setting of "1." The 1 Page Per Sheet button opens a menu where you can choose to print multiple pages on a single sheet of paper or to scale the printed page to a particular paper size. You can also use the navigation controls at the bottom of the screen to display other pages in a document. Refer to Figure 1–21.

Figure 1–21 Print settings in Backstage view

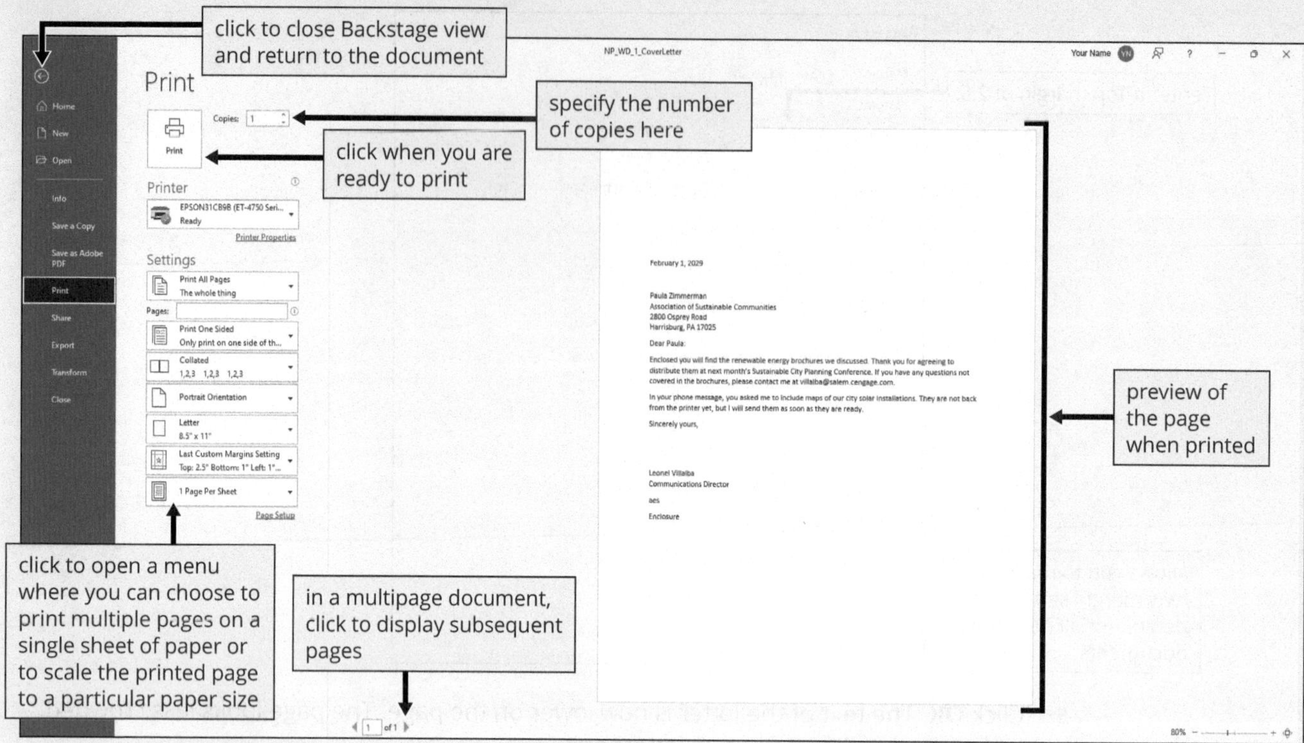
click to close Backstage view and return to the document
specify the number of copies here
click when you are ready to print
preview of the page when printed
click to open a menu where you can choose to print multiple pages on a single sheet of paper or to scale the printed page to a particular paper size
in a multipage document, click to display subsequent pages

4. Review your document and make sure its overall layout matches that of the document in Figure 1–21. If you notice a problem with paragraph breaks or spacing, click the **Back** button at the top of the navigation pane to return to the document, make any necessary changes, and then start again at Step 2.

At this point, you can print the document or you can leave Backstage view and return to the document in Print Layout view. In the following steps, you should print the document only if your instructor asks you to. If you will be printing the document, make sure your printer is turned on and contains paper.

To leave Backstage view or to print the document:

1. Click the **Back** button at the top of the navigation pane to leave Backstage view and return to the document in Print Layout view, or click the **Print** button. Backstage view closes, and the letter prints if you clicked the Print button.
2. sam Click the **File** tab, and then click **Close** in the navigation pane to close the document without closing Word.

Next, Leonel asks you to create an envelope he can use to send an energy conservation report to an environmental engineering publication.

Creating an Envelope

Before you can create the envelope, you need to open a new, blank document. To create a new document, you can start with a blank document—as you did with the letter to Paula Zimmerman—or you can start with one that already contains formatting and generic text commonly used in a variety of professional documents, such as a fax cover sheet or a memo. These preformatted files are called **templates**. You could use a template to create a formatted envelope, but to create a basic envelope for a business letter, it's better to start with a new, blank document.

To create a new document for the envelope:

1. Click the **File** tab, and then click **New** in the navigation pane. The New screen is similar to the one you saw when you first started Word, with a blank document in the upper-left corner, along with a variety of templates. Refer to Figure 1–22.

Figure 1–22 New options in Backstage view

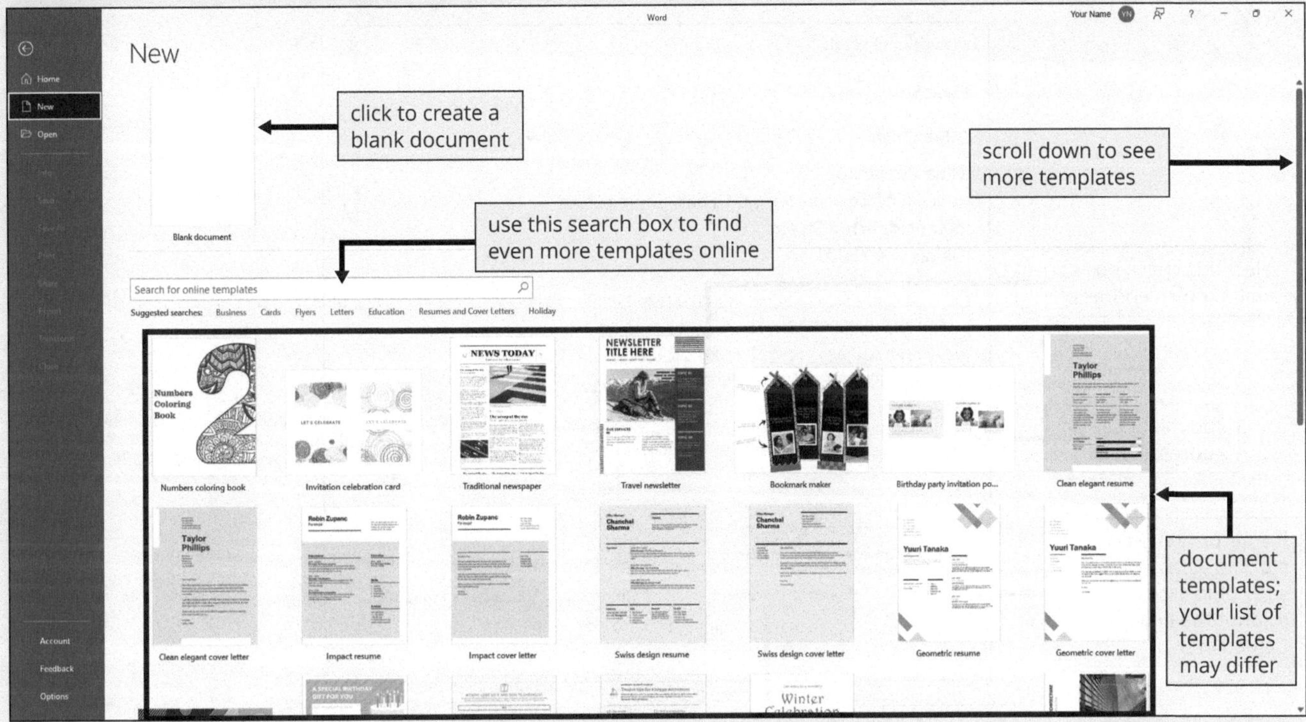

2. Click **Blank document**. A new document named Document2 opens in the document window, with the Home tab selected on the ribbon.
3. If necessary, display nonprinting characters and the rulers.
4. Save the new document as **NP_WD_1_JournalEnvelope** in the location specified by your instructor.

To create the envelope:

1. On the ribbon, click the **Mailings** tab. The ribbon changes to display the various Mailings options.
2. In the Create group, click the **Envelopes** button. The Envelopes and Labels dialog box opens, with the Envelopes tab displayed. The insertion point appears in the Delivery address box, ready for you to type the recipient's address. Depending on how your computer is set up, and whether you are working on your own computer or a school computer, the Return address box might contain an address.
3. In the Delivery address box, type the following address, pressing **ENTER** to start each new line:

   Nina Petrenko

   Journal of Environmental Urban Engineering

   600 Bridgerton Street

   Dallas, TX 75001

   Because Leonel will be using the department's printed envelopes, you don't need to print a return address on this envelope.

4. Click the **Omit** check box to insert a checkmark, if necessary.

   At this point, if you had a printer stocked with envelopes, you could click the Print button to print the envelope. To save an envelope for printing later, you need to add it to the document. Your Envelopes and Labels dialog box should match the one in Figure 1–23.

Figure 1–23 Envelopes and Labels dialog box

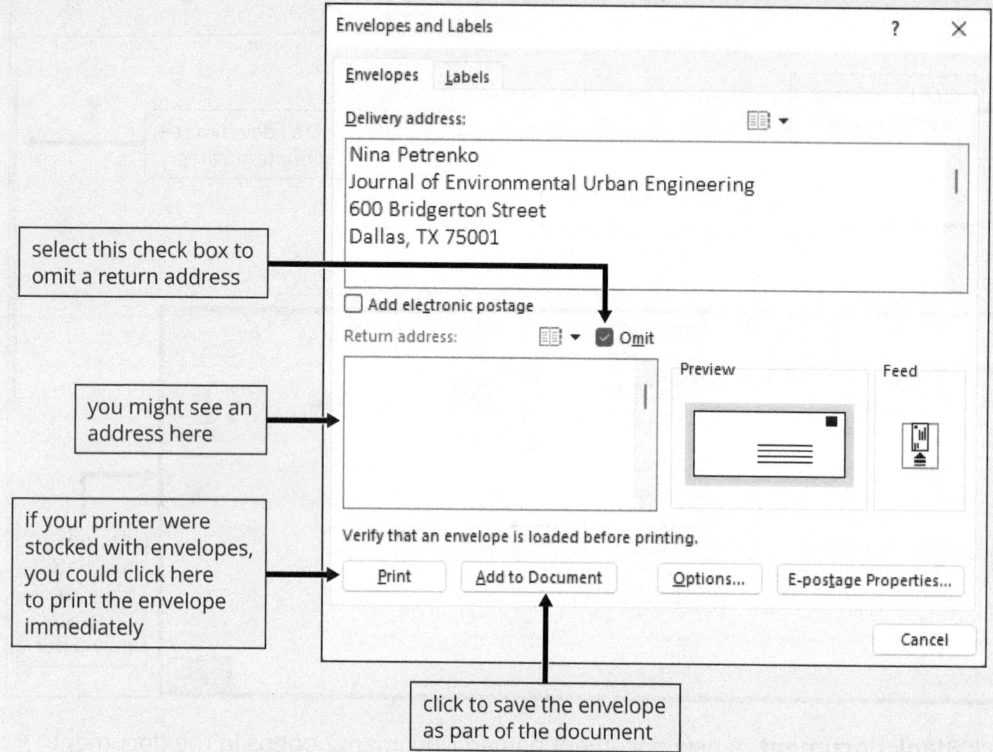

5. Click **Add to Document**. The dialog box closes, and you return to the document window. The envelope is inserted at the top of your document, with 1.0 line spacing. The double line with the words "Section Break (Next Page)" is related to how the envelope is formatted and will not be visible when you print the envelope. The envelope will print in the standard business envelope format. In this case, you added the envelope to a blank document, but you could also add an envelope to a completed letter, in which case Word adds the envelope as a new page before the letter.
6. Save the document. Leonel will print the envelope later, so you can close the document now.
7. Click the **File** tab, and then click **Close** in the navigation pane. The document closes, but Word remains open.

You're finished creating the cover letter and the envelope. In the next part of this module, you will modify a flyer by formatting the text and adding a photo.

Insight

Creating Documents with Templates

Microsoft offers predesigned templates for all kinds of documents, including calendars, reports, and thank-you cards. You can use the scroll bar on the right of the New screen (shown earlier in Figure 1–22) to scroll down to display more templates, or you can use the Search for online templates box in the New screen to search among thousands of other options available at Microsoft365.com. When you open a template, you actually open a new document containing the formatting and text stored in the template, leaving the original template untouched. A typical template includes placeholder text that you replace with your own information.

Templates allow you to create stylish, professional-looking documents quickly and easily. To use them effectively, however, you need to be knowledgeable about Word and its many options for manipulating text, graphics, and page layouts. Otherwise, the complicated formatting of some Word templates can be more frustrating than helpful. As you become a more experienced Word user, you'll learn how to create your own templates.

Part 1.1 Quick Check

1. What feature displays the rest of the word you are typing directly in the document and allows you to press the Tab key to accept the suggestion?
2. Explain how to display nonprinting characters.
3. In a block-style letter, does the date appear above or below inside address?
4. Explain how to remove a hyperlink from a Word document.
5. Define the term "paragraph spacing."
6. Explain how to display a shortcut menu with options for correcting a word with a wavy red underline.

Part 1.2 Visual Overview: Formatting a Document

Alignment buttons control the text's **alignment**—that is, the way it lines up horizontally between the left and right margins. Here, the Center button is selected because the text containing the insertion point is center-aligned.

You can click the Clear All Formatting button to restore selected text to the default font, font size, and color.

Clicking the Format Painter button displays the Format Painter pointer, which you can use to copy formatting from the selected text to other text in the document.

The Font group on the Home tab includes the Font box and the Font size box for setting the font and the font size, respectively. A **font** is a set of characters that uses the same typeface.

You click the Shading arrow to apply a colored background to a selected paragraph.

You use the Borders arrow to apply an outline to the selected paragraph. The image on the Borders button reflects the most recently used Border option.

The document has a landscape orientation, meaning it is wider than it is tall.

You can insert a photo or another type of picture in a document by using the **Pictures button** located on the Insert tab of the ribbon. After you insert a photo or another picture, you can format it with a style that adds a border or a shadow or changes its shape.

The boldface and blue font color applied to this text are examples of formatting that you should use sparingly to draw attention to a specific part of a document.

The white font color used on this text is an example of **character formatting** because it affects individual characters.

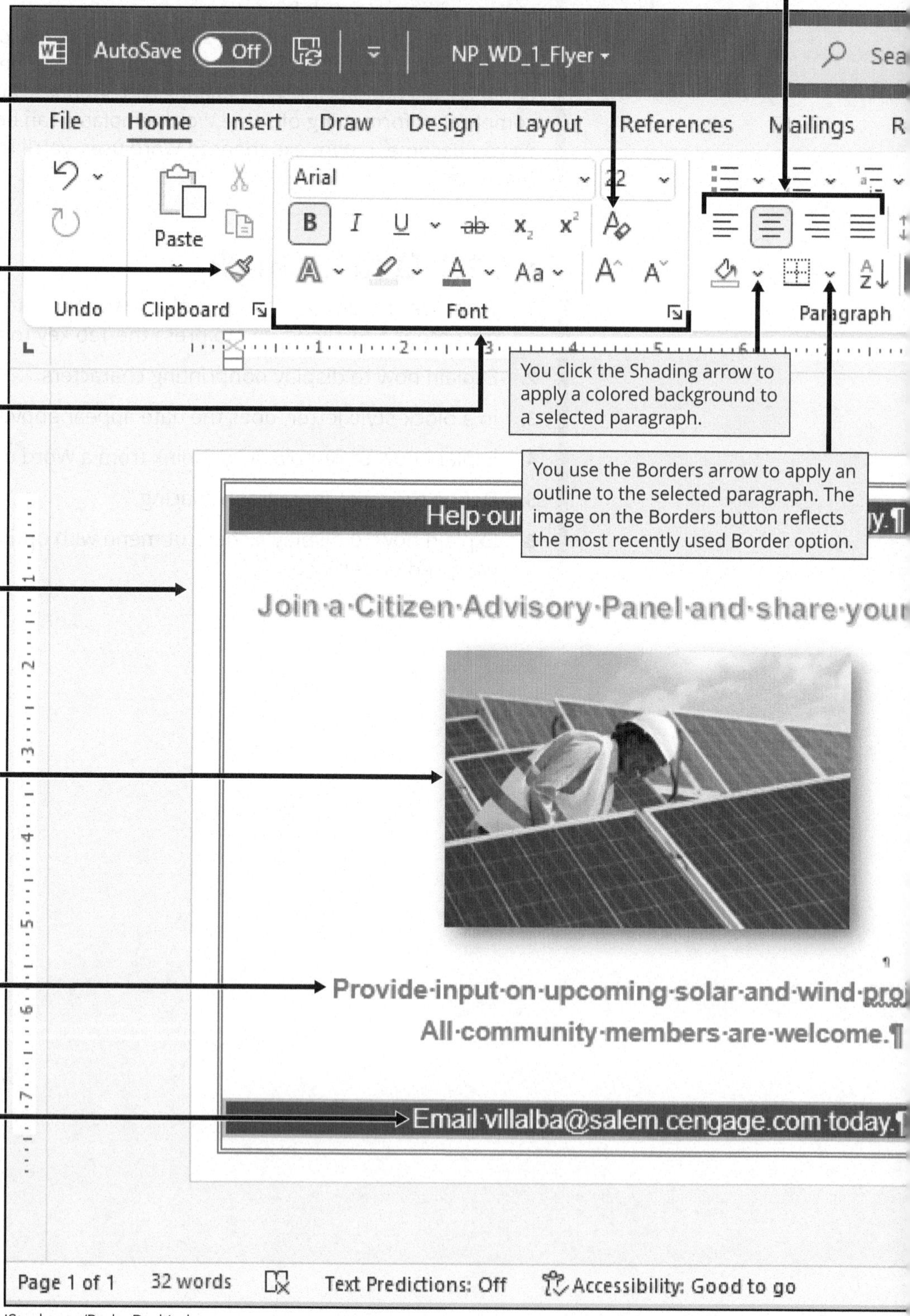

AutoSave Off NP_WD_1_Flyer Search
File Home Insert Draw Design Layout References Mailings R
Arial 22
Paste
Undo Clipboard Font Paragraph
Help·our ...y.¶
Join·a·Citizen·Advisory·Panel·and·share·your
Provide·input·on·upcoming·solar·and·wind·proj
All·community·members·are·welcome.¶
Email·villalba@salem.cengage.com·today.¶
Page 1 of 1 32 words Text Predictions: Off Accessibility: Good to go

iStock.com/RuslanDashinsky

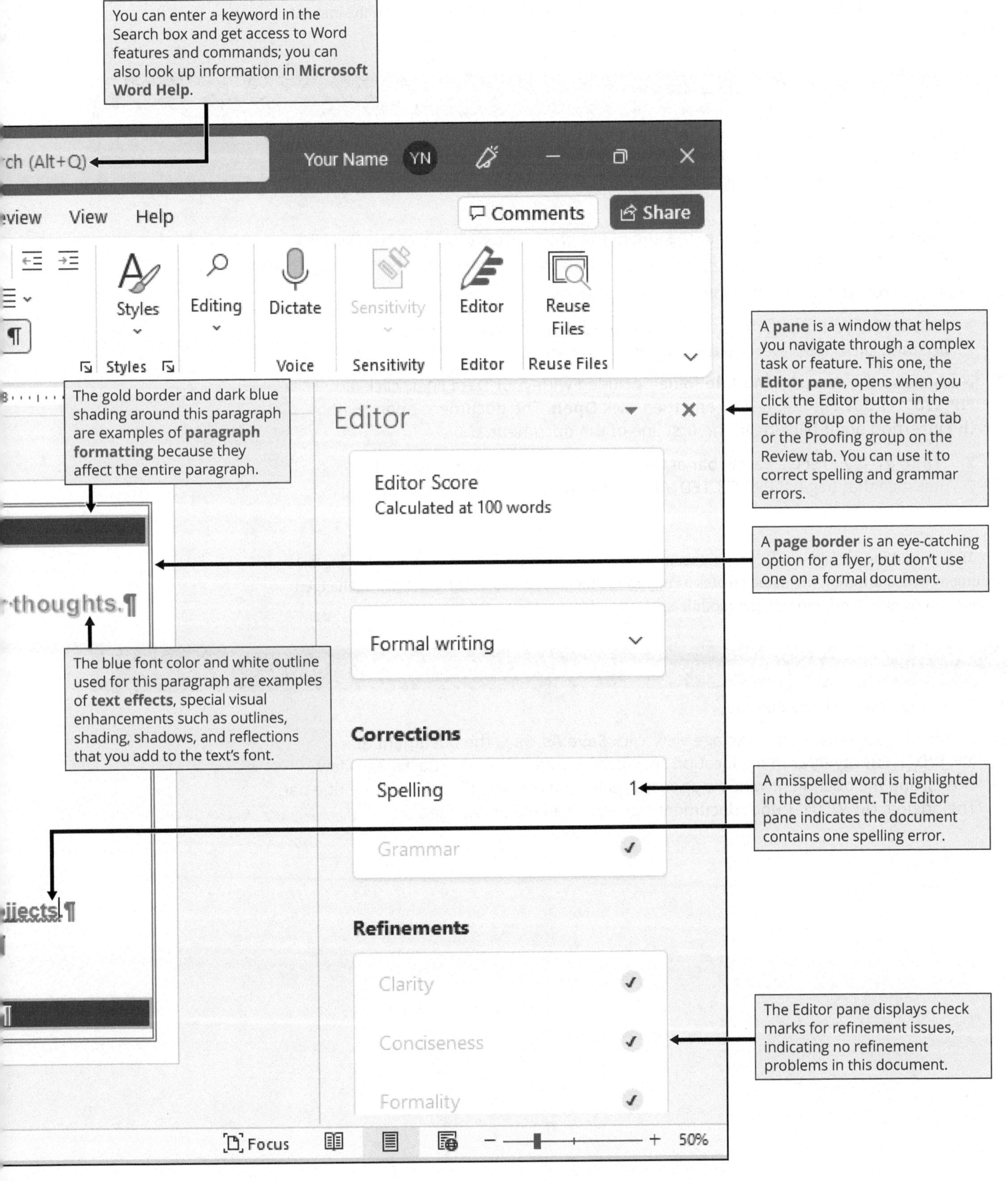
You can enter a keyword in the Search box and get access to Word features and commands; you can also look up information in Microsoft Word Help.
rch (Alt+Q)
Your Name
YN
eview
View
Help
Comments
Share
Styles
Editing
Dictate
Sensitivity
Editor
Reuse Files
Styles
Voice
Sensitivity
Editor
Reuse Files
A pane is a window that helps you navigate through a complex task or feature. This one, the Editor pane, opens when you click the Editor button in the Editor group on the Home tab or the Proofing group on the Review tab. You can use it to correct spelling and grammar errors.
The gold border and dark blue shading around this paragraph are examples of paragraph formatting because they affect the entire paragraph.
Editor
Editor Score
Calculated at 100 words
A page border is an eye-catching option for a flyer, but don't use one on a formal document.
r·thoughts.¶
Formal writing
The blue font color and white outline used for this paragraph are examples of text effects, special visual enhancements such as outlines, shading, shadows, and reflections that you add to the text's font.
Corrections
Spelling
1
Grammar
A misspelled word is highlighted in the document. The Editor pane indicates the document contains one spelling error.
jjects.¶
Refinements
Clarity
Conciseness
Formality
The Editor pane displays check marks for refinement issues, indicating no refinement problems in this document.
Focus
50%

Opening an Existing Document

In this part of the module, you'll complete a flyer encouraging community members to join a citizen advisory panel. Leonel has already typed the text of the flyer, inserted a photo into it, and saved it as a Word document. He would like you to check the document for spelling and grammar errors, format the flyer to make it eye-catching and accessible for all readers, and then replace the current photo with a new one. You'll start by opening the document.

To open the flyer document:

1. sam On the ribbon, click the **File** tab to open Backstage view, and then click **Open** in the navigation pane. On the left side of the Open screen is a list of places you can go to locate other documents, and on the right is a list of recently opened documents.

   Trouble? If you closed Word at the end of the previous part, start Word now, click Open in the navigation pane in Backstage view, and then begin with Step 2.

2. Click the **Browse** button. The Open dialog box opens.

   Trouble? If your instructor asked you to store your files to your OneDrive account, click OneDrive, and then log in to your account.

3. Navigate to the **Word1 > Module** folder included with your Data Files, click **NP_WD_1-1.docx** in the file list, and then click **Open**. The document opens with the insertion point blinking in the first line of the document.

   Trouble? If you see a yellow bar at the top of the document window with a message that begins "PROTECTED VIEW," click the Enable Editing button.

Before making changes to Leonel's document, you will save it with a new name. Saving the document with a different file name creates a copy of the file and leaves the original file unchanged in case you want to work through the module again.

To save the document with a new name:

1. On the ribbon, click the **File** tab.
2. In the navigation pane in Backstage view, click **Save As**. Save the document as **NP_WD_1_EnergyFlyer** in the location specified by your instructor. Backstage view closes, and the document window appears again with the new file name in the title bar. The original NP_WD_1-1.docx document closes, remaining unchanged.

Proskills

Decision Making: Creating Effective Documents

Before you create a new document or revise an existing document, take a moment to think about your audience. Ask yourself these questions:

- Who is your audience?
- What do they know?
- What do they need to know?
- How can the document you are creating change your audience's behavior or opinions?

Every decision you make about your document should be based on your answers to these questions. To take a simple example, if you are creating a flyer to announce an upcoming seminar on college financial aid, your audience would be students and their parents. They probably all know what the term "financial aid" means, so you don't need to explain that in your flyer. Instead, you can focus on telling them what they need to know—the date, time, and location of the seminar. The behavior you want to affect, in this case, is whether your audience will show up for the seminar. By making the flyer professional looking, you increase the chance that they will.

You might find it more challenging to answer these questions about your audience when creating more complicated documents, such as corporate reports. But the focus remains the same—connecting with the audience. As you are deciding what information to include in your document, remember that the goal of a professional document is to convey the information as effectively as possible to your target audience.

Before revising a document for someone else, it's a good idea to familiarize yourself with its overall structure.

To review the document:

1. Verify that the document is displayed in Print Layout view and that nonprinting characters and the rulers are displayed. For now, you can ignore the wavy underlines that appear in the document.
2. Change the Zoom level to **120%**, if necessary, and then scroll down, if necessary, so that you can read the last line of the document.

   At this point, the document is very simple. By the time you are finished, it will look like the document shown in the Part 1.2 Visual Overview, with the spelling and grammar errors corrected. Figure 1–24 summarizes the tasks you will perform.

Figure 1–24 Formatting changes requested by Leonel

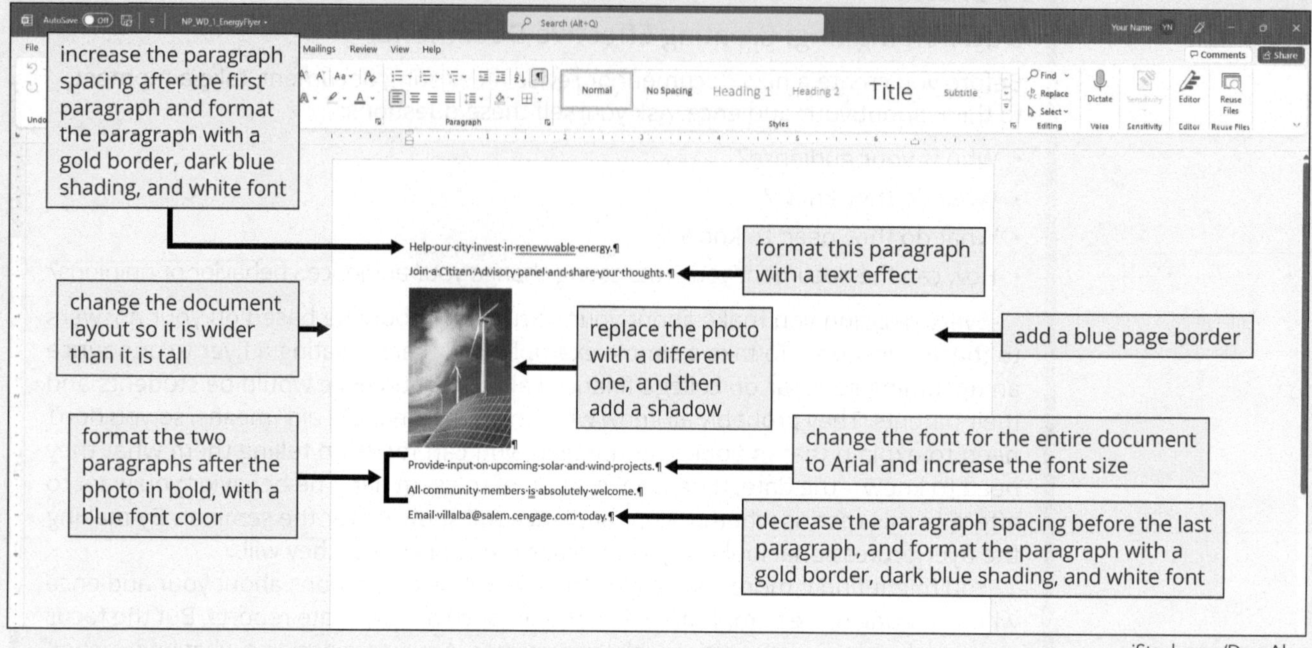

iStock.com/DaveAlan

You will start by correcting the spelling and grammar errors.

Using the Editor Pane

As you learned earlier in this module, Word marks possible spelling and grammar errors, as well as wordiness, with underlines so you can quickly go back and correct those errors. A more thorough way of checking the spelling in a document is to use the Editor pane to check a document word by word for a variety of errors. You can customize the spelling and grammar settings to add or ignore certain types of errors.

The suggestions displayed in the Editor pane are generated by **Microsoft Editor**, a feature built into all Microsoft 365 apps, including PowerPoint and Outlook. Microsoft Editor uses AI (artificial intelligence) to make specific suggestions appropriate for your document.

Leonel asks you to use the Editor pane to check the flyer for mistakes. Before you do, you'll review the various Spelling and Grammar settings.

To review the Spelling and Grammar settings:

1. On the ribbon, click the **File** tab, and then click **Options** in the navigation pane. (Note that depending on the size of your monitor, you might have to click More in the navigation pane and then click Options.) The Word Options dialog box opens. You can use this dialog box to change a variety of settings related to how Word looks and works.
2. In the left pane, click **Proofing**. The dialog box displays options for proofing a document. Note that there are two similar sections, one labeled "When correcting spelling in Microsoft Office programs" and one labeled "When correcting spelling and grammar in Word." Here you will focus on the Word settings.
3. Review the four selected options in the "When correcting spelling and grammar in Word" section. These options tell you that Word will check for misspellings, grammar errors, and frequently confused words as you type, marking them with wavy underlines as necessary.
4. Scroll down if necessary to display the two check boxes at the bottom of the dialog box, which you could select to hide any underlines in the current document calling attention to spelling or grammar errors.

> **Tip** It's never a good idea to select the "Hide spelling errors in this document only" check box. But if you find the Editor's suggestions about how to improve your writing style distracting, you could select the "Hide grammar errors in this document only" check box while you are writing a draft, and then deselect it later when you are ready to check the entire document all at once.

5. In the "When correcting spelling and grammar in Word" section, click **Settings**. The Grammar Settings dialog box opens, with "Grammar & Refinements" selected under "Writing style." Here you can control the types of errors Word checks for. Grammar errors include issues related to punctuation, subject-verb agreement, sentence fragments, and so on. Refinement errors include errors related to clarity, conciseness, formality, inclusive language, and vocabulary issues including cliches, profanity, and weak verbs.
6. Select all the check boxes in the Grammar section if they are not selected by default. Refer to Figure 1–25.

Figure 1–25 Grammar Settings dialog box

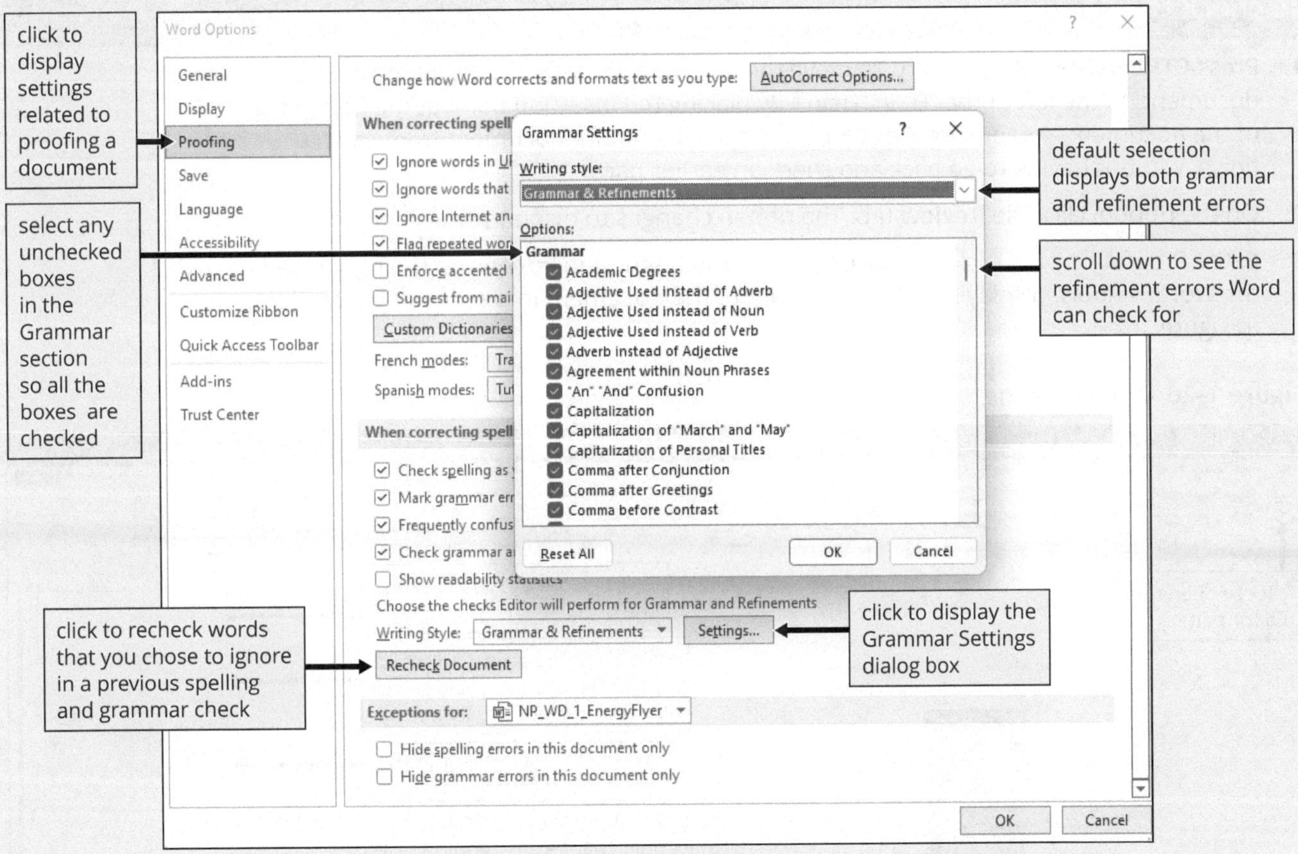

7. Scroll down and select all the Formality boxes if they are not selected by default.
8. Click **Cancel** to close the Grammar Settings dialog box and return to the Word Options dialog box.

   Note that the results displayed in the Editor pane are sometimes hard to predict. For example, in some documents Word will mark a misused word or duplicate punctuation as an error and then fail to mark the same items as errors in another document. Also, if you choose to ignore a misspelling in a document and then, without closing Word, type the same misspelled word in another document, Word will probably not mark it as an error. Sometimes, if you change a document's line or paragraph spacing, Word will mark text as errors that it previously did not. These issues can be especially problematic when working on a document typed by someone else. So to ensure that you get the best possible results, it's a good idea to click Recheck Document in the Word Options dialog box before you use the Editor pane.

9. Click the **Recheck Document** button, and then click **Yes** in the warning dialog box.
10. In the Word Options dialog box, click **OK** to close the dialog box. You return to the document.

Now you are ready to check the document's spelling and grammar. All errors marked with red underlines are considered spelling errors, while all errors marked with blue underlines are considered grammar errors. Errors marked with purple dotted underlines are considered errors related to a lack of conciseness. To begin checking the document, you'll use the Editor button in the Proofing group on the Review tab.

To check the document for spelling and grammar errors:

1. Press **CTRL+HOME**, if necessary, to move the insertion point to the beginning of the document, to the left of the "H" in "Help." By placing the insertion point at the beginning of the document, you ensure that Word will check the entire document from start to finish, without having to go back and check an earlier part.
2. On the ribbon, click the **Review** tab. The ribbon changes to display reviewing options.
3. In the Proofing group, click the **Editor** button. The Editor pane opens on the right side of the Word window, displaying information about the document in a series of boxes. Refer to Figure 1–26.

Figure 1–26 Editor pane

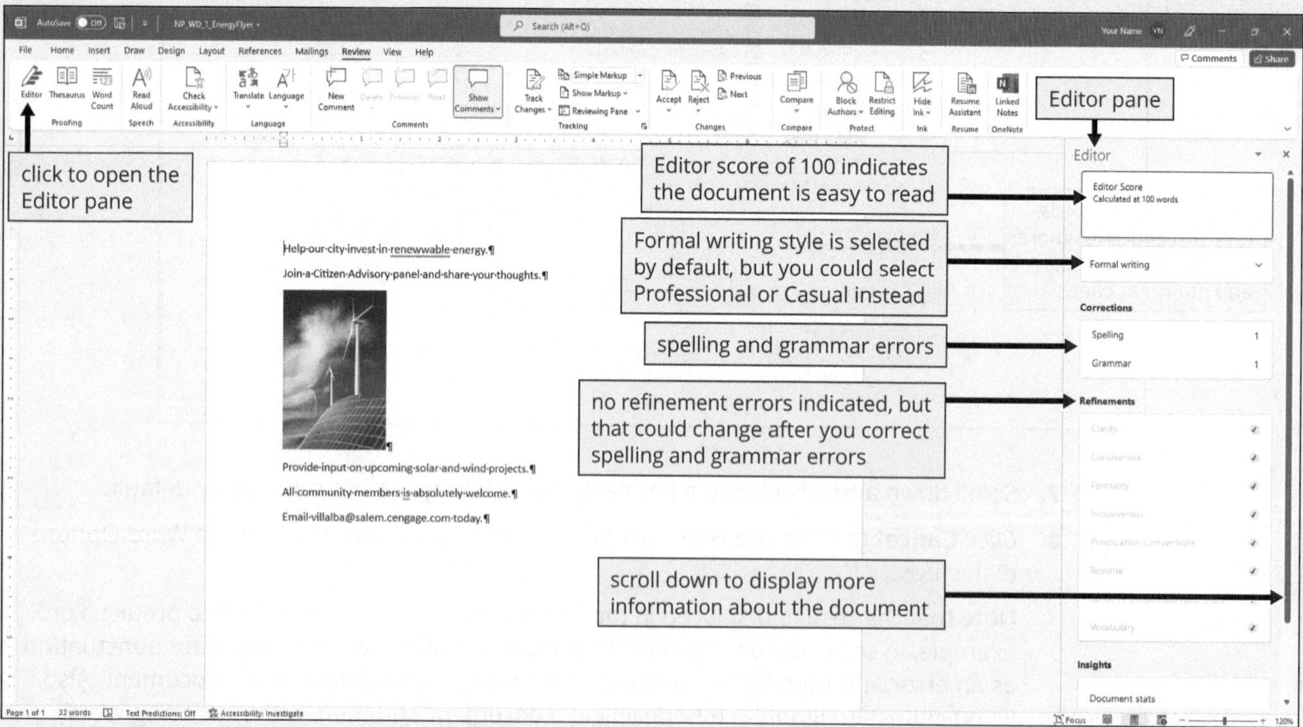

iStock.com/DaveAlan

Depending on the size of your monitor, you might have to scroll down to see all the parts of the Editor pane listed here:

- **Editor Score**—This score indicates how easy the document is to read on a scale of 1 to 100, with 1 meaning difficult to read and 100 meaning easy to read.
- **"How formal will this document be?" list box**—This setting determines how the Editor evaluates the document text. "Formal writing" is selected by default, indicating that the Editor is applying all the grammar and refinement rules selected in the Grammar Settings dialog box you reviewed earlier. You could click the arrow and select "Professional" (which applies most of the selected grammar and refinement rules) or "Casual" (which applies the fewest grammar and refinement rules) instead.
- **Corrections**—This section lists the number of spelling and grammar errors.
- **Refinements**—This section may indicate potential ways to improve the document text. The suggestions here may change after you correct any grammar and spelling errors.
- **Similarity**—Clicking "Check for similarity to online sources" initiates an online search for text that matches the document text. This can be useful if you suspect you are reviewing a document that contains text taken from another source without a citation. Note that this option might not be available in your installation of Word.
- **Insights**—You can click "Document stats" to view statistics about the current document, such as word and character counts and readability statistics.

To finish checking the document for spelling and grammar errors:

1. Scroll back up to the top of the Editor pane, if necessary, and then, in the Corrections box, click **Spelling**. Now the Editor pane displays information about the first error. As in the document, the word "renewwable" is underlined in red as a possible spelling error. To the right of the sentence in the Editor pane is a speaker icon, which you can click to hear the sentence read aloud. Below, in the Suggestions box, is the correctly spelled word "renewable." You might also see the definition of "renewable." The incorrectly spelled word "renewwable" is also highlighted in gray in the document. Note that below the Suggestions list, you also have the option to ignore the highlighted error once, ignore it every time it appears in the document, or add it to Word's dictionary. Refer to Figure 1–27.

Figure 1–27 Correcting errors in the Editor pane

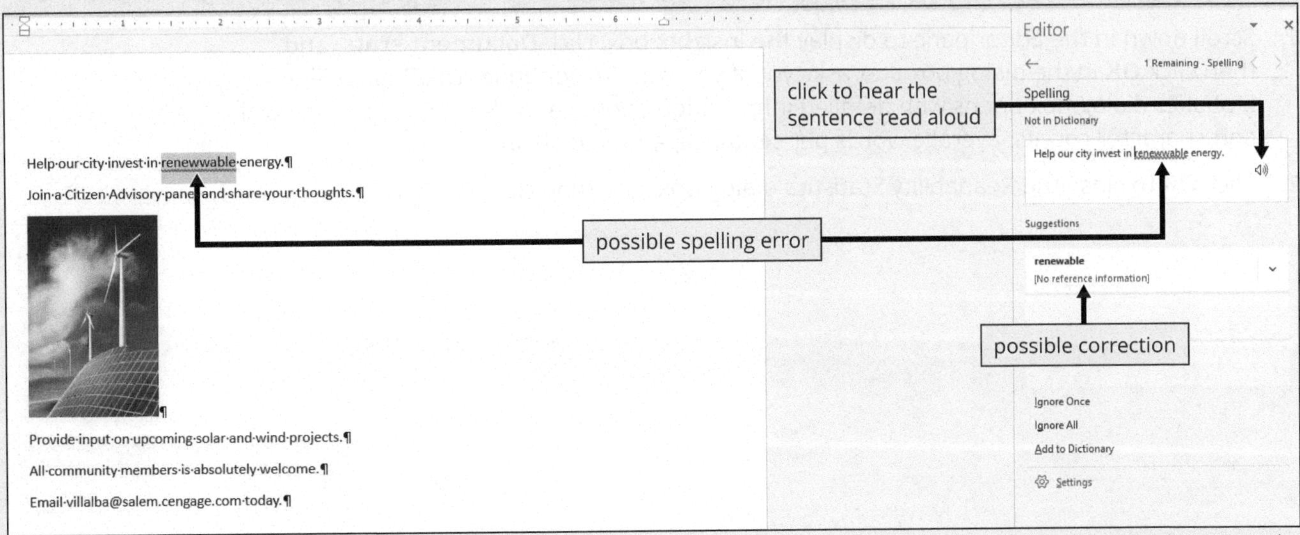

iStock.com/DaveAlan

2. In the Editor pane, click the arrow next to "renewable" in the Suggestions list. A menu of options allows you to hear the correction read aloud or spelled out, change all instances of the highlighted word in the document to "renewable," or add the highlighted word to the list of words that should be corrected automatically using the AutoCorrect feature.
3. Press **Esc** to close the menu, and then click the **renewable** suggestion. The misspelled word "renewwable" is replaced with "renewable," and "Grammar" is selected in the Corrections box, indicating that Word is ready to correct the grammar error next. Note that Word does not always correct errors in the order they are listed in the Editor pane; sometimes it's necessary to scroll up or down in the Editor pane to make sure you have responded to every error.
4. In the Corrections box, click **Grammar**. Word highlights the word "is" in the second to last paragraph, indicating another possible error. The explanation near the top of the pane indicates that Word has detected a problem related to using a singular or plural word.
5. In the Suggestions list, click **are**. The Refinements box now indicates that the document contains one conciseness error.
6. In the Refinements box, click **Conciseness**. In the document, Word highlights the phrase "absolutely welcome."
7. In Suggestions list in the Editor pane, click **welcome**. Word deletes the unnecessary word "absolutely," and a dialog box opens, indicating that you have finished reviewing the Editor's suggestions.

   Tip For any type of error, if the Editor pane does not display the correction you want, you can click the highlighted word in the document, type a correction, and then click Resume in the Editor pane.

8. Click **OK** to close the dialog box.

To review a document's readability statistics and learn even more about a document, you can use Editor pane's Insights box. Leonel wants you to try that now.

To review the document's readability statistics:

1. Scroll down in the Editor pane to display the Insights box, click **Document stats**, and then click **OK** in the dialog box that asks you if you want to continue. The Readability Statistics dialog box opens with detailed information about Leonel's flyer, including word and character counts, average words per sentence, and readability statistics.
2. Click **OK** to close the Readability Statistics dialog box, and then close the Editor pane.

Proskills

Written Communication: Proofreading Your Document

The many Grammar & Refinements options in the Grammar Settings dialog box allow you to fine-tune the issues you want the Editor to focus on. For example, you could use the Inclusiveness options to check for ethnic slurs or terms that make unnecessary assumptions about age, gender, and other issues. The Editor only makes suggestions, which you are free to accept or ignore. If you selected the Gender Bias check box, for example, the Editor would suggest replacing "mailman" with "mail carrier." Note that the items flagged by the Editor in response to your selections in the Grammar Settings dialog box may not be consistent from one document to another.

But no matter how carefully you adjust the options in the Grammar Settings dialog box, the Editor won't always catch every error in a document, and it sometimes flags "errors" that are actually correct. This means there is no substitute for careful proofreading. Always take the time to read through your document to check for errors the Editor pane might have missed. Keep in mind that the Editor pane cannot pinpoint inaccurate phrases or poorly chosen words. You'll have to find those yourself. To produce a professional document, you must read it carefully several times. It's a good idea to ask one or two other people to read your documents as well; they might catch something you missed.

Also keep in mind that the Readability scores displayed in the bottom section of the Readability Statistics dialog box are not always accurate, especially for a document like Leonel's flyer, which consists of short, one-sentence paragraphs. Ultimately, it's up to you to make sure your document is written at a level that your intended audience can understand.

You still need to proofread the document. You'll do that next.

To proofread the document:

1. Review the document text for any remaining errors. In the second paragraph, change the lowercase "p" in "panel" to an uppercase "P."
2. In the last line of text, replace "villalba" with your last name, and then save the document. Including your name in the document will make it easier for you to find your copy later if you print it on a shared printer.

Now you're ready to begin formatting the document. You will start by turning the page so it is wider than it is tall. In other words, you will change the document's **orientation**.

Changing Page Orientation

Portrait orientation, with the page taller than it is wide, is the default page orientation for Word documents because it is the orientation most commonly used for letters, reports, and other formal documents. However, Leonel wants you to format the flyer in **landscape orientation**—that is, with the page turned so it is wider than it is tall—to better accommodate the photo. You can accomplish this task by using the Orientation button located on the Layout tab on the ribbon. After you change the page orientation, you will select narrower margins so you can maximize the amount of color on the page.

To change the page orientation:

1. Change the document Zoom level to **One Page** so you can see the entire document.
2. On the ribbon, click the **Layout** tab. The ribbon changes to display options for formatting the overall layout of text and images in the document.
3. In the Page Setup group, click the **Orientation** button, and then click **Landscape** on the menu. The document changes to landscape orientation.
4. In the Page Setup group, click the **Margins** button, and then click the **Narrow** option on the menu. The margins shrink from 1 inch to .5 inch on all four sides. Refer to Figure 1–28.

Figure 1–28 Document in landscape orientation with narrow margins

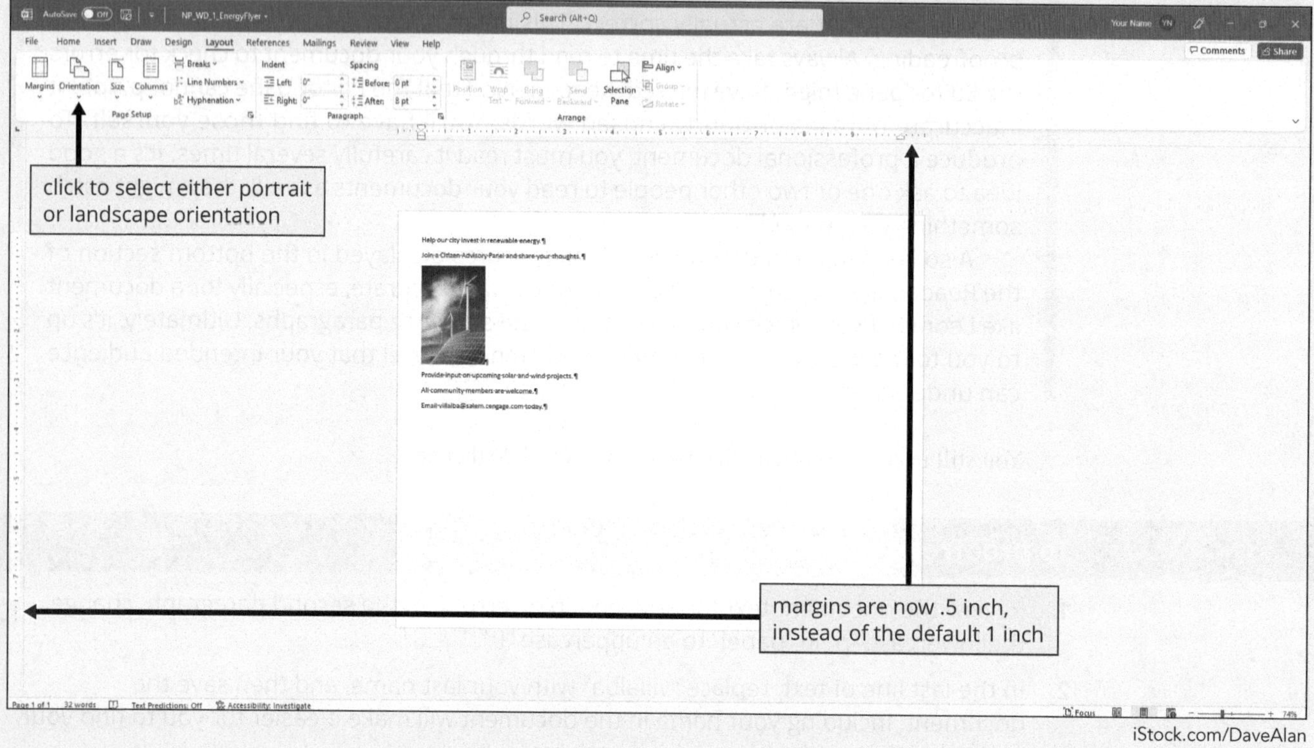

iStock.com/DaveAlan

Changing the Font and Font Size

Leonel typed the document in the default font size, 11 point, and the default font, Calibri, but he would like to switch to the Arial font instead. Also, he wants to increase the size of all five paragraphs of text. To apply these changes, you start by selecting the text you want to format. Then you select the options you want in the Font group on the Home tab.

To change the font and font size:

1. Change the document Zoom level to **120%**.
2. On the ribbon, click the **Home** tab.
3. To verify that the insertion point is located at the beginning of the document, press **CTRL+HOME**.
4. Press and hold **SHIFT**, and then click to the right of the second paragraph marker, at the end of the second paragraph of text. The first two paragraphs of text are selected, as shown in Figure 1–29.

Figure 1–29 Selected text, with default font displayed in Font box

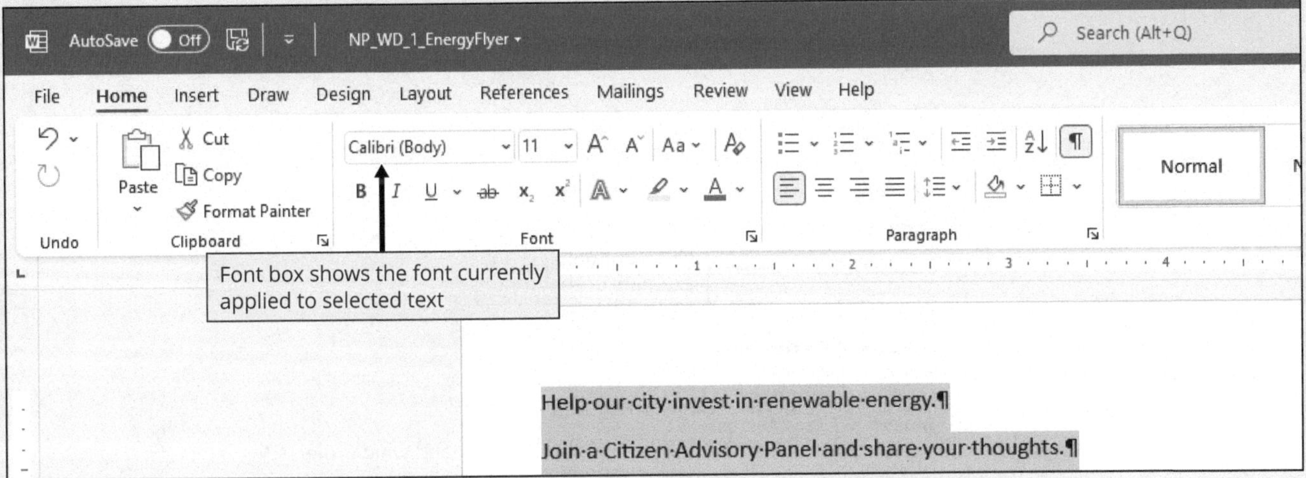

The Font box in the Font group displays the name of the font applied to the selected text, which in this case is Calibri. The word "Body" next to the font name indicates that the Calibri font is intended for formatting body text. **Body text** is ordinary text, as opposed to titles or headings.

5. In the Font group on the Home tab, click the **Font arrow**. A list of available fonts appears, with Calibri Light and Calibri at the top of the list. Calibri is highlighted in gray, indicating that this font is currently applied to the selected text. The word "Headings" next to the font name "Calibri Light" indicates that Calibri Light is intended for formatting headings.

   Below Calibri Light and Calibri, you might see a list of fonts that have been used recently on your computer, followed by a complete alphabetical list of all available fonts. (You won't see the list of recently used fonts if you just installed Word.) You need to scroll the list to see all the available fonts. Each name in the list is formatted with the relevant font. For example, the name "Arial" appears in the Arial font. Refer to Figure 1–30.

Figure 1–30 Font list

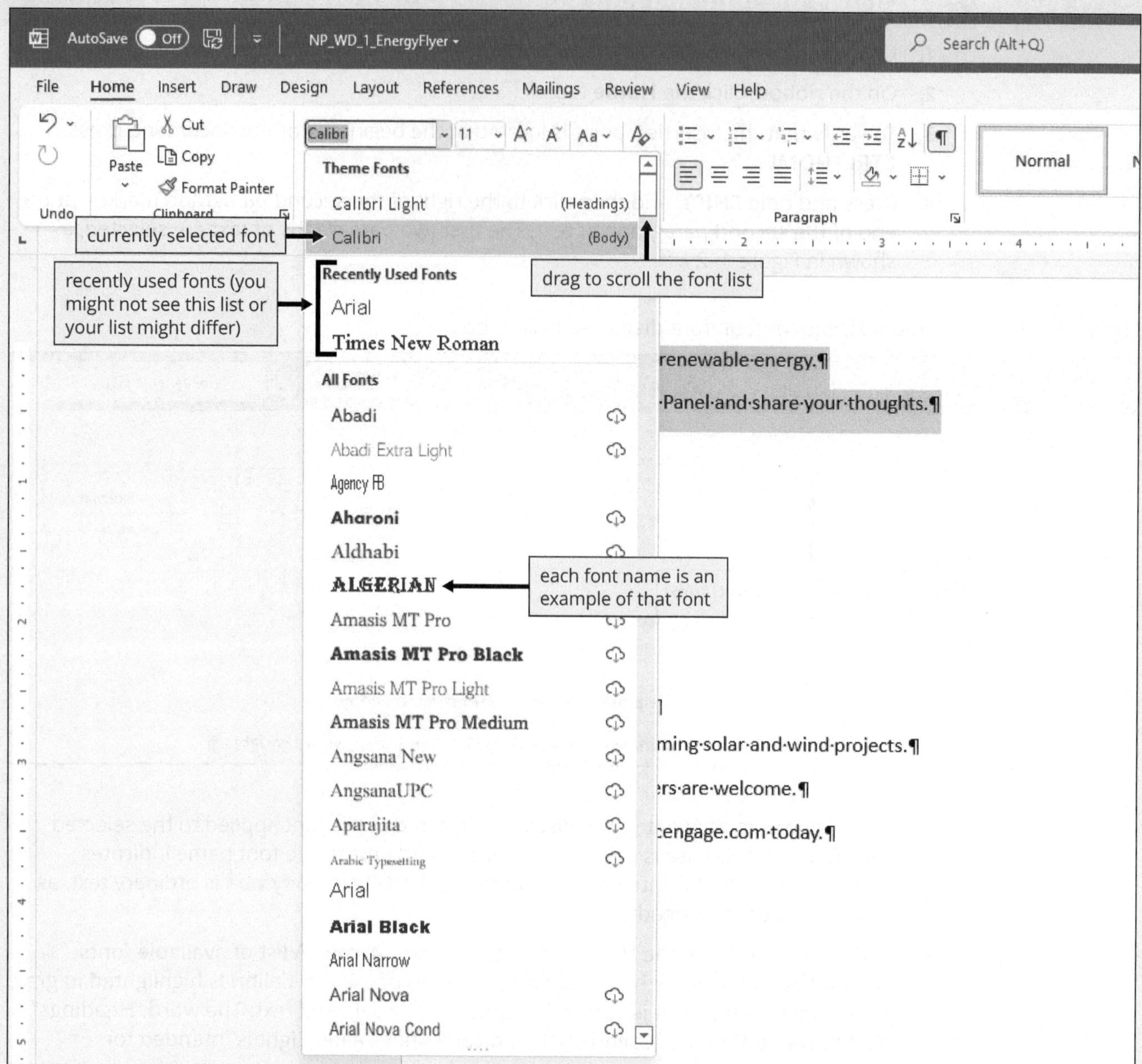

6. Without clicking, move the pointer over a dramatic-looking font in the font list, such as Algerian or Arial Black, and then move the pointer over another font.

   The selected text in the document changes to show a Live Preview of the font the pointer is resting on. **Live Preview** shows the results that would occur in your document if you clicked the option you are pointing to.

7. When you are finished reviewing the Font list, click **Arial**. The Font menu closes, and the selected text is formatted in Arial.

   Next, you will make the text more eye-catching by increasing the font size. The Font Size box currently displays the number "11," indicating that the selected text is formatted in 11-point font.

8. Verify that the first two paragraphs are still selected, and then click the **Font Size arrow** in the Font group to display a menu of font sizes. As with the Font menu, you can move the pointer over options in the Font Size menu to display a Live Preview of that option in the document.
9. On the Font Size menu, click **22**. The selected text increases significantly in size, and the Font Size menu closes.
10. Select the three paragraphs of text below the photo, format them in the Arial font, and then increase the paragraph's font size to 22 points.
11. Click a blank area of the document to deselect the text, and then save the document.

Keep in mind that to restore selected text to its default appearance, you can click the Clear All Formatting button in the Font group on the Home tab.

Leonel examines the flyer and decides he would like to apply more character formatting, which affects the appearance of individual characters, in the middle three paragraphs. After that, you can turn your attention to paragraph formatting, which affects the appearance of the entire paragraph.

Applying Text Effects, Font Colors, and Font Styles

For formal, professional documents, you typically only need to use **bold** or *italic* to make a word or paragraph stand out. Occasionally you might need to underline a word. To apply these forms of character formatting, select the text you want to format, and then click the Bold, Italic, or Underline button in the Font group on the Home tab. To really make text stand out, you can use text effects. You access these options by clicking the Text Effects and Typography button in the Font group on the Home tab. Keep in mind that text effects can be very dramatic.

Leonel suggests applying text effects to the second paragraph.

To apply text effects to the second paragraph:

1. Scroll up, if necessary, to display the beginning of the document, and then click in the selection bar to the left of the second paragraph. The entire second paragraph is selected.
2. In the Font group on the Home tab, click the **Text Effects and Typography** button [A].

   A gallery of text effects appears. Options that allow you to fine-tune a particular text effect, perhaps by changing the color or adding an even more pronounced shadow, are listed below the gallery. A **gallery** is a menu or grid that shows a visual representation of the options available when you click a button.
3. Place the pointer over the blue letter "A." This displays a ScreenTip with the text effect's full name: Fill: Blue, Accent color 5; Outline: White, Background color 1; Hard Shadow: Blue, Accent color 5. A Live Preview of the effect appears in the document. Refer to Figure 1–31.

Figure 1–31 Live Preview of a text effect

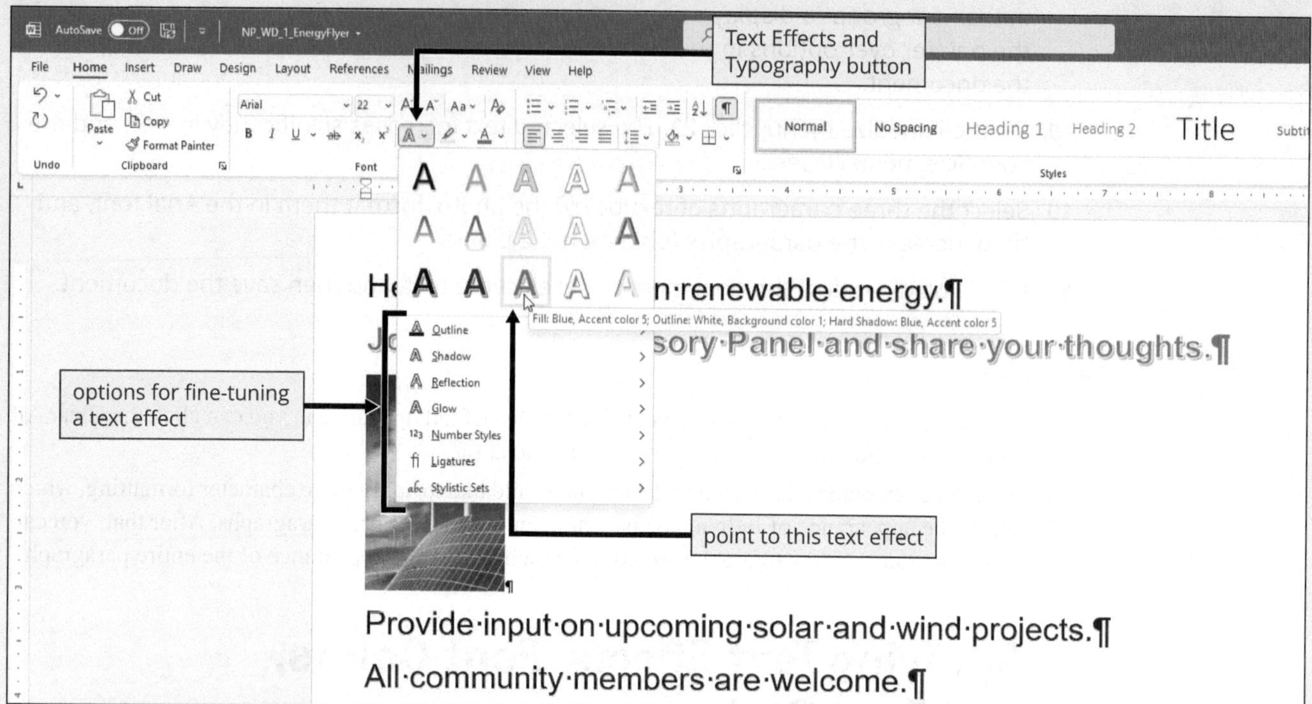

iStock.com/DaveAlan

4. Click the blue letter "A." The text effect is applied to the selected paragraph, and the Text Effects gallery closes. The second paragraph is formatted in blue with a white outline, as shown in the Part 1.2 Visual Overview. On the ribbon, the Bold button in the Font group is now highlighted because bold formatting is part of this text effect.

   Next, to make the text stand out a bit more, you'll increase the font size. This time, instead of using the Font Size button, you'll use a different method.

5. In the Font group, click the **Increase Font Size** button. The font size increases from 22 points to 24 points, which is the next higher font size on the Font menu.
6. Click the **Increase Font Size** button again. The font size increases to 26 points, which is the next higher font size on the Font menu. If you need to decrease the font size of selected text, you can use the Decrease Font Size button. Each time you click the Decrease Font Size button, the font decreases to the next lower font size on the Font menu.

Leonel asks you to emphasize the third and fourth paragraphs by adding bold and a blue font color.

To apply a font color and bold:

1. Select the third and fourth paragraphs of text, which contain the text "Provide input on upcoming solar and wind projects. All community members are welcome."
2. In the Font group on the Home tab, click the **Font Color arrow**. A gallery of font colors appears. Black is the default font color and appears at the top of the Font Color gallery, with the word "Automatic" next to it.

   The options in the Theme Colors section of the menu are complementary colors that work well when used together in a document. The options in the Standard Colors section are more limited. For more advanced color options, you could use the More Colors or Gradient options. Leonel prefers a simple blue.

   Trouble? If the third and fourth paragraphs turned red, you clicked the Font Color button instead of the arrow next to it. On the Quick Access Toolbar, click the Undo button, and then repeat Step 2.

3. In the Theme Colors section, place the pointer over the square that's second from the right in the top row. A ScreenTip with the color's name, "Blue, Accent 5," appears. A Live Preview of the color appears in the document, where the text you selected in Step 1 now appears formatted in blue. Refer to Figure 1–32.

Figure 1–32 Font Color gallery showing a Live Preview

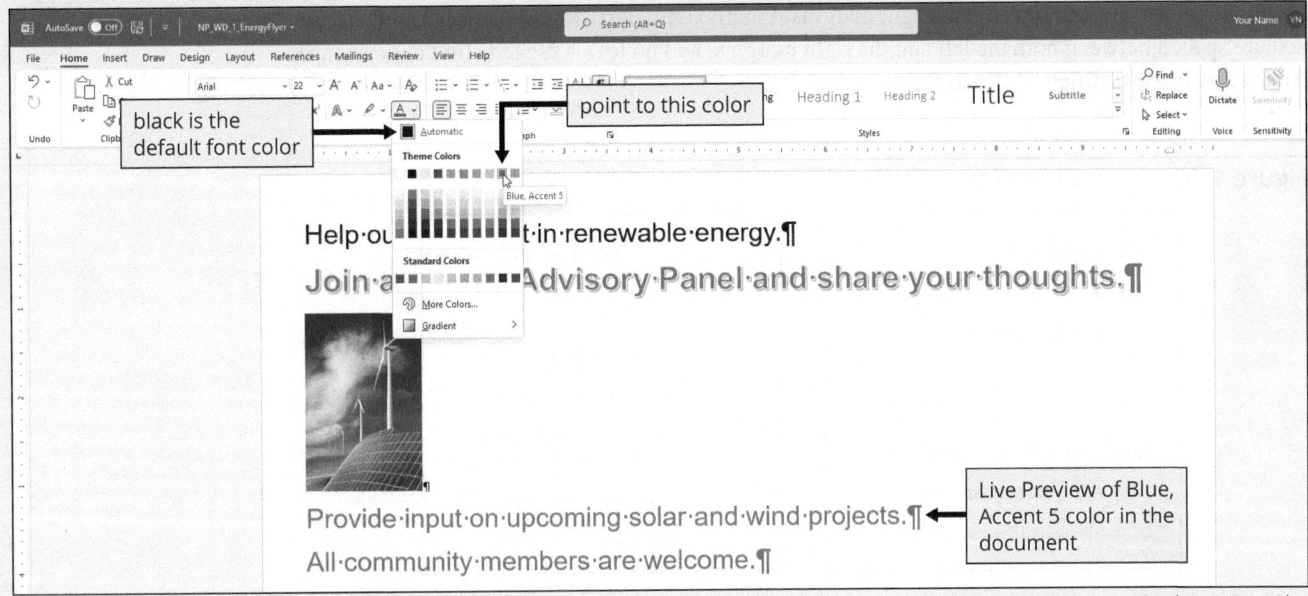

iStock.com/DaveAlan

4. Click the **Blue, Accent 5** square. The Font color gallery closes, and the selected text is formatted in blue. On the Font Color button, the bar below the letter "A" is now blue, indicating that if you select text and click the Font Color button, the text will automatically change to blue.
5. In the Font group, click the **Bold** button B. The selected text is now formatted in bold, with thicker, darker lettering.

Insight

Working with Theme Colors

You can display the name of a color by pointing to it. The colors in the top row of the Theme Colors section have names related to how Microsoft suggests using each color. For example, the white square in the top row (first on the left) is named "White, Background 1," and the light gray square in the top row (third from the left) is named "Gray, Background 2." This means they make good background colors in a document. The black square (second from the left in the top row), which is named "Black, Text 1," is the only theme color recommended for text. The remaining colors are considered good options for accent colors. For example, the green square (first on the right), is named "Green, Accent 6."

You will learn more about theme colors as you become a more experienced Word user. But for now, just keep in mind that the recommendations implied by the color names are just suggestions, and an informal document, like the flyer you are working on now, is a perfect opportunity to use accent colors for text. However, to make your document easy to read, it's important use a darker version of each theme color for text. The Theme Colors section in the color palette provide an array of colors in lighter and darker shades, with names that make that clear. For example, the light green square in the second row of the Themes color section (first on the right) is named "Green, Accent 6, Lighter 80%," while the dark green square in the bottom row of the Theme Colors section (first on the right), is named "Green, Accent 6, Darker 50%."

Next, you will complete some paragraph formatting, starting with paragraph alignment.

Aligning Text

Alignment refers to how text and graphics line up between the page margins. By default, text is **left-aligned** in Word. That is, the text is flush with the left margin, with the text along the right margin **ragged**, or uneven. By contrast, **right-aligned** text is aligned along the right margin and is ragged along the left margin. **Centered** text is positioned evenly between the left and right margins and is ragged along both the left and right margins. Finally, with **justified alignment**, full lines of text are spaced between both the left and the right margins, and no text is ragged. Text in newspaper columns is often justified. Refer to Figure 1–33.

Figure 1–33 Varieties of text alignment

left alignment
The term "alignment" refers to the way a paragraph lines up between the margins. The term "alignment" refers to the way a paragraph lines up between the margins.

right alignment
The term "alignment" refers to the way a paragraph lines up between the margins. The term "alignment" refers to the way a paragraph lines up between the margins.

center alignment
The term "alignment" refers to the way a paragraph lines up between the margins.

justified alignment
The term "alignment" refers to the way a paragraph lines up between the margins. The term "alignment" refers to the way a paragraph lines up between the margins.

The Paragraph group on the Home tab includes a button for each of the four major types of alignment described in Figure 1–33: the Align Left button, the Center button, the Align Right button, and the Justify button. To align a single paragraph, click anywhere in that paragraph, and then click the appropriate alignment button. To align multiple paragraphs, select the paragraphs first, and then click an alignment button.

You need to center all the text in the flyer now. You can center the photo at the same time.

To center-align the text:

1. Make sure the Home tab is still selected, and press **CTRL+A** to select the entire document.

   Key Step Use CTRL+A to select the entire document, instead of dragging the pointer. It's easy to miss part of the document when you drag the pointer.

2. In the Paragraph group, click the **Center** button, and then click a blank area of the document to deselect the selected paragraphs. The text and photo are now centered on the page, similar to the centered text shown earlier in the Part 1.2 Visual Overview.
3. Save the document.

Adding a Paragraph Border and Shading

A **paragraph border** is an outline that appears around one or more paragraphs in a document. You can choose to apply only a partial border—for example, a bottom border that appears as an underline under the last line of text in the paragraph—or an entire box around a paragraph. You can select different colors and line weights for the border as well, making it more or less prominent as needed. You apply paragraph borders using the Borders button in the Paragraph group on the Home tab. **Shading** is background color that you can apply to one or more paragraphs and that can be used in conjunction with a border for a more defined effect. You apply shading using the Shading button in the Paragraph group on the Home tab.

Now you will apply a border and shading to the first paragraph, as shown earlier in the Part 1.2 Visual Overview. Then you will use the Format Painter to copy this formatting to the last paragraph in the document.

To add shading and a paragraph border:

1. Scroll up if necessary and select the first paragraph. Be sure to select the paragraph mark at the end of the paragraph.
2. On the Home tab, in the Paragraph group, click the **Borders arrow**. A gallery of border options appears, as shown in Figure 1–34. To apply a complete outline around the selected text, you use the Outside Borders option.

Figure 1–34 Border gallery

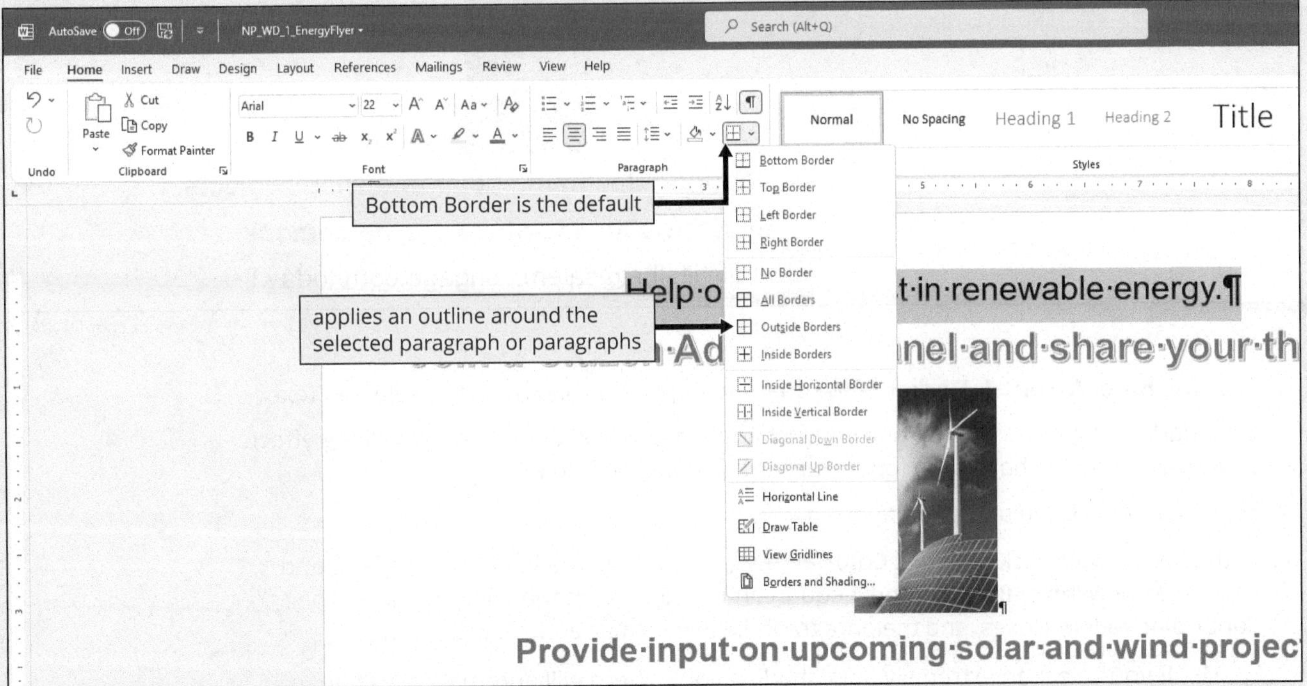

iStock.com/DaveAlan

> **Trouble?** If the gallery does not open and instead the paragraph becomes underlined with a single underline, you clicked the Borders button instead of the arrow next to it. On the Quick Access Toolbar, click the Undo button, and then repeat Step 2.

3. In the Border gallery, click **Outside Borders**. The menu closes and a black border appears around the selected paragraph, spanning the width of the page. In the Paragraph group, the Borders button changes to show the Outside Borders option.

Trouble? If the border around the first paragraph doesn't extend all the way to the left and right margins and instead encloses only the text, you didn't select the paragraph mark as directed in Step 1. Click the Undo button repeatedly to remove the border, and begin again with Step 1.

4. In the Paragraph group, click the **Shading arrow**. A gallery of shading options opens, divided into Theme Colors and Standard Colors. You will use a shade of dark blue in the fifth column from the left.
5. In the bottom row in the Theme Colors section, move the pointer over the square in the fifth column from the left to display a ScreenTip that reads "Blue, Accent 1, Darker 50%." A Live Preview of the color appears in the document. Refer to Figure 1–35.

Figure 1–35 Shading gallery with a Live Preview displayed

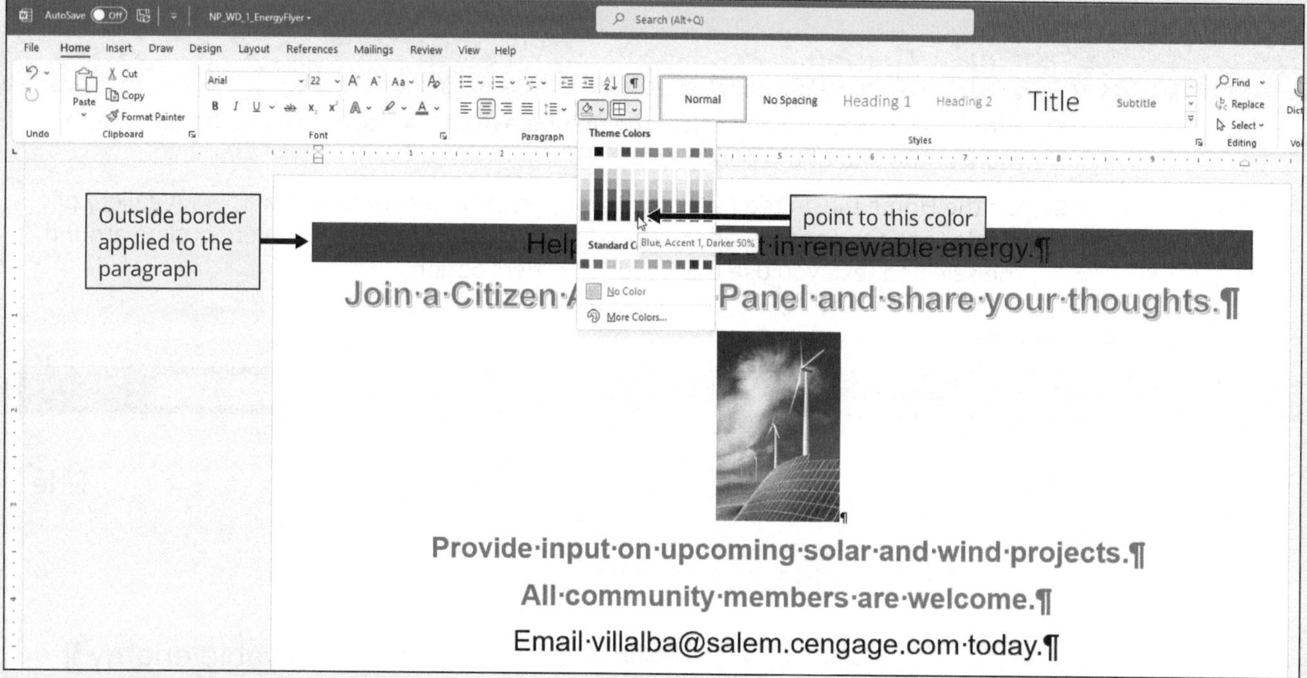

iStock.com/DaveAlan

6. Click the **Blue, Accent 1, Darker 50%** square to apply the shading to the selected text.

   On a dark background like the one you just applied, a white font creates a striking effect. Leonel asks you to change the font color for this paragraph to white.
7. Make sure the Home tab is still selected.
8. In the Font group, click the **Font Color arrow** to open the Font Color gallery, and then click the **White, Background 1** square in the top row of the Theme Colors. The Font Color gallery closes, and the paragraph is now formatted with white font.

   Tip If you select an extremely dark shading color, Word will automatically change the font color to white.

   The black paragraph border is hard to distinguish from the dark blue shading, so you will change the border to a different color. To make more advanced changes to borders or paragraph shading, you need to use the Borders and Shading dialog box.
9. Click the **Borders arrow** and then, at the bottom of the menu, click **Borders and Shading**. The Borders and Shading dialog box opens with the Borders tab displayed.
10. Click the **Color arrow** to open the Color gallery, and then click the **Gold, Accent 4** square, which is the third square from the right in the top row of the Theme Colors section.

    Next, to make the border more noticeable, you will increase its width.

11. Click the **Width arrow**, and then click **3 pt**. At this point, the settings in your Borders and Shading dialog box should match the settings in Figure 1–36.

Figure 1–36 Borders and Shading dialog box

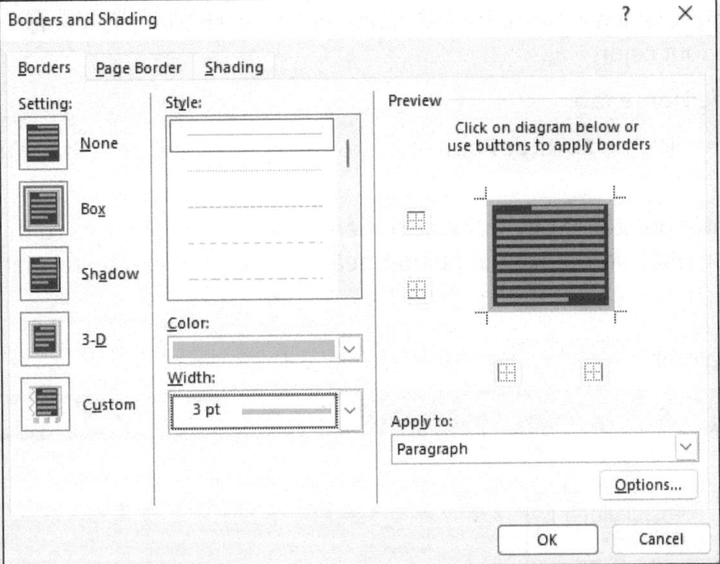

12. Click **OK** to close the Borders and Shading dialog box and return to the document.
13. Click a blank area of the document to deselect the text, review the change, and then save the document. The first paragraph is now formatted with a gold border, a dark blue background, and white text as shown in the Part 1.2 Visual Overview.

To add balance to the flyer, Leonel suggests formatting the last paragraph in the document with the same shading, border, and font color as the first paragraph. You'll do that next.

Copying Formatting with the Format Painter

You could select the last paragraph and then apply the border, shading, and font color one step at a time. But it's easier to copy all the formatting from the first paragraph to the last paragraph using the Format Painter button in the Clipboard group on the Home tab.

Reference

Using the Format Painter

- Select the text whose formatting you want to copy.
- On the Home tab, in the Clipboard group, click the Format Painter button, or to copy formatting to multiple sections of nonadjacent text, double-click the Format Painter button.
- The pointer changes to the Format Painter pointer, the I-beam pointer with a paintbrush.
- Click the words you want to format, or drag to select and format entire paragraphs.
- When you are finished formatting the text, click the Format Painter button again to turn off the Format Painter.

You'll use the Format Painter now.

To use the Format Painter:

1. Change the document Zoom level to **One Page** so you can easily see both the first and last paragraphs.
2. Select the first paragraph, which is formatted with the dark blue shading, the gold border, and the white font color.
3. On the ribbon, click the **Home** tab.
4. In the Clipboard group, click the **Format Painter** button to activate, or turn on, the Format Painter.
5. Move the Format Painter pointer over the document. The pointer changes to the Format Painter pointer when you move the pointer near an item that can be formatted. Refer to Figure 1–37.

Figure 1–37 Format Painter

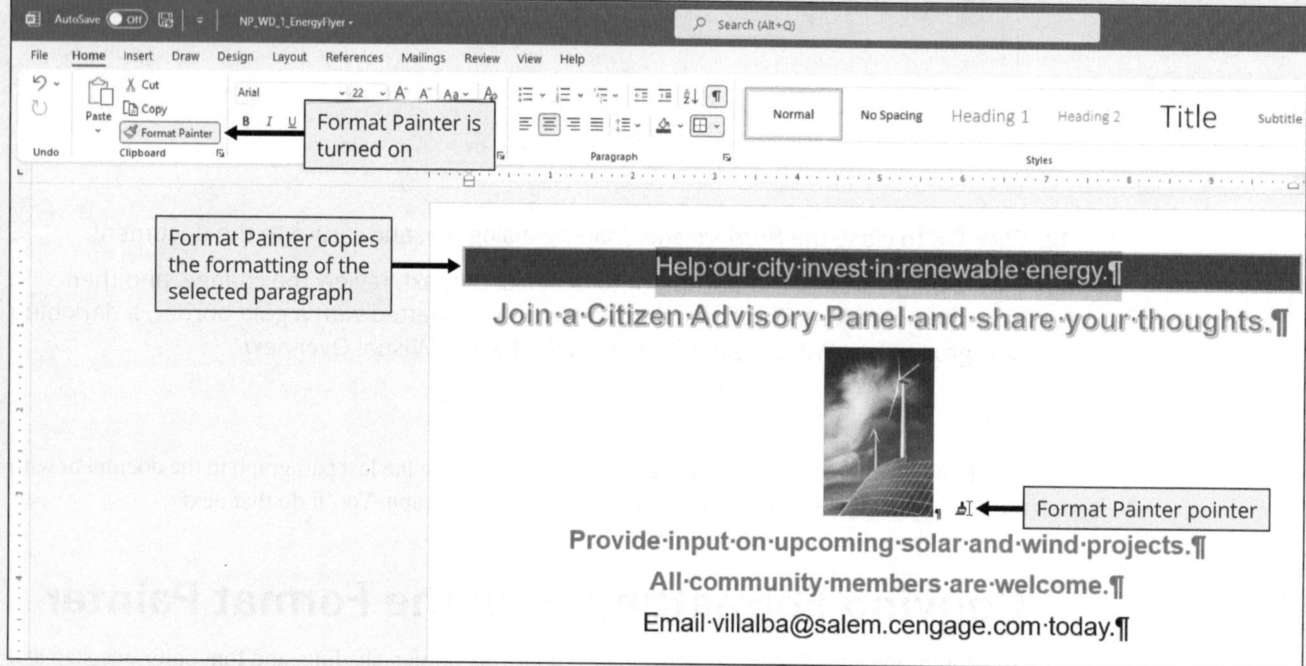

iStock.com/DaveAlan

6. Click and drag the Format Painter pointer to select the last paragraph in the document. The paragraph is now formatted with dark blue shading, a gold border, and white font. The pointer returns to its original I-beam shape.

   Trouble? If the text in the newly formatted paragraph wrapped to a second line, replace your last name with your first name, or, if necessary, use only your initials so the paragraph is only one-line long.

   Tip To turn off the Format Painter without using it, press ESC.

7. Click anywhere in the document to deselect the text, review the change, and then save the document.

Your next task is to increase the paragraph spacing below the first paragraph and above the last paragraph. This will give the shaded text even more weight on the page. To complete this task, you will use the settings on the Layout tab, which offer more options than the Line and Paragraph Spacing button on the Home tab.

To increase the paragraph spacing below the first paragraph and above the last paragraph:

1. Click anywhere in the first paragraph, and then click the **Layout** tab. On this tab, the Paragraph group contains settings that control paragraph spacing. Currently, the paragraph spacing for the first paragraph is set to the default 0 points before the paragraph and 8 points after.
2. In the Paragraph group, click the **After** box to select the current setting, type **42**, and then press **ENTER**. The added space causes the second paragraph to move down 42 points.
3. Click anywhere in the last paragraph.
4. On the Layout tab, in the Paragraph group, click the **Before** box to select the current setting, type **42**, and then press **ENTER**. The added space causes the last paragraph to move down 42 points.

Insight

Formatting Professional Documents

In more formal documents, use color and special effects sparingly. The goal of letters, reports, and many other types of documents is to convey important information, not to dazzle the reader with fancy fonts and colors. Such elements only serve to distract the reader from your main point, and can make documents difficult for people with dyslexia to read. So generally, it's a good idea to limit the number of colors to two and to stick with left alignment for text. In a document like the flyer you're currently working on, you have a little more leeway because the goal of the document is to attract attention. However, you still want it to look professional.

Next, Leonel wants you to replace the photo with one that will look better in the document's new landscape orientation. You'll replace the photo, and then you'll resize it so that the flyer fills the entire page.

Inserting a Picture and Adding Alt Text

A **picture** is a photo or another type of image that you insert into a document. To work with a picture, you first need to select it. Once a picture is selected, a contextual tab—the Picture Format tab—appears on the ribbon, with options for editing the picture and adding effects such as a border, a shadow, a reflection, or a new shape. A **contextual tab** appears on the ribbon only when an object is selected. It contains commands related to the selected object so that you can manipulate, edit, and format the selected object. You can also use the mouse to resize or move a selected picture. To insert a new picture, you use the Pictures button in the Illustrations group on the Insert tab.

To delete the current photo and insert a new one:

1. Click the photo to select it.

   The circles, called **sizing handles**, around the edge of the photo indicate the photo is selected. The Layout Options button, to the right of the photo, gives you access to options that control how the document text flows around the photo. You don't need to worry about these options now. Finally, note that the Picture Format tab appeared on the ribbon when you selected the photo. Refer to Figure 1–38.

Figure 1–38 Selected photo

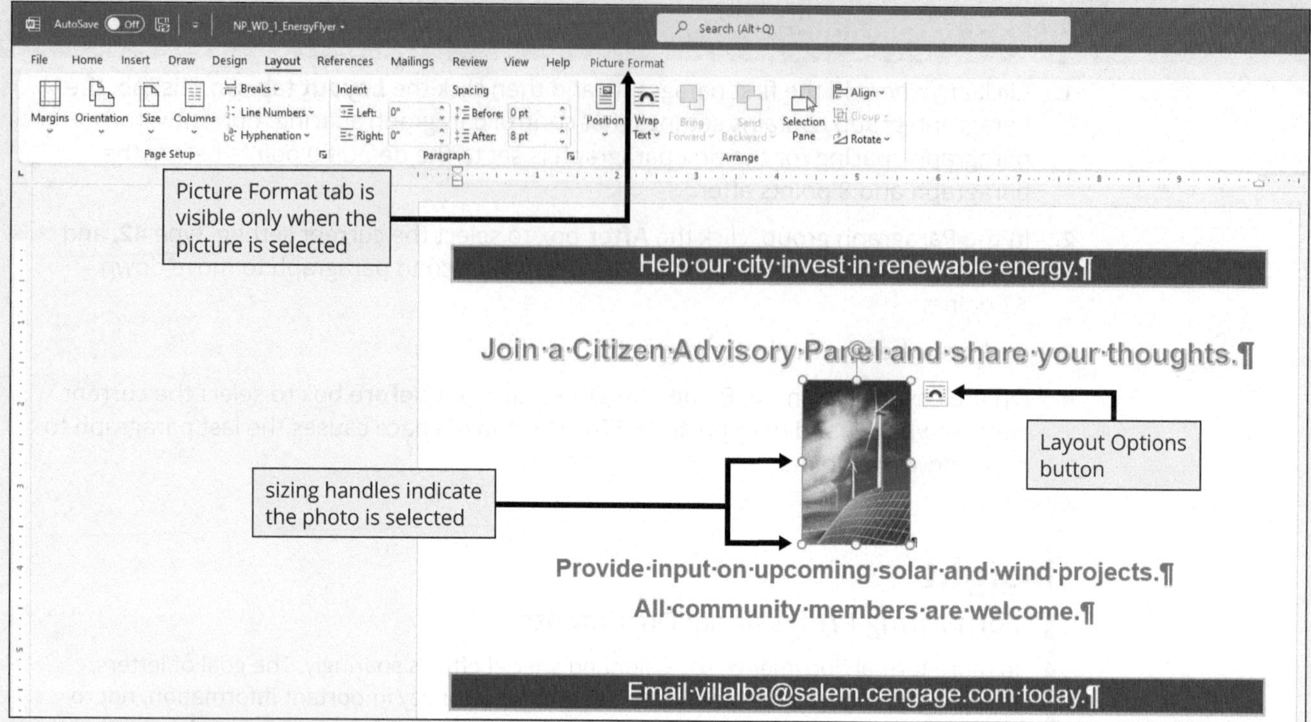
Picture Format tab is visible only when the picture is selected
Help·our·city·invest·in·renewable·energy.¶
Join·a·Citizen·Advisory·Panel·and·share·your·thoughts.¶
Layout Options button
sizing handles indicate the photo is selected
Provide·input·on·upcoming·solar·and·wind·projects.¶
All·community·members·are·welcome.¶
Email·villalba@salem.cengage.com·today.¶

iStock.com/DaveAlan

2. Press **DELETE**. The photo is deleted from the document. The insertion point blinks next to the paragraph symbol.

Now you are ready to insert the new photo in the paragraph containing the insertion point. When you do, you will briefly see a gray box at the bottom of the photo containing a description of the image. This description, which is called **alternative text** (or **alt text**, for short), makes it possible for a screen reader program to read a description of the image aloud. This is useful for people who are blind, visually impaired, or color blind, who would otherwise find it difficult or impossible to see an image. Popular screen reader programs include Freedom Scientific's JAWS and Microsoft Narrator.

Word automatically creates alt text for most photos, although it is often too generic to be really helpful (for example, "Two people"). To refine alt text created by Word so that it accurately describes an image, click the Alt Text button in the Accessibility group on the Picture Format tab. This opens the Alt Text pane, where you can edit the existing alt text. As you become a more experienced Word user, you'll have the chance to create new alt text for charts, tables, and other items. Before you can use automatic alt text, you need to make sure the automatic alt text option is turned on in the Word Options dialog box.

To turn on automatic alt text, insert a new photo, and edit its alt text:

1. Click **File**, and then click **Options** to open the Word Options dialog box with the General tab displayed.
2. In the navigation pane, click **Accessibility**. In the "Automatic Alt Text" section, click the **Automatically generate alt text for me** check box to insert a checkmark, if necessary, and then click **Ok** to close the Word Options dialog box.
3. On the ribbon, click the **Insert** tab. The ribbon changes to display the Insert options.

4. In the Illustrations group, click the **Pictures** button. The Insert Picture From gallery opens.

   Tip To swap one picture for another while retaining the formatting and size of the original, right-click the picture, click Change Picture, click From a File, and then select the photo you want to insert.

5. Click **This Device**. The Insert Picture dialog box opens.
6. Navigate to the **Word1 > Module** folder included with your Data Files, and then click **Support_WD_1_Solar.jpg** to select the file. The name of the selected file appears in the File name box.
7. Click the **Insert** button to close the Insert Picture dialog box and insert the photo. An image of a worker adjusting solar panels appears in the document, below the second paragraph. The photo is selected, as indicated by the sizing handles on its border, and the Picture Format tab is displayed. After a pause, a gray box with the text "Alt Text: A picture . . ." appears as shown in Figure 1–39, remains on the screen for about five seconds, and then disappears.

   Trouble? Don't be concerned if you don't see the gray box with the alt text. On some small monitors, this text doesn't always appear.

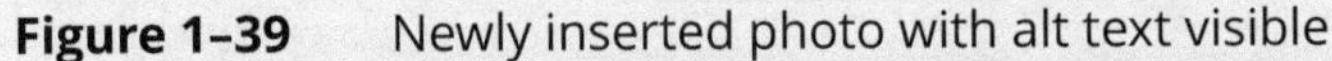

Figure 1–39 Newly inserted photo with alt text visible

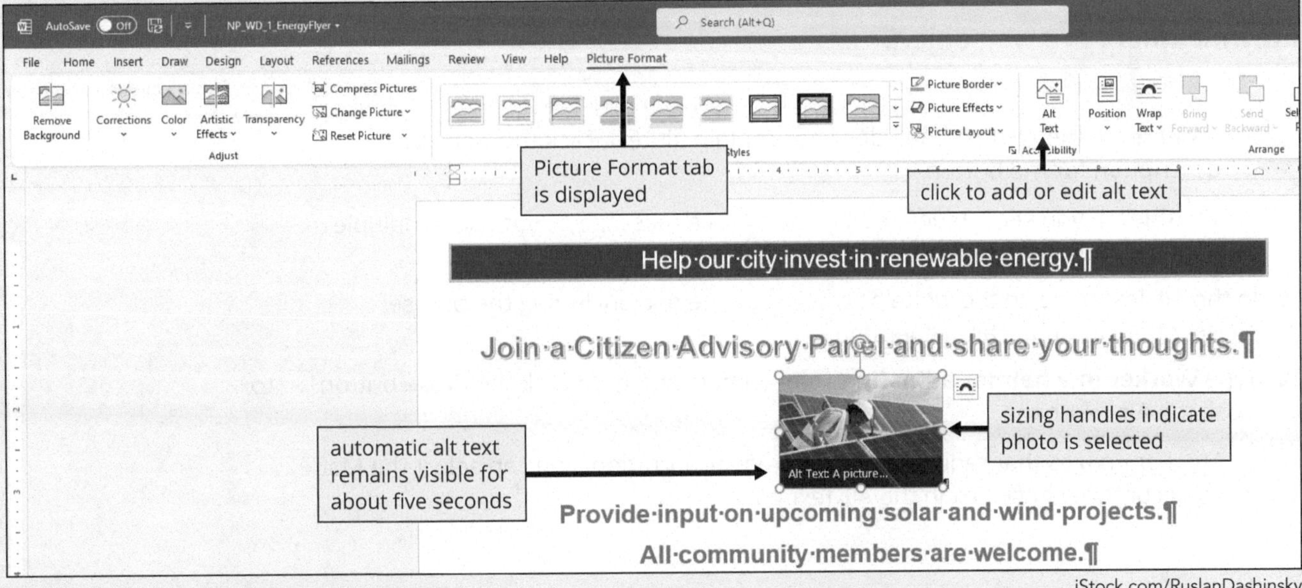

iStock.com/RuslanDashinsky

   Trouble? If you see a blue message box explaining how alt text works, click Got It to close the message box.

8. In the Accessibility group on the ribbon, click the **Alt Text** button to display the Alt Text pane, which displays the current alt text, as well as a note indicating the description was automatically generated. Refer to Figure 1–40.

Figure 1–40 Alt Text pane

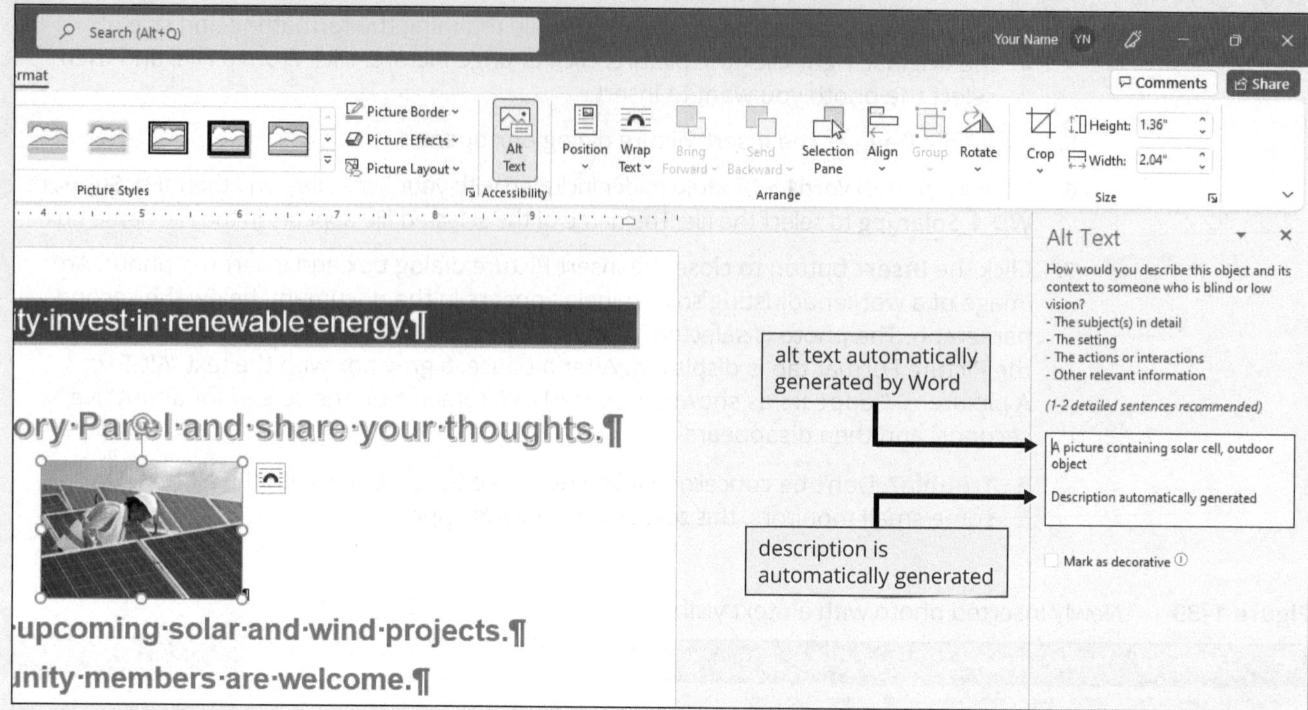

iStock.com/RuslanDashinsky

Trouble? If the Alt Text pane does not contain alt text, click the Generate a description for me button.

Trouble? If you see a blue message box with a message about using multiple panes, click Got It to close the message box.

9. In the Alt Text pane, in the white box, select all the text, including the phrase "Description automatically generated."
10. Type **Worker in a helmet adjusting solar panels** and then click the **Close** button ☒ to close the Alt Text pane.

Tip For images that require no screen reader narration, you can select the Mark as decorative check box in the Alt Text pane.

Now you need to resize the photo so it fills more space on the page. You could do so by clicking one of the picture's corner sizing handles, holding down the mouse button, and then dragging the sizing handle to resize the picture. But using the Shape Height and Shape Width boxes on the Picture Format tab gives you more precise results.

To resize the photo:

1. Make sure the Picture Format tab is still selected on the ribbon.
2. In the Size group on the far-right edge of the ribbon, locate the Shape Height box, which indicates that the height of the selected picture is currently 1.36". The Shape Width box indicates that the width of the picture is 2.04". As you'll see in the next step, when you change one of these measurements, the other changes accordingly, keeping the overall shape of the picture the same. Refer to Figure 1–41.

Figure 1–41 Shape Height and Shape Width boxes

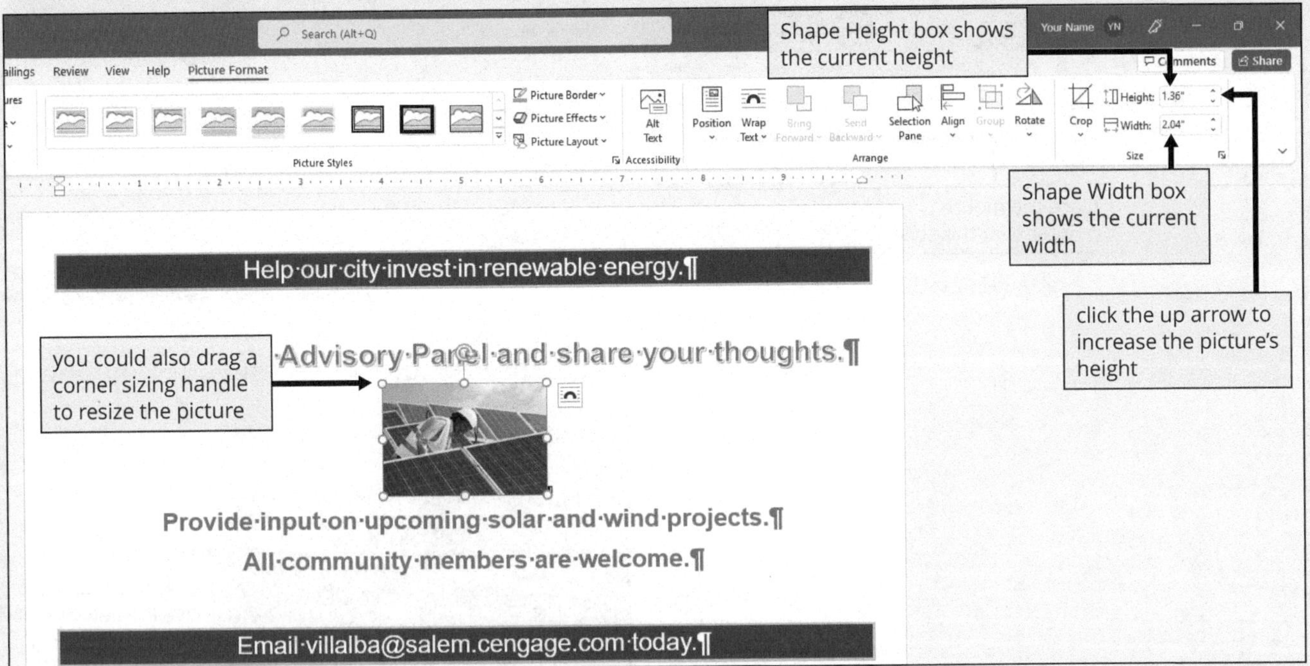

iStock.com/RuslanDashinsky

3. Click the **up arrow** in the Shape Height box in the Size group. The photo increases in size slightly. The measurement in the Shape Height box increases to 1.4", and the measurement in the Shape Width box increases to 2.1".
4. Click the **up arrow** in the Shape Height box repeatedly until the picture is 3.2" tall and 4.8" wide.

Formatting a Picture with a Style

A **picture style** is a collection of formatting options, such as a frame, a rounded shape, and a shadow. You can apply a picture style to a selected picture by clicking the style you want in the Picture Styles gallery on the Picture Format tab. Note that to return a picture to its original appearance, you can click the Reset Picture button in the Adjust group on the Picture Format tab. In the following steps, you'll start by displaying the Picture Styles gallery.

To add a style to the photo:

1. Make sure the Picture Format tab is still selected on the ribbon.
2. In the Picture Styles group, click the **More** button to the right of the Picture Styles gallery to open the gallery and display more picture styles. Some of the picture styles simply add a border, while others change the picture's shape. Other styles combine these options with effects such as a shadow or a reflection.
3. Place the pointer over various styles to observe the Live Previews in the document, and then place the pointer over the Drop Shadow Rectangle style, which is the fourth style from the left in the top row in Figure 1–42.

Figure 1–42 Previewing a picture style

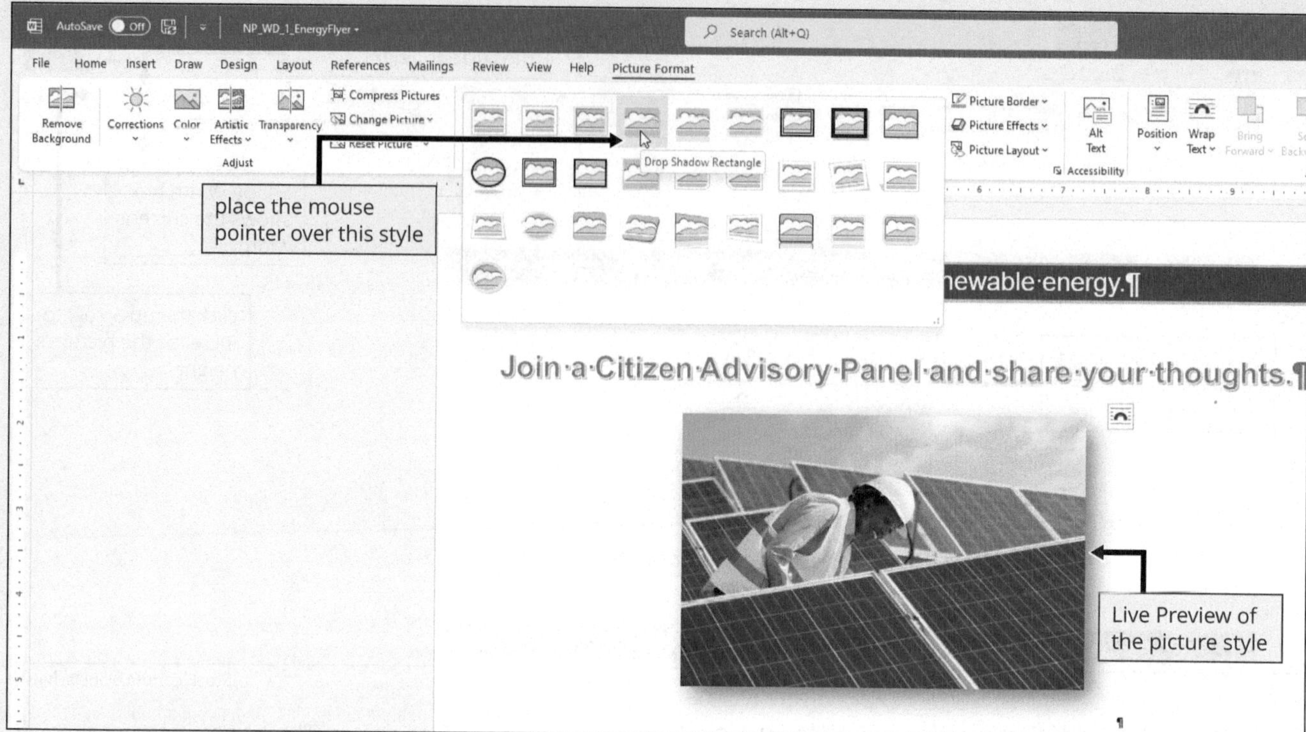

iStock.com/RuslanDashinsky

4. In the gallery, click the **Drop Shadow Rectangle** style to apply it to the photo and close the gallery. The photo is formatted with a shadow on the bottom and right sides, as shown earlier in the Part 1.2 Visual Overview.

   Tip To return a picture to its original appearance, click the Reset Picture button in the Adjust group on the Picture Format tab.

5. Click anywhere outside the photo to deselect it, and then save the document.

Insight

Working with Inline Pictures

By default, when you insert a picture in a document, it is treated as an inline object, which means its position changes in the document as you add or delete text. Also, because it is an inline object, you can align the picture just as you would align text, using the alignment buttons in the Paragraph group on the Home tab. Essentially, you can treat an inline picture as just another paragraph.

When you become a more advanced Word user, you'll learn how to wrap text around a picture so that the text flows around the picture—with the picture maintaining its position on the page no matter how much text you add to or delete from the document. The alignment buttons don't work on pictures that have text wrapped around them. Instead, you can drag the picture to the desired position on the page.

To complete the flyer, you need to add a border around the page.

Adding a Page Border

As with a paragraph border, the default style for a page border is a simple black line that forms a box around each page in the document. However, you can choose more elaborate options, including a dotted line, double lines, and, for informal documents, a border of graphical elements, such as stars or trees.

To insert a border around the flyer:

1. On the ribbon, click the **Design** tab.
2. In the Page Background group, click the **Page Borders** button. The Borders and Shading dialog box opens with the Page Border tab displayed. You can use the Setting options on the left side of this tab to specify the type of border you want. Because a document does not normally have a page border, the default setting is None. The Box setting is the most professional and least distracting choice, so you'll select that next.

   It's important to select the Box setting before you select other options for the border. Otherwise, when you click OK, your document won't have a page border, and you'll have to start over.
3. In the Setting section, click the **Box** setting. Selecting this option would add a simple line page border, but Leonel prefers a different line style.
4. In the Style box, scroll down and click the **double-line style**. Now you can select a different line color, just as you did when creating a paragraph border.
5. Click the **Color arrow** to open the Color gallery, and then click the **Blue, Accent 5** square, which is the second to the right square in the top row of the Theme Colors section. The Color gallery closes and the Blue, Accent 5 color is displayed in the Color box. At this point, you could change the line width as well, but Leonel prefers the default setting. Refer to Figure 1–43.

Figure 1–43 Adding a border to the flyer

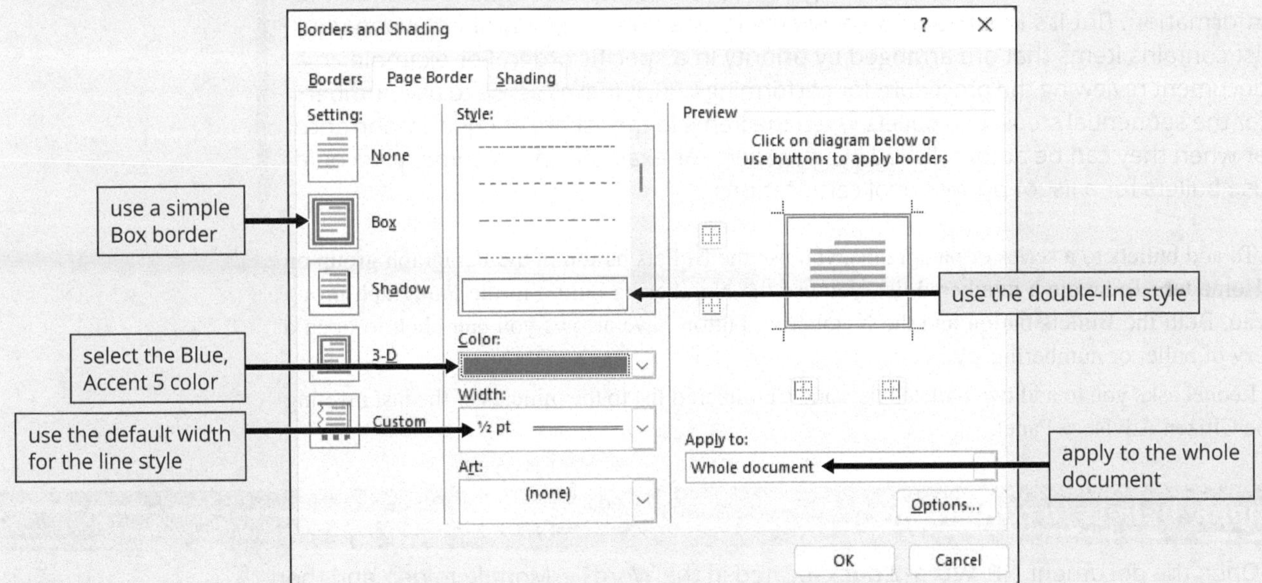

6. In the lower-right corner of the Borders and Shading dialog box, click the **Options** button. The Border and Shading Options dialog box opens.

   By default, the border is positioned 24 points from the edges of the page. If you plan to print your document on an older printer, it is sometimes necessary to change the Measure from setting to Text, so that the border is positioned relative to the outside edge of the text rather than the edge of the page. Alternatively, you can increase the settings in the Top, Bottom, Left, and Right boxes to move the border closer to the text. For most modern printers, however, the default settings are fine.

7. In the Border and Shading Options dialog box, click **Cancel**, and then click **OK** in the Borders and Shading dialog box. The flyer now has a double-line blue border, as shown earlier in the Part 1.2 Visual Overview.
8. Save the document.
9. Close the document without closing Word.

Leonel needs your help with one last task—adding bulleted and numbered lists to a document containing the minutes of the Citizen Advisory Panel's May meeting. After you finish formatting the document, Leonel can make the minutes available to the public through the department's website.

Creating Bulleted and Numbered Lists

A **bulleted list** is a group of related paragraphs with a black circle or other character to the left of each paragraph. For a group of related paragraphs that have a particular order (such as steps in a procedure), you can use consecutive numbers instead of bullets to create a **numbered list**. If you insert a new paragraph, delete a paragraph, or reorder the paragraphs in a numbered list, Word adjusts the numbers to make sure they remain consecutive.

Proskills

Written Communication: Organizing Information in Lists

Bulleted and numbered lists are both great ways to draw the reader's attention to information. But it's important to know how to use them. Use numbers when your list contains items that are arranged by priority in a specific order. For example, in a document reviewing the procedure for performing CPR, it makes sense to use numbers for the sequential steps. Use bullets when the items in the list are of equal importance or when they can be accomplished in any order. For example, in a resume, you could use bullets for a list of professional certifications.

To add bullets to a series of paragraphs, you use the Bullets button in the Paragraph group on the Home tab. To create a numbered list, you use the Numbering button in the Paragraph group instead. Both the Bullets button and the Numbering button have arrows you can click to open a gallery of bullet or numbering styles.

Leonel asks you to add two bulleted lists and a numbered list to the minutes of the last meeting of the Citizen Advisory Panel.

To apply bullets to paragraphs:

1. Open the document **NP_WD_1-2.docx** located in the Word1 > Module folder, and then save the document as **NP_WD_1_Meeting** in the location specified by your instructor.
2. Verify that the document is displayed in Print Layout view and that the rulers and nonprinting characters are displayed. Make sure the Zoom level is set to **120%**.
3. On page 1, select the complete list of members in attendance, starting with Jada Carter and concluding with Darius Holmes.
4. On the ribbon, click the **Home** tab, if necessary.
5. In the Paragraph group, click the **Bullets** button. Black circles appear as bullets before each item in the list. Also, the bulleted list is indented, and the paragraph spacing between the items is reduced.

   After reviewing the default, round bullet in the document, Leonel decides he would prefer square bullets.

6. In the Paragraph group, click the **Bullets arrow** . A gallery of bullet styles opens. Refer to Figure 1–44.

Figure 1–44 Bullets gallery

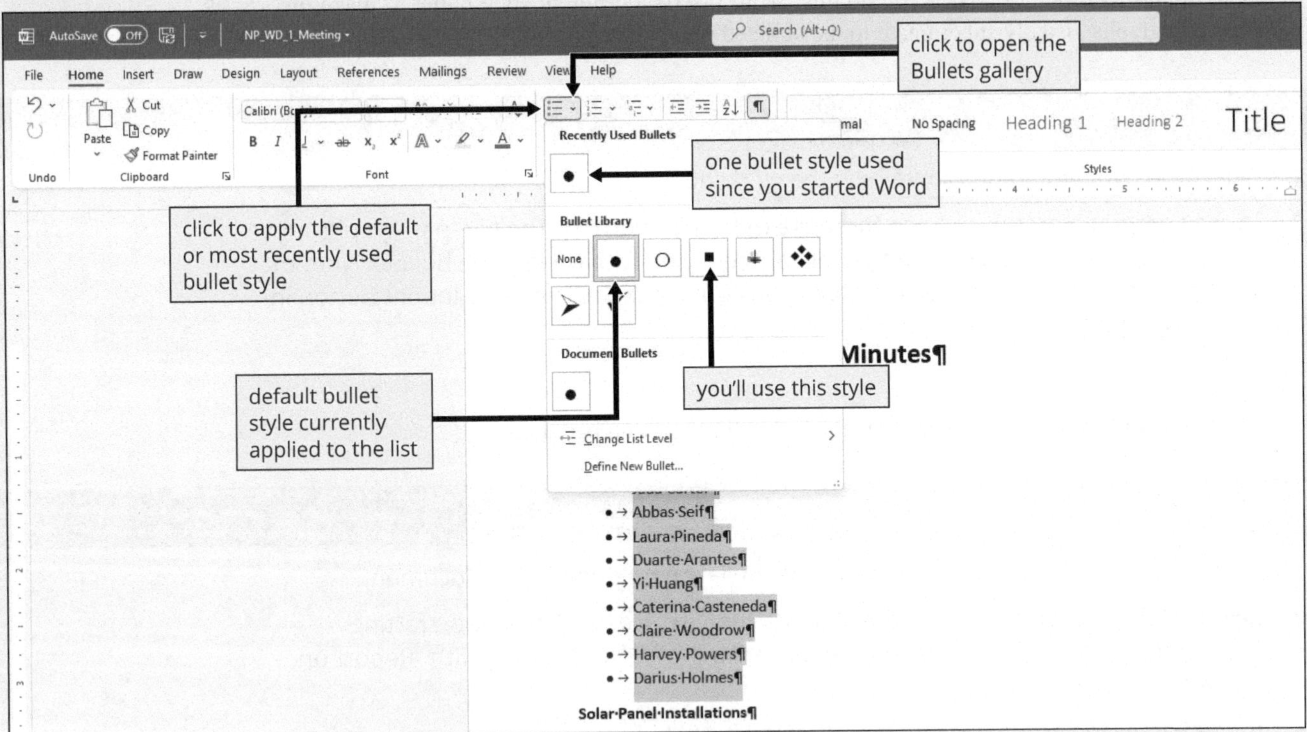

The Recently Used Bullets section appears at the top of the gallery of bullet styles; it displays the bullet styles that have been used since you started Word, which, in this case, is just the round black bullet style that was applied by default when you clicked the Bullets button. The **Bullet Library**, which offers a variety of bullet styles, is shown below the Recently Used Bullets. To create your own bullets from a picture file or from a set of predesigned symbols including diamonds, hearts, or Greek letters, click Define New Bullet, and then click Symbol or Picture in the Define New Bullet dialog box.

7. Move the pointer over the bullet styles in the Bullet Library to display a Live Preview of the bullet styles in the document. Leonel prefers the black square style.
8. In the Bullet Library, click the **black square**. The round bullets are replaced with square bullets.

Next, you need to format the list of information about solar panel installations with square bullets. When you first start Word, the Bullets button applies the default, round bullets you saw earlier. But after you select a new bullet style, the Bullets button applies the last bullet style you used. So, to add square bullets to the lead-reduction programs list, you just have to select the list and click the Bullets button.

To add bullets to the list of information about solar panel installations:

1. Scroll down in the document and select the paragraphs related to information about solar installations, starting with "Feasibility study and cost analysis" and ending with "Workshop 2: Long-term Cost Savings for Taxpayers."
2. In the Paragraph group, click the **Bullets** button . The list is now formatted with square black bullets.

The list is finished except for one issue. Below "Public workshops co-sponsored with the mayor's office" are two subordinate items listing the workshop titles. However, that's not clear because of the way the list is currently formatted.

To clarify this information, you can use the Increase Indent button in the Paragraph group to indent the last two bullets. When you do this, Word inserts a different style bullet to make the indented paragraphs visually subordinate to the bulleted paragraphs above.

To indent the last two bullets:

1. Select the two paragraphs containing the workshop titles.
2. In the Paragraph group, click the **Increase Indent** button. The two paragraphs move to the right, and the black square bullets are replaced with open circle bullets. Note that to remove the indent from selected text, you could click the Decrease Indent button in the Paragraph group.

Next, you will format the agenda for the next meeting as a numbered list.

To apply numbers to the list of agenda items:

1. Scroll down, if necessary, until you can see the last paragraph in the document.
2. Select all the paragraphs below the "Agenda for Next Meeting" heading, starting with "Opening remarks, public comments, and minutes" and ending with "Report on upcoming projects . . . ."
3. In the Paragraph group, click the **Numbering** button. Consecutive numbers appear in front of each item in the list. Refer to Figure 1–45.

Figure 1–45 Numbered list

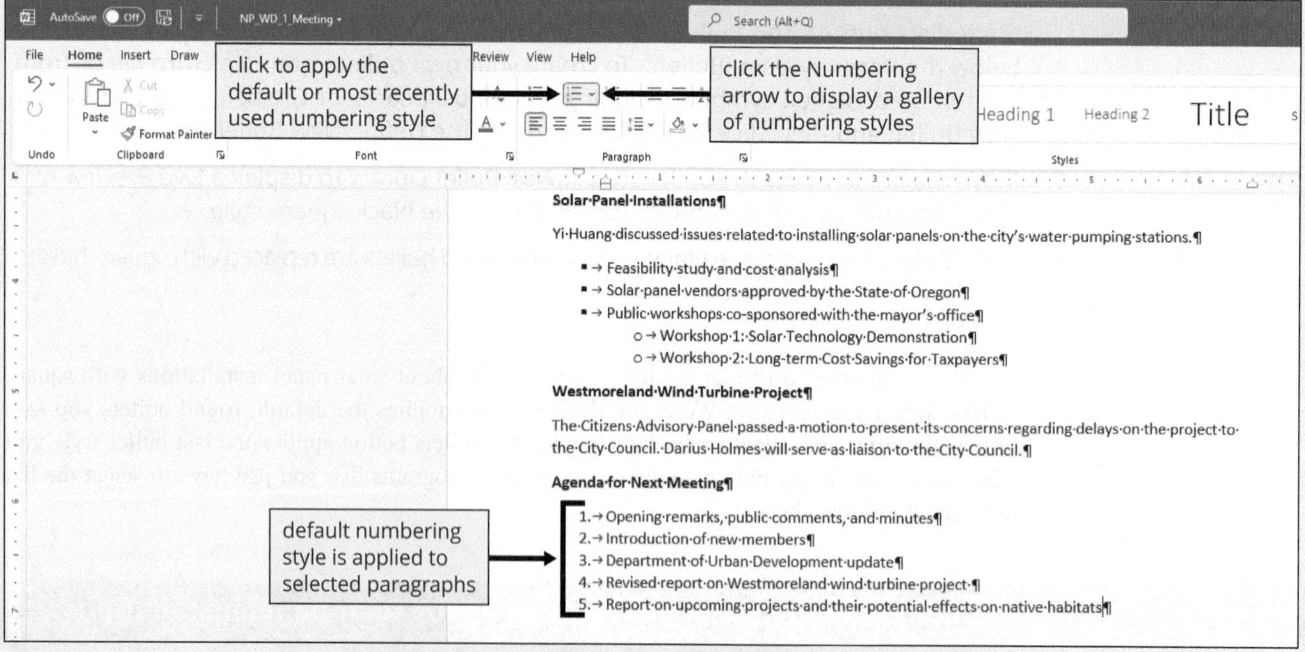

4. Click anywhere in the document to deselect the numbered list.
5. sam Save the document.

As with the Bullets arrow, you can click the Numbering arrow, and then select from a library of numbering styles. You can also indent paragraphs in a numbered list to create an outline, in which case the indented paragraphs will be preceded by lowercase letters instead of numbers. To apply a different list style to the outline (for example, with Roman numerals and uppercase letters), select the list, click the Multilevel List button in the Paragraph group, and then click a multilevel list style. Keep in mind that you can always add items to a bulleted or numbered list by moving the insertion point to the end of the last item in the list and pressing ENTER. The Bullets button is a **toggle button**, which means you can click it to add or remove bullets from selected text. The same is true of the Numbering button.

The document is complete and ready for Leonel to post to the department's website. Because Leonel is considering creating a promotional brochure that would include numerous photographs, he asks you to look up more information about inserting pictures. You can do that using Word Help.

Getting Help

To get the most out of Word Help, your computer must be connected to the Internet so it can access the reference information stored at Microsoft365.com. The quickest way to look up information is to use the Search box on the ribbon. You can also use the Search box to quickly access Word features.

Tip To display a menu of recent and suggested Help topics, click the Search box and wait for the menu to appear.

To look up information in Word Help:

1. Verify that your computer is connected to the Internet, and then, on the ribbon, click the **Search** box, and type **insert picture**. A menu of Help topics related to inserting pictures opens. You could click one of the items in the top part of the menu to access the relevant dialog box, menu, or other Word tool. For example, you could click Insert Picture to open the Insert Picture dialog box. Refer to Figure 1–46.

Figure 1–46 Word Help menu

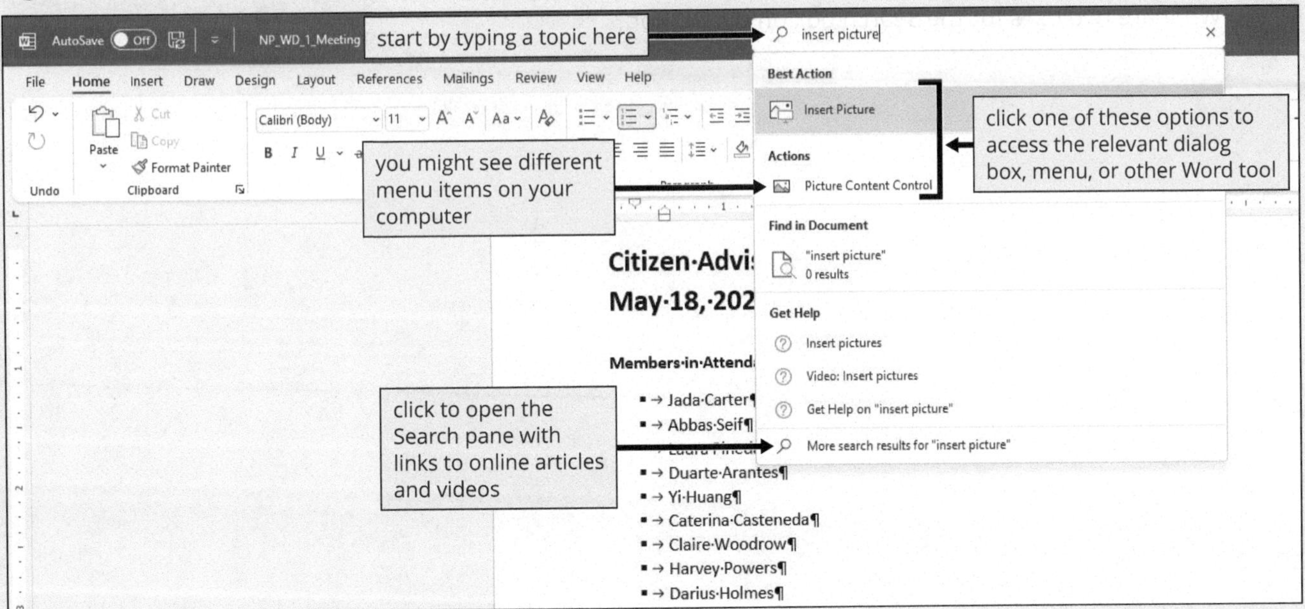

Tip To search the web for information on a word or phrase in a document, select the text, click the References tab, and then click the Search button in the Research group.

2. Click **More search results for "insert picture"** at the bottom of the menu. The Search pane opens with links to Help articles, definitions, and videos from Microsoft365.com as well as other items from the web. You might also see a list of files on your computer containing the phrase "insert picture." You could click any of the links in the search results to open the relevant article in a browser window.
3. Scroll down in the Search pane to read all the information. Note that you can type a new word or phrase in the text box at the top of the Search pane and then press **ENTER** to look up information on other topics.
4. Click the **Close** button [X] in the upper-right corner to close the Search pane.
5. Click the **File** tab, and then click **Close** in the navigation pane to close the document without closing Word.

Word Help is a great way to learn about and access Word's many features. Articles and videos on basic skills provide step-by-step guides for completing tasks, while more elaborate, online tutorials walk you through more complicated tasks. Be sure to take some time on your own to explore Word Help so you can find the information and features you want when you need it.

Part 1.2 Quick Check

1. Explain how to accept a grammar correction suggested by the Editor pane.
2. What orientation should you choose if you want your document to be narrower than it is wide?
3. What is the default font size?
4. Explain how to copy formatting from one paragraph to another.
5. What is the default text alignment?
6. Explain two important facts about a picture inserted as an inline object.
7. What are two uses for the Search box on the Ribbon?

Practice: Review Assignments

Data Files needed for the Review Assignments: NP_WD_1-3.docx, NP_WD_1-4.docx, Support_WD_1_House.jpg

Leonel asks you to write a cover letter to Nick Thorstad at the Iris Hill Neighborhood Center to accompany a pamphlet on heat pumps, an affordable form of alternative energy that will be discussed in an upcoming workshop for homeowners. After that, he wants you to create an envelope for the letter, and then format a flyer announcing free educational tours of solar panel installations in the Salem area. Finally, he needs you to add bulleted and numbered lists to the minutes for the Citizen Advisory Panel's July meeting. Change the Zoom level as necessary while you are working. Complete the following steps:

1. Open a new, blank document and then save the document as **NP_WD_1_ThorstadLetter** in the location specified by your instructor.
2. Type the date **February 15, 2029** using AutoComplete for "February."
3. Press ENTER twice, and then type the following inside address, using the default paragraph spacing and pressing ENTER once after each line:

   Nick Thorstad

   Iris Hill Neighborhood Center

   2500 Hannah Lane

   Salem, OR 97309
4. Type **Dear Nick:** as the salutation, press ENTER, and then type the following two paragraphs as the body of the letter:

   Enclosed you will find the heat pump pamphlet we discussed. I hope the homeowners taking part in your alternative energy workshop find this information useful. Additional information about heat pumps is available at www.energy.salem.cengage.com.

   Keep in mind that we also offer free educational tours of local solar panel installations. We can accommodate groups as large as thirty.
5. Press ENTER, type **Sincerely yours,** as the complimentary closing, press ENTER three times, type **Leonel Villalba** as the signature line, insert a manual line break, and type **Communications Director** as his title.
6. Press ENTER, type your initials, insert a manual line break, and then use the Undo button to make your initials all lowercase, if necessary.
7. Type **Enclosure** and save the document.
8. Scroll to the beginning of the document and proofread your work. Remove any wavy underlines by using a shortcut menu or by typing a correction yourself. Remove the hyperlink formatting from the web address.
9. Remove the paragraph spacing from the first three lines of the inside address.
10. Change the top margin to 2.75 inches. Leave the other margins at their default settings.
11. Save your changes to the letter, preview it, print it if your instructor asks you to, and then close it.
12. Create a new, blank document, and then create an envelope. Use Nick Thorstad's address (from Step 3) as the delivery address. Use your school's name and address for the return address. Add the envelope to the document. If you are asked if you want to save the return address as the new return address, click No.
13. Save the document as **NP_WD_1_ThorstadEnvelope** in the location specified by your instructor, and then close the document.
14. Open the document **NP_WD_1-3.docx**, located in the Word1 > Review folder included with your Data Files, and then check your screen to make sure your settings match those in the module.
15. Save the document as **NP_WD_1_SolarFlyer** in the location specified by your instructor.
16. Use the Recheck Document button in the Word Options dialog box, and then use the Editor pane to correct any errors. Ignore any items marked as errors that are in fact correct, and accept any suggestions regarding clarity and conciseness. If the Editor pane does not give you the opportunity to correct all the errors marked in the document, close the Editor pane and correct the errors using shortcut menus or by typing directly in the document.

17. Proofread the document and correct any other errors. Be sure to change "Today" to "**today**" in the last paragraph.
18. Change the page orientation to Landscape and the margins to Narrow.
19. Format the document text in 22-point Times New Roman font.
20. Center the text and the photo.
21. Format the first paragraph with an outside border using the default style, and change the border color to Green, Accent 6, and the border width to 1½ pt. Add blue shading to the paragraph, using the Blue, Accent 5 color in the Theme Colors section of the Shading gallery. Format the paragraph text in White, Background 1.
22. Format the last paragraph in the document using the same formatting you applied to the first paragraph.
23. Increase the paragraph spacing after the first paragraph to 42 points. Increase the paragraph spacing before the last paragraph in the document to 42 points.
24. Format the second paragraph with the Fill: Blue, Accent color 1; Shadow text effect. Add bold and increase the paragraph's font size to 24 points.
25. Format the text in the third and fourth paragraphs (the first two paragraphs below the photo) using the Blue, Accent 5 font color, and then add bold and italic.
26. Delete the photo and replace it with the **Support_WD_1_House.jpg** photo, located in the Word1 > Review folder.
27. Delete the existing alt text and the text indicating that the description was automatically generated, if necessary, and then type **Solar panels on a white house**. (Do not include the period after "house.")
28. Resize the new photo so that it is 3.8" tall, and then add the Soft Edge Rectangle style in the Pictures Styles gallery.
29. Add a page border using the Box setting, a double-line style, the default width, and the Green, Accent 6 color.
30. Save your changes to the flyer, preview it, and then close it.
31. Open the document **NP_WD_1-4.docx**, located in the Word1 > Review folder, and then check your screen to make sure your settings match those in the module.
32. Save the document as **NP_WD_1_MinutesJuly** in the location specified by your instructor.
33. Format the list of members in attendance as a bulleted list with square bullets, and then format the list of home-heating initiatives with square bullets (starting with "Rebate offered to . . ." and ending with "Workshop 2: Accessing Wind-Generated Power"). Indent the paragraphs for Workshop 1 and Workshop 2 so they are formatted with open circle bullets.
34. Format the five paragraphs below the "Agenda for Next Meeting" heading as a numbered list.
35. Use Search bar in the Ribbon to look up the topic **work with pictures**. Review the results in the Search pane, and then close the Search pane.

Apply: Case Problem 1

There are no Data Files needed for this Case Problem.

Paulson and Steel Real Estate You are an administrative assistant at Paulson and Steel Real Estate, in Rockford, Illinois. One of your company's agents recently sold a retail building, and you need to forward an extra key to the new owner. Create a cover letter to accompany the key by completing the following steps. Because your office is currently out of letterhead, you'll start the letter by typing a return address. As you type the letter, remember to include the appropriate number of blank paragraphs between the various parts of the letter. Complete the following steps:

1. Open a new, blank document, and then save the document as **NP_WD_1_Saelim** in the location specified by your instructor. If necessary, change the Zoom level to 120%.

2. Type the following return address, using the default paragraph spacing and replacing [Your Name] with your first and last names:

   [Your Name]

   Paulson and Steel Real Estate

   5388 Pomona Avenue, Suite 3

   Rockford, IL 61016
3. Type **November 16, 2029** as the date, leaving a blank paragraph between the last line of the return address and the date.
4. Type the following inside address, using the default paragraph spacing and leaving the appropriate number of blank paragraphs after the date:

   Mali Saelim

   Drucker Commercial Properties

   1021 Ash Avenue

   Belvidere, IL 61008
5. Type **Dear Ms. Saelim:** as the salutation.
6. To begin the body of the letter, type the following two paragraphs: **Please find enclosed the second key for the retail building you recently purchased at 534 Langley Road. This is the key we used for showing the building, and I can confirm that we kept it secure at all times.**

   I also wanted to remind you that, at the closing, the previous owner made these maintenance suggestions:
7. Add the following as separate paragraphs, using the default paragraph spacing:

   Use sidewalk salt to keep the front entrance free of ice during the winter.

   Clean the siding with a 2% bleach solution every fall.

   Replace the basement furnace filter twice a year.

   If you have any questions about your property, feel free to email me at admin@paulsonsteel.cengage.com.
8. Insert a new paragraph after the last paragraph, and then type the complimentary closing **Sincerely,** (including the comma).
9. Leave the appropriate amount of space for your signature, type your full name, insert a manual line break, and then type **Administrative Assistant**.
10. Type **Enclosure** in the appropriate place.
11. Remove the hyperlink formatting from the email address.
12. Use the Editor pane to correct any errors. Ignore any items marked as errors that are in fact correct (such as the last name "Saelim"), and ignore any suggestions regarding clarity and conciseness. If the Editor pane does not give you the opportunity to correct all the errors marked in the document, close the Editor pane and correct the errors using shortcut menus or by typing directly in the document.
13. Italicize the three paragraphs containing the maintenance suggestions (beginning with "Use sidewalk salt..." and ending with "Replace the basement furnace filter twice a year.").
14. Format the list of three maintenance suggestions as a bulleted list with square bullets.
15. Remove the paragraph spacing from the first three lines of the return address. Do the same for the first three paragraphs of the inside address.
16. Center the four paragraphs containing the return address, format them in 16-point Calibri, and then add the Fill: Black, Text color 1; Shadow text effect.
17. Deselect any selected text, and then create an envelope in the current document. Use Mali Saelim's address (from Step 4) as the delivery address. Edit the delivery address as necessary to remove any incorrect text. Use the return address shown in Step 2. Add the envelope to the NP_WD_1_Saelim.docx document. If you are asked if you want to save the return address as the default return address, click No.
18. Save the document, preview it, and close it.

Challenge: Case Problem 2

Data Files needed for this Case Problem: NP_WD_1-5.docx, Support_WD_1_Produce.jpg

Verona Health Cooperative You work as a marketing coordinator for Verona Health Cooperative. You need to create a flyer promoting a series of nutrition talks planned for November. Complete the following steps:

1. Open the document **NP_WD_1-5.docx** located in the Word1 > Case2 folder included with your Data Files, and then save the document as **NP_WD_1_Nutrition** in the location specified by your instructor.
2. In the document, replace "Student Name" with your first and last names.
3. Use the Editor pane to correct any errors, including adding a comma after the word "activity." Instruct the Editor pane to ignore your name if Word marks it with a wavy underline. If the Editor pane does not give you the opportunity to correct all the errors marked in the document, close the Editor pane and correct the errors using shortcut menus or by typing directly in the document.
4. Change the page margins to Narrow.
5. Complete the flyer as shown in Figure 1–47. Use the photo **Support_WD_1_Produce.jpg** located in the Word1 > Case2 folder. Use the default line spacing and paragraph spacing unless otherwise specified in Figure 1–47.

Figure 1–47 Formatted Verona Health Cooperative flyer

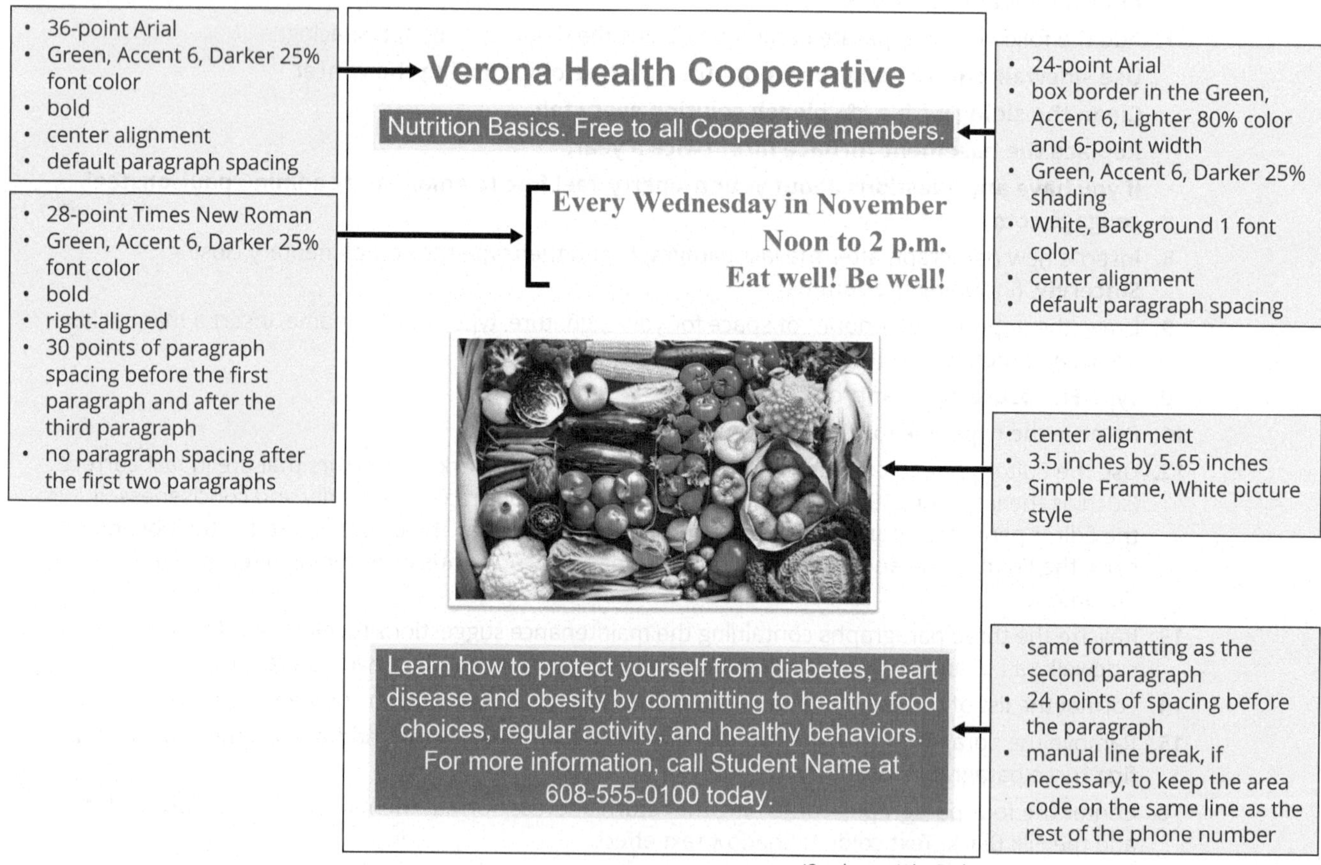

iStock.com/AlexRaths

6. If necessary, delete the existing alt text and the text indicating that the description was automatically generated, and then type **A picture of fresh fruits and vegetables.**
7. Save the document, preview it, and then close it.

Navigating and Formatting a Document

Editing an Academic Document According to MLA Style

Case: La Crosse Community College

Serena Rossi, a student at La Crosse Community College, is doing a student internship at Moraine Mortgage. She has written a handout that explains the process of getting a mortgage, and has asked you to help finish it. The text needs some reorganization and other editing, as well as some formatting so the finished document looks professional and is easy to read.

Serena is also taking a liberal arts class and is writing a research paper on ancient architecture. To complete the paper, she needs to follow a specific set of formatting and style guidelines, known as the MLA style for research papers.

Serena has asked you to help her edit these two very different documents. In Part 2.1, you will review and respond to some comments in the handout and then revise and format that document. In Part 2.2, you will review the MLA style and then format Serena's research paper to match the MLA specifications.

Starting Data Files: Word2

Module

NP_WD_2-1.docx
NP_WD_2-2.docx

Review Assignments

NP_WD_2-3.docx
NP_WD_2-4.docx

Case1

NP_WD_2-5.docx

Case2

NP_WD_2-6.docx

Objectives

Part 2.1

- Read, reply to, delete, and add comments
- Move text using drag and drop
- Cut and paste text
- Copy and paste text
- Navigate through a document using the Navigation pane
- Find and replace text
- Format text with styles

Part 2.2

- Format an MLA-style research paper
- Indent paragraphs
- Insert and modify page numbers
- Create footnotes and endnotes
- Create citations
- Create and update a bibliography
- Modify a source

Part 2.1 Visual Overview: The Navigation Pane and Styles

The **Navigation pane** allows you to search for text in the document, with the results highlighted in yellow in the document.

Click the **Search for more things button** to access advanced search tools, or to select something to search for besides text.

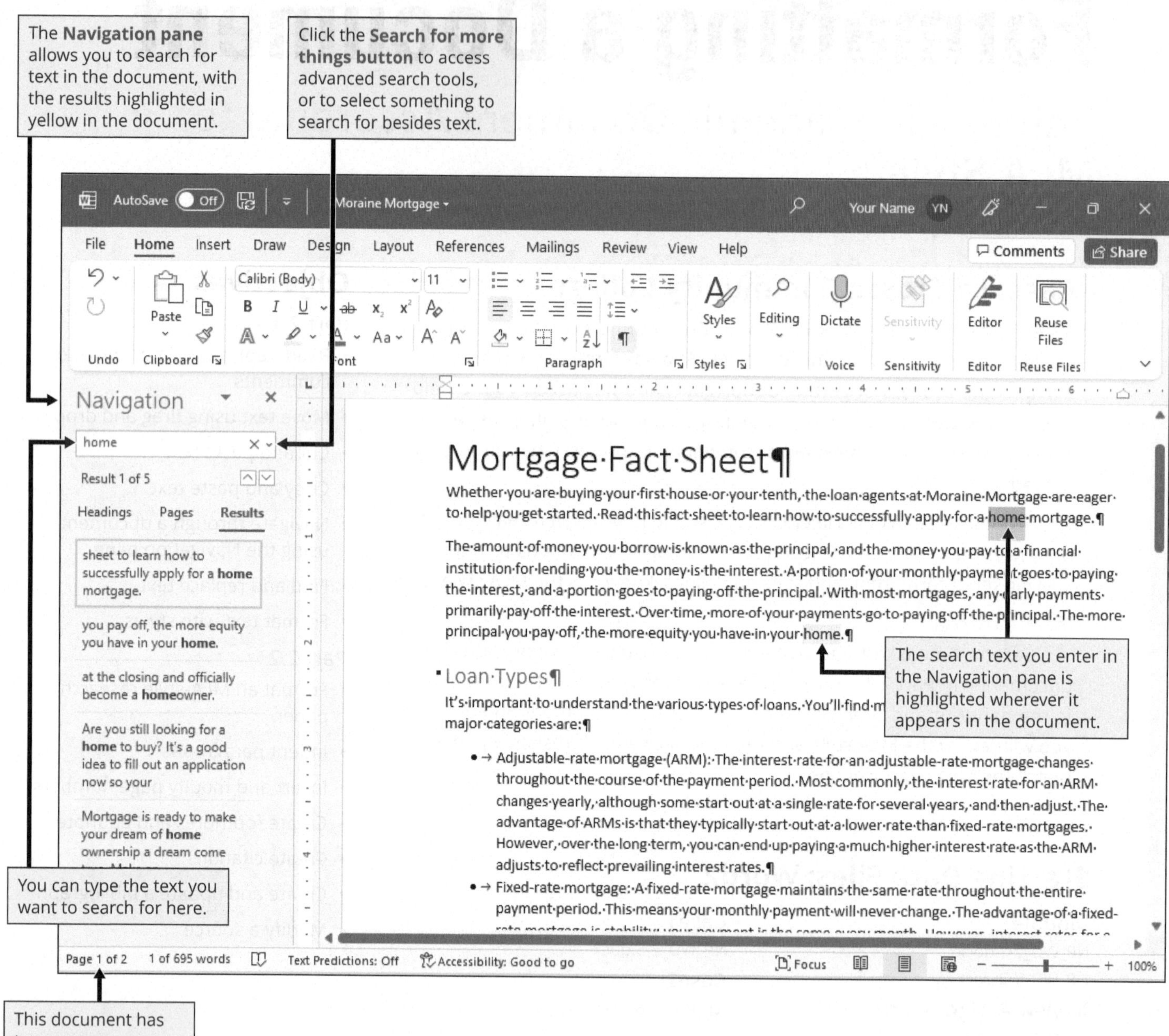

The search text you enter in the Navigation pane is highlighted wherever it appears in the document.

You can type the text you want to search for here.

This document has two pages; you can click here to open the Navigation pane.

This text is formatted in the Title style.

You can click a group's Dialog Box Launcher to open a dialog box or pane that gives you access to advanced settings.

Text styles allow you to apply a set of paragraph and character formatting options with one click in the Style Gallery.

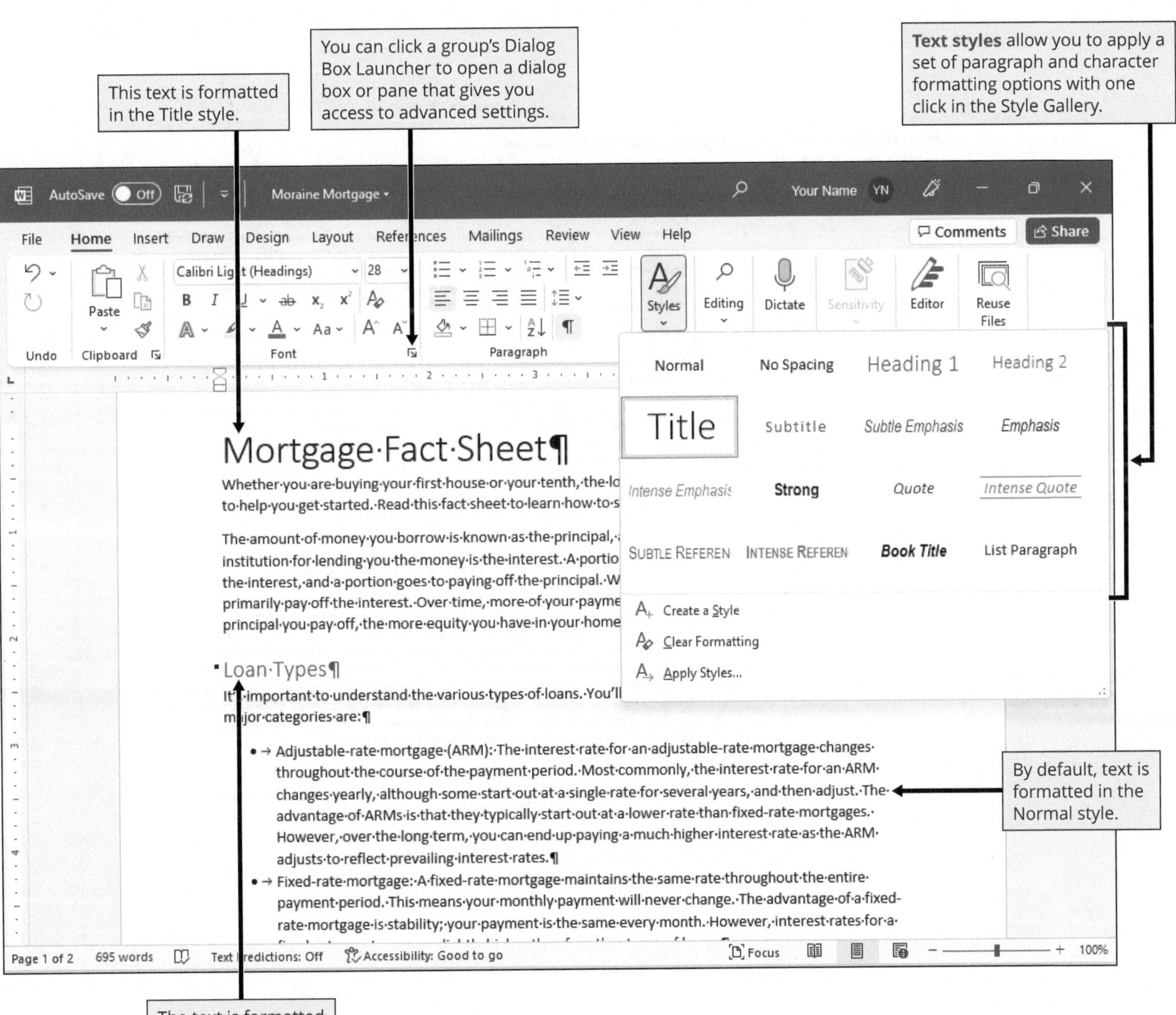

By default, text is formatted in the Normal style.

The text is formatted with the Heading 1 style for the Office theme.

Reviewing the Document

Before revising a document for someone else, it's a good idea to familiarize yourself with its overall structure and the revisions that need to be made. Take a moment to review Serena's notes, which are shown in Figure 2–1.

Figure 2–1 Draft of handout with Serena's notes (page 1)

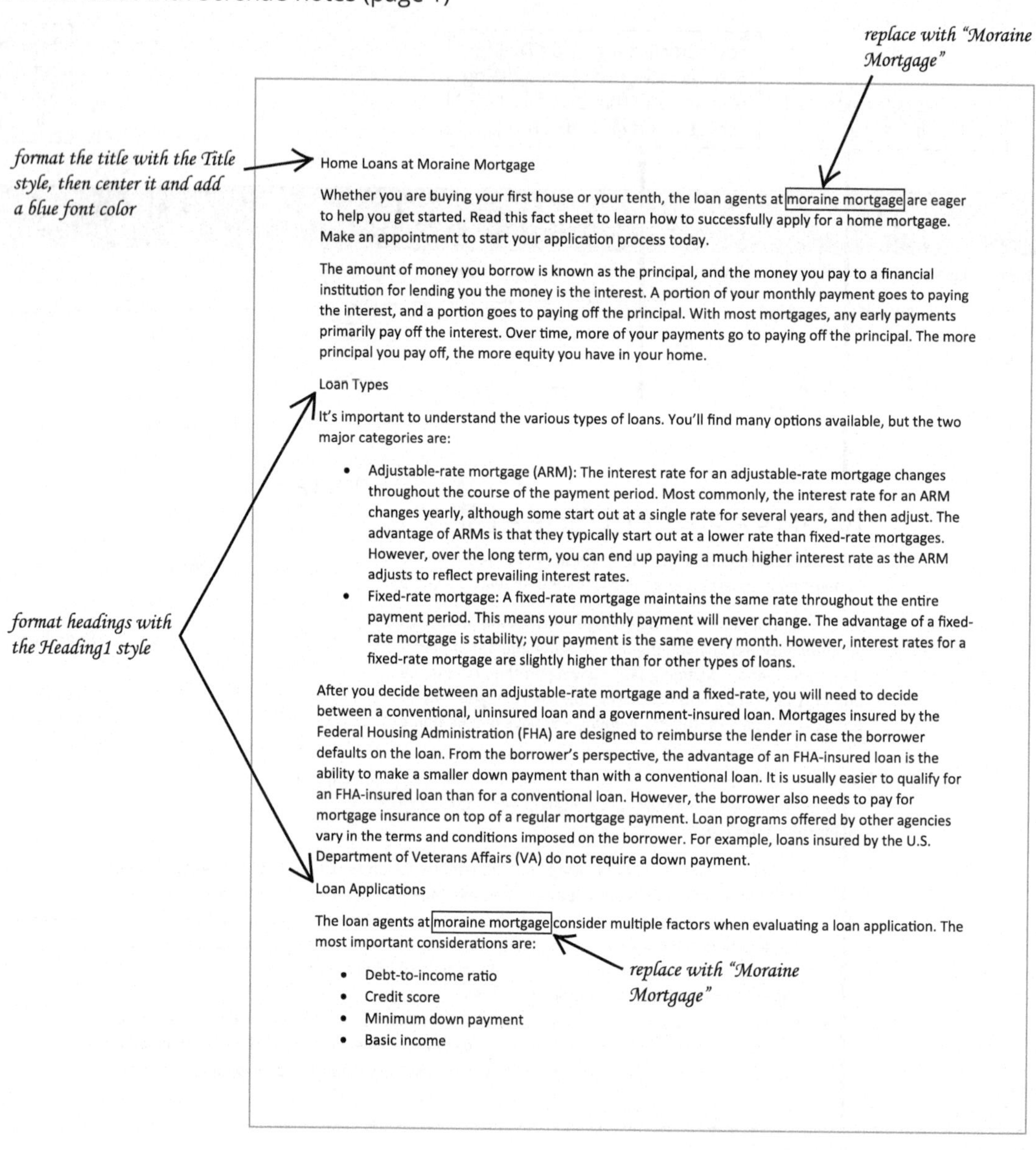

Home Loans at Moraine Mortgage

Whether you are buying your first house or your tenth, the loan agents at moraine mortgage are eager to help you get started. Read this fact sheet to learn how to successfully apply for a home mortgage. Make an appointment to start your application process today.

The amount of money you borrow is known as the principal, and the money you pay to a financial institution for lending you the money is the interest. A portion of your monthly payment goes to paying the interest, and a portion goes to paying off the principal. With most mortgages, any early payments primarily pay off the interest. Over time, more of your payments go to paying off the principal. The more principal you pay off, the more equity you have in your home.

Loan Types

It's important to understand the various types of loans. You'll find many options available, but the two major categories are:

- Adjustable-rate mortgage (ARM): The interest rate for an adjustable-rate mortgage changes throughout the course of the payment period. Most commonly, the interest rate for an ARM changes yearly, although some start out at a single rate for several years, and then adjust. The advantage of ARMs is that they typically start out at a lower rate than fixed-rate mortgages. However, over the long term, you can end up paying a much higher interest rate as the ARM adjusts to reflect prevailing interest rates.
- Fixed-rate mortgage: A fixed-rate mortgage maintains the same rate throughout the entire payment period. This means your monthly payment will never change. The advantage of a fixed-rate mortgage is stability; your payment is the same every month. However, interest rates for a fixed-rate mortgage are slightly higher than for other types of loans.

After you decide between an adjustable-rate mortgage and a fixed-rate, you will need to decide between a conventional, uninsured loan and a government-insured loan. Mortgages insured by the Federal Housing Administration (FHA) are designed to reimburse the lender in case the borrower defaults on the loan. From the borrower's perspective, the advantage of an FHA-insured loan is the ability to make a smaller down payment than with a conventional loan. It is usually easier to qualify for an FHA-insured loan than for a conventional loan. However, the borrower also needs to pay for mortgage insurance on top of a regular mortgage payment. Loan programs offered by other agencies vary in the terms and conditions imposed on the borrower. For example, loans insured by the U.S. Department of Veterans Affairs (VA) do not require a down payment.

Loan Applications

The loan agents at moraine mortgage consider multiple factors when evaluating a loan application. The most important considerations are:

- Debt-to-income ratio
- Credit score
- Minimum down payment
- Basic income

Figure 2–1 Draft of handout with Serena's notes (page 2)

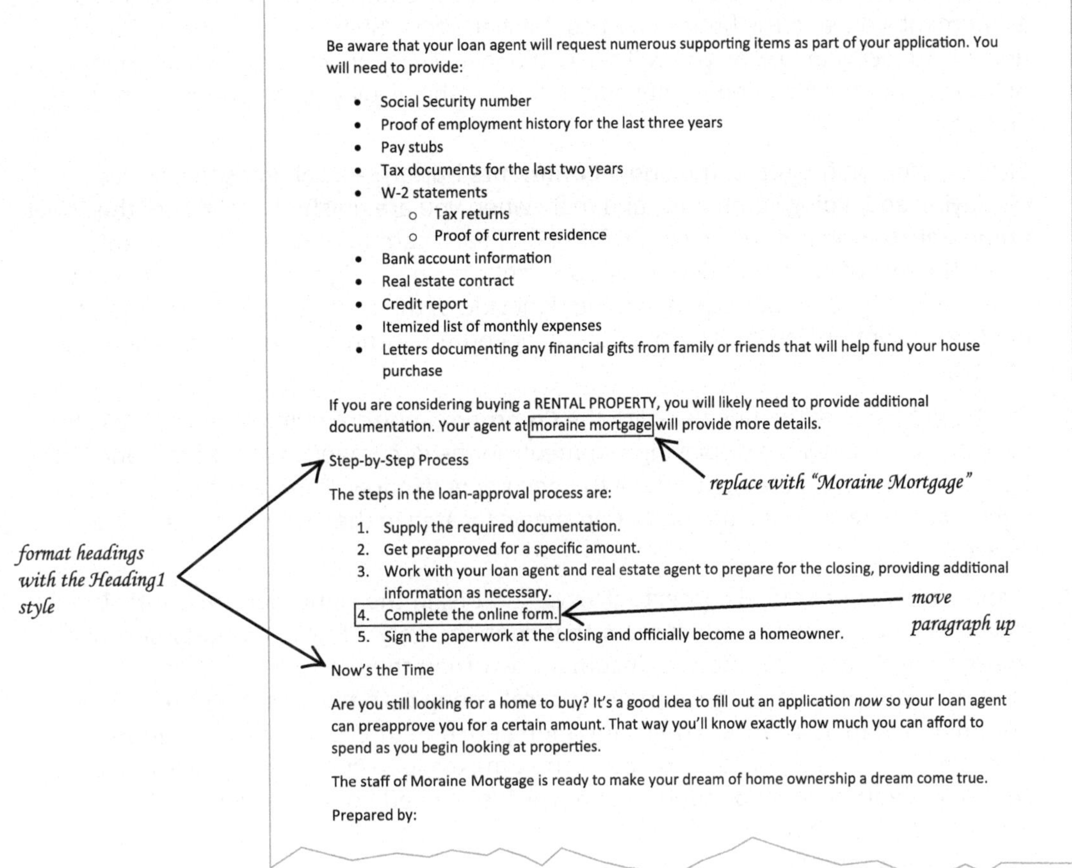
Be aware that your loan agent will request numerous supporting items as part of your application. You will need to provide:

- Social Security number
- Proof of employment history for the last three years
- Pay stubs
- Tax documents for the last two years
- W-2 statements
    - Tax returns
    - Proof of current residence
- Bank account information
- Real estate contract
- Credit report
- Itemized list of monthly expenses
- Letters documenting any financial gifts from family or friends that will help fund your house purchase

If you are considering buying a RENTAL PROPERTY, you will likely need to provide additional documentation. Your agent at moraine mortgage will provide more details.

Step-by-Step Process

The steps in the loan-approval process are:

1. Supply the required documentation.
2. Get preapproved for a specific amount.
3. Work with your loan agent and real estate agent to prepare for the closing, providing additional information as necessary.
4. Complete the online form.
5. Sign the paperwork at the closing and officially become a homeowner.

Now's the Time

Are you still looking for a home to buy? It's a good idea to fill out an application *now* so your loan agent can preapprove you for a certain amount. That way you'll know exactly how much you can afford to spend as you begin looking at properties.

The staff of Moraine Mortgage is ready to make your dream of home ownership a dream come true.

Prepared by:

Serena also included additional guidance in some comments she added to the document file. A **comment** is like an electronic sticky note attached to a word, phrase, or paragraph in a document. As you'll see in the following steps, you can adjust the appearance of comments in a document in several ways. No matter how you display comments, each comment includes the username of the person currently logged into your Office account. Within a single document, you can add new comments, edit or reply to existing comments, and delete comments.

You will open the document now, save it with a new name, and then review Serena's comments in Word.

To open and rename the document:

1. sam Open the document **NP_WD_2-1.docx** located in the Word2 > Module folder included with your Data Files.
2. Save the document as **NP_WD_2_Handout** in the location specified by your instructor.
3. Verify that the document is displayed in Print Layout view, that the Zoom level is set to **120%**, and that the rulers and nonprinting characters are displayed.
4. On the ribbon, click the **Review** tab to display the tools used for working with comments. Now you need to make sure the comments in the document are displayed to match the figures in this book. First, you need to make sure Simple Markup view is selected.
5. In the Tracking group, click the **Display for Review arrow**, and then click **Simple Markup** to select it, if necessary. At this point, you might see just comment icons to the right of the document text, or you might also see the full text of each comment.

6. In the Comments group, position the mouse pointer over the **Show Comments** button to display a horizontal line dividing the button into two parts. The top part contains a comment icon, and the bottom part contains the text "Show Comments" and a downward facing arrow. As you will see in the following step, clicking the comment icon on the top of the Show Comments button toggles the display of the comment text off and on.
7. Click the icon on the top of the **Show Comments** button several times to practice displaying and hiding comments, and then, when you are finished, make sure the Show Comments button is selected so the full text of each comment is displayed. At this point, the text of each comment might be displayed in the right margin, or it might be displayed in the Comments pane on the right side of the document window. You'll try out the two options next, using the Comments button located on the right side of the title bar.
8. On the right side of the title bar, click the **Comments** button multiple times to toggle back and forth between displaying comments in the document's right margin and in the Comments pane, on the right side of the document window. Comments located in the right margin are in contextual view. Comments located in the Comments pane are in list view.
9. Display the comments in contextual view—that is, in the right margin. Contextual view is the best view for a document that contains only a few comments because the comments are closer to the document text than they are when displayed in the Comment pane, and the comments scroll along with the document text. The Comments pane is a better choice for a long document that contains multiple comments per page because the list format makes it easier to keep track of which comments you have responded to and which still need your attention. Refer to Figure 2–2. Note that the comments on your screen might look different from the ones shown in the figure.

Figure 2–2 Comments displayed in contextual view

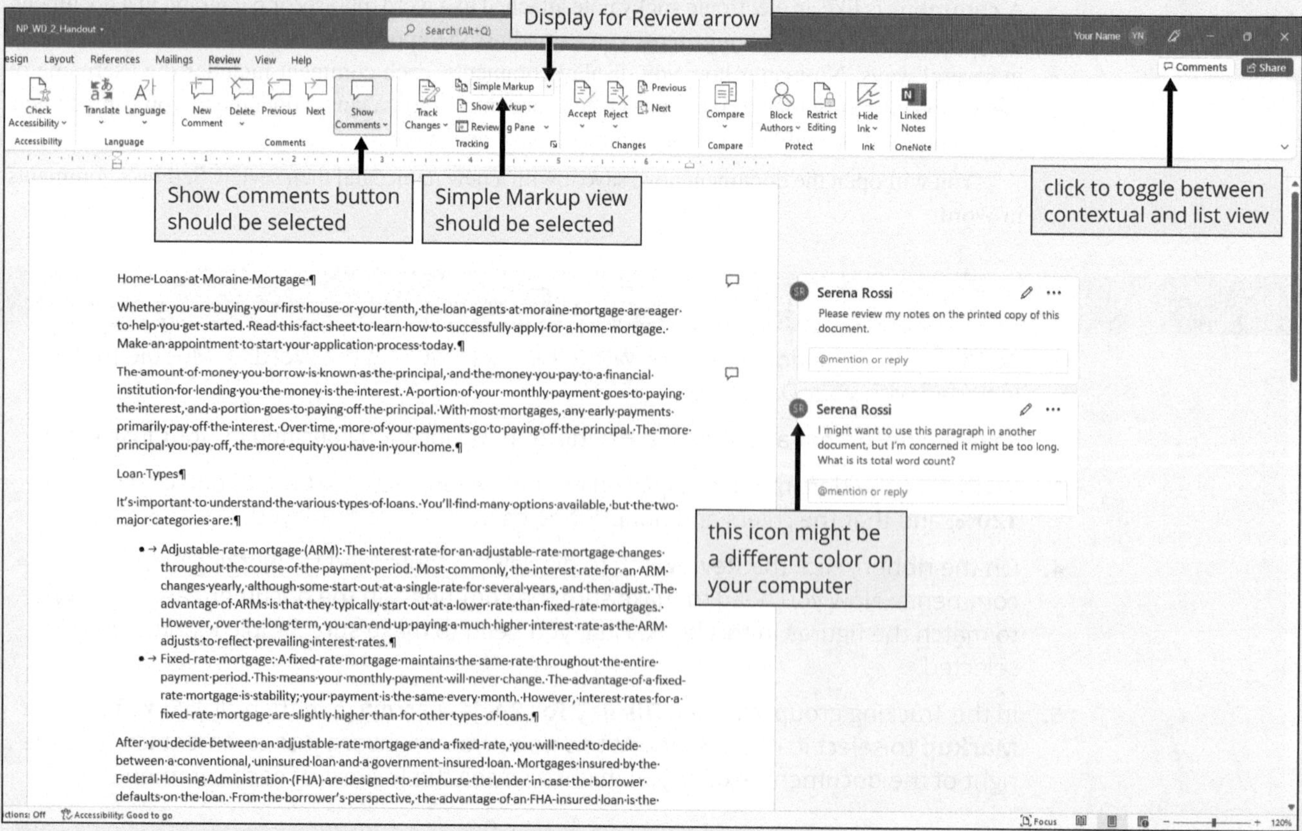

Trouble? Don't be concerned if your comments look different than those shown in the figures. You can still complete the steps.

Keep in mind that when working on a small monitor, it can be helpful to switch the document Zoom level to Page Width, in which case Word automatically reduces the width of the document to accommodate the comments.

10. Read the document, including the comments. The handout includes the title "Home Loans at Moraine Mortgage" at the top, as well as headings (such as "Loan Types" and "Loan Applications") that divide the document into parts. Right now, the headings are hard to spot because they don't look different from the surrounding text. Serena used the default font size, 11-point, and the default font, Calibri (Body), for all the text in the document.

11. Scroll down until you can see the first line on page 2 (which begins "Be aware that your loan agent..."), and then click anywhere in that sentence. The message "Page 2 of 2" in the status bar, in the lower-left corner of the Word window, tells you that the insertion point is currently located on page 2 of the two-page document. The shaded space between the first and second pages of the document indicates a page break. To hide the top and bottom margins in a document, as well as the space between pages, you can double-click the shaded space between any two pages.

12. Position the pointer over the shaded space between page 1 and page 2 until the pointer changes to the hide white space pointer, and then double-click. The shaded space disappears. Instead, the two pages are now separated by a gray, horizontal line.

Trouble? If the Header & Footer contextual tab appears on the ribbon, you double-clicked the top or bottom of one of the pages, instead of in the space between them. Click the Close Header and Footer button on the Header & Footer tab, and then repeat Step 10.

13. Use the show white space pointer to double-click the gray horizontal line between pages 1 and 2. The shaded space between the two pages is redisplayed.

Working with Comments

Now that you are familiar with Serena's handout, you can review and reply to her comments. A comment with one or more replies is known as a **thread**. The Comment group on the Review tab includes helpful tools for working with comments, but it is usually quicker to use the two buttons within a comment. The More thread actions button, which consists of three white dots, displays a menu with options for deleting a comment or a group of comments in a thread, among other things. The Edit comment button, which consists of a pencil icon, allows you to edit a comment's text.

Reference

Working with Comments

- On the ribbon, click the Review tab.
- To display comments in an easy-to-read view, in the Tracking group, click the Display for Review arrow, and then click Simple Markup.
- Use the Show Comments button in the Comments group to display or hide the text of the comments.
- To toggle between displaying the comments in the right margin (contextual view) and in the Comments pane (list view), click the Comments button on the right side of the title bar.
- To add a new comment, select the document text you want to comment on, click the New Comment button in the Comments group, type the comment text, and then click the Post comment button or press CTRL+ENTER.
- To reply to a comment, click the Reply box in the comment, type your reply, and then click the Post reply button.
- To edit a comment after it has been posted, click the Edit comment button in the comment, make the changes you want, and then click the Post comment button in the comment.
- To move the insertion point to the next or previous comment in the document, click the Next button or the Previous button in the Comments group.
- To delete an entire comment thread, click in the original comment, click the More thread actions button in the comment, and then click Delete thread.
- To delete one comment within a thread, click in the comment you want to delete, click the More thread actions button, and then click Delete comment.
- To delete all the comments in a document, click the Delete arrow in the Comments group, and then click Delete All Comments in Document.
- To indicate that a comment or a comment thread is no longer a concern, click the More thread actions button, and then click Resolve thread.
- To respond to a resolved comment, click the comment icon in the margin, if necessary, click the Reopen button in the comment, and then type your reply.

To review and respond to the comments in the document:

1. Press **CTRL+HOME** to move the insertion point to the beginning of the document.
2. On the Review tab, in the Comments group, click the **Next** button. The first comment now has an outline in a dark color, indicating that it is selected. The reply box below the comment contains the placeholder text "@mention or reply." Refer to Figure 2–3.

Figure 2–3 Comments attached to document text

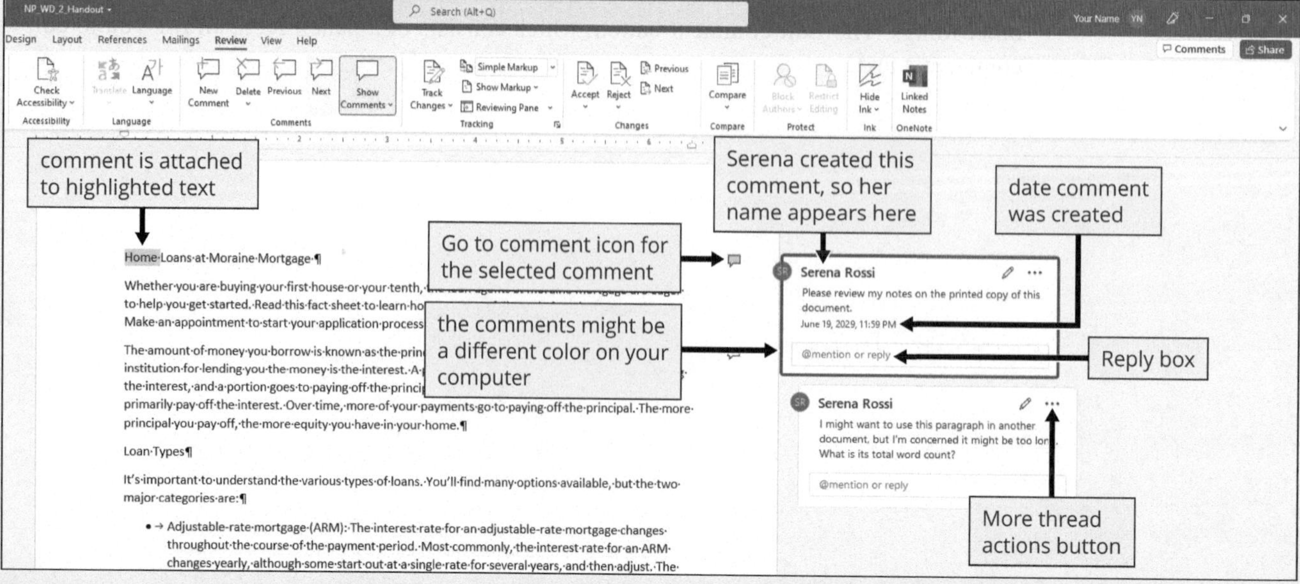

In the document, the text "Home" is highlighted. Because Serena created the comment, her name appears at the beginning of the comment.

3. Read the comment, and then in the Comments group, click the **Next** button to select the next comment. According to this comment, Serena wants to know the total word count of the paragraph the comment is attached to. You can get this information by selecting the entire paragraph and locating the word count in the status bar.
4. Triple-click anywhere in the second paragraph of the document (which begins "The amount of money you borrow...") to select the paragraph. In the status bar, the message "85 of 695 words" tells you that 85 of the document's 695 words are currently selected. So the answer to Serena's question is 85.

   Trouble? Don't be concerned if you see a slightly different word count in the status bar. No matter what you see, type the numeral 85 in Step 5.

5. In the second comment, click the **Reply** box, and type **85**. Finally, to add your comment to the document, you need to click the **Post reply** button.
6. Click the **Post reply** button in the comment. Your reply appears below Serena's original comment. The name that appears in your reply comment is the name associated with the Microsoft Office account running on your computer.

After you post a comment, you can go back and edit it at any time. You can also delete individual comments or comment threads.

1. Point to your reply to display the Edit comment button, and then click the **Edit comment** button. Your reply is displayed in a rectangular box, with the blinking insertion point ready for you to make any changes. In this case, you will change the numeral "85" to a complete sentence.
2. Use the Delete key to delete "85" and then type **The word count is 85**. Don't forget to include the period.
3. Click the **Post comment** button to post the comment.
4. In the Comments group, click the **Next** button to select the next comment, which asks you to insert your name after "Prepared by:" at the end of the document.
5. Click after the colon in "Prepared by:", press **SPACEBAR**, and then type your first and last names. To indicate that you have complied with Serena's request by adding your name, you could click the comment in the right margin, click the More thread actions button, and then click Resolve thread. However, in this case, you'll simply delete the comment. Serena also asks you to delete the first comment.
6. Click anywhere in the final comment, and then in the Comments group, click the **Delete** button.
7. In the Comments group, click the **Previous** button twice to select the comment at the beginning of the document.
8. In the selected comment, click the More thread actions button ··· and then click **Delete thread**.

Insight

Changing the Username

To change the username associated with your copy of Word, click the Dialog Box Launcher in the Tracking group on the Review tab, and then click Change User Name. From there, you can change the username and the initials associated with your copy of Word. To override the name associated with your Microsoft account and use the name that appears in the User name box in the Word Options dialog box instead, select the "Always use these values regardless of sign in to Office" check box. However, there is no need to change these settings for this module, and you should never change them on a shared computer at school unless specifically instructed to do so by your instructor.

As you reviewed the document, you might have noticed that, on page 2, a word appears in all uppercase letters. This is probably just a typing mistake. You can correct it and then add a comment that points out the change to Serena.

To correct the mistake and add a comment:

1. Scroll down to the middle of page 2, and then, in the paragraph above the "Step-by-Step Process" heading, select the text **RENTAL PROPERTY**.
2. On the ribbon, click the **Home** tab.
3. In the Font group, click the **Change Case** button Aa▾, and then click **lowercase**. The text changes to read "rental property." Note that you could select Capitalize Each Word to make the first letter in each word you have selected uppercase.
4. Verify that the text is still selected, and then click the **Review** tab on the ribbon.
5. In the Comments group, click the **New Comment** button. A new comment appears, with the insertion point ready for you to begin typing.
6. In the new comment, type **I assumed you didn't want this in all uppercase letters, so I changed it to lowercase.** (including the period) and then click the **Post comment** button ▷. Save the document.

   You can now close comments because you are finished working with comments.
7. In the Comments group, click the **Show Comments** button. The comments close, and the "Go to comment" icon in the right margin alerts you to the presence of a comment without taking up all the space required to display the comments. You can point to highlighted text to read a particular comment without displaying the comments.
8. Point to the phrase "rental property" on page 2. The phrase is highlighted, and the full comment is displayed, as shown in Figure 2–4.

Figure 2–4 Document with the Go to comment icon

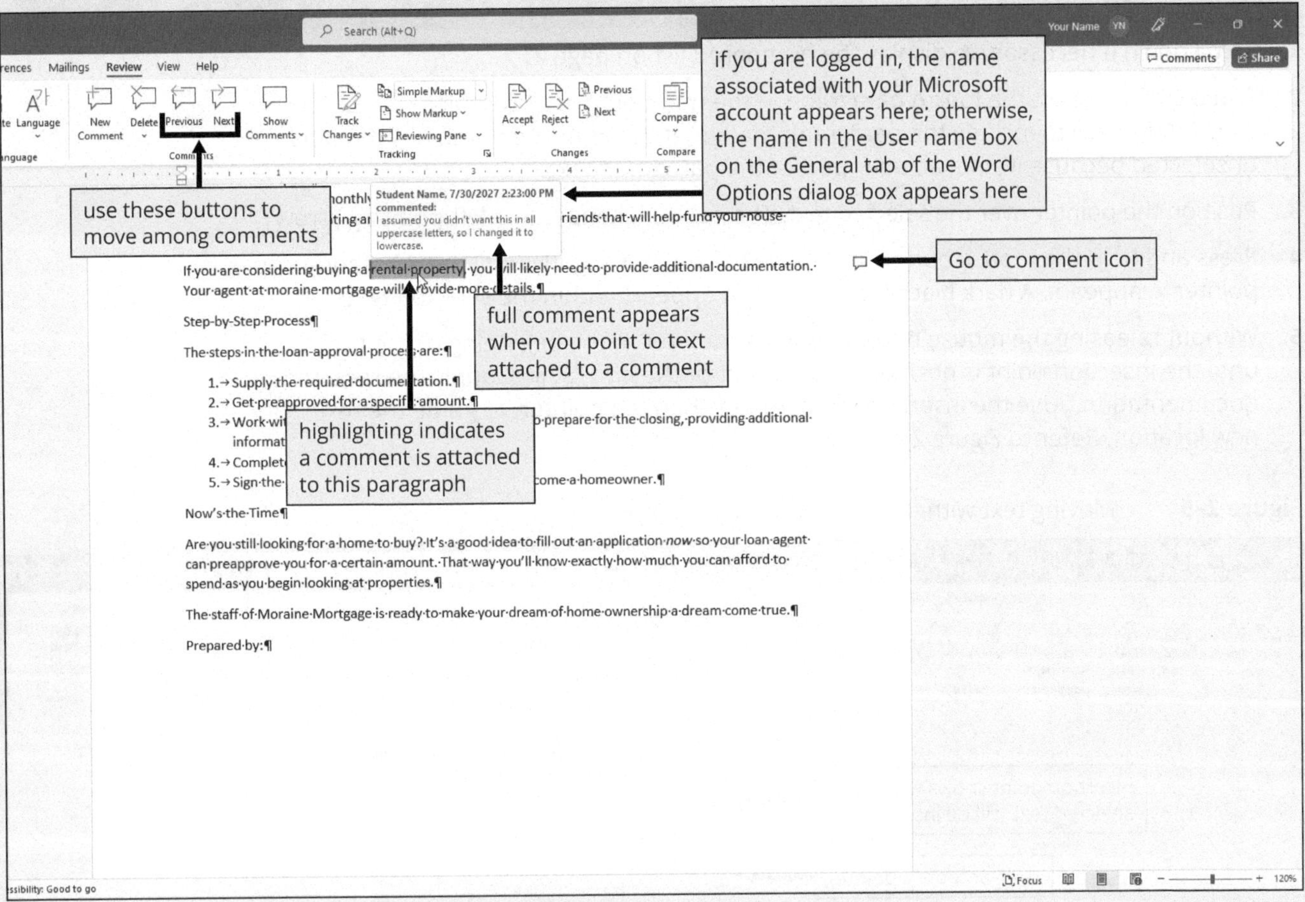

9. Move the mouse away from the phrase "rental property" to close the comment.

Insight

Comments allow you to communicate with coworkers about important issues in a document, but it's up to you to let your coworkers know if a document contains comments they need to review. However, if you work at a business or other organization that uses Microsoft SharePoint to allow coworkers to share files on OneDrive, you can save a Word document on OneDrive, and then send an email to a colleague from within a comment. Type the @ symbol in a comment followed by the first letters of the person's first or last name. This displays a list of people at your organization. Click the name of the person you want to see the comment, and then continue by adding any information you want to share. When you post the comment, Word sends an email informing the person about the comment. The combination of a person's name and the @ symbol is known as an **@mention**.

Moving Text in a Document

One of the most useful features of a word-processing program is the ability to move text easily. For example, Serena wants to reorder the information in the numbered list on page 2. You could do this by deleting a paragraph and then retyping it at a new location. However, it's easier to select and then move the text. Word provides several ways to move text—drag and drop, cut and paste, and copy and paste.

Dragging and Dropping Text

To move text with **drag and drop**, you select the text you want to move, press and hold the mouse button while you drag the selected text to a new location, and then release the mouse button.

In the numbered list on page 2, Serena wants you to move up the paragraph that reads "Complete the online form" so it is the first item in the list.

To move text using drag and drop:

1. Scroll down if necessary to display the numbered list on page 2.
2. Triple-click to select the fourth paragraph in the numbered list, "Complete the online form." Take care to include the paragraph marker at the end. The number 4 remains unselected because it's not actually part of the paragraph text.
3. Position the pointer over the selected text. The pointer changes to a left-pointing arrow.
4. Press and hold the mouse button and move the pointer slightly until the drag-and-drop pointer appears. A dark black insertion point appears within the selected text.
5. Without releasing the mouse button, drag the pointer to the beginning of the list until the insertion point is positioned to the left of the first "S" in "Supply the required documentation." Use the insertion point, rather than the pointer, to guide the text to its new location. Refer to Figure 2–5.

Figure 2–5 Moving text with the drag-and-drop pointer

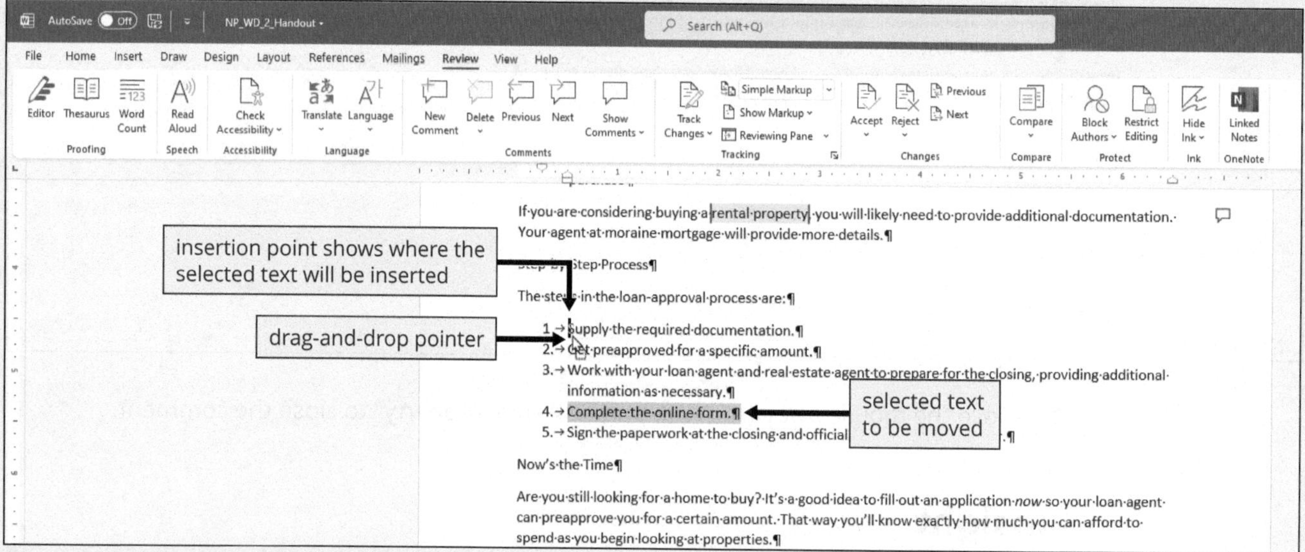

6. Release the mouse button, and then click a blank area of the document to deselect the text. The first item in the list is now "Complete the online form." The remaining paragraphs have been renumbered as paragraphs 2 through 5. Refer to Figure 2–6.

Figure 2–6 Text in new location

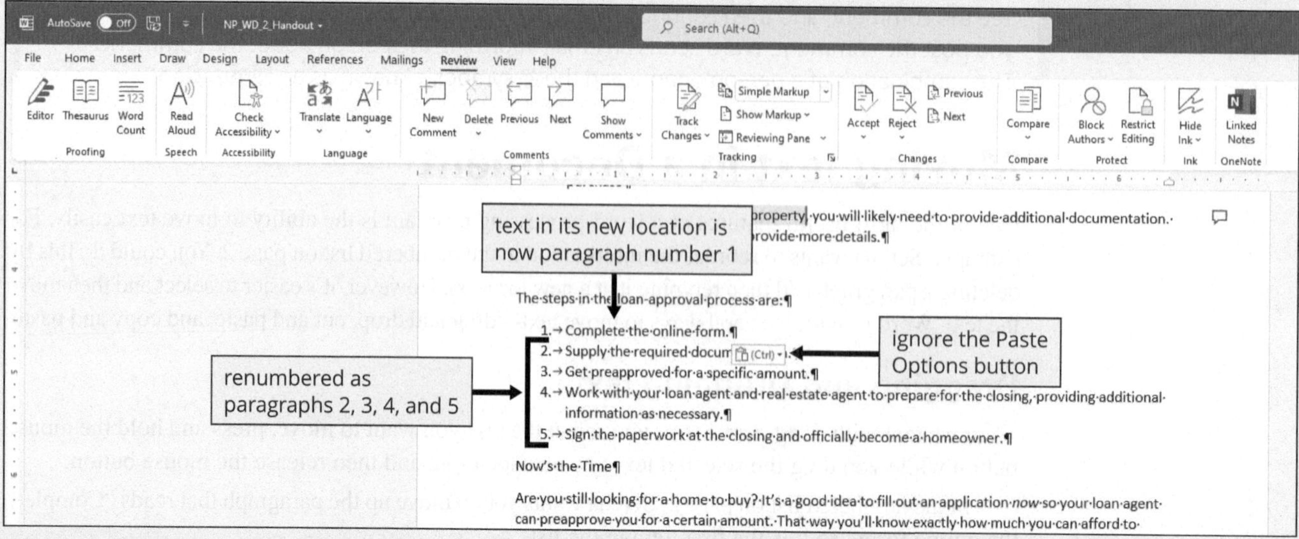

The Paste Options button appears near the newly inserted text, providing access to more advanced options related to pasting text. You don't need to use the Paste Options button right now; it will disappear when you start performing another task.

> **Trouble?** If the selected text moves to the wrong location, click the Undo button on the Home tab, and then repeat Steps 3 through 6.

7. Save the document.

Dragging and dropping works well when you are moving text a short distance. When you are moving text from one page to another, it's easier to cut, copy, and paste text using the Clipboard.

Cutting or Copying and Pasting Text Using the Clipboard

The **Office clipboard** is a temporary storage area on your computer that holds objects such as text or graphics until you need them. To **cut** means to remove text or another item from a document and place it on the Clipboard. Once you've cut something, you can paste it somewhere else. To **copy** means to copy a selected item to the Clipboard, leaving the item in its original location. To **paste** means to insert a copy of whatever is on the Clipboard into the document, at the insertion point. When you paste an item from the Clipboard into a document, the item remains on the Clipboard so you can paste it again somewhere else if you want. The buttons for cutting, copying, and pasting are located in the Clipboard group on the Home tab.

By default, Word pastes text in a new location in a document with the same formatting it had in its old location. To select other ways to paste text, you can use the Paste Options button, which appears next to newly pasted text, or the Paste arrow in the Clipboard group. Both buttons display a menu of paste options. Two particularly useful paste options are Merge Formatting, which combines the formatting of the copied text with the formatting of the text in the new location, and Keep Text Only, which inserts the text using the formatting of the surrounding text in the new location.

When you need to keep track of multiple pieces of cut or copied text, it's helpful to open the **Clipboard pane**, which displays the contents of the Clipboard. You open the Clipboard pane by clicking the Clipboard Dialog Box Launcher in the Clipboard group on the Home tab. When the Clipboard pane is displayed, the Clipboard can store up to 24 text items. When the Clipboard pane is not displayed, the Clipboard can hold only the most recently copied item.

Serena would like to move the last sentence in the second paragraph (the paragraph below the title "Home Loans at Moraine Mortgage"). You'll use cut and paste to move this sentence to a new location.

To move text using cut and paste:

1. Click the **Home** tab on the ribbon.
2. Scroll up until you can see the second paragraph in the document, just below the "Home Loans at Moraine Mortgage" title.
3. Press and hold **CTRL**, and then click anywhere in the last sentence of the second paragraph, which reads "Make an appointment to start your application process today." The entire sentence is selected, but not the space before it.
4. In the Clipboard group, click the **Cut** button. The selected text is removed from the document and copied to the Clipboard. The space that originally appeared before the sentence remains, so you have to delete it.

   > **Tip** You can also press CTRL+X to cut selected text. Press CTRL+V to paste the most recently copied item.

5. Press **BACKSPACE** to delete the space.
6. Scroll down to the bottom of page 2, and then click at the end of the second-to-last paragraph in the document, just to the right of the period after "true."

7. In the Clipboard group, click the **Paste** button. The sentence appears in the new location. Note that Word also inserts a space before the sentence. The Paste Options button appears near the newly inserted sentence.

   Trouble? If a menu opens below the Paste button, you clicked the Paste arrow instead of the Paste button. Press ESC to close the menu, and then repeat Step 7, taking care not to click the arrow below the Paste button.

8. Save the document.

Serena explains that she'll be using some text from the mortgage handout as the basis for another department handout. She asks you to copy that information and paste it into a new document. You can do this using the Clipboard pane.

To copy text to paste into a new document:

1. In the Clipboard group, click the **Clipboard Dialog Box Launcher**. The Clipboard pane opens on the left side of the document window, as shown in Figure 2–7.

Figure 2–7 Clipboard pane

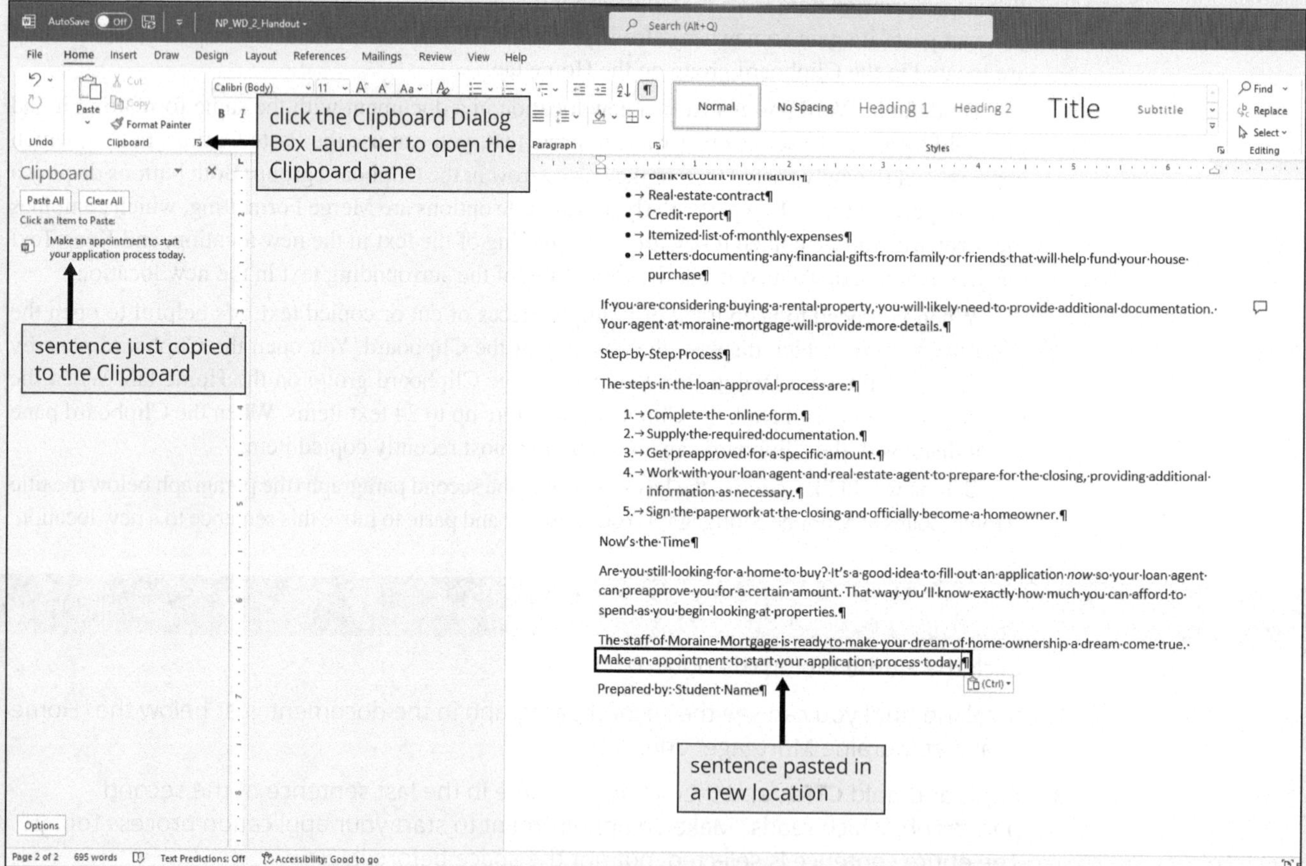

Notice the Clipboard contains the sentence you copied in the last set of steps. Now you can copy another sentence to the Clipboard.

2. Scroll up slightly, if necessary, and then locate the second sentence in the paragraph below the "Now's the Time" heading.
3. Press and hold **CTRL**, and then click anywhere in the sentence, which begins "It's a good idea to fill out an application *now*...." The sentence and the space following it are selected. Notice that the word "now" is italicized for emphasis.
4. In the Clipboard group, click the **Copy** button. The sentence appears at the top of the Clipboard pane, as shown in Figure 2–8. You can also copy selected text by pressing CTRL+C.

Figure 2–8 Items in the Clipboard pane

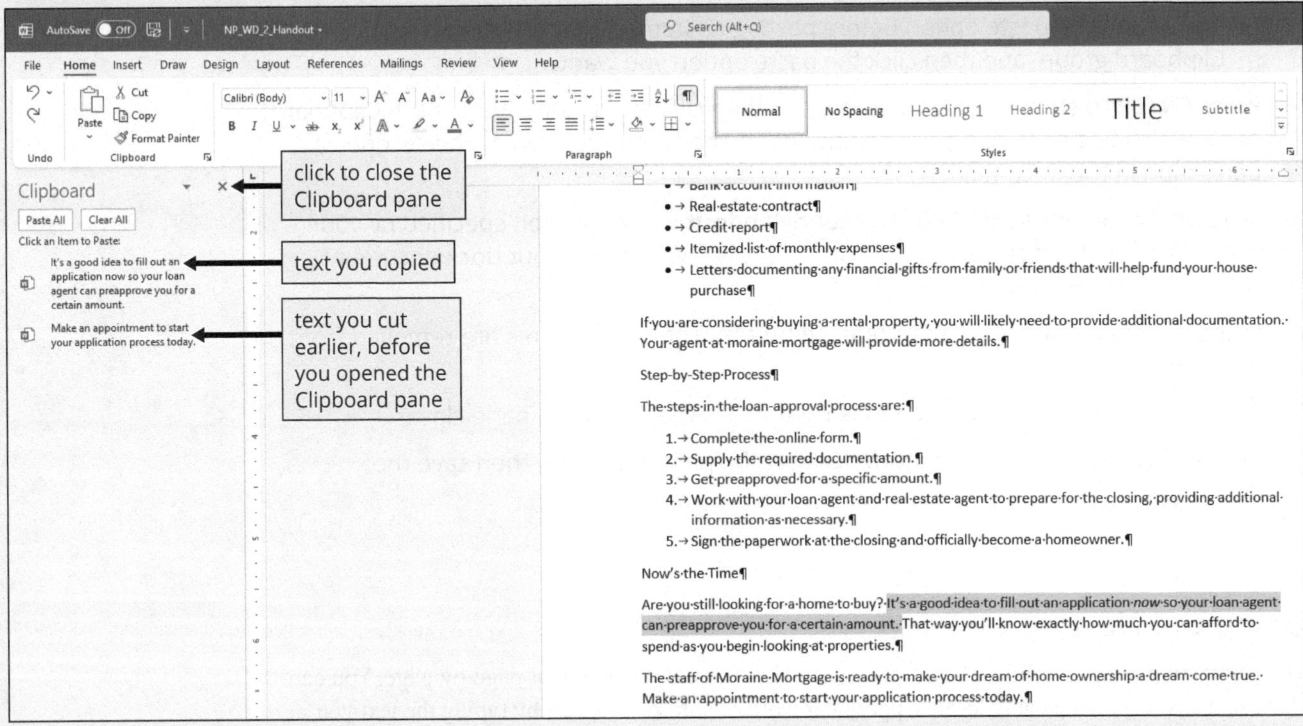

Now you can use the Clipboard pane to insert the copied text into a new document.

To insert the copied text into a new document:

1. Open a new, blank document. Open the Clipboard pane, if necessary. At this point, you could click the Paste All button in the Clipboard pane to paste the entire contents of the Clipboard into the document, but Serena wants to paste one item at a time.
2. In the Clipboard pane, click the first item in the list of copied items, which begins "It's a good idea to fill out an application now...." The text is inserted in the document, and the word "now" retains its italic formatting.

   Serena doesn't want to keep the italic formatting in the newly pasted text. You can remove this formatting by using the Paste Options button, which is visible just below the pasted text.
3. Click the **Paste Options** button (Ctrl) in the document. The Paste Options menu opens, as shown in Figure 2–9.

Figure 2–9 Paste Options menu

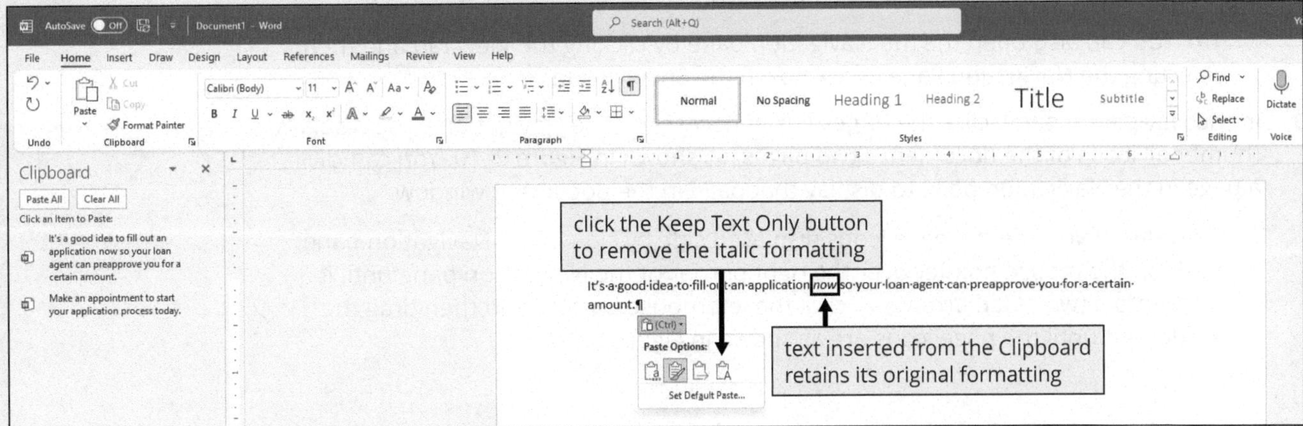

To paste the text without the italic formatting, you can click the Keep Text Only button.

4. Click the **Keep Text Only** button. Word removes the italic formatting from "now."

   Tip To select a paste option before pasting an item, click the Paste arrow in the Clipboard group, and then click the paste option you want.

5. Press **ENTER** to start a new paragraph, and then click the second item in the Clipboard pane, which begins "Make an appointment...." The text is inserted as the second paragraph in the document.
6. Save the document as **NP_WD_2_SecondHandout** in the location specified by your instructor, and then close it. You return to the NP_WD_2_Handout.docx document, where the Clipboard pane is still open.
7. In the Clipboard pane, click the **Clear All** button. The copied items are removed from the Clipboard.
8. In the Clipboard pane, click the **Close** button ✕. The Clipboard pane closes.
9. Click anywhere in the document to deselect the paragraph, and then save the document.

Using the Navigation Pane

The Navigation pane simplifies the process of moving through a document page by page. You can also use the Navigation pane to locate a particular word or phrase. You start by typing the text you're searching for—the **search text**—in the Search box at the top of the Navigation pane. As shown in the Part 2.1 Visual Overview, Word highlights every instance of the search text in the document. At the same time, a list of the **search results** appears in the Navigation pane. You can click a search result to go immediately to that location in the document.

To become familiar with the Navigation pane, you'll use it to navigate through the document page by page. You'll start by moving the insertion point to the beginning of the document.

To navigate through the document page by page:

1. Press **CTRL+HOME** to move the insertion point to the beginning of the document.
2. On the left edge of the task bar, click the page indicator (which currently reads "Page 1 of 2"). The Navigation pane opens on the left side of the Word window.
   In the box at the top, you can type the text you want to find. The three links below the Search document box—Headings, Pages, and Results—allow you to navigate through the document in different ways. As you become a more experienced Word user, you'll learn how to use the Headings link; for now, you'll ignore it. To move quickly among the pages of a document, you can use the Pages link.

   Tip You can also open the the Navigation pane by clicking the View tab and then selecting the Navigation Pane check box in the Show group.

3. In the Navigation pane, click the **Pages** link, if necessary. The Navigation pane displays thumbnail icons of the document's two pages, as shown in Figure 2–10. You can click a page in the Navigation pane to display that page in the document window.

   Trouble? If you see the page icons displayed side by side in the Navigation pane, position the mouse pointer over the right border of the Navigation pane until it turns into a two-sided arrow ⇔, click the left mouse button, and then drag the border left until the page icons are as shown in Figure 2–10.

Figure 2–10 Document pages displayed in the Navigation pane

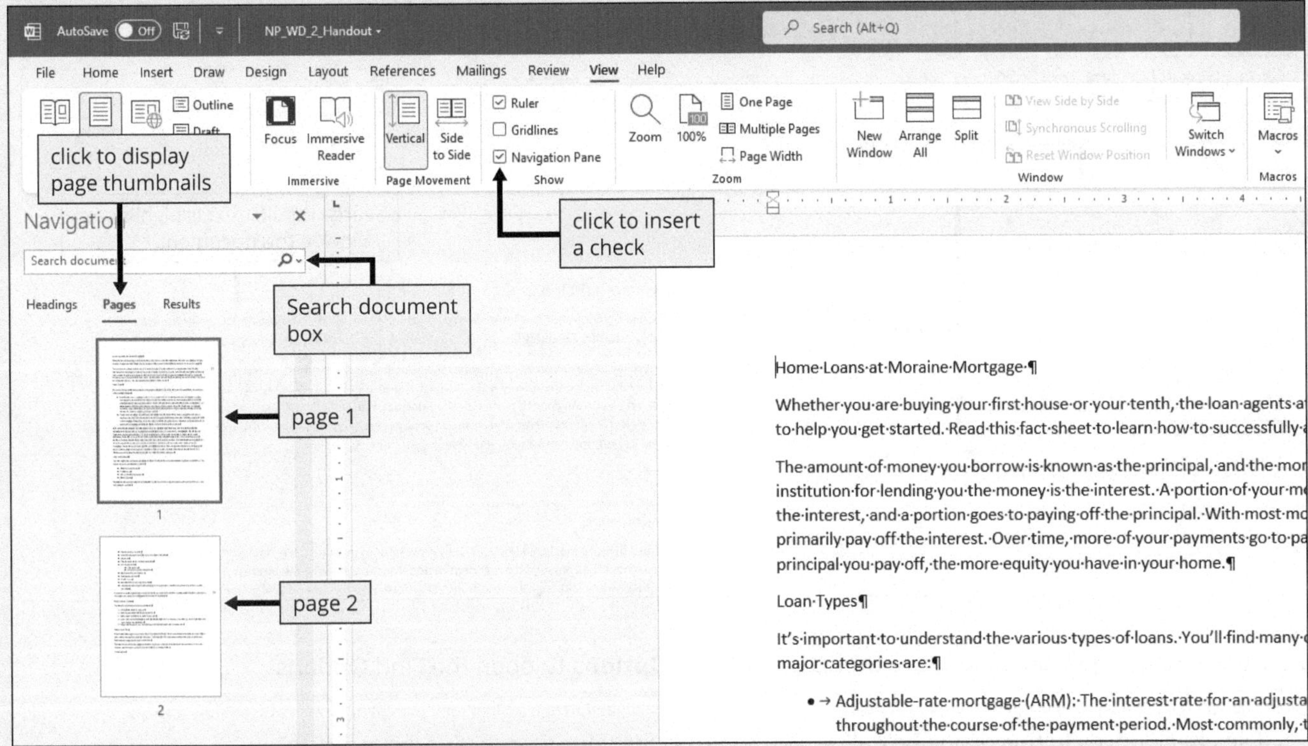

4. In the Navigation pane, click the **page 2** thumbnail. Page 2 is displayed in the document window, with the insertion point blinking at the beginning of the page.
5. In the Navigation pane, click the **page 1** thumbnail to move the insertion point back to the beginning of the document.

Serena thinks she might have mistakenly used "moraine mortgage" in some parts of the document when she actually meant to use "Moraine Mortgage." She asks you to use the Navigation pane to find all instances of "moraine mortgage."

To search for "moraine mortgage" in the document:

1. In the Navigation pane, click the **Results** link, click the **Search document** box, and then type **moraine mortgage**. You do not have to press ENTER.

   Every instance of the text "moraine mortgage" is highlighted in yellow in the document. The yellow highlight is only temporary; it will disappear as soon as you begin to perform any other task in the document. A full list of the five search results is displayed in the Navigation pane. Some of the search results contain "Moraine Mortgage" (with "M" uppercase), while others contain "moraine mortgage" (with all lowercase letters). To narrow the search results, you need to tell Word to match the case of the search text.
2. In the Navigation pane, click the **Search for more things** button. This displays a two-part menu. In the bottom part, you can select other items to search for, such as graphics or tables. The top part provides more advanced search tools. Refer to Figure 2–11.

Figure 2–11 Navigation pane with Search for more things menu

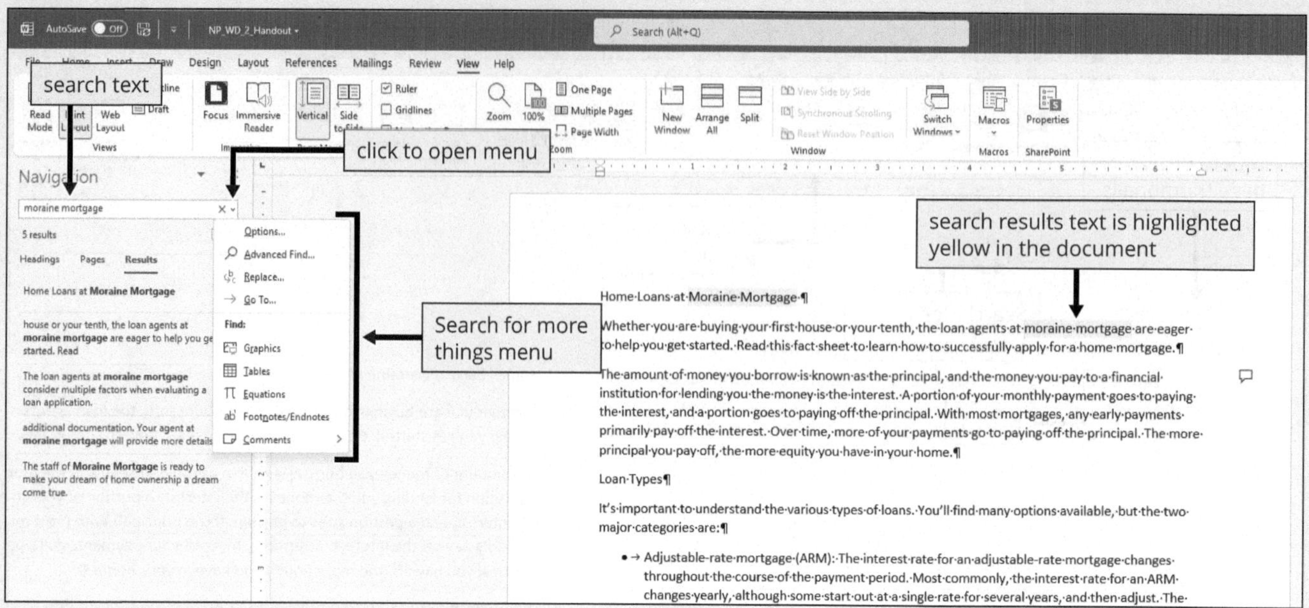

3. At the top of the Search for more things menu, click **Options** to open the Find Options dialog box.

   The check boxes in this dialog box allow you to fine-tune your search. For example, to ensure that Word finds the search text only when it appears as a separate word and not when it appears as part of another word, you could select the Find whole words only check box. Right now, you are concerned only with making sure the search results have the same case as the search text.

4. Click the **Match case** check box to select it, and then click **OK** to close the Find Options dialog box. Now you can search the document again.

5. Press **CTRL+HOME** to move the insertion point to the beginning of the document if it isn't there already, click the **Search document** box in the Navigation pane, and then type **moraine mortgage**. This time, only three search results appear in the Navigation pane, and they contain the lowercase text "moraine mortgage."

   To move among the search results, you can use the up and down arrows in the Navigation pane.

6. In the Navigation pane, click the **down arrow** button. Word selects the first instance of "moraine mortgage" in the Navigation pane, as indicated by a blue outline. Also, in the document, the first instance has a gray selection highlight over the yellow highlight. Refer to Figure 2–12.

Figure 2–12 Navigation pane with the first search result selected

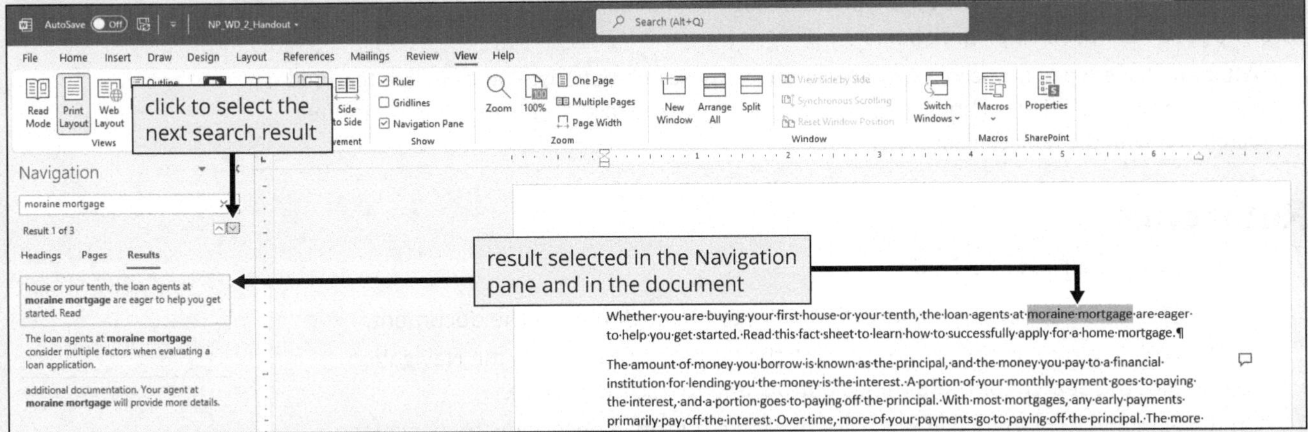

Trouble? If the second instance of "moraine mortgage" is selected in the Navigation pane, then you pressed the ENTER key after typing "moraine mortgage" in Step 5. Click the up arrow button to select the first instance.

7. In the Navigation pane, click the **down arrow** button. Word selects the second instance of "moraine mortgage" in the document and in the Navigation pane.
8. Click the **down arrow** button again to select the third search result, and then click the **up arrow** button to select the second search result again.

   You can also select a search result in the document by clicking a search result in the Navigation pane.
9. In the Navigation pane, click the third search result (which begins "additional documentation. Your agent..."). The third search result is selected in the document and in the Navigation pane.

After reviewing the search results, Serena decides she would like to replace the three instances of "moraine mortgage" with "Moraine Mortgage." You can do that by using the Find and Replace dialog box.

Insight

Using the Search Pane

You can also use the Search pane to search for text in a document. To open the Search pane, click the Find button in the Editing group on the Home tab or press CTRL+F. To look for text in the current document, verify that This file is selected at the top-left corner of the Search pane, type the text you want to find in the text box, and then press Enter. This displays a list of every instance of the search text, similar to the Navigation pane. You can also click the This file button, and select another search option. For example, you could click Web to look for the text on the web, or to look for images on the web related to the text. This makes the Search pane a very powerful tool, similar to a browser. But for working within a document, the Navigation pane is usually more convenient, in part because it allows you to switch back and forth between the document headings and search results.

Finding and Replacing Text

To open the Find and Replace dialog box from the Navigation pane, click the Search for more things button, and then click Replace. You can also click the Replace button in the Editing group on the Home tab. Either option opens the **Find and Replace dialog box**, with the Replace tab displayed by default. The Replace tab provides options for finding a specific word or phrase in the document and replacing it with another word or phrase. To use the Replace tab, type the search text in the Find what box, and then type the text you want to substitute in the Replace with box. You can also click the More button on the Replace tab to display the Search Options section, which includes the same options you saw earlier in the Find Options dialog box, including the Find whole words only check box and the Match case check box.

After you have typed the search text and selected any search options, you can click the Find Next button to select the first occurrence of the search text; you can then decide whether to substitute the search text with the replacement text.

Reference

Finding and Replacing Text

- Press CTRL+HOME to move the insertion point to the beginning of the document.
- In the Editing group on the Home tab, click the Replace button, or in the Navigation pane, click the Search for more things button, and then click Replace.
- In the Find and Replace dialog box, click the More button, if necessary, to display the Search Options section of the Replace tab.
- In the Find what box, type the search text.
- In the Replace with box, type the replacement text.
- Select the appropriate check boxes in the Search Options section of the dialog box to narrow your search.
- Click the Find Next button.
- Click the Replace button to substitute the found text with the replacement text and find the next occurrence.
- Click the Replace All button to substitute all occurrences of the found text with the replacement text without reviewing each occurrence. Use this option only if you are absolutely certain that the results will be what you expect.

You'll use the Find and Replace dialog box now to replace three instances of "moraine mortgage" with "Moraine Mortgage." You could use the Navigation pane, but when you don't have the Navigation pane open, it's more convenient to use the Replace button in the Editing group on the Home tab. You'll try that option in the following steps.

To replace three instances of "moraine mortgage" with "Moraine Mortgage":

1. Press **CTRL+HOME** to move the insertion point to the beginning of the document.
2. Click the **Home** tab, and then, in the Editing group, click the **Replace** button. The Find and Replace dialog box opens with the Replace tab on top.

   The search text you entered earlier in the Navigation pane, "moraine mortgage," appears in the Find what box. If you hadn't already conducted a search, you would need to type your search text now. Because you selected the Match case check box earlier in the Find Options dialog box, "Match Case" appears below the Find what box.
3. In the lower-left corner of the dialog box, click the **More** button to display the search options. Because you selected the Match case check box earlier in the Find Options dialog box, it is selected here.

   Trouble? If you see the Less button instead of the More button, the search options are already displayed.
4. Click the **Replace with** box, and then type **Moraine Mortgage**.
5. Click the **Find Next** button. Word highlights the first instance of "moraine mortgage" in the document. Refer to Figure 2–13.

Figure 2–13 Find and Replace dialog box

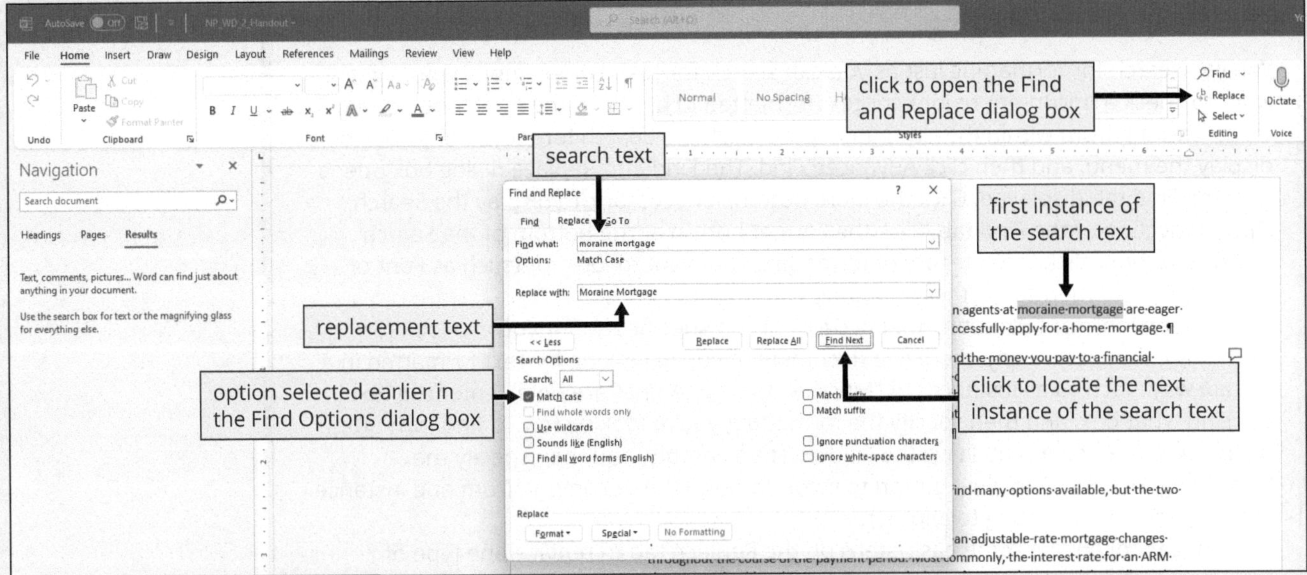

6. Click the **Replace** button. Word replaces "moraine mortgage" with "Moraine Mortgage" and then selects the next instance of "moraine mortgage." If you do not want to make a replacement, you can click the Find Next button to skip the current instance of the search text and move on to the next. In this case, however, you do want to make the replacement.
7. Click the **Replace** button. Word selects the last instance of "moraine mortgage."
8. Click the **Replace** button. Word makes the substitution and then displays a message box telling you that Word has finished searching the document.
9. Click **OK** to close the message box, and then in the Find and Replace dialog box, click **Close**.

You are finished with the Navigation pane, so you can close it. But first you need to restore the search options to their original settings. It's a good practice to restore the original search settings so that future searches are not affected by any settings you used for an earlier search.

To restore the search options to their original settings:

1. In the Navigation pane, open the **Find Options** dialog box, deselect the **Match case** check box, and then click **OK** to close the Find Options dialog box.
2. Click the **Close** button [X] in the upper-right corner of the Navigation pane.
3. Save the document.

Insight

Searching for Formatting

You can search for formatting just as you can search for text. For example, you might want to check a document to look for text formatted in bold and the Arial font. To search for formatting from within the Navigation pane, click the Search for more things button to display the menu, and then click Advanced Find. The Find and Replace dialog box opens with the Find tab displayed. Click the More button, if necessary, to display the Search Options section of the Find tab. Click the Format button at the bottom of the Search Options section, click the category of formatting you want to look for (such as Font or Paragraph), and then select the formatting you want to find.

You can look for formatting that occurs only on specific text, or you can look for formatting that occurs anywhere in a document. If you're looking for text formatted in a certain way (such as all instances of "Moraine Mortgage" that are bold), enter the text in the Find what box, and then specify the formatting you're looking for. To find formatting on any text in a document, leave the Find what box empty, and then specify the formatting. Use the Find Next button to move through the document, from one instance of the specified formatting to another.

You can follow the same basic steps on the Replace tab to replace one type of formatting with another. First, click the Find what box and select the desired formatting. Then click the Replace with box and select the desired formatting. If you want, type search text and replacement text in the appropriate boxes. Then proceed as with any Find and Replace operation.

Now that the text in the document is final, you will turn your attention to styles, which affect the look of the entire document.

Working with Styles

A style is a set of formatting options that you can apply by clicking an icon in the Style gallery on the Home tab. Each style is designed for a particular use. For example, the Title style is intended for formatting the title at the beginning of a document.

All the text you type in a document has a style applied to it. By default, text is formatted in the Normal style, which applies 11-point Calibri font, left alignment, 1.08 line spacing, and a small amount of extra space between paragraphs. In other words, the Normal style applies the default formatting you learned about when you first began typing a Word document.

There are two types of styles—character and paragraph. A **paragraph style** is a named set of paragraph and character format settings, such as line spacing, text alignment, and borders, that can be applied to a paragraph to format it all at once. The Normal, Heading, and Title styles all apply paragraph-level formatting. A **character style** is a named group of character format settings; character styles are set up to format only individual characters or words (for example, emphasizing a phrase by adding italic formatting and changing the font color).

Depending on the size of your monitor, one row of the Style gallery is usually visible on the Home tab. To display the entire Style gallery, click the More button in the Styles group. After you begin applying styles in a document, the visible row of the Style gallery changes to show the most recently used styles.

You are ready to use the Style gallery to format the document title with the Title style, which is a paragraph style.

To display the entire Style gallery and then format the document title with a style:

1. Press **CTRL+HOME** to scroll to the top of the document and to position the insertion point in the document's first paragraph, which contains the text "Home Loans at Moraine Mortgage."
2. In the Styles group, click the **More** button. The Style gallery opens, displaying styles arranged in rows and columns. Depending on the size of your screen and your screen resolution, the Style gallery on your screen might contain more or fewer rows than shown in Figure 2–14.

Figure 2–14 Displaying the Style gallery

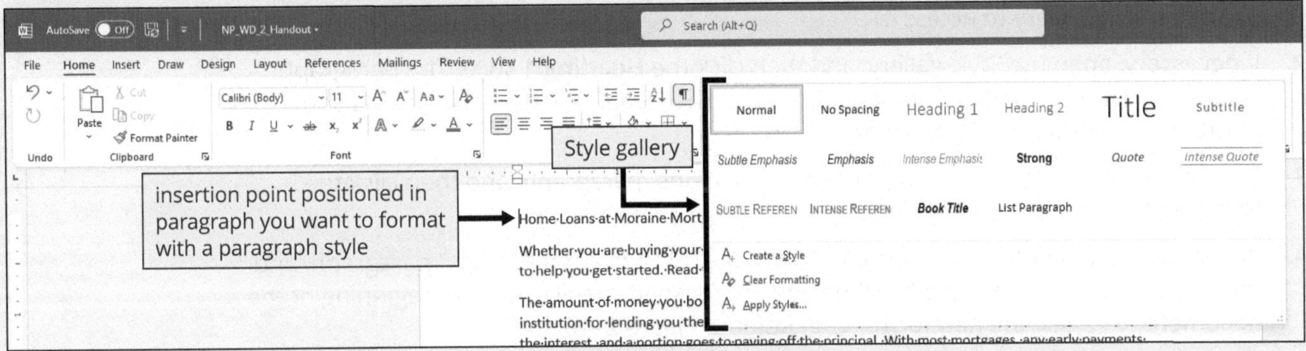

3. Point to (but don't click) the **Title** style. The ScreenTip "Title" is displayed, and a Live Preview of the style appears in the paragraph containing the insertion point, as shown in Figure 2–15. The Title style changes the font to 28-point Calibri Light.

   Tip To close the Style gallery without selecting a style, press ESC.

Figure 2–15 Title style in the Style gallery

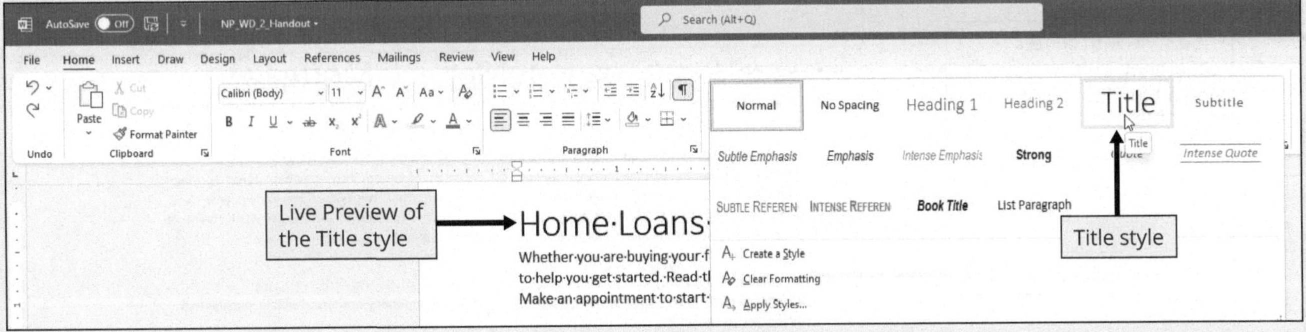

4. Click the **Title** style. The style is applied to the paragraph. After you apply a style, you can always add additional formatting. In this case, Serena would like you to center the title, change the font color, and add bold.
5. In the Paragraph group, click the **Center** button. The title is centered in the document.
6. Triple-click the title to select the entire paragraph.
7. In the Font group on the Home tab, click the **Bold** button, and then click the **Font Color arrow** and select the **Blue, Accent 5, Darker 25%** font color.

Next, you will format the document headings using the heading styles, which have different levels. The highest level, Heading 1, is used for the major headings in a document, and it applies the most noticeable formatting using a larger font than the other heading styles. (In heading styles, the highest, or most important, level has the lowest number.) The Heading 2 style is used for headings that are subordinate to the highest level headings; it applies slightly less dramatic formatting than the Heading 1 style.

The handout only has one level of headings, so you will apply only the Heading 1 style.

To format text with the Heading 1 style:

1. Click the **Home** tab to display it, if necessary, and then click anywhere in the "Loan Types" paragraph. Depending on the size of your monitor, the Heading 1 style might be visible in the portion of the Style gallery visible on the Home tab, or you might have to open the Style gallery to access it.
2. If necessary, open the Style gallery, and then click the **Heading 1** style. The paragraph is now formatted in blue, 16-point Calibri Light. The Heading 1 style also inserts some paragraph space above the heading.
3. Scroll down, click anywhere in the "Loan Applications" paragraph, and then click the **Heading 1** style in the Style gallery.
4. Repeat Step 3 to apply the Heading 1 style to the "Step-by-Step Process" paragraph, and the "Now's the Time" paragraph. When you are finished, scroll up to the beginning of the document to review the new formatting. Refer to Figure 2–16.
5. **sam** Save your changes and close the document.

Figure 2–16 Document with Title and Heading 1 styles

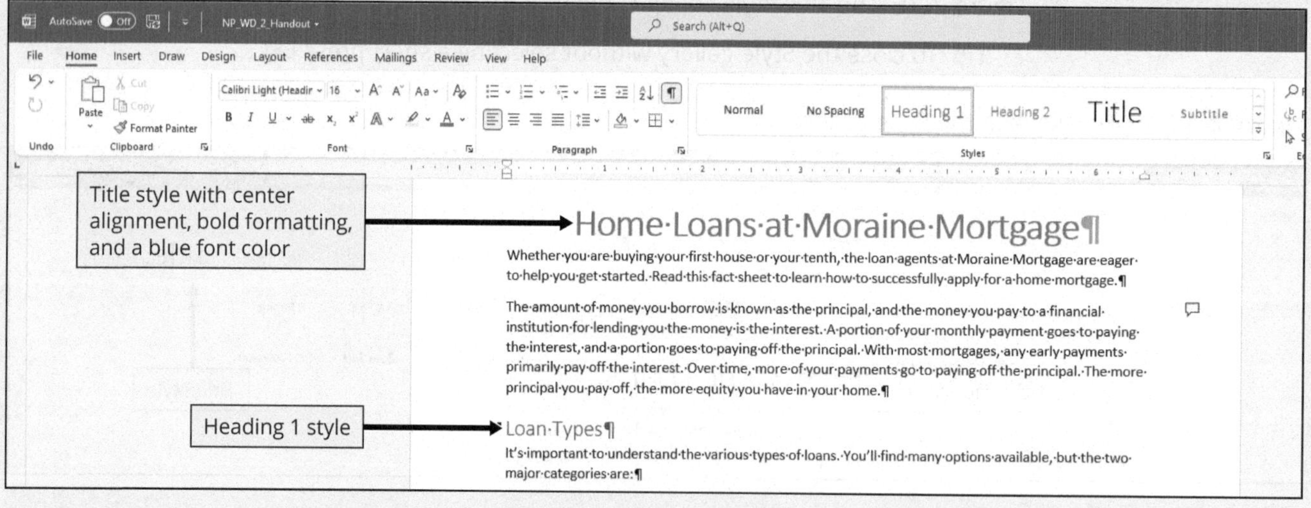

By default, the Style gallery offers 16 styles, each designed for a specific purpose. As you gain more experience with Word, you will learn how to use a wider array of styles. You'll also learn how to create your own styles. Styles allow you to change a document's formatting in an instant. But the benefits of heading styles go far beyond attractive formatting. Heading styles allow you to reorganize a document or generate a table of contents with a click of the mouse. Also, heading styles are set up to keep a heading and the body text that follows it together, so a heading is never separated from its body text by a page break. Each Word document includes nine levels of heading styles, although only the Heading 1 and Heading 2 styles are available by default in the Style gallery. Whenever you use the lowest heading style in the Style gallery, the next-lowest level is added to the Style gallery. For example, after you use the Heading 2 style, the Heading 3 style appears in the Styles group in the Style gallery.

Serena's mortgage handout is now finished. She will review it, delete the comments, and have copies printed for new homebuyers.

Part 2.1 Quick Check

1. Explain how to delete a comment from a document.
2. What should you select in the Find Options dialog box if you want to search for "Moraine Mortgage" but not "moraine mortgage"?
3. Which paste option inserts copied text using the formatting of the surrounding text?
4. What is a style?
5. Which style is applied to all text in a new document by default?

Part 2.2 Visual Overview: MLA Formatting Guidelines

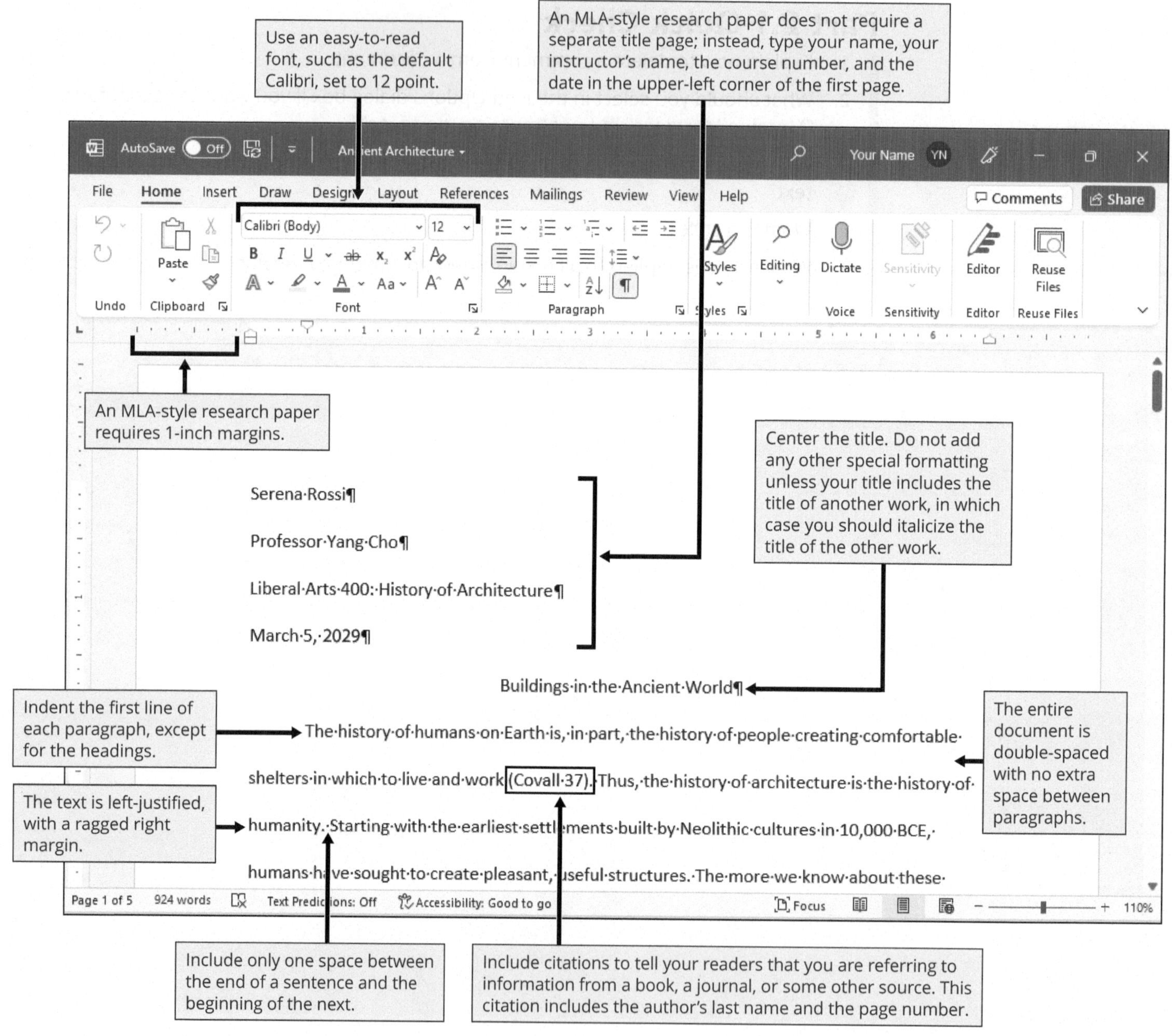

Use an easy-to-read font, such as the default Calibri, set to 12 point.
An MLA-style research paper does not require a separate title page; instead, type your name, your instructor's name, the course number, and the date in the upper-left corner of the first page.
An MLA-style research paper requires 1-inch margins.
Center the title. Do not add any other special formatting unless your title includes the title of another work, in which case you should italicize the title of the other work.
Serena·Rossi¶
Professor·Yang·Cho¶
Liberal·Arts·400:·History·of·Architecture¶
March·5,·2029¶
Buildings·in·the·Ancient·World¶
Indent the first line of each paragraph, except for the headings.
The·history·of·humans·on·Earth·is,·in·part,·the·history·of·people·creating·comfortable·shelters·in·which·to·live·and·work·(Covall·37).·Thus,·the·history·of·architecture·is·the·history·of·humanity.·Starting·with·the·earliest·settlements·built·by·Neolithic·cultures·in·10,000·BCE,·humans·have·sought·to·create·pleasant,·useful·structures.·The·more·we·know·about·these·
The entire document is double-spaced with no extra space between paragraphs.
The text is left-justified, with a ragged right margin.
Include only one space between the end of a sentence and the beginning of the next.
Include citations to tell your readers that you are referring to information from a book, a journal, or some other source. This citation includes the author's last name and the page number.

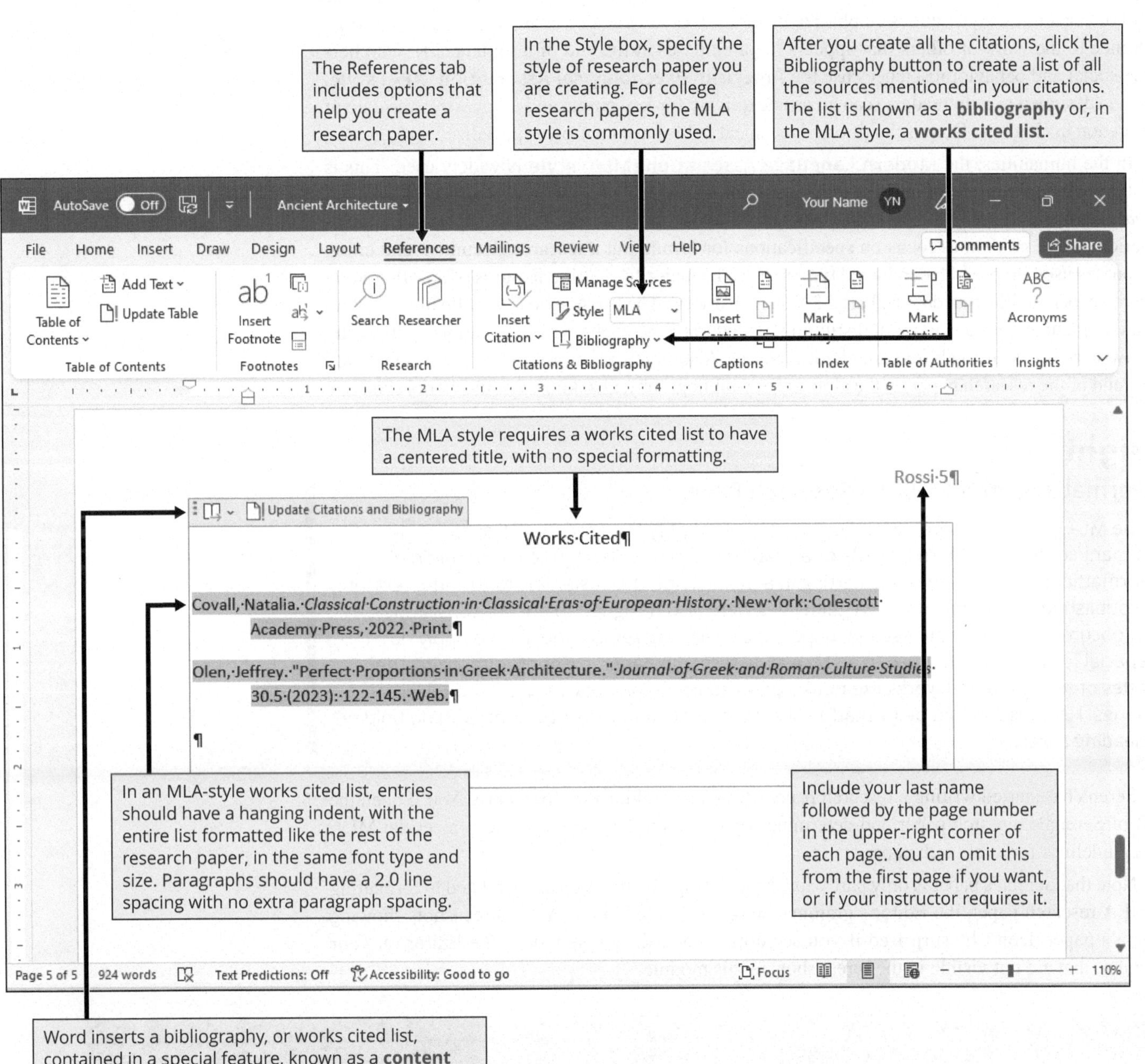
The References tab includes options that help you create a research paper.
In the Style box, specify the style of research paper you are creating. For college research papers, the MLA style is commonly used.
After you create all the citations, click the Bibliography button to create a list of all the sources mentioned in your citations. The list is known as a **bibliography** or, in the MLA style, a **works cited list**.
AutoSave Off
Ancient Architecture
Your Name
YN
File Home Insert Draw Design Layout References Mailings Review View Help
Comments
Share
Table of Contents
Add Text
Update Table
Insert Footnote
Search
Researcher
Insert Citation
Manage Sources
Style: MLA
Bibliography
Insert Caption
Mark Entry
Mark Citation
Acronyms
Table of Contents
Footnotes
Research
Citations & Bibliography
Captions
Index
Table of Authorities
Insights
The MLA style requires a works cited list to have a centered title, with no special formatting.
Rossi·5¶
Update Citations and Bibliography
Works·Cited¶
Covall,·Natalia.·Classical·Construction·in·Classical·Eras·of·European·History.·New·York:·Colescott·Academy·Press,·2022.·Print.¶
Olen,·Jeffrey.·"Perfect·Proportions·in·Greek·Architecture."·Journal·of·Greek·and·Roman·Culture·Studies·30.5·(2023):·122-145.·Web.¶
In an MLA-style works cited list, entries should have a hanging indent, with the entire list formatted like the rest of the research paper, in the same font type and size. Paragraphs should have a 2.0 line spacing with no extra paragraph spacing.
Include your last name followed by the page number in the upper-right corner of each page. You can omit this from the first page if you want, or if your instructor requires it.
Page 5 of 5
924 words
Text Predictions: Off
Accessibility: Good to go
Focus
110%
Word inserts a bibliography, or works cited list, contained in a special feature, known as a **content control**, used to display information that is inserted automatically and that may need to be updated later. You can use the buttons in the content control tab to make changes to material inside the content control.

Reviewing the MLA Style

A **style guide** is a set of rules that describe the preferred format and style for a certain type of writing. People in different fields use different style guides, with each style guide designed to suit the needs of a specific discipline. For example, journalists commonly use the *Associated Press Stylebook*, which focuses on the concise writing style common in magazines and newspapers. In the world of academics, style guides emphasize the proper way to create a **citation**, which is a formal reference to the work of others that appears in parentheses at the end of a sentence. Researchers in the social and behavioral sciences use the **American Psychological Association (APA) style**, which is designed to help readers scan an article quickly for key points and emphasizes the date of publication in citations. Other scientific and technical fields have their own specialized style guides.

In the humanities, the **Modern Language Association (MLA) style** is widely used. This is the style Serena has used for her research paper. She followed the guidelines specified in the *MLA Handbook for Writers of Research Papers*, published by the Modern Language Association of America. These guidelines focus on specifications for formatting a research document and citing the sources used in research conducted for a paper. The major formatting features of an MLA-style research paper are illustrated in the Part 2.2 Visual Overview. The MLA style is very flexible, making it easy to include citations without disrupting the natural flow of the writing. It allows you to cite other writers' works using brief parenthetical entries. A complete reference to each item is included at the end of the research paper, in the alphabetized bibliography, also known as the works cited list.

Insight

Formatting an MLA-Style Research Paper

The MLA guidelines were developed, in part, to simplify the process of transforming a manuscript into a journal article or a chapter of a book. The style calls for minimal formatting; the simpler the formatting in a manuscript, the easier it is to turn the text into a published document. The MLA guidelines were also designed to ensure consistency in documents, so that all research papers look alike. Therefore, you should apply no special formatting to the text in an MLA-style research paper, except for italicizing the titles of self-contained works like books, plays, journals, albums, movies, and television series. Headings should be formatted like the other text in the document, with no bold or heading styles.

Serena has started writing a research paper on ancient architecture for a class. You'll open the draft of Serena's research paper and determine what needs to be done to make it meet the MLA style guidelines for a research paper.

Note that Serena's paper is only partly finished. To help you focus on skills related to formatting an MLA research paper, the Editor's grammar suggestions are hidden in the screenshots showing Serena's paper. Don't be surprised if you see dotted underlines inserted by the Editor on your computer that are not visible in the screenshots in this module.

To open the document and review it for MLA style:

1. sam Open the document **NP_WD_2-2.docx** located in the Word2 > Module folder included with your Data Files, and then save the document as **NP_WD_2_Ancient** in the location specified by your instructor.
2. Verify that the document is displayed in Print Layout view and that the rulers and nonprinting characters are displayed. Set the Zoom level to at least **120%**.
3. Review the document to familiarize yourself with its structure. First, notice the parts of the document that already match the MLA style. Serena included a block of information in the upper-left corner of the first page, giving her name, her instructor's

name, the course name, and the date. The title at the top of the first page also meets the MLA guidelines in that it is centered and does not have any special formatting. The headings ("Neolithic Settlements," "Egyptian Construction," "The Civic-Minded Greeks," and "Roman Achievement") have no special formatting, but unlike the title, they are left-aligned. Finally, the body text is left-aligned with a ragged right margin, and the entire document is formatted in the same font, Calibri, which is easy to read.

What needs to be changed in order to make Serena's paper consistent with the MLA style? Currently, the entire document is formatted using the default settings, which are the Normal style for the Office theme. To transform the document into an MLA-style research paper, you need to complete the checklist shown in Figure 2–17.

Figure 2–17 Checklist for formatting a default Word document to match the MLA style

- ✓ Double-space the entire document.
- ✓ Remove extra paragraph spacing from the entire document.
- ✓ Increase the font size for the entire document to 12 points.
- ✓ Indent the first line of each body paragraph .5 inch from the left margin.
- ✓ Add the page number (preceded by your last name) in the upper-right corner of each page. If you prefer, you can omit this from the first page.

You'll take care of the first three items in the checklist now.

To begin applying MLA formatting to the document:

1. Press **CTRL+A** to select the entire document.
2. Make sure the Home tab is selected on the ribbon.
3. In the Paragraph group, click the **Line and Paragraph Spacing** button and then click **2.0**.
4. Click the **Line and Spacing** button again, and then click **Remove Space After Paragraph**. The entire document is now double-spaced, with no paragraph spacing, and the entire document is still selected.
5. In the Font group, click the **Font Size arrow**, and then click **12**. The entire document is formatted in 12-point font.
6. Click anywhere in the document to deselect the text.
7. In the first paragraph of the document, replace Serena's name with your first and last names, and then save the document.

Now you need to indent the first line of each body paragraph.

Indenting a Paragraph

Word offers a number of options for indenting a paragraph. You can move an entire paragraph to the right, or you can create specialized indents, such as a **hanging indent**, where all lines except the first line of the paragraph are indented from the left margin. As you saw in the Part 2.2 Visual Overview, all the body paragraphs (that is, all the paragraphs except the information in the upper-left corner of the first page, the title, and the headings) have a first-line indent in MLA research papers. Figure 2–18 shows some examples of other common paragraph indents.

Figure 2–18 Common paragraph indents

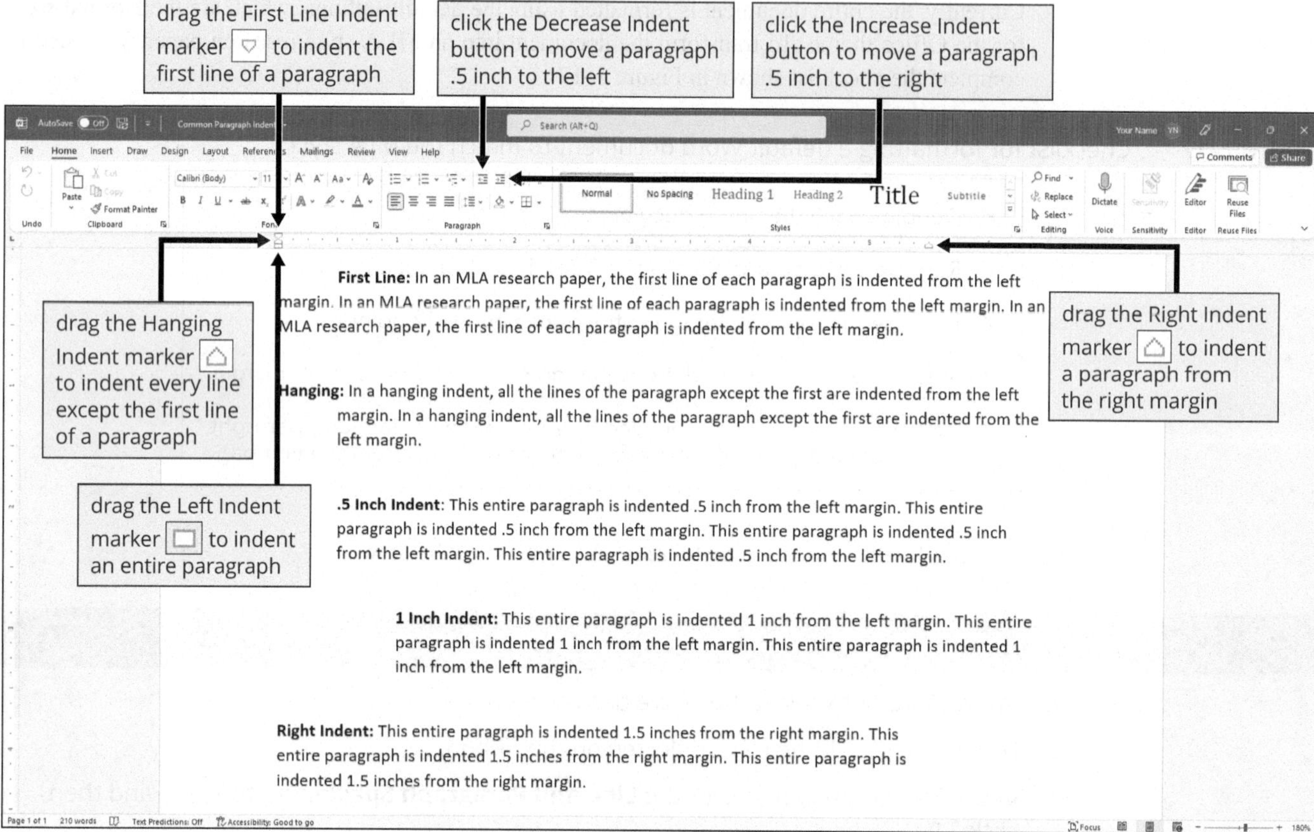

To quickly indent an entire paragraph .5 inch from the left, position the insertion point in the paragraph you want to indent, and then click the Increase Indent button in the Paragraph group on the Home tab. You can continue to indent the paragraph in increments of .5 inch by repeatedly clicking the Increase Indent button. To move an indented paragraph back to the left .5 inch, click the Decrease Indent button.

To create first-line, hanging, or right indents, you can use the indent markers on the ruler. First, click in the paragraph you want to indent or select multiple paragraphs. Then drag the appropriate indent marker to the left or right on the horizontal ruler. The indent markers are small and can be hard to see. As shown in Figure 2–18, the **First Line Indent marker** is triangle-shaped and looks like the top half of an hourglass; the **Hanging Indent marker** looks like the bottom half. The rectangle below the Hanging Indent marker is the **Left Indent marker**. The **Right Indent marker** looks just like the Hanging Indent marker except that it is located on the far-right side of the horizontal ruler.

Note that when you indent an entire paragraph using the Increase Indent button, the three indent markers move as a unit along with the paragraphs you are indenting. If you prefer, instead of dragging indent markers to indent a paragraph, you can click the Dialog Box Launcher in the Paragraph group on the Home tab, and then adjust the Indentation settings in the Paragraph dialog box.

In Serena's paper, you will indent the first lines of the body paragraphs .5 inch from the left margin, as specified by the MLA style.

To indent the first line of each paragraph:

1. On the first page of the document, just below the title, click anywhere in the first main paragraph, which begins "The history of humans...."
2. On the horizontal ruler, position the pointer over the First Line Indent marker ▽. When you see the ScreenTip that reads "First Line Indent," you know the mouse is positioned correctly.
3. Press and hold the mouse button as you drag the **First Line Indent** marker ▽ to the right, to the .5-inch mark on the horizontal ruler. As you drag, a vertical guideline appears over the document, and the first line of the paragraph moves right. Refer to Figure 2–19.

Figure 2–19 Dragging the First Line Indent marker

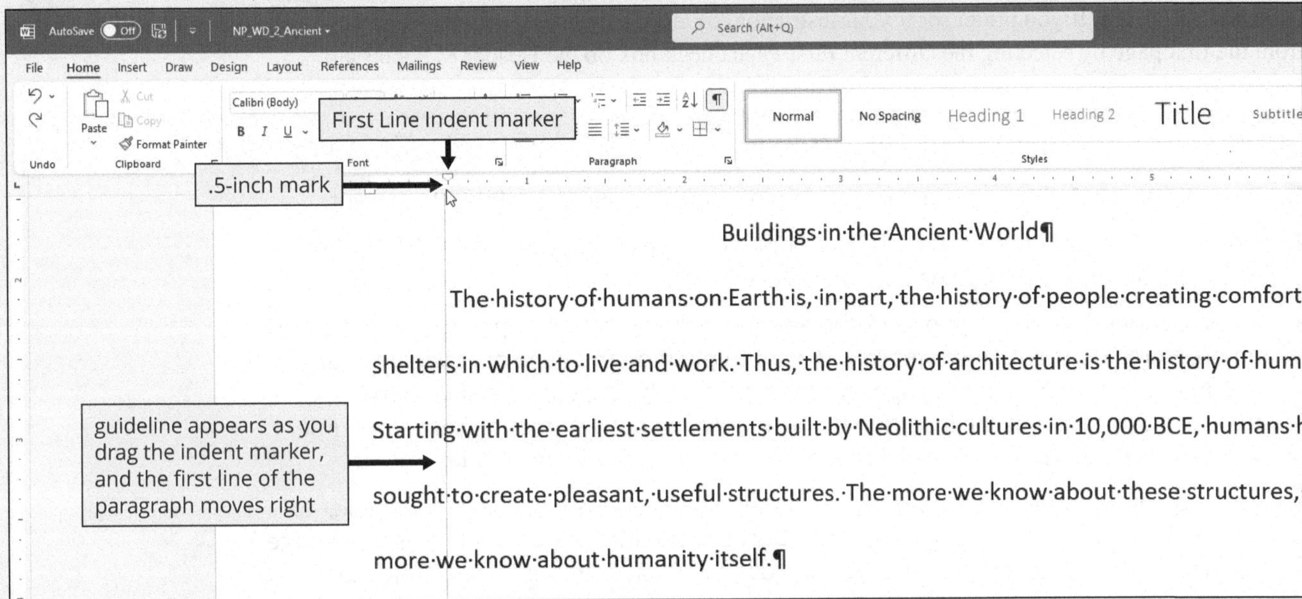
First Line Indent marker
.5-inch mark
guideline appears as you drag the indent marker, and the first line of the paragraph moves right
Buildings·in·the·Ancient·World¶
The·history·of·humans·on·Earth·is,·in·part,·the·history·of·people·creating·comfort
shelters·in·which·to·live·and·work.·Thus,·the·history·of·architecture·is·the·history·of·hum
Starting·with·the·earliest·settlements·built·by·Neolithic·cultures·in·10,000·BCE,·humans·h
sought·to·create·pleasant,·useful·structures.·The·more·we·know·about·these·structures,
more·we·know·about·humanity·itself.¶

> **Trouble?** If you see a black L-shaped icon on the ruler, you accidentally clicked the ruler and inserted a tab stop. Undo the change and start again with step 3.

4. When the First Line Indent marker ▽ is positioned at the .5-inch mark on the ruler, release the mouse button. The first line of the paragraph containing the insertion point indents .5 inch, and the vertical guideline disappears.
5. Scroll down, if necessary, click anywhere in the next paragraph in the document (which begins "In this paper, I will present..."), and then drag the **First Line Indent** marker ▽ to the right, to the .5-inch mark on the horizontal ruler. As you move the indent marker, you can use the vertical guideline to ensure that you match the first-line indent of the preceding paragraph.

   You could continue to drag the indent marker to indent the first line of the remaining body paragraphs, but it's faster to use the Repeat button on the Home tab.
6. Scroll down and click in the paragraph below the "Neolithic Settlements" heading, and then on the Home Tab, click the **Repeat** button. Note that, on most computers, you can press F4 instead to repeat an action, if you prefer.
7. Click in the next paragraph, at the top of page 2 (which begins "The rise of agriculture..."), and then click the **Repeat** button.
8. Continue using the **Repeat** button to indent the first line of all of the remaining body paragraphs, including the last paragraph on page 4. Take care not to indent the headings, which in this document are formatted just like the body text.
9. Scroll to the top of the document, verify that you have correctly indented the first line of each body paragraph, and then save the document.

Inserting and Modifying Page Numbers

When you insert page numbers in a document, you don't have to type a page number on each page. Instead, you can insert a **page number field**, which is an instruction that tells Word to insert a page number on each page, no matter how many pages you eventually add to the document. Word inserts page number fields above the top margin, in the blank area known as the **header**, or below the bottom margin, in the area known as the **footer**. You can also insert page numbers in the side margins, although for business or academic documents, it's customary to place them in the header or footer.

After you insert a page number field, Word switches to Header and Footer view. In this view, you can add your name or other text next to the page number field or use the Header & Footer contextual tab to change various settings related to headers and footers.

The MLA style requires a page number preceded by the student's last name in the upper-right corner of each page. If you prefer (or if your instructor requests it), you can omit the page number from the first page by selecting the Different First Page check box on the Header & Footer tab.

To add page numbers to the research paper:

1. Press **CTRL+HOME** to move the insertion point to the beginning of the document.
2. On the ribbon, click the **Insert** tab. The ribbon changes to display the Insert options, including options for inserting page numbers.
3. In the Header & Footer group, click the **Page Number** button to open the Page Number menu. Here you can choose where you want to position the page numbers in your document—at the top of the page, at the bottom of the page, in the side margins, or at the current location of the insertion point. To remove page numbers from a document, you can click the Remove Page Numbers command on the Page Number menu.
4. Point to **Top of Page**. A gallery of page number styles opens. You can scroll the list to review the many styles of page numbers. Because the MLA style calls for a simple page number in the upper-right corner, you will use the Plain Number 3 style. Refer to Figure 2–20.

Figure 2–20 Gallery of page number styles

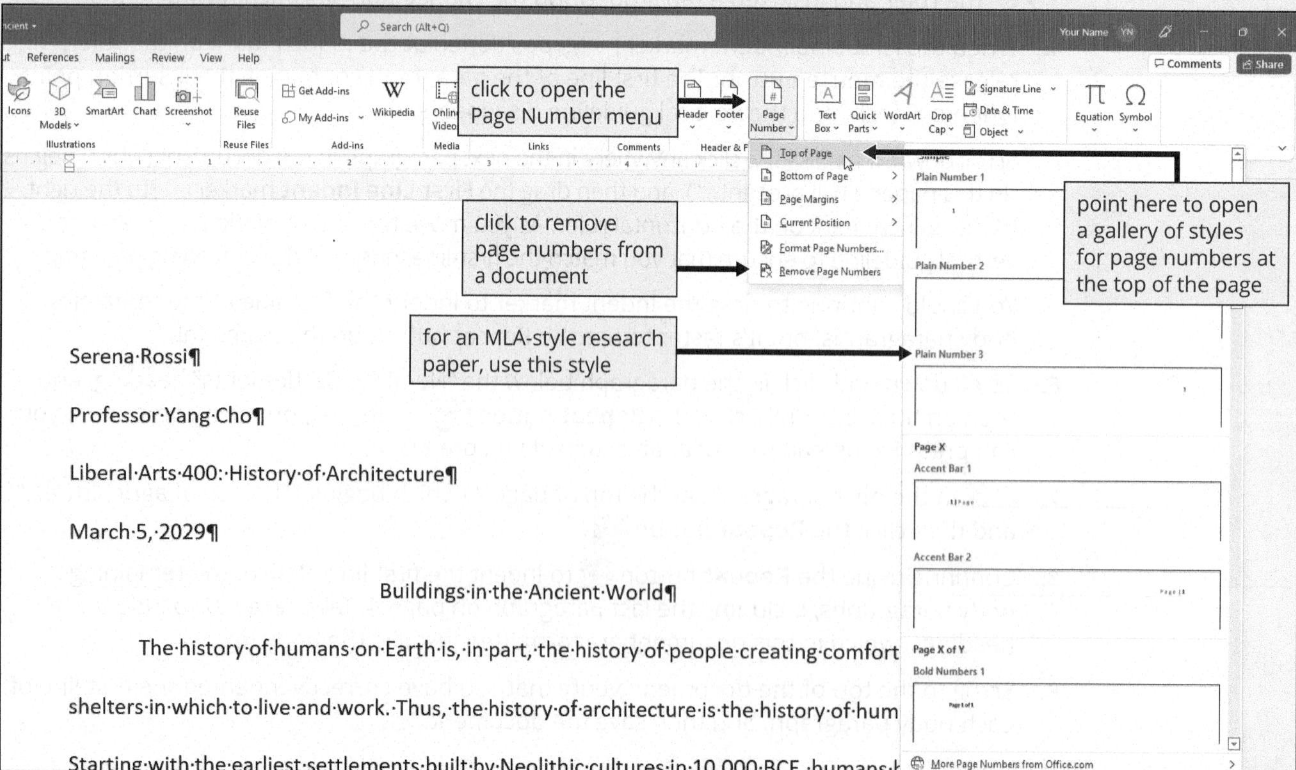

5. In the gallery, click the **Plain Number 3** style. The Word window switches to Header and Footer view, with the page number for the first page in the upper-right corner. The page number has a gray background, indicating that it is a page number field and not simply a number that you typed.

   The Header & Footer tab is displayed on the ribbon, giving you access to a variety of formatting options. The insertion point blinks to the left of the page number field, ready for you to add text to the header if you wish. Note that in Header and Footer view, you can type only in the header or footer areas. The text in the main document area is a lighter shade of gray, indicating that it cannot be edited in this view.
6. Type your last name, and then press **SPACEBAR**. If you see a wavy red line below your last name, right-click your name, and then click **Ignore All** on the Shortcut menu.
7. Select your last name and the page number field.
8. In the Mini toolbar, click the **Font Size arrow**, click **12**, and then click anywhere in the header to deselect the text. Now the header's font size matches the font size of the rest of the document. This isn't strictly necessary in an MLA research paper, but some instructors prefer it. The page number no longer has a gray background, but it is still a field, which you can verify by clicking it.
9. Click the **page number field** to display its gray background. Refer to Figure 2–21.

Figure 2–21 Last name inserted next to the page number field

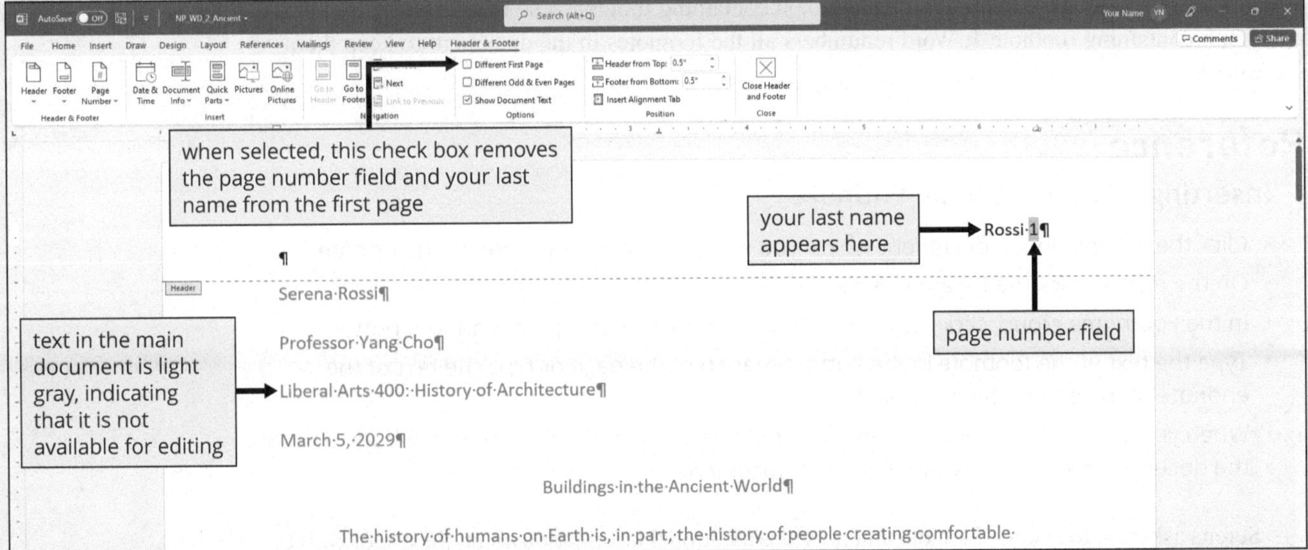

10. Scroll down and observe the page number (with your last name) at the top of pages 2, 3, and 4. As you can see, whatever you insert in the header on one page appears on every page of the document by default.
11. Scroll up to return to the header on the first page.
12. On the Header & Footer tab, in the Options group, click the **Different First Page** check box to insert a check. The page number field and your last name are removed from the first page header. The insertion point blinks at the header's left margin in case you want to insert something else for the first page header. In this case, you don't.
13. In the Close group, click the **Close Header and Footer** button. You return to Print Layout view, and the Header & Footer tab is no longer displayed on the ribbon.

Tip After you insert page numbers, you can reopen Header and Footer view by double-clicking a page number in Print Layout view.

14. Scroll down to review your last name and the page number in the headers for pages 2, 3, and 4. In Print Layout view, the text in the header is light gray, indicating that it is not currently available for editing.

You have finished all the tasks related to formatting the MLA-style research paper. Now Serena would like to add a footnote to provide some extra information.

Creating a Footnote

A **footnote** is an explanatory comment or reference that appears at the bottom of a page. When you create a footnote, Word inserts a small, superscript number (called a **marker**) in the text. The term **superscript** means that the number is raised slightly above the line of text. Word then inserts the same number in the page's bottom margin and positions the insertion point next to it so you can type the text of the footnote. **Endnotes** are similar, except that the text of an endnote appears at the end of a document. By default, the reference marker for an endnote is a lowercase Roman numeral, and the reference marker for a footnote is an ordinary, Arabic numeral.

Word automatically manages the reference markers for you, keeping them sequential from the beginning of the document to the end, no matter how many times you add, delete, or move footnotes or endnotes. For example, if you move a paragraph containing footnote 4 so that it falls before the paragraph containing footnote 1, Word renumbers all the footnotes in the document to keep them sequential.

Reference

Inserting a Footnote or an Endnote

- Click the location in the document where you want to insert a footnote or an endnote.
- On the ribbon, click the References tab.
- In the Footnotes group, click the Insert Footnote button or the Insert Endnote button.
- Type the text of the footnote in the bottom margin of the page or type the text of the endnote at the end of the document.
- When you are finished typing the text of a footnote or an endnote, click in the body of the document to continue working on the document.

Serena asks you to insert a footnote that provides additional information about the use of wood in ancient Egypt.

To add a footnote to the research paper:

1. Use the Navigation pane to find the sentence "Wood was scarce in ancient Egypt." on page 2, and then click to the right of the period after "Egypt."
2. Close the Navigation pane.
3. On the ribbon, click the **References** tab.
4. In the Footnotes group, click the **Insert Footnote** button. A superscript "1" is inserted to the right of the period after "Egypt." Word also inserts the number "1" in the bottom margin below a separator line. The insertion point is now located next to the number in the bottom margin, ready for you to type the text of the footnote.
5. Type **Wood was typically reserved for household objects.** Refer to Figure 2–22.

Figure 2–22 Inserting a footnote

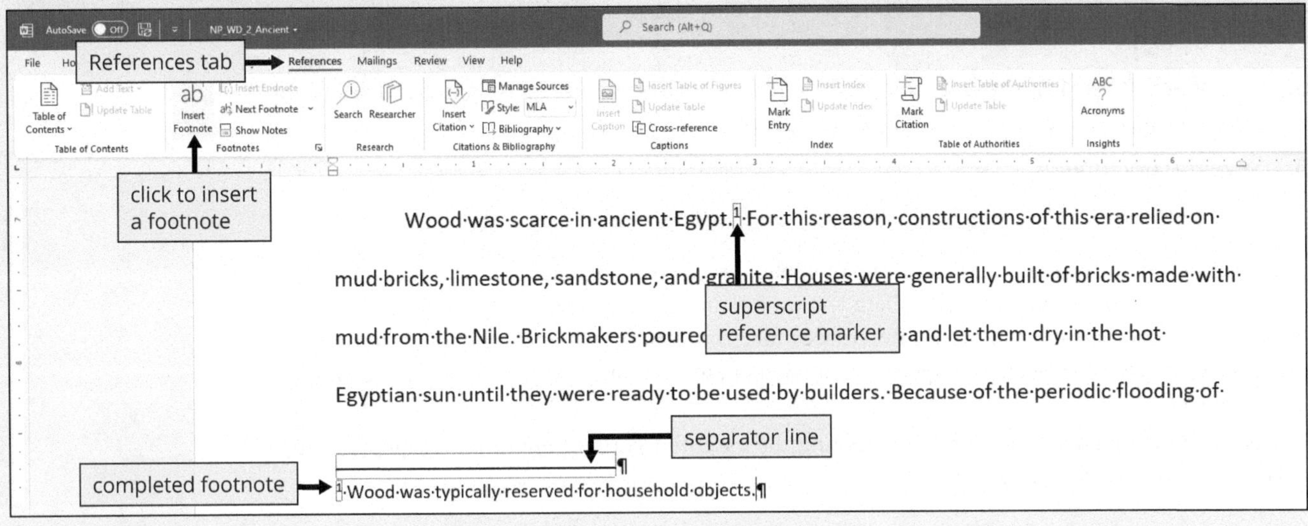

Now, Serena would like you to insert a second footnote about the rise of agriculture.

To insert a second footnote:

1. Scroll up to the first sentence on page 2, which begins "The rise of agriculture..." and ends with the phrase "family and communal life."
2. Click to the right of the period after "life."
3. In the Footnotes group, click the **Insert Footnote** button, and then type **Agriculture includes the domestication of both plants and animals.** Because you inserted the new footnote about agriculture earlier in the document than the footnote about wood, Word inserts a superscript "1" for the new footnote and then renumbers the other footnote as "2." Refer to Figure 2–23. You can easily move back and forth between superscript footnote numbers and footnote text, as you'll see in the next two steps.

Figure 2–23 Inserting a second footnote

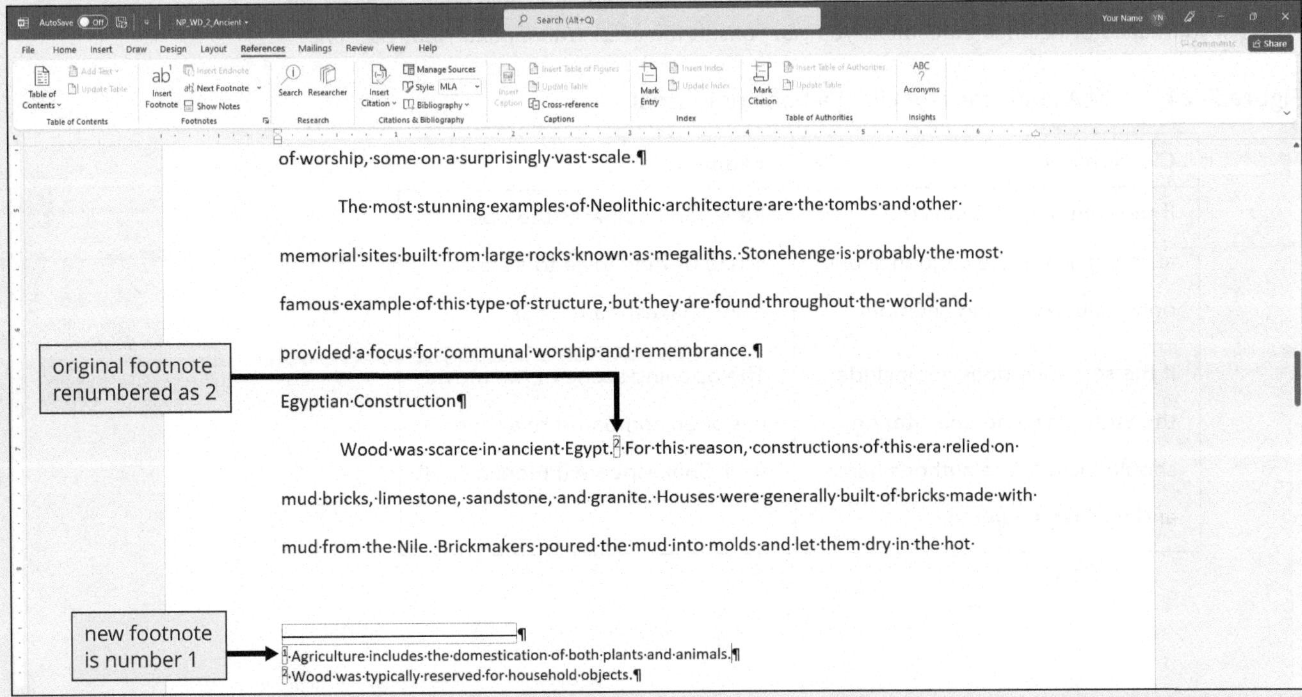

4. Scroll up to the first paragraph of page 2 and double-click the superscript **1** after the word "life." The screen scrolls down to display the footnote at the bottom of the page.
5. Double-click the **1** at the beginning of the footnote. The screen scrolls up to display the superscript number 1 in the first paragraph on page 2.
6. Save the document.

Inserting endnotes is similar to inserting footnotes, except that the notes appear at the end of the document. To insert an endnote, click where you want to insert it, and then click the Insert Endnote button in the Footnotes group on the References tab. You can double-click endnote numbers to move back and forth between the superscript numbers in the document and the notes at the end of the document.

Next Serena wants your help with creating the essential parts of any research paper—the citations and the bibliography.

Working With Citations and Bibliographies

A bibliography (or, as it is called in the MLA style, the works cited list) is an alphabetical list of all the books, magazine articles, websites, movies, and other works referred to in a research paper. The items listed in a bibliography are known as **sources**. The entry for each source includes information such as the author, the title of the work, the publication date, and the publisher.

Within the research paper itself, you include a parenthetical reference, or citation, every time you summarize, quote, or refer to a source. Every source included in your citations then has a corresponding entry in the works cited list. A citation should include enough information to identify the quote or referenced material, so the reader can easily locate the source in the accompanying works cited list. The exact form for a citation varies depending on the style guide you are using and the type of material you are referencing.

Some style guides are very rigid about the form and location of citations, but the MLA style offers quite a bit of flexibility. Typically, though, you insert an MLA citation at the end of a sentence in which you quote or refer to material from a source. For books or journals, the citation itself usually includes the author's last name and a page number. However, if the sentence containing the citation already includes the author's name, you need to include only the page number in the citation. Figure 2–24 provides some sample MLA citations; the format shown could be used for books or journals. For detailed guidelines, you can consult the *MLA Handbook, Ninth Edition*.

Figure 2–24 MLA guidelines for citing a book or journal

Citation Rule	Example
If the sentence includes the author's name, the citation should only include the page number.	Peterson compares the opening scene of the movie to a scene from Shakespeare (188).
If the sentence does not include the author's name, the citation should include the author's name and the page number.	The opening scene of the movie has been compared to a scene from Shakespeare (Peterson 188).

Note that Word's citation and bibliography tools correspond to the seventh edition of the *MLA Handbook*, which is not the most recent edition, but which is still up to date on essential features of the MLA style. Here's a link to the Modern Language Association website, where you can learn about the latest edition, which includes guidance on citing digital sources: www.mla.org.

Word greatly simplifies the process of creating citations and a bibliography. You specify the style you want to use, and then Word takes care of setting up the citation and the works cited list appropriately. Every time you create a citation for a new source, Word prompts you to enter the information needed to create the corresponding entry in the works cited list. If you don't have all your source information available, Word also allows you to insert a temporary, placeholder citation, which you can replace later with a complete citation. When you are finished creating your citations, Word generates the bibliography automatically. Note that placeholder citations are not included in the bibliography.

Proskills

Written Communication: Acknowledging Your Sources

A research paper is a means for you to explore the available information about a subject and then present this information, along with your own understanding of the subject, in an organized and interesting way. Acknowledging all the sources of the information presented in your research paper is essential. If you fail to do this, you might be subject to charges of plagiarism, or trying to pass off someone else's thoughts as your own. Plagiarism is an extremely serious accusation for which you could suffer academic consequences ranging from failing an assignment to being expelled from school.

To ensure that you don't forget to cite a source, you should be careful about creating citations in your document as you type. In this module, you will insert citations into completed paragraphs as practice, but in real life you should insert citations as you type your document. It's easy to forget to go back and cite all your sources correctly after you've finished typing a research paper. Failing to cite a source could lead to accusations of plagiarism and all the consequences that entails. If you don't have the complete information about a source available when you are typing your paper, you should at least insert a placeholder citation. But take care to go back later and substitute complete citations for any placeholders.

Creating Citations

Before you create citations, you need to select the style you want to use, which in the case of Serena's paper is the MLA style. Then, to insert a citation, you click the Insert Citation button in the Citations & Bibliography group on the References tab. If you are citing a source for the first time, Word prompts you to enter all the information required for the source's entry in the bibliography or works cited list. If you are citing an existing source, you simply select the source from the Insert Citation menu.

By default, an MLA citation includes only the author's name in parentheses. However, you can use the Edit Citation dialog box to add a page number. You can also use the Edit Citation dialog box to remove, or suppress, the author's name, so only the page number appears in the citation. However, in an MLA citation, Word will replace the suppressed author name with the title of the source, so you need to suppress the title as well, by selecting the Title check box in the Edit Citation dialog box.

Reference

Creating Citations

- On the ribbon, click the References tab. In the Citations & Bibliography group, click the Style arrow, and then select the style you want.
- Click in the document where you want to insert the citation. Typically, a citation goes at the end of a sentence, before the ending punctuation.
- To add a citation for a new source, click the Insert Citation button in the Citations & Bibliography group, click Add New Source, enter information in the Create Source dialog box, and then click OK.
- To add a citation for an existing source, click the Insert Citation button, and then click the source.
- To add a placeholder citation, click the Insert Citation button, click Add New Placeholder, and then, in the Placeholder Name dialog box, type placeholder text, such as the author's last name, that will serve as a reminder about which source you need to cite. Note that a placeholder citation cannot contain any spaces.
- To add a page number to a citation, click the citation in the document, click the Citation Options button, click Edit Citation, type the page number, and then click OK.
- To display only the page number in a citation, click the citation in the document, click the Citation Options button, and then click Edit Citation. In the Edit Citation dialog box, select the Author and Title check boxes to suppress this information, and then click OK.

So far, Serena has referenced information from two different sources in her research paper. You'll select a style and then begin adding the appropriate citations.

To select a style for the citation and bibliography:

1. On the ribbon, click the **References tab**. The ribbon changes to display references options.
2. In the Citations & Bibliography group, click the **Style arrow**, and then click **MLA Seventh Edition** if it is not already selected.

   Key Step Be sure to select the correct citation and bibliography style before you begin.

3. Click the page indicator in the Status Bar to open the Navigation pane.
4. Use the Navigation pane to find the phrase "As at least one historian," which appears on page 3, and then click in the document at the end of that sentence (between the end of the word "gone" and the closing period).
5. Close the **Navigation** pane, and then click the **References tab** on the ribbon. You need to add a citation that informs the reader that historian Natalia Koval made the observation described in the sentence. Refer to Figure 2–25.

Figure 2–25 MLA style selected and insertion point positioned for new citation

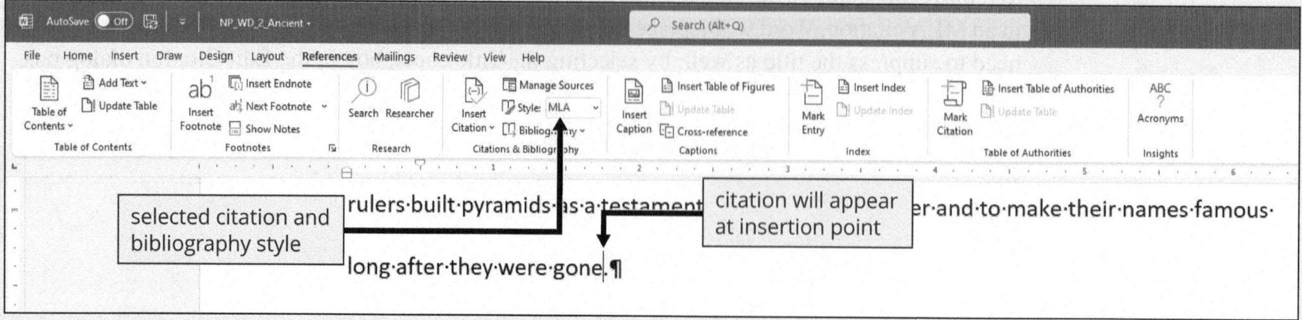

6. In the Citations & Bibliography group, click the **Insert Citation** button to open the menu. At this point, you could click Add New Placeholder on the menu to insert a temporary, placeholder citation. However, because you have all the necessary source information, you can go ahead and create a complete citation.
7. On the menu, click **Add New Source**. The Create Source dialog box opens, ready for you to add the information required to create a bibliography entry for Natalia Koval's book.
8. If necessary, click the **Type of Source arrow**, scroll up or down in the list, and then click **Book**.
9. In the Author box, type **Natalia Koval**.

   Tip When entering information in a dialog box, you can press TAB to move the insertion point from one box to another.

10. Click in the **Title** box, and then type **Classical Construction: An Ancient Perspective on Modern Design**.
11. Click in the **Year** box, and then type **2022**. This is the year the book was published. Next, you need to enter the name and location of the publisher.
12. Click the **City** box, type **New York**, click the **Publisher** box, and then type **Colescott Academy Press**.

    Finally, you need to indicate the medium used to publish the book. In this case, Serena used a printed copy, so the medium is "Print." For books or journals published online, the correct medium would be "Web."

13. Click the **Medium** box, and then type **Print**. Refer to Figure 2–26.

Figure 2–26 Create Source dialog box with information for the first source

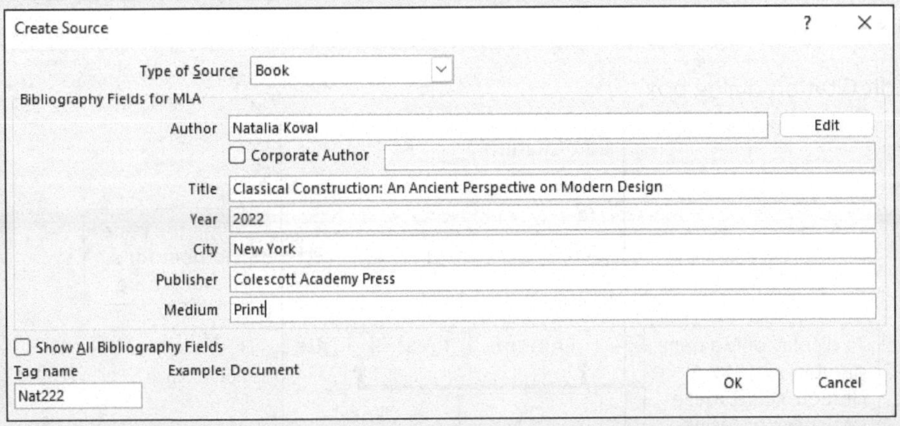

14. Click **OK**. Word inserts the parenthetical "(Koval)" at the end of the sentence in the document.

    Trouble? If the Researcher pane opens, close it.

Although the citation looks like ordinary text, it is actually contained inside a content control, a special feature used to display information that is inserted automatically and that may need to be updated later. You can see the content control itself only when it is selected. When it is unselected, you simply see the citation. In the next set of steps, you will select the content control and then edit the citation to add a page number.

To edit the citation:

1. In the document, click the citation **(Koval)**. The citation appears in a content control, which is a box with a tab on the left and an arrow button on the right. The arrow button is called the Citation Options button.
2. Click the **Citation Options** button. A menu of options related to editing a citation opens, as shown in Figure 2–27.

Figure 2–27 Citation Options menu

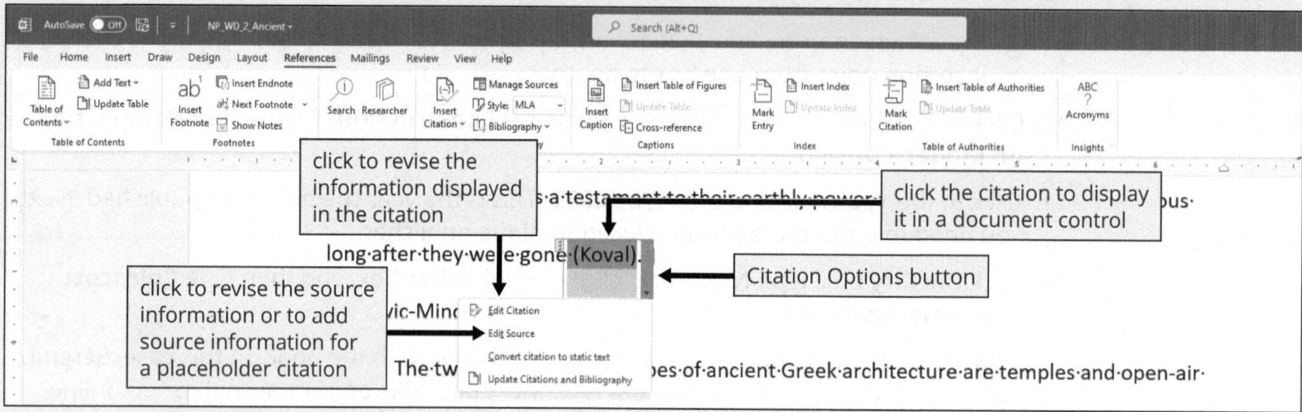

To edit the information about the source, you click Edit Source. To change the information that is displayed in the citation itself, you use the Edit Citation option.

3. On the Citation Options menu, click **Edit Citation**. The Edit Citation dialog box opens, as shown in Figure 2–28.

Figure 2–28 Edit Citation dialog box

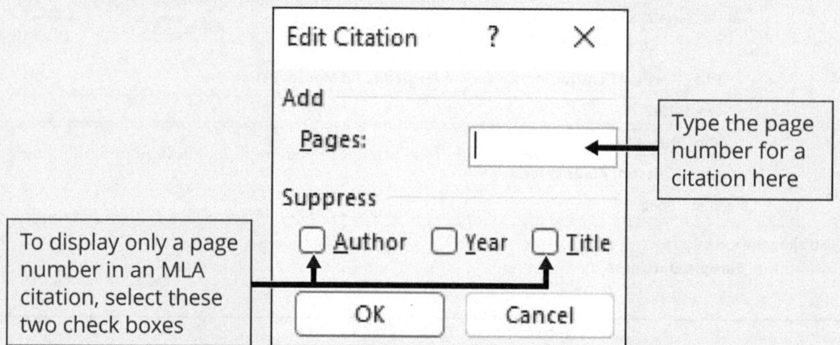

To add a page number for the citation, you type the page number in the Pages box. If you want to display only the page number in the citation (which would be necessary if you already mentioned the author's name in the same sentence in the text), then you would also select the Author and Title check boxes in this dialog box to suppress this information.

4. Type **37** to insert the page number in the Pages box, click **OK** to close the dialog box, and then click anywhere in the document outside the citation content control. The revised citation now reads "(Koval 37)."

Note that if you need to delete a citation, you can click the citation to display the content control, click the tab on the left side of the content control, and then press DELETE. Next, you will add two more citations, both for the same journal article.

To insert two more citations:

1. Scroll down to the second-to-last paragraph on page 3, and then click at the end of the last sentence in that paragraph (which begins "According to historian Jeffrey Olen..."), between the word "mean" and the period. Because this sentence mentions historian Jeffrey Olen, you need to add a citation to one of his journal articles.
2. In the Citations & Bibliography group, click the **Insert Citation** button to open the Insert Citation menu. Notice that Natalia Koval's book is now listed as a source on this menu. You could click Koval's book on the menu to add a citation to it, but right now you need to add a new source.
3. Click **Add New Source** to open the Create Source dialog box, click the **Type of Source arrow**, and then click **Journal Article**.

   The Create Source dialog box displays the boxes, or fields, appropriate for a journal article. The information required to cite a journal article differs from the information you entered earlier for the citation for the Koval book. For journal articles, you are prompted to enter the page numbers for the entire article. If you want to display a particular page number in the citation, you can add it later.

   By default, Word displays boxes, or fields, for the information most commonly included in a bibliography. In this case, you also want to include the volume and issue numbers for Jeffrey Olen's article, so you need to display more fields.
4. In the Create Source dialog box, click the **Show All Bibliography Fields** check box to select this option. The Create Source dialog box expands to allow you to enter more detailed information. Red asterisks highlight the fields that are recommended, but these recommended fields don't necessarily apply to every source.
5. Enter the following information, scrolling down to display the necessary boxes:

   Author: **Jeffrey Olen**

   Title: **Perfect Proportions in Greek Architecture**

   Journal Name: **Journal of Greek and Roman Culture Studies**

   Year: **2023**

   Pages: **122–145**

   Volume: **30**

   Issue: **5**

   Medium: **Web**

   When you are finished, your Create Source dialog box should look like the one shown in Figure 2–29.

Figure 2–29 Create Source dialog box with information for the journal article

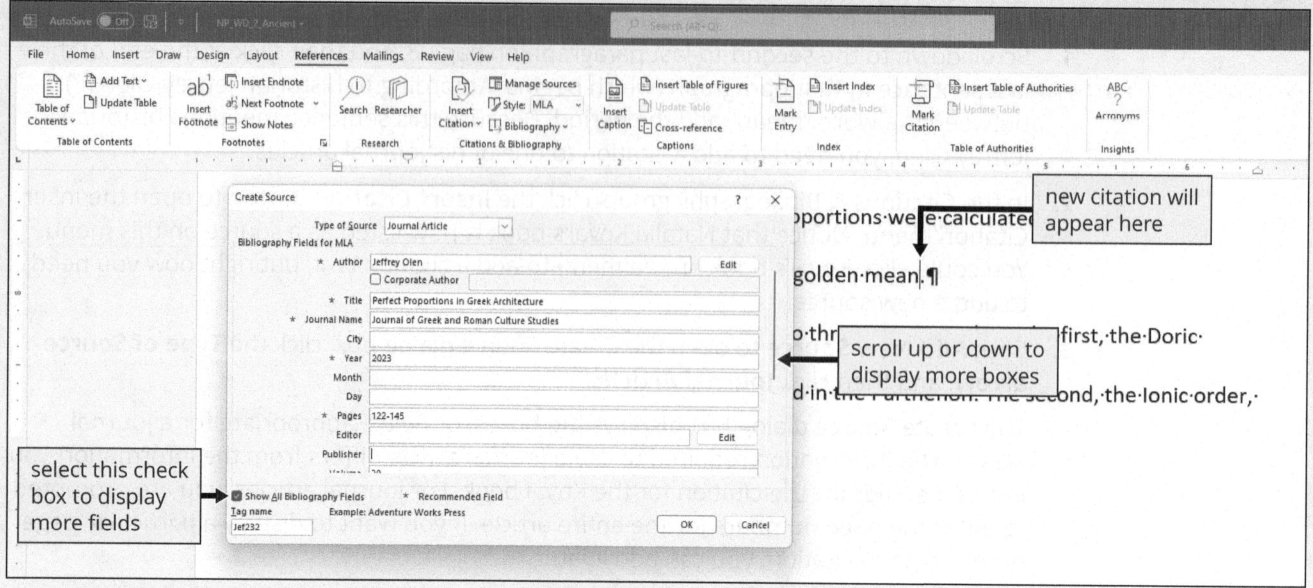

6. Click **OK**. The Create Source dialog box closes, and the citation "(Olen)" is inserted in the text. Because the sentence containing the citation already includes the author's name, you will edit the citation to include the page number and suppress the author's name.
7. Click the **(Olen)** citation to display the content control, click the **Citation Options** button, and then click **Edit Citation** to open the Edit Citation dialog box.
8. In the Pages box, type **142**, and then click the **Author** and **Title** check boxes to select them. You need to suppress both the author's name and the title because otherwise Word will replace the suppressed author name with the title. When using the MLA style, you don't ever have to suppress the year because the year is never included as part of an MLA citation. When working in other styles, however, you might need to suppress the year.
9. Click **OK** to close the Edit Citation dialog box, and then click anywhere outside the content control to deselect it. The end of the sentence now reads "...as the golden mean (142)."
10. Scroll down to the last sentence in the document. Click at the end of the sentence, to the left of the period after "bridges."
11. On the References tab, in the Citations & Bibliography group, click the **Insert Citation** button, and then click the **Olen, Jeffrey** source in the menu. You want the citation to refer to the entire article instead of just one page, so you will not edit the citation to add a specific page number.
12. Save the document.

You have entered the source information for two sources.

Insight

Distinguishing Between Endnotes, Footnotes, and Citations

It's easy to confuse footnotes with endnotes, and endnotes with citations. Remember, a footnote appears at the bottom, or foot, of a page and always on the same page as its reference marker. You might have one footnote at the bottom of page 3, three footnotes at the bottom of page 5, and one at the bottom of page 6. By contrast, an endnote appears at the end of the document, with all the endnotes compiled into a single list. Both endnotes and footnotes can contain any kind of information you think might be useful to your readers. Citations, however, are only used to list specific information about a book or other source you refer to or quote from in the document. A citation typically appears in parentheses at the end of the sentence containing information from the source you are citing, and the sources for all of the document's citations are listed in a bibliography, or a list of works cited, at the end of the document.

Inserting a Page Break

Once you have created a citation for a source in a document, you can generate a bibliography. In the MLA style, the bibliography (or works cited list) starts on a new page. So your first step is to insert a manual page break. A **manual page break** is one you insert at a specific location; it doesn't matter if the previous page is full or not. To insert a manual page break, use the Page Break button in the Pages group on the Insert tab.

To insert a manual page break:

1. Press **CTRL+END** to move the insertion point to the end of the document, if necessary.
2. On the ribbon, click the **Insert** tab.
3. In the Pages group, click the **Page Break** button. Word inserts a new, blank page at the end of the document, with the insertion point blinking at the top. Note that you could also use the CTRL+ENTER keyboard shortcut to insert a manual page break. To insert a new, blank page in the middle of a document, you would use the Blank Page button in the Pages group instead.
4. Scroll up to see the dotted line with the words "Page Break" at the bottom of the text on page 4. You can delete a manual page break just as you would delete any other nonprinting character, by clicking immediately to its left and then pressing DELETE. Refer to Figure 2–30.

Figure 2–30 Manual page break inserted into the document

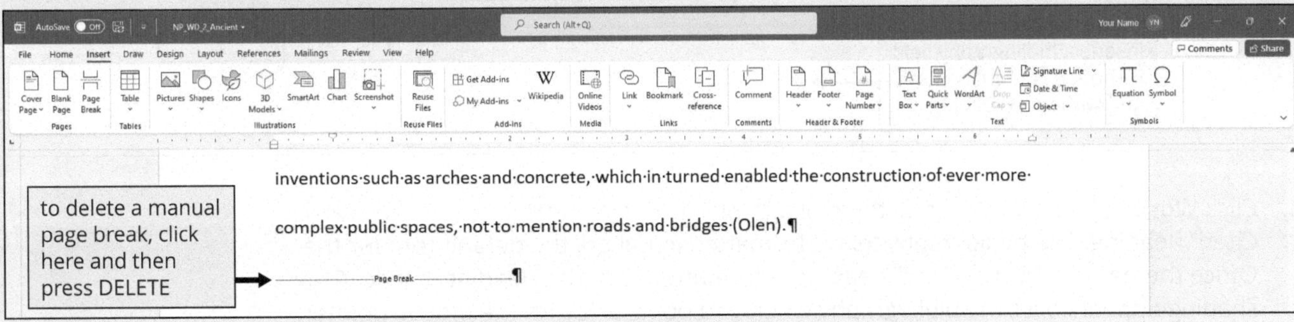

Now you can insert the bibliography on the new page 5.

Generating a Bibliography

When you generate a bibliography, Word scans all the citations in the document, collecting the source information for each citation, and then it creates a list of information for each unique source. The format of the entries in the bibliography will reflect the style you specified when you created your first citation, which in this case is the MLA style. The bibliography itself is a **field**, similar to the page number field you inserted. In other words, it is really an instruction that tells Word to display the source information for all the citations in the document. Because it is a field and not actual text, you can easily update the bibliography later to reflect any new citations you might add.

You can choose to insert a bibliography as a field directly in the document, or you can insert a bibliography enclosed within a content control that also includes the heading "Bibliography" or "Works Cited." Inserting a bibliography enclosed in a content control is best because the content control includes a useful button that you can use to update your bibliography if you make changes to the sources.

To insert the bibliography:

1. Scroll down so you can see the insertion point at the top of page 5.
2. On the ribbon, click the **References tab**.
3. In the Citations & Bibliography group, click the **Bibliography** button. The Bibliography menu opens, displaying three styles with preformatted headings—"Bibliography," "References," and "Works Cited." The Insert Bibliography command at the bottom inserts a bibliography directly in the document as a field, without a content control and without a preformatted heading. Refer to Figure 2–31.

Figure 2–31 Bibliography menu

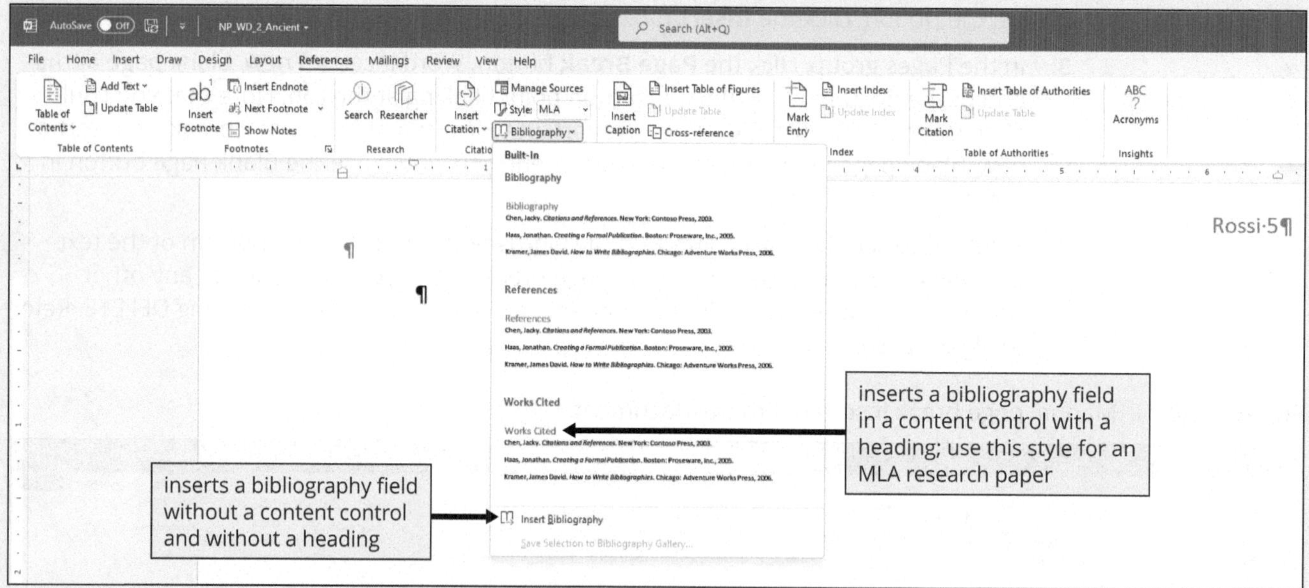

4. Click **Works Cited**. Word inserts the bibliography, with two entries, below the "Works Cited" heading. The bibliography text is formatted in Calibri, the default font for the Office theme. The "Works Cited" heading is formatted with the Heading 1 style. Gray shading appears over the bibliography when you point to it with the mouse pointer, indicating that the bibliography is more than simple text.

   To see the content control that contains the bibliography, you need to select it.
5. Click the **Works Cited** heading in the bibliography. The content control containing the bibliography is now visible in the form of a rectangular border and a tab with two buttons. Depending on where you clicked, some of the bibliography text might be highlighted in dark gray.

6. Click the Koval, Natalia entry, and then click the Olen, Jeffrey entry. Both entries are now highlighted in dark gray, indicating that the text of the bibliography is a field and not regular text. Refer to Figure 2–32.

Figure 2–32 Bibliography displayed in a content control

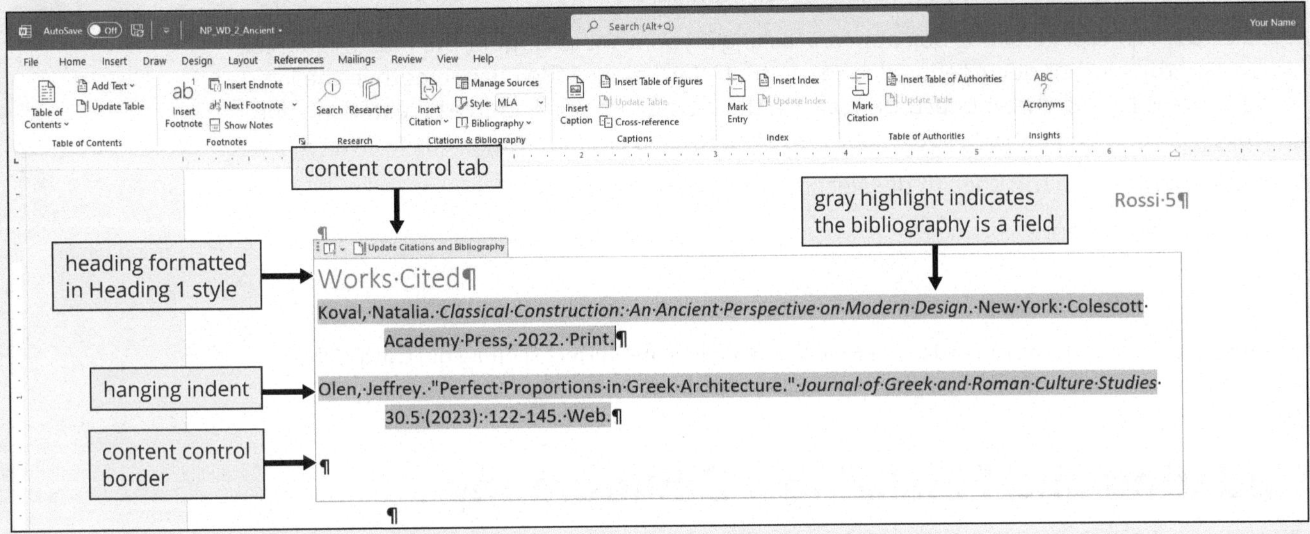

As Serena looks over the works cited list, she realizes that she misspelled the last name of one of the authors. You'll correct the error now and then update the bibliography.

Insight

Managing Sources

When you create a source, Word adds it to a Master List of all the sources created on your computer. Word also adds each new source to the Current List of sources for that document. Both the Master List and the Current List are accessible via the Source Manager dialog box, which you open by clicking the Manage Sources button in the Citations & Bibliography group on the References tab. Using this dialog box, you can copy sources from the Master List into the Current List and vice versa. As you begin to focus on a particular academic field and turn repeatedly to important works in your chosen field, you'll find this ability to reuse sources very helpful.

Modifying an Existing Source

To modify information about a source, you click a citation to that source in the document, click the Citation Options button on the content control, and then click Edit Source. Depending on how your computer is set up, after you are finished editing the source, Word may prompt you to update the Master List and the source information in the current document. In almost all cases, you should click Yes to ensure that the source information is correct in all the places it is stored on your computer.

> **Tip** To transform a placeholder citation into a regular citation, click the Citation Options button, click Edit Source, and then enter source information.

To edit a source in the research paper:

1. Click in the blank paragraph below the bibliography content control to deselect the bibliography.
2. Scroll up to display the end of the second paragraph on page 3, and then click the **(Koval 37)** citation you entered earlier in the ninth line from the top of the page. The content control appears around the citation.

3. Click the **Citation Options** button, and then click **Edit Source**. The Edit Source dialog box opens. Note that Word displays the author's last name first in the Author box, just as it would appear in a bibliography.
4. In the **Author** box, double-click **Koval** to select the author's last name, and then type **Covall**. The author's name now reads "Covall, Natalia."
5. Click **OK**. A message dialog box appears, asking if you want to update the master source list and the current document. Click **Yes** so that Word makes the change both in the list of sources for the current document and in the master list of all sources created in your copy of Word. The message box closes, and the revised citation now reads "(Covall 37)."
6. Click anywhere on the page to deselect the citation content control.
7. Save the document.

You've edited the document text and the citation to include the correct spelling of "Covall," but now you need to update the bibliography to correct the spelling.

Updating and Finalizing a Bibliography

The bibliography does not automatically change to reflect edits you make to existing citations or to show new citations. To incorporate the latest information stored in the citations, you need to update the bibliography. To update a bibliography in a content control, click the bibliography, and then, in the content control tab, click Update Citations and Bibliography. To update a bibliography field that is not contained in a content control, right-click the bibliography, and then click Update Field on the shortcut menu.

To update the bibliography:

1. Scroll down to page 5 and click anywhere in the works cited list to display the content control.
2. In the content control tab, click **Update Citations and Bibliography**. The works cited list is updated, with "Koval" changed to "Covall" in the first entry.

Serena still has a fair amount of work to do on her research paper. After she finishes writing it and adding all the citations, she will update the bibliography again to include all her cited sources. At that point, you might think the bibliography would be finished. However, a few steps remain to ensure that the works cited list matches the MLA style. To finalize Serena's works cited list to match the MLA style, you need to make the changes shown in Figure 2–33.

Figure 2–33 Steps for finalizing a Word bibliography to match MLA guidelines for the works cited list

1. Format the "Works Cited" heading to match the formatting of the rest of the text in the document.
2. Center the "Works Cited" heading.
3. Double-space the entire works cited list, including the heading, and remove extra space after the paragraphs.
4. Change the font size for the entire works cited list to 12 points.

To format the bibliography as an MLA-style works cited list:

1. Click in the **Works Cited** heading, and then click the **Home** tab on the ribbon.
2. In the Styles group, click the **Normal** style. The "Works Cited" heading is now formatted in Calibri body font like the rest of the document. The MLA style for a works cited list requires this heading to be centered.
3. In the Paragraph group, click the **Center** button.
4. Select the entire works cited list, including the heading. Change the font size to **12** points, change the line spacing to **2.0**, and then remove the paragraph spacing after each paragraph.
5. Click below the content control to deselect the works cited list, and then review your work. Refer to Figure 2–34.

Figure 2–34 MLA-style Works Cited list

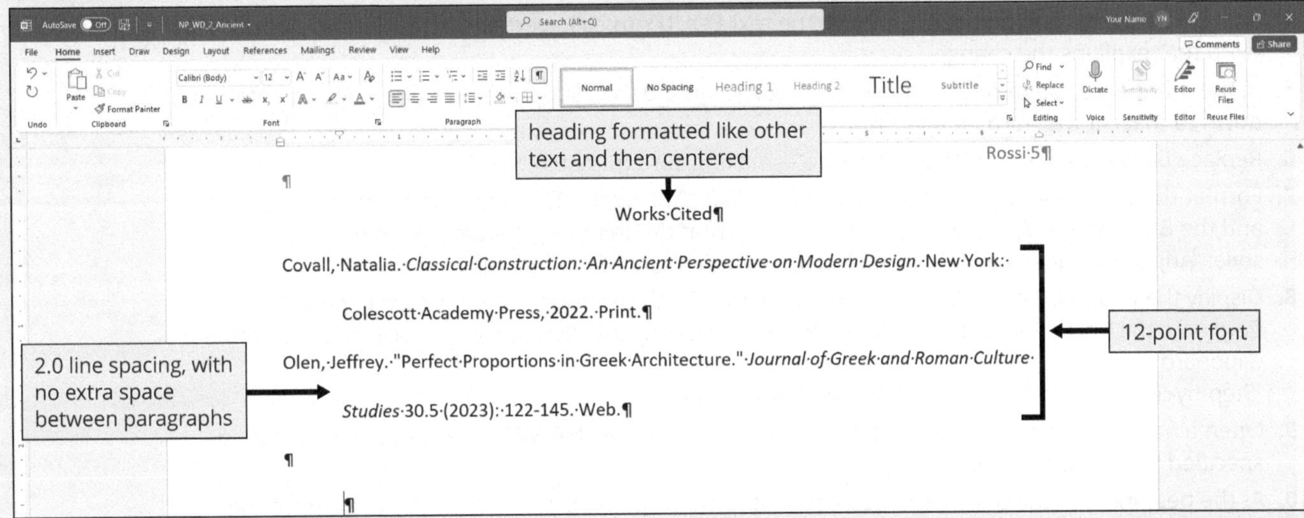

6. **sam** Save the document and close it.

Serena's research paper now meets the MLA style guidelines.

Part 2.2 Quick Check

1. Explain how to quickly indent a paragraph .5 inches from the left margin.
2. What is the default form of an MLA citation in Word?
3. List the five tasks you need to perform to make a default Word document match the MLA style.
4. What is a page number field?
5. Explain how to generate a works cited list.

Practice: Review Assignments

Data Files needed for the Review Assignments: NP_WD_2-3.docx, NP_WD_2-4.docx

Because the home mortgage handout turned out so well, Serena has been asked to create a fact sheet for customers who are considering refinancing their home mortgages. Serena asks you to help her revise and format the document. She also asks you to create a document listing the steps involved in refinancing a mortgage. Finally, Serena is working on another research paper on the history of international disaster movies for her film history class. She asks you to help her format the paper according to the MLA style and to create some citations and a bibliography. She has inserted the uppercase word "CITATION" wherever she needs to insert a citation. Complete the following steps:

1. Open the document **NP_WD_2-3.docx** located in the Word2 > Review folder included with your Data Files, and then save the document as **NP_WD_2_FactSheet** in the location specified by your instructor.
2. Read the first comment, which provides an overview of the changes you will be making to the document in the following steps, and then delete that comment.
3. Perform the task described in the remaining comment, and then delete that comment.
4. In the third paragraph on page 1, change the text EQUITY to all lowercase. Attach a comment to the word that explains the change.
5. In the numbered list on page 2, move the first item in the list ("Supply the required documentation.") down to make it the third item in the list.
6. Replace both instances of "Rate" with "rate"—making sure to match the case.
7. Format the title "Mortgage Refinancing: Just the Facts" using the Title style, with center alignment and the Blue, Accent 5, Darker 25% font color. Format the following headings with the Heading 1 style: "Adjustable or Fixed," "Required Documentation," and "Step-by-Step Process."
8. Display the Clipboard pane. On page 2, copy the list of refinancing five steps (which begins "1. Complete the online form") to the Clipboard, and then copy the "Step-by-Step Process" heading to the Clipboard. To ensure that you copy the heading formatting, be sure to select the paragraph mark after "Step-by-Step Process" before you click the Copy button.
9. Open a new, blank document, and then save the document as **NP_WD_2_Process** in the location specified by your instructor.
10. At the beginning of the document, paste the "Step-by-Step Process" heading and then, from the Paste Options menu, apply the Keep Text Only option. Paste the list of steps in a new paragraph below the heading. If necessary, reapply the numbered list formatting to the last item in the list.
11. At the end of the document, type **Prepared by:** followed by your first and last names.
12. Save the NP_WD_2_Process.docx document and close it.
13. In the NP_WD_2_FactSheet.docx document, clear the contents of the Clipboard pane, close the Clipboard pane, save the document, and then close it.
14. Open the document **NP_WD_2-4.docx** located in the Word2 > Review folder.
15. Save the document as **NP_WD_2_International** in the location specified by your instructor.
16. In the first paragraph, replace Serena's name with your own.
17. Adjust the font size, line spacing, paragraph spacing, and paragraph indents to match the MLA style.
18. Insert your last name and a page number in the upper-right corner of every page except the first. Use the same font size as in the rest of the document.
19. Locate the last sentence in the first main paragraph, which reads "In the hands of a true artist, this formula can create exciting, interesting drama." Insert a footnote at the end of the sentence that reads: **Many images and video clips from the movies mentioned in this paper are available on the web.**
20. Select MLA Seventh Edition as the citations and bibliography style.
21. Use the Navigation pane to highlight all instances of the uppercase word "CITATION." Keep the Navigation pane open so you can continue to use it to find the locations where you need to insert citations in Steps 22–26.

22. Delete the first instance of "CITATION" and the space before it, and then create a new source with the following information:
    Type of Source: **Book**
    Author: **Quinn Murphy**
    Title: **Silent Film: A History in Words and Photos**
    Year: **2021**
    City: **Cambridge**
    Publisher: **New Media Press**
    Medium: **Print**
23. Edit the citation to add **124** as the page number. Display only the page number in the citation.
24. Delete the second instance of "CITATION" and the space before it, and then create a new source with the following information:
    Type of Source: **Journal Article**
    Author: **Maya Suyemoto**
    Title: **Disaster Cinema on the Political Stage**
    Journal Name: **Media Signpost Quarterly: Criticism and Comment**
    Year: **2023**
    Pages: **48–71**
    Volume: **10**
    Issue: **2**
    Medium: **Web**
25. Edit the citation to add **75** as the page number.
26. Delete the third instance of "CITATION" and the space before it, and then insert a citation for the book by **Maya Suyemoto**.
27. At the end of the document, start a new page and insert a bibliography in a content control with the heading "Works Cited."
28. In the second source you created, change "**Suyemoto**" to "**Matsumoto**" and then update the bibliography.
29. Finalize the bibliography to create an MLA-style works cited list.
30. Save the document and close it.
31. Close any other open documents.

Apply: Case Problem 1

Data File needed for this Case Problem: NP_WD_2-5.docx

Paralegal Amisha Nur has more than a decade of experience in education services. After several years working at a small company, she is looking for a job as a sales representative at a global educational media firm. She has asked you to edit and format her resume. As part of the application process, she will have to upload her resume to employee recruitment websites. Because these sites typically request a simple page design, Amisha plans to rely primarily on heading styles to organize her information. When the resume is complete, she wants you to remove any color applied by the heading styles. She also needs help beginning a separate document that lists some of her current affiliations and certifications. Complete the following steps:

1. Open the document **NP_WD_2-5.docx** located in the Word2 > Case1 folder included with your Data Files, and then save the file as **NP_WD_2_Amisha** in the location specified by your instructor.
2. Read the comment included in the document, and then perform the task it specifies.
3. Respond to the comment with the response **If you like, I can show you how to remove hyperlink formatting the next time we meet.**, and then mark Amisha's comment as resolved.
4. Replace all occurrences of "MesaArizona" with **Mesa, Arizona**.

5. Format the document with styles as follows:
   - Amisha's name: Title style
   - Amisha's address, phone number, and email address: Subtitle style, 0 points of paragraph spacing
   - The "Objective," "Experience," "Education," and "Affiliations and Certifications" headings: Heading 1 style; Black, Text 1 font color; all uppercase
   - The paragraphs containing the names of the three organizations where Amisha used to work: Heading 2 style; Black, Text 1 font color
6. In the bulleted list for Edmunds and Dronzek Educational Media, move the bullet that begins "Resolve customer complaints..." up to make it the first bullet in the list.
7. Copy the "AFFILIATIONS AND CERTIFICATIONS" heading to the Clipboard, and then copy the last two bullets in the list of affiliations and certifications to the Clipboard.
8. Open a new, blank document, and then save the document as **NP_WD_2_Certifications** in the location specified by your instructor.
9. Paste the heading in the document as text only, and then paste the bulleted list starting in a new paragraph below the heading.
10. At the end of the document, type **Prepared by:** followed by your first and last names.
11. Save the NP_WD_2_Certifications.docx document and close it.
12. In the **NP_WD_2_Amisha.docx** document, clear the contents of the Clipboard pane, and close the Clipboard pane.
13. In the email address, replace "amishanur" with your first and last names in all lowercase, with no space between your first and last name.
14. Save and close the document.

Challenge: Case Problem 2

Data File needed for this Case Problem: NP_WD_2-6.docx

Albertine State College Marcel Wright is a student at St. Glastian College. He's working on a research paper about Louis Armstrong for a music history course, taught by Professor Suzette Harper. The research paper is only partly finished, but before Marcel does more work on it, he asks you to help format this early draft to match the MLA style. He also asks you to help create some citations, add a placeholder citation, and manage his sources. Complete the following steps:

1. Open the document **NP_WD_2-6.docx** located in the Word2 > Case2 folder included with your Data Files, and then save the document as **NP_WD_2_Armstrong** in the location specified by your instructor.
2. On the first page, replace "Marcel Wright" with your first and last name.
3. Revise the paper to match the MLA style, seventh edition, with a header on every page except the first. Use your last name in the header. Use the same font size for the header as for the rest of the document.
4. At the end of the appropriate sentence, add a citation for page 123 in the following book, omitting the author's name from the citation:

   Washington, Darius. *Louis Armstrong: Child of New Orleans, Titan of Jazz*. New York: Signature Academy Press, 2022. Print.
5. At the end of the appropriate sentence, add a citation for page 140 in the following journal article, omitting the author's name:

   Lumani, Haley. "Improvisation as Structured Expression." Journal of Modern Music, Culture, and Politics (2023): 133–155. Web.
6. At the end of the first sentence in the document (which begins "Many experts consider..."), insert a placeholder citation that reads "Wesley." At the end of the last sentence in the same paragraph (which begins "Groundbreaking recordings...), insert a placeholder citation that reads "Zhang."

7. **Explore:** Use Word Help to look up the topic "Add citations in a Word document," and then, within the Help article, read the section titled "Find a source." Then read the section "Edit a source," which includes a note about editing a placeholder.
8. **Explore:** Open the Source Manager, and search for the name "Washington." From within the Current List in the Source Manager, edit the Darius Washington citation to change "Titan" to "King" so the book title reads "*Louis Armstrong: Child of New Orleans, King of Jazz*." After you make the change, update the source in both lists. When you are finished, delete "Washington" from the Search box to redisplay all the sources in both lists.
9. **Explore:** From within the Source Manager, copy a source not included in the current document from the Master List to the Current List. Examine the sources in the Current List, and note the checkmarks next to the two sources for which you have already created citations and the question marks next to the placeholder sources. Sources in the Current List that are not actually cited in the text have no symbol next to them. For example, the source you copied from the Master List into your Current List has no symbol next to it in the Current List.
10. Close the Source Manager, create a bibliography on a new page with a "Works Cited" heading, and note which works appear in it.
11. **Explore:** Open the Source Manager, and then edit the Wesley placeholder source to include the following information about a journal article:

    Wesley, Alexander. "Louis Armstrong on the Global Stage." Music and Art International Journal (2024): 72–89. Web.
12. Update the bibliography.
13. **Explore:** Open Microsoft Edge and use the web to research the difference between a works cited list and a works consulted list. If necessary, open the Source Manager, and then delete any uncited sources from the Current List to ensure that your document contains a true works cited list, as specified by the MLA style, and not a works consulted list. (Marcel will create a full citation for the "Zhang" placeholder later.)
14. Update the bibliography, finalize it so it matches the MLA style, save the document, and close it.

Word **Module 3**

Creating Tables and a Multipage Report

Writing a Recommendation

Case: Totara Neighborhood Centers

Laila Jones is a project manager at Totara Neighborhood Centers, a nonprofit organization that provides social services and community programming for neighborhood centers in Chicago, Illinois. She has been working on a report for the organization's board of directors about computer literacy classes that will be offered at multiple locations throughout the year. She has asked you to finish formatting the report. Laila also needs your help with adding a table and a diagram to the end of the report.

In this module, you'll use the Navigation pane to review the document headings and reorganize the document. You will also insert a table and modify it by changing the structure and formatting, merging table cells, and adding a formula. Next, you'll create a watermark that indicates a document is a just a draft, set tab stops, hyphenate a document, and insert a section break. In addition, you'll create a SmartArt graphic and add headers and footers. Finally, you will insert a cover page, change the theme, and review the document in Read Mode and Immersive Reader.

Starting Data Files: Word3

Module
NP_WD_3-1.docx
NP_WD_3-2.docx

Review
NP_WD_3-3.docx

Case1
NP_WD_3-4.docx

Case2
NP_WD_3-5.docx

Objectives

Part 3.1

- Display document headings in the Navigation pane
- Reorganize document text using the Navigation pane
- Collapse and expand body text in a document
- Create and edit a table
- Sort rows in a table
- Modify a table's structure
- Format a table
- Merge cells and add a formula
- Create a watermark

Part 3.2

- Set tab stops
- Turn on automatic hyphenation
- Divide a document into sections
- Create a SmartArt graphic
- Create headers and footers
- Insert a cover page
- Change the document's theme
- Display a document in Read Mode
- Use Immersive Reader

Part 3.1 Visual Overview: Organizing Information in Tables

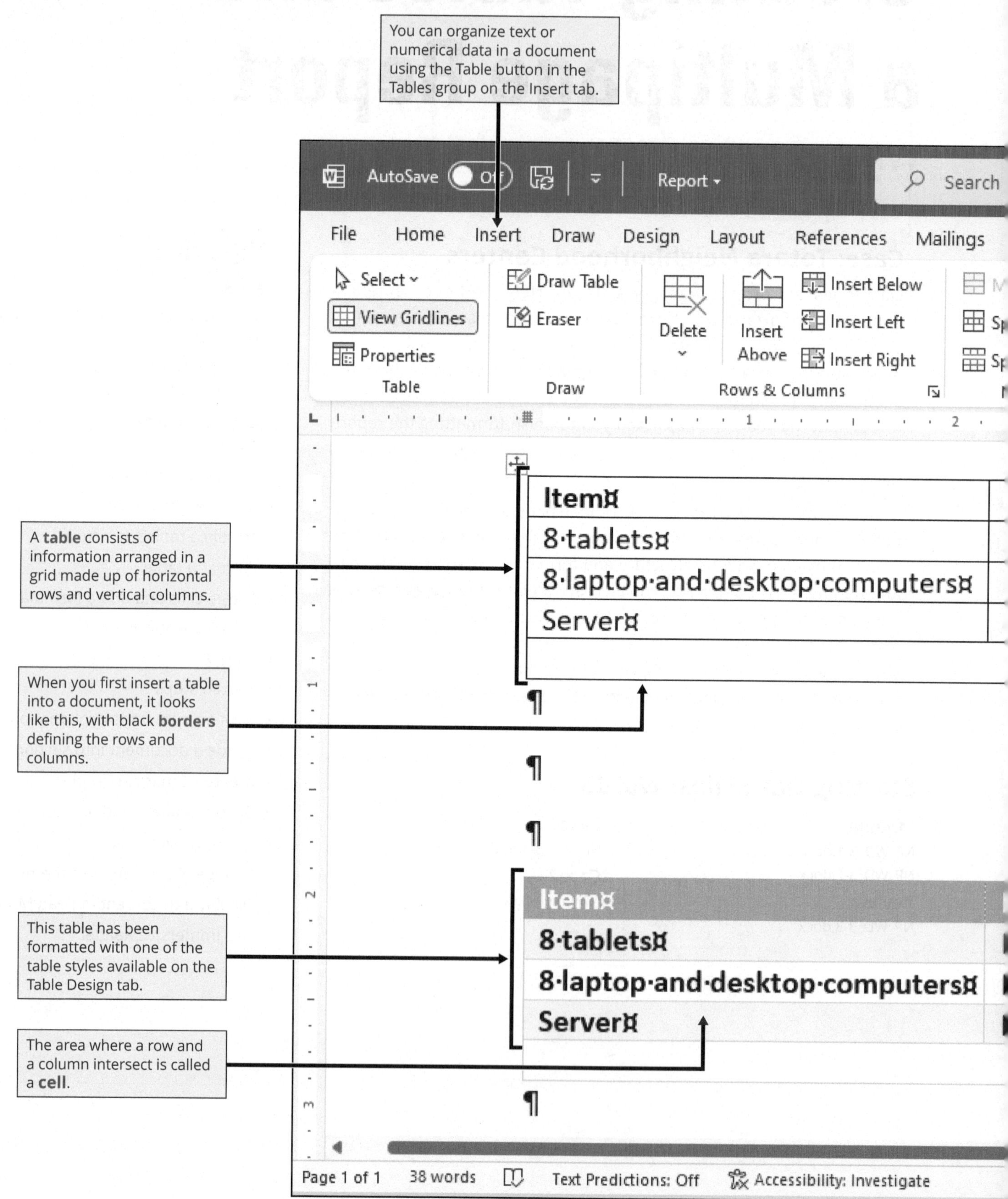

You can organize text or numerical data in a document using the Table button in the Tables group on the Insert tab.
A **table** consists of information arranged in a grid made up of horizontal rows and vertical columns.
When you first insert a table into a document, it looks like this, with black **borders** defining the rows and columns.
This table has been formatted with one of the table styles available on the Table Design tab.
The area where a row and a column intersect is called a **cell**.
AutoSave
Off
Report
Search
File
Home
Insert
Draw
Design
Layout
References
Mailings
Select
View Gridlines
Properties
Table
Draw Table
Eraser
Draw
Delete
Insert Above
Insert Below
Insert Left
Insert Right
Rows & Columns
Item¤
8·tablets¤
8·laptop·and·desktop·computers¤
Server¤
Page 1 of 1
38 words
Text Predictions: Off
Accessibility: Investigate

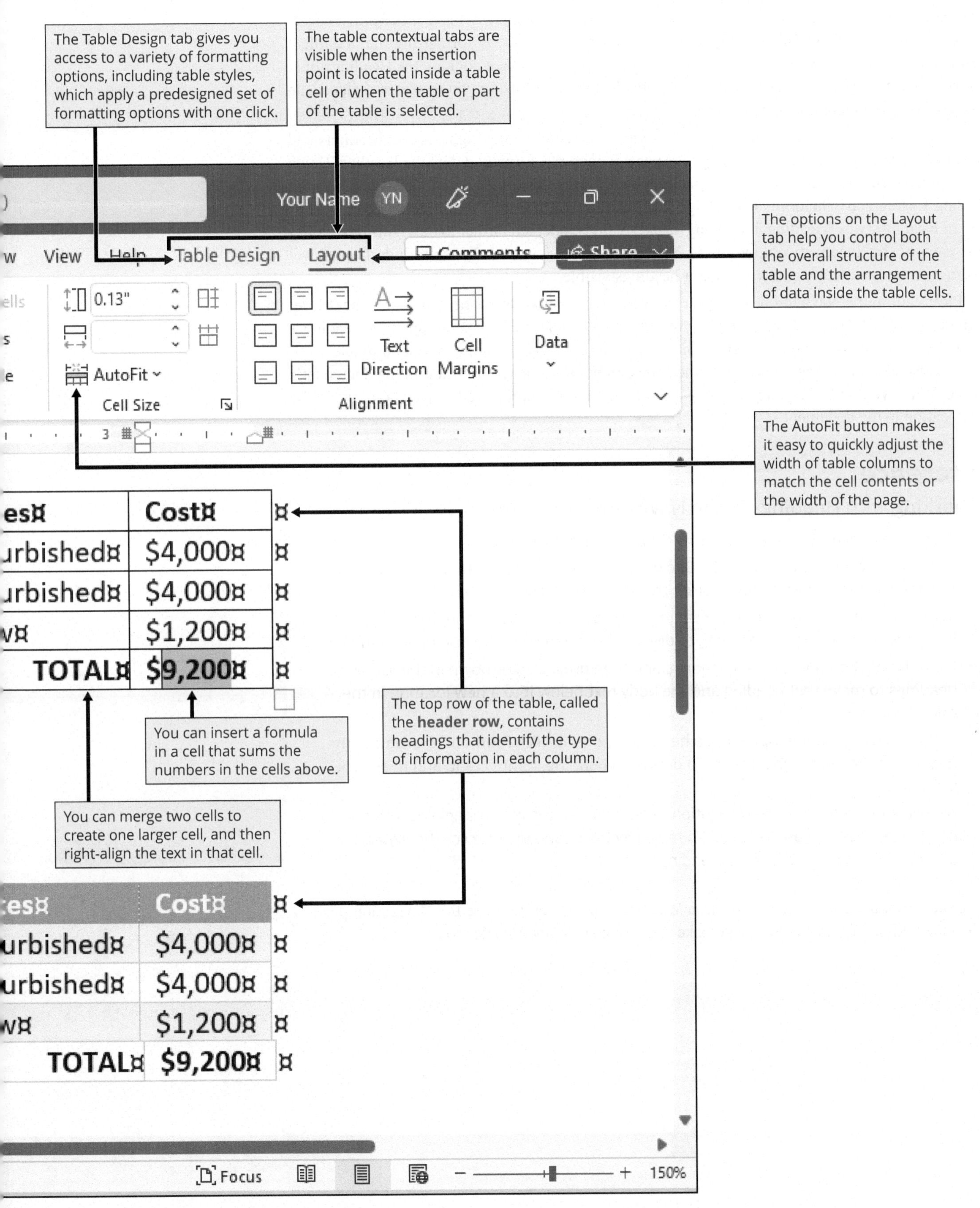
The Table Design tab gives you access to a variety of formatting options, including table styles, which apply a predesigned set of formatting options with one click.
The table contextual tabs are visible when the insertion point is located inside a table cell or when the table or part of the table is selected.
The options on the Layout tab help you control both the overall structure of the table and the arrangement of data inside the table cells.
The AutoFit button makes it easy to quickly adjust the width of table columns to match the cell contents or the width of the page.
The top row of the table, called the **header row**, contains headings that identify the type of information in each column.
You can insert a formula in a cell that sums the numbers in the cells above.
You can merge two cells to create one larger cell, and then right-align the text in that cell.
Your Name
YN
View
Help
Table Design
Layout
Comments
Share
0.13"
AutoFit
Cell Size
Text Direction
Cell Margins
Alignment
Data
Cost
$4,000
$1,200
TOTAL
$9,200
Focus
150%

Working with Headings in the Navigation Pane

When used in combination with the Navigation pane, Word's heading styles make it easier to navigate through a long document and to reorganize a document. You start by formatting the document headings with heading styles, displaying the Navigation pane, and then clicking the Headings link. This displays a hierarchy of all the headings in the document, allowing you to see, at a glance, an outline of the document headings.

Paragraphs formatted with the Heading 1 style are considered the highest-level headings and are aligned at the left margin of the Navigation pane. Paragraphs formatted with the Heading 2 style are considered subordinate to Heading 1 paragraphs and are indented slightly to the right below the Heading 1 paragraphs. Subordinate headings are often referred to as **subheadings**. Each successive level of heading styles (Heading 3, Heading 4, and so on) is indented farther to the right. To simplify your view of the document outline in the Navigation pane, you can choose to hide lower-level headings from view, leaving only the major headings visible.

From within the Navigation pane, you can **promote** a subordinate heading to the next level up in the heading hierarchy. For example, you can promote a Heading 2 paragraph to a Heading 1 paragraph. You can also do the opposite—that is, you can **demote** a heading to a subordinate level. You can also click and drag a heading in the Navigation pane to a new location in the document's outline. When you do so, any subheadings—along with their subordinate body text—move to the new location in the document.

Reference

Working with Headings in the Navigation Pane

- Format the document headings using Word's heading styles.
- Click the View tab, and then, in the Show group, select the Navigation Pane check box. Or click the page number indicator on the left edge of the status bar.
- In the Navigation pane, click the Headings link to display a list of the document headings, and then click a heading to display that heading in the document window.
- In the Navigation pane, click a heading, and then drag it up or down in the list of headings to move that heading and the body text below it to a new location in the document.
- In the Navigation pane, right-click a heading, and then click Promote to promote the heading to the next-highest level. To demote a heading, right-click it, and then click Demote.
- To hide subheadings in the Navigation pane, click the collapse triangle next to the higher level heading above them. To redisplay the subheadings, click the expand triangle next to the higher-level heading.

Laila saved the draft of her report as a Word document. You will use the Navigation pane to review the outline of Laila's report and make some changes to its organization.

To review the document headings in the Navigation pane:

1. **sam** Open the document **NP_WD_3-1.docx** located in the Word3 > Module folder included with your Data Files, and then save the file with the name **NP_WD_3_ComputerClasses** in the location specified by your instructor.
2. Verify that the document is displayed in Print Layout view and that the rulers and nonprinting characters are displayed.
3. Make sure the Zoom level is set to **120%**, and that the Home tab is selected on the ribbon.
4. Click the View tab and then select the **Navigation Pane** check box in the Show group to open the Navigation pane to the left of the document. Note that you could also click the page indicator in the status bar to open the Navigation pane.
5. In the Navigation pane, click the **Headings** link. The document headings are displayed in the Navigation pane, as shown in Figure 3–1. The blue highlighted heading ("Summary") indicates that part of the document currently contains the insertion point.

   Note: To ensure consistency between the figures in this book and your computer screen, the Check spelling as you type check box and the Mark grammar errors as you type check box in the Word Options dialog box were deselected before the figures in this module were created. The same is true for figures in subsequent modules.

Figure 3–1 Headings displayed in the Navigation pane

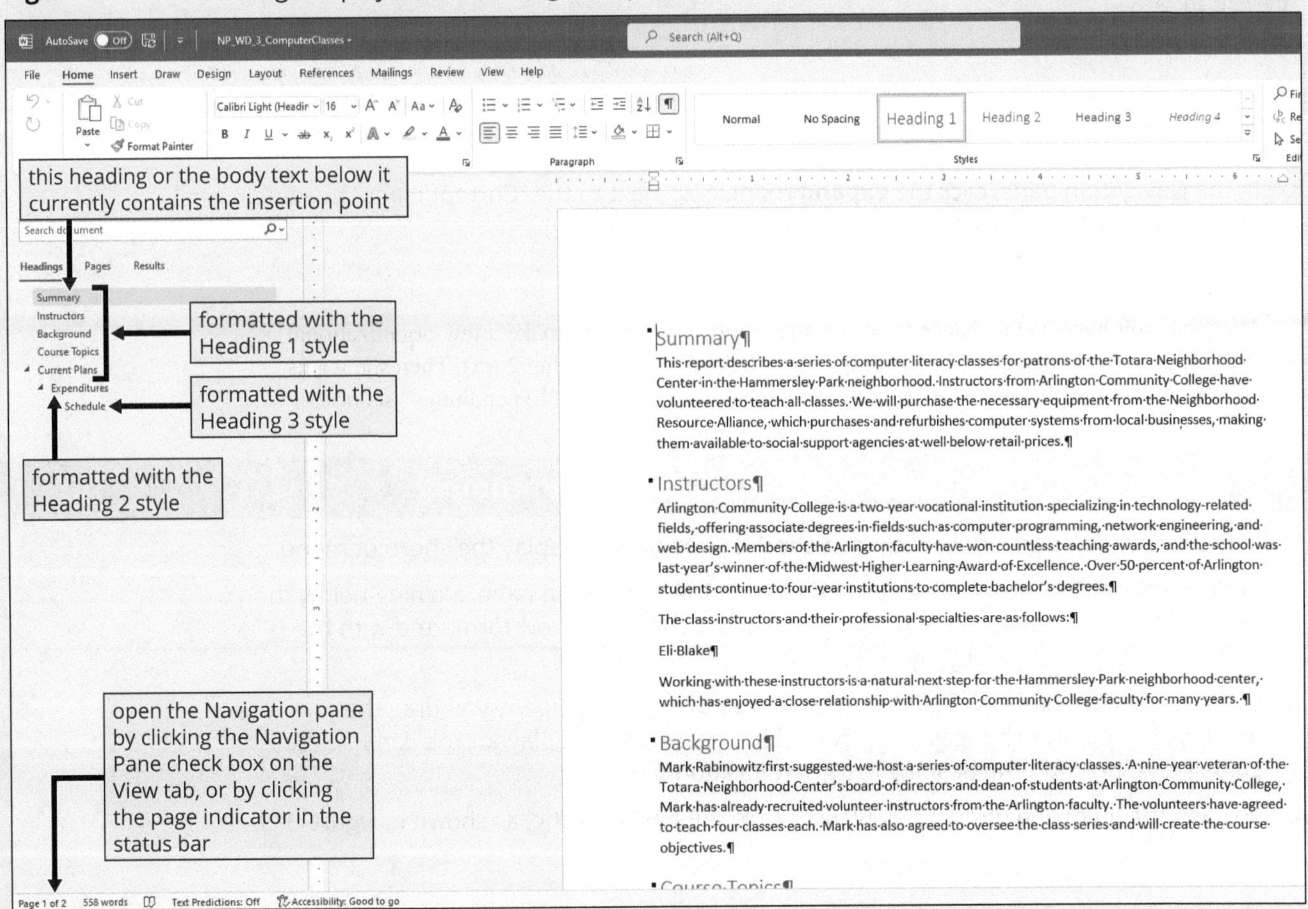

6. In the Navigation pane, click the **Current Plans** heading. Word displays the heading in the document window, with the insertion point at the beginning of the heading. The "Current Plans" heading is highlighted in blue in the Navigation pane. In the Navigation pane, you can see that there are subheadings below this heading.
7. In the Navigation pane, click the **collapse** triangle ◢ next to the "Current Plans" heading. The subheadings below this heading are no longer visible in the Navigation pane. This has no effect on the text in the actual document. Refer to Figure 3–2.

Figure 3–2 Heading 2 and Heading 3 text hidden in Navigation pane

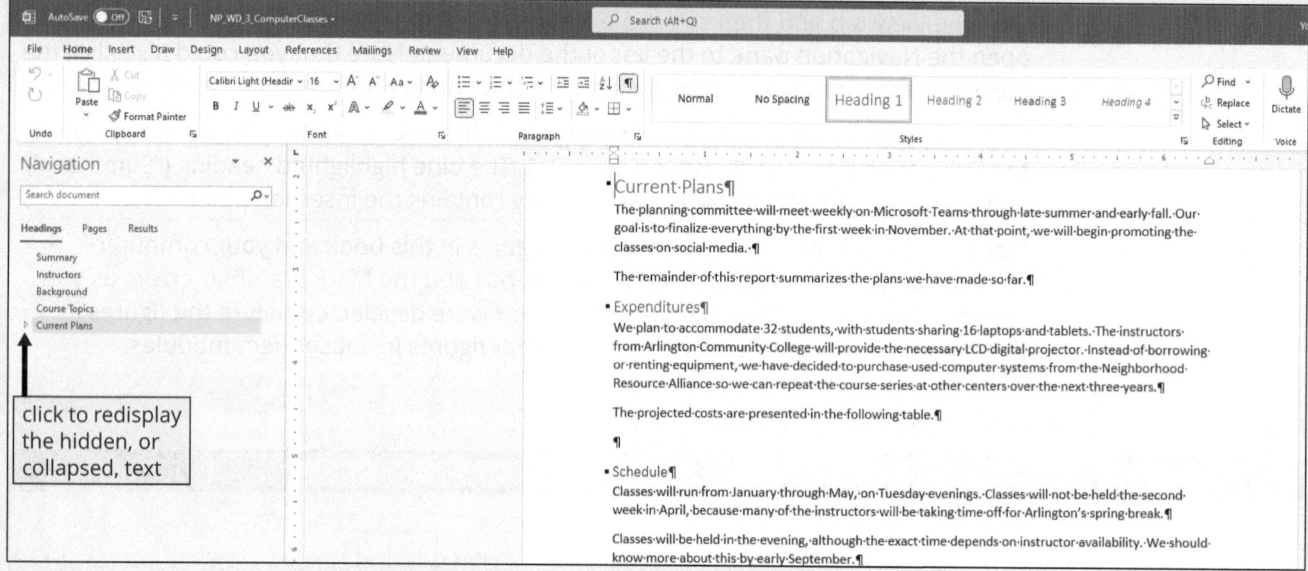

8. In the Navigation pane, click the **expand** triangle ▷ next to the "Current Plans" heading. The subheadings are again visible in the Navigation pane.

Now that you have had a chance to review the report, you need to make a few organizational changes. Laila wants to promote the Heading 3 text "Schedule" to Heading 2 text. Then she wants to move the "Schedule" heading and its body text up, so it precedes the "Expenditures" section.

To use the Navigation pane to reorganize text in the document:

1. In the Navigation pane, right-click the **Schedule** heading to display the shortcut menu.
2. Click **Promote**. The heading moves to the left in the Navigation pane, aligning below the "Expenditures" heading. In the document window, the text is now formatted with the Heading 2 style, with its slightly larger font.
3. In the Navigation pane, click and drag the **Schedule** heading up. As you drag the heading, the pointer changes to a move pointer, and a blue guideline is displayed. You can use the guideline to position the heading in its new location.
4. Position the guideline directly below the "Current Plans" heading, as shown in Figure 3–3.

Figure 3–3 Moving a heading in the Navigation pane

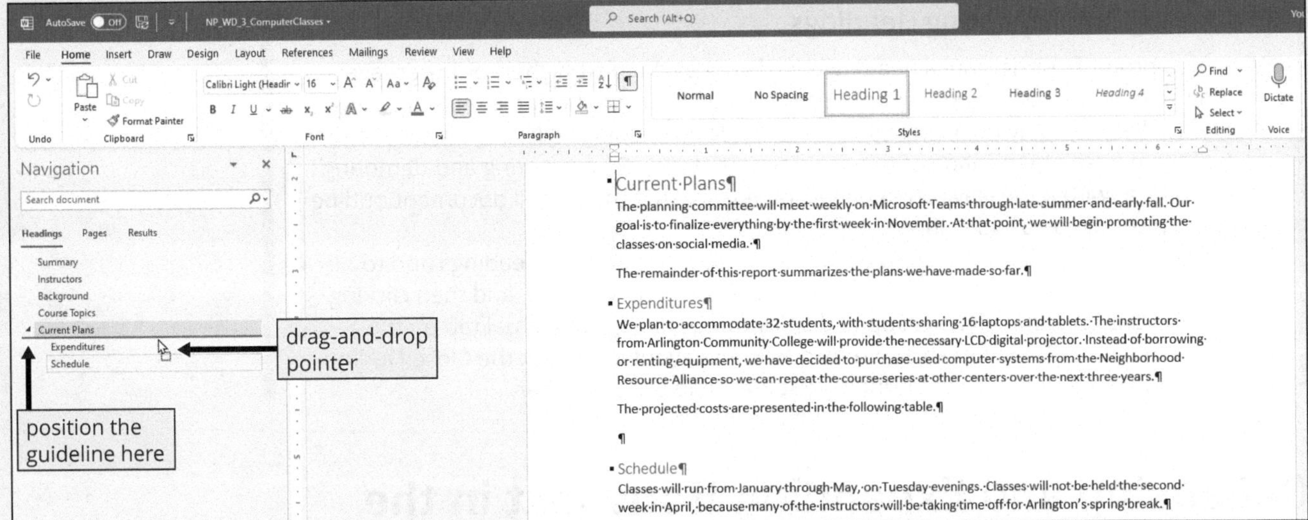

5. Release the mouse button. The "Schedule" heading is displayed in its new position in the Navigation pane, as the second-to-last heading in the outline. The heading and its body text are displayed in their new location in the document, before the "Expenditures" heading. Refer to Figure 3–4.

Figure 3–4 Heading and body text in new location

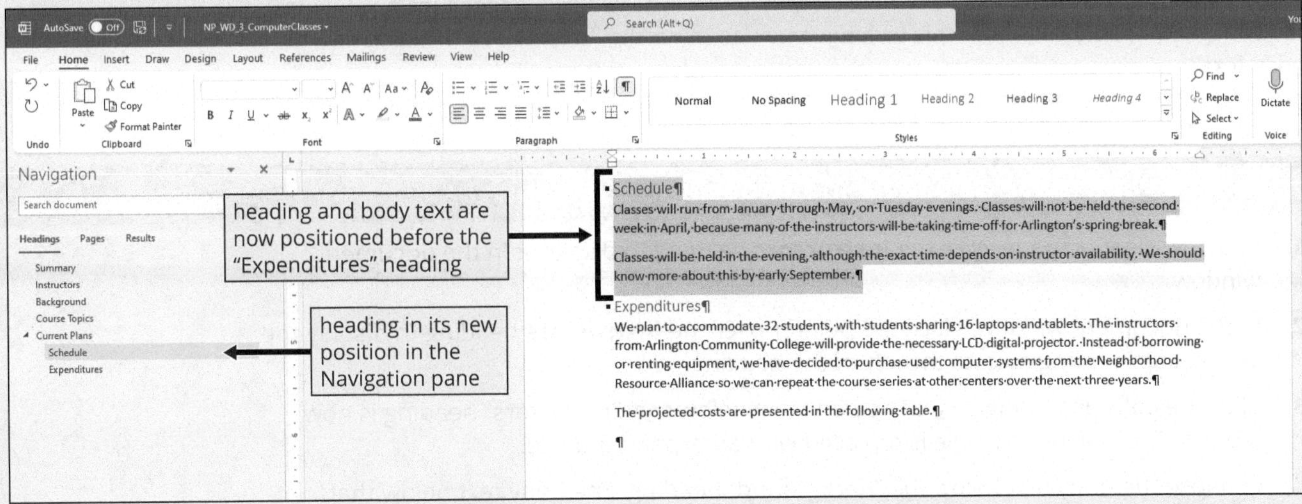

6. Click anywhere in the document to deselect the text, and then save the document.

Laila also wants you to move the "Instructors" heading and its accompanying body text. You'll do that in the next section, using a different method.

Insight

Promoting and Demoting Headings

When you promote or demote a heading, Word applies the next higher- or lower-level heading style to the heading paragraph. You could accomplish the same thing by using the Style gallery to apply the next higher- or lower-level heading style, but it's easy to lose track of the overall organization of the document that way. By promoting and demoting headings from within the Navigation pane, you ensure that the overall document outline is right in front of you as you work.

You can also use Outline view to display, promote, and demote headings and to reorganize a document. Turn on Outline view by clicking the View tab, and then clicking the Outline button in the Views group to display the Outlining contextual tab on the ribbon. To hide the Outlining tab and return to Print Layout view, click the Close Outline View button on the ribbon or the Print Layout button in the status bar.

Collapsing and Expanding Body Text in the Document

Because the Navigation pane gives you an overview of the entire document, dragging headings within the Navigation pane is the best way to reorganize a document. However, you can also reorganize a document from within the document window, without using the Navigation pane, by first hiding, or collapsing, the body text below a heading in a document. After you collapse the body text below a heading, you can drag the heading to a new location in the document. When you do, the body text moves along with the heading, just as if you had dragged the heading in the Navigation pane. You'll use this technique now to move the "Instructors" heading and its body text.

To collapse and move a heading in the document window:

1. In the Navigation pane, click the **Instructors** heading to display it in the document window.
2. In the document window, place the pointer over the **Instructors** heading to display the gray collapse triangle ◢ to the left of the heading.
3. Click the **collapse** triangle ◢. The body text below the "Instructors" heading is now hidden. The collapse triangle is replaced with an expand triangle.
4. Collapse the body text below the "Background" heading. The body text below that heading is no longer visible. Collapsing body text can be helpful when you want to hide details in a document temporarily, so you can focus on a particular part. Refer to Figure 3–5.

Figure 3–5 Body text collapsed in the document

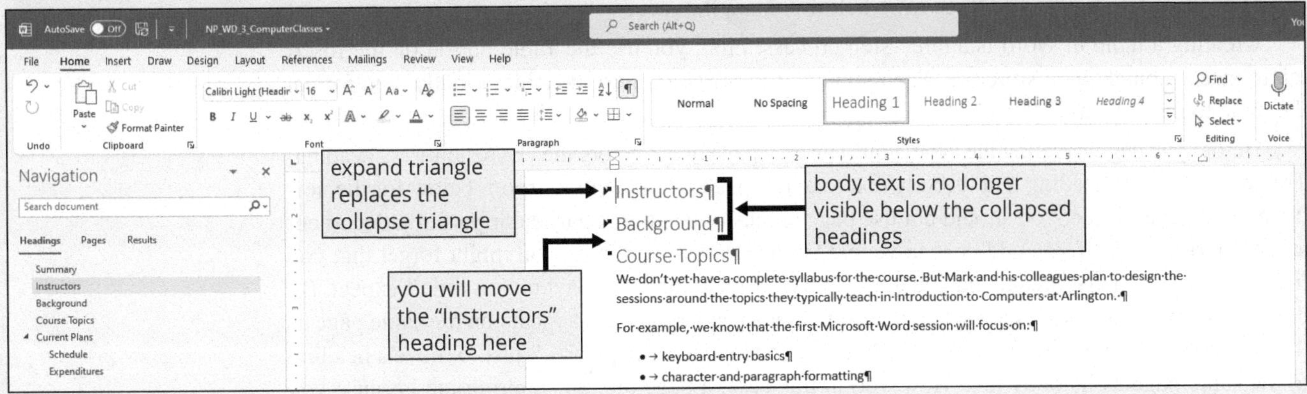

5. In the document, select the **Instructors** heading, including the paragraph mark at the end of the paragraph.
6. Click and drag the heading down. As you drag, a dark black insertion point moves along with the pointer.
7. Position the dark black insertion point to the left of the "C" in the "Course Topics" heading, and then release the mouse button. The "Instructors" heading and its body text move to the new location, before the "Course Topics" heading.

Finally, you need to expand the body text below the two collapsed headings.

8. Click anywhere in the document to deselect the text.
9. Click the **expand** triangle ▷ to redisplay the body text below the "Instructors" heading.
10. Click the **expand** triangle ▷ to the left of the "Background" heading to redisplay the body text below the heading.
11. Save the document.

The document is now organized the way Laila wants it. Next, you need to create a table summarizing her data on probable expenditures.

Inserting a Blank Table

A table is a useful way to present information that is organized into categories, or **fields**. For example, you could use a table to organize contact information for a list of clients. For each client, you could include information in the following fields: first name, last name, street address, city, state, and zip code. The complete set of information about a particular client is called a **record**. In a typical table, each column is a separate field, and each row is a record. A header row at the top contains the names of each field.

Tip The terms "table," "field," and "record" are also used to refer to information stored in database programs, such as Microsoft Access.

Figure 3–6 shows the information Laila wants to include in her table.

Figure 3–6 Information for Laila's table

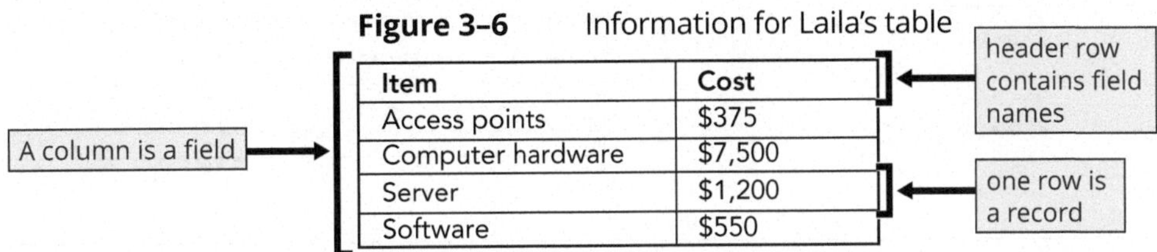

Item	Cost
Access points	$375
Computer hardware	$7,500
Server	$1,200
Software	$550

Laila's table includes two columns, or fields: "Item" and "Cost." The header row contains the names of these two fields. The three rows below contain the records.

Creating a table in Word is a three-step process. First, you use the Table button on the Insert tab to insert a blank table structure. Then you enter information into the table. Finally, you format the table to make it easy to read.

Before you begin creating the table, you'll insert a page break before the "Expenditures" heading. This will move the heading and its body text to a new page, with plenty of room below for the new table. As a general rule, you should not use page breaks to position a particular part of a document at the top of a page. If you add or remove text from the document later, you might forget that you inserted a manual page break, and you could end up with a document layout you didn't expect. By default, Word heading styles are set up to ensure that a heading always appears on the same page as the body text paragraph below it, so you'll never need to insert a page break just to move a heading to the same page as its body text. However, in this case, a page break is appropriate because you need the "Expenditures" heading to be displayed at the top of a page with room for the table below.

To insert a page break and insert a blank table:

1. In the Navigation pane, click **Expenditures** to display the heading in the document, with the insertion point to the left of the "E" in "Expenditures."
2. Close the Navigation pane, and then press **CTRL+ENTER** to insert a page break. The "Expenditures" heading and the body text following it move to a new, third page.
3. Scroll to position the "Expenditures" heading at the top of the Word window, and then press **CTRL+END** to move the insertion point to the blank paragraph at the end of the document.
4. On the ribbon, click the **Insert** tab.
5. In the Tables group, click the **Table** button. A table grid opens, with a menu at the bottom.

   Tip You can use the Quick Tables option to choose from preformatted tables that contain placeholder text.

6. Use the pointer to point to the **upper-left cell** of the grid, and then move the pointer down and across the grid to highlight two columns and four rows. (The outline of a cell turns orange when it is highlighted.) As you move the pointer across the grid, Word indicates the size of the table (columns by rows) at the top of the grid. A Live Preview of the table structure is displayed in the document. Refer to Figure 3–7.

Figure 3–7 Inserting a blank table

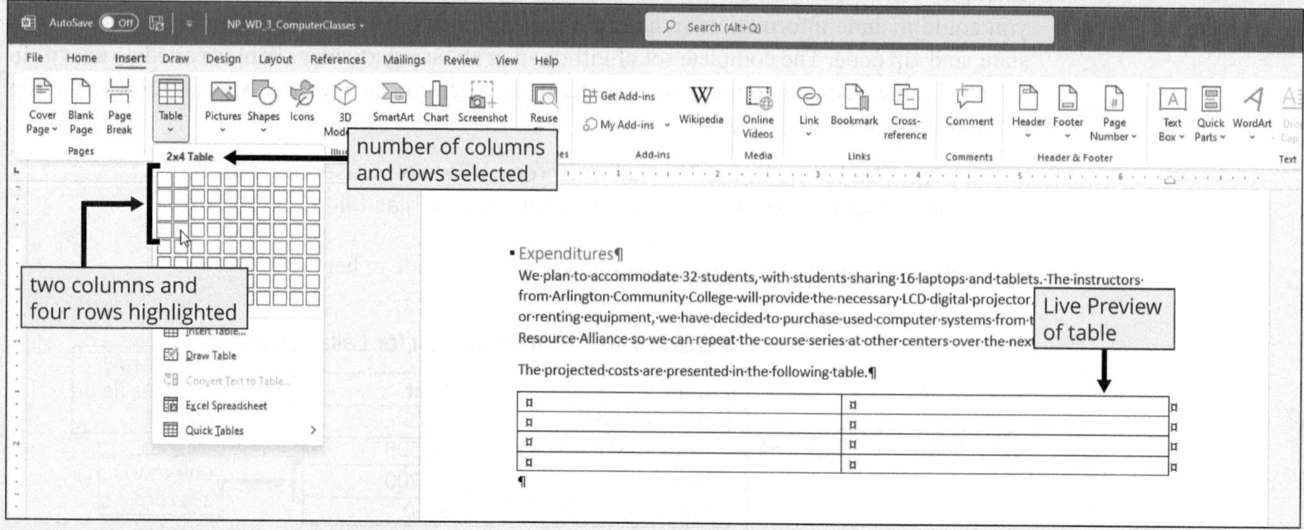

7. When the table size is 2 × 4, click the lower-right cell in the block of selected cells. An empty table consisting of two columns and four rows is inserted in the document, with the insertion point in the upper-left cell. Refer to Figure 3–8.

Figure 3–8 Blank table inserted in document

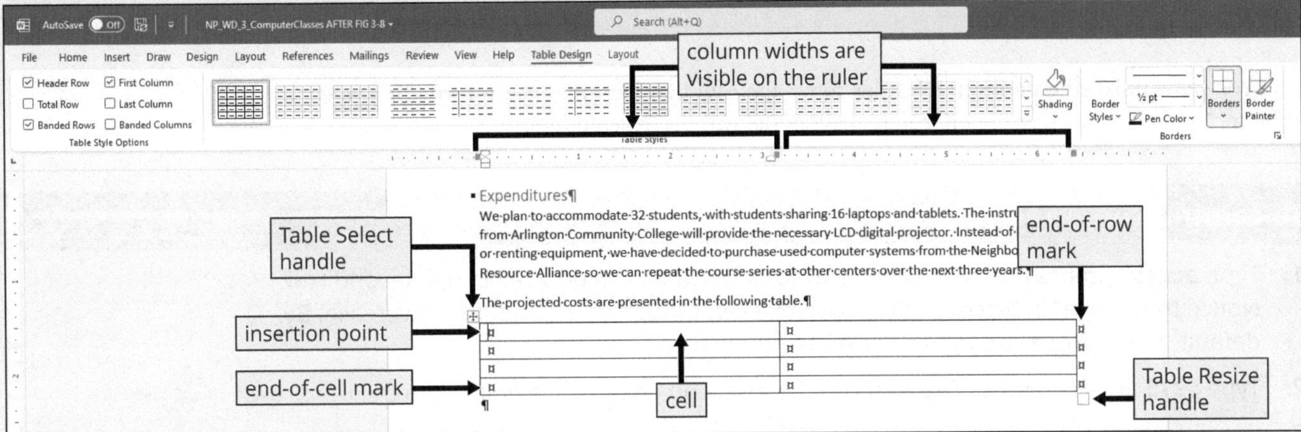

> **Trouble?** If you inserted a table with the wrong number of rows or columns, press Ctrl+Z to remove the table, and then repeat Steps 4 through 7.

The two columns are of equal width. Because nonprinting characters are displayed in the document, each cell contains an end-of-cell mark, and each row contains an end-of-row mark, which are important for selecting parts of a table. The Table Select handle ⊞ is displayed at the table's upper-left corner. You can click the Table Select handle ⊞ to select the entire table, and you can drag it to move the table. You can drag the Table Resize handle □, which is displayed at the lower-right corner, to change the size of the table.

The Table Design and Layout contextual tabs are currently displayed on the ribbon. Note that these tabs are only displayed when the insertion point is located in the table or when the table is selected. Also note that there are now two Layout tabs visible—one to the right of the Design tab, which you have used before to adjust paragraph spacing, and one to the right of the Table Design contextual tab.

The blank table is ready for you to begin entering information.

Entering Data in a Table

You can enter data in a table by moving the insertion point to a cell and typing. If the data takes up more than one line in the cell, Word automatically wraps the text to the next line and increases the height of that row. To move the insertion point to another cell in the table, you can click in that cell, use the arrow keys, or press TAB.

To enter information in the header row of the table:

1. Verify that the insertion point is located in the upper-left cell of the table.
2. Type **Item**. As you type, the end-of-cell mark moves right to accommodate the text.
3. Press **TAB** to move the insertion point to the next cell to the right.

Trouble? If Word created a new paragraph in the first cell rather than moving the insertion point to the second cell, you pressed ENTER instead of TAB. Press BACKSPACE to remove the paragraph mark, and then press TAB to move to the second cell in the first row.

4. Type **Cost** and then press **TAB** to move to the first cell in the second row.

You have finished entering the header row—the row that identifies the information in each column. Now you can enter the information about the various expenditures.

To continue entering information in the table:

1. Type **access points** and then press **TAB** to move to the second cell in the second row. Notice that the "a" in "Access" is capitalized, even though you typed it in lowercase. By default, AutoCorrect capitalizes the first letter in a cell entry.
2. Type **$375** and then press **TAB** to move the insertion point to the first cell in the third row.
3. Enter the following information in the bottom two rows, pressing **TAB** to move from cell to cell:

   Computer hardware **$10,500**

   Server **$1,200**

At this point, the table consists of a header row and three records. Laila realizes that she needs to add one more row to the table. You can add a new row to the bottom of a table by pressing TAB when the insertion point is in the rightmost cell in the bottom row.

To add a row to the table:

1. Verify that the insertion point is in the lower-right cell (which contains the value "$1,200"), and then press **TAB**. A new, blank row is added to the bottom of the table.
2. Type **Software**, press **TAB**, type **$550**, and then save the document. When you are finished, your table should look like the one shown in Figure 3–9.

Figure 3–9 Table with all data entered

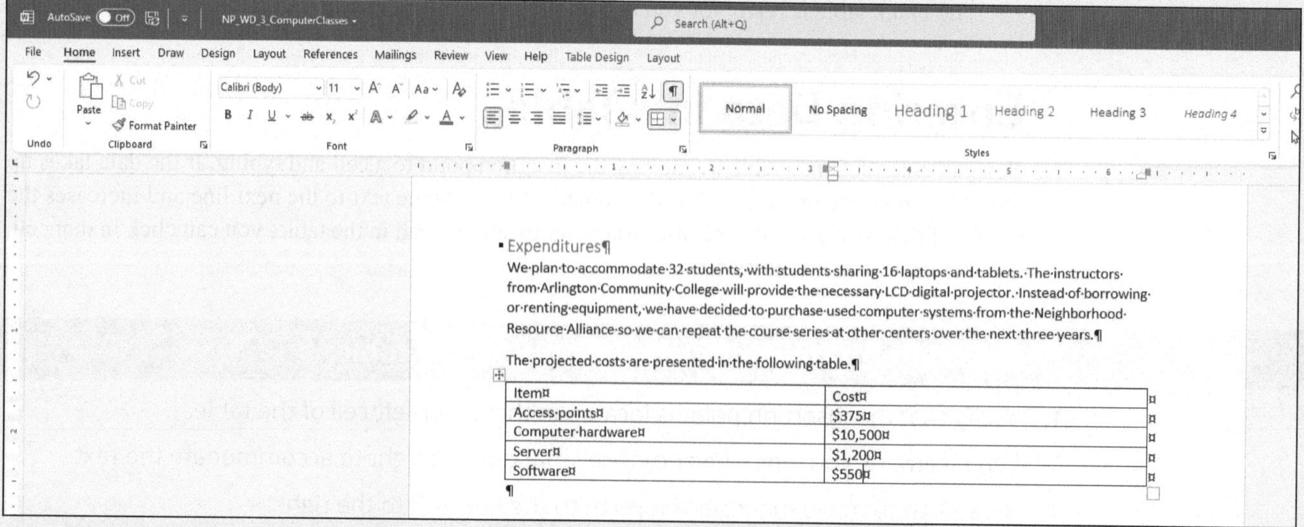

Trouble? If a new row is added to the bottom of your table, you pressed TAB after entering "$550". Press Ctrl+Z to remove the extra row from the table.

The table you've just created presents information about expenditures in an easy-to-read format. To make it even easier to read, you can format the header row in bold so it stands out from the rest of the table. To do that, you need to first select the header row.

Selecting Part of a Table

When selecting part of a table, you need to make sure you select the end-of-cell mark in a cell or the end-of-row mark at the end of a row. If you don't, the formatting changes you make next might not have the effect you expect. The foolproof way to select part of a table is to click in the cell, row, or column you want to select; click the Select button on the Layout contextual tab; and then click the appropriate command—Select Cell, Select Column, or Select Row. Or click Select Table to select the entire table. To select a row, you can also click in the left margin next to the row. Similarly, you can click just above a column to select it. After you've selected an entire row, column, or cell, you can drag the mouse to select adjacent rows, columns, or cells.

Note that in the following steps, you'll position the pointer until it takes on a particular shape so that you can then perform the task associated with that type of pointer. Pointer shapes are especially important when working with tables and graphics; in many cases, you can't perform a task until the pointer is the right shape. It takes some patience to get accustomed to positioning the pointer until it takes on the correct shape, but with practice you'll grow to rely on the pointer shapes as a quick visual cue to the options currently available to you.

To select and format the header row:

1. Position the pointer in the selection bar, to the left of the header row. The pointer changes to a right-pointing arrow.
2. Click the mouse button. The entire header row, including the end-of-cell mark in each cell and the end-of-row mark, is selected. Refer to Figure 3–10.

Figure 3–10 Header row selected

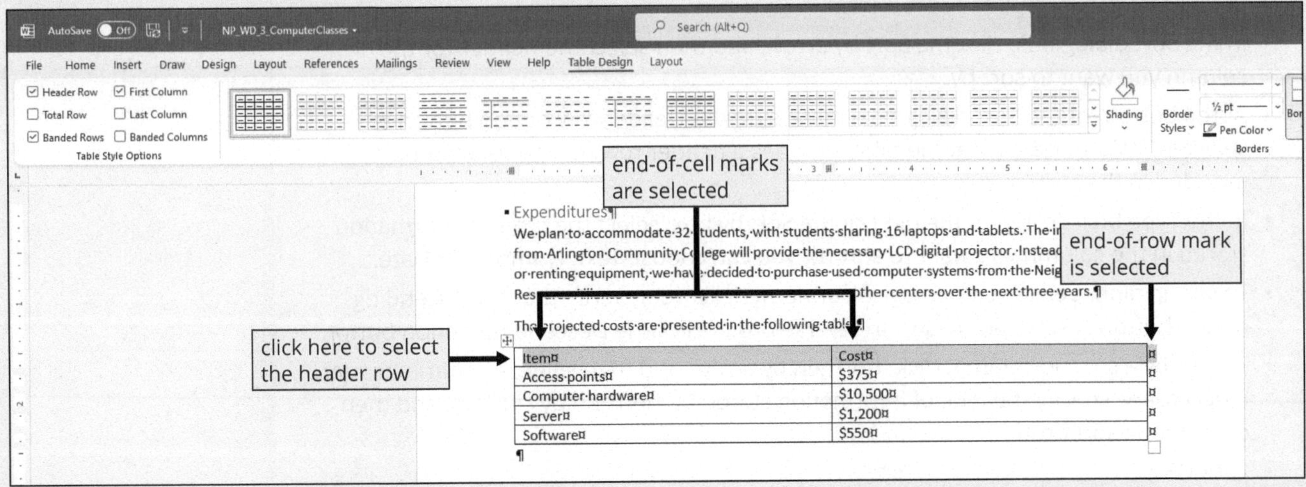

3. Press **CTRL+B** to apply bold to the text in the header row. You can also use the formatting options on the Home tab to format selected text in a table, including adding italic formatting, changing the font, aligning text within cells, or applying a style. However, text in a table that is formatted with a heading style will not show up as a heading in the Navigation pane.
4. Click anywhere in the table to deselect the header row, and then save the document.

Note that, in some documents, you might have a long table that extends across multiple pages. To make a multipage table easier to read, you can format the table header row to appear at the top of every page. To do so, click in the header row, click the Layout contextual tab to the right of the Table Design tab, and then click the Properties button in the Table group. In the Table Properties dialog box, click the Row tab, and then select the "Repeat as header row at the top of each page" check box.

Now that you have created a very basic table, you can sort the information in it and improve its appearance.

Sorting Rows in a Table

The term **sort** refers to the process of rearranging information in alphabetical, numerical, or chronological order. You can sort a series of paragraphs, including the contents of a bulleted list, or you can sort the rows of a table.

When you sort a table, you arrange the rows based on the contents of one of the columns. For example, you could sort the table you just created based on the contents of the "Item" column—either in ascending alphabetical order (from A to Z) or in descending alphabetical order (from Z to A). Alternatively, you could sort the table based on the contents of the "Cost" column—either in ascending numerical order (lowest to highest) or in descending numerical order (highest to lowest).

Clicking the Sort button in the Data group on the Layout contextual tab opens the Sort dialog box, which provides several options for fine-tuning the sort, including options for sorting a table by the contents of more than one column. This is useful if, for example, you want to organize the table rows by last name and then by first name within each last name. By default, Word assumes your table includes a header row that should remain at the top of the table—excluded from the sort.

Reference

Sorting the Rows of a Table

- Click anywhere within the table.
- On the ribbon, click the Layout contextual tab.
- In the Data group, click the Sort button.
- In the Sort dialog box, click the Sort by arrow, and then select the header for the column you want to sort by.
- At the bottom of the Sort dialog box, make sure the Header row option button is selected. This indicates that the table includes a header row that should not be included in the sort.
- In the Type box located to the right of the Sort by box, select the type of information stored in the column you want to sort by; you can choose Text, Number, or Date.
- To sort in alphabetical, chronological, or numerical order, verify that the Ascending option button is selected. To sort in reverse order, click the Descending option button.
- To sort by a second column, click the Then by arrow, and then select a column header. If necessary, specify the type of information stored in the Then by column, and then confirm the sort order.
- Click OK.

Laila would like you to sort the contents of the table in ascending numerical order based on the contents of the "Cost" column.

To sort the information in the table:

1. Make sure the insertion point is located somewhere in the table.
2. On the ribbon, click the **Layout** contextual tab.

3. In the Data group, click the **Sort** button. The Sort dialog box opens. Take a moment to review its default settings. The leftmost column in the table, the "Item" column, is selected in the Sort by box, indicating the sort will be based on the contents in this column. Because the "Item" column contains text, "Text" is selected in the Type box. The Ascending option button is selected by default, indicating that Word will sort the contents of the "Item" column from A to Z. The Header row option button is selected in the lower-left corner of the dialog box, ensuring the header row will not be included in the sort.

   You want to sort the column by the contents of the "Cost" column, so you need to change the Sort by setting.

4. Click the **Sort by arrow**, and then click **Cost**. Because the "Cost" column contains numbers, the Type box now displays "Number". The Ascending button is still selected, indicating that Word will sort the numbers in the "Cost" column from lowest to highest. At this point, if you wanted to sort by a second column, you could click the Then by arrow, and then select the Item header. Refer to Figure 3–11.

Figure 3–11 Sort dialog box

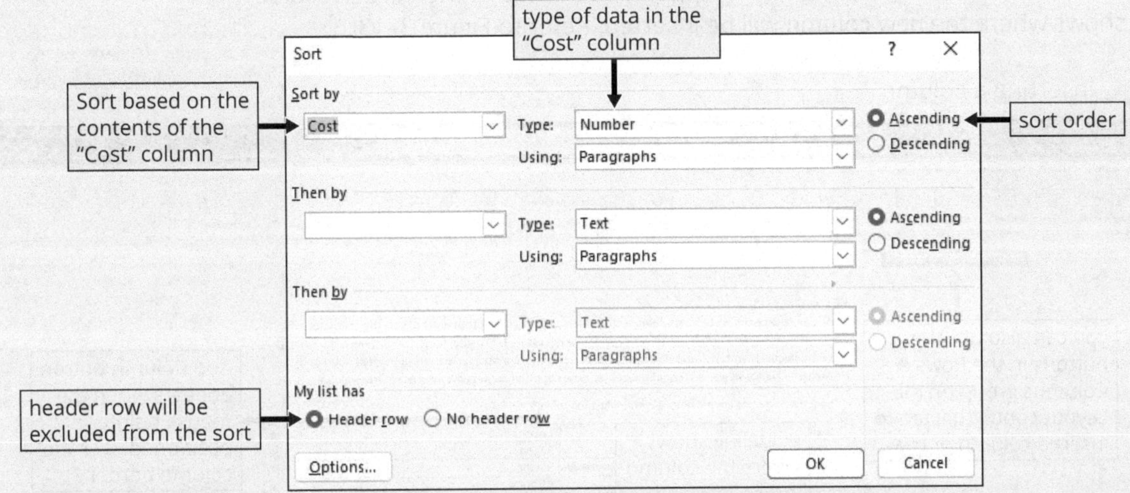

5. Click **OK** to close the Sort dialog box, and then click anywhere in the table to deselect it. Rows 2 through 5 are now arranged numerically from lowest to highest, according to the numbers in the "Cost" column, with the "Computer hardware" row at the bottom. Refer to Figure 3–12.

Figure 3–12 Table after being sorted

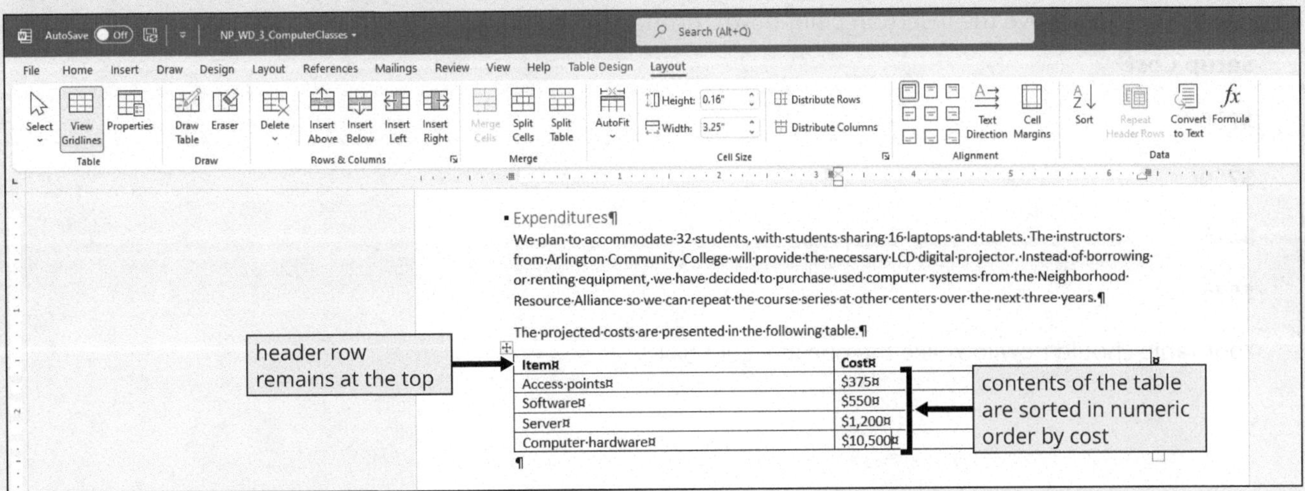

6. Save the document.

Laila decides that the table should also include the cost for installing each item. She asks you to insert a "Setup Cost" column.

Inserting Rows and Columns in a Table

To add a column to a table, you can use the tools in the Rows & Columns group on the Layout contextual tab, or you can use the Add Column button in the document window. To use the Add Column button, make sure the insertion point is located somewhere within the table. When you position the pointer at the top of the table, pointing to the border between two columns, the Add Column button is displayed. When you click that button, a new column is inserted between the two existing columns.

To insert a column in the table:

1. Verify that the insertion point is located anywhere in the table.
2. Position the pointer at the top of the table, so that it points to the border between the two columns. The Add Column button ⊕ appears at the top of the border. A blue guideline shows where the new column will be inserted. Refer to Figure 3–13.

Figure 3–13 Inserting a column

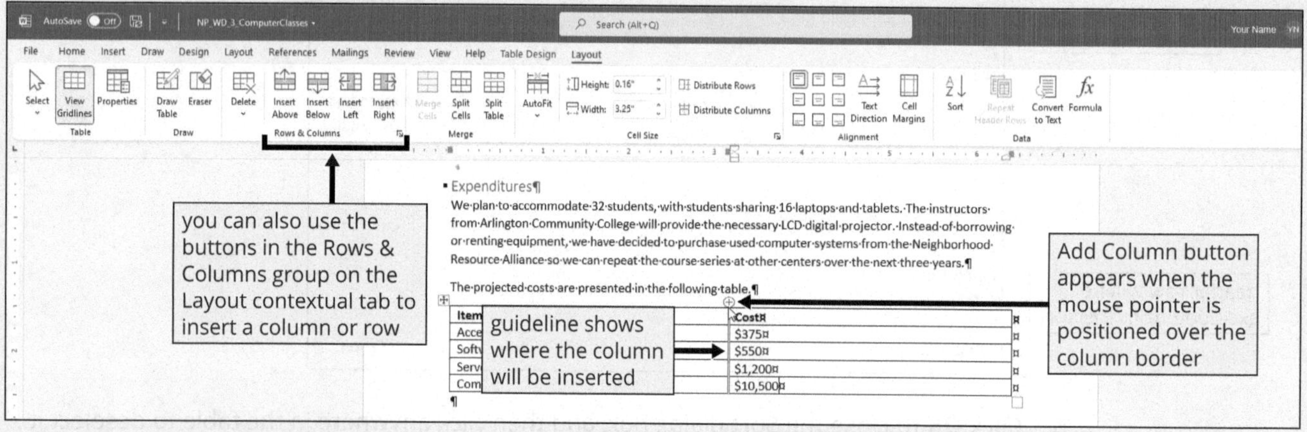

3. Click the **Add Column** button ⊕. A new, blank column is inserted between the "Item" and "Cost" columns. The three columns in the table are narrower than the original two columns, but the overall width of the table remains the same.
4. Click in the top cell of the new column, and then enter the following header and data. Use the ↓ key to move the insertion point down through the column.

   Setup Cost

   $250

   $750

   $275

   $825

   Your table should now look like the one in Figure 3–14.

Figure 3–14 New "Setup Cost" column

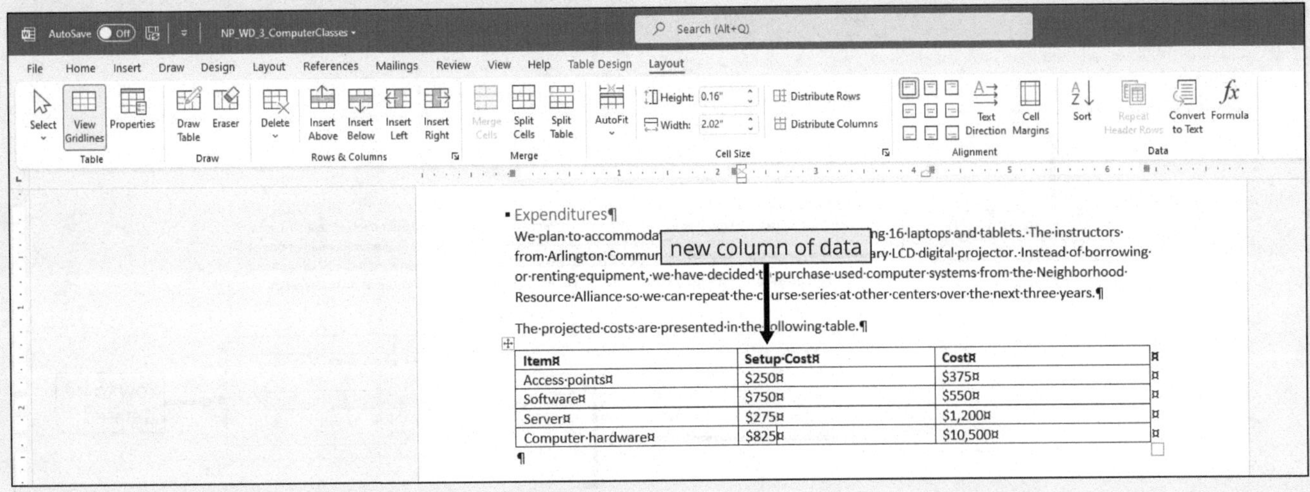

Because you selected the entire header row when you formatted the original headers in bold, the newly inserted header, "Setup Cost," is also formatted in bold.

Laila just learned that the costs listed for laptop computers actually cover all the necessary laptop computers plus the server. Therefore, she would like you to delete the "Server" row from the table.

Deleting Rows and Columns

When you consider deleting a row, you need to be clear about whether you want to delete just the contents of the row, or both the contents and the structure of the row. You can delete the contents of a row by selecting the row and pressing DELETE. This removes the information from the row but leaves the row structure intact. The same is true for deleting the contents of an individual cell, a column, or the entire table. To delete the structure of a row, a column, or the entire table—including its contents—you select the row (or column or the entire table), and then use the Delete button on the Mini toolbar or in the Rows & Columns group on the Layout tab. To delete multiple rows or columns, start by selecting all the rows or columns you want to delete.

Before you delete the "Server" row, you need to edit the contents in the last cell of the first column to indicate that the items in that row include laptops and servers.

To delete the "Server" row:

1. Triple-click the cell containing the text "Computer hardware" to select it and type **Laptop computers and server hardware**. Part of the text wraps to a second line within the cell. Note that you could also click anywhere in a cell, and then use BACKSPACE or DELETE to delete text, and then type new text. In other words, you can edit text in a table just as you would edit ordinary text in a document.

   Next, you need to delete the "Server" row, which is no longer necessary.

2. Click in the selection bar to the left of the **Server** row. The row is selected, with the Mini toolbar displayed on top of the selected row.
3. On the Mini toolbar, click the **Delete** button. The Delete menu opens, displaying options for deleting cells, columns, rows, or the entire table. Refer to Figure 3–15.

Figure 3–15 Deleting a row

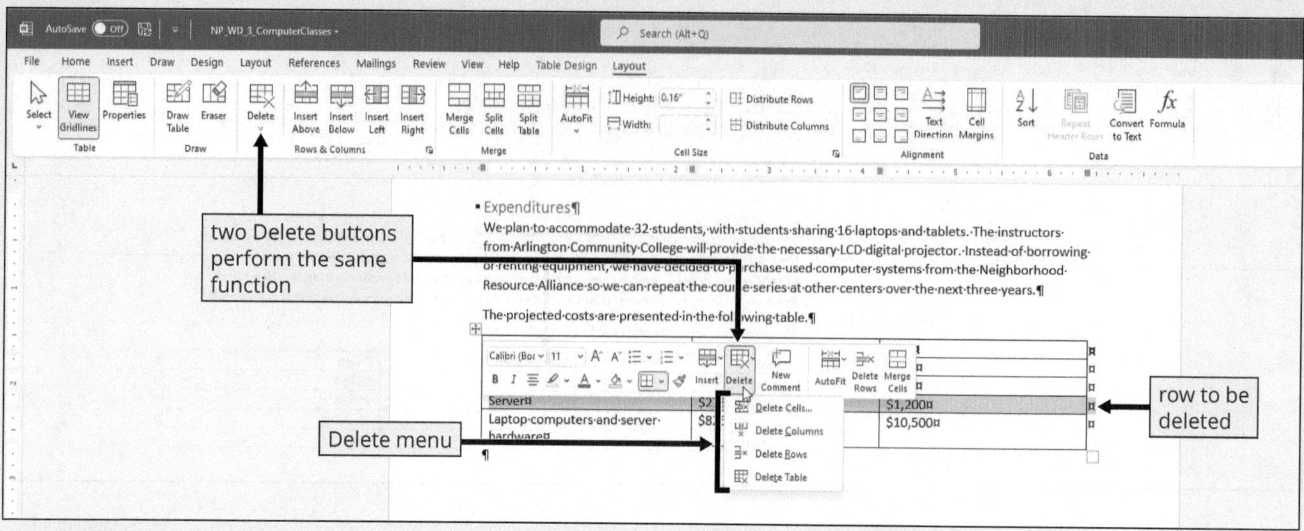

4. Click **Delete Rows**. The "Server" row is removed from the table, and the Mini toolbar disappears.
5. Save your work.

The table now contains all the information Laila wants to include. Next, you'll adjust the widths of the three columns.

Changing Column Widths and Row Heights

Word offers many ways to change the size of columns and rows. While it's good to know how to adjust row heights, in most cases, you'll only need to focus on column widths, because columns that are too wide for the material they contain can make a table hard to read.

You can change a column's width by dragging the column's right border to a new position. Or, if you prefer, you can double-click a column border to make the column width adjust automatically to accommodate the widest entry in the column. A more precise option is to click in the column you want to adjust, click the Layout contextual tab, and then change the setting in the Width box, just as you would adjust the width of a picture.

You can also adjust the height of rows and the width of the entire table. To change the height of a row, position the pointer over the bottom row border and drag the border up or down, or click in the row and change the setting in the Height box on the Layout contextual tab. You can change the width of the entire table by changing the width of all the columns and the height of all the rows at one time. To do this, drag the Table Resize handle (shown in Figure 3–8) or select the entire table and then adjust the settings in the Height and Width boxes on the Layout tab.

The AutoFit button in the Cell Size group on the Layout tab offers some additional options for changing the width of table columns. When you first create a table, its columns are all the same width, and the table stretches from the left to the right margin. If you enter data that is wider than the cell you are typing in, the data wraps in the cell to the next line. (Note that if the word you type is long and does not contain any spaces, the column will widen as much as needed to fit the word until the columns to its right are 0.15 inches wide, at which point the text will wrap in the cell.) If you want the columns to resize wider to accommodate data, you can select the table, click the AutoFit button, and then click AutoFit Contents. When you do this, columns that contain data that is longer than the width of the column will resize wider, if possible, to accommodate the widest entry. If the widest entry in a column is narrower than the column, the AutoFit Contents command will resize that column narrower to just fit that data. If you have adjusted column widths, either manually or by using the AutoFit Contents command, so that the table no longer stretches from the left to the right margin, you can click the AutoFit button and then click AutoFit Window. This will resize all the columns proportionally so that the table stretches from the left to the right margin. This command is useful if you paste a table copied from another file and it is too wide to fit on the page.

You'll use two methods to adjust the columns in Laila's table. You need to start by making sure that no part of the table is selected. Otherwise, when you double-click the border, only the width of the selected part of the table will change.

To change the width of the columns in the table:

1. Verify that no part of the table is selected, and then position the pointer over the right border of the "Setup Cost" column until the pointer changes to +||+. Refer to Figure 3–16.

Figure 3–16 Adjusting the column width

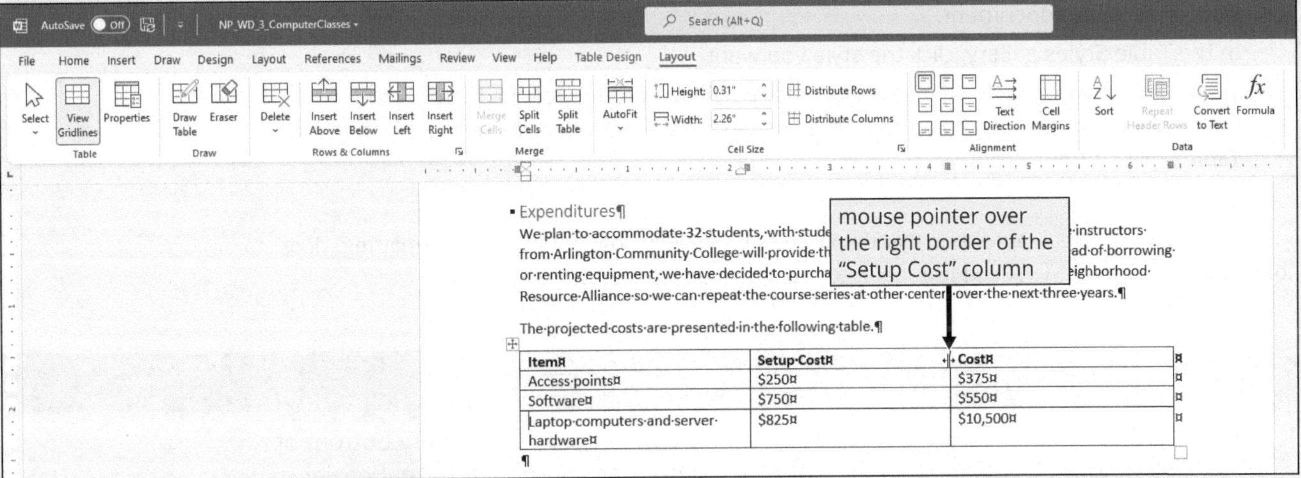

2. Double-click the mouse button. The right column border moves left so that the "Setup Cost" column is just wide enough to accommodate the widest entry in the column.
3. Verify that no part of the table is selected and that the insertion point is located in any cell in the table.
4. Make sure the Layout contextual tab is selected on the ribbon.
5. In the Cell Size group, click the **AutoFit** button, and then click **AutoFit Contents**. All of the table columns adjust so that each is just wide enough to accommodate its widest entry. The text "Laptop computers and server hardware" in row 4 no longer wraps to a second line.
6. Save the document.

To finish the table, you will add some formatting to improve the table's appearance.

Formatting Tables with Styles

To adjust a table's appearance, you can use any of the formatting options available on the Home tab. To change a table's appearance more dramatically, you can use table styles, which allow you to apply a collection of formatting options, including shading, color, borders, and other design elements, with a single click.

By default, a table is formatted with the Table Grid style, which includes only black borders between the rows and columns, no paragraph spacing, no shading, and the default black font color. You can select a more colorful table style from the Table Styles group on the Table Design tab. Whatever table style you choose, you'll give your document a more polished look if you use the same style consistently in all the tables in a single document.

Some table styles format rows in alternating colors, called **banded rows**, while others format the columns in alternating colors, called **banded columns**. You can choose a style that includes different formatting for the header row than for the rest of the table. Or, if the first column in your table is a header column—that is, if it contains headers identifying the type of information in each row—you can choose a style that instead applies different formatting to the first column.

Reference

Formatting a Table with a Table Style

- Click in the table you want to format.
- On the ribbon, click the Table Design tab.
- In the Table Styles group, click the More button to display the Table Styles gallery.
- Position the pointer over a style in the Table Styles gallery to see a Live Preview of the table style in the document.
- In the Table Styles gallery, click the style you want.
- To apply or remove style elements (such as special formatting for the header row, banded rows, or banded columns), select or deselect check boxes as necessary in the Table Style Options group.

Laila wants to use a table style that emphasizes the header row with special formatting, does not include column borders, and uses color to separate the rows.

To apply a table style to the Expenditures table:

1. Click anywhere in the table, and then scroll to position the table at the very bottom of the Word window. Depending on the size of your monitor, this might make it easier to see the Live Preview in the next few steps.
2. On the ribbon, click the **Table Design** tab. In the Table Styles group, the plain Table Grid style is highlighted, indicating that it is the table's current style.
3. In the Table Styles group, click the **More** button. The Table Styles gallery opens. The default Table Grid style now appears under the heading "Plain Tables." The more elaborate styles appear below, in the "Grid Tables" section of the gallery.
4. Review the complete collection of table styles. Depending on the size of your monitor, you might need to use the gallery's vertical scroll bar to display all the options. When you are finished, scroll up until you can see the "Grid Tables" heading again.
5. Move the pointer over the Grid Table 4 - Accent 6 style, which is located in the gallery's Grid Tables section. Refer to Figure 3–17.

Figure 3–17 Table styles gallery

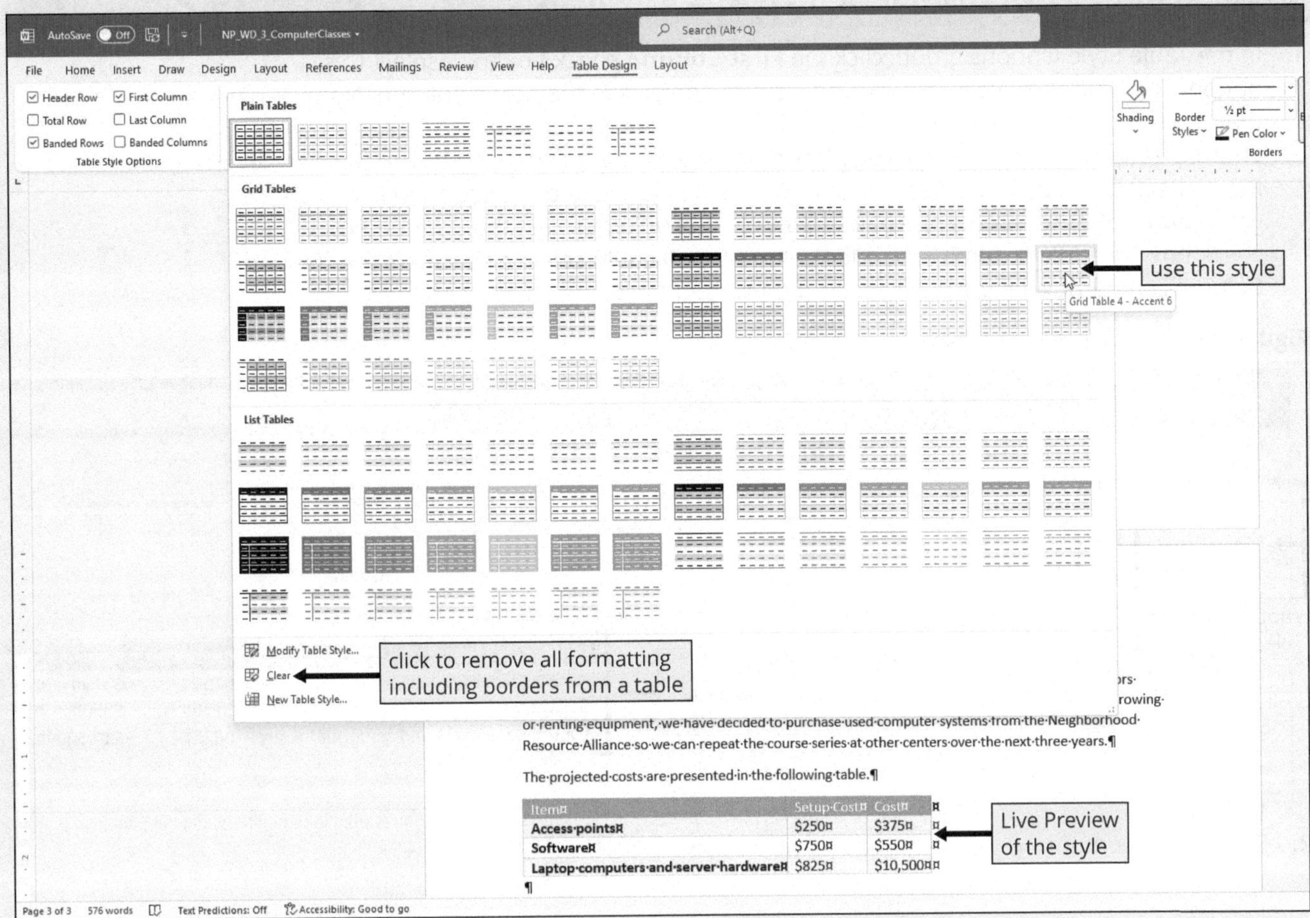

A ScreenTip displays the style's name, "Grid Table 4 - Accent 6." The style consists of a dark green heading row, with alternating rows of light green and white below. Depending on the size of your monitor, you might be able to see a Live Preview of the style in the document.

6. Click the **Grid Table 4 - Accent 6** style. The Table Styles gallery closes.
7. Scroll to position the table at the top of the Word window, so you can review it more easily. The table's header row is formatted with dark green shading and white text. The rows below appear in alternating colors of light green and white.

The only problem with the newly formatted table is that the text in the first column is formatted in bold. In tables where the first column contains row headers, bold would be appropriate—but this isn't the case with Laila's table. You'll fix this by deselecting the First Column check box in the Table Style Options group on the Table Design tab.

To remove the bold formatting from the first column:

1. In the Table Style Options group, click the **First Column** check box to deselect this option. The bold formatting is removed from the entries in the "Item" column. Note that the Header Row check box is selected. This indicates that the table's header row is emphasized with special formatting (dark green shading with white text). The Banded Rows check box is also selected because the table is formatted with banded rows of green and white. To remove the banded rows, you could deselect the Banded Rows check box. To apply or remove banded columns, you could select or deselect the Banded Columns check box. Figure 3–18 shows the finished table.

Figure 3–18 Completed table

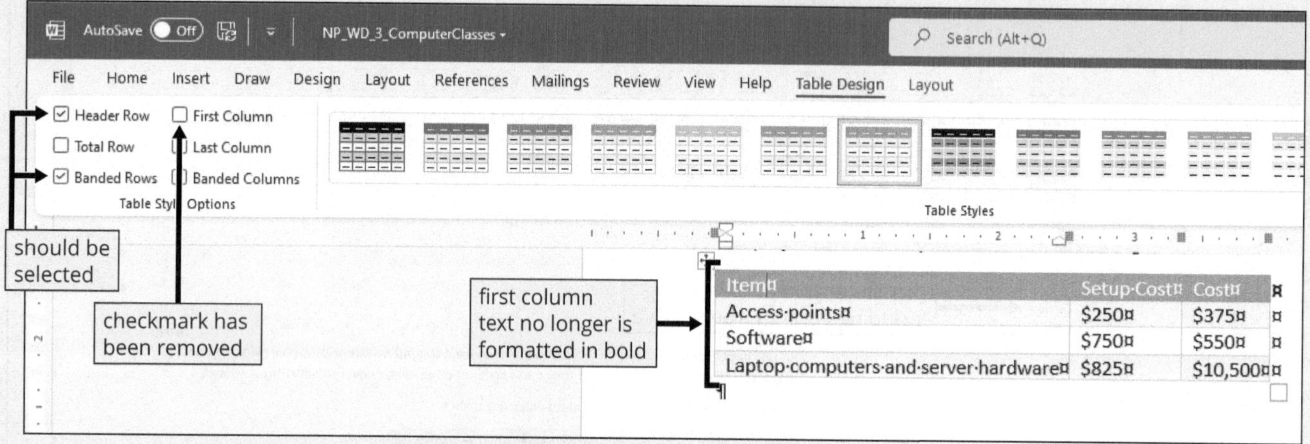

2. Save the document.

After you apply a table style, it's helpful to know how to remove it in case you want to start over from scratch. The Clear option on the menu below the Table Styles gallery removes the current style from a table, including the borders between cells. When a table has no borders, the rows and columns are defined by **gridlines**, which are useful as guidelines but do not appear when you print the table.

In the following steps, you'll experiment with clearing the table's style, displaying and hiding the gridlines, and removing the table's borders.

To experiment with table styles, gridlines, and borders:

1. In the Table Styles group, click the **More** button, and then click **Clear** in the menu below the gallery. The green shading and borders are removed from the table. Next, you need to make sure the table gridlines are displayed.
2. On the ribbon, click the **Layout** contextual tab.
3. In the Table group, click the **View Gridlines** button, if necessary, to select it. The table now looks much simpler, with no shading or font colors. Instead of the table borders, dotted gridlines separate the rows and columns. The text in the table is spaced farther apart because removing the table style restored the default paragraph and line spacing of the Normal style. The bold formatting that you applied earlier, which is not part of a table style, is visible again.

   It is helpful to clear a table's style and view only the gridlines if you want to use a table to lay out text and graphics on a page, but you want no visible indication of the table itself.

   Another option is to remove only the table borders, leaving the rest of the table style applied to the table. To do this, you have to select the entire table. But first you need to undo the style change.

4. Press **Ctrl+Z** to restore the Grid Table 4 - Accent 6 style, so that your table looks like the one in Figure 3–18.
5. In the upper-left corner of the table, click the **Table Select** handle to select the entire table, and then click the **Table Design** tab.
6. In the Borders group, click the **Borders arrow** to open the Borders gallery, click **No Border**, and then click anywhere in the table to deselect it. The borders are removed from the table, leaving only the nonprinting gridlines to separate the rows and columns. To add borders of any color to specific parts of a table, you can use the Border Painter.
7. In the Borders group, click the **Border Painter** button, and then click the **Pen Color** button to open the Pen Color gallery.
8. In the Pen Color gallery, click the **Orange, Accent 2** square in the sixth column of the first row of the gallery.
9. In the Borders group, click the **Line Weight arrow** ½ pt to open the Line Weight gallery, and then click **3 pt**.
10. Use the Border Painter pointer to click any gridline in the table. A thick orange border is added to the cell where you clicked.
11. Continue experimenting with the Border Painter pointer, and then press **ESC** to turn off the Border Painter pointer when you are finished.
12. Reapply the Grid Table 4 - Accent 6 table style to make your table match the one shown earlier in Figure 3–18.
13. Save the document and then close it.

Proskills

Problem Solving: Fine-Tuning Table Styles

After you apply a table style to a table, you might like the look of the table but find that it no longer effectively conveys your information or is not quite as easy to read. To fix this, you could apply a different table style or make formatting adjustments manually using the options on the Table Design tab. For example, you can change the thickness and color of the table borders using the options in the Borders group, and you can add shading using the Shading button in the Table Styles group. Also, if you don't like the appearance of table styles in your document, consider changing the document's theme (as explained later in this module) and previewing the table styles again. The table styles have a different appearance in each theme.

When using color in a table, it's a good rule of thumb to assume that 10 percent of your readers are colorblind. That means you should never use color to convey information. For example, don't format a row in a red font to indicate that the row is especially important, because some of your readers might not be able to distinguish a red font from another font color. Instead, you could add shading to a row, and then format the text so that it clearly contrasts with the shading.

Adding Formulas

Now that the Expenditures table is finished, Laila would like your help with a table containing her estimates for the cost of the server and laptop computers. She might add it to the report later, but for now it's stored in a separate document. The table is almost complete, but she still needs to add a formula field that calculates and displays the total cost of the new hardware.

The Formula button in the Data group on the Layout contextual tab allows you to insert a field that performs mathematical operations such as addition, subtraction, or division. By default, it inserts a formula field that sums the numbers in the rows above the cell containing the formula field. You'll see how that works in the following steps. In the process, you'll learn how to insert formulas that perform other operations.

To open the document and add a formula:

1. Open the document **NP_WD_3-2.docx** located in the Word3 > Module folder, and then save the file with the name **NP_WD_3_HardwareCosts** in the location specified by your instructor.
2. Verify that the document is displayed in Print Layout view and that the rulers and nonprinting characters are displayed.
3. Make sure the Zoom level is set to **120%**. Laila wants you to insert a formula that sums the three dollar amounts in the right-hand column.
4. Click the blank cell below "$1,200."
5. Click the **Layout** contextual tab, and then click the **Formula** button in the Data group. The Formula dialog box opens. By default, the Formula box contains =SUM(ABOVE), which tells Word to add together all the numbers in the cells above the cell that contains the insertion point, and then display the result of that calculation in the cell that contains the insertion point. You can use the Number format arrow to determine how the result of the formula will look in the cell. For example, you can choose to display it with no decimal places, with or without a dollar sign, or with a percentage sign. In this case, Laila wants the result of the calculation to display with no decimal places to match the dollar amounts in the cells above.
6. Click the **Number format arrow**, and then click **#,##0**. If you wanted to perform a calculation other than summing numbers, you could type a new formula in the Formula box, or you could select an option using the Paste function arrow. Using formulas other than the default SUM formula is an advanced skill, but you can learn how to incorporate them into your documents by searching Help for information on adding formulas to tables. Refer to Figure 3–19.

Figure 3–19 Formula dialog box

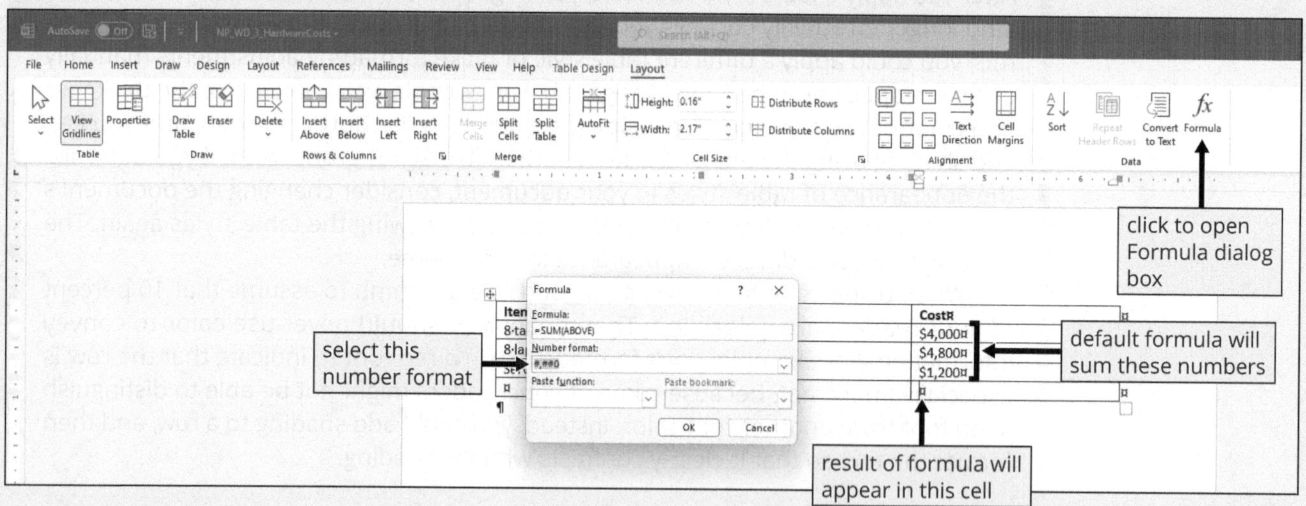

7. Click **OK**. The Formula dialog box closes, and the result of the calculation, 10,000, appears in the right-most cell in the bottom row. Next, you need to add a dollar sign to match the entries in the cells above.
8. Click to the left of the "1" in "10,000" and type **$**. When you click in the cell, gray shading appears behind the result of the formula. The shading indicates that the value is actually the result of a formula field rather than plain text.
9. Save the document.

The beauty of a formula field is that you can edit the numbers in a table, and then quickly update the result of the calculation. In this case, Laila wants to change the cost of the laptop computers from $4,800 to $4,000.

To change the cost of the new workstations and then update the formula:

1. Click the cell containing "$4,800," use the → or ← keys to move the insertion point to the left of the "8," press DELETE, and then type **0** to change the amount to $4,000. Now you need to update the formula to reflect the higher cost.
2. Right-click the cell containing the formula field, which currently displays the value $10,000. A shortcut menu opens, as shown in Figure 3–20. If the gray shading around the value $10,000 did not appear earlier, it appears now.

Figure 3–20 Updating the formula

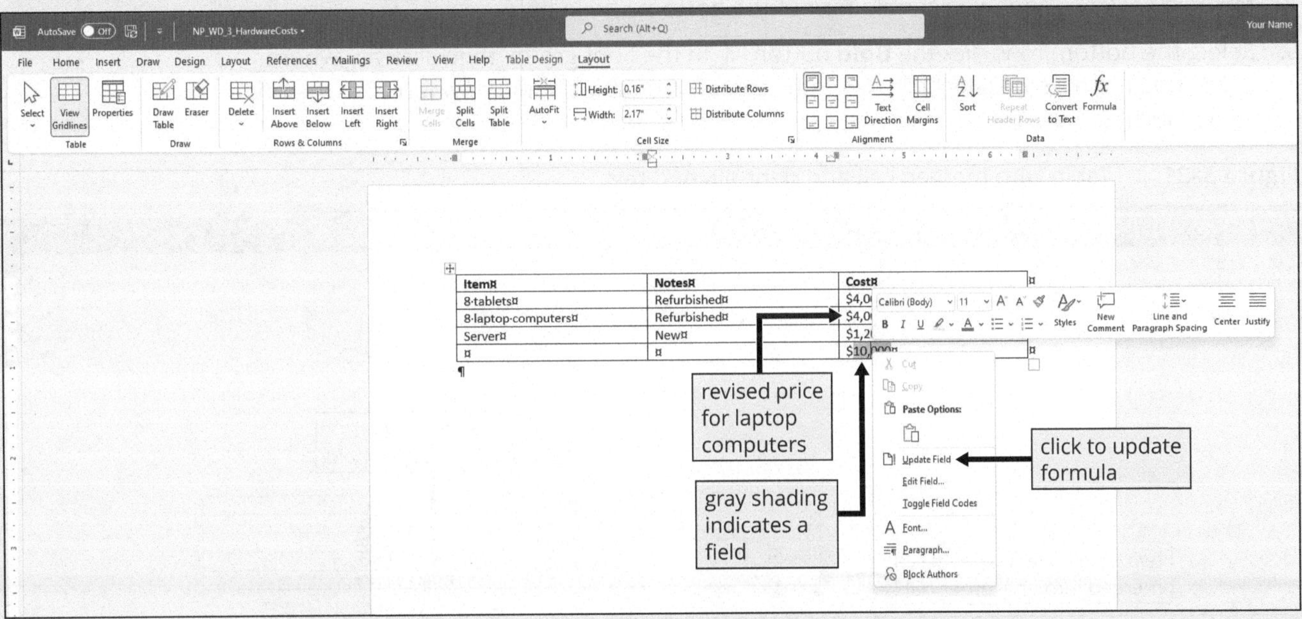

3. Click **Update Field** in the shortcut menu. The shortcut menu closes, and the value displayed in the cell changes to $9,200.

To finish the table, Laila would like to add "TOTAL" next to the cell containing the formula field.

Merging Cells

Currently, the table contains two blank cells in the bottom row. Laila could insert "TOTAL" in the cell next to the one containing the formula, but the table will look more polished if she combines, or **merges**, the two blank cells, and then inserts the text in the resulting new, larger cell. To merge one or more cells, select the cells, and then click the Merge Cells button in the Merge group on the Layout tab. Note that you can also split one cell into multiple cells by clicking the cell you want to split, clicking the Split Cells button in the Merge group to open the Split Cells dialog box, and then specifying the number of rows and columns you want to divide the cell into.

To merge the two blank cells and insert new text in the resulting cell:

1. Click and drag the mouse to select the two blank cells in the table's bottom row.
2. In the Merge group, click the **Merge Cells** button. The border dividing the two cells disappears, leaving one, larger cell.

   Tip You can also click the Eraser button in the Draw group on the Layout tab, and then click a gridline between cells to merge the two cells.

3. Click the new, larger cell to deselect it, and then type **TOTAL** in the cell. The new text is aligned on the left border of the cell. To move it closer to the cell containing the formula field, you need to right-align it.
4. Verify that the insertion point is located in the new, merged cell.
5. Click the **Home** tab, and then in the Paragraph group, click the **Align Right** button. The text moves to the right side of the merge cell. Finally, to make the new text and formula easier to spot, you should format the bottom row in bold.
6. Select the bottom row, click the **Bold** button B in the Font group, then click anywhere in the document to deselect the row. Your completed table should now look like the one shown in Figure 3–21.

Figure 3–21 Table with merged cell and right-aligned text

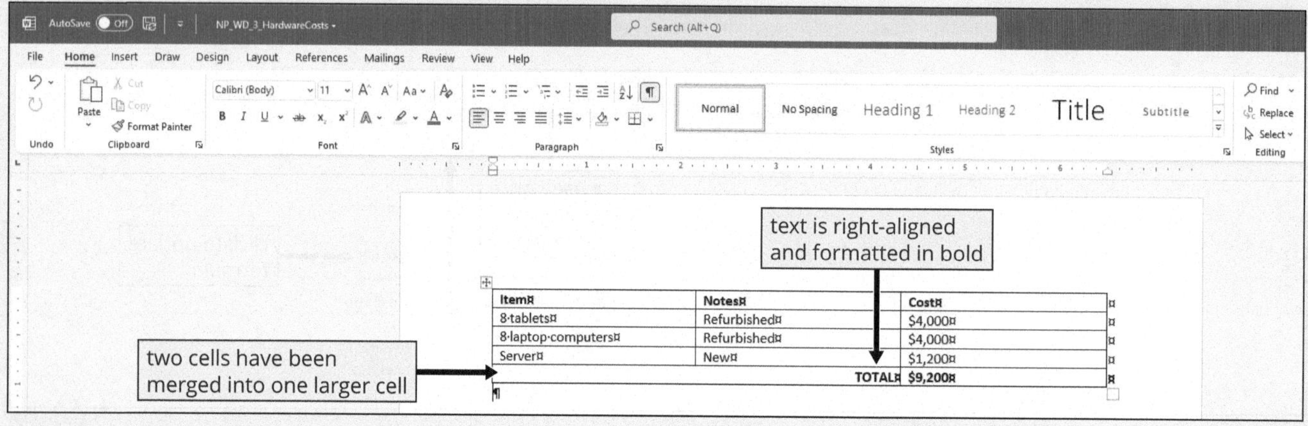

Insight

Using the Draw Table Pointer

Instead of inserting a blank table grid as a starting point, you can draw a table structure using the Draw Table pointer. This is especially useful when you want to use a table as a way to lay out the contents of a flyer or other specially formatted documents. You can insert titles, graphics, and other elements in the table cells, apply formatting to the cells, and then, when you are finished, remove all borders and hide the gridlines.

To get started, click the Insert tab, click the Table button in the Tables group, and then click Draw Table. This displays the Draw Table pointer, which looks like a pencil. You can click the mouse button and drag the Draw Table pointer to draw horizontal and vertical lines on the page. You can put row and column borders anywhere you want; there's no need to make all the cells in the table the same size. When you are finished drawing the table, turn off the Draw Table pointer by pressing ESC. To delete a border, click the Eraser button in the Draw group on the Layout tab, and click anywhere on the border you want to erase. Click the Eraser button again to turn it off.

Creating a Watermark

A **watermark** is text or a graphic that appears behind or in front of existing text on the printed pages of a document. Usually, the watermark appears in a light shade in the background of each printed page. You can select a predesigned watermark from the Watermark gallery or create your own, custom watermark.

Reference

Working with Watermarks

- To add a predesigned watermark, click the Design tab, click the Watermark button in the Page Background group, and then click the watermark you want to add to your document.
- To delete a watermark, click the Design tab, click the Watermark button in the Page Background group, and then click Remove Watermark.

To create a custom text watermark:

- On the ribbon, click the Design tab.
- In the Page Background group, click the Watermark button, and then click Custom Watermark to open the Printed Watermark dialog box.
- Click the Text watermark option button, click the Text arrow, and then click an option in the list; or delete the text in the Text box, and then type the text you want to use as the watermark.
- If desired, click the Font arrow, and then click a font; click the Size arrow, and then click a font size; and click the Color arrow, and then click a color.
- If desired, deselect the Semitransparent check box to make the text darker.
- If desired, click the Horizontal option button to lay out the text horizontally rather than diagonally.

Because the costs in the current document are not final, it's a good idea to add a "Draft" watermark. You'll do this next.

To add a watermark:

1. On the ribbon, click the **Design** tab, and then in the Page Background group, click the **Watermark** button. The Watermark gallery opens. Refer to Figure 3–22.

Figure 3–22 Watermark gallery and menu

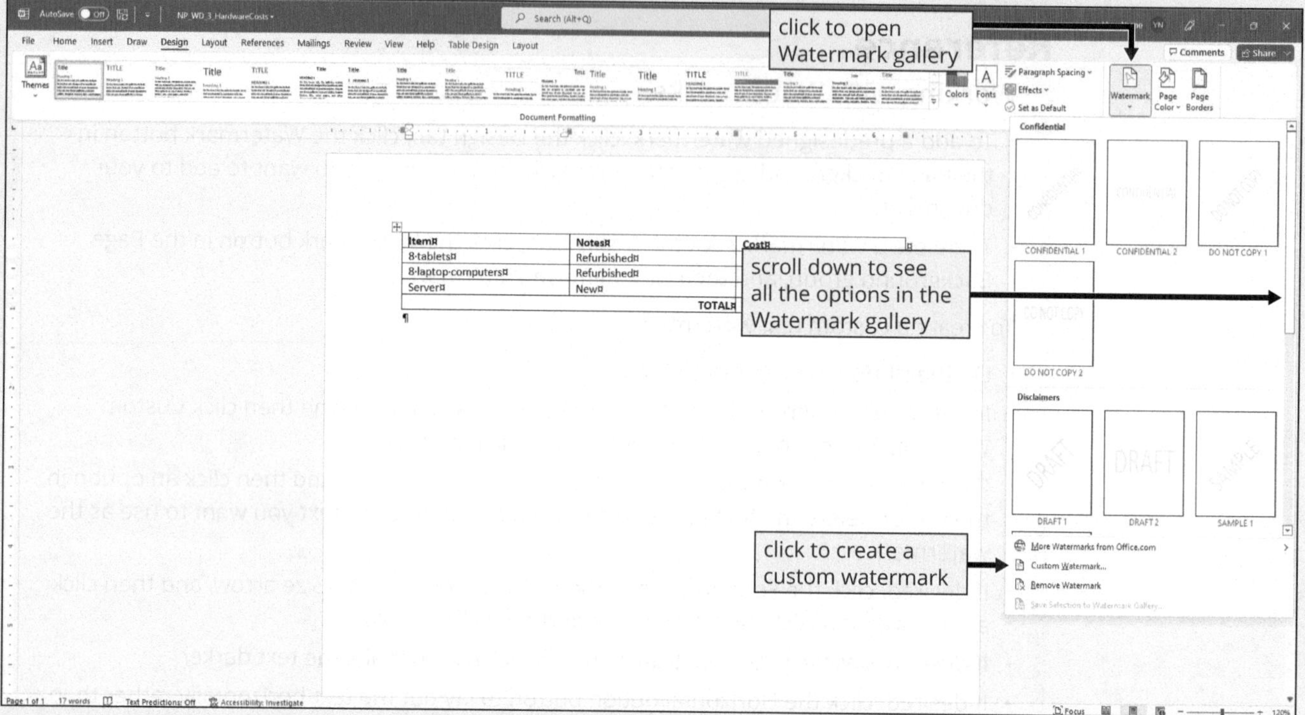

2. Scroll to the bottom of the gallery to view all the options. The gallery is divided into sections: Confidential, Disclaimers, and Urgent. Although the gallery does contain "DRAFT" both as a horizontal and a diagonal watermark, you will see what other options are available.
3. Below the gallery, click **Custom Watermark**. The Printed Watermark dialog box opens. The No watermark option button is selected, so none of the commands except the three option buttons are available to be selected. Refer to Figure 3–23.

Figure 3–23 Printed Watermark dialog box

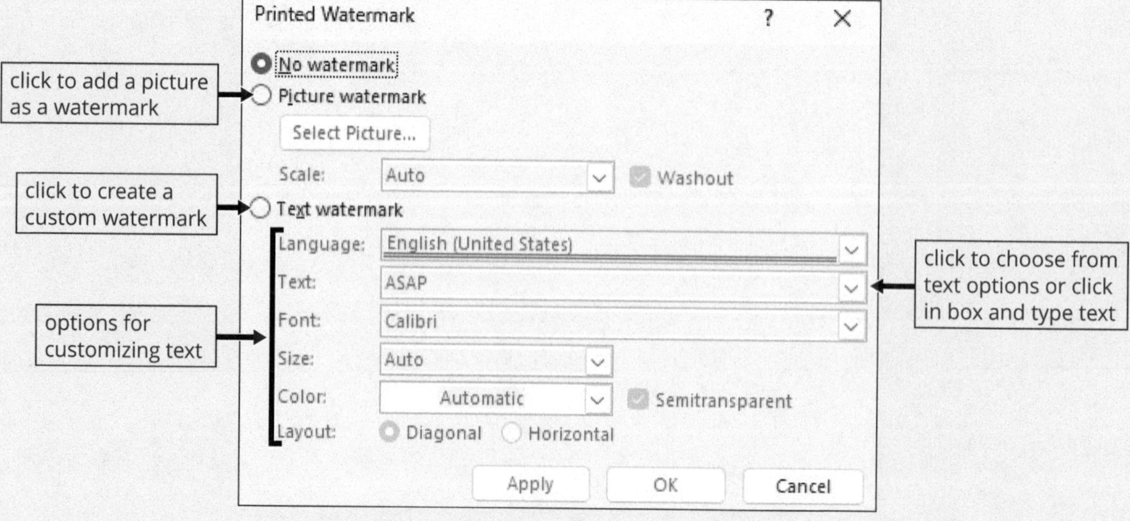

4. Click the **Text watermark** option button. The commands below that option button become available.

> **Tip** To insert a picture as a watermark, click the Picture watermark option button, and then click Select Picture.

5. Click the **Text arrow** to open a list of text watermarks. There are more options in this list than there were in the gallery. You can select one of these or type your own in the Text box.
6. Click **DRAFT**. You can customize text watermarks by changing the language, font, font size, font color, and transparency of the text. You can also change the direction of the text. With the default options, the text will be semitransparent, light gray, and slanted in a diagonal direction.
7. Click **OK**. "DRAFT" appears in light gray, arranged diagonally, as a watermark in the document.
8. Save the document and then close it.

Laila is waiting for confirmation on the information in the table. After she makes any necessary changes, she can delete the DRAFT watermark using the Remove Watermark command at the bottom of the Watermark gallery.

In the next part, you'll complete the rest of the report by organizing information using tab stops, dividing the document into sections, inserting headers and footers, inserting a cover page, and, finally, changing the document's theme.

Part 3.1 Quick Check

1. What style is considered the highest-level heading?
2. What are the three steps involved in creating a table in Word?
3. Explain how to delete a row from a table.
4. After you enter data in the last cell in the last row in a table, how can you insert a new row?
5. To adjust the width of a table's column to span the width of the page, would you use the AutoFit Contents option or the AutoFit Window option?
6. Explain how to add a predesigned watermark from the Watermark gallery.

Part 3.2 Visual Overview: Working with Headers and Footers

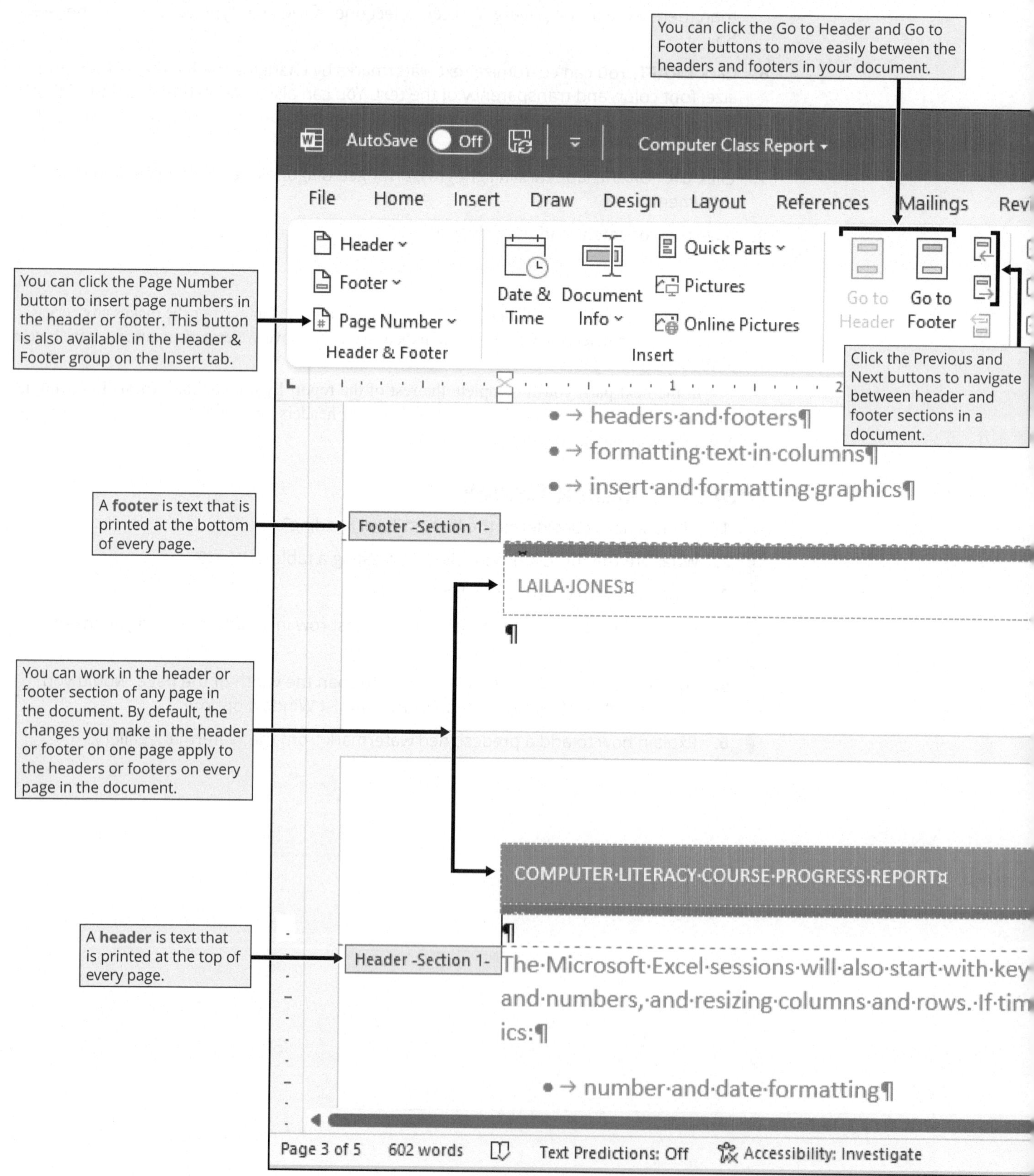
You can click the Go to Header and Go to Footer buttons to move easily between the headers and footers in your document.
AutoSave
Off
Computer Class Report
File
Home
Insert
Draw
Design
Layout
References
Mailings
Header
Footer
Page Number
Header & Footer
Date & Time
Document Info
Quick Parts
Pictures
Online Pictures
Insert
Go to Header
Go to Footer
You can click the Page Number button to insert page numbers in the header or footer. This button is also available in the Header & Footer group on the Insert tab.
Click the Previous and Next buttons to navigate between header and footer sections in a document.
headers·and·footers¶
formatting·text·in·columns¶
insert·and·formatting·graphics¶
A **footer** is text that is printed at the bottom of every page.
Footer -Section 1-
LAILA·JONES¤
You can work in the header or footer section of any page in the document. By default, the changes you make in the header or footer on one page apply to the headers or footers on every page in the document.
COMPUTER·LITERACY·COURSE·PROGRESS·REPORT¤
A **header** is text that is printed at the top of every page.
Header -Section 1-
The·Microsoft·Excel·sessions·will·also·start·with·key
and·numbers,·and·resizing·columns·and·rows.·If·tim
ics:¶
number·and·date·formatting¶
Page 3 of 5
602 words
Text Predictions: Off
Accessibility: Investigate

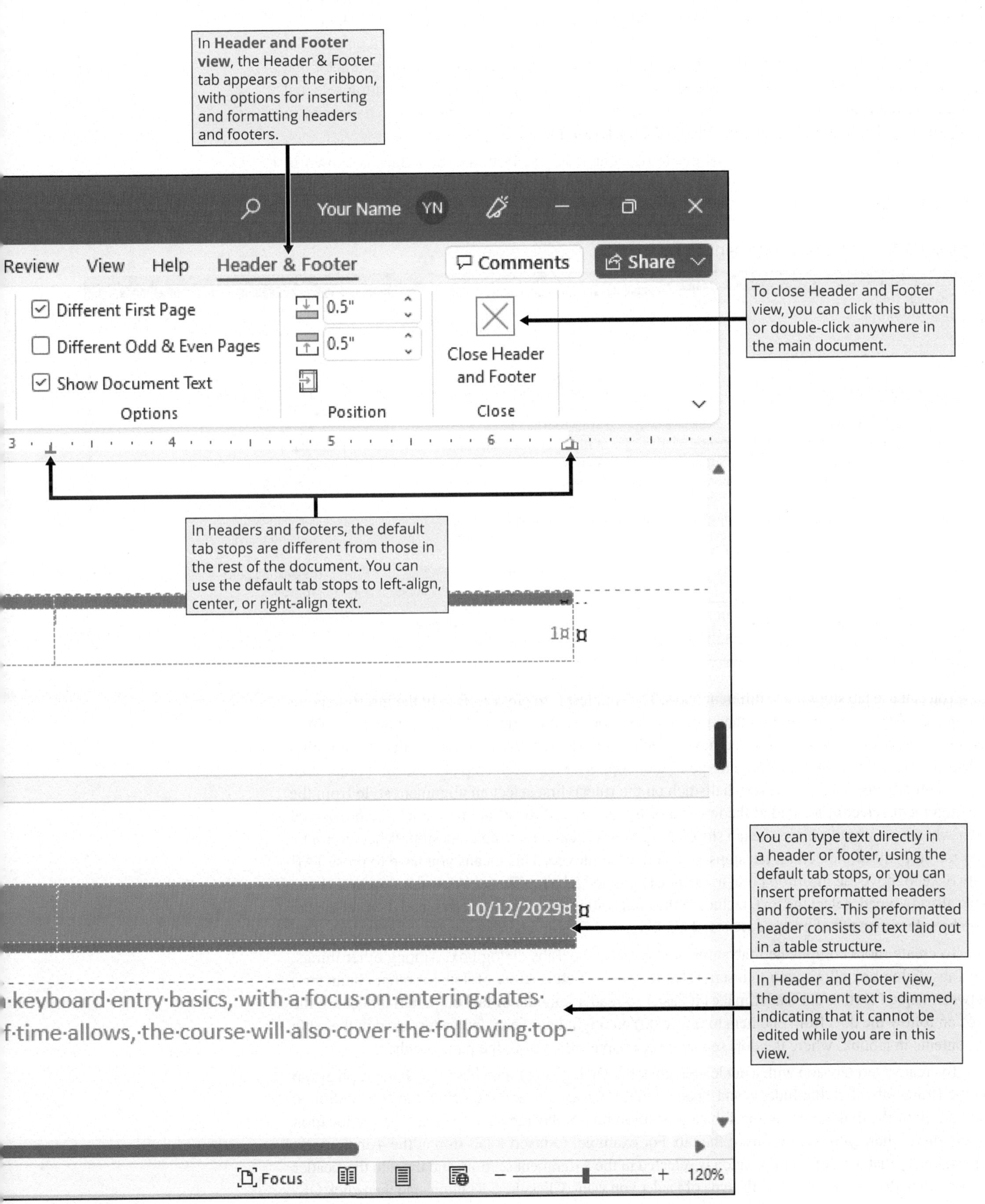
In **Header and Footer view**, the Header & Footer tab appears on the ribbon, with options for inserting and formatting headers and footers.
Your Name
YN
Review
View
Help
Header & Footer
Comments
Share
Different First Page
Different Odd & Even Pages
Show Document Text
Options
0.5"
0.5"
Position
Close Header and Footer
Close
To close Header and Footer view, you can click this button or double-click anywhere in the main document.
In headers and footers, the default tab stops are different from those in the rest of the document. You can use the default tab stops to left-align, center, or right-align text.
1
10/12/2029
You can type text directly in a header or footer, using the default tab stops, or you can insert preformatted headers and footers. This preformatted header consists of text laid out in a table structure.
In Header and Footer view, the document text is dimmed, indicating that it cannot be edited while you are in this view.
keyboard·entry·basics,·with·a·focus·on·entering·dates·
f·time·allows,·the·course·will·also·cover·the·following·top-
Focus
120%

Setting Tab Stops

A **tab stop** (often called a **tab**) is a location on the horizontal ruler where the insertion point moves when you press TAB. You can use tab stops to align small amounts of text or data. By default, a document contains tab stops every one-half inch on the horizontal ruler. There's no mark on the ruler indicating these default tab stops, but in the document you can see the nonprinting Tab character that appears every time you press TAB. (Of course, you need to have the Show/Hide ¶ button selected to see these nonprinting characters.) A nonprinting tab character is just like any other character you type; you can delete it by pressing BACKSPACE or DELETE.

The five major types of tab stops are Left, Center, Right, Decimal, and Bar, as shown in Figure 3–24. The default tab stops on the ruler are all left tab stops because that is the tab style used most often.

Figure 3–24 Tab stop alignment styles

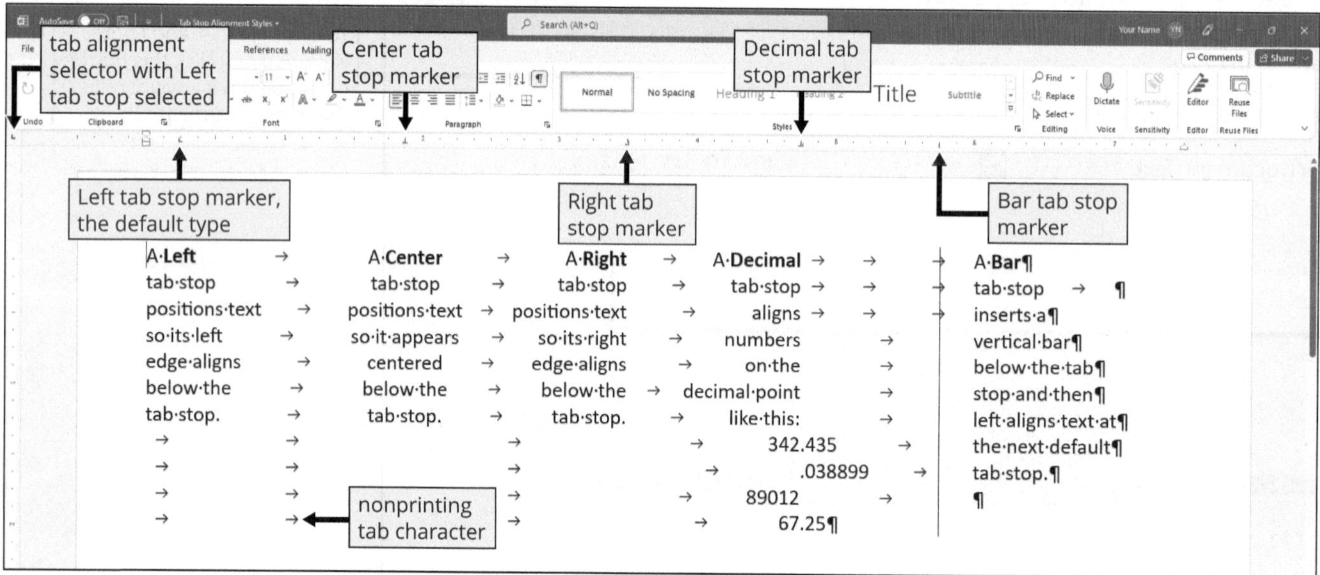

You can use tab stops a few different ways. The simplest is to press TAB until the insertion point is aligned where you want it, and then type the text you want to align. Each time you press TAB, the insertion point moves right to the next default tab stop, with the left edge of the text aligning below the tab stop. To use a different type of tab stop, or to use a tab stop at a location other than the default tab stop locations (every half-inch on the ruler), first select an alignment style from the tab alignment selector, located at the left end of the horizontal ruler, and then click the horizontal ruler where you want to insert the tab stop. This process is called setting a tab stop. When you set a new tab stop, all of the default tab stops to its left are removed. This means you have to press TAB only once to move the insertion point to the newly created tab stop. To set a new tab stop in text you have already typed, select the text, including the nonprinting tab stop characters, and then set the tab stop by selecting a tab alignment style and clicking on the ruler where you want to set the tab stop.

To create more complicated tab stops, you can use the Tabs dialog box. Among other things, the Tabs dialog box allows you to insert a **dot leader**, which is a row of dots (or other characters) between tabbed text. A dot leader makes it easier to read a long list of tabbed material because the eye can follow the dots from one item to the next. You might have seen dot leaders used in the table of contents in a book, where the dots separate the chapter titles from the page numbers.

To create a left tab stop with a dot leader, click the Dialog Box Launcher in the Paragraph group on the Home tab, click the Indents and Spacing tab, if necessary, and then click the Tabs button at the bottom of the dialog box. In the Tab stop position box in the Tabs dialog box, type the location on the ruler where you want to insert the tab. For example, to insert a tab stop at the 4-inch mark, type 4. Verify that the Left option button is selected in the Alignment section, and then, in the Leader section, click the option button for the type of leader you want. Click the Set button, and then click OK.

Reference

Setting, Moving, and Clearing Tab Stops

- To set a tab stop, click the tab alignment selector on the horizontal ruler until the appropriate tab stop alignment style is displayed, and then click the horizontal ruler where you want to position the tab stop.
- To move a tab stop, drag it to a new location on the ruler. If you have already typed text that is aligned by the tab stop, select the text before dragging the tab stop to a new location.
- To clear a tab stop, drag it off the ruler.

In the report you have been working on for Laila, you need to type the list of instructors and their specialties. You can use tab stops to quickly format this small amount of information in two columns. As you type, you'll discover whether Word's default tab stops are appropriate for this document or whether you need to set a new tab stop. Before you get started working with tabs, you'll take a moment to explore Word's Resume Reading feature.

To enter the list of instructors using tabs:

1. Open the **NP_WD_3_ComputerClasses.docx** document. The document opens with the "Summary" heading at the top of the Word window. On the right side, a "Welcome back!" message is displayed briefly and is then replaced with the Resume Reading button.
2. Point to the **Resume Reading** button to expand its "Welcome back!" message. Refer to Figure 3–25.

Figure 3–25 "Welcome back!" message displayed in reopened document

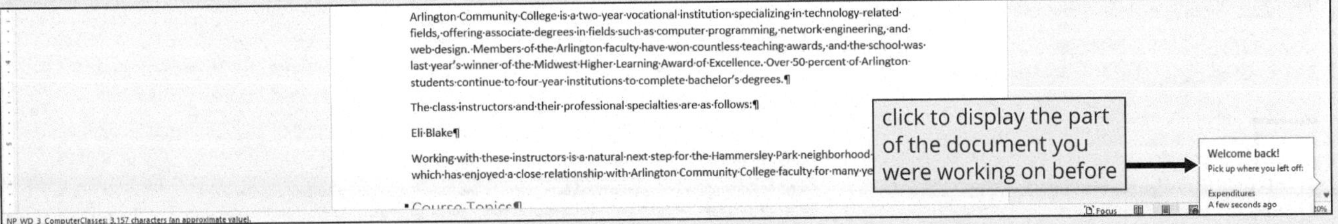

3. Click the **Welcome back!** message. The document window scrolls down to display the table, which you were working on just before you closed the document.
4. Scroll up to display the "Instructors" heading on page 1.
5. Confirm that the ruler and nonprinting characters are displayed, and that the document is displayed in **Print Layout** view, zoomed to **120%**.
6. Click to the right of the last "e" in "Eli Blake."
7. Press **TAB**. An arrow-shaped tab character appears, and the insertion point moves to the first tab stop after the "e" in "Blake." This tab stop is the default tab located at the 1-inch mark on the horizontal ruler. Refer to Figure 3–26.

Figure 3–26 Tab character

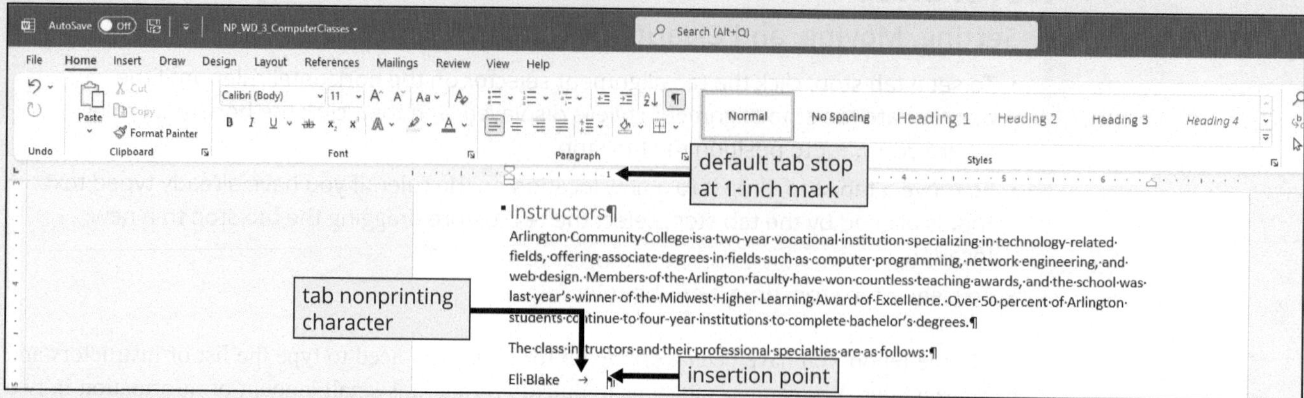

8. Type **database concepts**, and then press **ENTER** to move the insertion point to the next line.
9. Type **Alejandro J. Iglesias**, and then press **TAB**. The insertion point moves to the next available tab stop, this time located at the 1.5-inch mark on the ruler.
10. Type **word processing and spreadsheets**, and then press **ENTER** to move to the next line. Notice that Alejandro J. Iglesias's specialty does not align with Eli Blake's specialty on the line above it. You'll fix this after you type the last name in the list.
11. Type **Victoria Dikembe Habiba**, press **TAB**, and then type **networking and computer maintenance**. Refer to Figure 3–27.

Figure 3–27 List of instructors

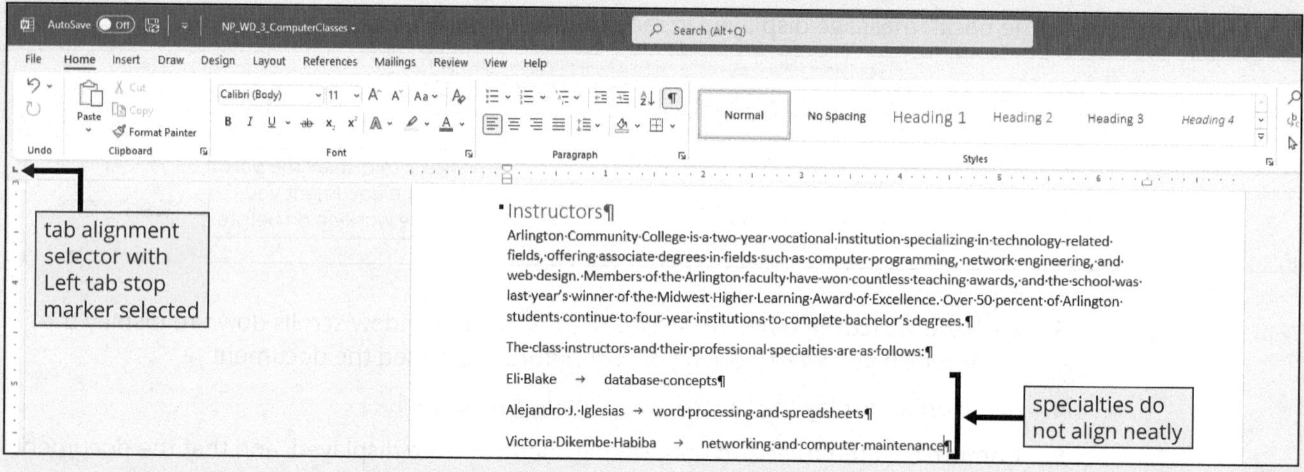

The list of names and specialties is not aligned properly. You could fix this by selecting the list of names and specialties, and then dragging a tab stop to a new location. Another option is to insert a new tab stop, which you will do next.

To add a new tab stop to the horizontal ruler:

1. Make sure the Home tab is displayed on the ribbon, and then select the list of instructors and their specialties.
2. On the horizontal ruler, click at the 2.5-inch mark. Because the current tab stop alignment style is Left tab, Word inserts a left tab stop at that location. Remember that when you set a new tab stop, all the default tab stops to its left are removed. The column of specialties shifts to the new tab stop. Note that if you needed to remove a tab stop, you could drag it off the ruler. Refer to Figure 3–28.

Figure 3–28 Titles aligned at new tab stop

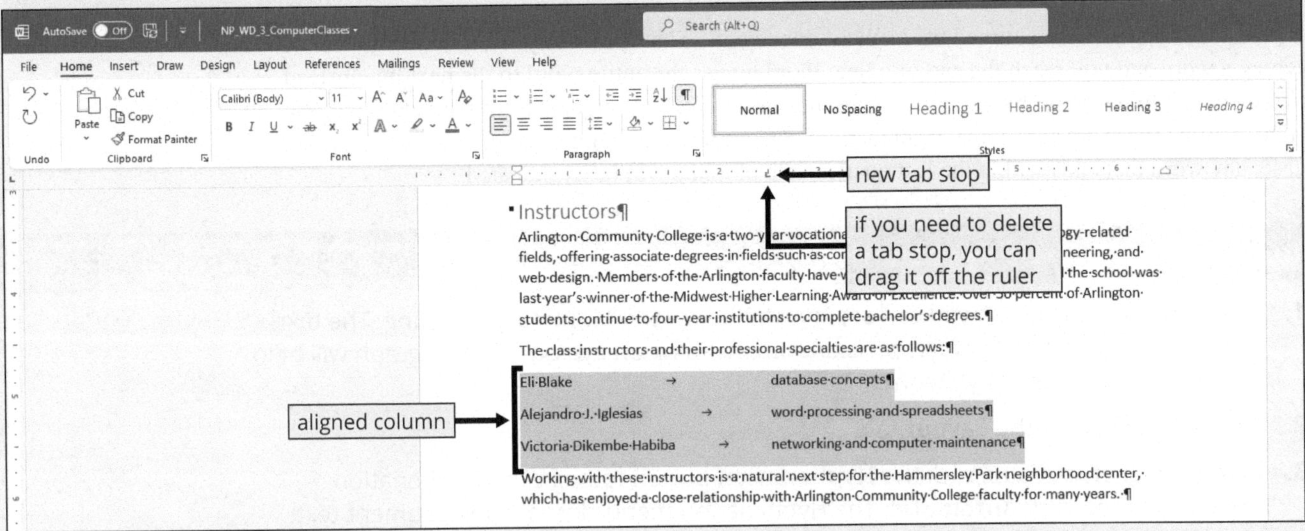

To complete the list, you need to remove the paragraph spacing after the first two paragraphs in the list, so the list looks like it's all one paragraph. You can quickly reduce paragraph and line spacing to 0 points by clicking the No Spacing style in the Styles group. In this case, you want to reduce only the paragraph spacing to 0 points, so you'll use the Line and Paragraph Spacing button instead.

3. Select the first two paragraphs in the list, which contain the names and specialties for Eli and Alejandro.
4. In the Paragraph group, click the **Line and Paragraph Spacing** button, and then click **Remove Space After Paragraph**.
5. Click anywhere in the document to deselect the list, and then save your work.

Proskills

Decision Making: Choosing Between Tabs and Tables

When you have information that you want to align in columns in your document, you need to decide whether to use tabs or tables. Whatever you do, don't try to align columns of data by pressing SPACEBAR to add extra spaces. Although the text might seem precisely aligned on the screen, it probably won't be aligned when you print the document. Furthermore, if you edit the text, the spaces you inserted to align your columns will be affected by your edits; they get moved just like regular text, ruining your alignment.

So what is the most efficient way to align text in columns? It depends. Inserting tabs works well for aligning small amounts of information in just a few columns and rows, such as two columns with three rows, but tabs become cumbersome when you need to organize a lot of data over multiple columns and rows. In that case, using a table to organize columns of information is better. Unlike with tabbed columns of data, it's easy to add data to tables by inserting columns. You might also choose tables over tab stops when you want to take advantage of the formatting options available with table styles. As mentioned earlier, if you don't want the table structure itself to be visible in the document, you can clear its table style and then hide its gridlines.

Now you're ready to address some other issues with the document. First, Laila has noticed that the right edges of most of the paragraphs in the document are uneven, and she'd like you to try to smooth them out. You'll correct this problem in the next section.

Hyphenating a Document

By default, hyphenation is turned off in Word documents. That means if you are in the middle of typing a word and you reach the end of a line, Word moves the entire word to the next line instead of inserting a hyphen and breaking the word into two parts. This can result in ragged text on the right margin. To ensure a smoother right margin, you can turn on automatic hyphenation—in which case, any word that ends within the last quarter-inch of a line will be hyphenated.

To turn on automatic hyphenation in the document:

1. Scroll up, if necessary, so you can see the text below the "Summary" heading. The text on the right side of this paragraph is uneven. Keeping an eye on this paragraph will help you see the benefits of hyphenation.
2. On the ribbon, click the **Layout** tab.
3. In the Page Setup group, click the **Hyphenation** button to open the Hyphenation menu, and then click **Automatic**. The Hyphenation menu closes. The document text shifts to account for the insertion of hyphens in words that break near the end of a line. For example, in the paragraph below the "Summary" heading, the words "Center," "volunteered," and "available" are now hyphenated. Refer to Figure 3–29.

Figure 3–29 Hyphenated document

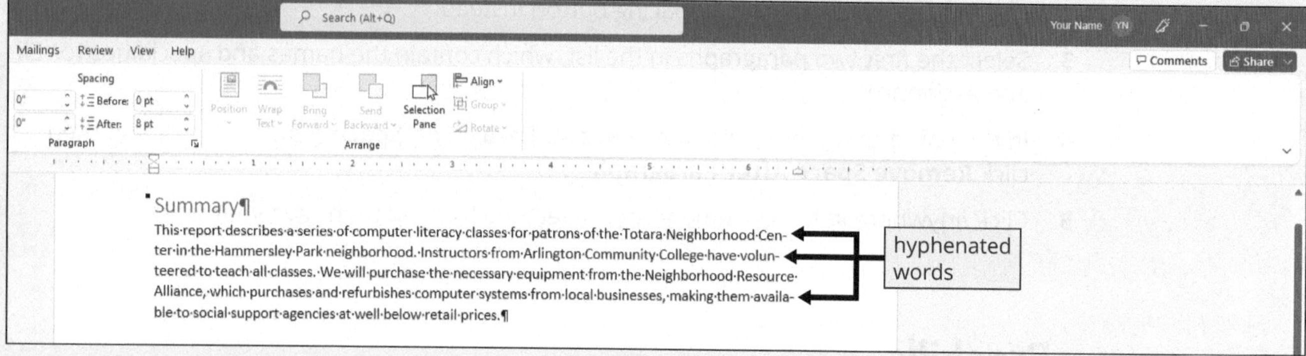

4. Save the document.

Note that text formatted in all uppercase letters can be difficult to read when hyphenated. If your document includes a title or other text formatted in all uppercase letters, you can turn off hyphenation for that text. Click Hyphenation in the Page Setup group on the Layout tab, click Hyphenation options, and then deselect the Hyphenate words in CAPS check box. As you will see later in this module, you can also select text you don't want to hyphenate, and then, on the Line and Page Breaks tab in the Paragraph dialog box, select the Don't hyphenate check box.

Laila plans to publicize the courses by posting handouts around the neighborhood, and she wants to include a sample handout in the report. Before you can add the sample handout, you need to divide the document into sections.

Formatting a Document into Sections

A **section** is a part of a document that can have its own page orientation, headers, footers, and so on. In other words, each section is like a document within a document. To divide a document into sections, you insert a **section break**. You can select from a few different types of section breaks. One of the most useful is a Next page section break, which inserts a page break and starts the new section on the next page. Another commonly used kind of section break, a Continuous section break, starts the section at the location of the insertion point without changing the page flow. To insert a section break, you click the Breaks button in the Page Setup group on the Layout tab and then select the type of section break you want to insert.

Tip If you insert an endnote in a document with sections, the endnote will appear at the end of the section containing the superscript endnote number, not at the end of the document.

Laila wants to format the handout in landscape orientation, but the report is currently formatted in portrait orientation. To format part of a document in an orientation different from the rest of the document, you need to divide the document into sections.

To insert a section break below the table:

1. Press **CTRL+END** to move the insertion point to the blank paragraph below the table, at the end of the document.
2. In the Page Setup group, click the **Breaks** button. The Breaks gallery opens, as shown in Figure 3–30.

Figure 3–30 Breaks gallery

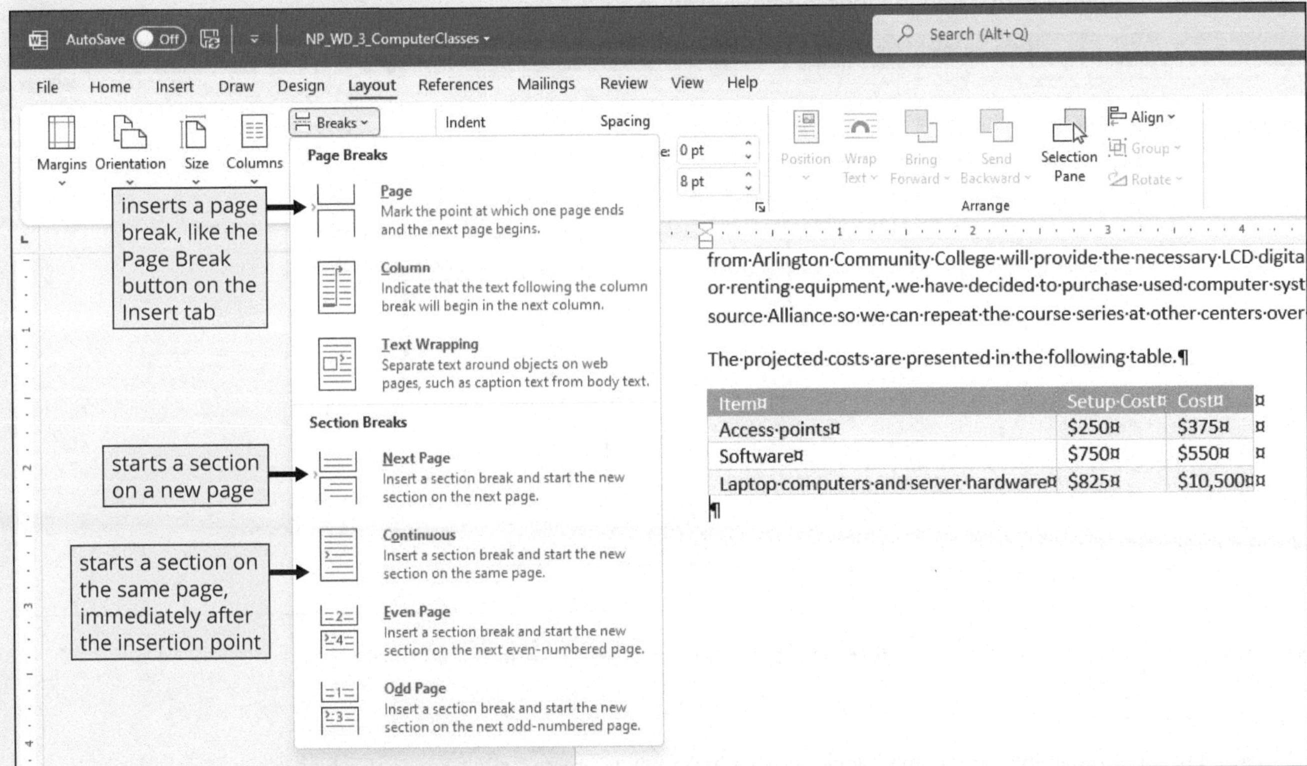

The Page Breaks section of the gallery includes options for controlling how the text flows from page to page. The first option, Page, inserts a page break. It has the same effect as clicking the Page Break button on the Insert tab or pressing CTRL+ENTER. The Section Breaks section of the gallery includes four types of section breaks. The two you'll use most often are Next Page and Continuous.

3. Under "Section Breaks," click **Next Page**. A section break is inserted in the document, and the insertion point moves to the top of the new page 4.
4. Scroll up, if necessary, until you can see the double dotted line and the words "Section Break (Next Page)" below the table on page 3. This line indicates that a new section begins on the next page.

   Tip To delete a section break, click to the left of the line representing the break, and then press DELETE.

5. Save the document.

You've created a new page that is a separate section from the rest of the report. The sections are numbered consecutively. The first part of the document is section 1, and the new page is section 2. Now you can format section 2 in landscape orientation without affecting the rest of the document.

To format section 2 in landscape orientation:

1. Scroll down and verify that the insertion point is positioned at the top of the new page 4.
2. On the ribbon, click the **View** tab.
3. In the Zoom group, click the **Multiple Pages** button, and then change the Zoom level to **30%** so you can see all four pages of the document displayed side by side.
4. On the ribbon, click the **Layout** tab.
5. In the Page Setup group, click the **Orientation** button, and then click **Landscape**. Section 2, which consists solely of page 4, changes to landscape orientation, as shown in Figure 3–31. Section 1, which consists of pages 1 through 3, remains in portrait orientation.

Figure 3–31 Page 4 formatted in landscape orientation

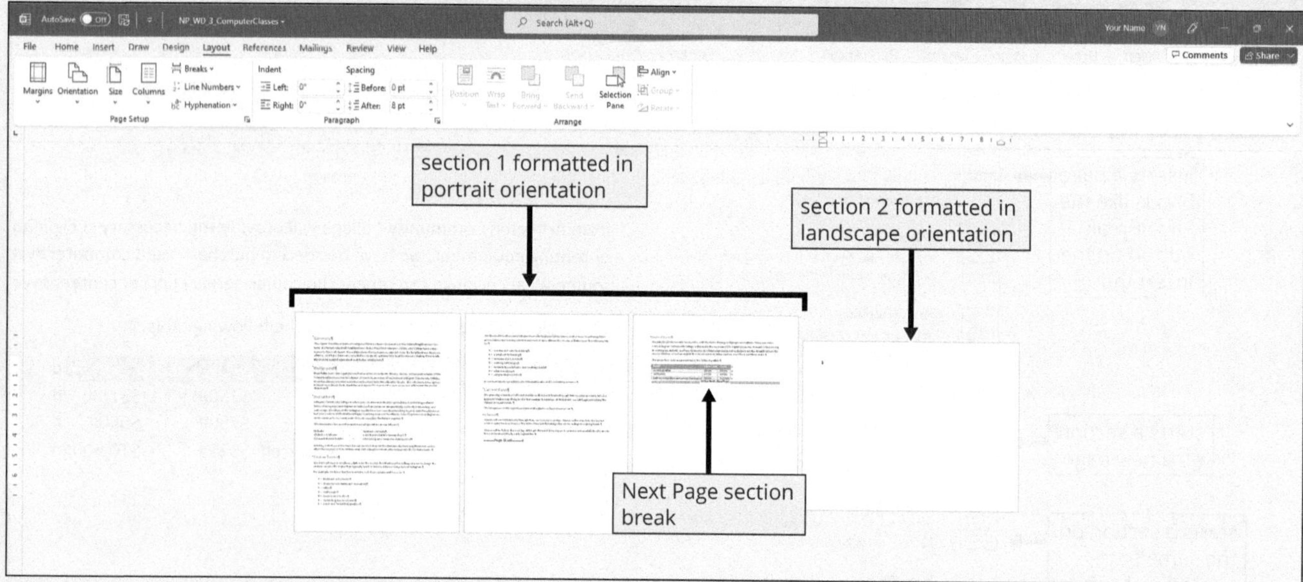

6. Change the Zoom level back to **120%**, and then save the document.

Page 4 is now formatted in landscape orientation, ready for you to create Laila's handout, which will consist of a graphic that shows the benefits of improving the company's wireless network. You'll use Word's SmartArt feature to create the graphic.

Creating SmartArt

A **SmartArt** graphic is a diagram of shapes, such as circles, squares, or arrows. A well-designed SmartArt graphic can illustrate concepts that might otherwise require several paragraphs of explanation. To create a SmartArt graphic, you switch to the Insert tab and then, in the Illustrations group, click the SmartArt button. This opens the Choose a SmartArt Graphic dialog box, where you can select from eight categories of graphics, including graphics designed to illustrate relationships, processes, and hierarchies. Within each category, you can choose from numerous designs. Once inserted into your document, a SmartArt graphic contains placeholder text that you replace with your own text. When a SmartArt graphic is selected, the SmartArt Design and Format tabs appear on the ribbon.

To create a SmartArt graphic:

1. Verify that the insertion point is located at the top of page 4, which is blank.
2. On the ribbon, click the **Insert** tab.
3. In the Illustrations group, click the **SmartArt** button. The Choose a SmartArt Graphic dialog box opens, with categories of SmartArt graphics in the left panel. The middle panel displays the graphics associated with the category currently selected in the left panel. The right panel displays a larger image of the graphic that is currently selected in the middle panel, along with an explanation of the graphic's purpose. By default, All is selected in the left panel.
4. Explore the Choose a SmartArt Graphic dialog box by selecting categories in the left panel and viewing the graphics displayed in the middle panel.
5. In the left panel, click **Relationship**, and then scroll down in the middle panel and click the **Converging Radial** graphic (in the first column, seventh row from the top), which shows three rectangles with arrows pointing to a circle. In the right panel, you see an explanation of the Converging Radial graphic. Refer to Figure 3–32.

Figure 3–32 Selecting a SmartArt graphic

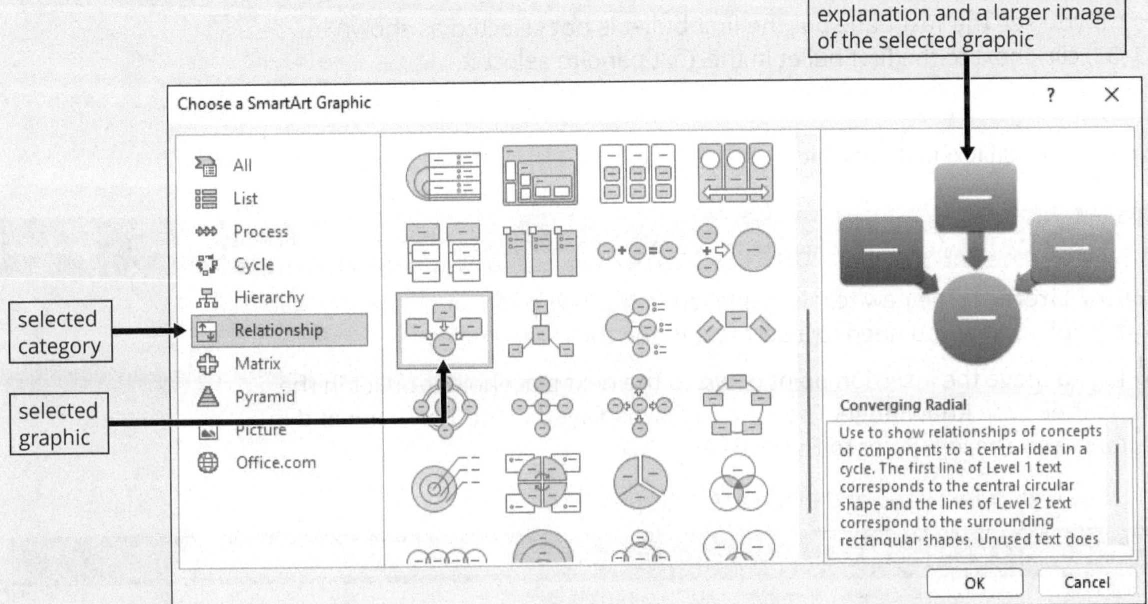

6. Click **OK**. The Converging Radial graphic, with placeholder text, is inserted at the top of page 4. The graphic is surrounded by a rectangular border, indicating that it is selected. The SmartArt contextual tabs appear on the ribbon. To the left of the graphic, you also see the Text pane, a small window with a title bar that contains the text "Type your text here." Refer to Figure 3–33.

   Trouble? If you do not see the Text pane, click the Text Pane button in the Create Graphic group on the SmartArt Design tab to select it.

   The insertion point is blinking next to the first bullet in the Text pane, which is selected with an orange rectangle. The circle at the bottom of the SmartArt graphic is also selected, as indicated by the border with sizing handles. At this point, anything you type next to the selected bullet in the Text pane will also appear in the selected circle in the SmartArt graphic.

Figure 3–33 SmartArt graphic with Text pane displayed

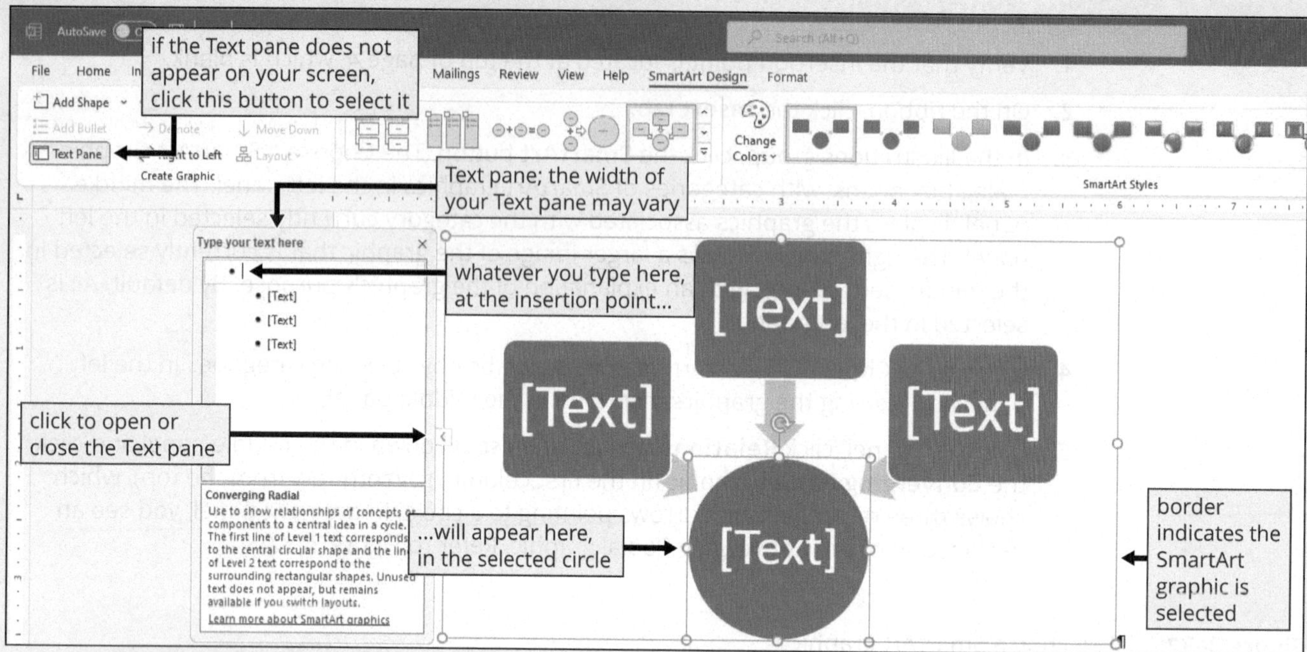

Trouble? If you see the Text pane but the first bullet is not selected as shown in Figure 3–33, click next to the first bullet in the Text pane to select it.

Now you are ready to add text to the graphic.

To add text to the SmartArt graphic:

1. Type **Computer Literacy**. The new text is displayed in the Text pane and in the circle in the SmartArt graphic. Now you need to insert text in the three rectangles.
2. Press the ↓ key to move the insertion point down to the next placeholder bullet in the Text pane, and then type **Knowledge**. The new text is displayed in the Text pane and in the blue rectangle on the left. Refer to Figure 3–34.

Figure 3–34 New text in Text pane and in SmartArt graphic

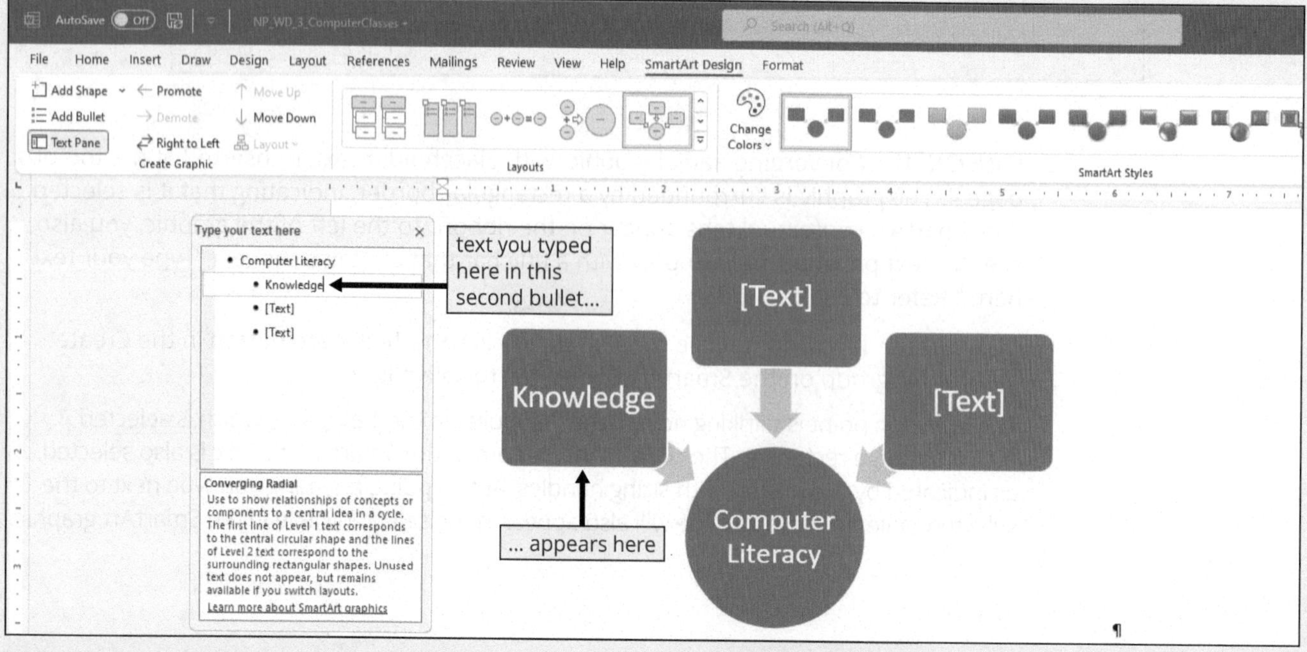

3. Press the ↓ key to move the insertion point down to the next placeholder bullet in the Text pane, and then type **Practical Skills**. The new text appears in the middle rectangle and in the Text pane. You don't need the third rectangle, so you'll delete it.
4. Click the third rectangle, on the right side of the SmartArt image, to display the SmartArt border, and then click the third rectangle again to select it. Make sure to click in the blue area and not on any letters. Then, press DELETE. The rectangle on the right is deleted from the SmartArt graphic. The two remaining rectangles and the circle enlarge and shift position. Note that if you wanted to add a shape to the diagram, you could click a shape in the SmartArt graphic, click the Add Shape arrow in the Create Graphic group on the SmartArt Design tab, and then click a placement option.
5. Make sure the SmartArt Design tab is still selected on the ribbon.
6. In the Create Graphic group, click the **Text Pane** button to deselect it. The Text pane closes.
7. Click the white area inside the SmartArt border to ensure that none of the individual shapes are selected.

Next, you need to resize the SmartArt graphic so it fills the page.

To adjust the size of the SmartArt graphic:

1. Zoom out so you can see the entire page. As you can see on the ruler, the SmartArt is currently 6 inches wide. You could drag the SmartArt border to resize it, just as you can with any graphic, but you will get more precise results using the Size button on the Format tab.
2. On the ribbon, click the **Format** tab.
3. On the right side of the Format tab, click the **Size** button, if necessary, to display the Height and Width boxes.
4. Click the **Height** box, type **6.5**, click the **Size** button again if necessary, click the **Width** box, type **9**, and then press ENTER. The SmartArt graphic resizes, so that it is now 9 inches wide and 6.5 inches high, taking up most of the page. Refer to Figure 3–35.

Figure 3–35 Resized SmartArt

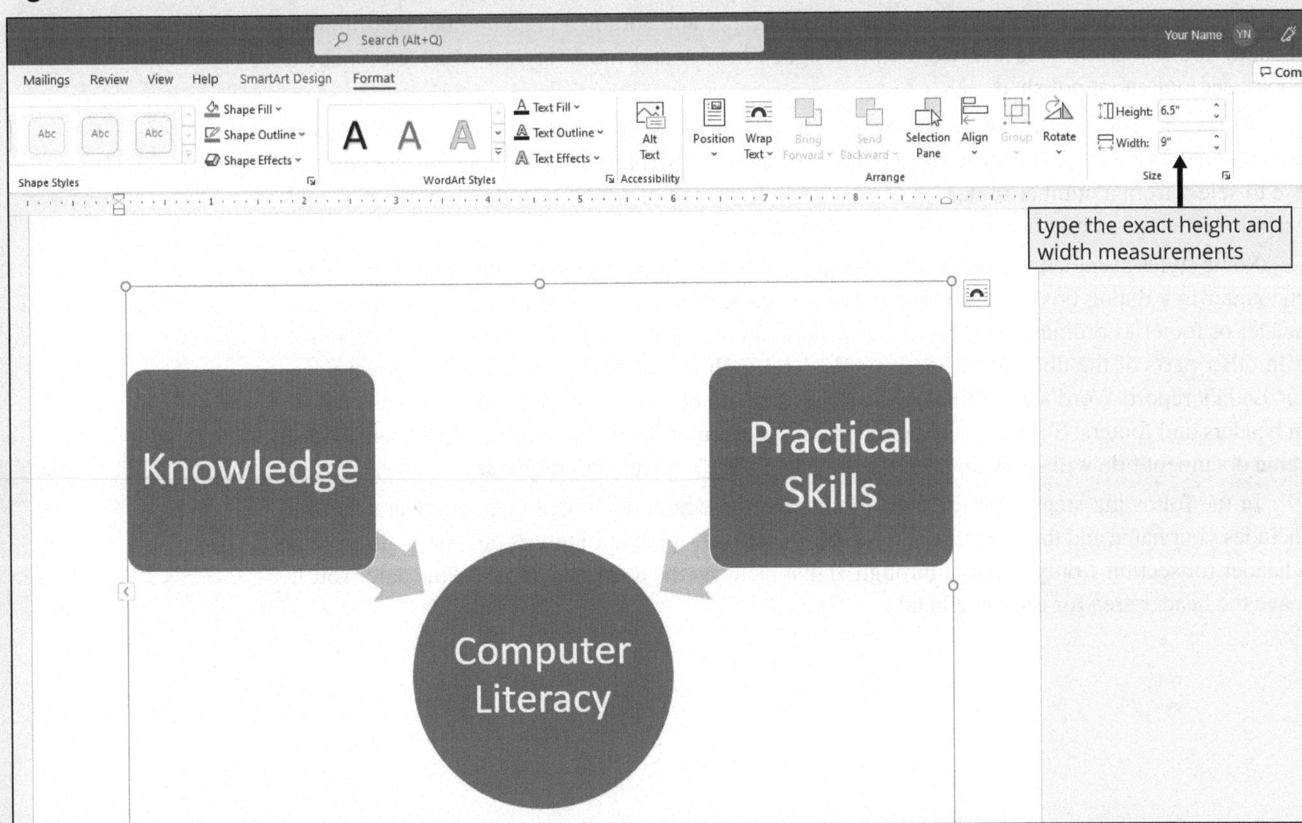

Trouble? If one of the shapes in the SmartArt graphic was resized, rather than the entire SmartArt graphic, the insertion point was located within the shape rather than in the white space. Press Ctrl+Z, click in the white area inside the SmartArt border, and then repeat Steps 3 and 4.

5. Click outside the SmartArt border to deselect it, and then review the graphic centered on the page.

Tip To add a border to a SmartArt graphic, click the Format tab, click the Shape Outline button in the Shape Styles group, and select an outline color.

Next, you need to insert a header at the top of each page in the report and a footer at the bottom of each page in the report.

Adding Headers and Footers

The first step to working with headers and footers is to open Header and Footer view. You can do that in three ways: (1) insert a page number using the Page Number button in the Header & Footer group on the Insert tab; (2) double-click in the header area (in a page's top margin) or in the footer area (in a page's bottom margin); or (3) click the Header button or the Footer button on the Insert tab.

By default, Word assumes that when you add something to the header or footer on any page of a document, you want the same text to appear on every page of the document. To create a different header or footer for the first page, you select the Different First Page check box in the Options group on the Header & Footer tab. When a document is divided into sections, like Laila's report, you can create a different header or footer for each section.

For a simple header or footer, double-click the header or footer area, and then type the text you want directly in the header or footer area, formatting the text as you would any other text in a document. You can also add a page number field using the Page Number button in the Header & Footer group on the Header & Footer tab.

When you add a page number field, you can select a simple page number, consisting only of the page number itself, or you can choose from a variety of more elaborate formatted options. You already have experience typing text in a document header and adding a page number field. In this section, you'll learn how to use Word's predesigned header and footer styles, which can make a document look more polished.

To choose from a selection of predesigned header or footer styles, use the Header and Footer buttons on the Header & Footer tab (or on the Insert tab). These buttons open galleries that you can use to select from a number of header and footer styles, some of which include page numbers and graphic elements such as horizontal lines or shaded boxes.

Some styles also include content controls that are similar to the kinds of controls that you might encounter in a dialog box. Any information that you enter in a content control is displayed in the header or footer as ordinary text, but it is also stored in the Word file so that Word can easily reuse it in other parts of the document. For example, later in this module, you will create a cover page for Laila's report. Word's predefined cover pages include content controls similar to those found in headers and footers. So if you use a content control to enter the document title in the header, the same document title will show up on the cover page; there's no need to retype it.

In the following steps, you'll create a footer for the whole document (sections 1 and 2) that includes your name and the page number. As shown in Laila's plan in Figure 3–36, you'll also create a header for section 1 only (pages 1 through 3) that includes the document title and the date. You'll leave the header area for section 2 blank.

Figure 3–36 Plan for headers and footers in Laila's report

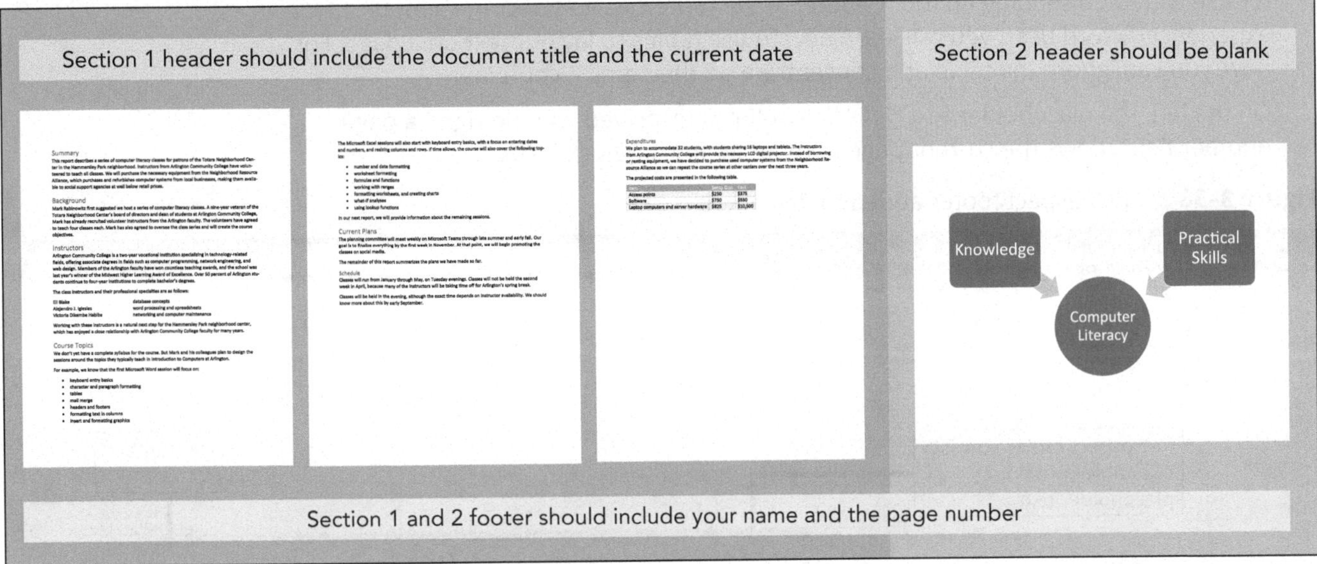

First you will create the footer on page 1.

To create a footer for the entire document:

1. Change the Zoom level to **120%**, and then scroll up until you can see the bottom of page 1 and the top of page 2.
2. Double-click in the white space at the bottom of page 1. The document switches to Header and Footer view. The Header & Footer tab is displayed on the ribbon. The insertion point is positioned on the left side of the footer area, ready for you to begin typing. The label "Footer -Section 1-" tells you that the insertion point is located in the footer for section 1. The document text is gray, indicating that you cannot edit it in Header and Footer view. The header area for section 1 is also visible at the top of page 2. The default footer tab stops (which are different from the default tab stops in the main document) are visible on the ruler. Refer to Figure 3–37.

Figure 3–37 Creating a footer

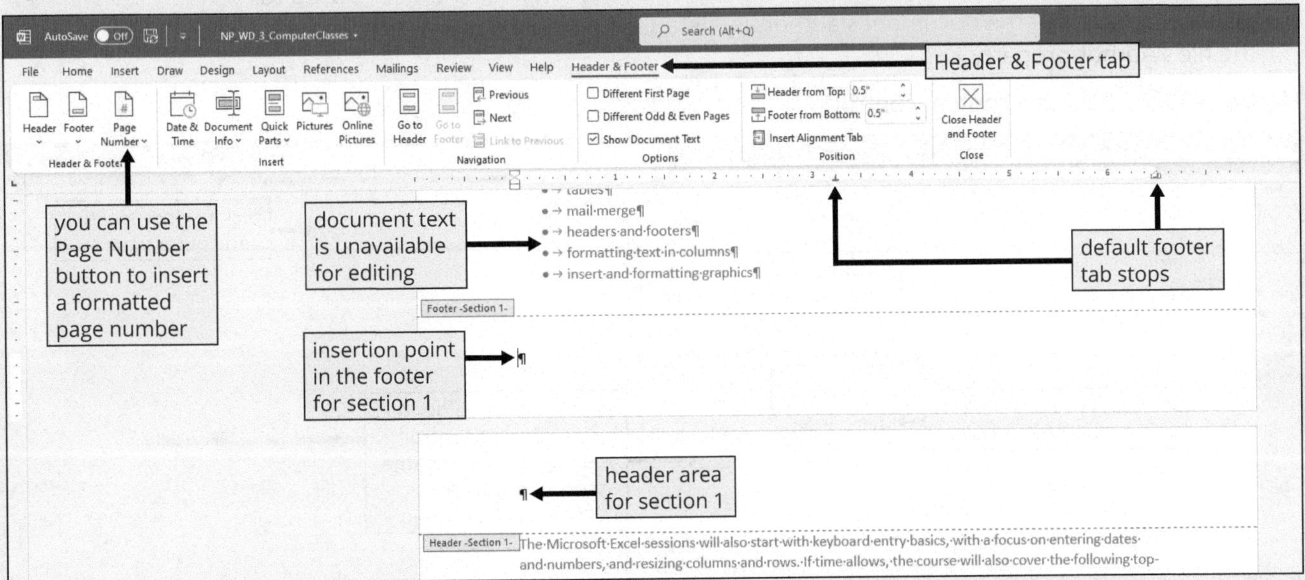

3. In the Header & Footer group, click the **Footer** button. A gallery of footer styles opens.

4. Scroll down and review the various footer styles, and then click the **Retrospect** style. A table with blue shading on top is added to the footer. As you become a more experienced Word user, you will learn how to use tables to lay out text on a page. For now, you can ignore the table and concentrate on the items it contains.

   On the left, the placeholder text "[YOUR NAME]" is displayed. On the right, a page number field shows the current page number. Refer to Figure 3–38.

Figure 3–38 Retrospect footer added to document

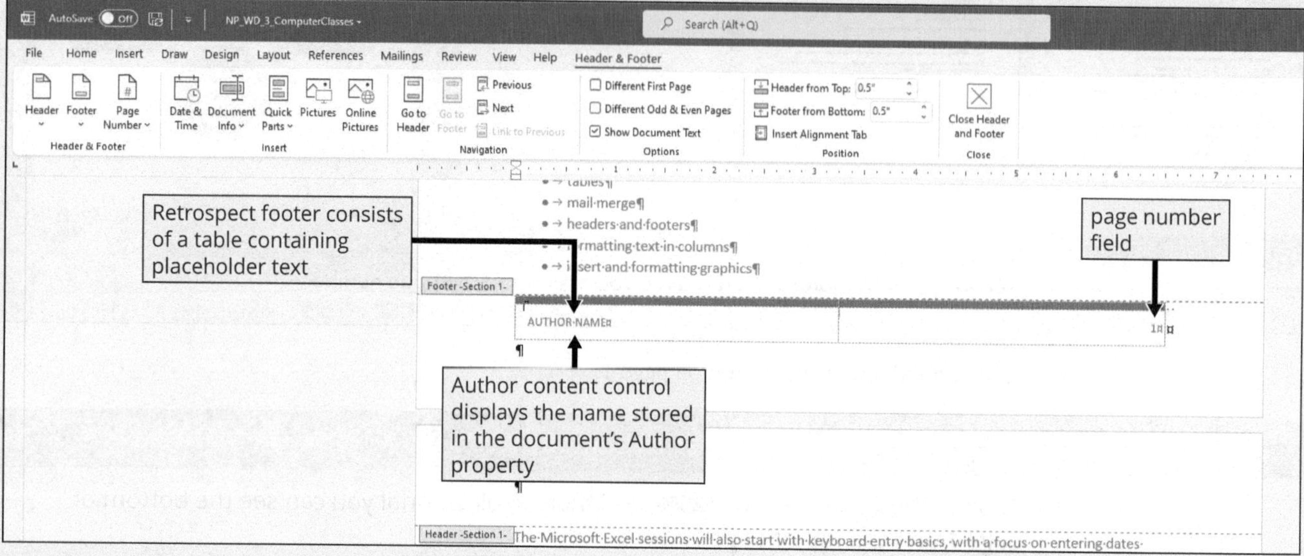

> **Trouble?** If something other than "YOUR NAME" appears on the left side of the header, that's fine.

5. Click the page number. Gray shading appears, indicating that the numeral is displayed by a field—in other words, an instruction that tells Word to display the correct page number. Laila doesn't want to make any changes to the page number, so you can turn your attention to adding your name to the footer instead. The text currently displayed on the left side of the footer is contained in a content control, as you'll see when you click it.

6. Click the text on the left side of the footer to display the content control. As shown in Figure 3–39, the content control's title tab contains "Author," indicating that it is used to display the name of the document's author. By default, it displays the name stored in the file's Author property.

Figure 3–39 Editing a content control

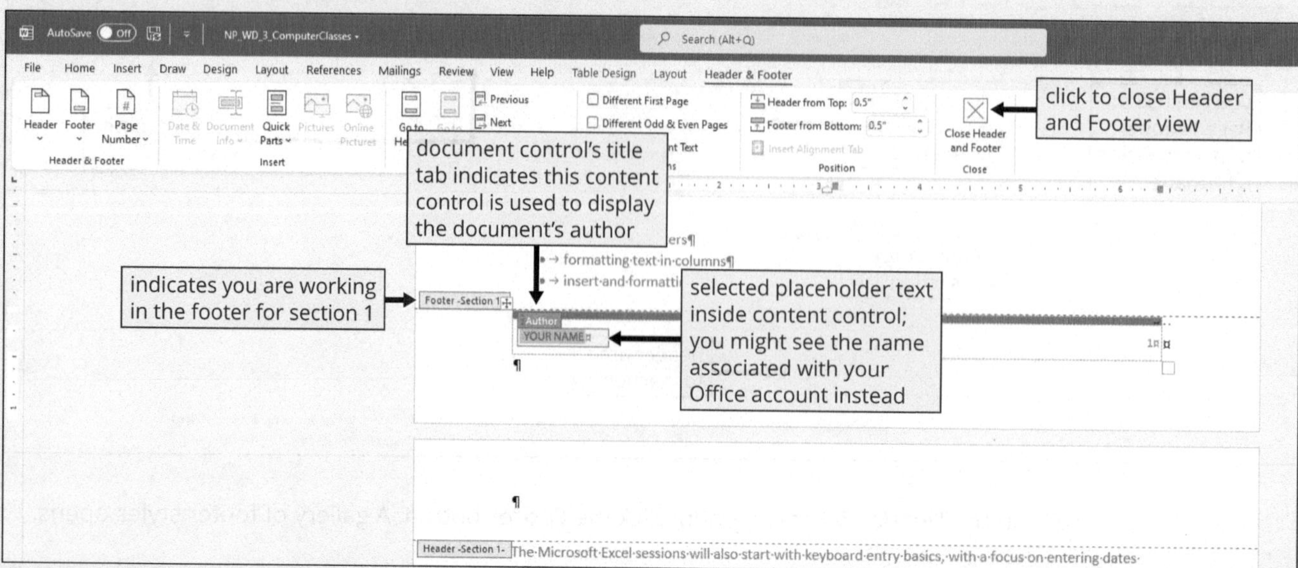

Tip To see a file's properties including the Author property, click the File tab, and then click Info.

7. Click the **Author** title tab to select the placeholder text within the content control, and then type your first and last name, capitalizing the first letter of each name, as you usually would. Your name appears in all uppercase letters, but the fact that you typed it with a mix of upper- and lowercase letters will be helpful later, when you insert the document's cover page.
8. Click in the blank paragraph below the table to deselect the content control.

   Next, you'll check to make sure that the footer you just created for section 1 also appears in section 2. To move between headers or footers in separate sections, you can use the buttons in the Navigation group on the Header & Footer tab.

   Tip To change the numbering style for a page number, or to specify a number to use as the first page number, right-click the page number field, and then click Format Page Numbers.

9. In the Navigation group, click the **Next** button. Word displays the footer for the next section in the document—that is, the footer for section 2, which appears at the bottom of page 4, the page containing the SmartArt graphic. The label at the top of the footer area reads "Footer -Section 2-" and contains the same text (your name and the page number) as in the section 1 footer. Word assumes, by default, that when you type text in one footer, you want it to appear in all the footers in the document.

Now you need to create a header for section 1. Laila does not want to include a header in section 2 because it would distract attention from the SmartArt graphic. So you will first separate the header for section 1 from the header for section 2.

To separate the headers for section 1 and section 2:

1. Verify that the insertion point is located in the section 2 footer area at the bottom of page 4 and that the Header & Footer tab is selected on the ribbon. To switch from the footer to the header in the current section, you can use the Go to Header button in the Navigation group.
2. In the Navigation group, click the **Go to Header** button. The insertion point moves to the section 2 header at the top of page 4. Refer to Figure 3–40.

Figure 3–40 Section 2 header is currently the same as the previous header, in section 1

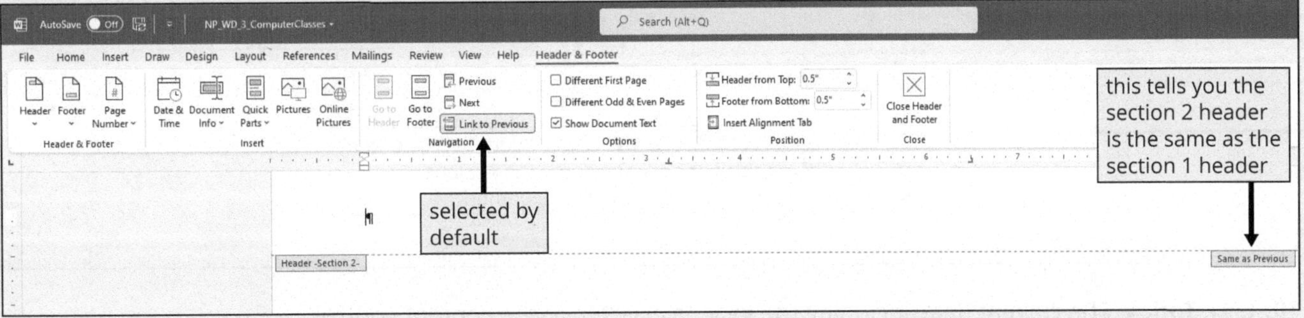

Notice that in the Navigation group, the Link to Previous button is selected. In the header area in the document window, the gray tab on the right side of the header border contains the message "Same as Previous," indicating that the section 2 header is set up to display the same text as the header in the previous section, which is section 1. To make the section 2 header a separate entity, you need to break the link between the section 1 and section 2 headers.

3. In the Navigation group, click the **Link to Previous** button to deselect it. The Same as Previous tab is removed from the right side of the section 2 header border.

> **Tip** When you create a header for a section, it doesn't matter what page you're working on as long as the insertion point is in a header in that section.

4. In the Navigation group, click the **Previous** button. The insertion point moves up to the nearest header in the previous section, which is the section 1 header at the top of page 3. The label "Header -Section 1-" identifies this as a section 1 header.
5. In the Header & Footer group, click the **Header** button. A gallery of header styles opens.
6. Scroll down and review the various header styles, and then click the **Retrospect** style. The placeholder text "[Document title]" is aligned at the left margin. The placeholder text "[Date]" is aligned at the right margin. The placeholder text appears in a white font, with orange shading in the background, and with a blue bar at the bottom. As with the footer, the header is actually a table, but you only need to focus on the table's contents.
7. Click the **[DOCUMENT TITLE]** placeholder text to select it inside the Title content control.
8. Type **Computer Literacy Course Progress Report**. The text you just typed appears in all uppercase letters, but the fact that you capitalized the only first letter of each word will be helpful later, when you insert the document's cover page. Next, you need to add the date. The header style you selected includes a date picker content control, which allows you to select the date from a calendar.
9. Click the **[Date]** placeholder text to display an arrow in the content control, and then click the arrow. A calendar for the current month appears, as shown in Figure 3–41. In the calendar, the current date is outlined in dark blue. You could click the arrow buttons on the top of the calendar to select a different month, and then click a date in the calendar. To insert the current date, you can click the Today button below the calendar.

Figure 3–41 Adding a date to the section 1 header

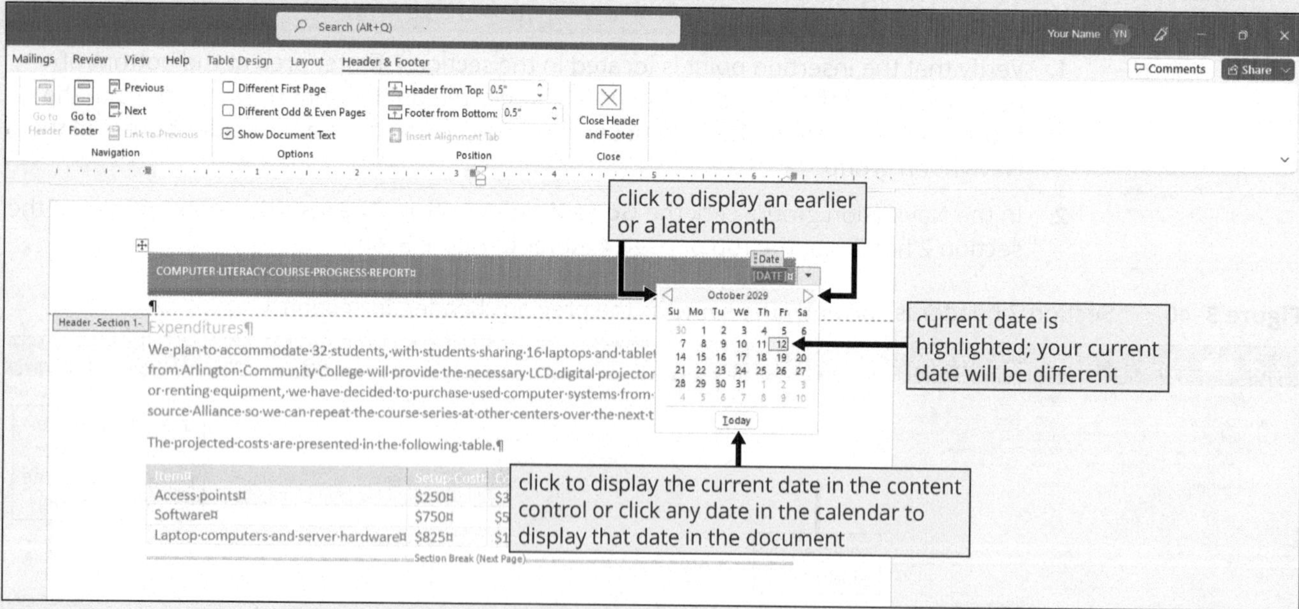

10. Click **Today**. The current date, including the year, is inserted in the content control.
11. Click in the blank paragraph below the header table to deselect the date content control. You are finished creating the header and footer for Laila's report, so you can close Header and Footer view and return to Print Layout view.
12. In the Close group, click the **Close Header and Footer** button, or double-click anywhere in the main document, and then save your work.
13. On the ribbon, click the **View** tab.

14. In the Zoom group, click the **Multiple Pages** button, and then change the Zoom level to **30%** so you can see all four pages of the document, including the header at the top of pages 1 through 3 and the footer at the bottom of pages 1 through 4. Take a moment to compare your completed headers and footers with Laila's plan for the headers and footers shown earlier in Figure 3–36.

Next, you need to insert a cover page for the report.

Inserting a Cover Page

A report's cover page typically includes the title and the name of the author. Some people also include a summary of the report on the cover page, which is commonly referred to as an abstract. In addition, you might include the date, the name and possibly the logo of your company or organization, and a subtitle. A cover page should not include the document header or footer.

To insert a preformatted cover page at the beginning of the document, you use the Cover Page button on the Insert tab. You can choose from a variety of cover page styles, all of which include content controls in which you can enter the document title, the document's author, the date, and so on. These content controls are linked to any other content controls in the document. For example, you already entered "Computer Literacy Course Progress Report" into a content control in the header of Laila's report. So if you use a cover page that contains a similar content control, "Computer Literacy Course Progress Report" will be displayed on the cover page automatically. Note that content controls sometimes display information entered when either Word or Windows was originally installed on your computer. If your computer has multiple user accounts, the information displayed in some content controls might reflect the information for the current user. In any case, you can easily edit the contents of a content control.

To insert a cover page at the beginning of the report:

1. Verify that the document is still zoomed so that you can see all four pages.
2. On the ribbon, click the **Insert** tab.
3. In the Pages group, click the **Cover Page** button. A gallery of cover page styles opens. Notice that the names of the cover page styles match the names of the preformatted header styles you saw earlier. For example, the list includes a Retrospect cover page, which is designed to match the Retrospect header and footer used in this document. To give a document a uniform look, it's helpful to use elements with the same style throughout.
4. Scroll down the gallery to see the cover page styles, and then locate the Retrospect cover page style.
5. Click the **Retrospect** cover page style. The new cover page is inserted at the beginning of the document.

   Tip To delete a cover page that you inserted from the Cover Page gallery, click the Cover Page button in the Pages group, and then click Remove Current Cover Page.

6. Change the Zoom display to **One Page**, increase the Zoom level to **100%**, and then scroll to display the cover page. The only difference between the title "Computer Literacy Course Progress Report" here and the title you entered in the document header is that here the title is displayed in upper- and lowercase letters, as you originally typed it in the header. Likewise, your name is included in the bottom part of the title page in upper- and lowercase letters, as you originally typed it in the footer.

Some content controls—are set up to display text in all uppercase letters, no matter how you type it. But it's a good idea to type text in a content control using the correct capitalization. That way, you can be sure the text will look right if it is reused in another content control that does not format text in all uppercase letters. The cover page also includes content controls for a subtitle, a company name, and a company address. Refer to Figure 3–42.

Figure 3–42 Newly inserted cover page

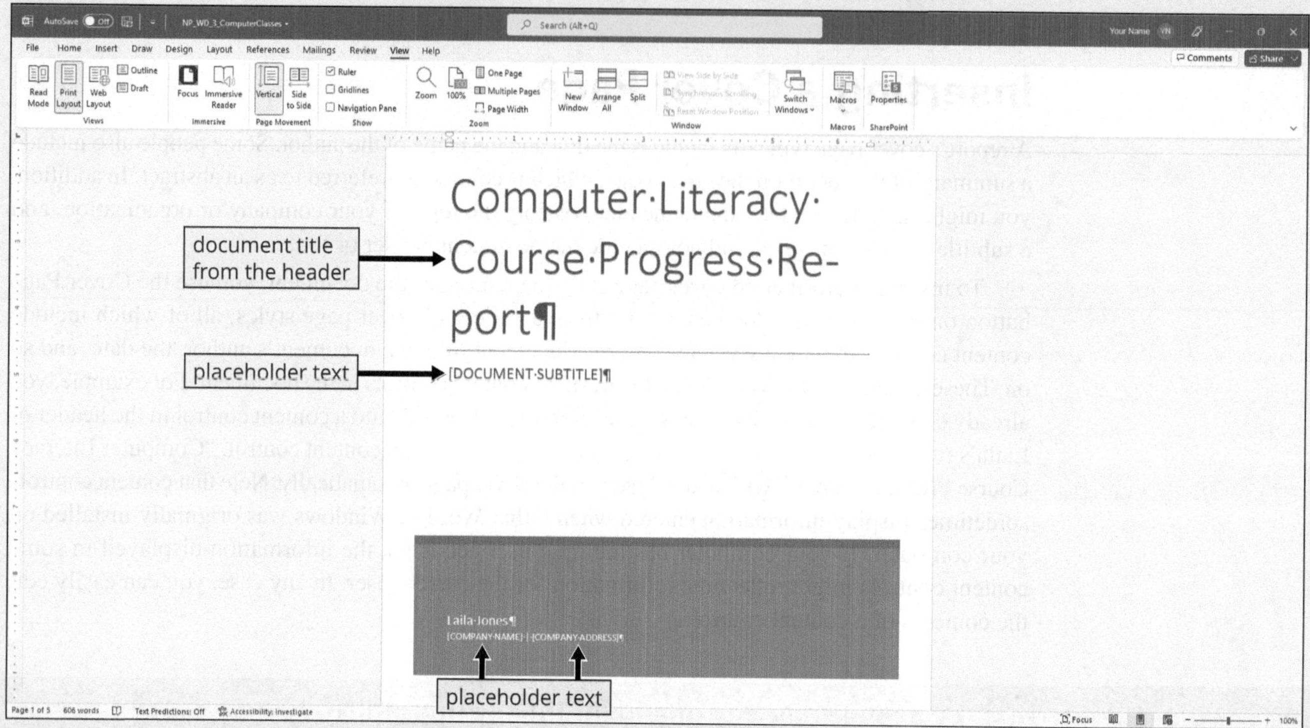

Trouble? If you see the document title or your name in all uppercase letters, edit the text in those content controls as necessary.

Because you turned on Automatic Hyphenation earlier, the word "Report" is hyphenated on the title page. You will fix that now by turning off hyphenation for just the title.

To turn off hyphenation for the title:

1. Click anywhere in the text "Computer Literacy Course Progress Report" to display the Title content control.
2. Select **Computer Literacy Course Progress Report**, right-click the selected text to display a shortcut menu, and then click Paragraph to open the **Paragraph** dialog box.
3. If necessary, click the **Line and Page Breaks** tab and then, in the Formatting exceptions section, select the **Don't hyphenate** check box.
4. Click **OK** to close the Paragraph dialog box. The word "Report" now appears on a third line, with no hyphen, in the Title content control. The rest of the document retains the hyphens inserted earlier when you turned on automatic hyphenation.

To complete the title page, you need to fill in the Subtitle content control, and then remove the remaining content controls.

To complete the title page:

1. Click the **[DOCUMENT SUBTITLE]** placeholder text, and then type **Totara Neighborhood Centers**. The text is displayed in all uppercase letters, even though you only capitalized the first letter of each word. Next, you will remove the Company and Address content controls because you do not need them in this report.
2. Below your name, right-click the **[COMPANY NAME]** placeholder text to display the shortcut menu, and then click **Remove Content Control**. The content control is removed from the cover page.
3. Press **DELETE** three times to remove the space, the vertical bar, and the second space, and then remove the Address content control, which displays the placeholder text "[COMPANY ADDRESS]."
4. Save the document.

Working with Themes

A **theme** is a coordinated collection of fonts, colors, and other visual effects designed to give a document a cohesive, polished look. A variety of themes are installed with Word, with more available online at templates.office.com. When you open a new, blank document in Word, the Office theme is applied by default. To change a document's theme, you click the Themes button, which is located in the Document Formatting group on the Design tab, and then click the theme you want. Pointing to the Themes button displays a ScreenTip that tells you what theme is currently applied to the document.

The **theme colors** are the colors you see in the Theme Colors section of any color gallery, such as the Font Color gallery. Theme colors are used in the document's styles to format headings, body text, and other elements. When applying color to a document, you usually have the option of selecting a color from a palette of colors designed to match the current theme or from a palette of standard colors. For instance, recall that the colors in the Font Color gallery are divided into Theme Colors and Standard Colors. When you select a Standard Color, such as Dark Red, that color remains the same no matter which theme you apply to the document. But when you click one of the Theme Colors, you are essentially telling Word to use the color located in that particular spot on the Theme Colors palette. Then, if you change the document's theme later, Word substitutes a color from the same location on the Theme Colors palette. This ensures that all the colors in a document are drawn from a group of colors coordinated to look good together. So as a rule, if you are going to use multiple colors in a document (perhaps for paragraph shading and font color), it's a good idea to stick with the Theme Colors.

> **Tip** Each document theme is designed to convey a specific look and feel. The Office theme is designed to be appropriate for standard business documents. Some themes are designed to give documents a flashier look.

A similar substitution takes place with fonts when you change the theme. However, to understand how this works, you need to understand the difference between headings and body text. Laila's document includes the headings "Summary," "Background," "Instructors," "Course Topics," "Current Plans," "Schedule," and "Expenditures"—all of which are formatted with heading styles. The text below the headings is considered body text. For example, the paragraph below the "Summary" heading is body text.

To ensure that your documents have a harmonious look, each theme assigns a font for headings and a font for body text. These two fonts are known as the document's **theme fonts**. They are used in the document's styles and appear at the top of the font list when you click the Font arrow in the Font group on the Home tab.

Typically, in a given theme, the same font is used for both headings and body text, but not always. In the Office theme, for instance, they are slightly different; the heading font is Calibri Light, and the body font is Calibri. These two fonts appear at the top of the Font list as "Calibri Light (Headings)" and "Calibri (Body)" when you click the Font arrow in the Font group on the Home tab. When you begin typing text in a new document with the Office theme, the text is formatted as body text with the Calibri font by default.

When applying a font to selected text, you can choose one of the two theme fonts at the top of the Font list, or you can choose one of the other fonts in the Font list. If you choose one of the other fonts and then change the document theme, that font remains the same. But if you use one of the theme fonts and then change the document theme, Word substitutes the appropriate font from the new theme. When you paste text into a document that has a different theme, Word applies the theme fonts and colors of the new document. To retain the original formatting, use the Keep Source Formatting option in the Paste Options menu.

Figure 3–43 compares elements of the default Office theme with the Integral theme. The Integral theme was chosen for this example because, like the Office theme, it has different heading and body fonts.

Figure 3–43 Comparing the Office theme to the Integral theme

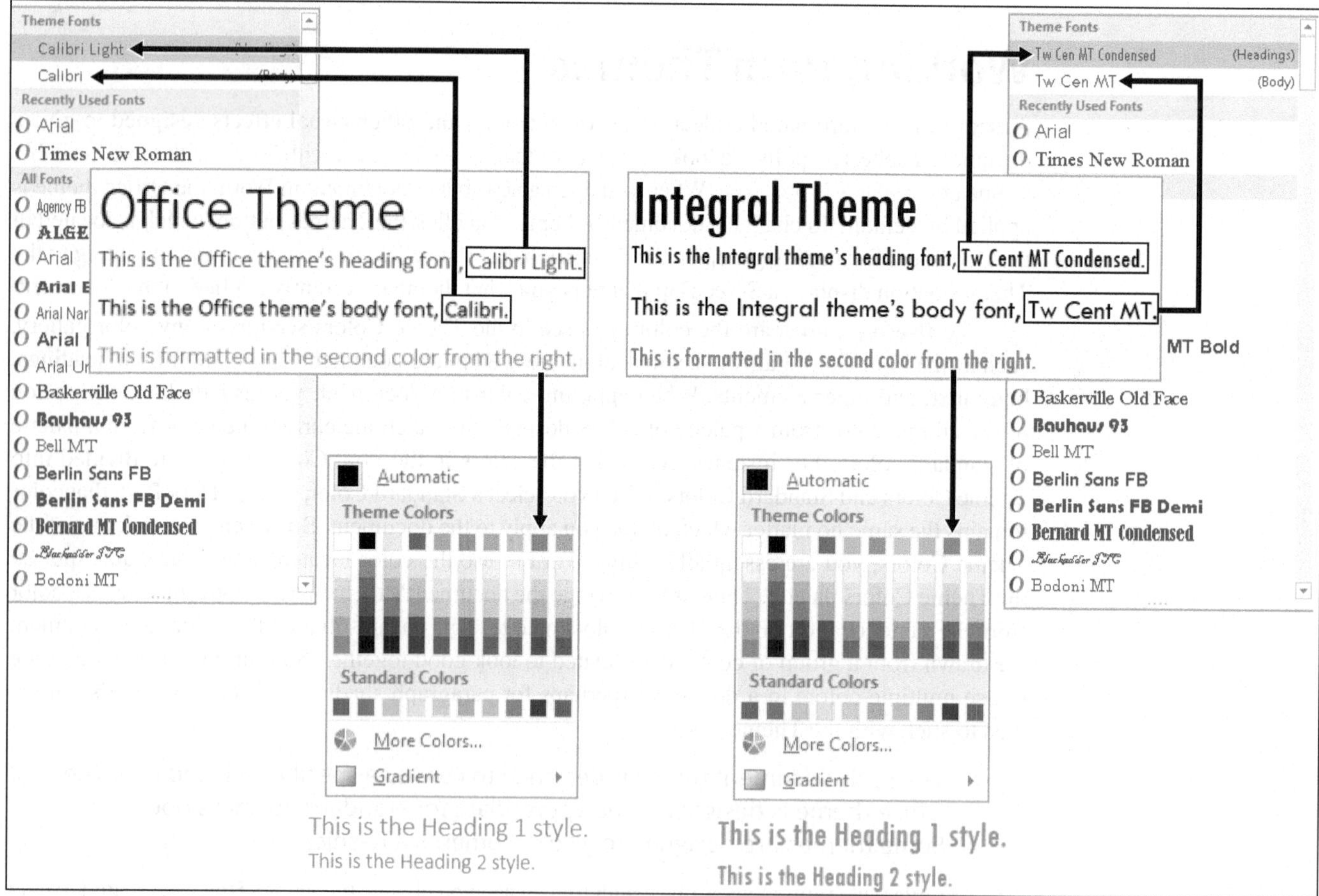

The default Office theme is currently applied to the document. However, Laila thinks the Facet theme might be more appropriate for the document. She asks you to apply it now.

To change the document's theme:

1. Change the zoom display to **Multiple Pages**, then scroll if necessary so you can see the first three pages of the document. This will allow you to quickly see how the document changes when you change the theme. Note that currently one section of the cover page is formatted with an orange background with a blue top border. The headers are formatted similarly, except with a blue bottom border. The footers are formatted with a white background and a blue top border.
2. On the ribbon, click the **Design** tab.
3. In the Document Formatting group, point to the **Themes** button. A ScreenTip appears containing the text "Current: Office Theme" as well as general information about themes.
4. In the Document Formatting group, click the **Themes** button. The Themes gallery opens. Because Microsoft occasionally updates the available themes, you might see a different list than the one shown in Figure 3–44.

Figure 3–44 Themes gallery

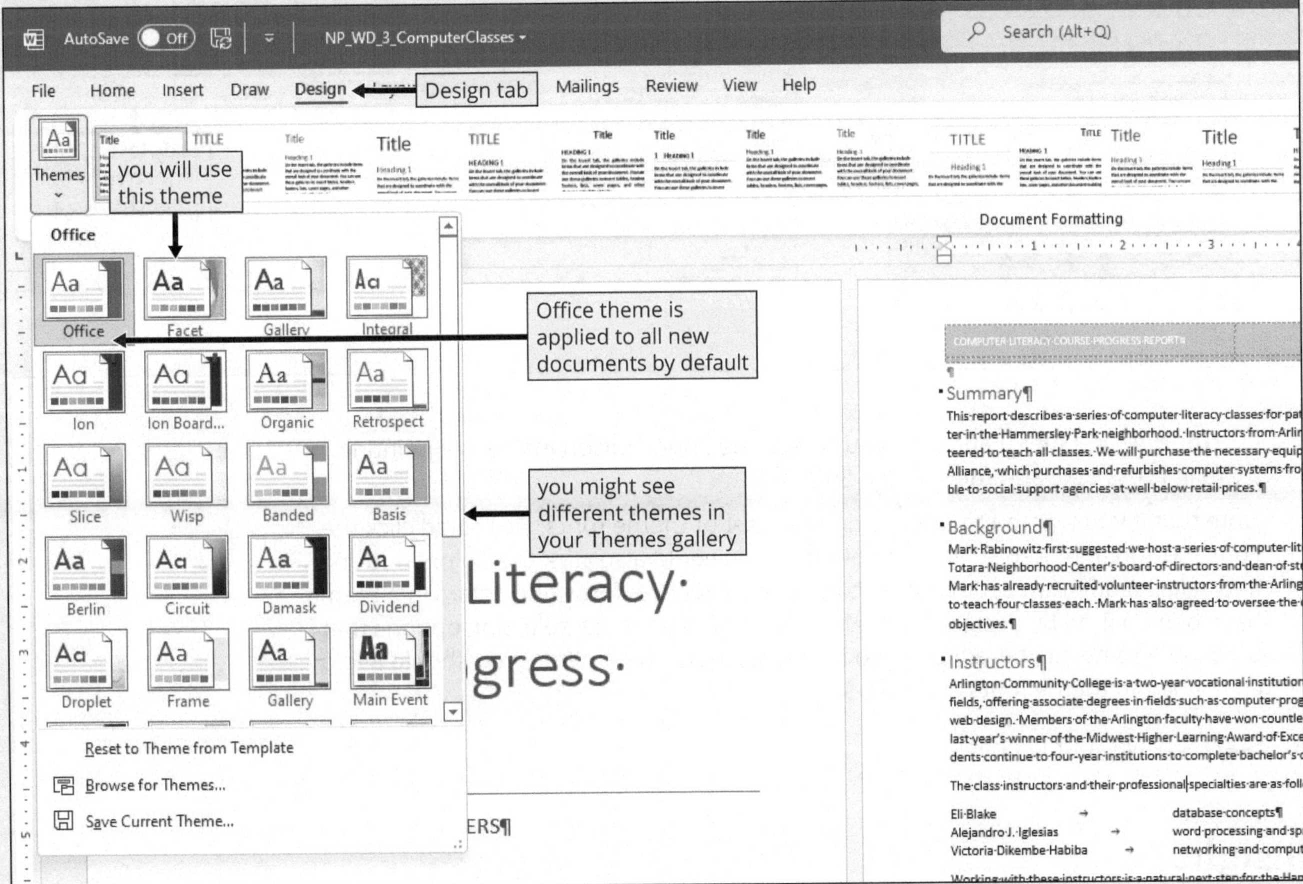

5. Move the pointer (without clicking it) over the various themes in the gallery to see a Live Preview of each theme in the document. The heading and body fonts as well as the heading colors change to reflect the fonts associated with the various themes.
6. In the Themes gallery, click the **Facet** theme, and then scroll down to review the document's new look. All the colors in the document have changed to shades of green, except the table, which is formatted in shades of brown. The document text is now formatted in the body and heading fonts of the Facet theme, with the headings formatted in green.

Trouble? If you do not see the Facet theme in your Themes gallery, click a different theme.

7. In the Document Formatting group, point to the **Fonts** button. A ScreenTip appears, listing the currently selected theme (Facet), the heading font (Trebuchet MS), and the body font (Trebuchet MS). Refer to Figure 3–45.

Figure 3–45 Fonts for the Facet theme

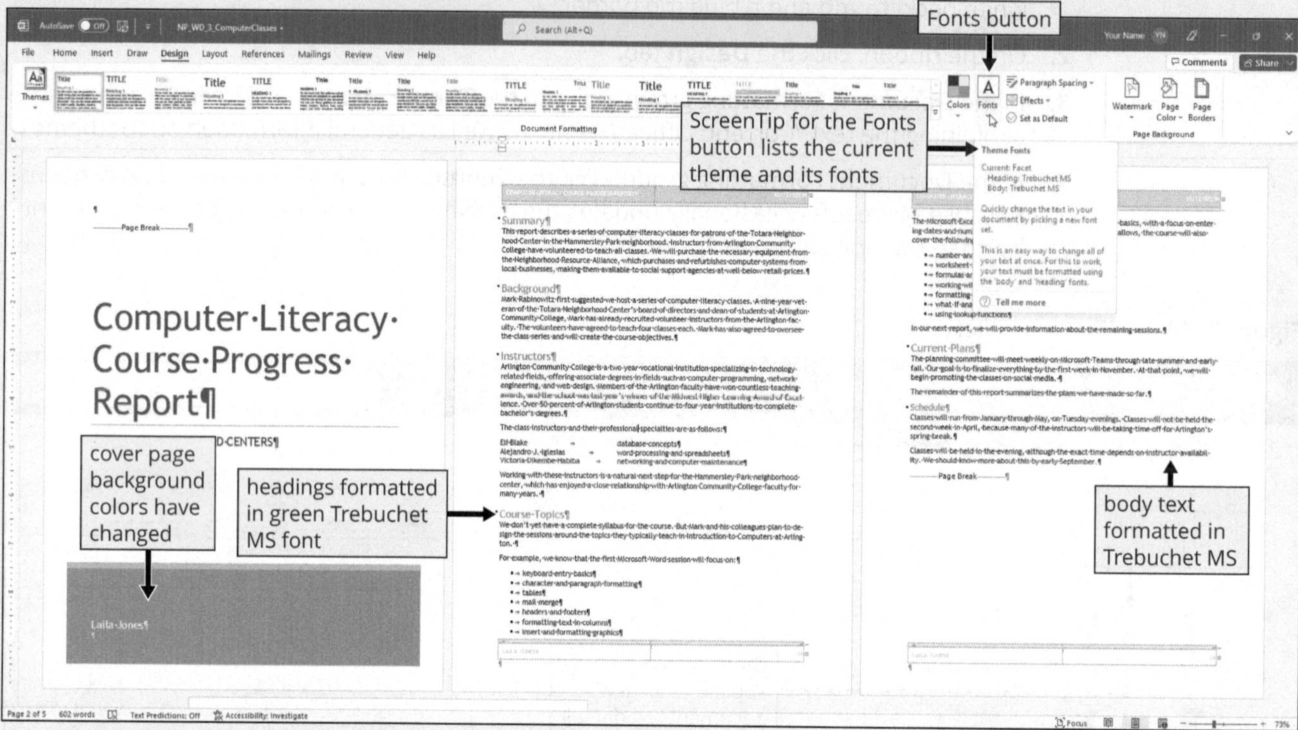

Trouble? If a menu appears, you clicked the Fonts button instead of pointing to it. Press ESC, and then repeat Step 7.

Note that if you wanted to select a different set of theme fonts, you could click the Fonts button and then select a set of fonts. You could also click the Colors button and select a different set of theme colors. However, the fonts and colors in a theme have been paired by designers who have a lot of experience selecting options that, together, create a coherent look. So for professional documents, you should avoid changing the theme fonts and colors.

8. sam Save your changes.

Insight

Personalizing the Word Interface

The Word Options dialog box allows you to change the look of the Word interface. For starters, you can set the Office Theme to Colorful, to Dark Gray, Black, or White. Some people find that the Black theme, which displays text in white on a black background, minimizes eye strain. The figures in this book were created using the Colorful them.

Note that in this context, "Office Theme" refers to the colors of the Word interface, and not the colors and fonts used in a Word document. You can also use the Office Background setting to add graphic designs, such as clouds or stars, to the Word interface. To get started, click the File tab, click Options in the navigation pane, make sure the General tab is displayed, and then select the options you want in the Personalize your copy of Microsoft Office section of the Word Options dialog box.

Your work on the report is finished. You should preview the report before closing it.

To preview the report:

1. On the ribbon, click the **File** tab.
2. In the navigation pane, click the **Print** tab. The report's cover page is displayed in the document preview in the right pane. Depending on the size of your monitor, you might also see the report's second page.
3. Examine the document preview, using the arrow buttons at the bottom of the pane to display the remaining pages.
4. If you need to make any changes to the report, return to Print Layout view, edit the document, preview the document again, and then save the document.
5. Display the document in Print Layout view.
6. Change the Zoom level back to **120%**, and then press **CTRL+HOME** to make sure the insertion point is located on the first page.

Proskills

Written Communication: Taking Notes

The process of writing a report or other long document usually involves taking notes. It's essential to organize your notes in a way that allows you to write about your topic logically and coherently. It's also important to retain your notes after you finish a first draft, so that you can incorporate additional material from your notes in subsequent drafts.

Clicking the Linked Notes button on the Review tab opens the Microsoft OneNote app in a window on the right side of the screen. (If you don't see the Linked Notes button, click the File tab to display Backstage view. Click Options in the navigation pane, and then click Add-ins. Click the arrow button in the Manage box, select Com Add-ins, if necessary, and then click the Go button. In the Com Add-ins dialog box, select OneNote Linked Notes Add-In, and then click OK.) In the Microsoft OneNote window, you can take notes that are linked to your Microsoft Word account. Every time you start Word and click the Linked Notes button, your notes are displayed in the OneNote window. You can copy material from a Word document and paste it in OneNote, and vice versa.

To get started, open a Word document, save it, make sure you are logged into your Microsoft account, click the Review tab, and then, in the OneNote group, click the Linked Notes button. This opens the Select Location in OneNote dialog box, where you can select a notebook, and then a page in that notebook. OneNote works best if you use a notebook stored on OneDrive, so unless you have a compelling reason to do otherwise, select a notebook stored on OneDrive. The full OneNote app opens, along with a pane for taking notes that you can use while Word is also open on the screen. Minimize the OneNote window, and maximize the Word window if necessary. Now you're ready to take notes. Start by typing a title for your notebook page at the insertion point in the OneNote pane, then click in the blank space below the title, and start taking notes. To display the OneNote ribbon, with a selection of tools for working with notes, click the ellipses at the top of the OneNote window. Click the Close button in the upper-right corner of the OneNote window pane when you are finished.

Displaying a Document in Read Mode

The members of Totara's board of directors could choose to print the report, but some might prefer to read it on their computers instead. In that case, they can take advantage of **Read Mode**, a document view designed to make reading on a screen as easy as possible. Unlike Print Layout view, which mimics the look of the printed page with its margins and page breaks, Read Mode focuses on the document's content. Read Mode displays as much content as possible on the screen at a time, with buttons that allow you to display more. Note that you can't edit text in Read Mode. To do that, you need to switch back to Page Layout view.

To display the document in Read Mode:

1. In the status bar, click the **Read Mode** button. The document switches to Read Mode, with a reduced version of the cover page on the left and the first part of the document text on the right. The text is arranged in columns, which are called screens. On the left edge of the status bar a message indicates the total number of screens, which can vary from one monitor to the next.

   To display more of the document, you can click the arrow button on the right. Refer to Figure 3–46.

Figure 3–46 Document displayed in Read Mode

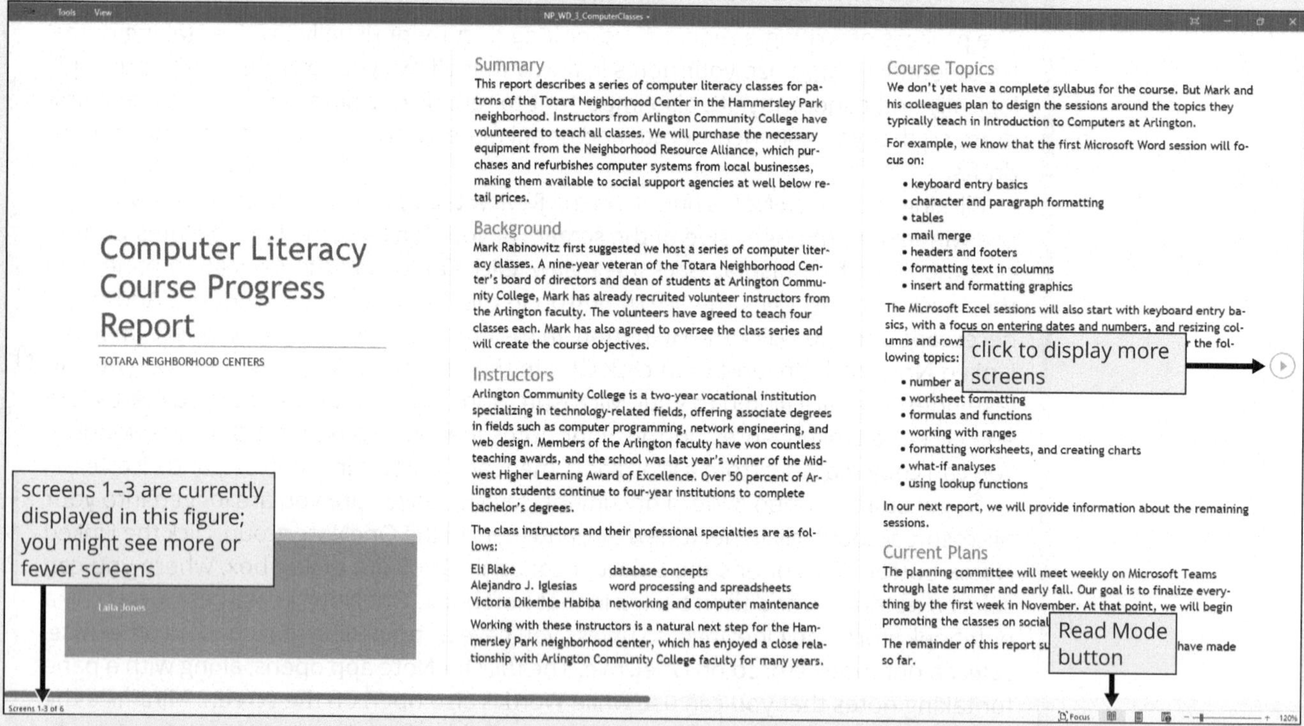

Trouble? If the pages on your screen are not laid out as shown in Figure 3–46, click View on the menu bar, point to Layout, and then click Column Layout.

2. Click the **right arrow** button on the right to display additional screens. A left arrow button is now displayed on the left side of the screen. You could click it to move back to the previous screens.
3. Continue to the **right arrow** button to display additional screens of text, until you reach the end of the document.

Tip To zoom in on a SmartArt graphic, you can double-click it. Click anywhere outside the object zoom window to return to the Read Mode screens.

4. Click the **left arrow** button on the left as necessary to return to the beginning of the document, and then click the **Print Layout** button in the status bar to return to Page Layout view.

Reading view is designed to allow readers to skim through a document quickly, much like flipping through the pages of a book. But when you want to focus more intensively, you can use Immersive Reader.

Using Immersive Reader

Immersive Reader is an accessibility feature designed to help with reading fluency and comprehension. You access it by clicking the Immersive Reader button on the View tab. This displays the Immersive Reader contextual tab, which includes the following buttons:

- **Column Width:** Allows you to alter the line length. For some people, reading short lines of text is easier than reading text that extends across the full width of the document.
- **Page Color:** Allows you to choose page colors other than white, which can help reduce eye strain. The page color you select is only visible on your screen, and has no effect on the document as it would appear in Print Layout view.
- **Line Focus:** Lets you highlight sets of one, three, or five lines to narrow your reading focus.
- **Text Spacing:** Adds more space between words, characters, and lines. Depending on your needs, you might find that this makes a block of text easier to read.
- **Syllables:** Inserts space between syllables, which can make it easier to pronounce unfamiliar words.
- **Read Aloud:** Begins an automated reading of the document text. As each word is pronounced, it is highlighted in the text.

In the following steps, you will explore some options in Immersive Reader.

To explore options in Immersive Reader:

1. Click the **View** tab, and then, in the Immersive group, click the **Immersive Reader** button. The document is displayed with darker background. People sometimes find that a black background with white text helps minimize eyestrain. You will try that next.
2. In Immersive Reader contextual tab, click the **Page Color** button to display a color palette, point to the black box in the top row to display a tooltip that reads "Inverse," and then click the black box. Word changes the document text to white, so it stands out against the black background. Refer to Figure 3–47.

Figure 3–47 Document displayed in Immersive Reader

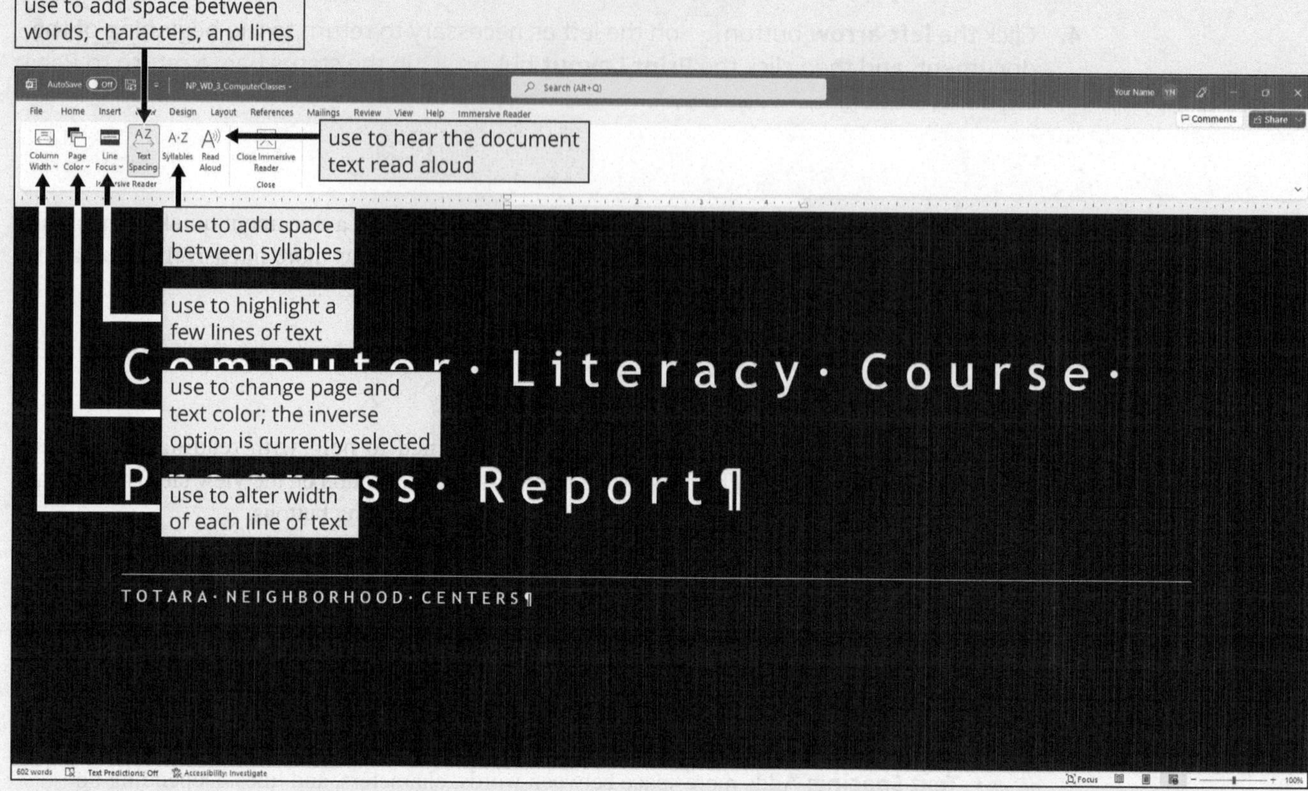

3. Explore the Immersive Reader features, trying out the buttons described in Figure 3–47. Nothing you do in Immersive Reader will affect the document itself, so don't be afraid to make lots of changes.
4. Click the Close Immersive Reader button. The document is again displayed in Print Layout view.
5. Close the document.

You now have a draft of the document, including a cover page, the report text, a nicely formatted table, and the SmartArt graphic (in landscape orientation).

Insight

Exploring Word's Accessibility Features

Word's accessibility tools, such as the features you explored in Immersive View, allow you to fine-tune the way Word works for you. To get the most out of out of Immersive Reader, try it out in various situations while you are working on different types of documents. You might find that a black background color is best when working on a laptop, while you prefer a white background on a larger, desktop monitor. If you are accustomed to listening to podcasts or audio books, you might be surprised by how helpful it is to use the Read Aloud feature to listen to something you've just written. Many people find that hearing their work read aloud makes it easier to notice things that need improvement.

Note that Read Aloud does not include all the features found in a dedicated screen reader program. For example, it does not narrate alt text attached to graphics. To learn more about Microsoft 365's support for dedicated screen reader programs such as Freedom Scientific's JAWS or Microsoft Narrator, open the Help pane and then search on "Use a screen reader to select and read text boxes and images in Word."

Keep in mind that while you'll find most of Word's accessibility features in Immersive Reader, a few are located on other tabs. The Dictate button in the Voice group on the Home tab is an accessibility option that can increase writing fluency for some people. If a microphone is installed on your computer, you can use the Dictate button to add text to a document by speaking rather than typing.

To get started, click the Dictate button, and wait for the button icon to change into a white microphone with a red circle next to it. Then speak clearly into your computer's microphone. The sentences you speak are immediately transcribed as document text. Note that you'll probably need to edit the text when you are finished dictating, but with practice, you can learn how to dictate in a way that produces fewer and fewer errors. Exactly how fast you need to talk, and how precisely, will vary from one microphone to another.

Focus mode displays the document similar to how it appears in Page Layout view, but without the Ribbon, so you can focus exclusively on its content. Display your document in Print Layout view, click the Focus button on the status bar or on the View tab in the Immersive group to hide everything in the Word window except for the document. To exit Focus mode, press ESC.

Part 3.2 Quick Check

1. How far apart are the default tab stops?
2. What is the default tab stop style?
3. By default, is hyphenation turned on or off in a Word document?
4. What is the first thing you need to do if you want to format part of a document in an orientation different from the rest of the document?
5. Explain how to create separate headers for a document with two sections.
6. What is the default theme in a new document?

Practice: Review Assignments

Data File needed for the Review Assignments: NP_WD_3-3.docx

At a recent meeting, the Totara board of directors requested a plan to reduce utility bills at the Hammersley Park facility. Laila Jones has begun working on a report for the board that summarizes progress toward this goal. You need to format the report, add a table at the end containing a preliminary schedule, add a formula to another table that summarizes costs associated with improving the facility's energy efficiency, and create a sample graphic that Laila could use in a handout announcing the energy efficiency project.

Complete the following steps:

1. Open the document **NP_WD_3-3.docx** located in the Word3 > Review folder included with your Data Files, and then save it as **NP_WD_3_Energy** in the location specified by your instructor.
2. Promote the "Expenditures" and "Repairs and Upgrades" headings from Heading 3 text to Heading 2 text, and then move the "Repairs and Upgrades" heading and its body text up above the "Expenditures" heading.
3. Insert a page break before the "Proposed Schedule" heading. In the blank paragraph at the bottom of the new page 3, insert a table using the information shown in Figure 3–48. Format the header row in bold.

Figure 3–48 Schedule for Laila's report

Date	**Item**
09/06/2029	On-site-audit
11/16/2029	Review audit results
4/4/2029	Meet with consultants
8/20/2029	Inform staff and patrons
7/8/2029	Submit grant application

4. Sort the table by the contents of the "Date" column in ascending order.
5. In the appropriate location in the table, insert a new row for **"Complete utility bill review"** on **10/5/2029**.
6. Delete the "Meet with consultants" row from the table.
7. Modify the widths of both columns to accommodate the widest entry in each.
8. Apply the Grid Table 4 - Accent 4 style to the table, and then remove the special formatting for the first column.
9. Locate the table on page 2, in the "Expenditures" section. In the table's lower-right cell, add a formula field that sums the total cost and displays the result in a format that matches the other numbers in the table, including a dollar sign ($).
10. Change the cost for Weather stripping and insulation to **$1,500** and then update the formula.
11. Merge the two blank cells, insert **TOTAL** in the new, merged cell, right-align the text in the cell, and then format the contents of the bottom row in bold.
12. Apply the Grid Table 4 - Accent 4 style to the table, and then remove the special formatting for the first column.
13. On page 1, replace the text "[consultant names]" with a tabbed list of consultants and their titles, using the following information: **Veronica Carrington-Brewster**, **Senior Consultant**; **Lia Kim**, **Project Manager**; **Yariel Delgado**, **Senior Engineer**. Insert a tab after each name, and don't include any punctuation in the list.
14. Use a left tab stop to align the consultants' titles 2.5 inches from the left margin, and then adjust the list's paragraph spacing so it appears to be a single paragraph.
15. Turn on automatic hyphenation.

16. After the table on page 3, insert a section break that starts a new, fourth page, and then format the new page in landscape orientation.
17. Insert a SmartArt graphic that illustrates the benefits of the energy audit project. Use the Circle Arrow Process graphic from the Process category, and, from left to right, include the following text in the SmartArt diagram: **Energy Audit**, **Repairs and Upgrades**, and **Energy Savings**. Do not include any punctuation in the SmartArt. Change the SmartArt graphic's height to 6.5 inches and the width to 9 inches.
18. Add the Retrospect footer to sections 1 and 2, and edit the Author content control so it displays your first and last name.
19. Separate the section 2 header from the section 1 header, and then create a header for section 1 using the Retrospect header style. Enter **Totara Energy Audit Project Summary Report** as the document title and select the current date. Note that the document title will be displayed in all uppercase.
20. Insert a cover page using the Retrospect style. Verify that the document title is displayed in title case, with the first letter of each word in uppercase. Change the hyphenation for the title so "Report" is no longer hyphenated. Add the following subtitle in all uppercase letters: **PREPARED BY *YOUR NAME***, replacing *YOUR NAME* with your first and last name. Delete the Author content control. Also delete the Company Name and Company Address content controls, as well as the vertical bar character between them.
21. Change the document theme to Retrospect, then save and preview the report. Laila will be adding more text to page 3, so don't be concerned that most of that page is blank.
22. Add a diagonal "DRAFT" watermark to the report using the default font, size, color and semitransparency settings in the Printed Watermark dialog box. (**Hint**: To ensure the insertion point is not located within a content control, click on the page after the cover page before adding the watermark.)
23. Close the document.

Apply: Case Problem 1

Data File needed for this Case Problem: NP_WD_3-4.docx

National Textile Manufacturers Council You are a member services representative at the National Textile Manufacturers Council, a professional organization for companies that manufacture fabric, fibers, chemicals, and other products used in the textile industry. You have been asked to help prepare an annual report for the organization's members. The current draft is not complete, but it contains enough for you to get started.

Complete the following steps:

1. Open the document **NP_WD_3-4.docx** located in the Word3 > Case1 folder included with your Data Files, and then save it as **NP_WD_3_Textile** in the location specified by your instructor.
2. Remove the watermark from the document.
3. Adjust the heading levels so that the "Regulatory Compliance Conferences" and "Fall and Spring Board Meetings" headings are formatted with the Heading 2 style.
4. Move the "Membership" heading and its body text down to the end of the report.
5. Format the Board of Directors list using a left tab stop with a dot leader at the 2.2-inch mark. (**Hint**: Use the Dialog Box Launcher in the Paragraph group on the Layout tab to open the Paragraph dialog box, and then click the Tabs button at the bottom of the Indents and Spacing tab to open the Tabs dialog box.)
6. Insert a page break that moves the "Membership" heading to the top of a new page, and then, below the body text on the new page, insert a table consisting of three columns and four rows.
7. In the table, enter the information shown in Figure 3–49. Format the column headings in bold.

Figure 3–49 Information for National Textile Manufacturers Council table

Type	Annual	Members
Affiliate	$2,000	1,250
Individual	$900	410
Enterprise	$10,000	5,678

8. Sort the table in descending order by Annual Fee.
9. In the appropriate location in the table, insert a row for a **Trial** membership type, with a **$325** fee, and **120** members.
10. Adjust the column widths so each column accommodates the widest entry.
11. Add a new row to the bottom of the table, and then insert a formula that sums the total number of members. Make sure the formula displays the result in the appropriate format.
12. Merge the two blank cells, add the right-aligned text **TOTAL** to the new, merged cell, and then format the bottom row in bold.
13. Format the table using the Grid Table 4 - Accent 3 table style without banded rows or special formatting in the first column.
14. Turn on automatic hyphenation.
15. Insert a Blank footer, and then type your name to replace the selected placeholder text "[Type here]" in the footer's left margin. In the right margin, insert a page number using the Large Color style or, if the Large Color style is not an option for you, insert a page number, and change its font size to 20. (**Hint**: Press TAB twice to move the insertion point to the right margin before inserting the page number, and then insert the page number at the current location.)
16. Insert a cover page using the Semaphore style. Select the current date. Enter the document title, **NATIONAL TEXTILE MANUFACTURERS COUNCIL MEMBER REPORT** in the appropriate content control. In the subtitle content control, enter **Prepared by [Your Name]**, but replace "[Your Name]" with your first and last names). (Note that the text you type is formatted in a special font format called small caps.) Delete the remaining content controls.
17. Change the document theme to Facet. If you did not use a page number style for the page number in the footer, format the page number in the Green, Accent 1, Darker 25% font color.
18. Save, preview, and then close the document.

Create: Case Problem 2

Data File needed for this Case Problem: NP_WD_3-5.docx

Brisbane Scientific Services Noah Macleod manages pickups and delivery for Brisbane Scientific Services, a company that sells and repairs laboratory equipment. A customer service agent has just emailed him a list of new researchers at Mendota State University who will need regular deliveries. Noah asks you to create and format a table containing the list of researchers. When you're finished with that project, you'll create a table detailing some of his recent repair expenses in the garage that houses Brisbane's fleet of trucks.

Complete the following steps:

1. Open the document **NP_WD_3-5.docx** located in the Word3 > Case2 folder included with your Data Files, and then save it as **NP_WD_3_Mendota** in the location specified by your instructor.
2. In the blank paragraph below the "Mendota State University New Researchers" heading, create the table shown in Figure 3–50.

Figure 3–50 Mendota State University New Researchers table

Contact	Department	Phone
Sarah Heitkamp	Engineering	555-555-5555
Lorenzo Rossi	Chemistry	555-555-5555
Rishi Patel	Chemistry	555-555-5555
Rose Tulika	Plant Pathology	555-555-5555
Caitlin Choy	Physics	555-555-5555

3. For the table style, start with the Grid Table 4 - Accent 4 table style, make any necessary changes to match Figure 3–50, and then change the theme to one that uses TW Cen MT (Condensed) for the heading font and TW Cen MT for the body font, and that formats the heading row with the Green, Accent 4 shading color. (Note that the text in the heading row is formatted with the theme's body font, which means it is displayed in TW CEN MT after you change the theme.) The final table should be about 5 inches wide and about 1.5 inches tall, as measured on the horizontal and vertical rulers. (**Hint**: Remember that you can drag the Table Resize handle to increase the table's overall size.)
4. Replace "Sarah Heitkamp" with your first and last names.
5. In the blank paragraph below the "Garage Repair Expenses" heading, create the table shown in Figure 3–51, using the same table style and modifications you used for the new researchers table. Use a formula for the total with a number format that includes a dollar sign but no decimal places. (**Hint**: You can edit the number format in the Formula dialog box to delete both instances of a decimal place with two trailing zeros.) The final table should be about 5.5 inches wide and about 1 inch tall, as measured on the horizontal and vertical rulers.

Figure 3–51 Noah's garage repair expenses

Item	Date	Expense
Install LED Lighting	April 14	$3,450
Replace weather stripping	April 20	$350
Replace back door lock	April 23	$50
	TOTAL	$3,850

6. Save, preview, and then close the document.

Enhancing Page Layout and Design

Creating a Newsletter

Case: Barboza Family Health Clinics

Stefan Nowak is a communications specialist for Barboza Family Health Clinics. He has decided to begin publishing a monthly wellness newsletter with articles about exercise, nutrition, and other wellness topics. He has already written the text of the first newsletter. Now he needs you to transform the text into a professional publication with a headline, pictures, drop caps, and other desktop-publishing elements. Stefan's budget doesn't allow him to hire a professional graphic designer to create the document using desktop-publishing software. But there's no need for that because you can do the work for him using the formatting, graphics, and page layout tools in Word. After you finish the newsletter, Stefan wants you to ensure the document is accessible to all types of people and then save the newsletter as a PDF so he can email it to the printing company. You also need to review another document that is currently available only as a PDF.

Starting Data Files: Word4

Module
NP_WD_4-1.docx
Support_WD_4_DinnerTable.png
Support_WD_4_Exercise.docx
Support_WD_4_OnlineClasses.pdf
Support_WD_4_WordCloud.jpg

Review
NP_WD_4-2.docx
Support_WD_4_Produce.jpg
Support_WD_4_Online.docx
Support_WD_4_Sunflower.jpg

Case1
NP_WD_4-3.docx
Support_WD_4_Bike.png
Support_WD_4_Bin.png
Support_WD_4_Recycle.docx

Case2
(none)

Objectives

Part 4.1
- Use continuous section breaks to format a document
- Format text in columns
- Insert symbols and special characters
- Distinguish between inline and floating objects
- Wrap text around an object
- Insert and format text boxes
- Insert drop caps
- Create and modify WordArt

Part 4.2
- Crop a picture
- Insert online pictures and 3D models
- Mark a picture as decorative
- Rotate a picture
- Adjust and compress a picture
- Remove a picture's background
- Insert stock images, icons, and other illustrations
- Format an icon with a graphics style

Part 4.3
- Balance columns
- Add a custom paragraph border
- Check a document for accessibility
- Save a document as a PDF
- Open a PDF in Word

Part 4.1 Visual Overview: Elements of Desktop Publishing

This picture is an example of an **object**—that is, something you can manipulate independently of the text. The dinner table picture, the apple icon, the WordArt headline, and the text boxes are also objects. To edit an object, you first have to click it to select it.

This specially formatted text is an example of **WordArt**, which is created using the WordArt button in the Text group on the Insert tab.

This is a text box, which is like a mini document within a document.

This dinner table picture was inserted from a file, but you can also use the Online Pictures command on the Pictures menu to search for photos and other illustrations on the web.

Pictures and text boxes are separate from the document text; you need to adjust the way text flows, or **wraps**, around those elements. Here, the Tight text wrap option is used to make text flow as closely as possible around the shape of the dinner table image.

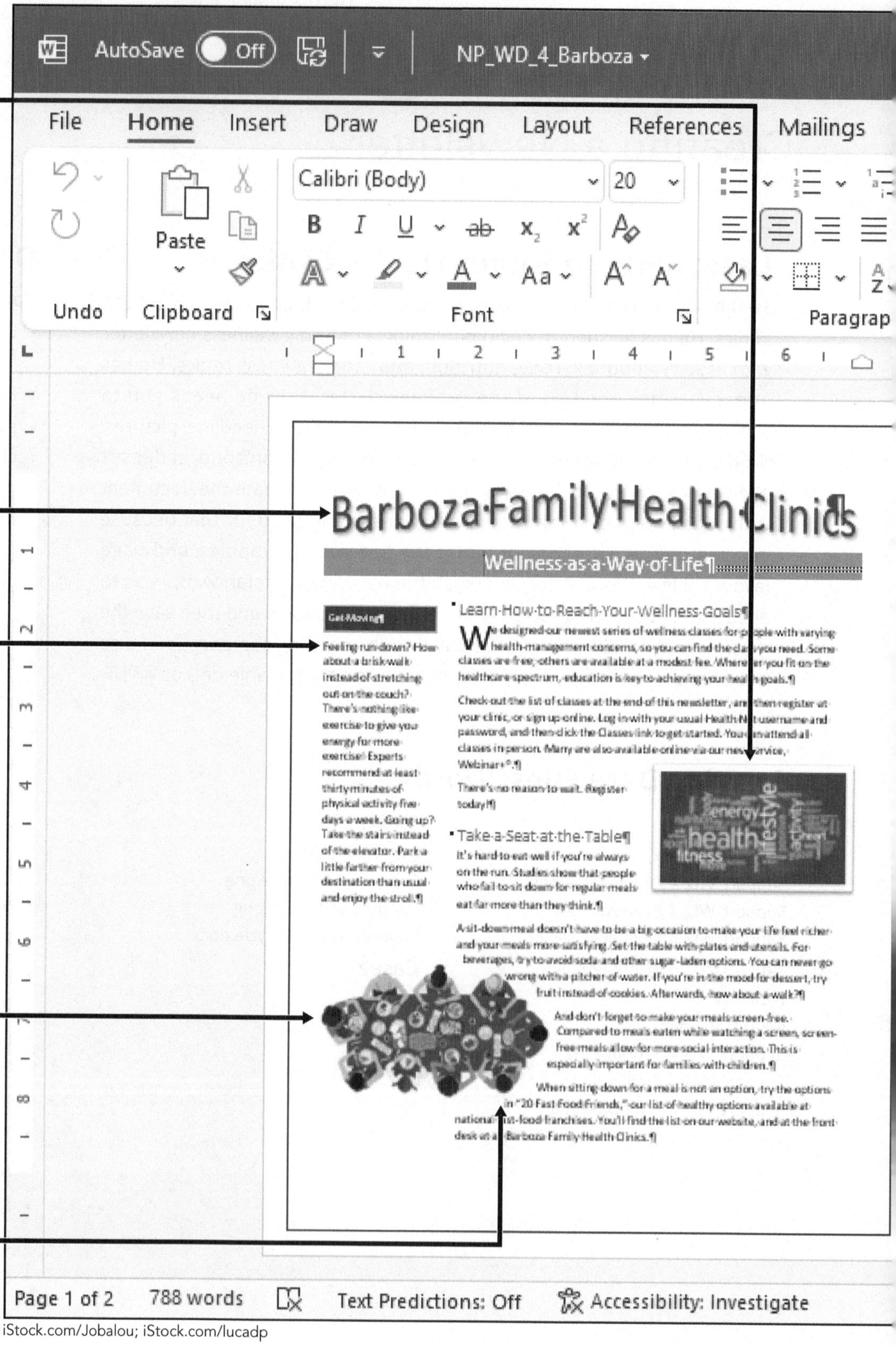

iStock.com/Jobalou; iStock.com/lucadp

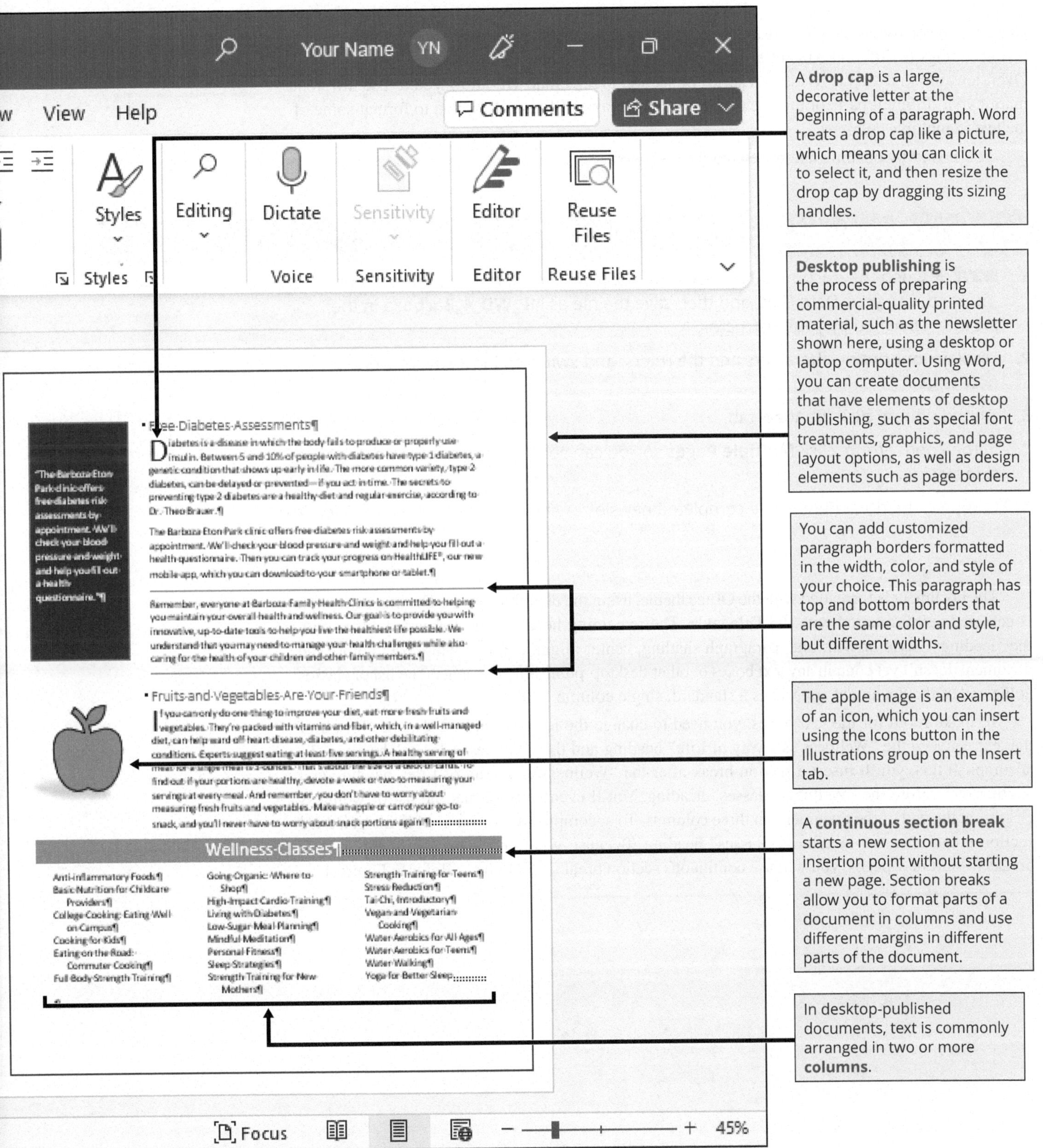
Your Name
YN
View
Help
Comments
Share
Styles
Editing
Dictate
Sensitivity
Editor
Reuse Files
Styles
Voice
Sensitivity
Editor
Reuse Files
Free Diabetes Assessments
Fruits and Vegetables Are Your Friends
Wellness Classes
Focus
45%
A **drop cap** is a large, decorative letter at the beginning of a paragraph. Word treats a drop cap like a picture, which means you can click it to select it, and then resize the drop cap by dragging its sizing handles.
Desktop publishing is the process of preparing commercial-quality printed material, such as the newsletter shown here, using a desktop or laptop computer. Using Word, you can create documents that have elements of desktop publishing, such as special font treatments, graphics, and page layout options, as well as design elements such as page borders.
You can add customized paragraph borders formatted in the width, color, and style of your choice. This paragraph has top and bottom borders that are the same color and style, but different widths.
The apple image is an example of an icon, which you can insert using the Icons button in the Illustrations group on the Insert tab.
A **continuous section break** starts a new section at the insertion point without starting a new page. Section breaks allow you to format parts of a document in columns and use different margins in different parts of the document.
In desktop-published documents, text is commonly arranged in two or more **columns**.

iStock.com/Jobalou; iStock.com/lucadp

Using Continuous Section Breaks to Enhance Page Layout

Newsletters and other desktop-published documents often incorporate multiple section breaks, with the various sections formatted with different margins, page orientations, column settings, and other page layout options. Continuous section breaks, which start a new section without starting a new page, are especially useful when creating a newsletter because they allow you to apply different page layout settings to different parts of a single page. To create the newsletter shown in Part 4.1 Visual Overview, the first step is to insert a series of section breaks that will allow you to use different margins for different parts of the document. Section breaks will also allow you to format some of the text in multiple columns.

You'll start by opening and reviewing the document.

To open and review the document:

1. sam Open the document **NP_WD_4-1.docx** from the Word4 > Module folder included with your Data Files, and then save the file as **NP_WD_4_Barboza** in the location specified by your instructor.
2. Display nonprinting characters and the rulers, and switch to Print Layout view, if necessary.
3. On the ribbon, click the **View** tab.
4. In the Zoom group, click **Multiple Pages** so you can see both pages of the document side by side.
5. Compare the document to the completed newsletter shown in Part 4.1 Visual Overview.

The document is formatted with the Office theme, using the default margins. The first paragraph is centered and formatted with the Title style. The remaining headings are formatted either with the Heading 1 style or with blue paragraph shading, center alignment, and white font color. The document doesn't yet contain any text boxes or other desktop-publishing elements. The list of classes at the end of the document appears as a standard, single column of text.

To make room for the text boxes, you need to change the left margin to 2.5 inches for all of the text between the "Wellness as a Way of Life" heading and the "Wellness Classes" heading. To accomplish this, you'll insert a section break after the "Wellness as a Way of Life" heading and another one before the "Wellness Classes" heading. You'll eventually format the list of wellness classes, at the end of the document, in three columns. To accomplish that, you need to insert a third section break after the "Wellness Classes" heading. Because you don't want any of the section breaks to start new pages, you will use continuous section breaks for all three. Refer to Figure 4–1.

Figure 4–1 Newsletter before adding section breaks

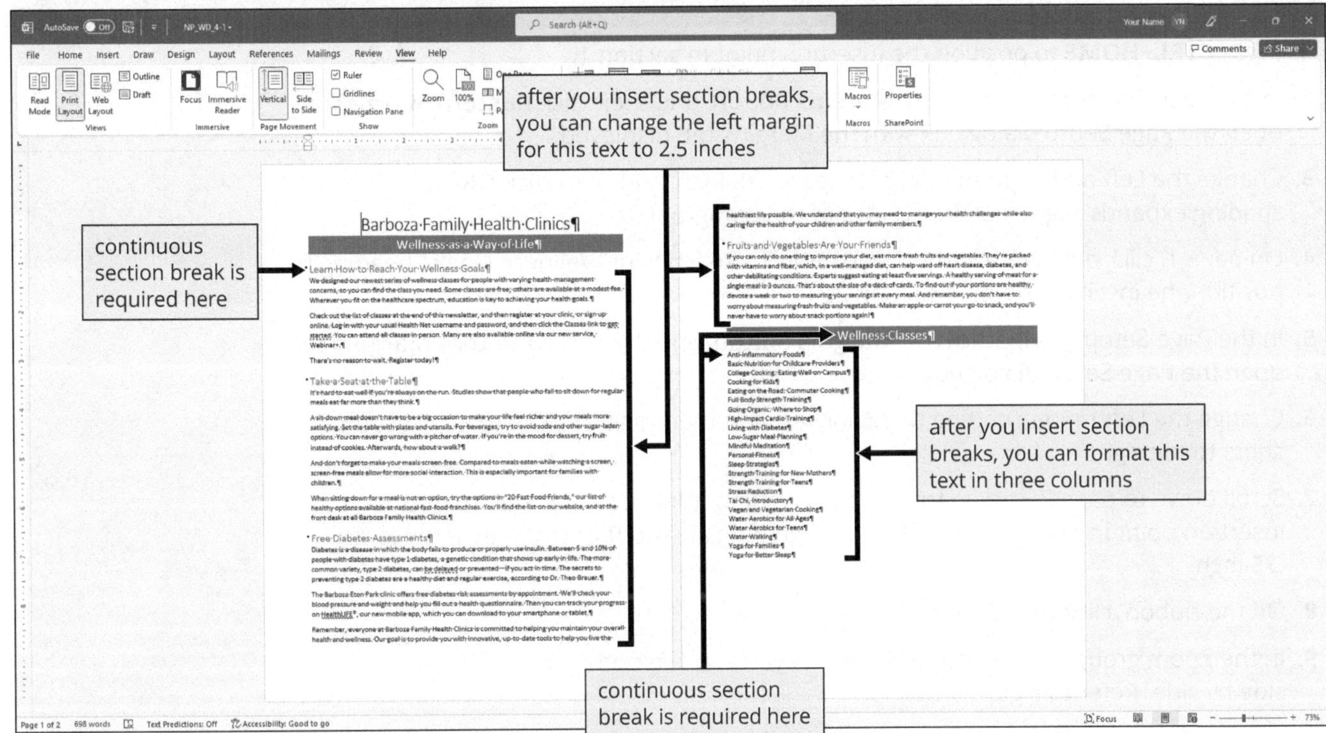

To insert continuous section breaks in the document:

1. Change the Zoom level to **120%**.
2. In the document, click at the beginning of the third paragraph, which contains the heading "Learn How to Reach Your Wellness Goals."
3. On the ribbon, click the **Layout** tab.
4. In the Page Setup group, click the **Breaks** button, and then click **Continuous**. The words "Section Break (Continuous)" with a dotted line on either side appears to the right of the "Wellness as a Way of Life" heading.
5. Scroll down to page 2, click at the beginning of the shaded paragraph "Wellness Classes," and then insert a continuous section break. A dotted line with the words "Section Break (Continuous)" appears at the end of the preceding paragraph.
6. Click at the beginning of the next paragraph, which contains the text "Anti-inflammatory Foods," and then insert a continuous section break. A dotted line with the words "Section Break (Continuous)" appears in the blue shading at the end of the preceding paragraph.

Now that you have created sections within the newsletter document, you can format the individual sections as if they were separate documents. In the following steps, you'll format the first and third sections by changing their left and right margins to .75 inch. You'll also format the second section by changing its left margin to 2.5 inches.

To set custom margins for sections 1, 2, and 3:

1. Press **CTRL+HOME** to position the insertion point in section 1.
2. In the Page Setup group, click the **Margins** button, and then click **Custom Margins** to open the Page Setup dialog box with the Margins tab displayed.
3. Change the Left and Right margin settings to **.75** inch, and then click **OK**. The blue shading expands slightly on both sides of the paragraph.
4. On page 1, click anywhere in the "Learn How to Reach Your Wellness Goals" heading to position the insertion point in section 2.
5. In the Page Setup group, click the **Margins** button, and then click **Custom Margins** to open the Page Setup dialog box.
6. Change the Left margin setting to **2.5** inches, and then click **OK**. The text in section 2 shifts to the right.
7. Scroll down to page 2, click in the shaded heading "**Wellness Classes**" to position the insertion point in section 3, and then change the Left and Right margin settings to **.75** inch.
8. On the ribbon, click the **View** tab.
9. In the Zoom group, click **Multiple Pages** so you can see both pages of the document side by side. Refer to Figure 4–2.

Figure 4–2 Sections 1, 2, and 3 with new margins

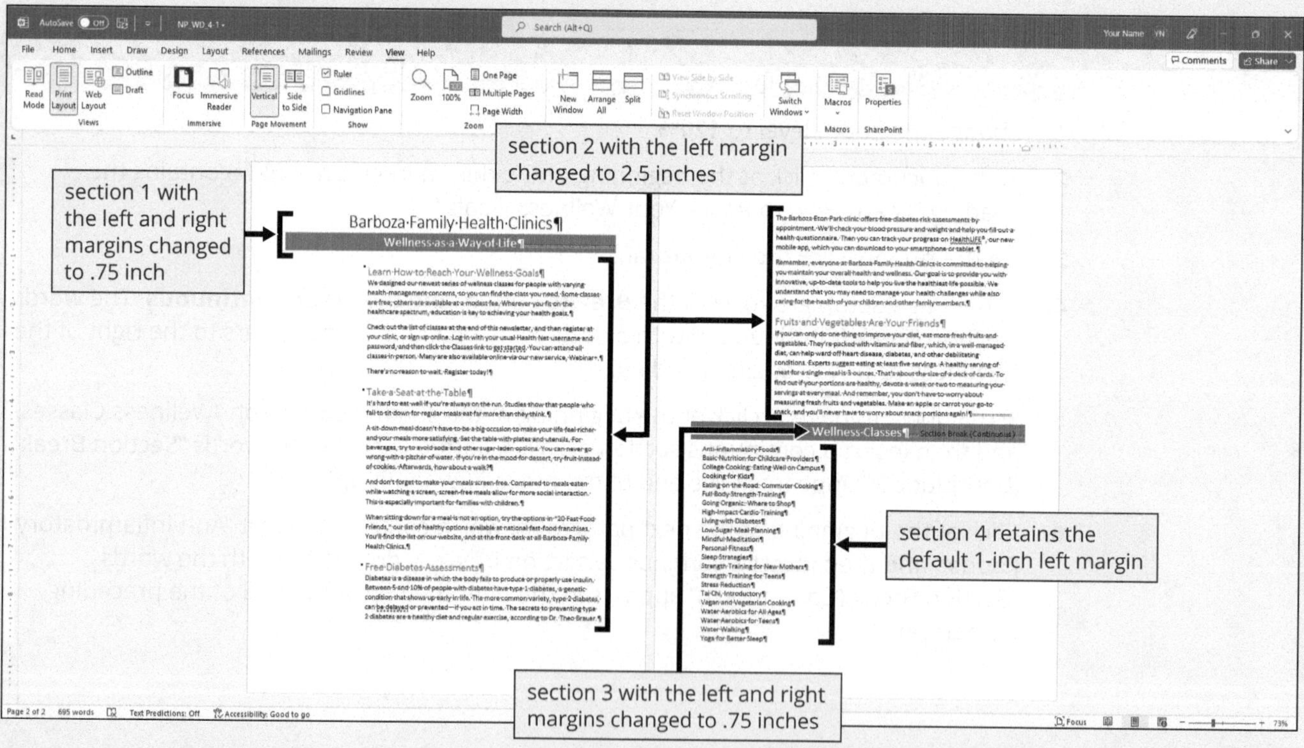

10. Save the document.

In addition to allowing you to format parts of a document with different margins, section breaks allow you to format part of a document in columns. You'll add some columns to section 4 next.

Formatting Text in Columns

Text meant for quick reading is often laid out in columns, with text flowing down one column, continuing at the top of the next column, flowing down that column, and so forth. To get started, click the Columns button in the Page Setup group on the Layout tab, and then click the number of columns you want in the Columns gallery. For more advanced column options, you can use the More Columns command to open the Columns dialog box. In this dialog box, you can adjust the column widths and the space between columns and choose to format either the entire document in columns or just the section that contains the insertion point.

> **Tip** When working with large amounts of text formatted in columns, it's helpful to hyphenate the document to avoid excessive white space caused by short lines. However, this is not an issue with the current document.

As shown in Part 4.1 Visual Overview, Stefan wants section 4 of the newsletter document, which consists of the wellness classes list, to be formatted in three columns.

To format section 4 in three columns:

1. Click anywhere in the list of wellness classes at the end of the document to position the insertion point in section 4.
2. On the ribbon, click the **Layout** tab.
3. In the Page Setup group, click the **Columns** button to display the Columns gallery. At this point, you could click Three to format section 4 in three columns of equal width. However, it's helpful to take a look at the columns dialog box so you can get familiar with some more advanced column options.
4. Click **More Columns** to open the Columns dialog box, and then in the Presets section, click **Three**. Refer to Figure 4–3.

Figure 4–3 Columns dialog box

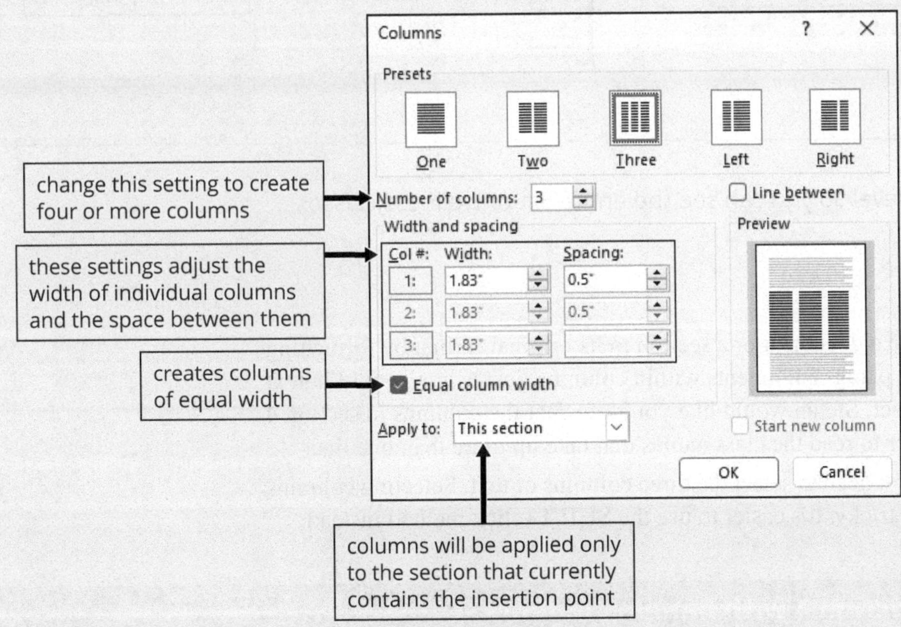

To format text in four or more columns, you can change the setting in the Number of columns box instead of selecting an option in the Presets section. By default, the Apply to box, in the lower-left corner, displays "This section," indicating that the three-column format will be applied only to the current section. To apply columns to the entire document, you could click the Apply to arrow and then click Whole document. To change the width of the individual columns or the spacing between the columns, you can use the settings in the Width and spacing section of the Columns dialog box.

5. Click **OK**. Section 4 is now formatted in three columns of the default width, although the third column is currently blank. This will change when you add more formatting elements to the newsletter. Refer to Figure 4–4.

Figure 4–4 Section 4 formatted in three columns

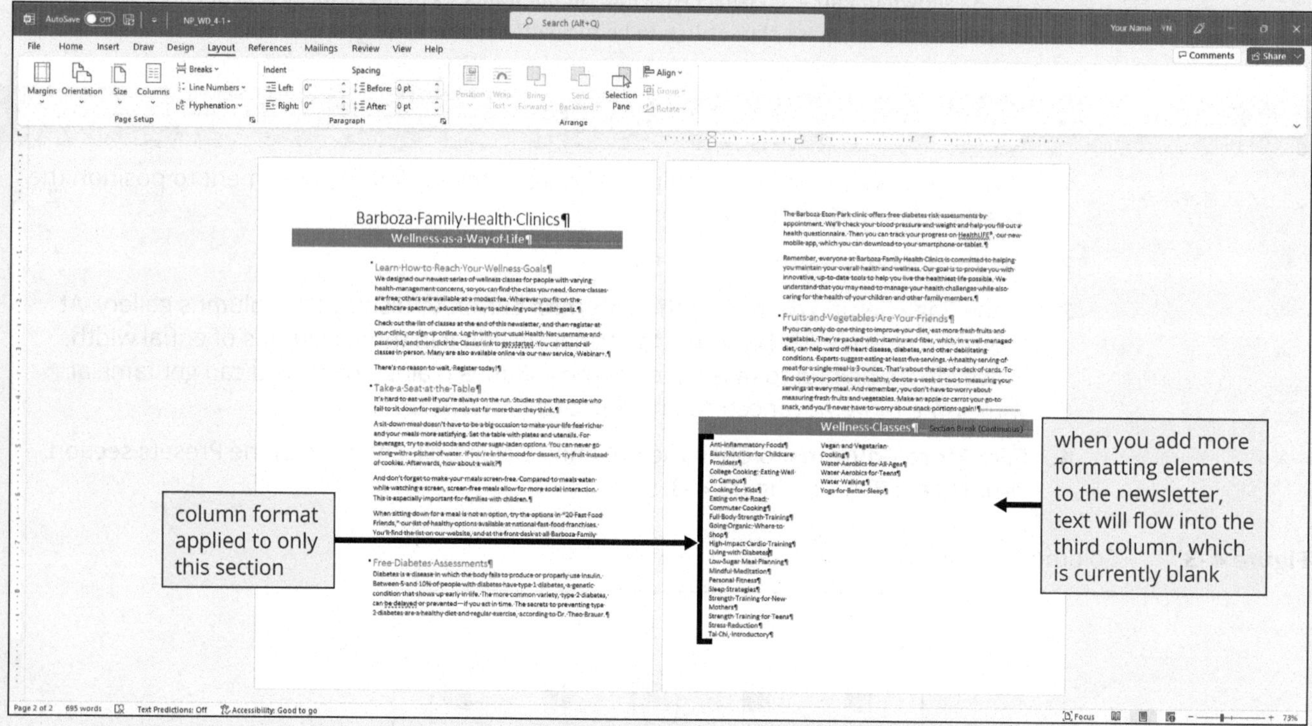

6. Change the document Zoom level so you can see the entire list of wellness classes, and then save the document.

Keep in mind that you can restore a document or a section to its original format by formatting it as one column. You can also adjust paragraph indents within columns, just as you would in text that is not formatted in columns. In fact, Stefan would like you to format the columns in section 4 with hanging indents so that it's easier to read the class names that take up more than one line.

To indent the class names, you first need to select the three columns of text. Selecting columns of text by dragging the mouse can be tricky. It's easier to use the SHIFT+click method instead.

To format the columns in section 4 with hanging indents:

1. Make sure the **Layout** tab is selected on the ribbon.
2. Click at the beginning of the first class name ("Anti-inflammatory Foods"), press and hold **SHIFT**, and then click at the end of the last class name ("Yoga for Better Sleep"). The entire list of wellness classes is selected.

3. In the Paragraph group, click the **Paragraph Dialog Box Launcher** to open the Paragraph dialog box with the Indents and Spacing tab displayed.
4. In the Indentation section, click the **Special** arrow, click **Hanging**, and then change the By setting to **0.2"**.
5. Click **OK** to close the Paragraph dialog box, and then click anywhere in the list to deselect it. The list of wellness classes is now formatted with a hanging indent, so the second line of each paragraph is indented .2 inches. Refer to Figure 4–5.

Figure 4–5 Text formatted in columns with hanging indent

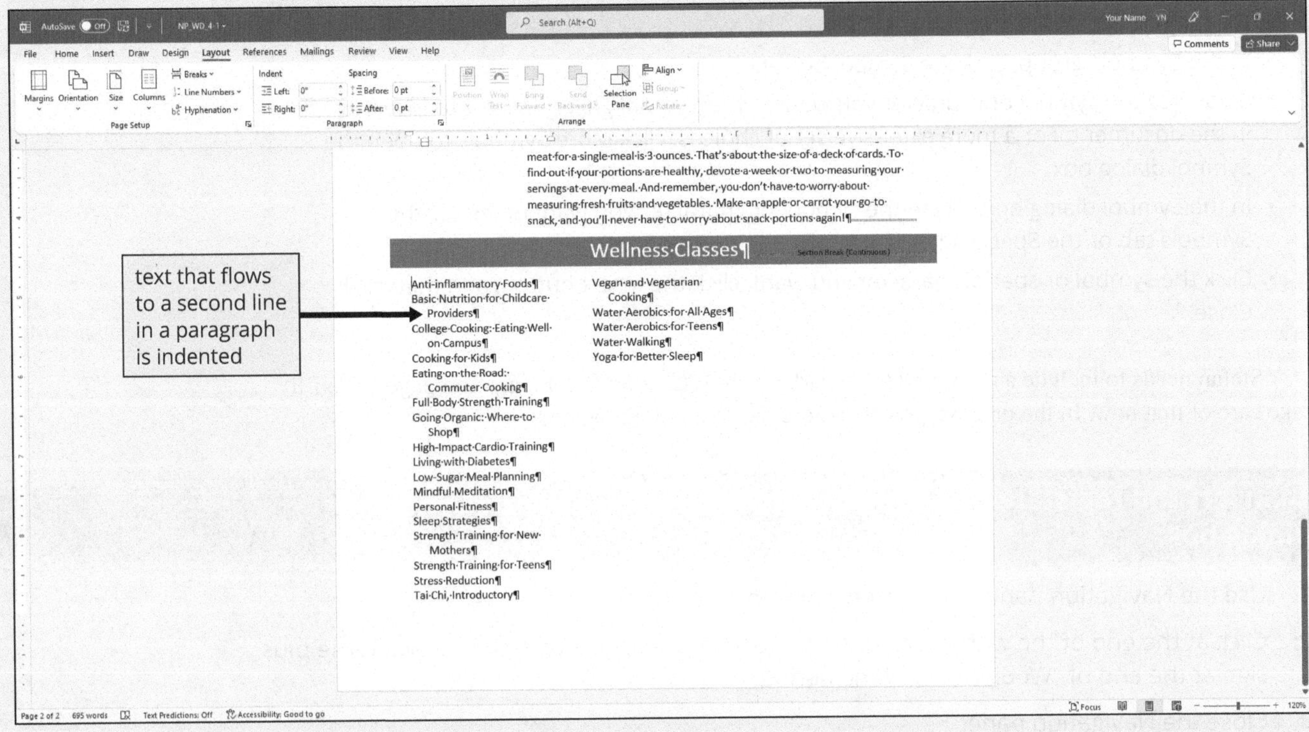

Inserting Symbols and Special Characters

When creating documents in Word, you can change some of the characters available on the standard keyboard into special characters or symbols called **typographic characters**. The AutoCorrect feature in Word automatically converts some standard characters into typographic characters as you type. In some cases, you need to press SPACEBAR and type more characters before Word inserts the appropriate typographic character. If Word inserts a typographic character that you don't want, you can click the Undo button to revert to the characters you originally typed. Refer to Figure 4–6.

Figure 4–6 Common typographic characters

To insert This Symbol or Character	Type	Word Converts To
Em dash	word--word	word—word
Smiley face	:)	😊
Copyright Symbol	(c)	©
Trademark symbol	(tm)	™
Registered trademark symbol	(r)	®
Fraction	1/2, 1/4	½, ¼
Arrows	<-- or -->	← or →

Most of the typographic characters in Figure 4–6 can also be inserted using the Symbol button on the Insert tab, which opens a gallery of commonly used symbols, and the More Symbols command, which opens the Symbol dialog box. The Symbol dialog box provides access to all the symbols and special characters you can insert into a Word document.

Reference

Inserting Symbols and Special Characters from the Symbol Dialog Box

- Move the insertion point to the location in the document where you want to insert a particular symbol or special character.
- On the ribbon, click the Insert tab.
- In the Symbols group, click the Symbol button.
- If you see the symbol or character you want in the Symbol gallery, click it to insert it in the document. For a more extensive set of choices, click More Symbols to open the Symbol dialog box.
- In the Symbol dialog box, locate the symbol or character you want on either the Symbols tab or the Special Characters tab.
- Click the symbol or special character you want, click the Insert button, and then click Close.

Stefan needs to include a registered trademark symbol (®) after "Webinar+" on page 1. You'll take care of that now. In the process, you'll explore the Symbol dialog box.

To insert the registered trademark symbol and explore the Symbol dialog box:

1. Use the Navigation pane to find **Webinar+** on page 1.
2. Click at the end of the word "Webinar+" to position the insertion point between the plus sign at the end of "Webinar+" and the period.
3. Close the Navigation pane.
4. Type **(r)**. AutoCorrect converts the "r" in parentheses into the superscript ® symbol.

   If you don't know which characters to type to insert a symbol or special character, you can review the AutoCorrect replacements in the AutoCorrect: English (United States) dialog box.
5. On the ribbon, click the **File** tab.
6. In the navigation pane, click **Options** to open the Word Options dialog box.
7. In the left pane, click **Proofing**, and then click the **AutoCorrect Options** button. The AutoCorrect: English (United States) dialog box opens, with the AutoCorrect tab displayed.
8. Review the table at the bottom of the AutoCorrect tab. The column on the left shows the characters you can type, and the column on the right shows what AutoCorrect inserts as a replacement. Refer to Figure 4–7.

Figure 4-7 AutoCorrect: English (United States) dialog box

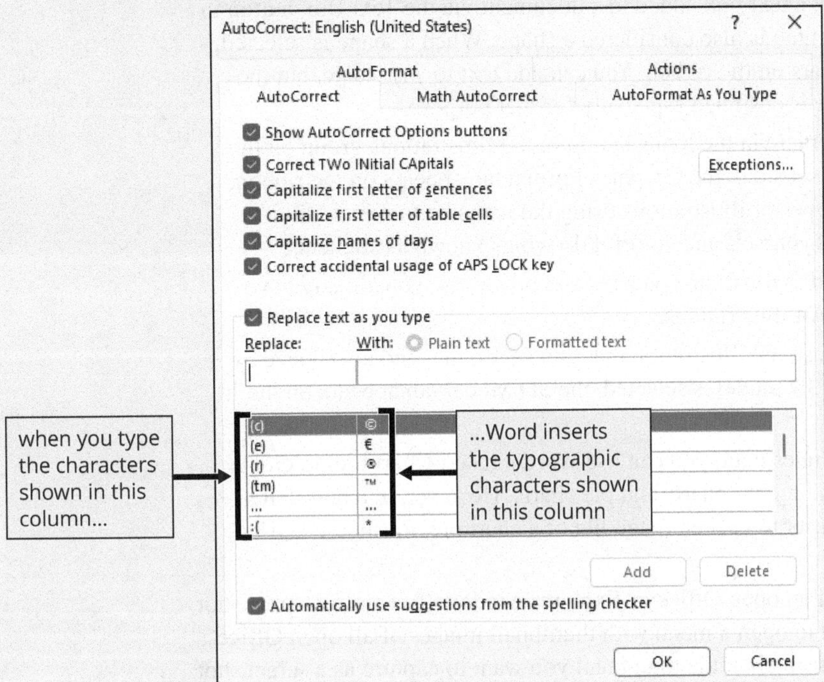

9. Scroll down to review the AutoCorrect replacements, click **Cancel** to close the AutoCorrect: English (United States) dialog box, and then click **Cancel** to close the Word Options dialog box.

   Now you can explore the Symbol dialog box, which offers another way to insert symbols and special characters.

10. On the ribbon, click the **Insert** tab.
11. In the Symbols group, click the **Symbol** button, and then click **More Symbols**. The Symbol dialog box opens with the Symbols tab displayed.
12. Scroll down the gallery of symbols on the Symbols tab to review the many symbols you can insert into a document. To insert one, you would click it, and then click the Insert button.
13. Click the **Special Characters** tab. The characters available on this tab are often used in desktop publishing. Notice the shortcut keys that you can use to insert many of the special characters.
14. Click **Cancel** to close the Symbol dialog box.

Introduction to Working with Objects

An object is something that you can manipulate independently of the document text. In desktop publishing, you will commonly work with two types of objects—illustrations and text objects. The starting point for adding these types of objects is the Insert tab.

People who work in online or print publishing often refer to illustrations as **graphic objects**, or simply **graphics**. However, Word has more specific vocabulary for the various types of illustrations, with separate contextual tabs for formatting each type. The following list summarizes the illustrations you can insert using the buttons in the Illustrations group on the Insert tab:

- **Picture**—An image stored as an electronic file, downloaded from a website or the Microsoft 365 library of stock images; when a picture is selected, the Picture Format contextual tab appears on the ribbon.

- **Shape**—A geometric object, like a rectangle or a circle, created using the Shapes command on the Insert tab; a text box added to a document via the Text Box button in the Text group on the Insert tab is also considered a shape. When a shape is selected, the Shape Format tab appears on the ribbon. You can add text to any shape, but the rectangular Text Box shape is designed especially for that purpose.
- **Icon**—A line drawing inserted via the Icons button in the Illustrations group on the Insert tab; when an icon is selected, the Graphics Format tab appears on the ribbon. You can also insert other types of illustrations using the Icons button, including cartoons that you can build yourself and colorful drawings known as stickers.
- **SmartArt**—Diagrams used to illustrate concepts and processes; you already have experience creating SmartArt illustrations.
- **3D model**—A three-dimensional illustration that you can rotate, and also resize by zooming in or out; when a 3D model is selected, the 3D Model tab appears on the ribbon.
- **Chart**—A graph that illustrates data; you can use Word's Insert Chart tool to create many kinds of charts, including bar charts and pie charts. However, in a newsletter, where space is tight, it's easier to use an image file of a chart previously created in Microsoft Excel.
- **Screenshot**—An image of an open Office or Explorer window. To create a screenshot, click the Screenshot button to open a menu with thumbnail images of all open Office or Explorer windows, and then click the thumbnail you want to capture as a screenshot. Word inserts the screenshot you choose at the insertion point in the document currently displayed on the screen. You can use the Screen Clipping command on the Screenshot menu to capture part of a screen, but it's typically easier to capture an entire screen, and then crop it to display only the part you want to focus on.

The following list summarizes some text objects you can insert in a document using the options in the Text group on the Insert tab:

- **Text box**—A preformatted rectangular shape, with shading and other features, to which you can add text.
- **WordArt**—Text in a text box that is formatted with text effects such as shadows and transformations that cause the text to bend or inflate.
- **Drop cap**—A large decorative letter that replaces the first letter of a paragraph.

Word treats illustrations and text objects as either inline or floating objects. Understanding the difference between inline and floating objects gives you the power to position them wherever you want on a page.

Distinguishing Between Inline and Floating Objects

An **inline object** behaves as if it were text. Like an individual letter, it has a specific location within a line of text, and its position changes as you add or delete text. You can align an inline object just as you would align text, using the alignment buttons in the Paragraph group on the Home tab. In a document consisting mostly of text, like a letter, inline objects are a good choice. However, in more complicated documents, inline objects are difficult to work with because every time you add or remove paragraphs of text, the object moves to a new position.

In contrast, you can position a **floating object** anywhere on the page, with the text flowing, or wrapping, around it. Unlike an inline object, which has a specific position in a line of text, a floating object has a more fluid connection to the document text. It is attached, or **anchored**, to an entire paragraph—so if you delete that paragraph, you will also delete the object. However, you can also move the object independently of that paragraph. An anchor symbol next to an object tells you that the object is a floating object rather than an inline object, as illustrated in Figure 4–8. As a general rule, you'll usually want to transform inline objects into floating objects, because floating objects are far more flexible.

Figure 4–8 An inline object compared to a floating object

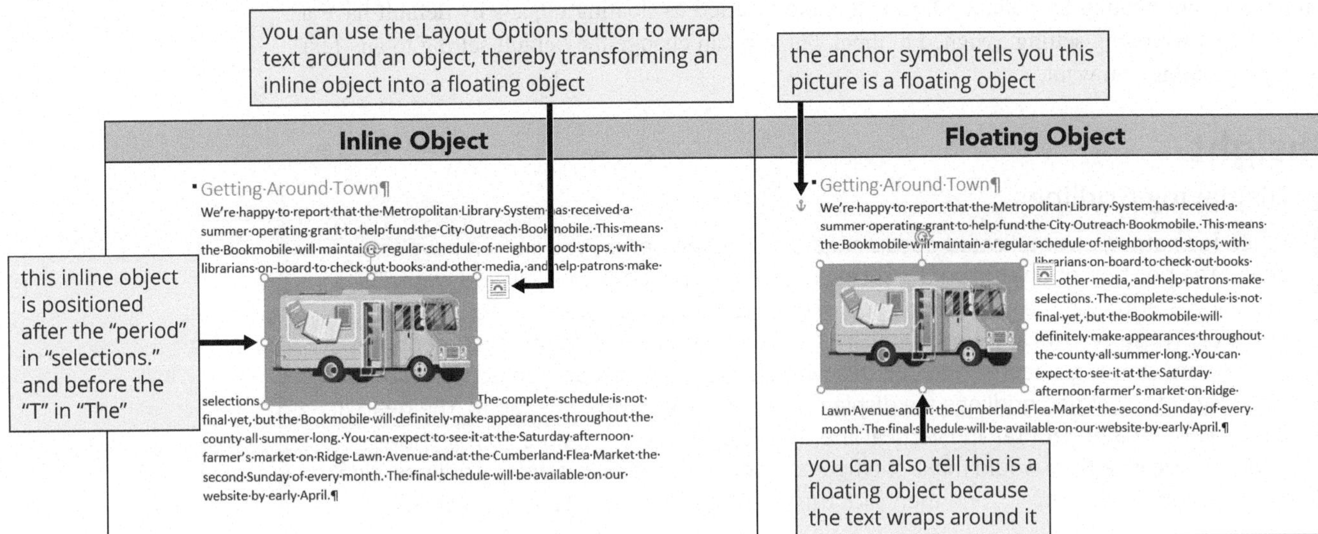

Mascha Tace/Shutterstock.com

Wrapping Text Around an Object

To transform an inline object into a floating object, you apply a **text wrapping setting** to it. First, click the object to select it, click the Layout Options button next to the object, and then click an option in the Layout Options gallery. For example, you can select Square text wrapping to make the text follow a square outline as it flows around the object, or you can select Tight text wrapping to make the text follow the shape of the object more exactly. Figure 4–9 describes the different types of wrapping. Note that you can also transform a floating object into an inline object by selecting the Inline with Text option in the Layout Options gallery.

Figure 4–9 Text wrapping options in the Layout Options gallery

Menu Icon	Type of Wrapping	Description
	In Line with Text	The object behaves as if it were text, and has a specific position within a paragraph. You can align inline objects using the alignment buttons on the Home tab, just as you would align text.
	Square	Text flows in a square outline around the object, regardless of the shape of the object; by default, Square text wrapping is applied to preformatted text boxes inserted via the Text Box button on the Insert tab.
	Tight	Text follows the exact outline of the object; if you want the text to flow around an object, this is usually the best option.
	Through	Text flows through the object, filling up any open areas; this type is similar to Tight text wrapping.
	Top and Bottom	Text stops above the object and then starts again below the object.
	Behind Text	The object is layered behind the text, with the text flowing over it.
	In Front of Text	The object is layered in front of the text, with the text flowing behind it; if you want to position an object in white space next to the text, this option gives you the greatest control over its exact position. By default, In Front of Text wrapping is applied to any shapes inserted via the Shapes button in the Illustrations group on the Insert tab.

Most illustrations, including photos and SmartArt, are inline by default; however, all text boxes and shapes are floating by default. Objects that are inserted as floating objects by default have a specific text wrapping setting assigned to them, but you can change the default setting to any text wrapping setting you want.

Insight

Displaying Gridlines

When formatting a complicated document such as a newsletter, you'll often have to adjust the position of objects on the page until everything looks the way you want. To make it easier to see the relative position of objects, you can display the document's gridlines. These vertical and horizontal lines are not actually part of the document.

They are simply guidelines you can use when positioning text and objects on the page. By default, when gridlines are displayed, objects align with, or snap to, the nearest intersection of a horizontal and vertical line. The figures in this module do not show gridlines because they would make the figures difficult to read. To display gridlines, click the View tab on the ribbon, and then click the Gridlines check box to insert a check.

Inserting Text Boxes

You can choose to add a preformatted text box shape to a document, or you can draw your own text box shape and adjust its appearance. Although some screen readers can read a text box formatted as an inline object, others will skip over those as well. For that reason, you need to think carefully about how you use text boxes in a document. You will learn more about this and other accessibility issues later in this module.

Reference

Inserting a Text Box

To insert a preformatted, rectangular text box, click in the document where you want to insert the text box.

- On the ribbon, click the Insert tab.
- In the Text group, click the Text Box button to open the Text Box gallery, and then click a text box style to select it.
- In the text box in the document, delete the placeholder text, type the text you want to include, and then format the text using the options on the Home tab.

or

- To insert and format your own rectangular text box, click the Insert tab on the ribbon.
- In the Illustrations group, click the Shapes button to open the Shapes gallery, and then click the Text Box icon.
- In the document, position the pointer where you want to insert the text box, press and hold the mouse button, and then drag the pointer to draw the text box.
- In the text box, type the text you want to include, and then format the text using the options on the Home tab.
- Format the text box using the options in the Shape Styles group on the Shape Format tab.

Inserting a Preformatted Text Box

The newsletter requires two text boxes. For the text box on page 1, you'll use the Text Box button in the Text group on the Insert tab. Text boxes inserted this way include placeholder text that you can replace with your own text. Preformatted text boxes come with preset font and paragraph options that are designed to match the text box's overall look. However, you can change the appearance of the text in the text box by using the options on the Home tab, just as you would for ordinary text. Many preformatted text boxes look good positioned alongside the main document text and are designed to be used as sidebars. A **sidebar** is typically used to draw attention to important information.

To insert a preformatted text box in the document:

1. Scroll up to the top of page 1, and then click anywhere in the "Learn How to Reach Your Wellness Goals" heading.
2. Change the Zoom level to **Multiple Pages** so you can see both pages of the document.
3. On the ribbon, click the **Insert** tab.
4. In the Text group, click the **Text Box** button to display the Text Box gallery, and then use the scroll bar to scroll down the gallery to locate the Ion Sidebar 1 text box.
5. Click **Ion Sidebar 1**. The text box is inserted in the left margin of page 1. Refer to Figure 4–10.

Figure 4–10 Text box inserted on page 1

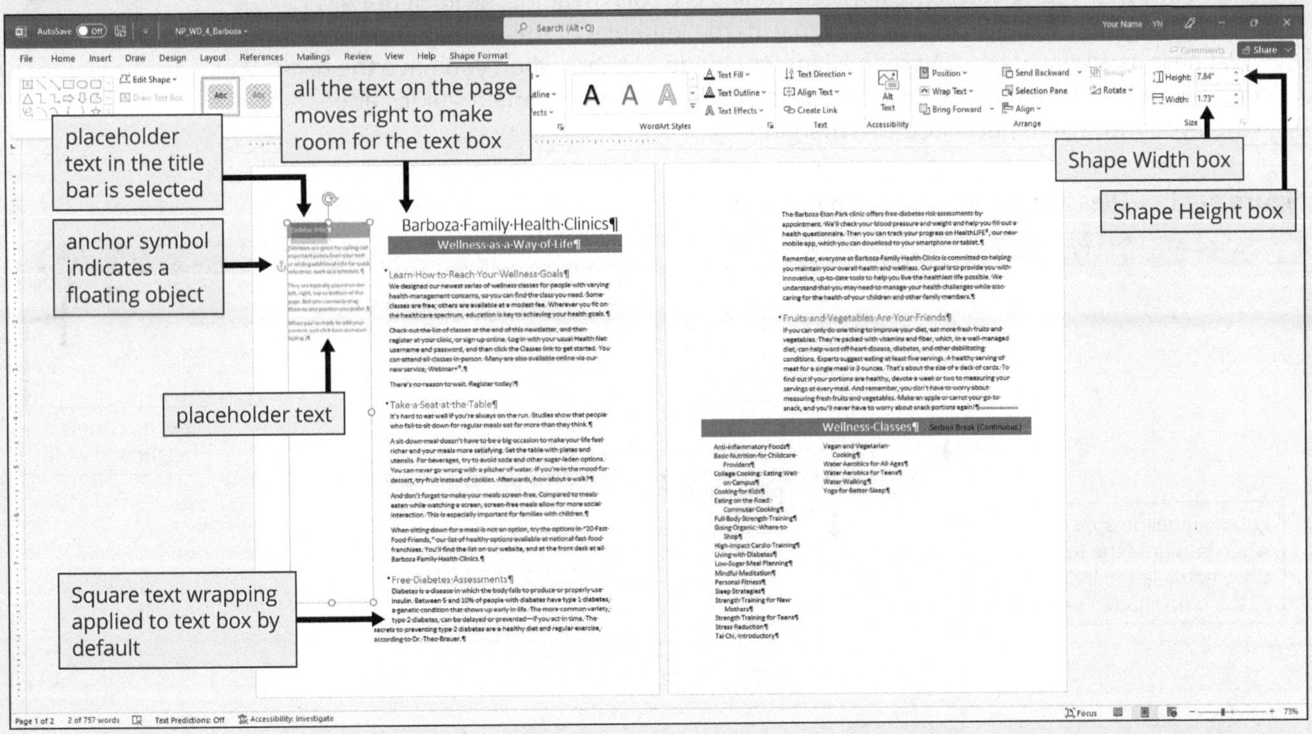

Most of the text on page 1 moves right to make room for the text box because Square text wrapping is applied to the text box by default. Later, after you resize and move the text box, the first two paragraphs will resume their original positions, centered at the top of the page. The anchor symbol next to the text box tells you it is a floating object.

The text box consists of a blue title box at the top that contains placeholder text, with additional placeholder text below the title bar. The dotted outline with sizing handles indicates the borders of the text box. When you first insert a text box, the placeholder text in the title box is selected, ready for you to type your own title. In this case, however, before you add any text, you'll resize and reposition the text box.

6. On the ribbon, click the **Shape Format** tab, if necessary.
7. In the Size group, click the **Shape Height** box, type **4**, click the **Shape Width** box, type **1.5**, and then press **ENTER**. The text box is now shorter and narrower.
8. Change the Zoom level to **120%**.

   Next, you need to drag the text box down below the first two paragraphs. To make this easier, you will make use of Word's alignment guides to help you position the text box. You will verify that those guides are turned on next.
9. Click the **Shape Format** contextual tab if necessary, and then, in the Arrange group, click the **Align** button, and then click **Use Alignment Guides**, if necessary, to insert a check, or, if it is already checked, press **ESC** to close the menu. Now you are ready to move the text box, but first you need to select the entire text box. Currently, only the placeholder text in the text box title bar is selected.
10. Position the pointer somewhere over the text box border until the pointer changes to ✥.
11. Click the **text box border** to select the entire text box. The text box border changes from dotted to solid, and the Layout Options button appears to the right of the text box.
12. With the pointer positioned over the border, press and hold the **mouse button**, and then drag the text box down so that the top of the text box aligns with the first line of text below the "Learn How to Reach Your Wellness Goals" heading, as in Figure 4–11. The left edge of the text box should align with the left edge of the blue-shaded heading "Wellness as a Way of Life." A green alignment guide appears when you have the text box aligned with the left edge of the blue-shaded heading. Alignment guides appear when you move an object close to a margin.

Figure 4–11 Resized and repositioned text box

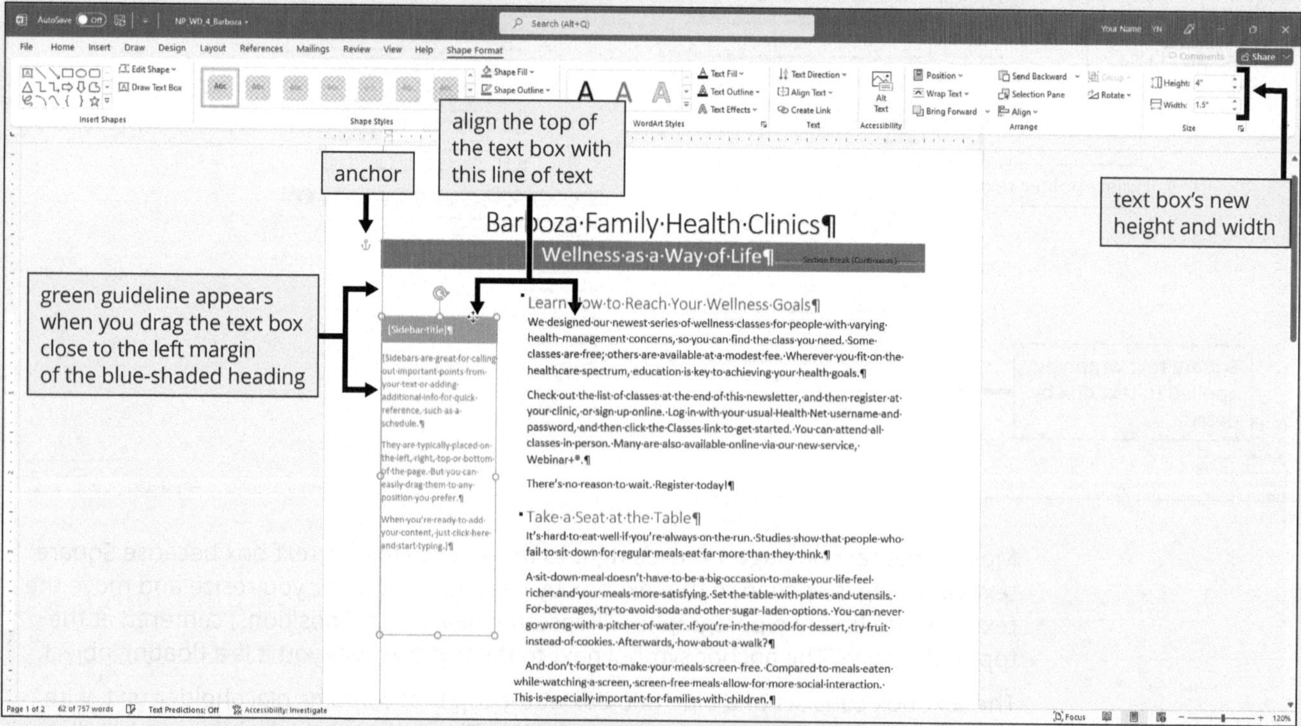

13. Release the mouse button.

After you insert a text box or other object, you usually need to adjust its relationship to the surrounding text; that is, you need to adjust its text wrapping setting.

Changing the Text Wrapping Setting for the Text Box

A preformatted text box inserted via the Text Box button on the Insert tab is, by default, a floating object formatted with Square text wrapping. You will verify this when you open the Layout Options gallery in the following steps. Then you'll select the In Front of Text option instead to gain more control over the exact position of the text box on the page.

To open the Layout Options gallery and change the wrapping option:

1. If necessary, drag the anchor icon to position it to the left of the blue-shaded paragraph containing the heading "Wellness as a Way of Life."
2. Click the **Layout Options** button. The Layout Options gallery opens with the Square option selected. Refer to Figure 4–12.

Figure 4–12 Square text wrapping currently applied to text box

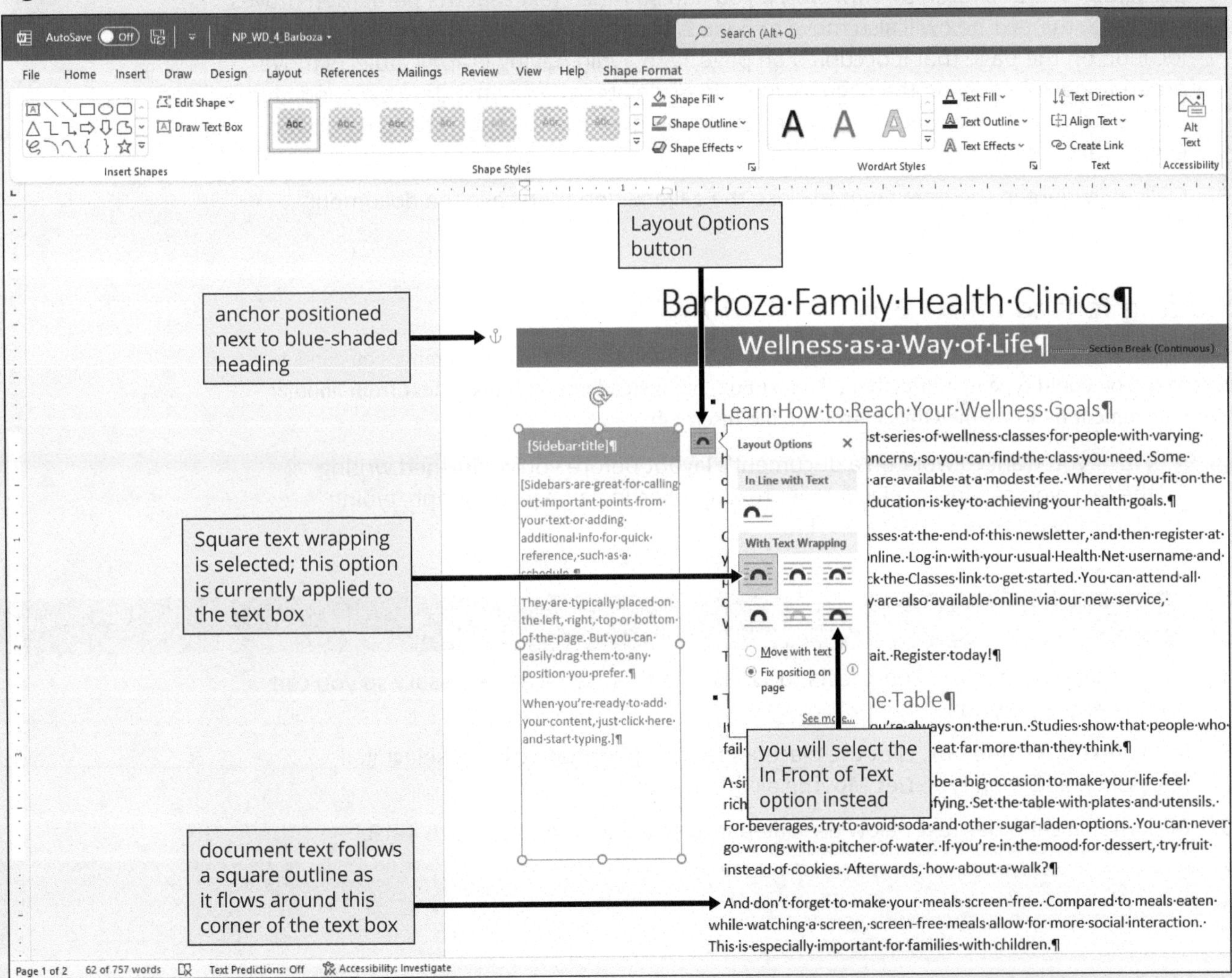

Square text wrapping is currently applied to the text box. You can see evidence of Square text wrapping where the document text flows around the lower-right corner of the text box. You'll have a chance to see some more dramatic examples of text wrapping later in this module, but it's important to be able to identify subtle examples of it.

3. Click any of the other options in the Layout Options gallery and observe how the document text and the text box shift position. Continue exploring the Layout Options gallery, trying out several of the options.
4. Click the **In Front of Text** option, and then click the **Close** button in the upper-right corner of the Layout Options gallery to close the gallery. The document text shifts so that it now flows directly down the left margin, without wrapping around the text box.

   Your next formatting task is to make sure the text box is assigned a fixed position on the page. You could check this setting using the Layout Options button, but you'll instead use the Wrap Text button in the Arrange group on the Shape Format tab to get some practice with that option.
5. On the ribbon, click the **Shape Format** tab, if necessary.
6. In the Arrange group, click the **Wrap Text** button. The Wrap Text menu gives you access to all the options in the Layout Options gallery, plus some more advanced settings.
7. Verify that **Fix Position on Page** has a checkmark next to it. This setting helps ensure that the text box will remain in its position on page 1, even if you add text above the paragraph it is anchored to. However, if you add so much text that the paragraph moves to page 2, the text box will also move to page 2, but it will be positioned in the same location on the page that it occupied on page 1. To avoid having graphic objects move around unexpectedly on the page as you add or delete other elements, it's a good idea to check this setting either in the Wrap Text menu or in the Layout Options menu for every graphic object.
8. Click anywhere in the document to close the gallery, and then save the document.

Adding Text to a Text Box

Now that the text box is positioned where you want it, with the correct text wrapping, you can add text to it. You could type text directly in the text box, but instead you will insert text from another Word document by using the Object arrow on the Insert tab.

> **Tip** If you want to work on a document's layout before you've finished writing the text, you can insert placeholder text by inserting a new paragraph, typing =lorem() and then pressing ENTER.

To insert text in the text box:

1. If necessary, change the Zoom level to **120%**, and then scroll as necessary so you can see the entire text box.
2. In the text box's title box, click the placeholder text **[Sidebar title]** to select it, if necessary, and then type **Get Moving** as the new title.
3. Click the placeholder text below the title bar to select it. Refer to Figure 4–13.

Figure 4–13 Text box with placeholder text selected

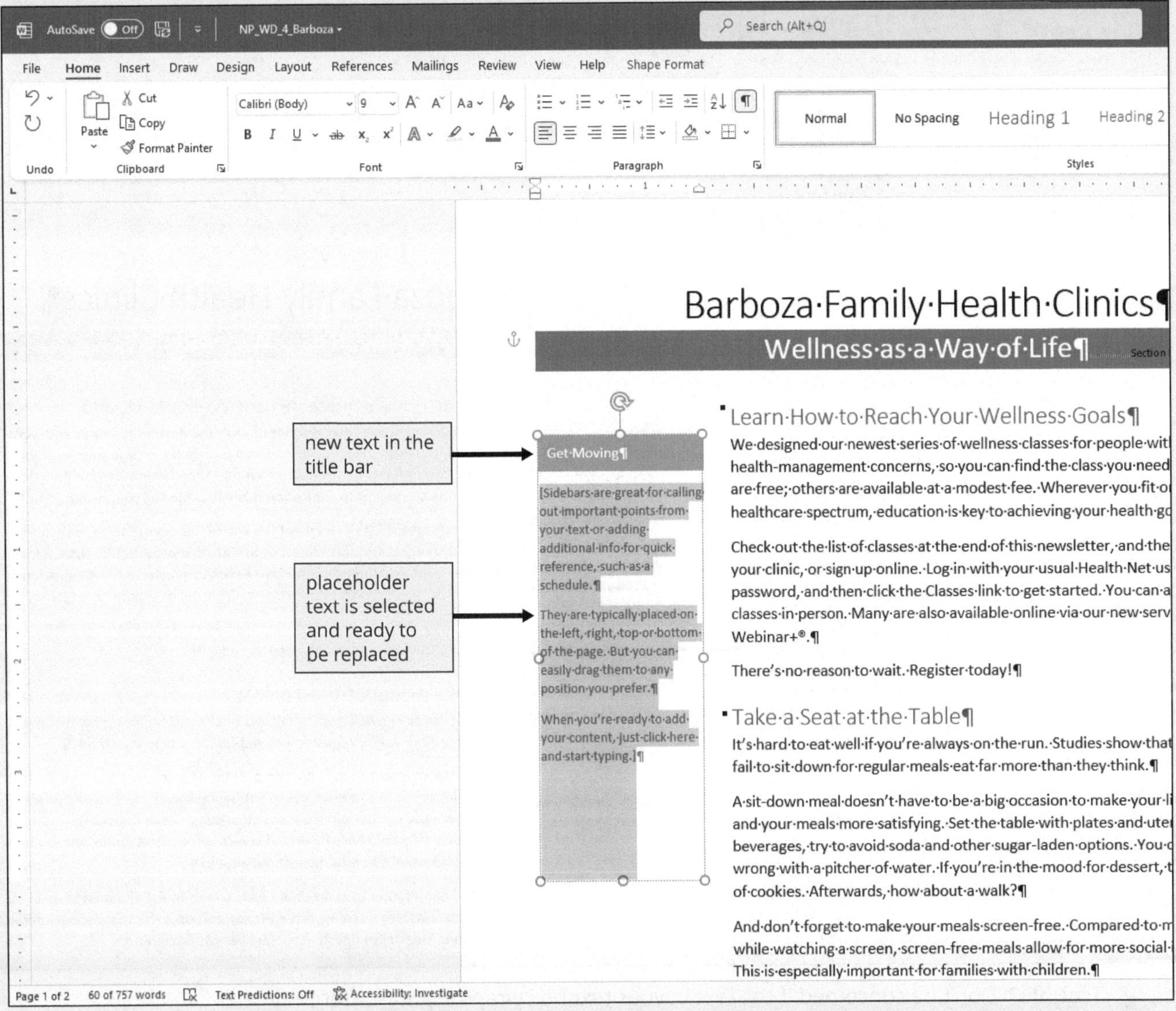

4. Press **DELETE** to delete the placeholder text. Now you can insert new text from another Word document.
5. On the ribbon, click the **Insert** tab.
6. In the Text group, click the **Object arrow** to open the Object menu, and then click **Text from File**. The Insert File dialog box opens. Selecting a Word document to insert is just like selecting a document in the Open dialog box.
7. Navigate to the **Word4 > Module** folder, click **Support_WD_4_Exercise.docx** to select the file, and then click the **Insert** button. The article about getting more exercise is inserted directly into the text box. The inserted text was formatted in 9-point Calibri in the Support_WD_4_Exercise.docx document, and it retains that formatting when you paste it into the newsletter document. To make the text easier to read, you'll increase the font size to 11 points.
8. With the insertion point located in the last paragraph in the text box (which is blank), press **BACKSPACE** to delete the blank paragraph, and then click and drag the pointer to select all the text in the text box, including the title in the shaded title box.
9. On the ribbon, click the **Home** tab.
10. In the Font group, click the **Font Size** arrow, and then click **11**. The size of the text in the text box increases to 11 points. Refer to Figure 4–14.

Figure 4–14 Text inserted in text box

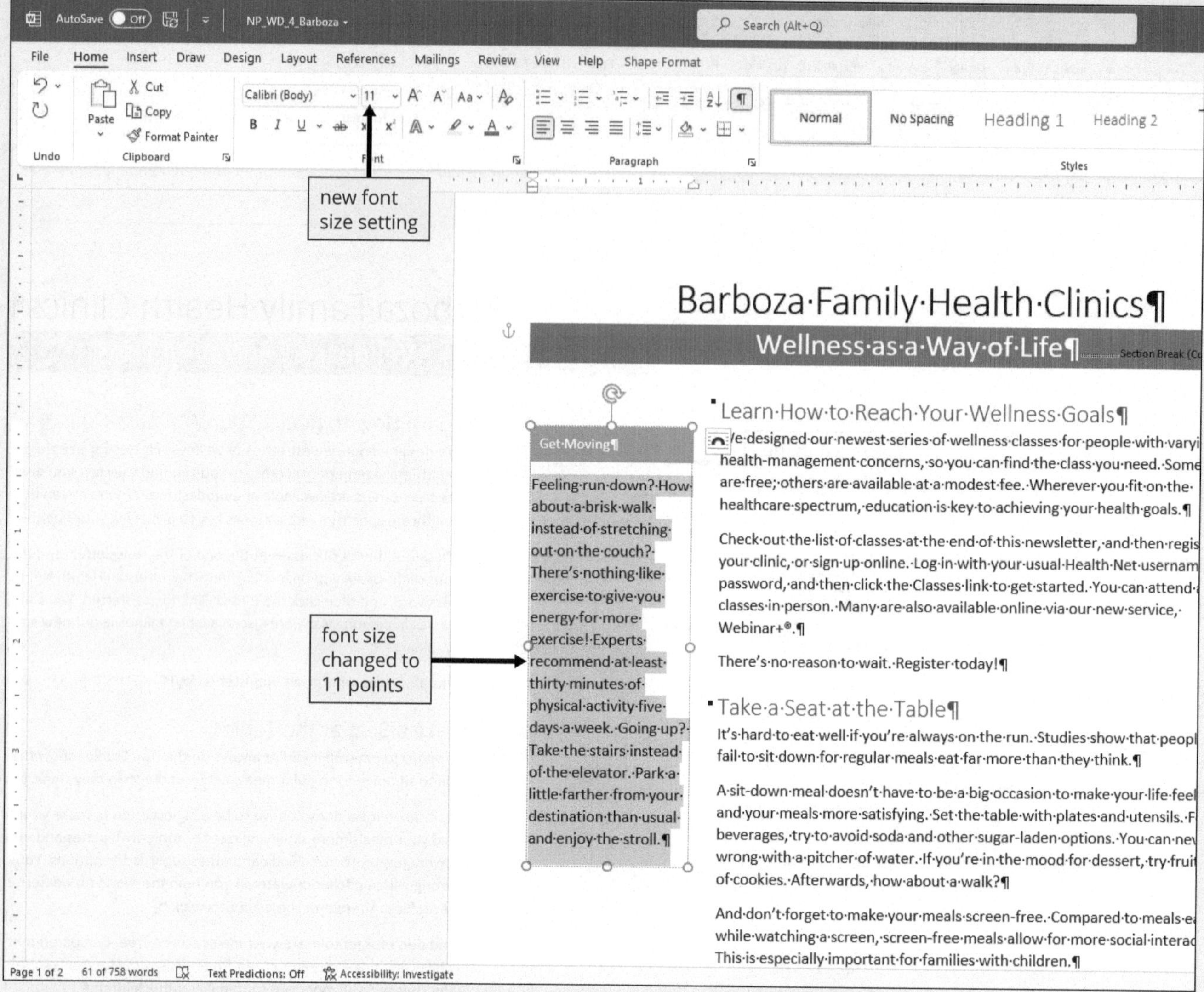
new font size setting
font size changed to 11 points
Barboza·Family·Health·Clinics¶
Wellness·as·a·Way·of·Life¶
Get·Moving¶
Feeling·run·down?·How·about·a·brisk·walk·instead·of·stretching·out·on·the·couch?·There's·nothing·like·exercise·to·give·you·energy·for·more·exercise!·Experts·recommend·at·least·thirty·minutes·of·physical·activity·five·days·a·week.·Going·up?·Take·the·stairs·instead·of·the·elevator.·Park·a·little·farther·from·your·destination·than·usual·and·enjoy·the·stroll.¶
Learn·How·to·Reach·Your·Wellness·Goals¶
Take·a·Seat·at·the·Table¶

Trouble? Don't be concerned if the text in your text box wraps slightly differently from the text shown in Figure 4–14. The same fonts can vary slightly from one computer to another, causing slight differences in the way text wraps within and around text boxes.

11. Click anywhere outside the text box to deselect it, and then save the document.

The first text box is complete. Now you need to add one more on page 2. As you saw in Part 4.1 Visual Overview, the second text box will have a different look from the first one. You can draw it using the Text Box option on the Shapes menu.

Drawing and Formatting a Text Box Using the Shapes Menu

If you don't like the preformatted text box options available via the Text Box button in the Text group on the Insert tab, you can use the Shapes button in the Illustrations group to draw an unformatted text box and then adjust its appearance by using the Shape Styles options on the Shape Format tab. You can type any text you want inside the text box at the insertion point. When you are finished, you can format the text using the options on the Home tab, just as you would ordinary text.

While text boxes are typically rectangular, you can turn any shape into a text box. Start by using the Shapes button to draw a shape of your choice, and then, with the shape selected, type any text you want. You won't see an insertion point inside the shape, but you can still type text inside it and then format it. You can format the shape itself by using the Shape Styles options on the Shape Format tab. Stars and circles can make especially dramatic text boxes for flyers or posters.

To draw and format a text box:

1. Scroll down to display the top of page 2 and click anywhere in the paragraph that begins "Remember, everyone at Barboza Family Health Clinics...".
2. On the ribbon, click the **Insert** tab.
3. In the Illustrations group, click the **Shapes** button to display the Shapes gallery. Refer to Figure 4–15.

Figure 4–15 Shapes gallery

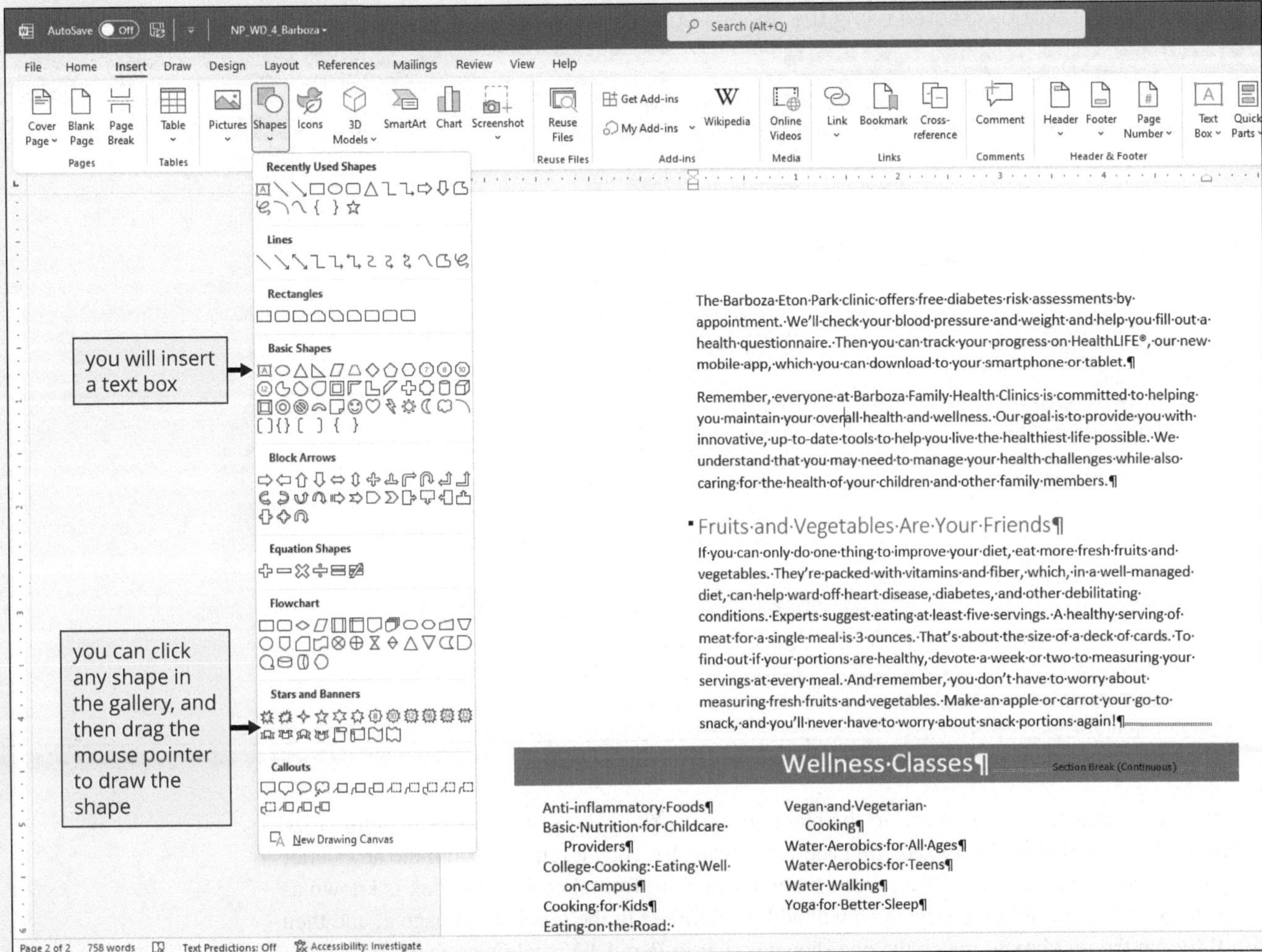

At this point, you could click any shape in the gallery, and then drag the pointer in the document to draw that shape. Then, after you finish drawing the shape, you could start typing in the selected shape to insert text.

4. In the Basic Shapes section of the Shapes gallery, click the **Text Box** icon. The gallery closes, and the pointer turns into a black cross.
5. Position the pointer in the blank area in the left margin, aligned with the first line of text on page 2, and then click and drag down and to the right to draw a text box approximately 1.5 inches wide and 2.5 inches tall. When you are satisfied with the text box, release the mouse button.

   Don't be concerned about the text box's exact dimensions or position on the page. For now, just make sure it fits in the blank space to the left of the last two paragraphs on the page.

   The new text box is selected, with sizing handles on its border and the insertion point blinking inside. The Layout Options button is visible, and the text box's anchor symbol is visible either next to the top paragraph of text on the page or next to the upper-left corner of the text box.

6. Use the Shape Height and Shape Width boxes on the Shape Format tab to set the height to **3.5** inches and the width to **1.5** inches.
7. Drag the text box as necessary to align its top border with the first line of text on the page. By default, a shape is always anchored to the nearest paragraph that begins above or next to the shape's top border. It doesn't matter if the paragraph is located to the shape's left or right. Note that as you add additional elements to page 1, the text on page 2 will change position. When you are finished adding elements to the newsletter, you'll need to review it and make any necessary adjustments to account for the text's final location. Refer to Figure 4–16.

Figure 4–16 Text box created using the Shapes button

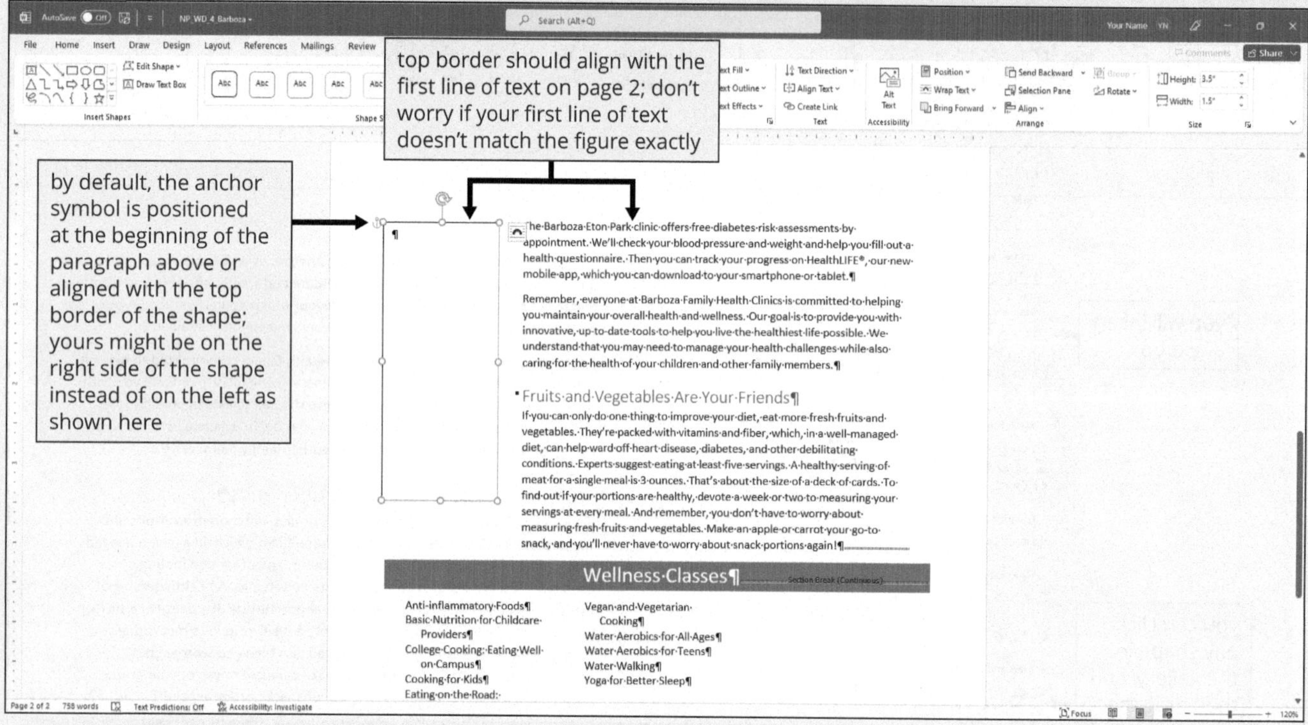

Now you need to add some text to the blank text box. You can use text boxes to summarize information, as you did in the text box on page 1. You can also copy a sentence from the newsletter and paste it into the text box. A direct quote from a document formatted in a text box is known as a **pull quote**. In the following steps, you will add a pull quote to the text box on page 2, and then you'll format the text box to match the one shown earlier in Part 4.1 Visual Overview.

To copy text from the newsletter and paste it into the text box:

1. Select the first two sentences in the paragraph that begins "The Barboza Eton Park clinic offers..." The complete selection should read: "The Barboza Eton Park clinic offers free diabetes risk assessments by appointment. We'll check your blood pressure and weight and help you fill out a health questionnaire."
2. Press **CTRL+C** to copy the selected text to the Office Clipboard.
3. Click in the blank text box, and then press **CTRL+V** to paste the copied sentence into the text box. The newly inserted sentence is formatted in 11-point Calibri, just as it was in the main document.
4. Add quotation marks at the beginning and end of the text, so it's clear the text box is a pull quote. Your next task is to center the sentence between the top and bottom borders of the text box. Then you'll add some color.
5. On the ribbon, click the **Shape Format** tab, if necessary.

6. In the Text group, click the **Align Text** button to display the Align text menu, and then click **Middle**. The text is now centered between the top and bottom borders of the text box. Next, you need to change the text's font color and add a background color. But first you'll make sure the text box is positioned so that you can see a Live Preview when you open the Shape Styles gallery.

> **Tip** Note that you can use the Text Direction button in the Text group to rotate text within a text box.

7. Scroll down, if necessary, so that the bottom of the text box is positioned just above the bottom of the Word screen.
8. In the Shape Styles group, click the **More** button to display the Shape Styles gallery. Like the text styles you have used to format text, shape styles allow you to apply a collection of formatting options, including font color and shading, with one click.
9. Move the pointer over the various options in the Shape Styles gallery and observe the Live Previews in the document. If your monitor is too small to allow you to see the Live Previews, that's fine. Just continue with these steps.
10. When you are finished, position the pointer over the **Colored Fill - Blue, Accent 5** style, which is a blue box, the second from the right in the second row. Refer to Figure 4–17.

Figure 4–17 Shape Styles gallery

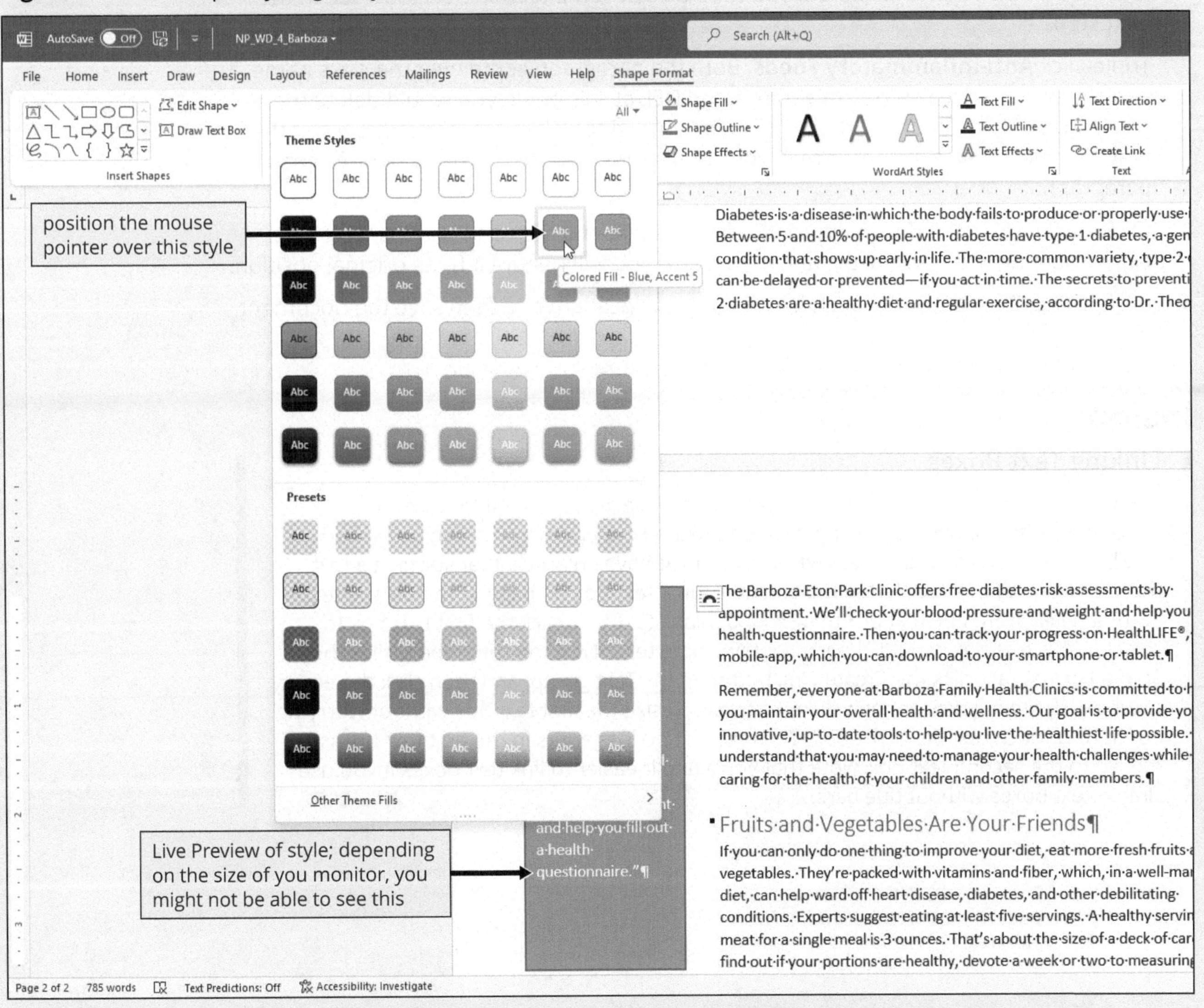

11. In the Shape Styles gallery, click the **Colored Fill - Blue, Accent 5** style. The style is applied to the text box, and the Shape Styles gallery closes.

Now, you need to make sure the text box is located in a fixed position on the page. In the following steps, you'll also experiment with the text box's anchor symbol. It's important to understand the role the anchor symbol plays in the document's overall layout.

To fix the text box's position on the page and experiment with the anchor symbol:

1. Verify that the text box is still selected, with the Shape Format tab displayed on the ribbon.
2. In the Arrange group, click the **Wrap Text** button. A checkmark appears next to Move with Text because that is the default setting for shapes.
3. Click **Fix Position on Page** to add a checkmark and close the Wrap Text menu.
4. Scroll up if necessary to display the beginning of the list of classes.
5. Reduce the Zoom setting if necessary so that you can see the text box's anchor and the beginning of the list of classes on the same screen.
6. Drag the text box's anchor down to the list of wellness classes and position it to the left of the first class in the list ("Anti-inflammatory Foods"). If you select the entire paragraph to which the text box is anchored, you will also select the text box, as you'll see in the next step.
7. Triple-click **Anti-inflammatory Foods**. Both the paragraph containing the class name and the text box are selected. If you pressed DEL at this point, you would delete the paragraph of text and the text box. If you ever need to delete a paragraph but not the graphic object that is anchored to it, you should first drag the anchor to a different paragraph.
8. Click anywhere in the document to deselect the text and the text box. You were just experimenting with moving the anchor, so now you will restore it to its original position.
9. Press **CTRL+Z** to return the anchor to its original location, and then save the document.

Insight

Linking Text Boxes

If you have a large amount of text that you want to place in different locations in a document, with the text continuing from one text box to another, you can use linked text boxes. For example, in a newsletter, you might have an article that starts in a text box on page 3 of the newsletter and continues in a text box on page 4. To flow the text automatically from one text box to a second, blank text box, click the first text box to select it (this text box should already contain some text). Next, on the ribbon, click the Shape Format tab, click the Create Link button in the Text group, and then click the empty text box. The text boxes are now linked. You can resize the first text box without worrying about how much text fits in the box. The text that no longer fits in the first text box is moved to the second text box. Note that you'll find it easier to link text boxes if you use simple text boxes without title bars.

Part 4.1 Quick Check

1. What is the first thing you need to do when formatting the second half of a document in columns?
2. What feature automatically converts some standard characters into typographic characters as you type?
3. How do you convert an inline object into a floating object?
4. What does the anchor symbol indicate?
5. What two buttons can you use to insert a text box in a document?

Part 4.2 Visual Overview: Editing Pictures

You can use the Remove Background button to remove a picture's background.

You can click the Crop button arrow to access more advanced cropping options, including cropping to a shape such as an oval or an arrow.

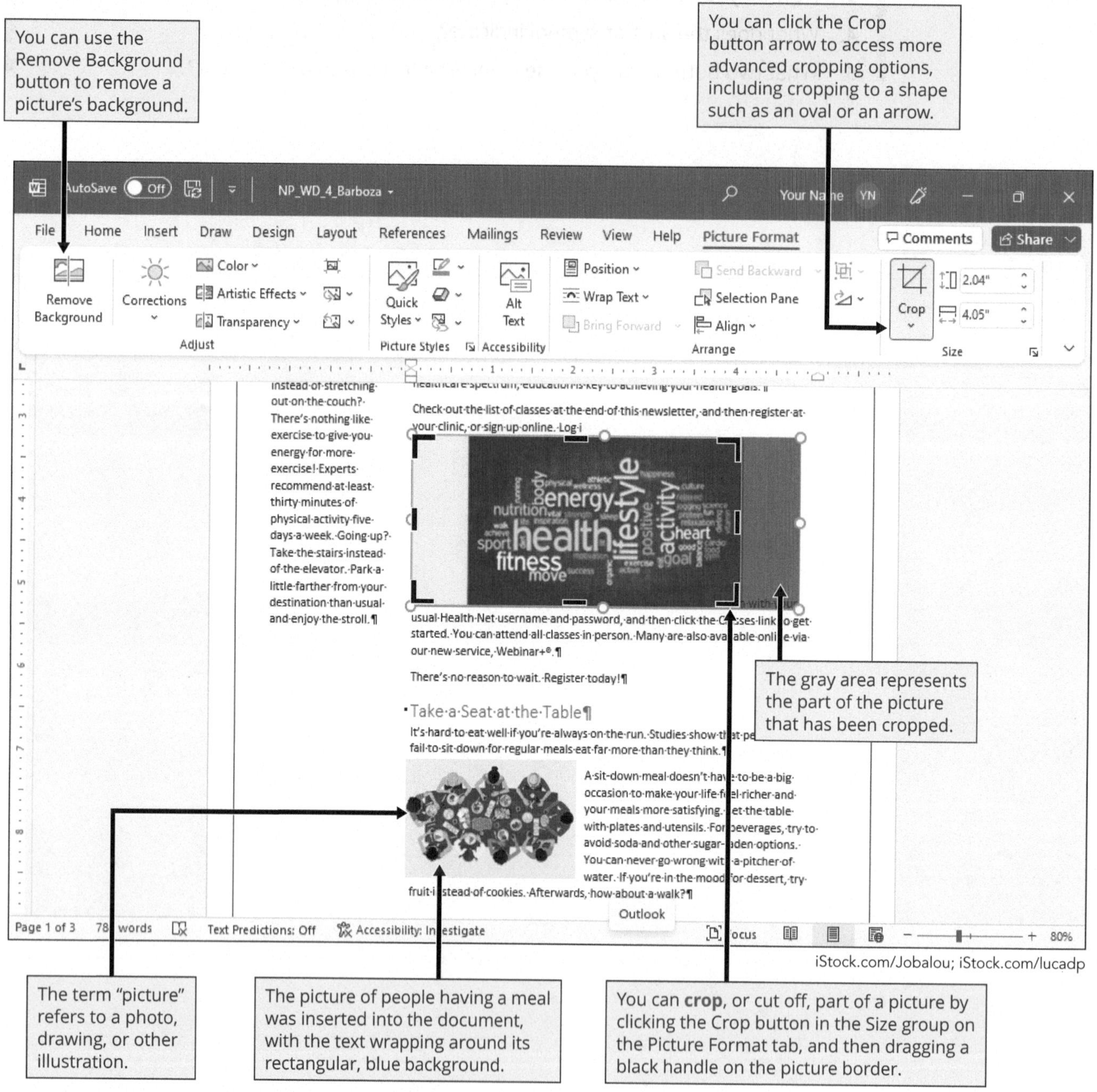

iStock.com/Jobalou; iStock.com/lucadp

The gray area represents the part of the picture that has been cropped.

The term "picture" refers to a photo, drawing, or other illustration.

The picture of people having a meal was inserted into the document, with the text wrapping around its rectangular, blue background.

You can **crop**, or cut off, part of a picture by clicking the Crop button in the Size group on the Picture Format tab, and then dragging a black handle on the picture border.

Clicking the Remove Background button in the Adjust group on the Picture Format tab displays the Background Removal tab, with tools for removing a picture's background.

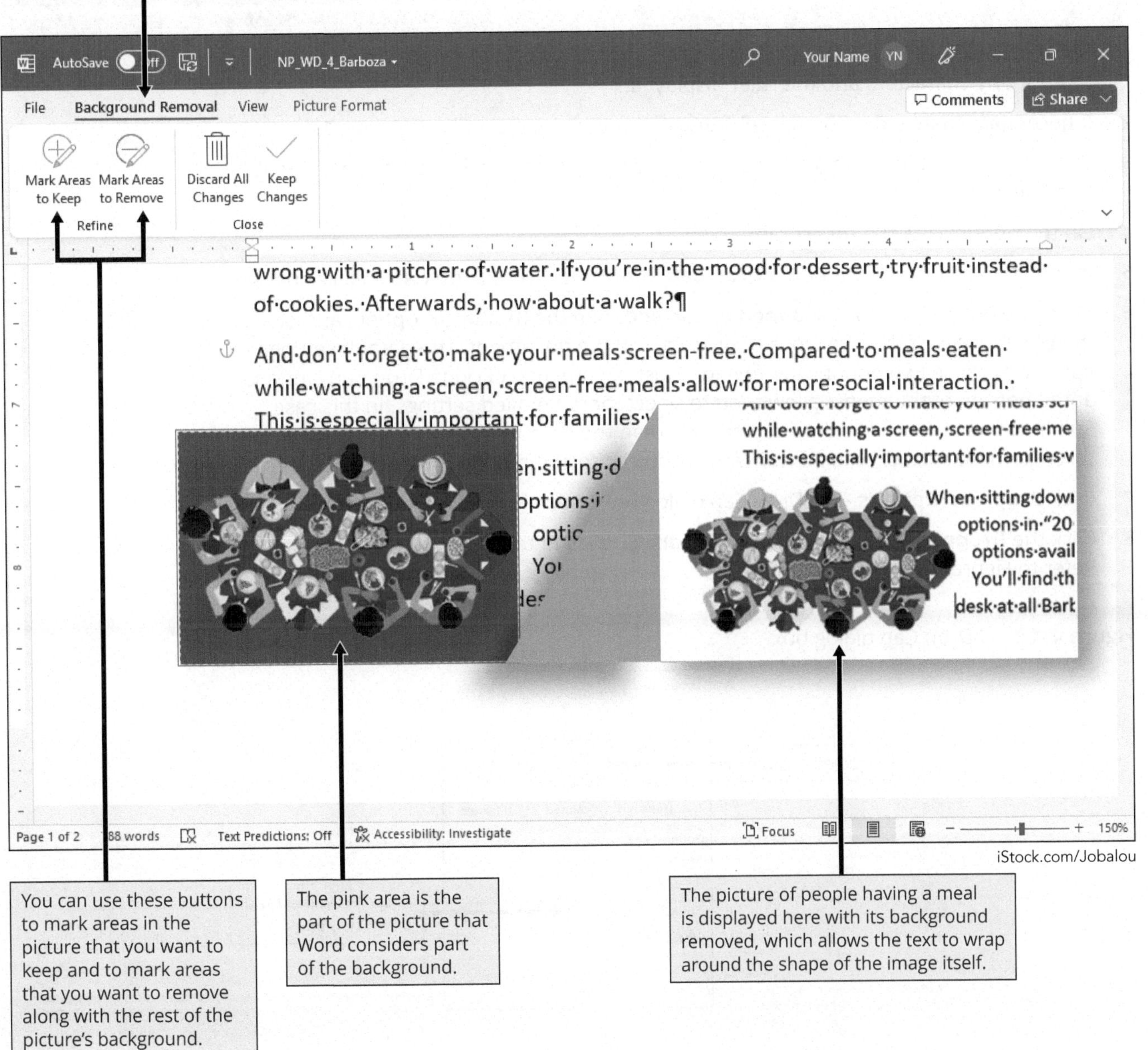
AutoSave
Off
NP_WD_4_Barboza
Your Name
YN
File
Background Removal
View
Picture Format
Comments
Share
Mark Areas to Keep
Mark Areas to Remove
Refine
Discard All Changes
Keep Changes
Close
wrong·with·a·pitcher·of·water.·If·you're·in·the·mood·for·dessert,·try·fruit·instead· of·cookies.·Afterwards,·how·about·a·walk?¶
And·don't·forget·to·make·your·meals·screen-free.·Compared·to·meals·eaten· while·watching·a·screen,·screen-free·meals·allow·for·more·social·interaction.· This·is·especially·important·for·families·
while·watching·a·screen,·screen-free·me
This·is·especially·important·for·families·v
When·sitting·dowi
options·in·"20
options·avail
You'll·find·th
desk·at·all·Bark
Page 1 of 2
88 words
Text Predictions: Off
Accessibility: Investigate
Focus
150%

iStock.com/Jobalou

You can use these buttons to mark areas in the picture that you want to keep and to mark areas that you want to remove along with the rest of the picture's background.

The pink area is the part of the picture that Word considers part of the background.

The picture of people having a meal is displayed here with its background removed, which allows the text to wrap around the shape of the image itself.

Inserting Drop Caps

As you saw in Part 4.1 Visual Overview, a drop cap is a large decorative letter that replaces the first letter of a paragraph. Drop caps are commonly used in newspapers, magazines, and newsletters to draw the reader's attention to the beginning of an article. You can place a drop cap next to the paragraph, in the margin, or you can place a drop cap in the paragraph, with the text wrapping around it. By default, a drop cap extends down three lines, but you can change that setting in the Drop Cap dialog box.

Stefan asks you to create a drop cap for some of the paragraphs that follow the headings. He prefers the drop cap to extend two lines into the paragraph, with the text wrapping around it.

To insert drop caps in the newsletter:

1. Make sure the NP_WD_4_Barboza.docx document is open in Print Layout view with the nonprinting characters and the ruler displayed.
2. If necessary, change the Zoom level **120%** if necessary and scroll up to page 1.
3. Click anywhere in the paragraph below the "Learn How to Reach Your Wellness Goals" heading.
4. On the ribbon, click the **Insert** tab.
5. In the Text group, click the **Add a Drop Cap** button. The Drop Cap gallery opens.
6. Move the pointer over the **Dropped** option and then the **In margin** option, and observe the Live Preview of the two types of drop caps in the document. The default settings applied by these two options are fine for most documents. Clicking Drop Cap Options, at the bottom of the menu, allows you to select more detailed settings. In this case, Stefan wants to make the drop cap smaller than the default. Instead of extending down through three lines of text, he wants the drop cap to extend only two lines.
7. Click **Drop Cap Options**. The Drop Cap dialog box opens.
8. Click the **Dropped** icon, click the **Lines to drop** box, and then change the setting to **2**. Refer to Figure 4–18.

Figure 4–18 Drop Cap dialog box

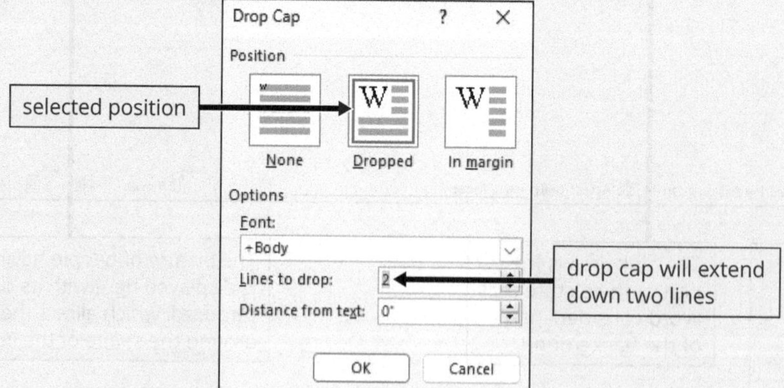

9. Click **OK**. Word formats the first character of the paragraph as a drop cap "W," as shown in Part 4.1 Visual Overview. The dotted box with selection handles around the drop cap indicates it is selected. Refer to Figure 4–19.

Figure 4–19 Drop Cap inserted in document

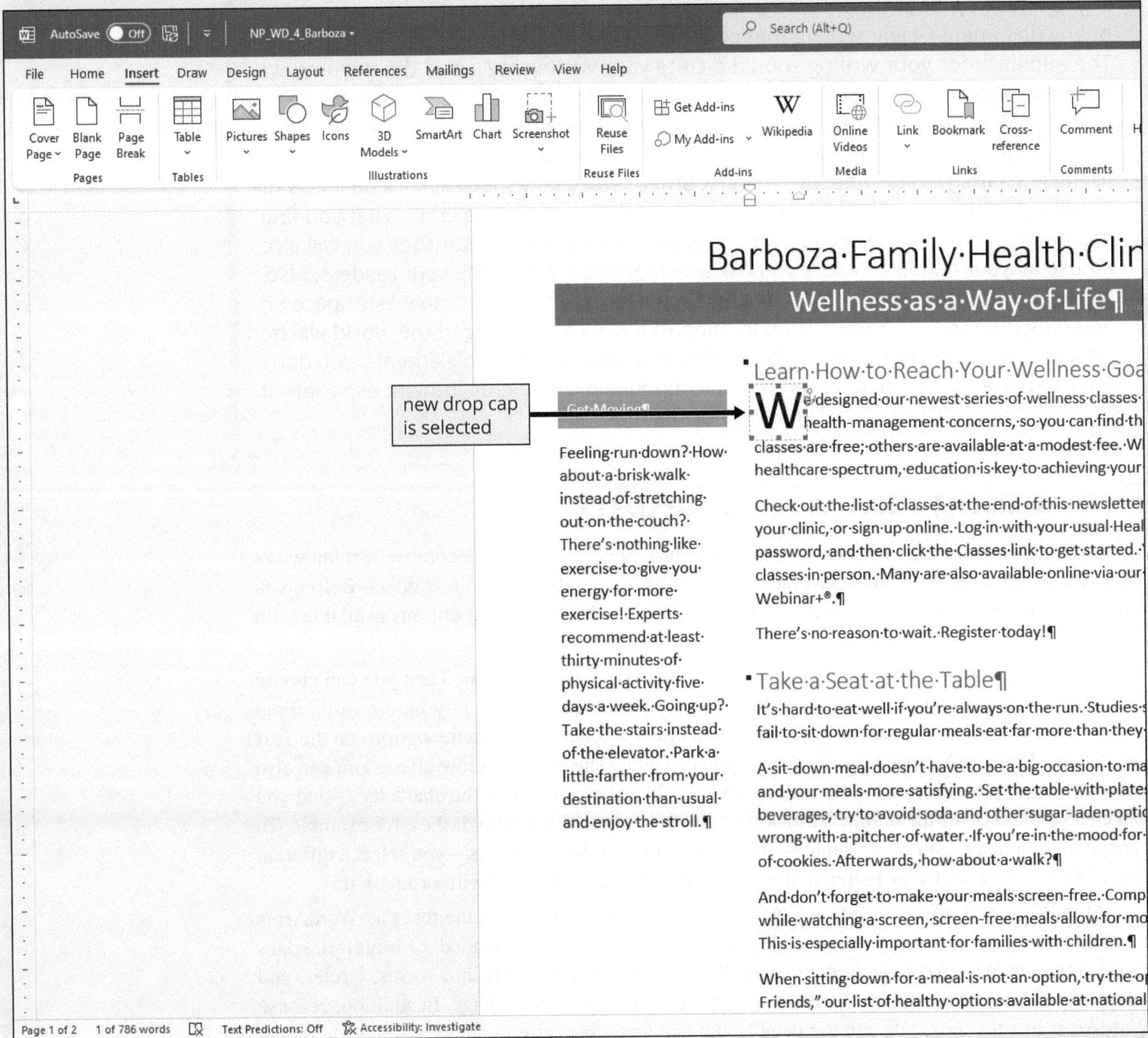

Tip To delete a drop cap, click the paragraph that contains it, open the Drop Cap dialog box, and then click None.

10. Near the bottom of page 1, insert a similar drop cap in the paragraph following the "Free Diabetes Assessments" heading. You skipped the paragraph following the "Take a Seat at the Table" heading because you'll eventually insert a graphic there. Including a drop cap there would make the paragraph look too cluttered.
11. On page 2, insert a similar drop cap in the paragraph following the "Fruits and Vegetables Are Your Friends" heading.
12. Click anywhere in the text to deselect the drop cap, and then save your work.

Proskills

Written Communication: Writing for Your Audience

Pictures, WordArt, and other design elements can make a newsletter appealing to readers. They can also be a lot of fun to create and edit. But don't let the design elements in your desktop-published documents distract you from the most important aspect of any document—clear writing that conveys your message to a particular audience. The audience for your writing should dictate your writing style and the document's overall design.

Because the newsletter format feels less formal than a report or letter, it's tempting to use a casual tone. If you are creating a newsletter for an audience consisting of friends or family, that's fine. But in most other settings—especially in a business or academic setting—you should strive for a professional tone, similar to what you find in a newspaper. Avoid jokes; you can never be certain that what amuses you will also amuse all your readers. Worse, you risk unintentionally offending your readers. Also, space is typically at a premium in any document, so you don't want to waste space on anything unessential. Finally, keep in mind that the best writing in the world will be wasted in a document that is overburdened with too many design elements. You don't have to use every element covered in this module in a single document, especially if they create accessibility problems for your readers.

Formatting Text with WordArt

To create special text elements such as a newsletter headline, you can use decorative text known as WordArt. Essentially, WordArt is text in a text box that is formatted with a text effect. Before you move on to learning about WordArt, it's helpful to review the formatting options available with text effects.

To begin applying a text effect, you select the text you want to format. Then you can choose from several preformatted text effects via the Text Effects and Typography button in the Font group on the Home tab. You can also modify a text effect by choosing from the options on the Text Effects and Typography menu. For example, you can add a shadow or a glow effect. You can also change the **outline color** of the characters—that is, the exterior color of the characters—and you can change the style of the outline by making it thicker or breaking it into dashes, for example. To change the character's **fill color**—that is, the interior color of the characters—you select a different font color via the Font Color button in the Font group, just as you would with ordinary text.

All of these text effect options are available with WordArt. However, the fact that WordArt is in a text box allows you to add some additional effects. You can add rounded, or **beveled**, edges to the letters in WordArt, format the text in 3D, and transform the text into waves, circles, and other shapes. You can also rotate WordArt text so it lies vertically on the page. In addition, because WordArt is in a text box, you can use page layout and text wrap settings to place it anywhere you want on a page, with text wrapped around it.

To start creating WordArt, you can select the text you want to transform into WordArt, and then click the WordArt button in the Text group on the Insert tab. Alternatively, you can start by clicking the WordArt button without selecting text first. In that case, Word inserts a text box with placeholder WordArt text, which you can then replace with something new. In the following steps, you'll select the first paragraph and format it as WordArt to create the newsletter title.

To create the title of the newsletter using WordArt:

1. On page 1, select the entire newsletter title **Barboza Family Health Clinics**, including the paragraph mark.

   Key Step Be sure to select the paragraph mark so the page layout in your newsletter matches the figures.

2. To avoid unexpected results, you should start by clearing any formatting from the text you want to format as WordArt, so you'll do that next.
3. On the ribbon, click the **Home** tab, if necessary.
4. In the Font group, click the **Clear All Formatting** button. The paragraph reverts to the Normal style. Now you can convert the text into WordArt.
5. On the ribbon, click the **Insert** tab.
6. In the Text group, click the **Insert WordArt** button. The WordArt gallery opens.
7. Position the pointer over the WordArt style that is second from the left in the top row. A ScreenTip describes some elements of this WordArt style—"Fill: Blue, Accent color 1; Shadow." Refer to Figure 4–20.

Figure 4–20 WordArt gallery

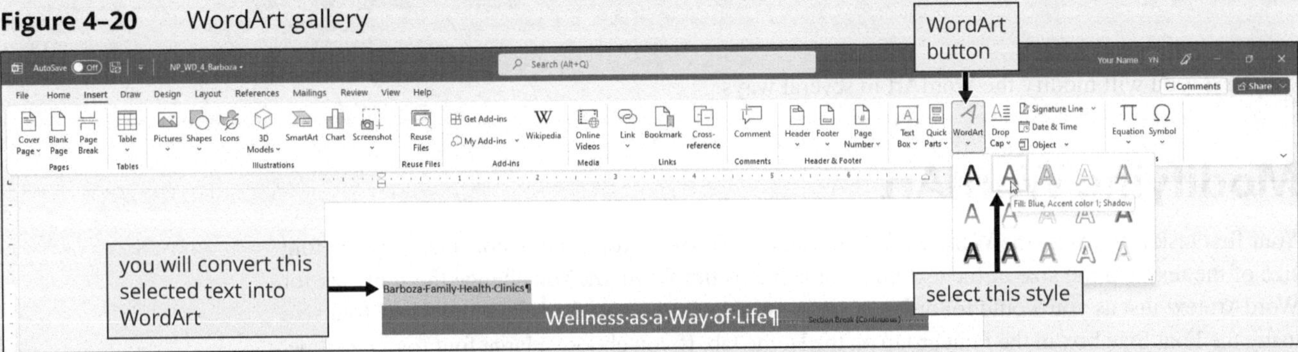

8. Click the WordArt style **Fill: Blue, Accent color 1; Shadow**. The gallery closes, and a text box containing the formatted text is displayed in the document. Refer to Figure 4–21.

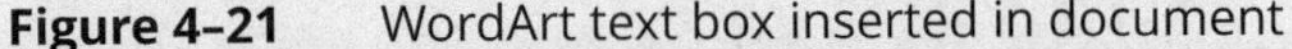

Figure 4–21 WordArt text box inserted in document

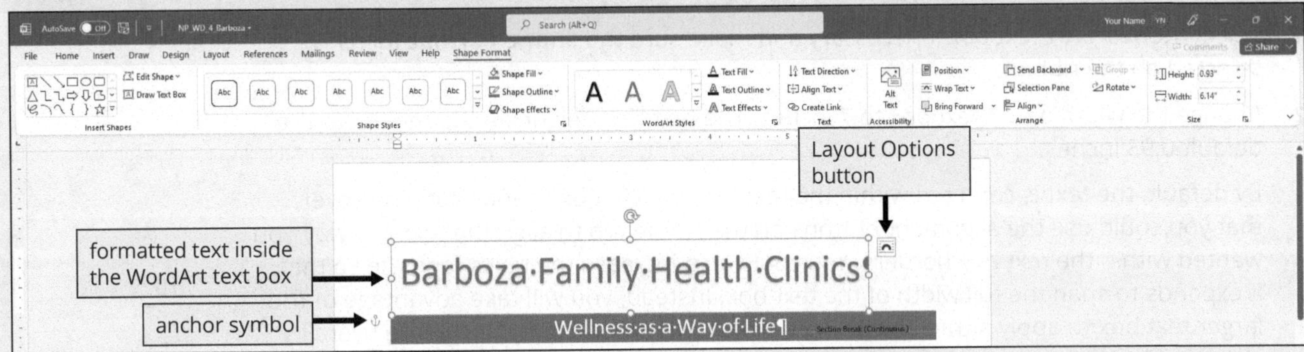

The Shape Format tab appears as the active tab on the ribbon, displaying a variety of tools that you can use to edit the WordArt. Before you change the look of the WordArt, you need to fix its position on the page and change its text wrap setting. You will use the Top and Bottom option, which is only available via the Wrap Text button in the Wrap Text group.

9. Make sure the **Shape Format** tab is selected on the ribbon.
10. In the Arrange group, click the **Wrap Text** button to open the Wrap Text menu, then click **Top and Bottom**. Note that for a WordArt text box that contains fewer characters, you might find that the Square text wrap option works better. When wrapping text around an object on a page, it's often necessary to experiment until you find the best option.
11. Click the **Wrap Text** button again and then click **Fix Position on Page** to insert a check.
12. If necessary, drag the WordArt text box up to position it above the shaded paragraph, using the top and left green guidelines as necessary, and then drag the "Get Moving" text box down, if necessary, so its top border aligns with the "Learn How to Reach Your Wellness Goals" heading.
13. Save the document.

Next, you will modify the WordArt in several ways.

Modifying WordArt

Your first task is to resize the WordArt. When resizing WordArt, you need to consider both the font size of the text and the size of the text box that contains the WordArt. You change the font size for WordArt text just as you would for ordinary text—by selecting it and then choosing a new font size using the Font Size box in the Font group on the Home tab. If you choose a large font for a headline, you might also need to resize the text box to ensure that the resized text appears on a single line. In this case, the font size of the new WordArt headline looks good; you only need to adjust the size of the text box so it spans the width of the page. The larger text box will make it possible for you to add some more effects.

To resize the WordArt text box and add some effects:

1. Select the WordArt text box if necessary and make sure the **Shape Format** tab is selected on the ribbon.
2. Change the width of the text box to **7** inches. The text box height should remain at the default 0.93 inches.

   By default, the text is centered within the text box, which looks good. Note, however, that you could use the alignment buttons on the Home tab to align the text any way you wanted within the text box borders. You could also increase the text's font size so that it expands to span the full width of the text box. Instead, you will take advantage of the larger text box to apply a transform effect, which will expand and change the overall shape of the WordArt text. Then you'll make some additional modifications.
3. Make sure the border of the **WordArt** text box is a solid line, indicating that the text box is selected. If you see a dotted line instead, click the border to change it to a solid line.

4. In the WordArt Styles group, click the **Text Effects** button [A] to display the Text Effects gallery, and then point to **Transform**. The Transform gallery displays options for changing the WordArt's shape.
5. Move the pointer over the options in the Transform gallery and observe the Live Previews in the WordArt text box. Note that you can always remove an effect that has been previously applied by clicking the None option at the top of a gallery. For example, to remove a transform effect, you could click the None option in the No Transform section at the top of the gallery. When you are finished, position the pointer over the **Chevron: Up** effect. Refer to Figure 4–22.

Figure 4–22 Applying a transform text effect

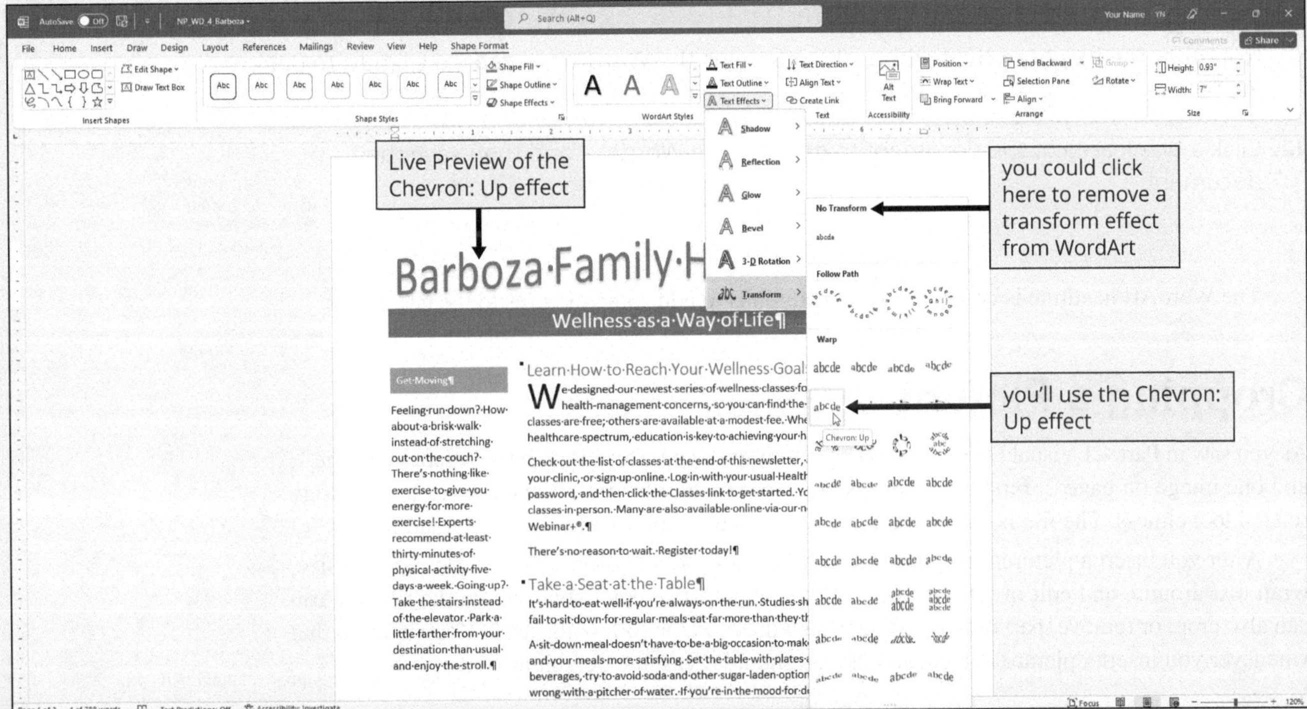

6. Click the **Chevron: Up** effect. The Transform menu closes, and the effect is applied to the WordArt. Now you will make some additional changes using the options in the WordArt Styles group. You'll start by changing the fill color.
7. In the WordArt Styles group, click the **Text Fill arrow** [A] to display the Text Fill color gallery.
8. In the Theme Colors section of the gallery, click the square that is fifth from the left in the bottom row to select the **Blue, Accent 1, Darker 50%** color. The Text Fill gallery closes, and the WordArt is formatted in a darker shade of blue. Next, you'll add a shadow to make the headline more dramatic.
9. In the WordArt Styles group, click the **Text Effects** button [A] to display the Text Effects gallery, and then point to **Shadow** to display the Shadow gallery, which is divided into several sections.
10. In the Outer section, point to the top-left option to display a ScreenTip that reads "Offset: Bottom Right."
11. Click the **Offset: Bottom Right** shadow style. A shadow is added to the WordArt text. Refer to Figure 4–23.

Figure 4–23 Completed WordArt headline

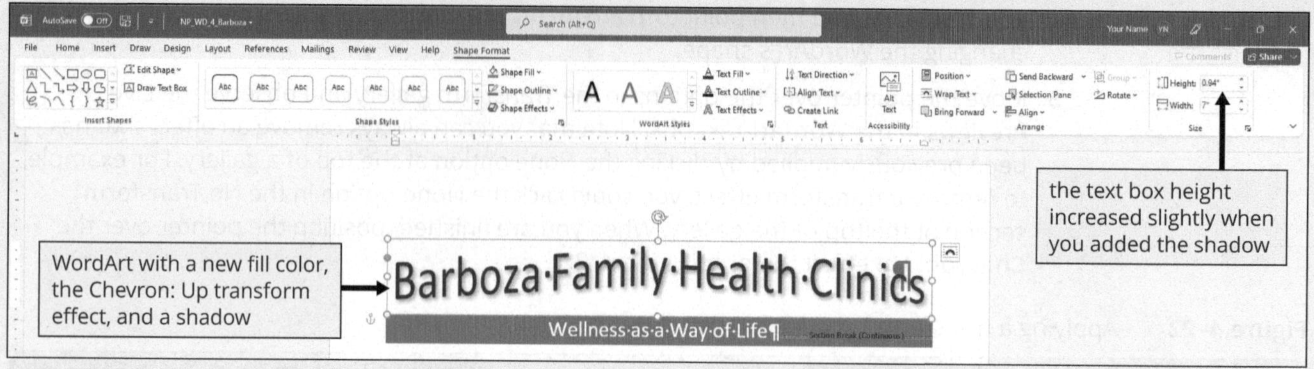

Note that the height of the text box that contains the WordArt increased slightly, to 0.94 inches.

12. Click a blank area of the document to deselect the WordArt, and then save the document.

The WordArt headline is complete. Your next job is to add some pictures to the newsletter.

Cropping a Picture

As you saw in Part 4.1 Visual Overview, you need to insert two images into the newsletter on page 1, and one image on page 2. First, you will insert a word cloud illustration made up of terminology related to wellness. The file is saved as a PNG file named Support_WD_4_WordCloud.jpg.

After you insert a picture into a document, it functions as an object that you can move, resize, wrap text around, and edit in other ways using the appropriate contextual tab on the ribbon. You can also crop, or remove, part of a picture, as you will see in the following steps. Keep in mind that whenever you insert a picture in a document, you should revise the default alt text.

To insert the picture on page 1:

1. On page 1, click at the end of the first paragraph below the "Learn How to Reach Your Wellness Goals" heading to position the insertion point between ". . . your health goals." and the paragraph mark. Typically, there's no need to be so precise about where you click before inserting a picture but doing so here will ensure that your results match the results described in these steps exactly.
2. On the ribbon, click the **Insert** tab.
3. In the Illustrations group, click the **Pictures** button to display the Pictures menu.
4. Click **This Device** to open the Insert Picture dialog box.
5. Navigate to the **Word4 > Module** folder included with your Data Files, and then insert the picture file named **Support_WD_4_WordCloud.jpg**. The picture is inserted in the document as an inline object. It is selected, and the Picture Format tab is displayed on the ribbon. For a few seconds, the default alt text appears at the bottom of the picture.
6. In the Accessibility group, click the **Alt Text** button to open the Alt Text pane, and replace the default alt text with the following: **A design made of words related to the word health, including lifestyle, nutrition, and activity**. Notice the Mark as decorative check box, which you will use later in this module. In this case, you should leave it unchecked.
7. Close the Alt Text pane and then scroll as necessary so you can see the entire picture.

The picture is wider than it needs to be, with a yellow rectangle on each side of the word cloud. You need to cut off, or crop, the yellow rectangles. In addition to cropping part of a picture, you can take advantage of Word's more advanced cropping options. One option is to crop to a shape, which means trimming the edges of a picture so it fits into a star, an oval, an arrow, or another shape. You can also crop to a specific ratio of height to width.

Whatever method you use, once you crop a picture, the part you cropped is hidden from view. However, it remains a part of the picture in case you change your mind and want to restore the cropped picture to its original form.

Before you crop off the sides of the picture, you'll try cropping it to a specific shape.

To crop the picture:

1. In the Size group, click the **Crop arrow** to display the Crop menu, and then point to **Crop to Shape**. A gallery of shapes is displayed, similar to the gallery you saw in Figure 4–15.
2. In the Basic Shapes section of the gallery, click the **Lightning Bolt** shape (in the third row from the top). The picture takes on the shape of a lightning bolt, with everything outside the lightning bolt shape cropped off.

   This isn't a useful option for this picture but cropping to shapes can be very effective with pictures in informal documents, such as party invitations or posters, especially if you then use the Behind Text wrapping option, so that the document text flows over the picture.
3. Press **CTRL+Z** to undo the cropping.
4. In the Size group, click the **Crop** button (not the Crop arrow). Dark black sizing handles appear around the picture borders.
5. Position the pointer directly over the middle sizing handle on the right border. The pointer changes to ⊢.
6. Press and hold down the mouse button, and drag the pointer slightly left. The pointer changes to +.
7. Drag the pointer toward the left until the picture border aligns with the right edge of the word cloud image (at about the 4-inch mark on the horizontal ruler), and then release the mouse button. At this point, your word cloud image should match the one in Figure 4–24. If it doesn't, undo the change and try again. In the cropped picture, the right portion is no longer visible. It is temporarily replaced with a gray background. You can ignore the text wrapping for now. The original border remains, indicating that the cropped portion is still saved as part of the picture in case you want to undo the cropping.

Figure 4–24 Cropping a picture

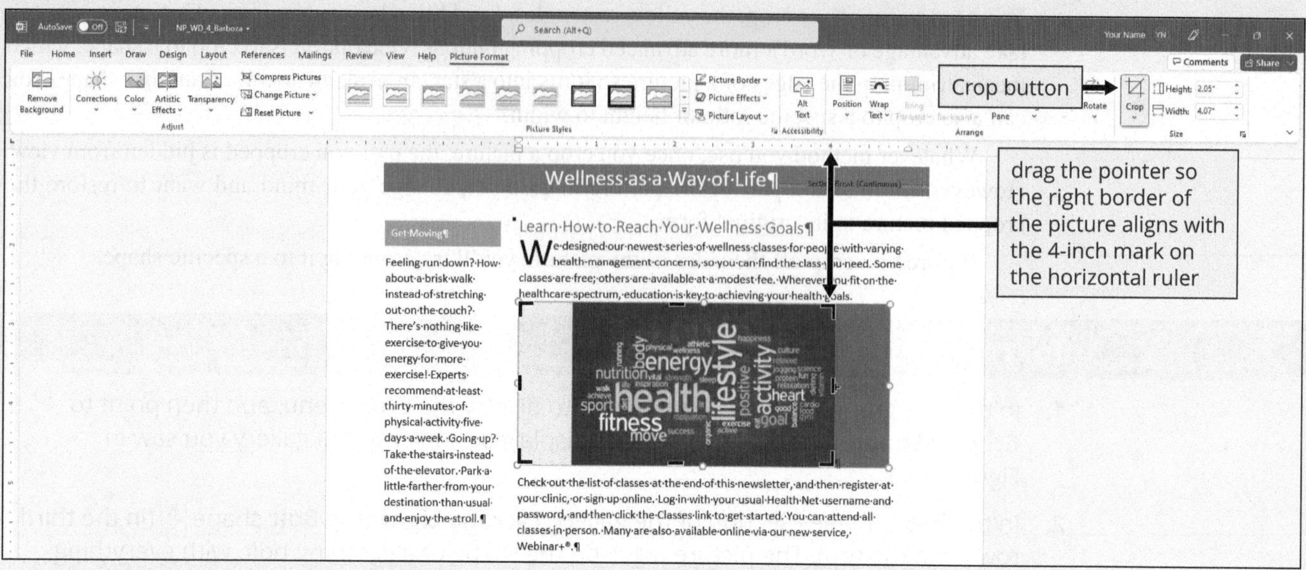

iStock.com/lucadp

8. Drag the middle sizing handle on the left border to the right until the left border aligns with the left edge of the word cloud image, at about the 0.75-inch mark on the horizontal ruler.

   The picture now takes up less space, and it shifts to the left. To ensure a specific ratio, you can also crop a picture by changing its **aspect ratio**—that is, the ratio of width to height. You'll try that next. But first, you'll restore the picture to its original state.

9. In the Adjust group, click the **Reset Picture arrow** to display the Reset Picture menu, and then click **Reset Picture & Size**. The picture returns to its original state.

10. In the Size group, click the **Crop arrow**, and then point to **Aspect Ratio** to display the Aspect Ratio menu, which lists various ratios of width to height. To make a picture a square, with all sides the same length, you could click the 1-to-1 ratio at the top of the menu. In this case, however, you want to crop the image to a rectangle shape in landscape orientation.

11. Under "Landscape," click **5:3**. The picture is cropped to a rectangle shape. Refer to Figure 4–25.

Figure 4–25 Picture cropped to a 5:3 aspect ratio

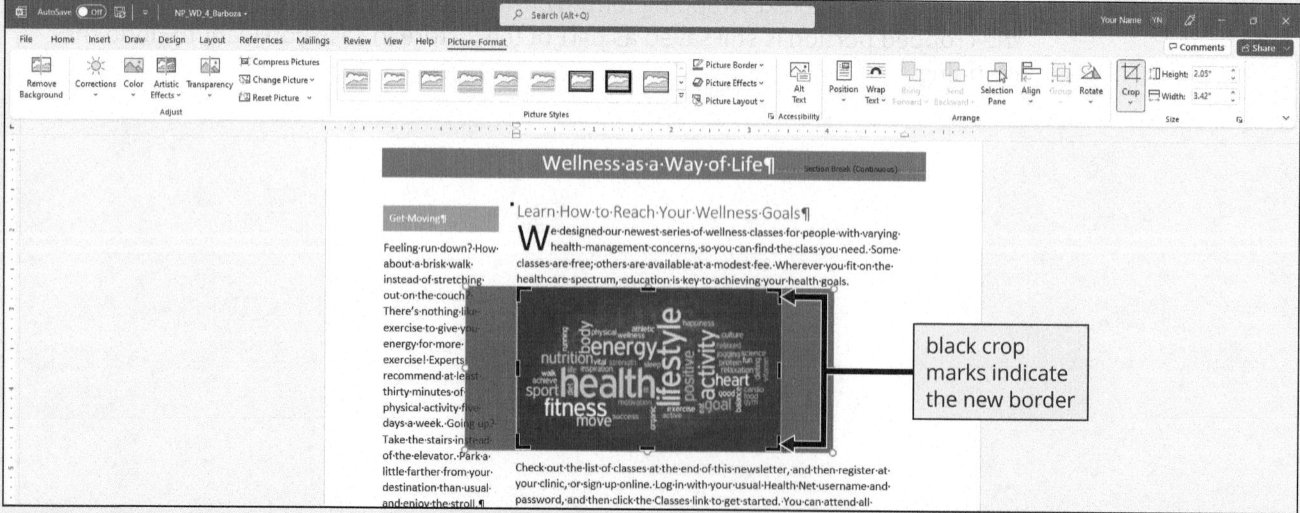

iStock.com/lucadp

12. Click anywhere outside the picture to deselect it and complete the cropping procedure.

Next, you need to change the picture from an inline object to a floating object by wrapping text around it. You also need to position it on the page. You can complete both tasks at the same time by using the Position button in the Arrange group.

To change the picture's position and wrapping:

1. Change the Zoom level to **One Page**, and then click the **picture** to select it.
2. On the ribbon, click the **Picture Format** tab.
3. In the Arrange group, click the **Position** button to display the Position gallery. You can click an icon in the "With Text Wrapping" section to move the selected picture to one of nine preset positions on the page. As with any gallery, you can see a Live Preview of the options before you actually select one.

   Tip When you select an option in the Position gallery, Fix Position on Page is also selected on the Wrap Text menu by default.

4. Move the pointer over the various icons, and observe the changing Live Preview in the document, with the picture moving to different locations on the page and the text wrapping around it.
5. Point to the icon in the middle row on the far right side to display a ScreenTip that reads "Position in Middle Right with Square Text Wrapping," and then click the **Position in Middle Right with Square Text Wrapping** icon. The picture moves to the middle of the page along the right margin. By default, it is formatted with Square text wrapping, so the text wraps to its left, following its square outline. Next, you'll add a picture style.
6. In the Pictures Styles group, click the **Simple Frame, White** style, which is the left-most style in the top row of the Picture Styles gallery. A frame and a shadow are applied to the picture. Refer to Figure 4–26.

Figure 4–26 Picture style added to picture

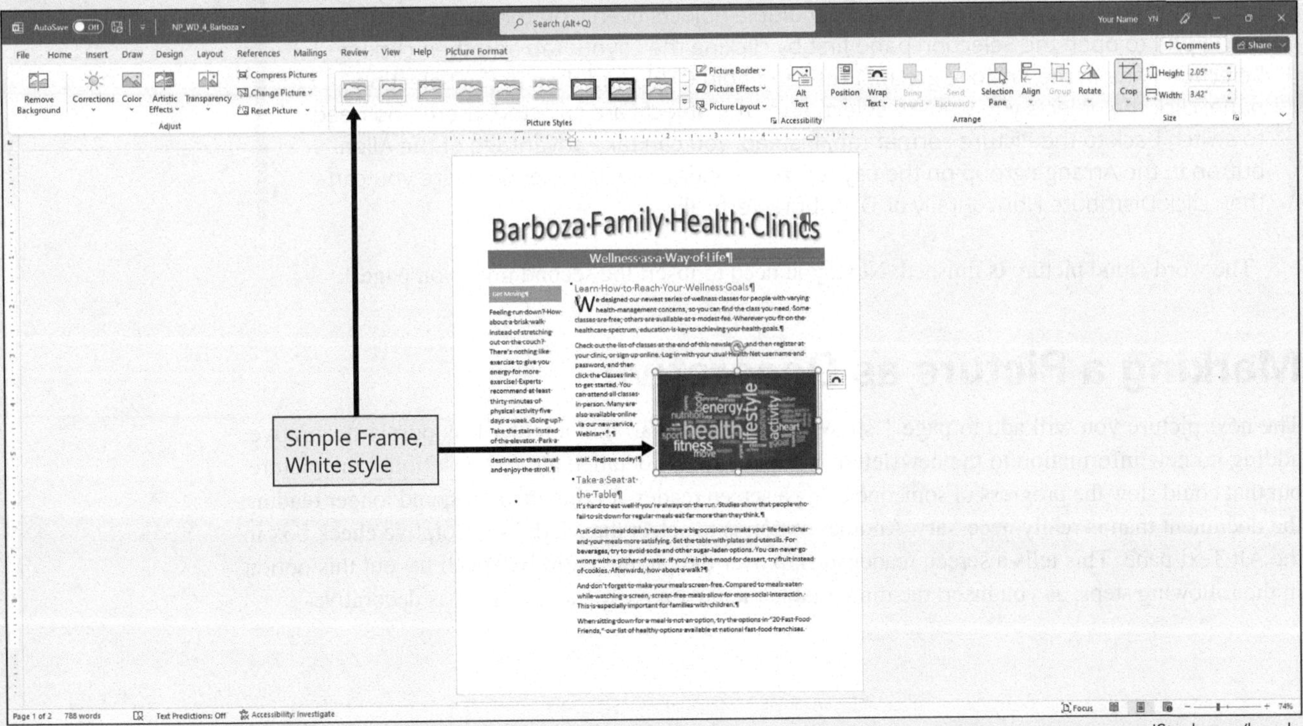

iStock.com/lucadp

Tip To add a simple border without adding a style, click the Picture Border button, and then click a color in the color gallery.

Tip If you aren't sure what formatting has been applied to a picture, and you want to start over with the formatting but not change the picture's size, use the Reset Picture button in the Adjust group on the Picture Format tab.

Your final step is to resize the picture to make it a bit smaller.

7. In the Size group, click the **Shape Height** box, type **1.5**, and then press **ENTER**. For most types of graphics, the aspect ratio is locked, meaning that when you change one dimension, the other changes to match. In this case, because the aspect ratio of the picture is 5:3, when you changed the height to 1.5 inches, the width changed to 2.5 inches.
8. Click anywhere in the document to deselect the picture, and then save the document.

Insight

Aligning Graphic Objects and Using the Selection Pane

The steps in this module provide precise directions about where to position graphic objects in the document. However, when you are creating a document on your own, you might find it helpful to use the Align button in the Arrange group on the Picture Format tab to align objects relative to the margin or the edge of the page. Aligning a graphic relative to the margin, rather than the edge of the page, is usually the best choice because it ensures that you don't accidentally position a graphic outside the page margins, causing the graphic to get cut off when the page is printed.

After you choose whether to align to the page or margin, you can open the Align menu again and choose an alignment option. For example, you can align the top of an object at the top of the page or align the bottom of an object at the bottom of the page. You can also choose to have Word distribute multiple objects evenly on the page. To do this, it's helpful to open the Selection pane first by clicking the Layout tab and then clicking Selection Pane in the Arrange group. Press and hold CTRL, and then in the Selection pane, click the objects you want to select. After the objects are selected, there's no need to switch back to the Picture Format tab. Instead, you can take advantage of the Align button in the Arrange group on the Layout tab to open the Align menu, where you can then click Distribute Horizontally or Distribute Vertically.

The word cloud picture is finished. Next, you need to insert the second image on page 1.

Marking a Picture as Decorative

The next picture you will add to page 1 shows people eating around a table. It is purely decorative, adding no new information to the newsletter. You could write detailed alt text describing the picture, but that could slow the progress of someone using a screen reader, forcing them to spend longer reading the document than is really necessary. Another option is to select the Mark as decorative check box in the Alt Text pane. This tells a screen reader to skip over the picture entirely. You'll try out this option in the following steps, as you insert the dinner table picture on page 1 and mark it as decorative.

To insert a picture and mark it as decorative:

1. Zoom in so you can read the document text at the bottom of page 1, and then click at the end of the first paragraph below the "Take a Seat at the Table" heading to position the insertion point between "they think." and the paragraph mark.
2. Change the Zoom level to **Multiple Pages** so you can see the entire document.
3. On the ribbon, click the **Insert** tab.
4. In the Illustrations group, click the **Pictures** button, click **This Device** to display the Insert Picture dialog box, and then navigate to the **Word4 > Module** folder.
5. Click the image **Support_WD_4_DinnerTable.png**, and then click the **Insert** button. The dialog box closes, and the picture of a people sharing a meal around a table is inserted as an inline object at the current location of the insertion point. Because it is an inline object, Word treats the image as part of the sentence that ends "they think," moving the next paragraph to the top of the next page to make room for the picture.
6. Open the Alt Text pane, delete the default alt text, select the **Mark as decorative** check box, and then close the Alt Text pane. The picture is selected, as indicated by its border with handles. The Picture Format tab is displayed on the ribbon. Now you can wrap text around the picture and position it on the page.
7. In the Arrange group, click the **Wrap Text** button, and then click **Tight**. The picture is now a floating object, positioned on page 1, with text wrapped to its right.
8. Drag the picture to the lower-left corner of page 1, centered below the text box. It should be positioned roughly as in Figure 4–27, but don't worry about exactly matching the figure. The anchor symbol for the picture might be positioned on either side of the picture, or somewhere else.

Figure 4–27 Resized picture as a floating object

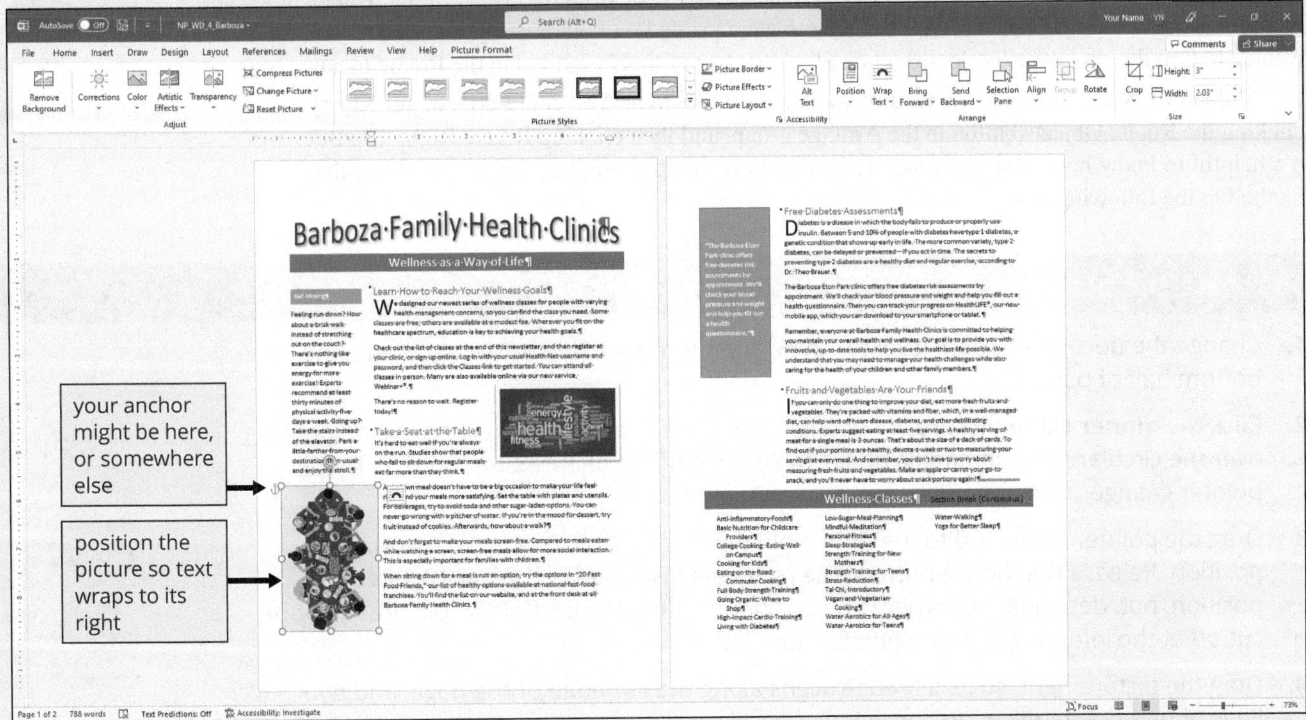

iStock.com/Jobalou; iStock.com/lucadp

9. Click the **Layout Options** button, click **Fix position on page**, and then close the Layout Options gallery.

Stefan reviews your work and is very happy with the newsletter so far. He likes the picture but would like you to make a few changes. First, he wants you to rotate the picture to the right, so it has a horizontal orientation.

Insight

Using the Draw Tab

You can use the tools on the Draw tab to draw on a touch screen, using your finger or a stylus. If you do not have a touch screen, you can use the mouse instead. When the Draw with Touch button is selected, you can choose to draw with a pen, a pencil, or a highlighter. For each drawing tool, you can choose from different colors, and you can adjust any of the drawing tools to create a wider or more narrow line. You can select different effects, such as Galaxy, which creates a glitter effect. To begin selecting an effect, click a pen in the Drawing Tools group on the Draw tab, and then click the down arrow button on the pen's icon to display a menu of options.

The Ink-to-Shape button in the Convert group lets you incorporate hand-drawn text edits (including common copy-editing symbols such as an inverted V to indicate an insertion) into regular document text. Likewise, you can use the Ink to Math button to convert hand-drawn mathematical equations into document text, which you can then edit using the Equation tab. After you have finished drawing, you can "replay" the drawing action and watch the characters and shapes you drew get redrawn in the document. To hide something you drew in a document, click the Hide Ink button in the Ink group on the Review tab.

Rotating a Picture

You can quickly rotate a picture by dragging the Rotation handle that appears on the picture's border when the picture is selected. To access some preset rotation options, you can click the Rotate Objects button in the Arrange group on the Picture Format tab to open the Rotate menu. To quickly rotate a picture 90 degrees, click Rotate Right 90° or Rotate Left 90° in the Rotate menu. You can also flip a picture, as if the picture were printed on both sides of a card and you wanted to turn the card over. To do this, click Flip Vertical or Flip Horizontal in the Rotate menu.

Stefan only wants to rotate the picture 90 degrees to the right. You could do that quickly by clicking the Rotate Objects button in the Arrange group, and then clicking Rotate Right 90°. But it's helpful to know how to rotate a picture by dragging the Rotation handle, so you'll use that method in the following steps.

To rotate the picture:

1. Change the document Zoom level to **120%**, and then scroll down so you can see the bottom half of page 1.
2. Click the **dinner table picture**, if necessary, to select it, and then position the pointer over the circular rotation handle above the middle of the picture's top border. The pointer changes to .
3. Drag the pointer down and to the right, until the dinner table rotates to a horizontal position. Release the mouse button. The picture is displayed in the new, rotated position, but, depending on where you positioned it earlier, part of the picture might be cut off at the left margin. That's fine for now.
4. Drag the picture right, so its left edge aligns along the left edge of the page, and two lines of paragraph text wrap above it. Refer to Figure 4–28.

Figure 4–28 Dragging the Rotation handle

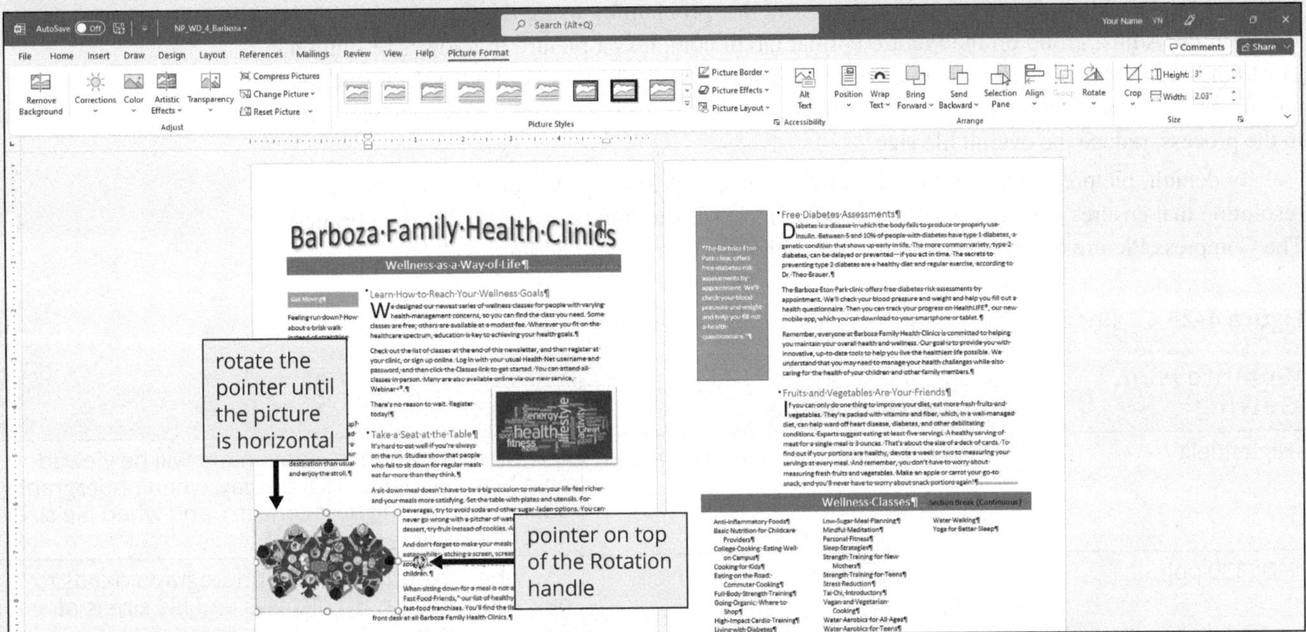

iStock.com/Jobalou; iStock.com/lucadp

5. Release the mouse button and save the document.

You're almost finished editing the picture. Your next task is to remove its background, but first you'll explore the options in the Adjust group.

Adjusting and Compressing a Picture

The Adjust group on the Picture Format tab provides several tools for adjusting a picture's overall look. You'll explore some of these options in the following steps.

To try out some options in the Adjust group:

1. Make sure that the **dinner table picture** is still selected, and that the **Picture Format** tab is selected on the ribbon.
2. In the Adjust group, click the **Corrections** button, and then move the pointer over the various options in the Corrections gallery and observe the Live Preview in the document. You can use the Corrections gallery to sharpen or soften a picture's focus or to adjust its brightness.
3. Press **ESC** to close the Corrections gallery.
4. In the Adjust group, click the **Color** button, and then move the pointer over the options in the Color gallery, and observe the Live Preview in the document. You can adjust a picture's color saturation and tone. You can also use the Recolor options to completely change a picture's colors.
5. Press **ESC** to close the Color gallery.
6. In the Adjust group, click the **Artistic Effects** button, and then move the pointer over the options in the Artistic Effects gallery, and observe the Live Preview in the document.
7. Press **ESC** to close the Artistic Effects gallery.

Inserting a picture file into a document can increase the size of the document file, making it difficult to share via email or online. You can avoid that problem by using the Compress Pictures button in the Adjust group on the Picture Format tab to compress a picture to a lower resolution. The term **resolution** refers to the amount of detail contained in an image. The higher the resolution, the more detail visible in an image. When you compress an image, you reduce its resolution, and in the process, reduce the overall file size.

By default, pictures added to Word documents are compressed to 220 pixels per inch (ppi), a resolution that ensures a picture will look good on most screens and reproduce well when printed. The Compress Picture dialog box offers the resolution options shown in Figure 4–29.

Figure 4–29 Photo compression settings

Compression Setting	Compression Value	When to Use
High fidelity	Photos are compressed very minimally.	Use when a picture in a document will be viewed on a high-definition (HD) display, when photograph quality is of the highest concern, and when file size is not an issue.
HD (330 ppi)	Photos are compressed to 330 pixels per inch.	Use when the quality of the photograph needs to be maintained on HD displays and file size is of some concern.
Print (220 ppi)	Photos are compressed to 220 pixels per inch.	Use when the quality of the photograph needs to be maintained when printed. This is the default resolution.
Web (150 ppi)	Photos are compressed to 150 pixels per inch.	Use when a picture in a document will be viewed on a low-definition display or uploaded to a webpage.
E-mail (96 ppi)	Photos are compressed to 96 pixels per inch.	Use when it is important to keep the overall file size small, such as for documents that need to be emailed.
Use default resolution	Photos are compressed to the resolution specified on the Advanced tab in the Word Options dialog box. (The default setting is 220 ppi.)	Use when file size is not an issue, or when the quality of the photo display is more important than file size.
Do not compress images in file	Photos are not compressed at all.	Use when it is critical that photos remain at their original resolution.

To ensure that the newsletter is easy to email, you will reduce the compression setting for the pictures in the document to 96 ppi. You'll start by checking the document's current file size. When you are finished, you will check the file size again to see how it has changed.

Reference

Modifying Photo Compression Settings

- Click a photo to select it.
- On the ribbon, click the Picture Format tab.
- In the Adjust group, click the Compress Pictures button to open the Compress Pictures dialog box.
- Click the option button next to the resolution you want to use.
- To apply the new compression settings to all the photos in the file, click the Apply only to this picture check box to deselect it.
- To keep cropped areas of photos, click the Delete cropped areas of pictures check box to deselect it.
- Click OK.

To change the dining table picture resolution to 96 ppi:

1. Click the **File** tab to switch to Backstage view, and then click **Info**. On the right side of the screen, under the "Properties" heading, the Size is listed as 193 KB. (Don't be concerned if yours is slightly higher or lower.)
2. Close Backstage view.
3. Verify that the dining table picture is selected, and then click the **Picture Format** tab if necessary.
4. In the Adjust group, click the **Compress Pictures** button. The Compress Pictures dialog box opens. Under Resolution, the Use default resolution option button is selected.
5. Click the **E-mail (96 ppi)** option button, which compresses pictures to the smallest possible size.
6. At the top of the dialog box, under Compression options, deselect the Apply only to this picture check box. This will ensure that the new compression settings are also applied to the word cloud image.
7. Verify that the Delete cropped areas of pictures check box is selected. This will ensure that the cropped areas of the word cloud image are permanently removed from the document. Refer to Figure 4–30.

Figure 4–30 Compress Pictures dialog box

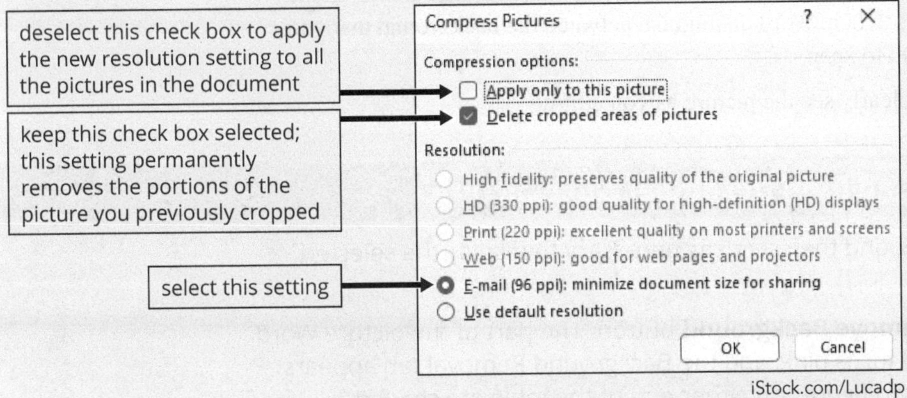

iStock.com/Lucadp

8. Click **OK**. The two pictures are compressed to 96 ppi, and the cropped areas of the word cloud image are removed from the document. Because you are reviewing the picture on a computer screen, it looks the same as it did at the default resolution.
9. Click the **File** tab, and then click **Info**. Note that the document's file size has been reduced from 193 KB to 142 KB. The picture files you used in this module were already quite small, so this reduction in file size wouldn't make a big difference when emailing the document. However, if you find yourself working with larger picture files, compressing pictures in a document will be much more important.

Insight

Changing the Default Compression Setting

By default, Word compresses all newly inserted pictures to 220 ppi. To change the default compression setting, open the Word Options dialog box and then, in the navigation pane, click Advanced. Scroll down until you can see the Image Size and Quality section. By default, the Image Size and Quality list box contains the name of the current document, which means any changes to the compression settings will apply only to the current document. To change the default settings for all new documents, you could select All New Documents instead.

To select a default resolution other than 220 ppi, click the Default resolution arrow and click the resolution you want. To turn off compression for all images, select the Do not compress images in file check box.

Now you are ready to remove the blue background from the dinner table picture.

Removing a Picture's Background

Removing a picture's background can be tricky, especially if you are working on a photo with a background that is not clearly differentiated from the foreground image. For example, you might find it difficult to remove a white, snowy background from a photo of an equally white snowman. Removing a background from a drawing, like the dinner table picture, is usually much easier than removing a background from a photo. You start by clicking the Remove Background button in the Adjust group, and then making changes to help Word distinguish between the background that you want to exclude and the image you want to keep.

You'll start by zooming in so you can clearly see the picture as you edit it.

To remove the blue background from the dinner table picture:

1. Change the Zoom level to **180%**, and then scroll as necessary to display the selected dinner table picture.
2. In the Adjust group, click the **Remove Background** button. The part of the picture Word considers to be the background turns pink, and the Background Removal tab appears on the ribbon. Notice that the two figures on either end of the table are shaded, indicating that Word considers them to be part of the background. Refer to Figure 4–31.

Figure 4–31 Removing a picture's background

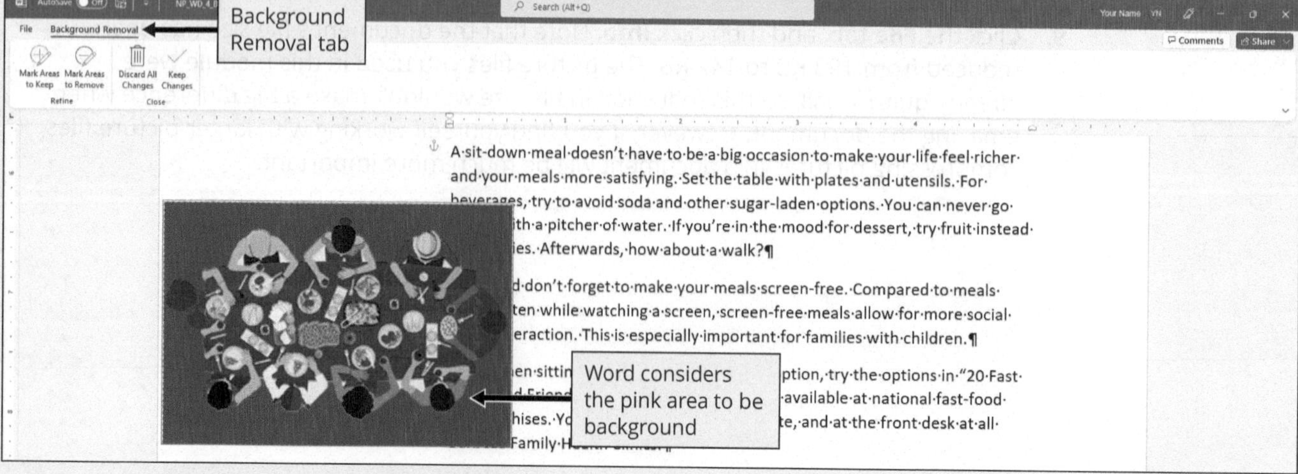

iStock.com/Jobalou

3. On the Background Removal tab, click the **Mark Areas to Keep** button in the Refine group to select it, if necessary, and then move the drawing pointer over the dinner table. You can use this pointer to click any areas you want to keep.
4. Move the pointer over the person on the left side of the dinner table. Refer to Figure 4–32.

Figure 4–32 Marking an area to keep

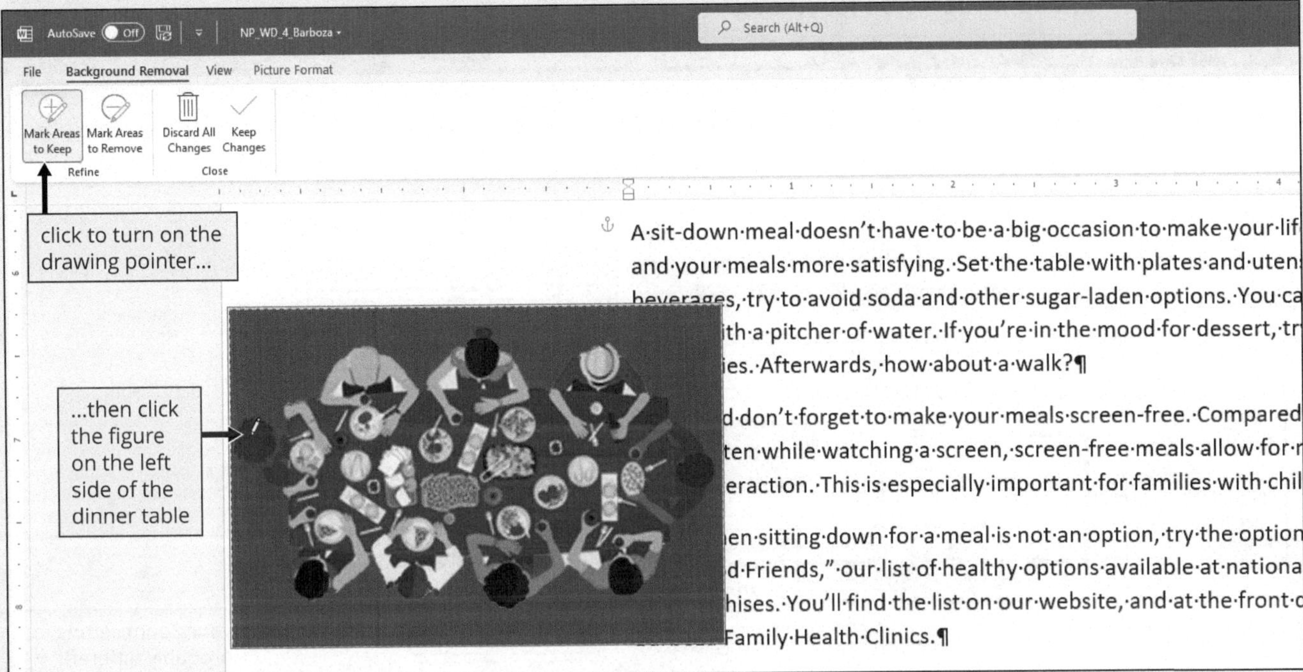

AutoSave Off
NP_WD_4_Barboza
Search (Alt+Q)
File
Background Removal
View
Picture Format
Mark Areas to Keep
Mark Areas to Remove
Discard All Changes
Keep Changes
Refine
Close
click to turn on the drawing pointer...
...then click the figure on the left side of the dinner table
A·sit-down·meal·doesn't·have·to·be·a·big·occasion·to·make·your·lif
and·your·meals·more·satisfying.·Set·the·table·with·plates·and·uten
beverages,·try·to·avoid·soda·and·other·sugar-laden·options.·You·ca
ith·a·pitcher·of·water.·If·you're·in·the·mood·for·dessert,·tr
ies.·Afterwards,·how·about·a·walk?¶
d·don't·forget·to·make·your·meals·screen-free.·Compared
ten·while·watching·a·screen,·screen-free·meals·allow·for·r
eraction.·This·is·especially·important·for·families·with·chil
en·sitting·down·for·a·meal·is·not·an·option,·try·the·option
d·Friends,"·our·list·of·healthy·options·available·at·nationa
hises.·You'll·find·the·list·on·our·website,·and·at·the·front·c
Family·Health·Clinics.¶

iStock.com/Jobalou

5. Click the mouse button. The area you clicked loses the shading, so you can see the person sitting at the table more clearly. Depending on exactly where you clicked, however, part of the figure might still be shaded.
6. Continue clicking the shaded parts of the dinner table image as indicated in Figure 4–32, until all the people sitting around the table appear without shading. You might need to click some parts of the picture multiple times to convert all of the dinner table image from background to foreground. Although it might be hard to tell, the hair on many of the figures is marked as background by default. Use CTRL+Z as necessary to undo changes and start again. Removing a picture's background can be tricky, and it often takes several tries to get it right.

   Note that you could click the Mark Areas to Remove button and then use the pointer in a similar way to mark parts of the picture that you want to remove, rather than retain. In an image with a larger background, you could also click and drag the Mark Areas to Remove pointer or the Mark Areas to Keep pointer to select a larger area of the picture for deletion or retention.

   Now you will accept the changes you made to the picture.
7. In the Close group, click the **Keep Changes** button. The background is removed from the picture, leaving only the image of the dinner table, with no green background. Now the text wrapping follows the curved shape of the dinner table, although the dinner table might overlap some letters.

   Trouble? If parts of the image are missing, click the Remove Background button and then use the Mark Areas to Keep pointer to make any corrections.
8. Change the Zoom level to **100%**.

9. Drag the picture right so its left edge aligns with the left edge of the text box, using the green alignment line for guidance. Feel free to zoom in or out if that makes it easier for you to move the picture. When you are finished, the text should wrap similarly to the text shown in Figure 4–33. Note that in Figure 4–43, the document is zoomed so you can see both pages, but your zoom setting will probably be different.

Figure 4–33 Picture with background removed

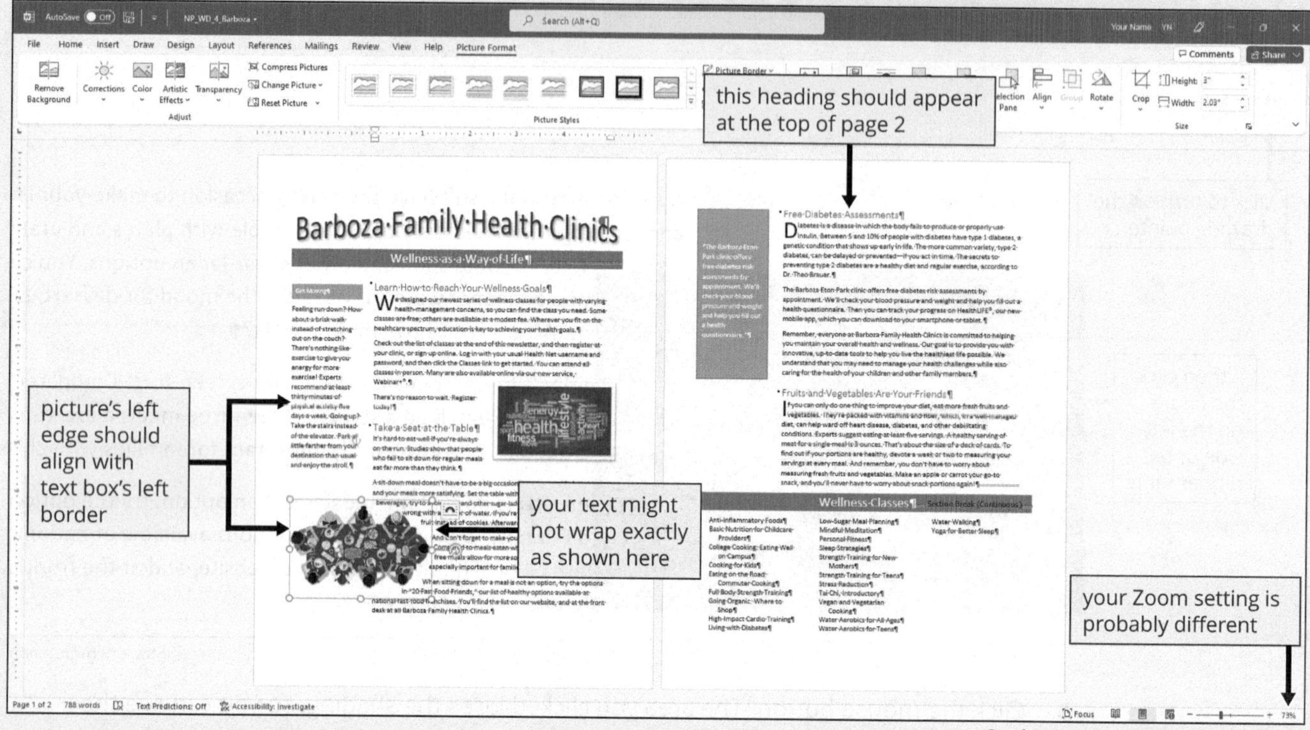

iStock.com/Jobalou; iStock.com/lucadp

Don't be concerned if you can't get the text wrapping to match exactly. The most important thing is that when you are finished, the "Free Diabetes Assessments" heading should be positioned at the top of page 2. Finally, you might need to adjust the dinner table's position slightly, so it doesn't overlap any text.

10. Click outside the picture to deselect it, and then save the document.

You're finished with your work on the dinner table picture. Now Stefan asks you to add an apple icon to accompany the article about fruits and vegetables. Before you do that, you will explore some sources for illustrations designed to be used in a Word document.

Inserting Stock Images, Icons, and Other Illustrations

If you don't already have the pictures you need for a document stored as image files and you have an active Microsoft 365 subscription, you can look for pictures in the Microsoft 365 library. To get started, click the Pictures button in the Illustrations group on the Insert tab and then click Stock Images. You can choose from the following options:

- **Images**—Microsoft 365 stock photo images, which are also available via the Pictures button in the Illustrations group on the Insert tab.
- **Icons**—Symbolic images, such as smiley faces or lightbulbs, drawn in black and white; after you insert an icon in a document, you can fine-tune it by changing its fill and outline colors.

- **Cutout People**—Photos of people with backgrounds removed.
- **Stickers**—Colorful images similar to phone emojis.
- **Illustrations**—Line drawings in gray, white, and yellow; after you insert an illustration in a document, you can change the yellow to another color by changing the image's Graphics Fill color.
- **Cartoon People**—Black-and-white cartoon drawings of people, along with parts of cartoon drawings that you can combine to create your own characters and background scenes where you can place your cartoon characters; after you insert a cartoon in a document, you can fine-tune it by changing its fill and outline colors.

Note that your computer must be connected to the Internet to access these illustrations. A notice at the bottom of the gallery explains that all Microsoft 365 subscribers have full access to the entire library of images. However, it's possible that copyright restrictions might apply to pictures in the Microsoft 365 library if you use them in a document you plan to publish and sell. Before you use an image, go to Office.com and search on "What am I allowed to use premium creative content for?"

> **Tip** You can use the Online Video button in the Media group on the Insert tab to insert an online video in a document from YouTube or elsewhere on the web. Use this option sparingly, though, because inserting an online video introduces code that hackers could manipulate to import malware into your computer.

If you can't find the image you need in the Microsoft 365 library, you can search for images on the web. But keep in mind that ownership of all forms of media, including text, drawings, photographs, and video, is governed by copyright laws. To get started, click the Pictures button in the Illustrations group on the Insert tab, and then click Online Pictures. This opens the Online Pictures dialog box, where you can use the Search Bing box at the top to look for images or click categories such as "Animals" to see a collection of related images.

To start a search, you would type keywords, such as "walking a dog," in the search box, and then press ENTER. Images from all over the web that have the keywords "walking a dog." By default, Word displays only images that are available for use under Creative Commons, a public copyright license that allows the free distribution of work that would otherwise be restricted by copyright law. Typically, the search results include photos and premade pictures known as **clip art**, which can be used to illustrate a wide variety of publications. To insert one of those images, you would click it, and then click the Insert button. To widen your search to all the images on the web (the vast majority of which are subject to strict copyright restrictions), you could deselect the Creative Commons only check box.

You can also search the Microsoft 365 library for **3D models**, which are illustrations created using 3D animation techniques that you can rotate in three dimensions. To insert a 3D model in a document, click the 3D Models button in the Illustrations group on the Insert tab. This opens the Online 3D Models dialog box, where you can type some key words, or click categories such as "Animals" to see a collection of related 3D models. Click the model you want, click the Insert button, and then use the handles on the image in the document to resize or rotate it. You can wrap text around a 3D model just as you would wrap text around any type of picture. Like other pictures, 3D models are typically copyright protected. After you insert a 3D model, you can use the tools on the 3D Model tab to select other options and to add alt text. You can use the More button in the 3D Model Views group to choose from a variety of views for your model. For example, you could choose to display an astronaut 3D model as seen from above or below.

Proskills

Written Communication: Understanding Copyright Laws

You should assume that any image, video, or other item you find on the web is owned by someone who has a right to control its use. It's your responsibility to make sure you understand copyright laws and to abide by them. The U.S. Copyright Office maintains a Frequently Asked Questions page that should answer any questions you might have: www.copyright.gov/help/faq.

Generally, copyright laws allow a student to reuse a photo, drawing, or other item for educational purposes, on a one-time basis, without getting permission from the owner. However, to avoid charges of plagiarism, students must acknowledge the source of the item in their work. Any person or organization looking to use copyright material in order to make a profit faces much more stringent copyright restrictions. In those instances, you must request permission from the owner, and you will often need to pay a fee.

When you search for images by clicking the Pictures button in the Illustrations group on the Insert tab, and then clicking Online Pictures, all of the images that initially appear as a result of your search are licensed under a Creative Commons license, as indicated by the checkmark in the Creative Commons only check box. There are several types of Creative Commons licenses. One type allows you to use an image for any reason, including commercial use, and to modify the image, as long as the photographer is credited or attributed (similar to the credits under the photos in some figures in this book). Another type of license allows you to use an image with an attribution as long as it is not for commercial purposes and as long as you do not modify the image. You can learn more about Creative Commons licenses at creativecommons.org.

Even if an image has a Creative Commons license, you must still review the exact license on the website on which the image is stored. When you point to an image in the search results in the Online Pictures window, the More information and actions button appears in the lower-right corner of the image. Click the icon to display more information about the image, including its website. Note that you can also click the Learn more here link, at the bottom of the Online Pictures dialog box, to read an in-depth explanation of copyright regulations.

Even if you have verified that the copyright restrictions governing a picture do not require you to include a credit acknowledging its source, it's a good idea to include one anyhow. You never want to appear to be claiming ownership of something you did not create. To allow you to focus on the skills taught in this module, you will not take the time to add credits in the newsletter you are creating. But the sources of the images are credited next to the module figures.

Stefan would like to add an apple icon to the newsletter to illustrate the article about fruits and vegetables. In the process of adding it, you will explore some of the other picture options.

To insert an icon:

1. Verify that your computer is connected to the Internet, change the Zoom level to **120%**, and then scroll to display the middle of page 2.
2. On page 2, click the border of the text box to select it, and then, if necessary, drag the text box up so the top border aligns with the "Free Diabetes Assessments" heading. Make sure its left border aligns with the left border of the blue-shaded paragraph below. You'll insert the icon in the white space below the text box.
3. Click at the end of the paragraph below the "Fruits and Vegetables Are Your Friends" heading.
4. On the ribbon, click the **Insert** tab.

5. In the Illustrations group, click the **Pictures** button and then click **Stock Images**. The Microsoft 365 library opens, displaying a gallery of images. You can use the options in the library to find a wide array of other types of pictures. You start by clicking the type of picture you want at the top, then clicking a category, and then scrolling down to review the related pictures. Or you can select a picture type and then search for a specific picture using the Search box. Refer to Figure 4–34.

Figure 4–34 Microsoft 365 Illustrations library

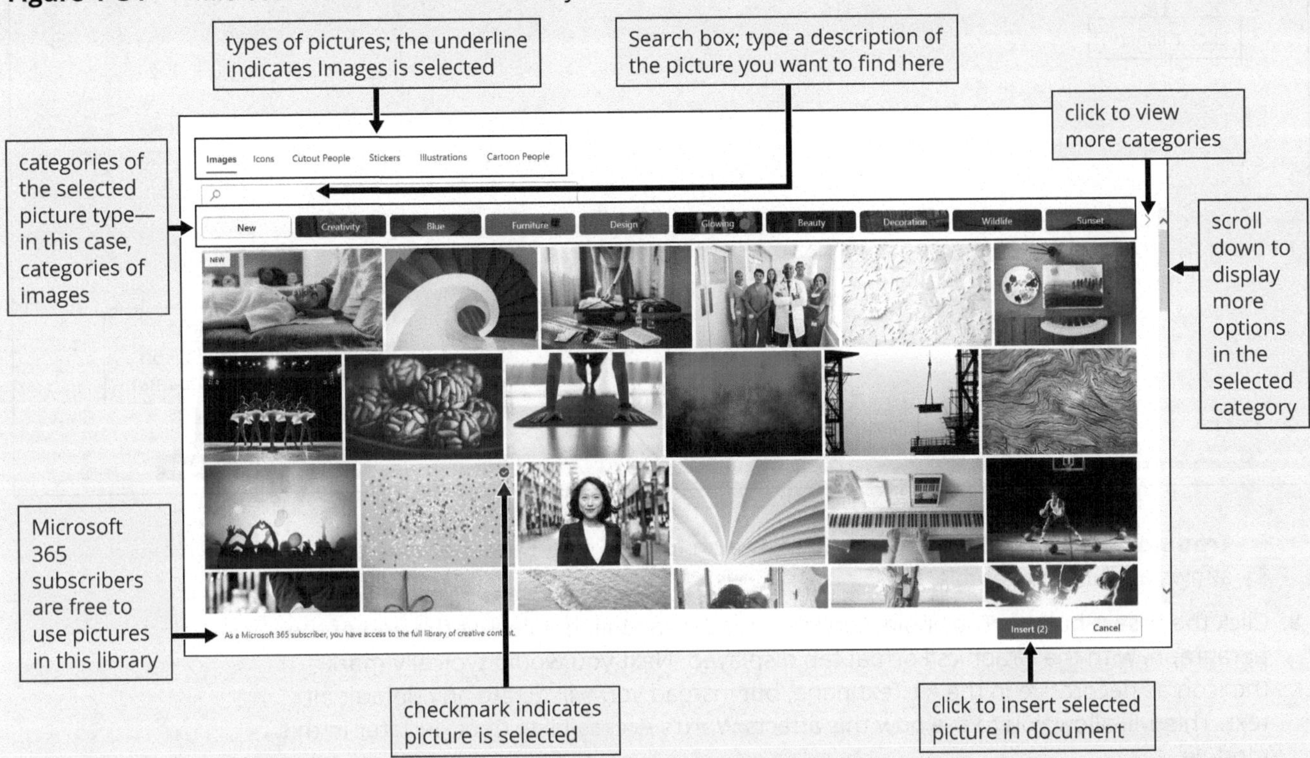

> **Tip** To open the Microsoft 365 library with the Icons tab displayed, you could click the Icons button in the Illustrations group instead.

6. Explore the options in the Microsoft 365 library, clicking each content type at the top of the library, and then using the arrows to scroll to the right and left to view additional categories. Click any category, and then scroll down in the gallery to view the related illustrations.

7. Click **Icons** at the top of the library, click the Search box, type **apple**, and then click the icon showing an apple with black fill. A checkmark indicates that the icon is selected, as shown in Figure 4–35.

Figure 4–35 Selected icon

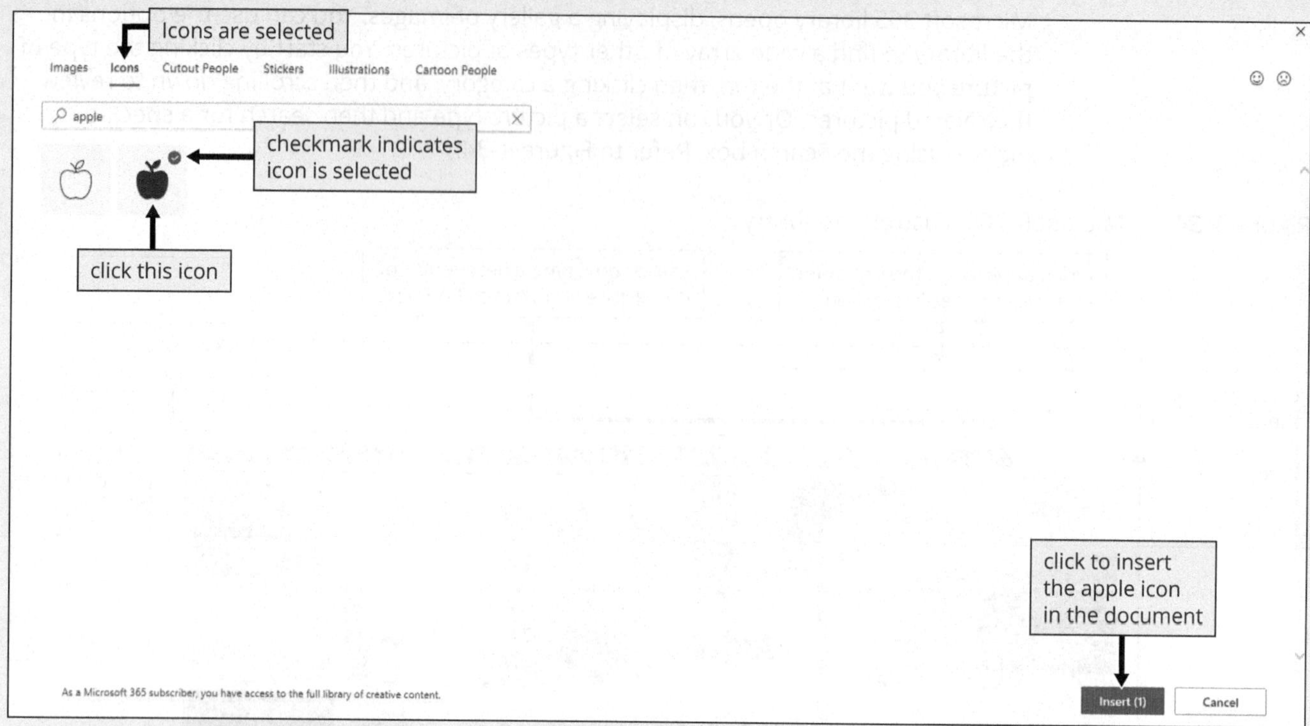

Trouble? If you don't see an apple icon, search for and select another icon that shows a fruit or vegetable.

8. Click the **Insert** button. The apple icon is inserted as an inline object at the end of the paragraph, with the Graphics Format tab displayed. Next you would typically mark the icon as decorative in the Alt Text pane, but instead you will delete any default alt text. This will allow you to see how this affects Word's Accessibility Checker later in this module.
9. In the Accessibility group on the Graphics Format tab, click the **Alt Text** button to open the Alt Text pane and delete any alt text. Make sure the **Mark as decorative** check box is not selected, and then close the Alt Text pane.

   By default, an icon is inserted as an inline object, so you need to apply text wrapping to it.
10. In the Arrange group, click the **Wrap Text** button to open the Wrap Text menu and then click **In Front of Text**.
11. Click the **Wrap Text** button again, and then click **Fix Position on Page**.
12. Drag the icon left to center it in the white space below the text box in the margin.

Formatting an Icon with a Graphics Style

To make the icon more interesting, you can change its fill and outline colors. You could do that by using the Graphics Fill button and the Graphics Outline button in the Graphics Styles group on the Graphics Format tab. You can also change both options at once by applying a graphics style. You'll try that option next, and then you'll enlarge the icon.

To apply a graphics style and enlarge the icon:

1. In the Graphics Styles group, click the **More** button to open the Graphics Styles gallery, point to some of the style icons and view the Live Previews in the document, and then click the **Colored Fill - Accent 1, Dark 1 Outline** style, which is in the second row from the bottom, second style from the left. The style applies a blue fill with a black outline to the icon.
2. In the Graphics Styles group, click the **Graphics Effects** button to open the Graphics Effects menu, point to **Shadow** to open the Shadow Effects gallery, and then point to the **Perspective: Upper Left** effect, which is in the top row of the Perspectives section, first effect on the left. A Live Preview appears in the document, as in Figure 4–36.

Figure 4–36 Icon with Live Preview of graphics style

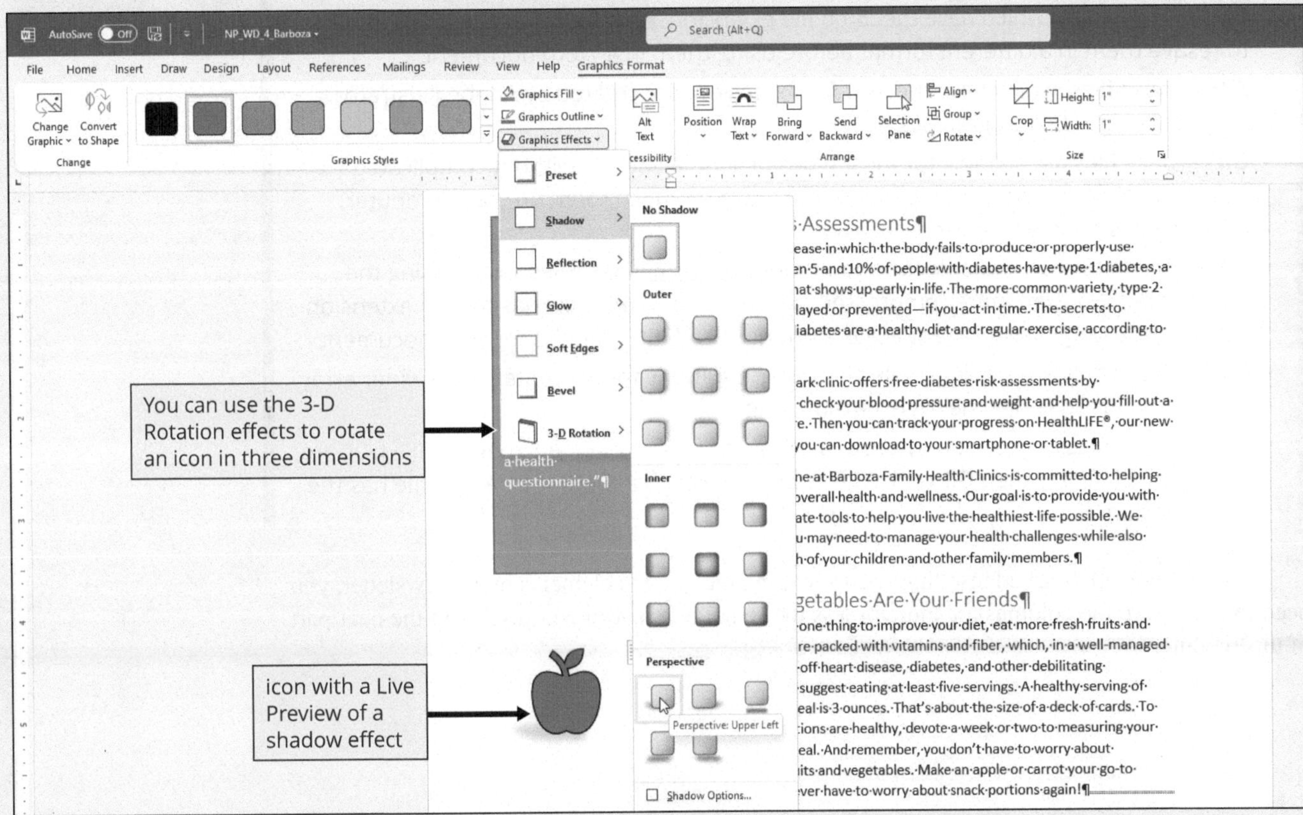

Tip You can use the 3-D Rotation effects to rotate an icon in three dimensions.

3. Click the **Perspective: Upper Left** effect. A shadow appears around the bottom of the icon.
4. In the Size group, change the icon's height to 1.5 inches. Because the icon has a square aspect ratio, its width also changes to 1.5 inches.
5. Drag the icon as necessary to make sure it is centered in the white space below the text box in the margin, click anywhere in the document to deselect the icon, and then save the document.

Tip To edit an icon using the tools on the Shape Format tab, select the icon, click the Convert to Shape button in the Change group on the Graphics Format tab, and then click the icon or one of its shapes.

Insight

Working with Digital Picture Files

Digital picture files come in two main types—vector graphics and raster graphics. A vector graphics file stores an image as a mathematical formula, which means you can increase or decrease the size of the image as much as you want without affecting its overall quality. Vector graphics are often used for line drawings and, because the file sizes tend to be small, are widely used on the web. File types for vector graphics are often proprietary, which means they work only in specific graphics programs. In Word, you will sometimes encounter files with the .wmf file extension, which is short for Windows Metafiles. A WMF file is a type of vector graphics file created specifically for Windows. In most cases, though, you'll work with raster graphics, also known as bitmap graphics. A **bitmap** is a grid of square colored dots, called **pixels**, that form a picture. A bitmap graphic, then, is essentially a collection of pixels. The most common types of bitmap files are as follows:

- **BMP**—These files, which have the .bmp file extension, tend to be very large, so it's best to resave them in a different format before using them in a Word document.
- **EPS**—These files, which have the .eps file extension, are created by Adobe Illustrator and can contain text as graphics.
- **GIF**—These files are suitable for most types of simple line art, without complicated colors. A GIF file is compressed, so it doesn't take up much room on your computer. A GIF file has the file extension .gif.
- **JPEG**—These files are suitable for photographs and drawings. Files stored using the JPEG format are even more compressed than GIF files. A JPEG file has the file extension .jpg. If conserving file storage space is a priority, use JPEG graphics for your document.
- **PNG**—These files are similar to GIF files but are suitable for art containing a wider array of colors. A PNG file has the file extension .png.
- **TIFF**—These files are commonly used for photographs or scanned images. TIFF files are usually much larger than GIF or JPEG files but smaller than BMP files. A TIFF file has the file extension .tif.

Now that you are finished inserting and formatting the graphic elements in the newsletter, you need to make sure the columns are more or less the same length. You will do that in the next part of this module.

Part 4.2 Quick Check

1. What two things do you need to consider when resizing WordArt?
2. When cropping a picture, how can you maintain a specific ratio of width to height?
3. What should you assume about any image, video, or other item you find on the web?
4. Name two types of illustrations you can add to a document via the Stock Images command on the Pictures menu.
5. Explain two ways to change an icon's fill color and outline color.

Part 4.3 Visual Overview: Checking a Document for Accessibility

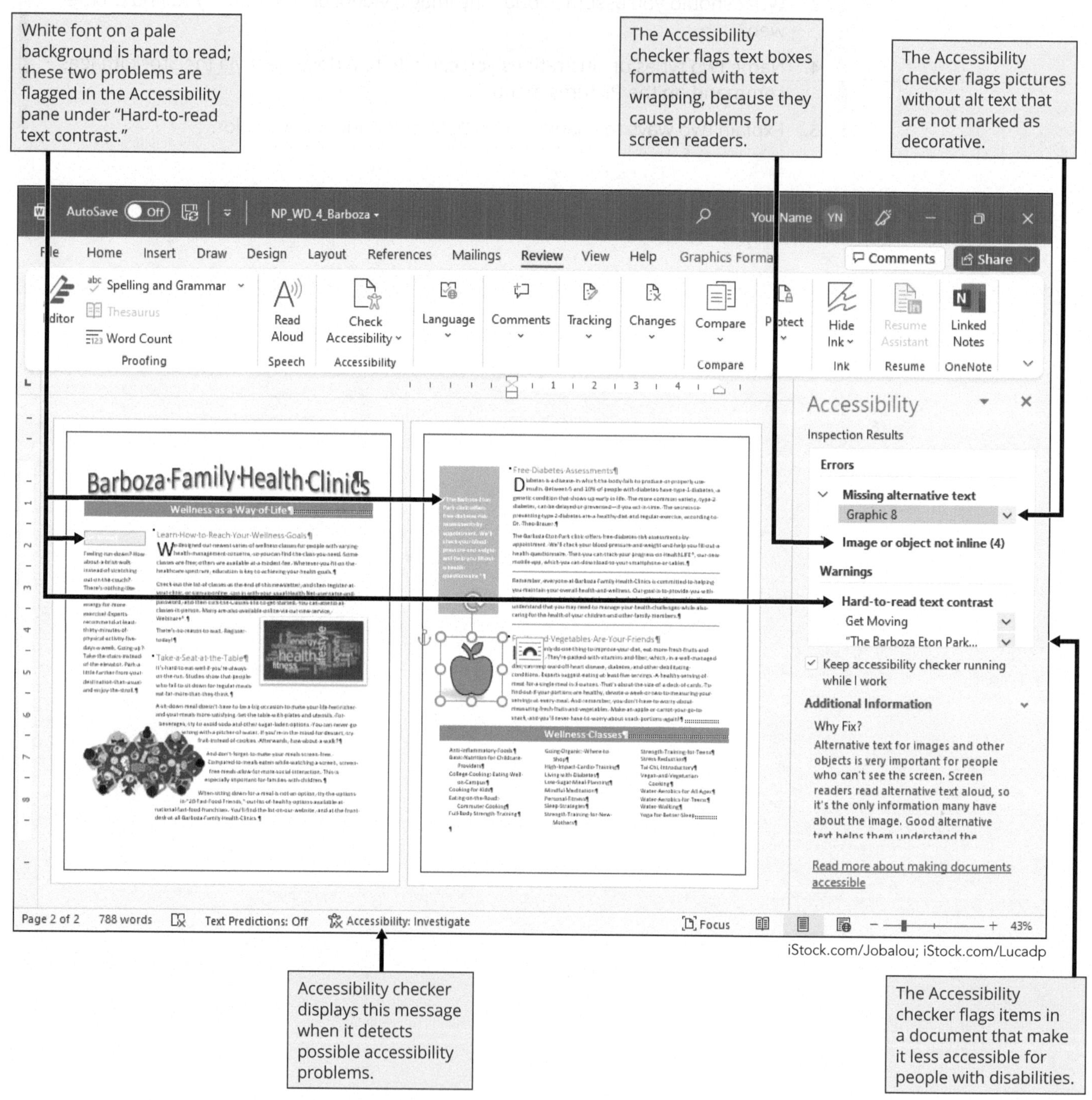

iStock.com/Jobalou; iStock.com/Lucadp

Clicking the Check Accessibility button opens the Accessibility pane.

You can click an item in the Accessibility pane, then click its arrow button to display a list of recommended actions...

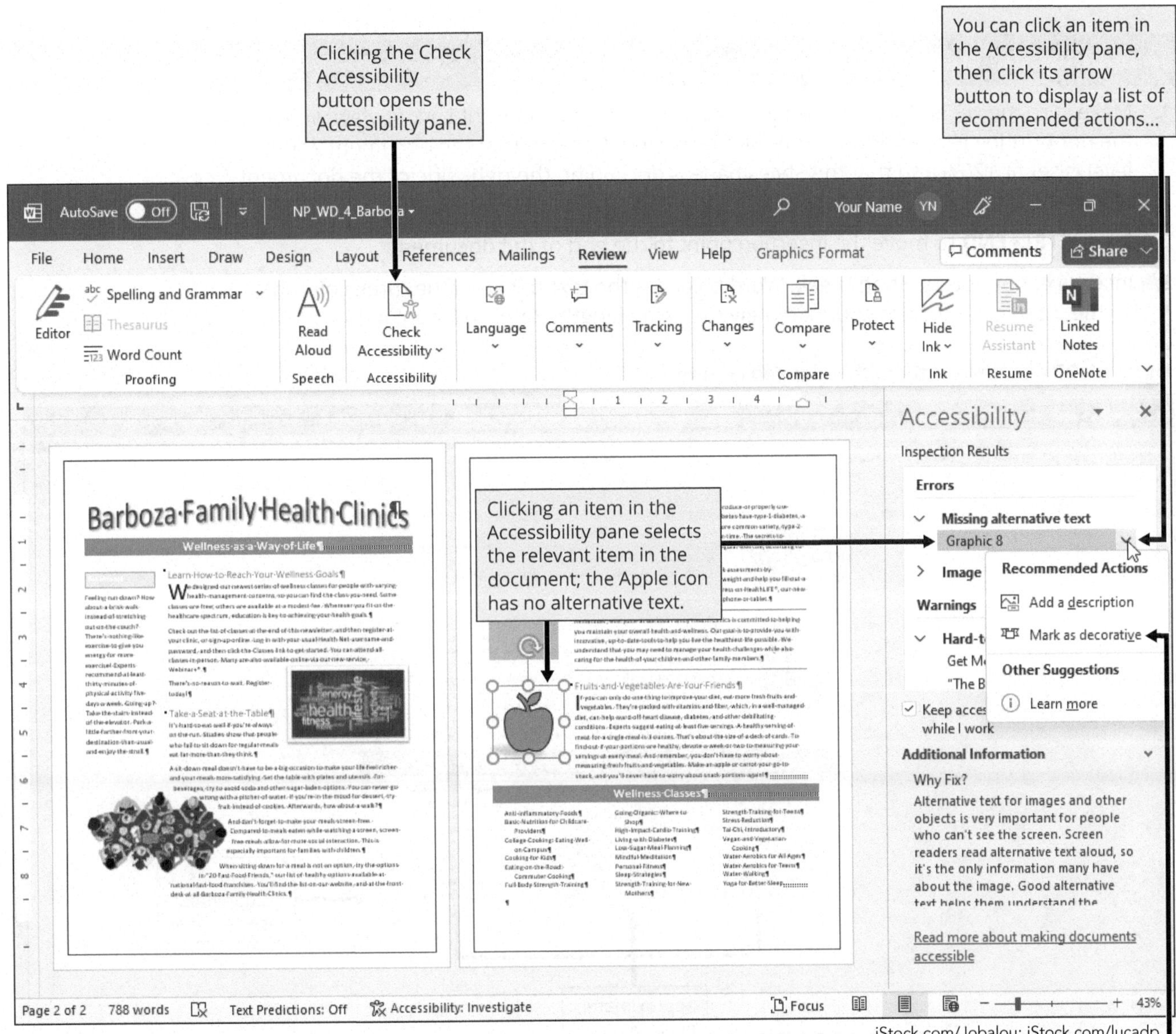

Clicking an item in the Accessibility pane selects the relevant item in the document; the Apple icon has no alternative text.

iStock.com/Jobalou; iStock.com/lucadp

...and then click the action you want to perform; here, "Mark as decorative" is a good choice for the apple icon.

Balancing Columns

To **balance** columns on a page—that is, to make them equal length—you insert a continuous section break at the end of the last column. Word then adjusts the flow of content between the columns so they are of equal or near-equal length. The columns remain balanced no matter how much material you remove from any of the columns later. The columns also remain balanced if you add material that causes the columns to flow to a new page; the overflow will also be formatted in balanced columns.

To balance the columns:

1. Make sure the NP_WD_4_ Barboza.docx document is open in Print Layout view with the nonprinting characters and the ruler displayed. Confirm that the document Zoom level is set at 120% and that the Styles pane is docked on the right side of the document window.
2. Press **CTRL+END** to move the insertion point to the end of the document.
3. Insert a continuous section break. Word balances the text between the three columns, so the three columns are approximately the same length. Refer to Figure 4–37.

Figure 4–37 Newsletter with balanced columns

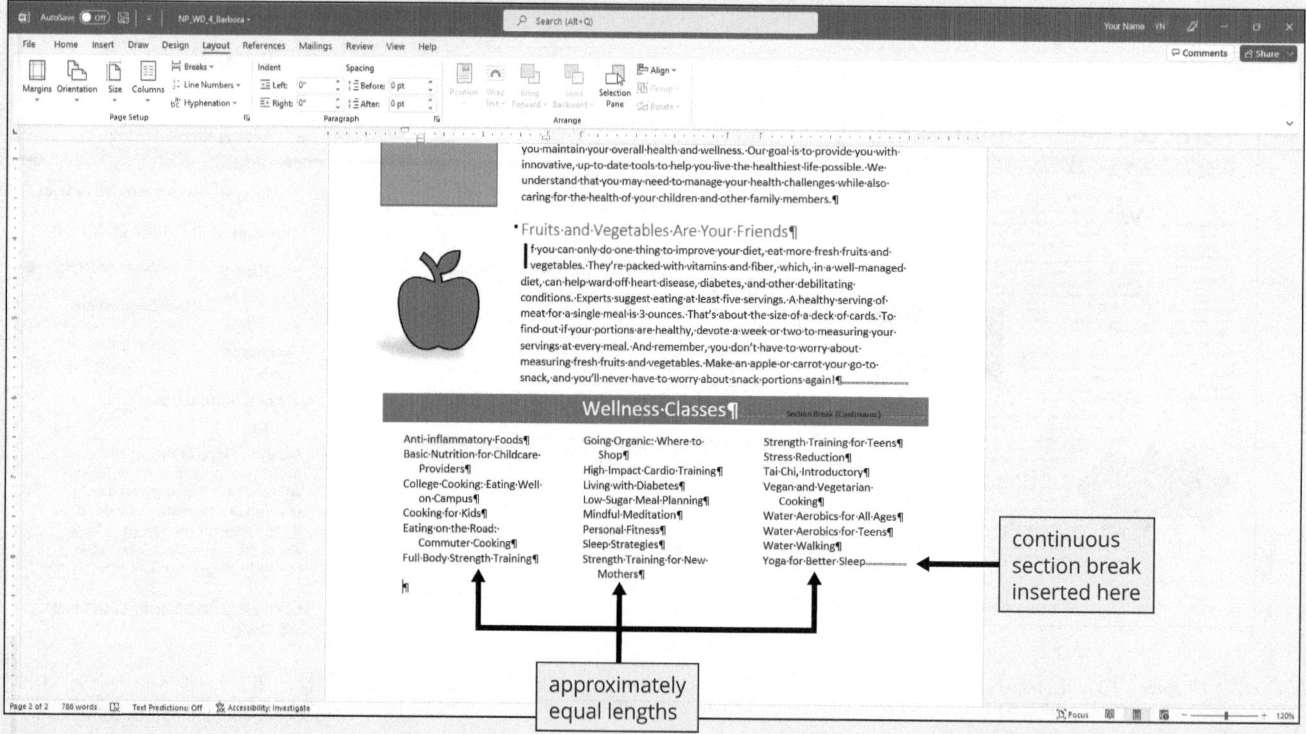

Note that you can also adjust the length of a column by inserting a column break using the Breaks button in the Page Setup group on the Layout tab. A column break moves all the text and graphics following it to the next column. Column breaks are useful when you have a multipage document formatted in three or more columns, with only enough text on the last page to fill some of the columns. In that case, balancing columns on the last page won't work. Instead, you can use a column break to distribute an equal amount of text over all the columns on the page. However, as with page breaks, you need to be careful with column breaks because it's easy to forget that you inserted them. Then, if you add or remove text from the document, or change it in some other significant way, you might end up with a page layout you didn't expect.

Adding a Custom Paragraph Border

Paragraph borders are useful for drawing attention to text and also for separating parts of a document, so it is easier to read. You already know how to add a basic box border around a paragraph. You can also create a custom border consisting of one or more border lines, and then change the style, line width (sometimes called thickness or weight), and color.

Reference

Adding a Custom Border

- Position the insertion point in the paragraph to which you want to add a custom border.
- On the ribbon, click the Home tab.
- In the Paragraph group, click the Borders arrow, and then click Borders and Shading to open the Borders tab in the Borders and Shading dialog box.
- In the Setting list, click the Custom button.
- In the Preview area, click where you want to insert a border. For example, you could click below the paragraph to insert a bottom border. Or you could click above and below the paragraph to insert top and bottom borders.
- Click the Color arrow, click a border color, and then, in the Preview area, click the border or borders you want to format in that color. You can format different borders in different colors.
- Click the Width arrow, click a border width and then, in the Preview area, click the border or borders you want to format with that line width. You can format different borders with different widths.
- Click OK.

Stefan wants to make sure readers pay special attention to the second paragraph on page 2. You can help with that by adding a custom border.

To insert a custom border in the newsletter:

1. On page 2, scroll up if necessary to display the paragraph above the heading "Fruits and Vegetables Are Your Friends," which begins "Remember, everyone at Barboza Family Health Clinics..."
2. Click anywhere in the paragraph that begins "Remember, everyone at Barboza Family Health Clinics..."
3. Click the **Home** tab.
4. In the Paragraph group, click the **Borders arrow**, and then click **Borders and Shading**. The Borders and Shading dialog box opens with the Borders tab selected.
5. In the Setting list on the left, click the **Custom** button. Now you will add top and bottom borders to the paragraph. The Preview area on the right side of the dialog box contains a block of gray lines meant to simulate a paragraph of text. You can add borders by selecting style, color and width settings, and then clicking above, below, or to the left or right of the gray lines.
6. Click the **Width** arrow, click **1 ½ pt**, click the **Color** arrow, and then click the **Blue, Accent 1** square in the top row of the Theme colors section, fifth square from the left.

   The default style setting is appropriate for this document, so you are finished selecting the border options for the paragraph's top border.

7. In the Preview area, click the top border to add a blue border with the 1 ½ pt width. For the bottom border, you will retain the Blue, Accent 1 color, but increase the width.
8. Click the **Width** arrow, click **3 pt**, and then, in the Preview area, click the bottom border to add a blue border with a 3 pt width.
   Refer to Figure 4–38.

Figure 4–38 Borders tab in the Borders and Shading dialog box

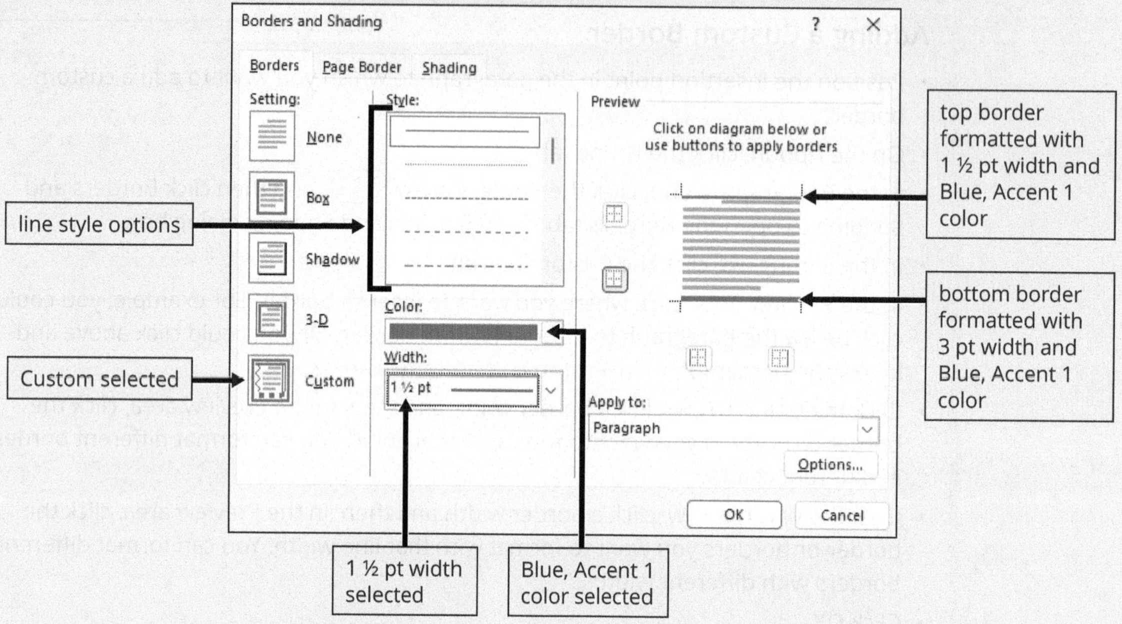

9. Click **OK**. The custom borders you created appear above and below the paragraph, reminding newsletter readers that Barboza Family Health is committed to their health and wellness.

To give the paragraph even more emphasis, you can add some space between the borders and the paragraph text.

To change the space between the borders and the paragraph text:

1. Make sure the insertion point is still in the paragraph that begins "Remember, everyone at Barboza Family Health Clinics...."
2. On the Home tab, in the Paragraph group, click the **Borders arrow**, and then click **Borders and Shading**. The Borders and Shading dialog box opens.
3. In the dialog box, click **Options**. The Border and Shading Options dialog box opens.
4. Change the values in the Top box and the Bottom box to **8 pt**.

5. Click **OK**, and then click **OK** in the Borders and Shading dialog box. The borders you added are now separated from the paragraph text by eight points of space. Refer to Figure 4–39.

Figure 4–39 Paragraph with eight points of space between it and the custom borders

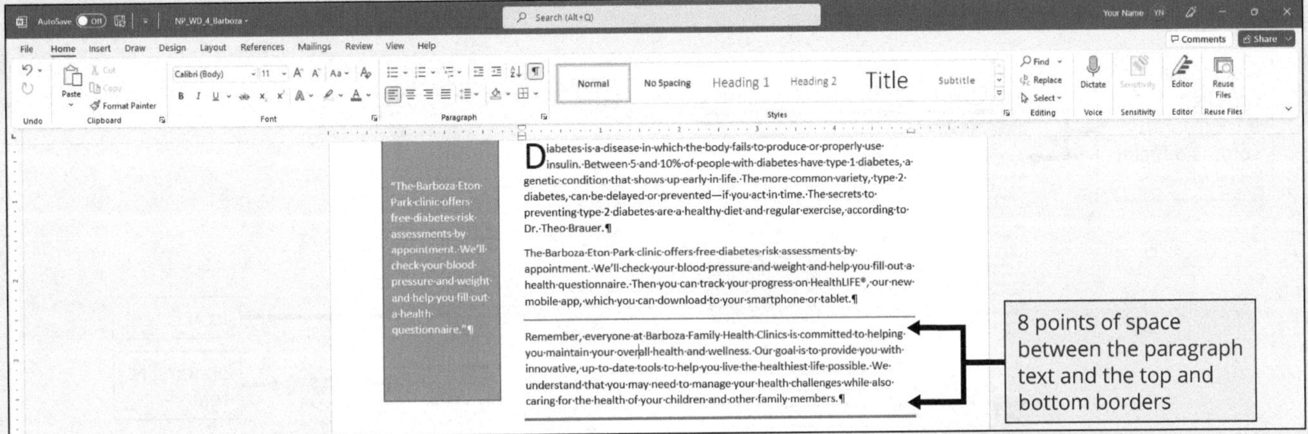

Tip You can use the Format Painter to copy custom borders from one paragraph to another.

6. Scroll down to review the columns at the end of page 2 and notice that even though you just added 16 points of space to the document text, the balanced columns did not change.
7. Save your work.

Enhancing the Newsletter's Formatting

A newsletter is a good opportunity to take advantage of some of Word's flashier formatting options, such as adding a page border and changing the theme colors. Stefan asks you to do both to give the newsletter a little more polish.

To change the theme colors and insert a border around both pages of the newsletter:

1. Change the Zoom level to **Multiple Pages**.
2. On the ribbon, click the **Design** tab.
3. In the Document Formatting group, click the **Colors** button, scroll down, and then click **Blue Green**. The colors of the various document elements—such as the text boxes, icon, and headings—change to reflect the new theme colors.

   The lighter background colors in the text boxes make the white font harder to read. You will address that issue in the next section, when you check the document for accessibility. Refer to Figure 4–40.

Figure 4–40 Newsletter with new theme colors

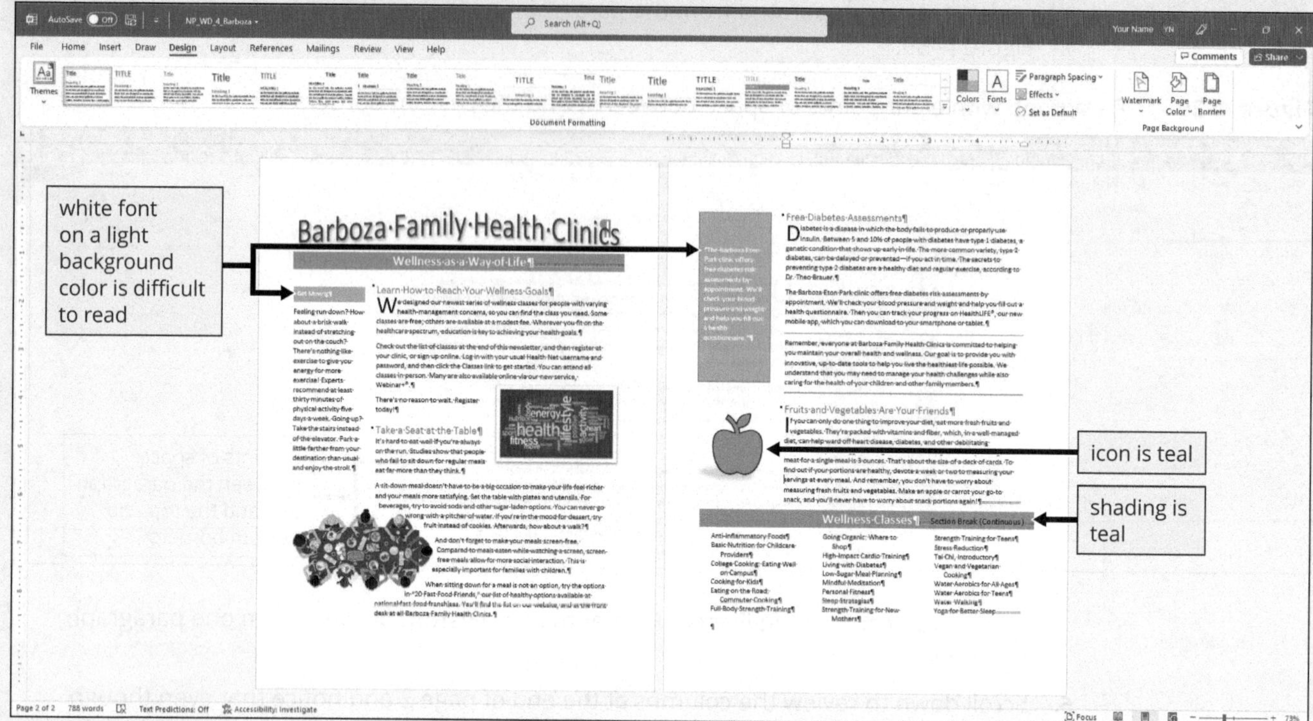

iStock.com/Jobalou; iStock.com/lucadp

4. In the Page Background group, click the **Page Borders** button. The Borders and Shading dialog box opens with the Page Border tab displayed.
5. In the Setting section, click the **Box** setting.

   Stefan is happy with all the default page border settings, except one; he wants to use a dark blue border color.
6. Click the **Color** arrow to open the Color gallery, and then click the **Blue, Accent 6, Darker 50%** square, which is in the bottom row, first box on the right in the Theme Colors section.
7. Click **OK**. The newsletter now has a dark blue border, as shown earlier in Part 4.1 Visual Overview.
8. Compare the newsletter to Part 4.1 Visual Overview and adjust the position of the various elements as necessary, to make your newsletter match the layout of the Visual Overview as closely as possible. Note that you can click a text box or graphic object to select it, and then use the arrow keys on your keyboard to nudge the item up, down, left, or right. Don't be concerned with trying to get the text to wrap around the dinner table image exactly as it does in Part 4.1 Visual Overview. Just make sure it does not obscure any text, and that the heading "Free Diabetes Assessments" appears at the top of page 2.
9. Save the document. Finally, to get a better sense of how the document with complicated formatting will look when printed, it's a good idea to review it with nonprinting characters turned off.
10. On the ribbon, click the **Home** tab.
11. In the Paragraph group, click the **Show/Hide** button ¶ to turn off nonprinting characters.
12. Change the Zoom level to **120%**, and then scroll to display page 2.
13. On page 2, at the end of the first paragraph after the "Free Diabetes Assessments" heading, replace "Theo Brauer" with your first and last names.
14. Save the document.

Before you call a document finished, you should check it for issues that make it inaccessible—that is, difficult for people to read. You can do that by using Word's Accessibility Checker.

Checking a Document for Accessibility

An **accessible document** is a document designed to be read by people with a wide range of abilities and disabilities, with or without assistive technology such as a screen reader. A truly accessible document is as easy for someone with blindness, visual impairments, color blindness, dyslexia, or a learning disability to read via a screen reader as it is for any person to read without a screen reader. The United States federal government requires all government documents (and documents produced by businesses that work for the government) to adhere to specific standards that ensure a document can be read by a screen reader. You can learn more about these requirements here: section 508.gov. More and more, businesses and other organizations are also enforcing accessibility standards.

As you have learned, one way to make documents accessible is to add alt text describing the contents of graphics. If a graphic contains no actual information, and instead merely adds design interest, you should delete any default alt text and then select the Mark as decorative check box in the Alt Text pane, as you did for the pictures in this module. This tells a screen reader to ignore the decorative item. As you work on more advanced Word documents, you will gain practice adding alt text that allows a screen reader to narrate the contents of charts, tables, SmartArt, and other more complicated items.

You can also make a document easier for people to read by paying attention to the contrast between font colors and background colors. It's important to choose paragraph shading and font colors that contrast clearly. For example, you should avoid using a white font on a pale blue background.

But no matter how hard you try to make a document accessible, you might not catch everything. To help you to identify accessibility issues in a document, you can use Word's **Accessibility Checker**, which checks for potential problems. Content flagged as an error is content that is difficult or impossible for some readers to access. Content flagged with a warning is content that might be difficult for some readers to access. By default, the Accessibility Checker runs in the background continuously while you work on a document. If the Accessibility Checker does not identify any accessibility issues, the status bar displays the message "Accessibility: Good to go." But if the Accessibility Checker detects a potential issue, it displays the message: "Accessibility: Investigate."

Some screen readers (such as Word's Read Aloud tool) cannot access text in a text box at all, while more powerful screen readers can access text boxes, but only if they are formatted as inline objects. For that reason, the Accessibility Checker will flag any text boxes that are not formatted as inline objects. Earlier in this module, you formatted text boxes with text wrapping so you could gain experience working with floating objects and sidebars, which are typical elements of desktop published documents. As you check the newsletter for accessibility issues in the next set of steps, you will retain text wrapping for text boxes because one goal of this module is to give you an opportunity to learn how text wrapping works. But keep in mind that when you choose to use text boxes that are not inline objects, you are making your document less accessible for people using screen readers.

In the following steps, you will use the Accessibility Checker to see what adjustments could make the newsletter more accessible. Note that the results of the Accessibility Checker can vary from one computer to another, and from one time to another.

To check the newsletter for accessibility issues:

1. Change View setting to **Multiple Pages**, so you can see the entire newsletter at once. Notice that the status bar displays the message "Accessibility: Investigate," indicating that the newsletter contains some potential accessibility problems. You could click the message to open the Accessibility pane, but in the next step you will use another option.
2. On the ribbon, click the **Review** tab, and then click the **Check Accessibility** button in the Accessibility group to display the Accessibility pane to the right of the document window. Figure 4–41 shows two categories of results—errors and warnings—but you might see something different on your screen. The number next to an item tells you how many instances of that issue the document contains. The number of instances on your computer might not match the number in Figure 4–41. You can click the arrow button next to an item to display more information. The bottom of the Accessibility pane provides additional information about some of the items in the list.

Figure 4–41 Errors and warning in the Accessibility pane

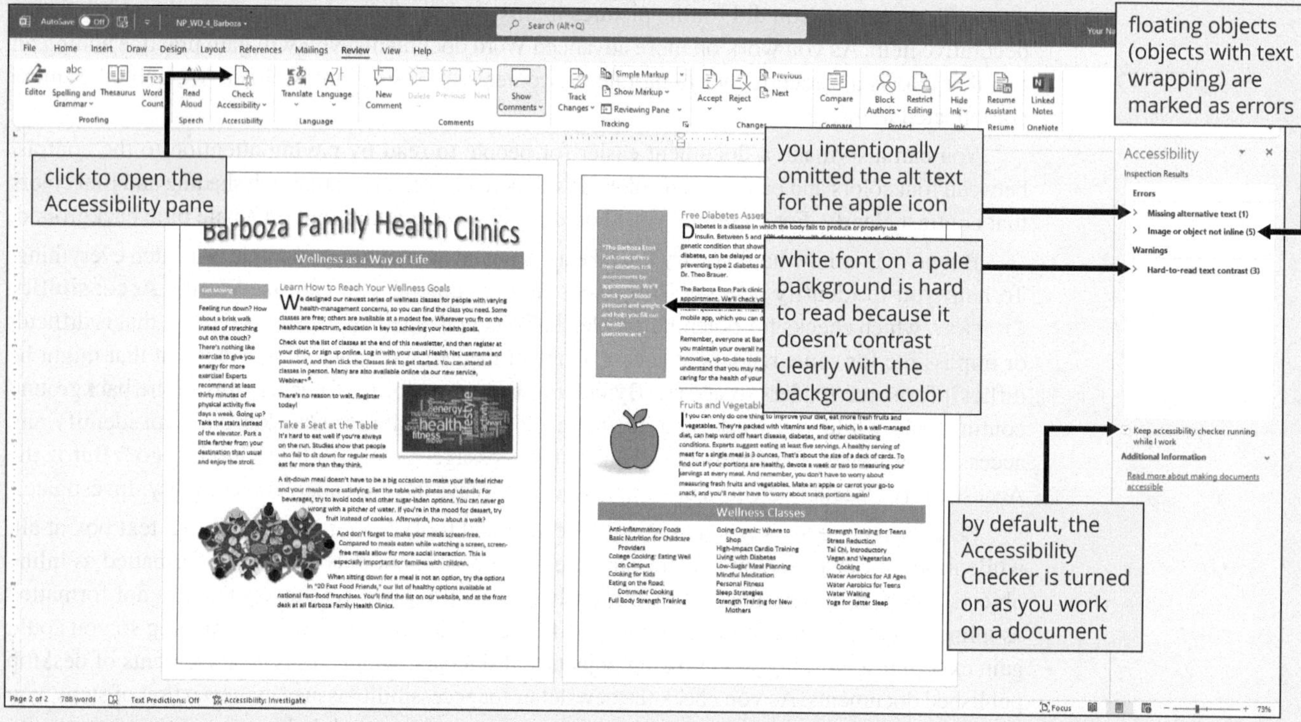

iStock.com/Jobalou; iStock.com/lucadp

Tip The Accessibility Checker is a feature that will continue to evolve over time. It's difficult to predict exactly what you might see at any one time.

3. In the Accessibility pane, click **Missing alternative text** to display the word "Graphic" with a number following it. (The exact number doesn't matter.) Recall that you did not create any alt text for the apple icon earlier in this module, so the Accessibility pane flagged it as an accessibility error.
4. Click **Graphic** to select it and display a down arrow to its right. The apple icon is selected in the document.

Trouble? You might see a number after "Graphic" in the Accessibility pane. That's fine. Just click "Graphic," as described in Step 4.

5. Click the down arrow next to **Graphic** to display the Recommended Actions menu, with options for correcting the error. Because the apple icon contains no information, you will mark it as decorative. Refer to Figure 4–42.

Figure 4–42 Options for correcting an accessibility error

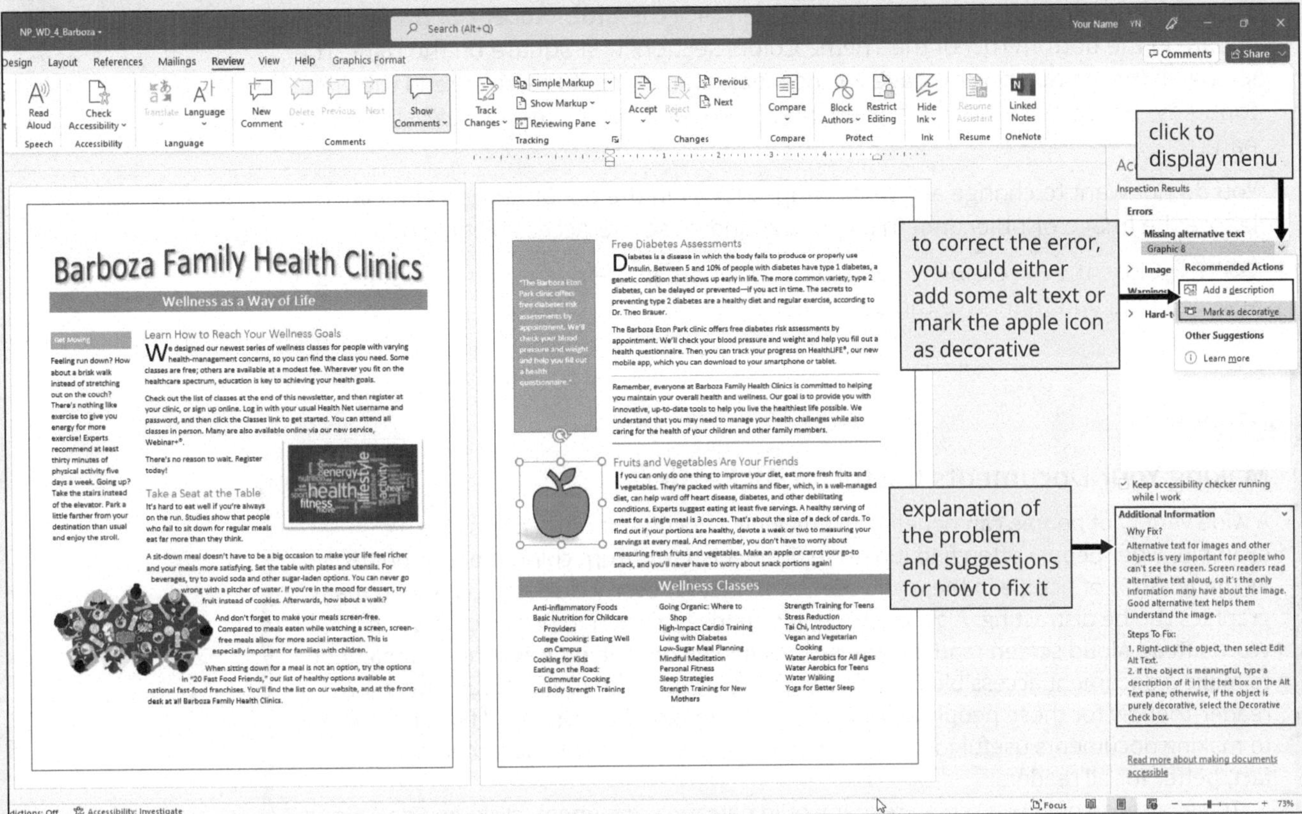

iStock.com/Jobalou; iStock.com/lucadp

6. Click **Mark as decorative**. Word marks the apple icon as decorative, and the Missing alternative text error no longer appears in the Accessibility pane. You can verify that the icon is now marked as decorative by opening the Alt Text pane.

> **Trouble?** If you make a mistake by clicking the wrong command in the Accessibility pane, click the Undo button in the Undo group on the Home tab to undo it. If that doesn't reverse the change, close the Accessibility pane, click the Undo button in the Undo group on the Home tab, and then open the Accessibility pane again.

7. Verify that the apple icon is selected in the document and then open the Alt Text pane. The Accessibility pane minimizes to an icon to the right of the Alt Text pane.
8. Note that the Mark as decorative check box is selected, and then close the Alt Text pane. The Accessibility pane is again displayed on the right side of the document window.
9. Under Warnings, click **hard-to-read text contrast** to display a list of items with text that is hard to read. Word flagged the title of the text box on page 1 and the text box on page 2 because the light teal text does not contrast clearly with the white font. (Don't be concerned if your Accessibility pane displays more than one entry for the text box on page 2.) You can fix these problems by selecting darker shading.
10. Click the down arrow to the right of **Get** to select the word "Get" in the "Get Moving" title on page 1 and open the Recommended Actions menu.
11. In the Recommended Actions menu, point to the arrow to the right of **Paragraph Shading** to open the Paragraph Shading palette, and then click the **Blue, Accent 6, Darker 50%** square in the bottom row of the Theme Colors section, first square on the right. The title box in the text box on page 1 is now formatted with dark blue shading, making the white font easier to read. Now you need to fix the problem with the text on page 2.
12. Click the down arrow to the right of **"The Barboza..."** to select that text in the text box on page 2 and open the Recommended Actions menu.

13. In the Recommended Actions menu, point to the arrow to the right of **Shape Fill** to open the Paragraph Shading palette, and then click the **Blue, Accent 6, Darker 50%** square in the bottom row of the Theme Colors section, first square on the right. The shape fill for the text box on page 2 is now darker, making it easier to read the white font. Any mentions of the text box on page 2 are removed from the Accessibility pane.

    You do not want to change any word wrap settings in the document, so you can ignore the Image or object not in line errors and close the Accessibility pane.

14. **sam** Close the Accessibility pane, click anywhere in the document to deselect any selected text, and then save the document.

Insight

Making Your Documents Useful for All Readers

A wide variety of people can benefit from making a document more accessible. For example, older people often find it hard to distinguish text from colored backgrounds. As many as 8% of people in the world are colorblind. An overly cluttered page with many graphics can be distracting. Also, many people choose to listen to documents using Word's Read Aloud screen reader because they find it convenient. Anything you might do to make a document accessible for a screen reader would also make documents more reader-friendly for these people as well. So, while the term "accessibility" typically refers to making documents useful for people with disabilities, accessible documents are, in fact, better for all readers.

To get a sense of how a screen reader would narrate a document, click the Read Aloud button in the Voice group on the Home tab and listen to the Read Aloud narration. Note any items that the Read Aloud screen reader skips. People with vision impairments would typically use more powerful screen readers than Word's Read Aloud tool but experimenting with it will give you a sense of how a screen reader works.

Now that you've made the newsletter more accessible, you are ready to export it as a PDF that Stefan can email to the printer.

Saving a Document as a PDF

A **PDF**, or **Portable Document Format file**, contains an image showing exactly how a document will look when printed. Exporting a document as a PDF ensures it can be opened on any computer. This is especially useful when you need to email a document to people who might not have Word installed on their computers. All PDFs have a file extension of .pdf. By default, PDFs open in your default browser, unless you have a PDF reader or editor installed, such as Adobe Acrobat Reader, a free program installed on most computers for reading PDFs, or Adobe Acrobat, a PDF-editing program available for purchase from Adobe.

To save the newsletter document as a PDF:

1. On the ribbon, click the **File** tab to open Backstage view.
2. In the navigation pane, click **Export** to display the Export screen with Create PDF/XPS Document selected. You can ignore the Investigate Accessibility button because you have already made the accessibility-related changes you want to make.
3. Click the **Create PDF/XPS** button. The Publish as PDF or XPS dialog box opens.

4. If necessary, navigate to the location specified by your instructor for saving your files, and then verify that "NP_WD_4_Barboza" appears in the File name box. Below the Save as type box, verify that the "Open file after publishing" check box is selected. The "Standard (publishing online and printing)" button might be selected by default. This generates a PDF suitable for printing. If you plan to distribute a PDF only via email or over the web, you should select the "Minimum size (publishing online)" button instead. Refer to Figure 4–43.

Figure 4–43 Publish as PDF or XPS dialog box

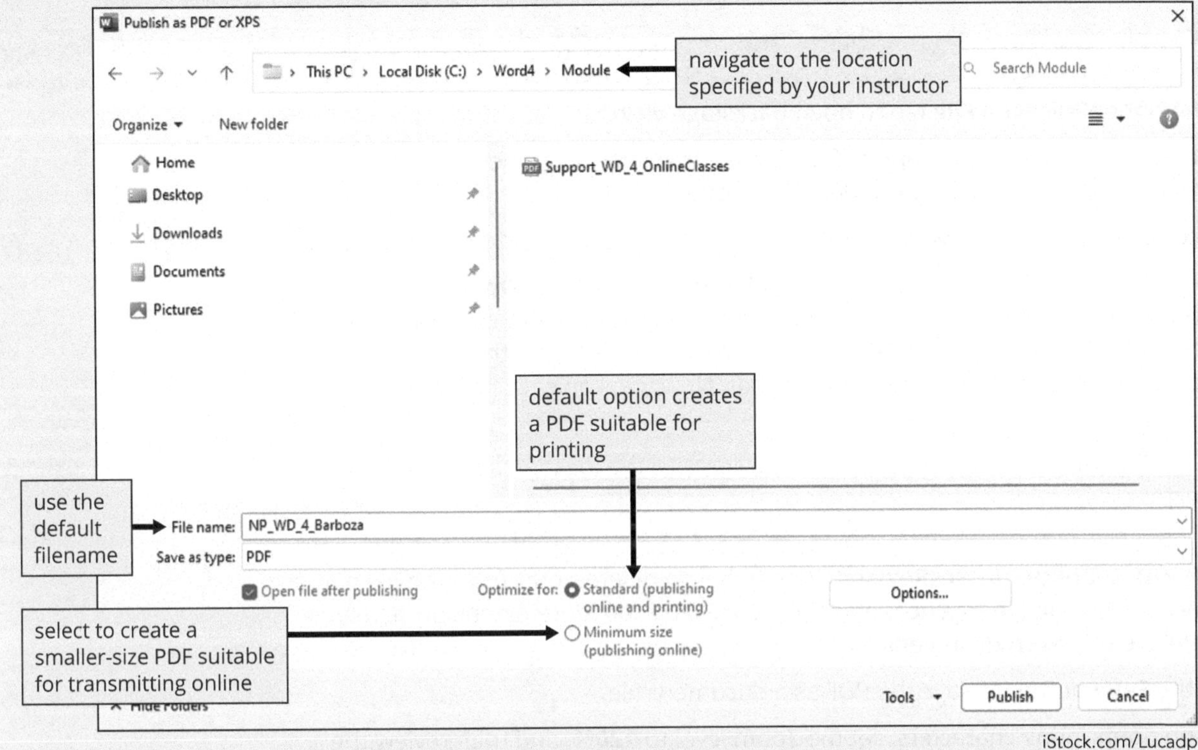

iStock.com/Lucadp

5. Click the **Publish** button. The Publish as PDF or XPS dialog box closes, and, after a pause, your default browser or a PDF reader or editor application opens with the NP_WD_4_Barboza.pdf file displayed.
6. Scroll down and review the PDF. Note that results can vary from one computer to another when you save a Word document as a PDF. Sometimes you might need to go back to the Word document, make some adjustments, and then re-save the document as a PDF.
7. Close Adobe Acrobat Reader or Adobe Acrobat.
8. In Word, close the document, saving changes if necessary, but keep Word running.

In addition to saving a Word document as a PDF, you can convert a PDF to a Word document.

Converting a PDF to a Word Document

You may sometimes need to use text from a PDF in your own Word documents. Before you can do this, of course, you need to make sure you have permission to do so. Assuming you do, you can open the PDF in a browser or PDF reader, drag the pointer to select the text you want to copy, press CTRL+C, return to your Word document, and then press CTRL+V to paste the text into your document. If you need to reuse or edit the entire contents of a PDF, it's easier to convert it to a Word document. This is a very useful option with PDFs that consist mostly of text. For more complicated PDFs, such as the NP_WD_4_Barboza.pdf file you just created, the results are less predictable.

> **Tip** If the PDF's creator restricted the file's security using, you will not be able to copy text from the PDF or convert it to a Word document.

Stefan has a PDF containing some text about online classes. He asks you to open it in Word and convert it back to a Word document file.

To open the PDF in Word:

1. On the ribbon, click the **File** tab to open Backstage view.
2. In the navigation pane, click **Open**, if necessary, to display the Open screen, click **Browse**, and then navigate to the **Word4 > Module** folder.
3. If necessary, click the **arrow** to the right of the File name box, and then click **All Files**.
4. In the file list, click **Support_WD_4_OnlineClasses.pdf**, click the **Open** button, and then, if you see a dialog box explaining that Word is about to convert a PDF to a Word document, click **OK**. The PDF opens in Word, with the name "Support_WD_4_OnlineClasses" in the title bar. Now you can save it as a Word document.
5. Click the **File** tab, click **Save As**, and then navigate to the location specified by your instructor.
6. Verify that "Word Document" appears in the Save as type box, change the file name to **NP_WD_4_OnlineClassesRevised**. Remember to delete ".pdf" from the file name. When you save the file as a document, Word will add the .docx extension signifying that the file is a Word document.
7. Click the **Save** button to save the PDF as a document file.
8. Turn on nonprinting characters, set the Zoom level to **120%**, and then review the document, which consists of a WordArt headline and a paragraph of text formatted in the Normal style. If you see one or more extra spaces at the end of the paragraph of text, they were added during the conversion from a PDF to a Word document. In a more complicated document, you might see graphics overlaid on top of text, or columns broken across multiple pages.
9. Close the **NP_WD_4_OnlineClassesRevised.docx** document.

Part 4.3 Quick Check

1. How do you balance columns on a page?
2. What is the first step in creating a custom paragraph border?
3. Define "accessible document."
4. What should you keep in mind when formatting a paragraph with paragraph shading?
5. Do you have to turn the Accessibility Checker on, or does it check a document in the background?

Practice: Review Assignments

Data Files needed for the Review Assignments: NP_WD_4-2.docx, Support_WD_4_Online.docx, Support_WD_4_Produce.jpg, Support_WD_4_Sunflower.jpg

Stefan is working on another wellness newsletter. He has already written the document's text, and he asks you to help him transform it into a professional-looking newsletter. He also asks you to save the newsletter as a PDF so he can email it to the printer and to edit some text currently available only as a PDF. The finished newsletter should match the one shown in Figure 4–44.

Figure 4–44 Completed newsletter

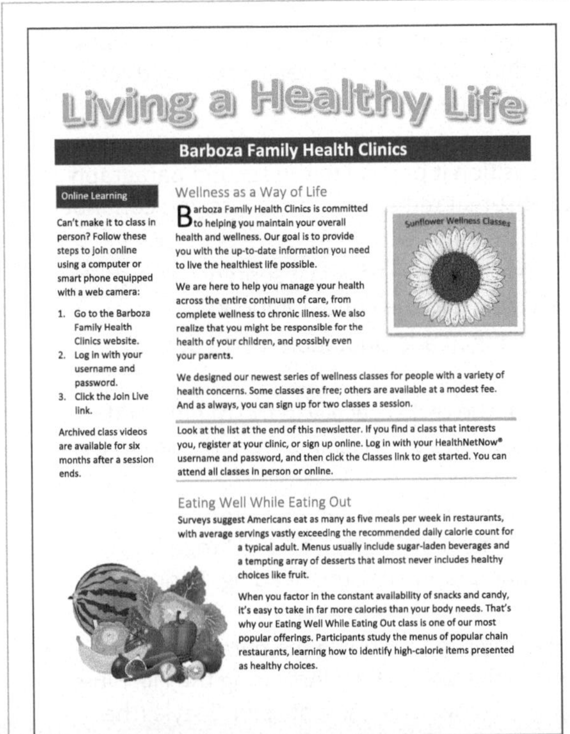

Living a Healthy Life

Barboza Family Health Clinics

Online Learning

Can't make it to class in person? Follow these steps to join online using a computer or smart phone equipped with a web camera:

1. Go to the Barboza Family Health Clinics website.
2. Log in with your username and password.
3. Click the Join Live link.

Archived class videos are available for six months after a session ends.

Wellness as a Way of Life

Barboza Family Health Clinics is committed to helping you maintain your overall health and wellness. Our goal is to provide you with the up-to-date information you need to live the healthiest life possible.

We are here to help you manage your health across the entire continuum of care, from complete wellness to chronic illness. We also realize that you might be responsible for the health of your children, and possibly even your parents.

We designed our newest series of wellness classes for people with a variety of health concerns. Some classes are free; others are available at a modest fee. And as always, you can sign up for two classes a session.

Look at the list at the end of this newsletter. If you find a class that interests you, register at your clinic, or sign up online. Log in with your HealthNetNow® username and password, and then click the Classes link to get started. You can attend all classes in person or online.

Eating Well While Eating Out

Surveys suggest Americans eat as many as five meals per week in restaurants, with average servings vastly exceeding the recommended daily calorie count for a typical adult. Menus usually include sugar-laden beverages and a tempting array of desserts that almost never includes healthy choices like fruit.

When you factor in the constant availability of snacks and candy, it's easy to take in far more calories than your body needs. That's why our Eating Well While Eating Out class is one of our most popular offerings. Participants study the menus of popular chain restaurants, learning how to identify high-calorie items presented as healthy choices.

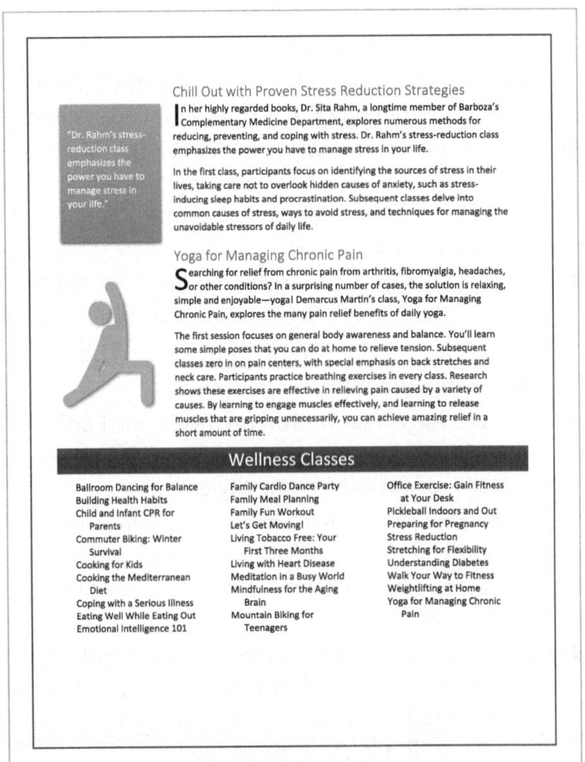

"Dr. Rahm's stress-reduction class emphasizes the power you have to manage stress in your life."

Chill Out with Proven Stress Reduction Strategies

In her highly regarded books, Dr. Sita Rahm, a longtime member of Barboza's Complementary Medicine Department, explores numerous methods for reducing, preventing, and coping with stress. Dr. Rahm's stress-reduction class emphasizes the power you have to manage stress in your life.

In the first class, participants focus on identifying the sources of stress in their lives, taking care not to overlook hidden causes of anxiety, such as stress-inducing sleep habits and procrastination. Subsequent classes delve into common causes of stress, ways to avoid stress, and techniques for managing the unavoidable stressors of daily life.

Yoga for Managing Chronic Pain

Searching for relief from chronic pain from arthritis, fibromyalgia, headaches, or other conditions? In a surprising number of cases, the solution is relaxing, simple and enjoyable—yoga! Demarcus Martin's class, Yoga for Managing Chronic Pain, explores the many pain relief benefits of daily yoga.

The first session focuses on general body awareness and balance. You'll learn some simple poses that you can do at home to relieve tension. Subsequent classes zero in on pain centers, with special emphasis on back stretches and neck care. Participants practice breathing exercises in every class. Research shows these exercises are effective in relieving pain caused by a variety of causes. By learning to engage muscles effectively, and learning to release muscles that are gripping unnecessarily, you can achieve amazing relief in a short amount of time.

Wellness Classes

Ballroom Dancing for Balance
Building Health Habits
Child and Infant CPR for Parents
Commuter Biking: Winter Survival
Cooking for Kids
Cooking the Mediterranean Diet
Coping with a Serious Illness
Eating Well While Eating Out
Emotional Intelligence 101
Family Cardio Dance Party
Family Meal Planning
Family Fun Workout
Let's Get Moving!
Living Tobacco Free: Your First Three Months
Living with Heart Disease
Meditation in a Busy World
Mindfulness for the Aging Brain
Mountain Biking for Teenagers
Office Exercise: Gain Fitness at Your Desk
Pickleball Indoors and Out
Preparing for Pregnancy
Stress Reduction
Stretching for Flexibility
Understanding Diabetes
Walk Your Way to Fitness
Weightlifting at Home
Yoga for Managing Chronic Pain

PurpleChicken/Pixabay; OpenClipart-Vectors/Pixabay

Complete the following steps:

1. Open the file **NP_WD_4-2.docx** from the Word4 > Review folder included with your Data Files, and then save the document as **NP_WD_4_Wellness** in the location specified by your instructor.
2. Insert continuous section breaks in the following locations:
   a. On page 1, at the beginning of the "Wellness as a Way of Life" heading, to the left of the "W" in "Wellness."
   b. On page 2, at the beginning of the shaded heading "Wellness Classes" to the left of the "W" in "Wellness."
   c. On page 2, at the beginning of the first class name, to the left of the "B" in "Ballroom"
3. In section 1 (the newsletter title and shaded heading on page 1) and section 3 (the shaded heading on page 2), change the left and right margins to .75 inches. In section 2 (the main newsletter text), change the left margin to 2.5 inches.
4. Format section 4 (the class list) in three columns of equal width, and then format the entire list of class names with a 0.2-inch hanging indent.

5. Search for the term **HealthNetNow** in the newsletter, and then add the ® symbol to the right of the "w."
6. On page 1, click anywhere in the "Wellness as a Way of Life" heading, and then insert a preformatted text box using the Ion Sidebar 1 option.
7. Change the text wrapping setting for the text box to In Front of Text. Change the height of the text box to 4.5 inches and its width to 1.5 inches, and then drag it to position it in the white space in the left margin, with its top edge aligned with the top the "Wellness as a Way of Life" heading. The left border of the text box should align with the left edge of the shaded paragraph above. Verify that the text box's position is fixed on the page.
8. Change the text box title to **Online Learning**. Delete all the placeholder text in the text box, and then insert the text of the Word document **Support_WD_4_Online.docx**, which is located in the Word4 > Review folder. Delete the extra paragraph mark at the end of the text and change the font size for the text and text box title to 11.
9. Use the Shapes button on the Insert tab to draw a rectangular text box that roughly fills the blank space in the upper-left margin of page 2. When you are finished, adjust the height and width as necessary to make the text box 2 inches tall and 1.5 inches wide.
10. Make sure the text wrap setting for the text box is set to In Front of Text and that the text box has a fixed position on the page. Drag the anchor down to position it parallel to the second paragraph after the "Yoga for Managing Chronic Pain" heading to ensure it remains on page 2 as you continue revising the newsletter.
11. On page 1, in the paragraph below the "Chill Out With" heading, select the last sentence (which begins "Dr. Rahm's stress reduction class. . . "), and then copy it to the Office Clipboard.
12. Paste the copied sentence into the text box on page 2, and then add quotation marks at the beginning and end.
13. Use the Align Text button on the Shape Format tab to align the text vertically in the middle of the text box, and then apply the Intense Effect - Blue, Accent 1 shape style (second from the left in the bottom row of the Theme Styles).
14. In the first line of text after each of the following headings, insert a drop cap that drops two lines: "Wellness as a Way of Life," "Chill Out with Proven Stress Reduction Strategies," and "Yoga for Managing Chronic Pain." Do not insert a drop cap in the paragraph after the heading "Eating Well While Eating Out."
15. On page 1, select the entire first paragraph, "Living a Healthy Life," including the paragraph mark. Clear the formatting from the paragraph, and then format the text as WordArt, using the Fill: Blue, Accent color 5; Outline: White, Background color 1; Hard Shadow: Blue, Accent color 5 style (the middle option in the bottom row).
16. Change the WordArt text box width to 7 inches and retain the default height.
17. Retain the Square text wrapping, and fix its position on the page. Drag the WordArt text box up above the shaded paragraph if necessary, so it appears at the top of page 1.
18. Apply the Chevron: Up transform text effect, and then add a shadow text effect using the Offset: Bottom Right style (the left-most option in the top row of the Outer section).
19. Click at the end of the paragraph below the "Wellness as a Way of Life" heading, insert the picture file named **Support_WD_4_Sunflower.jpg** from the Word4 > Review folder, delete the picture's default alt text and mark it as decorative.
20. Practice cropping the picture to a shape, and then try cropping it by selecting various aspect ratios. Use the Reset Picture button as necessary to restore the picture to its original appearance. When you are finished, crop the picture by dragging the handles to remove the black background on either side of the blue square.
21. Change the picture's height to 1.75 inches; do not change the width. Use the Position button to place the picture in the middle of the right side of page 1 with square text wrapping, and then add the Simple Frame, White picture style.
22. On page 1, click at the end of the "Eating Well While Eating Out" heading, and then insert the picture **Support_WD_4_Produce.jpg** from the Word4 > Review folder.
23. Delete the picture's default alt text and mark it as decorative, and then rotate the picture 90 degrees to the left.

24. Remove the picture's background, change its height to 2.5 inches; do not change the width. Apply Square text wrapping, position it to the left of the paragraph below the "Eating Well While Eating Out" heading, with two lines of text wrapped above it as in Figure 4–44 and then fix its position on the page.
25. Add top and bottom custom borders to the paragraph above the "Eating Well While Eating Out" heading (which begins "Look at the list..."). For the top border, use the Blue, Accent 5 color and 3 pt width. For the bottom border, use the Blue, Accent 5 color and 1 ½ pt width.
26. Drag the sunflower picture up above the paragraph with the borders. Position the picture so the second paragraph under the heading "Sunflower Wellness Classes" wraps to its left. If necessary, drag the text box on page 1 down to align it with the "Wellness as a Way of Life" heading. Refer to Figure 4–44.
27. On page 2, drag the text box to align its top border with the top of the drop cap "I" in the paragraph below the heading "Chill Out with Proven Stress Reduction Strategies."
28. Click at the end of the paragraph below the "Yoga for Managing Chronic Pain" heading and insert a yoga icon with black fill that shows a figure leaning left, with one arm raised. Delete the default alt text and mark it as decorative.
29. Apply In Front of Text text wrapping, fix its position on the page, change the icon's height to 2 inches, then drag the icon to center it in the white space below the text box.
30. Apply the Colored Fill – Accent 5, No Outline graphics style (second row, second from the right in the Graphics style gallery).
31. Add the Offset: Bottom Right shadow graphics effect (upper-left effect in the Outer section of the Shadow gallery).
32. Compress all the pictures in the newsletter. Delete cropped areas and use a resolution recommended for webpages and projectors.
33. Balance the columns at the bottom of page 2.
34. Change the theme colors to Blue Green.
35. Insert a page border using the Box setting and the default style and width. For the border color, use Blue, Accent 6, Darker 50% (bottom row, first on the right in the Theme Colors section).
36. Check the document for accessibility. Ignore errors related to inline objects. If you forgot to mark a picture or other graphic as decorative, do that now. Correct the hard-to-read text by changing the paragraph shading for those items to Blue, Accent 6, Darker 50% (bottom row, first on the right in the Theme Colors section). If no text is marked as hard-to-read, make this shading change to the heading "Barboza Family Health Clinics" on page 1, the "Online Learning" text box title on page 1, and the "Wellness Classes" heading on page 2.
37. Make any additional adjustments necessary to ensure that your newsletter matches the one shown in Figure 4–44.
38. In the text box page 2, replace "Dr. Rahm" with your first and last names.
39. Save the document, and then export it as a PDF named **NP_WD_4_WellnessPrinter** in the location specified by your instructor.
40. In Word, open the **NP_WD_4_WellnessPrinter.pdf** file, save it as a Word document named **NP_WD_4_ConvertedPDF.** Review the document's appearance, note the problems with the formatting that you would have to correct if you actually wanted to use this new DOCX file, and also note that the three pictures are no longer marked as decorative in the Alt Text pane. Close the document.

Apply: Case Problem 1

Data Files needed for this Case Problem: NP_WD_4-3.docx, Support_WD_4_Bike.png, Support_WD_4_Bin.png, Support_WD_4_Recycle.docx

Solana Homes You are a human resources specialist at Garmin and Shield Insurance in Jackson, Mississippi. Your manager has asked you to complete a flyer about community events that might interest company employees and their families. The finished flyer should match the one shown in Figure 4–45.

Figure 4–45 Completed flyer

Garmin and Shield Insurance

Supporting Our Community

Time to Recycle

The new recycling pavilion is designed to make separating recyclable materials quick and easy. Studies show that minimizing the time required to recycle household materials increases participation in community recycling programs.

New Recycling Pavilion

We're happy to announce that the recycling pavilion built with the support of Garmin and Shields employees and their families is now open. Located on Berners Avenue, just outside our corporate office, the recycling pavilion offers state-of-the art collection facilities, with bi-weekly pickups. The pavilion is designed to make recycling easy in all kinds of weather, for all Jackson community members. The design crew was motivated by numerous studies demonstrating that community support and accessible facilities greatly increase the number of families committed to recycling.

New recycling bins will also be installed throughout our offices. Garmin and Shields contracted with Jackson Waste Disposal and Recycling to handle trash and recycling pickups. Company owner Rosco Lehan has been recognized numerous times as an innovator in co-mingling reuse and recycling.

Register for the River View Ride by September 15

River View Ride

The annual River View Ride, a popular community bike ride and fundraiser, is set for October 15-20. Garmin and Shield will sponsor all interested employees, with donations to local charities of up to $200 per person. We encourage all participants to register before the September 15 deadline. The registration fee is $125. Online registration opens August 15. The registration fee entitles you to breakfast, lunch, and dinner.

Each rider is allowed one medium-sized backpack and one sleeping bag on the baggage truck. Once again accounts manager Charlie Yellow Feather has volunteered to manage on-the-road logistics for all Garmin and Shield employees, including reserving camp sites. Thanks, Charlie!

Congratulations to Our Community Service Award Winners

Student Name
Michael Paul Bethke
Kashif Chaibi
Elina Compere
Layla Carrington
Bruce Williams
Jasmin Erickson
Seki Taro
J.T. Sreedharan
Clarissa Fey-Esperanza
Haiyan Jiang
Makayla Jeschke
Tia Morello-Jimenez
Jalen Harjo
Eileen Jasper-Schwartz
Harriet Schaefer
Sandra Carmel
Teo Andre Nesaule
Suzette Plishka

u_kncwyxd5/Pixabay;Clker-Free-Vector-Images/Pixabay

Complete the following steps:

1. Open the file **NP_WD_4-3.docx** located in the Word4 > Case1 folder included with your Data Files, and then save it as **NP_WD_4_Garmin** in the location specified by your instructor.
2. Change the document margins to Narrow, and then, where indicated in the document, insert continuous section breaks. Remember to delete each instance of the highlighted text "[Insert SECTION BREAK]" before you insert a section break.
3. In section 2 (the main flyer text), change the left margin to 3 inches, and then format section 4 (the list of award winners) in four columns of equal width.
4. Format the second paragraph in the document ("Supporting Our Community") as WordArt, using the Gradient Fill: Dark Green, Accent color 5; Reflection style (second from the left in the middle row of the WordArt gallery). Change the text box height to approximately 0.9 inches and the width to 7 inches. Change the text wrapping setting to Top and Bottom and fix its position on the page. If necessary, drag the WordArt to position it between the headings "Garmin and Shield Insurance" and "New Recycling Pavilion."

5. Insert drop caps that drop two lines in the first paragraph after the "New Recycling Pavilion" heading and in the first paragraph after the "River View Ride" heading.
6. Click in the fourth paragraph in the document (the one with the drop cap "W"), and then insert a preformatted text box using the Grid Sidebar option. Change the text wrapping setting for the text box to In Front of Text, and then change its height to 3.5 inches and its width to 2.3 inches.
7. Drag the text box to position it in the white space on the left side of the page, and then align its top border with the "New Recycling Pavilion" heading.
8. Delete the title placeholder text in the text box, and type **Time to Recycle**. Delete the placeholder paragraphs and insert the text of the Word document **Support_WD_4_Recycle** from the Word4 > Case1 folder. Delete the blank paragraph.
9. In the blank space below the text box, draw a rectangular text box. When you are finished, adjust the height and width to make the text box 1.3 inches tall and 2 inches wide. Apply the Intense Effect – Dark Green, Accent 5 shape style (bottom row, second from the right in the Themes Styles section), and then position the text box as in Figure 4–45, leaving room for the bike picture you will add later.
10. In the text box, type **Register for the River View Ride by September 15.** Align the text in the middle of the text box, and then use the Center button on the Home tab to center the text between the text box's left and right borders.
11. At the end of the paragraph with the drop cap "W," (which begins "We're happy to announce . . ."), insert the picture **Support_WD_4_Bin.png** from the Word4 > Case1 folder.
12. Delete the default alt text and mark the picture as decorative in the Alt Text pane and then crop the picture to an oval shape.
13. Apply Square text wrapping, fix its position on the page, and then change its height to 1 inch. Drag the picture to position it so the drop cap "W" and one more line of text wrap above it, as in Figure 4–45.
14. At the end of the paragraph with the drop cap "T," (which begins "The annual River View Ride, a popular. . ."), insert the picture **Support_WD_4_Bike.png** from the Word4 > Case1 folder.
15. Delete the default alt text and then mark the picture as decorative in the Alt Text pane. Apply Square text wrapping, change the picture's height to 1 inch, add the Center Shadow Rectangle picture style, and then position the picture in the left margin, centered between the two text boxes, with a fixed position on the page, as in Figure 4–45.
16. Compress all pictures in the document. Delete cropped areas and use a resolution recommended for webpages and projectors
17. Balance the columns at the end of the flyer and then replace the first name in the list of award winners (Casey Ann Ramirez) with your first and last names.
18. Make any adjustments necessary so that your newsletter matches the one shown in Figure 4–45, and then save the document.
19. Export the document as a PDF named **NP_WD_4_GarminPDF** in the location specified by your instructor. Review the PDF, and then close the program in which it opened.
20. In Word, open the PDF named **NP_WD_4_GarminPDF.pdf**, save it as **NP_WD_4_GarminFromPDF**, review its contents, note the corrections you would have to make if you actually wanted to use this document. Close all open documents.

Research: Case Problem 2

There are no Data Files needed for this Case Problem.

Emma Mae Cottages and Suites You are an administrative assistant at Emma Mae Cottages and Suites, a chain of beach resorts that specializes in accommodations for families. Among other amenities, the chain's properties offer fun classes for children. As part of your training, your supervisor asks you to review online examples of flyers announcing art classes for kids and then re-create the first page of a flyer on art classes for kids as a Word document. Instead of writing the complete text of the flyer, you can use placeholder text. Next, your manager asks you to experiment with the options for building a cartoon from scratch using the Icons button in the Illustrations group on the Insert tab. Complete the following steps:

1. Open a new, blank document, and then save it as **NP_WD_4_Art** in the location specified by your instructor.
2. Open your browser and search online for images of flyers by searching for the keywords **art classes for kids flyer**. Review at least a dozen images of flyers before picking a style that you want to re-create in a Word document. The style you choose should contain at least two pictures and should feature text that clearly contrasts with any background colors to ensure it is easy to read. Keep the image of the flyer visible in your browser so you can return to it for reference as you work.
3. In your Word document, create the first page of the flyer. Compose your own WordArt headlines and other headings or replicate the headlines and headings in the sample flyer. To generate text that you can use to fill the space below the headings, type **=lorem()** and then press ENTER. Change the document theme, theme fonts, and theme colors as necessary to replicate the colors and fonts in the flyer you are trying to copy. Don't worry about the flyer's background color; white is fine. When choosing colors for text boxes, focus on picking a fill color that contrasts with the font color. White font with a dark background is always a good choice.
4. Add at least two pictures, using pictures that you find online. Rotate or flip pictures and remove their backgrounds as necessary to make them work in the flyer layout. Add an artistic effect to one picture. Mark the pictures as decorative or add descriptive alt text, depending on whether they contain information.
5. Add at least one 3D model to the flyer. Revise the model's alt text if necessary.
6. Make any other changes necessary so that the layout and style of your document match the flyer example that you found online.
7. Somewhere in the document, attach a comment that reads **I used the following webpage as a model for this flyer design:**, and then include the web address for the flyer image you used as a model. To copy a web address from a browser window, click the web address in the browser's Address bar, and then press CTRL+C.
8. Save the document, close it, and then close your browser.
9. Open a new, blank document, and save it as **NP_WD_4_Cartoon**. Switch to Landscape orientation, and then use the Pictures button in the Illustrations group on the Insert tab to access the Cartoon People options and experiment with creating your own cartoon. Focus on creating a picture that you could share with your manager in a professional setting. Add a scene, format it with Square text wrapping, and then size it to fill the page. Next, add at least two characters, remembering to apply Square text wrapping for each character and sizing them appropriately. By default, you can place characters formatted with text wrapping on top of the scene, but if you want one character to overlap another to create a crowd scene, you can experiment with the Bring Forward and Send Backward buttons in the Arrange group on the Graphics Format tab. You can also use the Rotate button in the Arrange group on the Graphics Format tab to change the direction of a character's face. Add at least three fill or outline colors to the scene and characters. Finally, use the Icons button again to add at least one sticker to the scene. Apply Square text wrapping so you can position it somewhere in the scene.
10. Save the document and close it.

Getting Started with Excel

Developing a Purchase Order Report

Case: Insight Video Solutions

Sofi Feng is an account assistant for Insight Video Solutions, a startup company that designs and installs high-end video equipment for video conferencing and online seminars. One of Sofi's responsibilities is to maintain documentation on customer accounts, relating that information to the general financial health of the company. Sofi wants to use Excel to create purchase order reports for Insight Video Solution customers. You'll help her to develop those reports.

Starting Data Files

Excel1

Module

NP_EX_1-1.xlsx

Review

NP_EX_1-2.xlsx

Case1

NP_EX_1-3.xlsx

Case2

NP_EX_1-4.xlsx

Objectives

Part 1.1

- Open and close a workbook
- Navigate through a workbook and worksheet
- Select cells and ranges
- Plan and create a workbook
- Insert, rename, and move worksheets
- Enter text, dates, and numbers
- Undo and redo actions
- Resize columns and rows

Part 1.2

- Enter formulas and the SUM and COUNT functions
- Copy and paste formulas
- Move or copy cells and ranges
- Insert and delete rows, columns, and ranges
- Create patterned text with Flash Fill
- Add cell borders and change font size
- Change worksheet views
- Prepare a workbook for printing

Part 1.1 Visual Overview: The Excel Workbook

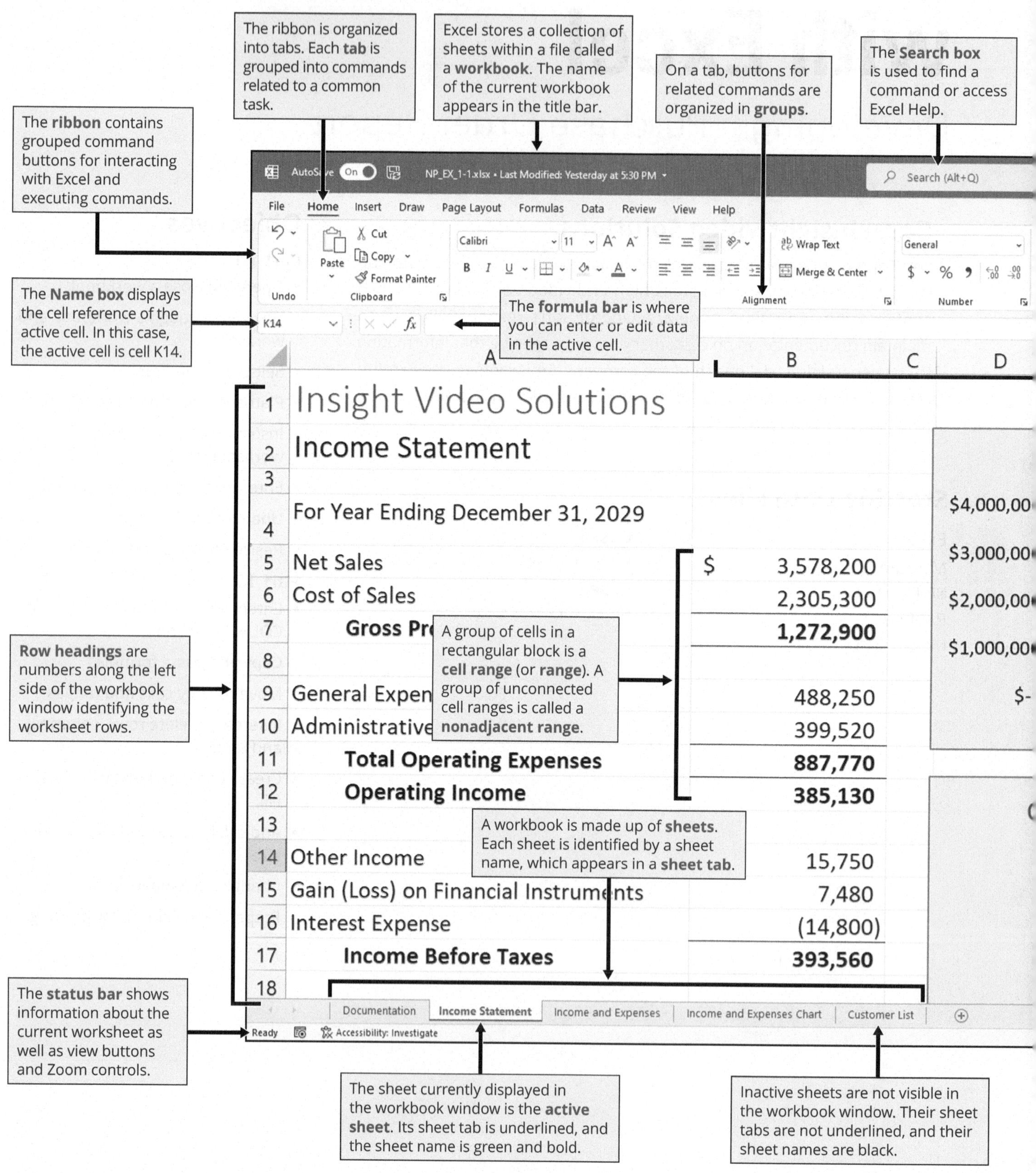

The ribbon is organized into tabs. Each tab is grouped into commands related to a common task.
Excel stores a collection of sheets within a file called a workbook. The name of the current workbook appears in the title bar.
On a tab, buttons for related commands are organized in groups.
The Search box is used to find a command or access Excel Help.
The ribbon contains grouped command buttons for interacting with Excel and executing commands.
AutoSave On
NP_EX_1-1.xlsx • Last Modified: Yesterday at 5:30 PM
Search (Alt+Q)
File
Home
Insert
Draw
Page Layout
Formulas
Data
Review
View
Help
Cut
Copy
Paste
Format Painter
Undo
Clipboard
Calibri
11
Wrap Text
Merge & Center
General
Alignment
Number
The Name box displays the cell reference of the active cell. In this case, the active cell is cell K14.
K14
The formula bar is where you can enter or edit data in the active cell.
A
B
C
D
1 Insight Video Solutions
2 Income Statement
3
4 For Year Ending December 31, 2029
5 Net Sales $ 3,578,200
6 Cost of Sales 2,305,300
7 Gross Pr 1,272,900
8
9 General Expen 488,250
10 Administrative 399,520
11 Total Operating Expenses 887,770
12 Operating Income 385,130
13
14 Other Income 15,750
15 Gain (Loss) on Financial Instruments 7,480
16 Interest Expense (14,800)
17 Income Before Taxes 393,560
18
$4,000,00
$3,000,00
$2,000,00
$1,000,00
$-
A group of cells in a rectangular block is a cell range (or range). A group of unconnected cell ranges is called a nonadjacent range.
Row headings are numbers along the left side of the workbook window identifying the worksheet rows.
A workbook is made up of sheets. Each sheet is identified by a sheet name, which appears in a sheet tab.
Documentation
Income Statement
Income and Expenses
Income and Expenses Chart
Customer List
Ready
Accessibility: Investigate
The status bar shows information about the current worksheet as well as view buttons and Zoom controls.
The sheet currently displayed in the workbook window is the active sheet. Its sheet tab is underlined, and the sheet name is green and bold.
Inactive sheets are not visible in the workbook window. Their sheet tabs are not underlined, and their sheet names are black.

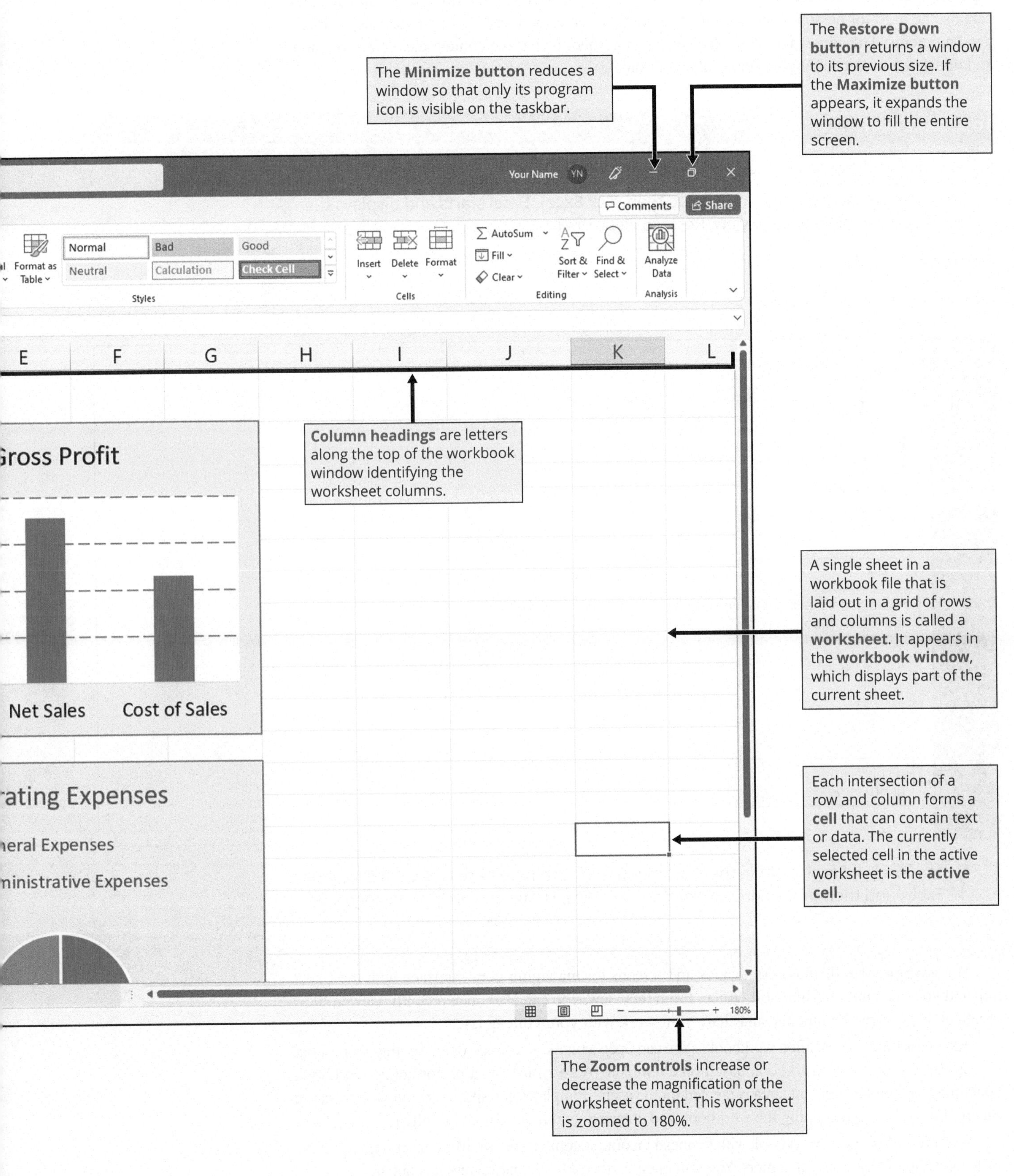
The **Minimize button** reduces a window so that only its program icon is visible on the taskbar.
The **Restore Down button** returns a window to its previous size. If the **Maximize button** appears, it expands the window to fill the entire screen.
Your Name
YN
Comments
Share
Format as Table
Normal
Bad
Good
Neutral
Calculation
Check Cell
Styles
Insert
Delete
Format
Cells
AutoSum
Fill
Clear
Sort & Filter
Find & Select
Editing
Analyze Data
Analysis
E
F
G
H
I
J
K
L
Column headings are letters along the top of the workbook window identifying the worksheet columns.
Gross Profit
Net Sales
Cost of Sales
A single sheet in a workbook file that is laid out in a grid of rows and columns is called a **worksheet**. It appears in the **workbook window**, which displays part of the current sheet.
ating Expenses
neral Expenses
ministrative Expenses
Each intersection of a row and column forms a **cell** that can contain text or data. The currently selected cell in the active worksheet is the **active cell**.
180%
The **Zoom controls** increase or decrease the magnification of the worksheet content. This worksheet is zoomed to 180%.

Using the Excel Interface

Microsoft Excel (or just **Excel**) is a program to store, analyze, and report data arranged in the form of a spreadsheet. A **spreadsheet** is a grouping of text and numbers in a rectangular grid or table. Spreadsheets are often used in business for budgeting, inventory management, and financial reporting because they unite text, numbers, and graphics within a single document. Spreadsheets can also be used for personal needs such as planning a family budget, tracking expenses, or listing personal items. The advantage of an electronic spreadsheet is that the content can be easily edited and updated to reflect changing financial conditions.

To start Excel:

1. On the Windows taskbar, click the **Start** button. The Start menu opens.
2. On the Start menu, scroll the list, and then click **Excel.** Excel starts and displays the Home screen in Backstage view. Refer to Figure 1–1.

Figure 1–1 Backstage view

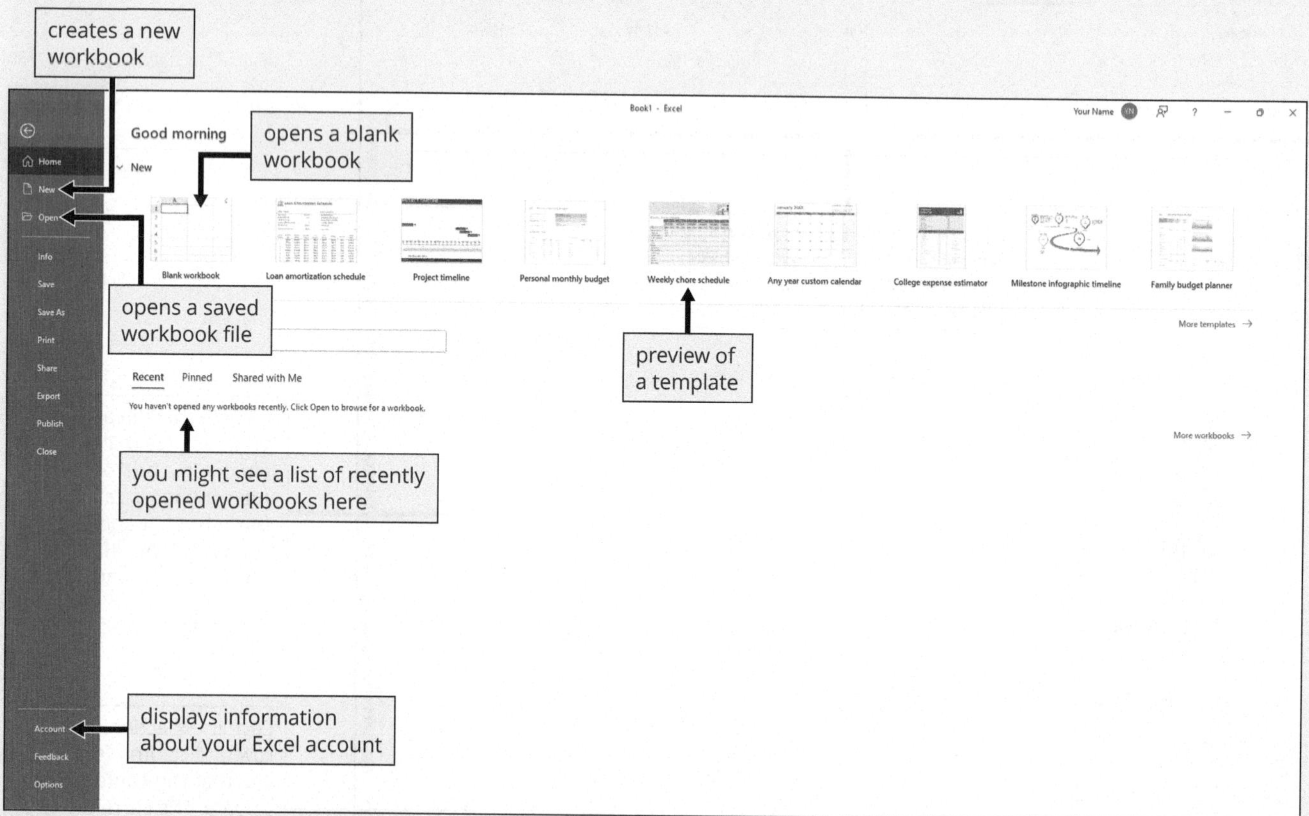

Trouble? If Excel is not in the Start menu, click the Type here to search box, type Excel, and then press Enter. Excel starts with the Home screen in Backstage view.

Backstage view displays commands and screens for managing your interface with the Excel app and your account on Microsoft Office. From this view, you can also open recently viewed files, create and save new documents, and share your work with your colleagues.

Excel documents are called workbooks. You can open a blank workbook or an existing workbook, or you can create a new workbook based on a template. A **template** is a preformatted workbook containing designs and content already created for the users. Templates can speed up your work because much of the effort in designing the workbook and entering its initial content has already been done.

Sofi created an Excel workbook with financial income statements drawn from the current accounts of Insight Video Solutions customers. You will open that workbook and review its contents.

To open the Income Statement workbook:

1. In Backstage view, click **Open**. The Open screen is displayed, providing access to locations where workbooks might be saved.
2. Click **Browse**. The Open dialog box appears.
3. Navigate to the **Excel1 > Module** folder included with your Data Files.

    Trouble? If you don't have the starting Data Files, you need to get them before you can proceed. Your instructor will either give you the Data Files or indicate how to access them. If you have any questions about the Data Files, ask your instructor or technical support person for assistance.

4. Click **NP_EX_1-1.xlsx** in the file list to select it.

    If your instructor wants you to submit your work as a SAM Project for automatic grading, you must download the Data File in Step 4 from the assignment launch page.

5. Click the **Open** button. The workbook opens in Excel.

    Trouble? If only the tab names appear at the top of the Excel window instead of the full ribbon as it appears in the Part 1.1 Visual Overview, right-click any tab name to display a shortcut menu, and then click Collapse the Ribbon to display the full ribbon.

6. If the Excel window doesn't fill the screen, click the **Maximize** button ☐ in the upper-right corner of the title bar. Refer to Figure 1–2.

Figure 1–2 Financial workbook

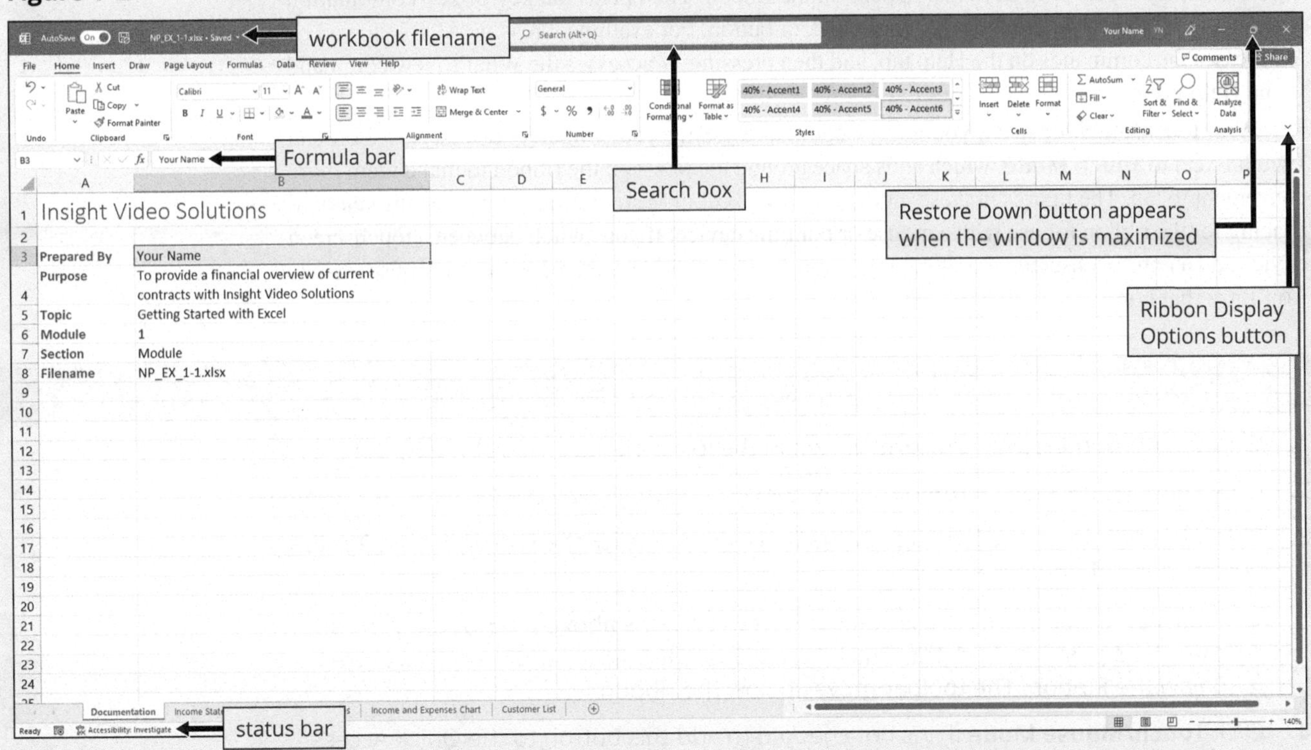

Nearly everything you do in Excel uses a command. You can access Excel commands on the ribbon using a mouse or pointing device. Or, you can use keyboard shortcuts.

Tip If you want help with a task, you can use Excel Help. To access Help, press F1. You can also enter a descriptive phrase or keyword in the Search box on the title bar to view help on that topic.

A **keyboard shortcut** is a key or combination of keys that you press together to perform a command or access a feature. For example, the keyboard shortcut to save a document is CTRL+S, which means you press the CTRL and S keys at the same time. When available, a keyboard shortcut is listed next to the command's name in a ScreenTip. A **ScreenTip** is a label that appears next to an object, providing information about that object or giving a link to additional information in Excel Help. Figure 1–3 lists some of the keyboard shortcuts commonly used in Excel.

Figure 1–3 Excel keyboard shortcuts

Press	To	Press	To
ALT	Display the Key Tips for the commands and tools on the ribbon	CTRL+V	Paste content that was cut or copied
CTRL+A	Select all objects in a range	CTRL+W	Close the current workbook
CTRL+C	Copy the selected object(s)	CTRL+X	Cut the selected object(s)
CTRL+G	Go to a location in the workbook	CTRL+Y	Repeat the last command
CTRL+N	Open a new blank workbook	CTRL+Z	Undo the last command
CTRL+O	Open a saved workbook file	F1	Open the Excel Help window
CTRL+P	Print the current workbook	F5	Go to a location in the workbook
CTRL+S	Save the current workbook	F12	Save the current workbook with a new name or to a new location

You can also use the keyboard to access commands on the ribbon. Press ALT to display **Key Tips**, which are labels with keys that appear on the ribbon. Then press the key or key combination listed to access the corresponding tab, command, or button. For example, pressing ALT followed by Y accesses the commands on the Help tab, and then pressing W accesses the What's New command in the Help group.

With touchscreen devices, you access commands using your finger(s) or a stylus. You can switch Excel to **Touch Mode**, which adds space around the icons on the ribbon to make them more convenient to tap. The figures in these modules show Excel in **Mouse Mode**, which is the standard spacing for the ribbon for use with a mouse or pointing device. If you switch between a touchscreen device and a non-touchscreen monitor, you might want to switch between Touch and Mouse modes. You'll try that now.

To switch between Mouse Mode and Touch Mode:

1. Click the **Ribbon Display Options** button in the lower-right corner of the ribbon.
2. Click **Show Quick Access Toolbar** if it is not checked to display the Quick Access Toolbar.
3. Below the ribbon on the left edge of the Excel window, click the **Quick Access Toolbar** button. A list of options appears.

   Trouble? If the Quick Access Toolbar button appears above the ribbon, you can change its position. Click the Quick Access Toolbar button, and then click Show Below the Ribbon. The toolbar moves below the ribbon.

4. Click **Touch/Mouse Mode** if it is not checked to add this button to the Quick Access Toolbar.
5. On the Quick Access Toolbar, click the **Touch/Mouse Mode** button, and then click **Touch**. The display is in Touch Mode with more space between the commands and buttons on the ribbon. Refer to Figure 1–4.

Figure 1-4 Excel displayed in Touch Mode

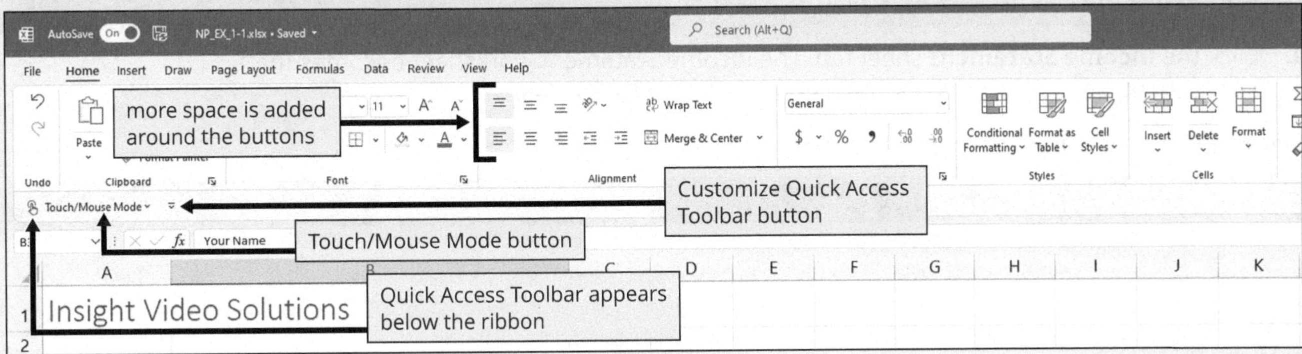

Trouble? If the screen display doesn't change, you were already in Touch mode. Continue with the next step.

Next, you will switch back to Mouse Mode. If you are working with a touchscreen and want to continue using Touch Mode, skip Step 6.

6. On the Quick Access Toolbar, click the **Touch/Mouse Mode** button, and then click **Mouse**. The display returns to Mouse Mode (refer to Figure 1–2). The figures in these modules show the ribbon in Mouse Mode.
7. To remove the Touch/Mouse Mode button from the Quick Access Toolbar, click the **Customize Quick Access Toolbar** button, and then click **Touch/Mouse Mode** to deselect it. The Touch/Mouse Mode button is removed from the Quick Access Toolbar.
8. To hide the Quick Access Toolbar, click the **Ribbon Display Options** button, and then click **Hide Quick Access Toolbar**.

The Quick Access Toolbar is useful for accessing commands that might take several clicks to access on the ribbon. However, these modules do not use the Quick Access Toolbar.

Navigating Between Sheets

The contents of a workbook are displayed in the workbook window located below the ribbon. Workbooks are organized into separate pages called sheets. Excel supports two types of sheets: worksheets and chart sheets. A worksheet contains a grid of rows and columns organized into cells in which you can enter text, numbers, dates, and formulas. Worksheets can also contain graphical elements such as charts, maps, and clip art. A **chart sheet** contains a single chart linked to data within a workbook. A chart sheet can also contain other graphical elements like clip art, but it doesn't contain a grid for entering data values.

Worksheets and chart sheets are identified by the sheet tabs at the bottom of the workbook window. Sofi's workbook contains five sheets labeled Documentation, Income Statement, Income and Expenses, Income and Expenses Chart, and Customer List. If a workbook contains more sheet tabs than can fit in the workbook window, the list of tabs will end with an ellipsis (…), indicating there are additional sheets. You can use the sheet tab scrolling buttons, located to the left of the sheet tabs, to scroll through the complete sheet tab list. Scrolling through the tab list does not change the active sheet; it changes only which sheet tabs are visible within the workbook window.

The sheet currently displayed in the workbook window is the active sheet, which in this case is the Documentation sheet. The sheet tab of the active sheet has a green underline, and the sheet name appears in bold. To change the active sheet, you click its sheet tab.

Tip Some workbooks have hidden sheets; even though these sheets aren't displayed, they are still part of the workbook.

You will view the different sheets in Sofi's workbook.

To view the sheets in Sofi's workbook:

1. Click the **Income Statement** sheet tab. The Income Statement worksheet becomes the active sheet, and its name is now bold green. Refer to Figure 1–5.

Figure 1–5 Income Statement worksheet

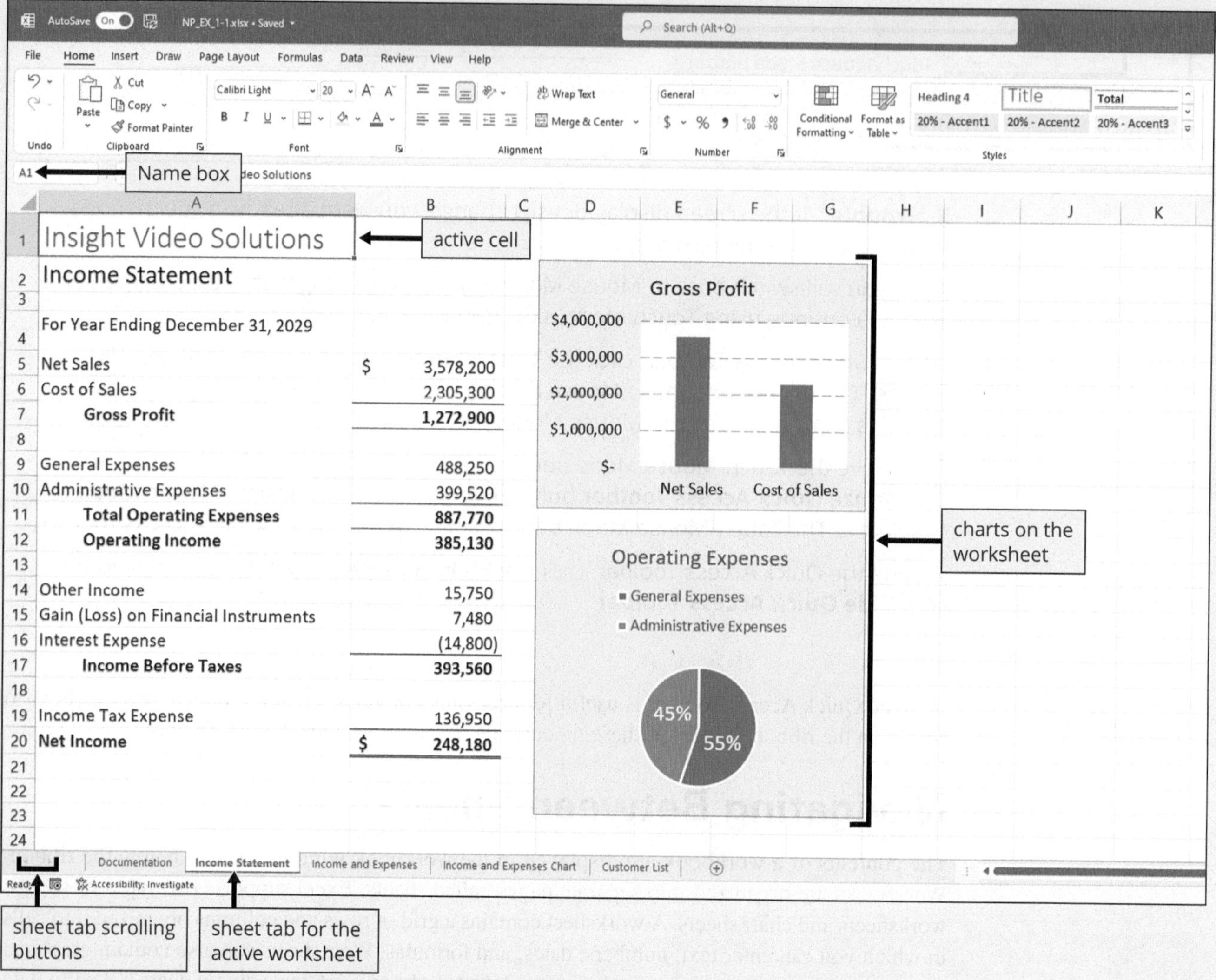

The Income Statement worksheet sheet contains financial data on the company's sales, profit, expenses, and net income. The sheet also contains a chart comparing the company's net sales to its cost of sales and a chart that breaks down the company's operating expense into general and administrative expenses. The charts provide a visual interpretation of the data contained in the income statement.

2. Click the **Income and Expenses** sheet tab. The active sheet displays sales and expense data for each month of the fiscal year. From viewing the final data in this worksheet, you can learn that the company showed a negative operating income for the first three months of the year but a positive income for the remaining months as sales increased.
3. Click the **Income and Expenses Chart** sheet tab. The active chart sheet shows the monthly profit and expenses for the company and the operating income. The chart provides a visual summary of the data in the Income and Expenses worksheet. Refer to Figure 1–6.

Figure 1–6 Income and Expenses Chart sheet

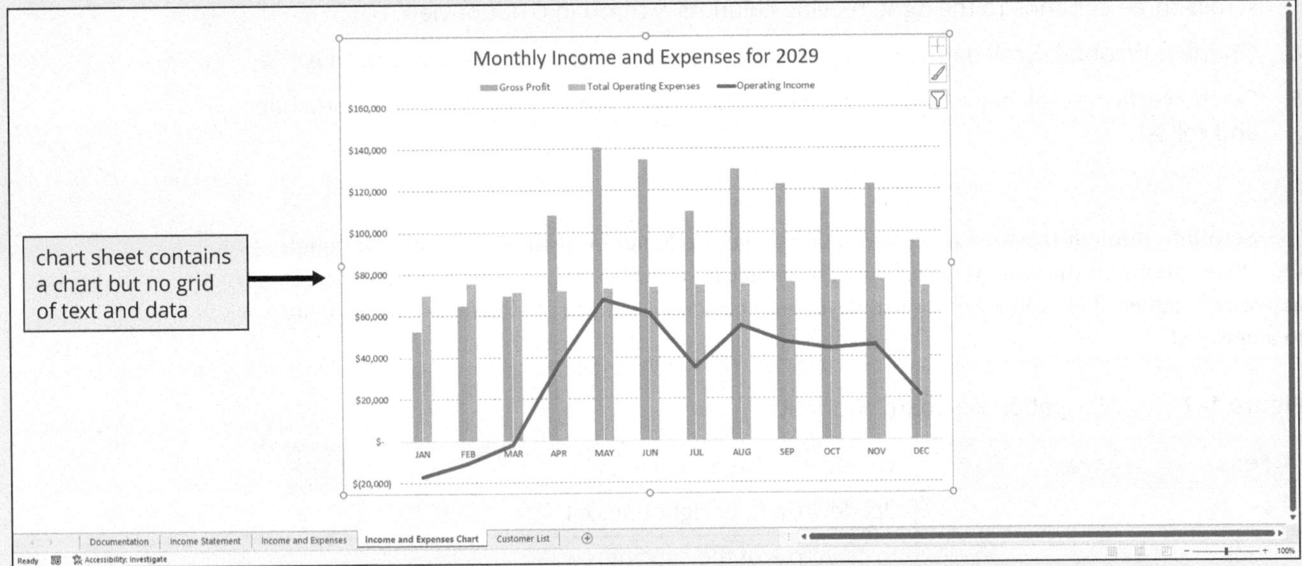

4. Click the **Customer List** sheet tab. The active sheet shows a list of Insight Video Solutions customers from the current fiscal year. The worksheet provides contact information for each customer as well as the order total from each customer's account with the company.

Selecting Worksheet Cells and Cell Ranges

Rows within a worksheet are identified by numbers; the columns are identified by letters. Row headings range from 1 to 1,048,576. Column headings start with letters from A to Z. After Z, the next columns are labeled AA, AB, AC, and so forth. The last possible column heading is XFD, which means there are 16,384 available columns in a worksheet. The total number of possible cells in a single Excel worksheet is more than 17 billion, providing an extremely large working space for reports.

Each cell is identified by a **cell reference** that indicates the column and row of that cell. The company's net income of $248,180 (refer to Figure 1–5) is in cell B20, which is the intersection of row B and column 20. In every cell reference, the column letter always appears first.

The cell currently selected in the worksheet is the active cell, indicated by a thick green border. The corresponding column and row headings for the active cell are shaded. The cell reference of the active cell appears in the Name box, which is on the left edge of the window just below the ribbon. The active cell in Figure 1–5 is cell A1, containing the company name, Insight Video Solutions.

To move different parts of the worksheet into view, use the horizontal and vertical scroll bars located at the bottom and right edges of the workbook window. Each scroll bar has clickable arrow buttons to move the worksheet one column or row and a scroll box that can be dragged to shift the worksheet larger amounts in the direction you choose.

You will use these tools to scroll through the contents of the Customer List worksheet.

To scroll through the Customer List worksheet:

1. On the Customer List worksheet, click the **down arrow** button ▾ on the vertical scroll bar three times to scroll down the worksheet three rows.
2. Drag the vertical scroll box down until you reach row 140 containing information on the last customer in the list (Zohne & Haus Group).

3. On the horizontal scroll bar, click the **right arrow** button ▶ three times. The worksheet scrolls three columns to the right, moving columns A through C out of view.
4. On the horizontal scroll bar, drag the scroll box to the left until you reach column A.
5. On the vertical scroll bar, drag the scroll box up until you reach the top of the worksheet and cell A1.

Scrolling through the worksheet does not change the location of the active cell. Although the active cell might shift out of view, its cell reference is in the Name box. To choose a different active cell, either click a new cell or use keyboard shortcuts describe in Figure 1–7 to navigate to a new cell.

Figure 1–7 Navigation keyboard shortcuts

Press	To move the active cell
↑↓←→	Up, down, left, or right one cell
HOME	To column A of the current row
CTRL+HOME	To cell A1
CTRL+END	To the last cell in the worksheet that contains data
ENTER	Down one row or to the start of the next row of data
SHIFT+ENTER	Up one row
TAB	One column to the right
SHIFT+TAB	One column to the left
PGUP, PGDN	Up or down one screen
CTRL+PGUP, CTRL+PGDN	To the previous or next sheet in the workbook

Keyboard shortcuts are especially useful in large scientific and financial worksheets in which data is spread across hundreds or thousands of rows and columns. You will use keyboard shortcuts to change the active cell in the Customer List worksheet.

To change the active cell using keyboard shortcuts:

1. On the Customer List worksheet, move the pointer over cell D10 containing the text "Detroit," and then click the mouse button. The active cell moves from cell A1 to cell D10. A green border appears around cell D10 indicating that it's now the active cell. The labels for row 10 and column D are shaded, and the cell reference in the Name box changes to D10.
2. Press **TAB**. The active cell moves one column to the right to cell E10 containing the text "MI".
3. Press **PGDN**. The active cell moves down one full screen.
4. Press **PGUP**. The active cell moves up one full screen, returning to cell E10.
5. Press **CTRL+END**. The active cell is cell L140, the last worksheet cell containing data.
6. Press **CTRL+HOME**. The active cell returns to the first cell in the worksheet, cell A1.

To change the active cell to a specific cell location, you can enter the cell's address in either the Go To dialog box or the Name box. You'll try both methods.

To change the active cell using the Go To dialog box and Name box:

1. On the Home tab, in the Editing group, click the **Find & Select** button, and then click **Go To** on the menu that opens (or press **CTRL+G** or **F5**). The Go To dialog box opens.
2. Type **A104** in the Reference box. Refer to Figure 1–8.

Figure 1–8 Go To dialog box

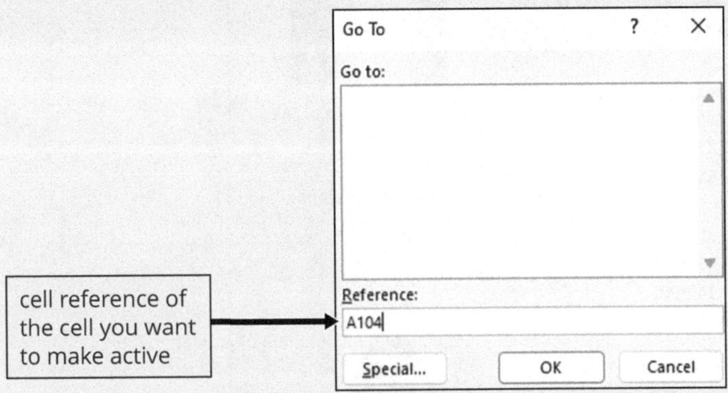

3. Click **OK**. Cell A104 becomes the active cell, showing account information for customer CD7586, New Tech Construction.
4. Click the **Name** box, type **A42**, and then press **ENTER**. Cell A42 becomes the active cell of the row showing account information for customer CD2939, Reed & Stribling Financial.

Many tasks in Excel involve working with groups of cells, called a cell range or simply a range. Cell ranges are identified with a **range reference** that specify which cells are included in the range. Cells in an adjacent range are in a rectangular block. The reference for an adjacent range includes the reference for the top-left and bottom-right cells separated by a colon. For example, A1:G5 references a rectangular block including all cells from cell A1 through cell G5.

As with individual cells, you can select cell ranges using your mouse or pointing device, the keyboard, or commands. You will select a cell range in the Income Statement worksheet.

To select a cell range in the Income Statement worksheet:

1. Click the **Income Statement** sheet tab. The Income Statement worksheet is the active sheet.
2. Click cell **A5** to select it and, without releasing the mouse button, drag down and right to cell **B7**.
3. Release the mouse button. All cells from cell A5 down to cell B7 are selected, and the block of cells is surrounded by a green border. The first cell selected, A5, is the active cell in the worksheet. The Quick Analysis button appears next to the selected range, providing options for analyzing the data in the selected range. Refer to Figure 1–9.

Figure 1–9 Range A5:B7 selected in the worksheet

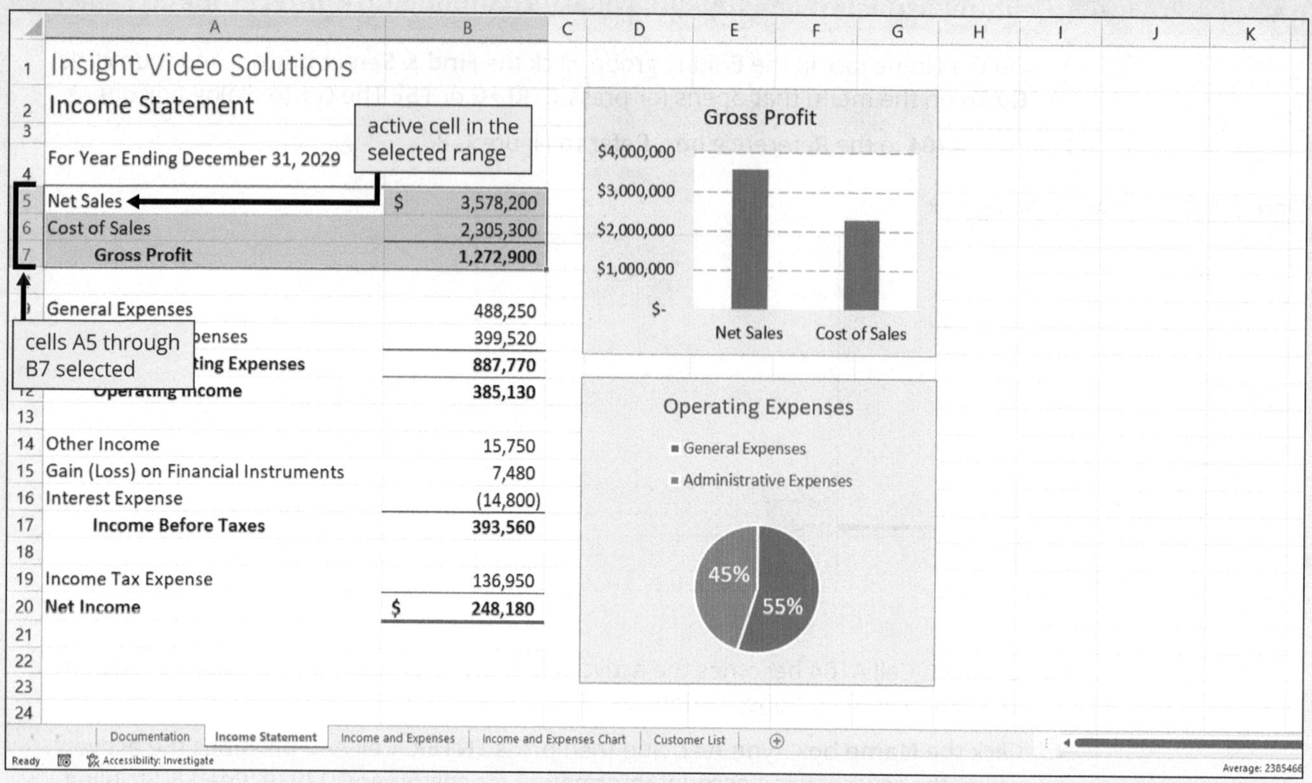

Tip You can also select a range by clicking the top-left cell in the range, holding down SHIFT, clicking the bottom-right cell in the range, and then releasing SHIFT.

4. Click cell **A1** to deselect the range.

You can select separate adjacent ranges, known as a nonadjacent range. References for nonadjacent ranges includes the reference to each adjacent range separated by commas. For example, the reference A1:G5,A10:G15 includes two ranges—the first is the rectangular block of cells from cell A1 to cell G5, and the second is the rectangular block of cells from cell A10 to cell G15.

To reference entire rows or columns, you include only the row or column headings. For example, the reference A:B includes all cells in columns A and B, and the reference 10:12,15:18 includes all cells in rows 10 through 12 and 15 through 18. To reference all cells in a single row or column, repeat the row or column heading. For example, the reference A:A selects all cells in column A, and the reference 20:20 selects all cells in row 20.

You will use select cells in a nonadjacent range in the Income Statement worksheet.

To select a nonadjacent range in the Income Statement worksheet:

1. Click cell **A5**, hold down **SHIFT** as you click cell **B7**, and then release **SHIFT** to select the range A5:B7.
2. Hold down **CTRL** as you drag to select the range **A9:B12**, and then release **CTRL**. The two separate blocks of cells in the nonadjacent range A5:B7, A9:B12 are selected. Refer to Figure 1–10.

Figure 1–10 Nonadjacent range A5:B7, A9:B12 selected

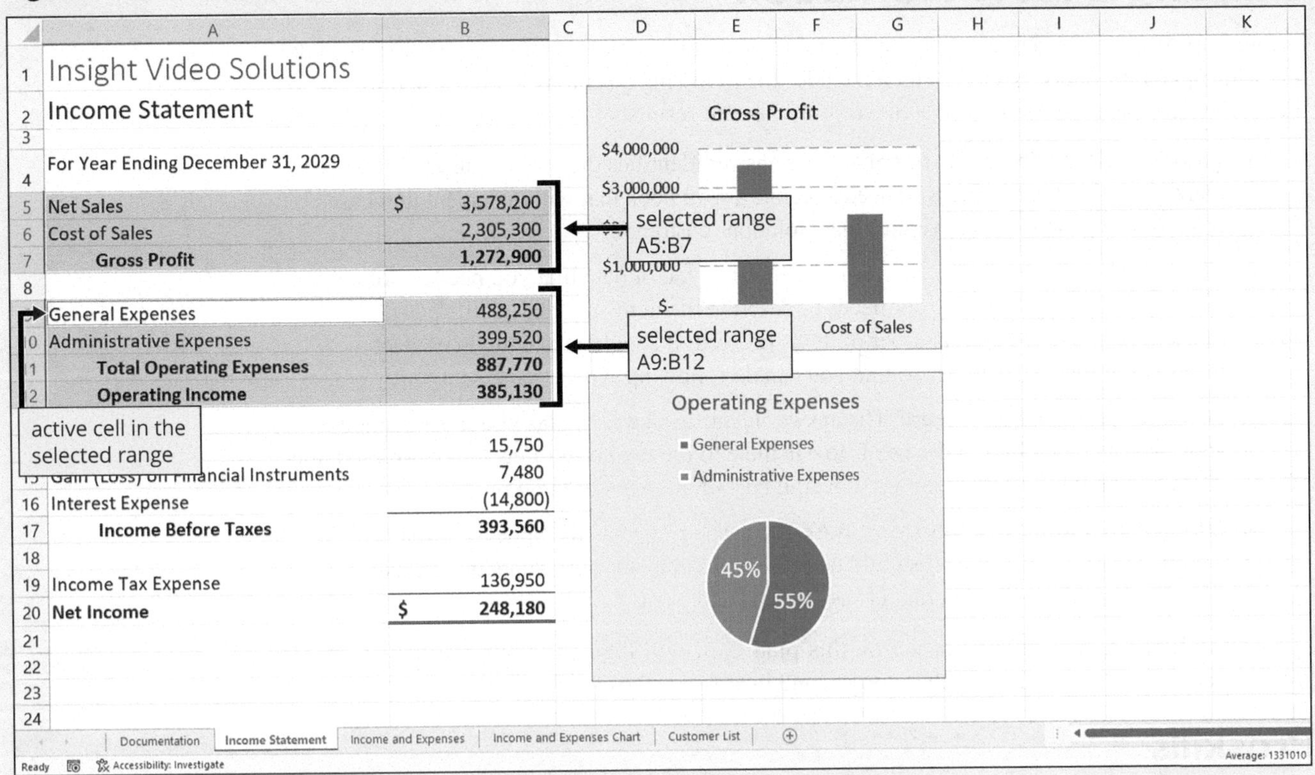

Tip You can select a range by typing its reference, such as A5:B7, A9:B12, in the Go To dialog box or the Name box and pressing ENTER.

Closing a Workbook

When you are finished with a workbook, you should close it. A dialog box might appear, asking whether you want to save any changes made to the workbook. If you have made changes that you want to keep, save the workbook with the changes. Because you have finished reviewing Sofi's workbook for the company, you will close the workbook without saving any changes you may have inadvertently made to its contents.

To close Sofi's workbook:

1. On the ribbon, click the **File** tab to display Backstage view, and then click **Close** in the navigation bar (or press **CTRL+W**).
2. If a dialog box opens, asking whether you want to save your changes to the workbook, click **Don't Save**. The workbook closes without saving any changes. Excel remains opens, ready for you to create or open another workbook.

Now that you've reviewed Sofi's workbook of the company's incomes and expenses, you are ready to create your own workbook. Sofi wants you to create a workbook providing details on a purchase order made by an Insight Video Solutions customer.

Starting a New Workbook

Before starting a new workbook, it is often useful to plan out its contents and structure. You can do this with a planning analysis sheet, which includes the following questions to help you think about the workbook's purpose and how to achieve your intended results:

1. **What problems do I want to solve?** The answer identifies the goal or purpose of the workbook. For this module, you need to create a workbook that will document purchase order information from an Insight Video Solutions customer.
2. **What data do I need?** The answer identifies the type of data that you need to collect for the workbook. A purchase order needs to describe the items purchased, the per-unit cost of each item, and the total number of items ordered. It should also contain contact information for the customer so that you can do follow up if necessary.
3. **What calculations do I need?** The answer identifies the formulas you need to apply to your data. The purchase order needs to calculate to the total cost of each item ordered, the tax levied on the order, and the final overall cost of all items ordered plus tax.
4. **What form should my solution take?** The answer impacts the appearance of the workbook content and how it should be presented to others. Sofi wants the estimates stored in a single worksheet that is easy to read and prints clearly.

You will create a workbook based on this plan. Sofi will then use your solution in other workbooks that track customer purchase orders and income for the company.

Proskills

Written Communication: Creating Effective Workbooks

Workbooks convey information in written form. As with any type of writing, the final product creates an impression and provides an indicator of your interest, knowledge, and attention to detail. To create the best impression, all workbooks—especially those you intend to share with others such as coworkers and clients—should be well planned, well organized, and well written.

A well-designed workbook should clearly identify its overall goal and present information in an organized format. The data it includes—both the entered values and the calculated values—should be accurate. The process of developing an effective workbook includes the following steps:

1. Determine the workbook's purpose, content, and organization before you start.
2. Create a list of the sheets used in the workbook, noting each sheet's purpose.
3. Insert a documentation sheet that describes the workbook's purpose and organization. Include the name of the workbook's author, the date the workbook was created, and any additional information that will help others to track the workbook to its source.
4. Enter all the data in the workbook. Add labels to indicate what the values represent and, if possible, where they originated so others can view the source of your data.
5. Enter formulas for calculated items rather than entering the calculated values into the workbook. For more complicated calculations, provide documentation explaining them.
6. Test the workbook with a variety of values; edit the data and formulas to correct errors.
7. Save the workbook and create a backup copy when the project is completed. Print the workbook's contents if you need to provide a hard-copy version to others or for your files.
8. Maintain a history of your workbook as it goes through different versions, so that you and others can quickly review how the workbook has changed during revisions.

By including clearly written documentation, explanatory text, a logical organization, and accurate data and formulas, you will create effective workbooks that others can easily use.

You create new workbooks from the New screen in Backstage view. The New screen includes template icons that preview different types of workbooks with preplaced content and formatting. You will create a workbook from the Blank workbook template and then add all the content Sofi wants.

To start a new, blank workbook for a customer purchase order:

1. sam On the ribbon, click the **File** tab to display Backstage view.
2. Click **New** in the navigation bar to display the New screen, which includes access to templates for a variety of workbooks.
3. Click **Blank workbook**. A blank workbook opens.

   Tip You can also create a new blank workbook by pressing CTRL+N.

   In these modules, the workbook window is zoomed to 140% for better readability. If you want to zoom your workbook window to match the figures, complete Step 4. If you prefer to work in the default zoom of 100% or at another zoom level, read but do not complete Step 4; more or less of the worksheet might display on your screen, but this will not affect your work in the modules.
4. If you want your workbook window zoomed to 140% to match the figures, on the Zoom slider at the lower-right of the Excel window, click the **Zoom In** button + four times to increase the percentage to **140%**. The 140% magnification increases the size of each cell but reduces the number of worksheet cells visible in the workbook window. Refer to Figure 1–11.

Figure 1–11 Blank workbook

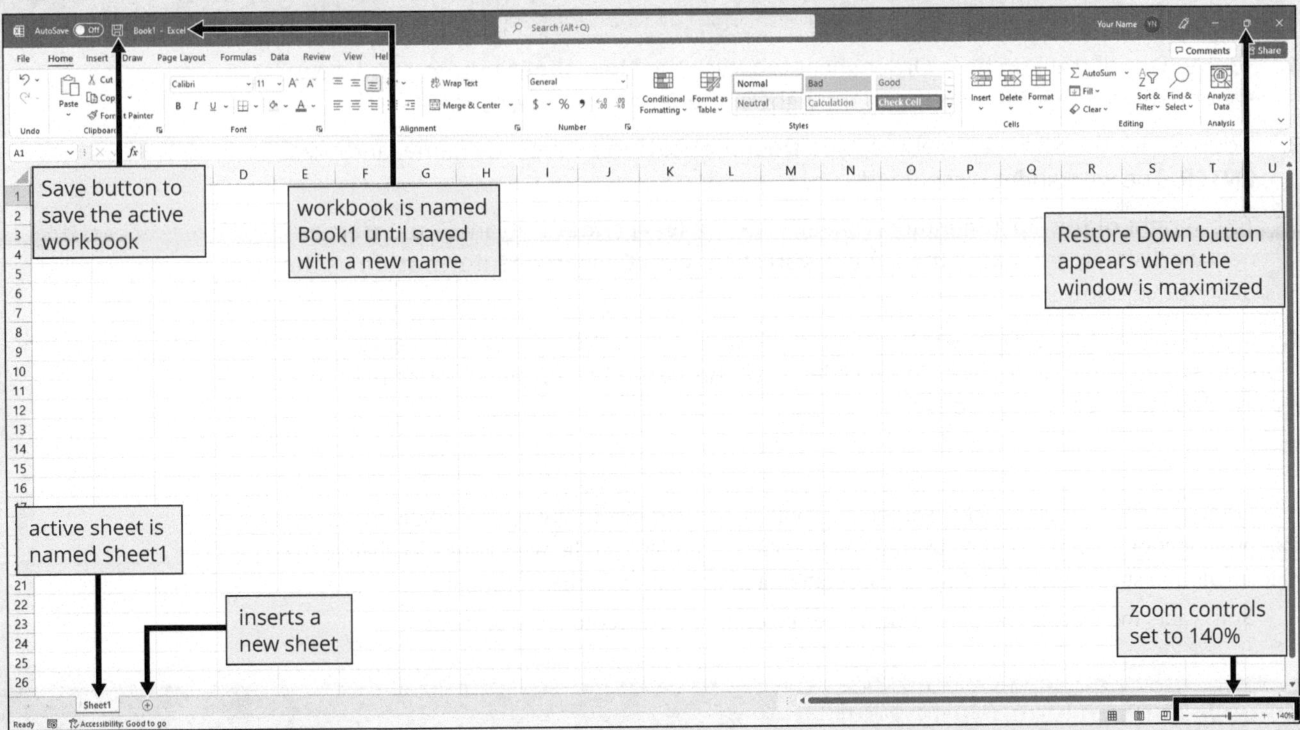

The name of the active workbook, Book1, appears in the title bar. If you open multiple blank workbooks, they are named Book1, Book2, Book3, and so forth until you save them with more descriptive names.

Inserting, Naming, and Moving Worksheets

Blank workbooks open with a single blank worksheet named Sheet1. It's a good practice to give sheets more descriptive names that indicate the purpose and content of each sheet. Sheet names cannot exceed 31 characters, but they can contain blank spaces and include uppercase and lowercase letters.

Because Sheet1 is not a descriptive name, Sofi asks you to rename the worksheet as Purchase Order.

To rename the Sheet1 worksheet:

1. Double-click the **Sheet1** tab to select the text of the sheet name.
2. Type **Purchase Order** as the new name, and then press **ENTER**. The width of the sheet tab expands to fit the longer sheet name

Many workbooks include multiple sheets to organize the report into logical sections. A common practice is to include a documentation worksheet containing a description of the workbook, the name of the person who prepared the workbook, and the date it was created.

Sofi wants you to create two new worksheets and name them Documentation and Customer Information. The Customer Information worksheet will store information about the customer making the purchase.

To insert and name the Documentation and Customer Information worksheets:

1. To the right of the Purchase Order sheet tab, click the **New sheet** button ⊕. A new sheet named Sheet2 is inserted to the right of the Purchase Order sheet.
2. Double-click the **Sheet2** sheet tab, type **Documentation** as the new name, and press **ENTER**. The worksheet is renamed.
3. To the right of the Documentation sheet, click the **New sheet** button ⊕ to insert a new worksheet, and name the Sheet3 worksheet with **Customer Information** as the descriptive name.
4. If you want these worksheets zoomed to 140% to match the figures, go to each worksheet, and then on the Zoom slider, click the **Zoom In** button + four times to increase the percentage to 140%.

Often the first worksheet in a workbook provides an overview of the book's contents. Sheets that provide more specific or detailed information are placed later in the workbook. To change the placement of a sheet, click and drag its sheet tab to a new location in the workbook.

Sofi wants the Documentation worksheet to be of the first sheet in the workbook.

To move the Documentation worksheet:

1. Point to the **Documentation** sheet tab. The sheet tab name changes to bold.
2. Press and hold the mouse button. The pointer changes to the move sheet pointer, and a small arrow appears in the upper-left corner of the sheet tab.

3. Drag to the left until the small arrow appears in the upper-left corner of the Purchase Order sheet tab, and then release the mouse button. The Documentation worksheet is now the first sheet in the workbook.

    Tip You can make a copy of a worksheet by holding down CTRL as you drag and drop the sheet tab.

You might find a workbook has sheets that can be deleted. The easiest way to delete a sheet is by using a **shortcut menu**, which is a list of commands related to an object that opens when you right-click the object. Sofi asks you to include customer information on the Purchase Order worksheet. The Customer Information worksheet is no longer needed and can be removed.

To delete the Customer Information worksheet:

1. Right-click the **Customer Information** sheet tab. A shortcut menu opens.
2. Click **Delete**. The Customer Information worksheet is removed from the workbook.

When you delete a sheet, you also delete any text and data it contains. So be careful that you do not remove important and irretrievable information.

Save changes to your workbook frequently so that you don't lose any work. The first time you save a workbook, the Save As dialog box opens so you can name the file and choose where to save it. You can save the workbook on your computer or network or to your account on OneDrive.

If you save a file to your OneDrive account, you can turn on AutoSave. The workbook is then saved to your OneDrive account every few seconds. You can also access a previously saved version of the file using the version history in OneDrive. If you do not turn on AutoSave, remember to save your workbook periodically so you do not lose any work.

You'll save the workbook you just created.

To save the workbook you created for the first time:

1. On the title bar, click the **Save** button (or press **CTRL+S**). The Save this file dialog box opens.
2. Click **More options**. The Save As screen in Backstage view appears.
3. Click the **Browse** button. The Save As dialog box opens.
4. Navigate to the location specified by your instructor for your saved files.
5. In the File name box, select **Book1.xlsx** (the default file name assigned to your workbook) if it is not already selected, and then type **NP_EX_1_Order** as the new name.
6. Verify that **Excel Workbook** appears in the Save as type box.
7. Click **Save**. The workbook is saved, the dialog box closes, and the workbook window reappears with the new file name in the title bar.

As you modify a workbook, you will need to resave the file. Because you already saved the workbook with a file name, the next time you click the Save button, the changes you made to the workbook are saved without opening the Save As dialog box.

Tip You can save a workbook to your OneDrive account by clicking its file name in the title bar and then clicking Upload.

Sometimes you will want to save a workbook with a new file name. This is useful when you want to modify a workbook but keep a copy with the original content and structure or when you want to save a copy of the workbook to a new location. To save a workbook with a new name, click the File tab to return to Backstage view, click Save As on the navigation bar, specify the new file name and location, and then click Save.

Entering Text into a Worksheet

Worksheet cells can contain text, numbers, dates, and times. **Text data** is any combination of letters, numbers, and symbols. A **text string** is a series of text data characters. **Numeric data** is any number that can be used in a mathematical operation. **Date data** and **time data** are values displayed in commonly recognized date and time formats. For example, Excel interprets the cell entry April 15, 2029, as a date and not as text. By default, text is left-aligned within worksheet cells, and numbers, dates, and times are right-aligned.

Text is often used in worksheets as labels for the numeric values and calculations displayed in the workbook. Sofi wants you to enter text content into the Documentation sheet.

To enter text into the Documentation sheet:

1. Go to the **Documentation** sheet, and then press **CTRL+HOME** to make sure cell A1 is the active cell.
2. Type **Insight Video Solutions** in cell A1. As you type, the text appears in the cell and in the formula bar.
3. Press **ENTER** twice. The text is entered into cell A1, and the active cell moves down two rows to cell A3.
4. Type **Author** in cell A3, and then press **TAB**. The text is entered, and the active cell moves one column to the right to cell B3.
5. Type your name in cell B3, and then press **ENTER**. The text is entered, and the active cell moves one cell down and to the left to cell A4.
6. Type **Date** in cell A4, and then press **TAB**. The text is entered, and the active cell moves one column to the right to cell B4, where you would enter the date on which the workbook is created. For now, you will leave the cell for the date blank.
7. Press **ENTER** to make cell A5 the active cell, type **Purpose** in the cell, and then press **TAB**. The active cell moves one column to the right to cell B5.
8. Type **To display a purchase order** in cell B5, and then press **ENTER**.

The text entered in cells A1, B3, and B5 is displayed over their adjacent cells. Though the company name in cell A1 appears to occupy three cells, it is still only entered in cell A1. If the adjacent cells also contain content, only the text that fits into the cell is displayed while the remaining text is hidden. You will learn how to increase the width of cell to accommodate its extended content in the next session.

Editing Cells and Using AutoComplete

Excel keeps a list of the actions you took during your current session. If you need to undo an action, you can use the Undo button on the Home tab of the ribbon or press CTRL+Z to reverse your most recent action. To reverse addition actions, continue to click the Undo button (or press CTRL+Z), and each action stored in the list will be reversed one at a time.

You will undo the most recent change you made to the Documentation sheet—the text you entered in cell B5. Then you will enter a different description of the workbook's purpose in that cell.

To undo the text entry in cell B5:

1. On the Home tab in the Undo group, click the **Undo** button (or press **CTRL+Z**). The last action is reversed, removing the text you entered in cell B5.
2. In cell B5, type **To document a purchase order for the company** and then press **ENTER**. The new purpose statement is entered in cell B5. Figure 1–12 shows the text entered in the Documentation sheet.

Figure 1–12 Text entered in the Documentation sheet

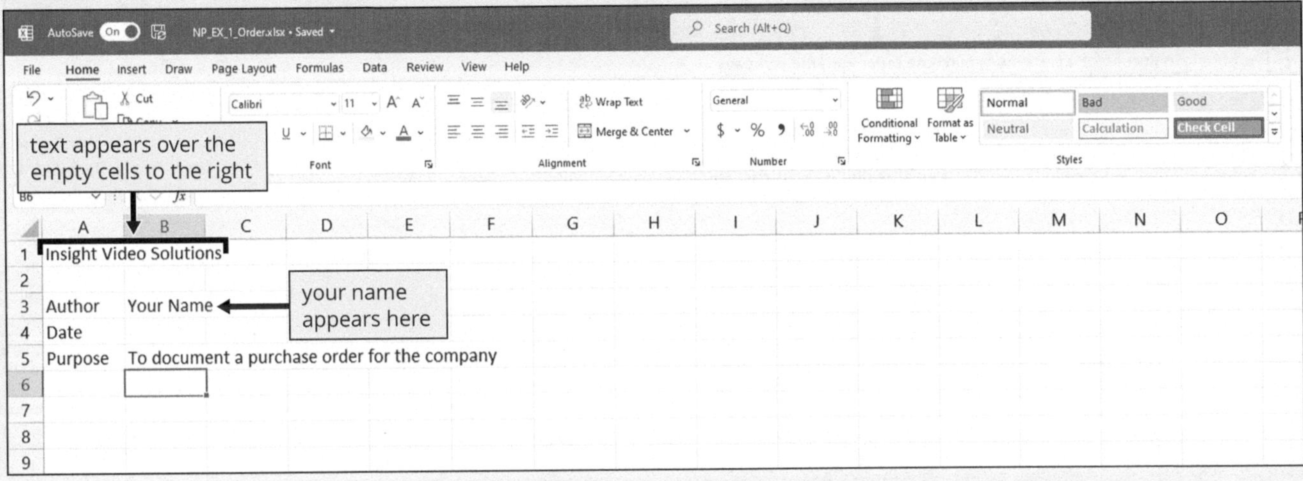

If you need to restore actions you have undone, you can redo them. To redo one action at a time, click the Redo button in the Undo group on the Home tab or press CTRL+Y. To redo additional actions, continue click the Redo button or press CTRL+Y. After you undo or redo an action, Excel continues the action list, starting with the new changes you make to the workbook.

To replace an entire cell entry, you can overwrite the previous entry. Select the cell and then type the new entry. If you want to replace only part of the entry, you can switch to Edit mode to make the changes directly in the cell. To switch to Edit mode, double-click the cell. A blinking insertion point indicates where the new content will be inserted. In the cell or formula bar, the pointer changes to an I-beam, which you can use to select sections of text with the cell. Anything you type replaces the selected content.

Sofi wants you rewrite the purpose statement to clarify that the workbook documents a customer's purchase order with the company.

To edit the text in cell B5:

1. Double-click cell **B5** to select the cell and switch to Edit mode. A blinking insertion point appears within the text of cell B5. The status bar displays Edit instead of Ready to indicate that the cell is in Edit mode.
2. Press **LEFT ARROW** or **RIGHT ARROW** as needed to move the insertion point directly to the left of the word "purchase" in the cell text.
3. Type **customer's** following by a space to change the text to "To document a customer's purchase order for the company" in the cell.
4. Select the word **for** and then type **with** to change the text to "To document a customer's purchase order with the company" in cell B5. Refer to Figure 1–13.

Figure 1–13 Edited text in the Documentation sheet

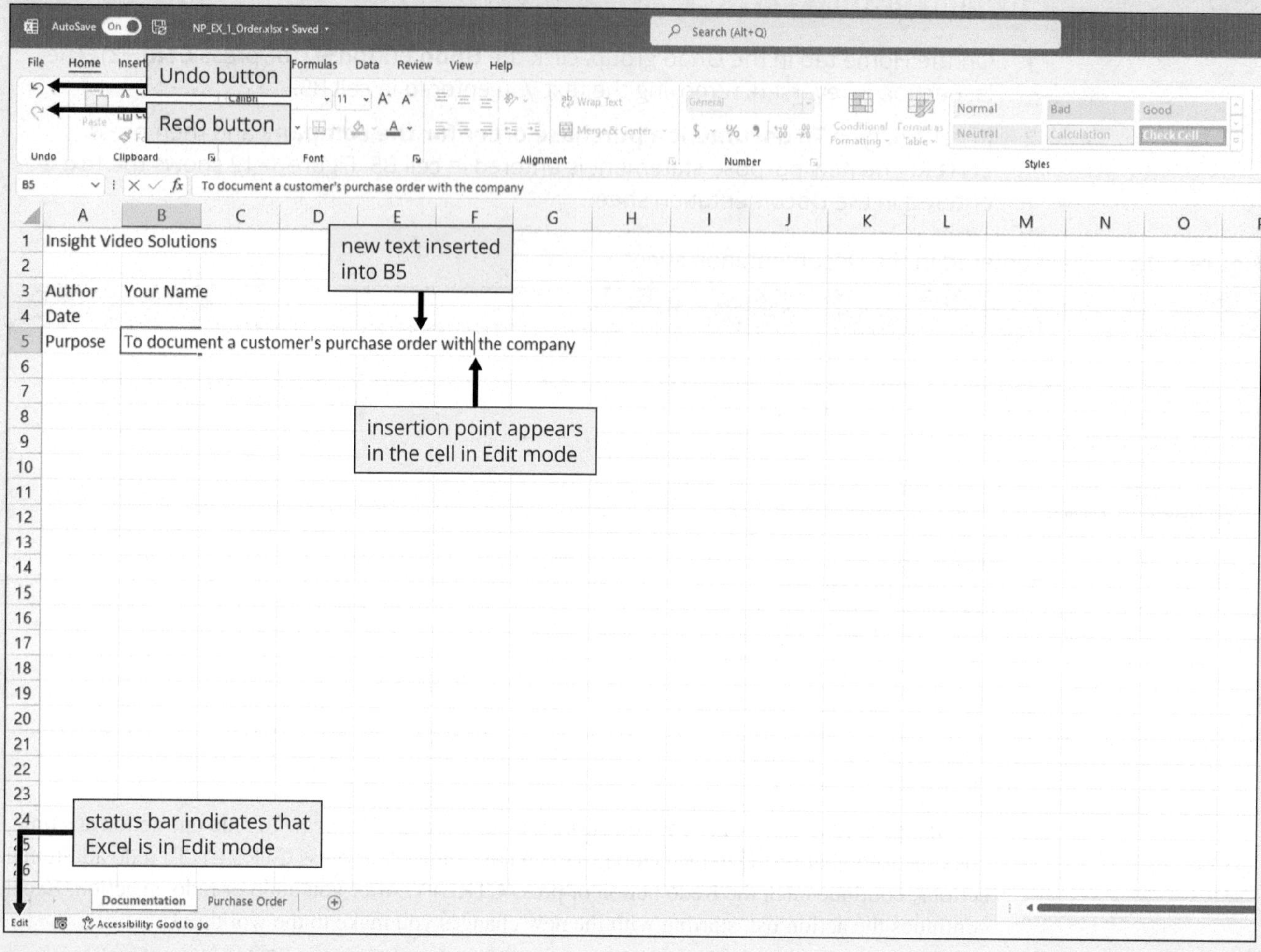

5. Press **ENTER** to accept the edits.

As you type text into the active cell, Excel anticipates the remaining characters by displaying text that begins with the same letters as a previous entry of the same column. This feature, known as **AutoComplete**, makes entering repetitive text easier and reduces data entry errors. To accept the suggested text, press TAB or ENTER. To override the suggested text, continue to type the text you want to enter in the cell. AutoComplete does not work with dates or numbers or when a blank cell is positioned between the previous entry and the text you are typing.

AutoComplete entries might appear as you enter descriptive text about the customer's order in the Purchase Order worksheet.

To enter information about the purchase order:

1. Click the **Purchase Order** sheet tab to make it the active sheet.
2. In cell **A1**, type **Insight Video Solutions** as the worksheet title, and then press **ENTER**.
3. In cell **A2**, type **Purchase Order** and then press **ENTER** twice to move the insertion point to cell A4.

   First, enter the labels for the customer information in column A.
4. In the range **A4:A8**, enter the following text labels, pressing **ENTER** after each entry: **Customer**, **Street**, **City**, **State**, and **Postal Code**.

5. In the range **A10:A12**, enter the following text labels: **Contact**, **Phone**, and **Email**.

   Next, enter the customer data in column B alongside each category label.

6. In the range **B4:B8**, enter the customer's name and address using the following text values: **Davis Financial Services**, **45 West Lancet Drive**, **Boston**, **MA**, and **02109**.

7. In the range **B10:B12**, enter information about the customer's contact person using the following text values: **Lishan Zola**, **800-555-1048**, and **l.zola@example.com**. Figure 1–14 shows the completed customer information for the purchase order.

Figure 1–14 Customer information in the Purchase Order worksheet

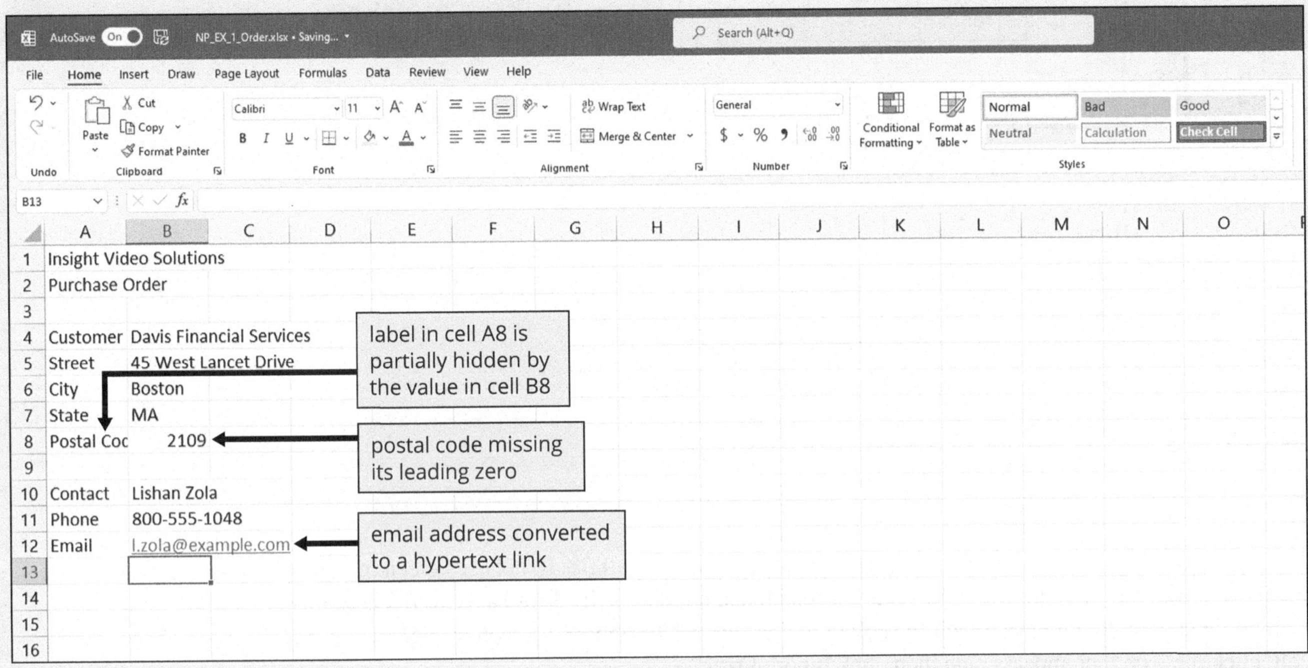

Excel converts any email or website address into a hypertext link, which opens in an email app or web browser when clicked. An email link, like the one in cell B12, is displayed in blue and underlined.

When you enter a number in a cell, Excel removes leading zeroes from integer values. So, the postal code value 02109 you entered in cell B7 appears as 2109. Excel removed the zero because it treated the postal code as number rather than text. To correct this problem, you can instruct Excel to treat a number as text so its leading zero is not dropped. You'll make this change for the postal code in cell B8.

To display the postal code as text:

1. Click cell **B8** to select the cell. The value is right-aligned, indicating that Excel considers it a number.
2. On the Home tab, in the Number group, click the **Number Format arrow**. A list of number format options appears.
3. Scroll down the list, and then click **Text**. Anything entered in the cell will be treated by Excel as text. The value in B8 is left-aligned, indicating that Excel considers it text.

   Tip You can also display a number as text by typing an apostrophe (') before the number.

4. Type **02109** and press **ENTER**. The cell retains the leading zero. Refer to Figure 1–15.

Figure 1–15 Postal code displayed as text

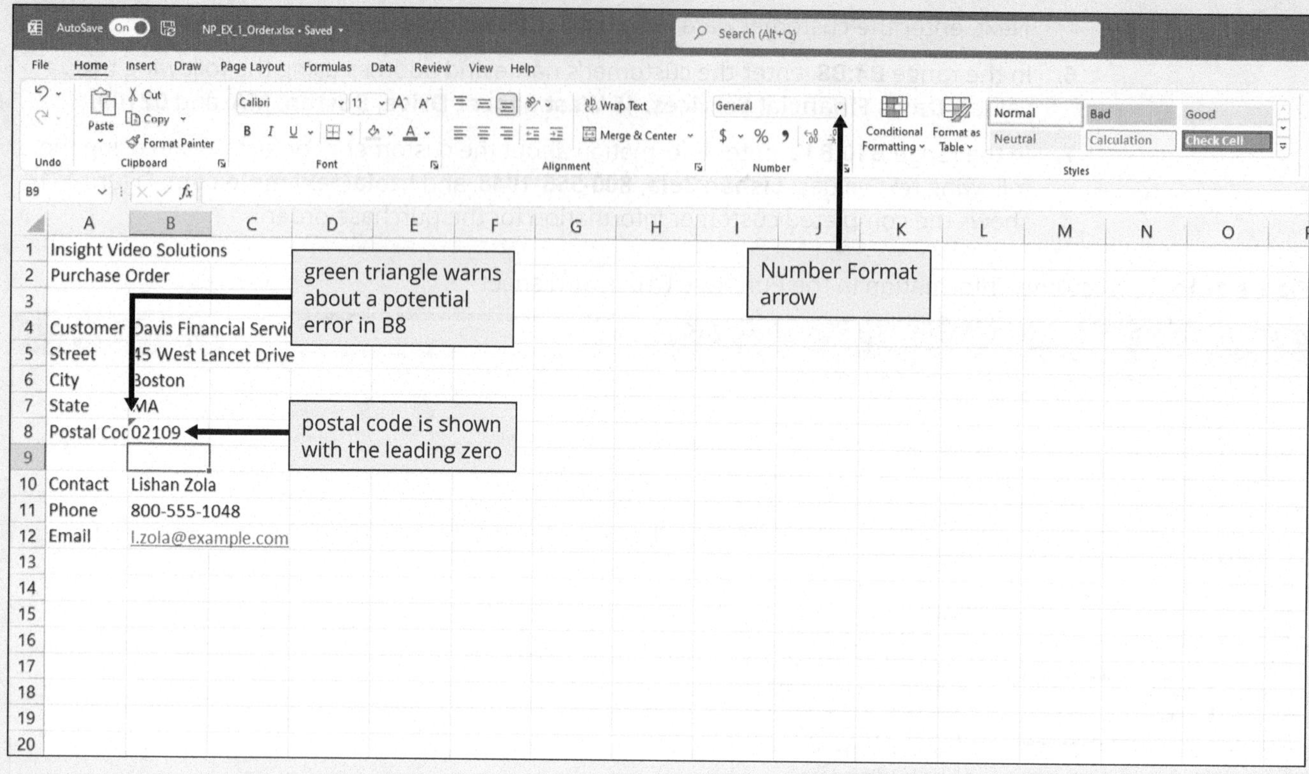

Notice that a green triangle appears in the upper-left corner of cell B8. Excel uses green triangles to flag potential errors. In this case, Excel is warning that a number is displayed as text. Because this is intentional, you do not have to edit the cell to fix the "error." To remove a green triangle, click the cell, click the icon that appears, and then click Ignore Error.

Entering Dates and Numeric Values

Excel recognizes dates in any of the following standard date formats:

- 4/6/2029
- 4/6/29
- 4-6-2029
- April 6, 2029
- 6-Apr-29

Even though dates appear as text, they are stored as numbers equal to the number of days between the specified date and January 0, 1900. Times also appear as text but are stored as numbers equal to fractions of a 24-hour day. For example, a date and time of April 15, 2029, 6:00 PM is stored as the number 47,223.75, which is 47,223 days after January 0, 1900, plus three-quarters of one day. Excel stores dates and times as numbers so they can be used for date and time calculations, such as determining the elapsed time between two dates.

Based on how your computer displays dates, Excel might change the appearance of a date after you type it. For example, if you enter the date 4/15/29 into the active cell, Excel might display the date with the four-digit year value, 4/15/2029. If you enter the text April 15, 2029, Excel might change the date format to 15-Apr-29. Changing the date format does not affect the underlying date or time value.

Insight

International Date Formats

For international business transactions, you may need to adopt international standards for expressing dates, times, and currency values in your workbooks. For example, a worksheet cell might contain the date 06/05/29, which could be interpreted as either the 5th of June 2029, or the 6th of May 2029.

The interpretation depends on which country the workbook has been designed for. You can avoid this problem by entering the full date, as in June 5, 2029. However, this might not work with documents written in foreign languages, such as Japanese, that use different character symbols.

To solve this problem, many international businesses adopt ISO (International Organization for Standardization) dates in the format *yyyy-mm-dd*, where *yyyy* is the four-digit year value, *mm* is the two-digit month value, and *dd* is the two-digit day value. A date such as June 5, 2029, is entered as 2029/06/05. If you choose to use this international date format, make sure that everyone else using your workbook understands this format so they interpret dates correctly. You can include information about the date format in the Documentation sheet.

The purchase order report needs the date of the customer order. For your work, you will enter dates in the format *mm/dd/yyyy*, where *mm* is the two-digit month number, *dd* is the two-digit day number, and *yyyy* is the four-digit year number. You also need to enter the order ID.

To enter the order date and order ID:

1. In cell A14, type **Order Date** and then press **TAB** to make B14 the active cell.
2. Type **1/6/2029** in cell B14, and then press **ENTER** to make A15 the active cell.

   Trouble? Depending on your system configuration, Excel might change the date to the date format *dd-mmm-yy*. This difference will not affect your work.

3. Type **Order ID** in cell A15. AutoComplete feature will suggest inserting Order Date into the cell. Ignore the suggestion and press **TAB** to make B15 the active cell.
4. Type **OR2055-1506** in cell B15 and press **ENTER**. Figure 1–16 shows the completed customer information.

Figure 1–16 Customer order date and ID

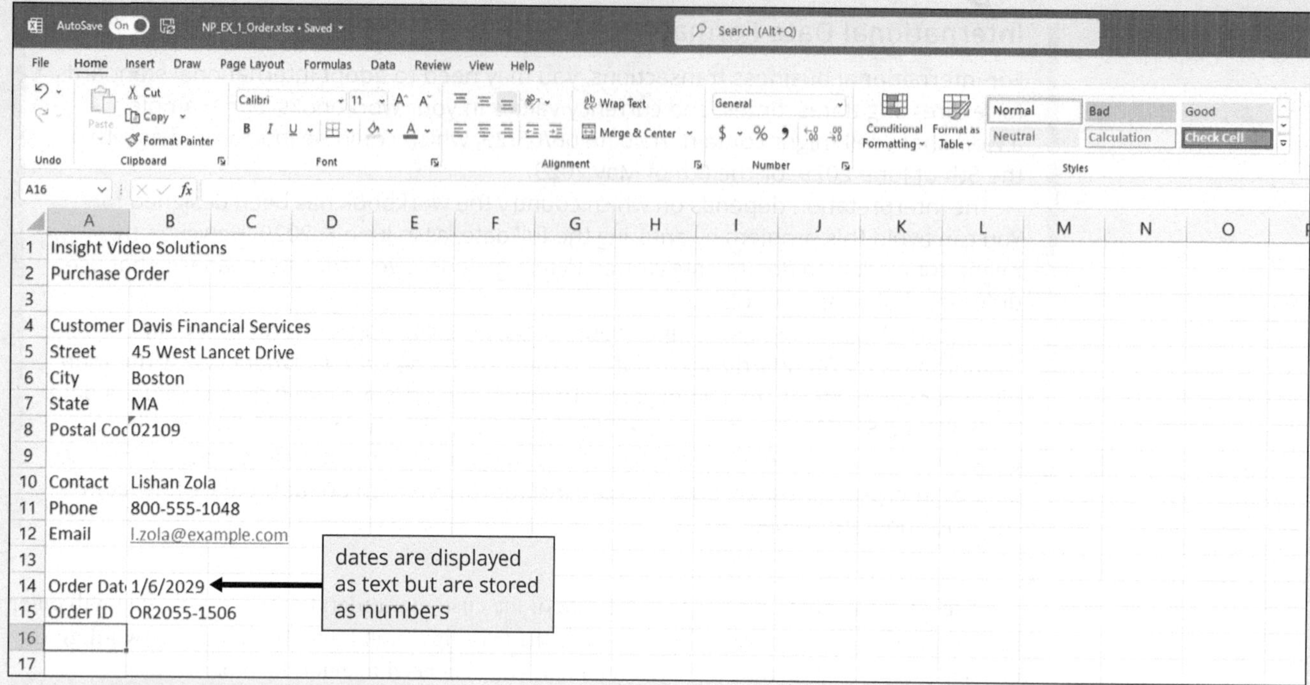

5. Click the **Documentation** sheet tab, and then enter the current date in cell B4.

The next part of the Purchase Order worksheet will document what products and services the customer ordered from Insight Video Solutions. Figure 1–17 lists the data you will add to the worksheet.

Figure 1–17 Customer order data

Category	Subcategory	Description	QTY	Cost
AUD	9010	TruSound AT100T wireless audio transmitter	12	$24.50
AUD	9020	TruSound AT100R wireless audio receiver	12	$28.00
VID	7050	TruVideo SCX5G green screen backdrop and storage case	1	$45.50
AUD	5100	TruSound TS100 wireless headset	20	$65.50
VID	4020	Eagleview EV45W conference camera	5	$325.50
TEL	7010	SureTalk V9200 VOIP conference phone with wiring harness and control board	5	$475.50
SER	4020	Installation and wiring	1	$650.00

You'll enter the first three columns of this list into the worksheet.

To enter the first of the list of purchased items:

1. Click the **Purchase Order** sheet tab to return to the Purchase Order worksheet.
2. Click **A17** to make it the active cell, type **Category** as the column label, and then press **TAB** to move to cell B17.
3. Type **Subcategory** in B17, press **TAB** to move to C17, type **Description** and then press **ENTER**. Note that the Subcategory label in cell B17 is only partially visible because of the text in cell C17.
4. In the range **A18:C24**, enter the Category, Subcategory, and Description text for the seven products and services listed in Figure 1–17, pressing **TAB** to move from one column to next and pressing **ENTER** to move to the start of the next row. Refer to Figure 1–18.

Figure 1–18 Products and services on the purchase order

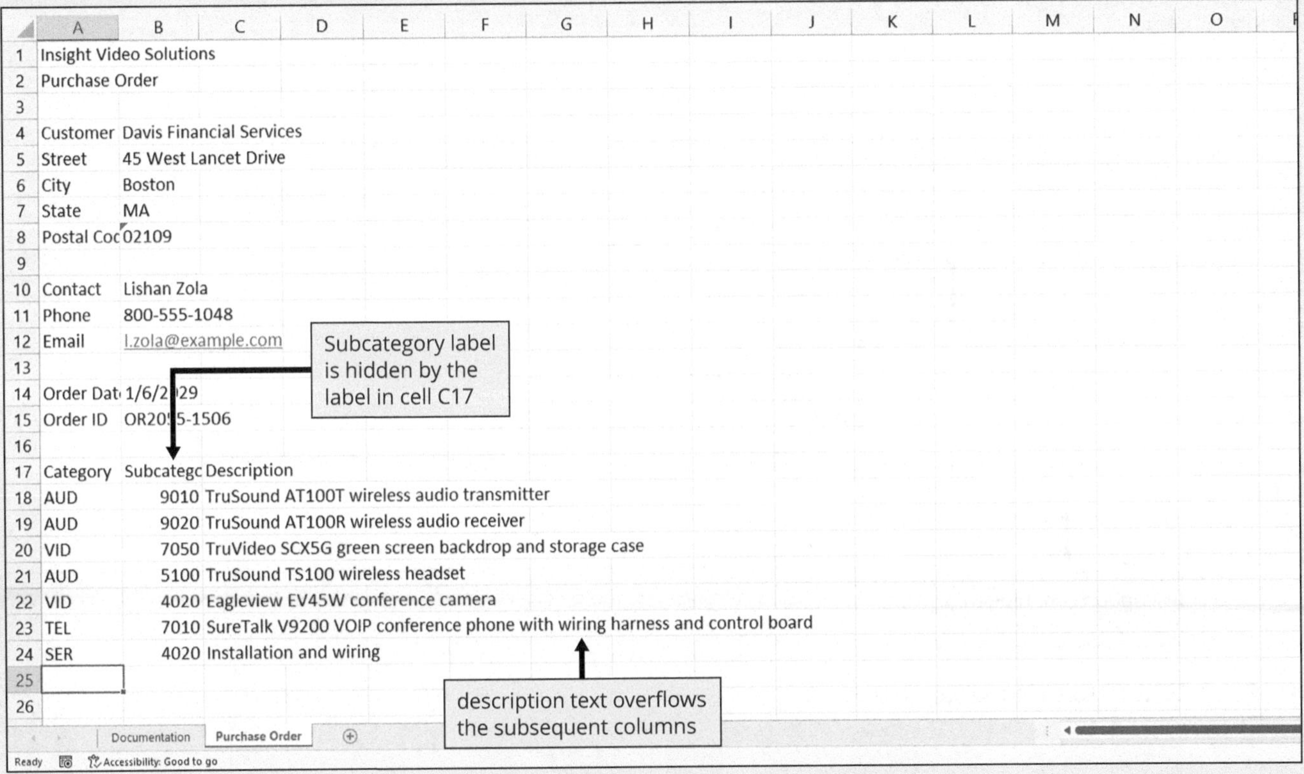

Numbers are entered in a worksheet in a variety of formats, including integers (378), decimals (3.14), negative numbers (–4.27), and scientific notation (1.25E3 for 1.25×10^3). Currency values like $125.50 or percentages like 95% are special number formats. As with dates, currency and percentages entered in a cell are displayed with their symbols but stored as numbers. For example, a currency value such as $87.25 is stored as the number 87.25, and a percentage such as 95% is stored as 0.95.

An integer that is too long to fit in a cell is displayed in scientific notation. A decimal value with too many decimal places is rounded (but its full value is stored). Hashtag symbols (#####) in a cell indicate the cell is too narrow to display its stored number.

You'll complete the purchase order by entering the quantity and cost of each product or service ordered by the customer.

To enter the quantity and cost of each product or service:

1. Click cell **D17**, type **QTY** as the label, and then press **TAB**. Cell E17 becomes the active cell.
2. Type **Cost** in cell E17, and then press **ENTER**. Cell D18 becomes the active cell.
3. In the range **D18:E24**, enter the quantity and cost of the products and services ordered by the customer (refer to Figure 1–17). Note that as you enter this information, the description values in column C will be hidden. Refer to Figure 1–19.

Figure 1–19 Quantities and costs on the purchase order

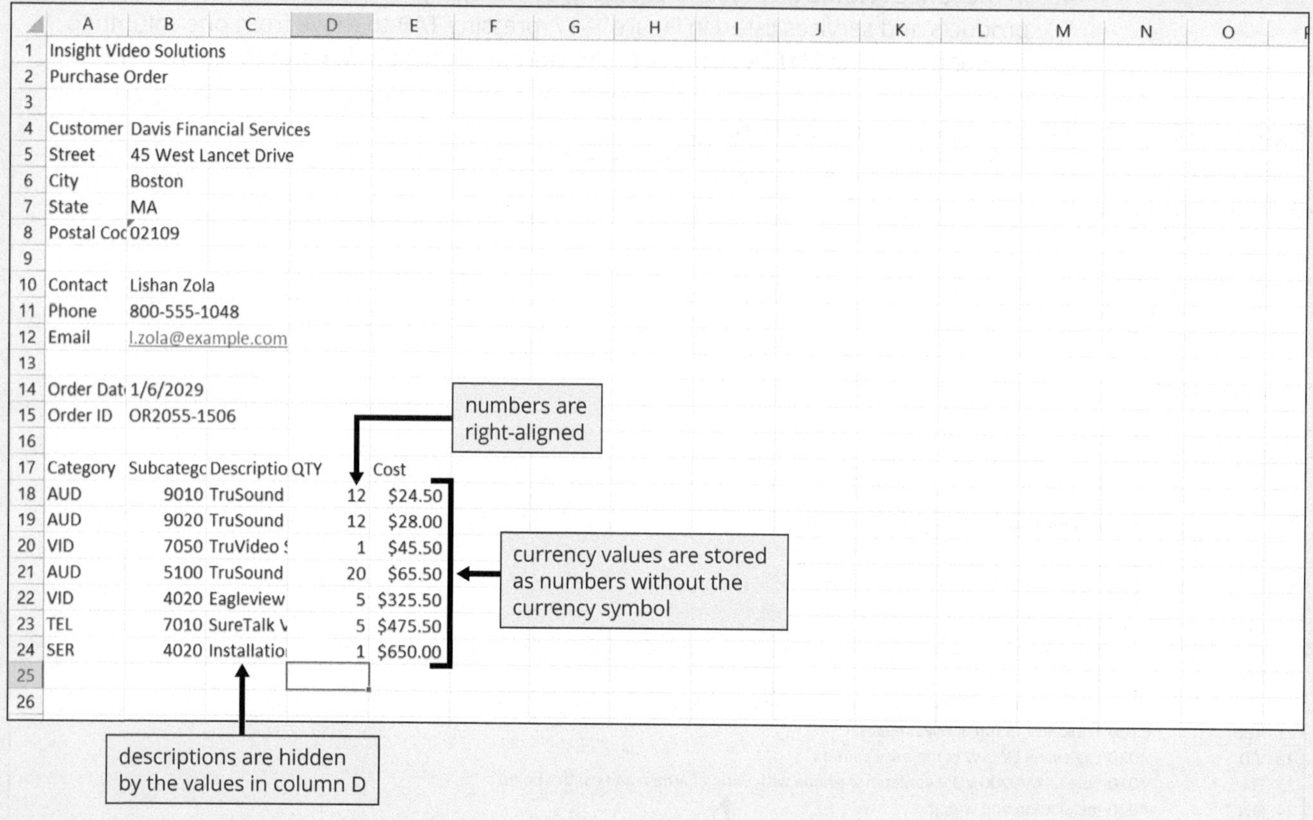

4. Press **CTRL+S** to save the workbook.

Some of the labels and all the descriptions are hidden by the text and values entered in adjacent cells, making the worksheet unreadable. You can display the hidden cell content by increasing the column widths.

Resizing Worksheet Columns and Rows

Resizing columns and rows in worksheet let you modify the worksheet layout to create the best fit for your data.

Resizing Worksheet Columns

Column widths are expressed as the number of characters a column can fit. The default column width is 8.43 standard-sized characters. In general, this means that you can type eight characters in a cell. Any additional text will overlap the adjacent cell or be hidden by it. Column widths are also expressed in terms of pixels. A **pixel** is an individual point on a computer monitor or printout. A column width of 8.43 characters is equivalent to 64 pixels.

Insight

Column Widths and Pixels

On a computer monitor, pixel size is based on screen resolution. As a result, cell content that looks fine on one screen might appear differently when viewed on a screen with a different resolution. If you work on multiple computers or share workbooks with others, you should set column widths based on the maximum number of characters you want displayed in the cells rather than pixel size. This ensures that everyone sees the cell contents the way you intended.

You will increase the width of column A so that all the text labels in that column are completely displayed.

To increase the width of column A:

1. Point to the **right border** of the column A heading until the pointer changes to the column resize pointer ✛.
2. Click and drag to the right until the width of the column heading reaches **12** characters, but do not release the mouse button. The ScreenTip that appears as you resize the column shows the new column width in characters and in pixels. Refer to Figure 1–20.

Figure 1–20 Width of column A increased to 12 characters

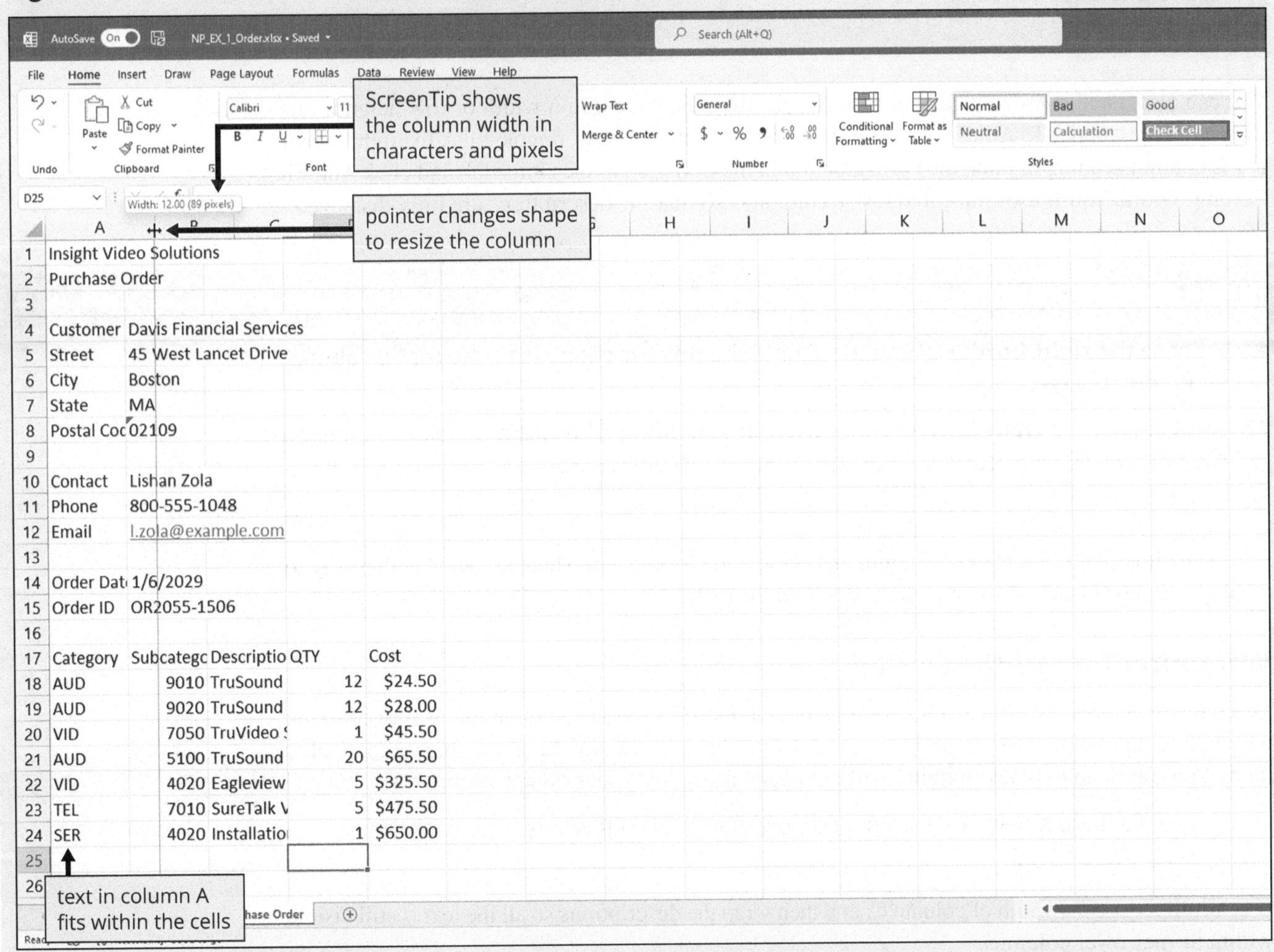

3. Release the mouse button. The width of column A expands to 12 characters, and all the text in that column is visible.

You can change the widths of multiple columns at once. When you change the width of one column in a group of selected columns, the widths of all the columns in that group are similarly resized.

To select a group of adjacent columns, click the first column heading in the group, hold down SHIFT, and then click the last column heading in the group. Another way to select a group of adjacent columns is to hold down the mouse button as you drag the pointer over the headings of the columns you want to include in the group. To select nonadjacent columns, hold down CTRL and click the heading of each column in the group.

Using the click-and-drag method to resize columns can be imprecise. Instead, you can use the Format command in the Cells group on the Home tab to set an exact column width and row height. You'll use the Format command to set the width of column B to 14 characters so all the text in column B is visible.

To set the width of column B using the Format command:

1. Click the **column B** heading. The entire column is selected.
2. On the Home tab, in the Cells group, click the **Format** button, and then click **Column Width**. The Column Width dialog box opens.
3. Type **14** in the Column width box to set the width to 14 characters.
4. Click **OK**. The width of column B is increased to 14 characters.
5. Click **A2** to deselect column B.

You can also use the **AutoFit** feature to automatically adjust a column width or row height to its widest or tallest entry. To AutoFit a column to the width of its contents, double-click the right border of the column heading or click the Format button in the Cells group the Home tab and click AutoFit Column Width. You'll use AutoFit to resize column C so that the descriptions are fully displayed.

To use AutoFit to resize the width of column C:

1. Point to the **right border** of column C until the pointer changes to the resize column width pointer ✥.
2. Double-click the **right border** of the column C heading. The width of column C increases to about 70.86 characters so that the longest item description is completely visible.

Sometimes AutoFit creates a column that is too wide for the worksheet layout. Another way to display long text entries is to wrap the text within the cell.

Wrapping Text Within a Cell

When text is wrapped within a cell, any content that doesn't fit along a single line is moved to the next line within the cell. As more lines are added to the cell, the row height increases to display them. You can wrap only text within a cell; numbers, dates, and times do not wrap.

> **Tip** To force a new line within a cell, press ALT+ENTER where you want the new line created.

You'll reduce the width of column C, and then wrap the descriptions so all the text is still visible within the narrower columns.

To wrap text in column C:

1. Resize the width of column C to **30** characters.
2. Select the range **C18:C24**. These cells contain descriptions of the products and services.
3. On the Home tab, in the Alignment group, click the **Wrap Text** button. The Wrap Text button is highlighted, indicating that it is applied to the selected range. Any text in the selected cells that exceeds the column width wraps to a new line in those cells.
4. Click **C17** to make it the active cell. Refer to Figure 1–21.

Figure 1–21 Text wrapped within cells

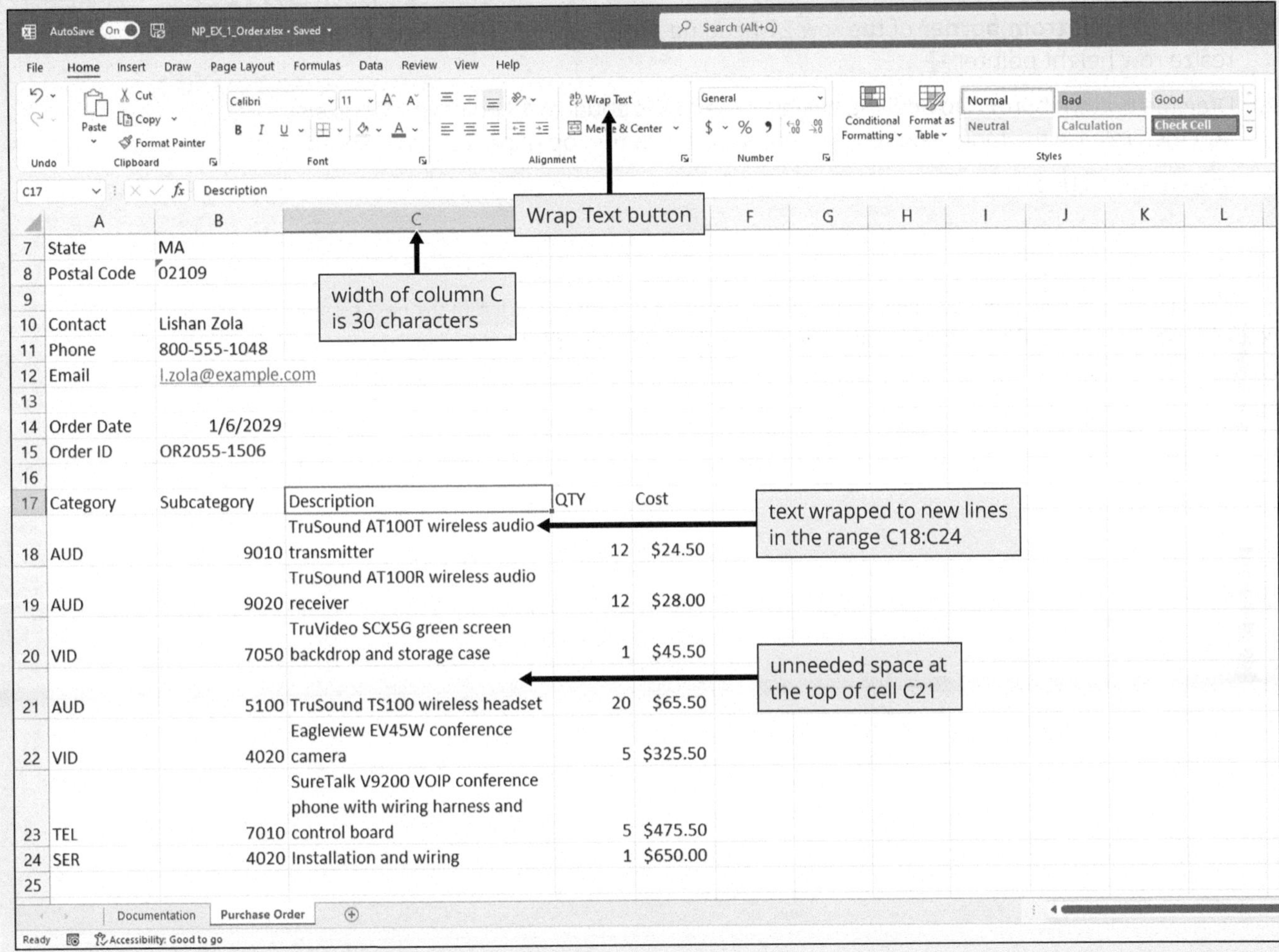

Resizing Worksheet Rows

Row heights are measured in points or pixels. A **point** is approximately 1/72 of an inch. The default row height is 15 points or 20 pixels. There are several ways to change row height. You can drag the bottom border of the row heading to a new height. You can click the Format button in the Cells group on the Home tab, click Row Height, and then set an exact row height. Also, you can double-click the bottom border of the row to AutoFit the row to its contents.

After you wrapped the text in the range C18:C24, row 21 has unneeded space above the description. You'll decrease the height of row 21 to remove the extra space at the top of cell C21.

To change a row height of cell C21:

1. Point to the **bottom border** of the row 21 heading until the pointer changes to the resize row height pointer ╪.
2. Drag the bottom border up until the height of the row is equal to **18** points (or **24** pixels), and then release the mouse button. The empty space at the top of cell C21 is removed.
3. Save the workbook.

You have entered the products and services in the customer's purchase order. In the next session, you will use formulas and functions to calculate the total cost of that order.

Part 1.1 Quick Check

1. How do worksheets and chart sheets differ?
2. What is the cell reference for the cell located in the fourth column and fifth row of a worksheet?
3. What is the range reference for the block of cells A10 through D15?
4. What is the range reference for cells A10 through C20 and cells A22 through C32?
5. Text entered in cell A3 exceeds the cell's width. If the cell to the right is empty, how is the text displayed? If the cell to the right contains content, how is that text displayed?
6. Cell B10 contains the percentage 75%. What numeric value is stored in the cell?
7. Cell C10 contains the date May 3, 2029. Is this content stored as a text string or a number?
8. What does a series of hashtag symbols (#####) in a cell indicate?

Part 1.2 Visual Overview: Excel Formulas and Functions

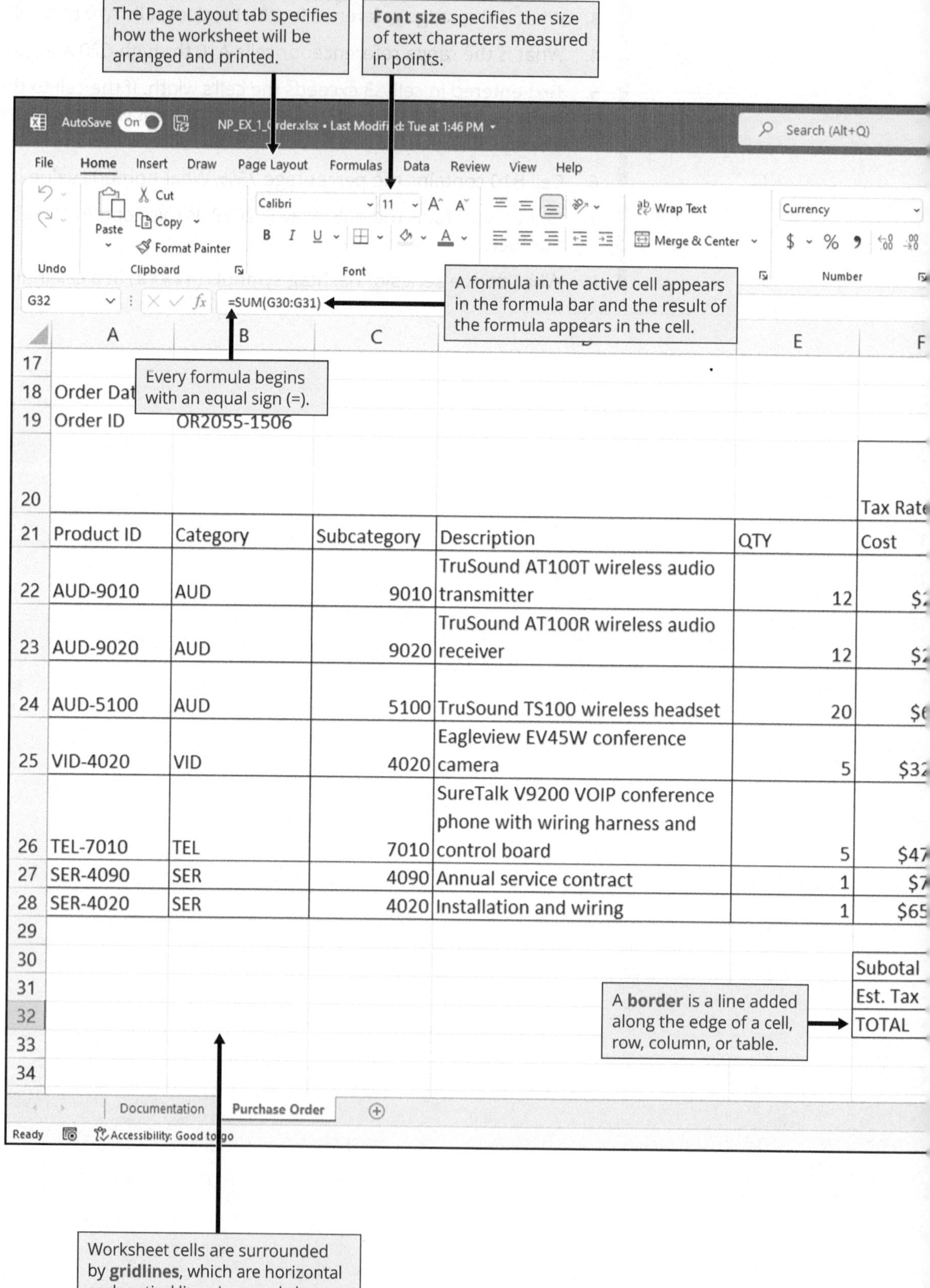

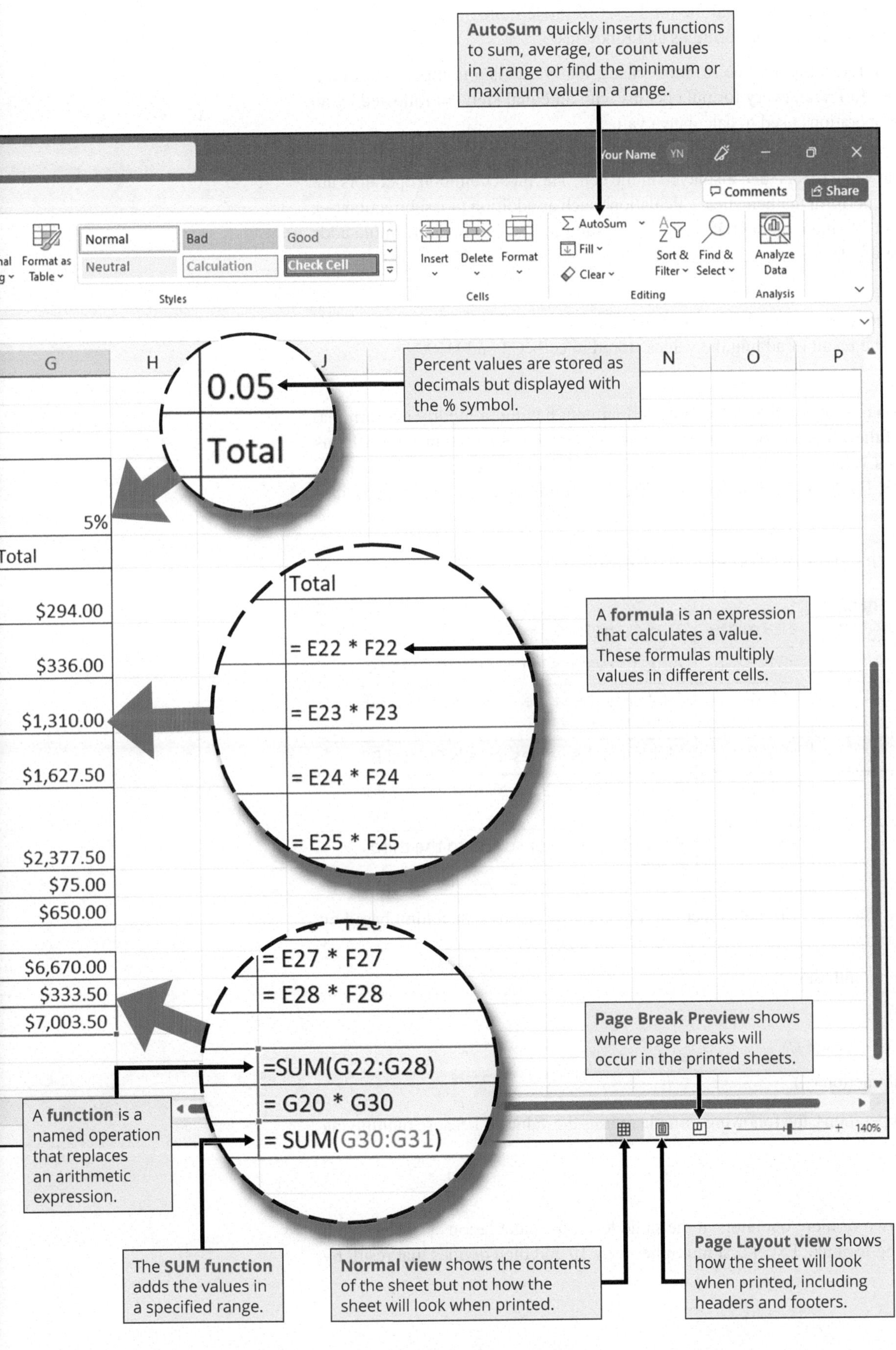
AutoSum quickly inserts functions to sum, average, or count values in a range or find the minimum or maximum value in a range.
Percent values are stored as decimals but displayed with the % symbol.
0.05
Total
5%
Total
$294.00
$336.00
$1,310.00
$1,627.50
$2,377.50
$75.00
$650.00
$6,670.00
$333.50
$7,003.50
= E22 * F22
= E23 * F23
= E24 * F24
= E25 * F25
= E27 * F27
= E28 * F28
=SUM(G22:G28)
= G20 * G30
= SUM(G30:G31)
A **formula** is an expression that calculates a value. These formulas multiply values in different cells.
Page Break Preview shows where page breaks will occur in the printed sheets.
A **function** is a named operation that replaces an arithmetic expression.
The **SUM function** adds the values in a specified range.
Normal view shows the contents of the sheet but not how the sheet will look when printed.
Page Layout view shows how the sheet will look when printed, including headers and footers.

Calculating with Formulas

So far you have entered text, numbers, and dates in the worksheet. However, the main reason for using Excel is to perform calculations and analysis on data. Sofi wants the workbook to report on the number of items in the purchase order and the total cost of those items including tax. Such calculations are added to a worksheet using formulas and functions.

A formula is an expression returning a value. In most cases, that value is a number—though it could also be text or a date. In Excel, every formula begins with an equal sign (=) followed by an expression containing the operations used to calculate a value.

A formula is written using **operators**, or mathematical symbols, that combine different values, resulting in a single value that is then displayed in the cell. The most common operators are **arithmetic operators** that perform mathematical calculations such as addition (+), subtraction (–), multiplication (*), division (/), and exponentiation (^). For example, the following formula adds 3 and 8, returning a value of 11:

```
=3+8
```

Most Excel formulas contain references to cells rather than specific values. For example, the following formula returns the result of adding the values stored in cells C3 and D10:

```
=C3+D10
```

If a value changes, you can update that value in its cell without having to modify the formula. Continuing the example, if the value 3 is stored in cell C3 and the value 8 is stored in cell D10, this formula would also return a value of 11. If the value in cell C3 is later changed to 10, the formula would return a value of 18. Figure 1–22 describes the different arithmetic operators and provides examples of formulas.

Figure 1–22 Arithmetic operators and example formulas

Operation	Arithmetic Operator	Example	Description
Addition	+	=B1+B2+B3	Adds the values in cells B1, B2, and B3
Subtraction	–	=C9-B2	Subtracts the value in cell B2 from the value in cell C9
Multiplication	*	=C9*B9	Multiplies the values in cells C9 and B9
Division	/	=C9/B9	Divides the value in cell C9 by the value in cell B9
Exponentiation	^	=B5^3	Raises the value of cell B5 to the third power

If a formula contains more than one arithmetic operator, Excel performs the calculation based on the following order of operations:

1. Operations within parentheses
2. Exponentiation (^)
3. Multiplication (*) or division (/)
4. Addition (+) or subtraction (–)

Based on the order of operations, the following formula returns the value 23 because multiplying 4 by 5 is done before adding 3:

```
=3+4*5
```

If a formula contains two or more operators at the same level, the calculations are done from left to right. In the following formula, Excel first multiplies 4 by 10 and then divides that result by 8 to return the value 5:

```
=4*10/8
```

When parentheses are used, the expression inside them is calculated first. In the following formula, Excel calculates (3+4) first, and then multiplies that result by 5 to return the value 35:

```
=(3+4)*5
```

Figure 1–23 shows how changes in a formula affect the order of operations and the result of the formula.

Figure 1–23 Order of operations applied to formulas

Formula	Order of Operations	Result
=50+10*5	10 * 5 calculated first and then 50 is added	100
=(50+10)*5	(50 + 10) calculated first and then 60 is multiplied by 5	300
=50/10–5	50/10 calculated first and then 5 is subtracted	0
=50/(10–5)	(10 – 5) calculated first and then 50 is divided by that value	10
=50/10*5	Two operators at same precedence level, so the calculation is done left to right with 50/10 calculated first and that value is then multiplied by 5	25
=50/(10*5)	(10 * 5) is calculated first and then 50 is divided by that value	1

The purchase order report should calculate the total cost of each product or service ordered by the customer. The total cost is equal to the number of units ordered multiplied by the cost per unit. You already entered this information in columns D and E. Now you will enter a formula in cell F11 to calculate the total cost of each product or service.

To enter a formula calculating the total for wireless audio transmitters:

1. If you took a break after the previous session, make sure the NP_EX_1_Order.xlsx workbook is open and the Purchase Order worksheet is active.
2. Click cell **F17**, type **Total** as the label, and then press **ENTER**. The label is entered in the cell, and cell F18 becomes the active cell.
3. In cell F18, type **=D18 * E18** (the quantity multiplied by the cost of each item). As you type the formula, a list of Excel function names appears in a ScreenTip, which provides a quick method for entering functions. The list will close when you complete the formula. You will learn more about Excel functions shortly. Also, Excel color codes each cell reference and its corresponding cell with the same color. Refer to Figure 1–24.

Figure 1–24 Formula with cell references

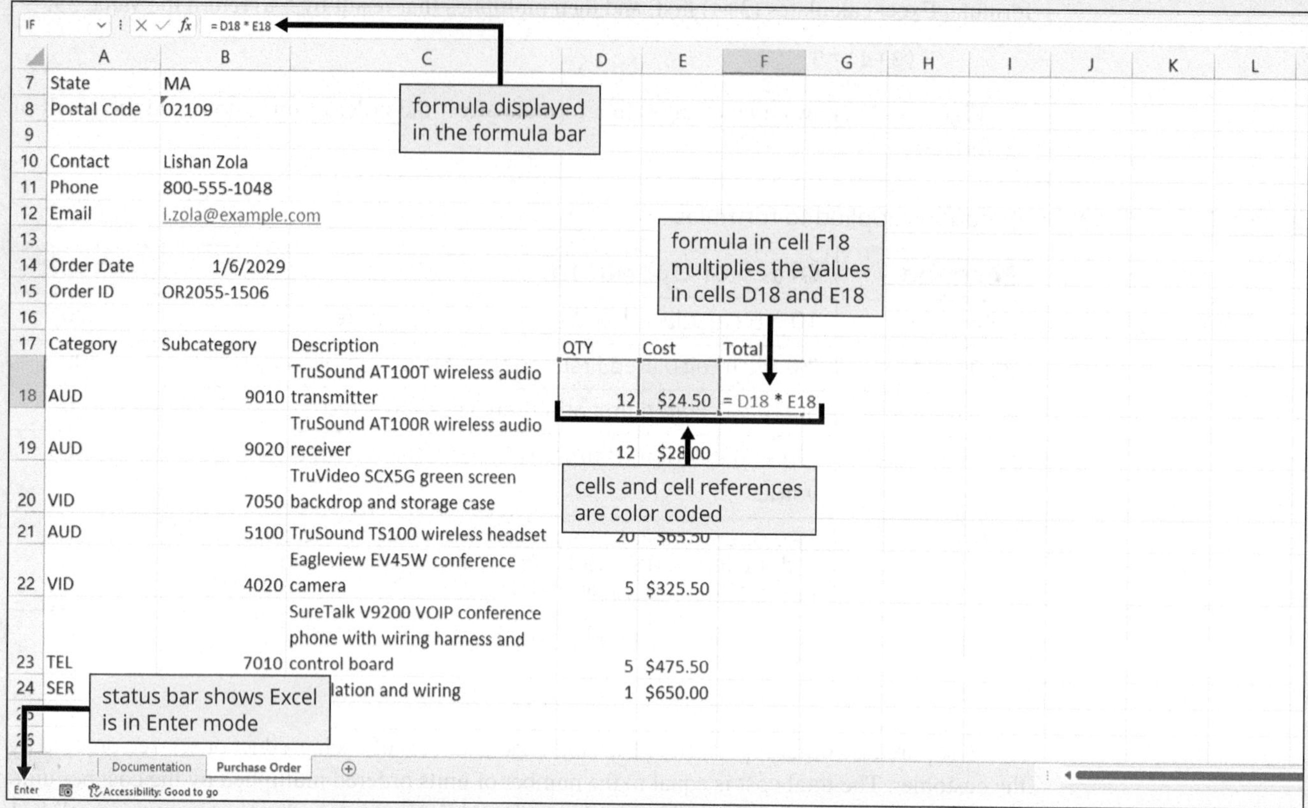

4. Press **ENTER**. The formula result $294.00 appears in cell F18, which is the total cost of purchasing 12 wireless audio transmitters at a cost of $24.50 each. The result is displayed as currency because cell E18, which is referenced in the formula, contains a currency value.
5. Click cell **F18** to make it the active cell. The cell displays the result of the formula, but the formula bar displays the formula you entered so that you can review both the formula and its value.

For the first item, you entered the formula by typing each cell reference in the expression. You can also insert a cell reference by clicking the cell as you type the formula. This technique reduces the possibility of error caused by typing an incorrect cell reference. You will use this method to enter the formula to calculate the cost of ordering 12 wireless audio receivers.

To enter a formula for purchasing wireless audio receivers using a mouse:

1. Click cell **F19** to make it active cell.
2. Type = to indicate the beginning of a formula. Excel will insert the cell reference to any cell you click.

   Key Step Be sure to type = first; otherwise, Excel will not recognize the entry as a formula.

3. Click cell **D19**. The cell reference is inserted into the formula in the formula bar. At this point, any cell you click changes the cell reference used in the formula. The cell reference isn't locked until you type an operator.
4. Type * to enter the multiplication operator. The cell reference for cell D19 is locked in the formula, and the next cell you click will be inserted after the operator.

5. Click cell **E19** to enter its cell reference in the formula. The formula, =D19*E19, is complete.
6. Press **ENTER**. A total cost of $336.00 for the 12 wireless audio receivers appears in F19.

Next, you will enter formulas to complete the calculations of the remaining items in the purchase order.

Copying and Pasting a Formula

Many worksheets have the same formula repeated across several rows or columns. Rather than retyping the formula, you can copy a formula from one cell and paste it into another cell or an entire range of cells. When you copy a formula, Excel places the formula onto the **Clipboard**, which is a temporary storage area for selections you copy or cut. When you **paste**, Excel retrieves the formula from the Clipboard and places it into its new location in the workbook.

The cell references in the copied formula change to reflect the formula's new location. A formula from a cell in column C that add values from other cells in column C will change its reference to column E when copied to a cell in that column. In this way, Excel makes it easier to reuse the same general formula in different locations in your workbook.

You will calculate the cost of the remaining items on the purchase order by copying the formula in cell F19 and pasting it into the range F20:F24.

To copy and paste the formula in F19:

1. Click cell **F19** to make it the active cell. This is the cell with the formula you want to copy.
2. On the Home tab, in the Clipboard group, click the **Copy** button (or press **CTRL+C**). Excel copies the formula to the Clipboard. A blinking green box surrounds the cell being copied.
3. Select the range **F20:F24**. These are the cells where you will paste the formula.
4. In the Clipboard group, click the **Paste** button (or press **CTRL+V**). Excel pastes the formula into the selected cells, adjusting each formula so that the total cost of each item is based on the quantity and cost values in that row. Hashtag symbols appear in the range F21:F23 because those cells are not wide enough to display the currency values. The Paste Options button, containing additional options for pasting the contents of the Clipboard, appears in the lower-right corner of the selected range.
5. Increase the width of column F to **15** characters. All the values in column F are visible. Refer to Figure 1–25.

Figure 1–25 Copied and pasted formula

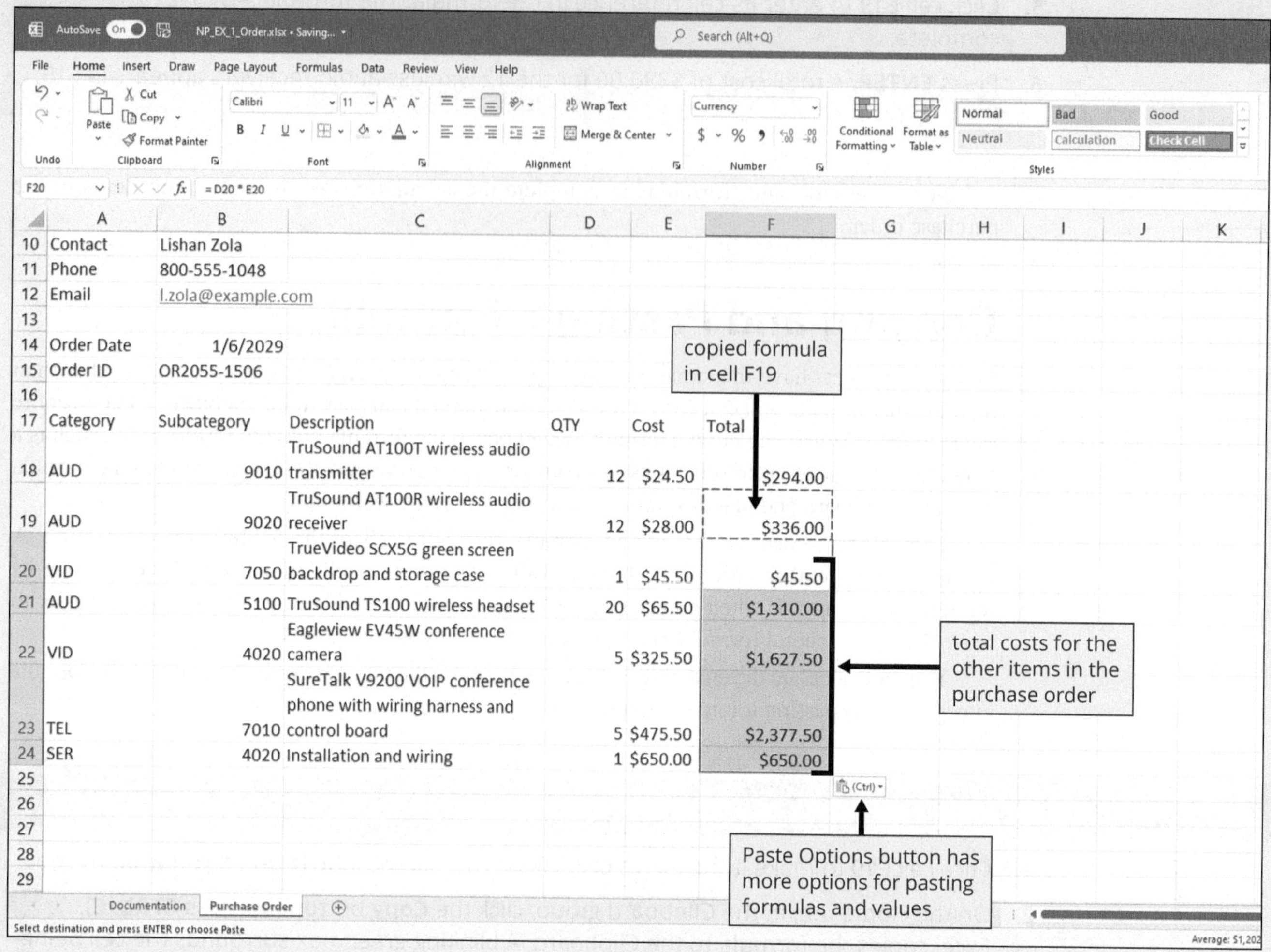

6. Click **F20** to make it the active cell. The formula =D20*E20 appears in the formula bar. Notice that the cell references from the copied formula are updated to reflect its new location in the worksheet.
7. Examine the remaining formulas from cells in the range F21:F24 to verify that the copied formula in each cell has been updated to reflect that cell's location in the worksheet.

As more cell references are included, the formula becomes more and more complicated. One way of simplifying a formula is with a function.

Calculating with Functions

A function is a named operation that returns a value. Every function follows a set of rules, or **syntax**, specifying how the function should be written. The general syntax of all Excel functions is

FUNCTION(*arg1*, *arg2*, [*arg3*], [*arg4*], ...)

where *FUNCTION* is the function name, and *arg1*, *arg2*, and so forth are arguments. An **argument** is information the function uses to return a value. Arguments required by the function are listed first. Optional arguments, indicated by the brackets in the function syntax, are listed last. If an optional argument is not included, Excel might assign it a default value (depending on the function). For example, the syntax of the SUM function used to calculate totals is

SUM(*number1*, [*number2*], [*number3*], ...)

where *number1* is a required argument containing a number or range of values to sum and *number2*, *number3*, and so on are optional arguments for other numbers or ranges to add to that sum. To calculate the sum of values from nine worksheet cells, you could enter the following long formula:

```
=A1+A2+A3+C11+C12+C13+E21+E22+E23
```

Or you can do the same calculation with a SUM function that references those cells as arguments of the function.

```
=SUM(A1:A3, C11:C13, E21:E23)
```

Both expressions return the same value, but the formula with the SUM function is more compact and less prone to a typing error. Excel supports more than 300 functions from the fields of finance, business, science, and engineering, including functions that work with numbers, text, and dates.

> **Tip** If a function does not have any arguments, enter the function name followed by an empty parentheses, such as = NOW() for the NOW function to display the current time.

The syntax of every Excel function is described in Excel Help, including examples and a summary of the required and optional arguments.

Inserting Functions with AutoSum

A fast and convenient way to enter some commonly used functions is with AutoSum. The AutoSum button, located in the Editing group on the Home tab of the ribbon, can insert the following functions into a selected cell or range:

- SUM—Adds the values in a specified range
- AVERAGE—Averages the values in a specified range
- COUNT—Counts the total numeric values in a specified range
- MAX—Returns the maximum value in a specified range
- MIN—Returns the minimum value in a specified range

After you select one of the AutoSum options, Excel includes the most likely range from the adjacent data and enters it as the argument. You should always verify that the range included in the AutoSum function matches the range that you want to use.

You'll use AutoSum to calculate the total cost of all items on the purchase order.

To calculate the total cost of all items on the purchase order:

1. Click cell **E25** to make it the active cell, type **Subtotal** as the label, and then press **TAB**. Cell F25 is the active cell.
2. On the Home tab, in the Editing group, click the **AutoSum arrow**. The button's menu opens and displays five common functions: Sum, Average, Count Numbers, Max, and Min.
3. On the AutoSum menu, point to Sum.
4. Click **Sum** to enter the SUM function. The formula =SUM(F18:F24) is entered in cell F25. The cells being summed are selected and highlighted in the worksheet so you can quickly confirm that Excel selected the appropriate range from the available data. A ScreenTip appears below the formula describing the function's syntax. Refer to Figure 1–26.

> **Tip** You can quickly insert the SUM function by clicking the worksheet cell where the sum should be calculated and pressing ALT+=.

Figure 1–26 SUM function entered using the AutoSum button

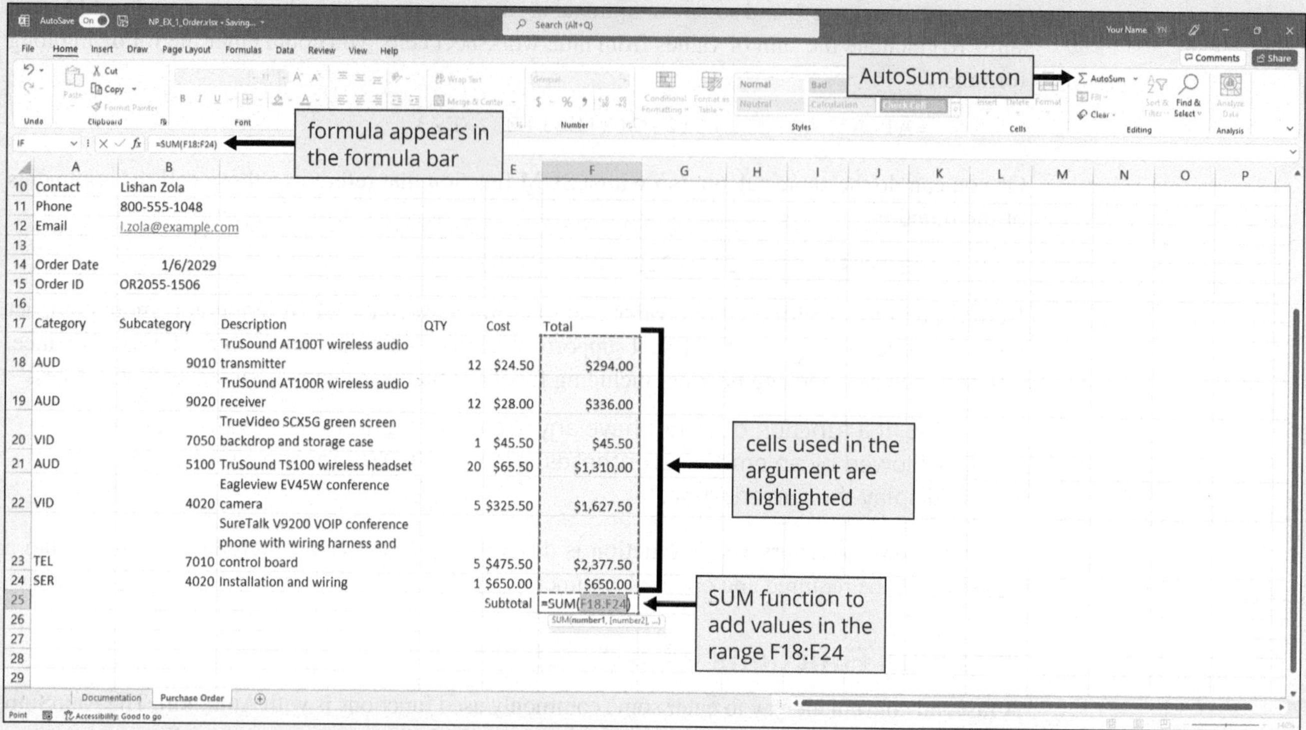

5. Press **ENTER** to accept the formula. Cell F25 shows the total cost of the seven items on the purchase order, which is $6,640.50.

Every order from Insight Video Solutions is subject to a 5% sales tax. You'll add formulas to calculate the amount of tax due on this order and then add the subtotal value to the tax.

To calculate the sales tax and total expenses:

1. Click cell **E16**, type **Tax Rate** as the label, and then press **TAB**. Cell F16 is the active cell.
2. Type **5%** in cell F16, and then press **ENTER**. The 5% value is displayed in the cell, but the stored value is 0.05.
3. Click cell **E26** to make it the active cell, type **Est. Tax** as the label, and then press **TAB**. Cell F26 is the active cell.
4. Type the formula **=F16*F25** in cell F26 to calculate the tax on all items bought in the purchase order, and then press **ENTER**. The formula multiplies the tax rate in cell F16 (0.05) by the subtotal in cell F25 ($6,640.56). The estimated tax is $332.03.
5. Click cell **E27**, type **TOTAL** as the label, and then press **TAB**. Cell F27 is the active cell.
6. Type the formula = **SUM(F25:F26)** in cell F27 to calculate the total cost of the purchase order, adding the subtotal to the estimate text, and then press **ENTER**. The total for the purchase order of $6,972.53.
7. Click cell **F27**. Refer to Figure 1–27.

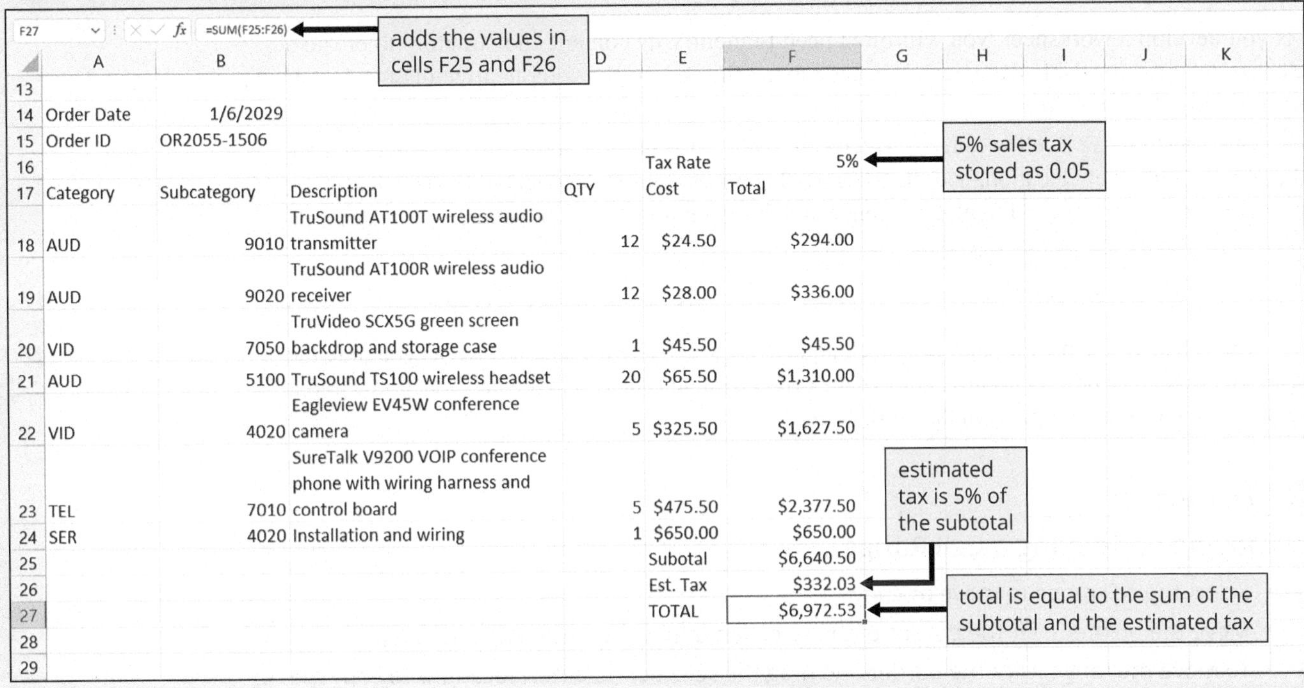

	A	B	C	D	E	F
13						
14	Order Date	1/6/2029				
15	Order ID	OR2055-1506				
16					Tax Rate	5%
17	Category	Subcategory	Description	QTY	Cost	Total
18	AUD	9010	TruSound AT100T wireless audio transmitter	12	$24.50	$294.00
19	AUD	9020	TruSound AT100R wireless audio receiver	12	$28.00	$336.00
20	VID	7050	TruVideo SCX5G green screen backdrop and storage case	1	$45.50	$45.50
21	AUD	5100	TruSound TS100 wireless headset	20	$65.50	$1,310.00
22	VID	4020	Eagleview EV45W conference camera	5	$325.50	$1,627.50
23	TEL	7010	SureTalk V9200 VOIP conference phone with wiring harness and control board	5	$475.50	$2,377.50
24	SER	4020	Installation and wiring	1	$650.00	$650.00
25					Subotal	$6,640.50
26					Est. Tax	$332.03
27					TOTAL	$6,972.53
28						
29						

Figure 1–27 Total cost of the purchase order

If you want to add all the numbers in a column or row, you need to reference the entire column or row in the SUM function. For example, SUM(E:E) will return the sum of all numeric values in column E and SUM(5:5) will return the sum of all numeric values in row 5. Any cells with text in those columns or rows will be ignored.

Proskills

Problem Solving: Writing Effective Formulas

You can use formulas to quickly perform calculations and solve problems. First, identify the problem you need to solve. Then, gather the data needed to solve the problem. Finally, create accurate and effective formulas that use the data to answer or resolve the problem. To write effective and useful formulas, consider these guidelines:

- **Keep your formulas simple.** Use functions in place of long, complex formulas whenever possible. For example, use the SUM function instead of entering a formula that adds individual cells, making it easier to confirm that the formula is providing accurate information.
- **Do not hide data values within formulas.** The worksheet displays formula results, not the actual formula. For example, to calculate a 5% interest rate on a currency value in cell A5, you could enter the formula =0.05*A5. However, this approach doesn't reveal how the value is calculated. A better practice places the 5% value in a cell accompanied by a descriptive label and uses the cell reference in the formula, making it clear to others what calculation is being performed.
- **Break up long formulas to display intermediate results.** Long formulas can be difficult to interpret and are prone to error. For example, the formula =SUM(A1:A10)/SUM(B1:B10) calculates the ratio of two sums but hides the two sum values. Consider calculating each sum in separate cells, such as A11 and B11, and use the formula =A11/B11 to calculate the ratio. The worksheet will then include both the sums and the calculation of their ratio.
- **Test complicated formulas with simple values.** Use values you can calculate in your head to confirm that your formula works as intended. For example, using 1s or 10s as the input values makes it easier to verify that your formula is working as intended.

Finding a solution to a problem requires accurate data and analysis. In a workbook, this means using formulas for calculations, showing all the values used in the formulas clearly in the worksheet, and testing to verify their accuracy.

Moving Worksheet Cells

As you develop a worksheet, you will often need to modify its content and structure to create a cleaner and more readable document. You can move cells and ranges without affecting the data or the formulas they contain.

One way to move a cell or range is to select it, point to the bottom border of the selection, drag the selection to a new location, and then release the mouse button. This technique is called **drag and drop** because you are dragging the range and dropping it in a new location.

> **Tip** If the drop location is not visible, drag the selection to the edge of the workbook window to scroll the worksheet, and then drop the selection.

You can also use the drag-and-drop technique to copy cells by pressing CTRL as you drag the selected range to its new location. A copy of the original range is placed in the new location without removing the original range from the worksheet.

Reference

Moving or Copying a Cell Range

- Select the cell range to move or copy.
- Move the pointer over the border of the selection until the pointer changes shape.
- To move the range, click the border and drag the selection to a new location. To copy the range, hold down CTRL and drag the selection to a new location.

or

- Select the cell range to move or copy.
- On the Home tab, in the Clipboard group, click the Cut or Copy button; or right-click the selection, and then click Cut or Copy on the shortcut menu; or press CTRL+X or CTRL+C.
- Select the cell or the upper-left cell of the range where you want to paste the copied content.
- In the Clipboard group, click the Paste button; or right-click the selection and then click Paste on the shortcut menu; or press CTRL+V.

Sofi wants the labels and values in the range E25:F27 moved down one row to the range E26:F28 to set those calculations off from the list of purchase order items. You will use the drag-and-drop method to move the range.

To drag and drop the range E25:F27:

1. Select the range **E25:F27**. This is the range you want to move.
2. Point to the **bottom border** of the selected range so that the pointer changes to the move pointer.
3. Press and hold the mouse button to change the pointer to the arrow pointer, and then drag the selection down one row. Do not release the mouse button. A ScreenTip appears, indicating that the new range of the selected cells will be E26:F28. A dark green border also appears around the new range. Refer to Figure 1–28.

Figure 1–28 Range being moved with drag and drop

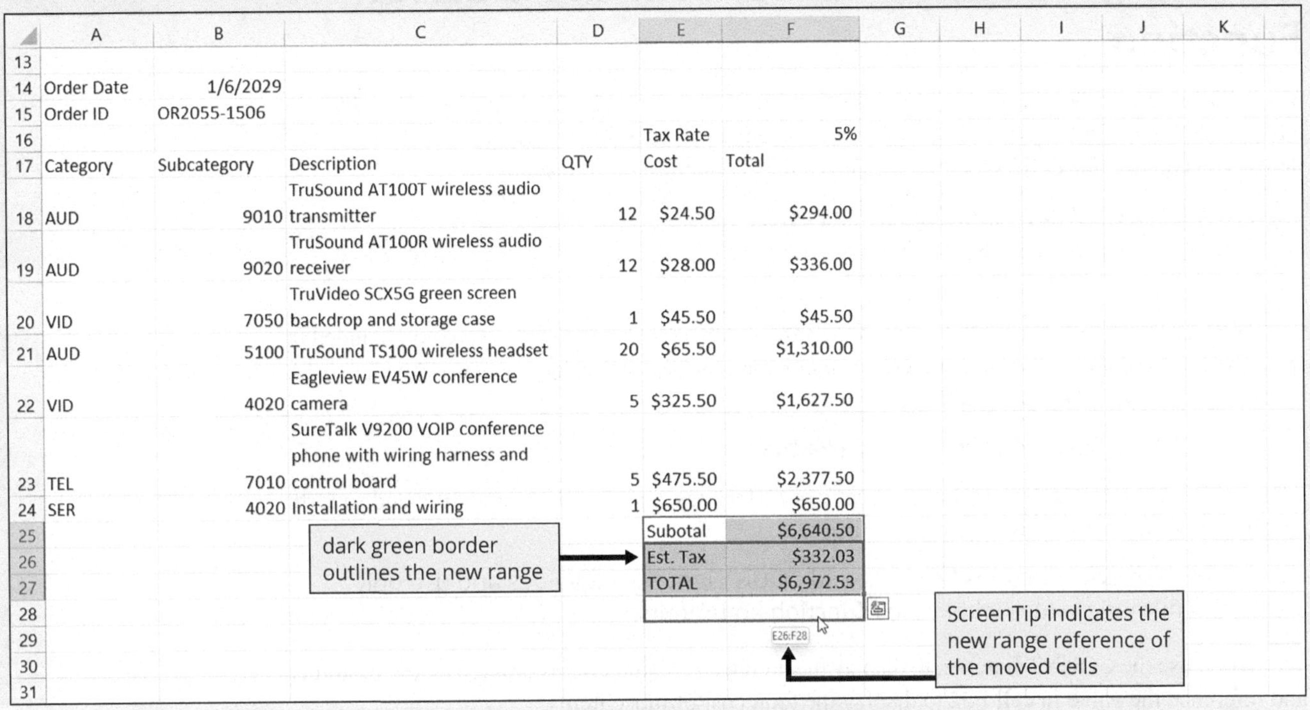

	A	B	C	D	E	F
13						
14	Order Date	1/6/2029				
15	Order ID	OR2055-1506				
16					Tax Rate	5%
17	Category	Subcategory	Description	QTY	Cost	Total
18	AUD	9010	TruSound AT100T wireless audio transmitter	12	$24.50	$294.00
19	AUD	9020	TruSound AT100R wireless audio receiver	12	$28.00	$336.00
20	VID	7050	TruVideo SCX5G green screen backdrop and storage case	1	$45.50	$45.50
21	AUD	5100	TruSound TS100 wireless headset	20	$65.50	$1,310.00
22	VID	4020	Eagleview EV45W conference camera	5	$325.50	$1,627.50
23	TEL	7010	SureTalk V9200 VOIP conference phone with wiring harness and control board	5	$475.50	$2,377.50
24	SER	4020	Installation and wiring	1	$650.00	$650.00
25					Subotal	$6,640.50
26					Est. Tax	$332.03
27					TOTAL	$6,972.53
28						
29						
30						
31						

dark green border outlines the new range

E26:F28

ScreenTip indicates the new range reference of the moved cells

4. Verify that the ScreenTip displays the range E26:F28, and then release the mouse button. The selected cells move to their new location.

The drag-and-drop technique can be slow and awkward in larger worksheets. In that situation, it is often more efficient to cut or copy a selected range and then paste it into the new location. Cutting moves the selected content. Copying duplicates the selected content in the new location.

Sofi wants to include a summary of the purchase order totals at the top of the worksheet. To free up space for this summary, you'll cut the contents of the range A4:F28 and paste it into the range A8:F32.

To move the range A4:F28 using cut and copy:

1. Click the **Name** box to the left of the formula bar, type **A4:F28** as the range to select, and then press **ENTER**. The range A4:F28 is selected.
2. On the Home tab, in the Clipboard group, click the **Cut** button (or press **CTRL+X**). The range is surrounded by a moving border, indicating that it has been cut.
3. Click cell **A8** to select it. This is the upper-left corner of the range where you want to paste the selection that you cut.
4. In the Clipboard group, click the **Paste** button (or press **CTRL+V**). The range A4:F28 is pasted into the range A8:F32. Note that the cell references in the formulas were automatically updated to reflect the new location of those cells in the worksheet.

Next you will add a summary of the purchase order to top of the worksheet, starting with a count of the total items ordered by the customer.

Counting Numeric Values with the COUNT Function

Many financial workbooks need to report the number of entries, such as the number of products in an order or the number of items in an expense or revenue category. To calculate the total number of items, you can use the COUNT function. The COUNT function has the syntax

```
COUNT(value1, [value2], [value3],…)
```

where *value1* is the range of numeric values to count and *value2*, *value3*, and so forth are optional arguments to specify other numbers and ranges.

The COUNT function counts only numeric values. Any cells containing text are not included in the tally. To also count cells containing nonnumeric data such as text strings, you use the COUNTA function. The COUNTA function has the syntax

```
COUNTA(value1, [value2], [value3],…)
```

where *value1* is the range containing numeric or text values, and *value2*, *value3*, and so forth specify other ranges to be included in the tally.

> **Tip** Numeric functions like SUM and COUNT ignore text values and use only the numeric values within their function arguments.

You'll use the COUNT function to display the number of distinct items ordered by the customer and reference the value in cell F32 to display the total cost of those items.

To apply the COUNT function:

1. Scroll up the worksheet, click cell **A4** to make it the active cell, type **Summary** as the label, and then press **ENTER** to make cell A5 the active cell.
2. In cell A5, type **Products** as the label, and press **TAB** to make cell B5 the active cell.
3. In cell B5, type **= COUNT(** to begin the COUNT function.
4. Select the range **F22:F28**. The range reference F22:F28 is entered as the first (and only argument) of the COUNT function.
5. Type **)** to complete the function, and then press **ENTER** to make cell A6 the active cell. Cell B5 displays 7, indicating that the purchase order contains seven distinct items.
6. In cell A6, type **Total Charge** as the label, and then press **TAB** to make cell B6 the active cell.
7. In cell B6, type **= F32** as the formula, and then press **ENTER**. This formula displays $6,972.53, which is the total cost of the order calculated in cell F32. Refer to Figure 1–29.

Figure 1–29 Purchase Order summary

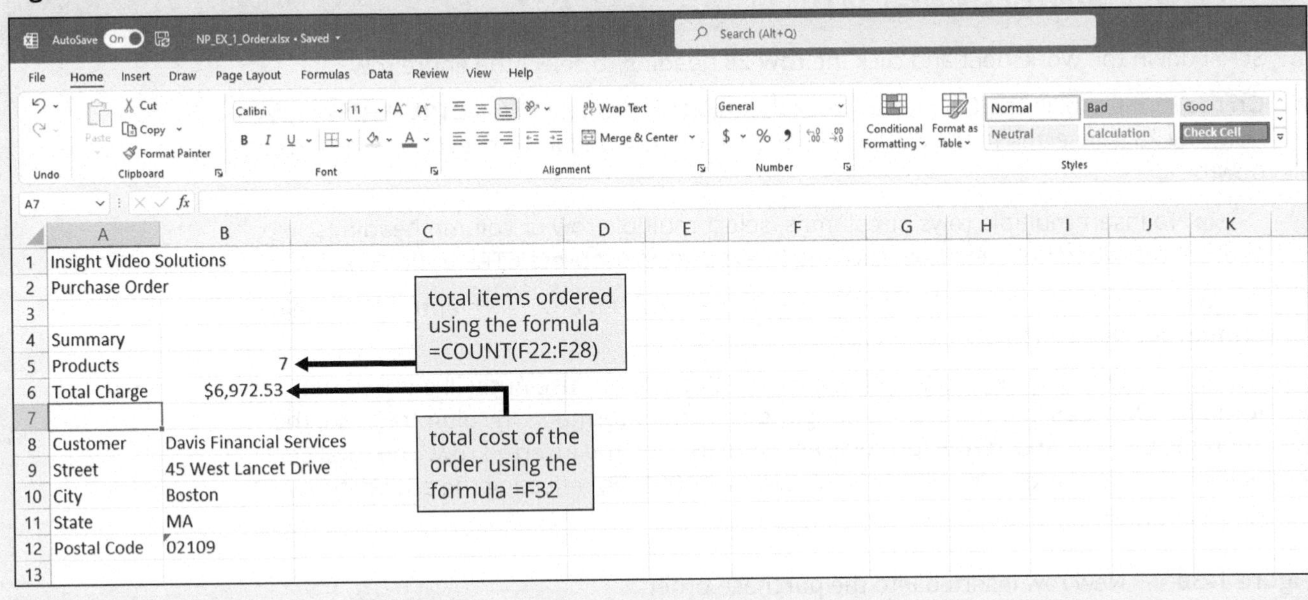

The formula in cell B6 displaying the total cost of the order as calculated in cell F32 illustrates an important practice: Don't repeat the same formula multiple times. Instead, reference the cell containing the formula. If the formula is changed later, the new results will appear throughout the workbook.

Inserting and Deleting Rows and Columns

Another way to modify the structure of a workbook is to insert or remove whole rows and columns from a worksheet. When you insert a new column, the existing columns are shifted to the right, and the new column has the same width as the column directly to its left. When you insert a new row, the existing rows are shifted down, and the new row has the same height as the row above it. Because inserting a new row or column moves the location of the other cells in the worksheet, any cell references in a formula or function are updated to reflect the new layout.

Reference

Inserting and Deleting Rows and Columns

- Select the row or column headings where you want to insert or delete content.
- To insert rows and columns, on the Home tab, in the Cells group, click the Insert button; or right-click the selected headings and click Insert on the shortcut menu; or press CTRL+SHIFT+ =.
- To delete rows or columns, on the Home tab, in the Cells group, click the Delete button; or right-click the selecting headings, and then click Delete on the shortcut menu; or press CTRL+ -.

Davis Financial Services has decided to purchase an annual service contract for technical support and maintenance. Sofi wants you to add the new item to the purchase order. You'll insert a new row in the worksheet and enter the new item in the list.

To enter a new purchased item in the list:

1. Scroll down the worksheet and click the **row 28** heading to select the entire row.
2. On the Home tab, in the Cells group, click the **Insert** button (or press **CTRL+SHIFT+=**). A new row 28 is inserted in the worksheet, and all the rows below the new row are shifted down.

   Tip To insert multiple rows or columns, select multiple row or column headings from the worksheet and then click the Insert button (or press CTRL+SHIFT+=).

3. In the range A28:E28, enter the following data pressing TAB after each entry: **SER**, **4090**, **Annual service contract**, **1**, and **$75.00**.

   Cell F28 is the active cell and $75.00 appears in the cell because AutoFill entered the formula =D28*E28 into the cell following the pattern of formulas in column F. Also, the Subtotal, Est. Tax, and TOTAL formulas adjust to include the inserted row. The total cost of the purchase order in cell F33 is increased to $7,051.28, reflecting the added item. Refer to Figure 1–30.

Figure 1–30 New row inserted into the purchase order

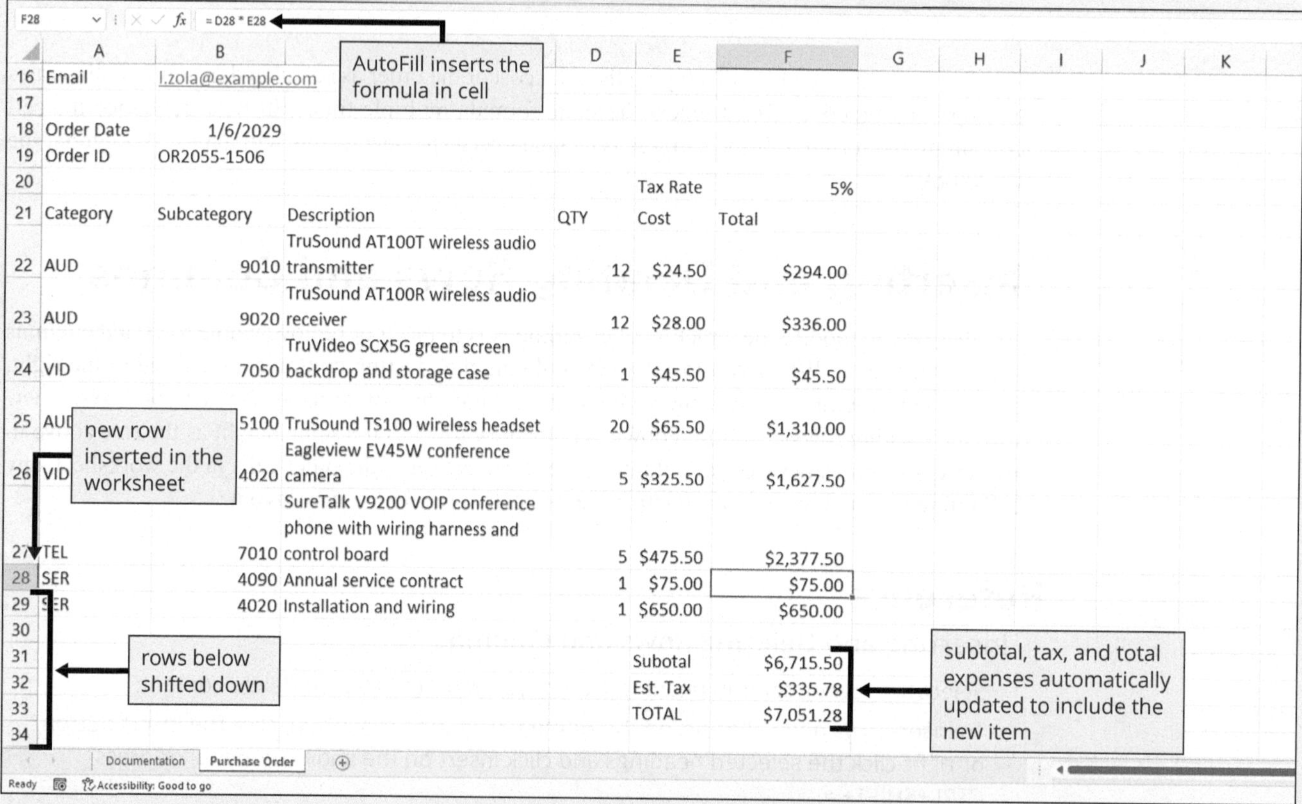

4. Scroll to the top of the worksheet and verify that the number of items in the purchase order in cell B5 is now eight.

There are two ways to remove content from a worksheet: deleting and clearing. **Deleting** removes both the data and rows or columns from the worksheet. The rows below the deleted row shift up to fill the vacated space. Likewise, the columns to the right of the deleted column shift left to fill the vacated space. Also, all cell references in worksheet formulas are adjusted to reflect the change that removing the row or column makes to the worksheet structure. To delete a selected row or column, click the Delete button in the Cells group on the Home tab.

Clearing removes the data from the selected cells, leaving those cells blank but preserving the worksheet structure. No formulas in the worksheet are modified when data is cleared. To clear data from a selected cell or range, press DELETE.

Sofi tells you that the customer did not order the green screen backdrop. You'll correct the purchase order by deleting row 24 from worksheet.

To delete the green screen row from the worksheet:

1. Click the **row 24** heading to select the entire row containing the order of the green screen backdrop.
2. On the Home tab, in the Cells group, click the **Delete** button (or press **CTRL+ -**). Row 24 is deleted, and the rows below it shift up to fill the space.

Tip To delete multiple rows or columns, select multiple row or column headings from the worksheet and click the Delete button (or press CTRL+ -).

All cell references in the formulas are updated to reflect the deleted row. The subtotal value in cell F30 changes to $6,670.00, which is the sum of the range F22:F28. The estimated tax in cell F31 decreases to $333.50. The total cost of the purchase order drops to $7,003.50. Also, the result of the COUNT function in cell B7 shows that seven items were purchased by the customer.

Inserting and Deleting a Range

You can also insert or delete cell ranges within a worksheet. By default, inserting a range shifts cells to right when the selected range is longer than it is wide and shift cells down when the selected range is wider than it is long. You can specify the direction shifted cells move using the Insert command in the Cells group on the Home tab. All cell references in formulas are automatically changed to reflect the new structure of the worksheet. Refer to Figure 1–31.

Figure 1–31 Cell range inserted into a worksheet

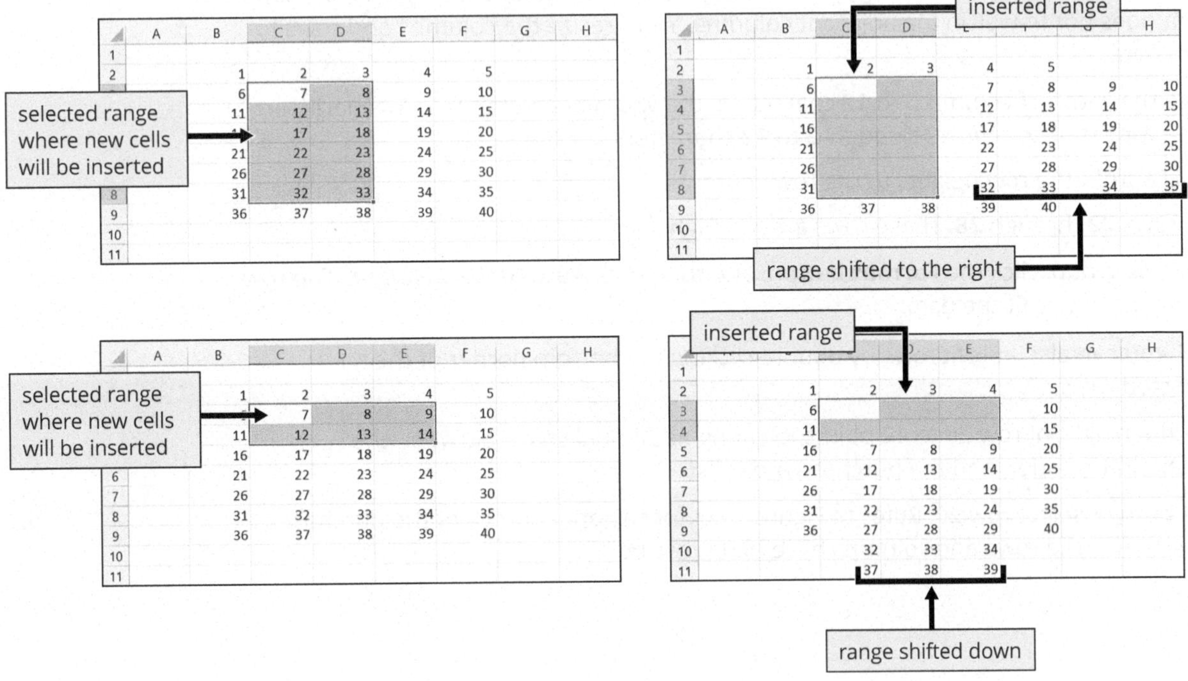

The process works in reverse when you delete a range. Cells adjacent to the deleted range either move up or left to fill in the space vacated by the deleted cells. You can specify the direction shifted cells move using the Delete command in the Cells group on the Home tab. Whether you insert or delete a range, cells shifting to a new location adopt the widths of the columns and heights of the rows that they shift into. As a result, you may need to resize column widths and row heights after inserting or deleting cells.

Reference

Inserting or Deleting a Range

- Select a range that matches the area you want to insert or delete.
- On the Home tab, in the Cells group, click the Insert button or the Delete button.

or

- Select the range that matches the range you want to insert or delete.
- On the Home tab, in the Cells group, click the Insert arrow and then click Insert Cells or click the Delete arrow and then click Delete Cells; or right-click the selected range, and then click Insert or Delete on the shortcut menu.
- Click the option button for the direction to shift the cells, columns, or rows.
- Click OK.

Insight Video Solutions assigns a product ID for each item appearing in a purchase order. Sofi asks you to insert a new range of cells into the purchase order list for this data.

To insert a new range to enter the product IDs:

1. Select the range **A20:A32**.
2. On the Home tab, in the Cells group, click the **Insert arrow**. A menu of insert options appears.
3. Click **Insert Cells**. The Insert dialog box opens.
4. Verify that the **Shift cells right** option button is selected, and then click **OK**. New cells are inserted into the selected range, and the adjacent cells move to the right. The shifted content does not fit well in the adjacent columns. You'll resize the columns and rows to fit their data.
5. Change the width of column C to **12** characters, the width of column D to **30** characters, and the widths of columns E through G to **12** characters.

   You will autofit the row heights to the row contents.
6. Select rows **22** through **28**. These rows are too high.
7. In the Cells group, click the **Format** button, and then click **AutoFit Row Height**. The row heights now better fit the data.

   Tip You can also autofit rows by double-clicking the bottom border of the selected rows.
8. Resize the height of row 20 to **42** points, creating additional space between the summary information and the purchase order list.
9. Click **A21** to deselect row 20. Refer to Figure 1–32 for the appearance of the purchase order list after the rows and columns have been resized.

Figure 1–32 New range inserted in the purchase order

row 20 height increased to 42 points

adjacent cells shifted to the right

inserted range A20:A32

	A	B	C	D	E	F	G
18	Order Date						
19	Order ID						
20						Tax Rate	5%
21		Category	Subcategory	Description	QTY	Cost	Total
22		AUD	9010	TruSound AT100T wireless audio transmitter	12	$24.50	$294.00
23		AUD	9020	TruSound AT100R wireless audio receiver	12	$28.00	$336.00
24		AUD	5100	TruSound TS100 wireless headset	20	$65.50	$1,310.00
25		VID	4020	Eagleview EV45W conference camera	5	$325.50	$1,627.50
26		TEL	7010	SureTalk V9200 VOIP conference phone with wiring harness and control board	5	$475.50	$2,377.50
27		SER	4090	Annual service contract	1	$75.00	$75.00
28		SER	4020	Installation and wiring	1	$650.00	$650.00
29							
30						Subotal	$6,670.00
31						Est. Tax	$333.50
32						TOTAL	$7,003.50
33							
34							
35							

Documentation | Purchase Order

Ready | Accessibility: Good to go

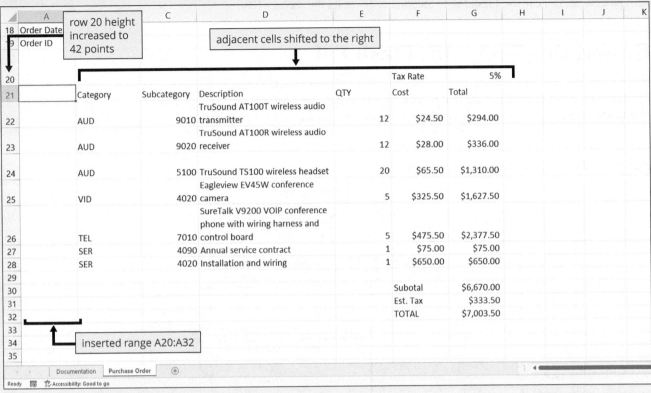

Notice that even though the product IDs will be entered in the range A21:A28, you inserted new cells in the range A20:A32 to retain the layout of the worksheet contents. Selecting the additional rows ensures that the tax rate and summary values still line up with the Cost and Total columns. Whenever you insert a new range, be sure to consider its impact on the entire layout of the worksheet.

Insight

Hiding and Unhiding Rows, Columns, and Worksheets

Workbooks can become long and complicated, filled with formulas and data that are important for performing calculations but are of little interest to readers. In those situations, you can simplify your workbooks by hiding rows, columns, and even worksheets. Although the contents of hidden cells cannot be seen, the data in those cells is still available for use in formulas and functions throughout the workbook.

Hiding removes a row or column from view while keeping it part of the worksheet. To hide a row or column, select the row or column heading, click the Format button in the Cells group on the Home tab, point to Hide & Unhide on the menu that appears, and then click Hide Rows or Hide Columns. The border of the row or column heading is doubled to mark the location of hidden rows or columns.

A worksheet is hidden when the entire worksheet contains data that is not of interest to the reader and is better summarized elsewhere in the workbook. To hide a worksheet, make that worksheet active, click the Format button in the Cells group, point to Hide & Unhide, and then click Hide Sheet.

Unhiding redisplays the hidden content in the workbook. To unhide a row or column, click in a cell below the hidden row or to the right of the hidden column, click the Format button, point to Hide & Unhide, and then click Unhide Rows or Unhide Columns. To unhide a worksheet, click the Format button, point to Hide & Unhide, and then click Unhide Sheet. The Unhide dialog box opens. Click the sheets you want to unhide, and then click OK. The hidden content is redisplayed in the workbook.

Although hiding data can make a worksheet and workbook easier to read, be sure never to hide information that is important to the reader.

You will complete the content of the purchase order list by adding the product IDs for each item purchased. You can use Flash Fill to automatically create the account IDs.

Generating Text with Flash Fill

Flash Fill enters text based on patterns it finds from preceding rows in the same columns of data. For example, Flash Fill can use the first names, middle initials, and last names stored in separate columns to display complete names in another column (refer to Figure 1–33). To accept the suggested full names, press ENTER. To reject the suggested text, continue typing the text you want to enter.

Figure 1–33 Text automatically entered with Flash Fill

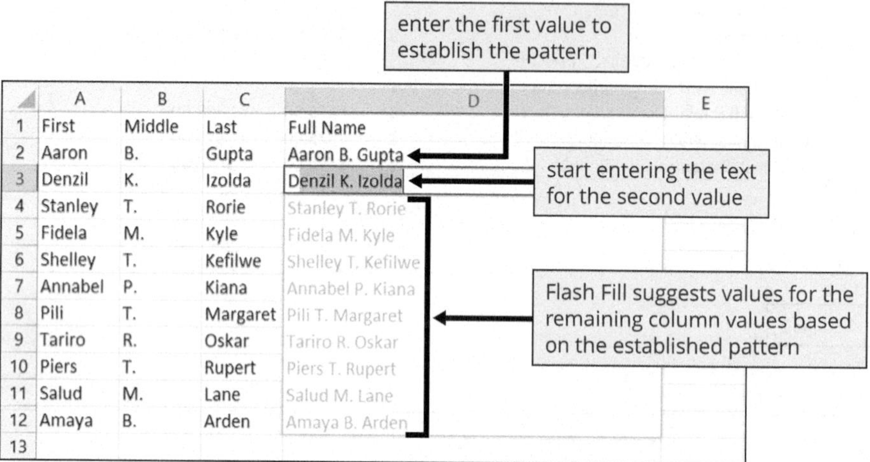

	A	B	C	D	E
1	First	Middle	Last	Full Name	
2	Aaron	B.	Gupta	Aaron B. Gupta	
3	Denzil	K.	Izolda	Denzil K. Izolda	
4	Stanley	T.	Rorie	Stanley T. Rorie	
5	Fidela	M.	Kyle	Fidela M. Kyle	
6	Shelley	T.	Kefilwe	Shelley T. Kefilwe	
7	Annabel	P.	Kiana	Annabel P. Kiana	
8	Pili	T.	Margaret	Pili T. Margaret	
9	Tariro	R.	Oskar	Tariro R. Oskar	
10	Piers	T.	Rupert	Piers T. Rupert	
11	Salud	M.	Lane	Salud M. Lane	
12	Amaya	B.	Arden	Amaya B. Arden	
13					

Flash Fill works best when the pattern is clearly recognized from the values in the data. Be sure to enter the data pattern in the column or row next to the related data. The data used to generate the pattern must be in a rectangular grid and cannot have blank columns or rows.

Insight Video Solution generates product IDs by combining the text of the Category and Subcategory columns. For example, installation and wiring, in the SER category and 4020 subcategory, has a product ID of SER-4020. You'll use Flash Fill to generate the product ID values for all items on the purchase order.

To generate product IDs using Flash Fill:

1. In cell A21, type **Product ID** and then press **ENTER**. Cell A22 becomes the active cell.
2. Type **AUD-9010** in cell A22, and then press **ENTER** to establish the pattern for the product IDs. Cell A23 is the active cell.
3. Type **AUD-9020** in cell A23. After you type 2, Flash Fill generates the remaining entries in column based on the established pattern. Refer to Figure 1–34.

Figure 1–34 Product IDs generated by Flash Fill

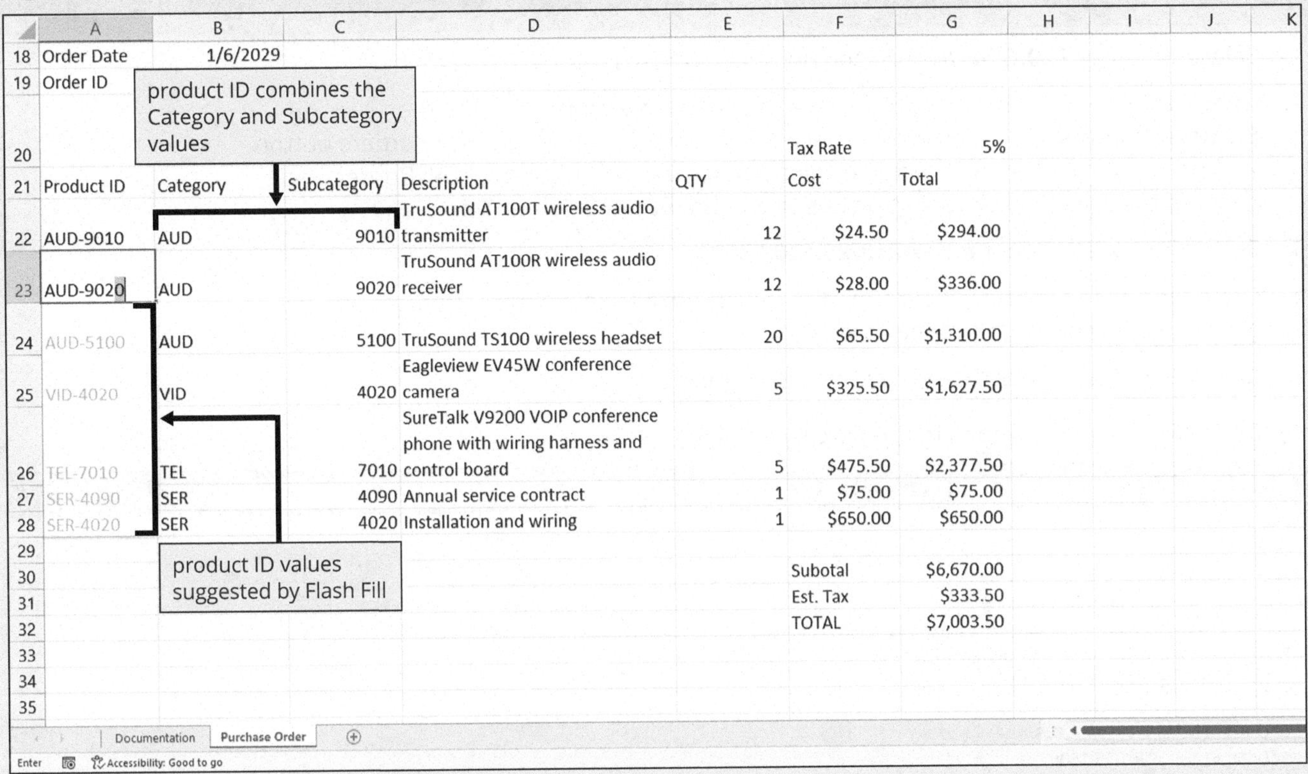

4. Press **ENTER** to accept the suggested text values.

> **Trouble?** If you pause for an extended time between entering text to establish the pattern, Flash Fill might not extend the pattern for you. Delete the text you entered in the cell, and then repeat Steps 3 and 4.

Flash Fill generates text, not formulas. If you edit or replace the entry originally used to create the Flash Fill pattern, the other entries generated by Flash Fill in the column will not be updated.

Formatting a Worksheet

Formatting enhances the appearance of the worksheet data by changing its font, size, color, or alignment or adding cell borders. Two common formatting changes are adding cell borders and changing the font size of text.

Adding Cell Borders

You can make worksheet content easier to read by adding borders around the worksheet cells. Borders can be added to the left, top, right, or bottom edge of any cell or range. You can set the color, thickness of and the number of lines in each border. Borders are especially useful when you print a worksheet because the gridlines that surround the cells in the workbook window are not printed by default. They appear only in the worksheet window as a guide.

Sofi wants borders around the cells listing the items in the purchase order to make the content easier to read.

To add borders around cells in the purchase order:

1. Select the range **F20:G20**. You will add borders to these cells.
2. On the Home tab, in the Font group, click the **Borders arrow**, and then click **All Borders**. Borders are added around each cell in the selected range. The Borders button changes to reflect the last selected border option, which in this case is All Borders. The name of the selected border option appears in the button's ScreenTip.
3. Select the nonadjacent range **A21:G28,F30:F32**.
4. On the Home tab, in the Font group, click the **All Borders** button. Borders appear around all the cells in this range as well.
5. Click cell **A32** to deselect the range. Refer to Figure 1–35.

Figure 1–35 Borders added to the purchase order

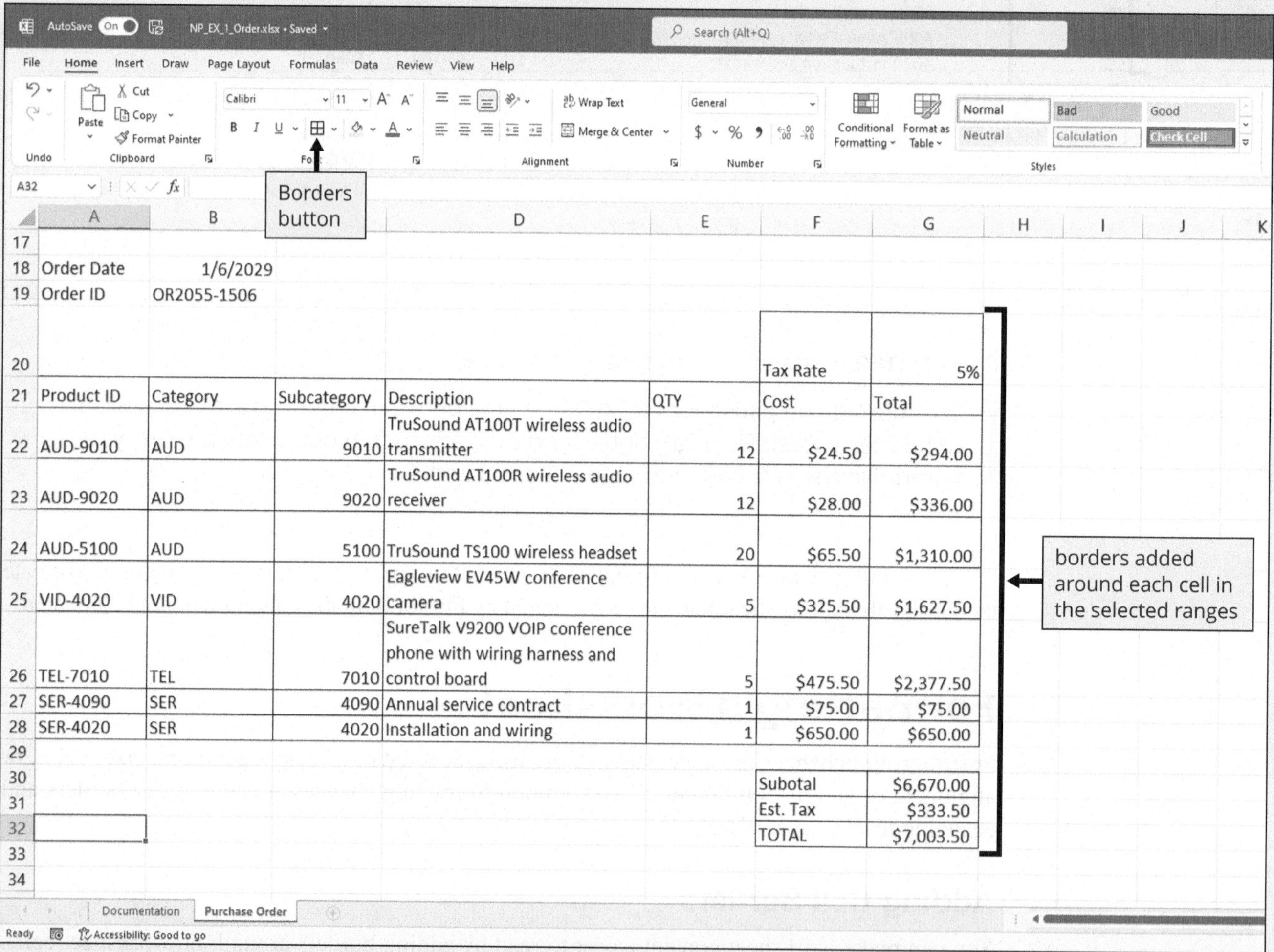

Changing the Font Size

Changing the size of text in a sheet provides a way to identify different parts of a worksheet, such as distinguishing a title or section heading from data. The size of the text is referred to as the font size and is measured in points. The default font size for worksheets is 11 points, but it can be made larger or smaller as needed. You can resize text in selected cells using the Font Size button in the Font group on the Home tab. You can also use the Increase Font Size and Decrease Font Size buttons to resize cell content to the next higher or lower standard font size.

Sofi wants you to increase the size of the worksheet title to 36 points and the subtitle to 22 points to make them more visible and stand out from the rest of the worksheet content.

To change font sizes of worksheet title and subtitle:

1. Scroll up the worksheet and click cell **A1** to select the worksheet title.
2. On the Home tab, in the Font group, click the **Font Size arrow** [11 ▾] to display a list of font sizes, and then click **36.** The worksheet title changes to 36 points.
3. Click cell **A2**, and then in the Font group, click the **Increase Font Size** button [A^] six times until the font size is **22** points. Refer to Figure 1–36.

Figure 1–36 Font sizes increased for worksheet text

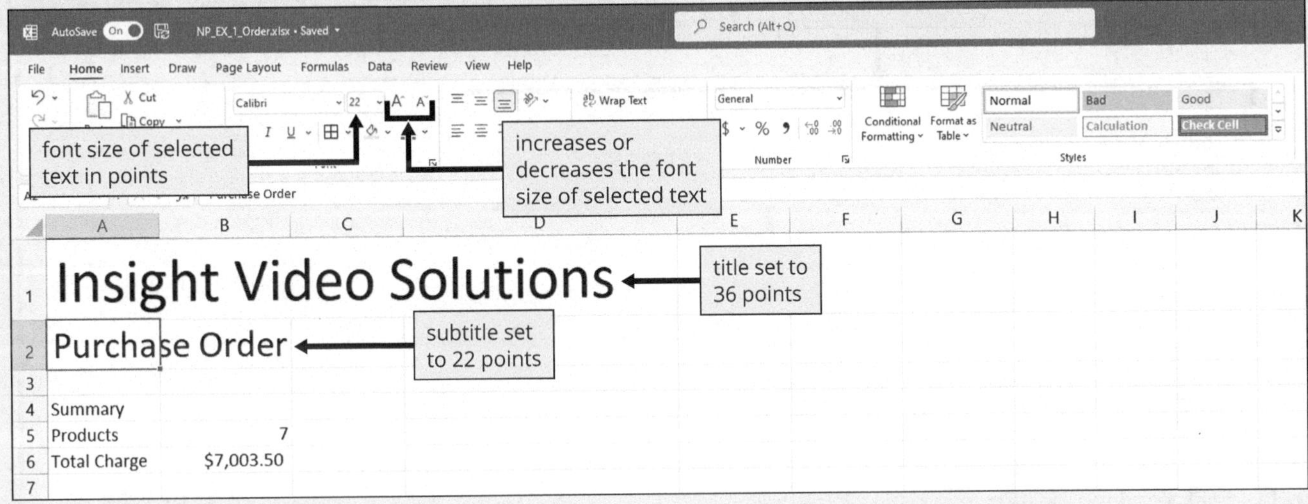

4. Press **CTRL+S** to save the workbook.

Now that the workbook content and formatting are final, you can print the report on the customer's purchase order.

Printing a Workbook

Excel has many tools to control the print layout and appearance of a workbook. Before printing a worksheet, you will want to preview the printout to make sure that it will print correctly.

Changing Worksheet Views

You can view a workbook in three ways. Normal view, which you have been using throughout this module, shows the contents of the worksheet. Page Layout view shows how the worksheet will appear when printed. Page Break Preview displays the location of the different page breaks within the worksheet. This view is useful when a worksheet spans several printed pages, and you need to control what content appears on each page.

Sofi wants you to preview the print version of the Purchase Order worksheet. You will do this by switching between views.

To switch worksheet views:

1. Click the **Page Layout** button on the status bar. The page layout of the worksheet appears in the workbook window.
2. On the Zoom slider at the lower-right corner of the workbook window, click the **Zoom Out** button until the percentage is **70%**. The reduced magnification makes it clear that the worksheet will spread over two pages when printed. Refer to Figure 1–37.

Figure 1–37 Worksheet in Page Layout view

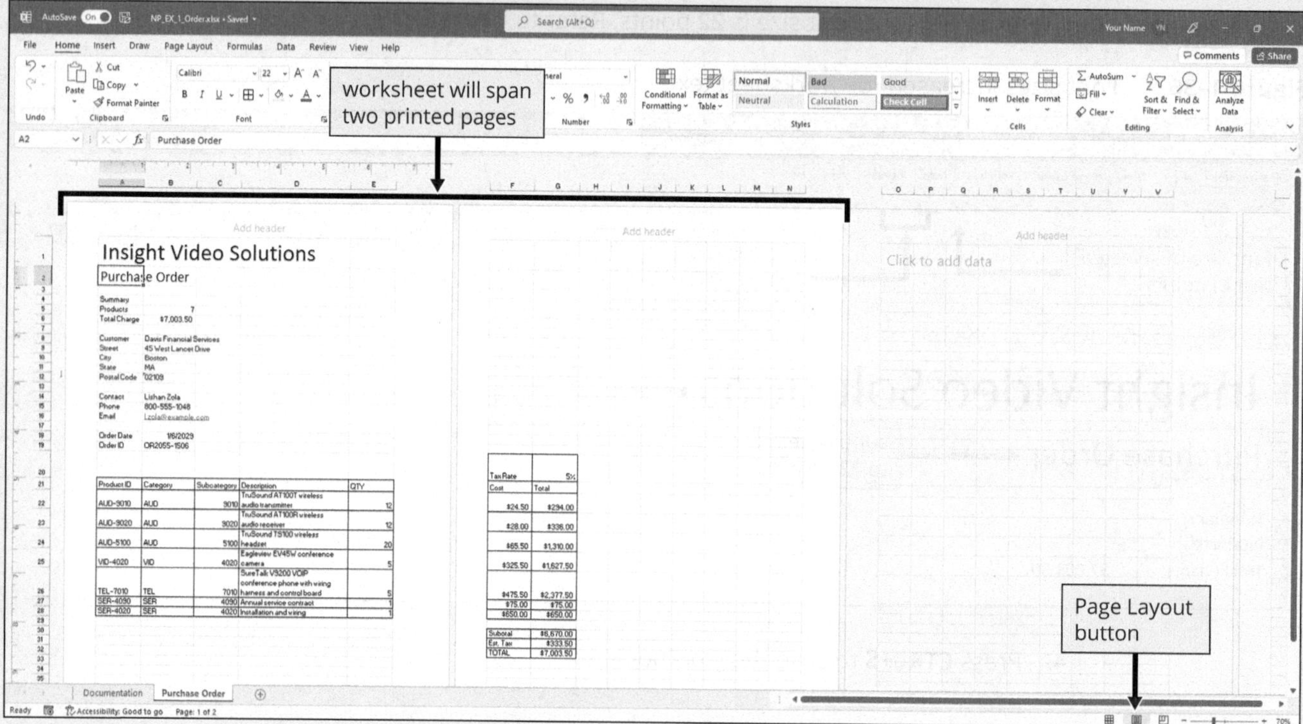

3. Click the **Page Break Preview** button on the status bar. The view switches to Page Break Preview, which shows only those parts of the current worksheet that will print. A dotted blue border separates one page from another.

   Tip You can relocate a page break by dragging the dotted blue border in the Page Break Preview window.

4. On the Zoom slider, drag the slider button to the right until the percentage is **90%**. You can now more easily read the contents of the worksheet. Refer to Figure 1–38.

Figure 1–38 Worksheet in Page Break Preview view

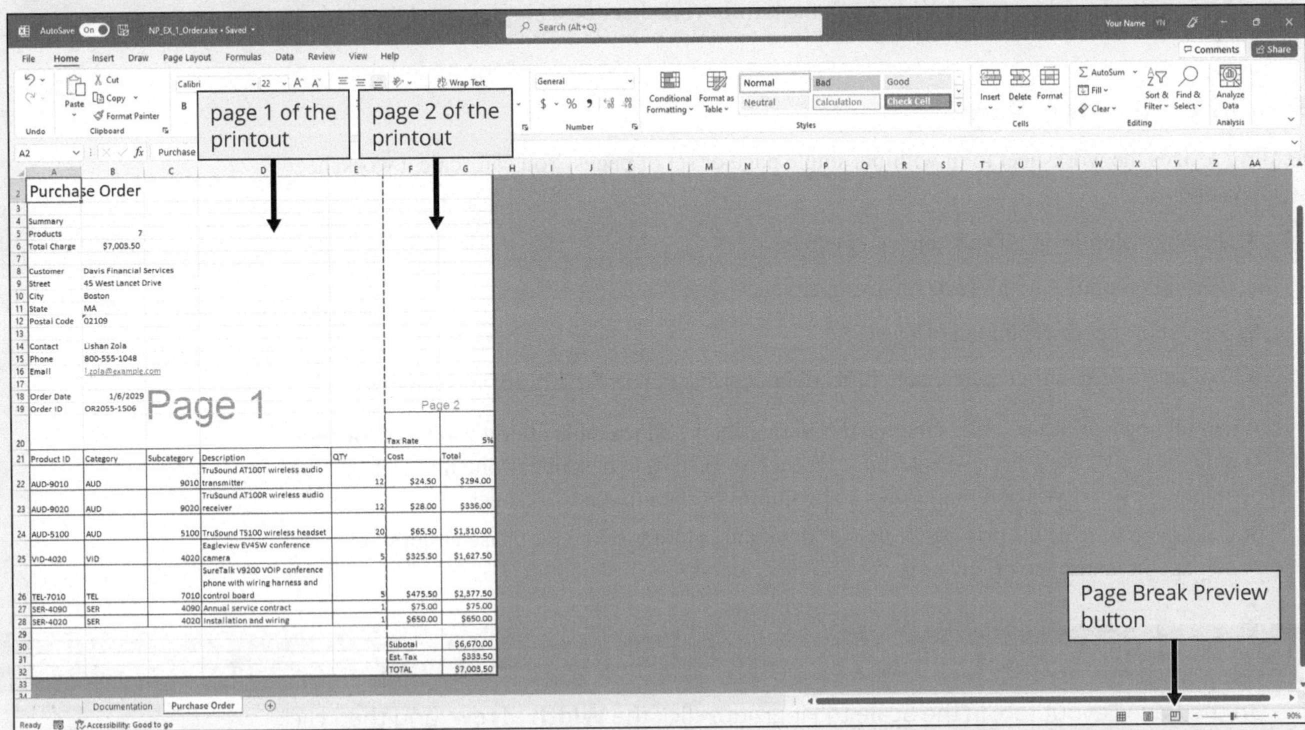

5. Click the **Normal** button on the status bar. The worksheet returns to Normal view. After viewing the worksheet in Page Layout or Page Break Preview, a dotted black line appears between columns D and E in Normal view to indicate where the page breaks occur.

Changing the Page Orientation

Page orientation specifies in which direction content is printed on the page. In **portrait orientation**, the page is taller than it is wide. In **landscape orientation**, the page is wider than it is tall. By default, Excel displays pages in portrait orientation. Changing the page orientation affects only the active sheet in the workbook and not the other, unselected, sheets.

As you saw in Page Layout view and Page Break Preview, the Purchase Order worksheet will print on two pages—columns A through E will print on the first page, while columns F and G will print on the second page. Keep in mind that the columns that print on each page may differ slightly depending on the printer. Sofi wants the entire worksheet to print on a single page, so you'll change the page orientation from portrait to landscape.

To change the page orientation of the Purchase Order worksheet:

1. On the ribbon, click the **Page Layout** tab. The tab includes options for changing how the worksheet is arranged.
2. In the Page Setup group, click the **Orientation** button, and then click **Landscape**. The worksheet switches to landscape orientation, though you cannot tell this change occurred in Normal view.
3. Click the **Page Layout** button on the status bar to switch to Page Layout view.

The worksheet will still print on two pages with rows 1 through 25 on the first page and rows 26 through 32 on the second. You can fit the entire worksheet on a single page by rescaling the page.

Scaling a Printed Page

Scaling resizes the worksheet to fit within a single page or set of pages. You can scale a worksheet so the printout:

1. Fits all columns or all rows on a single page.
2. Fits all columns and all rows on a single page.
3. Fits on a specified number of pages.
4. Adjusts to a specified percentage of its default size, such as 50% of its normal size.

When scaling a printout, make sure that the worksheet is still readable after it is resized. Scaling affects only the active worksheet, so you can scale each worksheet to best fit its contents. That scaling will be retained even if you add more rows and columns of data to the worksheet.

Sofi asks you to scale the printout so that all rows and columns of the Purchase Order worksheet fit on one page in landscape orientation.

To scale the printout of the worksheet:

1. On the Page Layout tab, in the Scale to Fit group, click the **Width arrow**, and then click **1 page**. All the columns in the worksheet fit on one page.
2. In the Scale to Fit group, click the **Height arrow**, and then click **1 page**. All the rows in the worksheet fit on one page. Refer to Figure 1–39.

Figure 1–39 Printout scaled to fit on one page

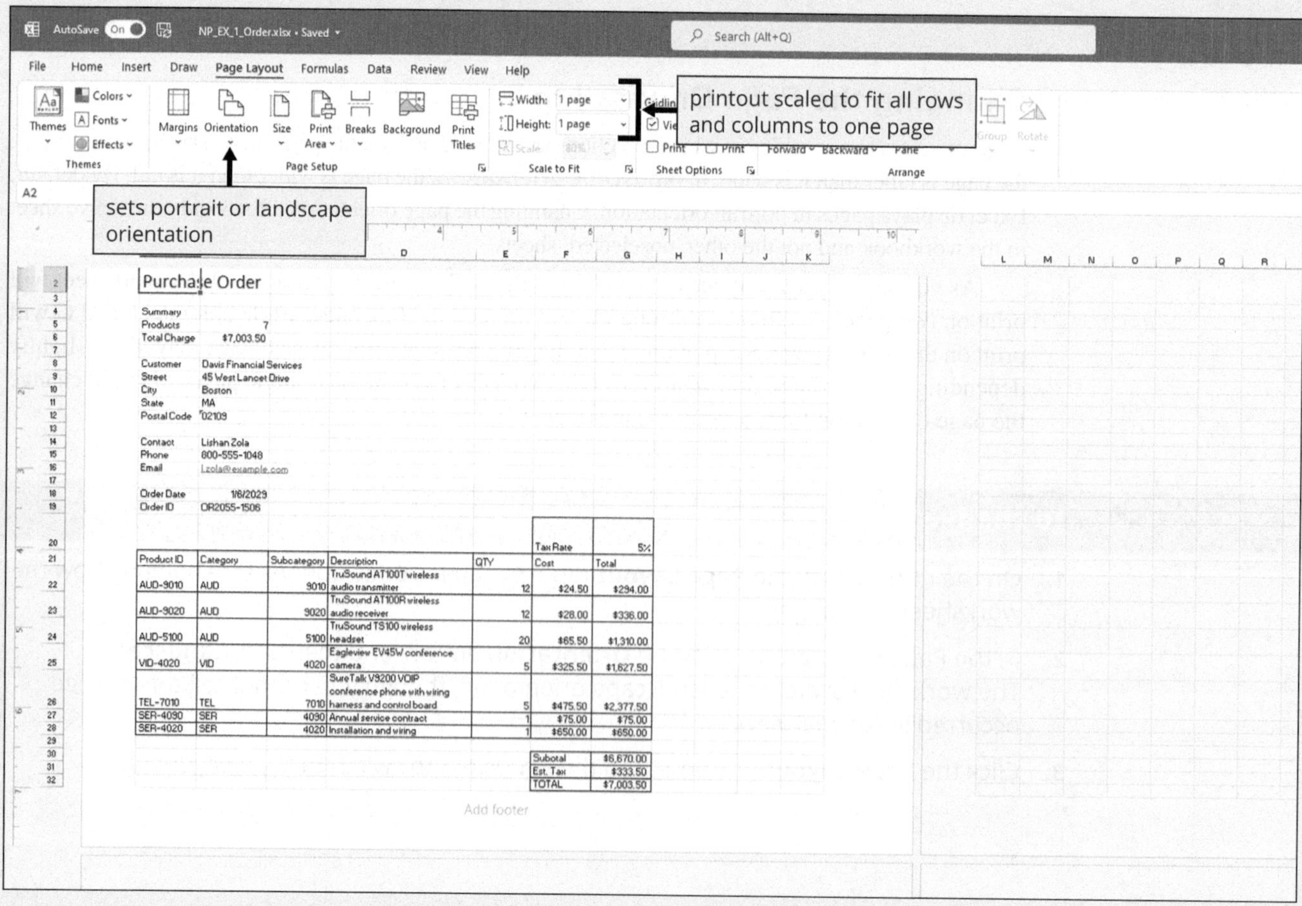

Setting the Print Options

You can print the contents of a workbook by using the Print screen in Backstage view. The Print screen provides options for choosing where to print, how many copies to print, and what to print. You can choose to print only a selected range of cells, only the currently active sheet, or all the worksheets in the workbook.

By default, a printout includes only the worksheet content. The other elements of the Excel window, such as the row and column headings and the gridlines, will not be printed. The print preview shows you exactly how the printed pages will look with the current settings. You should always preview before printing to ensure that the printout looks exactly as you intend.

> **Tip** To print the gridlines or the column and row headings, click the corresponding Print check box in the Sheet Options group on the Page Layout tab.

Sofi asks you to preview and print the workbook containing the purchase order for the customer.

To preview and print the workbook:

1. On the ribbon, click the **File** tab to display Backstage view.
2. Click **Print** in the navigation bar. The Print screen appears with the print options and a preview of the printout of the Purchase Order worksheet. Refer to Figure 1–40.

Figure 1–40 Print screen in Backstage view

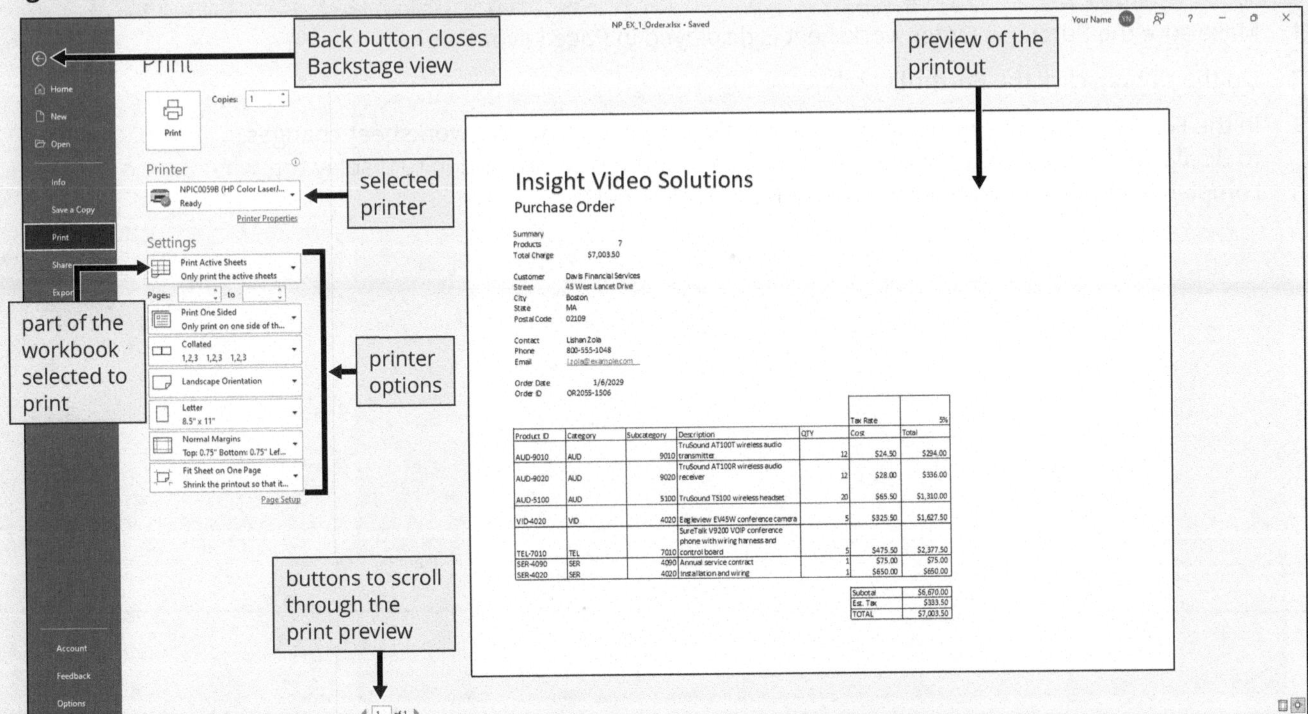

3. Click the **Printer** button, and then click the printer you want to print to, if it is not already selected. By default, Excel will print only the active sheet.
4. In the Settings options, click the top button, and then click **Print Entire Workbook** to print all sheets in the workbook—in this case, both the Documentation and the Purchase Order worksheets. The preview shows the first sheet in the workbook—the Documentation worksheet. Note that this sheet is still in portrait orientation.

5. Below the preview, click the **Next Page** button ▶ to view the print preview for the Purchase Order worksheet, which will print on a single page in landscape orientation.
6. If you are instructed to print, click the **Print** button to send the contents of the workbook to the specified printer. If you are not instructed to print, click the **Back** button ⊖ in the navigation bar to exit Backstage view.

Viewing Worksheet Formulas

Most of the time, you will be interested viewing and printing the data and formula results, not the formulas used to calculate those results. However, in some cases, you might want to view the formulas contained within a worksheet. Displaying that information is useful when you encounter unexpected results and need to examine the underlying formulas, or when you want to discuss the formulas with a colleague. You can view a worksheet in **formula view**, which displays the formulas in place of the results.

In formula view, any printout will include the formulas instead of the values. To make the printout easier to interpret, you should also print the worksheet gridlines, row headings, and column headings, so that cell references from the formulas are easy locate.

You'll look at the formulas in the Purchase Order worksheet.

To view the formulas in the Purchase Order worksheet:

1. Make sure the Purchase Order worksheet is displayed in Page Layout view.
2. On the ribbon, click the **Formulas** tab.
3. In the Formula Auditing group, click the **Show Formulas** button. The worksheet changes to display formulas instead of the values. Notice that the columns widen to display the complete formula text within each cell. Refer to Figure 1–41.

Figure 1–41 Worksheet with formulas displayed

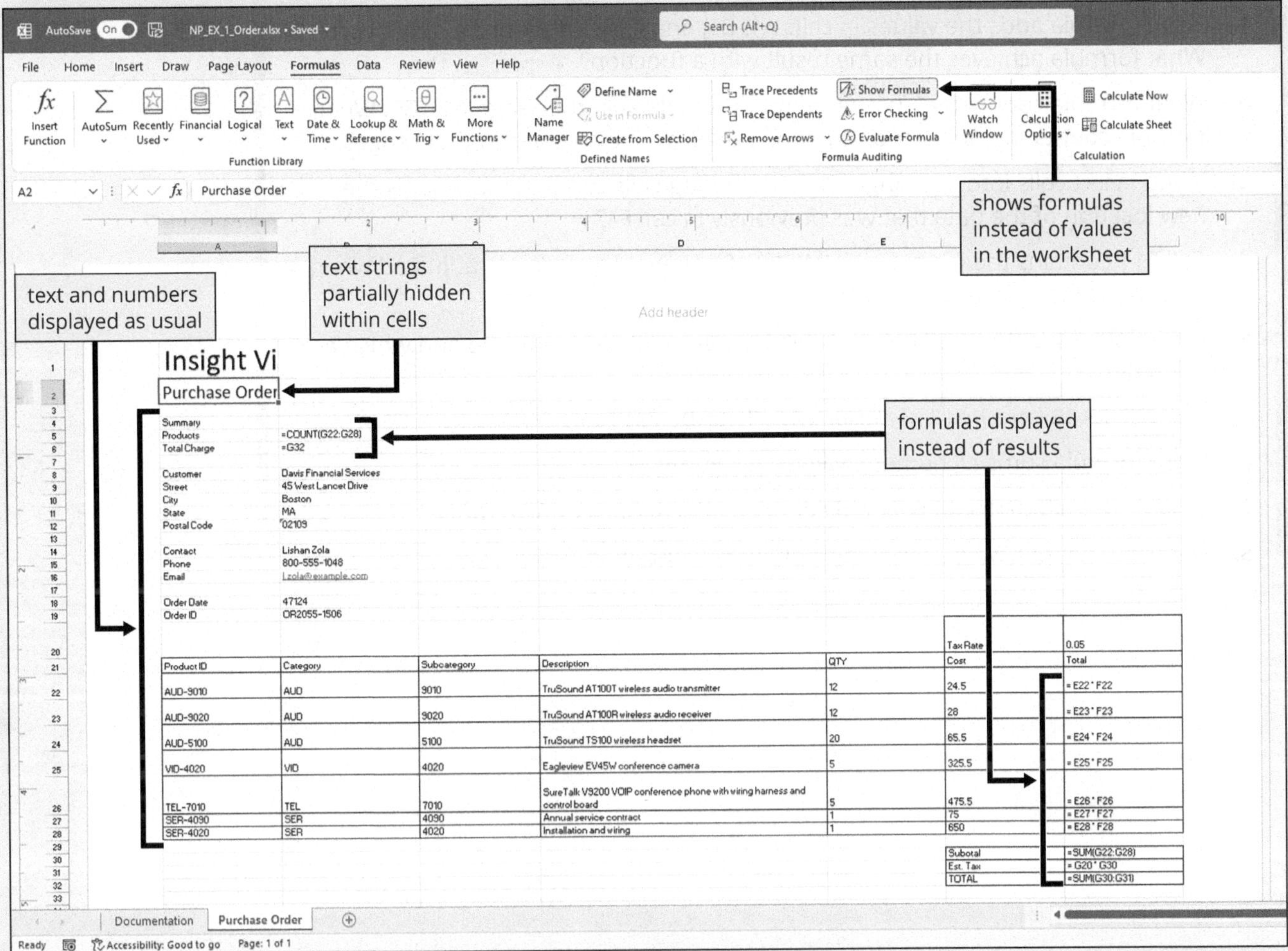

4. When you are done reviewing the formulas, click the **Show Formulas** button again to hide the formulas and display the resulting values.

   Tip You can also toggle between formula view and Normal view by pressing CTRL+` (the grave accent symbol ` is usually located above TAB).

5. Click the **Normal** button on the status bar to return the workbook to Normal view.
6. On the Zoom slider, drag the slider button to the right until the percentage is **140%** (or the magnification you want to use).
7. sam Save the workbook, and then close it.

Sofi is pleased with the workbook you created and will use it to create purchase orders for other customer of Insight Video Solutions.

Part 1.2 Quick Check

1. What formula adds the values in cells A1, B1, and C1 without using a function? What formula achieves the same result with a function?
2. What formula counts the number of numeric values in the range A1:A30. What formula counts the number of numeric values and text values in that range?
3. If you insert cells into the range C1:D10, shifting cells to the right, what is the new location of the data that was previously in cell F4?
4. Cell E11 contains the formula =SUM(E1:E10). How is the formula adjusted when a new row is inserted above row 5?
5. In the following AVERAGE function, which arguments are required and which are optional?

   AVERAGE(*number1*, [*number2*], [*number3*],...)
6. What formula sums all numeric values in column E?
7. What is the difference between deleting a range and clearing a range?
8. Describe the four ways of viewing worksheet content in Excel.

Practice: Review Assignments

Data File needed for the Review Assignments: NP_EX_1-2.xlsx

Sofi wants you to create a workbook to provide quarterly summaries of the Insight Video Solutions income and expenses. The report should also provide the total income and expenses from the entire fiscal year and the percent change in operating income from one quarter to the next. Complete the following:

1. Open the **NP_EX_1-2.xlsx** workbook located in the Excel1 > Review folder included with your Data Files, and then save the workbook as **NP_EX_2_Quarterly** in the location specified by your instructor.
2. Move the Documentation sheet to from the last to the first sheet in the workbook, and then enter your name in cell B3 and the current date in cell B4.
3. Edit the purpose statement in cell B5 by adding the phrase **in the current fiscal year** to the end of the text.
4. Wrap the text in cell B5, set the width of column B to **30** characters and the height of row 5 to **60** points.
5. Set the font size of the title in cell A1 to **26** points.
6. Add all borders around the range A3:B5.
7. Remove the Notes about the Company worksheet from the workbook.
8. Change the name of the Income worksheet to **Quarterly Report**.
9. In the ranges B5:E6 and B9:E10, enter the data from Figure 1–42.

Figure 1–42 Quarterly income and expenses

	QTR 1	QTR 2	QTR 3	QTR 4
Net Sales	$648,150	$988,750	$982,750	$1,018,550
Cost of Sales	$401,200	$604,950	$619,650	$679,500
General Expenses	$99,400	$120,000	$123,650	$125,200
Administrative Expenses	$77,350	$98,300	$101,620	$102,250

10. In the range B7:E7, enter a formula to calculate the gross profit per quarter by subtracting the cost of sales from the net sales.
11. In the range B11:E11, enter a formula to calculate the total operating expenses per quarter by adding the general and administrative expenses.
12. In the range B13:E13, enter a formula to calculate the operating income per quarter by subtracting total operating expenses from gross profit.
13. In the range C14:E14, enter the following formula to calculate the percent change in operating income from one quarter to the next:

$$\%\text{ change} = \frac{\text{current operating income} - \text{previous operating income}}{\text{previous operating income}} \times 100$$

14. Move the range A4:E14 to the range A17:E27.
15. Copy the labels from the range A18:A26 into the range A5:A13. Enter **End-of-Year Total** in cell B4 and **Average per Quarter** in cell C4. Wrap the text in cells B4 and C4.
16. In cell B5, use the SUM function to calculate the sum of all net sales in the range B18:E18.
17. In cell C5, enter a formula that divides the value in cell B5 by 4.
18. Copy the formulas in the range B5:C5 into the nonadjacent range B6:C7,B9:C11,B13:C13 to calculate the end-of-year totals and quarterly averages for each income and expense category.
19. Change the page orientation of the Quarterly Report worksheet to landscape.
20. Scale the Quarterly Report worksheet so that all the columns and rows print on one page.
21. Save the workbook. If you are instructed to print the workbook, print both sheets in the document.
22. Display the formula used in the Quarterly Report worksheet. If you are instructed to print the formulas, print the entire sheet. Hide the formulas.
23. Save the workbook, and then close it.

Apply: Case Problem 1

Data File needed for this Case Problem: NP_EX_1-3.xlsx

Boxes Express Kiran Avanti manages delivery drivers in the southwest region for Boxes Express, a shipping company specializing in overnight and two-day deliveries. One of Kiran's monthly responsibilities is to monitor the distances and hours traveled by Boxes Express drivers to ensure that they follow safety regulations for distance and travel times. Kiran also monitors the driving costs incurred by each driver. Kiran asks you to work on an Excel report detailing the trips and costs of a typical Boxes Express driver. Complete the following:

1. Open the **NP_EX_1-3.xlsx** workbook located in the Excel1 > Case1 folder included with your Data Files, and then save the workbook as **NP_EX_1_Boxes** in the location specified by your instructor.
2. On the Documentation sheet, enter your name in cell B3 and the current date in cell B4.
3. Change the name of the Log worksheet to **Driving Log**.
4. In the Driving Log worksheet, move the data in the range D1:O23 to the range D4:O26.
5. Increase the font size of cell A1 to **24** points. Increase the font size of cells A2, A4, D4, and L4 to **16** points. Increase the font size of row 5 to **12** points.
6. Use AutoFit to increase the width of columns E and F to match their contents.
7. In the range J6:J26, determine the miles driven by entering formulas to calculate the difference between the ending and beginning mileage for each day.
8. In the range N6:N26, determine the cost of fuel each day by entering formulas to multiply the number of gallons used by the cost per gallon.
9. Summarize the driving time during the month by entering the following calculations:
   a. In cell B5, use the COUNT function to count the number of numeric values in column D.
   b. In cell B6, use the SUM function to determine the total driving hours from column G.
   c. In cell B7, determine the average hours of driving per day by entering a formula to divide the value in cell B6 by the value in cell B5.
10. Summarize the expenses incurred during the month by entering the following calculations:
    a. In cell B9, use the SUM function to calculate the total expenses in column range N:O.
    b. In cell B10, use the SUM function to calculate the total spent on fuel in column N.
    c. In cell B11, use the SUM function to calculate the total miscellaneous expenses from column O.
11. Summarize the data on fuel consumption by entering the following calculations:
    a. In cell B13, use the SUM function to add up the gallons consumed in column L.
    b. In cell B14, use the SUM function to add up the total mileage from column J.
    c. In cell B15, calculate the miles per gallon by dividing the total mileage by the total gallons consumed.
    d. In cell B16, calculate the cost of delivery by dividing the total expenses incurred during the month by the total mileage driven.
12. The company wants to keep the cost per mile of delivery packages to the hubs and distribution centers to $1 or less per mile. In cell B18, enter **over budget** if the cost per mile is over this goal or **under budget** if it meets this goal.
13. Add all borders around the cells in the nonadjacent ranges D5:J26,L5:O26.
14. Change the page orientation of the Driving Log worksheet to landscape.
15. Scale the Driving Log worksheet so that all rows and columns fit on one page. If you are instructed to print your solution, print the contents of the entire workbook.
16. Save the workbook, and then close it.

Challenge: Case Problem 2

Data File needed for this Case Problem: NP_EX_1-4.xlsx

Eat Well, Inc. Marta Arlet works in the Human Resources Department of the national grocery store chain Eat Well, Inc. Marta is finalizing a workbook that summarizes data from almost 500 employees from all stores in the chain. The report will include information on the employee's average salaries, years of employment with the company, personal days, sicks days, and performance evaluation.

To complete Marta's workbook, you will use the AVERAGE function to calculate averages from ranges of numeric values. The syntax of the AVERAGE function is:

`AVERAGE(`*`number1`*`, [`*`number2`*`], [`*`number3`*`],...)`

You will also combine employee first and last names into a single text string using the & operator. To apply the & operator to create a full name from a first and last name, you use the formula

`= `*`first`*` &" "& `*`last`*

where *`first`* is the cell reference to the employee's first name and *`last`* is the cell reference to the employee's last name. Complete the following:

1. Open the **NP_EX_1-4.xlsx** workbook located in the Excel1 > Case2 folder included with your Data Files, and then save the workbook as **NP_EX_1_EatWell** in the location specified by your instructor.
2. In the Documentation sheet, enter your name and the current date in cells B3 and B4.
3. Wrap the text in cell B5 and set the width of column B to **25** characters and the height of row 5 to **80** points.
4. In the Employees worksheet, AutoFit the width of column A. Set the width of column B to **16** characters.
5. In cell J4, enter a formula to determine the first employee's number of days employed by subtracting the date hired from the current date value.
6. In cell K4, enter a formula to determine the years hired for the first employee by dividing the value in cell J4 by 365.25.
7. Copy the formulas from the range J4:K4 into the range J5:K495 to estimate the days and years hired for the rest of the employees.
8. **Explore:** In cell F4, enter the formula **= D4 &" "& E4** to display the full name for the first employee.
9. Copy the formula in cell F4 into the range F5:F495 to display the other employee full names.
10. Summarize the employee data for the company by entering the following calculations into the worksheet:
    a. In cell B4, use the COUNT function to count the number of values in column I.
    b. In cell B5, use the SUM function with the values in column L to calculate the total of employee salaries to the company.
    c. In cell B6, use the SUM function with the values in column M to calculate the total number of personal days taken by company employees.
    d. In cell B7, use the SUM function with the values in column N to calculate the total number of sick days taken by company employees.
11. **Explore:** Calculate employee averages by inserting the following calculations into the worksheet:
    a. In cell B10, use the AVERAGE function to calculate the average salary using the values from column L.
    b. In cell B11, use the AVERAGE function to calculate the average years employed using values from column K.
    c. In cell B12, use the AVERAGE function to calculate the average number of personal days using the values from column M.
    d. In cell B13, use the AVERAGE function to calculate the average number of sicks days using the values from column N.
    e. In cell B14, use the AVERAGE function to calculate the average performance rating using the values from column O.

12. A new employee was hired at Eat Well. Insert cells into the range D10:O10, shifting the current cells down the worksheet.
13. Enter the following information about the new employee: **Andrew** in cell D10, **Alito** in cell E10, **IT** in cell G10, **3/31/2029** in cell H10, **3/23/2029** in cell I10, **$81,000** in cell L10, **0** in cell M10, **0** in cell N10, and **75** in cell O10. (Note that the formulas will automatically be inserted into cells F10, J10, and K10.)
14. In the range D3:O496, add all borders around the cells.
15. Change the page orientation of the worksheet to landscape.
16. Change the page scaling of the worksheet so that all the columns fit on one page.
17. **Explore:** Select the range A1:B14, and then using the Print Settings options on the Print page in Backstage View, print only the selected cells (not the entire worksheet or workbook).
18. Save the workbook, and then close it.

Formatting a Workbook

Creating a Sales Report

Case: Hook and Line Seafood

Robert Coby is a sales manager for Hook and Line Seafood, a chain of seafood restaurants in Florida, Georgia, and Alabama. Robert creates an annual sales report using data from 12 restaurants in the Hook and Line chain. The report includes monthly summaries of each restaurant's total revenue, total expenses, net profit, and profit margin. That is a lot of data on a single worksheet. You will format the worksheet for Robert to improve its readability and to highlight important results such as months when a restaurant had a net loss instead of a profit. The workbook will also be released in a print version, so you will need to format the workbook for print as well as for the screen.

Starting Data Files

Excel2 Module
NP_EX_2-1.xlsx
Support_EX_2_Background.jpg

Review
NP_EX_2-2.xlsx
Support_EX_2_Texture.jpg

Case1
NP_EX_2-3.xlsx

Case2
NP_EX_2-4.xlsx
Support_EX_2_Home.thmx

Objectives

Part 2.1
- Change fonts, font style, and font color
- Add fill colors and a background image
- Format numbers as currency and percentages
- Format dates and times
- Copy and paste formats with the Format Painter
- Align, indent, and rotate cell contents
- Merge a group of cells

Part 2.2
- Use the AVERAGE function
- Apply cell styles
- Find and replace text and formatting
- Change workbook themes
- Highlight cells with conditional formats
- Format a worksheet for printing

Part 2.1 Visual Overview: Formatting a Worksheet

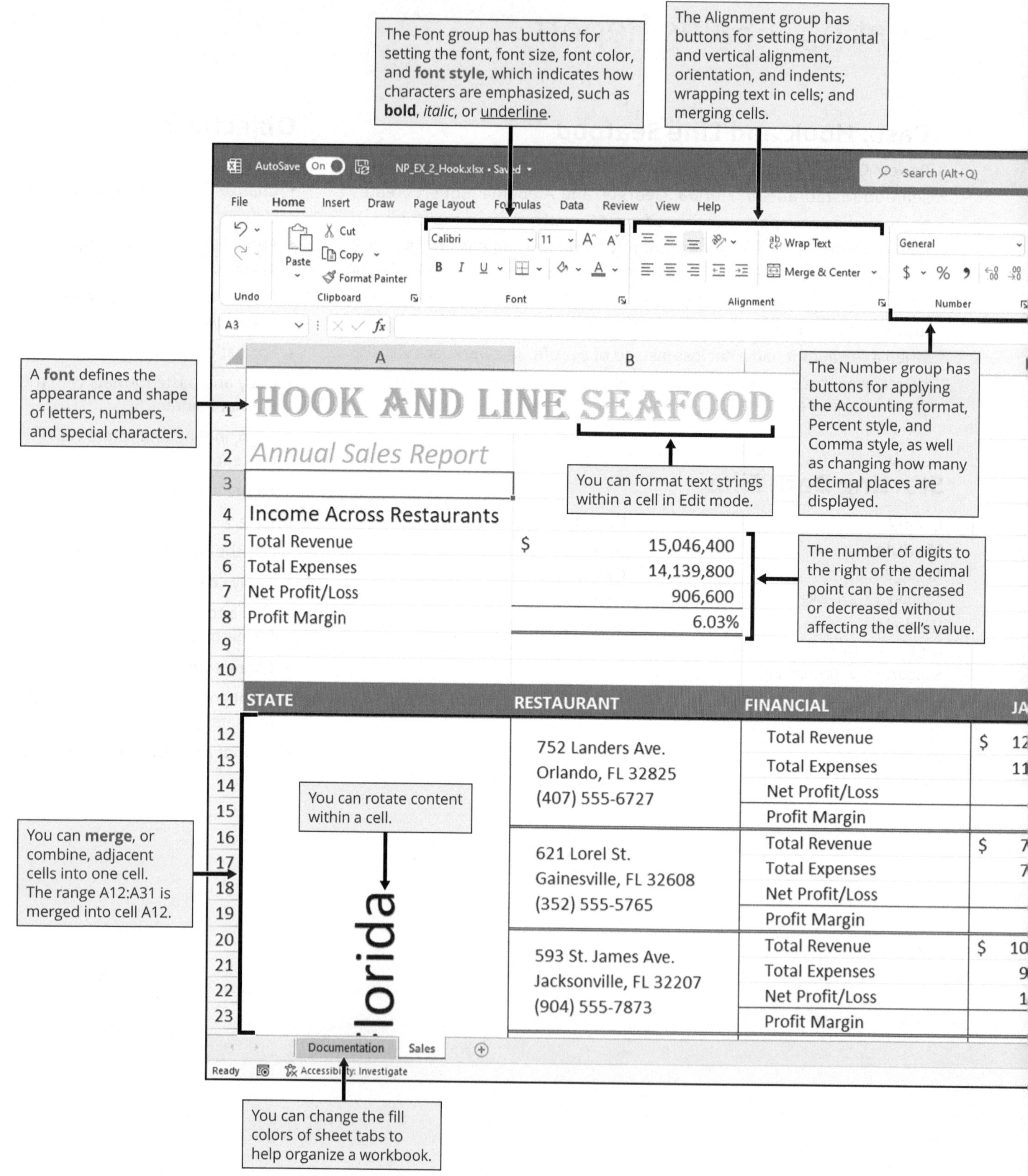
The Font group has buttons for setting the font, font size, font color, and **font style**, which indicates how characters are emphasized, such as **bold**, *italic*, or underline.
The Alignment group has buttons for setting horizontal and vertical alignment, orientation, and indents; wrapping text in cells; and merging cells.
A **font** defines the appearance and shape of letters, numbers, and special characters.
You can format text strings within a cell in Edit mode.
The Number group has buttons for applying the Accounting format, Percent style, and Comma style, as well as changing how many decimal places are displayed.
The number of digits to the right of the decimal point can be increased or decreased without affecting the cell's value.
You can rotate content within a cell.
You can **merge**, or combine, adjacent cells into one cell. The range A12:A31 is merged into cell A12.
You can change the fill colors of sheet tabs to help organize a workbook.
HOOK AND LINE SEAFOOD
Annual Sales Report
Income Across Restaurants
Total Revenue $ 15,046,400
Total Expenses 14,139,800
Net Profit/Loss 906,600
Profit Margin 6.03%
STATE
RESTAURANT
FINANCIAL
752 Landers Ave.
Orlando, FL 32825
(407) 555-6727
621 Lorel St.
Gainesville, FL 32608
(352) 555-5765
593 St. James Ave.
Jacksonville, FL 32207
(904) 555-7873
Total Revenue
Total Expenses
Net Profit/Loss
Profit Margin
lorida
Documentation
Sales

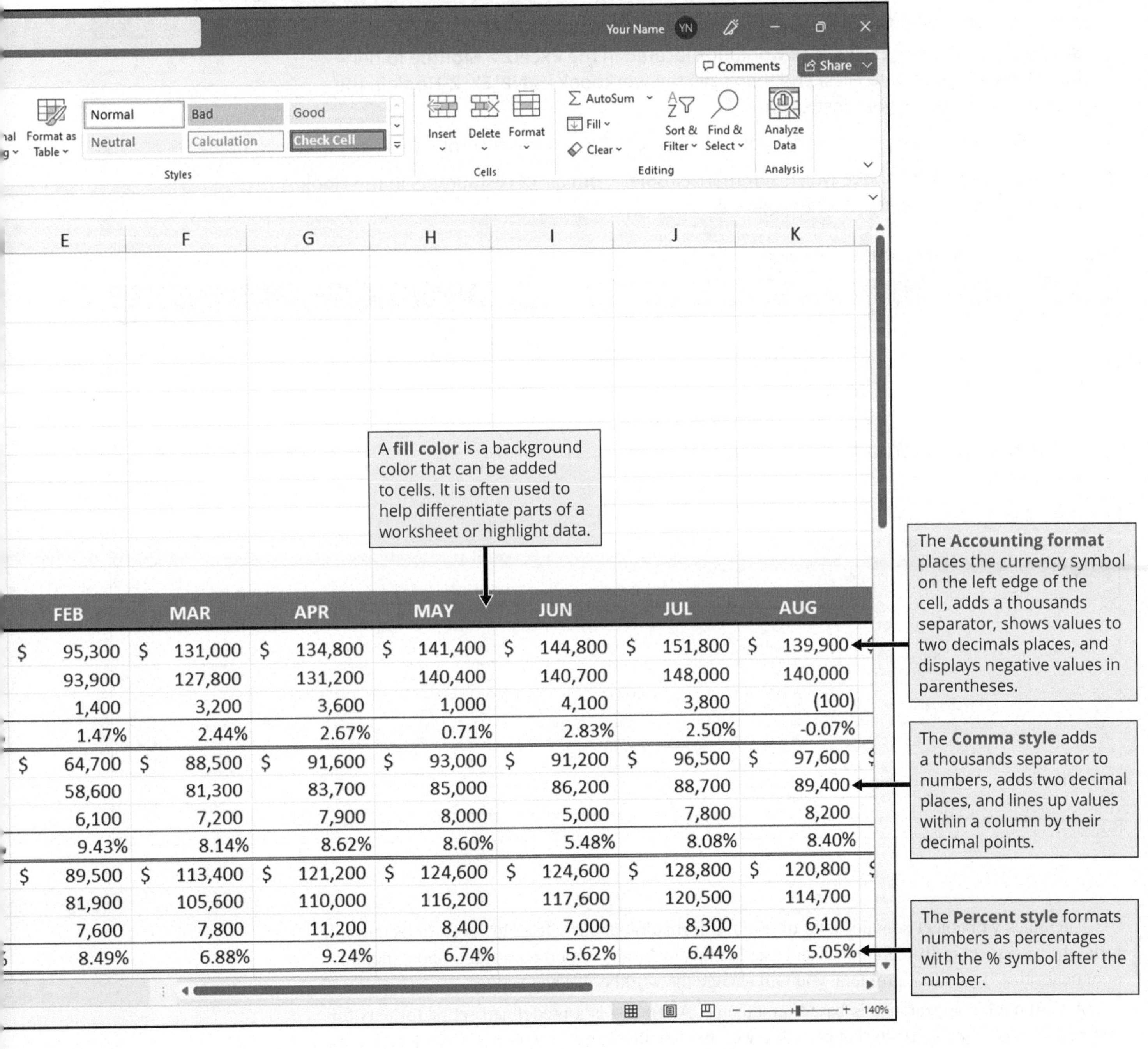
Your Name
Comments
Share
Normal
Bad
Good
Neutral
Calculation
Check Cell
Format as Table
Styles
Insert
Delete
Format
Cells
AutoSum
Fill
Clear
Sort & Filter
Find & Select
Editing
Analyze Data
Analysis
A fill color is a background color that can be added to cells. It is often used to help differentiate parts of a worksheet or highlight data.
FEB MAR APR MAY JUN JUL AUG
The Accounting format places the currency symbol on the left edge of the cell, adds a thousands separator, shows values to two decimals places, and displays negative values in parentheses.
The Comma style adds a thousands separator to numbers, adds two decimal places, and lines up values within a column by their decimal points.
The Percent style formats numbers as percentages with the % symbol after the number.
140%

FEB	MAR	APR	MAY	JUN	JUL	AUG
$ 95,300	$ 131,000	$ 134,800	$ 141,400	$ 144,800	$ 151,800	$ 139,900
93,900	127,800	131,200	140,400	140,700	148,000	140,000
1,400	3,200	3,600	1,000	4,100	3,800	(100)
1.47%	2.44%	2.67%	0.71%	2.83%	2.50%	-0.07%
$ 64,700	$ 88,500	$ 91,600	$ 93,000	$ 91,200	$ 96,500	$ 97,600
58,600	81,300	83,700	85,000	86,200	88,700	89,400
6,100	7,200	7,900	8,000	5,000	7,800	8,200
9.43%	8.14%	8.62%	8.60%	5.48%	8.08%	8.40%
$ 89,500	$ 113,400	$ 121,200	$ 124,600	$ 124,600	$ 128,800	$ 120,800
81,900	105,600	110,000	116,200	117,600	120,500	114,700
7,600	7,800	11,200	8,400	7,000	8,300	6,100
8.49%	6.88%	9.24%	6.74%	5.62%	6.44%	5.05%

Formatting Text

The appearance of a workbook is often as important as the calculations it contains. A poorly organized and formatted workbook can obscure useful information and insights. A well-formatted workbook helps make data accessible for users to analyze and review. Note that formatting changes only the appearance of data. It does not alter the content of the data.

Robert has sales information for the restaurant chain stored in a workbook. He wants you to turn the data into a document that will be both insightful and impactful. You'll start by reviewing the data in Robert's workbook.

To open and review Robert's workbook:

1. sam Open the **NP_EX_2-1.xlsx** workbook located in the **Excel2 > Module** folder included with your Data Files, and then save the workbook as **NP_EX_2_Hook** in the location specified by your instructor.
2. In the Documentation sheet, enter your name in cell B4 and the current date in cell B5.
3. Go to the **Sales** worksheet, which summarizes sales from all 12 restaurants in the Hook and Line Seafood chain. Refer to Figure 2–1.

Figure 2–1 Unformatted Sales worksheet

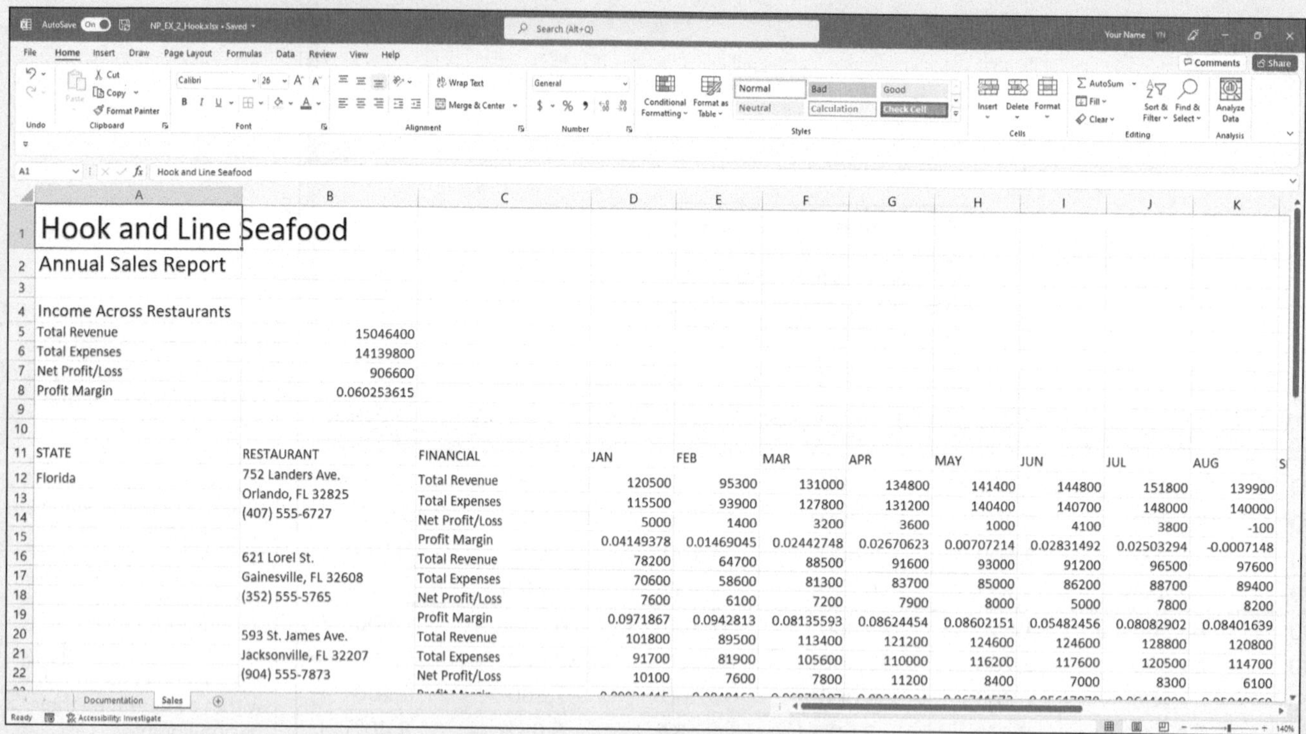

The Sales worksheet contains a lot of useful information about sales. However, in its current form, the worksheet is difficult to read and users cannot make any important insights about monthly or annual sales. To fix that problem, you will change the workbook's appearance.

A workbook's appearance is based on a theme. A **theme** is a predefined set of formats for text, colors, and graphic effects that provide a workbook with a consistent, professional look that is informative for the user. All new workbooks use the Office theme, but you can choose a different theme from the Excel library or create your own. Themes are saved as files, so that the same theme can be shared by multiple workbooks.

The theme impacts the appearance of text used in the workbook. Text design is based on fonts, which are sets of characters that share a common appearance and shape. **Serif fonts**, such as Times New Roman, have extra strokes at the end of each character. **Sans serif fonts**, such as Arial, do not include these flourishes. Other fonts are purely decorative, such as a font associated with a company's logo.

Excel organizes fonts into theme fonts and standard fonts. A **theme font** is associated with a particular theme and is used to format headings and body text within the workbook. If you change a workbook's theme, text formatted with a theme font will also change. A **standard font** is not associated with any theme and retains its appearance no matter what theme the workbook uses.

Every font can be formatted with a font style that can add special emphasis to the characters, such as *italic*, **bold**, ***bold italic***, underline, and color. You can also increase or decrease the font size to change its impact.

Reference

Formatting Text

- To choose the font, select the cell or range. On the Home tab, in the Font group, click the Font arrow, and then select a font name.
- To set the font size, select the cell or range. On the Home tab, in the Font group, click the Font Size arrow, and then select a size.
- To set the font style, select the cell or range. On the Home tab, in the Font group, click the Bold, Italic, or Underline button; or press CTRL+B, CTRL+I, or CTRL+U.
- To set the font color, select the cell or range. On the Home tab, in the Font group, click the Font Color arrow, and then select a color.
- To format a text selection, double-click the cell to enter Edit mode, select the text to format, change the font, size, style, or color, and then press ENTER.

As you design a workbook, you can test different formatting options using **Live Preview**, which shows the results of a format change before it is selected. Robert wants the company name to use the same font as the corporate logo. He also wants other text in the Documentation sheet to stand out more.

To format text in the Documentation sheet:

1. Go to the **Documentation** sheet, and then click cell **A1** if necessary to select it.
2. On the Home tab, in the Font group, click the **Font arrow** to display a gallery of available fonts. Each name is previewed in its font typeface. The first two fonts listed are the Office theme fonts for headings and body text—Calibri Light and Calibri. The remaining fonts are standard fonts not associated with any theme.
3. In the Font gallery, scroll down as needed and point to **Algerian**. Live Preview shows the effect of the font on the text in cell A1. Refer to Figure 2–2.

Figure 2–2 Font gallery

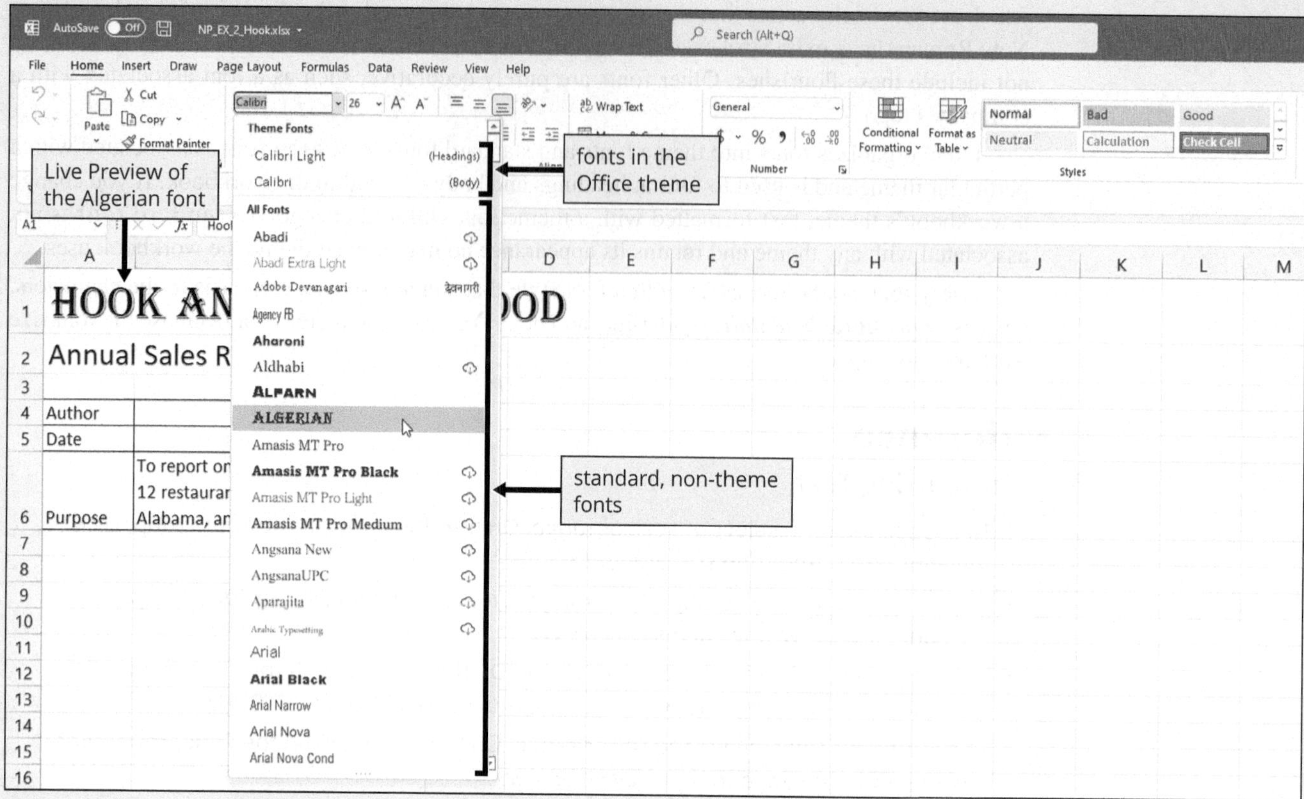

Trouble? If Algerian is not in your list of standard fonts, use a font suggested by your instructor or choose a different decorative font.

4. Click **Algerian** in the list of standard fonts. The text in cell A1 changes to the selected font.
5. In the Font group, click the **Bold** button B (or press **CTRL+B**). The text changes to a bold font.
6. Click cell **A2** containing the subtitle for the worksheet.
7. In the Font group, click the **Italic** button I (or press **CTRL+I**). The Annual Sales Report subtitle is italicized.
8. Select the range **A4:A6** containing the labels, and then press **CTRL+B**. The text in the selected range changes to bold.
9. Click cell **A8** to deselect the range. Refer to Figure 2–3.

Figure 2–3 Font styles applied to text

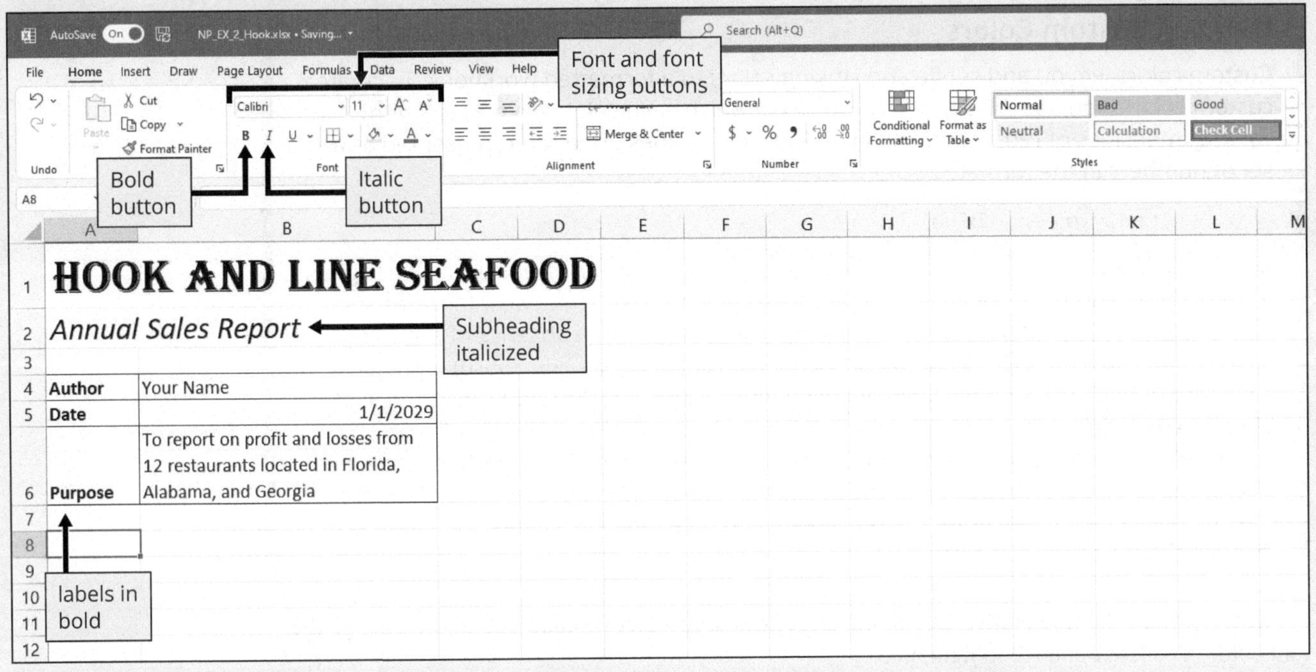

Applying a Font Color

Color can transform a plain workbook filled with numbers and text into a powerful presentation that captures the user's attention. Color can also emphasize important points in a data analysis.

Like fonts, colors are organized into theme and standard colors. **Theme colors** are a set of 12 coordinated colors that belong to the workbook's theme. Four colors are designated for text and backgrounds, six colors are used for accents and highlights, and two colors are used for hyperlinks (followed and not followed links). These 12 colors are designed to complement each other while remaining readable when used in combination. Each theme color has five variations, or accents, with a different tint of shading of the color.

Ten **standard colors**—dark red, red, orange, yellow, light green, green, light blue, blue, dark blue, and purple—are always available regardless of the workbook's theme. Beyond these easily accessible standard colors is an extended palette of 134 colors. You can also create a custom color by specifying a mixture of red, blue, and green color values, making available 16.7 million custom color combinations, which are more colors than the human eye can distinguish. Some dialog boxes have an automatic color option that uses your Windows default text and background colors, usually black text on a white background.

Insight

Creating Custom Colors

Custom colors let you add subtle and striking colors to a formatted workbook. To create custom colors, you use the **RGB Color model** in which each color is expressed with varying intensities of red, green, and blue. RGB color values are often represented as a set of numbers in the format

`(red, green, blue)`

where `red` is an intensity value assigned to red light, `green` is an intensity value assigned to green light, and `blue` is an intensity value assigned to blue light. The intensities are measured on a scale of 0 to 255—0 indicates no intensity (or the absence of the color) and 255 indicates the highest intensity. So, the RGB color value (255, 255, 0) represents a mixture of high-intensity red (255) and high-intensity green (255) with the absence of blue (0), creating yellow.

To create colors in Excel using the RGB model, click the More Colors option located in a color menu or dialog box to open the Colors dialog box. In the Colors dialog box, click the Custom tab, and then enter the red, green, and blue intensity values. A preview box displays the resulting RGB color.

Robert wants the title and subtitle in the Documentation sheet to stand out. You'll change the font color in cells A1 and A2 to light blue.

To change the text color of the title and subtitle:

1. In the Documentation sheet, select the range **A1:A2** containing the title and subtitle.
2. On the Home tab, in the Font group, click the **Font Color arrow** [A ⌄]. The gallery of theme and standard colors opens.
3. In the Standard Colors section, point to the **Light Blue** color (the seventh color). The color name appears in a ScreenTip, and Live Preview shows the text with the light blue font color. Refer to Figure 2–4.

Figure 2–4 Font color gallery

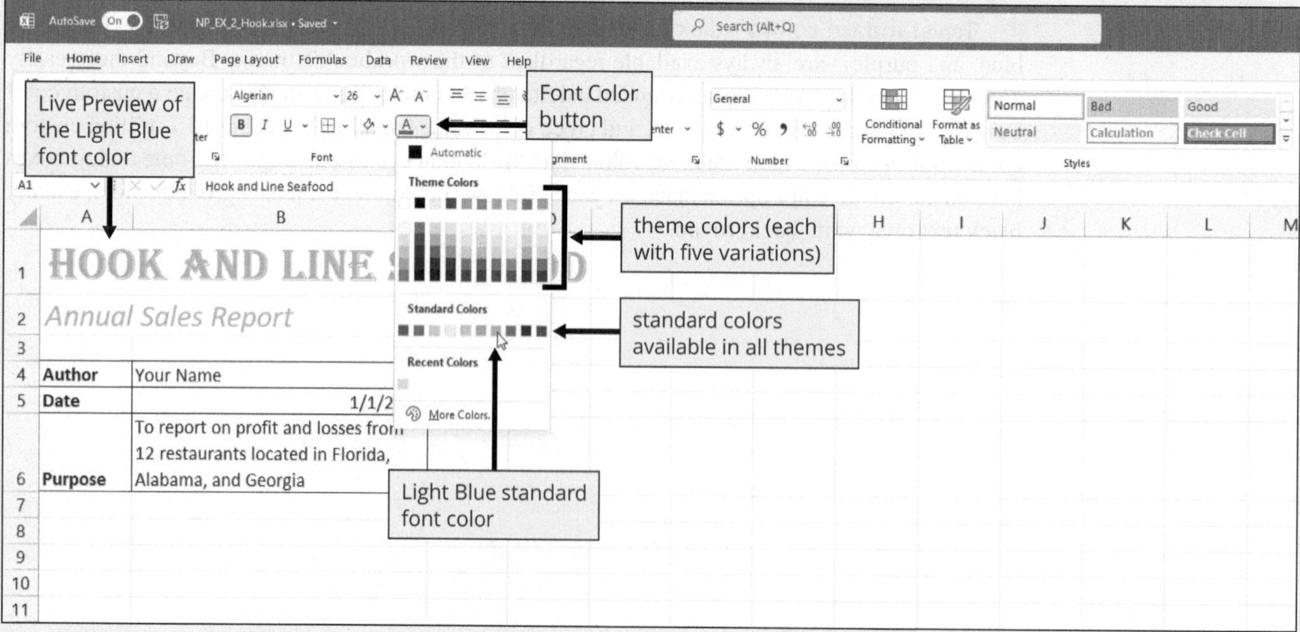

4. Click the **Light Blue** standard color. The title and subtitle text change that font color.

Formatting Text Selections Within a Cell

Not all text in a cell must be the same color. In Edit mode, you can select and format selections of text within a cell. You can make these changes to selected text from the ribbon or from the Mini toolbar. The **Mini toolbar** is a small toolbar that appears next to selected content, containing the most frequently used formatting commands for that content.

Robert asks you to format the company name in cell A1 so that "Seafood" is light green.

To change the color of "Seafood" in cell A1 to light green:

1. Double-click cell **A1** to select the cell and enter Edit mode. The status bar reads "Edit" and the insertion point changes to the I-beam pointer to indicate that you are working with the cell in Edit mode.

   Tip You can also enter Edit mode by clicking a cell and pressing F2.

2. Drag the pointer over the word **Seafood** to select it. The Mini toolbar appears next to the selected text with button to change the font, size, style, and color of the selected text.
3. On the Mini toolbar, click the **Font Color arrow** A, and then in the Standard Colors section, point to the **Light Green** color (the fifth color). Live Preview changes the color of the selected text to light green. Refer to Figure 2–5.

Figure 2–5 Mini toolbar in Edit mode

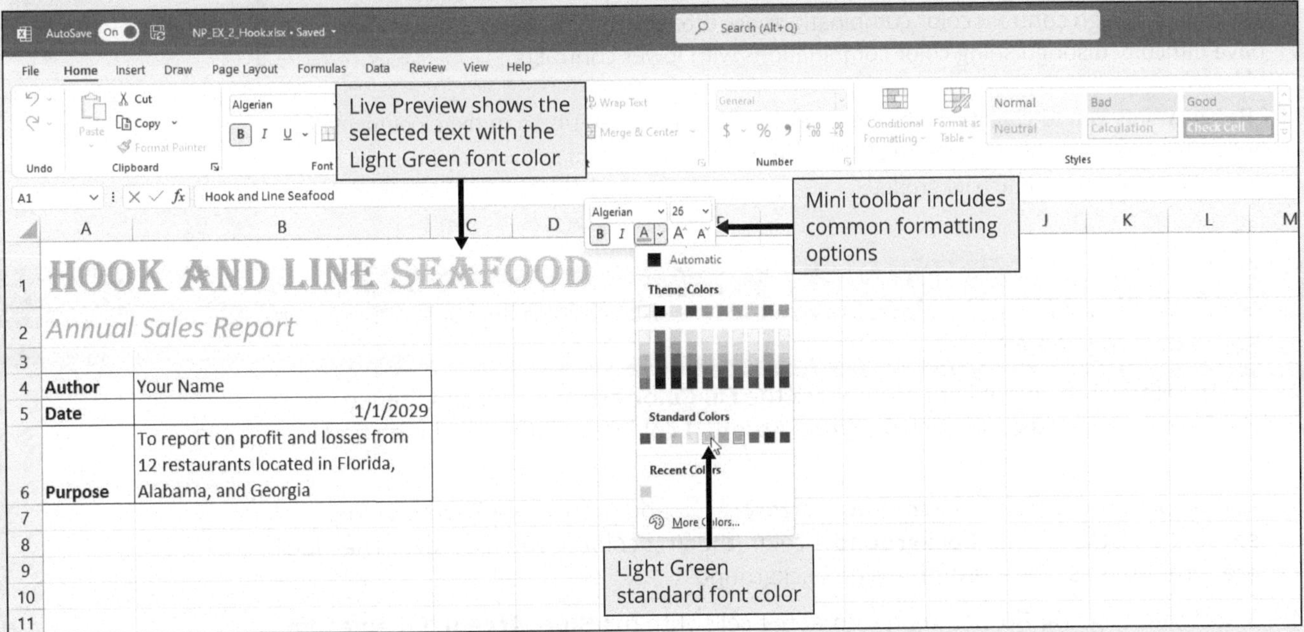

4. Click the **Light Green** standard color. The Mini toolbar closes and the selected text changes to light green.

Working with Fill Colors and Backgrounds

Another way to distinguish sections of a worksheet is by formatting the cell backgrounds. You can fill the cell background with color or with an image.

Changing a Fill Color

In the Office theme, worksheet cells do not include any background color. But filling a cell's background with color, also known as a fill color, can be helpful for highlighting data, differentiating parts of a worksheet, or adding visual interest to a report. The colors available for fonts are also available for cell backgrounds.

Insight

Using Color to Enhance a Workbook

When used wisely, color can enhance any workbook. However, when used improperly, color can distract the user, making the workbook difficult to read. As you add color to a workbook, keep in mind the following tips:

- Use colors from the same theme to maintain a consistent look and feel across the worksheets. If the built-in themes do not fit your needs, you can create a custom theme.
- Use colors to differentiate types of cell content and to direct users where to enter data. For example, format a worksheet so that formula results appear in cells without a fill color and users enter data in cells with a light gray fill color.
- Avoid color combinations that are difficult to read.
- Print the workbook in both color and black-and-white to ensure the printed copy is readable in both versions.
- Understand your printer's limitations and features. Colors that look good on your monitor might not look as good when printed.
- Don't overdo it. Too many color choices will distract rather than enhance your document.

Be sensitive to your audience. About 8% of all men and 0.5% of all women have some type of color vision impairment and might not be able to distinguish the text when certain color combinations are used. Red–green color vision impairment is the most common, so avoid using red text on a green background or green text on a red background. High contrast color combinations are often better choices for users who have difficulty distinguishing color combinations with lower contrasts.

Robert wants you to change the background color of the range A4:A6 in the Documentation sheet to white text on a blue background. He also wants you to change the content in the range B4:B6 to blue text on a white background.

To change the font and fill colors on the Documentation sheet:

1. Select the range **A4:A6**.
2. On the Home tab, in the Font group, click the **Fill Color arrow**, and then in the Theme Colors section, click the **Blue, Accent 1** color (the fifth color in the first row).
3. In the Font group, click the **Font Color arrow** A, and then in the Theme Colors section, click the **White, Background 1** color (the first color in the first row). The labels are formatted as white text on a blue background.
4. Select the range **B4:B6**, and then format the cells with the **Blue, Accent 1** theme font color and the **White, Background 1** theme fill color.
5. Click cell **A8** to deselect the range. Refer to Figure 2–6.

Figure 2–6 Font and fill colors applied to ranges

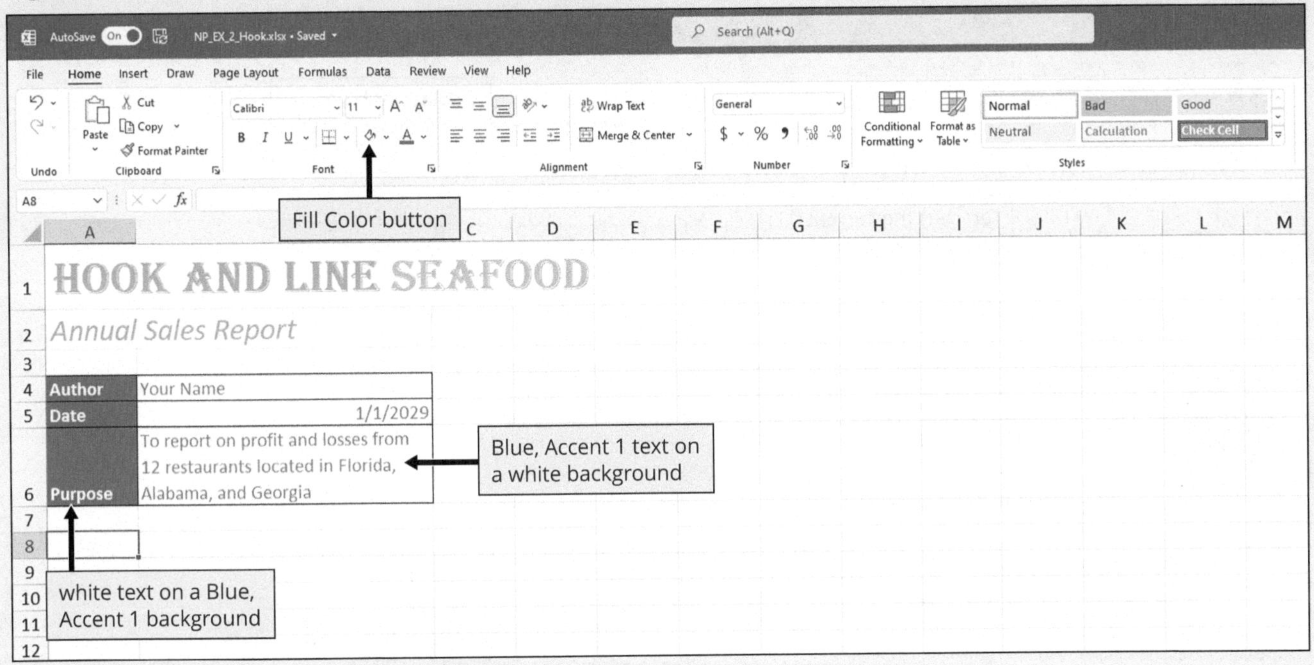

You can change the background color of an entire worksheet by first selecting all the cells in the sheet and then changing the fill color. To select all cells in a worksheet, click the Select All button above the row headers or press CTRL+A.

Adding a Background Image

Another way to format the worksheet background is with a background image. Background images are usually based on image files of textures such as granite, wood, or fibered paper. The image does not need to match the size of the worksheet. A small image repeats, or tiles, until it fills the entire sheet. Background images do not affect any cell's format or content. Any fill colors will appear on top of the background image.

> **Tip** A background image appears only in the workbook window. It is not printed. To print a graphic image, add it to the worksheet as a graphic object.

Robert has an image file he wants to use as the background for the Documentation sheet. You'll add that background image now.

To add a background image to the Documentation sheet:

1. On the ribbon, click the **Page Layout** tab to display the page layout options.
2. In the Page Setup group, click the **Background** button. The Insert Pictures dialog box opens with options to search for an image from a file on your computer, from the Bing Image server, or on your OneDrive account.
3. Click the **From a file** option. The Sheet Background dialog box opens.
4. Navigate to the **Excel2 > Module** folder included with your Data Files, click the **Support_EX_2_Background.jpg** image file, and then click **Insert**. The image is added to the background of the Documentation sheet. The worksheet gridlines remain visible on the background image.
5. In the Sheet Options group, in the Gridlines list, click the **View** checkbox to deselect it. The gridlines for the Documentation sheet are hidden, creating a cleaner background. Hiding the gridlines in this worksheet does not affect the gridlines in other worksheets. Refer to Figure 2–7.

Figure 2–7 Background image added to the worksheet

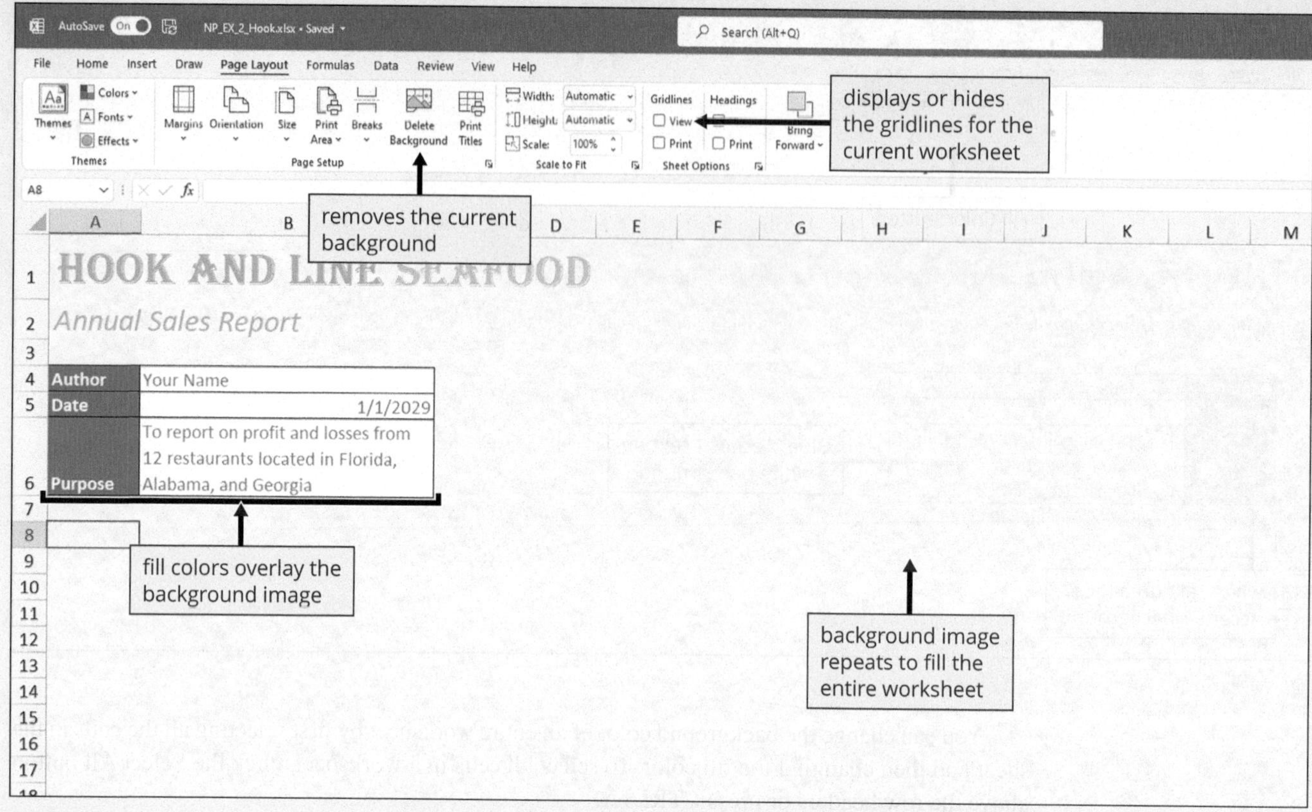

To remove a background image from a worksheet, click the Delete Background button in the Page Setup group on the Page Layout tab.

Changing the Sheet Tab Color

You can add colors to sheet tabs to visually group worksheets sharing a common topic. Although you can change the sheet tab fill color, you cannot change its text color or text style. Robert wants you to change the fill color of the Documentation sheet tab to gold.

To change the tab color of the Documentation sheet:

1. Right-click the **Documentation** sheet tab. A shortcut menu appears with options related to the sheet tab.
2. On the shortcut menu, point to **Tab Color** to display the palette of theme and standard colors.
3. In the Theme Colors section, click **Gold, Accent 4** (the eighth color in the first row). The Documentation sheet tab has a gold highlight.
4. Click the **Sales** sheet tab to make that the active sheet. The Documentation sheet tab has a solid gold fill color.

Formatting Numbers

Formatting the numerical values in a worksheet makes them easier to read. All cells start out in the **General format**, which displays the value stored in the cell without any extra characters (such as currency symbols or commas) or specialized formatting. The General format is fine for some values, but other numbers are easier to interpret with additional formatting, such as:

- Adding commas to separate thousands within larger numbers
- Changing the number of digits displayed to the right of the decimal point
- Including currency symbols to identify the monetary unit of exchange
- Identifying percentages with the % symbol

All the numbers in the Sales worksheet are in the General format. It is not immediately apparent whether the values represent currency or quantities. Also, values without commas, such as the total revenue 15046400 in cell B5, may be misread.

Applying the Accounting and Currency Formats

Excel supports two monetary formats—Accounting and Currency. Both formats add thousands separators to the values and display two digits to the right of the decimal point. The **Accounting format** places the currency symbol at the left edge of the cell and displays negative numbers within parentheses and zero values with a dash. It also slightly indents the values from the right edge of the cell to allow room for parentheses around negative values. The **Currency format** places the currency symbol directly to the left of the first digit of the monetary value and displays negative numbers with a negative sign. Figure 2–8 compares the two formats for the same set of numbers.

Figure 2–8 Accounting and Currency format

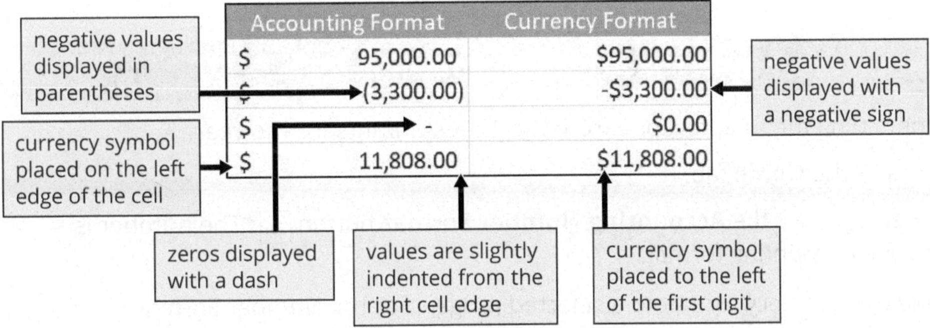

When choosing between the Accounting format and the Currency format, consider accounting principles that govern how financial data should be formatted and displayed. Note that changing the number format does not alter the value stored in the cell.

Proskills

Written Communication: Formatting Monetary Values

Spreadsheets commonly include monetary values. To make these values more readable and comprehensible, keep in mind the following guidelines when formatting the currency data in a worksheet:

- **Format for your audience.** General financial reports often round values to the nearest hundred, thousand, or million. Investors are more interested in the big picture than in exact values. However, for accounting reports, accuracy is important and often legally required. For those reports, be sure to display the exact monetary value.
- **Use thousands separators.** A long string of numbers can be challenging to read. Use the thousands separator to make the number easier to comprehend.
- **Apply the Accounting format to columns of monetary values.** The Accounting format makes columns of numbers easier to read than the Currency format. Use the Currency format for individual cells that are not part of long columns of numbers.
- **Use only two currency symbols in a column of monetary values.** Standard accounting format displays one currency symbol with the first monetary value in the column and optionally displays a second currency symbol with the last value in that column. Use the Accounting format to fix the currency symbols, aligning them in the column.

Following these standard accounting principles will make financial data easier to read both on the screen and in printouts.

Robert wants you to format the total revenue value in cell B5 with the Accounting format.

To display the total revenue in the Accounting format:

1. Click cell **B5** containing the total revenue from the 12 restaurants for the year.
2. On the ribbon, click the **Home** tab.
3. In the Number group, click the **Accounting Number Format** button [$]. The number is formatted with the Accounting format.

   Tip To apply the Currency format to a selected range, click the Number Format arrow and then click Currency (or press CTRL+SHIFT+$).

The value $15,046,400.00 in cell B5 indicates that the total revenue for all the restaurants is more than $15 million. The Accounting format displays both dollars and cents, but that level of precision is not needed in this sales report. You can decrease or increase the number of decimal places displayed without affecting the underlying cell value. To choose a different currency symbol, click the Accounting Number Format arrow and then click the currency symbol you want.

Robert wants you to hide the digits to the right of the decimal point.

To change the number of decimal places displayed in cell B5:

1. Make sure cell **B5** is still selected. You'll change remove the decimal places from this cell.
2. Click the **Decrease Decimal** button [.00→.0] twice. The cents value for the total revenue are hidden, and cell B5 displays $15,046,400.

The Comma style is identical to the Accounting format except that it does not place a currency symbol on the left edge of the cell. A general approach with financial reports is to apply the Accounting format only to the top and bottom values of a long column and then format the other values with the Comma style to add comma separators and cents values. The advantage of using the Comma style and the Accounting format together is that the numbers and the commas will be aligned within the column. Also, this approach streamlines the worksheet, since the same currency symbols are not repeated down an entire column of financial data.

The next two values in column B are the total expenses from the 12 restaurants and those restaurants' total net profit or loss (equal to the total revenue minus the total expenses). You'll format the total expenses and net profit/loss values with the Comma style, which adds a thousands separator and cents values to numbers. Then you'll decrease the number of decimal places to hide the cents values.

To apply the Comma style to financial data:

1. Select the range **B6:B7** containing the total expenses and net profit/loss values.
2. On the Home tab, in the Number group, click the **Comma Style** button. A comma separator and cent values are added to the numbers.
3. Click the **Decrease Decimal** button twice to hide the two digits to the right of the decimal point.
4. Click cell **B8** to deselect the range. Refer to Figure 2–9.

Figure 2–9 Accounting format and Comma style added to financial data

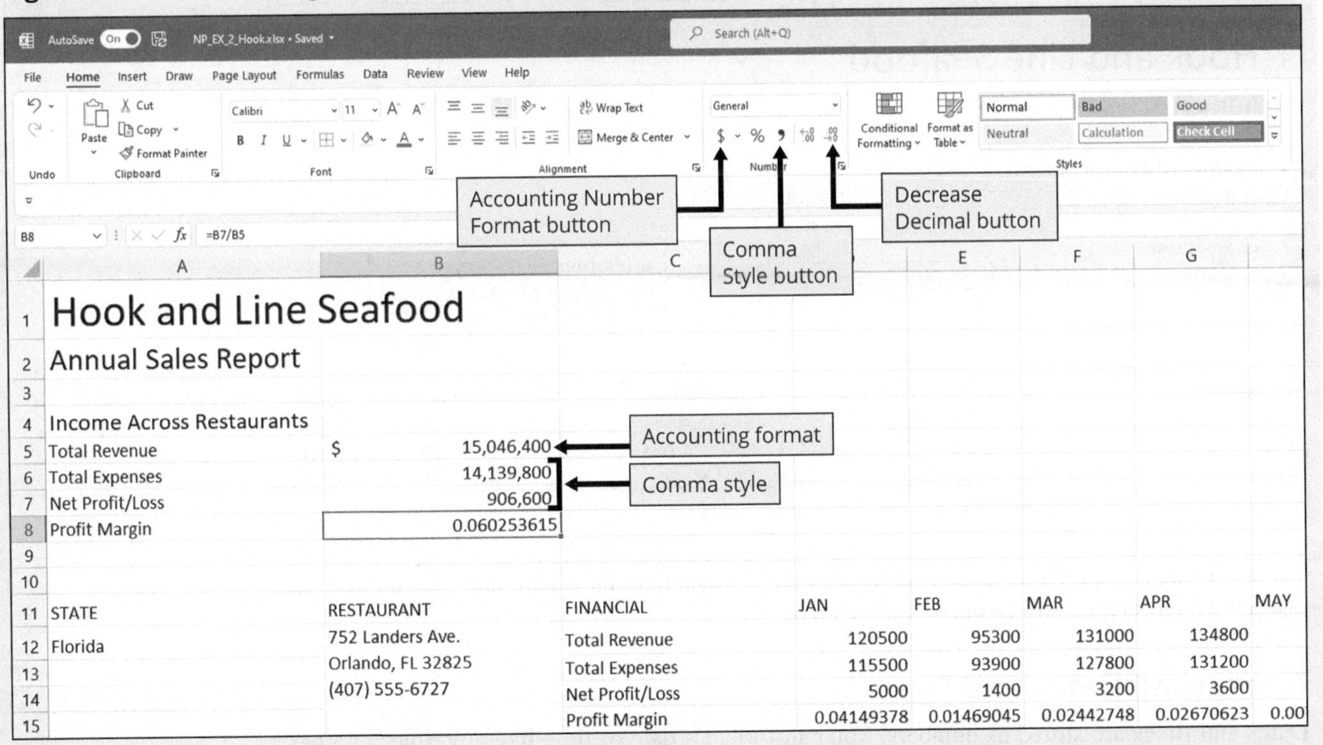

Formatting Percentages

To format a percentage with no decimal places, you use the Percent Style button. For example, the number 0.124 would be formatted as 12%. You can change how many decimal places are displayed in the cell by increasing the number of decimal places displayed in the cell.

The final entry in the Income Across Restaurants section of the worksheet is the company's profit margin. A company's profit margin is equal to the net profit or loss divided by the total revenue. Profit margins are displayed as percentages (the percentage of total revenue that is profit). Restaurants often achieve profit margins of 4% to 7% on their sales. The financial statement already includes a formula to calculate profit margin for the entire franchise and for each restaurant's monthly sales. You'll format this value as a percentage.

To format the overall profit margin as a percentage:

1. If it is not already selected, click cell **B8** to select it.
2. On the Home tab in the Number group, click the **Percent Style** button. The profit margin is displayed as 6%.
3. In the Number group, click the **Increase Decimal** button twice. The percentage now includes two decimal places—6.03%. Refer to Figure 2–10.

Figure 2–10 Percent style applied

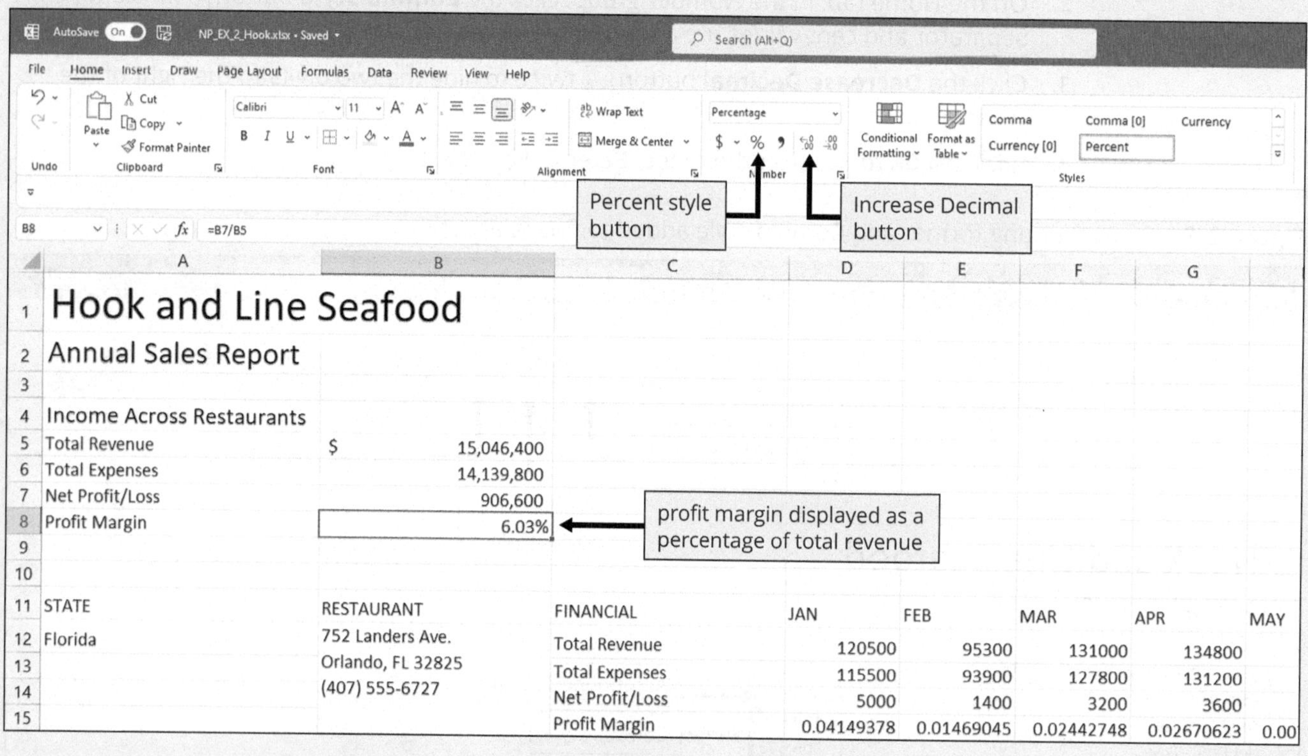

The financial report more clearly reveals that the 12 restaurants have a bit more than a 6% profit margin, which is typical for businesses of this type.

Formatting Dates and Times

Dates and times are stored as numbers. You can format a date or time like any other number without affecting its underlying value in the cell. The **Short Date format** displays dates in the form *mm/dd/yyyy* and the **Long Date format** displays dates with day of the week and the full month name as a text and the day and the year in numbers.

Robert wants you to display the date in the Documentation sheet in the Long Date format.

To format the date in the Documentation sheet with the Long Date format:

1. Go to the **Documentation** sheet, and then select cell **B5**.
2. On the Home tab, in the Number group, click the **Number Format arrow** to display a list of number formats, and then click **Long Date**. The weekday, month name, day, and year appear in cell B5.

   Tip To view the numeric value of a date and time, apply the General format to the cell.

Other built-in numeric formats in Excel include:

- **Time** for displaying time values in a 12-hour time format
- **Fraction** for displaying decimals as fractions to a specified number of digits
- **Scientific** for displaying numeric values in scientific notation
- **Text** for displaying numeric values as text

Excel also has customizable formats that you can modify to fit a wide variety of situations. In the Number group, click the Number Format arrow, and then click More Number Formats to create a custom format.

Copying and Pasting Formats

You formatted the overall sales values in the range B5:B8, but the monthly sales figures for each restaurant in the range D12:P59 are still in the General format. Rather than repeat the same steps to format the monthly sales results, you can copy and paste the formats you just applied.

Copying Formats with the Format Painter

The **Format Painter** copies and pastes formatting from one cell or range to another. The cells with the formatting you want to copy are called the **source range**. The cells where you want to paste the formatting are called the **destination range**. The Format Painter does not copy formulas or values. If the destination range is larger than the source range, the copied format will be repeated across and down the destination range until all cells in the range are formatted.

You will use the Format Painter to copy the formats from the range B5:B8 into the table of monthly sales for the restaurants in the chain.

To copy and paste monthly sales formats with the Format Painter:

1. Go to the **Sales** worksheet, and then select the range **B5:B8**. This is the source range with formats you want to copy.
2. On the Home tab, in the Clipboard group, click the **Format Painter** button. The pointer changes to the Format Painter pointer.
3. Select the range **D12:P59** containing the monthly sales data for each restaurant. This the destination range where the copied formats will be pasted. The copied format is repeated until it fills the entire range. Refer to Figure 2-11.

Figure 2–11 Formats copied and pasted

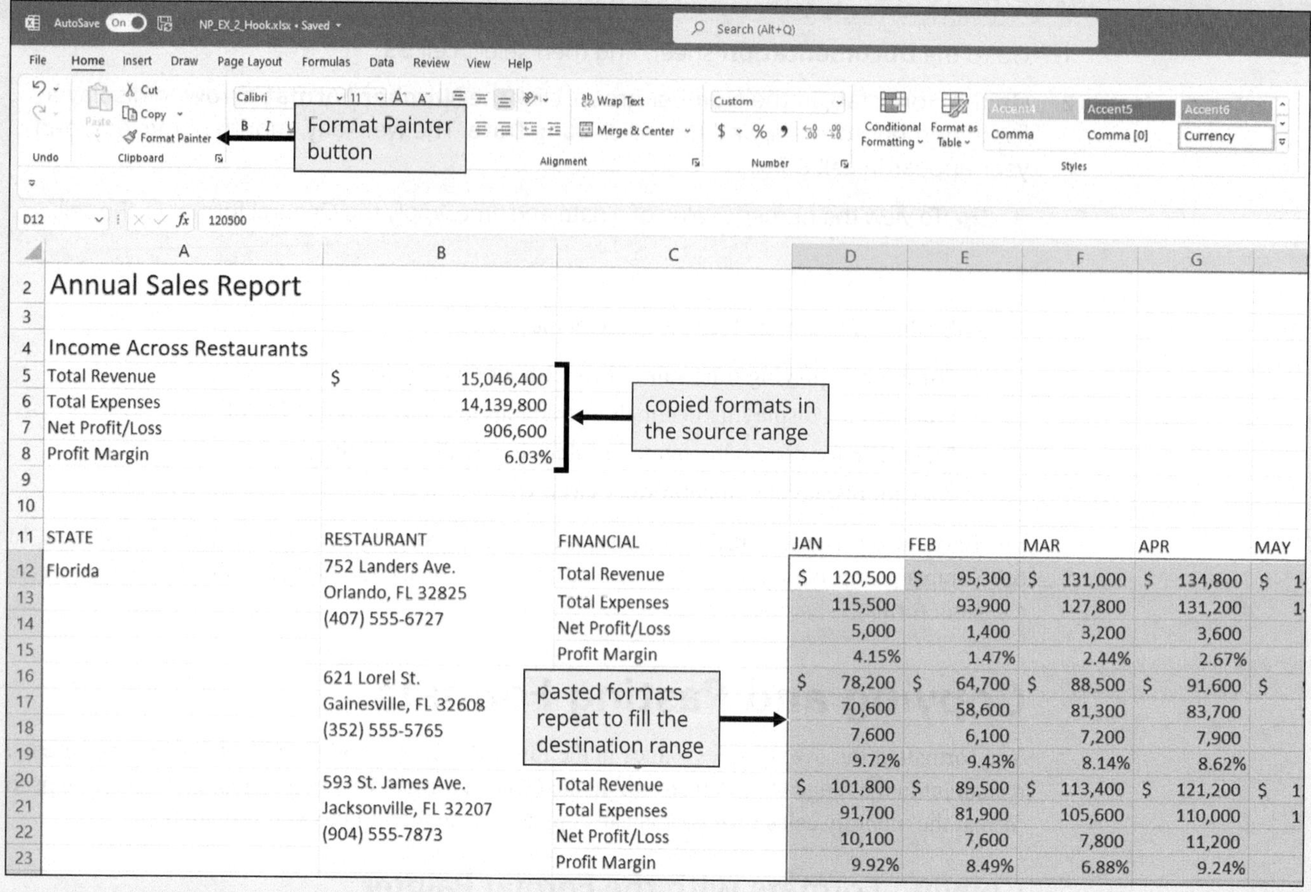

Tip To copy and paste the formats into several nonadjacent ranges, select the source range, double-click the Format Painter button, select destination ranges, and then press ESC to turn off the Format Painter.

You can also use the Format Painter to copy and paste formats between worksheets. You'll use the Format Painter to copy the title and subheading formats in the Documentation sheet to the same title and subheading in the Sales worksheet.

To copy and paste formats between worksheets:

1. Go to the **Documentation** sheet.
2. Select the range **A1:A2** containing the formatted title and subheading.
3. On the Home tab, in the Clipboard group, click the **Format Painter** button. The selected formats are copied.
4. Go to the **Sales** worksheet, and then select the range **A1:A2** to paste the formats. The title and subheading formats match the Documentation sheet.

   The green font color from the word "Seafood" was not included in the pasted formats because the Format Painter does not copy and paste formats of text within a cell. You'll add that formatting to the cell A1.
5. Double-click cell **A1** to enter Edit mode, select **Seafood**, and then change the font color to the **Light Green** standard color.
6. Press **ENTER** to exit Edit mode and select cell A2.

The format of the company title and the subheading on the Sales worksheet now matches the title and subheading in the Documentation sheet.

Copying Formats with the Paste Options Button

Another way to copy and paste formats is with the Paste Options button (Ctrl), which provides options for pasting only values, only formats, or a combination of values and formats. Each time a copied range is pasted, the Paste Options button appears in the lower-right corner of the destination range. Clicking the Paste Options buttons opens a list of options; refer to Figure 2–12. When you point to an icon in the Paste Options list, a ScreenTip will appear explaining the meaning of the icon and its impact on pasting the copied cell range.

Figure 2–12 Paste Options list

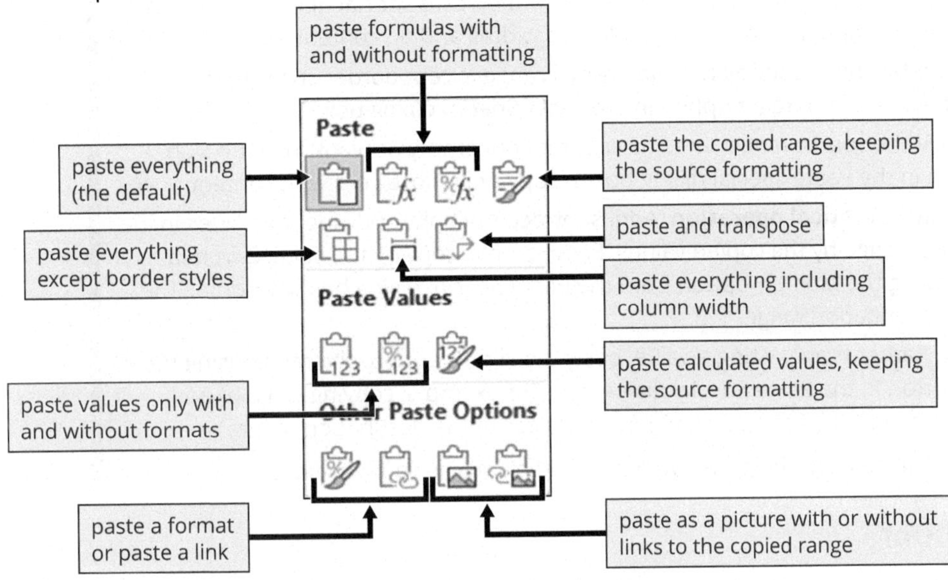

Copying Formats with Paste Special

Paste Special give you more control over what is pasted. To use Paste Special, copy a range of cells, select the range to paste the copied content, click the Paste arrow in the Clipboard group on the Home tab or right-click the selected range, and then click Paste Special. The Paste Special dialog box opens; refer to Figure 2–13.

Figure 2–13 Paste Special options

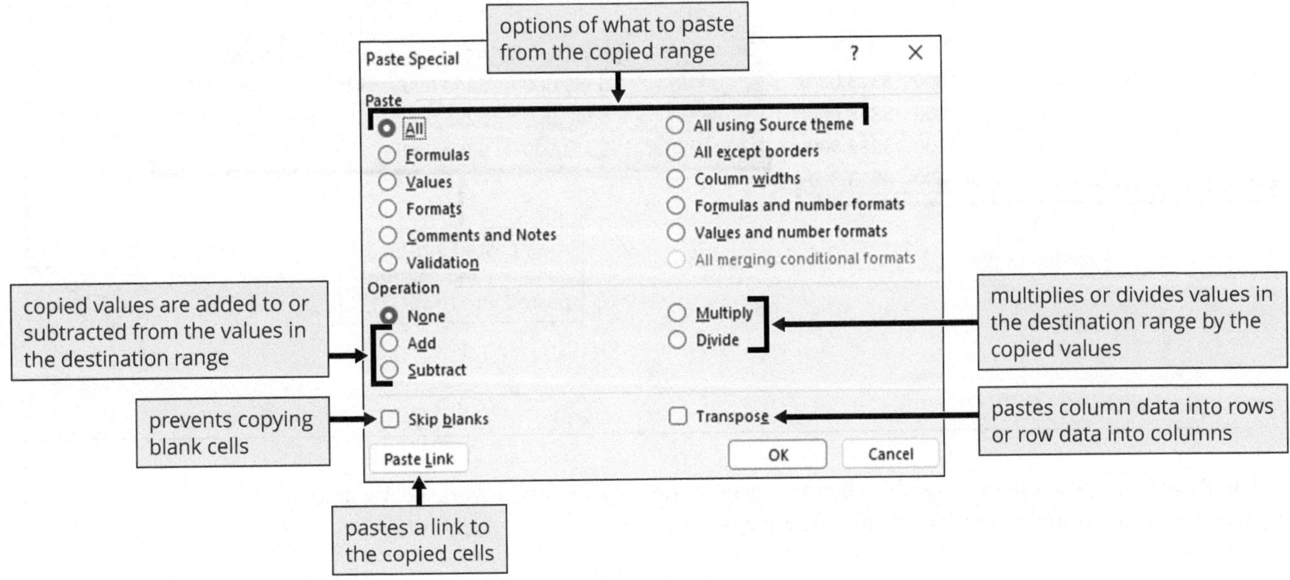

By default, Excel pastes everything except column widths.

Insight

Performing Special Tasks with Paste Special

Paste Special gives you a large amount of control over what is pasted into a range. You can also use Paste Special to modify cell values and formulas. The following are a few special tasks you can perform using Paste Special:

- **Paste values only.** Rather than pasting cell formulas and formatting, paste only the calculated values from the source range by selecting the Values option in the Paste Special dialog box. Any formatting already applied to the destination range is unaffected.
- **Paste column widths.** Copy the source range containing the column widths to duplicate and then select the destination range. In the Paste Special dialog box, select the Column widths option to paste only columns widths and no content.
- **Paste with no borders.** Copy all formats from a range except border styles by selecting the All except borders option in the Paste Special dialog box.
- **Skip blanks.** If the source range contains cells that are empty or blank, use the Skip Blanks option in the Paste Special dialog box to copy only those cells with content.
- **Perform a mathematical operation.** Add, subtract, multiply, or divide the values in the destination range by the copied values. For example, copying the value 2 from a cell and choosing the Multiply option from the Paste Special dialog box will double the values in the destination range.
- **Paste a link.** Rather than pasting a value, paste a cell reference to the range using the Paste Link button in the Paste Special dialog box. For example, copying cell B10 and pasting a link, places the formula =B10 into every cell of the destination range.

These Paste Special features help you work more efficiently as you worksheets.

Transposing Data

Data values are often arranged in a rectangular grid. However, you might want to change the orientation of that grid, switching rows for columns and columns for row. You can do this with the Transpose option. In Figure 2–14, a range of sales data that was copied and then pasted so that the rows and columns are transposed with the store data switched from the rows to the columns and the month data switched from columns to rows. Cell formulas and formats are automatically adjusted for the data's new orientation.

Figure 2–14 Pasted range transposed

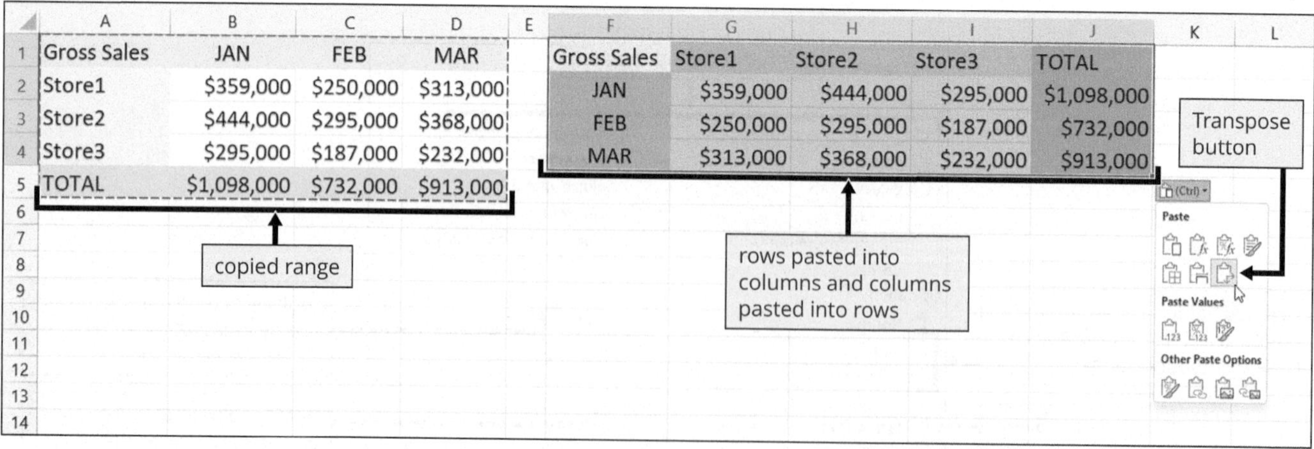

The Paste Transpose option is useful when you want to quickly modify a worksheet's layout without redoing the formulas and formats to reflect the new layout.

Working with Border Styles

Accountants follow specific style rules to distinguish financial figures representing raw data from those figures representing calculated values. Subtotals calculated from a column of values are underlined. A grand total calculated from several subtotals has a double underline. The financial term "the bottom line" refers to this accounting practice of using underlines to indicate the final and most important calculation from a column of figures. You can use borders to apply these accounting practices to workbooks.

To add borders to cells, you use the Borders button in the Font group on the Home tab. You can also use your mouse or stylus to draw borders around a cell or range by clicking the Borders arrow, and then clicking Draw Border or Draw Border Grid.

You will use border styles to format Robert's financial report, adding a single bottom border to the net profit and loss value calculated from all restaurants in the Hook and Line Seafood chain and a double bottom border to the profit margin from all the chain restaurants. The profit margin represents "the bottom line" for Robert's financial analysis.

To add border styles to the restaurants' financial summaries:

1. Click cell **B7** containing the net profit and loss for the company across all restaurants.
2. On the Home tab, in the Font group, click the **Border arrow** to display a list of border style options.
3. Click **Bottom Border**. A single black line is added at the bottom of the cell.
4. Click cell **B8** containing the profit margin for the company.
5. In the Font group, click the **Border arrow**, and then click **Bottom Double Border**. A double black line is added to the bottom of the cell.
6. Select the range **B5:B8** containing the cells you just formatted. You'll copy these border styles to the table of monthly sales for each restaurant.
7. On the Home tab, in the Clipboard group, click the **Format Painter** button.
8. Select the range **D12:P59** to paste the copied formats into the table.
9. Click cell **A10** to deselect the range. Refer to Figure 2–15.

Figure 2–15 Border styles copied and pasted

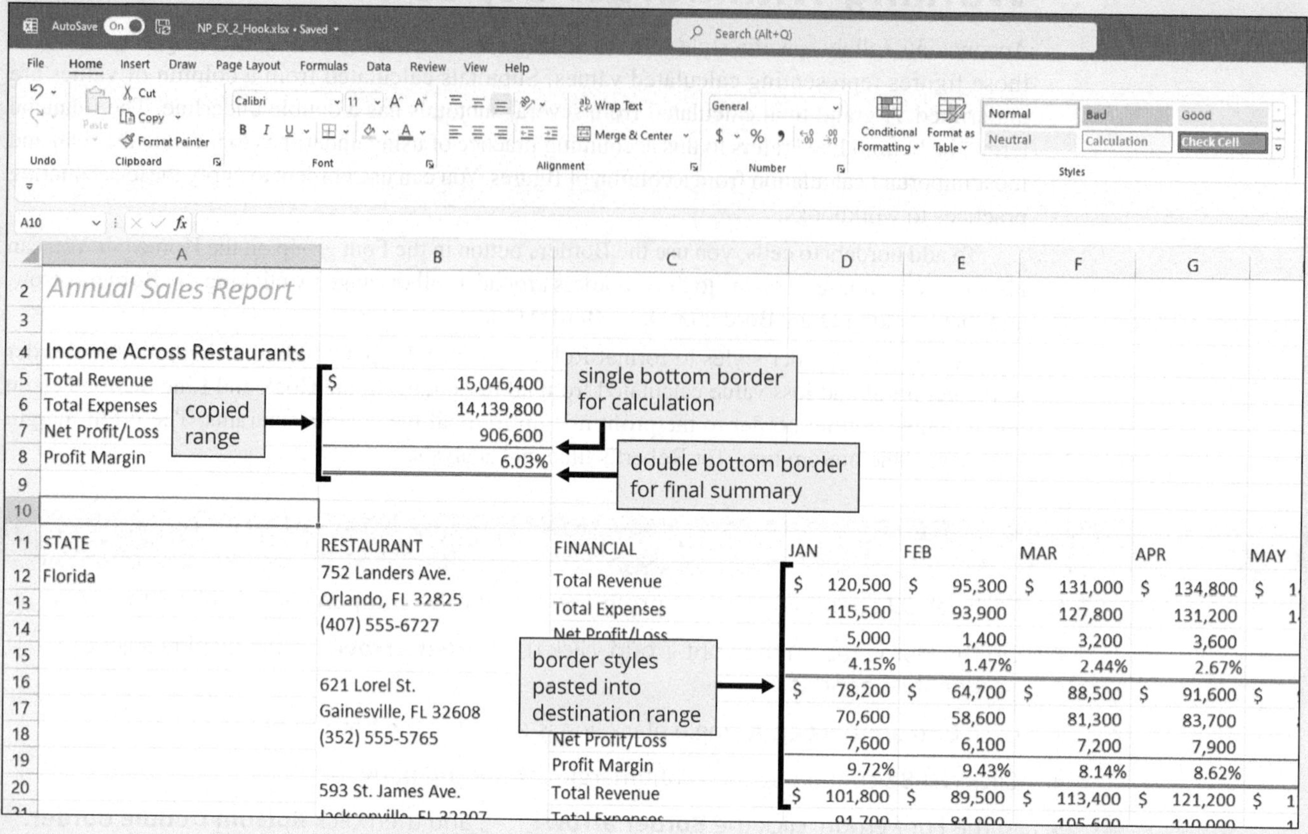

Border styles can be customized by changing their color, thickness, and placement within a range of cells. You can also add different border styles to a range of cells using the More Borders option from the Border button.

Robert wants to add borders around the financial labels, the address of each restaurant and state name. You will use the More Borders option to set a border style for those cells.

To add borders to the financial labels and restaurant names and addresses:

1. Click cell **C14** containing the Net Profit/Loss label.
2. On the Home tab, in the Font group, click the **Border arrow** to display the list of border options, and then click **Bottom Border**. A bottom border is added to that cell.
3. Select the range **A12:C15** containing the labels of the state name, restaurant address, and financial category.
4. In the Font group, click the **Border arrow** to display the list of border options, and then click **More Borders**. The Format Cells dialog box opens to the Border tab, displaying a preview of the border appearance.
5. In the Line Style section, click the **single border line** at the bottom of the first column of border styles to select it, if necessary.

6. In the Border section, click the outside left line, vertical middle line, and outside right line of the border preview to apply the border style to those edges.

7. In the Line Style section, click the **double border line** at the bottom of the second column of border styles to select it.

8. In the Border section, click the bottom edge of the border preview to add a double bottom to the cells. Refer to Figure 2–16.

Figure 2–16 Border tab in the Format Cells dialog box

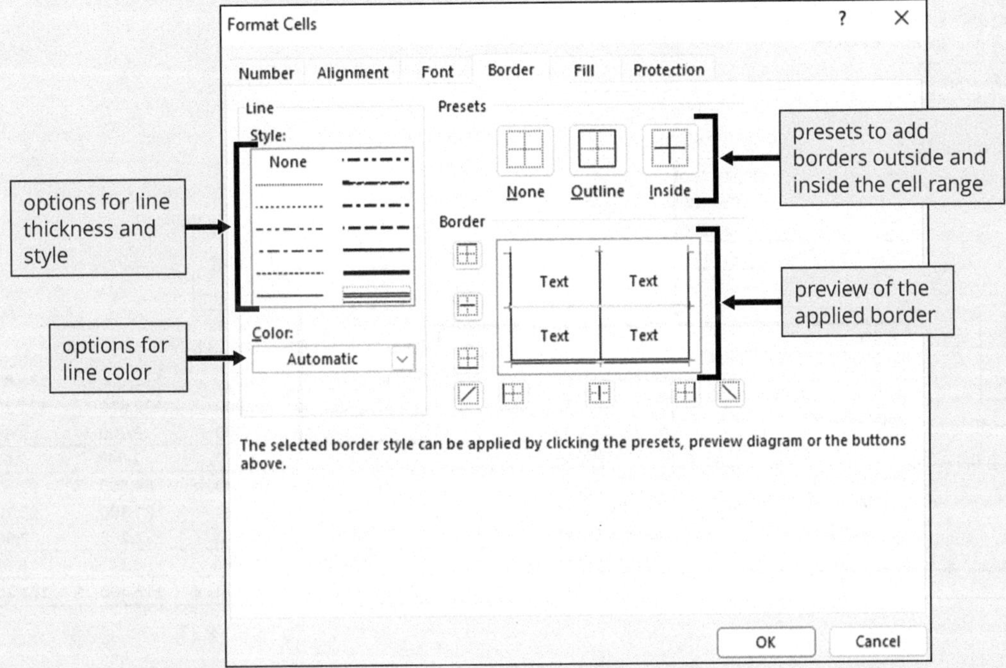

9. Click **OK**. The border styles are applied to the range A12:C15.

> **Trouble?** If you make a mistake, you can erase borders from the worksheet. On the Home tab, in the Font group, click the Border button, and then click Erase Border. The pointer changes to an eraser. Drag the eraser over any border you want to remove.

10. Make sure the range A12:C15 is still selected, and then use the Format Painter to copy the format from the selected range to the range **A16:C59**. The border styles are applied to all the labels in the financial table.

11. Click cell **A1** to deselect the range. Refer to Figure 2–17.

Figure 2–17 Borders applied to the table labels

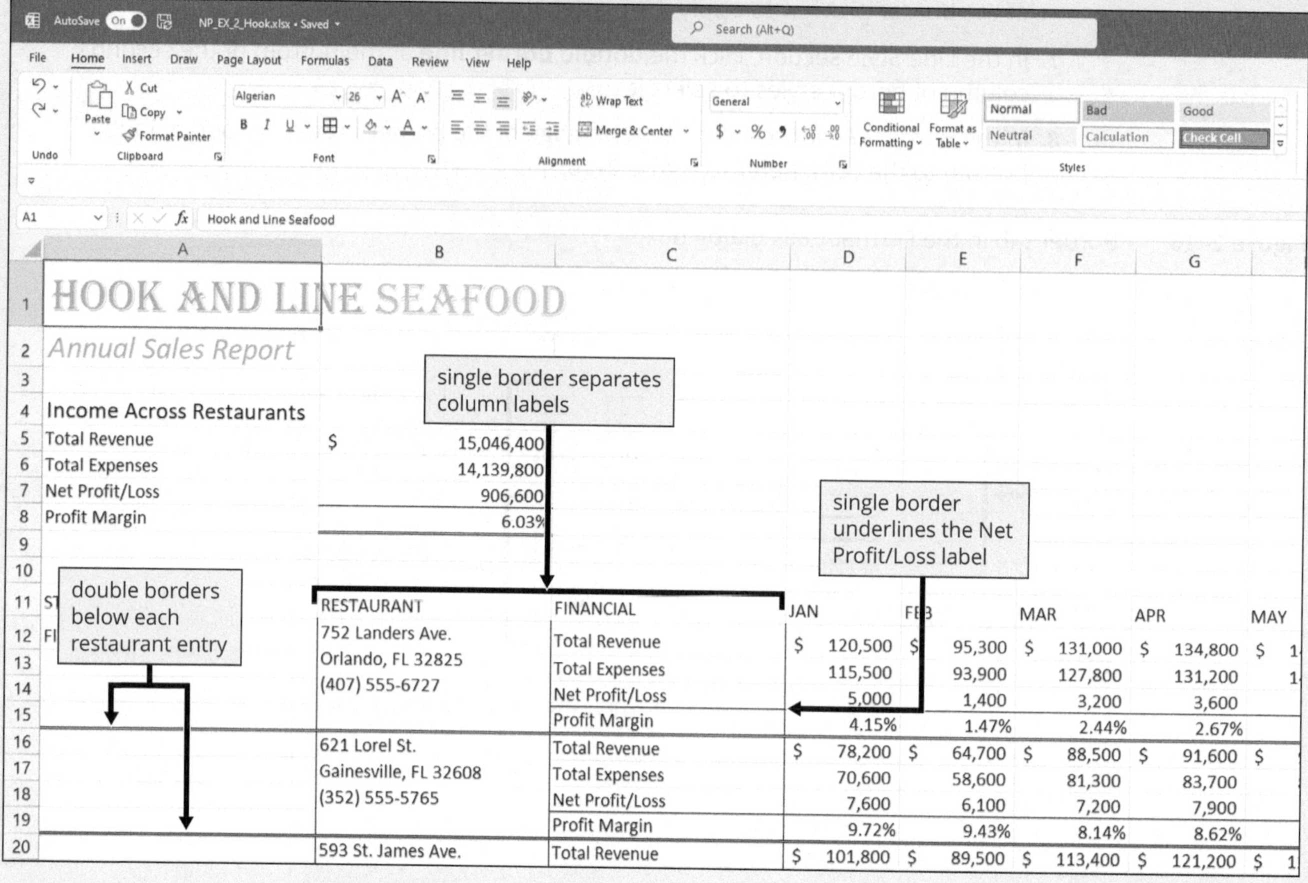

Aligning Cell Contents

By default, text aligns with the left edge of the cell and numbers align with the right edge. Both text and numbers are aligned vertically at the bottom edge of the cell. You might want to change the alignment to make the text and numbers more readable or visually appealing. In general, you should center column titles, left-align other text, and right-align numbers to keep their decimal places lined up within a column. Figure 2–18 describes the buttons located in the Alignment group on the Home tab that you use to set these alignment options.

Figure 2–18 Cell alignment options

Button	Name	Description
	Top Align	Aligns the cell content with the cell's top edge
	Middle Align	Vertically centers the cell content within the cell
	Bottom Align	Aligns the cell content with the cell's bottom edge
	Align Left	Aligns the cell content with the cell's left edge
	Align Center	Horizontally centers the cell content within the cell
	Align Right	Aligns the cell content with the cell's right edge
	Decrease Indent	Decreases the size of the indentation used in the cell
	Increase Indent	Increases the size of the indentation used in the cell
	Orientation	Rotates the cell content to any angle within the cell
	Wrap Text	Forces the cell text to wrap within the cell borders
	Merge & Center	Merges the selected cells into a single cell

The date in the Documentation sheet is right aligned in cell B5 because Excel treats dates and times as numbers. Robert wants you to left-align the date in the Documentation sheet and center some of the column titles in the Sales worksheet.

To left-align the date and center labels:

1. Go to the **Documentation** sheet, and then click cell **B5**.
2. On the Home tab, in the Alignment group, click the **Align Left** button. The date shifts to the left edge of the cell, matching the other entries.
3. Go to the **Sales** worksheet, and then select the range **D11:P11** containing some of the column labels in the financial table.
4. In the Alignment group, click the **Center** button. The column labels are centered horizontally within their cells.

Indenting Cell Text

Text at the left edge of a cell or numbers at the right edge of a cell can appear crowded at the cell's border. You can add more space between a cell's content and border by indenting. Increasing the indent moves cell content away from the border. Decreasing the indent moves cell content closer to the border.

Robert wants the restaurant addresses in column B and the financial categories in column C to be indented two spaces from the left borders of their cells. He also wants that text to be vertically aligned in the middle of their cells.

To indent the content of the addresses and financial categories:

1. In the Sales worksheet, select the range **B12:C59** containing the restaurant addresses and the financial categories.
2. On the Home tab, in the Alignment group, click the **Increase Indent** button twice. The selected text moves two spaces to the right within their cells.

   Tip To shift cell contents closer to the border, click the Decrease Indent button in the Alignment group on the Home tab.

3. In the Alignment group, click the **Middle Align** button. The text is vertically centered in the middle of the cells.
4. Click cell **A10** to deselect the range. Refer to Figure 2–19.

Figure 2–19 Cell content aligned in the worksheet

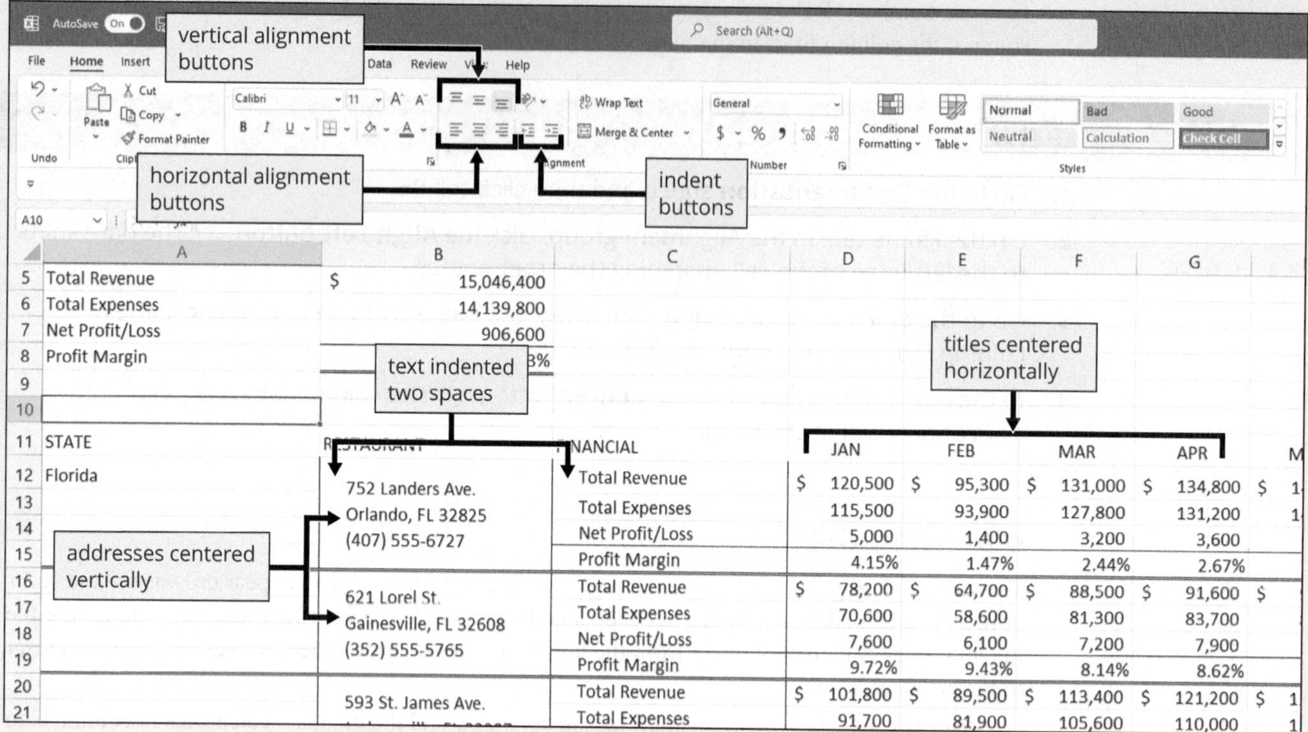

Merging Cells

So far, every cell is in a single row and column. You can also merge, or combine, a range of cells into a single cell. The merged cell can span multiple rows and/or columns. When a range is merged, only the content from the upper-left cell of the range is retained. The upper-left cell also becomes the cell reference for the merged range. For example, if you merge the range A10:C15 into a single cell, its merged cell reference is A10. References to cells below and to the right of the merged cell do not change. Below the merged cell A10, the cell references for the next three cells remain A16, B16, and C16, and the references to the five cells to the right remain D10 through D15. But no cells that have the reference B11 or C12 because those cells are merged into cell A10.

You can align the content of a merged cell by clicking the Merge & Center arrow in the Alignment group on the Home tab, and then using one of the following options:

- **Merge & Center**—merges the range into one cell and horizontally centers the content
- **Merge Across**—merges each row in the selected range across the columns in the range
- **Merge Cells**—merges the range into a single cell but does not horizontally center the cell merged
- **Unmerge Cells**—reverses a merge, returning the merged cell to a range of individual cells

The Sales worksheet already has some merged cells. For example, the address for the first restaurant spans the range B12:B15 but is merged into the single cell B12. Similarly, the address for second restaurant is in the merged cell B16, which includes range B16:B19. The merged cells allow the restaurant addresses to line up with the rows containing their financial information. This makes the connection between the data clearer.

Column A in the table of monthly restaurant financials contains the names of the three states in the report. Robert wants you to merge those cells so that the state name is in a single cell.

To merge each state into a single cell:

1. In the Sales worksheet, select the range **A12:A31** containing the cells for the five Florida restaurants.
2. On the Home tab, in the Alignment group, click the **Merge & Center** button. The five cells are merged into a single cell with the reference A12. "Florida" is centered horizontally in the cell and aligned with the bottom border.
3. Select the range **A32:A43** containing the Georgia restaurants, and then click the **Merge & Center** button. The cells associated with the three Georgia restaurants merge into cell A32. "Georgia" is centered at the bottom of the merged cell.
4. Select the range **A44:A59** containing the Alabama restaurants, and then click the **Merge & Center** button. The cells associated with the four Alabama restaurants are merged and centered into cell A44. Refer to Figure 2–20.

Figure 2–20 Ranges merged into single cells

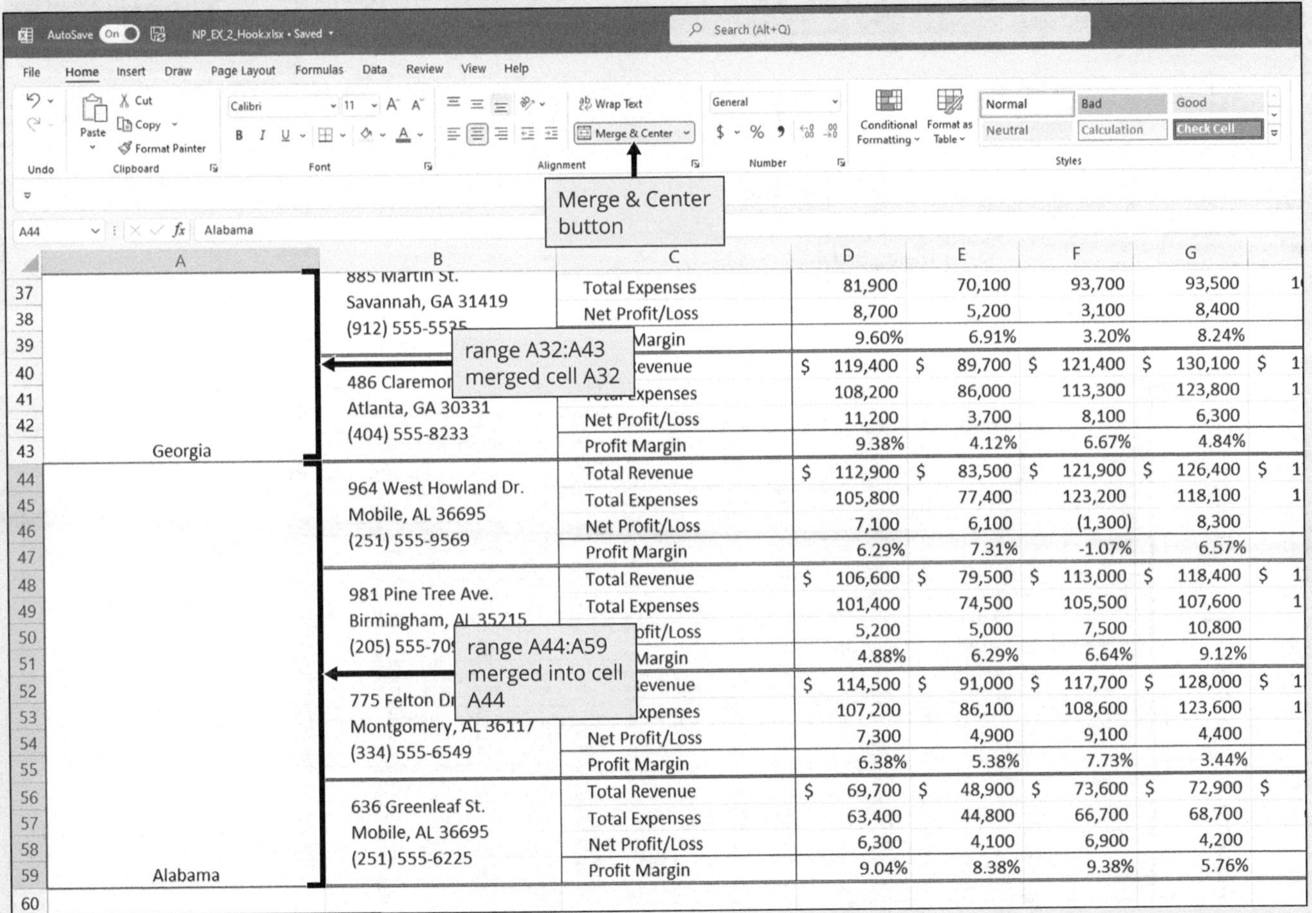

Rotating Text

Text and numbers are displayed horizontally within cells. However, you can rotate cell text to any angle to save space, better connect data, or to visual interest to a worksheet. Merging the state cells better connected the state name with its restaurants. However, the merged cells take up a lot of room. You will remove the extra space by rotating the state names vertically within their cells. You will also increase the font size of the state names.

To rotate and resize the state names in the merged cells:

1. Select the range **A12:A59** containing the three merged cells for the state names of Florida, Georgia, and Alabama.
2. On the Home tab, in the Alignment group, click the **Orientation** button to display a list of rotation options.
3. Click **Rotate Text Up**. The state names rotate 90 degrees counterclockwise.
4. In the Alignment group, click the **Middle Align** button to vertically center the rotated state name.
5. Change the font size to **36** points.
6. Click cell **A1** to select it.
7. Zoom the worksheet to **60%** so the entire formatted table is visible. Refer to Figure 2–21.

Figure 2–21 Rotated cell contents

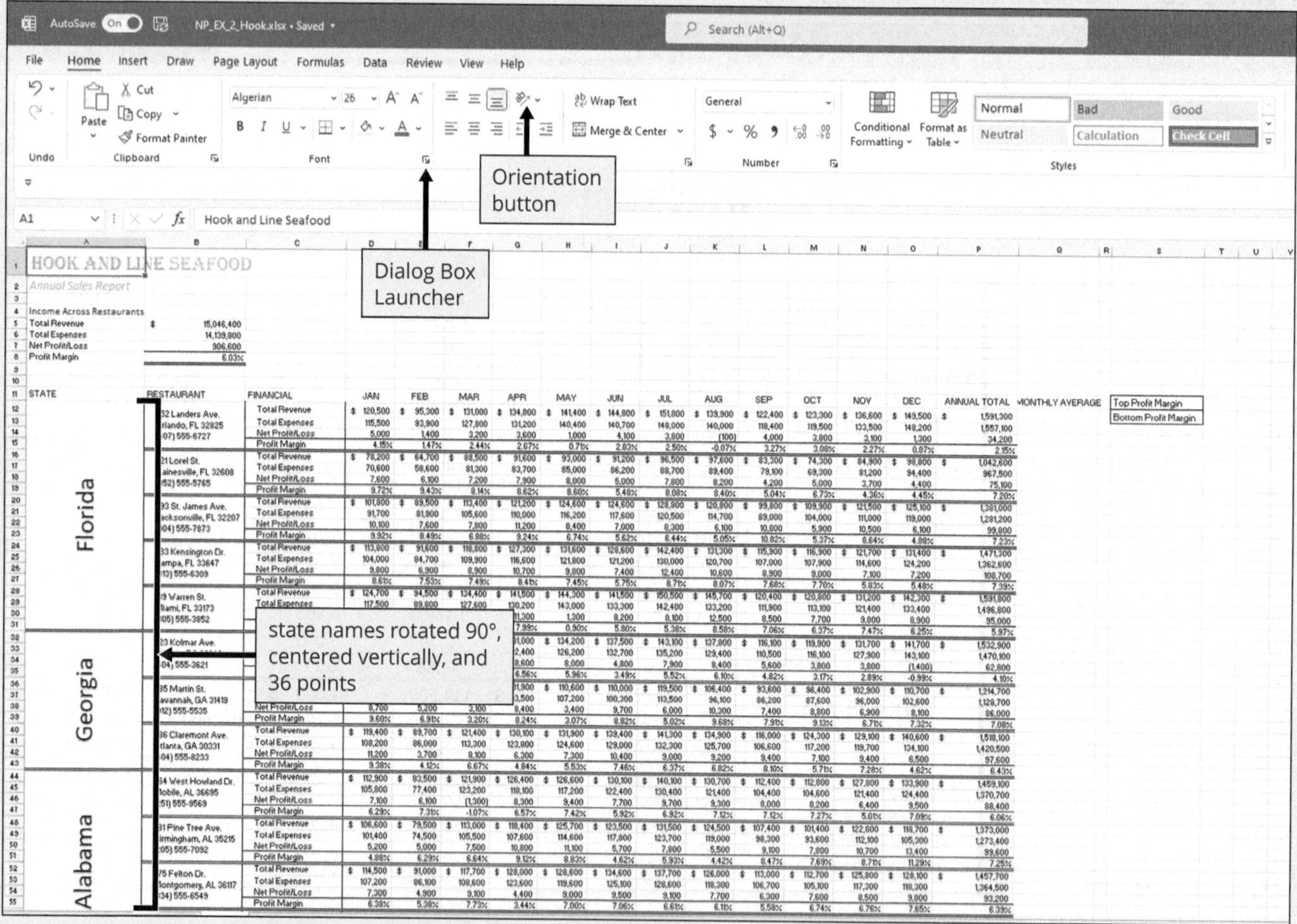

8. Zoom the worksheet back to **140%**.

Exploring the Format Cells Dialog Box

Although many formatting options appear on the ribbon, all these options and more are available in the Format Cells dialog box. The dialog box contains the following six tabs, each focusing on different formatting options:

- **Number**—options for formatting the appearance of numbers, including dates and numbers treated as text such as telephone or Social Security numbers
- **Alignment**—options for how data is aligned within a cell

- **Font**—options for selecting font types, sizes, styles, and other formatting attributes such as underlining and font colors
- **Border**—options for adding and removing cell borders as well as selecting a line style and color
- **Fill**—options for creating and applying background colors and patterns to cells
- **Protection**—options for locking or hiding cells to prevent other users from modifying their contents

You can open the Format Cells dialog box in a variety of ways. You can access it from options on the ribbon, such as when you used the Border tab earlier. You can right-click a selected range and then click Format Cells on the shortcut menu. Or you can click the Dialog Box launcher in the lower-right corner of the Font, Alignment, or Number group on the Home tab.

The final part of the table of monthly restaurants revenue and expenses to be formatted are the column labels in row 11. You will use the Format Cells dialog box to format the labels in white font on a light blue background with a thick bottom border.

To format the revenue and expenses labels with the Format Cells dialog box:

1. Select the range **A11:P11** containing the labels for the table of monthly revenue and expenses for the restaurants.
2. On the Home tab, in the Font group, click the **Dialog Box Launcher** located to the right of the group name (refer to Figure 2–21). The Format Cells dialog box opens with the Font tab displayed.
3. Click the **Color** box to display the available colors, and then click the **White, Background 1** theme color (the first color in the first row).
4. In the Font style list, click **Bold**. Refer to Figure 2–22.

Figure 2–22 Font tab in the Format Cells dialog box

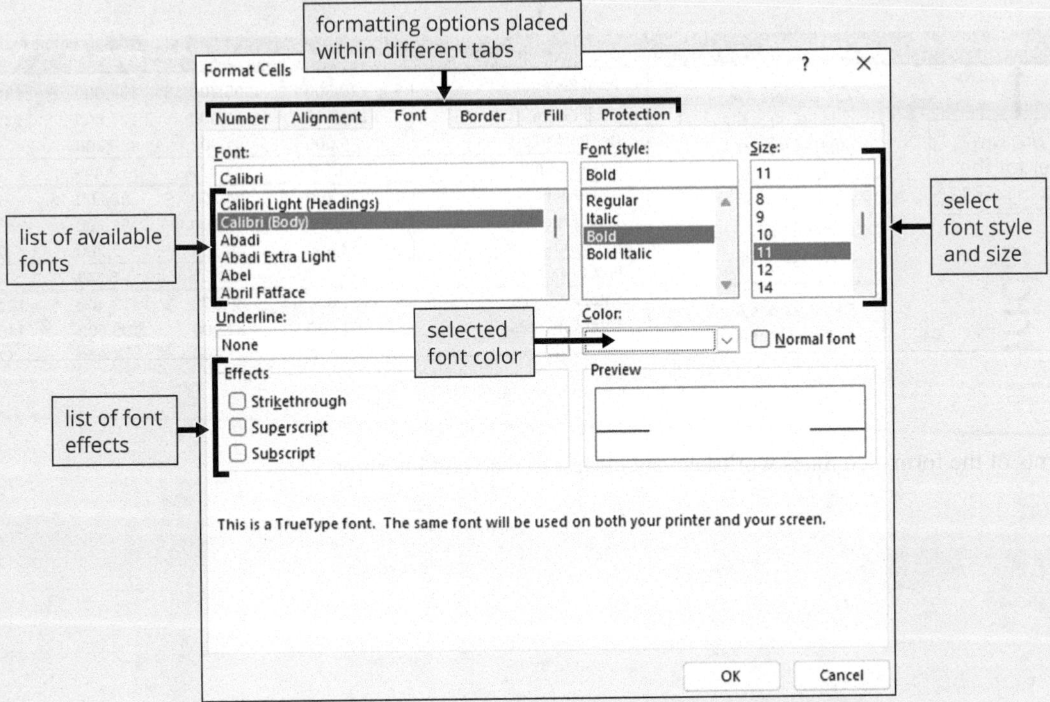

5. Click the **Fill** tab to display background color options.
6. In the Background Color section, click the **Blue, Accent 1** theme color (the fifth color in the first row). The background is set to blue, as previewed in the Sample box.
7. Click the **Border** tab, and then in the Style box, click the **Thick** line (the sixth line in the second column).
8. In the Border section, click the bottom border of the border preview. The thick line style is set for the bottom border.
9. Click **OK** to apply the formatting choices you made in the dialog box to the range A11:P11.
10. Click cell **A1**. Refer to Figure 2–23.

Figure 2–23 Column labels formatted in the worksheet

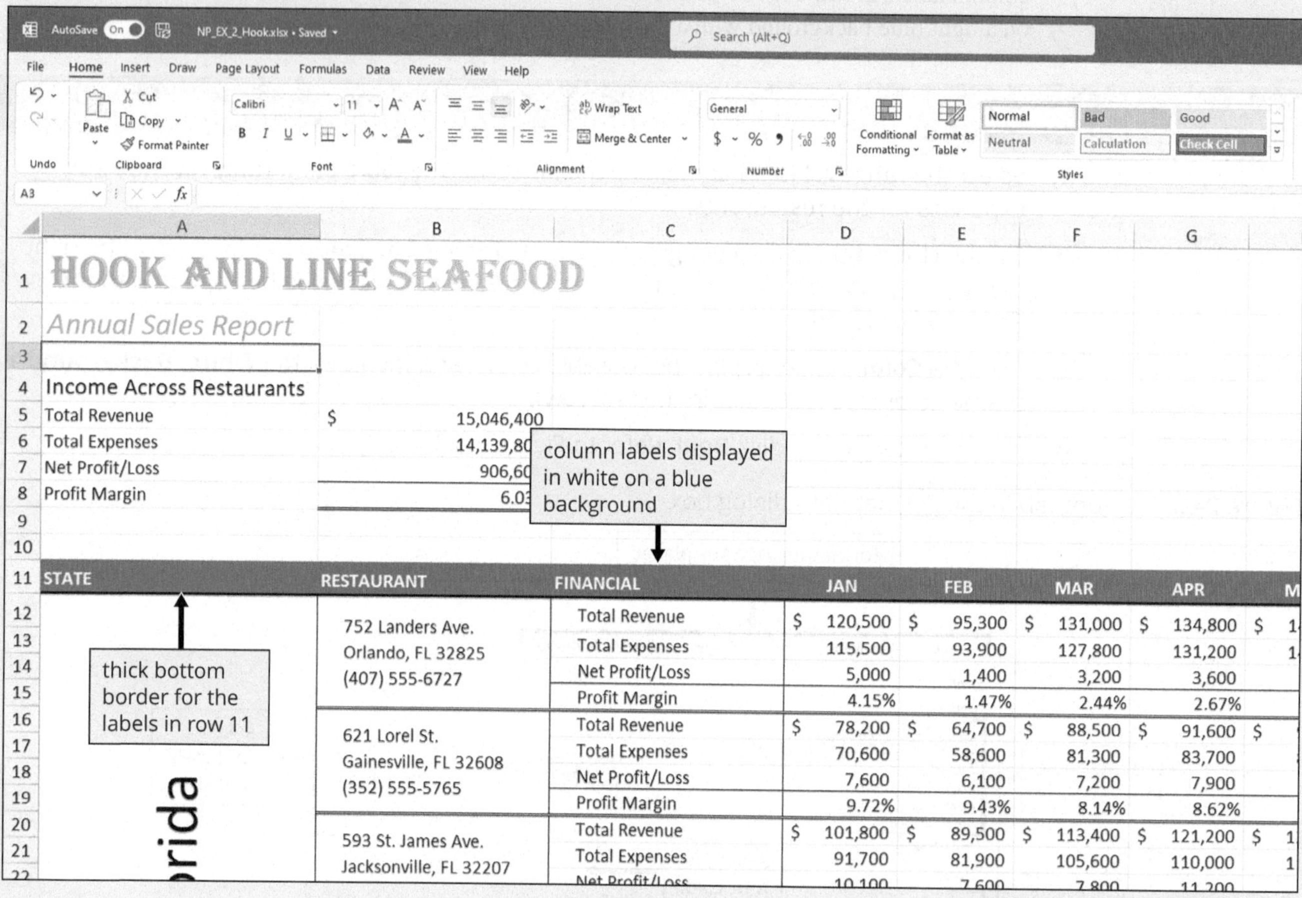

The contents of the formatted Sales worksheet are clearer to read and interpret.

Proskills

Written Communication: Formatting Workbooks for Readability and Appeal

Designing a workbook requires the same care as designing any written document or report. A well-formatted workbook provides a structure and establishes a sense of professionalism with readers. You can improve the readability of your worksheets with the following guidelines:

- **Clearly identify each worksheet's purpose.** Include column or row titles and a descriptive sheet name.
- **Include only one or two topics on each worksheet.** Do not crowd individual worksheets with too much information. Place extra topics on separate sheets. Readers should be able to interpret each worksheet with minimal horizontal and vertical scrolling.
- **Organize worksheets in order of importance.** Place worksheets summarizing findings near the front of the workbook. Place worksheets with detailed and involved analysis near the end as an appendix.
- **Use consistent formatting throughout the workbook.** If negative values appear in red in one worksheet, format them in the same way in all sheets. Also, be consistent in the use of thousands separators, decimal places, and percentages.
- **Pay attention to the format of the printed workbook.** Make sure printouts are legible with informative headers and footers. Check that the printed content is scaled correctly to the page size and that page breaks divide the information into logical sections.

Be aware that much formatting can be intrusive, overwhelming data and making the document less readable. Remember that the goal of formatting is not to make a "pretty workbook" but to accentuate important trends and relationships in the data. A well-formatted workbook should seamlessly convey information to the reader. If the reader is thinking about how the workbook looks, the reader is not thinking about the data.

You have made great progress in formatting Robert's sales report. You will continue this process in the next part of this module. You will apply cell styles and workbook themes to the workbook. You will also use conditional formatting to highlight important results from Robert's financial analysis. Finally, you will explore formatting print versions of workbooks.

Part 2.1 Quick Check

1. What is the difference between a serif font and a sans serif font?
2. What is the difference between a theme color and a standard color?
3. If you need to display a graphic image with your printed workbook, explain why you should not insert the graphic as a background image on the worksheet.
4. What is the General format?
5. How does the Accounting format differ from the Currency format?
6. How do the Short Date format and the Long Date format display dates?
7. Describe three ways of copying a format from one range to another.
8. The range C5:E7 is merged into a single cell. What is the cell reference of the merged cell? What are the cell references to the cells directly below and directly to the right of the merged cell?

Part 2.2 Visual Overview: Designing a Printed Worksheet

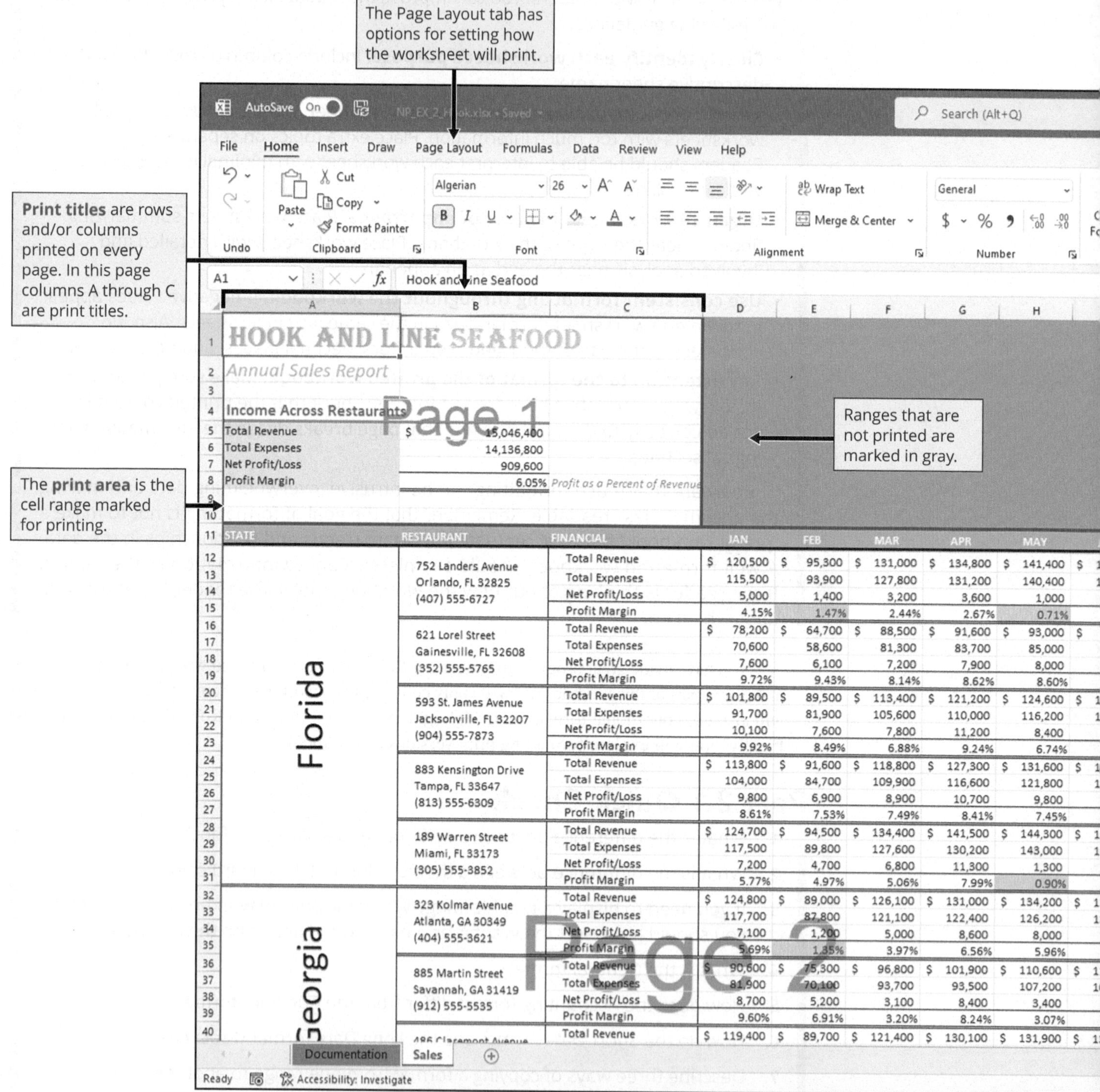

The Page Layout tab has options for setting how the worksheet will print.
Print titles are rows and/or columns printed on every page. In this page columns A through C are print titles.
The **print area** is the cell range marked for printing.
Ranges that are not printed are marked in gray.
Page 1
Page 2

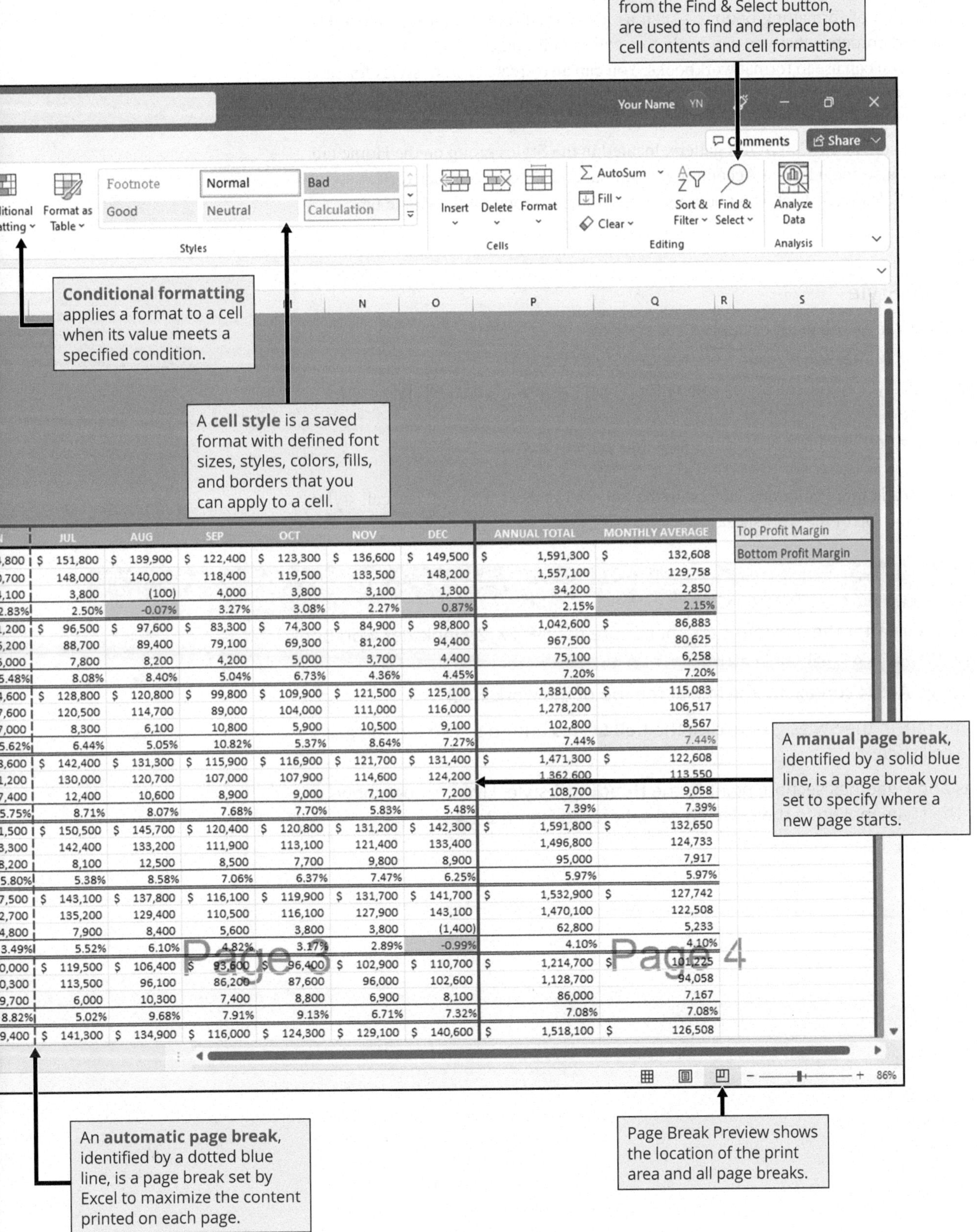
The Find and Replace commands, which are available from the Find & Select button, are used to find and replace both cell contents and cell formatting.
Your Name YN
Comments
Share
Format as Table
Footnote
Normal
Bad
Good
Neutral
Calculation
Styles
Insert
Delete
Format
Cells
AutoSum
Fill
Clear
Sort & Filter
Find & Select
Editing
Analyze Data
Analysis
Conditional formatting applies a format to a cell when its value meets a specified condition.
A **cell style** is a saved format with defined font sizes, styles, colors, fills, and borders that you can apply to a cell.
JUL
AUG
SEP
OCT
NOV
DEC
ANNUAL TOTAL
MONTHLY AVERAGE
Top Profit Margin
Bottom Profit Margin
A **manual page break**, identified by a solid blue line, is a page break you set to specify where a new page starts.
Page 3
Page 4
An **automatic page break**, identified by a dotted blue line, is a page break set by Excel to maximize the content printed on each page.
Page Break Preview shows the location of the print area and all page breaks.

Applying Cell Styles

Cells throughout a workbook often store the same type of data. For example, cells in each worksheet might contain the same heading and subheading, or several worksheets might contain related tables of financial figures. A good design practice is to apply a common format to cells that contain the same type of data.

One way to ensure that similar data is displayed with a consistent format is with cell styles. A cell style is a collection of formatting options—such as a specified font, font size, font styles, font color, fill color, and borders—that you can apply to a cell or cell range. Excel has a library of built-in cell styles that you can use to format workbooks. You can also create custom styles for each workbook. When you apply a cell style, any formatting that is part of the cell style override any formatting previously applied to that range.

All cell styles are listed in the Cell Styles gallery, located in the Styles group on the Home tab. The Cell Styles gallery also includes the Accounting, Comma, and Percent number format styles that you applied to the Sales worksheet using buttons in the Number group on the Home tab.

Reference

Applying a Cell Style

- Select the cell or range you want to apply a cell style to.
- On the Home tab, in the Styles group, click the Cell Styles button.
- Point to each cell style in the Cell Styles gallery for a Live Preview of that cell style on the selected cell or range.
- Click the cell style you want to apply to the selected cell or range.

Robert asks you to add more color and interest to the Sales worksheet. You will use cell styles to format the labels at the top of the worksheet.

To apply cell styles to the labels:

1. If you took a break after the previous part, make sure the NP_EX_2_Hook.xlsx workbook is open and the Sales worksheet is active.
2. Select the range **A4:B4** containing the title at the top of the worksheet.
3. On the Home tab, in the Styles group, click the **Cell Styles** button to expand the gallery of available cell styles.
4. In the Titles and Headings section, point to the **Heading 1** style. Live Preview shows a preview of the style applied to the selected cells. Refer to Figure 2–24.

Figure 2–24 Cell Styles gallery

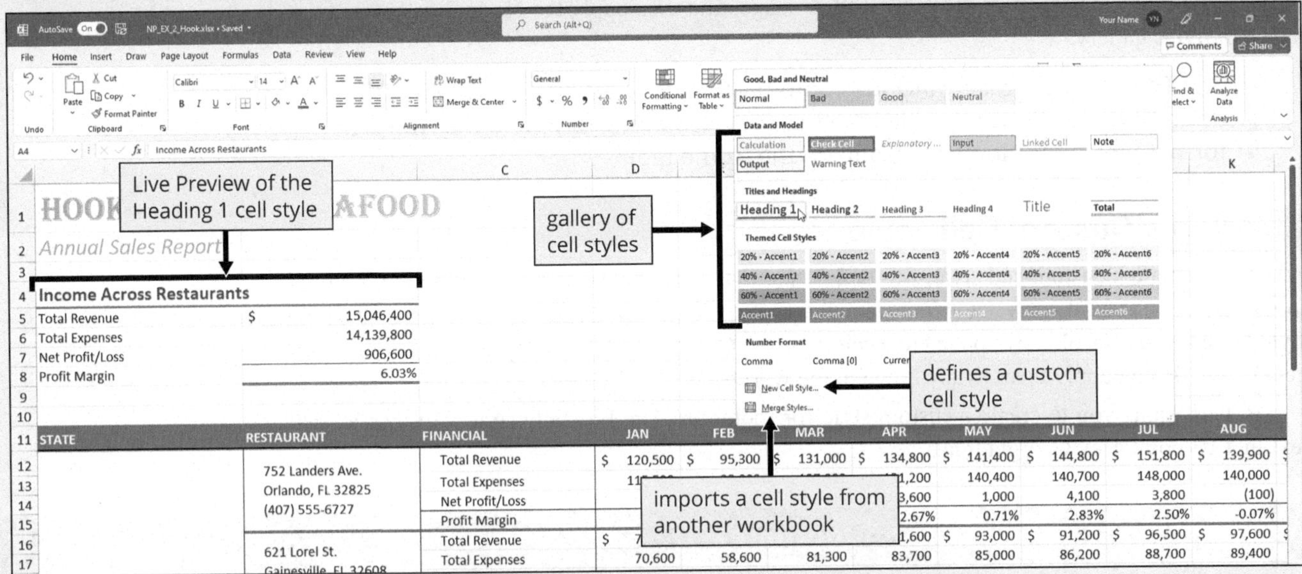

5. Click the **Heading 1** style to apply the style to the range A4:B4.
6. Select the range **A5:A8** containing the financial category labels.
7. In the Styles group, click the **Cell Styles** button, and then click the **20% - Accent 3** style in the Cell Styles gallery.
8. In cell **C8**, enter **Profit as a Percent of Revenue** to add an explanatory note about the meaning of profit margin.
9. Click cell **C8** to select it, click the **Cell Styles** button to open the Cell Styles gallery, and then in the Data and Model section, click the **Explanatory** style. The new note is formatted.
10. Click cell **A1**. Refer to Figure 2–25.

Figure 2–25 Worksheet formatted with cell styles

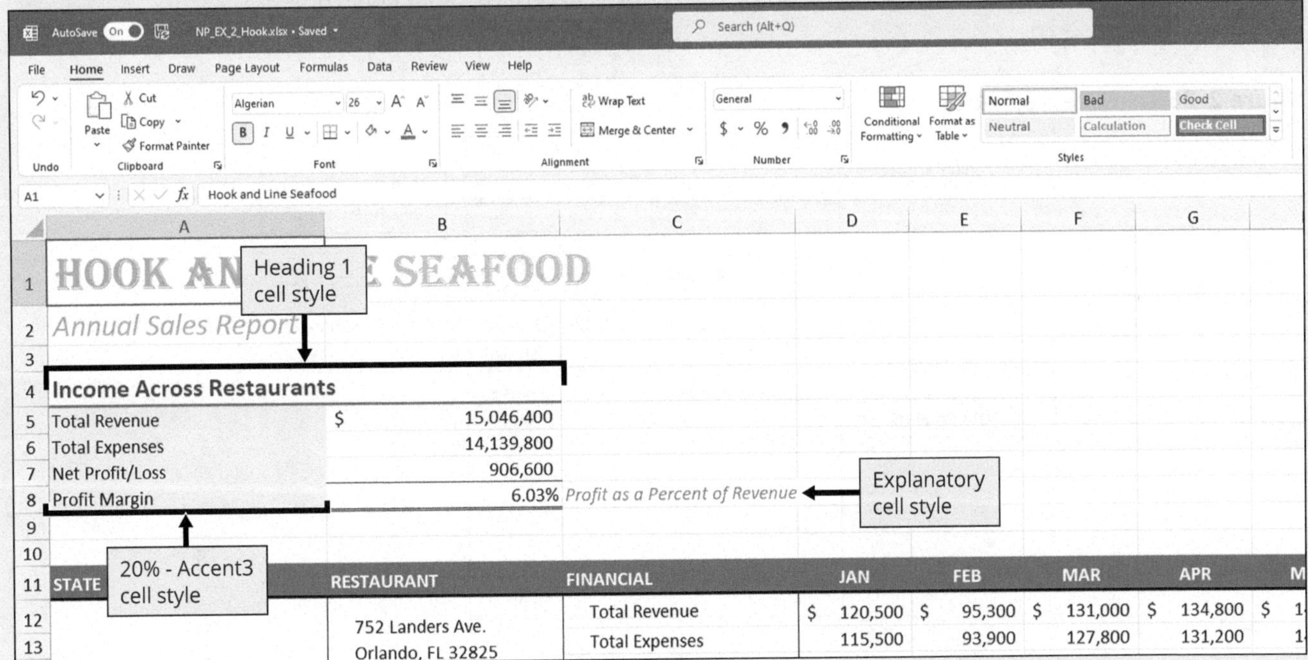

All cells start out formatted with the Normal cell style. To restore cells with other added formatting to the Normal style, select the cell or range, and then apply the Normal cell style from the Cell Styles gallery.

> **Tip** The Cell Style gallery includes Comma, Currency, and Percent styles. Be aware that this Currency style matches the Accounting format in the Number format box in the Numbers group on the Home tab!

Creating a Custom Cell Style

When you create a custom cell style, you define the font, font size, font styles, alignment, number format, borders, and fill you want to include in that style. You can base a new cell style on an existing style or on formatting already applied to a cell or range. Custom cell styles appear in the Cell Styles gallery so you can apply them to any range in the workbook.

Robert wants you to create a custom style for footnotes. The Footnote style will display cell text in a 10-point gray Georgia font.

To create a custom cell style for footnotes:

1. In cell **A61**, enter **Financial figures rounded to nearest hundred dollars.** as the footnote text.
2. Right-click cell **A61**, and then click **Format Cells** on the shortcut menu. The Format Cells dialog box opens.
3. Click the **Font** tab, click **Georgia** in the Font box, and then click **10** in the Size box.
4. Click the **Color** box, and then click the **White, Background 1, Darker 50%** theme color (the last color in the first column).
5. Click **OK** to close the Format Cells dialog box. Cell A61 is still selected.
6. On the Home tab, in the Styles group, click the **Cell Styles** button, and then click **New Cell Style**. The Style dialog box opens. From this dialog box, you name the custom style and select which formatting of the selected cell to include in the custom style.
7. In the Style name box, type **Footnote** as the name for the custom style.
8. In the Style includes section, deselect all of the checkboxes except the Font checkbox. Refer to Figure 2–26.

Figure 2–26 Style dialog box

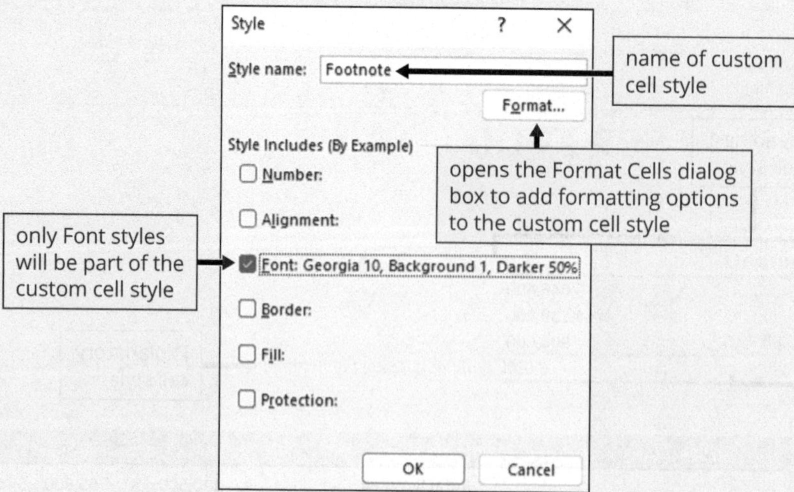

9. Click **OK**. The new style is created and added to the Cell Style gallery.
10. In the Styles group, click the **Cell Styles** button to display the Cell Style gallery, and verify that the Footnote cell style appears in the Custom section at the top of the gallery.
11. With cell A61 still selected, click **Footnote** to apply the custom style to the cell.

You can apply custom cell styles to any cell in the workbook. Robert wants you to add a footnote for the Documentation sheet and format it with the new Footnote style.

To apply the Footnote cell style in the Documentation sheet:

1. Go to the **Documentation** sheet.
2. In cell **A10**, enter **Report presented at the sales conference in Orlando, FL.** as the new footnote text.
3. Click cell **A10**, and then on the Home tab, in the Styles group, click the **Cell Styles** button. The Cell Styles gallery opens and includes the custom Footnote cell style.
4. In the Custom section, click **Footnote**. The text you just entered is formatted in the Footnote cell style. Refer to Figure 2–27.

Figure 2–27 Custom cell style applied to the worksheet

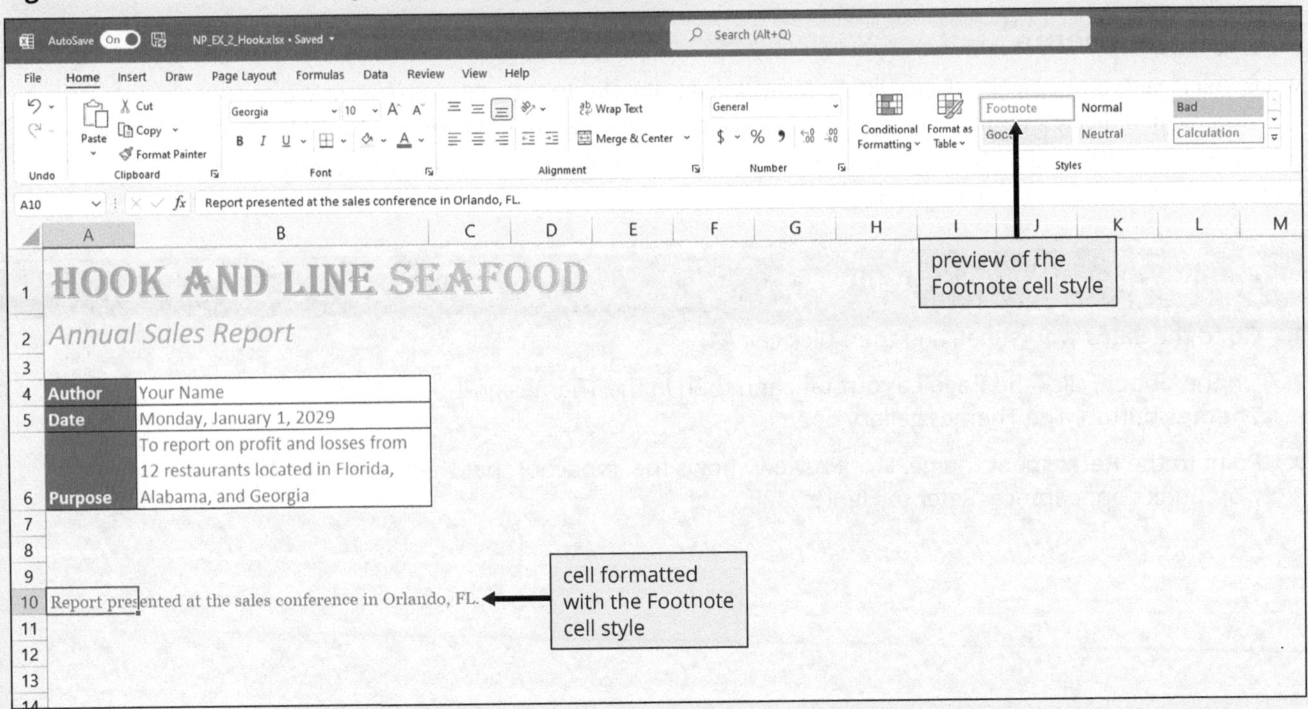

To change the formatting included in a custom cell style, right-click the style's name in the Cell Styles gallery and then click Modify on the shortcut menu. In the Style dialog box, enter the new formatting options. Any cells in the workbook formatted with that style automatically update to reflect the latest style.

Merging Custom Cell Styles

Custom cell styles are part of the workbook in which they are created. To use a custom cell style in another workbook, it must be copied from one workbook to another. Copying cells styles is useful for companies and organizations that need a consistent format in their workbooks and reports. To copy custom cell styles from one workbook to another, do the following:

1. Open the workbook containing the custom cell styles (the source workbook) and the workbook that will receive the custom cell style (the destination workbook).
2. In the destination workbook, open the Cell Styles gallery, and then click Merge Styles at the bottom of the gallery.
3. In the Merge Styles dialog box, select the source workbook containing the custom cell styles, and then click OK.

The custom cell styles from the source workbook are then copied into the destination workbook. Note that if the custom cell style in the source workbook is changed, that change will not appear in the destination workbook until the merge process is repeated.

Working with Themes

Another way to make multiple changes to the formats used in a workbook is with themes. Recall that a theme is a predefined set of formats that are applied throughout a workbook to give it a consistent, professional look.

Applying a Theme

When you change a workbook's theme, all the formats and cell styles based on that theme change to reflect the new theme's formats. Formats based on standard fonts and colors remain unchanged.

Many of the formatted choices applied to Robert's workbook use theme fonts and colors. Robert wants you to change to workbook's theme.

To change the workbook's theme:

1. Go to the **Sales** worksheet, and then click cell **A1**.
2. On the ribbon, click the **Page Layout** tab, and then in the Themes group, click the **Themes** button. The Themes gallery opens.
3. Point to the **Retrospect** theme. Live Preview shows the impact of that theme on the workbook's appearance. Refer to Figure 2–28.

Figure 2–28 Live Preview of the Retrospect theme

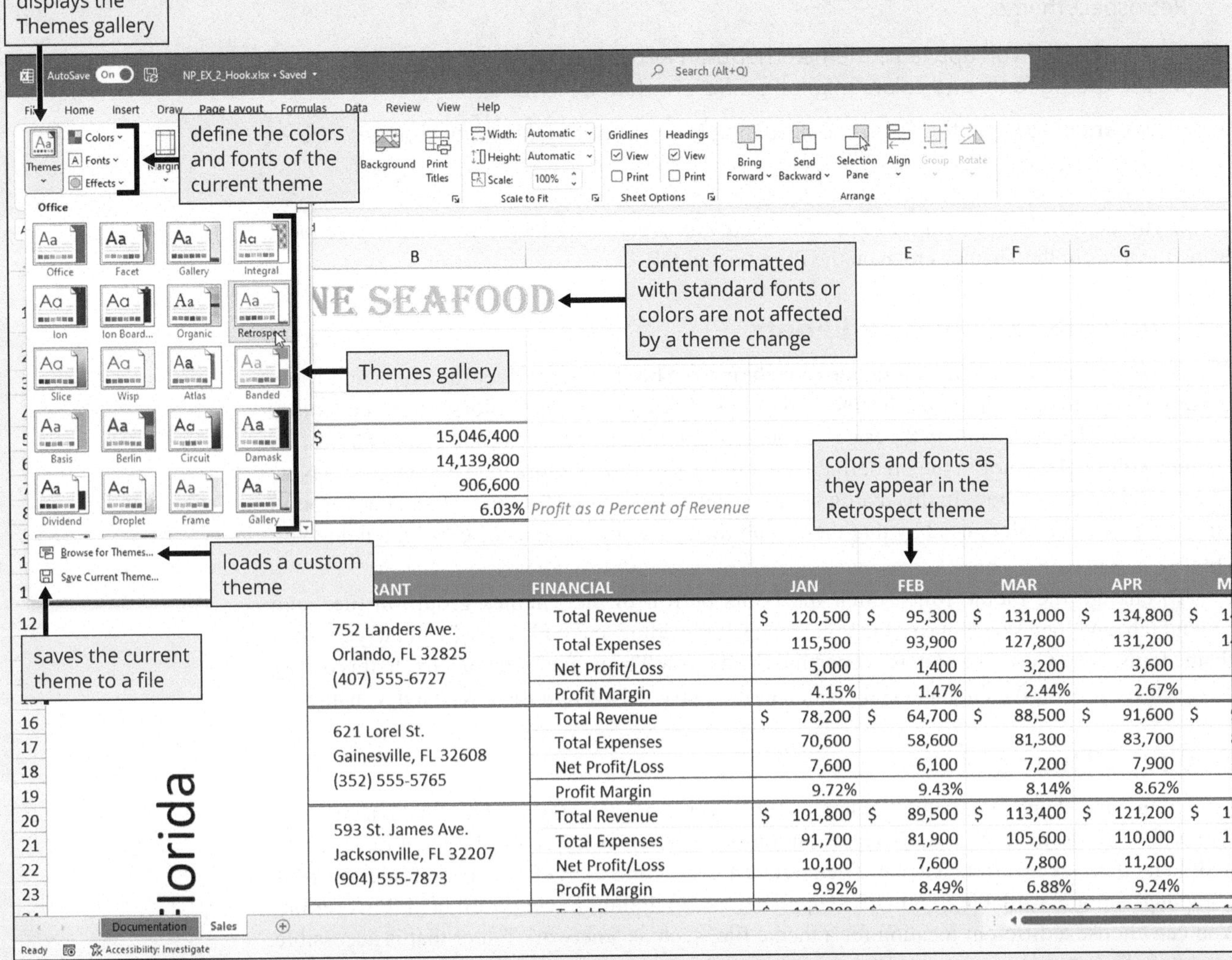

4. Click **Retrospect** to apply that theme to the workbook.

   Trouble? If Retrospect does not appear in the gallery, choose a different theme to apply to the workbook. Note that the colors and fonts in your workbook might differ from those in the figures.

Changing the theme made a significant difference in the worksheet's appearance. The most obvious changes to the worksheet are the fill colors and the fonts. The font and text colors for the company name in cell A1 did not change because they use standard fonts and colors. You can view the fonts and colors used by the Retrospect theme in the Format Cells dialog box.

To view the theme font and colors for the current theme:

1. Right-click cell **A11**, and then click **Format Cells** on the shortcut menu. The Format Cells dialog box opens.
2. Click the **Font** tab, if necessary. The first two fonts in the font list are always the theme fonts. In this case, the fonts used by the Retrospect theme are Calibri Light for headings and Calibri for body—the same fonts that the Office theme uses.

3. Click the **Fill** tab. The theme colors at the top of the color gallery range from ice blue to orange to green. A fill color that was blue in the Office theme is orange in the Retrospect theme.

   Trouble? If you applied a theme other than Retrospect for your workbook, the theme fonts and colors might be different than described.

4. Click **Cancel** to close the Format Cells dialog box without making any changes.

If you do not like the color or fonts associated with a particular theme you can change them using the tools in the Themes group on the Page Layout tab.

Setting Theme Colors and Fonts

Businesses often design custom themes for their workbooks that reflect the color and fonts used in the company's logo and business mailings. To change theme colors, click the Colors button in the Themes group on the Page Layout tab, and then select one of the color palettes. To create a color palette not in the predefined list, click Customize Colors to open the Create New Theme Colors dialog box. In this dialog box, you can select colors for the text and background and the six accent colors used by that theme and then save the custom colors with a name you choose.

To change the theme fonts, click the Fonts button in the Themes group on the Page Layout tab, and then select one of the font themes for heading and body text. To create your own theme fonts, click Customize Fonts to open the Create New Theme Fonts dialog box. In this dialog box, select fonts for heading and body text, and then save the custom fonts with a new name.

Saving a Theme

Once you have changed a theme's colors or fonts, you can save your custom theme as its own theme file. To do this, click the Themes button in the Themes group on the Page Layout tab, and then click Save Current Theme. Theme files are stored in the Office Theme folder on your computer and are available to all Office applications, including Excel, Word, and PowerPoint. You can choose a different location for a theme file, such as a network folder that is accessible to your colleagues.

Finding and Replacing Text and Formats

You can use Find and Replace to make global changes to formats that do not involve cell styles or themes. Find and Replace searches through the current cell selection, worksheet, or workbook, looking for content that matches a set of search criteria. The criteria can be based on text, numbers, formats, or some combination of all three. When cells are found matching the search criteria, their contents or formats can be replaced with new content or formats. You can review each match found one at a time, deciding whether to replace its content or formats. You can also highlight all matches found in the workbook. Or you can replace all matches at once without reviewing them.

Robert wants you to replace all street title abbreviations (such as St. or Ave.) in the restaurant addresses with the full street titles (such as Street or Avenue). You'll use Find and Replace to make these changes.

To find and replace the street title abbreviations:

1. On the ribbon, click the **Home** tab. In the Editing group, click the **Find & Select** button, and then click **Replace** (or press **CTRL+H**). The Find and Replace dialog box opens.
2. In the Find what box, type **St.** as the text to locate.
3. Press **TAB** to move the insertion point to the Replace with box, and then type **Street** as the new text.
4. Click the **Options** button, if necessary, to expand the list of find and replace options. Refer to Figure 2–29.

Figure 2–29 Find and Replace dialog box

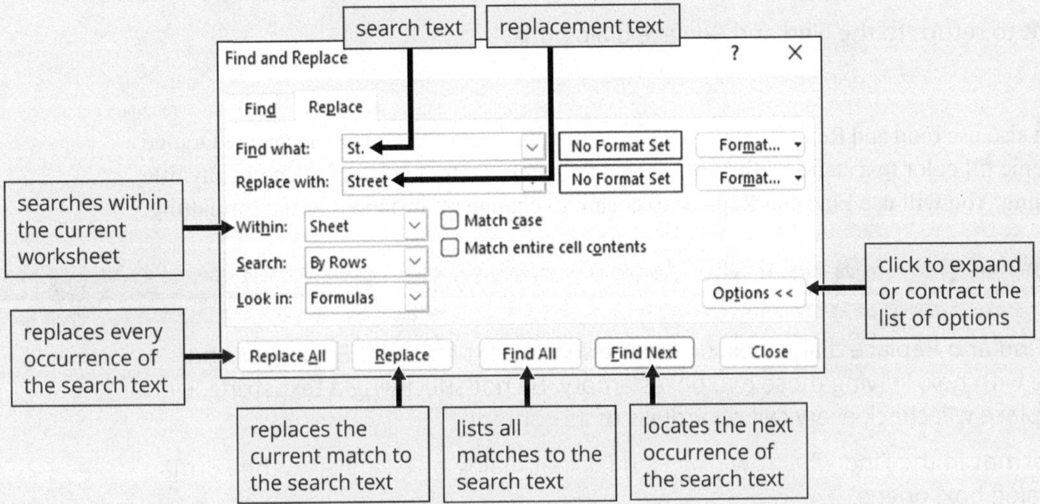

5. Click **Find Next** to locate the next occurrence of "St." in the Sales worksheet. Cell B16 containing the address "621 Lorel St." is selected.

   Key Step Always check the matched text so that you do not inadvertently replace text that should not be replaced.

6. Click **Replace** to replace "St." with "Street" in cell B16. Cell B20, containing the address "593 St. James Ave." is selected as the next matching cell. You do not want to replace "St." in this address because it is not an abbreviation for Street.
7. Click **Find Next**. Cell B28 containing the address "189 Warren St." is selected.
8. Click **Replace** to change the address to 189 Warren Street.
9. Click **Replace** twice to change the remaining two occurrences of "St." with "Street" in the range B36:B56. When you have finished, the Find and Replace dialog box remains open.

Rather than reviewing each possible replacement, you can use the Replace All button in the Find and Replace dialog box to make all the replacements at once. You should do this only if you are sure there is no chance for a replacement error. You will use the Replace All button to change all instances of "Ave." in the store addresses with "Avenue" and all instances of "Dr." with "Drive."

To replace all matches of "Ave." and "Dr.":

1. In the Find and Replace dialog box, type **Ave.** in the Find what box, and then type **Avenue** in the Replace with box.
2. Click **Replace All**. A dialog box appears, indicating that five matches were replaced.
3. Click **OK** to return to the Find and Replace dialog box.

> **Tip** By default, searches do not differentiate between uppercase and lowercase letters. To search using uppercase and lowercase letters, select the Match Case check box.

4. Type **Dr.** in the Find what box, and then type **Drive** in the Replace with box.
5. Click **Replace All**. A dialog box appears, indicating that three replacements were made.
6. Click **OK** to return to the Find and Replace dialog box.

You can also use Find and Replace to replace formatting. Robert want you to change the Orange Accent 1 theme fill color to a standard light blue color to match the font color of the company title and subheading. You will use Find and Replace to ensure to change all instances of the formatting.

To find and replace the fill color throughout the workbook:

1. In the Find and Replace dialog box, delete the search text from the Find what and Replace with box, leaving those two boxes empty. By not specifying a text string, Find and Replace will check every cell regardless of its content.
2. Click **Format** in the Find what row. The Find Format dialog box, similar to the Format Cells dialog box, opens.
3. Click the **Fill** tab, and then click the **Orange, Accent 1** theme color (the fifth color in the first row).
4. Click **OK** to return to the Find and Replace dialog box.
5. Click **Format** in the Replace with row. The Find Format dialog box opens.
6. On the Fill tab, click the **Light Blue** standard color (the seventh color in the non-theme colors) and then click **OK**.
7. Click the Within box, and then click **Workbook** to search throughout the entire workbook. Refer to Figure 2–30.

Figure 2–30 Format replacement

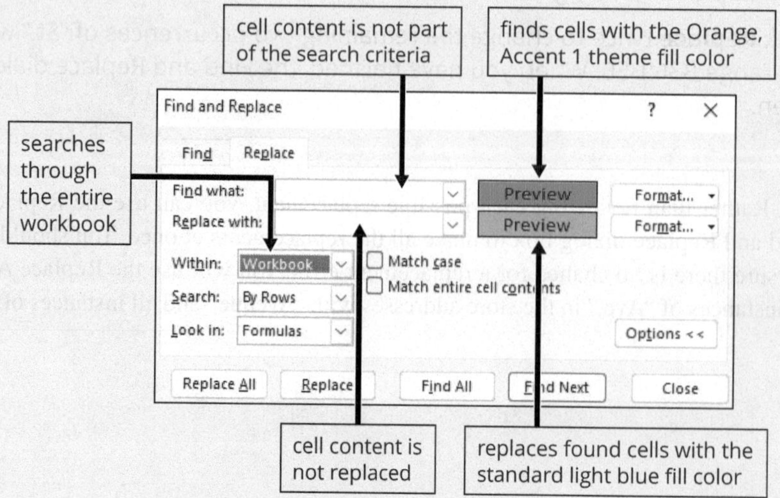

8. Click **Replace All**. A dialog box indicates that 19 cells were reformatted. The column labels in the Sales worksheet are displayed with the light blue fill color.
9. Click **OK** to return to the Find and Replace dialog box, and then **Close** to return to the worksheet.
10. Go the **Documentation** sheet and verify that the labels in A4:A6 are also displayed with a light blue fill.

A good practice is to clear find-and-replace formats from the Find and Replace dialog box after you are done so they won't affect any future searches and replacements. You will do this now.

To clear the find and replace options:

1. On the Home tab, in the Editing group, click the **Find & Select** button, and then click **Replace**. The Find and Replace dialog box opens.
2. In the Find what row, click the **Format arrow**, and then click **Clear Find Format**. The search format is removed.
3. In the Replace with row, click the **Format arrow**, and then click **Clear Replace Format**. The replacement format is also removed.
4. Click **Close**. The Find and Replace dialog box closes.

When finding and replacing a format, any formatting options you choose in the Find Format dialog box will be part of the search criteria, but formatting within a selected cell that is not part of that search criteria (such a font size of border style) will not be affected.

Proskills

Using Wildcards with Find and Replace

You can create flexible searches by adding wildcards to your search criteria. A **wildcard** is a symbol that represents any character or combination of characters. Two useful wildcards are the question mark (?) character representing any single character and the asterisk character (*) representing any string of characters.

For example, the search string St?ck would match Stack, Stick, Stock, Stuck, or any text string with a single character between the "St" and "ck" characters. The text string St*k would match Stock, Streak, Stack, or any text string that begins with "St" and ends with "k."

Calculating Averages

The monthly sales table includes the annual overall total for each restaurant in the Hook and Line Seafood chain. Robert is aware that monthly sales vary throughout the year, but he wants to know what a typical month looks like for each restaurant. You'll calculate each restaurant's monthly average revenue, expenses, and net profit or loss.

The AVERAGE function calculates the average value from a collection of numbers. Its syntax is

```
AVERAGE(number1, [number2], [number3], ...)
```

where *number1*, *number2*, *number3*, and so forth are either numbers or references to ranges containing numbers. For example, the following formula calculates the average of the numbers in the ranges B2:B10 and D2:D10:

```
=AVERAGE(B2:B10, D2:D10)
```

Only numeric values in the ranges are included in the calculations. Nonnumeric content is ignored.

You will use the AVERAGE function to calculate the monthly average revenue, expenses, and net profit/loss for each restaurant and then calculate the profit margin for a typical month.

To calculate the monthly financial averages for the restaurants:

1. Go to the **Sales** worksheet.
2. In cell **Q11**, enter **MONTHLY AVERAGE** as the column title. The cell is automatically formatted to match the adjacent cell P11.
3. In cell **Q12**, type **= AVERAGE(** to begin the function, select the range **D12:O12** as the range to average, type **)** to close the function arguments, and then press **ENTER**. The average monthly revenue for the first restaurant is $132,608.

   Trouble? If cell Q12 returns $244,815, you included cell P12 in the range reference. You do not want to include the annual total in the average calculation. Edit the function in cell Q11 so that the range reference is D12:O12.

4. In cell **Q13**, enter the formula **= AVERAGE(D13:O13)** to calculate the average monthly expenses for the first restaurant, and then press **ENTER**. The restaurant's average monthly expenses are 129,758 (dollars).
5. In cell **Q14**, enter the formula **= Q12 – Q13** to subtract the first restaurant's average monthly expenses from its average monthly revenue, and then press **ENTER**. The first restaurant's expected monthly profit is $2,850.
6. In cell **Q15**, enter the formula **= Q14/Q12** to divide the restaurant's monthly profits by its monthly revenue, and press **ENTER**. The first restaurant's typical monthly profit margin is 2.15%.

   Excel formatted the calculations but didn't include the border styles and didn't format the net profit/loss value in cell Q13 in the Accounting format.

7. Use the Format Painter to copy the formats from the range **P11:P15** to the range **Q11:Q15**. The formats in the two columns should now match.
8. Copy the range **Q12:Q15** containing the monthly averages for the first restaurant and paste them to the range **Q16:Q59**. The monthly averages for the remaining restaurants appear in column Q.

   Trouble? If the column label was duplicated, you copied the range Q11:Q15. Press CTRL+Z to under the paste. Then redo Step 8, being sure to copy the range Q12:Q15 without the column label.

9. Click cell **Q12** to deselect the pasted range. Refer to Figure 2–31.

Figure 2–31 Monthly averages across restaurants

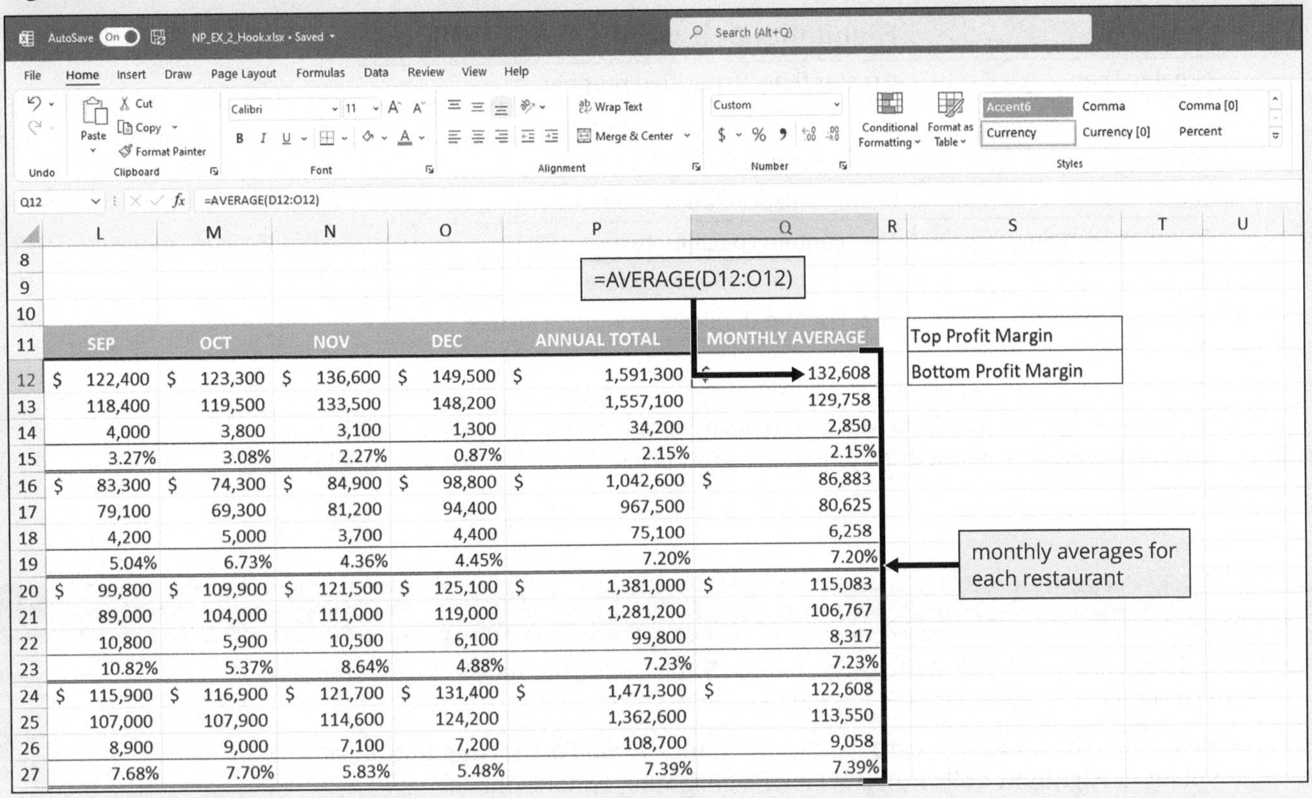

Q12 =AVERAGE(D12:O12)

=AVERAGE(D12:O12)

	SEP	OCT	NOV	DEC	ANNUAL TOTAL	MONTHLY AVERAGE
12	$ 122,400	$ 123,300	$ 136,600	$ 149,500	$ 1,591,300	$ 132,608
13	118,400	119,500	133,500	148,200	1,557,100	129,758
14	4,000	3,800	3,100	1,300	34,200	2,850
15	3.27%	3.08%	2.27%	0.87%	2.15%	2.15%
16	$ 83,300	$ 74,300	$ 84,900	$ 98,800	$ 1,042,600	$ 86,883
17	79,100	69,300	81,200	94,400	967,500	80,625
18	4,200	5,000	3,700	4,400	75,100	6,258
19	5.04%	6.73%	4.36%	4.45%	7.20%	7.20%
20	$ 99,800	$ 109,900	$ 121,500	$ 125,100	$ 1,381,000	$ 115,083
21	89,000	104,000	111,000	119,000	1,281,200	106,767
22	10,800	5,900	10,500	6,100	99,800	8,317
23	10.82%	5.37%	8.64%	4.88%	7.23%	7.23%
24	$ 115,900	$ 116,900	$ 121,700	$ 131,400	$ 1,471,300	$ 122,608
25	107,000	107,900	114,600	124,200	1,362,600	113,550
26	8,900	9,000	7,100	7,200	108,700	9,058
27	7.68%	7.70%	5.83%	5.48%	7.39%	7.39%

Top Profit Margin

Bottom Profit Margin

monthly averages for each restaurant

The monthly averages indicate that a typical restaurant in the Hook and Line Seafood chain can expect monthly profit margins in the range of 2% to 7% and higher. Sometimes restaurants in smaller markets can outperform restaurants in larger markets in terms of their profit margins. However, large revenues are no guarantee of financial success if they are accompanied by large expenses.

Highlighting Data with Conditional Formats

A conditional format is applied to a cell based on the cell's content. As the cell's content changes, the format of the cell might change in response. Conditional formats draw attention to important or unusual results, such as a sales total that exceeds a specified goal or an unusually large expense from a company's balance sheet.

The four types of conditional formats in Excel are data bars, highlighting, color scales, and icon sets. In this module, you will use conditional formats to highlight cells based on their content.

Reference

Highlighting Cells with Conditional Formats

- Select the range in which you want to highlight cells.
- On the Home tab, in the Styles group, click the Conditional Formatting button, point to Highlight Cells Rules or Top/Bottom Rules, and then click the appropriate rule.
- Select the appropriate options in the dialog box.
- Click OK.

Figure 2–32 describes the seven ways a conditional format can highlight a cell based on content.

Figure 2–32 Conditional Format highlighting rules

Rule	Highlights Cell Values
Greater Than	Greater than a specified number
Less Than	Less than a specified number
Between	Between two specified numbers
Equal To	Equal to a specified number
Text that Contains	That contain specified text
A Date Occurring	That contain a specified date
Duplicate Values	That contain duplicate or unique values

Robert wants to highlight months in which a restaurant's profit margin dropped below 2%. You will create a conditional format that displays profit margins below 2% in dark red text on a light red background.

To create a conditional format to highlight profit margins below 2%:

1. In the Sales worksheet, select the range **D15:O15** containing the monthly profit margins from January to December for the Orlando location.
2. On the Home tab, in the Styles group, click the **Conditional Formatting** button, and then point to **Highlight Cells Rules**. A list of highlighting options opens.
3. Click **Less Than**. The Less Than dialog box opens.
4. Type **2%** in the left box, and then press **TAB**. The right box lists the formatting options you can apply to cells whose value is less than 2%.
5. Verify that **Light Red Fill with Dark Red Text**, the first formatting option in the list, is selected. Refer to Figure 2–33.

Figure 2–33 Less than dialog box

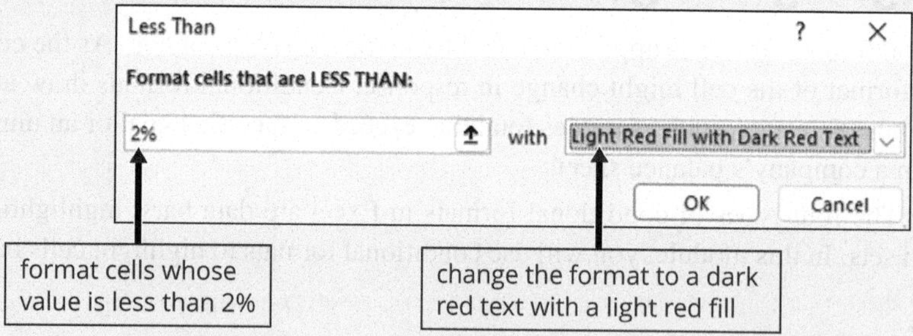

Tip To create your own format for highlighting cells, select Custom Format in the formats list and then choose formatting options in the Format Cells dialog box.

6. Click **OK** to apply the conditional format.
7. Click cell **O9** to deselect the range. Refer to Figure 2–34.

Figure 2–34 Conditional format highlighting cells less than 2%

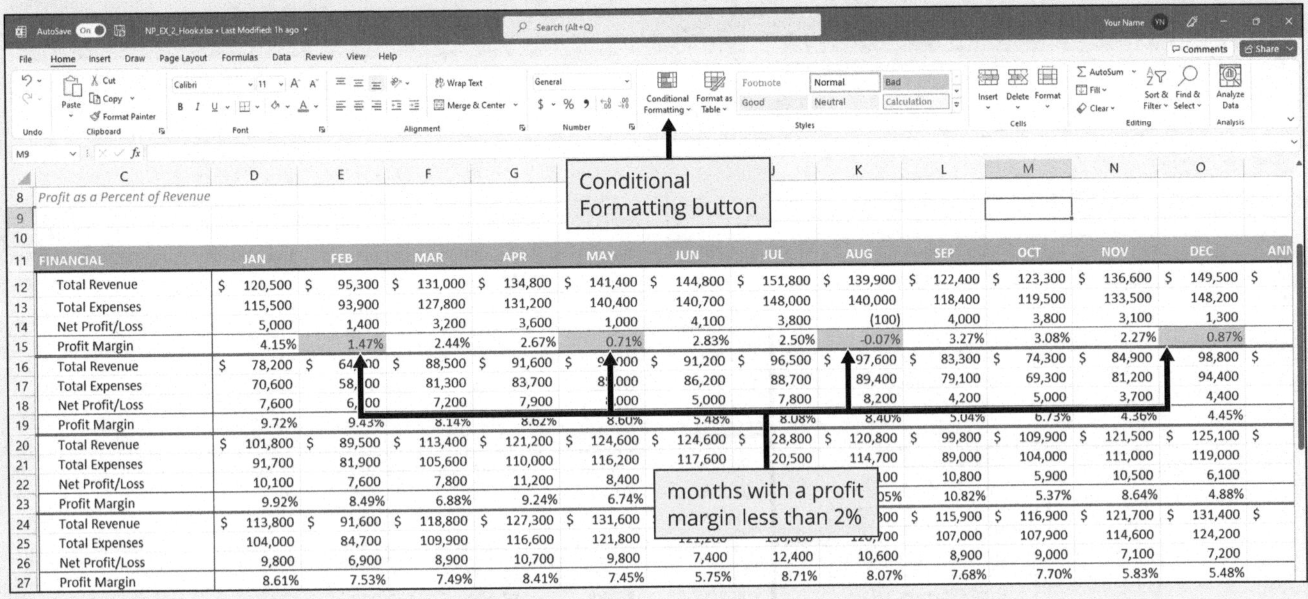

With the conditional format, Robert can quickly locate the months when the Orlando restaurant reported a profit margin of less than 2%: cell E15 (February), cell H15 (May), cell K15 (August), and cell O15 (December).

Like other formats, a conditional format can be copied and pasted from one cell range to another. You'll copy the conditional format you just defined and paste it into the range containing the monthly profit margins of the other 11 restaurants.

To copy and paste the Less than conditional format:

1. Select the range **D12:O15** containing the formats applied to the financial figures for the Orlando restaurant (including the conditional formats in row 15).
2. On the Home tab, in the Clipboard group, click the **Format Painter** button.
3. Select the range **D16:O59** containing the monthly financial data for the other restaurants.
4. Click cell **A1** to deselect the range, and then scroll down the worksheet to view the other months that have profit margins of below 2%. Refer to Figure 2–35.

Figure 2–35 Low monthly profit margins for other restaurants highlighted

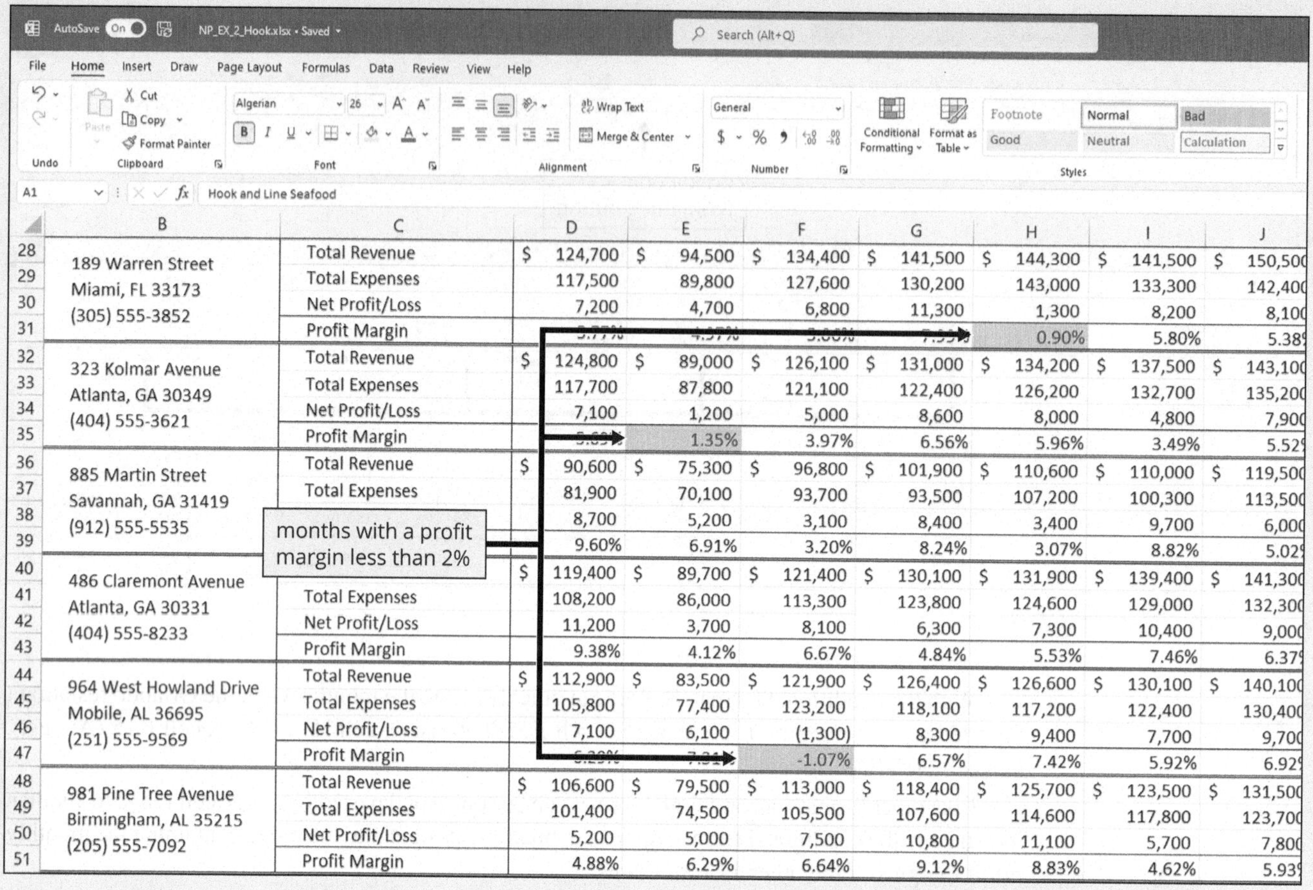

A1 Hook and Line Seafood

	B	C	D	E	F	G	H	I	J
28	189 Warren Street	Total Revenue	$ 124,700	$ 94,500	$ 134,400	$ 141,500	$ 144,300	$ 141,500	$ 150,50
29	Miami, FL 33173	Total Expenses	117,500	89,800	127,600	130,200	143,000	133,300	142,40
30	(305) 555-3852	Net Profit/Loss	7,200	4,700	6,800	11,300	1,300	8,200	8,10
31		Profit Margin	[illegible]	[illegible]	[illegible]	[illegible]	0.90%	5.80%	5.38
32	323 Kolmar Avenue	Total Revenue	$ 124,800	$ 89,000	$ 126,100	$ 131,000	$ 134,200	$ 137,500	$ 143,10
33	Atlanta, GA 30349	Total Expenses	117,700	87,800	121,100	122,400	126,200	132,700	135,20
34	(404) 555-3621	Net Profit/Loss	7,100	1,200	5,000	8,600	8,000	4,800	7,90
35		Profit Margin	[illegible]	1.35%	3.97%	6.56%	5.96%	3.49%	5.52
36	885 Martin Street	Total Revenue	$ 90,600	$ 75,300	$ 96,800	$ 101,900	$ 110,600	$ 110,000	$ 119,50
37	Savannah, GA 31419	Total Expenses	81,900	70,100	93,700	93,500	107,200	100,300	113,50
38	(912) 555-5535		8,700	5,200	3,100	8,400	3,400	9,700	6,00
39			9.60%	6.91%	3.20%	8.24%	3.07%	8.82%	5.02
40	486 Claremont Avenue		$ 119,400	$ 89,700	$ 121,400	$ 130,100	$ 131,900	$ 139,400	$ 141,30
41	Atlanta, GA 30331	Total Expenses	108,200	86,000	113,300	123,800	124,600	129,000	132,30
42	(404) 555-8233	Net Profit/Loss	11,200	3,700	8,100	6,300	7,300	10,400	9,00
43		Profit Margin	9.38%	4.12%	6.67%	4.84%	5.53%	7.46%	6.37
44	964 West Howland Drive	Total Revenue	$ 112,900	$ 83,500	$ 121,900	$ 126,400	$ 126,600	$ 130,100	$ 140,10
45	Mobile, AL 36695	Total Expenses	105,800	77,400	123,200	118,100	117,200	122,400	130,40
46	(251) 555-9569	Net Profit/Loss	7,100	6,100	(1,300)	8,300	9,400	7,700	9,70
47		Profit Margin	[illegible]	[illegible]	-1.07%	6.57%	7.42%	5.92%	6.92
48	981 Pine Tree Avenue	Total Revenue	$ 106,600	$ 79,500	$ 113,000	$ 118,400	$ 125,700	$ 123,500	$ 131,50
49	Birmingham, AL 35215	Total Expenses	101,400	74,500	105,500	107,600	114,600	117,800	123,70
50	(205) 555-7092	Net Profit/Loss	5,200	5,000	7,500	10,800	11,100	5,700	7,80
51		Profit Margin	4.88%	6.29%	6.64%	9.12%	8.83%	4.62%	5.93

months with a profit margin less than 2%

Trouble? If you make a mistake applying the formats with the Format Painter button, click the Undo button in the Undo group on the Home tab (or press CTRL+Z) to undo your actions and repeat Steps 1 through 4.

The conditional format reveals to Robert that the only months in which profit margins dropped below 2% occurred with the May sales of the Miami restaurant (cell H31), the February and December sales of the Atlanta restaurant (cells E35 and O35), the March sales of the first Mobile restaurant (cell F47), and the August sales of the second Mobile restaurant cell (K59).

Conditional formats highlight that four of the nine monthly profit margins that dropped below 2% occurred in the Orlando restaurant. This result could indicate problems with management or the economic challenges of the Orlando location.

Highlighting Cells with a Top/Bottom Rule

A top/bottom rule formats cells with the highest or lowest numbers in the selected range. Robert wants you to use this rule to highlight the restaurants with the best three average profit margins. You will create this conditional format.

To highlight the restaurants the best average profit margins by a top/bottom rule:

1. Select the nonadjacent range **Q15,Q19,Q23,Q27,Q31,Q35,Q39,Q43,Q47,Q51,Q55,Q59** containing the average monthly profit margins for the restaurants.
2. On the Home tab, in the Styles group, click the **Conditional Formatting** button, click **Top/Bottom Rules**, and then click **Top 10 Items.** the Top 10 Items dialog box opens.

3. In the left box from 10 to **3**, and then press **TAB**.
4. In the right box, select **Green Fill with Dark Green Text**. Refer to Figure 2–36.

Figure 2–36 Top 10 Items dialog box

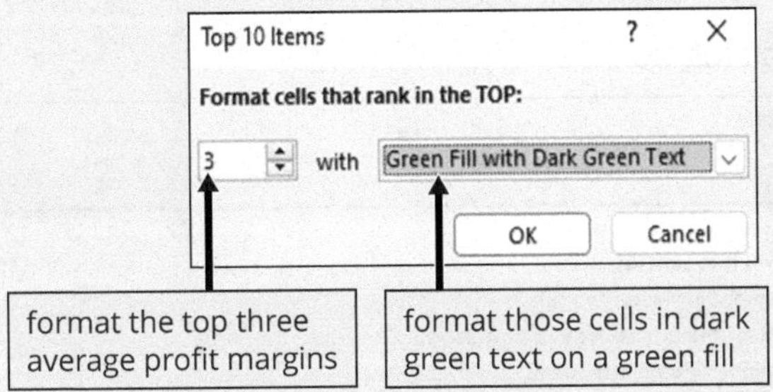

5. Click **OK**. The profit margins for the top three restaurants are displayed in a dark green text on a green file.

The restaurants with the top three average profit margins are Jacksonville with a profit margin of 7.23% (cell Q23), Tampa with a profit margin of 7.39% (cell Q27), and Birmingham with a profit margin of 7.25% (cell Q51).

Editing a Conditional Format

You can modify a conditional format by changing what is being highlighted or the format applied to those cells. With only 12 restaurants, Robert wants to highlight only the top restaurant in the chain. You'll use the Manage Rules command to edit the conditional format.

To edit the top conditional format rule:

1. Make sure the nonadjacent range **Q15,Q19,Q23,Q27,Q31,Q35,Q39,Q43,Q47,Q51,Q55,Q59** containing the profit margins for each restaurant is still selected.
2. On the Home tab, in the Styles group, click the **Conditional Formatting** button, and then click **Manage Rules**. The Conditional Formatting Rules Manager dialog box opens, listing all the conditional formats applied to the current selection. Refer to Figure 2–37.

Figure 2–37 Conditional Formatting Rule Manager dialog box

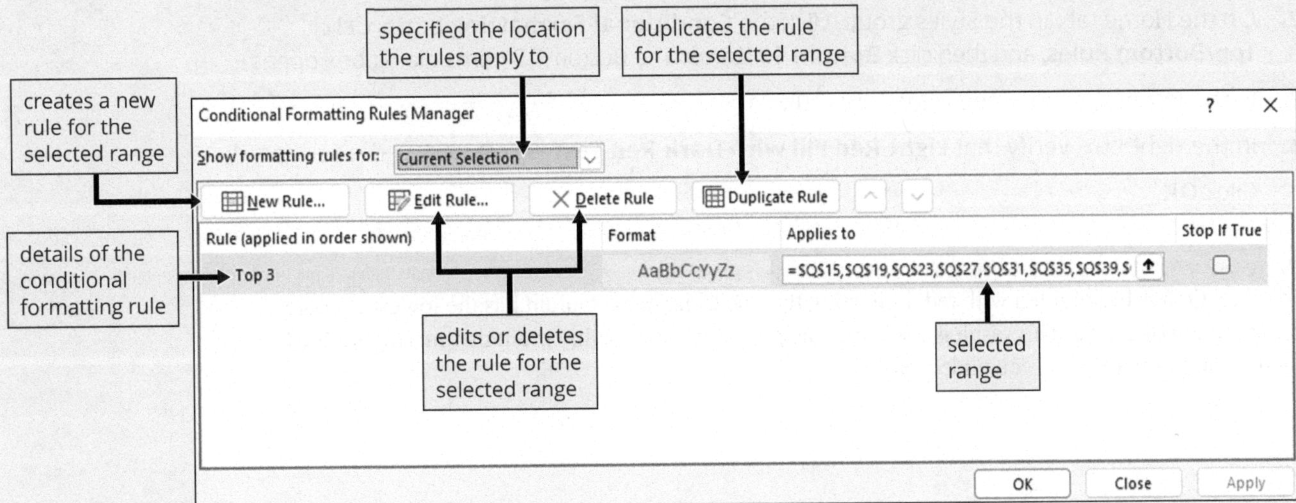

3. Click **Edit Rule** to edit the rule selected in the dialog box. The Edit Formatting Rule dialog box opens.
4. In the Edit the Rule Description section, change the value in the middle box from 3 to **1** so that only the top profit margin is highlighted. Refer to Figure 2–38.

Figure 2–38 Edit Formatting Rule dialog box

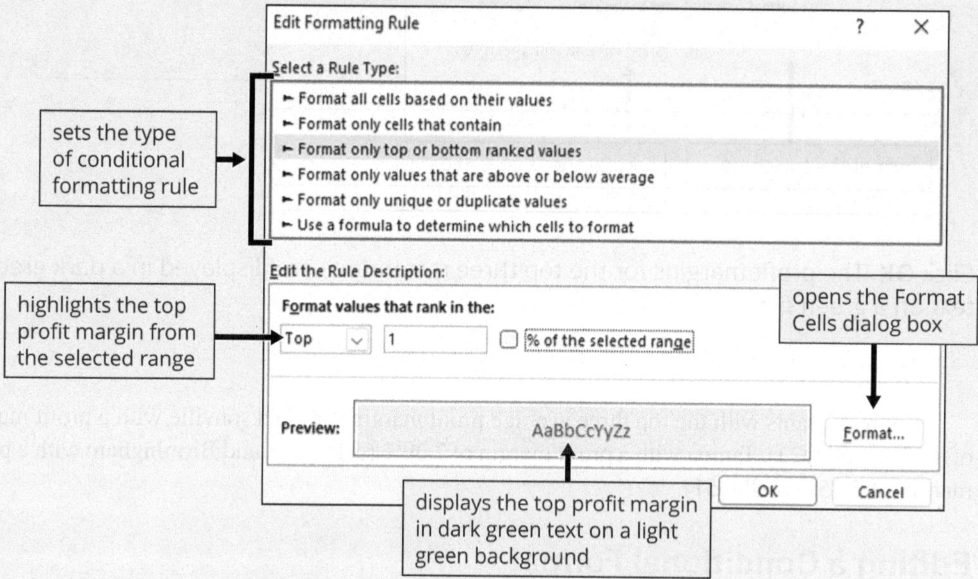

5. Click **OK** in each dialog box to return to the worksheet.

The only cell highlighted in green is cell Q27, containing the 7.39% monthly average profit margin for the Tampa location, which is the restaurant with the best in the chain.

A cell range can contain multiple conditional formats. You'll add another rule to the selected cells to highlight the restaurant with the lowest average profit margin in the chain.

To highlight the restaurant with the lowest profit margin:

1. Make sure the nonadjacent range **Q15,O19,Q23,Q27,Q31,Q35,Q39,Q43,Q47,Q51,Q55,Q59** is still selected.
2. On the Home tab, in the Styles group, click the **Conditional Formatting** button, click **Top/Bottom Rules**, and then click **Bottom 10 Items**. The Bottom 10 Items dialog box opens.
3. In the left box, change the value from 10 to **1**.
4. In the right box, verify that **Light Red Fill with Dark Red Text** is selected as the format.
5. Click **OK**.

Cell Q15 is highlighted with red, indicating that the Orlando restaurant has the lowest average profit margin of 2.15%. This result is not surprising given the low monthly profit margins highlighted by the conditional format you added earlier.

Insight

Conditional Formatting with Cell References

Conditional formats can be based on cell references. For example, you can use a conditional format to highlight all cells whose value is greater than the value stored in cell B10 by doing the following:

1. Select the range to be formatted.
2. On the Home tab, in the Styles group, click the Conditional Formatting button, click Highlight Cells Rules, and then click Greater Than.
3. In the Greater Than dialog box, enter = $B$10 in the Format cells that are GREATER THAN box.
4. Click OK.

All cells in the selected range that are greater than the value in cell B10 are highlighted. If the value in cell B10 changes, the cells highlighted with the conditional format will also change. The $ symbol in the cell reference locks the reference so that the formula always points to cell B10 for every cell in the selected range. If the formula was entered as = B10, the cell reference would change for every cell.

A conditional format is based on the current cell values. If any cell value changes, the highlighted cells can also change. Robert notices an incorrect data entry for the Jacksonville restaurant. December expenses were $116,000 and not $119,000. You'll edit the value in cell O21 and check how this change impacts the results of the conditional format.

To correct the value in cell O21 and check the impact on the conditional format:

1. Click cell **O21** containing the incorrect expense value.
2. Type **116,000** as the corrected December expense value.
3. Press **ENTER**. The average monthly profit margin for the Jacksonville location in cell Q23 increases to 7.44%, making it the top restaurant in the chain instead of Tampa.

Because a cell can have several conditional formats, the rule listed last in the Conditional Formatting Rules Manager take precedence over any other rule. To allow an earlier conditional formatting rule to take precedence over later rules, click the Stop if True checkbox next to the rule you want to have precedence.

Documenting Conditional Formats

You should document all the conditional formats used in a workbook to ensure that users understand why some cells are formatted differently than others. A legend is an effective way to document the conditional format rules in a workbook.

In cells S11 and S12 of the Sales worksheet, Robert created the legend text for the top and bottom profit margins. You will format those cells to match the conditional formats you applied to the restaurant profit margins.

To document the top and bottom conditional formats:

1. In the Sales worksheet, click cell **S11** to select it.
2. On the Home tab, in the Styles group, click the **Conditional Formatting** button, click **Highlight Cell Rules**, and then click **Text that Contains**. The Text That Contains Dialog box opens.
3. Verify that **Top Profit Margin** (the text in cell S11) appears in the left box, select **Green Fill with Dark Green Text** as the format in the right box, and then click **OK**. The format of cell S11 matches the top profit margin conditional format.
4. Click cell **S12** to select it.
5. Click the **Conditional Formatting** button, click **Highlight Cell Rules**, and then click **Text that Contains**. The Text That Contains Dialog box opens.
6. Verify that **Bottom Profit Margin** (the text entered in cell S12) appears in the left box, select **Light Red Fill with Dark Red Text** format is selected in the right box, and then click **OK**. The format of cell S12 matches the bottom profit margin conditional format.
7. Click cell **S9** to deselect the legend text. Refer to Figure 2–39.

Figure 2–39 Highlighting the top and bottom profit margins

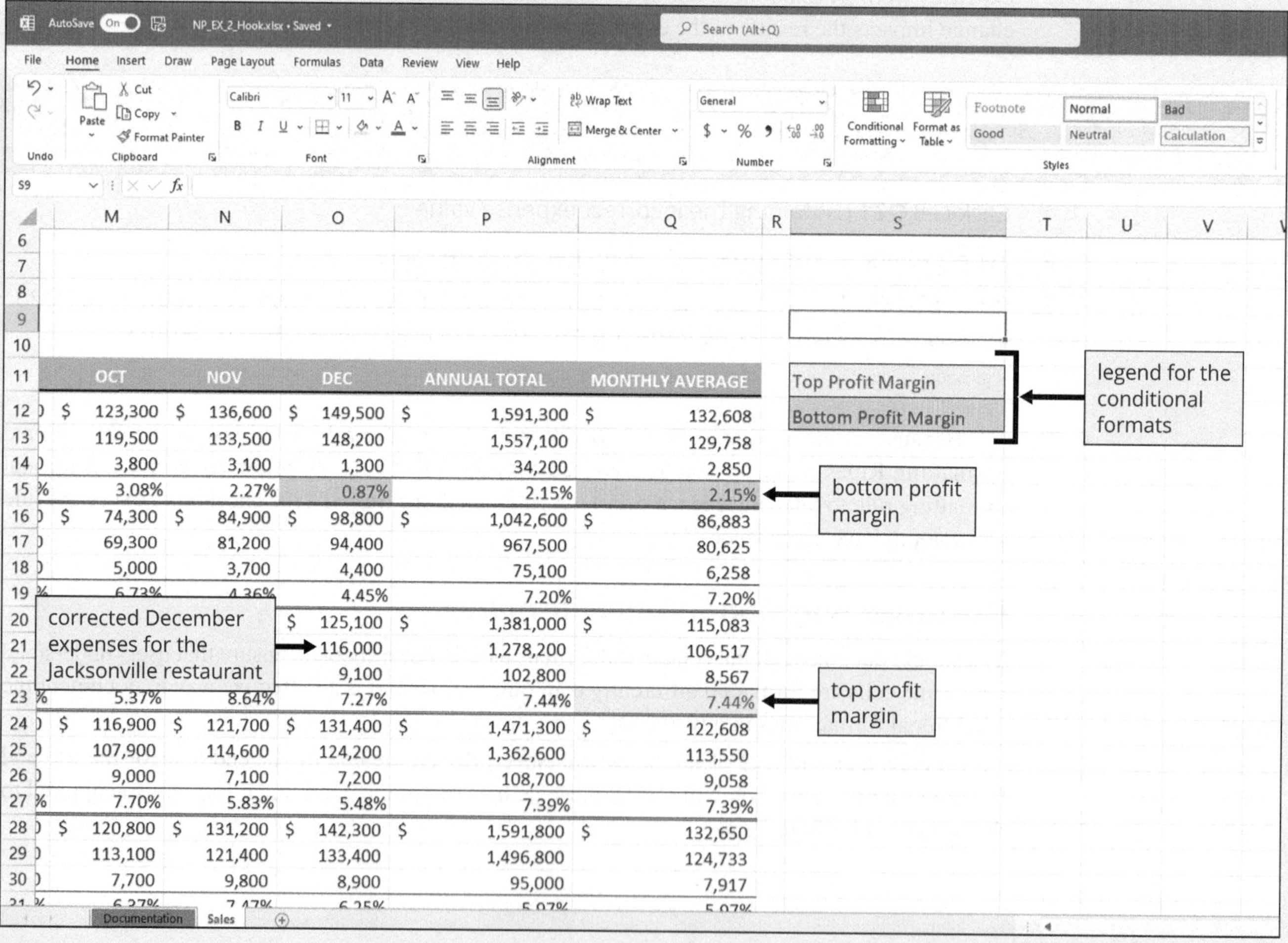

Clearing Conditional Formatting Rules

You can remove a conditional format at any time without affecting the underlying data. Select the range containing the conditional format, click the Conditional Formatting button in the Styles group on the Home tab, and then click Clear Rules. A menu opens, providing options to clear the conditional formatting rules from the selected cells or the entire worksheet.

Proskills

Written Communication: Using Conditional Formats Effectively

Conditional formats are an excellent way to highlight important trends and data values to clients and colleagues. However, be sure to use them judiciously. Overusing conditional formats might obscure the very data you want to emphasize. Keep in mind the following tips as you make decisions about what to highlight and how it should be highlighted:

- **Document the conditional formats you use.** If a bold, green font means that a sales number is in the top 10% of all sales, document that information in the worksheet.
- **Do not clutter data with too much highlighting.** Limit highlighting rules to one or two per data set. Highlights are designed to draw attention to points of interest. If you use too many, you will end up highlighting everything—and, therefore, nothing.
- **Consider alternatives to conditional formats.** If you want to highlight the top 10 sales regions, it might be more effective to simply sort the data with the best-selling regions at the top of the list.

Remember that the goal of highlighting is to showcase important data or results. Careful use of conditional formats helps readers to focus on the important points you want to make rather than distracting them with secondary issues and facts.

Formatting a Workbook for Printing

Many workbooks are distributed in print versions. In addition to formatting workbooks for the computer screen, you also need to consider how they appear when printed. The requirements for a printed worksheet are different than the requirements for the same worksheet viewed on a monitor. For printed page, consider how the data appears on each page. If the content spans several pages, you do not want column and row labels printed on one page while financial figures end up on a different page without any context or explanation.

The Page Layout tab includes many tools to format and lay out the print version of workbooks. You can change the page orientation, set the print area, add page breaks, and create headers and footers. The print settings can be applied to the entire workbook or to individual sheets within the workbook.

Using Page Break Preview

As you begin formatting the printed version of a workbook, you want to check how the sheets will print. Page Break Preview shows how many total pages will be printed and what will be printed on each page. In Page Break Preview, a solid or dotted blue order indicates that the page boundaries and page numbers appear in the workbook window. As you develop the print version of a workbook, you can refer to Page Break Preview to ensure that each page contains the appropriate content in a clear and informative design.

Robert wants you to check how the Sales worksheet would print in portrait orientation. You'll use Page Break Preview to review the page layout.

To preview the print layout in Page Break Preview:

1. Click cell **A1** to select it.
2. On the ribbon, click the **Page Layout** tab.
3. In the Page Setup group, verify that page orientation is set to **Portrait**.
4. On the status bar, click the **Page Break Preview** button. The worksheet switches to Page Break Preview.
5. Change the zoom level so all pages of the printed report are displayed the workbook window. Refer to Figure 2–40.

Figure 2–40 Sales worksheet in Page Break Preview

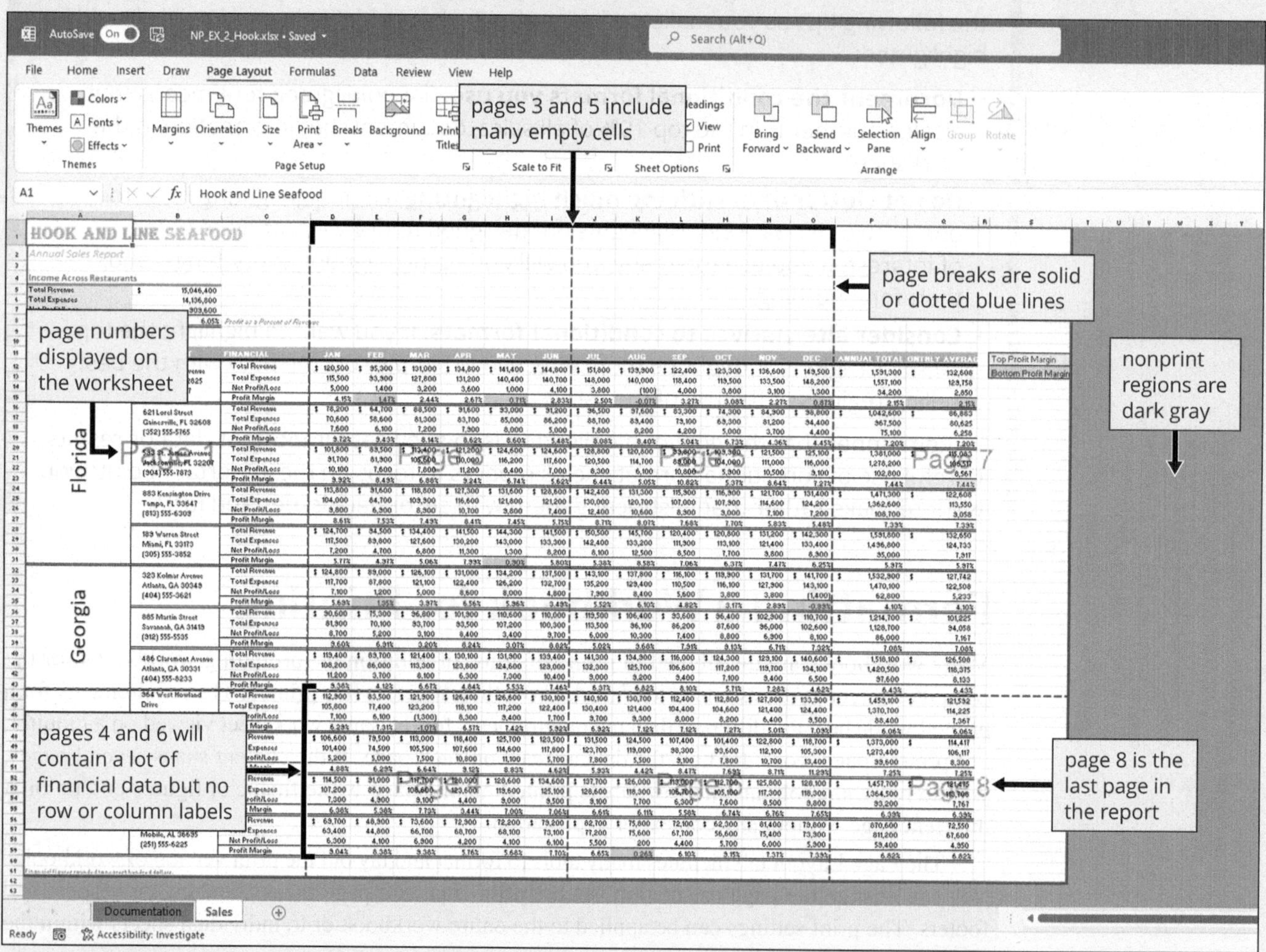

Trouble? If your layout is different than Figure 2–40, don't worry. The layout depends on your printer and monitor.

Page Break Preview reveals that the printed Sales worksheet would require eight pages. Some of the pages would be very confusing to a reader. For example, pages 4 and 6 are filled with financial data without any labels identifying the month or the restaurant. Half of pages 3 and 5 contain empty cells, wasting space. The report needs reformatting before it is suitable for printing.

Defining the Print Area

The print area specifies which range or ranges in a worksheet will be printed. The default print area is the range that extends from cell A1 to the rightmost column and lowest row containing printable content. In many worksheets, this includes a lot of empty cells. For example, in the Sales worksheet, the range D1:S10 has no content, and the printed report would be more effective without those cells. To remove cells from a printed worksheet, you can set a more different print area that includes nonadjacent ranges. Each worksheet has its own print area.

Robert wants you to define a print area for the Sales worksheet that eliminates the blank cells. You'll do that in Page Break Preview, which clearly indicates what areas will print.

To define the print area for the Sales worksheet:

1. Increase the zoom level of the workbook window to **90%** to make it easier to select cells and cell ranges.
2. Select the nonadjacent range **A1:C10,A11:S61** covering the summary information at the top of the worksheet and the complete financial table including the conditional formatting legends and the footnote.
3. On the Page Layout tab, in the Page Setup group, click the **Print Area** button, and then click **Set Print Area**. The print area covers an L-shaped region for the nonadjacent range A1:C10,A11:S61. The rest of the worksheet is shaded dark gray, indicating that those cells are not part of the printout.
4. Click **A1** to deselect the range.
5. Reduce the zoom level until the complete preview of the printed report is displayed in the workbook window. Refer to Figure 2–41.

Figure 2–41 Print area set for the Sales worksheet

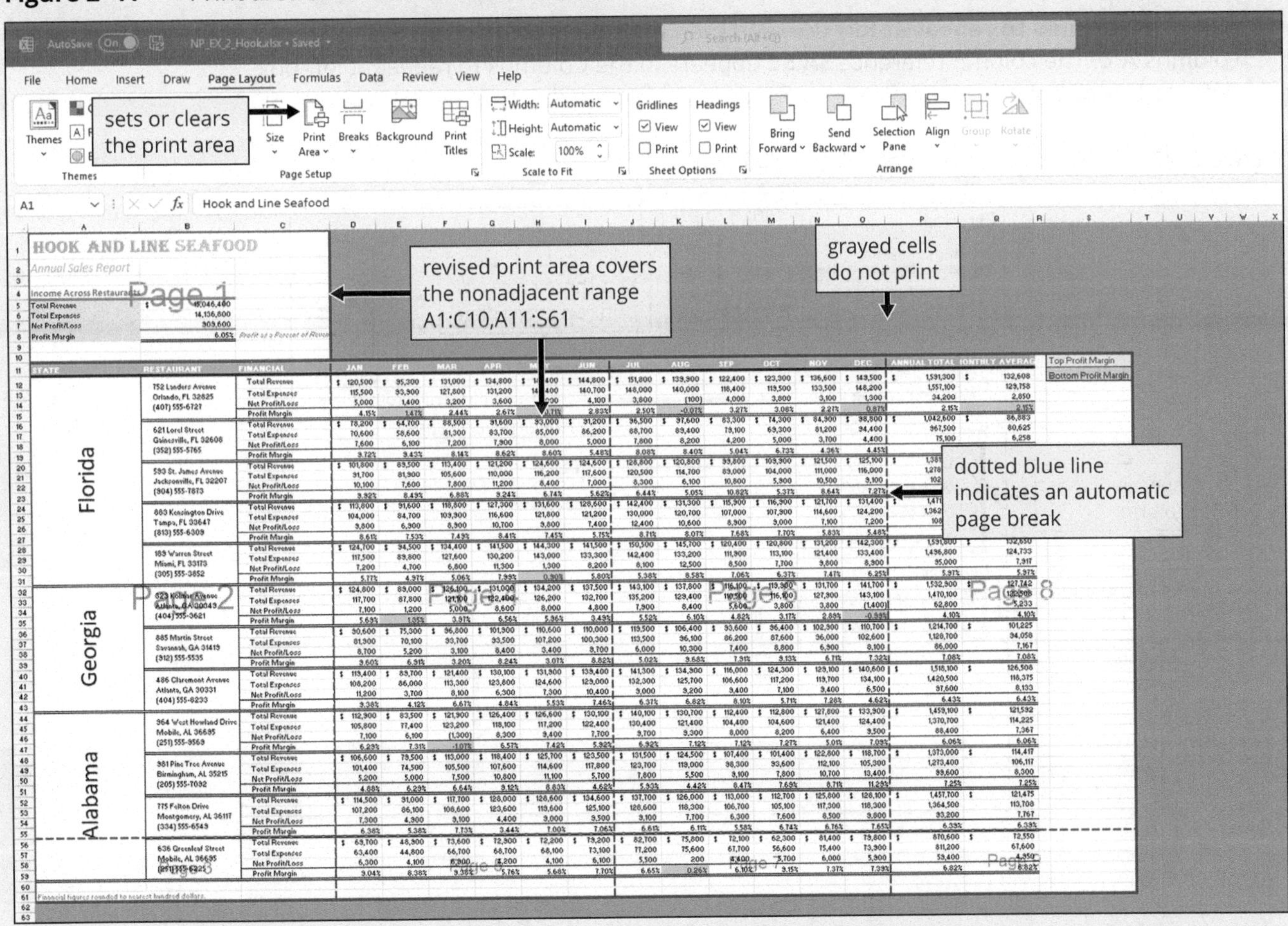

To reset the print area, click the Print Area button in the Page Setup group on the Page Layout tab, and then click Clear Print Area. The print area returns to its original setting, a rectangle extending from cell A1 to the right and bottom edges of the sheet content.

Setting the Print Titles

A good practice is for every page of a printed report to include descriptive text such as the company's name, titles and subheadings, and row and column labels for any content. You can repeat important information like this on every page by specifying which rows and columns in the worksheet should print on all pages. Those rows and columns act as print titles, adding context to every printed page.

In the Sales worksheet, as currently set, the company name and report subheading will be printed only on the first page and many pages will have financial data with no labels. Robert wants the company name and report subheading in rows 1 and 2 and the labels containing the state name, restaurant location, and financial category in columns A through C repeated on every page. You will mark them as print titles.

To define the print titles for the Sales worksheet:

1. On the Page Layout tab, in the Page Setup group, click the **Print Titles** button. The Page Setup dialog box opens with the Sheet tab displayed.

   Tip You can also open the Page Setup dialog box by clicking the Dialog Box Launcher in the Page Setup group on the Page Layout tab.

2. In the Print titles section, click the **Rows to repeat at top** box, and then in the Sales worksheet, select rows **1:3**. The row reference $1:$3 appears in the Rows to repeat at top box. A flashing border appears around the three rows of the worksheet to indicate that the contents of these rows will be repeated on each page of the printout.
3. Click the **Columns to repeat at left** box, and then in the Sales worksheet, select columns **A:C**. The column reference **$A:$C** appears in the Columns to repeat at left box. Refer to Figure 2–42.

Figure 2–42 Sheet tab in the Page Setup dialog box

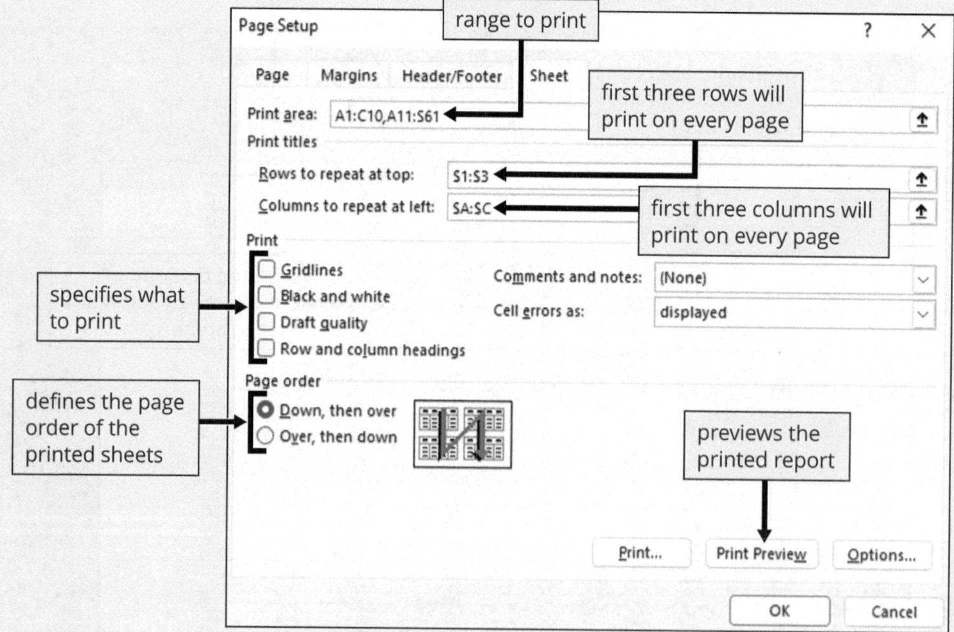

4. Click **Print Preview** to preview the current format of the printed report. The printed report will be 35 pages.
5. Click the **Next Page** button ▶ to go through the printout page by page. The content of rows 1 through 3 and columns A through C appear on every page.
6. In the page number box, enter **4** to return to the preview of that page. Refer to Figure 2–43.

Figure 2–43 Page 4 printout with page titles

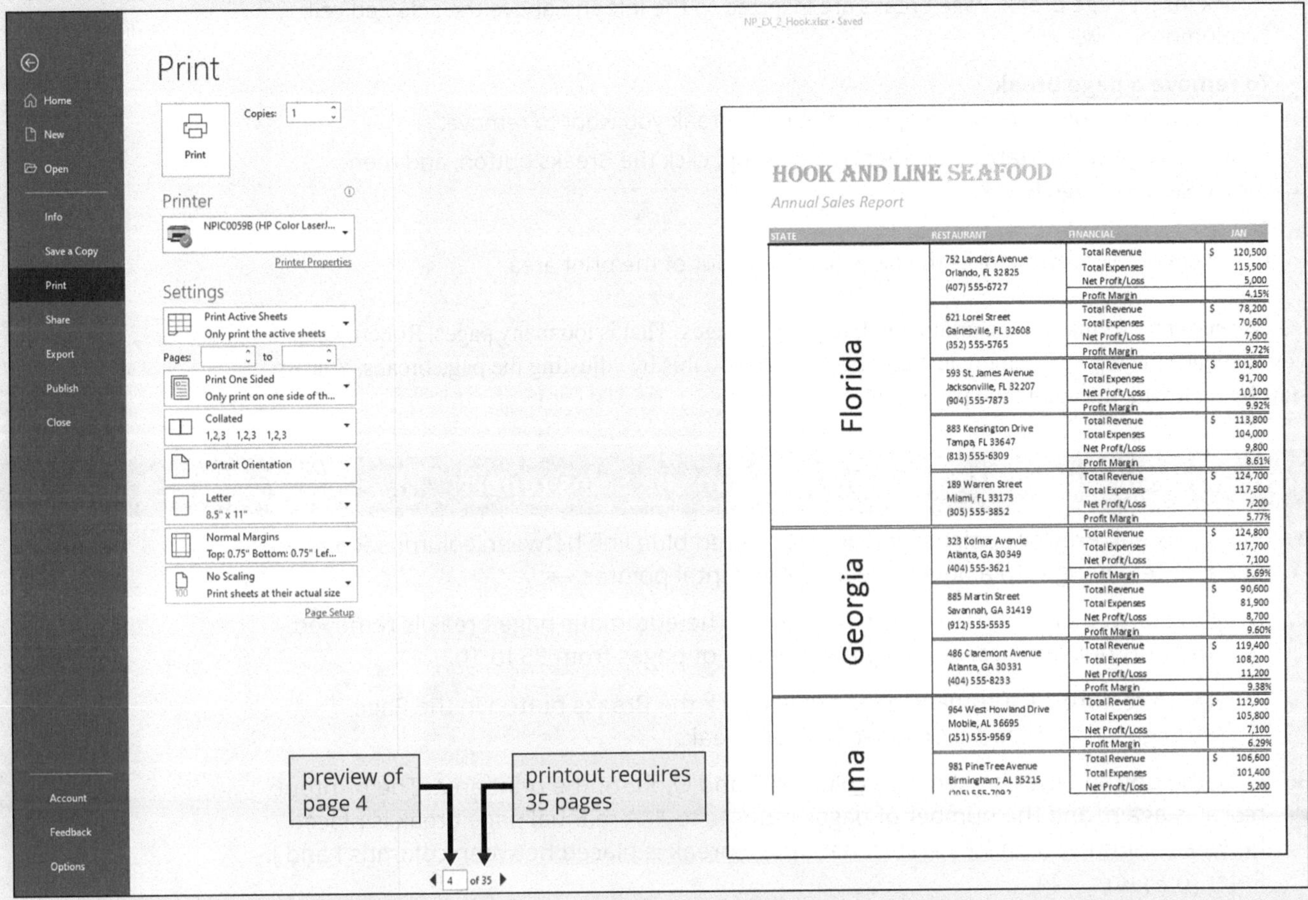

Trouble? Depending on your printer, the content of your printed pages might be slightly different.

7. Click the **Back** button to exit Backstage view and return to the Sales worksheet.

Moving, Adding, and Removing Page Breaks

When a worksheet will not fit on to a single printed page, Excel adds page breaks throughout the worksheet. These automatic page breaks are placed to fit the most content possible on each printed page. However, automatic page breaks can split pages at awkward locations, such as within the middle of a table. They can also create long and unwieldy printouts.

To better split a printout into logical segments, you can manually set page breaks. In Page Break Preview, automatic page breaks are dotted blue lines and manual page breaks are solid blue lines. You encountered these page breaks when you set the print area for the Sales worksheet. To move a page break, you click and drag the break to a new row or new column. Each time you move, add, or remove a page break, the printout rescales to adjust to the new page layout.

Reference

Moving, Adding, and Removing Page Breaks

To move a page break:

- Drag a page break line to a new location within the print area.

To add a page break:

- Click the worksheet where you want to insert a page break.
- On the Page Layout tab, in the Page Setup group, click the Breaks button, and then click Insert Page Break. Page breaks are inserted to the left and above the selected cell, column, or row.

To remove a page break:

- Select any cell below or to the right of the page break you want to remove.
- On the Page Layout tab, in the Page Setup group, click the Breaks button, and then click Remove Page Break.

or

- In Page Break Preview, drag the page break line out of the print area.

As currently formatted, the printout will require 35 pages. That is too many pages. Robert wants you to reduce the report to a more manageable size. You do this by adjusting the page breaks. You'll start by removing the automatic page breaks.

To remove the automatic page breaks from the Sales report:

1. In Page Break Preview, point to the vertical dotted blue line between columns R and S. The pointer changes to a double-headed horizontal pointer ↔.
2. Drag the dotted blue line out of the print area. The automatic page break is removed, and the printout rescales, reducing the number of pages from 35 to 10.

   Tip To restore all automatic page breaks, click the Breaks button in the Page Setup group and then click Reset All Page Breaks.

3. Drag the dotted blue line between columns P and Q out of the print area. The printout rescales again, and the number of pages reduces to 4. A manual page break is placed between columns O and P. An automatic page break is placed between columns I and J. Refer to Figure 2–44.

Figure 2–44 Rescaled printout of the Sales report after removing automatic breaks

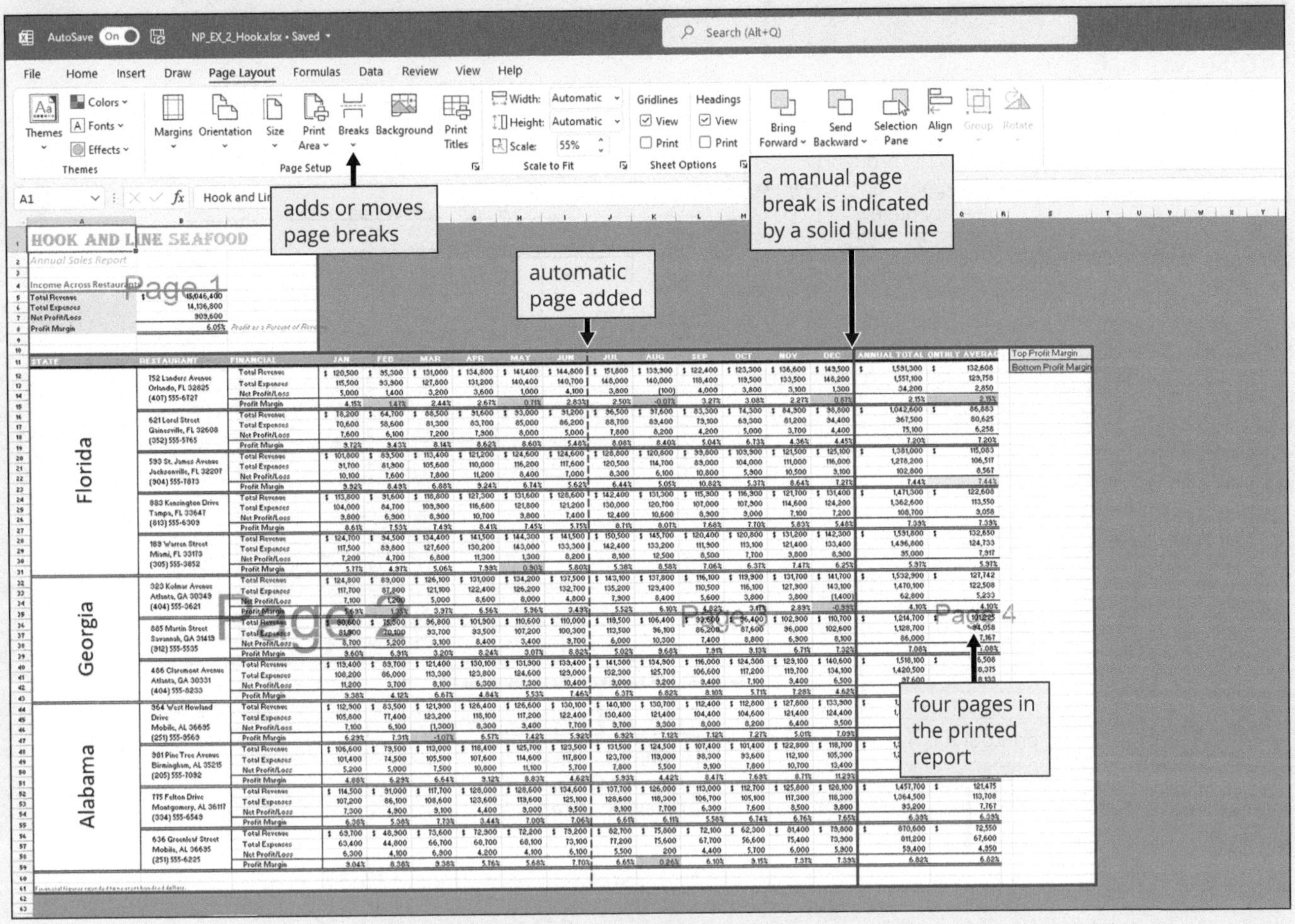

adds or moves page breaks

a manual page break is indicated by a solid blue line

automatic page added

four pages in the printed report

The printout of the Sales worksheet now has four pages. Robert wants the summary data from the 12 restaurants on page 1, the financial figures of all the restaurants from January to June on page 2, the July to December figures on page 3, and the final totals and monthly averages on page 4. The automatic page breaks match Robert's the report layout. To ensure that the page breaks stay in place, you will change the automatic page break between column I and J to a manual break.

To move and insert page breaks:

1. In Page Break Preview, click the column **J** column header containing the July figures.
2. On the Page Layout tab, in the Page Setup group, click the **Breaks** button, and then click **Insert Page Break**. The page break between column I and column J changes to a solid blue line, indicating a manual page break.
3. Click cell **A1** to deselect column J and then verify that manual page break appears between columns I and J.
4. In the lower-right corner of the Page Setup group, click the **Dialog Box Launcher**. The Page Setup dialog box opens.
5. Click **Print Preview** to preview the printed report, and then verify that the report is four pages and the last three pages display the company name, subheading, state name, restaurant address, and financial labels. Refer to Figure 2–45.

Figure 2–45 Preview of page 2 of the Sales report printout

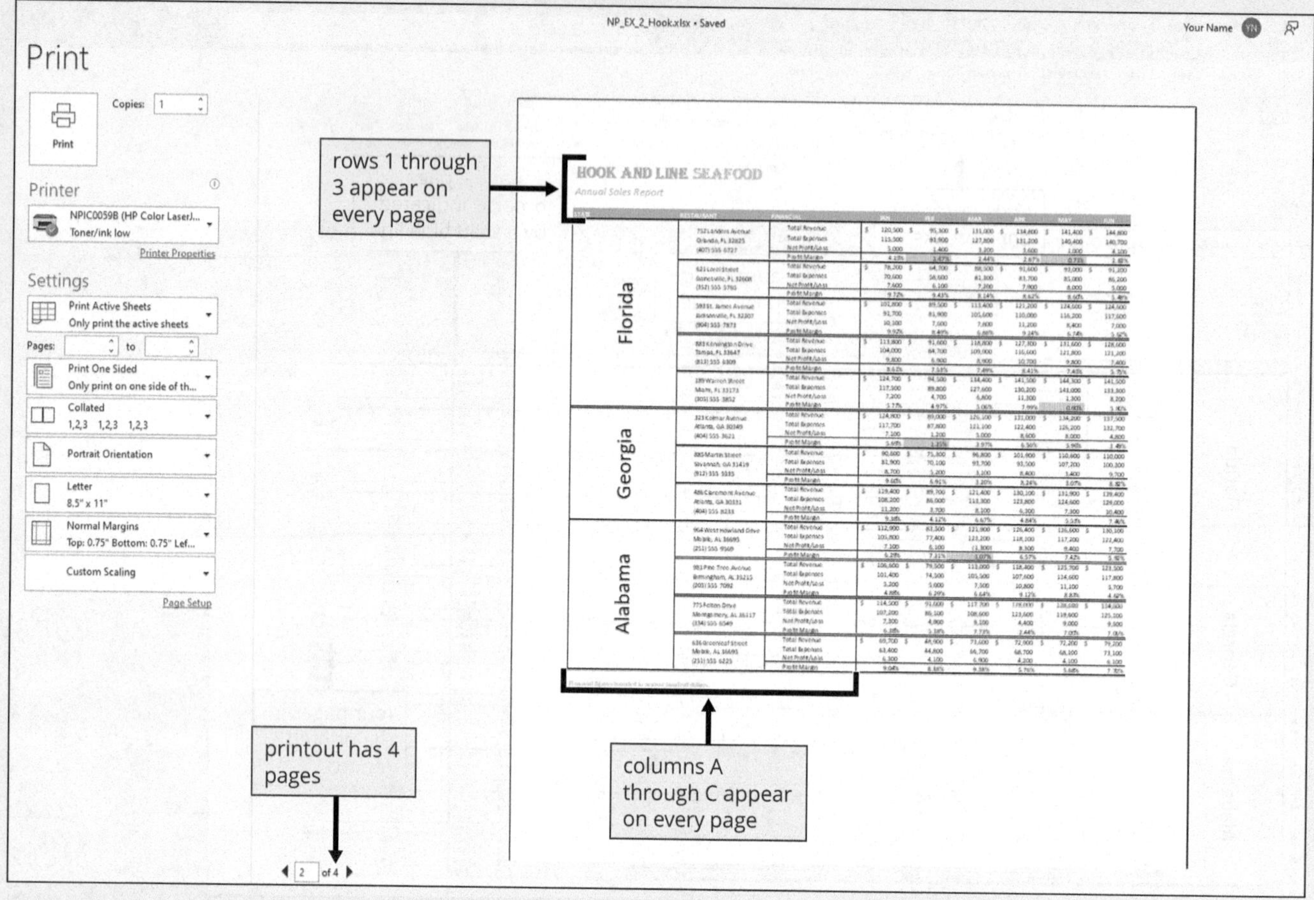

Trouble? If your report is not four pages, return to Page Break Preview and insert, move, or remove page breaks as needed until the printout is four pages with titles on each page.

Adding Headers and Footers

Headers and footers appear only on printed pages. A **header** is text placed at the top of a printed page, and a **footer** is text placed at the page bottom of a printed page. Headers and footers are divided into three sections—left, center, and right—into which you can enter information.

Headers and footers often contain information that does not appear in the workbook itself. The information can be dynamic, such as the workbook or worksheet name, page numbers, the total number of pages, or the date the pages printed. If you later change the workbook name or the number of pages in the report, the header and footer will reflect that change. You can also enter text into the header and footer that doesn't change, such as your name as the report's author.

A printout can contain different sets of headers and footers. You can design one set for the first page of the report. Then, you can create another set for the remaining pages or for odd- and even-numbered pages.

Robert wants you to add headers and footers to the report. For the header, you'll display workbook's file name in left section and the current date in the right section. For the footer, you'll display the current page number and the total number of pages in the center section and your name in the right section.

To set up the page header for the Sales report:

1. In Print Preview, at the bottom of the Settings section, click the **Page Setup** link. The Page Setup dialog box opens.
2. Click the **Header/Footer** tab to display options for the header and footer.

   Tip You can create or edit headers and footers in Page Layout view by clicking in the Header & Footer section and using the tools on the Design tab.

3. Click the **Different first page** check box to select it, creating one set of headers and footers for the first page and another set for subsequent pages.
4. Click the **Customer Header** button. The Header dialog box opens. Because you selected the Different first page option, the dialog box contains a Header tab and a First Page Header tab.
5. Click the **First Page Header** tab.
6. Click in the Left section box, type **File name:** and press **SPACEBAR**, and then click the **Insert File Name** button. The code &[File], representing the file name of the current workbook, is added to the header text.
7. Press **TAB** twice to move to the Right section box, and then click the **Insert Date** button. The code &[Date] is added to the right section. Refer to Figure 2–46.

Figure 2–46 Header dialog box

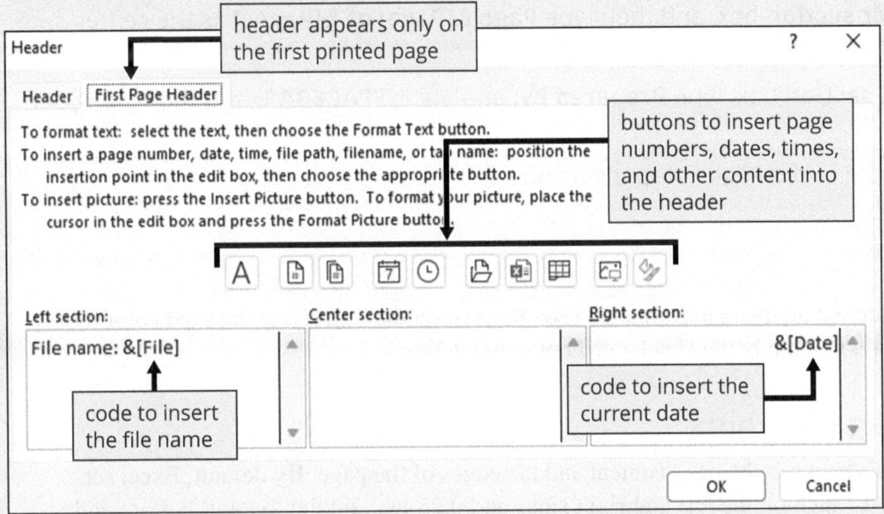

8. Click **OK** to return to the Page Setup dialog box.

The header text you just created will print only on the first page of the report. Robert wants a footer to print on all pages. Because you selected different headers and footers for the first page, you will create one footer for the first page and another footer for subsequent pages.

To create footers for the printed report:

1. In the Page Setup dialog box, on the Header/Footer tab, click the **Custom Footer** button. The Footer dialog box opens.
2. On the Footer tab, click the **Center section** box, type **Page** and press **SPACEBAR**, and then click the **Insert Page Number** button. The code &[Page] is added to the center footer.

3. Press **SPACEBAR**, type **of** and press **SPACEBAR**, and then click the **Insert Number of Pages** button. The code &[Pages] is added to the center footer. Refer to Figure 2–47.

Figure 2–47 Footer dialog box

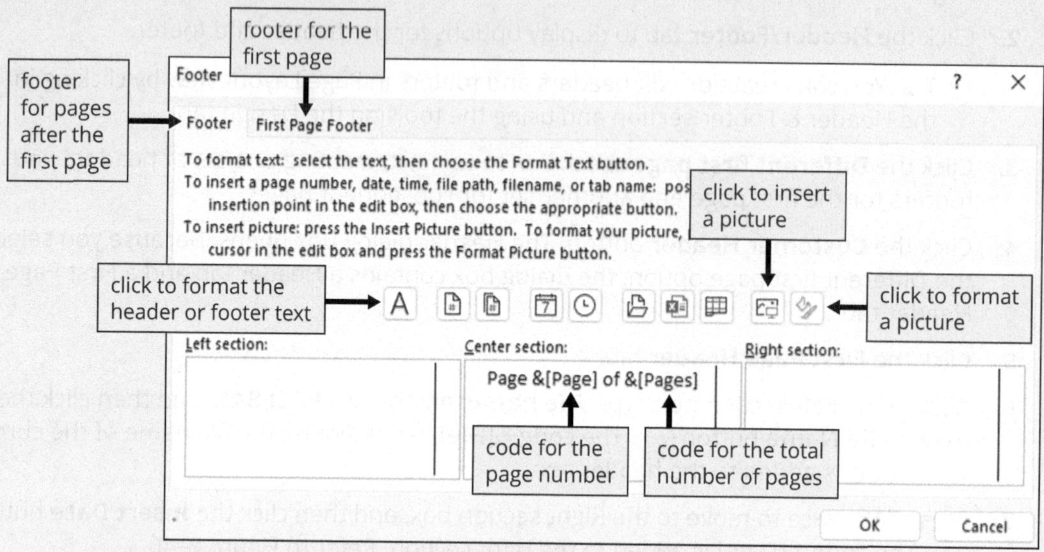

4. Click the **First Page Footer** tab to design the footer of the first page.
5. Click the **Center section** box, and then type **Page &[Page] of &[Pages]** as the center footer of the first page.
6. Click the **Right section** box, type **Prepared by:** and press **SPACEBAR**, and then type your name.
7. Click **OK** to return to the Page Setup dialog box.

Header and footer text are plain unformatted text. You can set the font style, size, and color by clicking the Format Text button in the Header or Footer dialog box.

Setting the Page Margins

A **margin** is the space between the page content and the edges of the page. By default, Excel sets the page margins to 0.7 inch on the left and right sides and 0.75 inch on the top and bottom and allows for 0.3-inch margins around the header and footer. You can reduce or increase these margins as needed by selecting predefined margin sizes or setting your own.

Hook and Line Seafood requires all company reports to use larger top margins to accommodate the company letterhead. You will increase the top margin to 1.5 inches.

To set the top margin for the printed report:

1. In the Page Setup dialog box, click the **Margins** tab to display options for changing the page margins.

   Tip To apply preset margins, click the Margins button in the Page Setup group on the Page Layout tab.

2. Double-click the **Top** box to select the current setting, and then type **1.5** to increase the size of the top margin to 1.5 inches. Refer to Figure 2–48.

Figure 2–48 Margin tab of the Page Setup dialog box

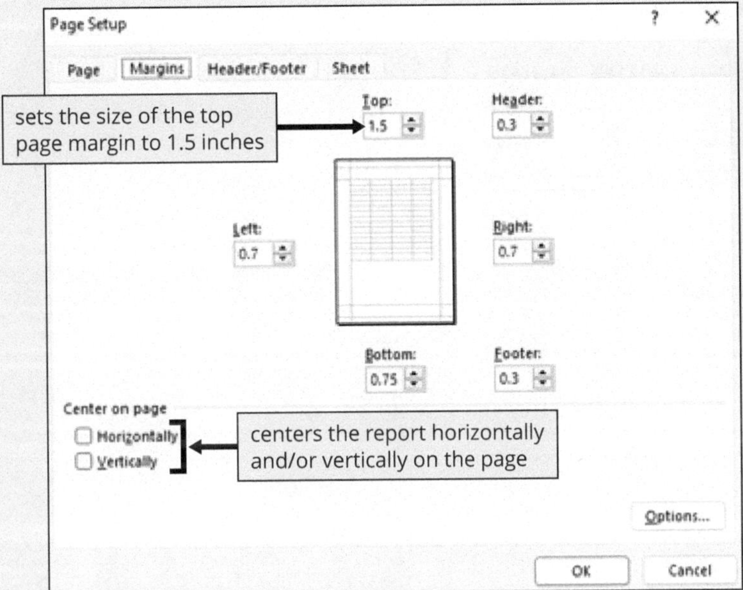

3. Click **OK**. The Page Setup dialog box closes. The new margin appears in the preview.

Page content can be centered both horizontally and vertically on the page. You can do this in the Page Setup dialog box on the Margins tab by selecting the Horizontally and Vertically check boxes.

Robert wants you to print the final version of the Sales report. Before you print, you'll preview the formatted pages.

To preview and print the Sales report:

1. On the Print screen in Backstage view, click the **Zoom to Page** button located in the lower-right corner of the preview window. The display changes to include the entire first page. Refer to Figure 2–49.

Figure 2–49 Preview of the first page

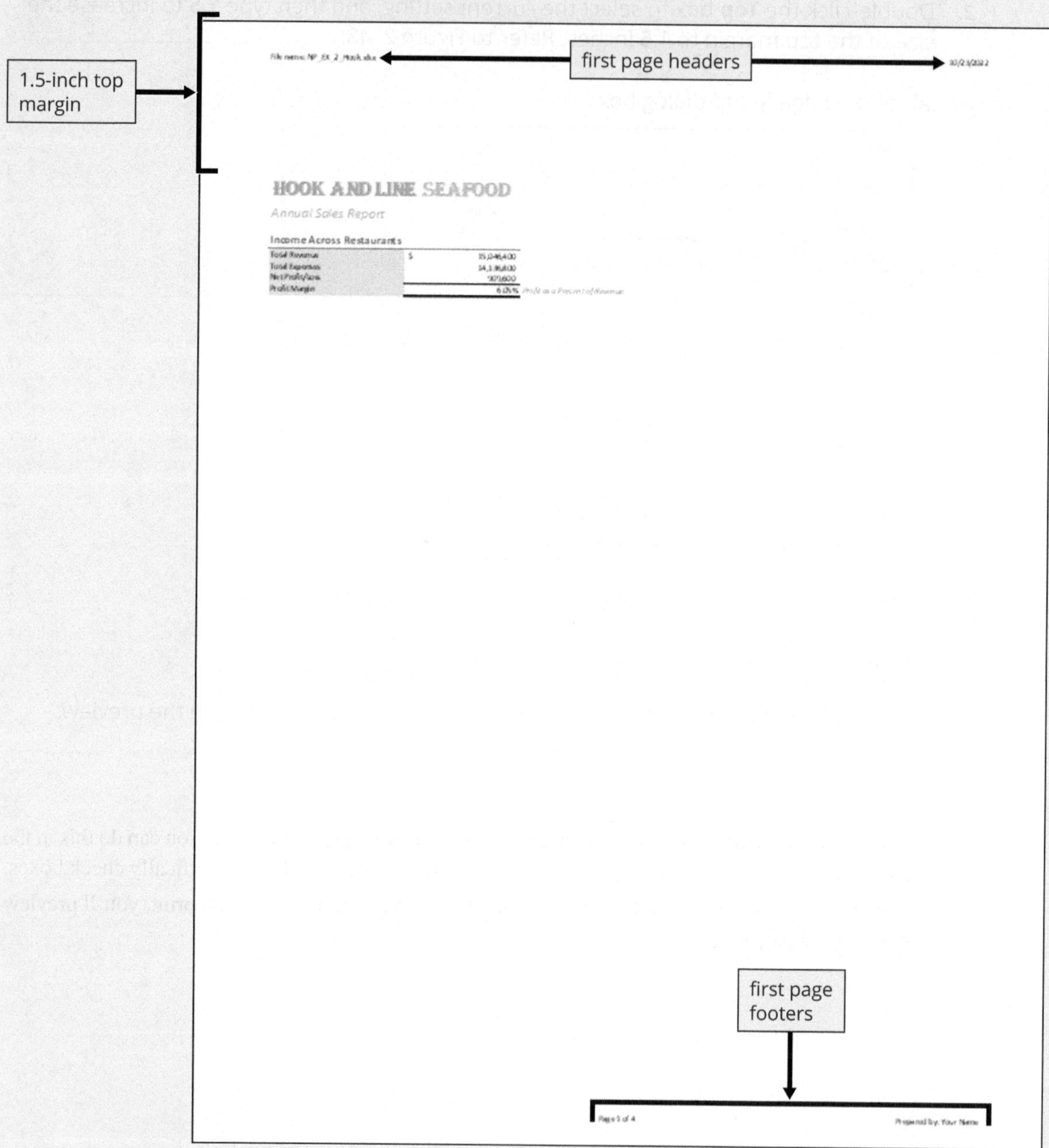

2. Navigate through the rest of the four pages in the Print Preview window.
3. On the Print screen, in the Settings section, click the first box, and then click **Print Entire Workbook**. The printout will include five pages—one page for the Documentation sheet and four pages for the Sales worksheet.
4. If you are instructed to print, click the **Print** button to print the entire workbook. If you are not instructed to print, click the **Back** button on the Backstage view navigation bar to return to the workbook window.
5. Click the **Normal** button on the status bar to return the view of the workbook to normal.
6. **sam** Save the workbook, and then close it.

Robert is pleased that your work formatting the workbook has made the sales report more readable and the data more accessible.

Part 2.2 Quick Check

1. If you change the definition of a custom cell style, what impact does that have on cells formatted with that style in the workbook?
2. If you change the definition of a custom cell style, what impact does that have on cells formatted with that style in other workbooks?
3. If you change a workbook's theme, what impact does that have on a cell whose background is filled with a standard color?
4. What is the formula to calculate the average of the values in columns F through H?
5. Why would you use a conditional format to highlight cells rather than formatting those cells directly?
6. What are print titles?
7. In Page Break Preview, how can you tell the difference between automatic page breaks and manual page breaks?
8. What is the code to display the text "Page *number* of *total*" in a page header or footer where *number* is the page number and *total* is the total number of pages?

Practice: Review Assignments

Data Files needed for the Review Assignments: NP_EX_2-2.xlsx, Support_EX_2_Texture.jpg

The Hook and Line Seafood chain wants to expand its market and increase its visibility. It has started a fleet of mobile food trucks to cater to parks, beaches, and festivals in southern Florida. Robert is working on a report analyzing August revenue from Food Truck 3. His analysis has four sections: a summary section, a table of revenue by weekday, a table of revenue by location, and a calendar of daily revenue by location during August. Robert wants each section to print on a separate page. He also wants the report to highlight the days and the locations with the highest and lowest revenue. The worksheet has almost no formatting. You'll format the report for both the computer screen and the printed page. Complete the following:

1. Open the **NP_EX_2-2.xlsx** workbook located in the Excel2 > Review folder included with your Data Files, and then save the workbook as **NP_EX_2_Truck** in the location specified by your instructor.
2. In the Documentation sheet, enter your name in cell B4 and the date in cell B5.
3. Set the background of the Documentation sheet to the **Support_EX_2_Texture.jpg** image file located in the Excel2 > Review folder included with your Data Files.
4. In the August worksheet, format the calendar as follows:
   a. Format cell A39 with the Title cell style.
   b. Merge and center the range B40:H40 containing the month and year, and then format the merged cell with the 60% – Accent4 cell style.
   c. In the range B41:H41, format the day abbreviations with the Accent6 cell style, and then center the text in each cell.
   d. In cell B42, format containing the day number with the 20% – Accent3 cell style.
   e. Format cell B44 containing the day's revenue with Currency format and decrease the decimal to remove the cents value.
   f. Add an outside border around the range B42:B44.
   g. Use the Format Painter to copy the format from the range B42:B44 to the rest of the calendar days in the range B42:H56.
   h. In the range A42:A44, merge and center the title, middle-align the text vertically, increase the font size to 14 points, orient the text Angle Counterclockwise, and then add a border around the merged cell.
   i. Copy the format from the merged cell A42 to the range A45:A56.
5. Format the Revenue by Location summary as follows:
   a. Format cell A22 using the Title cell style and format the range A23:C23 using the Accent6 cell style.
   b. In the range A24:A37 containing the addresses, decrease the font to 9 points and increase the indent twice.
6. Copy and paste the format in the range A22:C23 into the range A12:C13. Copy and paste the format in the range A24:C24 into the range A14:C20.
7. Apply the following formatting to the Revenue by Day summary:
   a. Apply the Title cell style to cell A4.
   b. In cell B5, apply the Accounting format and reduce the number of decimals to hide the cents values.
   c. In the range B6:B7, apply the Comma format and hide the cents values.
   d. In cell B8, apply the Percent and display two decimal places.
   e. In cell B8, add a single border line above the cell and a double border line below the cell.
8. Create a custom style for the August summary by doing the following:
   a. In cell C6, format the note in 9 points, italic, Gray, Accent3 font and increase the indent one space.
   b. Save the format you applied to cell C6 as custom cell style named **sidenote** and include only the Alignment and Font settings in the style.
   c. Apply the sidenote custom cell style to the range C5:C8.

9. Highlight the top and bottom days in August by selecting the range B44:H44,B47:H47,B50:H50,B53:H53,B56:H56 containing the daily revenue totals. Create a conditional format to display the top day in green fill with dark green text. Create another conditional format to display the bottom day in light red fill with dark red text.
10. Use conditional formats to highlight the best and worst locations by selecting the range C24:C37 and changing the top location to a green fill with dark green text and the worst location to a light red fill with dark red text.
11. Repeat Step 10 for the weekday averages in the range C14:C20.
12. Format the print version of the August worksheet as follows:
    a. Verify that sheet will print in portrait orientation.
    b. Set the print area of the report to A1:C38,A39:H56.
    c. Repeat rows 1 through 3 as print titles on every page of the report.
    d. Insert a manual page break directly above rows 12, 22, and 39. Remove all automatic page breaks from the document so that it prints on four pages.
    e. Add a different first page for headers and footers. On the first page header, enter your name in the left section, the file name in center, and the date in the right section.
    f. For the first page footer and subsequent page footers, enter the code **Page &[Page] of &[Pages]** in the center section.
13. Preview the printed version of the August worksheet. Verify that the report has four pages, the first rows of the worksheet will print on each page, the overall summary is on page 1, the revenue by day of the week is on page 2, the revenue by location is on page 3, and the revenue for day in the calendar is on page 4. Make sure your name, the file name, and the date appear on the first page header and that the page number and total number of pages appear on every footer.
14. If you are instructed to print, print the entire workbook.
15. Save the workbook, and then close it.

Apply: Case Problem 1

Data File needed for this Case Problem: NP_EX_2-3.xlsx

Thrill Managers Alya Jannat is an analyst for Thrill Managers, a web company that analyzes usage data for theme parks and thrill rides. One of the services provided by Thrill Managers is an hourly analysis of wait times at different parks. Using their reports, park visitors can arrange their visits to minimize wait times and park owners can distribute their resources to improve the customer experience. Alya wants you to finish formatting a worksheet displaying hourly wait times for a popular theme park over the past month. You will use conditional formats to create a "heat map" that shows the times during each day and across each week where wait times increase in response to customer demand. Complete the following:

1. Open the **NP_EX_2-3.xlsx** workbook located in the Excel2 > Case1 folder included with your Data Files, and then save the workbook as **NP_EX_2_Thrill** in the location specified by your instructor.
2. In the Documentation sheet, enter your name in cell B4 and the current date in cell B5. Format the date in cell B5 using the Long Date format and left-align it in the cell.
3. Copy the format from the range A1:A2 of the Documentation sheet into the range A1:A2 of the Wait Times worksheet.
4. In the Wait Times worksheet, in the range J21:K21, merge and center the title and apply the Accent1 cell style. In the range J22:J28, indent the wait times one space to the right. In the range J21:K28, add a thick outside border.
5. Define the color scale for the range of wait times with the following fill colors:
    a. In cell K22, set the fill color to Olive Green, Accent 3.
    b. In cell K23, set the fill color to Olive Green, Accent 3, Lighter 40%.
    c. In cell K24, set the fill color to Olive Green, Accent 3, Lighter 60%.
    d. In cell K25, set the fill color to Orange, Accent 6, Lighter 60%.
    e. In cell K26, set the fill color to Red, Accent 2, Lighter 60%.
    f. In cell K27, set the fill color to Red, Accent 2, Lighter 40%.
    g. In cell K28, set the fill color to Red, Accent 2.

6. In the range B22:H34, create the following conditional formats in the order specified:
   a. Highlight values greater than 60 with the Red, Accent 2 fill color. (Note: Use the Custom Format option in the Greater Than dialog box and then set the fill color in the Fill tab.)
   b. Highlight values less than 10 with an Olive Green, Accent 3 fill (seventh color in the first row).
   c. Highlight values between 10 and 20 with an Olive Green, Accent 3, Lighter 40% fill (seventh color in the fourth row).
   d. Highlight values between 20 and 30 with an Olive Green, Accent 3, Lighter 60% fill (seventh color in the third row).
   e. Highlight values between 30 and 40 with an Orange, Accent 6, Lighter 60% fill (last color in the third row).
   f. Highlight values between 40 and 50 with Red, Accent 2, Lighter 60% fill (sixth color in the third row).
   g. Highlight values between 50 and 60 with Red, Accent 2, Lighter 40% fill (sixth color in the fourth row).
7. In the range B21:H21, apply the Accent1 cell style to the day abbreviations and center the text horizontally.
8. In the range B20:H20, merge and center the date range and increase the font size to 14 points.
9. In the range A22:A34, right-align the hour values and increase the indent one space (to move the values the left).
10. In the range B21:H34, add thick outside borders.
11. Use the Format Painter to copy the formats in the range A20:K34 and paste the formats to the ranges A36:K50, A52:K66, and A68:K82.
12. Enter the following calculations to determine the average wait times during each of the four weeks in June:
    a. In cell B5, use the AVERAGE function to calculate the average ride wait time for values in the range B22:H34.
    b. In cell B6, calculate the average wait time for values in the range B38:H50.
    c. In cell B7, calculate the average wait time for values in the range B54:H66.
    d. In cell B8, calculate the average wait time for values in the range B70:H82.
    e. In the range A5:A8, decrease the font size to 10 points and indent the text one space to the right.
    f. Merge and center the range A4:C4, apply the Accent1 cell style to the merged cell, and then add thick outside borders to the range A4:C8.
13. Enter the following calculations to determine average wait times from Sunday to Saturday:
    a. In cell B11, calculate the average of value in the nonadjacent range B22:B34, B38:B50, B54:B66, B70:B82.
    b. In cell B12 calculate the average of values in the range C22:C34, C38:C50, C54:C66, C70:C82.
    c. In cell B13, calculate the average of values in the range D22:D34, D38:D50, D54:D66, D70:D82.
    d. In cells B14 through B17, calculate the averages of the wait times for Wednesday through Saturday, revising the cell references to point to in columns E through H.
    e. In the range A11:A17, decrease the font size to 10 points and indent the text one space to the right.
    f. Merge and center the range A10:C10, apply the Accent1 cell style to the merged cell, and then add thick outside borders to the range A10:C17.
14. Format the print version of the report as follows:
    a. Repeat rows 1 through 3 on every page.
    b. Remove all automatic page breaks from the printout and add manual page breaks above rows 20, 36, 52, and 68.
    c. Verify that the orientation is portrait and scale the printout to 75%.
    d. Display your name and the date in the right section of the first page header.
    e. On every page after the first page, display the text Page *page* of *number* in the center footer, where *page* is the page number and *total* is the number of pages.
15. Preview the printout to verify that the report is printed on five pages, your name and the date are on the right side in the header of the first page, and that the page number and total number of pages are centered in the footer on the remaining pages.
16. If you are instructed to print, print the entire workbook.
17. Save the workbook, and then close it.

Challenge: Case Problem 2

Data Files needed for this Case Problem: NP_EX_2-4.xlsx, Support_EX_2_Home.thmx

Home Tracker Samuel Javier is an analyst for Home Tracker, a property listing service. Part of Samuel's job is to maintain a current listing of homes in different markets. Each listing includes the home address, market price, square footage, number of bedrooms, and the number of bathrooms. Samuel stores this information in a workbook and wants to add search tools he can use to highlight the entire row of each property that matches specified criteria.

To highlight those properties, you will use a conditional format based on a formula. These formulas need locked cell references so that the format can be copied across a range of cells without the cell references changing. To lock a cell reference, include the $ symbol before the row and/or column addresses. The following formula highlights cells when the values in column E (starting with cell E2) are less than or equal to the value in cell K2 and the values in column G (starting with cell G2) are equal to the value in cell K3.

```
= AND($E2 <= $K$2, $G2 = $K$3)
```

As the values stored in cells K2 and K3 change, the cells matched by this formula also change. You will use a similar formula for Samuel's workbook to highlight properties with a specified price, number of bedrooms, and number of bathrooms. Complete the following:

1. Open the **NP_EX_2-4.xlsx** workbook located in the Excel2 > Case2 folder included with your Data Files, and then save the workbook as **NP_EX_2_Tracker** in the location specified by your instructor.
2. In the Documentation sheet, in the range B3:B4, enter your name and the date.
3. **Explore:** On the Page Layout tab, in the Themes group, click the Themes button, and click Browse for Themes. Open the **Support_EX_2_Home.thmx** theme file located in the Excel2 > Case2 folder included with your Data Files. Verify that the colors and fonts in the Documentation sheet change.
4. In the Home Listings worksheet, apply the following formatting to the range containing criteria for the conditional format:
   a. In the range A4:B4, merge and center the contents of the cells, and then apply the Accent2 cell style.
   b. Format cell B5 in Currency format (*not* the Currency cell style) with no digits to the right of the decimal point.
   c. In the range A5:A7, change the fill color of to the theme color Gold, Accent3, Lighter 80%.
   d. In the range A4:B7, add thick outside borders with the Orange, Accent2 color and a dotted inside border in black.
5. Insert the following formulas and formats to summarize the home listing data:
   a. In cell B10, use the COUNT function to count the number of values in column H.
   b. In cell B11, use the AVERAGE function to display the average listing price from column H.
   c. In cell B12, use the AVERAGE function to calculate the average square footage in column I.
   d. Copy the formats from the range A4:B7 and paste them into the range A9:B12.
   e. In cell B10, change the format to General. In cell B11, change the format to Currency with no digits to the right of the decimal point. In cell B12, change the format to Comma with no digits to the right of the decimal point.
6. Apply the following formatting to the property listings:
   a. In the range D1:K1, apply the Accent6 cell style to the column labels.
   b. In the range G1:G226, apply the Text format to the postal code values. In the range H1:H226, apply the Currency format with no decimal places to the listed prices. In the range I1:I226, apply the Comma Style format with no decimal places to the square footage.
   c. Add a dotted border around all cells in the range D2:K226.
7. **Explore:** Select the range D2:K226 containing information on each property, and then apply the following conditional format:
   a. On the Home tab, in the Styles group, click the Conditional Formatting button, click Highlight Cell Rules, and then click More Rules.
   b. In the New Formatting Rule dialog box, click Use a formula to determine which cells to format.

c. In the Format values where this formula is true box, enter the following formula (exactly as written):

```
= AND($H2 <= $B$5, $J2 = $B$6, $K2 = $B$7)
```

d. Click the Format button, and then in the Format Cells dialog box, format the font as bold, standard red, and format the fill to the Light Yellow, Background 2 theme color (the third color in the first row).

e. Close the dialog box, and then verify that only one property (524 East Lakewood Street, Coraopolis, PA) matches the search criteria and that the entire row of data for that property is highlighted.

8. Change the values in the range B5:B7 to highlight properties listed for $300,000 or less with three bedrooms and two baths. Verify that nine properties are highlighted in the table.
9. Apply the following print formats to the worksheet:
   a. Set the orientation of the printout to landscape.
   b. Set the print area to the nonadjacent range A1:B12,D1:K226.
   c. Set the print titles to display row 1 on every page.
   d. Remove any automatic page breaks from printout. Add manual page breaks above rows 50, 100, 150, and 200.
   e. Add a header to the first page displaying your name, the date, and the name of the workbook on separate lines in the right section of the header.
   f. **Explore:** In the Header dialog box, select the code for the header and click the Format Text button to open the Font dialog box. Set the font size of the header text to 20 points.
   g. On each page, display a center footer displaying the word **Page** followed by the page number and the number of pages in the printed report.
10. Preview the printout to verify that the report is printed on six pages and that your name, the date, and the workbook file name are in right header of the first page. Verify that the page number and total number of pages are centered in the footer on every page.
11. If you are instructed to print, print the entire workbook.
12. Save the workbook, and then close it.

Calculating with Formulas and Functions

Staffing a Call Center

Case: MediCOH

Chryssa Fontini manages the national call center for MediCOH, a nationwide health care insurer based in central Ohio. The call center is open Monday through Friday from 8 AM to 6 PM, Central Time. It is Chryssa's responsibility to ensure that the center is adequately staffed to handle customer queries and requests. To accomplish that task, Chryssa analyzes the volume of calls made to the center, paying particular attention to the amount of time customers wait on hold. If the hold times are too long or if too many customers hang up before reaching an operator, MediCOH will lose business and the trust of its customers. Chryssa has created an Excel workbook of call data. You will analyze this data to help Chryssa meet the staffing needs of the call center.

Starting Data Files

Excel3

Module

NP_EX_3-1.xlsx

NP_EX_3-2.xlsx

Review

NP_EX_3-3.xlsx

Case1

NP_EX_3-4.xlsx

Case2

NP_EX_3-5.xlsx

Objectives

Part 3.1

- Perform calculations on dates and times
- Extend a formula or data series with AutoFill
- Use relative, absolute, and mixed cell references
- Write formulas using dynamic arrays
- Analyze data with the Quick Analysis tool
- Interpret an error value

Part 3.2

- Calculate minimums, maximums, averages, medians, and modes
- Round a value to a specified number of digits
- Write a logical formula with the IF function
- Retrieve data with XLOOKUP, VLOOKUP, and HLOOKUP
- Use Goal Seek to do a What-If Analysis

Part 3.1 Visual Overview: References and Ranges

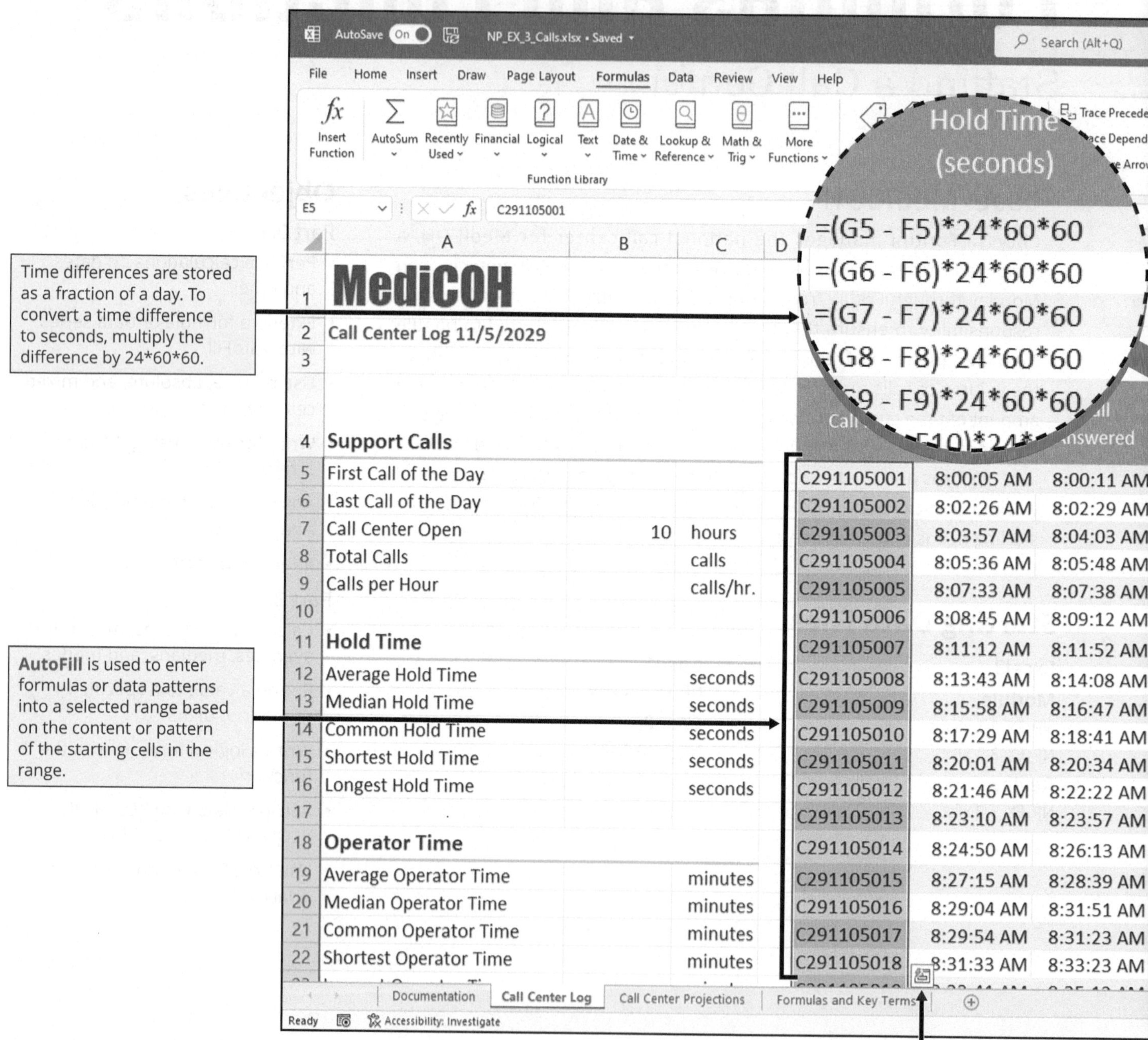

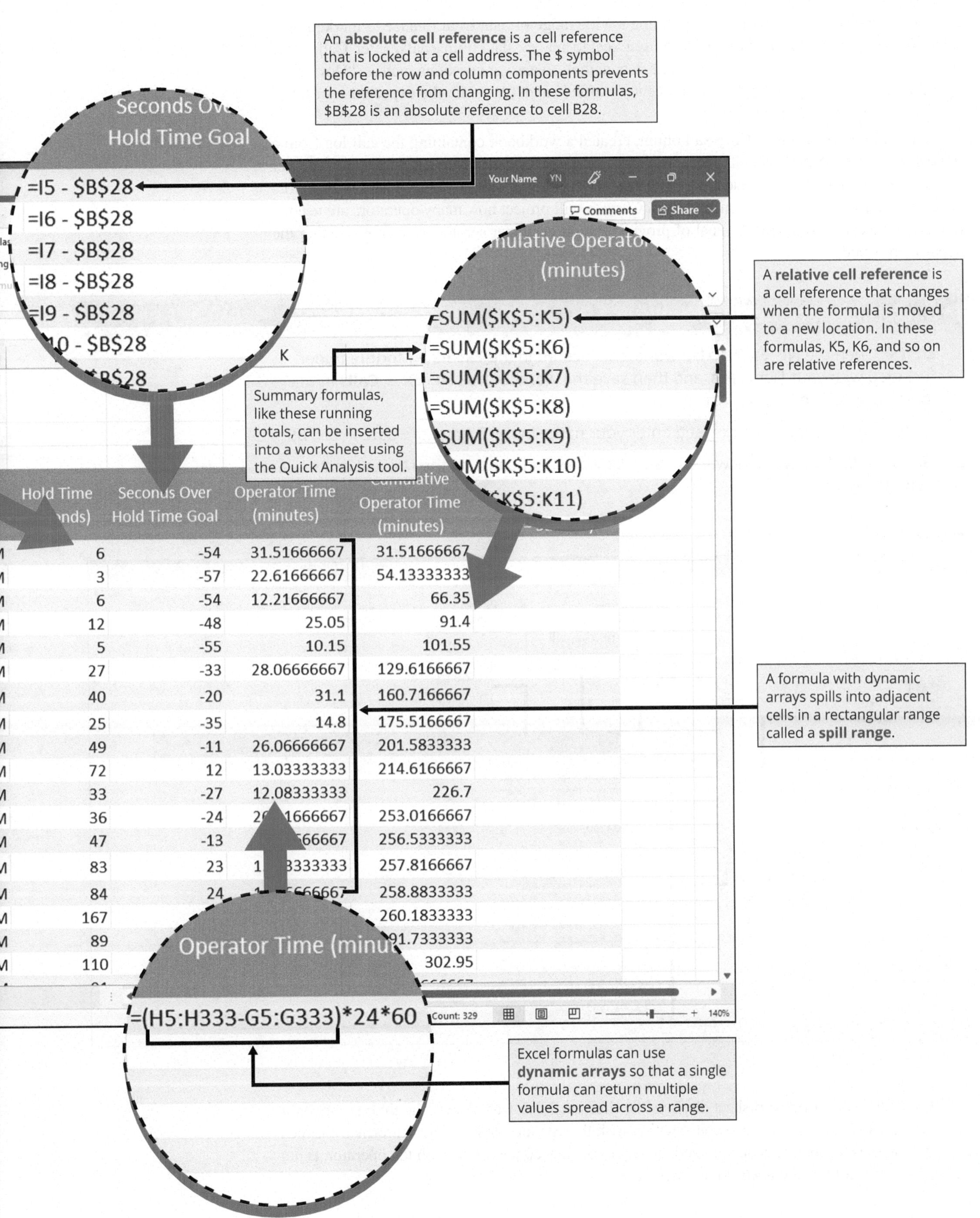
An **absolute cell reference** is a cell reference that is locked at a cell address. The $ symbol before the row and column components prevents the reference from changing. In these formulas, $B$28 is an absolute reference to cell B28.
Seconds Over Hold Time Goal
=I5 - $B$28
=I6 - $B$28
=I7 - $B$28
=I8 - $B$28
=I9 - $B$28
Cumulative Operator Time (minutes)
=SUM($K$5:K5)
=SUM($K$5:K6)
=SUM($K$5:K7)
=SUM($K$5:K8)
A **relative cell reference** is a cell reference that changes when the formula is moved to a new location. In these formulas, K5, K6, and so on are relative references.
Summary formulas, like these running totals, can be inserted into a worksheet using the Quick Analysis tool.
Your Name
Comments
Share
Hold Time
Seconds Over Hold Time Goal
Operator Time (minutes)
Operator Time (minutes)
A formula with dynamic arrays spills into adjacent cells in a rectangular range called a **spill range**.
Operator Time (minu
=(H5:H333-G5:G333)*24*60
Count: 329
140%
Excel formulas can use **dynamic arrays** so that a single formula can return multiple values spread across a range.

Designing a Workbook for Calculations

Excel is a powerful application for interpreting a wide range of data from finance to marketing to scientific research. In this module, you will use Excel to analyze data from a call center. Call center science is a rich field of research using mathematical tools to answer questions such as, "How many operators are necessary to handle the call center traffic?" and "What are the expected wait times with a given number of operators?"

The call center manager, Chryssa Fontini, created a workbook containing the call log from a typical day at the MediCOH call center. You will use this data to determine how long a customer typically waits on hold before reaching an operator and how long conversations with those operators last. Based on your calculations and analysis, Chryssa will project how many operators are needed to handle the call traffic with the goal of providing good customer service without exceeding the department's budget.

To open the call center workbook:

1. sam Open the **NP_EX_3-1.xlsx** workbook located in the **Excel3 > Module** folder included with your Data Files, and then save the workbook as **NP_EX_3_Calls** in the location specified by your instructor.
2. In the Documentation worksheet, enter your name in cell B4 and the date in cell B5.
3. Go to the **Call Center Log** worksheet. This worksheet contains the raw call center data. Refer to Figure 3–1.

Figure 3–1 Call center log

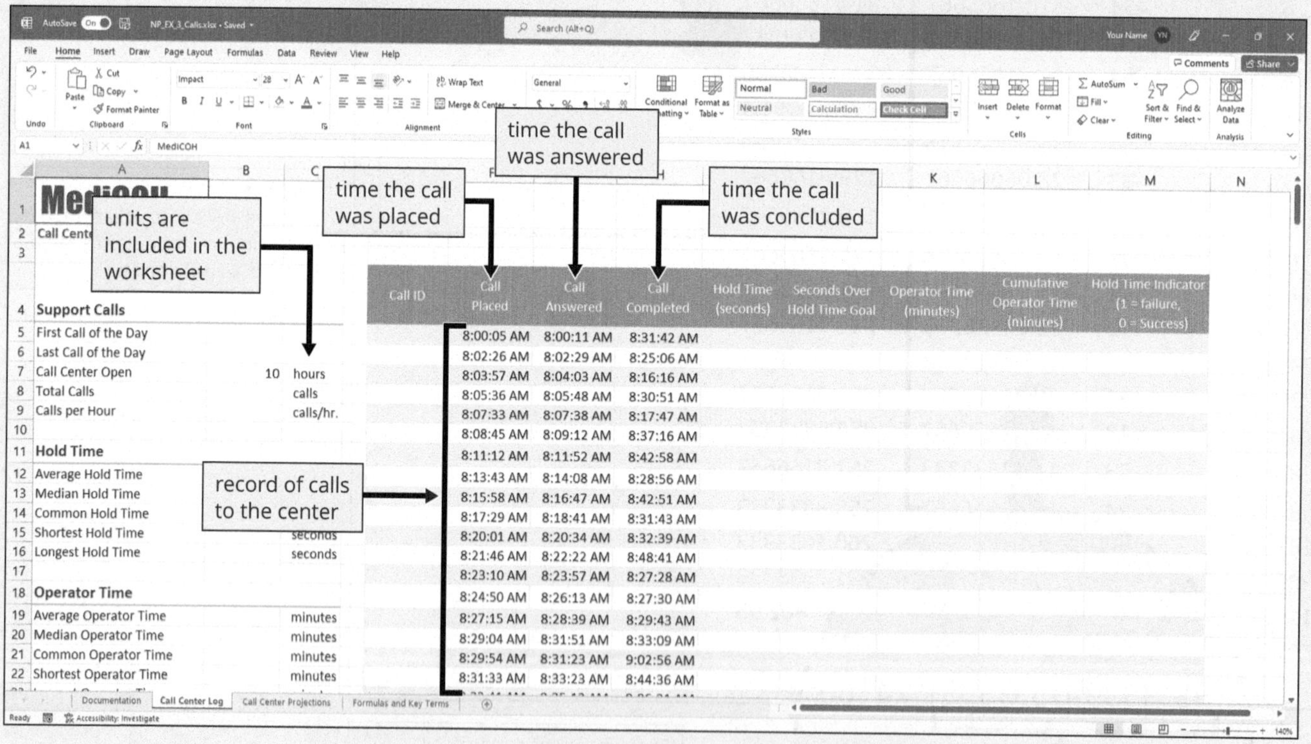

time the call was answered
time the call was placed
time the call was concluded
units are included in the worksheet
record of calls to the center

Call ID	Call Placed	Call Answered	Call Completed	Hold Time (seconds)	Seconds Over Hold Time Goal	Operator Time (minutes)	Cumulative Operator Time (minutes)	Hold Time Indicator (1 = failure, 0 = Success)
	8:00:05 AM	8:00:11 AM	8:31:42 AM					
	8:02:26 AM	8:02:29 AM	8:25:06 AM					
	8:03:57 AM	8:04:03 AM	8:16:16 AM					
	8:05:36 AM	8:05:48 AM	8:30:51 AM					
	8:07:33 AM	8:07:38 AM	8:17:47 AM					
	8:08:45 AM	8:09:12 AM	8:37:16 AM					
	8:11:12 AM	8:11:52 AM	8:42:58 AM					
	8:13:43 AM	8:14:08 AM	8:28:56 AM					
	8:15:58 AM	8:16:47 AM	8:42:51 AM					
	8:17:29 AM	8:18:41 AM	8:31:43 AM					
	8:20:01 AM	8:20:34 AM	8:32:39 AM					
	8:21:46 AM	8:22:22 AM	8:48:41 AM					
	8:23:10 AM	8:23:57 AM	8:27:28 AM					
	8:24:50 AM	8:26:13 AM	8:27:30 AM					
	8:27:15 AM	8:28:39 AM	8:29:43 AM					
	8:29:04 AM	8:31:51 AM	8:33:09 AM					
	8:29:54 AM	8:31:23 AM	9:02:56 AM					
	8:31:33 AM	8:33:23 AM	8:44:36 AM					

Row	A	B	C
1	MediCOH		
2	Call Center		
4	Support Calls		
5	First Call of the Day		
6	Last Call of the Day		
7	Call Center Open	10	hours
8	Total Calls		calls
9	Calls per Hour		calls/hr.
11	Hold Time		
12	Average Hold Time		
13	Median Hold Time		
14	Common Hold Time		
15	Shortest Hold Time		seconds
16	Longest Hold Time		seconds
18	Operator Time		
19	Average Operator Time		minutes
20	Median Operator Time		minutes
21	Common Operator Time		minutes
22	Shortest Operator Time		minutes

Documentation | Call Center Log | Call Center Projections | Formulas and Key Terms

The Call Center Log worksheet displays the time each call was placed, the time an operator answered the call, and the time the conversation with the operator ended. Other information, such as how long the customer was on hold and the length of each conversation with the operator, is not included in the call log and needs to be calculated.

Documenting Calculations

A workbook with many calculations and formulas can be challenging to interpret. It is helpful to list the formulas used in the workbook and explain the assumptions and key terms behind those formulas. These can be placed in a separate worksheet.

Chryssa included a worksheet containing explanations of the equations and key terms that are used in this workbook. You will review the formulas and key terms used in the workbook.

To review the workbook's formulas and key terms:

1. Go to the **Formulas and Key Terms** worksheet.
2. Review the worksheet contents, paying attention to the equations and key terms that you will be using in this workbook.
3. Go to the **Call Center Log** worksheet.

Constants and Units

An important Excel skill is the ability to translate a mathematical equation into an Excel formula. Some equations use **constants**, which are terms in an equation whose values don't change. For example, the following equation converts a time interval measured in days to an interval measured in seconds by multiplying the *day* value by three constants—24, 60, and 60, because there are 24 hours in a day, 60 minutes in each hour, and 60 seconds in each minute:

```
seconds = day × 24 × 60 × 60
```

A good practice is to include the units in any calculation next to the calculated value. In some situations, the unit is obvious, such as when a currency value is formatted with the appropriate currency symbol. In other situations, such as reporting time intervals, the unit is unknown unless you include it (hours, minutes, or seconds) as text in the worksheet.

Insight

Deciding Where to Place a Constant

Constants can be placed in an Excel formula or in a worksheet cell referenced by the formula. Which approach is better?

The answer depends on the constant being used, the purpose of the workbook, and the intended audience. Placing constants in separate cells referenced by the formulas can help users better understand the worksheet because all the values are visible. You can also add explanatory text next to each constant, documenting its meaning and use within the calculations. On the other hand, you don't want anyone to inadvertently change the value of a constant, which then alters a calculation.

You will need to evaluate how important it is for other people to immediately locate the constant and whether the constant requires any explanation for other people to understand the formula. In general, if the constant is commonly known, such as the constant 60 used to multiply hour values into minutes, you can place the constant directly in a formula. However, if the constant is less well-known, such as a tax rate, it is better to place the constant in its own cell, making it more visible. If you decide to place a constant in a cell, you can lock that cell value to ensure that the constant remains unchanged and unchangeable.

You will use constants to calculate each customer's hold time during their call to the center.

Calculating with Dates and Times

Excel stores dates and times as the number of days since January 0, 1900. Full days are a whole number. Partial days are a fraction, such as 0.5 for a half day or 12 hours. Storing dates and times as numbers makes it easier to calculate time and date intervals.

Chryssa wants you to calculate the length of time the first customer in the call log spent on hold.

To calculate the first customer's hold time:

1. In cell **I5**, enter the formula **= G5 – F5** to calculate the hold time of the first call, equal to the difference between the time when the call was placed and the time when the call was answered by an operator. The time 12:00:06 AM appears in this cell.
2. Click cell **I5** to select it. When Excel performs calculations with dates and times, it retains the date/time format. In this instance, you want to display the numerical difference between the time values and not the time.
3. On the Home tab, in the Number group, click the **Number Format arrow**, and then click **General**. The General number format changes the value displayed in the cell to 6.9444E-05.

The value 6.9444E-05 is a decimal value in scientific notation, equal to 6.9444×10^{-5} or 0.000069444. Because Excel measures times in days, this value represents the fractional part of one day. You will convert this value to seconds by multiplying it by 24 times 60 times 60 (the total number of seconds in a single day).

To convert the first customer's hold time to seconds:

1. In cell **I5**, change the formula to **= (G5 – F5)*24*60*60** to convert the value to seconds.
2. Click cell **I5** to select it, and then change the number format to **General**. The value 6 appears in the cell, indicating that the first customer was on hold for 6 seconds.

Now that you have calculated the hold time for the first customer, you will apply this formula and number format to the rest of calls in the log. Although you could copy and paste the formula for the remaining entries in the log, you will use a more efficient method to enter the formulas and formats.

AutoFilling Formulas and Data Patterns

One way to efficiently enter long columns or rows of formulas and data values is with AutoFill. AutoFill extends a formula or a pattern of data values into a selected range. This method is often faster than copying and pasting, which requires two distinct actions.

AutoFilling a Formula

To extend a formula into a range with AutoFill, you select the cell containing the formula. When the cell is selected, a **fill handle** appears as a green square in the lower-right corner of the cell. Double-clicking or dragging the fill handle over a range extends the formula and format of the selected cell into the range.

> **Tip** You can also click the Fill button in the Editing group on the Home tab, and then select the direction to fill.

You will use AutoFill to extend the formula in cell I5 down the remaining cells in the Hold Time column.

To extend the formula and format in cell I5 with AutoFill:

1. Verify that cell **I5** is still selected. The fill handle, the small green square, appears in the lower-right corner of the cell.
2. Point to the **fill handle** in the lower-right corner of the cell. The pointer changes to a plus pointer **+**.
3. Double-click the **fill handle**. The formula and format in cell I5 extend through the rest of the hold time cells in the range I5:I333. Refer to Figure 3–2.

Figure 3–2 Formula and format extended with AutoFill

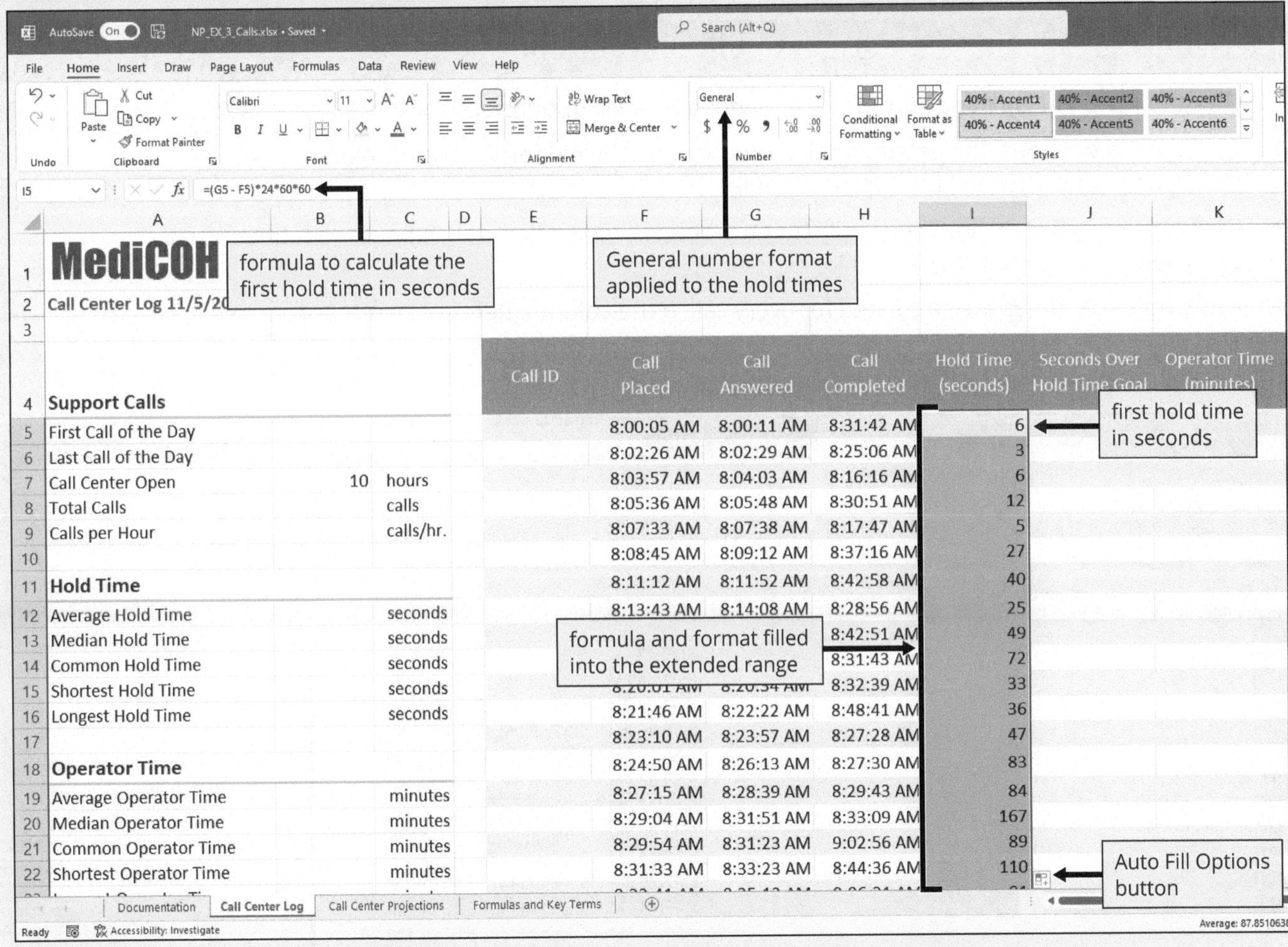

AutoFill also extends formulas and formats from a range. You select the range with the formulas and formats you want to extend, and then either drag the fill handle over the range you want to fill or double-click the fill handle.

Exploring Auto Fill Options

AutoFill extends both the formulas and the formatting of the initial cell or range. However, you might want to extend only the formulas or only the formatting from the initial cells. You use the Auto Fill Options button that appears after AutoFill is complete to do that. The Auto Fill Options button lets you specify what to extend. Refer to Figure 3–3.

Figure 3–3 Auto Fill Options menu

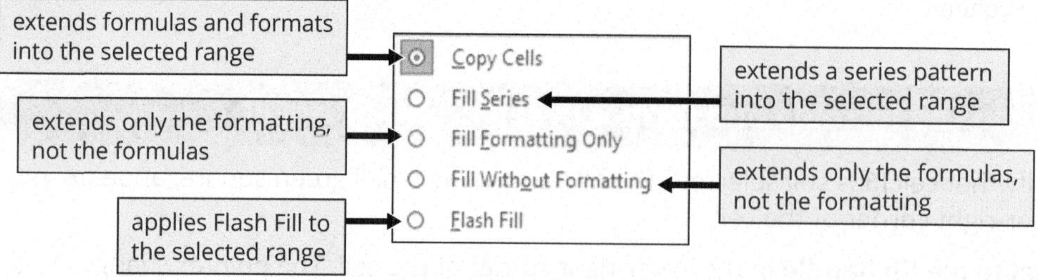

Chryssa used banded rows to make the call log easier to read. By extending cell I5 into the rest column I, you copied cell I5's formatting as well as its formula, removing the banded row effect for column I. You will use the Auto Fill Options button to restore the banded row effect to column I.

To use the Auto Fill Options button to copy only formulas:

1. Click the **Auto Fill Options** button. A menu of AutoFill options appears.
2. Click the **Fill Without Formatting** option button. The original formatting of the range is restored without affecting the copied formulas.
3. Click cell **I5** to select it, and then verify that the banded rows effect still appears with the calculated hold times from column I.
4. Verify that hold times are calculated for every call in the column. Refer to Figure 3–4.

Figure 3–4 Hold times for the last calls of the day

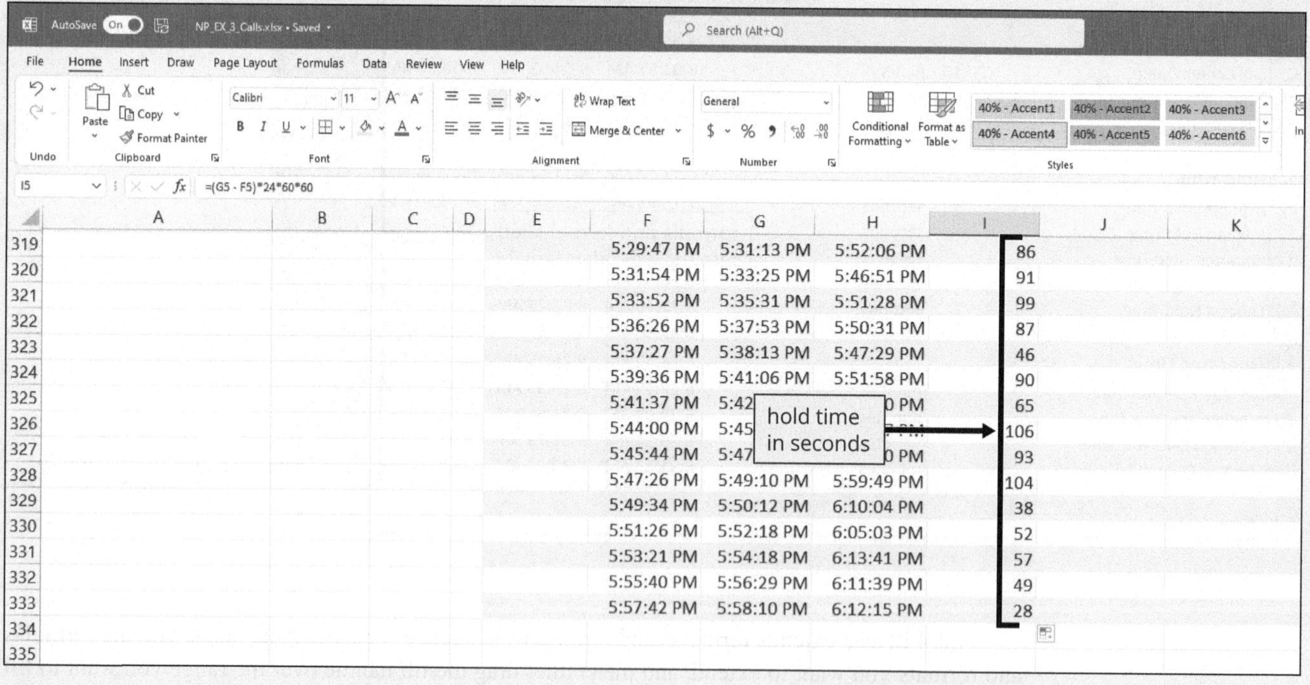

	F	G	H	I
319	5:29:47 PM	5:31:13 PM	5:52:06 PM	86
320	5:31:54 PM	5:33:25 PM	5:46:51 PM	91
321	5:33:52 PM	5:35:31 PM	5:51:28 PM	99
322	5:36:26 PM	5:37:53 PM	5:50:31 PM	87
323	5:37:27 PM	5:38:13 PM	5:47:29 PM	46
324	5:39:36 PM	5:41:06 PM	5:51:58 PM	90
325	5:41:37 PM	5:42	0 PM	65
326	5:44:00 PM	5:45		106
327	5:45:44 PM	5:47	0 PM	93
328	5:47:26 PM	5:49:10 PM	5:59:49 PM	104
329	5:49:34 PM	5:50:12 PM	6:10:04 PM	38
330	5:51:26 PM	5:52:18 PM	6:05:03 PM	52
331	5:53:21 PM	5:54:18 PM	6:13:41 PM	57
332	5:55:40 PM	5:56:29 PM	6:11:39 PM	49
333	5:57:42 PM	5:58:10 PM	6:12:15 PM	28

Filling a Series

AutoFill can extend any data pattern involving dates, times, numbers, and text. To extend a series of data values based on a pattern, enter enough values to establish the pattern, select the cells containing the pattern, and then drag the fill handle into a larger range. Figure 3–5 shows how AutoFill can be used to extend an initial series of odd numbers established in cells A2 and A3 into the range A2:A9.

Figure 3–5 AutoFill used to extend a series

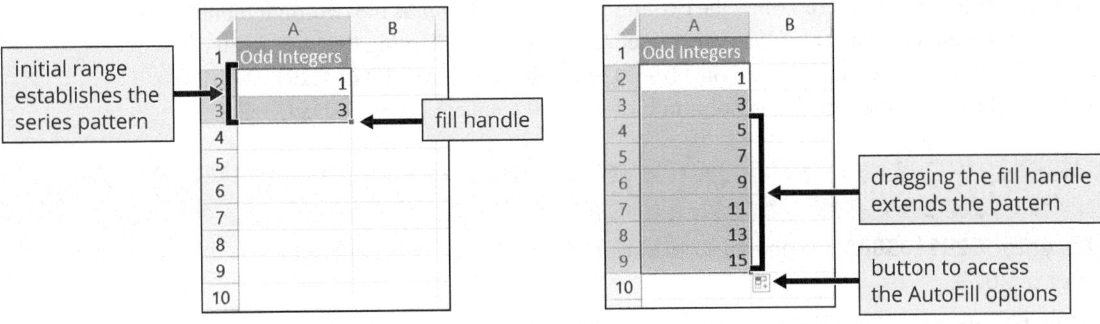

Figure 3–6 describes other extended patterns created with AutoFill. In each case, you must provide enough information to identify the pattern. AutoFill recognizes some patterns from only a single entry—such as Jan or January to create a series of month abbreviations or names, and Mon or Monday to create a series of the days of the week. A text pattern that includes text and a number such as Region 1, Region 2, and so on can also be automatically extended using AutoFill. You can start the series at any point, such as Weds, June, or Region 10, and AutoFill will continue with the next days, months, or text.

Figure 3–6 Series patterns extended with AutoFill

Type	Initial Value(s)	Extended Values
Numbers	1, 2, 3	4, 5, 6, ...
	2, 4, 6	8, 10, 12, ...
Dates and Times	Jan	Feb, Mar, Apr, ...
	January	February, March, April, ...
	15-Jan, 15-Feb	15-Mar, 15-Apr, 15-May, ...
	12/30/2029	12/31/2029, 1/1/2029, 1/2/2029, ...
	1/31/2029, 2/28/2029	3/31/2029, 4/30/2029, 5/31/2029, ...
	Mon	Tue, Wed, Thu, ...
	Monday	Tuesday, Wednesday, Thursday, ...
	11:00 AM	12:00 PM, 1:00 PM, 2:00 PM, ...
	11:58 AM, 11:59 AM	12:00 PM, 12:01 PM, 12:02 PM, ...
Patterned Text	1st period	2nd period, 3rd period, 4th period, ...
	Region 1	Region 2, Region 3, Region 4, ...
	Quarter 3	Quarter 4, Quarter 1, Quarter 2, ...
	Qtr3	Qtr4, Qtr1, Qtr2, ...

AutoFill can extend patterns either horizontally across columns within a single row or vertically across rows within a single column.

Reference

Extending a Series with AutoFill

- Enter the first few values of the series into a range.
- Select the range, and then drag the fill handle over the cells you want to fill; or double-click to fill handle to extend the series alongside the adjacent data.
- To copy only the formats or only the formulas, click the Auto Fill Options button and select the appropriate option.

or

- Enter the first few values of the series into a range.
- Select the entire range into which you want to extend the series.
- On the Home tab, in the Editing group, click the Fill button, and then click Down, Right, Up, Left, Series, or Justify.

At the MediCOH call center, calls are automatically assigned a sequential call ID number with the pattern C*YearMonthDateNumber*, where *Year* is the two-digit year value, *Month* is the two-digit month value, *Date* is the two-digit day value, and *Number* is three-digit number indicating the placement of the call on that day. For example, the 12th call on 11/9/2029 would have a call ID of C291109012. You will use AutoFill to insert the call IDs in column E of the Call Center Log worksheet.

To insert the call ID number series in the call log:

1. In cell **E5**, enter **C291105001** as the call ID number for the first call received on November 5, 2029.
2. Click cell **E5** to select it, and then double-click the **fill handle** in the lower-right corner of the cell. The text series extends through remaining cells in the Call ID column.
3. At the bottom of the Call ID column, click the **Auto Fill Options** button, and then click **Fill Without Formatting**. The original formatting is retained.

> **Tip** Another way to retain banded rows in a table is to select the two cells in the column and then autofill the series.

4. Go to cell **E333** and verify that the last call ID is C291105329.
5. Click cell **E5** to select it. Refer to Figure 3–7.

Figure 3–7 Text pattern extended with AutoFill

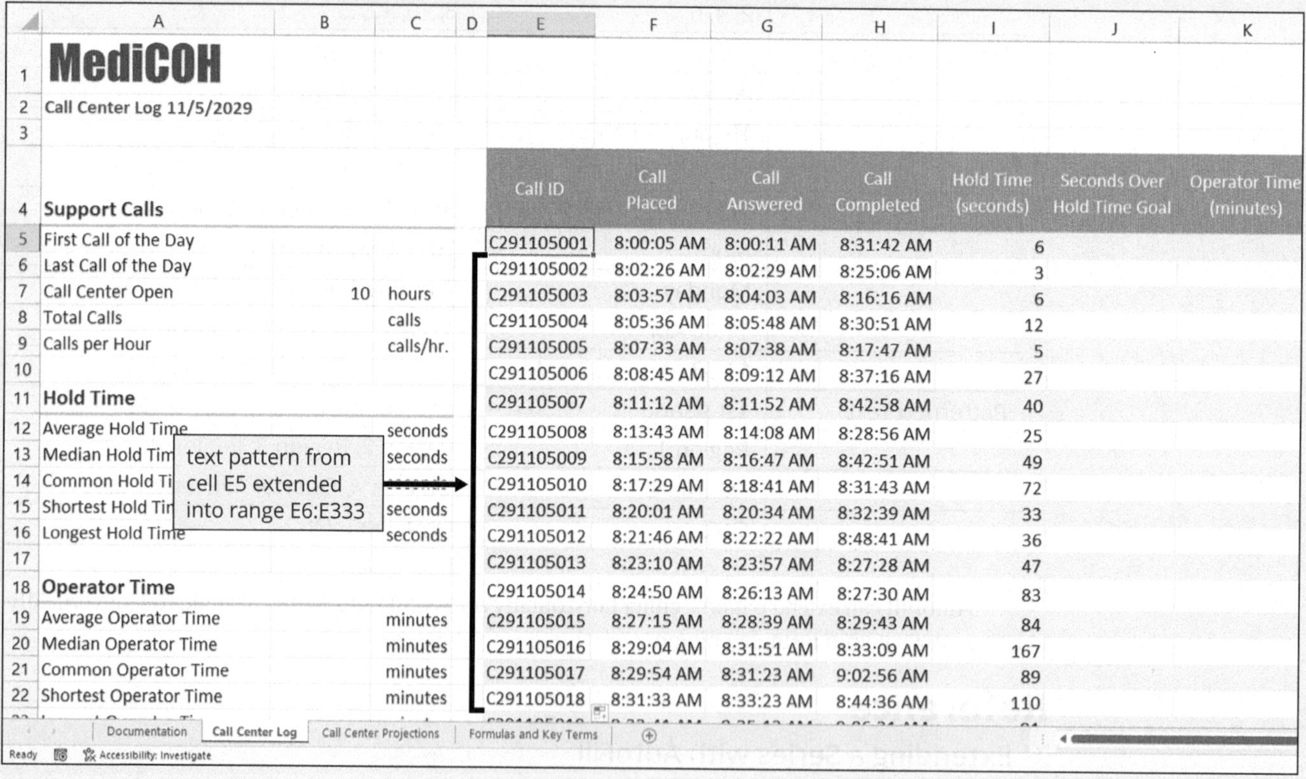

6. Save the workbook.

Another way to define a series is with the Series dialog box; refer to Figure 3–8. To access the Series dialog box, select the range in which you want to place a series of values, click the Fill button in the Editing group on the Home tab, and then select Series. You can specify a linear or growth series for numbers; a date series for dates that increase by day, weekday, month, or year; or an AutoFill series for patterned text. With numbers, you can also specify the step value (how much each number increases over the previous entry) and a stop value (the endpoint for the entire series).

Figure 3–8 Series dialog box

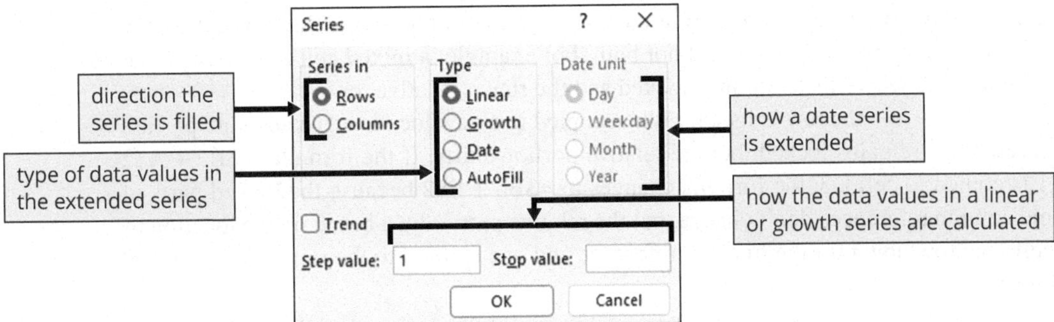

Exploring Cell References

You entered the formula = (G5 – F5)*24*60*60 in cell E5. When you extended the formula, AutoFill not only copied the formula but also adjusted the cell references in the formula to reflect the formula's new location in the worksheet. For example, AutoFill entered the formula = (G6 – F6)*24*60*60 in cell E6. If you do not want Excel to adjust cell references, you need to modify the type of cell reference used.

Excel has four types of cell references: relative, absolute, mixed, and spill. Each type of cell reference reacts differently when a formula or function is copied and pasted to a new location.

Relative Cell References

A relative cell reference changes based on its position to the cell containing the formula. For example, if cell A1 contains the formula = B1 + A2, Excel interprets that formula as, "Add the value of the cell one column to the right of cell A1 (cell B1) to the value of the cell one row down from cell A1 (cell A2)." This relative interpretation of the references is retained when the formula is copied to a new location. If the formula in cell A1 is copied to cell D3, the cell that is one column to the right is cell E3 and the cell that is one row down is cell D4. The formula copied from cell A1 = B1 + A2 into cell D3 becomes = E3 + D4.

Similarly, the hold time formula = (G5 – F5)*24*60*60 in cell E5 instructed Excel to calculate the difference of the cell one column to the left (cell F5) and the cell two columns to the left (cell G5). Because the formula uses relative references, the other hold time calculations used the same pattern. For example, the formula in cell E6 is = (G6 – F6)*24*60*60 and so on. But with some formulas, you don't want the cell references to change. This is when an absolute cell reference is useful.

Absolute Cell References

An absolute cell reference remains locked to a cell even when the formula it's used in is copied to a new location. Absolute references use the dollar sign symbol, $, before each column and row designation. For example, B8 is a relative reference to cell B8, while $B$8 is an absolute reference to that cell. If cell A1 contains the formula = $B$8 + $A$2, Excel interprets that formula as, "Add the value of cell B8 to the value of cell A2." That interpretation is always the same no matter where the formula is copied.

Mixed Cell References

A **mixed cell reference** contains both relative and absolute components, locking either the column reference or the row reference, but not both. For example, a mixed cell reference to cell A2 can be either $A2 where the column is locked and the row is relative, or it can be A$2 where the column is relative and the row is locked. When copied to a new location, the absolute portion of the cell reference remains locked, but the relative portion shifts. If the formula = $B2 + A$2 in cell A1 is copied to cell D3, the formula changes to =$B4 + E$2 because the locked parts of the row and column references don't change, but the relative parts adjust based on the location of the new cell (one row down for the first cell reference and one column to the right for the second cell reference).

You can cycle between relative, absolute, and mixed references using the F4 key. After you type a cell reference, such as A1, in a formula, pressing F4 once changes it to the absolute reference $A$1, pressing F4 again changes it to the mixed reference A$1, and pressing F4 a third time changes it to the mixed reference $A1. Pressing F4 a fourth time repeats the cycle with the relative reference A1.

Proskills

Problem Solving: When to Use Relative, Absolute, and Mixed Cell References

Part of effective workbook design is knowing when to use relative, absolute, and mixed cell references. Use relative references when you want to apply the same formula with input cells that share a common layout or pattern. Relative references are commonly used when copying a formula that calculates summary statistics across columns or rows of data values. Use absolute references when you want copied formulas to always refer to the same cell. This usually occurs when a cell contains a constant value, such as a tax rate, that will be referenced in formulas throughout the worksheet. Mixed references are seldom used other than when creating tables of calculated values such as a multiplication table in which the values of the formula or function can be found at the intersection of the rows and columns of the table.

Mixed references are useful in tables where the first row and column contain data applied to every cell within table. You will use mixed cell reference to create a multiplication table.

To use mixed references to formulas in a table:

1. Open the **NP_EX_3-2.xlsx** workbook located in the **Excel3 > Module** folder included with your Data Files, and then save the workbook as **NP_EX_3_Explore** in the location specified by your instructor.
2. In the Documentation worksheet, enter your name in cell B3 and the date in cell B4.
3. Go to the **Mixed References** worksheet, and then click cell **B5**. This cell will contain the first entry in the multiplication table.
4. Type the equal sign = to begin the formula.
5. Click cell **A5**, and then press the **F4** key three times. The cell reference changes to the mixed reference $A5.
6. Type * as the operator.
7. Click cell **B4**, and then press the **F4** key twice. The cell reference changes to B$4.
8. Press **ENTER**. The formula =$A5*B$4 is entered in the cell, returning the value 1.

9. Use AutoFill to extend the formula in cell B5 down to cell **B14** and then across the range B5:F14. The multiplication table is complete.
10. Click cell **B5**, and then click the **Formulas** tab on the ribbon.
11. In the Formula Auditing group, click the **Show Formulas** button. The formulas with the mixed references copied across the multiplication table appear in the worksheet. Refer to Figure 3–9.

Figure 3–9 Multiplication table formulas with mixed references

	A	B	C	D	E	F	G	H	I
1	Mixed Ref								
2	Multiplication T								
3									
4		1	2	3	4	5			
5	1	=$A5*B$4	=$A5*C$4	=$A5*D$4	=$A5*E$4	=$A5*F$4			
6	2	=$A6*B$4	=$A6*C$4	=$A6*D$4	=$A6*E$4	=$A6*F$4			
7	3	=$A7*B$4	=$A7*C$4	=$A7*D$4	=$A7*E$4	=$A7*F$4			
8	4	=$A8*B$4	=$A8*C$4	=$A8*D$4	=$A8*E$4	=$A8*F$4			
9	5	=$A9*B$4	=$A9*C$4	=$A9*D$4	=$A9*E$4	=$A9*F$4			
10	6	=$A10*B$4	=$A10*C$4	=$A10*D$4	=$A10*E$4	=$A10*F$4			
11	7	=$A11*B$4	=$A11*C$4	=$A11*D$4	=$A11*E$4	=$A11*F$4			
12	8	=$A12*B$4	=$A12*C$4	=$A12*D$4	=$A12*E$4	=$A12*F$4			
13	9	=$A13*B$4	=$A13*C$4	=$A13*D$4	=$A13*E$4	=$A13*F$4			
14	10	=$A14*B$4	=$A14*C$4	=$A14*D$4	=$A14*E$4	=$A14*F$4			
15									

12. Click the **Show Formulas** button again. The calculated values are displayed.
13. Save the workbook.

Now that you've worked with relative, absolute, and mixed cell references, you will return to the call center log.

Chryssa's goal for the call center is to have every call answered within one minute. To document how well the call center is meeting that goal, you will determine by how much each call meets or exceeds that 60-second challenge.

To calculate the difference between each hold time and the 60-second goal:

1. Return to the **NP_EX_Calls** workbook, and make sure the Call Center Log worksheet is active.
2. In cell **B28**, enter **60** as the hold-time goal.
3. In cell **J5**, enter the formula **= I5 – $B$28** to subtract the 60-second goal from the first call of the day. The calculated value is –54, indicating that the first call had a hold time that was 54 seconds below the call center goal.

   Key Step Be sure to enter the absolute cell reference $B$28 rather than the relative reference so the reference is locked when you extend the formula down the column.

4. Click cell **J5** to select it, and then double-click the **fill handle** to autofill the Seconds Over Hold Time Goal column.
5. Click the **Auto Fill Options** button, and then click the **Fill Without Formatting** option to retain the banded rows.
6. Click cell **J5** to deselect the range. Refer to Figure 3–10.

Figure 3–10 Formulas with absolute cell references

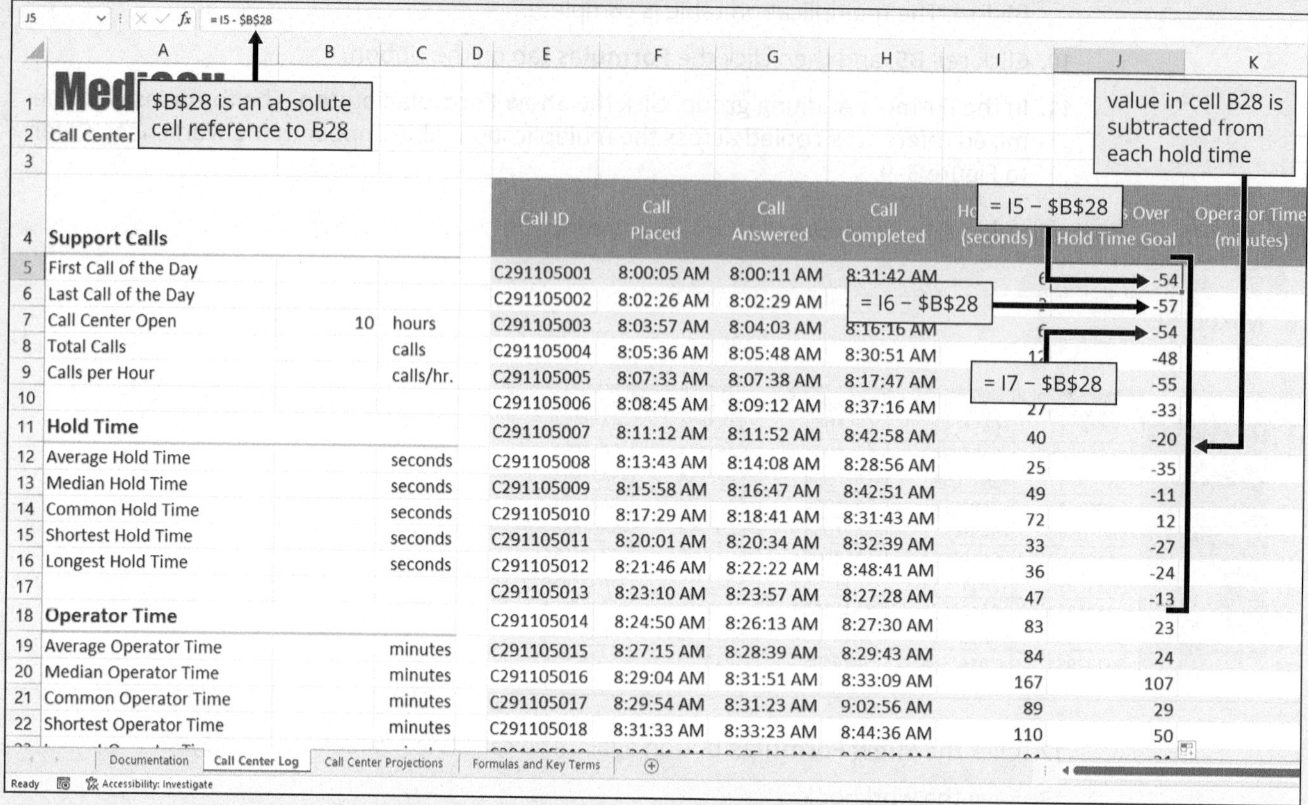

7. Save the workbook.

Because the formula uses an absolute reference to cell B28, it will always point to cell B28 even when extended through the range J5:J333. For example, the formula in cell J6 is = I6 – $B$28, the formula in J7 is = I7 – $B$28, and so forth.

Calculating with Dynamic Arrays

So far you have entered formulas that return a single value in a single cell. You can also enter formulas that use dynamic arrays to return multiple values across multiple cells. An **array** is a collection of elements or data values. A **dynamic array** is an array that automatically increases in size as more values are added to it.

An Excel formula with dynamic arrays populates multiple cells in a rectangular range of cells. You enter the formula only once in the upper-left cell of the range, and then Excel automatically applies the formula across and down the rectangular range. You don't have to copy or paste the formula. Excel determines where to place the calculated values based on the arrays specified in that single formula.

You will return to the Explore workbook and use a dynamic array to create another multiplication table.

To create a multiplication table with dynamic arrays:

1. Go to the **NP_EX_3_Explore** workbook, and then go to the **Dynamic Arrays** worksheet.
2. In cell **B5**, type the equal sign = to begin a formula.
3. Select the range **A5:A14** containing the first array of values for the multiplication table.
4. Type * as the multiplication operator, and then select the range **B4:F4** containing the second array of values for the multiplication table. The formula =A5:A14*B4:F4 is displayed in the formula bar.

5. Press **ENTER**. The dynamic array formula is applied to the rest of table, showing the multiplication of each combination of row and column values.
6. Click cell **B5** to select it. Refer to Figure 3–11.

Figure 3–11 Multiplication table with a dynamic array

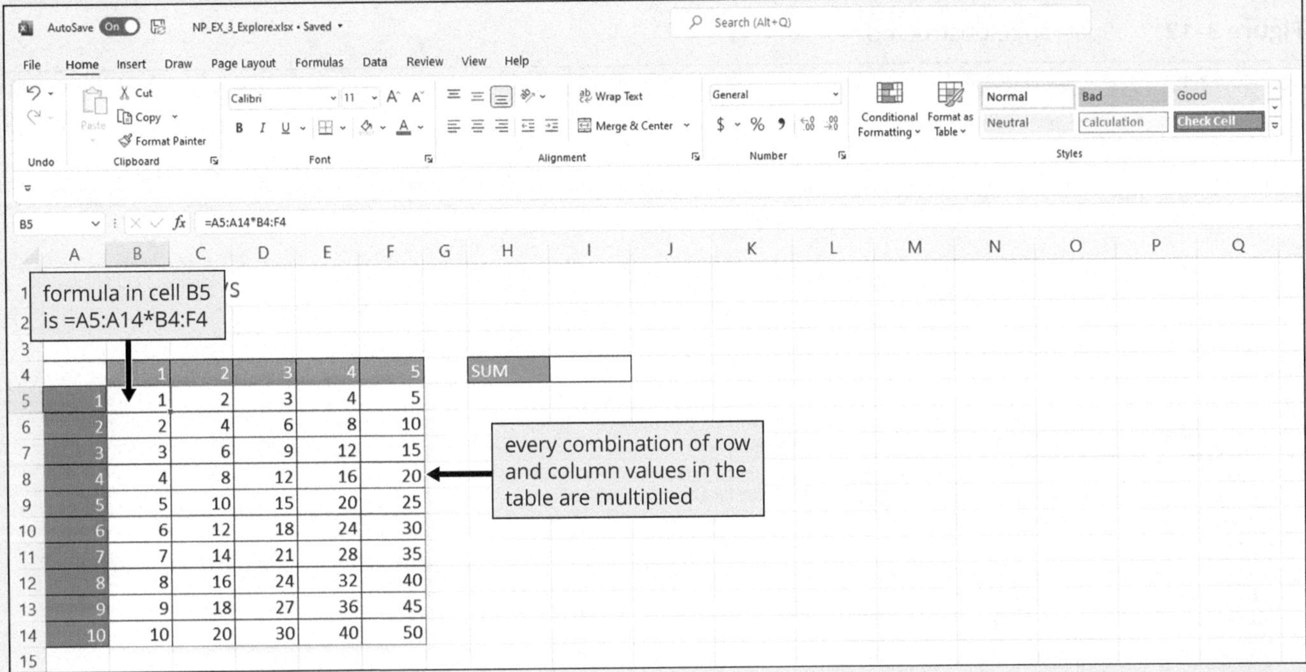

7. Click cell **E10** displaying the value 24 (the product of 6 and 4). This cell displays the same formula you entered in cell B5, =A5:A14*B4:F4, but grayed out. This is because the formula only exists in cell B5 but is applied everywhere in the table.

   As with other formulas, when you change a cell value, the calculated values update to reflect that change.

8. In cell **F4**, enter **6** as the new value. Column F now displays multiples of 6 instead of 5.
9. In cell **F4**, return cell value to **5**.

Every formula or function that uses a single value can be turned into a dynamic array. You just replace the single values with arrays to return multiple values. For example, the formula = A1 + B1 returns a single value containing the sum of cells A1 and B1. But the formula = A1:A10 + B1:B10 returns a column of 10 values: the first cell contains the sum of cells A1 and B1, the second cell contains the sum of cells A2 and B2, and so on.

Spill Ranges

The range of values returned by a dynamic array formula is called a spill range because the formula in the upper-left corner of the rectangular range "spills" into the other cells. All the cells in the spill range use the same formula, but only the formula in the upper-left cell can be edited.

Dynamic array formulas can only spill into empty cells, ensuring that any content in the path of the spill range is not overwritten. If a dynamic array formula cannot be spilled because one of the cells in the dynamic array already contains content, #SPILL! appears in upper-left cell. You'll try this now.

To change the spill range for the multiplication table:

1. In cell **E10**, enter **Excel**. The values are removed from the original spill range. Cell B5 displays #SPILL! indicating that the spill range could not be generated because the range contains other content. Refer to Figure 3–12.

Figure 3–12 Spill range obstructed

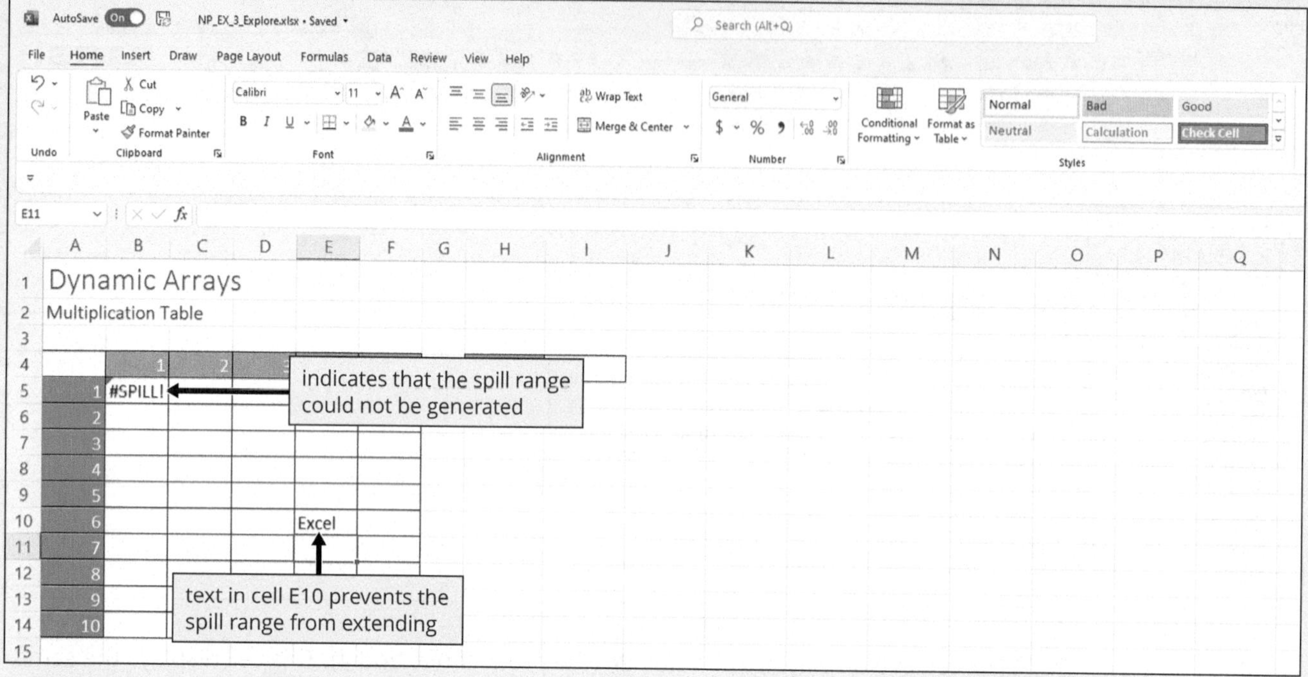

2. Click cell **E10**, and then press **DELETE** to remove the text in the cell. The dynamic array formula once again fills the multiplication table with values.

Referencing a Spill Range

A spill range reference includes the reference of the upper-left cell of the spill range followed by the pound sign (#). For example, A10# references a spill range that starts from cell A10. Because the size of the spill range is determined by the dynamic array formula, you do not need to specify the exact rows and columns in the range. Excel will automatically include all cells that contain the formula spilled from cell A10.

You'll use the SUM function with a spill range reference to calculate the sum of the values in the multiplication table.

To calculate the sum of the values in the multiplication table with a spill range:

1. In the Dynamic Arrays worksheet, click cell **I4** to select it.
2. Type **= SUM(B5#)** as the formula, and then press **ENTER**. Excel returns a value of 825, the total sum of the values in the spill range of the multiplication table.
3. Click cell **I4** to select it. Refer to Figure 3–13.

Figure 3–13 Function with a spill range reference

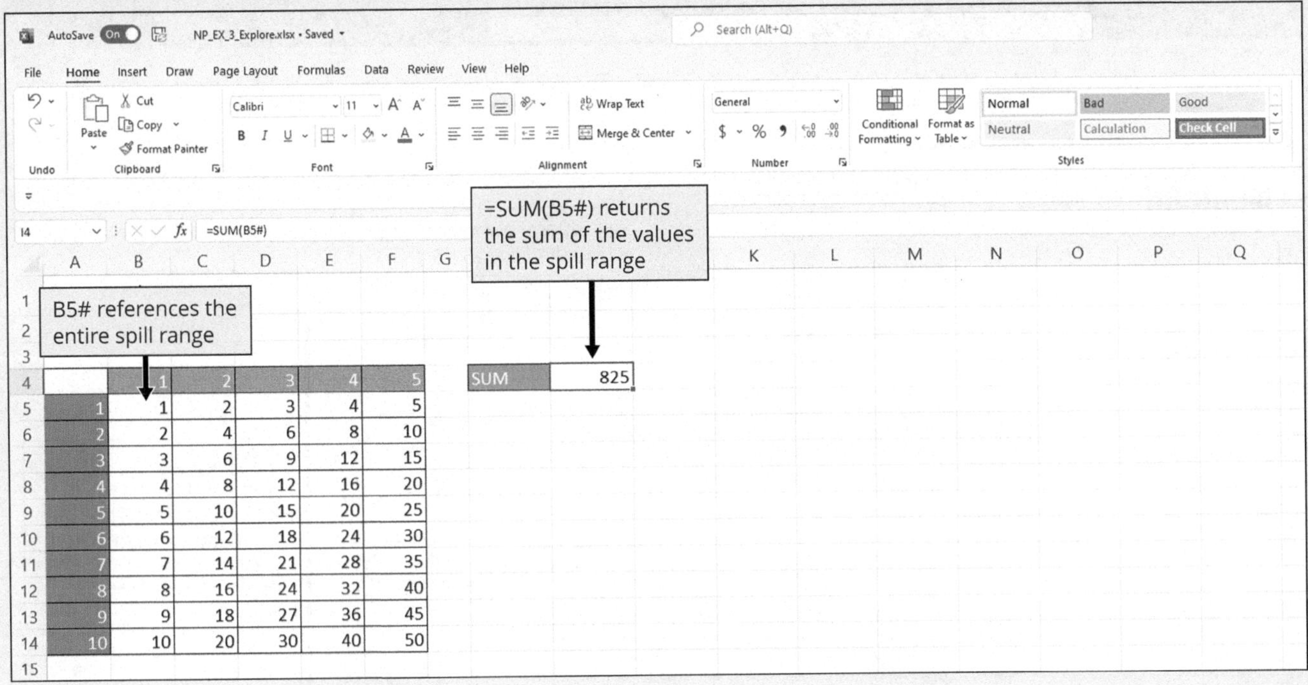

4. Save the workbook, and then close it

The next column in the call log calculates the number of minutes operators spend on the phone with customers. You will use dynamic arrays to calculate the difference between the time each call was completed and the time the call was answered. Because this difference is expressed in days, you will multiply the difference by 24 times 60 to convert it to minutes.

To calculate the operator time in minutes:

1. Go to the **NP_EX_3_Calls** workbook, and make sure the **Call Center Log** worksheet is active.
2. In cell **K5**, enter **= (H5:H333 – G5:G333)*24*60** as the dynamic array formula. The difference in minutes for each call is displayed in the spill range K5:K333. A thin blue border surrounds the cells in the spill as a reminder that the dynamic array formula in cell K5 is spilled into these cells.
3. Click cell **K5** to select it. The duration of the first call in this cell is displayed as a time value.
4. On the Home tab, in the Number group, click the **Number Format arrow**, and then click **General** to apply the General number format to cell K5. Refer to Figure 3–14.

Figure 3–14 Duration of each call with an operator

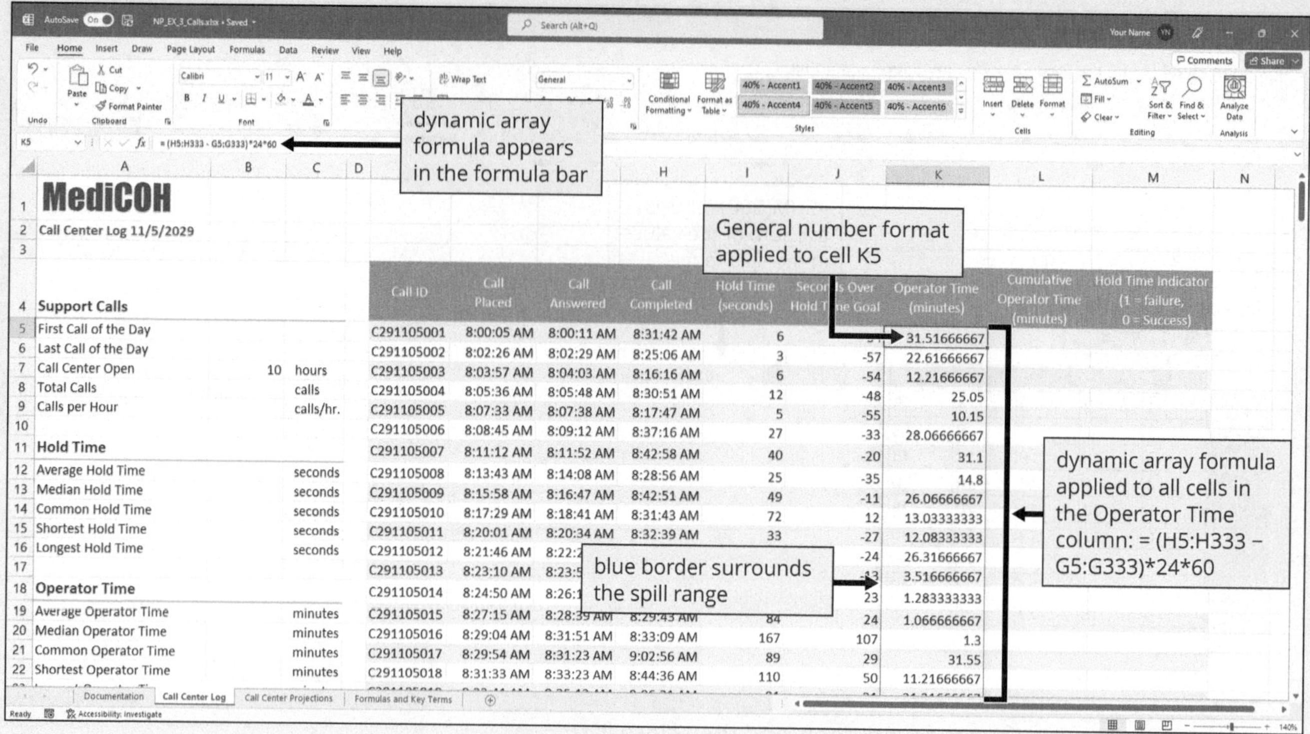

Performing Calculations with the Quick Analysis Tool

When you select a range of cells, the Quick Analysis tool appears to provide quick access to tools for data analysis, chart creation, and conditional formatting. The tool is organized into the following five categories:

- **Formatting** to apply conditional formats to the selected range
- **Charts** to create charts from the data in the range
- **Totals** to calculate sums, counts, and averages of the selected data
- **Tables** to convert the selected range into an Excel table
- **Sparklines** to create sparkline charts from the selected data

Many of the Quick Analysis tools are also accessible in other ways. For example, the conditional formatting commands are also available in the Styles group on the Home tab, and the SUM function is also available in the Editing group on the Home tab or in the Function Library group on the Formulas tab as well as by typing it in the cell.

Chryssa wants a running total of the time that operators spend on the phone as the day progresses. Although you can calculate the total from this column of data by directly entering the SUM function into a cell, you will use the Quick Analysis tool to apply that calculation to the values in column K.

To calculate a running total with the Quick Analysis tool:

1. Select the range **K5:K333** containing the operator time in minutes for each call.
2. In the lower-right corner of the selected range, click the **Quick Analysis** button (or press **CTRL+Q**). A menu of Quick Analysis categories and buttons appears.
3. In the Quick Analysis tool categories, click **Totals**. The tools for calculating summary statistics in the selected range appear. Refer to Figure 3–15.

Figure 3–15 Totals category on the Quick Analysis tool

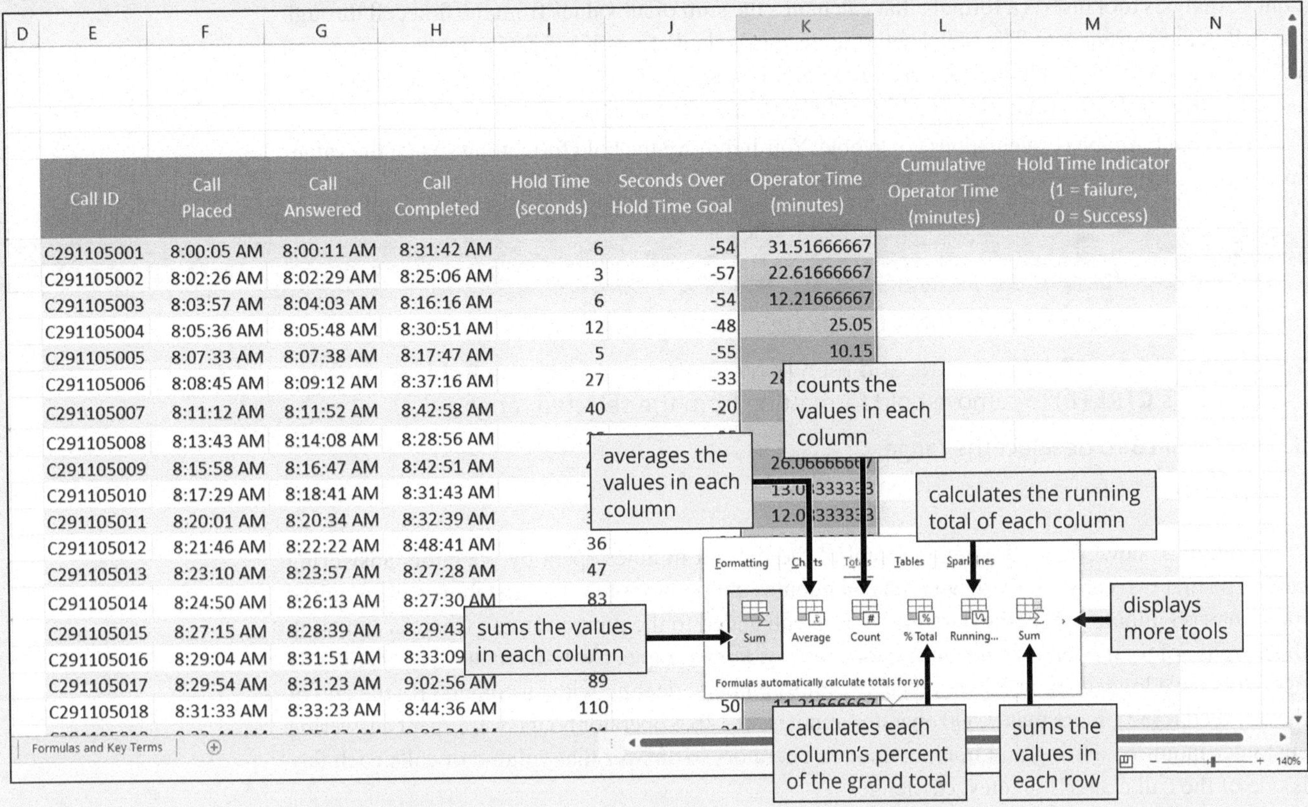

4. Click the **right arrow** to access additional Quick Analysis tools.
5. Click the **Running** tool (the last icon in the list). The running total of call durations is added to the adjacent range L5:L333.
6. Scroll up and click cell **L5**. Refer to Figure 3–16.

Figure 3–16 Running total of operator time

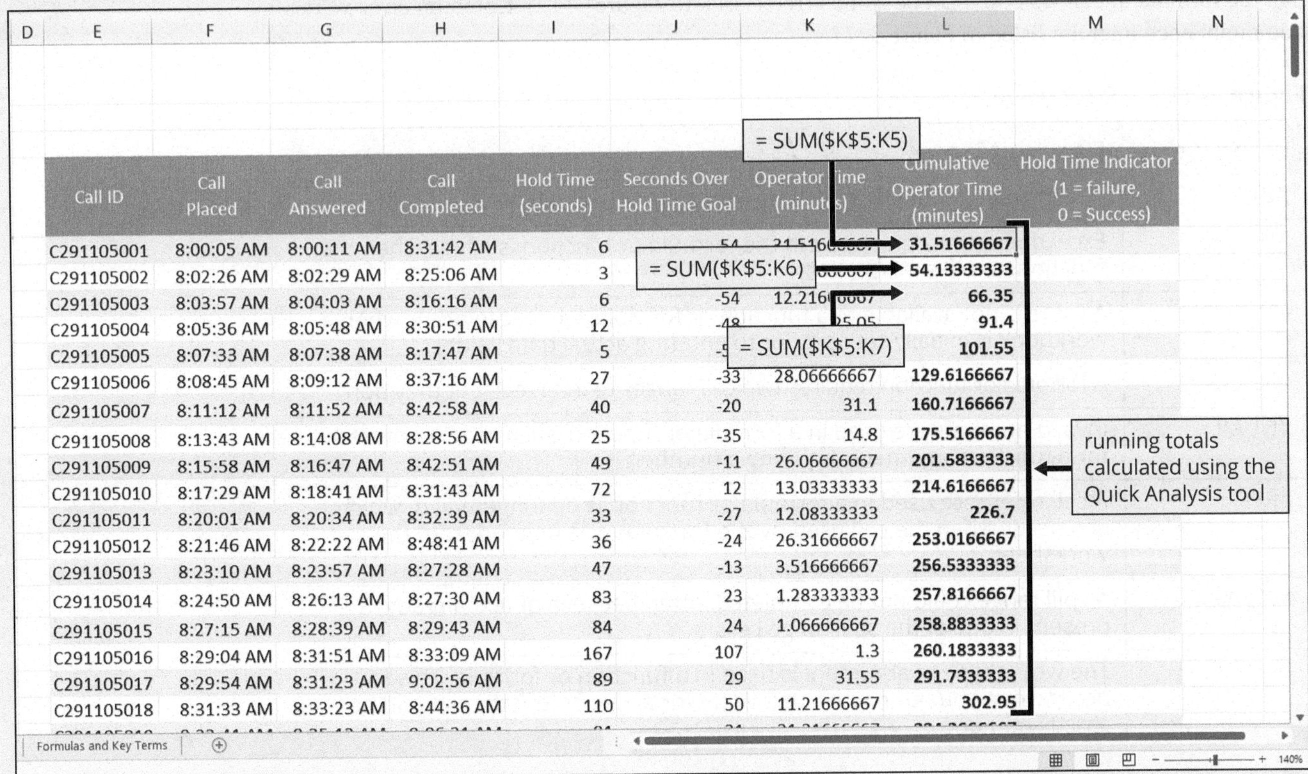

Column L shows the running totals of operator time in minutes. For each cell in column L, the Quick Analysis tool inserts a formula that calculates the sum of all values from the first cell through the cell in the current row. The initial cell reference is locked at cell K5 ($K$5), but the second cell reference is relative and changes for each row (K5, K6, K7, and so on). So, the function in cell L5 is SUM($K$5:K5), the function in cell L6 is SUM(KK:K6), and so on.

The Quick Analysis calculations are in bold. You'll remove the bold formatting so that the values in column L have same formatting as column K.

To remove bold formatting from the running totals:

1. Select the range **L5:L333** containing the running totals.
2. On the ribbon, click **Home** tab, and then in the Font group, click the **Bold** button B (or press **CTRL+B**) to remove bold formatting from the selected range.
3. Click cell **L5** to deselect the range.

Column L now shows the running total of the time in minutes spent by operators answering calls. The first two calls required more than 54 minutes of operator time. The first three calls required more than 66 minutes. With the duration of each call added to the previous total, Chryssa can track the increase of total operator time throughout the day. For example, by 9 AM (cell L24), MediCOH operators have logged about 359 minutes, or almost 6 hours, dealing with customers. By the end of the day (cell L333), more than 7,590 operator minutes, or 126.5 operator hours, were spent answering customer inquiries. Hiring and training enough operators to answer that volume of calls each day is one of the call center's greatest challenges.

Interpreting Error Values

When Excel encounters a formula that it cannot resolve, it returns an **error value** indicating that no results can be returned from the formula. For example, when Excel could not complete the dynamic array earlier because of the obstructing text in cell E10, it returned the error value #SPILL! to indicate that the formula in cell B5 could not be spilled (refer back to Figure 3–12). Common error values you might encounter are listed in Figure 3–17.

Figure 3–17 Error values

Error Value	Description
#DIV/0!	The formula or function contains a number divided by 0.
#NAME?	Excel doesn't recognize text in the formula or function, such as when the function name is misspelled.
#N/A	A value is not available to a function or formula, which can occur when a workbook is initially set up prior to entering actual data values.
#NULL!	A formula or function requires two cell ranges to intersect, but they don't.
#NUM!	Invalid numbers are used in a formula or function, such as text entered for a function argument requiring a number.
#REF!	A cell reference used in a formula or function is no longer valid, which can occur when the cell used by the function was deleted from the worksheet.
#SPILL!	A spill range could not be completed, often because of text already present in one of the spill range cells
#VALUE!	The wrong type of argument is used in a function or formula. This can occur when you reference a text value for an argument that should be strictly numeric.

When a formula returns an error, an error indicator appears in the upper-left corner of that cell. You can point to the error indicator to display a ScreenTip with more information about the error. Although the ScreenTips provide hints as to the reason for the error, you usually need to examine the formula to determine exactly what went wrong and how to fix it.

You have completed your initial work on the call center log by calculating the hold time experienced by each customer and the total time operators spent helping customers during a typical day. In the next part, you will use functions to summarize this data. Your analysis will help Chryssa develop a plan for the center's staffing needs.

Part 3.1 Quick Check

1. Write a formula to convert the number of days entered in cell B10 to seconds.
2. If 4/30/2029 and 5/31/2029 are the initial values in a range, what are the next two values that AutoFill will insert?
3. You need to reference cell Q57 in a formula. What is its relative reference? What is its absolute reference? What are its two mixed references?
4. If cell R10 contains the formula =R1+R2 that is then copied to cell S20, what formula is entered in cell S20?
5. If cell R10 contains the formula =$R1+R$2 that is then copied to cell S20, what formula is entered in cell S20?
6. The range A1:A10 contains the integers from 1 to 10. If you enter the dynamic array formula =2*A1:A10 in cell B1, what will be the result?
7. The range A2:A11 contains the integers from 1 to 10. The range B1:D1 contains the values 10, 20, and 30. If the dynamic array formula =A2:A11+B1:D1 is entered in cell B2, what will be the result?
8. Cell A10 displays the #SPILL! error value. What might have caused that error?
9. Cell B2 contains the formula =SUME(A1:A100) with the name of the SUM function misspelled as SUME. What error value will appear in cell B2?

Part 3.2 Visual Overview: Formulas and Functions

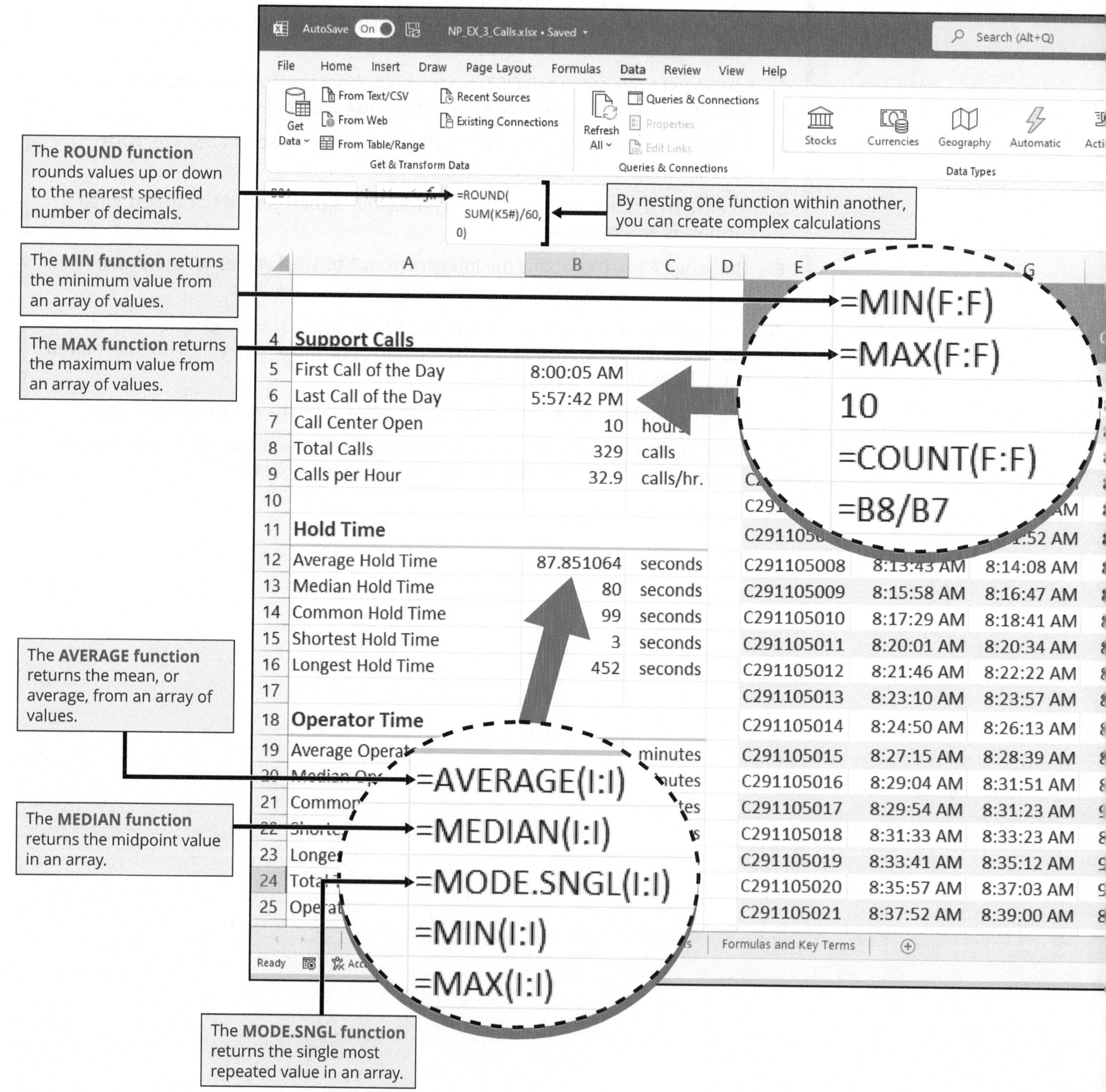
The **ROUND function** rounds values up or down to the nearest specified number of decimals.
=ROUND(SUM(K5#)/60, 0)
By nesting one function within another, you can create complex calculations
The **MIN function** returns the minimum value from an array of values.
=MIN(F:F)
The **MAX function** returns the maximum value from an array of values.
=MAX(F:F)
10
=COUNT(F:F)
=B8/B7
Support Calls
First Call of the Day 8:00:05 AM
Last Call of the Day 5:57:42 PM
Call Center Open 10
Total Calls 329 calls
Calls per Hour 32.9 calls/hr.
Hold Time
Average Hold Time 87.851064 seconds
Median Hold Time 80 seconds
Common Hold Time 99 seconds
Shortest Hold Time 3 seconds
Longest Hold Time 452 seconds
Operator Time
The **AVERAGE function** returns the mean, or average, from an array of values.
=AVERAGE(I:I)
The **MEDIAN function** returns the midpoint value in an array.
=MEDIAN(I:I)
=MODE.SNGL(I:I)
=MIN(I:I)
=MAX(I:I)
The **MODE.SNGL function** returns the single most repeated value in an array.

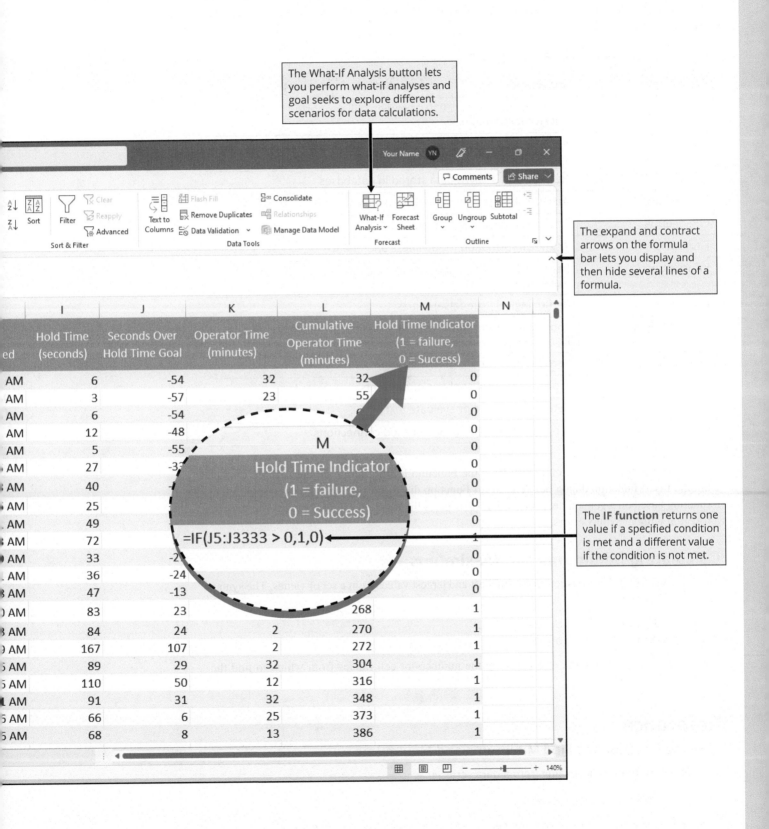

The What-If Analysis button lets you perform what-if analyses and goal seeks to explore different scenarios for data calculations.

The expand and contract arrows on the formula bar lets you display and then hide several lines of a formula.

The **IF function** returns one value if a specified condition is met and a different value if the condition is not met.

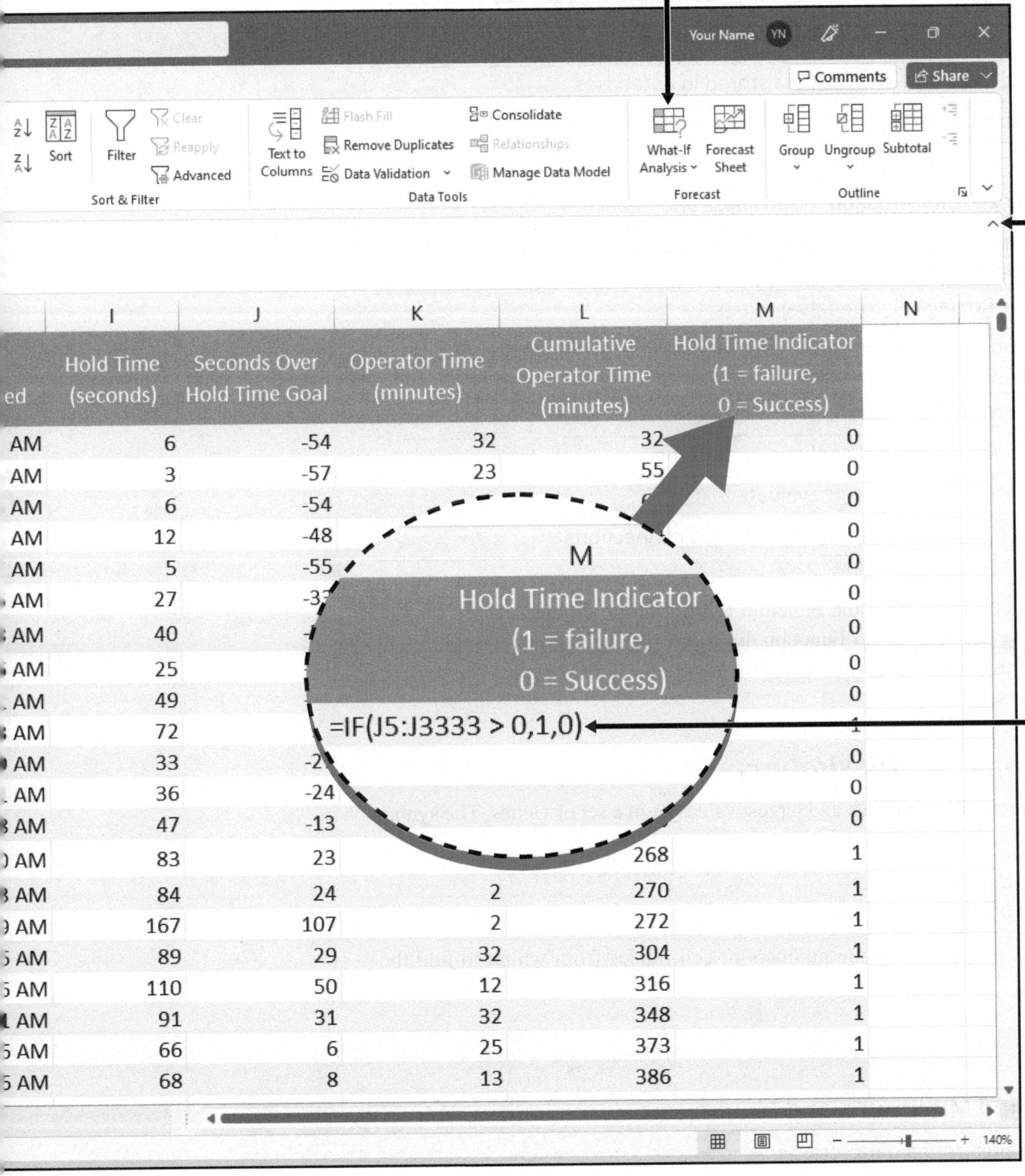
Your Name
Comments
Share
Sort
Filter
Clear
Reapply
Advanced
Sort & Filter
Text to Columns
Flash Fill
Remove Duplicates
Data Validation
Consolidate
Relationships
Manage Data Model
Data Tools
What-If Analysis
Forecast Sheet
Forecast
Group
Ungroup
Subtotal
Outline
Hold Time (seconds)
Seconds Over Hold Time Goal
Operator Time (minutes)
Cumulative Operator Time (minutes)
Hold Time Indicator (1 = failure, 0 = Success)
M
Hold Time Indicator
(1 = failure,
0 = Success)
=IF(J5:J3333 > 0,1,0)
140%

Analyzing Data with Excel Functions

Excel supports several hundred functions covering a wide range of topics, including finance, statistics, and engineering. With so many functions, it can be challenging to find the function you need. To help you locate functions, Excel organizes the functions into a function library with the 13 categories described in Figure 3–18.

Figure 3–18 Function library categories

Category	Description
Compatibility	Functions from Excel 2010 or earlier, still supported to provide backward compatibility
Cube	Retrieve data from multidimensional databases involving online analytical processing (OLAP)
Database	Retrieve and analyze data stored in databases
Date & Time	Analyze or create date and time values and time intervals
Engineering	Analyze engineering problems
Financial	Analyze information for business and finance
Information	Return information about the format, location, or contents of worksheet cells
Logical	Return logical (true-false) values
Lookup & Reference	Look up and return data matching a set of specified conditions from a range
Math & Trig	Perform math and trigonometry calculations
Statistical	Provide statistical analyses of data sets
Text	Return text values or evaluate text
Web	Provide information on web-based connections

You can access the function library from the Function Library group on the Formulas tab or from the Insert Function dialog box. The Insert Function dialog box includes a search tool to find a function based on a general description. It also displays the function syntax, helping you to enter a function without syntax errors.

Calculating Minimums and Maximums

The MIN and MAX functions return the smallest and largest values from a set of values. The syntax of the two functions is:

```
MIN(number1, [number2], …)
MAX(number1, [number2], …)
```

where *number1*, *number2*, and so on are the numbers or cell ranges from which to find the smallest or largest value.

Reference

Using Functions to Find Minimums and Maximums

- To return the smallest value from a data series, use

```
MIN(number1, [number2], …)
```

where *number1*, *number2* … are the cell ranges or numbers in the data series.

- To return the largest value from a data series, use

```
MAX(number1, [number2], …)
```

Chryssa wants the call center report to note the times of the first and last calls of the day. You will do that calculation with the MIN and MAX functions.

To calculate the first and last calls of the day:

1. If you took a break after the previous part, make sure the NP_EX_3_Calls.xlsx workbook is open and the Call Center Log worksheet is active.
2. Click cell **B5** to select it.
3. On the ribbon, click the **Formulas** tab. In the Function Library group, click the **More Functions** button, and then point to **Statistical** to display a list of all the statistical functions.
4. Scroll down the list, and then click **MIN**. The Function Arguments dialog box for the MIN function opens.
5. In the Number1 box, type **F:F** to return the smallest value from all of the time values in column F. You won't enter anything in the Number2 box because you want to search only this range of cells.
6. Click **OK**. The function returns 0.3333912, which is the numeric value of the minimum time value in column F.
7. On the ribbon, click the **Home** tab. In the Number group, click the **Number Format arrow**, and then click **Time**. The value displayed in cell B5 changes to 8:00:05 AM (the time of the first call).
8. Click cell **B6**, and then repeat Steps 2 through 7, clicking the **MAX** function in Step 4 to return the time of the last call of the day. Cell B6 displays 5:57:42 PM, indicating that the last call was placed just before the call center closed.

The Call Center Log worksheet should also display the number of calls received and the number of calls per hour. You'll add these calculations to the worksheet.

To count the number of calls during the day and per hour:

1. In cell **B8**, enter the formula **= COUNT(F:F)** to count all the cells containing numbers in column F. A total of 329 calls were made that day.
2. In cell **B9**, enter the formula **= B8/B7** to calculate the number of calls per hour. Cell B9 displays 32.9, indicating that the national call center received almost 33 calls per hour. Refer to Figure 3–19.

Figure 3–19 Completed support calls calculations

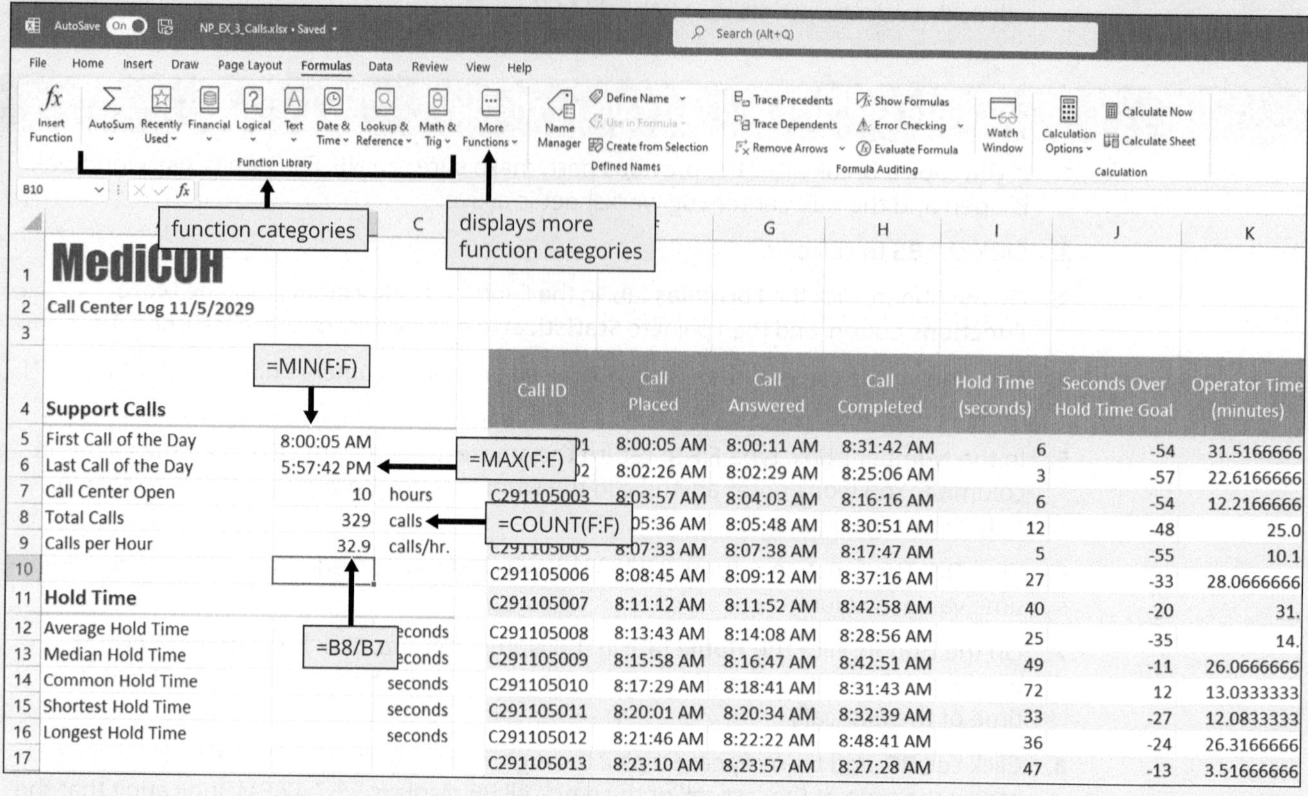

Chryssa now has a better picture of the level of traffic at the call center. Next, you will calculate how long a typical caller will wait on hold before reaching an operator.

Measures of Central Tendency

Central tendency is a single measurement from a data series that returns the most typical or "central" data value. There are several measures of central tendency. This module focuses on the three most used measures—average, median, and mode. The **average**, also known as the **mean**, is equal to the sum of the data values divided by their count. The **median** is the center data value so that half the values are less than the median and half are greater. Finally, the **mode** is the value repeated most often in the data series. A data series can have several modes if different values are repeated the same number of times. These three measures are calculated using the following functions

```
AVERAGE(number1, [number2], ...)
MEDIAN(number1, [number2], ...)
MODE.SNGL(number1, [number2], ...)
MODE.MULT(number1, [number2], ...)
MODE(number1, [number2], ...)
```

where *number1*, *number2*, and so on reference the data values. Notice that Excel includes three different mode functions. The MODE.SNGL function returns a single value representing the mode of the data. The **MODE.MULT function** returns either a single value or a list of values if more than one value is repeated the same number of times. The MODE function is the older version of the function for calculating modes and is equivalent to the MODE.SNGL function.

> **Tip** If there are several possible modes, both the MODE.SNGL and MODE functions return the first mode value listed in the data series.

The average, while the most used measure of central tendency, can be adversely affected by extreme values. Consider an exam in which every student receives a 90 except one student who receives a zero. That single zero value will cause the class average to drop, making it appear that class did poorly on the exam. On the other hand, the median and the mode will both be 90, providing a more accurate assessment of a typical student's performance on the exam. However, the median and the mode are also limited because they obscure information that might be useful. The instructor might want to know that one student did extremely poorly on the exam, which only the average indicates. For these reasons, it is often best to compare the results of all three measures.

Reference

Calculating Measures of Central Tendency

- To calculate the average from a data series, use

  `AVERAGE(number1, [number2], ...)`

- To calculate the median or midpoint from a data series, use

  `MEDIAN(number1, [number2], ...)`

- To return a single value that is repeated most often in a data series, use

  `MODE.SNGL(number1, [number2], ...)`

- To return the value or list of values that is repeated most often in a data series, use

  `MODE.MULT(number1, [number2], ...)`

Chryssa wants to know the typical hold time that customers will experience at the call center based on the average, median, and mode measures of the hold-time data. Chryssa also wants to know the shortest and longest hold times that customers experienced during the day. You'll calculate these measures using the AVERAGE, MEDIAN, MODE.SNGL, MIN, and MAX functions.

To calculate the average, median, and mode hold times:

1. Click cell **B12**, and then click the **Formulas** tab on the ribbon.
2. In the Function Library group, click the **More Functions** button, and then point to **Statistical** in the list of function categories. A list of statistical functions appears.
3. Click **AVERAGE**. The Function Arguments dialog box opens.
4. In the Number1 box, type **I:I** to reference the column containing the calculated hold times, and then click **OK**. The average hold time of was about 87.85 seconds, or almost a minute and a half.
5. Click cell **B13**, and the repeat Steps 2 through 4, selecting **MEDIAN** as the statistical function in Step 3. The medium hold time was 80 seconds.
6. Click cell **B14**, and then repeat Steps 2 through 4, selecting **MODE.SNGL** as the function in Step 3. the most common hold time was 99 seconds.
7. In cell **B15**, enter the formula **=MIN(I:I)** to calculate the minimum hold-time value in column I. The shortest hold time was 3 seconds.
8. In cell **B16**, enter the formula **= MAX(I:I)** to calculate the longest hold time. The longest hold time of the day was 452 seconds, or about seven and a half minutes. Refer to Figure 3–20.

Figure 3–20 Hold-time summary statistics

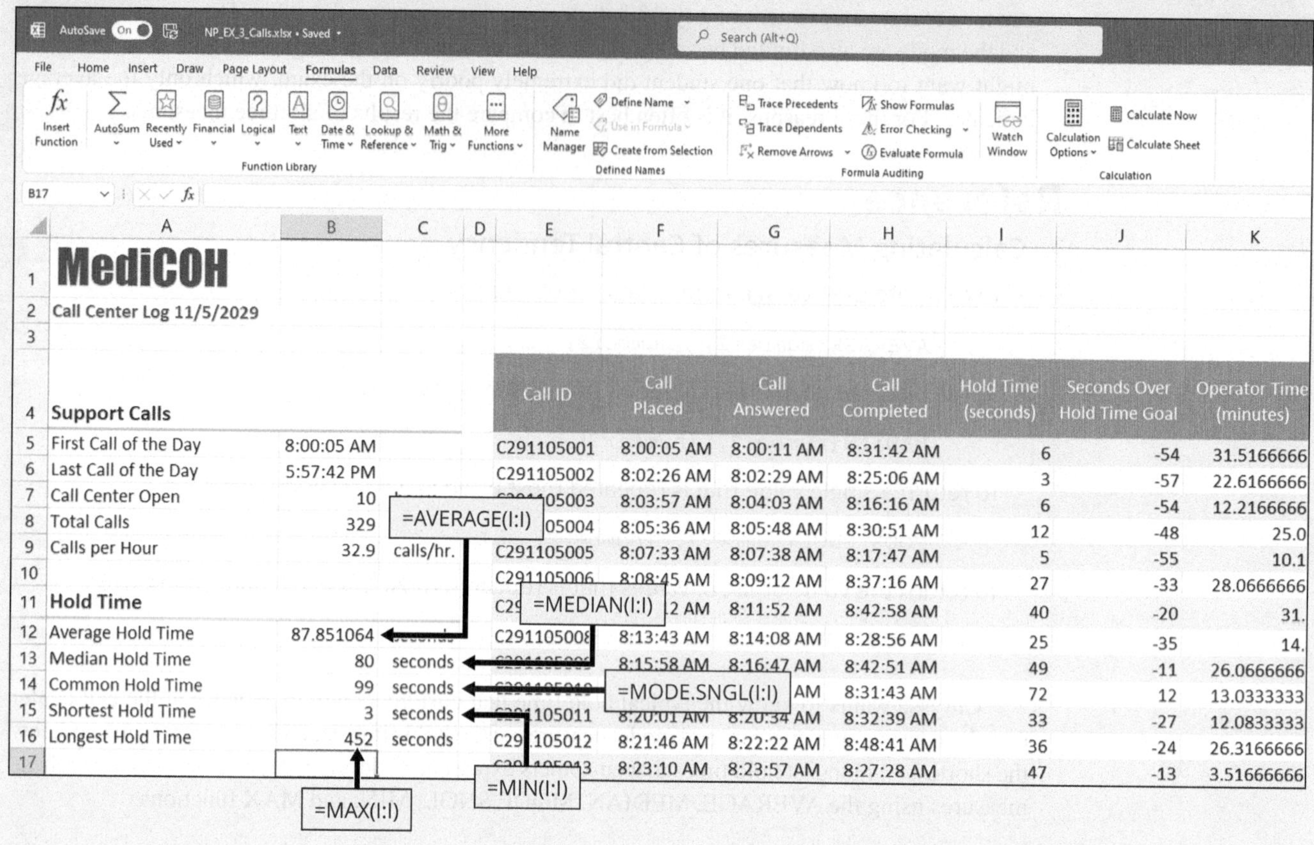

The average, median, and mode values all indicate that a typical customer will wait on hold for about a minute and a half, though it can be much longer. Chryssa wants you to do a similar analysis for the length of time an operator spends on a call. Recall that the operator time calculations in column K were done using a dynamic array formula, so you will reference the data values in that column using the spill range reference K5#.

To calculate the typical length of an operator conversation:

1. In cell **B19**, enter the formula **= AVERAGE(K5#)** to calculate the average length of the conversations. The average conversation lasted 25.471125 minutes.
2. In cell **B20**, enter the formula **= MEDIAN(K5#)** to return the midpoint value. The median conversation lasted 22.75 minutes.
3. In cell **B21**, enter the formula **= MODE.SNGL(K5#)** to return the most common conversation length. Conversations most commonly lasted 13.25 minutes.
4. In cell **B22**, enter the formula **= MIN(K5#)** to return the shortest operator conversation. The shortest conversation lasted 1.0666 minutes.
5. In cell **B23**, enter the formula **= MAX(K5#)** to determine the duration of the longest conversation. of the longest conversation lasted 109.46667 minutes, or about1 hour and 50 minutes. Refer to Figure 3–21.

Figure 3–21 Operator time summary statistics

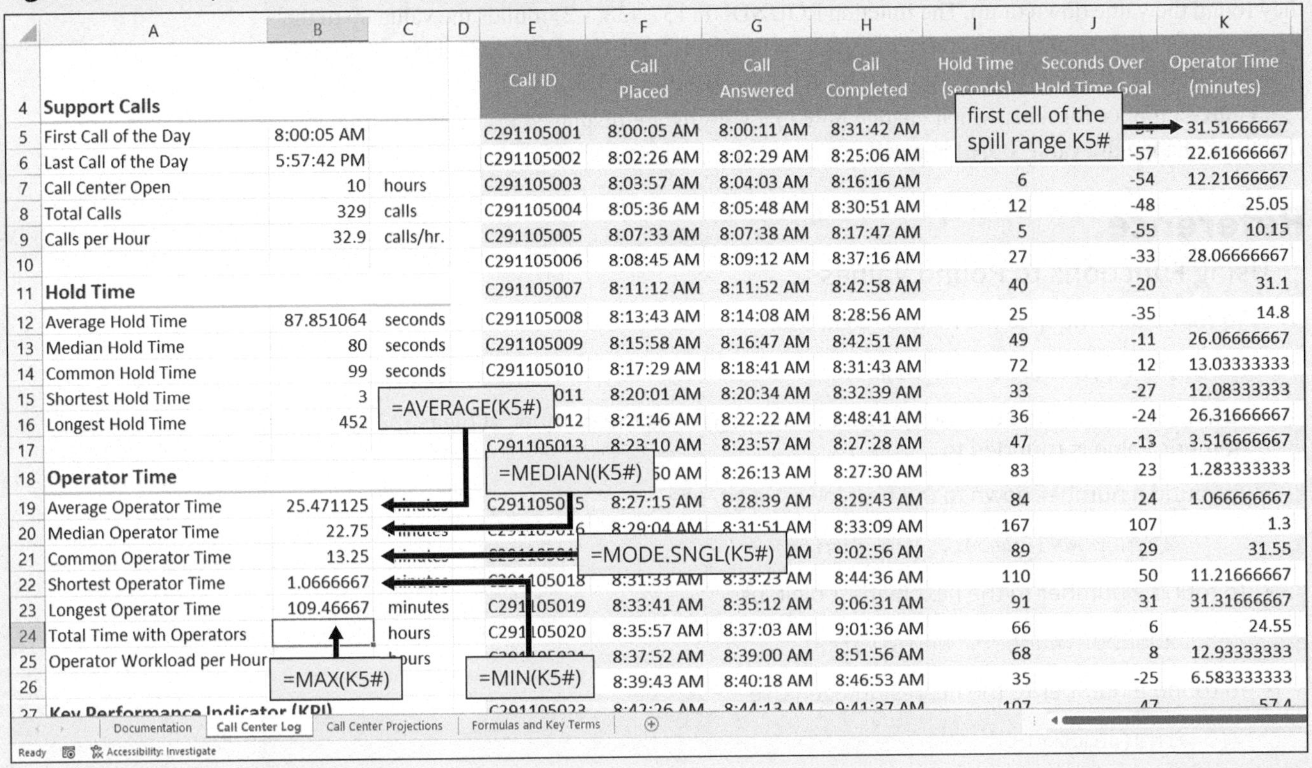

	A	B	C	D	E	F	G	H	I	J	K
					Call ID	Call Placed	Call Answered	Call Completed	Hold Time (seconds)	Seconds Over Hold Time Goal	Operator Time (minutes)
4	**Support Calls**										
5	First Call of the Day	8:00:05 AM			C291105001	8:00:05 AM	8:00:11 AM	8:31:42 AM			31.51666667
6	Last Call of the Day	5:57:42 PM			C291105002	8:02:26 AM	8:02:29 AM	8:25:06 AM		-57	22.61666667
7	Call Center Open	10	hours		C291105003	8:03:57 AM	8:04:03 AM	8:16:16 AM	6	-54	12.21666667
8	Total Calls	329	calls		C291105004	8:05:36 AM	8:05:48 AM	8:30:51 AM	12	-48	25.05
9	Calls per Hour	32.9	calls/hr.		C291105005	8:07:33 AM	8:07:38 AM	8:17:47 AM	5	-55	10.15
10					C291105006	8:08:45 AM	8:09:12 AM	8:37:16 AM	27	-33	28.06666667
11	**Hold Time**				C291105007	8:11:12 AM	8:11:52 AM	8:42:58 AM	40	-20	31.1
12	Average Hold Time	87.851064	seconds		C291105008	8:13:43 AM	8:14:08 AM	8:28:56 AM	25	-35	14.8
13	Median Hold Time	80	seconds		C291105009	8:15:58 AM	8:16:47 AM	8:42:51 AM	49	-11	26.06666667
14	Common Hold Time	99	seconds		C291105010	8:17:29 AM	8:18:41 AM	8:31:43 AM	72	12	13.03333333
15	Shortest Hold Time	3			011	8:20:01 AM	8:20:34 AM	8:32:39 AM	33	-27	12.08333333
16	Longest Hold Time	452			012	8:21:46 AM	8:22:22 AM	8:48:41 AM	36	-24	26.31666667
17					C291105013	8:23:10 AM	8:23:57 AM	8:27:28 AM	47	-13	3.516666667
18	**Operator Time**					50 AM	8:26:13 AM	8:27:30 AM	83	23	1.283333333
19	Average Operator Time	25.471125			C2911050 5	8:27:15 AM	8:28:39 AM	8:29:43 AM	84	24	1.066666667
20	Median Operator Time	22.75			6	8:29:04 AM	8:31:51 AM	8:33:09 AM	167	107	1.3
21	Common Operator Time	13.25					AM	9:02:56 AM	89	29	31.55
22	Shortest Operator Time	1.0666667			105018	8:31:33 AM	8:33:23 AM	8:44:36 AM	110	50	11.21666667
23	Longest Operator Time	109.46667	minutes		C291105019	8:33:41 AM	8:35:12 AM	9:06:31 AM	91	31	31.31666667
24	Total Time with Operators		hours		C291105020	8:35:57 AM	8:37:03 AM	9:01:36 AM	66	6	24.55
25	Operator Workload per Hour		hours			8:37:52 AM	8:39:00 AM	8:51:56 AM	68	8	12.93333333
26						8:39:43 AM	8:40:18 AM	8:46:53 AM	35	-25	6.583333333
27	Key Performance Indicator (KPI)				C291105023	8:42:26 AM	8:44:13 AM	9:41:37 AM	107	47	57.4

The three measures of central tendency for the length of the conversations show distinctly different values. The average conversation with an operator lasts about 25 and half minutes, but the most common conversation length, as indicated by the mode, is 13.25 minutes with a median of 22.75 minutes. One interpretation is that many calls could be dealt with in a short time, although some longer calls (up to almost 110 minutes) require more operator time, bringing up the average. This information tells Chryssa that the call center might handle calls more efficiently by routing more difficult, time-consuming calls to the most experienced operators.

Rounding Data Values

Three rounding functions supported by Excel are ROUND, ROUNDDOWN, and ROUNDUP. The ROUND function rounds a value to the nearest digit, the **ROUNDDOWN function** rounds the value to the next lowest digit, and the **ROUNDUP function** rounds the value up to the next highest digit. These syntax of these three functions are

```
ROUND(number, Num_digits)
ROUNDDOWN(number, Num_digits)
ROUNDUP(number, Num_digits)
```

where `number` is the number to be rounded and `Num_digits` is the digit to round the number to. A positive `Num_digits` rounds values to the right of the decimal point and a negative `Num_digits` rounds digits to the left of decimal point. A `Num_digits` value of zero rounds the number to the nearest integer. Refer to Figure 3–22 for examples of rounding a value to different digits.

Figure 3–22 ROUND function examples

Formula	Interpretation	Result
= ROUND(137.438, 2)	Round to the nearest hundredth	137.44
= ROUND(137.438, 1)	Round to the nearest tenth	137.4
= ROUND(137.438, 0)	Round to the nearest integer	137
= ROUND(137.438, −1)	Round to nearest multiple of ten	140
= ROUND(137.438, −2)	Round to the nearest multiple of one hundred	100

Values returned from the ROUNDDOWN and ROUNDUP functions are similar except that they round the value down or up. The function ROUNDUP(137.438, –2) rounds the value up to the next multiple of 100, returning a value of 200. The function ROUNDDOWN(132.438, –1) rounds the value down to the previous multiple of 10, returning a value of 130.

Unlike number formats, which change how many digits are displayed in a cell, the rounding functions change the value stored in a cell.

Reference

Using Functions to Round Values

- To round a number to the nearest digit, use

  `ROUND(number, Num_digits)`

  where *number* is the numeric value and *Num_digits* is the number of digits the numeric value is rounded to.
- To round a number down to the next lowest digit, use

  `ROUNDDOWN(number, Num_digits)`
- To round a number to the next highest digit, use

  `ROUNDUP(number, Num_digits)`
- To round a number to the nearest integer, use

  `INT(number)`
- To round a number to the nearest multiple of a value, use

  `MROUND(number, multiple)`

  where *multiple* is a multiple to be rounded to.

The operator time values in column K show time values to fractions of a minute. Chryssa doesn't need that kind of accuracy in the analysis. Instead, she wants the call durations to be rounded to whole minutes. For example, a call lasting 12.2 minutes would round up to 13 minutes. You will use rounding functions to round up the operator times.

To roundup the operator times:

1. Click cell **K5**, and then press **DELETE** to remove the dynamic array formula. The multiple values in column K disappear and the running totals in column L change to zero.
2. On the Formulas tab, in the Function Library group, click the **Insert Function** button. The Insert Function dialog box opens.
3. In the Search for a function box, type **round** to describe the function you want to use, and then click **Go**. Functions related to rounding appear in the search results. Refer to Figure 3–23.

Figure 3–23 Insert Function dialog box

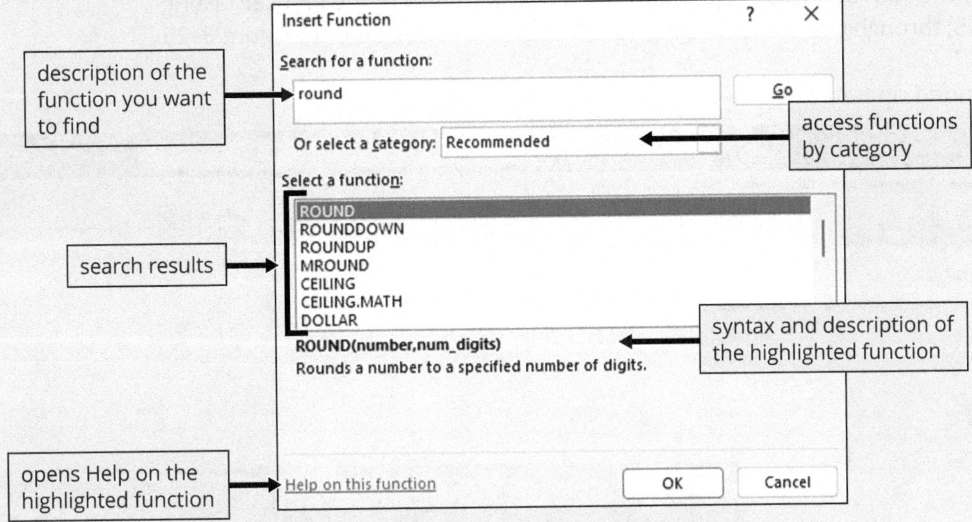

4. In the Select a function box, click **ROUNDUP**, and then click **OK**. The Function Arguments dialog box opens, describing the arguments used by the function.
5. In the Number box, type the formula **(H5:H333 – G5:G333)*24*60** to calculate the duration of the operator times in minutes.
6. Press **TAB**, and then type **0** in the Num_digits box to round up the calculated value to the next highest integer. For cell K5, the formula result 31.51666667 will be rounded up to 32. Refer to Figure 3–24.

Figure 3–24 Function Arguments dialog box

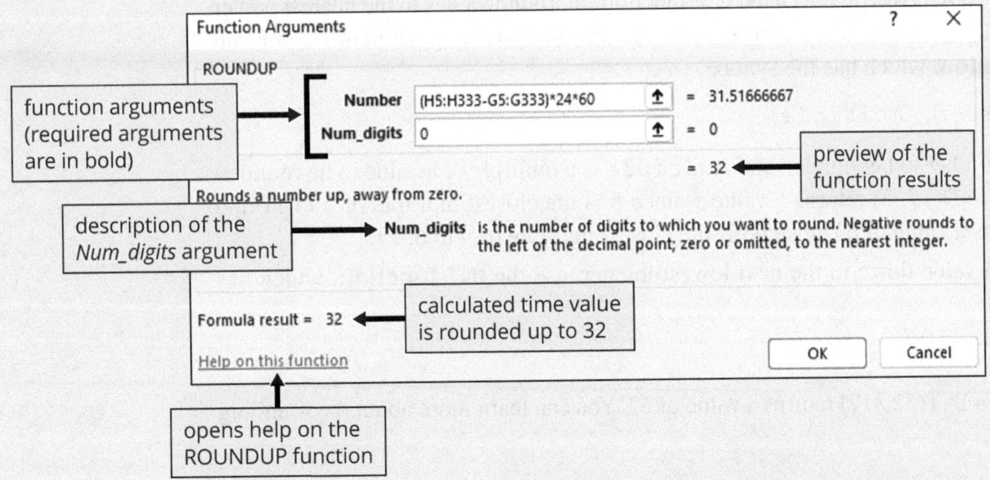

7. Click **OK** to close the dialog box. The formula =ROUNDUP((H5:H333 – G5:G333)*24*60, 0) is entered in cell K5. The rounded values appear in column K starting with the first call lasting 32 minutes (cell K5) through the last call lasting 15 minutes (cell K333). Refer to Figure 3–25.

Figure 3–25 Rounded operator times

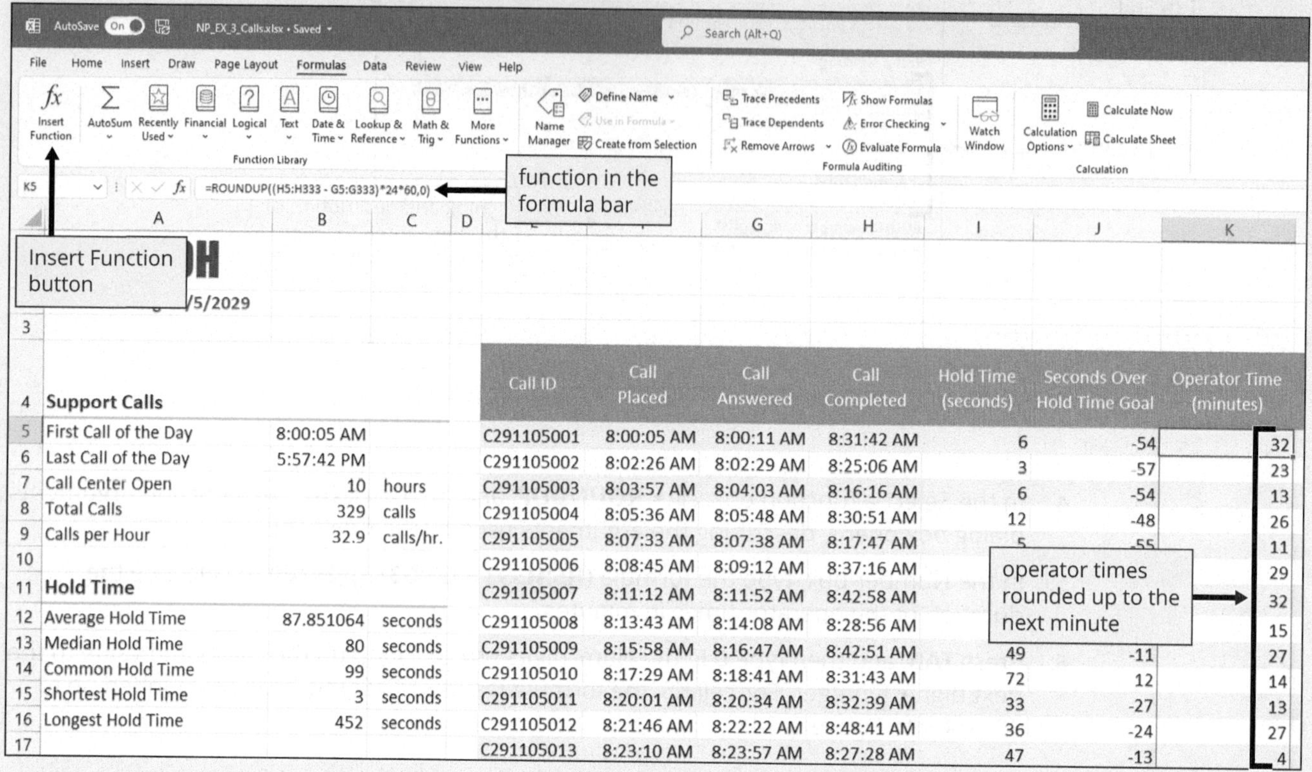

The ROUND, ROUNDDOWN, and ROUNDUP functions all round values to the nearest power of 10 such as 1/100, 1/10, 1, 10, 100, and so forth. To round values to powers other than 10, you can use the **MROUND function**, which has the syntax

MROUND(*number*, *multiple*)

where *number* is the number to be rounded and *multiple* is a multiple of a value to be rounded to. For example, MROUND(17, 5) returns a value 5 since 5 is the closest multiple of 5 to 17 and MROUND(60, 9) returns a value of 63 since 63 is the closest multiple of 9 to 60.

To always rounds a value down to the next lowest integer, use the **INT function**, which has the syntax

INT(*number*)

For example, the function INT(52.817) returns a value of 52. You can learn more about the rounding functions in Excel Help.

Proskills

Written Communication: Displaying Significant Digits

Excel stores numbers with a precision up to 15 digits and displays as many digits as will fit into the cell. So even the result of a simple formula such as =10/3 will display 3.33333333333333 if the cell is wide enough.

A number with 15-digit accuracy is difficult to read, and calculations rarely need that level of precision. Many scientific disciplines, such as chemistry or physics, have rules specifying exactly how many digits should be displayed with any calculation. These digits are called **significant digits** because they indicate the accuracy of the measured and calculated values. For example, the value 19.32 has four significant digits.

The rules for determining the number of significant digits reported in a calculation vary between disciplines. Generally, a calculated value should display no more digits than are found in any of the values used in the calculation. For example, any calculations based on the value 19.32 should have no more than four significant digits even if other numbers are measured with greater precision. Showing more digits would be misleading because it implies a level of accuracy beyond what was measured.

Because Excel displays calculated values with as many digits as can fit into a cell, you need to know the standards of your profession to report the number of digits correctly.

Nesting Functions

Functions can be **nested**, or placed inside within, other functions. When functions are nested, Excel evaluates the innermost function first and then moves outward, evaluating the remaining functions with the inner function acting as an argument for the next outer function. For example, the following expression nests the AVERAGE function within the ROUND function. In this expression, the average of the values in the range A1:A100 is calculated first, and then that average is rounded to the nearest integer:

```
ROUND(AVERAGE(A1:A100),0)
```

Formulas that involve several layers of nested functions can be challenging to read. The more nested functions there are, the more difficult it becomes to associate each set of arguments with its corresponding function. To help interpret nested functions, Excel displays the opening and closing parentheses of each function level in a different color. You can also expand the formula bar and then enter different levels of nested functions on separate lines, making each function clearer.

The last part of the Operator Time section in the Call Center Log worksheet calculates the total time operators spend on the phone during the day. Knowing how long operators are actively engaged with customers is important to determining the call center's staffing needs. Chryssa wants the total support time rounded to the nearest hour. To do that, you will use both the SUM function and the ROUND function nested in a single formula. Chyrssa also wants to know the total operator time per hour. You will calculate this value by dividing the total operator time by the total number of hours the call center is open.

To calculate and round the total operator time and the operator time per hour:

1. Click cell **B24** to make it the active cell.
2. Click the **down arrow** in the bottom-right corner of the formula bar. The formula bar expands in height.
3. Type **=ROUND(** to begin the formula. As you type the formula, the syntax of the ROUND function appears in a ScreenTip. The number argument is in bold to indicate that you are entering this part of the function.
4. Press **ALT+ENTER** to create a new line on the formula bar.

5. Press the **SPACEBAR** three times to indent the line three spaces.
6. Type **SUM(K5#)/60,** to calculate the total operator, divided by 60 to convert that sum to hours.
7. Press **ALT+ENTER** to create a new line on the formula bar.
8. Type **0)** to end the ROUND function, rounding the sum to the nearest hour, and then press **ENTER**.

   Key Step To round a value to the nearest integer, specify 0 as the last argument in the function to indicate that the value is rounded to zero digits.

9. Click cell **B24** to make it the active cell. The value 142 appears in cell B24, indicating that center operators have logged about 142 hours during the day dealing with customer inquiries. Refer to Figure 3–26.

Figure 3–26 Rounded sum of total operator hours

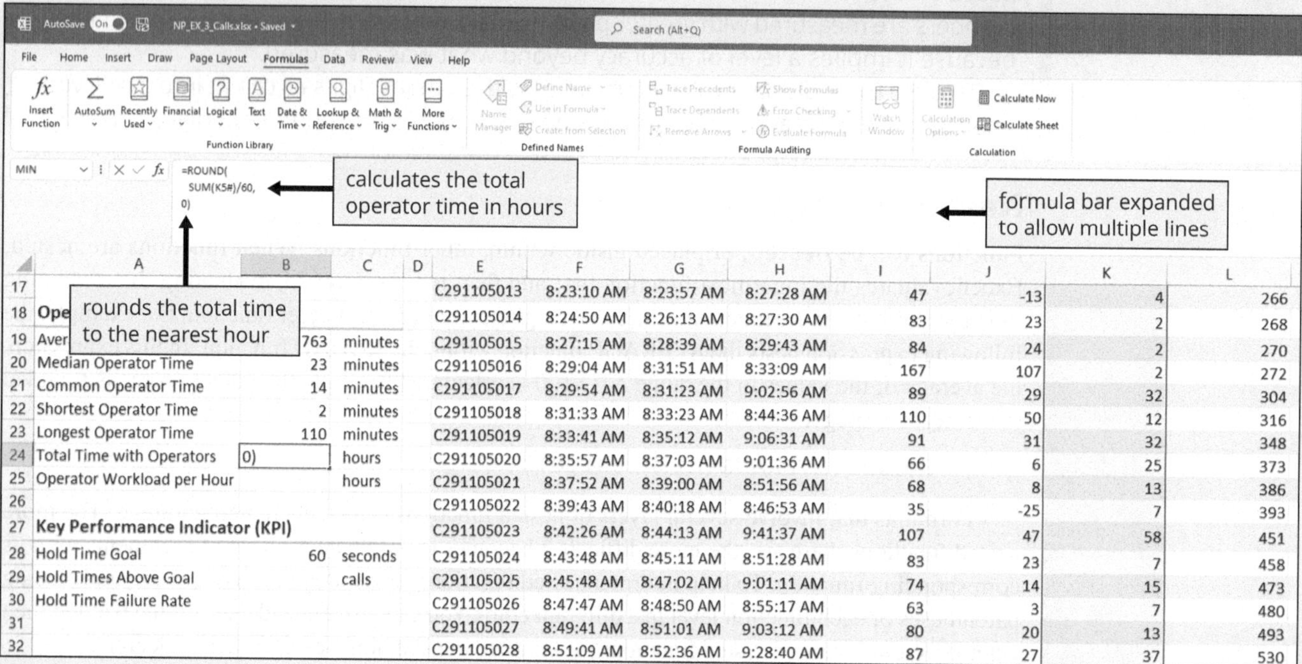

10. Click the **up arrow** in the upper-right corner of the expanded formula bar. The formula bar collapses to one line.
11. In cell **B25**, enter the formula **=B24/B7** to divide the total operator time by the number of hours the call center is open. The total operator time per hour is 14.2.

Chryssa learns that on average, the call center staff spends 14.2 hours with customers every hour. In other words, the call center needs at least 15 operators available every hour to keep up with call volume. Fewer than 15 operators will result in a backlog that would increase throughout the day as more calls pile up in the queue.

The Role of Blanks and Zeroes

The functions you've entered were applied to whole columns of data even though those columns contained empty cells and cells with text strings. Mathematical and statistical functions such as SUM, COUNT, AVERAGE, and MEDIAN include only numeric data in their calculations, ignoring empty cells and text entries. A blank cell is considered a text entry and is not treated as the number zero. Refer to Figure 3–27 for how the results differ when a blank replaces a zero in a data series.

Figure 3–27 Calculations with blanks and zeroes

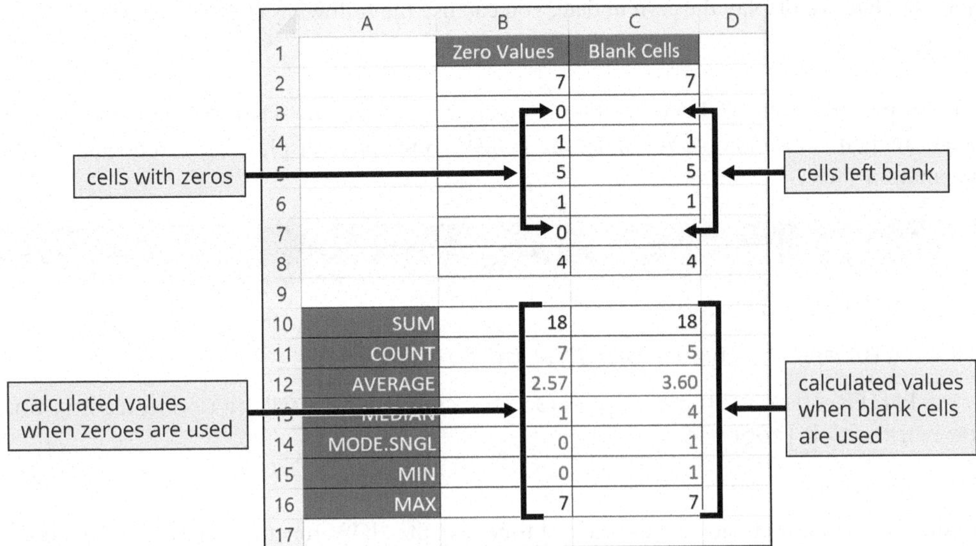

Whether you use a blank cell or a zero in a data series depends on what you are trying to measure. For example, to calculate the average number of hours per day that the call center is open, Chryssa could enter 0 or a blank for days that the call center is closed. Using a zero returns the average hours worked across all calendar days and gives a good overall summary of the company's annual staffing needs. Using a blank cell would summarize staffing needs only for the days that the call center is open. Both approaches have their uses. Consider the purpose of your calculations and choose the approach that best achieves your goal.

Date and Time Functions

Excel supports a large collection of date and time functions. Figure 3–28 summarizes some of the most useful ones.

Figure 3–28 Date and time functions

Function	Description
DATE(*year*,*month*,*day*)	Creates a date value for the date represented by the *year*, *month*, and *day* arguments
DAY(*serial_number*)	Extracts the day of the month from a date value stored as *serial_number*
MONTH(*serial_number*)	Extracts the month number from a date value stored as serial_number, where 1=January, 2=February, and so on
YEAR(*serial_number*)	Extracts the 4-digit year value from a date value stored as *serial_number*
NETWORKDAYS(*start_date*, *end_date*,[*holidays*])	Calculates the number of whole working days between *start_date* and *end_date*; to exclude holidays, add the optional holidays argument containing a list of holiday dates to skip
WEEKDAY(*serial_number*, [*return_type*])	Calculates the weekday from a date value stored as *serial_number*, where 1=Sunday, 2=Monday, and so forth; to choose a different numbering scheme, set *return_type* to 1 (1=Sunday, 2=Monday, ...), 2 (1=Monday, 2=Tuesday, ...), or 3 (0=Monday, 1=Tuesday, ...)
WORKDAY(*start_date*, *days*,[*holidays*])	Returns the workday after *days* workdays have passed since the *start_date*; to exclude holidays, add the optional holidays argument containing a list of holiday dates to skip
NOW( )	Returns the current date and time
TODAY( )	Returns the current date

Many workbooks include the current date so that any reports generated by the workbook are identified by date. To display the current date, you can use the following **TODAY function**:

```
TODAY()
```

The date displayed by the TODAY function is updated automatically whenever you enter a new formula or reopen the workbook. You'll use the TODAY function to display the current date on the Documentation sheet.

To display the current date:

1. Go to the **Documentation** sheet.
2. Click cell **B5**, and then type **=TODAY()** as the formula
3. Press **ENTER**. The current date appears in the cell. The date will be updated every time the workbook is reopened.

To display the current date and the current time, use the NOW function. The NOW function, like the TODAY function, is automatically updated whenever you add a new calculation to the workbook or reopen it.

Insight

Date Calculations with Working Days

Businesses are often more interested in workdays rather than calendar days. For example, to estimate a delivery date in which packages are not shipped or delivered on weekends, it is more useful to know the date of the next weekday rather than the date of the next day.

To display the date of a working day that is a specified number of workdays past a start date, use the **WORKDAY function** with the syntax

```
WORKDAY(start_date, days, [holidays])
```

where *start_date* is the starting date, *days* is the number of workdays after that starting date, and *holidays* is an optional list of holiday dates to skip. For example, if cell A1 contains the date 12/20/2029, a Thursday, the following formula displays the date 1/2/2029, a Wednesday that is nine working days later:

```
WORKDAY(A1,9)
```

The optional *holidays* argument references a series of dates that the WORKDAY function will skip in performing its calculations. So, if 12/24/2029, 12/25/2029, and 1/1/2030 are entered in the range B1:B2 as holidays, the following function will return the date 1/4/2030, a Friday, that is nine working days (excluding the holidays) after 12/20/2029:

```
WORKDAY(A1,9,B1:B3)
```

To reverse the process and calculate the number of working days between two dates, use the **NETWORKDAYS function**, which has the syntax

```
NETWORKDAYS(start_date, end_date, [holidays])
```

where *start_date* is the starting date, *end_date* is the ending date, and *holidays* is an optional list of holiday dates to skip. So, if cell A1 contains the date 12/20/2029 and cell A2 contains the date 1/7/2030, the following function returns the value 11, indicating that there are 11 working days between the start and ending date, excluding the holidays specified in the range B1:B3:

```
NETWORKDAYS(A1,A2,B1:B3)
```

For international applications, which might have a different definition of working day, Excel supports the WORKDAY.INTL function. Refer to Excel Help for more information.

Chryssa wants to keep hold times down to a minute or less. She wants to know how many calls in the call log meet this goal. You can use logical functions to find the answer.

Working with the Logical IF Function

A **logical function** is a function that returns one of two possible values depending on whether a given condition is true or false. The condition is entered as an expression, such as A5 = 3. If cell A5 is equal to 3, the condition is true; if cell A5 is not equal to 3, the condition is false. A common logical function is the following IF function:

```
IF(logical_test, value_if_true, [value_if_false])
```

where `logical_test` is a condition that is either true or false, `value_if_true` is the value returned by the function if the condition is true, and `value_if_false` is an optional argument containing the value if the condition is false.

> **Tip** If no `value_if_false` argument is provided, the IF function returns the value FALSE when the condition is false.

For example, the following function returns a value of 100 if A1 = B1. Otherwise, it returns a value of 50:

```
IF(A1 = B1, 100, 50)
```

The `value_if_true` and the `value_if_false` arguments in the IF function can also be cell references. For example, the following function returns the value of cell C1 if the condition is true, otherwise it returns the value of cell D1:

```
IF(A1 = B1, C1, D1)
```

The = symbol in IF function is a **comparison operator**, which is an operator expressing the relationship between two values. Figure 3–29 describes other comparison operators that can be used with logical functions.

Figure 3–29 Logical comparison operators

Operator	Expression	Tests
=	A1 = B1	If value in cell A1 is equal to the value in cell B1
>	A1 > B1	If the value in cell A1 is greater than the value in cell B1
<	A1 < B1	If the value in cell A1 is less than the value in cell B1
>=	A1 >= B1	If the value in cell A1 is greater than or equal to the value in cell B1
<=	A1 <= B1	If the value in cell A1 is less than or equal to the value in cell B1
<>	A1 <> B1	If the value in cell A1 is not equal to the value in cell B1

The following function returns the text string "goal met" if the value in cell A1 is less than or equal to the value of cell B1. Otherwise, it returns the text string "goal failed":

```
IF(A1 <= B1, "goal met", "goal failed")
```

> **Tip** To apply multiple logical conditions, you can nest one IF function within another.

To determine whether a customer was on hold longer than a minute, you will use the IF function to test the values in column J, containing the difference between each customer's hold time and the hold time goal of 60 seconds. If the difference is positive (indicating a hold time longer than 60 seconds), the IF function will return a value of 1. Otherwise, it will return a value of zero.

To use the IF function to indicate that a call has exceed the hold-time goal:

1. Go to the **Call Center Log** worksheet.
2. Click cell **M5** to select that cell.
3. On the Formulas tab, in the Function Library group, click the **Logical** button to display a list of all the logical functions.
4. Click **IF** to open the Function Arguments dialog box for the IF function.
5. In the Logical_test box, type the **J5:J333 > 0** to test whether the array of values in column J are greater than zero.
6. In the Value_if_true box, type **1** as the value to display if the hold time is over 60 seconds.
7. In the Value_if_false box, type **0** as the value to display if the hold time is 60 seconds or less.
8. Click **OK** to enter the formula = IF(J5:J333 > 0, 1, 0) in cell M5. An array of 0s and 1s appear in column M. The tenth call, in cell M14, is the first call that exceeds the 1-minute hold-time goal. Refer to Figure 3–30.

Figure 3–30 Hold times exceeding 1 minute

seconds above or below the 60-second goal

=IF(J5:J333 > 0,1,0)

0 indicates a hold time of 60 seconds or less

1 indicates a hold time greater than 60 seconds

Call ID	Call Placed	Call Answered	Call Completed	Hold Time (seconds)	Seconds Over Hold Time Goal	Operator Time (minutes)	Cumulative Operator Time (minutes)	Hold Time Indicator (1 = failure, 0 = Success)
C291105001	8:00:05 AM	8:00:11 AM	8:31:42 AM	6	-54	32	32	0
C291105002	8:02:26 AM	8:02:29 AM	8:25:06 AM	3	-57			0
C291105003	8:03:57 AM	8:04:03 AM	8:16:16 AM	6	-54			0
C291105004	8:05:36 AM	8:05:48 AM	8:30:51 AM	12	-48			0
C291105005	8:07:33 AM	8:07:38 AM	8:17:47 AM	5	-55	11	105	0
C291105006	8:08:45 AM	8:09:12 AM	8:37:16 AM	27	-33	29	134	0
C291105007	8:11:12 AM	8:11:52 AM	8:42:58 AM	40	-20	32	166	0
C291105008	8:13:43 AM	8:14:08 AM	8:28:56 AM	25	-35	15	181	0
C291105009	8:15:58 AM	8:16:47 AM	8:42:51 AM	49	-11			0
C291105010	8:17:29 AM	8:18:41 AM	8:31:43 AM	72	12			1
C291105011	8:20:01 AM	8:20:34 AM	8:32:39 AM	33	-27			0
C291105012	8:21:46 AM	8:22:22 AM	8:48:41 AM	36	-24	27	262	0
C291105013	8:23:10 AM	8:23:57 AM	8:27:28 AM	47	-13	4	266	0
C291105014	8:24:50 AM	8:26:13 AM	8:27:30 AM	83	23	2	268	1
C291105015	8:27:15 AM	8:28:39 AM	8:29:43 AM	84	24	2	270	1
C291105016	8:29:04 AM	8:31:51 AM	8:33:09 AM	167	107	2	272	1
C291105017	8:29:54 AM	8:31:23 AM	9:02:56 AM	89	29	32	304	1
C291105018	8:31:33 AM	8:33:23 AM	8:44:36 AM	110	50	12	316	1

Formulas and Key Terms

Businesses often track success with a **key performance indicator (KPI)**, which compares a measured outcome to an established norm or baseline. The percentage of customers experiencing long hold times is one KPI that Chryssa uses to measure the success of the call center. A high percentage of long hold times indicates that the call center needs to improve its service.

Since every call is graded as either a failure (1) or a success (0), you can calculate the percent of calls with long hold times by summing the values in column M and dividing that sum by the total number of calls.

To calculate the number and percent of long hold times:

1. In cell **B29**, enter the formula **= SUM(M5#)** to add the values in column M. Cell B29 displays 265, indicating that 265 callers experienced hold times of longer than a minute.
2. In cell **B30**, enter the formula **= B29/B8** to calculate the percentage of calls with long hold times.
3. Click cell **B30**. You'll format cell B30 to display the value as a percentage to two decimal places.
4. On the ribbon, click the **Home** tab. In the Number group, click the **Number Format** box, and then click **Percentage**. The result of 80.55% indicates that more than 80% of callers experienced a long hold time based on the 60-second standard that Chryssa is trying to maintain for the center. Refer to Figure 3–31.

Figure 3–31 Percentage of failed calls with long hold times

B30 = B29/B8

	A	B	C	D	E	F	G	H	I	J	K
18	**Operator Time**				C291105014	8:24:50 AM	8:26:13 AM	8:27:30 AM	83	23	
19	Average Operator Time	25.981763	minutes		C291105015	8:27:15 AM	8:28:39 AM	8:29:43 AM	84	24	
20	Median Operator Time	23	minutes		C291105016	8:29:04 AM	8:31:51 AM	8:33:09 AM	167	107	
21	Common Operator Time	14	minutes		C291105017	8:29:54 AM	8:31:23 AM	9:02:56 AM	89	29	3
22	Shortest Operator Time	2	minutes		C291105018	8:31:33 AM	8:33:23 AM	8:44:36 AM	110	50	1
23	Longest Operator Time	110	minutes		C291105019	8:33:41 AM	8:35:12 AM	9:06:31 AM	91	31	3
24	Total Time with Operators	142	hours		C291105020	8:35:57 AM	8:37:03 AM	9:01:36 AM	66	6	2
25	Operator Workload per Hour	14.2	hours		C291105021	8:37:52 AM	8:39:00 AM	8:51:56 AM	68	8	1
26					C291105022	8:39:43 AM	8:40:18 AM	8:46:53 AM	35	-25	
27	**Key Performance Indicator (KPI)**				C291105023	8:42:26 AM	8:44:13 AM	9:41:37 AM	107	47	5
28	Hold Time Goal	60	seconds		C291105024	8:43:48 AM	8:45:11 AM	8:51:28 AM	83	23	
29	Hold Times Above Goal	265			5025	8:45:48 AM	8:47:02 AM	9:01:11 AM	74	14	1
30	Hold Time Failure Rate	80.55%			C291105026	8:47:47 AM	8:48:50 AM	8:55:17 AM	63	3	
31					C291105027	8:49:41 AM	8:51:01 AM	9:03:12 AM	80	20	1
32					C291105028	8:51:09 AM	8:52:36 AM	9:28:40 AM	87	27	3
33					C291105029	8:52:20 AM	8:53:45 AM	9:16:03 AM	85	25	2

=SUM(M5#)

=B29/B8

You have compiled a lot of useful information about the call center. Based on your analysis, you know the following:

- The national call center receives about 33 calls per hour.
- Callers wait on hold for an average of about 88 seconds with more than 80% of the callers waiting longer than a minute to reach an operator.
- Operators spend an average of about 26 minutes on each call with some calls lasting up to an hour and a half.
- At least 15 operators must be available every hour to handle the call volume.

More operators will reduce the hold times, but Chryssa wants to know how many more operators are needed to make a significant difference. To answer this question, you will enter what you have learned about the call center.

To enter the call center metrics:

1. Go to the **Call Center Projections** worksheet.
2. In cell **B6**, enter **33** as the anticipated calls per hour to the center.
3. In cell **B7**, enter **15** as the number of operators available to answer calls.
4. In cell **B8**, enter **60** as the hold time goal in seconds.
5. In cell **B9**, enter **26** as the average call duration in minutes.
6. In cell **B12**, enter the formula **= B9/60** to calculate the average call duration in hours. The average call duration is 0.43 hours.

   Tip A green triangle appears next to some calculated values in this worksheet. You can ignore them. They do not affect the calculated values and just indicate some calculations in the workbook use custom functions created specifically for this report.

7. In cell **B13**, enter the formula **= B6*B12** to calculate the number of operators required each hour to handle the call volume. The number of operators hours per workload is 14.30. The Hold Time Lookup Table entries are generated based on the value in cell B13. You will use this table shortly.
8. In cell **B14**, enter the formula **= B13/B7** to calculate the anticipated percentage of operators occupied with callers. At the current call volume and 15 operators, 95.33% of the operators will be occupied with a call at any one time.
9. In cell **B15**, enter the formula **= 1 – B14** to calculate the percent of operators who are free to answer calls. The percentage of available operators is 4.67%. Refer to Figure 3–32.

Figure 3–32 Metrics of the call center

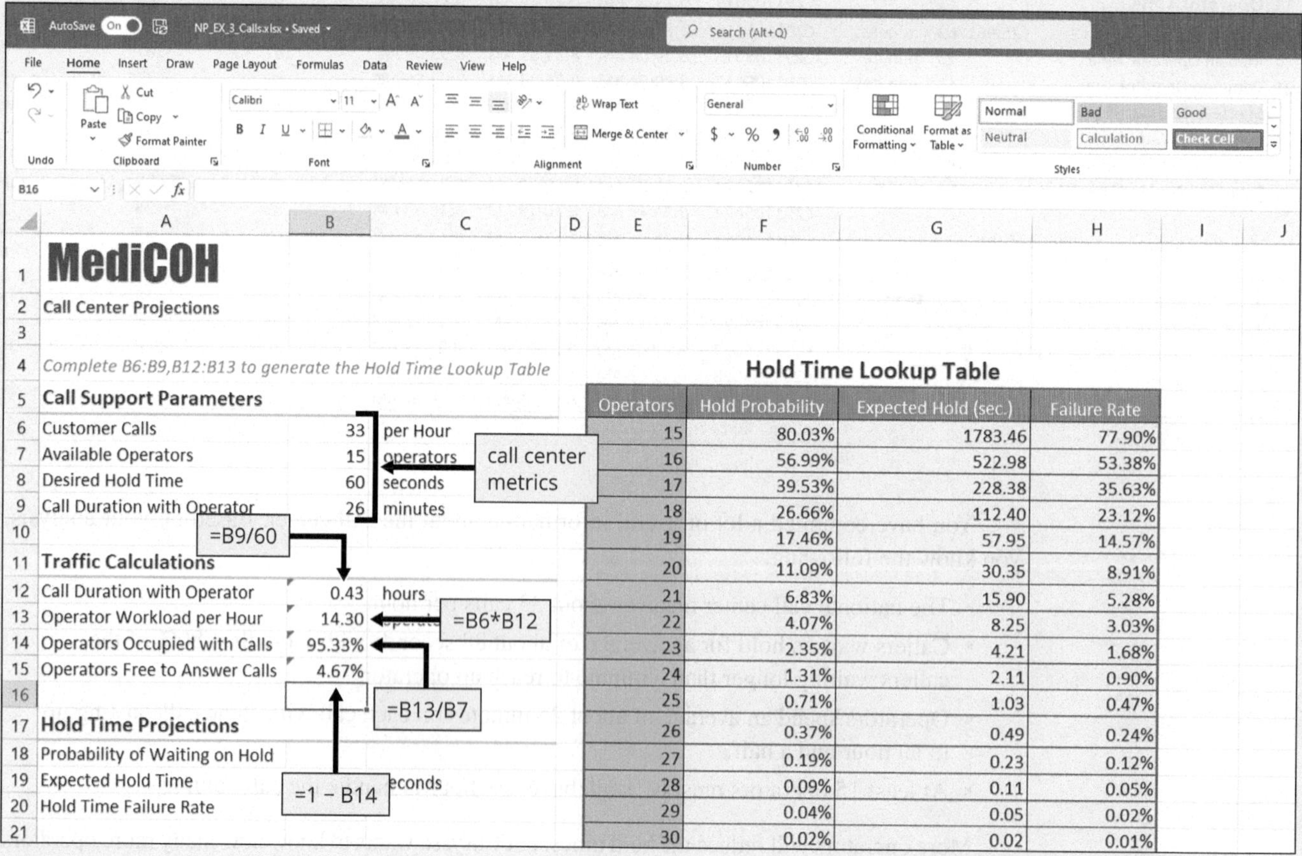

Operators	Hold Probability	Expected Hold (sec.)	Failure Rate
15	80.03%	1783.46	77.90%
16	56.99%	522.98	53.38%
17	39.53%	228.38	35.63%
18	26.66%	112.40	23.12%
19	17.46%	57.95	14.57%
20	11.09%	30.35	8.91%
21	6.83%	15.90	5.28%
22	4.07%	8.25	3.03%
23	2.35%	4.21	1.68%
24	1.31%	2.11	0.90%
25	0.71%	1.03	0.47%
26	0.37%	0.49	0.24%
27	0.19%	0.23	0.12%
28	0.09%	0.11	0.05%
29	0.04%	0.05	0.02%
30	0.02%	0.02	0.01%

As you entered the call center data, a table of hold time probabilities and projections was populated in the range E5:H32. The table was generated by MediCOH statisticians using a branch of mathematics called "queuing theory" to predict call center performance based on call volume, the number of available operators, and the average length of each call. A study of queueing theory is beyond the scope of this module, but you can extract information from the table using lookup functions, answering questions about the optimal number of operators required at the center.

Insight

Using the IFERROR Function to Catch Error Values

An error value does not mean that your formula is wrong. Some errors appear simply because you have not yet entered any data into the workbook. For example, if you apply the AVERAGE function to a range that does not yet contain any data values, the #DIV/0! error value appears because Excel cannot calculate averages without data. However, as soon as you enter your data, the #DIV/0! error value disappears, replaced with the calculated average.

Error values of this type can make your workbook confusing and difficult to read. One way to hide them is with the following **IFERROR function**

```
IFERROR (Value, Value_if_error)
```

where `Value` is the value to be calculated and `Value_if_error` is the value returned by Excel if any error is encountered in the function. For example, the following IFERROR function returns the average of the values in column F, but if no values have yet been entered in that column, it returns a blank text string (" "):

```
IFERROR(AVERAGE(F:F), "")
```

Using this logical function results in a cleaner workbook that is more usable without distracting error values.

Looking Up Data

A **lookup function** retrieves a value matching a specified condition from a table of data. For example, a lookup function can be used to retrieve a shipping rate given a package's size and destination or a tax rate for a specified income.

The table storing the data to be retrieved is called a **lookup table**. The row or column with values to be matched is called the **lookup array**. If the values in the lookup array are organized in a row, the table is a **horizontal lookup table**; if the values are arranged in a column, the table is a **vertical lookup table**. The remaining rows or columns contain the **return array**, which are values retrieved from the lookup table when a match is found.

Figure 3–33 displays a vertical lookup table for retrieving data about MediCOH employees. The first column contains the lookup array (Employee ID), and the other columns contain return arrays (First Name, Last Name, Department). In this example, a lookup value for the employee ID "E86-2-2044" is supplied to the lookup table. A matching ID is found in cell A6—the fifth entry in the lookup array. The fifth entry from the return array for employee last names is returned, which in this case is "Aziz" located in cell C6.

Figure 3–33 Exact match returned from a lookup table

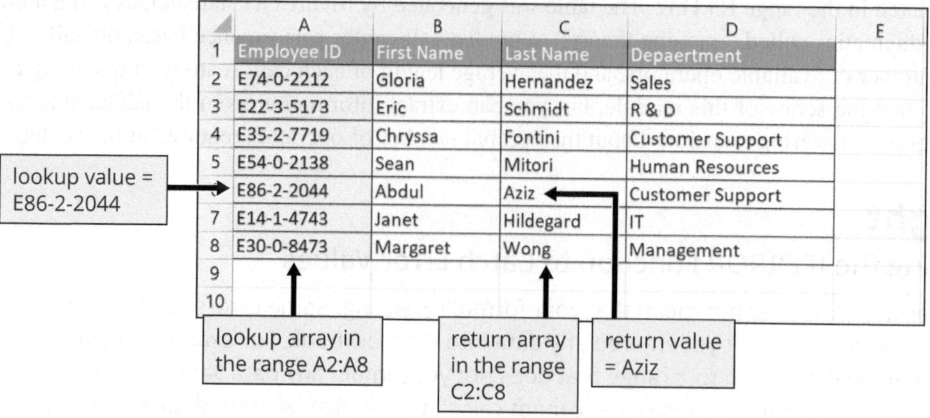

Lookup tables can be constructed for exact matches or approximate matches. In an **exact match lookup**, like the one in Figure 3–33, the lookup value must exactly match one of the values in the lookup array. If the lookup value falls within a range of values in the lookup arrow, you use an **approximate match lookup**. For example, in an approximate match lookup, you might match each employee's salary not to a specific amount but to a range of values, such as salaries between $70,000 and $80,000. Any salary falling within that range would constitute a match. In this module you will work with only exact match lookups.

Finding an Exact Match with the XLOOKUP Function

To retrieve a value from a lookup table, you use the following **XLOOKUP function**, which matches a supplied value to the lookup array and retrieves a corresponding value in the return array

```
XLOOKUP(lookup_value, lookup_array, return_array,
[if_not_found], [match_mode], [search_mode])
```

where `lookup_value` is the value to match, `lookup_array` is the column or row containing the lookup values, `return_array` is the column or row containing the return values, `if_not_found` is an optional value returned if no match is found, `match_mode` is the type of match, and `search_mode` specifies how the lookup array will be searched for matches.

The optional `match_mode` argument supports the following values defining what constitutes a match:

- match = 0 (default) Exact match. If none is found, returns the error value #N/A or the value specified by the `if_not_found` argument.
- match = –1 Exact match. If none is found, returns the next smaller value in the lookup array.
- match = 1 Exact match. If none is found, returns the next larger value in the lookup array.
- match = 2 Wildcard match using the *, ? and ~ symbols to locate a match within the lookup array.

The optional `search_mode` argument supports the following values defining how Excel will search through the lookup array:

- search = 1 (default) Perform a search starting down from the first value in the lookup array.
- search = –1 Perform a reverse search, starting up from the last value in the lookup array.
- search = 2 Perform a binary search that relies on lookup values being sorted in ascending order. If not sorted, invalid results will be returned.
- search = –2 Perform a binary search that relies on lookup values being sorted in descending order. If not sorted, invalid results will be returned.

If you do not include values for the `match_mode` and `search_mode` arguments, the XLOOKUP function performs an exact match lookup starting down from the first value in the lookup array.

The following XLOOKUP function performs the exact match lookup presented in Figure 3–33 with "E86-2-2044"as the lookup value, the range A2:A8 as the lookup array, and the range C2:C8 as the return array. If no employee with that ID is found in the lookup array, the text string "No employee found" is returned by the function.

```
XLOOKUP("E86-2-2044", A2:A8, C2:C8, "No employee found")
```

The Call Center Projection worksheet contains the following lookup and return arrays:

- **Operators.** The number of operators available to answer calls.
- **Hold Probability.** The probability that a customer will be placed on hold.
- **Expected Hold (sec).** The expected hold time in seconds for a customer calling the support center.
- **Failure Rate.** The probability that the customer's hold time will exceed the hold-time goal.

The number of operators in the lookup table starts with 15 operators. This is due to the mathematics of queueing theory. If the number of operators answering calls is less than the workload, the call center is understaffed and cannot keep up with demand. The workload of the call center was estimated in cell B13 as 14.30 operator hours every hour so the center must have at least 15 operators available to always answer calls.

You will use the XLOOKUP function to return the probability that a customer will have to wait on hold if 15 operators are staffing the call center.

To determine customers' hold probability with exact match lookup with XLOOKUP:

1. Click cell **B18** to select it.
2. On the ribbon, click the **Formulas** tab. In the Function Library group, click the **Lookup & Reference** button, and then click **XLOOKUP**. The Function Arguments dialog box opens.
3. In the Lookup_value box, enter **B7** as the cell containing the number of available operators.
4. In the Lookup_array box, enter **E6:E32** as the range containing the array of possible lookup matches.
5. In the Return_array box, enter **F6:F32** as the range containing the array of possible return values. You will not enter any other arguments for the XLOOKUP function, but instead will use their default values. Refer to Figure 3–34.

Figure 3–34 Function Arguments dialog box for the XLOOKUP function

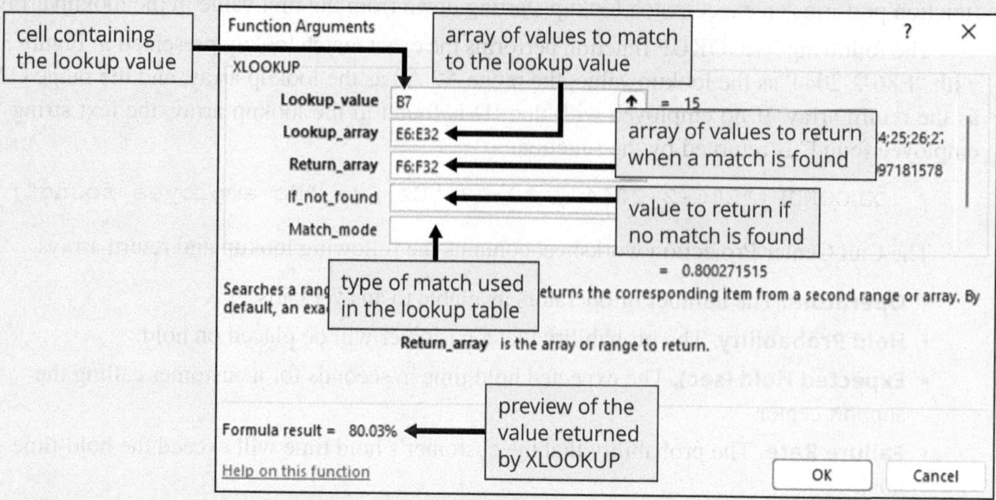

6. Click **OK**. The formula = XLOOKUP(B7, E6:E32, F6:F32) is entered in cell B18, returning the value 80.03%.

The value 80.03% indicates that with 15 operators, there is slightly more than an 80% probability that a customer will be placed on hold.

Next, you will use the XLOOKUP function to return the expected hold time and the probability that a hold time will exceed the 60-second goal set by Chryssa.

To use the XLOOKUP function with other call center metrics:

1. In cell **B19**, enter the formula **= XLOOKUP(B7, E6:E32, G6:G32)** to return the expected hold time with 15 operators. The return value is 1783.46 seconds, or about 30 minutes.
2. In cell **B20**, enter the formula **= XLOOKUP(B7, E6:E32, H6:H32)** to return the hold time failure rate, indicating that probability that a customer will wait on hold longer than 60 seconds. The return value is 77.90%, indicating that almost 78% of callers will wait on hold longer than a minute. Refer to Figure 3–35.

Figure 3–35 XLOOKUP results from the Hold Time lookup table

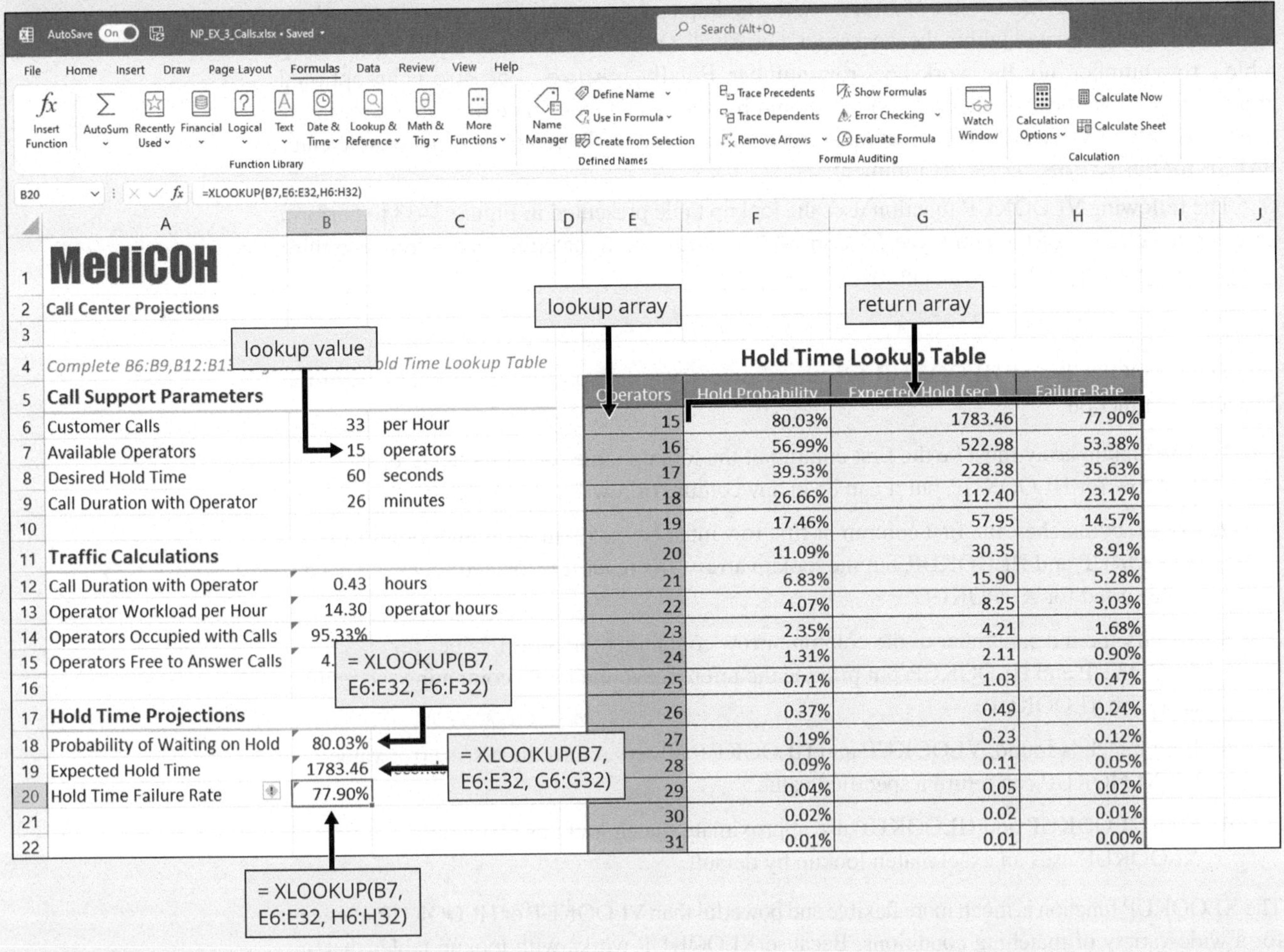

Fifteen operators are barely enough to handle the expected call volume, resulting in unacceptable hold times of almost 30 minutes. This problem could be fixed by increasing the number of available operators. You'll need to figure out how many operators would be required to bring the hold times down to acceptable levels.

Finding an Exact Match with VLOOKUP and HLOOKUP

The XLOOKUP function is the current standard for retrieving values from lookup tables. The previous standard, which you might encounter in older workbooks, uses the **VLOOKUP function** (vertical lookup function) or the **HLOOKUP function** (horizontal lookup function). The VLOOKUP and HLOOKUP functions are identical except for the orientation of the lookup table. The VLOOKUP function arranges the lookup and return arrays in columns of the lookup table. The HLOOKUP function arranges the lookup and return arrays in rows rather than columns.

The VLOOKUP and HLOOKUP functions have similar syntax:

```
VLOOKUP(lookup_value, table_array, col_index_num,
[range_lookup])

HLOOKUP(lookup_value, table_array, row_index_num,
[range_lookup])
```

In both, `lookup_value` is the lookup value to find in the first column of the lookup table, and `table_array` is the reference to the lookup table. In the VLOOKUP function, `col_index_num` is the number of the column in the lookup table that contains the return value. In the HLOOKUP function, `row_index_num` is the number of the row in the lookup table that contains the return value. The *col_index_num* refers to the column number of the lookup table, not the worksheet column. So, a *col_index_num* of 2 refers to the lookup table's second column no matter where the lookup table is located within the worksheet. For the HLOOKUP function, you enter the lookup table's row number, not the worksheet row number. Finally, *range_lookup* is an optional argument that specifies whether the lookup should be done as an exact match or an approximate match. Its default value is TRUE, creating an approximate match. To create an exact match, enter FALSE for the *range_lookup* argument.

The following VLOOKUP function uses the lookup table presented in Figure 3–33 to perform an exact match look of the employee ID E86-2-2044, returning a matching value from the third column of the lookup table located in the A2:D8 range:

```
VLOOKUP("E86-2-2044", A2:D8, 3, FALSE)
```

The VLOOKUP and HLOOKUP functions have several important differences from the XLOOKUP function:

1. The lookup array must be the first column of the lookup table for VLOOKUP or the first row for HLOOKUP, but it can be in any column or row for XLOOKUP.
2. For exact matches, the first column or first row must be sorted in ascending order for VLOOKUP and HLOOKUP, but the lookup array (wherever it is located) does not need to be sorted for XLOOKUP.
3. Specify the index number of the column or row containing the return values for VLOOKUP and HLOOKUP, but provide the reference to the range containing the return array for XLOOKUP.
4. If no match is found, VLOOKUP and HLOOKUP always return the #N/A error value, but XLOOKUP can return a specified value.
5. Both VLOOKUP and HLOOKUP use approximate match lookups by default; XLOOKUP uses an exact match lookup by default.

The XLOOKUP function is much more flexible and powerful than VLOOKUP or HLOOKUP, allowing for a wide variety of matching conditions. Because XLOOKUP works with lookup tables that are arranged by column or by row, it can replace both VLOOKUP and HLOOKUP. However, VLOOKUP and HLOOKUP have been the established standard. So, you should be comfortable with both approaches.

Insight

Generating Random Data

For some projects, you will want to simulate scenarios using randomly generated data. The following RAND function can generate a random decimal number between 0 and 1:

```
RAND()
```

To convert this random number to any decimal within a given range, include the function within the formula

```
(top - bottom)*RAND() + bottom
```

where *bottom* is the bottom of the range and *top* is the top of the range. For example, the following expression generates a random decimal number between 10 and 50:

```
(50-10)*RAND()+10
```

To limit the random numbers to integers, use the following RANDBETWEEN function:

```
RANDBETWEEN(bottom, top)
```

For example, the following formula generates a random integer between 10 and 50:

```
RANDBETWEEN(10, 50)
```

Random number functions are **volatile functions** in that they will automatically recalculate their values every time Excel does any calculation in the workbook. This means a different set of random numbers will appear with every new calculation in the workbook.

Performing What-If Analysis with Formulas and Functions

A **what-if analysis** explores the impact that changing input values has on calculated values and output values. By exploring a wide range of different input values, you will achieve a better understanding of data and its implications.

Using Trial and Error

One way to perform a what-if analysis is by **trial and error** where you change one or more of the input values to explore how they impact the calculated values in the workbook. Trial and error requires some guesswork and patience as you estimate which values to change and by how much. You'll use trial and error to investigate how changing the number of available operators impacts the hold-time projections.

To use trial and error to evaluate the impact changing the number of operators:

1. In cell **B7**, enter **16**. With one additional operator on call, the probability of waiting on hold drops to about 57% (cell B18), the expected hold time decreases to about 523 seconds (cell B19), and the hold time failure rate falls to 53.38% (cell B20).
2. In cell **B7**, enter **17**. With 17 operators available to answer calls, the probability of waiting on hold drops to about 40%, the expected hold time decreases to about 228 seconds, and the hold time failure rate falls to 35.63%.
3. In cell **B7**, enter **19**. With 19 available operators, the expected hold time drops just below one minute to about 58 seconds. Refer to Figure 3–36.

Figure 3–36 Using trial and error to determine the number of operators

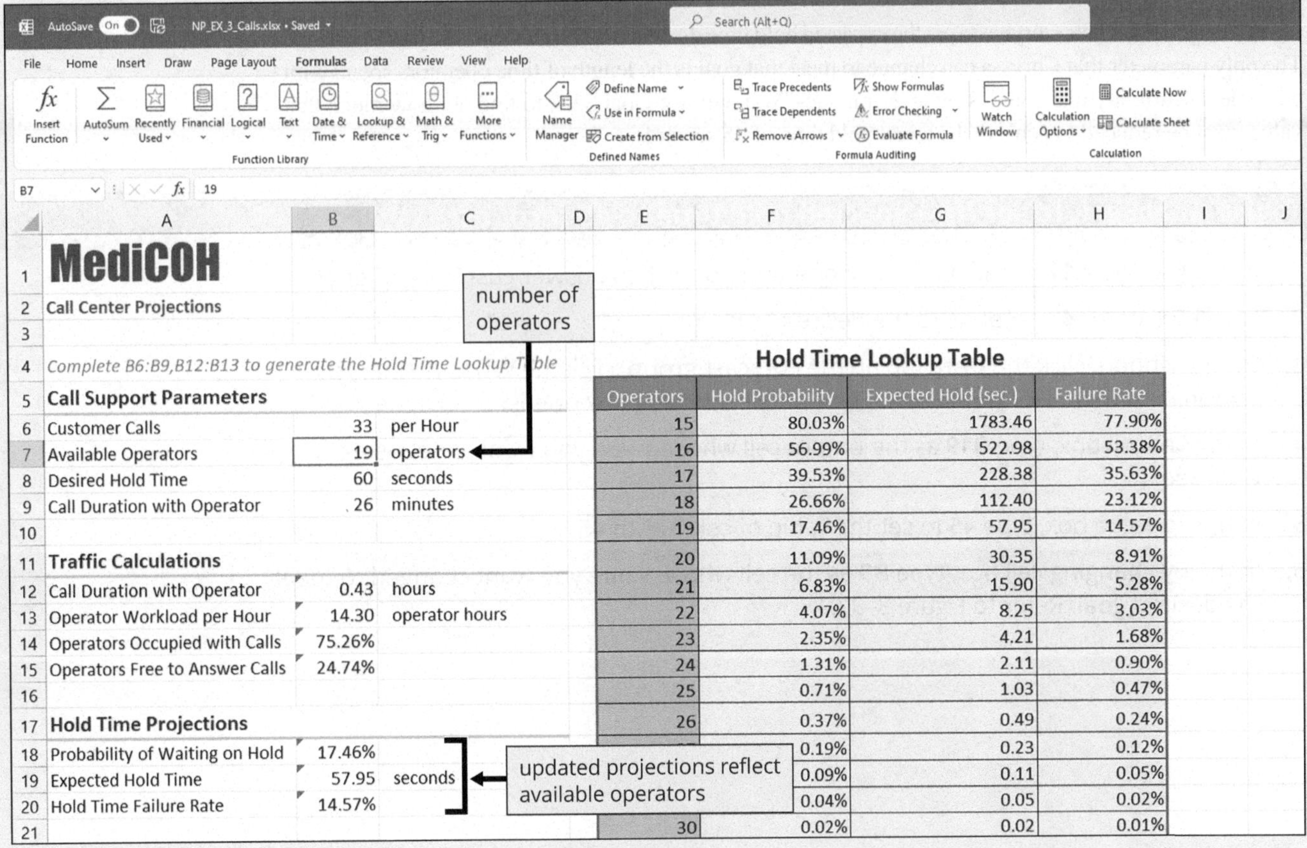

Based on the trial-and-error analysis, Chryssa recommended to management that the call center staff be expanded to 19 operators. However, the company does not have the budget to staff the call center to that level. Chryssa must come up with another solution. Other than hiring more staff, the only other factor in the company's control is how long operators spend on calls. If operators could handle calls more efficiently without sacrificing quality, the same number of operators could handle more callers. Chryssa needs to know by how much time each call would have to be trimmed to accommodate the daily call volume. That calculation can be done using Goal Seek.

Using Goal Seek

Goal Seek reverses the trial-and-error process by specifying an output value and working backward to find the input value needed to reach that goal. The output is always a calculated value, and the input is always a constant that can be changed using the Goal Seek tool. Goal Seek can be used only with calculated numbers, not with text.

Reference

Performing What-If Analysis and Goal Seek

To perform a what-if analysis by trial and error:

- Change the value of a worksheet cell (the input cell).
- Observe its impact on one or more calculated cells (the result cells).
- Repeat until the desired results are achieved.

To perform a what-if analysis using Goal Seek:

- On the Data tab, in the Forecast group, click the What-If Analysis button, and then click Goal Seek.
- Select the result cell in the Set cell box, and then specify its value (goal) in the To value box.
- In the By changing cell box, specify the input cell.
- Click OK. The value of the input cell changes to set the value of the result cell.

Management wants Chryssa to get the expected hold time down to 45 seconds with only 17 operators. The only parameter that Chryssa can change to meet that goal is the length of time operators spend with customers. Currently that value is set to 26 minutes. You will use Goal Seek to find out how much that value must be reduced to achieve the target hold time of 45 seconds.

To use Goal Seek to set the expected hold time to 45 seconds:

1. In cell **B7**, enter **17** as the number of operators on-call to answer customer queries.
2. In cell **B8**, enter **45** seconds as the desired hold time.
3. On the ribbon, click the **Data** tab. In the Forecast group, click the **What-If Analysis** button, and then click **Goal Seek**. The Goal Seek dialog box opens.
4. In the Set cell box, type **B19** as the output cell whose value you want to set using Goal Seek.
5. In the To value box, type **45** to set the value of cell B19 to 45.
6. In the By changing cell box, type **B9** as the cell whose value you want changed to meet the desired goal. Refer to Figure 3–37.

Figure 3–37 Goal Seek dialog box

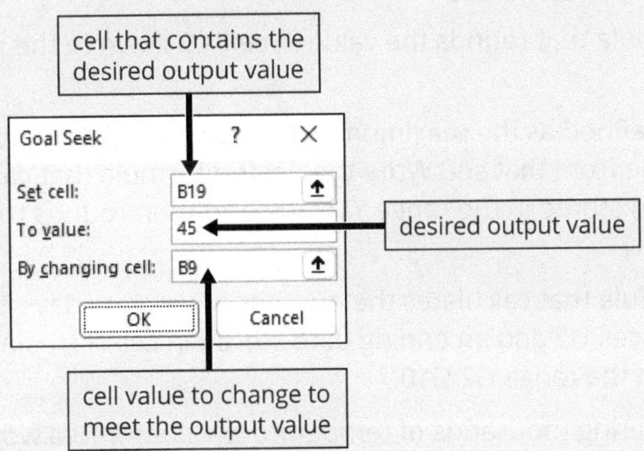

7. Click **OK**. The Goal Seek dialog box closes and the Goal Seek Status dialog box opens, indicating that Goal Seek has found a solution.
8. Click **OK**. The value in cell B9 changes from 26 to 22.4611 minutes and the value in cell B19 changes to the goal value of 45 seconds. Refer to Figure 3–38.

Figure 3–38 Goal Seek solution

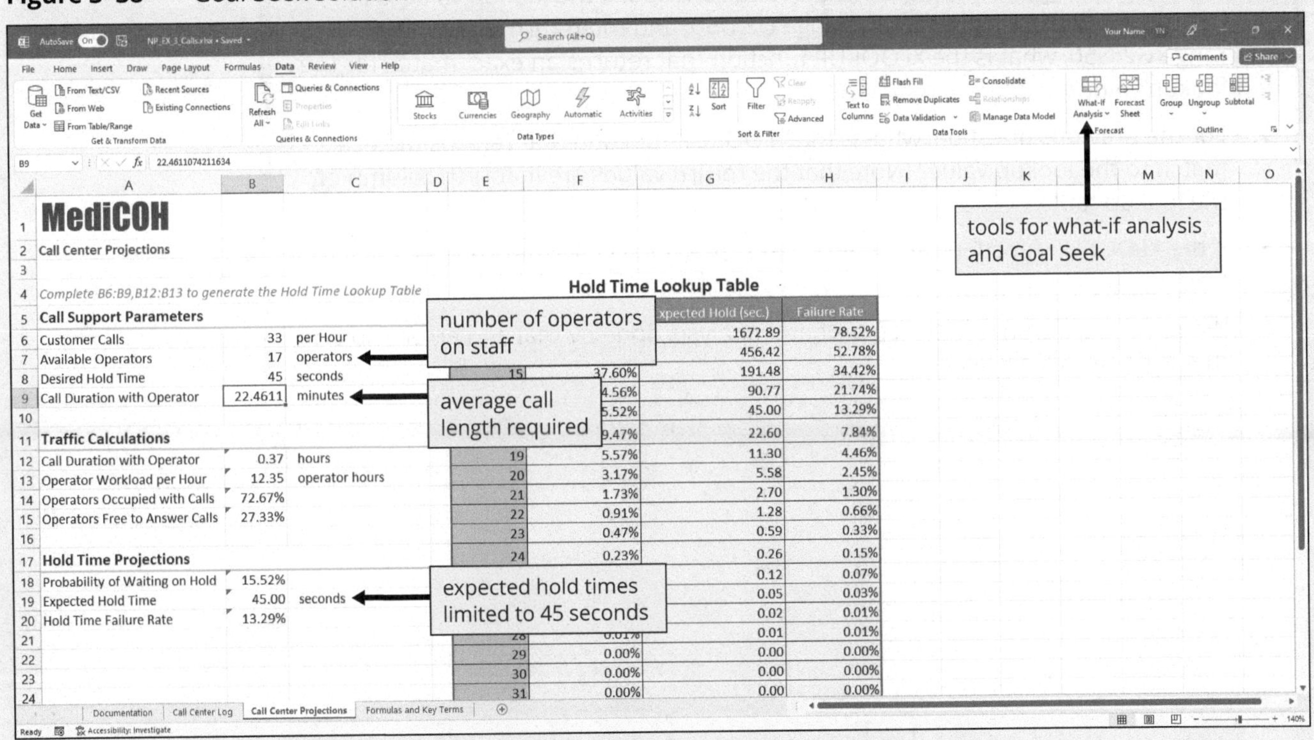

9. **sam** Save the workbook, and then close it.

The Goal Seek results tell Chryssa that if the average length of calls can be reduced to about 22.46 minutes (rough 22 and half minutes), 17 operators can handle the call volume with an expected hold time of 45 seconds.

Your analysis of the call center log has provided Chryssa a better understanding of the challenges facing the call center and how to meet those challenges. If the call center could route the most difficult calls to the most experienced operators, the average call length could be reduced, resulting in shorter hold times for MediCOH customers. With increased efficiency in handling calls, operators could be given more breaks so that they remain fresh and alert when helping customers.

Part 3.2 Quick Check

1. Write the formula that rounds the value in cell A5 down to the nearest multiple of 1000.
2. The range is defined as the maximum value from a set of numbers minus the minimum value from that set. Write the nested formula that calculates the range of the values in stored in the range Y1:Y100 and then rounds that value to the nearest integer.
3. Write the formula that calculates the number of working days between a starting date stored in cell H2 and an ending date stored in cell H3, using a list of holiday dates stored in the range G2:G10.
4. Stephen is entering thousands of temperature values into a worksheet for a climate research project and wants to speed up data entry by entering blanks rather than typing zeroes. Why will this cause complications in the calculation of the average temperature.
5. If the value in cell Q3 is greater than the value in cell Q4, you want to display the text "OK"; otherwise, display the text "RETRY". Write the formula that accomplishes this.
6. A vertical lookup table is placed in the range D1:H50. If the lookup value is in cell B2, the lookup array is in the range D2:D50, and the return array is in the range G2:G50, what is the XLOOKUP function that returns an exact match for the lookup value?
7. For the previous question, what is the VLOOKUP function that returns the exact match to the lookup value? (Note that the return values are in fourth column of the lookup table.)
8. If the XLOOKUP function cannot find a match, what value is returned by default from the function?
9. What is the difference between a what-if analysis done by trial and error and one that is done by Goal Seek?

Practice: Review Assignments

Data File needed for the Review Assignments: NP_EX_3-3.xlsx

Chryssa needs you to perform another analysis of the call center log. Callers who wait on hold often hang up before reaching an operator. Chryssa wants to examine the relationship between abandoned calls and the length of the hold time. To explore that relationship, you will analyze a call center log that lists all calls made on a typical day with information on whether the caller hung up before reaching an operator. Complete the following:

1. Open the **NP_EX_3-3.xlsx** workbook located in the Excel3 > Review folder included with your Data Files, and then save the workbook as **NP_EX_3_Abandon** in the location specified by your instructor.
2. In the Documentation sheet, enter your name in cell B4 and use the TODAY function to enter the current date in cell B5.
3. In the Caller Log worksheet, in cell E5, enter **C291208001**. Calls that were answered by an operator have the ID format C*YearMonthDateNumber*, where *Year* is the two-digit year value, *Month* is the two-digit month value, *Date* is the two-digit day value, and *Number* is three-digit number indicating the placement of the call on that day.
4. Drag the fill handle from cell E5 to cell E306 to enter the IDs of the rest of the answered calls. Fill the IDs without formatting.
5. Calls that were abandoned before reaching an operator have the ID format X*yearMonthDateNumber*. Use AutoFill to fill in the abandoned call IDs in the range E307:E344, starting with X291208001 in cell E307. Again, fill without formatting.
6. In cell I5, calculate the time in seconds that clients were on hold before reaching an operator or hanging up by entering the following dynamic array formula:

   ```
   =(G5:G344 - F5:F344)*24*60*60
   ```

7. The hold time goal is 45 seconds. In cell J5, enter the following dynamic array formula and absolute cell reference to calculate the number seconds above or below the hold time goal for every call made that day to the center:

   ```
   =I5:I344 - $B$8
   ```

8. Create indicator values that determine whether a hold time is greater or less than 1 minute and whether a call was abandoned by entering the following formulas and functions:
   a. In cell K5, enter an IF function with dynamic arrays to return a value of 1 if the corresponding values in the range I5:I344 are less than or equal to 60, and return 0 if otherwise.
   b. In cell L5, enter an IF function with dynamic arrays to return a value of 1 if the corresponding values in the range I5:I344 are greater than 60, and return a value of 0 if otherwise.
   c. In cell M5, enter an IF function with dynamic arrays to return a value of 1 if the corresponding values in the range H5:H344 are equal to "hung up" and 0 if otherwise.
   d. In cell N5, enter a dynamic array formula that multiplies the values in the range K5:K344 by the values in the range M5:M344. In the results, the value 1 indicates the caller hung up within 1 minute and 0 otherwise.
   e. In cell O5, enter a dynamic array formula that multiplies the values in the range L5:L344 by the values in the range M5:M344. In the results, the value 1 indicates the caller hung up after 1 minute and 0 otherwise.
9. Summarize the calls made that day to the center by entering the following formulas and functions:
   a. In cell B5, enter the COUNT function to count the values in column F.
   b. In cell B6, enter the SUM function to sum up the values in the spill range starting with the cell M5#.
   c. In cell B7, calculate the difference between the value in cell B5 and the value in cell B6.
   d. In cell C6, calculate the percent of calls abandoned by dividing the value in cell B6 by the value in cell B5.
   e. In cell C7, calculate the percent of calls answered by dividing the value in cell B7 by the value in cell B5.

10. Summarize information on the call that were answered or abandoned within the first minute by entering the following formulas and functions:
    a. In cell B11, use the SUM function to sum up the values in the spill range starting with the cell K5#.
    b. In cell B12, use the SUM function to sum up the values in the spill range starting with the cell N5#.
    c. In cell B13, calculate the difference between the values of cell B11 and cell B12.
    d. In cell C12, calculate the percent of calls abandoned in the first minute by dividing the value in cell B12 by the value in cell B11.
    e. In cell C13, calculate the percent of calls answered by dividing the value in cell B13 by the value in cell B11.
11. In the range B16:B18, repeat Step 10 to perform the same calculations for calls with hold times longer than 1 minute. The total number of calls with hold times longer than 1 minute are in the spill range starting with cell L5#. The total number of calls abandoned after 1 minute are in the spill range starting with cell O5#.
12. Provide summary statistics on the abandoned calls by entering the following functions:
    a. In cell B21, use the AVERAGE function with the range I307:I344 to calculate the average time at which calls were abandoned. Nest the AVERAGE function within the ROUND function and round the calculated average to the nearest second.
    b. In cell B22, use the MEDIAN function with the range I307:I344 to calculate the midpoint time of the abandoned calls.
    c. In cell B23, use the MIN function with the range I307:I344 to calculate the quickest a client abandoned a call.
    d. In cell B24, use the MAX function with the range I307:I344 to calculate the longest a client waited before abandoning a call.
13. Perform the following steps to retrieve information on a specified call by the call ID:
    a. In cell B27, enter **X291208027** as the call ID.
    b. In cell B28, use the XLOOKUP function with cell B27 as the lookup value, column E as the lookup array, and column F as the return array. If no match is found, return the value "No call with that ID".
    c. In cell B29, enter the same function as in cell B28, except use column G as the return array.
    d. In cell B30, enter the same function as in cell B28 except use column H as the return array.
    e. Verify that the return values match the values for call X291208027 located in row 333.
14. Statisticians employed by MediCOH have derived an equation to predict the probability that a client will abandon a call after a specified number of seconds. Chryssa wants you to determine the length of time at which the probability of a client hanging up is 50%.
    a. Do a what-if analysis by entering **60** in cell B33 as an initial guess for probability of waiting on hold. Confirm that cell B34 shows a probability that 10% of customers will hang up if put on hold for one minute.
    b. Use Goal Seek to set cell B34 to the value 50% by changing cell B33.
15. Save the workbook, and then close it.

Apply: Case Problem 1

Data File needed for this Case Problem: NP_EX_3-4.xlsx

Curbside Thai Sajja Adulet is the owner and master chef of Curbside Thai, a popular food truck that operates in Charlotte, North Carolina. Sajja has compiled daily sales figures from the most recent fiscal year. You will analyze the data to calculate both the annual total and daily average of the restaurant's sales and expenses. You also will calculate the daily net income. You will also compare weekend and weekday sales. Finally, you will use Goal Seek to determine how to increase the restaurant's profit margin by reducing costs on space rental in downtown Charlotte. Complete the following:

1. Open the **NP_EX_3-4.xlsx** workbook located in the Excel3 > Case1 folder included with your Data Files, and then save the workbook as **NP_EX_3_Thai** in the location specified by your instructor.
2. In the Documentation sheet, enter your name and the date.

3. In the Daily Sales worksheet, in cell G5, calculate the net income for the first day using the sales in cell E5 minus the sum of cell F5 and the daily rental fee in cell B13. Use an absolute cell reference to cell B13 in your formula.
4. AutoFill the formula in cell G5 to the range G5:G368 and fill without formatting.
5. In cell H5, enter a number representing the day of the week using the formula = WEEKDAY(D5, 2) so that Mondays have the value 1, Tuesdays have the value 2, and so on. AutoFill the formula in cell H5 to the range H5:H368 and fill without formatting.
6. Sajja also wants to display the name of the day of the week. In cell I5, use the XLOOKUP function to retrieve the weekday name with cell H5 as the lookup value, the range M5:M11 as the lookup array, and the range N5:N11 as the return array. Use absolute cell references to the range M5:M11 and the range N5:N11. AutoFill the formula to range I5:I368 and fill without formatting.
7. In cell J5, enter the dynamic array formula = IF(H5:H368 < 6, E5:E368, "") to return the sales values from column E when the weekday numbers in column H are less than 6 (Monday through Friday) and a blank text string if otherwise.
8. In cell K5, enter the dynamic array formula = IF(H5:H368 >= 6, E5:E368, "") to return the sales values from column E when the weekday numbers in column H are greater than 6 (Saturday and Sunday) and a blank text string if otherwise.
9. Summarize the total sales figures by entering the following formulas:
   a. In cell B5, calculate the sum of the values in column E to estimate the total sales for the year.
   b. In cell B6, calculate the sum of the values in column F to estimate the total cost of goods sold for the year.
   c. In cell B7, multiply the value in cell B13 by the count of values in column D to estimate the annual cost of renting public space for the year.
   d. In cell B8, calculate the value of cell B5 minus the sum of cells B6 and B7 to determine the net income for the year.
   e. In cell B9, divide cell B8 by cell B5 to display the company's profit margin for the year.
10. Estimate daily averages for food truck sales by entering the following formulas:
    a. In cell B12, calculate the average of the values in column E to estimate the average daily sales.
    b. In cell B14, calculate the average of the values in column F to estimate the average daily cost of goods sold.
    c. In cell B15, enter cell B12 minus the sum of cell B13 and B14 to estimate the daily net income.
11. Compare average daily sales between the weekday and weekend by entering the following calculations:
    a. In cell B18, use the AVERAGE function to calculate the average sales values in column J.
    b. In cell B19, use the AVERAGE function to calculate the average sales value in column K.
    c. In cell B20, calculate the difference in weekend and weekday sales by subtracting the value in cell B18 from the value in cell B19.
12. Sajja wants to increase the company's profit margin. One way of doing this might be to find ways of renting public space at a reduced cost. Use Goal Seek to determine how low the space rental fee would have been to achieve a profit margin of 8.5%. Set the value in cell B9 to 8.5% by changing the value of cell B13.
13. Save the workbook, and then close it.

Challenge: Case Problem 2

Data File needed for this Case Problem: NP_EX_3-5.xlsx

Up Range Construction Owen Meuric is a production manager for Up Range Construction, a builder of homes and office spaces in Missouri. Building projects need to follow carefully designed construction schedules involving several different phases often occurring at the same time. Each construction phase requires a set number of days to complete and cannot be started until a specified prior phase is done. For example, painting cannot be started until the drywall work is completed, and drywall work can't be started until the insulation is in. Some construction phases also must be delayed several days before they can be started to allow materials to dry and settle.

Owen has created a workbook within information on a proposed building project, listing the construction phases, the number of days allotted for each phase, and the delay required before each phase can be begin. You will use this raw data to calculate the ending date for the entire building project. To create the production schedule, you will use the WORKDAY and NETWORKDAYS functions described in Figure 3–28 and in the Insight box, "Date Calculations with Working Days." Complete the following:

1. Open the **NP_EX_3-5.xlsx** workbook located in the Excel3 > Review folder included with your Data Files, and then save the workbook as **NP_EX_3_Schedule1** in the location specified by your instructor.
2. In the Documentation sheet, enter your name and the current date.
3. Go to the Production Schedule worksheet. Owen has set a starting date for the project of 2/5/2029. The client wants the building completed by 12/7/2029. Owen has listed all the phases of the project, the number of days to complete each phase, the prior phase that must be completed first, and the delay before each phase can begin.
4. **Explore:** In cell C13, use the WORKDAY function to calculate the ending date for the Site Work phase. Use cell B13 as the starting date, cell D13 as the number days, and the dates in the range I13:I28 as the holiday dates. Enter the holiday dates using an absolute cell reference.
5. AutoFill the formula in cell C13 across the range C13:C34 without formatting. The dates won't make sense because not all the information for the production schedule has been calculated yet.
6. Retrieve the ending date for the prior phase of each construction phase. In cell F14, use an XLOOKUP function with cell E14 as the lookup value, the range A13:A34 as the lookup array, and the range C13:C34 as the return array. Use absolute cell references to the ranges A13:A34 and C13:C34.
7. AutoFill the formula in cell F14 to the range F14:F34 without formatting.
8. **Explore:** Calculate the starting date of each construction phase. In cell B14, use the WORKDAY function with cell F14 (the ending date of the prior phase) as the starting date, cell G14 as the number of days delayed from the prior phase, and the range I13:I28 as the list of holiday dates. Enter the range I13:I28 as absolute cell references.
9. AutoFill the formula in cell B14 to the range B14:B34 without formatting. The worksheet now displays the starting and ending dates for each phase of the project as well as the completion date for the entire building.
10. In cell B5, enter a reference to cell C34 to display the ending date of the project.
11. Indicate if the building will be completed at or before the client's deadline. In cell B7, use the IF function to display the text "Acceptable" if cell B5 is less than or equal to cell B6 and "Unacceptable" otherwise.
12. Create two conditional formatting rules for cell B7. If the cell value is equal to "Acceptable" display the contents in a dark green font on a green background. If the value is "Unacceptable" display the cell in a dark red font on a light red background.
13. **Explore:** In cell B9, use the NETWORKDAYS function to calculate the number of working days spent on the project, using cell B4 as the starting date, cell B5 as the ending date, and the range I13:I28 as the holiday dates.
14. In cell B10, calculate the difference between cell B5 and cell B4 to display number of calendars days between the start of the project and the ending.
15. Save the workbook. The completion date on the project will not satisfy the client, and so you will draw up a new schedule.
16. Save the workbook as **NP_EX_3_Schedule2** in the same folder.
17. The company should be able to meet the client's deadline by starting the project earlier. Use Goal Seek to determine the starting date that will meet the client's deadline, setting the value of cell B5 (completion date) to 12/7/2029 by changing the value in cell B4 (start date).
18. Save the workbook, and then close it.

Analyzing and Charting Financial Data

Preparing an Investment Report

Case: Proxis Financial

Lydia Adessa is an analyst for Proxis Financial, an investment firm located in Grand Rapids, Michigan. Lydia needs to prepare financial reports that the company's clients will receive at meetings with a Proxis Financial advisor. One of the products handled by the company is the Hamilton Fund, a large-growth/large-risk investment fund. Lydia needs to summarize the fund's financial holdings as well as document its recent and long-term performance. Lydia has already entered the financial data into a workbook but wants you to finish the report. Because many clients are overwhelmed by tables of numbers, you will summarize the data using Excel financial charts and graphics.

Starting Data Files

Excel4

Module
NP_EX_4-1.xlsx

Review
NP_EX_4-2.xlsx

Case1
NP_EX_4-3.xlsx

Case2
NP_EX_4-4.xlsx

Objectives

Part 4.1

- Create a pie chart
- Format chart elements
- Create a line chart
- Work with chart legends
- Create a combination chart

Part 4.2

- Create a scatter chart
- Edit a chart data source
- Create a data callout
- Insert a text box into a chart
- Create and edit a data bar
- Create and edit a group of sparklines

Part 4.1 Visual Overview: Charts and Chart Elements

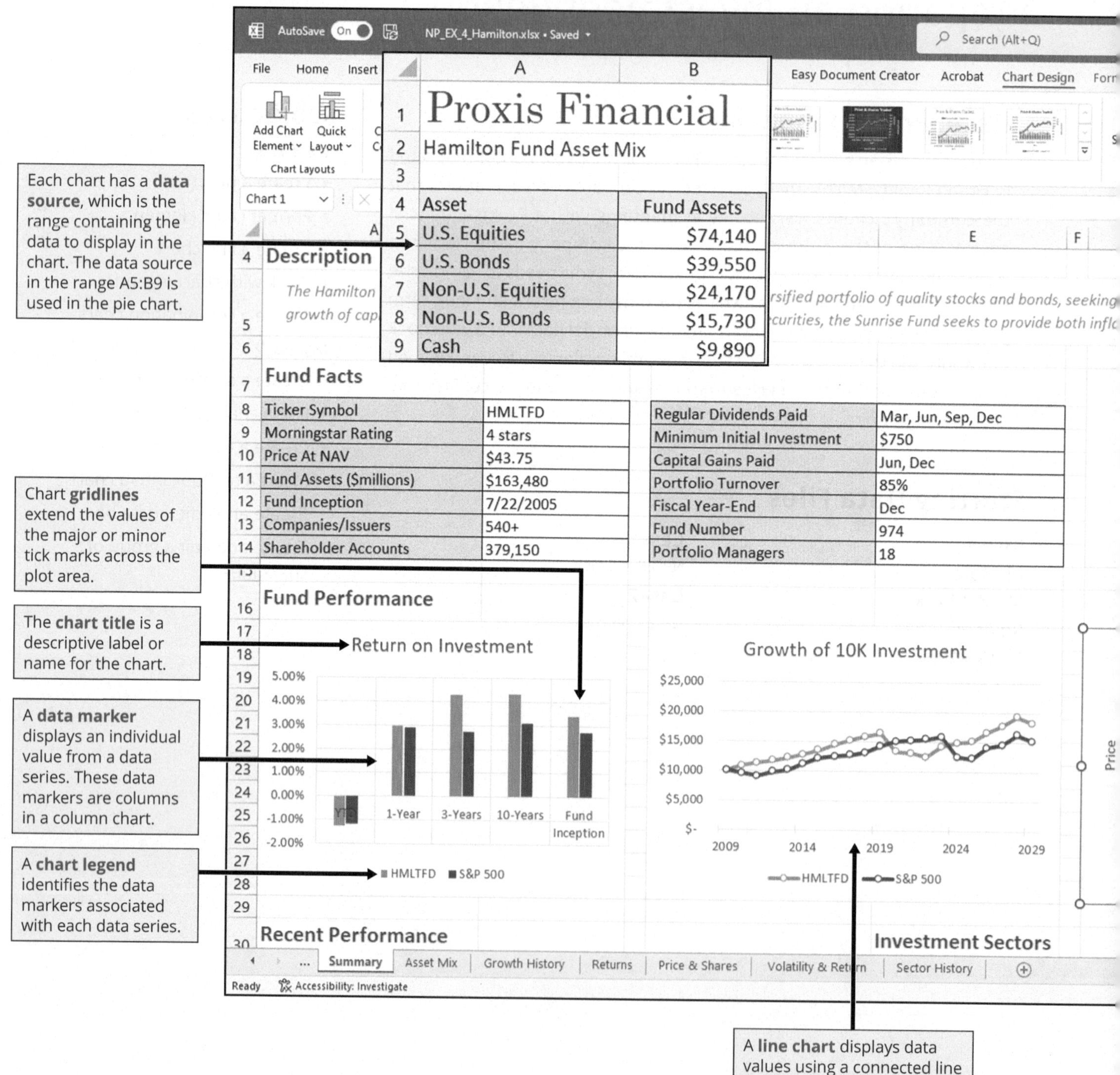

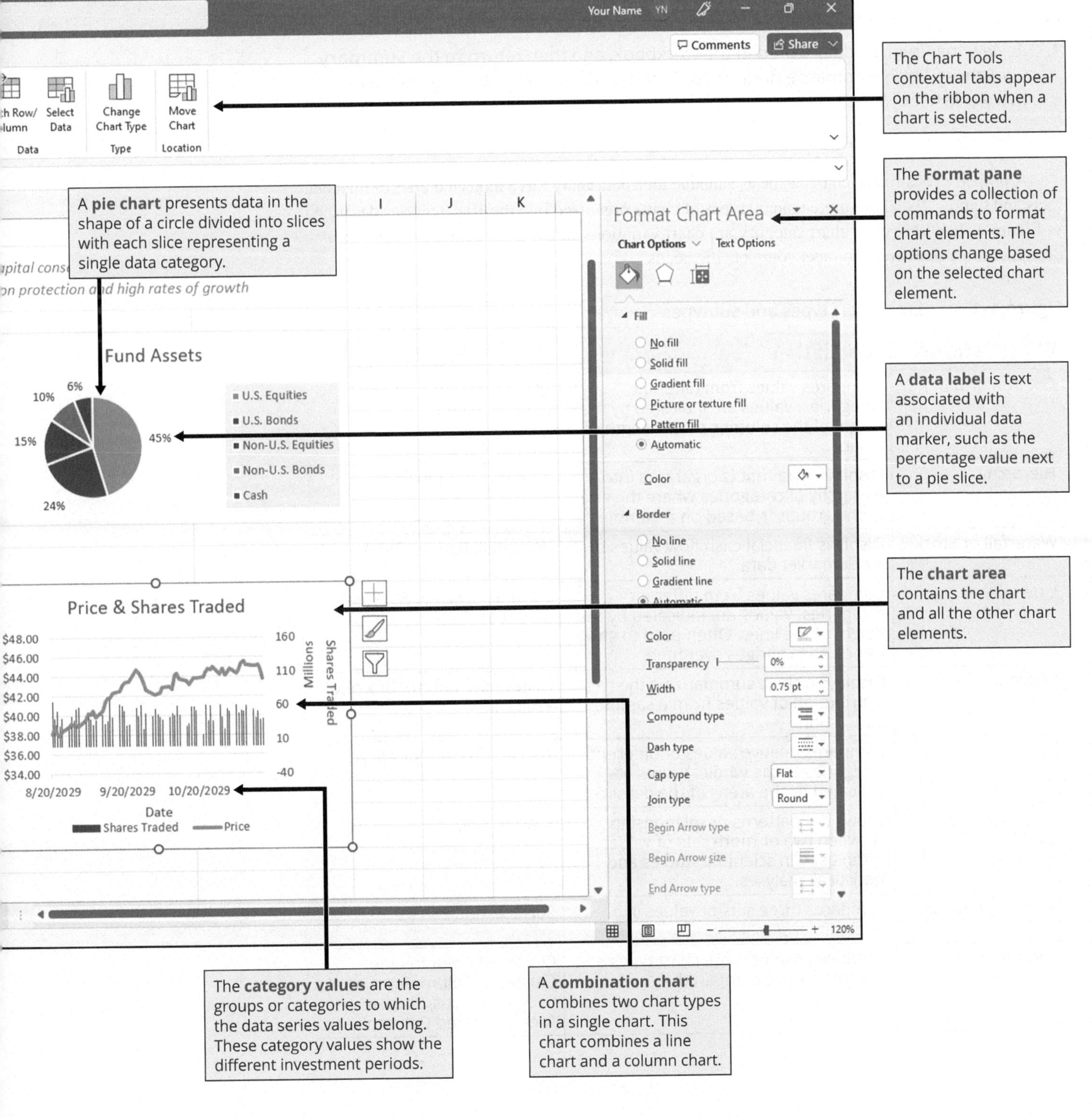
The Chart Tools contextual tabs appear on the ribbon when a chart is selected.
The **Format pane** provides a collection of commands to format chart elements. The options change based on the selected chart element.
A **pie chart** presents data in the shape of a circle divided into slices with each slice representing a single data category.
A **data label** is text associated with an individual data marker, such as the percentage value next to a pie slice.
The **chart area** contains the chart and all the other chart elements.
The **category values** are the groups or categories to which the data series values belong. These category values show the different investment periods.
A **combination chart** combines two chart types in a single chart. This chart combines a line chart and a column chart.
Your Name
Comments
Share
Select Data
Change Chart Type
Move Chart
Data
Type
Location
Format Chart Area
Chart Options
Text Options
Fill
No fill
Solid fill
Gradient fill
Picture or texture fill
Pattern fill
Automatic
Color
Border
No line
Solid line
Gradient line
Color
Transparency
0%
Width
0.75 pt
Compound type
Dash type
Cap type
Flat
Join type
Round
Begin Arrow type
Begin Arrow size
End Arrow type
120%
Fund Assets
6%
10%
15%
45%
24%
U.S. Equities
U.S. Bonds
Non-U.S. Equities
Non-U.S. Bonds
Cash
Price & Shares Traded
$48.00
$46.00
$44.00
$42.00
$40.00
$38.00
$36.00
$34.00
160
110
60
10
-40
Millions
Shares Traded
8/20/2029
9/20/2029
10/20/2029
Date
Shares Traded
Price

Getting Started with Excel Charts

In this module, you will learn how to analyze financial data using Excel charts and graphics. Lydia Adessa from Proxis Financial has already entered the financial data you need into an Excel workbook. You'll open and review that workbook now.

To open Lydia's financial workbook:

1. **sam** Open the **NP_EX_4-1.xlsx** workbook located in the **Excel4 > Module** folder included with your Data Files, and then save the workbook as **NP_EX_4_Hamilton** in the location specified by your instructor.
2. In the Documentation sheet, enter your name in cell B3 and the date in cell B4.
3. Review the financial data stored in the workbook, and then return to the **Summary** worksheet. You'll summarize data stored in the other sheets of the workbook in this worksheet.

A properly constructed chart can be as valuable for a data analyst as a thousand lines of financial facts and figures. Excel has more than 60 types of charts organized into the 10 categories described in Figure 4–1. Within each chart category are chart variations called chart subtypes. You can also design custom chart types to meet your specific needs.

Figure 4–1 Excel chart types and subtypes

Chart Category	Description	Chart Subtypes
Column or Bar	Compares values from different categories. Values are indicated by the height of the columns or the length of a bar.	2D Column, 3D Column, 2D Bar, 3D Bar
Hierarchy	Displays data that is organized into a hierarchy of categories where the size of the groups is based on a number.	Treemap, Sunburst
Waterfall or Stock	Displays financial cash flow values or stock market data.	Waterfall, Funnel, Stock
Line or Area	Compares values from different categories. Values are indicated by the height of the lines. Often used to show trends and changes over time.	2D Line, 3D Line, 2D Area, 3D Area
Statistic	Displays a chart summarizing the distribution of values from a sample population.	Histogram, Pareto, Box and Whisker
Pie	Compares relative values of different categories to the whole. Values are indicated by the areas of the pie slices.	2D Pie, 3D Pie, Doughnut
X Y (Scatter) or Bubble	Shows the patterns or relationship between two or more sets of values. Often used in scientific studies and statistical analyses.	Scatter, Bubble
Surface or Radar	Compares three sets of values in a three-dimensional chart.	Surface, Radar
Combo	Combines two or more chart types so the data can be compared.	Clustered Column-Line, Clustered Column-Line on Secondary Axis, Stacked Area-Clustered Column

Each chart type provides a different insight into data. Figure 4–2 presents the same financial data displayed in different Excel charts—a pie chart, a column chart, a treemap chart, and a map chart. The chart you choose depends on what aspect of the data you are trying to highlight.

Figure 4–2 Data displayed in different Excel chart types

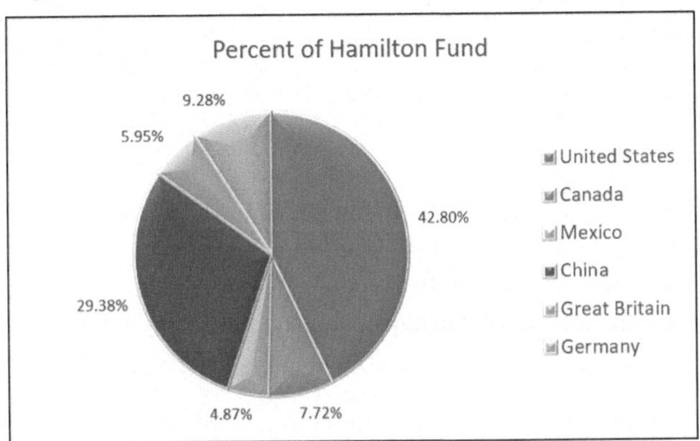

Pie chart

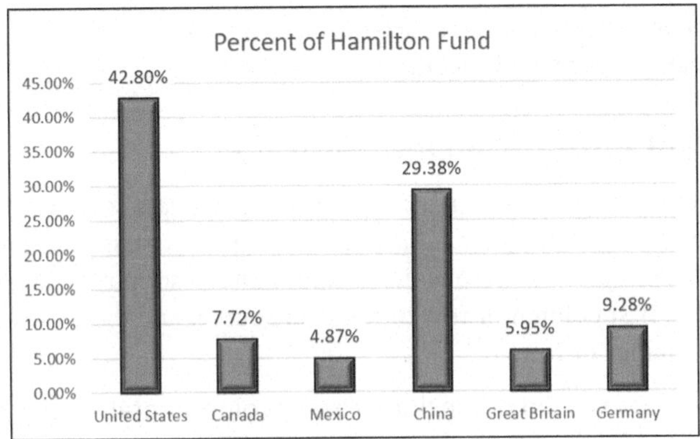

Column chart

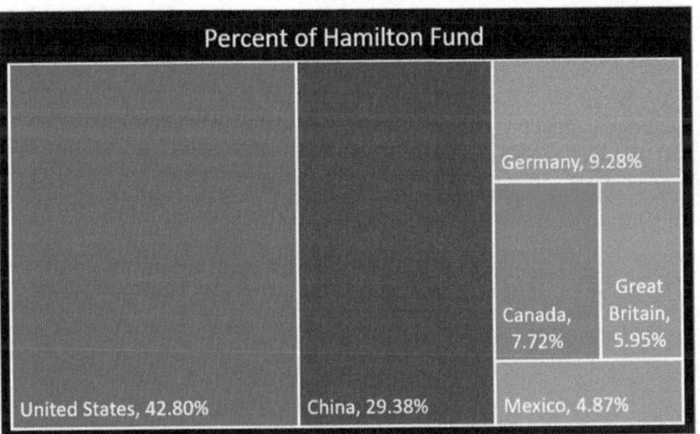

Treemap chart

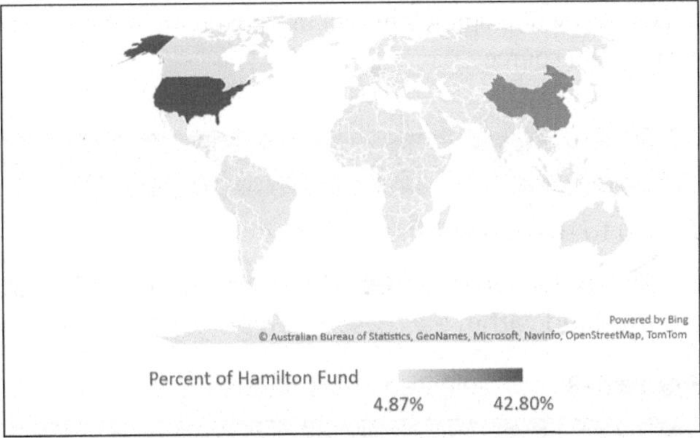

Map chart

Creating a chart is a multistep process. First, you select the data to display. Then, you choose the chart type best suited to that data. Finally, you format the chart's appearance to make it clearer to read and interpret. The first chart you will create for the Hamilton Fund report is a pie chart depicting the different assets of the fund.

Reference

Creating a Chart

- Select the range containing the data you want to chart.
- On the Insert tab, in the Charts group, click the Recommended Charts button or a button representing the general chart type, and then click the chart you want to create; or click the Quick Analysis button, click the Charts category, and then click the chart you want to create.
- On the Chart Design tab, in the Location group, click the Move Chart button, select whether to embed the chart in a worksheet or place it in a chart sheet, and then click OK.
- Use the chart tools to format the appearance of individual chart elements.

Creating a Pie Chart

A pie chart presents data in a circle graph divided into slices with each slice representing a single data category. Categories whose data values take up larger percentages of the whole are represented with larger slices; categories that take up a smaller percentage of the whole are presented as smaller slices. Pie charts are most effective when the data can be divided into six or fewer categories. With more categories, each slice becomes a smaller part of the whole, making comparisons between categories more difficult.

Selecting the Data Source

The data displayed in a chart come from a data source, which includes one or more data series and a set of category values. A **data series** contains the data values plotted within the chart. The category values groups those values into descriptive categories. Categories are usually listed in the first column or row of the data source, and the data series values are placed in subsequent columns or rows.

> **Tip** Do not include row or column totals in the pie chart data because Excel will treat those totals as another category.

The Asset Mix worksheet in Lydia's workbook breaks down the assets in the Hamilton Fund. The assets are organized into equities, bonds, and cash from sources within and outside of the United States. You will display this data in a pie chart. You will start creating the pie chart by selecting the chart's data source.

To select the data source for the pie chart:

1. Go to the **Asset Mix** worksheet.
2. Select the range **A4:B9**. This range contains the names of the assets and the amount invested within each asset category. Refer to Figure 4–3.

Figure 4–3 Selected chart data source

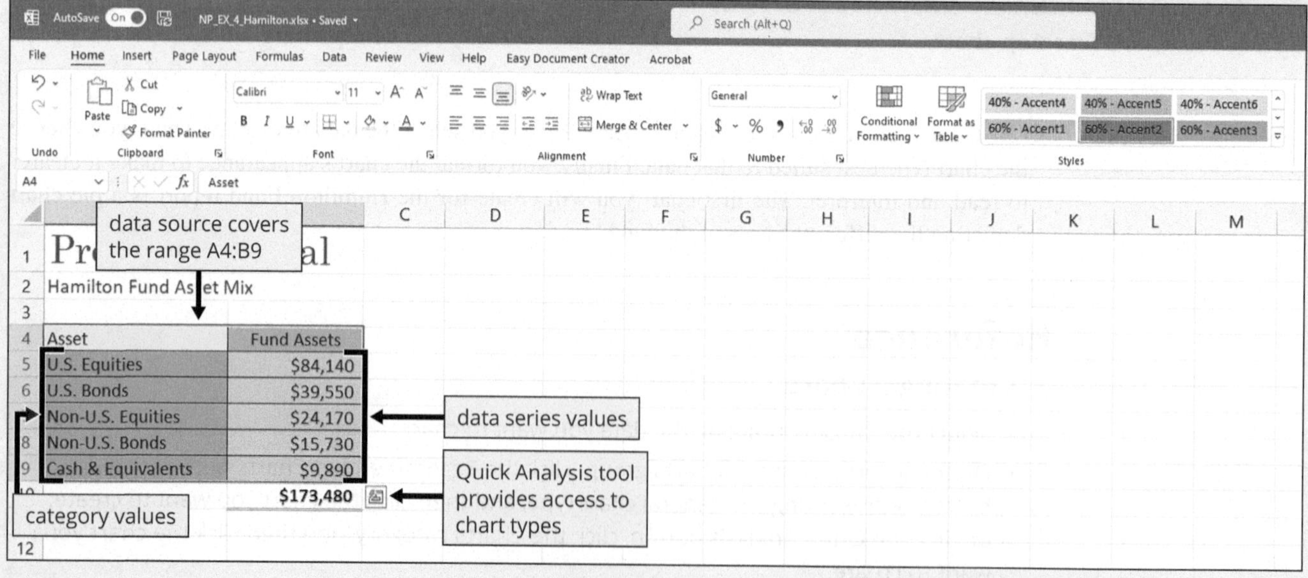

The selected data source covers two columns. The categories in the first column (Asset) identify each pie slice. The data series in the second column (Fund Assets) sets the size of each slice.

Charting with the Quick Analysis Tool

After you select a data source, the Quick Analysis tool appears in the lower-right corner of the selection. The Charts category in the Quick Analysis tool displays chart types that are appropriate for the selected data source. For this data source, a pie chart provides a good way to compare the relative amount that the Hamilton Fund invests in five asset categories. You'll use the Quick Analysis tool to generate the pie chart for Lydia.

To create a pie chart with the Quick Analysis tool:

1. With the range A4:B9 still selected, click the **Quick Analysis** button in the lower-right corner of the selected range (or press **CTRL+Q**) to open the Quick Analysis tool.
2. Click the **Charts** category. The chart types you will most likely want to use with the selected data source are listed.
3. Point to each chart type to preview that type of chart and a description of the data rendered as that chart. Refer to Figure 4–4.

Figure 4–4 Charts category of the Quick Analysis tool

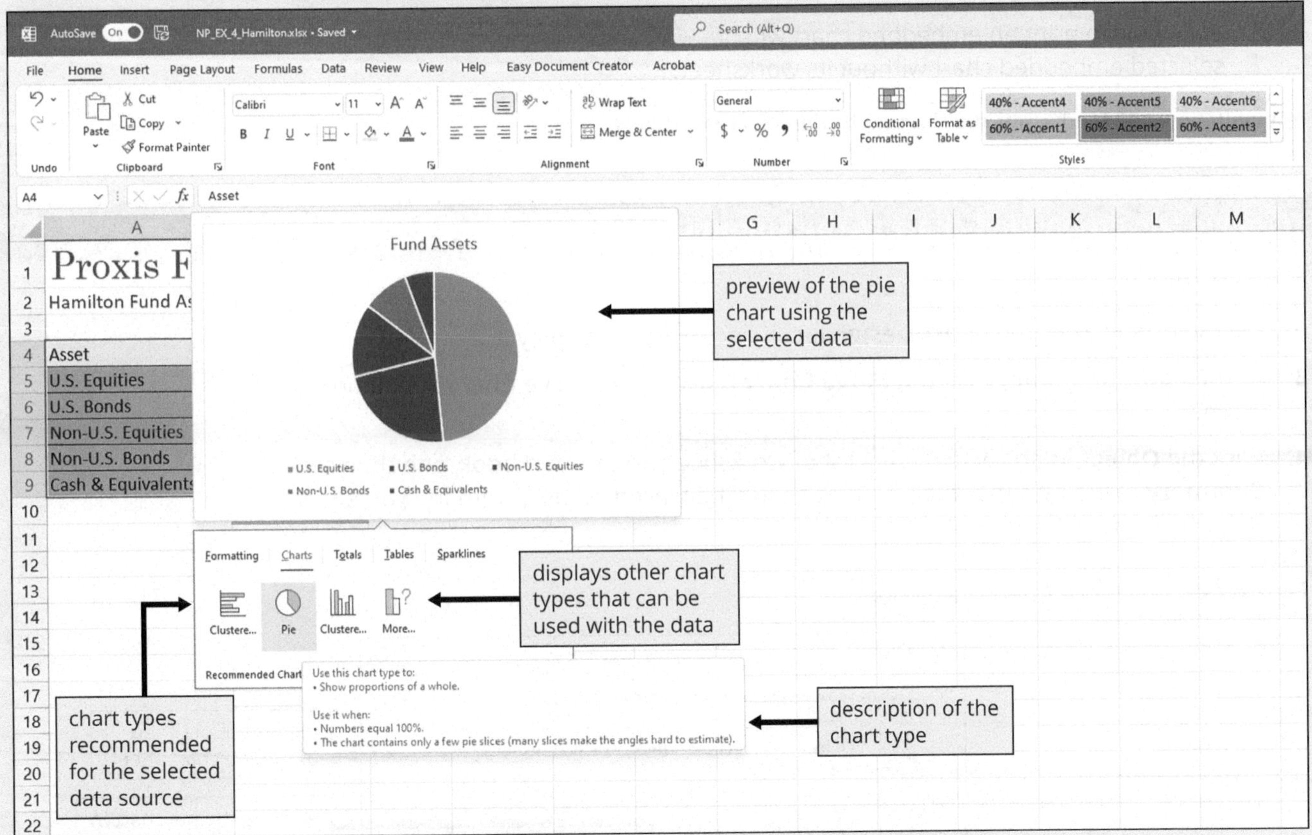

4. Click **Pie**. A pie chart appears in the Asset Mix worksheet.

Tip You can also insert a chart by selecting a chart type in the Charts group on the Insert tab.

Excel identifies the slice categories and the slice values from the data source. When the selected range is taller than it is wide, Excel assumes that the category values and data series are laid out in columns. Conversely, a data source that is wider than it is tall is assumed to have the category values and data series laid out in rows. The biggest slice in this pie chart represents the amount of the fund invested in U.S. equities, and the smallest slice represents the amount invested in cash and equivalents. Slices start at the top of the pie and are added to the right around the pie.

Each new chart is given a reference name, which appears in the Reference box at the upper-left corner of the worksheet. The initial chart names are Chart 1, Chart 2, and so forth, but you can click the Reference box and enter a different, more descriptive name. When a chart is selected, two chart contextual tabs appear on the ribbon. The Chart Design tab contains tools to modify the chart's overall design and its data source, and the Format tab contains tools to format the individual parts of the chart, such as the chart's title, border, or background. When the chart is not selected, the contextual tabs disappear.

Moving and Resizing a Chart

A chart is placed in its own chart sheet or embedded in a worksheet. The advantage of an embedded chart is that it can be displayed alongside relevant text and tables in the worksheet. Chart sheets are best used for charts that occupy a single page in a report or printout. In this report, you will embed all the charts in the Summary worksheet.

Tip You can print an embedded chart with its worksheet, or you can print the selected embedded chart without its worksheet.

You will move the fund assets pie chart to the Summary worksheet.

To move the embedded chart to the Summary worksheet:

1. Verify that the pie chart is selected.
2. On the ribbon, click the **Chart Design** tab, if necessary, to display it.
3. In the Location group, click the **Move Chart** button. The Move Chart dialog box opens.
4. Click the **Object in** arrow to open a list of worksheets in the workbook, and then click **Summary** to indicate that the pie chart should be placed in the Summary worksheet. Refer to Figure 4–5.

Figure 4–5 Move Chart dialog box

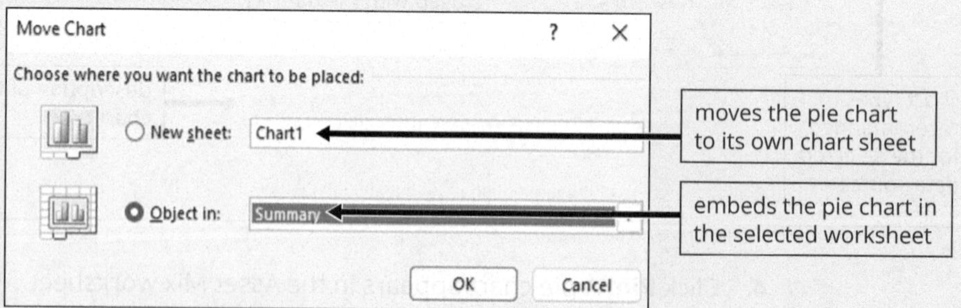

5. Click **OK** to close the Move Chart dialog box and move the chart to the Summary worksheet.

You can also use cut and paste to move an embedded chart to a different worksheet. Select the chart, click the Cut button in the Clipboard group on the Home tab, and then select the worksheet cell where you want to place the chart. Click the Paste button to place the upper-left corner of the chart at the selected cell.

Because an embedded chart covers the worksheet grid, it can obscure some of the content. You can fix that problem by moving the chart to an empty location and resizing it. To move and resize a chart, the chart must be selected, which adds a selection box around the chart. The selection box has sizing handles to change the chart's width and height. As you move and resize a chart, holding down ALT snaps the chart to the worksheet grid. If you do not hold down ALT, you can move and resize the chart to any location on the grid.

Lydia wants the pie chart to cover the range G7:H14 in the Summary worksheet. You'll move and resize the chart to fit this space.

To move and resize the pie chart:

1. Move the pointer over an empty part of the chart so that the pointer changes to the Move pointer and the ScreenTip displays "Chart Area."

   Key Step Make sure the ScreenTip shows "Chart Area" so that the entire chart moves when you drag.

2. Hold down **ALT**, drag the chart to cell **G7** until its upper-left corner snaps to the upper-left corner of the cell, and then release the mouse button and **ALT**. The upper-left corner of the chart now aligns with the upper-left corner of cell G7.

   Trouble? If the pie chart resizes or does not move to the new location, you probably didn't drag the chart from an empty part of the chart area. Press CTRL+Z to undo your last action, and then repeat Steps 1 and 2, being sure to drag the pie chart from the chart area.

3. Point to the sizing handle in the lower-right corner of the selection box until the pointer changes to the Resizing pointer.

4. Hold down **ALT**, drag the sizing handle up to the lower-right corner of cell **H14**, and then release the mouse button and **ALT**. The chart resizes to cover the range G7:H14 and remains selected. Refer to Figure 4–6.

Figure 4–6 Moved and resized pie chart

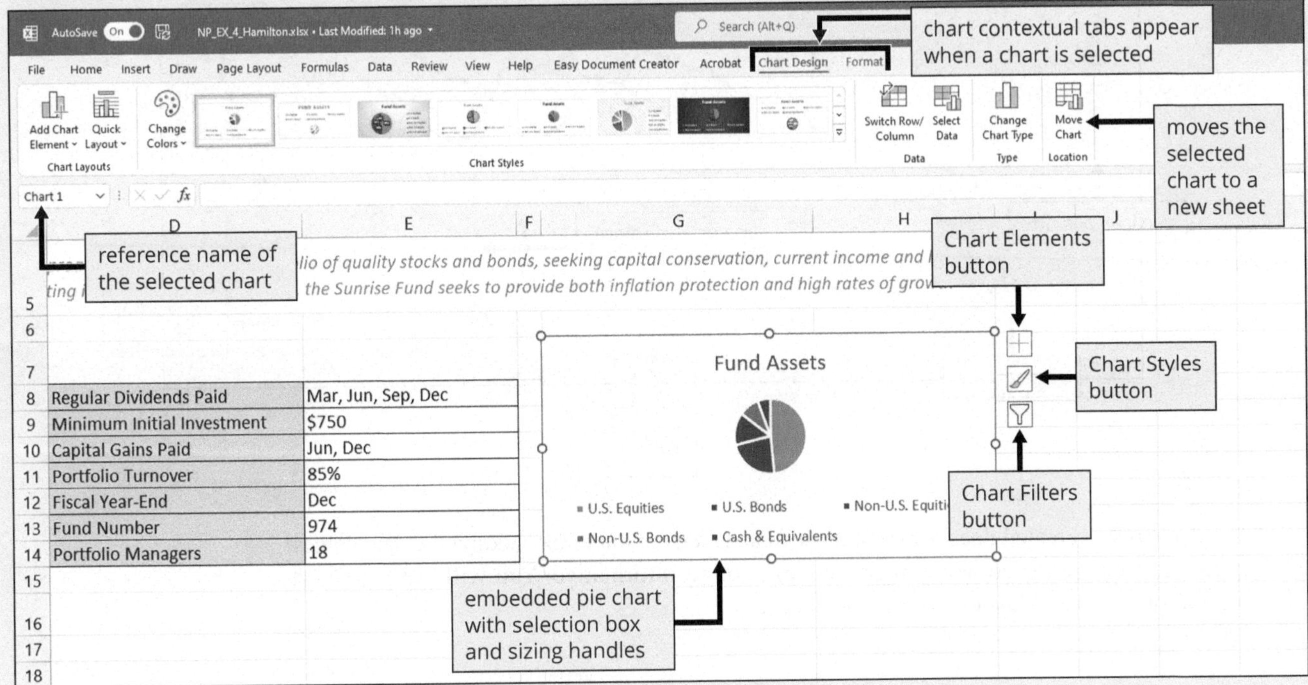

Even though a chart is not part of the worksheet grid, it resizes with the grid. If the size of a column or row is changed, the chart's width and height will also change, ensuring that an embedded chart will stay in the same location relative to other worksheet content.

Insight

Exploding a Pie Chart

Pie slices do not need to be fixed within the pie. An **exploded pie chart** moves one slice away from the others as if someone were taking the piece away from the pie. Exploded pie charts are useful for emphasizing one category above the others. For example, to emphasize the fact that Hamilton Fund invests heavily in U.S. equities, you could explode that single slice, moving it away from the other slices.

To explode a pie slice, first click the pie to select it, and then click the single slice you want to move. Make sure that a selection box appears around only that slice. Drag the slice away from the other slices in the pie. You can explode multiple slices by selecting each slice in turn and dragging them away. To explode all the slices, select the entire pie and drag the pointer away from the pie's center. Although you can explode more than one slice, the resulting pie chart is rarely effective at conveying information to the reader.

Working with Chart Elements

The individual parts of the chart are called **chart elements**. Figure 4–7 shows elements that are common to many charts. You can access the properties of these chart elements by clicking the Chart Elements button ⊞ that appears to the right of the chart.

Figure 4–7 Common chart elements

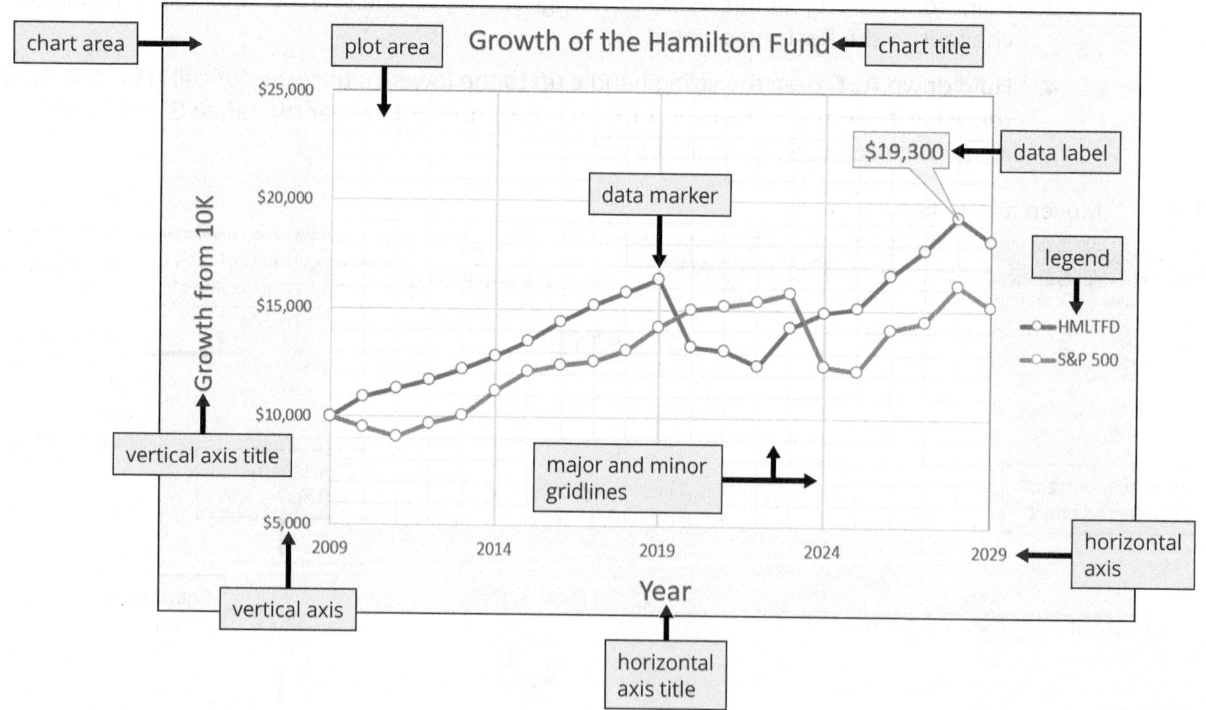

The pie chart you created does not contain any data labels. Lydia thinks adding the data values associated with each pie slice would make the chart more informative. You will use the Chart Elements button ⊞ to add that element to the pie chart.

To add the data labels chart element to the pie chart:

1. With the pie chart still selected, click the **Chart Elements** button ⊞. A menu of chart elements associated with the pie chart opens. As the checkmarks indicate, only the chart title and the chart legend are displayed in the pie chart.

   Tip You can also add and remove chart elements with the Add Chart Element button in the Chart Layouts group on the Chart Design tab.

2. Point to the **Data Labels** check box. Live Preview displays the chart with data labels of the dollar amount (in millions) invested within each category.
3. Click the **Data Labels** check box to select it. The data labels are added to the chart. Refer to Figure 4–8.

Figure 4–8 Data labels added to the pie chart

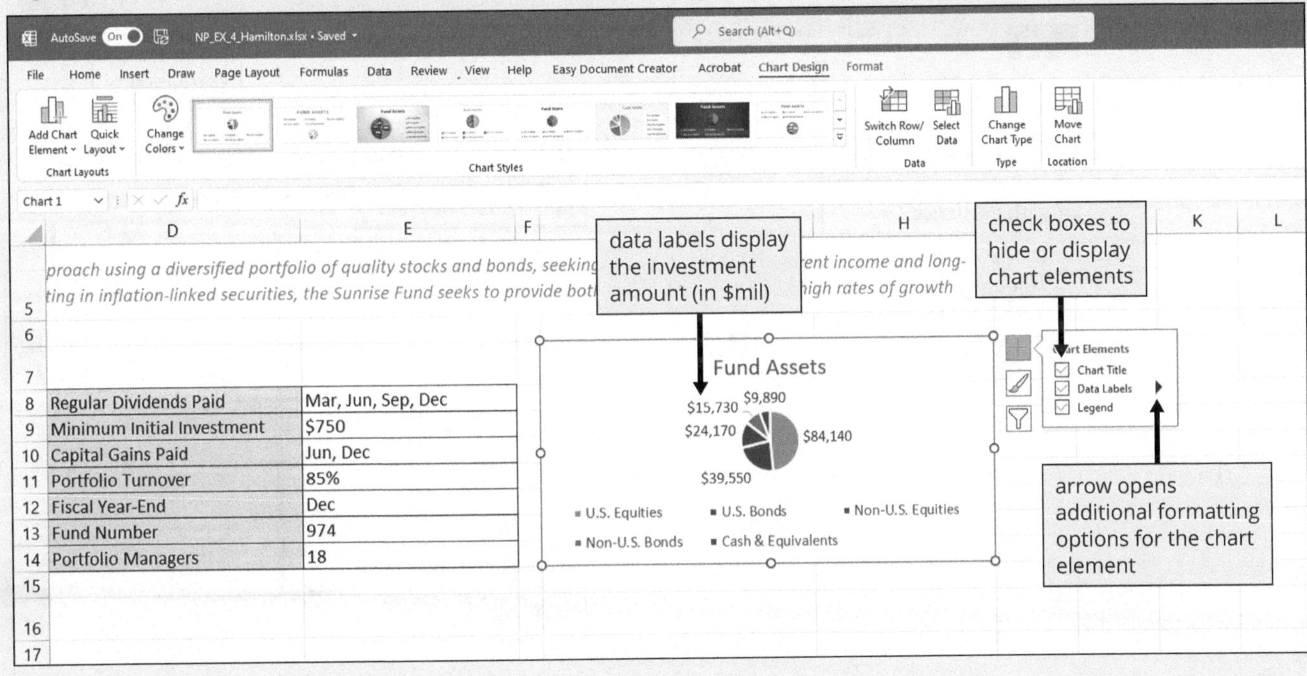

Lydia does not want the data labels to show the amount invested in each asset, but rather the percentage of the total invested in each asset. You can make that change by editing the Data Labels element.

Formatting a Chart Element

Each element listed in the Chart Elements button contains a submenu of common formatting choices. Explore the formatting choices available with data labels now to move the placement of the data labels.

To format a data label:

1. With the pie chart still selected, click the **Chart Elements** button ⊞ if necessary to display the menu, point to **Data Labels**, and then click the **right arrow** icon ▶ to display the list of common formatting choices for data labels.
2. Point to each of the following options for a Live Preview of data labels positioned at different locations around the pie chart: **Center, Inside End**, **Outside End**, **Best Fit**, and **Data Callout**.

3. Click **More Options** to view the extensive menu of formatting options for data labels in the Format Data Labels pane. The Format Data Labels pane is divided into different sections indicated by the icons near the top of the pane. The formatting options for the data labels is selected by default.
4. Click the **Percentage** check box to add percentages to the data labels for each pie slice.
5. Click the **Value** check box to deselect it, removing the data values from the data labels.
6. In the Label Position section, click the **Outside End** option button in the Label Position section to always place the data labels outside and at the end of each pie slice. Refer to Figure 4–9.

Figure 4–9 Format Data Labels pane

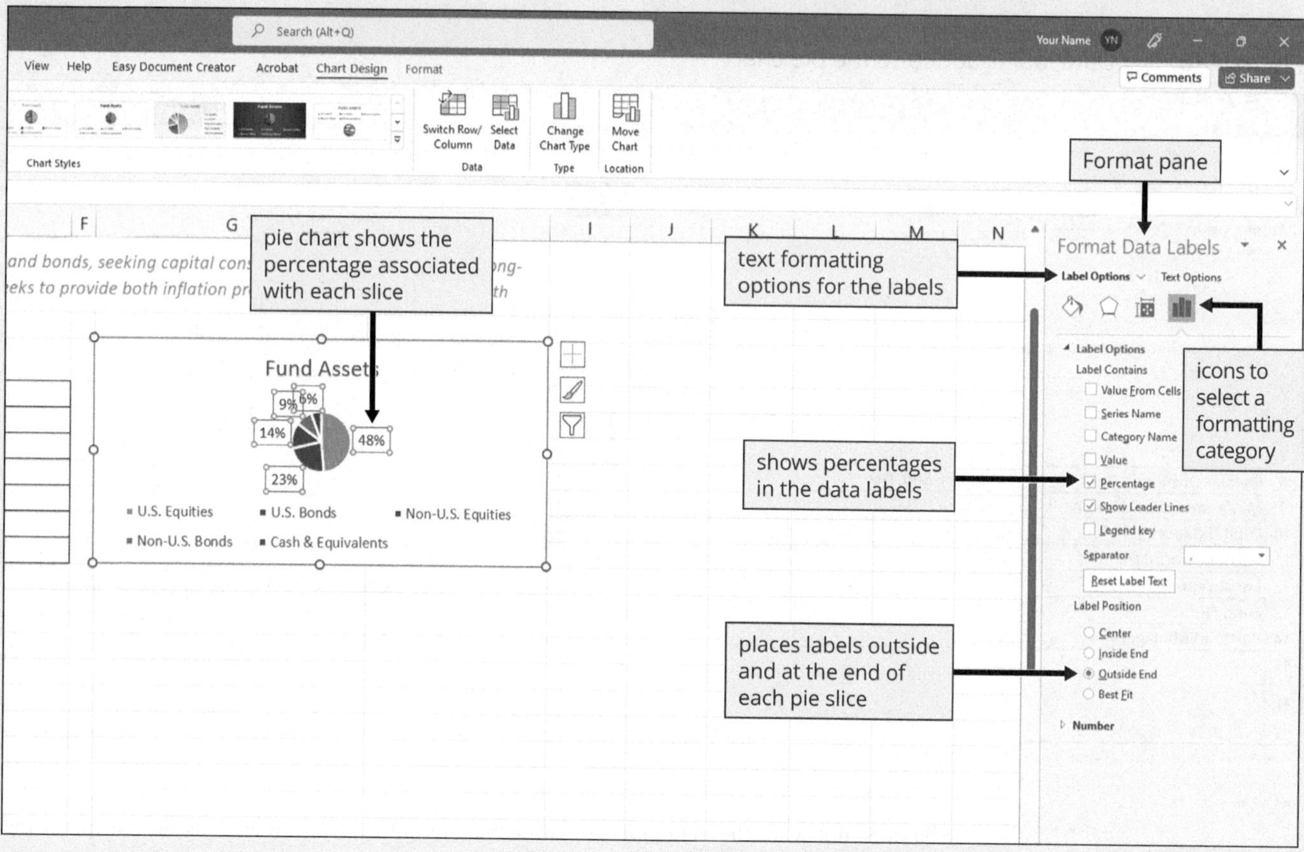

The Format pane is attached, or docked, to the right side of the workbook window. You can undock the pane so that it floats free above the worksheet grid by pointing to a blank area of the pane until the pointer changes to the Move pointer and then clicking and dragging the pane over the worksheet grid. To redock the pane, point to the floating pane until the pointer changes to the Move pointer and then drag to the right until the pane reattaches to the workbook window.

From the Format pane, you can format other chart elements. Lydia thinks the pie chart would be more effective if the legend were aligned with the right edge of the chart area rather than its current position at the bottom. Lydia also wants the background of the legend to be a light tan color. You'll use the Format pane to make those changes now.

To move and format the pie chart legend:

1. In the Format Data Labels pane, click the **Label Options arrow** directly below the Format Data Labels title, and then click **Legend** in the list of chart elements. The name of the Format pane changes to Format Legend and options for formatting the pie chart legend appear in the pane.

   Tip You can also double-click any chart element to open its Format pane.

2. In the Legend Options section, click the **Right** option button to place the pie chart legend on the right side of the chart area. Refer to Figure 4–10.

Figure 4–10 Chart legend in chart area

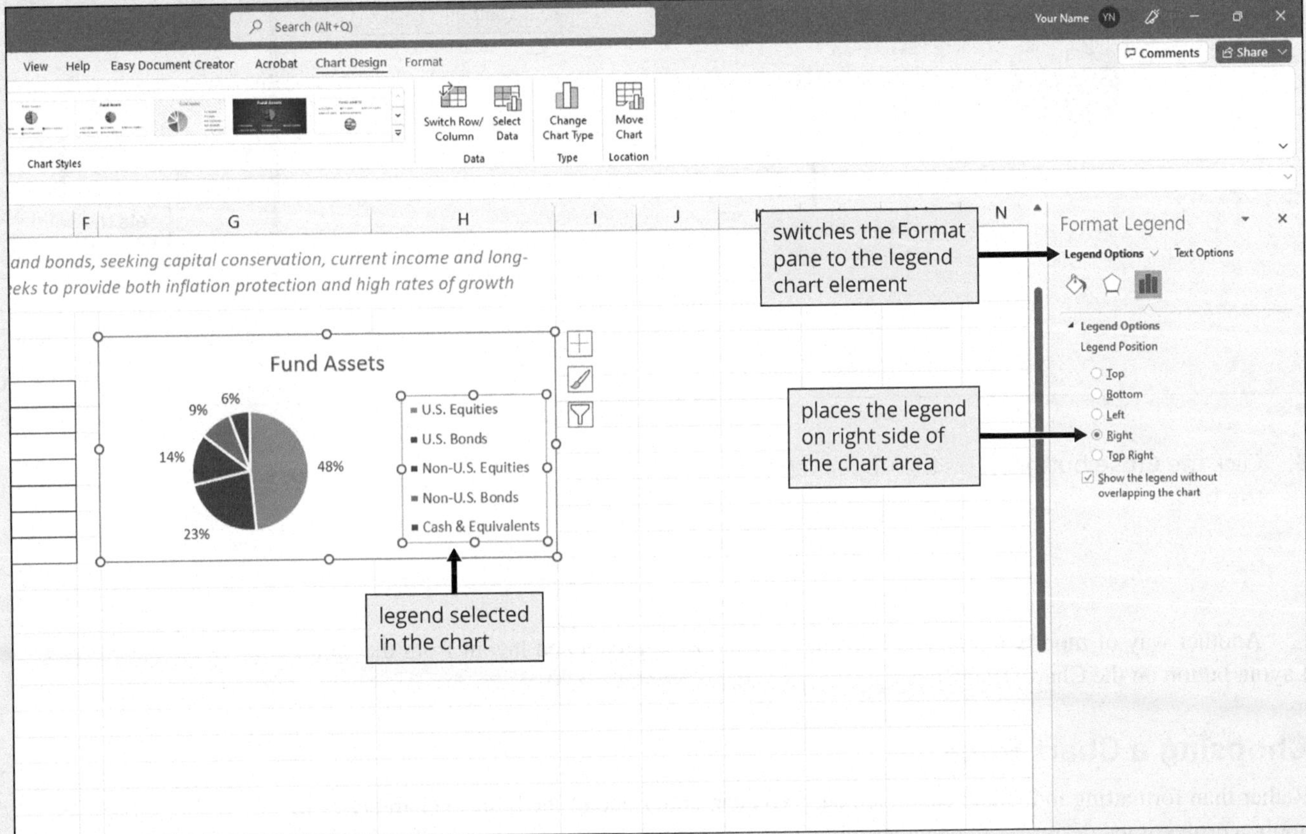

3. Click the **Fill & Line** icon, and then click the **Fill** heading to expand the fill options for the legend.
4. Click the **Solid fill** option button, click the **Color** button, and then click **Tan, Accent 6, Lighter 80%** (the last theme color in the second row) in the color palette. Refer to Figure 4–11.

Figure 4–11 Fill color for the chart legend

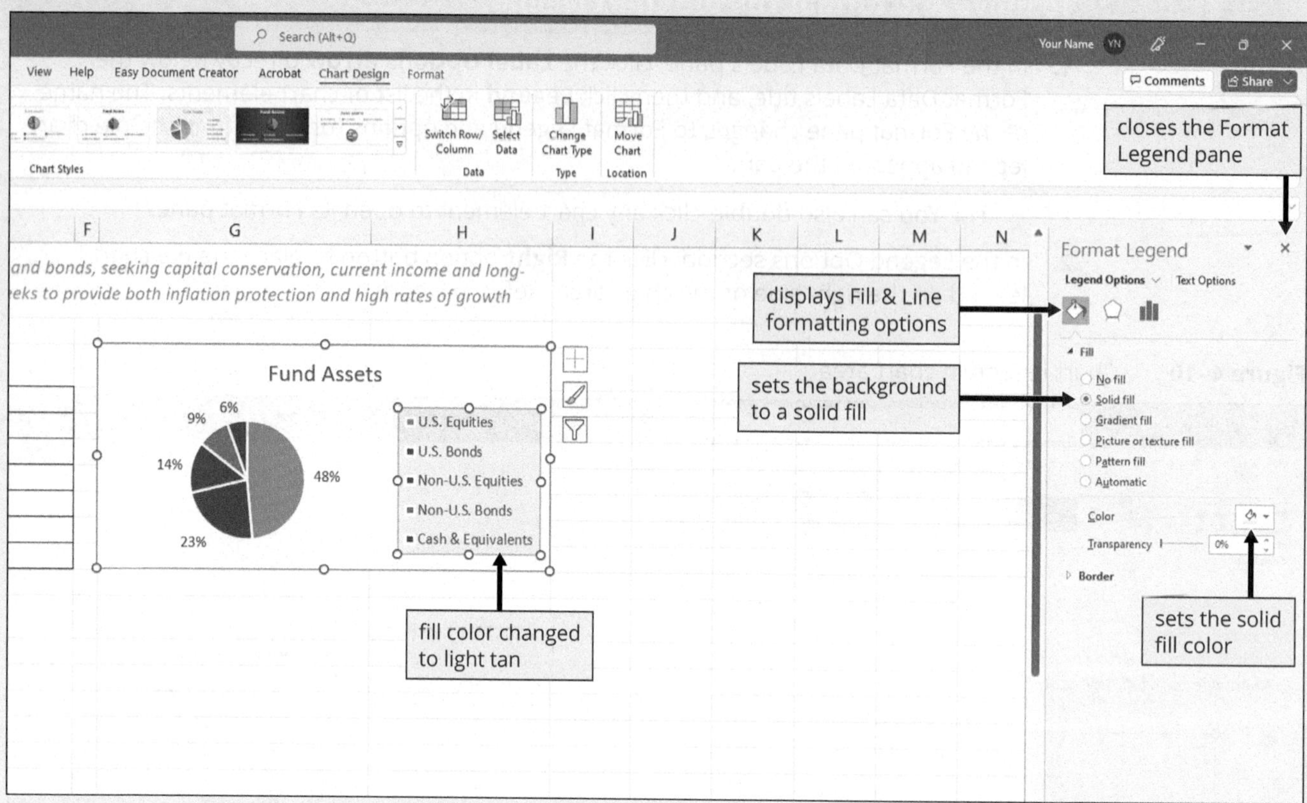

5. Click the **Close** button in the upper-right corner of the Format Legend pane to close the pane.

Another way of modifying the chart layout is to choose a predefined layout from the Quick Layout button on the Chart Design tab.

Choosing a Chart Style

Rather than formatting individual chart elements, you can apply one of the built-in chart styles to apply a professional design to all elements of the chart. You can access chart styles either from the Chart Styles button next to a selected chart or in the Chart Styles gallery on the Chart Tools tab. You'll use Live Preview to test different chart styles you can apply to pie charts.

To use the built-in pie chart styles:

1. With the pie chart still selected, click the **Chart Styles** button next to the chart.
2. Scroll through the gallery of chart styles, pointing to each entry in the gallery to see a preview of the chart with that style. Figure 4–12 shows a preview of design of the Style 6 chart style applied to the Asset Mix pie chart.

Figure 4–12 Preview of a chart style

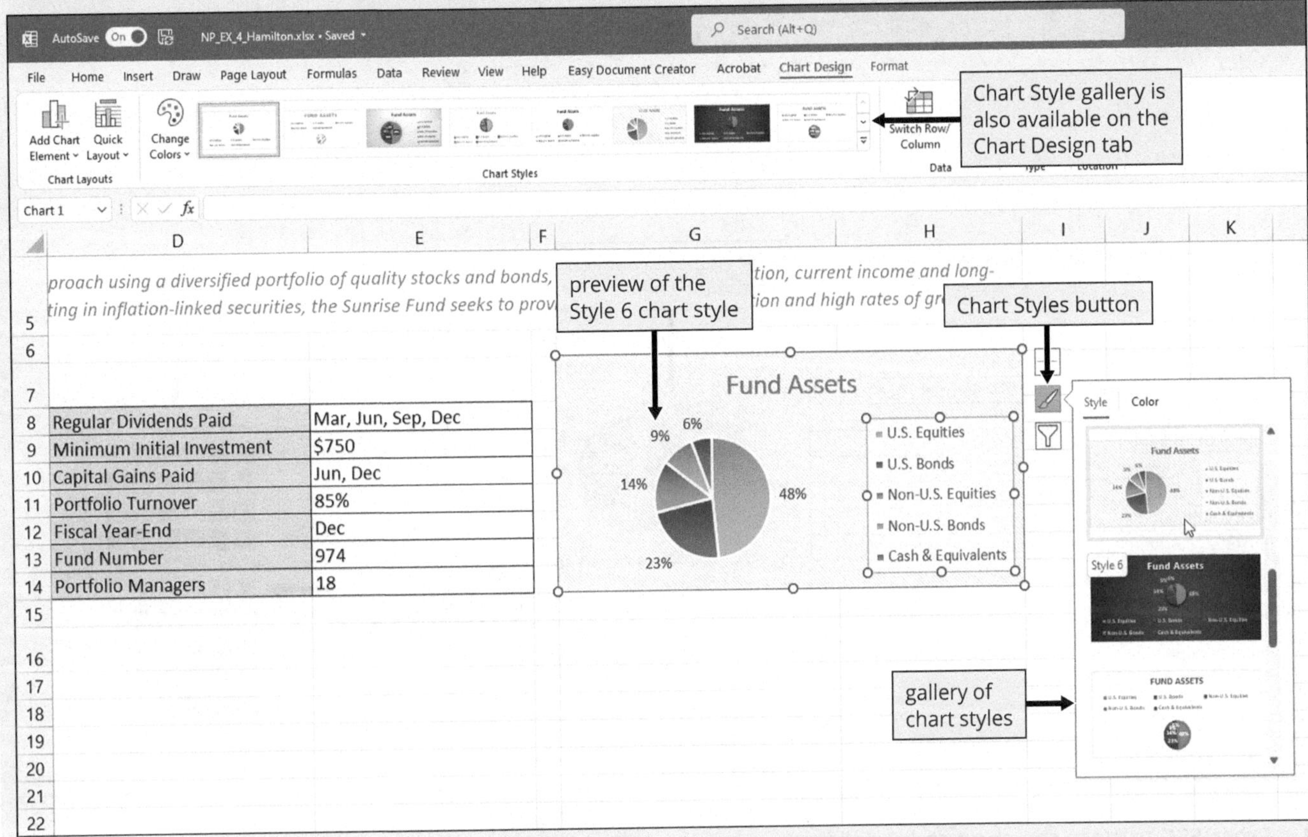

3. Press **ESC** to close the chart style gallery without changing the style of the Asset Mix pie chart.

   Trouble? If you accidentally apply a chart style, click the Undo button on the Quick Access Toolbar to restore the chart to its previous style.

Although Lydia does not want you to change the chart style of the Asset Mix pie chart, she is concerned that the pie chart is challenging to interpret with its mix of colors. You can eliminate this issue by choosing a different color scheme.

Changing the Color Scheme

By default, Excel applies a color scheme to a chart using theme colors. You can select a different color scheme from the Chart Styles button in the Colors submenu. Lydia wants you to use colors in the same orange hue but with different levels of saturation so that the largest slice is displayed in dark orange and the smallest slice displayed in a light orange. You will apply this color scheme to the Asset Mix pie chart.

To change the pie slice colors:

1. Click the **Chart Styles** button to reopen the gallery of chart styles.

   Tip You can also use the Change Colors button in the Chart Styles group on the Chart Design tab.

2. Click the **Color** tab to display a gallery of possible color schemes.
3. In the Monochromatic section, click the orange monochromatic color scheme labeled **Monochromatic Palette 1**. Refer to Figure 4–13.

Figure 4–13 Pie chart with updated color scheme

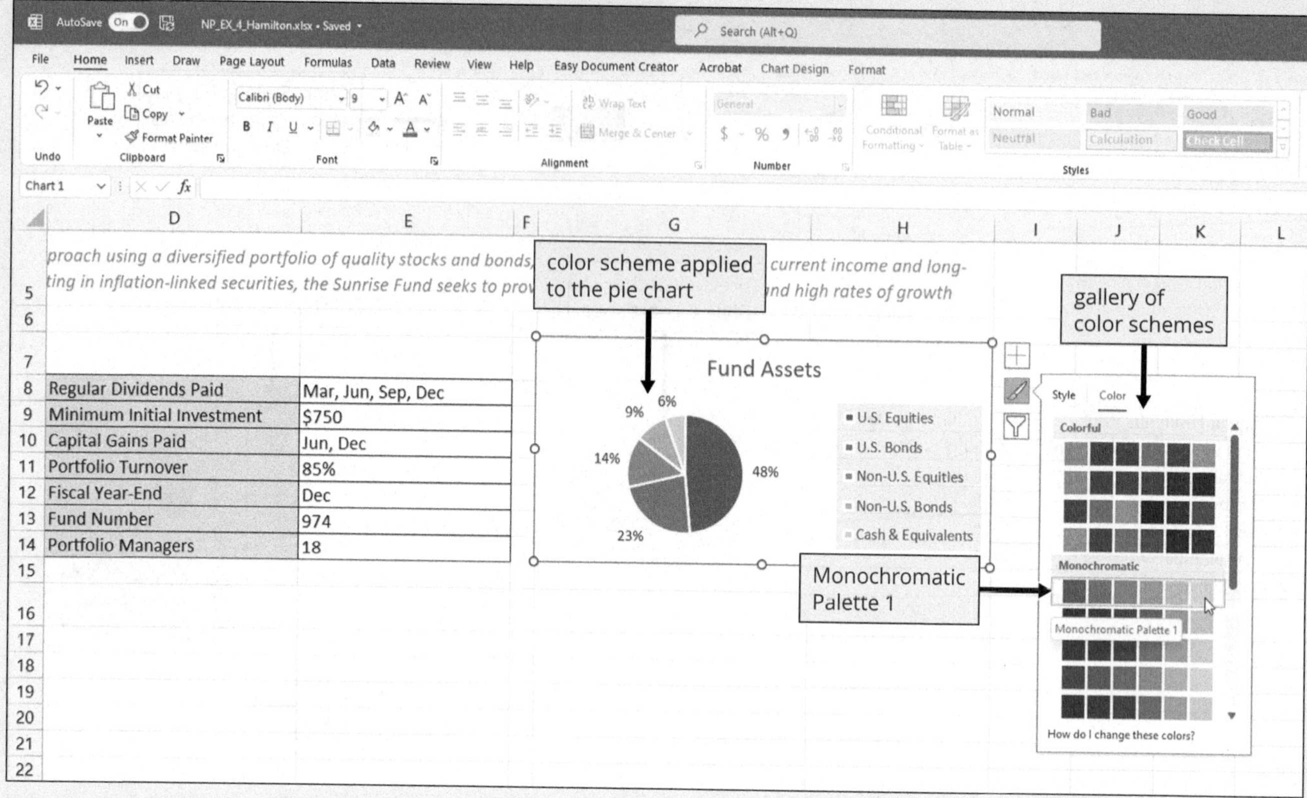

4. Press **ESC** to close the chart styles gallery.

Because the color schemes are based on the theme colors, you can change the color schemes by selecting new theme colors from the Colors box in the Themes group on the Page Layout tab. If you don't want to change the workbook's color theme, you can change the color of individual pie slices. To change a pie slice to another color, double-click the slice to select only that slice (and no other elements on the chart), and then choose a color from the Fill Color button in the Font group on the Home tab.

Filtering a Chart

If you want a chart to focus on fewer categories, you can filter the chart by removing one or more categories. To remove a category, click the Filter button next to the chart, opening a list of data categories. Check the data categories you want to appear in chart, and then click the Apply button. Removing a data category has no effect on the data source. It affects only the categories that Excel will display in the chart.

The pie chart in Figure 4–14 is filtered and does not display all its possible categories. The size of the slices is modified to match the number of categories that appear in the chart, not the total number of possible categories and their values.

Figure 4–14 Filtered pie chart

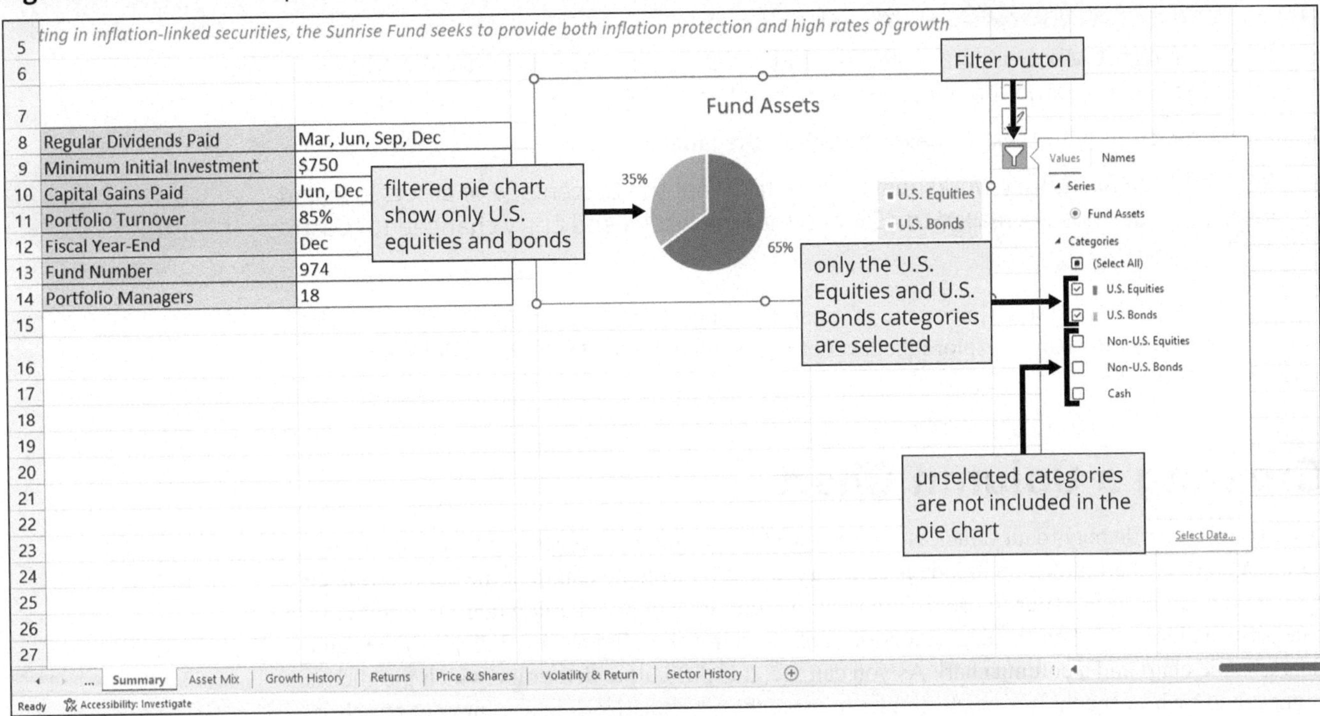

To redisplay a data category, click its check box to select it, and then click the Apply button. You can also use Live Preview to review the effects of filtering without applying the filter to the pie chart.

Insight

Overlaying Chart Elements

An embedded chart takes up less space than a chart sheet. However, it can be challenging to fit all the chart elements into that smaller space. One solution is to overlay one element on top of another. The most commonly overlaid elements are the chart title and the chart legend. To overlay the chart title, click the Chart Title arrow in the Chart Elements list and select Centered Overlay as the position option. Excel will place the chart title on top of the plot area, freeing up more space for other chart elements. Chart legends can also be overlaid by opening the Format pane for the legend and deselecting the Show the legend without overlapping the chart check box in the Legend Options section. Other chart elements can be overlaid by dragging them to new locations in the chart area and then resizing the plot area to recover the empty space.

Do not overuse the technique of overlaying chart elements. Too much overlaying of chart elements can make a chart difficult to understand.

Performing What-If Analyses with Charts

Because a chart is linked to its data source, any changes in the data source values will be reflected in the chart. This link between a chart and its data source provides a powerful tool for data exploration. For the Asset Mix pie chart, the chart title is linked to the text in cell B4 of the Asset Mix worksheet, the size of the pie slices is based on values in the range B5:B9, and the category names are linked to the category values in the range A4:A9.

Lydia notes that the value in cell B5 for the amount invested in U.S. equities should be $74,140 instead of $84,140. You will change the value in the cell and change the category name in cell B9 from "Cash & Equivalents" to simply "Cash."

To modify the pie chart's data:

1. Go to the **Asset Mix** worksheet, and then in cell **B5**, change the value to **$74,140** to reflect the correct amount invested in U.S. equities.
2. In cell **A9**, change the text to **Cash** to update the label.
3. Return to the **Summary** worksheet and confirm that the percentage of assets invested in U.S. equities has decreased to 45% and that the last legend entry changed to "Cash."

The pie chart revealed some important information about the assets of the Hamilton Fund. Next, you will use a column chart to explore the level of returns that the fund has provided for investors over the past 10 years.

Creating a Column Chart

A **column chart** displays data values as columns with the height of each column based on the data value. A column chart turned on its side is called a **bar chart**, with the length of the bar determined by the data value. It is better to use column and bar charts than pie charts when the number of categories is large or when the data categories are close in value. Figure 4–15 displays the same data as a pie chart and a column chart. As you can see, it is difficult to determine which pie slice is biggest and by how much. It is much simpler to make those comparisons in a column or bar chart.

Figure 4–15 Pie and column charts with the same data

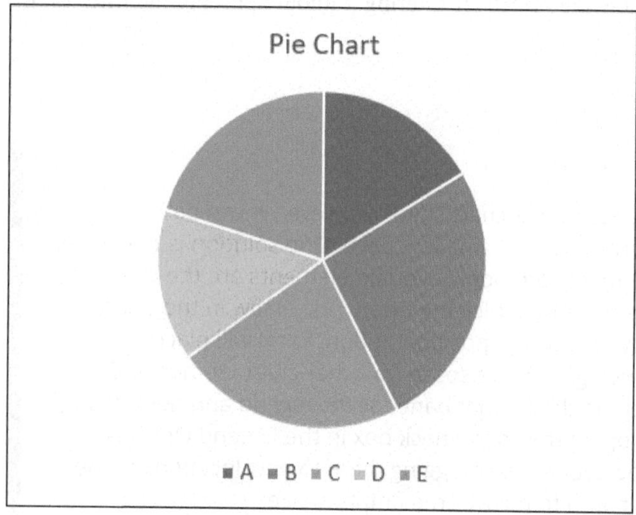

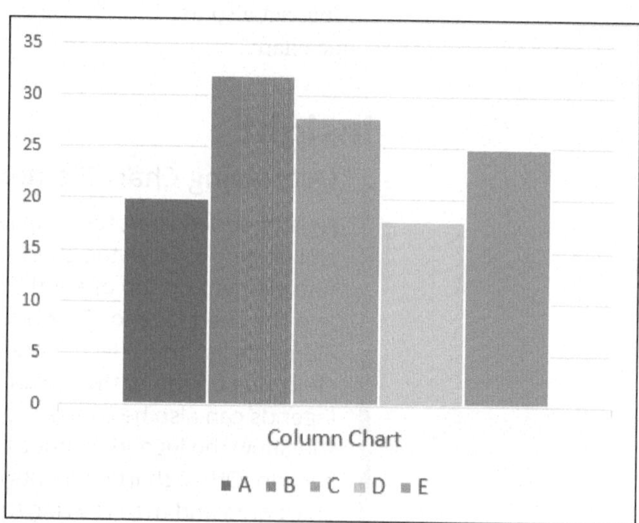

Comparing Column Chart Subtypes

Unlike pie charts, which have only one data series, column and bar charts can include multiple data series. Figure 4–16 presents three examples of column charts in which five data series (U.S. Equities, U.S. Bonds, Non-U.S. Equities, Non-U.S. Bonds, and Cash) are plotted against one category series (Years). Column charts are plotted against a **value axis** along the vertical side of the chart displaying the values from the data series and a **category axis** along the horizontal side of the chart displaying the category values associated with each data series.

Figure 4–16 Column chart subtypes

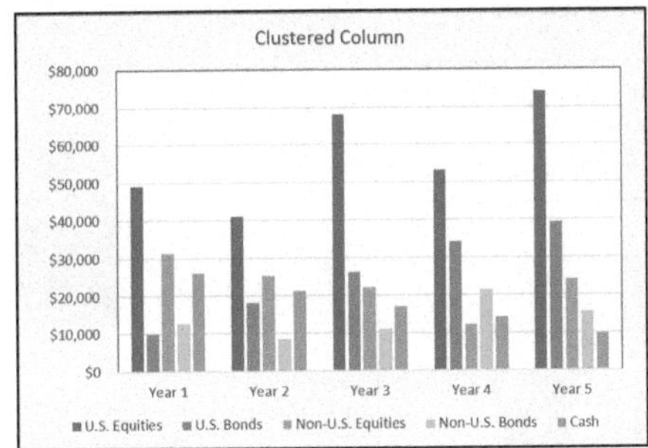

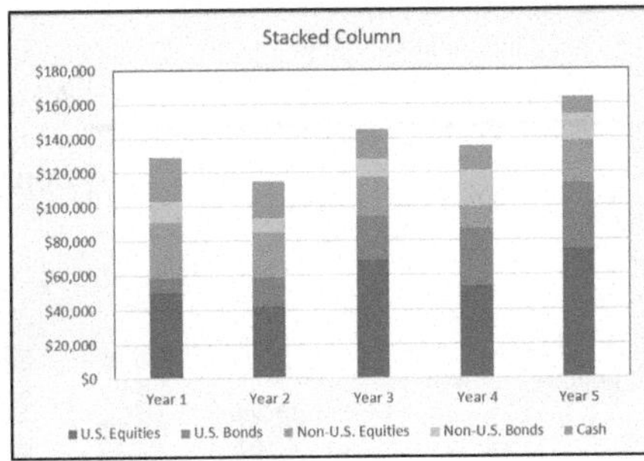

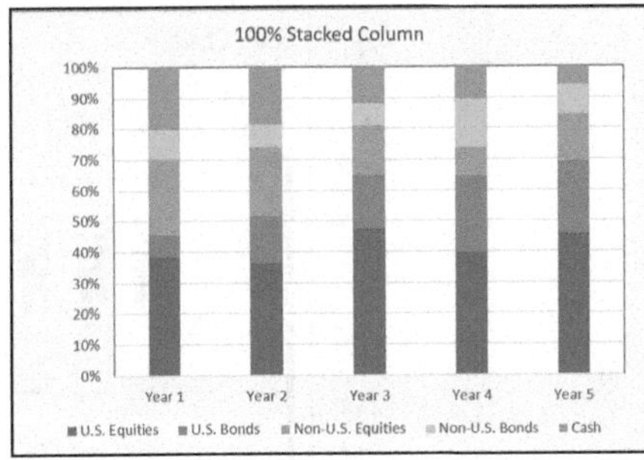

A **clustered column chart** displays the data series values in separate columns side by side so that you can compare the relative heights of values across categories. The clustered column chart in Figure 4–16 compares the amount invested in each category in Year 1 through Year 5. Note that the amount invested in U.S. bonds steadily increases as the amount invested in cash decreases over the same period.

A **stacked column chart** combines the data series values within a single column to show how much of the total is contributed by each item. The stacked column chart in Figure 4–16 gives information on the total amount invested each year in the fund and how each year's investment is split among five investment categories. This chart makes it clear that the total investment in the fund dropped from Year 3 to Year 4 before rising again in Year 5.

Finally, a **100% stacked column chart** makes the same comparison as the stacked column chart except that the stacked sections are expressed as percentages of the whole. As you can see from the 100% stacked column chart in Figure 4–16, the investment in U.S. equities and bonds starts out at about 45% in the first year and steadily increases to about 70% by Year 5. Each chart, while working with the same data source, reveals something different about the activity of the investment fund over the five-year period.

Creating a Clustered Column Chart

The process for creating a column chart is the same as for creating a pie chart: Select the data source and then choose a chart type and subtype. After the chart is embedded in the worksheet, you can move and resize the chart and change the chart's design, layout, and format.

Lydia wants a column chart presenting the returns of the Hamilton Fund adjusted over 1-year, 3-year, and 10-year periods, as well as year-to-date (YTD) and since the fund's inception. The column chart will include the returns from the Standard & Poor's 500 index (S&P 500) to indicate how the fund compares to an industry standard. You will create that chart now.

To create a clustered column chart:

1. Go to the **Returns** worksheet containing the returns based on month-end values.
2. Select the range **A4:C9** containing the categories and values to chart.
3. On the ribbon, click the **Insert** tab, and then in the Charts group, click the **Recommended Charts** button. The Insert Chart dialog box opens to the Recommended Charts tab. From this tab, you can preview and select a chart best suited to the data source. Refer to Figure 4–17.

Figure 4–17 Recommended Charts tab in the Insert Chart dialog box

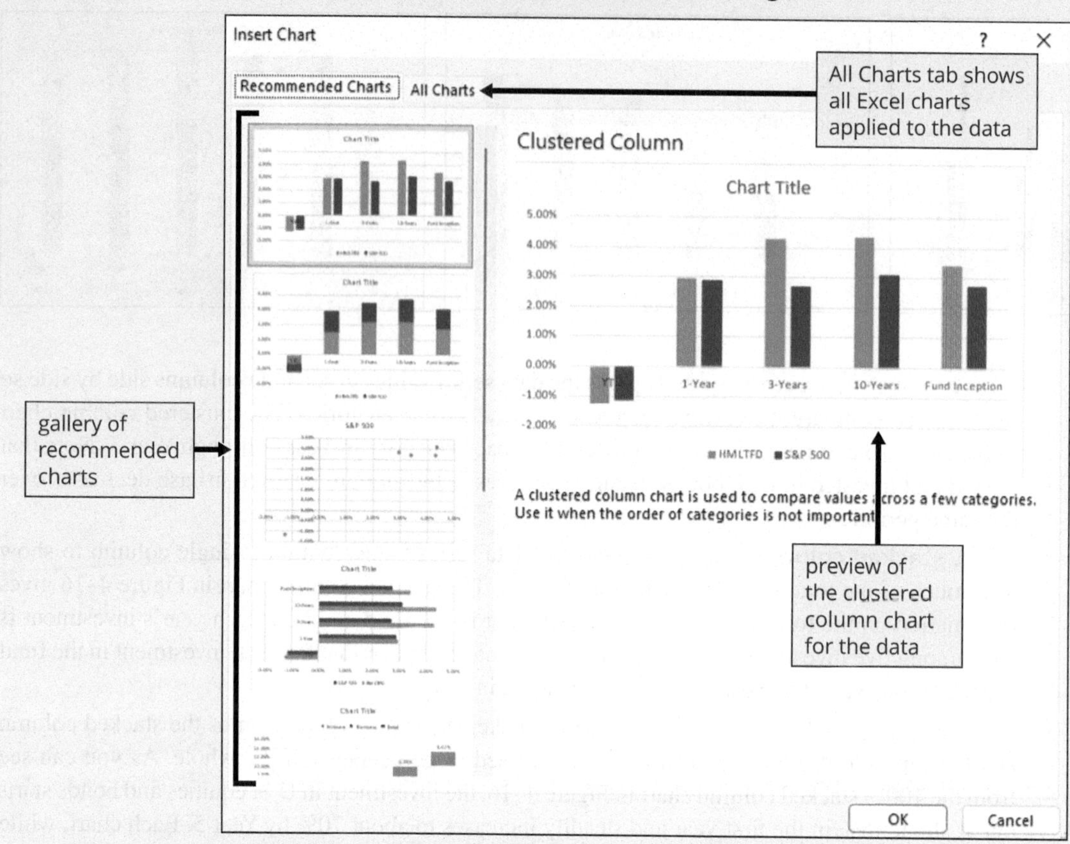

4. Confirm that the **Clustered Column** chart is selected, and then click **OK**.
5. On the Chart Design tab, in the Location group, click the **Move Chart** button.
6. From the Object in box, click **Summary**.
7. Click **OK** to move the column chart to the Summary worksheet.

> **Tip** To set an exact chart size, enter the height and width values in the Size group on the Format tab.

8. In the Summary worksheet, move and resize the chart to cover the range **A17:B28**, using **ALT** to snap the chart to the grid. Refer to Figure 4–18.

Figure 4–18 Clustered column chart

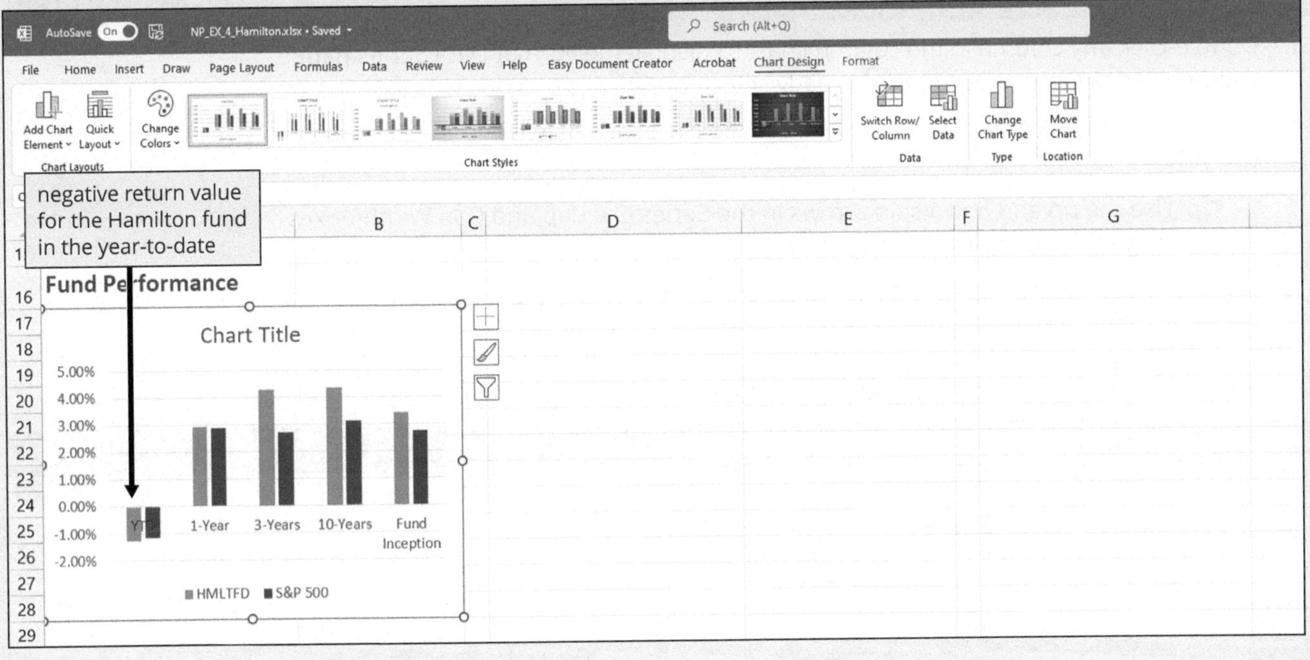

The column chart shows that the Hamilton Fund has generally outperformed the S&P 500 index for most of its life and especially during the previous 3-year and 10-year periods. However, in the current year-to-date, the fund is performing worse than the S&P 500 and, in fact, is showing a negative return in value.

Editing a Chart Title

When a chart has a single data series, the name of the data series is used for the chart title. When a chart has more than one data series, "Chart Title" is used as the temporary title of the chart. Lydia wants you to change the chart title to "Return on Investment." You will edit the chart title now.

To change the title of the column chart:

1. At the top of the column chart, click **Chart Title** to select it.

   Tip You can change the font size and style of the chart title by clicking the formatting buttons in the Font group on the Home tab.

2. Type **Return on Investment** as the new title, and then press **ENTER**. The new title is inserted into the chart.

Because the chart title is not linked to any worksheet cell, the title will not be updated if changes are made to the data source.

Setting the Gap Width

Excel automatically sets the space between the data series in a column chart as well as the gap width between one category value and the next. If a column chart contains several data series, there might be too little room between the categories, making it difficult to know when one category ends and the next begins. You can modify the space between the data series and gap width using the Format pane.

Lydia wants you to reduce the space between the two data series and increase the interval width between the Year categories.

To set the column chart gap and interval widths:

1. Double-click any column in the column chart to display the Format Data Series pane with the Series Options section already selected.
2. Select the **Series Overlap** box, and then change the space between the data series to **−10%**.

   Tip Use the up and down spin arrows in the Series Overlap and Gap Width boxes to change the values in 1% increments.

3. Select the **Gap Width** box, and then increase the value of the gap between the category values to **300%**. Refer to Figure 4–19.

Figure 4–19 Series overlap and gap width values

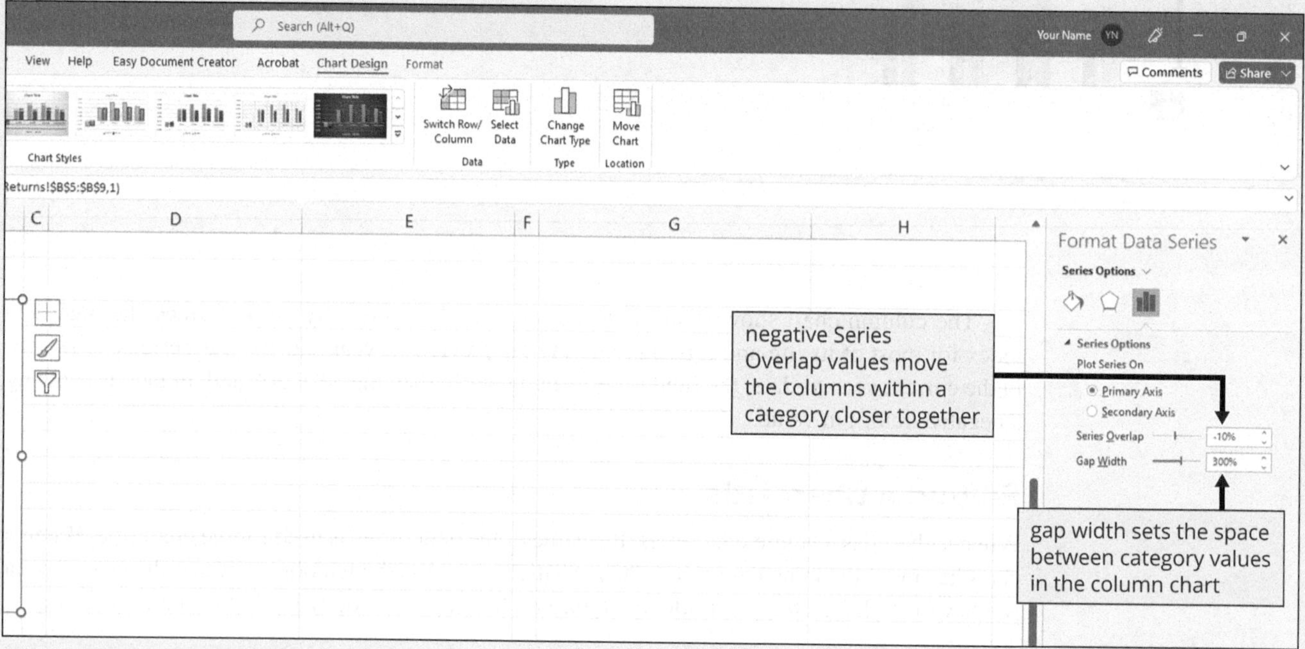

4. Close the Format Data Series pane.

Adding Gridlines to a Chart

Another way of distinguishing columns in separate categories is with gridlines. A gridline is a line that extends from the chart's horizontal and vertical axis into the plot area, making it easier to identify the values or categories associated with the chart's data markers. For example, the horizontal gridlines in the Return on Investment chart make it clearer that the return from the Hamilton Fund exceeds 4% growth for the 3-year and 10-year time periods.

Lydia wants you to add vertical gridlines to provide an additional visual aid for separating the time intervals from each other.

To add vertical gridlines to the chart:

1. With the column chart still selected, click the **Chart Elements** button [+] to the right of chart to display the list of chart elements associated with column charts.
2. To the right of Gridlines, click the **arrow** [▶] to display the gridline options, and then click **Primary Major Vertical** to add vertical gridlines to the chart. Refer to Figure 4–20.

Figure 4–20 Gridlines added to the column chart

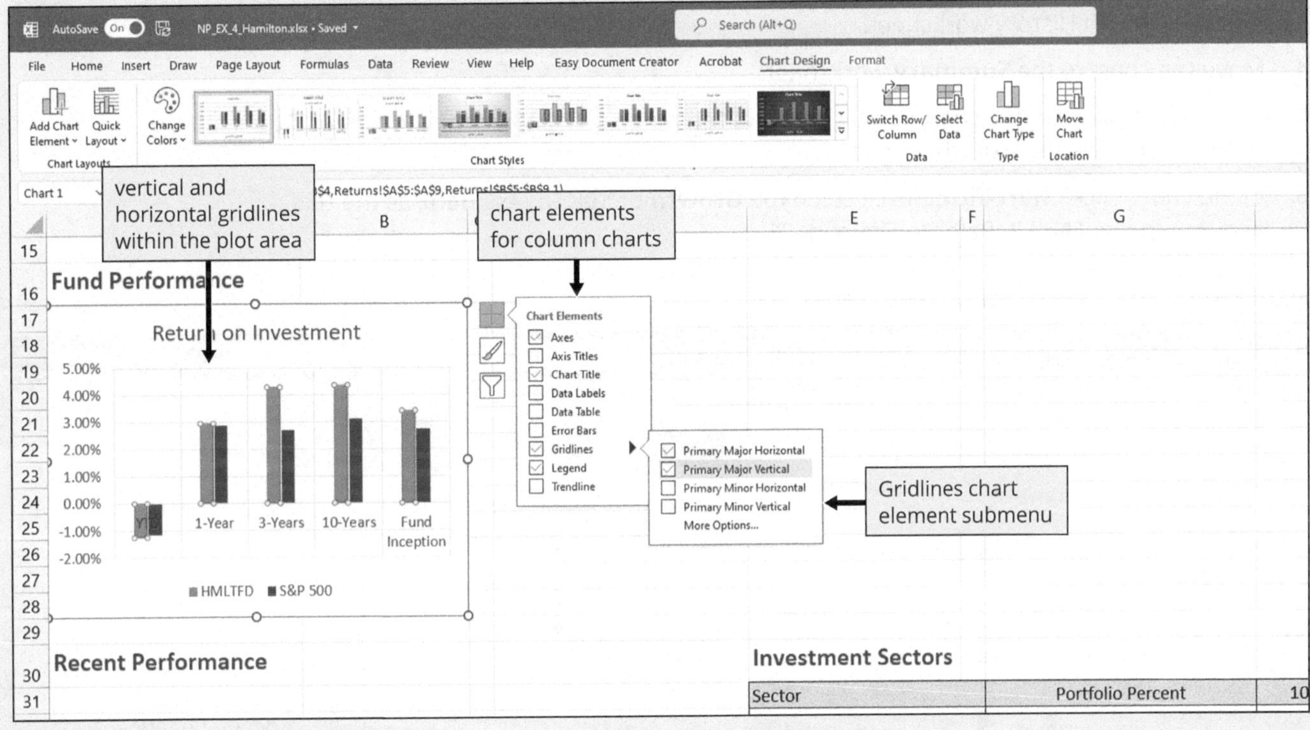

The column chart is complete. The next chart that Lydia wants added to the Summary worksheet analyzes how the value of the fund has changed over the past 20 years.

Insight

Adding Data Tables to Charts

You can use data labels to add data directly to a chart. Another way of viewing the data values associated with a chart is by adding a data table. The data table will be inserted within the chart area directly below the plot area. Each data series will appear as a separate row within the data table with category values placed in the first column of the table.

Creating a Line Chart

A line chart uses lines to plot one or more data series against a set of categories. The categories should follow a sequential order that is evenly spaced. For example, if the categories represent calendar months, the space between one month and the next must be constant. Otherwise, the line chart will give an inaccurate depiction of change over time.

Lydia wants a line chart comparing the growth of an investment in the Hamilton Fund over the past 20 years to the same investment in the Standard & Poor's 500 index. You will create this line chart using the data in the Growth History worksheet.

To create the growth history line chart:

1. Go to the **Growth History** worksheet, and then select the range **A4:C25** containing the growth of the Hamilton Fund and the S&P 500 index from a hypothetical $10,000 initial investment.
2. On the ribbon, click the **Insert** tab, and then in the Charts group, click the **Recommended Charts** button. The Insert Chart dialog box opens to the Recommended Charts tab.
3. Confirm that the **Line** chart type is selected, and then click **OK** to insert the line chart into the Growth History worksheet.
4. Move the chart to the **Summary** worksheet.
5. Move and resize the line chart so that it covers the range **D17:E28**, holding down **ALT** to snap the chart to the worksheet grid.
6. In the chart, click **Chart Title** to select it, type **Growth of 10K Investment** as the title, and then press **ENTER**. Refer to Figure 4–21.

Figure 4–21 Line chart of two data series

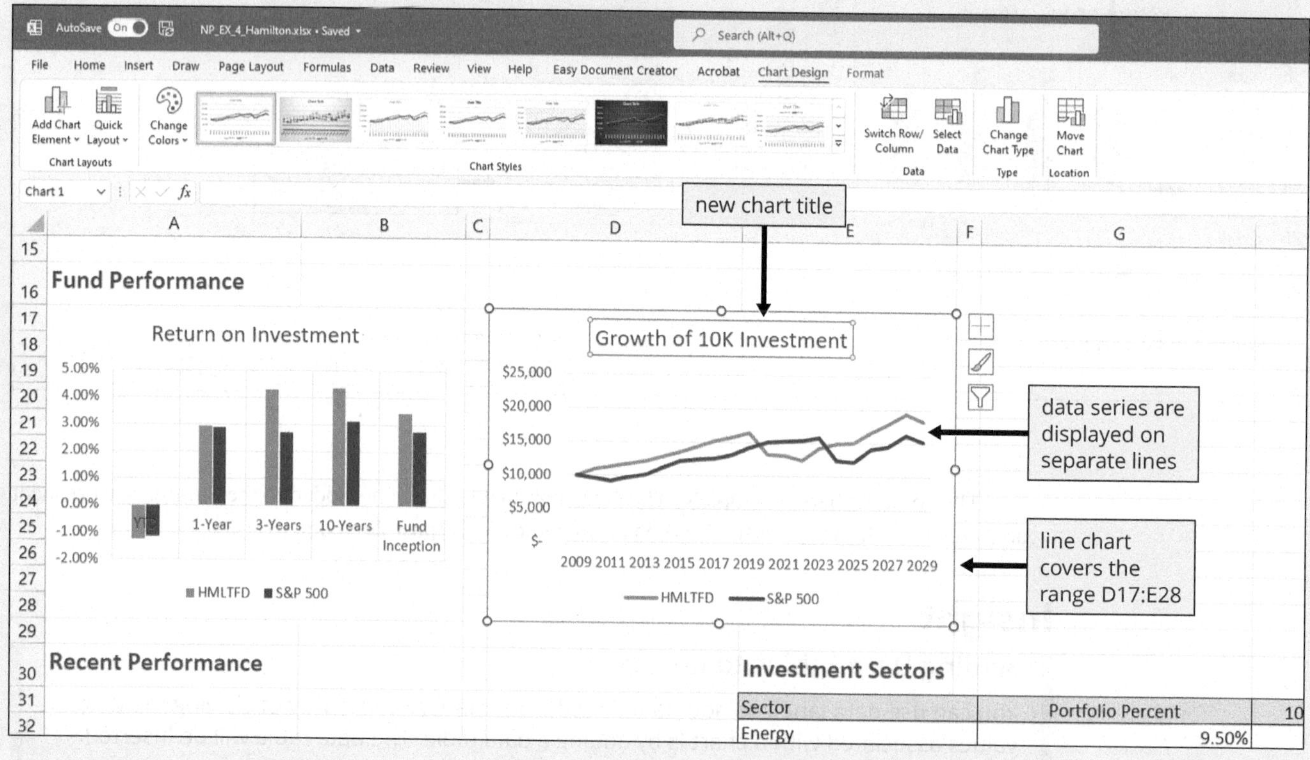

The line chart shows that the value of the Hamilton Fund exceeds the S&P 500 index for most of the past 20 years except between 2019 and 2023 when the index performed better. Lydia also notes that in the last year both the Hamilton Fund and the index have lost value.

Editing the Category Axis

You can modify the axis labels and tick marks to change which category values are displayed in the chart. The year values in the horizontal axis of the line chart are crowded, making the dates unclear. Lydia wants you to revise the axis so that it lists years in 5-year increments.

To format the horizontal axis:

1. Double-click one of the years on the horizontal axis to open the Format Axis pane.
2. If necessary, at the top of the Format pane, click the **Axis Options** button to select it.
3. Click **Tick Marks** to view options for modifying the tick marks on the category axis.
4. In the Interval between marks box, change the value to **5** so that the tick marks are laid out in 5-year intervals.
5. Click the **Major type** arrow, and then click **Cross** so that the tick marks are displayed as crosses.
6. Click **Labels** to expand that section, click the **Specify interval unit** option button, enter **5** in the Specify interval unit box, and then press **ENTER**. The year labels appear at 5-year intervals. Refer to Figure 4–22.

Figure 4–22 New category intervals for the horizontal axis

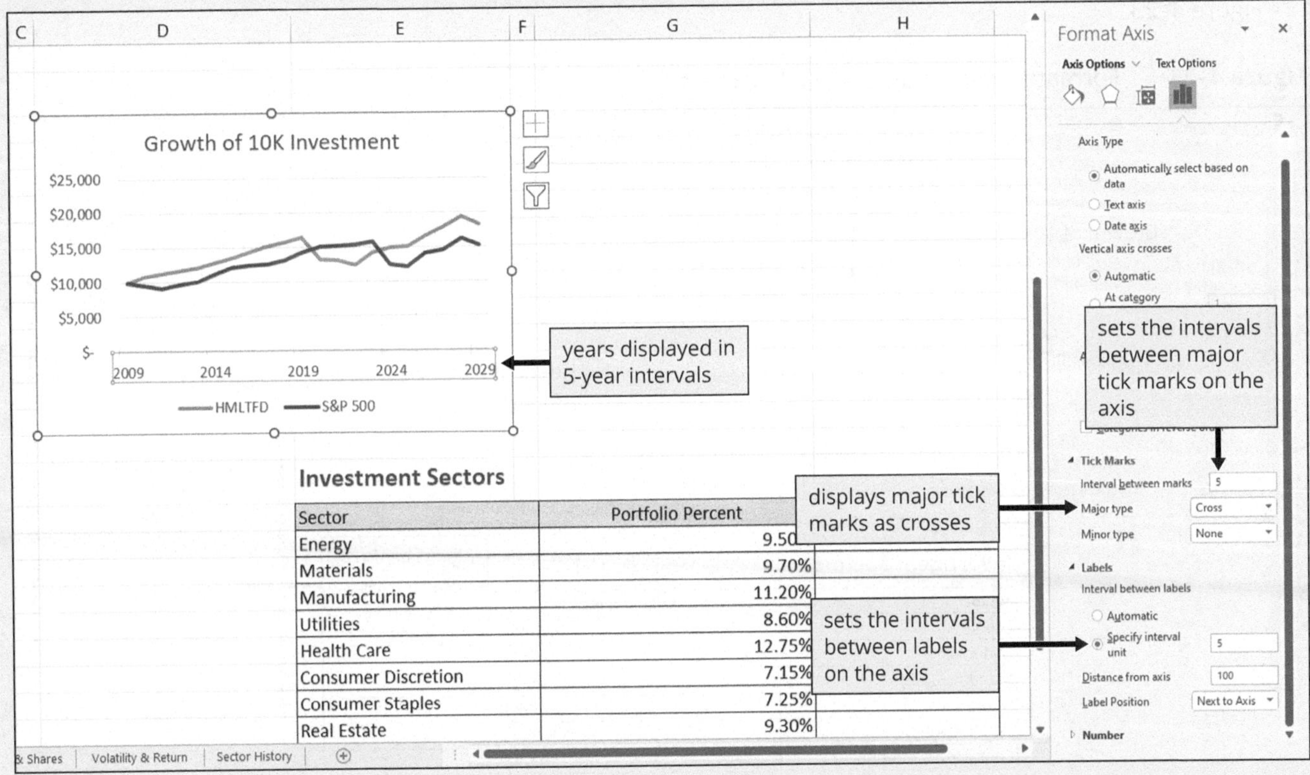

You can modify date categories by clicking the Date axis option button in the Axis Type section of the Format Axis pane. The pane will then show an input box from which you specify the number of days, weeks, months, and so forth between date values.

Formatting Data Markers

Each value from a data series is represented by a data marker. In pie charts, the data markers are the individual pie slices. In column charts, the columns are the data markers. In a line chart, the data markers are the points connected by the line. Depending on the line chart style, these data marker points can be displayed or hidden.

In the line chart you created, the data marker points are hidden, and only the line connecting those markers is visible. Lydia wants you to display those data markers and change their fill color to white so that they stand out, making the data values obvious.

To display and format the line chart data markers:

1. In the line chart, double-click the orange line for the Hamilton Fund (HMLTFD) to display the Format Data Series pane.
2. At the top of the Format pane, click the **Fill & Line** button.
3. At the top of the pane, click **Marker**, and then click **Marker Options** to display options specific to data markers.
4. Click the **Automatic** option button to automatically display the markers along with the line for the Hamilton Fund data series. The data markers are now visible in the line chart, but they have an orange fill color. You will change this fill color to white.
5. In the Fill section, click the **Solid fill** option button, click the **Color** button, and then select the **White, Background 1** theme color. The fill color for the data markers for the Hamilton Fund line changes to white.
6. Repeat Steps 1 through 5 for the maroon line representing the S&P 500 index. Refer to Figure 4–23.

Figure 4–23 Formatted data markers in a line chart

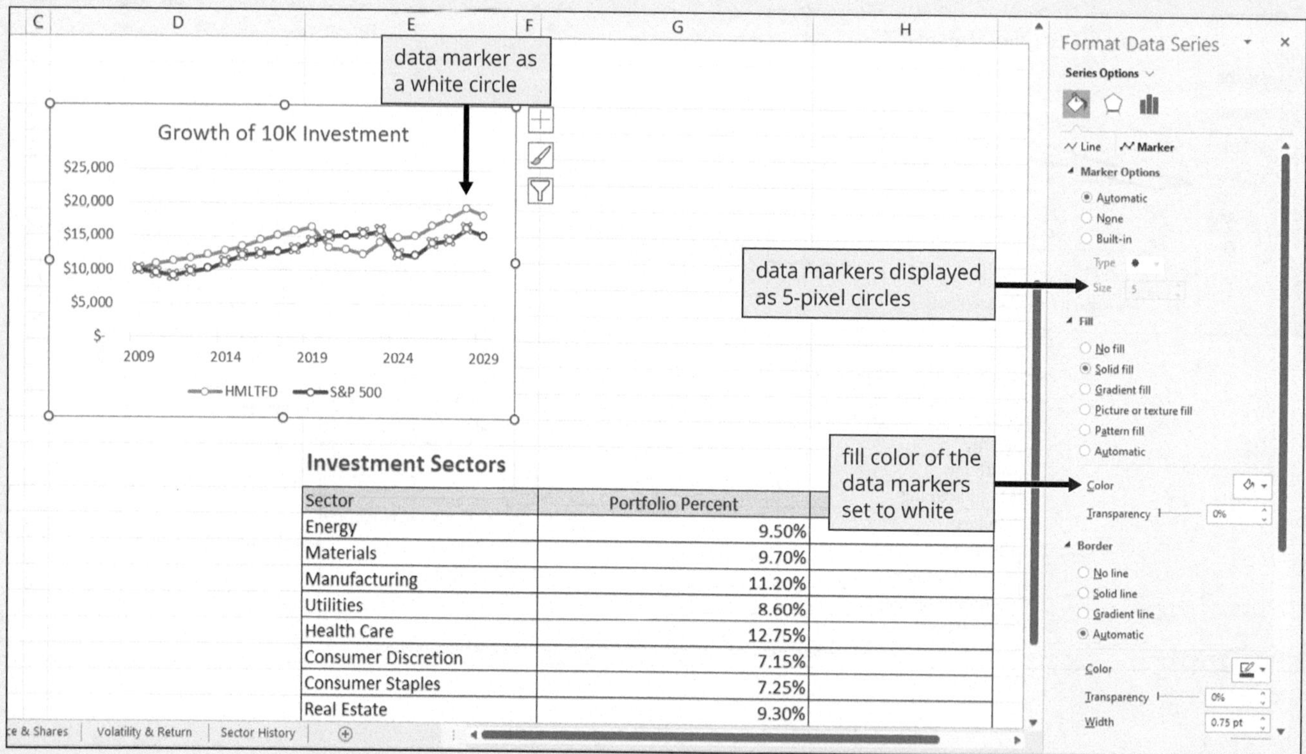

Sector	Portfolio Percent
Energy	9.50%
Materials	9.70%
Manufacturing	11.20%
Utilities	8.60%
Health Care	12.75%
Consumer Discretion	7.15%
Consumer Staples	7.25%
Real Estate	9.30%

7. Close the Format Data Series pane.

By adding the data markers, you now have a better view of individual values in plotted in the line chart.

Proskills

Written Communication: Communicating Effectively with Charts

Studies show that people better interpret information when it is presented as a graphic rather than in a table. As a result, charts can help communicate the real story underlying the facts and figures you present to colleagues and clients. A well-designed chart can illuminate the bigger picture that might be hidden by viewing only the numbers. However, poorly designed charts can mislead readers and make it more difficult to interpret data.

To create effective and useful charts, keep in mind the following tips as you design your charts:

- **Keep it simple.** Do not clutter a chart with too many graphical elements. Focus attention on the data rather than on decorative elements that do not inform.
- **Focus on the message.** Design the chart to highlight the points you want to convey to readers.
- **Limit the number of data series.** Most charts should display no more than four or five data series. Pie charts should have no more than six slices.
- **Choose colors carefully.** Display different data series in contrasting colors to make it easier to distinguish one series from another. Modify the default colors as needed to make them distinct on the screen and in the printed copy.
- **Limit text styles.** Use a maximum of two or three different text styles in the same chart. Too many text styles in one chart can distract attention from the data.

The goal of written communication is always to inform the reader in the simplest, most accurate, and most direct way possible. Everything in your workbook should be directed toward that aim.

Creating a Combination Chart

So far, the charts you created are based on one chart type. A combination chart combines two chart types, enabling you to display each data series using the chart type best suited for it.

When the data series values cover vastly different ranges, you can plot one data series against the **primary axis**, the vertical axis appearing along the left edge of the chart, and the other data series against the **secondary axis**, the vertical axis on the chart's right edge.

The next chart that Lydia wants added to the Summary worksheet will display the recent performance of the Hamilton Fund, showing its daily selling price and the number of shares traded over the past three months. You'll display the daily selling price in a line chart plotted against the primary axis and the number of shares traded in a column chart plotted against the secondary axis.

To create a combination chart:

1. Go to the **Price & Shares** worksheet, and then select the range **A4:C69**.
2. On the ribbon, click the **Insert** tab, and then in the Charts group, click the **Recommended Charts** button. The Insert Chart dialog box opens showing the recommended Line chart.
3. Click the **All Charts** tab for a list of all Excel chart types.
4. In the list of chart types, click **Combo**.
5. Click the **Custom Combination** chart subtype (the last subtype listed for the Combo chart). At the bottom of the dialog box, the "Choose the chart type and axis for your data series" box lists two data series in the selected data.
6. In the "Choose the chart type and axis for your data series" box, click the **Price** Chart Type arrow, and then in the Line section, click **Line**. The Price data series will be displayed as a line chart.

7. Click the **Shares Traded** Chart Type arrow, and then in the Column section, click **Clustered Column**. The Shares Traded data series will be displayed as a column chart.
8. In the Shares Traded row, click the **Secondary Axis** check box to plot the Shares Traded values on the secondary axis. Refer to Figure 4–24.

Figure 4–24 Combination chart preview

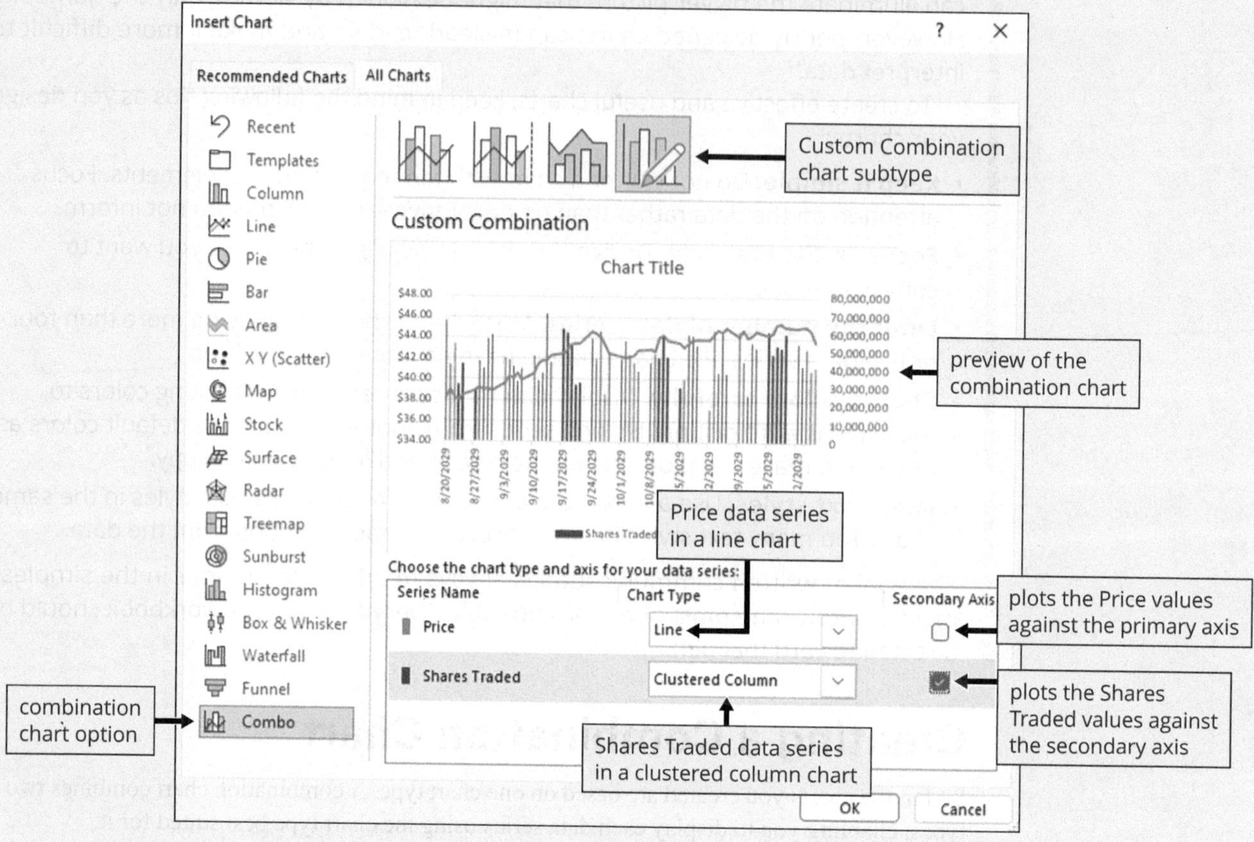

9. Click **OK** to embed the chart into the Price & Shares worksheet.

As with the other charts you created, you need to move the combination chart to the Summary worksheet. Then you will format it.

To move and format the combination chart:

1. Move the combination chart to the Summary worksheet. You may have to scroll through the worksheet to find the chart.
2. Move and resize the chart to cover the range **A31:D43**, holding down the **ALT** key to snap the worksheet to the grid.

   Tip To retain a chart's proportions as it is resized, hold down SHIFT as you drag the resizing handle.

3. Click **Chart Title** in the combination chart to select it, type **Price & Shares Traded** as the new title, and then press **ENTER** to insert the new chart title.
4. Click the **Chart Elements** button and then click the **Legend arrow** next to display a submenu of options for the chart legend.
5. Click **Right** to move the legend to the right of the chart area. Refer to Figure 4–25.

Figure 4–25 Combination chart of Price and Shares traded

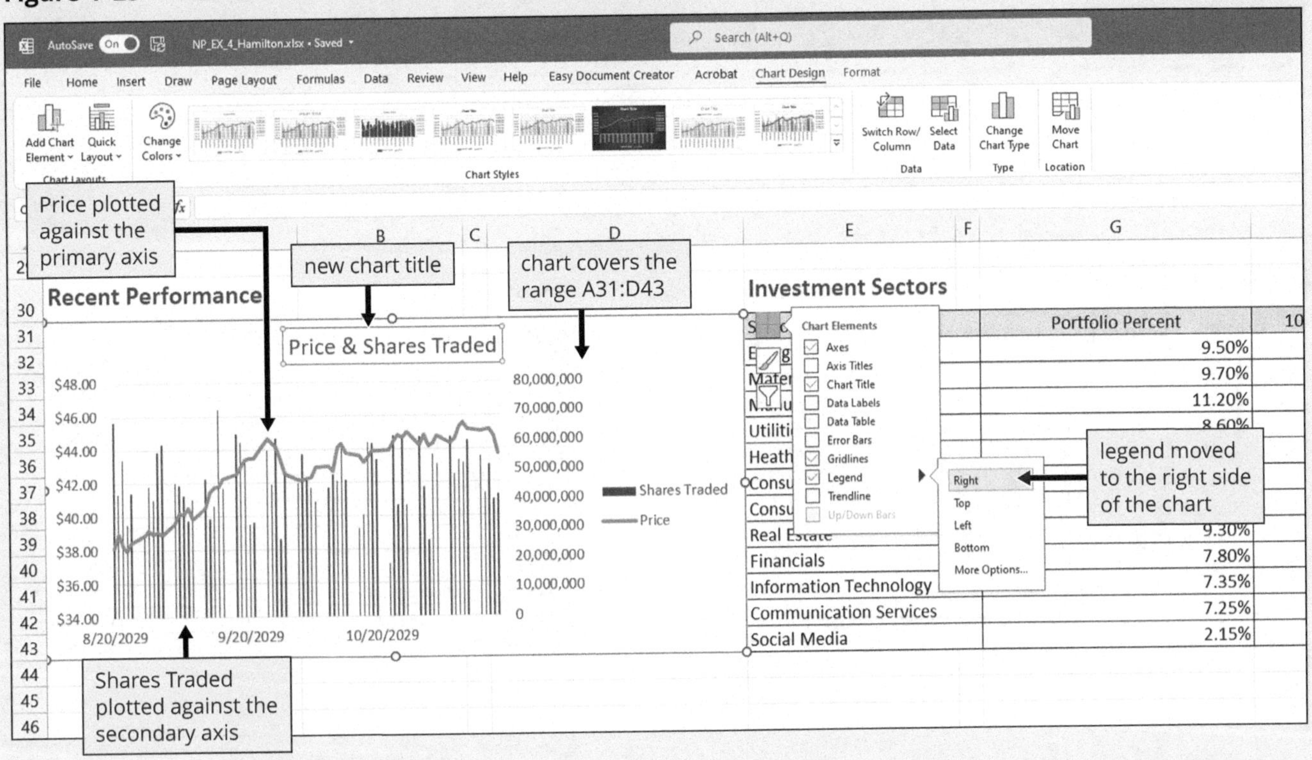

The combination chart clearly shows a downward trend in prices over the past three months. There does not seem to be any pattern in the number of shares traded each day during that time.

Adding an Axis Title

An **axis title** is descriptive text that appears next to a chart's horizontal or vertical axis. With data plotted against two axes, the chart would be clearer if axis titles were added describing the values displayed on those axes. Lydia wants you to make that change.

To add axis titles to the chart:

1. With the combination chart still selected, click the **Chart Elements** button if necessary, and then click the **Axis Titles** check box to select it. Titles are added to all three axes.
2. Click **Axis Title** next to the primary axis (on the left side of the chart), type **Price** as the axis title, and then press **ENTER**. The primary axis title is changed to Price.
3. Click **Axis Title** along the category (bottom) axis, type **Date** as the axis title, and then press **ENTER**. The category axis title is changed to Date.
4. Click **Axis Title** next to the secondary axis (on the right side of the chart), type **Shares Traded** as the axis title, and then press **ENTER**. The secondary axis title is changed to Shares Traded.
5. With the Shares Traded title still selected, click the **Home** tab on the ribbon. In the Alignment group, click the **Orientation** button, and then click **Rotate Text Down**. The secondary axis title is rotated for better readability. Refer to Figure 4–26.

Figure 4–26 Axis titles added to a chart

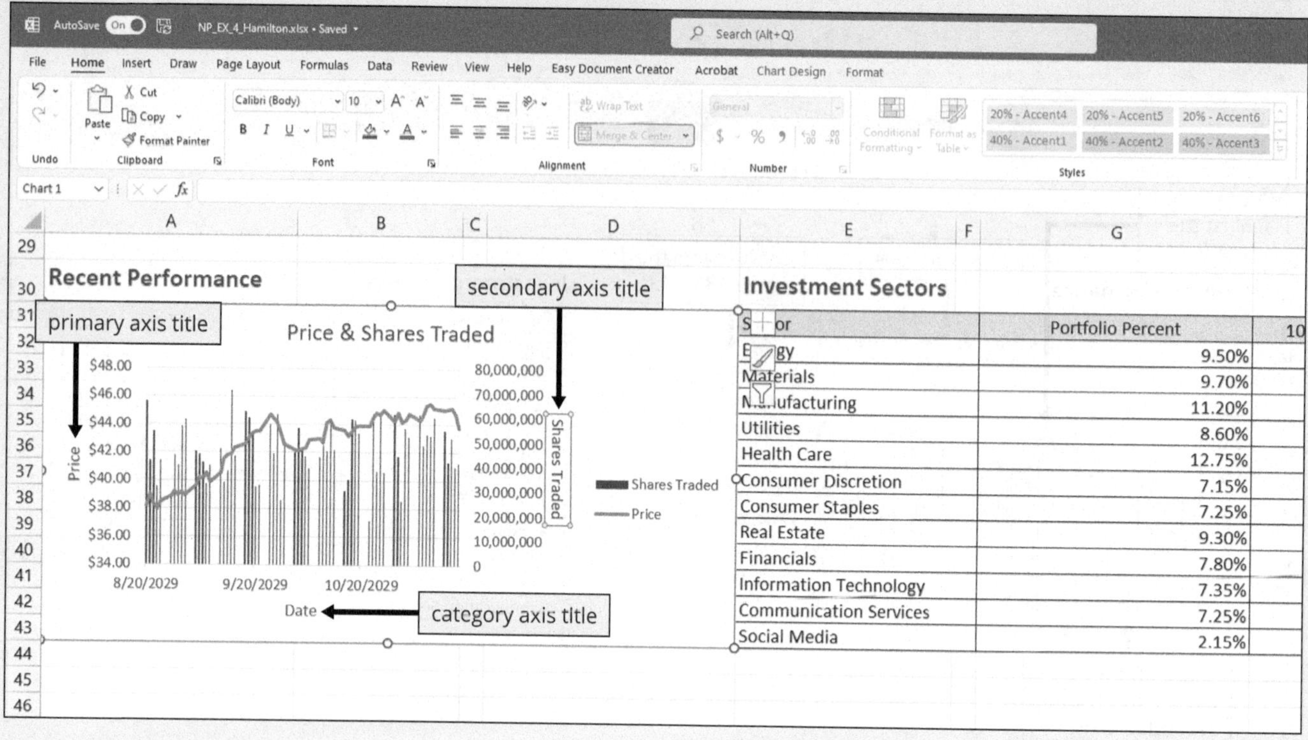

Editing a Value Axis Scale

Excel chooses the range of values, or **scale**, for the primary and secondary axes. For the Price data series, the scale ranges from $34 to $48. For the Shares Traded data series, the scale ranges from 0 to 80,000,000.

Excel divides the scale into regular intervals, marked on the axis with tick marks and labels. **Major tick marks** identify the main units on the chart axis while **minor tick marks** identify the smaller intervals between the major tick marks. The major tick marks for the Price series are placed at intervals of $2, and the major tick marks for the Shares Traded Series are placed at intervals of 10,000,000 shares. There are no minor tick marks in the combination chart. Tick marks placed too close together can make the scale difficult to read. On the other hand, increasing the gap between tick marks could make the chart less informative.

Lydia wants you to specify a different scale for the secondary axis, changing the size of the scale used with the Shares Traded data. Lydia also wants the scale of the secondary axis expanded so that the data markers for the column chart do not overlap the contents of the line chart. You will use the Format Axis pane to make these changes.

To set the scale of the secondary axis:

1. Double-click the secondary axis values on the right side of the chart to open the Format Axis pane.
2. Click the **Axis Options** button if necessary to display its options in the Format Axis pane, and then click the **Axis Options** label.
3. In the Bounds section at the top of the list of Axis Options, click the **Maximum** box, and then enter **1.6E08** (representing 160,000,000 in exponential notation) as the top end of the scale for the secondary axis.
4. Press **TAB** to enter the new scale value. The scale of the secondary axis expands so that the column chart is displayed below the line chart.

When the range of the axis covers values of a large magnitude, you can simplify the axis labels by including the units as part of the scale. Lydia thinks the secondary axis numbers will be clearer without all the zeros in the axis values. You will display the secondary axis values in units of one million.

To set the display units for the secondary axis:

1. In the Format Axis pane, click the **Display units** arrow, and then click **Millions**. The Unit Label "Millions" is added to the secondary axis and the axis displays the axis values in units of one million. Refer to Figure 4–27.

Figure 4–27 Scale of the secondary axis

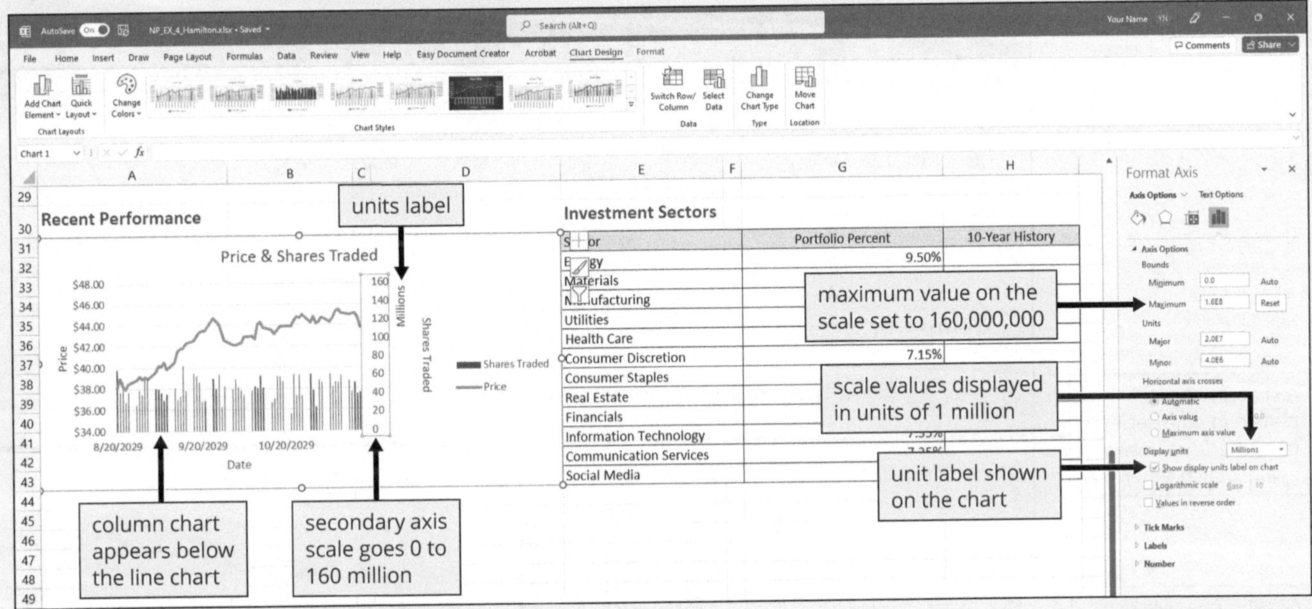

2. Close the Format Axis pane, and then save the workbook.

The combination chart comparing the yearly value of the Hamilton Fund to the S&P 500 index is complete. In the next session, you will create other charts and graphics that reveal valuable information about the Hamilton Fund.

Part 4.1 Quick Check

1. In a chart's data source, where does Excel assume that category values are placed?
2. What three chart elements are included in a pie chart?
3. A data series contains values grouped into 12 categories. Would this data be better displayed as a pie chart or a column chart? Explain why.
4. Which column chart should you use to display the values from each data series grouped into separate columns?
5. Which column chart should you use to display the values from each data series within each column?
6. Which column chart should you use to display the values from each data series as percentages within each column?
7. A researcher wants to track the average annual global temperature and the total global population over a 50-year period on a single chart. Why would a combination chart be a good choice for these data?
8. What are major tick marks and minor tick marks?

Part 4.2 Visual Overview: Scatter Charts, Data Bars, and Sparklines

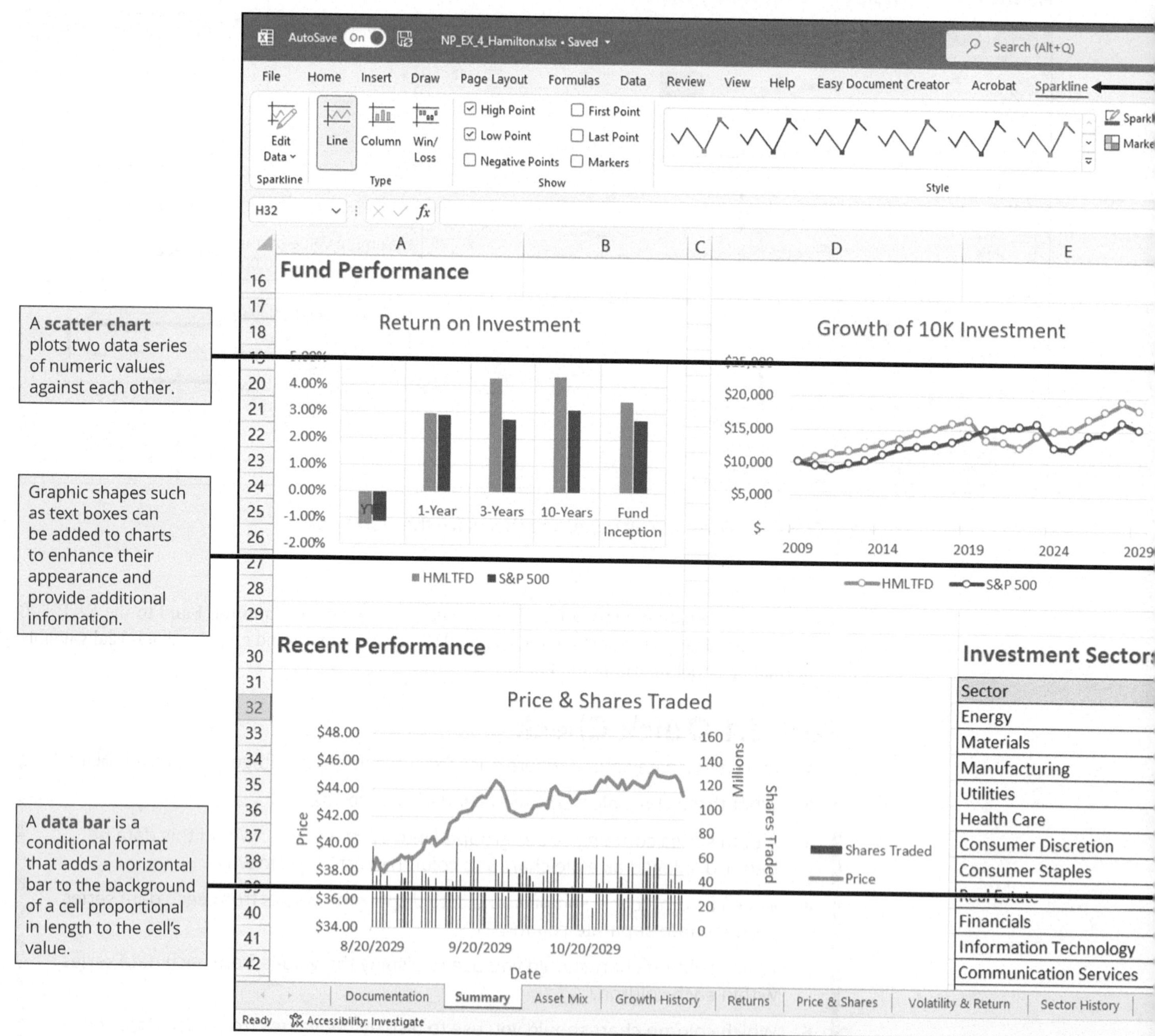

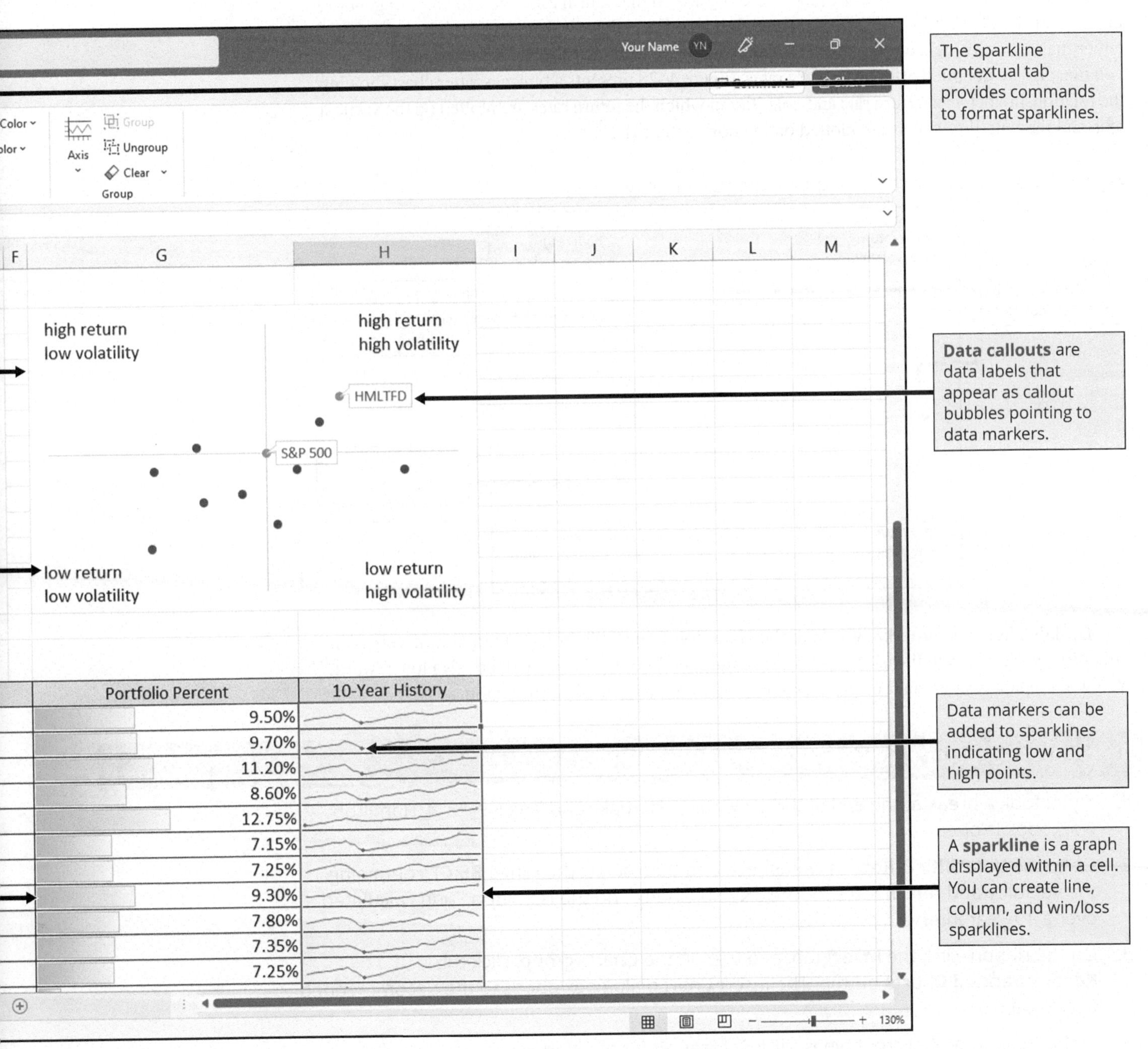
Your Name
Group
Ungroup
Clear
Axis
Group
high return
low volatility
high return
high volatility
HMLTFD
S&P 500
low return
low volatility
low return
high volatility
Portfolio Percent
10-Year History
9.50%
9.70%
11.20%
8.60%
12.75%
7.15%
7.25%
9.30%
7.80%
7.35%
7.25%
130%
The Sparkline contextual tab provides commands to format sparklines.
Data callouts are data labels that appear as callout bubbles pointing to data markers.
Data markers can be added to sparklines indicating low and high points.
A sparkline is a graph displayed within a cell. You can create line, column, and win/loss sparklines.

Creating a Scatter Chart

The charts you created so far all involve plotting numeric data against categorical data. Another important type of chart is the scatter chart, which plots two data series of numeric values against each other. Scatter charts are widely used in science and engineering applications when investigators want to discover how two numeric variables are related. For example, an economist might want to investigate the effect of high tax rates on tax revenue or the effect of increasing the minimum wage on the unemployment rate.

Lydia wants you to create a scatter chart exploring the relationship between the Hamilton Fund's rate of return and its volatility. The rate of return indicates how much an investment can earn for the investor while volatility measures the degree by which that return estimate can vary. In general, investments that have high rates of return are often volatile so that the investor faces the prospect of either making or losing a lot of money. On the other hand, safe investments, while usually not very volatile, also do not often offer high return rates. Figure 4–28 presents a typical scatter chart showing the relationship between return rate and volatility in which the return rates are plotted on the vertical axis and the volatility values are plotted on the horizontal axis.

Figure 4–28 Scatter chart of return rate vs. volatility

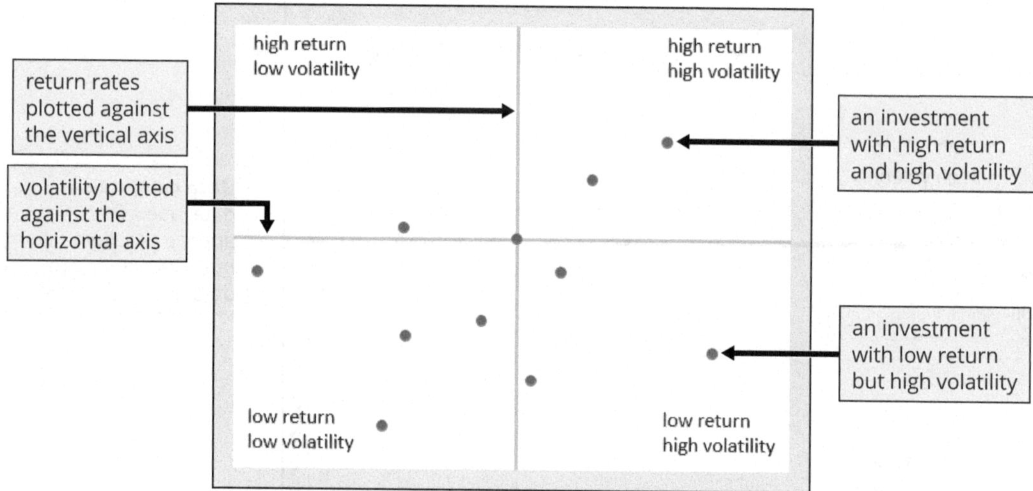

Lydia's clients want to know where the Hamilton Fund falls in its rate of return versus its volatility. Is the fund a high-risk/high-reward venture, or does it offer low risk but also low reward? You will create a scatter chart of those two data series to provide this information.

To create a scatter chart for the Hamilton Fund:

1. If you took a break at the end of the previous part, make sure the NP_EX_4_Hamilton workbook is open.
2. Go to the **Volatility & Return** worksheet, and then select the range **B5:C7** containing the volatility and return rates for the S&P 500 index and the Hamilton Fund calculated over a 10-year interval.
3. On the ribbon, click the **Insert** tab, and then in the Charts group, click the **Recommended Charts** button. The Insert Chart dialog box opens to the Recommended Charts tab.
4. In the recommended chart types, click **Scatter**. Refer to Figure 4–29.

Figure 4–29 Scatter chart preview

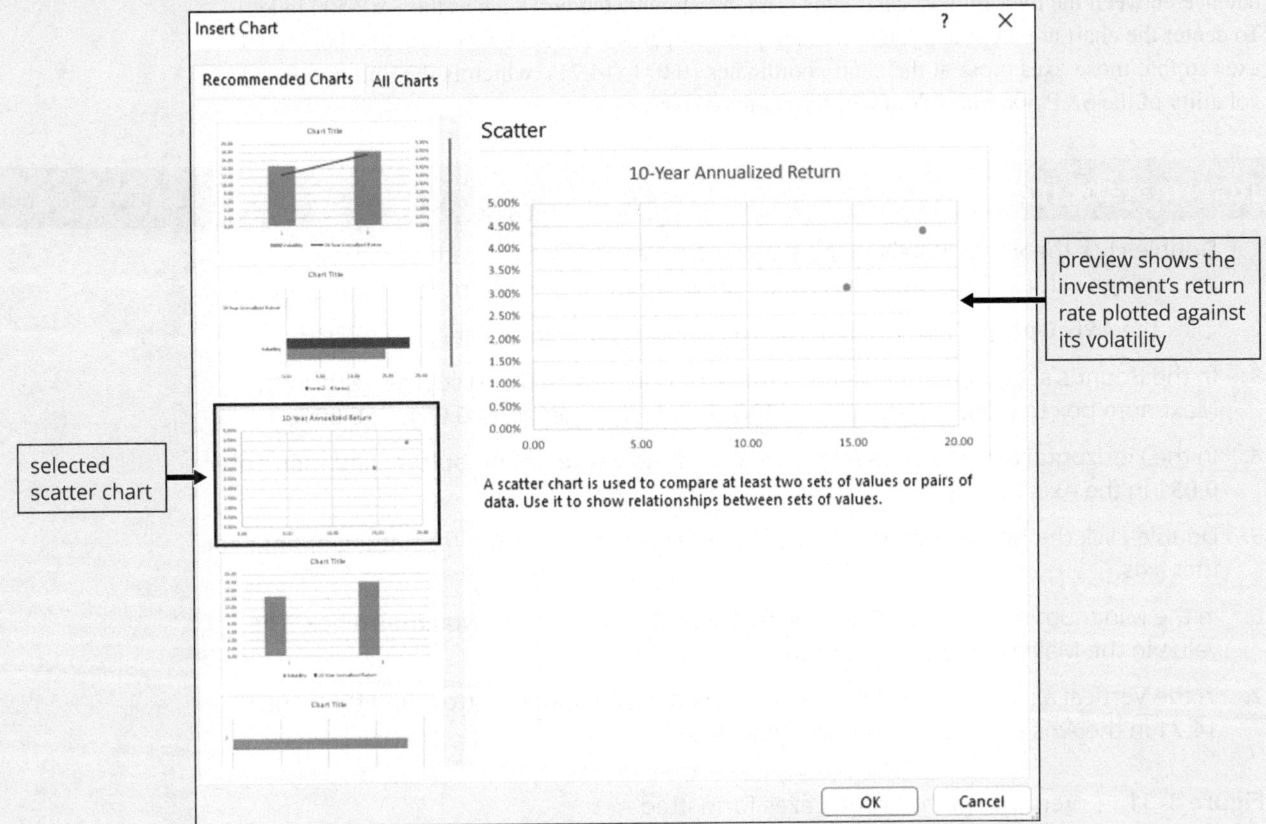

5. Click **OK** to insert the scatter chart.
6. Move the scatter chart to the Summary worksheet.
7. Move and resize the scatter chart to cover the range **G17:H28**, holding down the **ALT** key to snap the chart to the worksheet grid. Refer to Figure 4–30.

Figure 4–30 Scatter chart

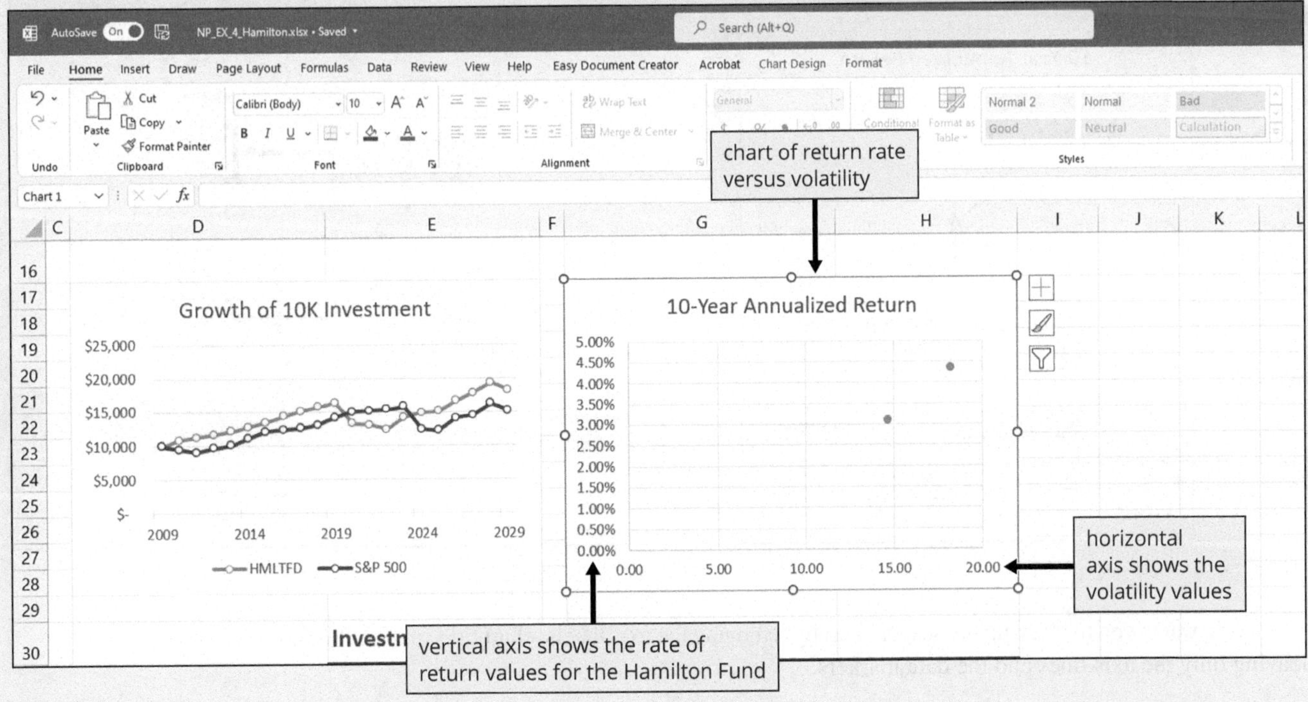

Scatter charts comparing return rates to volatility are usually centered at a point representing a balance between the two. In most cases, this is an investment standard such as the S&P 500 index. To center the chart at that point, you will modify the properties of both the vertical and horizontal axes so that those axes cross at the chart coordinates (0.031, 14.71), which is the return rate and volatility of the S&P 500 index. You will format these axes now.

To format the horizontal and vertical axes:

1. Double-click the **vertical axis** in the scatter chart containing the rate of return percentage values. The Format Axis pane opens to the Axis Options formatting choices.
2. Click the **Axis Options** button in the Format Axis pane to select it, if necessary.
3. In the Bounds section, set the value in the Minimum box to **0** and set the value in the Maximum box to **0.06**, and then press **TAB**. The axis ranges from 0.00% to 6.00%.
4. In the Horizontal axis crosses section, click the **Axis value** option button, and then enter **0.031** in the Axis value box.
5. Double-click the **horizontal axis** in the scatter chart to access the formatting options for that axis.
6. In the Minimum box, change the value to **4**, and then click in the **Maximum** box. The value in the Maximum box changes to 24.
7. In the Vertical axis crosses section, click the **Axis value** option button, and then enter **14.71** in the Axis value box. Refer to Figure 4–31.

Figure 4–31 Vertical and horizontal axes formatted

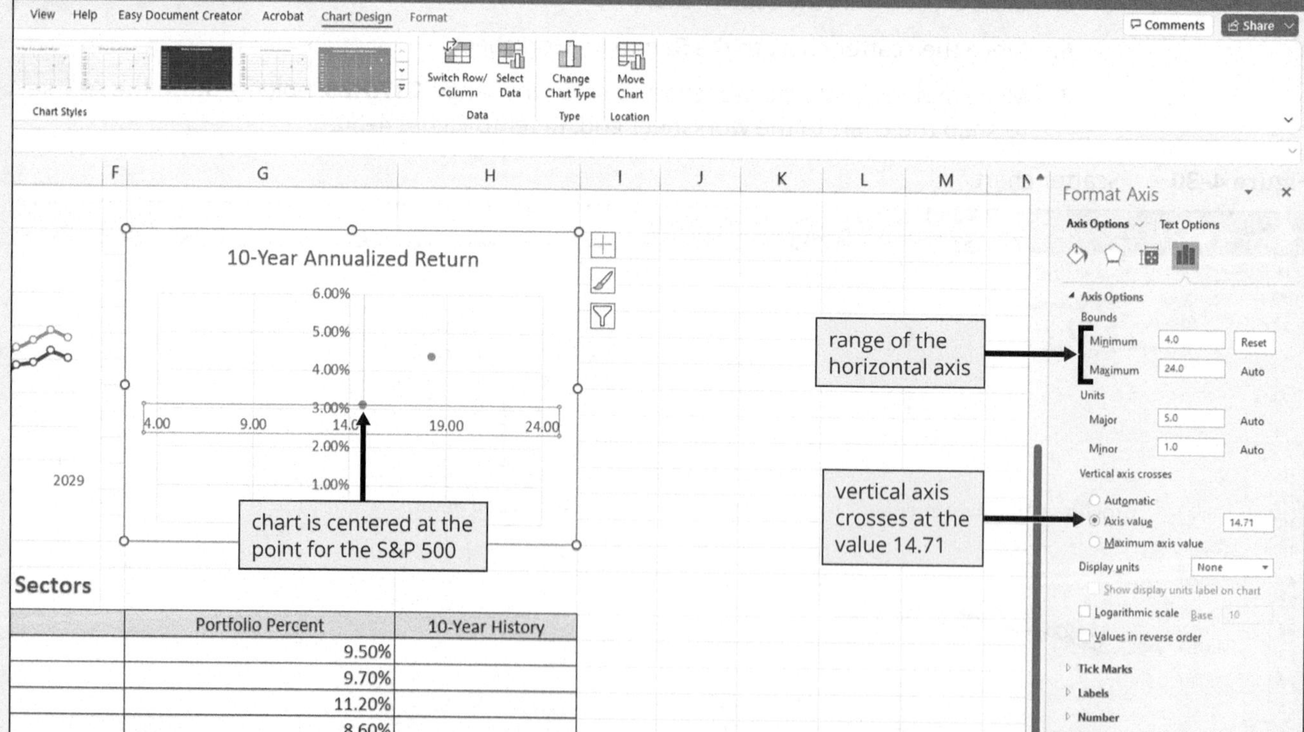

Lydia wants you to clean up the scatter chart by removing the axis labels, chart title, and gridlines, leaving only the axis lines and the data markers.

To remove elements from the scatter chart:

1. In the Format Axis pane for the horizontal axis, click the **Labels** section head, and then in the Label Position box, select **None** to remove the axis labels from the chart.
2. Double-click the labels for the vertical axis to display the Format Axis pane for the vertical axis.
3. Scroll down to the Labels section for that axis, click the **Label Position** box, and then click **None** to remove the vertical axis labels.
4. On the Chart Design tab, in the Chart Layouts group, click the **Add Chart Element** button, point to **Chart Title**, and then click **None** to remove the chart title.
5. In the Chart Layouts group, click the **Add Chart Element** button, point to **Gridlines**, and then click **Primary Major Horizontal** to deselect the option.
6. Click the **Add Chart Element** button, point to **Gridlines**, and then click **Primary Major Vertical** to deselect the option. Both the primary major horizontal and vertical gridlines are removed from the scatter chart.
7. Close the Format Axis pane.

Scatter chart data markers are all the same size. To glean useful information, you can set the size of each data marker relative to the size of a third variable. This type of chart is called a **bubble chart** and is a scatter chart subtype. The bubble chart in Figure 4–32 plots the annualized return versus the volatility for several funds. The size of the data markers is based on each fund's investment rating, with larger bubbles representing funds with better ratings.

Figure 4–32 Bubble chart

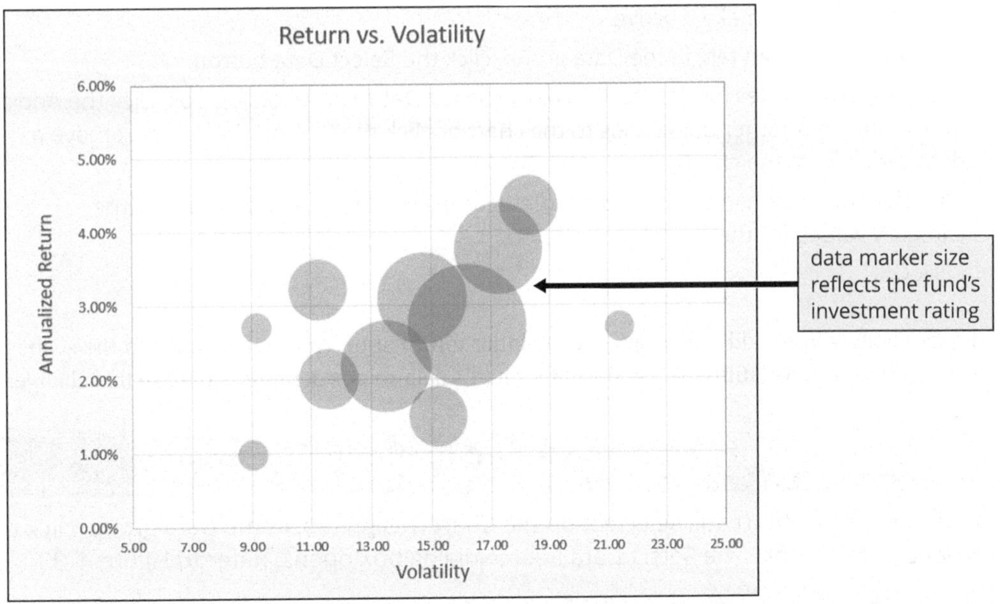

Having visual information about each fund's annualized return, volatility, and rating within a single chart can be useful for the company's investors.

Insight

Copying and Pasting Chart Formats

You will often want to repeat the same design for the charts in your worksheet. Rather than repeat the same steps, you can copy the formatting from one chart to another. To copy a chart format, first select the chart with the existing design that you want to replicate, and then click the Copy button in the Clipboard group on the Home tab (or press CTRL+C). Next, select the chart that you want to format, click the Paste arrow in the Clipboard group, and then click Paste Special to open the Paste Special dialog box. In the Paste Special dialog box, select the Formats option button, and then click OK. All the copied formats from the original chart—including fill colors, font styles, axis scales, and chart types—are then pasted into the new chart. Be aware that the pasted formats will overwrite any formats previously used in the new chart.

The scatter chart now contains only the two data points and the two axis lines. But with only two data markers in the chart, there is not a lot of basis for comparison with other investments. Lydia asks you to add data markers representing other funds to the scatter chart.

Editing the Chart Data Source

Excel automates most of the process of assigning a data source to the chart. However, sometimes the completed chart is not what you want, and you need to edit the chart's data source. At any time, you can modify the chart's data source to add more data series or change the current data series in the chart.

Reference

Modifying a Chart's Data Source

- Select the chart to make it active.
- On the Chart Design tab, in the Data group, click the Select Data button.
- In the Legend Entries (Series) section of the Select Data Source dialog box, click the Add button to add another data series to the chart or click the Remove button to remove a data series from the chart.
- Click the Edit button in the Horizontal (Category) Axis Labels section to select the category values for the chart.
- Click OK.

Lydia wants you to add a data series containing information from other funds to the scatter chart of returns versus volatility. You will edit the chart's data source definition to make that change.

To edit the chart's data source:

1. With the scatter chart still selected, on the Chart Design tab, in the Data group, click the **Select Data** button. The Select Data Source dialog box opens. Refer to Figure 4–33.

Figure 4–33 Select Data Source dialog box

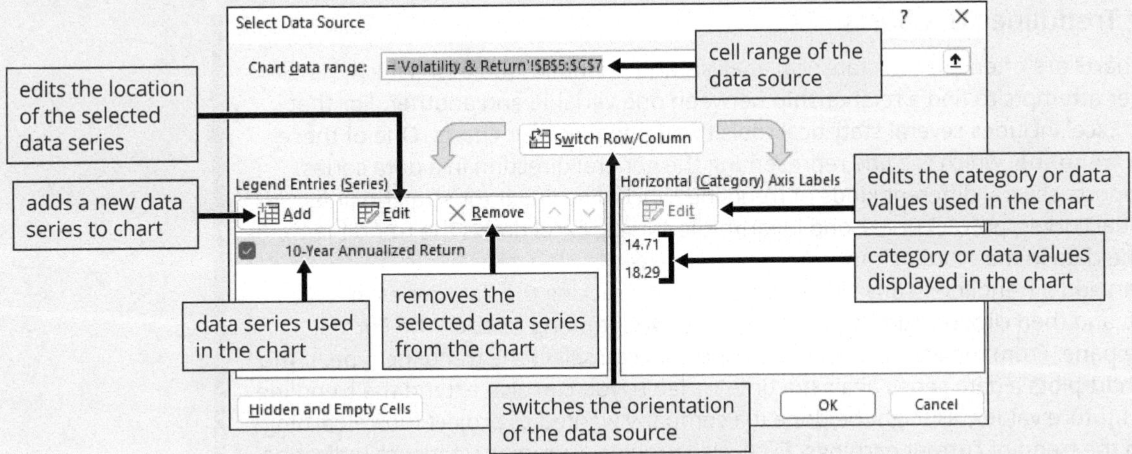

2. Click **Add** to open the Edit Series dialog box. You can add another data series to the chart from here.

   Tip To organize a chart's data source by rows rather than columns (or vice versa), click the Switch Row/Column button in the Select Data Source dialog box.

3. With the insertion point in the Series name box, click the **Volatility & Return** sheet tab, and then click cell **G5** in that worksheet. The expression `='Volatility & Return'!$G$5` is entered into the Series name box.
4. Click the **Series X values** box, and then in the Volatility & Return worksheet, select the range **F6:F14** to enter the expression `='Volatility & Return'!$F$6:$F$14.`
5. Click the **Series Y values** box, delete the expression in that box, and then in the Volatility & Return worksheet, select the range **G6:G14** to enter the expression `='Volatility & Return!'$G$6:$G$14`. Refer to Figure 4–34.

Figure 4–34 Edit Series dialog box

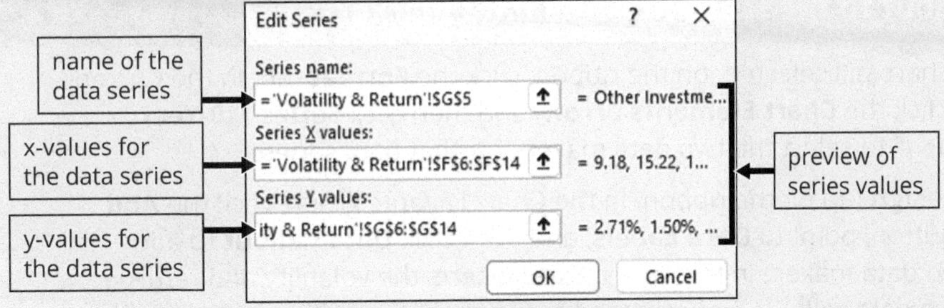

   Key Step Values or expressions might already be entered into the Edit Series dialog box, so you must delete any expressions before inserting a new reference.

6. Click **OK** to return to Select Data Source dialog box. Note that the data series "Other Investment Fund Returns" has been added to the list of data series.
7. Click **OK** to return to the Summary worksheet. Data markers for the second data series are added to the scatter chart.

You have simplified the scatter chart by removing elements that Lydia thinks will not be of interest to the company's investors (such as the exact values of the stock's volatility). However, the chart still needs some descriptive information to aid in its interpretation. You will add this additional text and graphics to the chart and worksheet next.

Insight

Adding Trendlines to Charts

Scatter charts are often used in statistical analysis and scientific studies in which the researcher attempts to find a relationship between one variable and another. For that purpose, Excel includes several statistical tools to augment scatter charts. One of these tools is a **trendline**, which is a line representing the general direction in a data series. Excel supports several different kinds of trendlines, including linear (or straight) lines, exponential curves, power curves, and logarithmic curves. Excel draws the trendline to best fit the data in the scatter chart.

You can add a trendline to any scatter chart by right-clicking the data series in the chart, and then clicking Add Trendline on the shortcut menu to open the Format Trendline pane. From the Format Trendline pane, you can select the trendline type. If the scatter chart plots a data series against a time variable, you can also extend the trendline to project future values, as might be done if a company wanted to project future earnings based on the trend of current earnings. Excel also provides summary statistics indicating how well the trendline fits the data.

Adding Graphic Objects to a Workbook

Another way of enhancing your workbooks is with graphic art. Excel supports a large gallery of clip art and icons to supplement your charts and worksheet data. One graphic feature you can add to charts is a data callout.

Adding a Data Callout to a Chart

Earlier, you used a data label to display percentage values in a pie chart. Another type of data label is a **data callout**, which is a label that appears as a text bubble attached to a data marker. Lydia wants you add data callouts to the S&P 500 and Hamilton Fund data markers. The data callouts should contain the abbreviated names of those two investments so that they can be easily identified by clients viewing the report.

To add a data callout to the scatter chart's data markers:

1. With the scatter chart still selected, on the ribbon, click the **Format** tab. In the Current Selection group, click the **Chart Elements arrow**, and then click **Series "10-Year Annualized Return"** to select the two data makers for that data series.
2. Click the **Chart Design** tab on the ribbon. In the Chart Layouts group, click the **Add Chart Element** button, point to **Data Labels**, and then click **Data Callout** to add callouts to the two data makers in the series. Excel inserts the volatility and return values into the two data callouts. You will change those values, so they reference the abbreviated names of the two investments.
3. Right-click one of the data labels, and then click **Format Data Labels** on the shortcut menu. The Format Data Labels pane opens.
4. In the Label contains section, click the **Value from Cells** check box. The Data Label Range dialog box opens.

   Tip You can change the shape of the callout by right-clicking the data callout, clicking Change Data Label Shapes, and choosing a callout shape.

5. Click the **Volatility & Return** sheet tab, and then select the range **A6:A7** to enter the expression `='Volatility & Return!'$A$6:$A7` in the Select Data Label Range box.
6. Click **OK**. The data labels now include the abbreviated investment names.

7. In the Format Data Labels pane, in the Label Contains section, click the **X Value** and **Y Value** check boxes to deselect them. The data labels only display the abbreviated investment names. Refer to Figure 4–35.

Figure 4–35 Data callouts added to the scatter chart

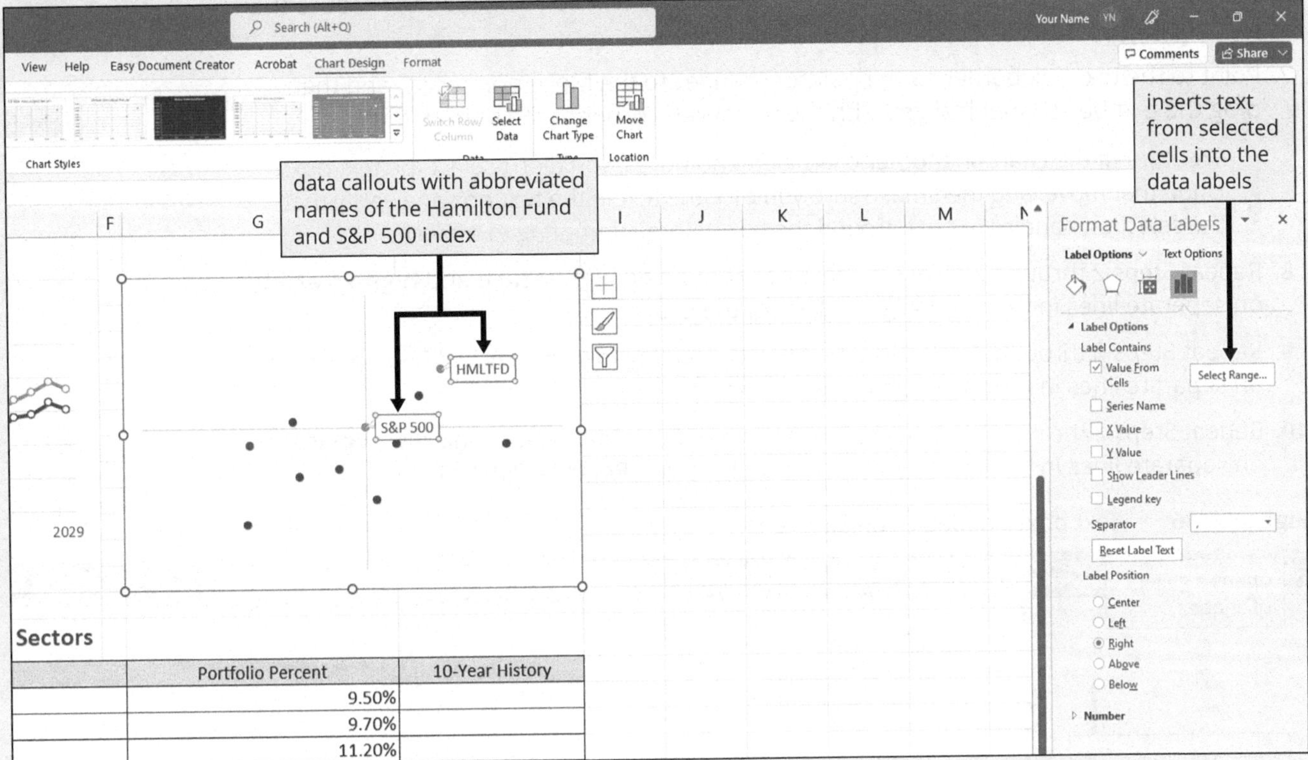

8. Close the Format Data Labels pane.

Inserting a Graphic Shape

Microsoft Office supports a gallery of over 160 shapes that can be added to any workbook or other Office document. The Shapes gallery includes rectangles, circles, arrows, stars, flow chart symbols, and text boxes. Each shape can be resized and formatted with a wide selection of colors, line styles, and special effects such as drop shadows and glowing borders. You can insert text strings, including numbered and bulleted lists, to any graphic shape.

Lydia asks you to complete the return rate/volatility scatter chart by inserting text boxes in the four corners of the chart, indicating which chart quadrant corresponds to high or low return rates and high or low volatility. You will insert the text boxes from the Shapes gallery.

To insert a text box:

1. With the scatter chart still selected, click the **Insert** tab on the ribbon.
2. In the Illustrations group, click the **Shapes** button. The Shapes gallery opens, organized into the categories of Recently Used Shapes, Lines, Rectangles, Basic Shapes, Block Arrows, Equations Shapes, Flowchart, Stars and Banners, and Callouts.

   Trouble? Depending on your monitor and settings, you may not see the Shapes button in the Illustrations group. In that case, click the Illustrations button in the Illustrations group, and then click the Shapes button.

3. In the Basic Shapes group, click the **Text Box** shape. The pointer changes to the Create Text pointer.

4. Click near the upper-left corner of the scatter chart. A text box is added. You will enter text here.
5. Type **high return** as the first line of text in the text box, press **ENTER**, and then type **low volatility** as the second line of text in the text box.
6. Click and drag the **sizing handles** around the selected text box as needed to reduce the text box to fit the text.
7. Point to the text box border so the pointer changes to the Move pointer, and then drag the text box so that it aligns with the upper-left corner of the scatter chart.

    Trouble? If the chart or another chart element moves, you didn't select the text box. Undo that move, and then make sure you click the text in the text box and verify that the selection handles appear around the box before attempting to move it.

8. Repeat Steps 2 through 7 to insert a text box containing **high return** and **high volatility** on separate lines in the upper-right corner of the chart.
9. Repeat Steps 2 through 7 to insert a text box containing **low return** and **low volatility** on separate lines in the lower-left corner of the chart.
10. Repeat Steps 2 through 7 to insert a text box containing **low return** and **high volatility** on separate lines in the lower-right corner of the chart. Refer to Figure 4–36.

Figure 4–36 Text boxes added to an Excel chart

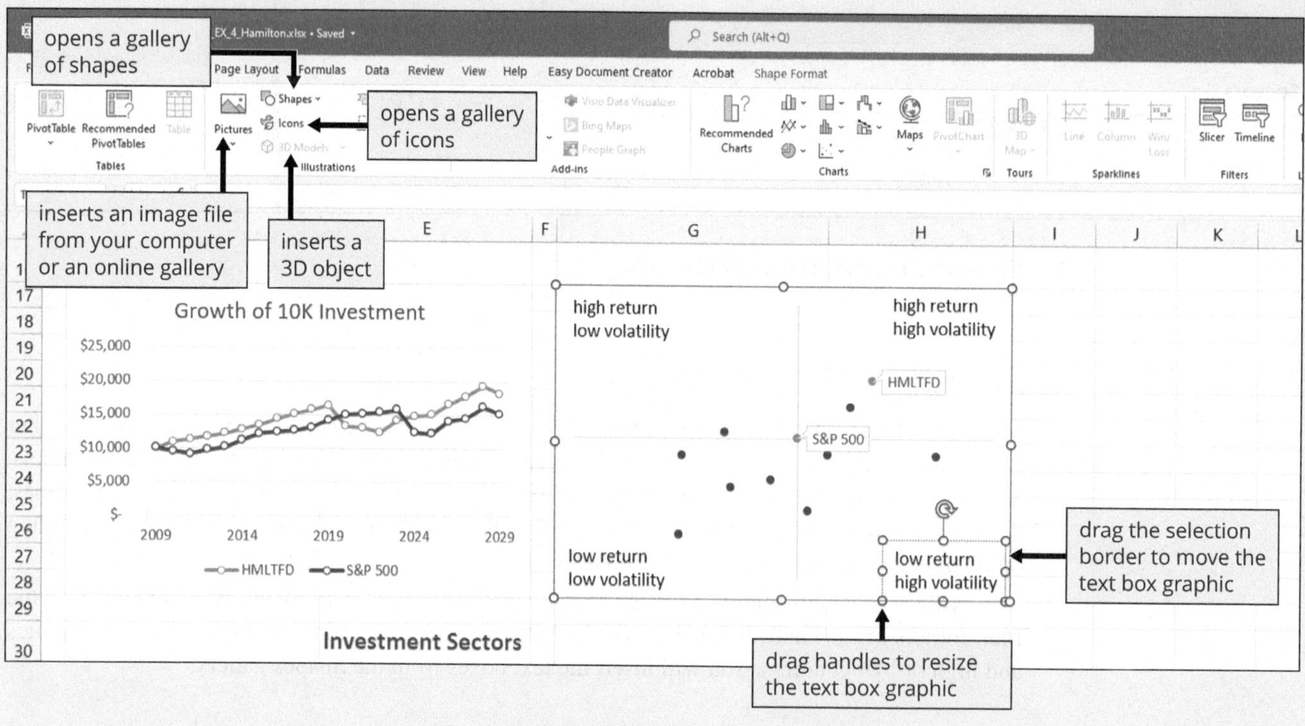

With the final version of the scatter chart, Lydia's clients can quickly identify the Hamilton Fund as a high return, high volatility investment, particularly when compared to the S&P 500 index and other sample investments.

Exploring Other Chart Types

At this point, you have used only a few of the many Excel chart types. Excel has other chart types that are useful for financial and scientific research, which you can access from the Charts group on the Insert tab. If you want to change the chart type of an existing chart, click the Change Chart Type button in the Type group on the Chart Design tab and then select the new chart type from the dialog box.

Hierarchy Charts

Hierarchy charts are like pie charts in that they show the relative contribution of groups to a whole. Unlike pie charts, a hierarchy chart also shows the organizational structure of the data with subcategories displayed within main categories. Excel supports two types of hierarchy charts: treemap charts and sunburst charts.

In a **treemap chart**, each category is placed within a rectangle, and subcategories are nested as rectangles within those rectangles. The rectangles are sized to show the relative proportions of the two groups based on values from a data series. The treemap chart in Figure 4–37 shows the investor sectors of the Hamilton Fund broken down by group and category. You can create a treemap chart by clicking the Recommended Charts button and then selecting Treemap from the list of chart types on the All Charts tab.

Figure 4–37 Treemap and Sunburst charts

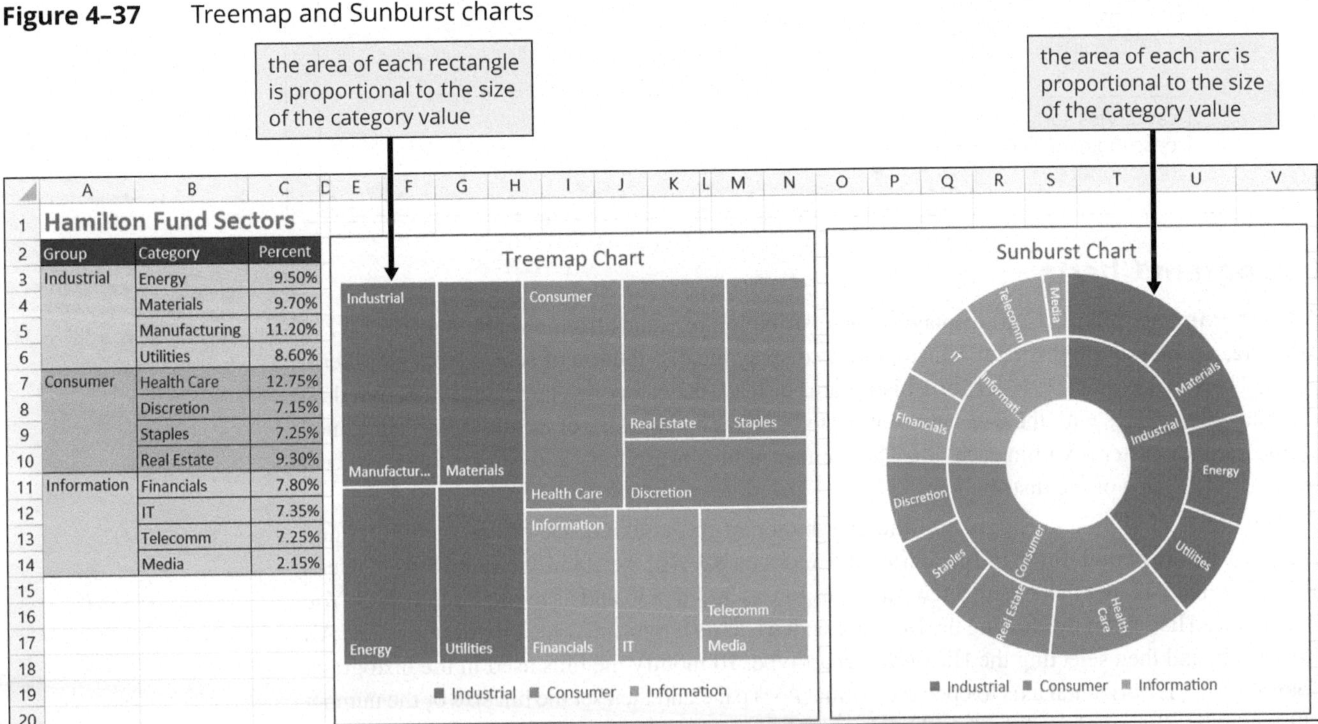

Hamilton Fund Sectors

Group	Category	Percent
Industrial	Energy	9.50%
	Materials	9.70%
	Manufacturing	11.20%
	Utilities	8.60%
Consumer	Health Care	12.75%
	Discretion	7.15%
	Staples	7.25%
	Real Estate	9.30%
Information	Financials	7.80%
	IT	7.35%
	Telecomm	7.25%
	Media	2.15%

A **sunburst chart** organizes hierarchical data through a series of concentric rings with the innermost rings showing the highest category levels and the outer rings showing categories from lower levels. The size of the rings indicates the relative proportions of the different groups and categories within groups. Refer back to Figure 4–37. Sunburst charts are better than treemap charts at conveying information from multiple levels of nested groups. But treemaps are better at displaying the relative sizes of the categories within each group level. You can create a sunburst chart by clicking the Recommended Charts button and then selecting Sunburst from the list of chart types on the All Charts tab.

Pareto Charts

A special kind of combination chart is the **Pareto chart**, which combines a column chart and a line chart to indicate which factors are the largest contributors to the whole. Figure 4–38 shows a Pareto chart of investment categories. The categories are sorted in descending order of importance so that the largest investment category, Health Care, is listed first followed by Manufacturing, Materials, Energy, and so forth. The line chart provides a running total of the percentage that each category adds to the overall total. Roughly 50% of the Hamilton Fund is invested in the first five categories listed in the chart.

Pareto charts are often used in quality control studies to isolate the most significant factors in the failure of a manufacturer process. They are also used in market research to indicate which factors and combination of factors are the most crucial in consumer choices. You can create a Pareto chart by clicking the Recommended Charts button, clicking Histogram on the All Charts tab, and then clicking the Pareto chart type.

Figure 4–38 Pareto chart

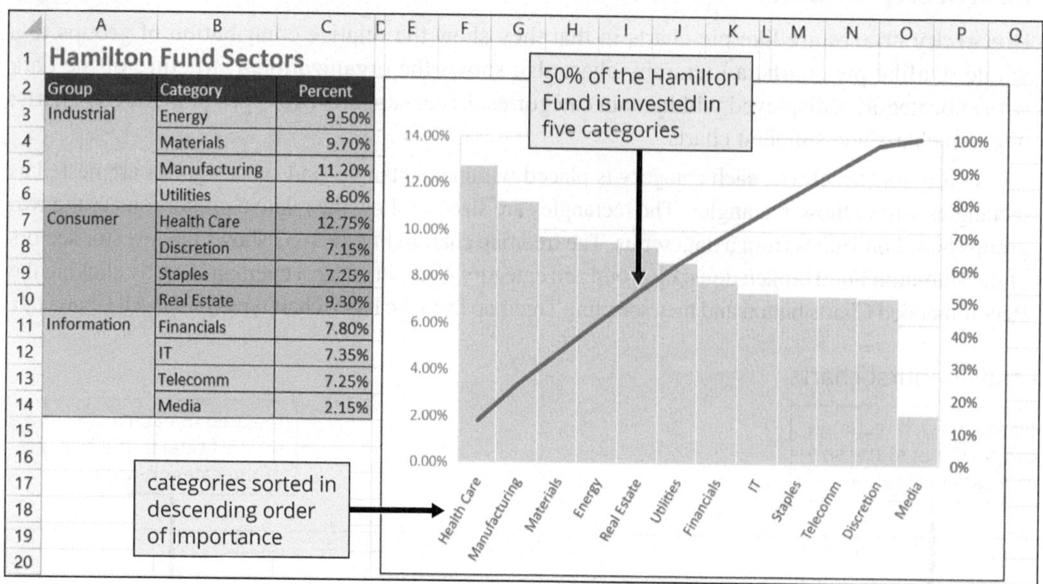

Histogram Charts

A **histogram** is a column chart displaying the distribution of values from a single data series. For example, a professor might create a histogram to display the distribution of scores from a midterm exam. There is no category series for a histogram. Instead, the categories are determined based on the data series values with the data values allocated to **bins** and the size of the columns determined by the number of items within each bin. The number of bins is arbitrary and can be chosen to best represent the shape of the distribution.

Figure 4–39 shows a histogram of the distribution of the weekly price of the Hamilton Fund over a 15-month period. From the histogram the midpoint price of the Hamilton Fund falls between about $41 and $42, but there were a few values as low as $35 to $36 and as high as $48 to $49. You can create a Histogram by clicking the Recommended Charts button, clicking Histogram on the All Charts tab, and then selecting the Histogram chart type. To modify the bins used in the histogram, double-click the horizontal axis to open the Format Axis pane and then set the bin size or the number of bins in the Bins section of the Axis Options section.

Figure 4–39 Histogram chart

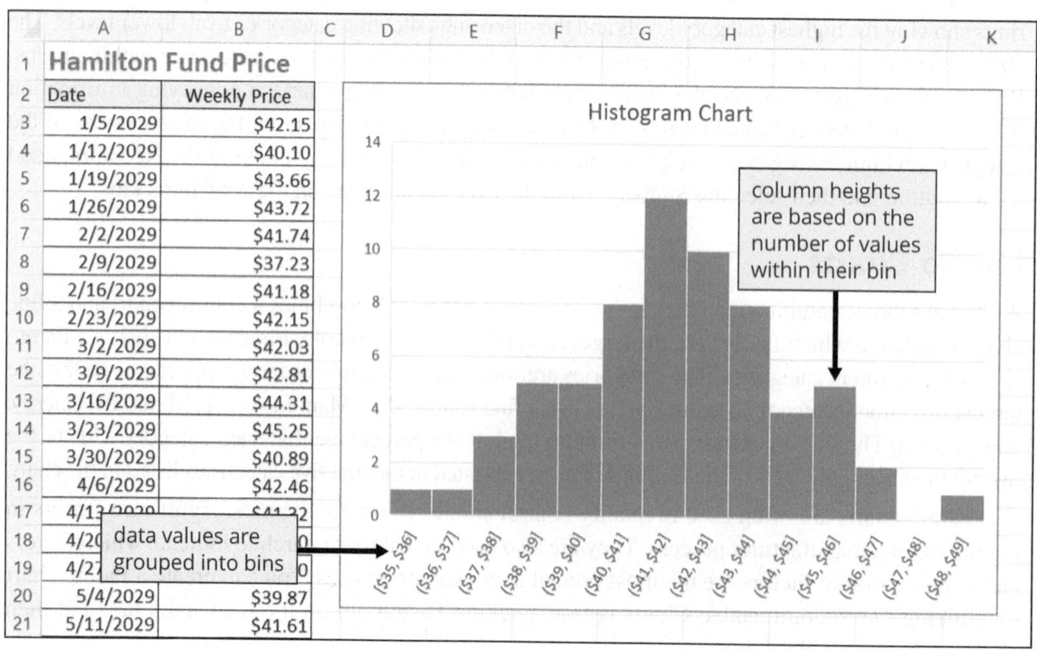

Waterfall Charts

A **waterfall chart** tracks the addition and subtraction of values within a sum. Figure 4–40 shows a waterfall chart of the value of an investment in the Hamilton Fund over 10 years. The initial and final value of the fund are shown in dark gray. Positive changes in the fund's value are shown in green. Years in which the fund decreased in value are shown in red. The waterfall chart is so named because the increasing and decreasing steps in the graph resemble a waterfall. Waterfall charts are often used with Profit and Loss statements to track the impact of revenue and expenses on a company's net profit.

Figure 4–40 Waterfall chart

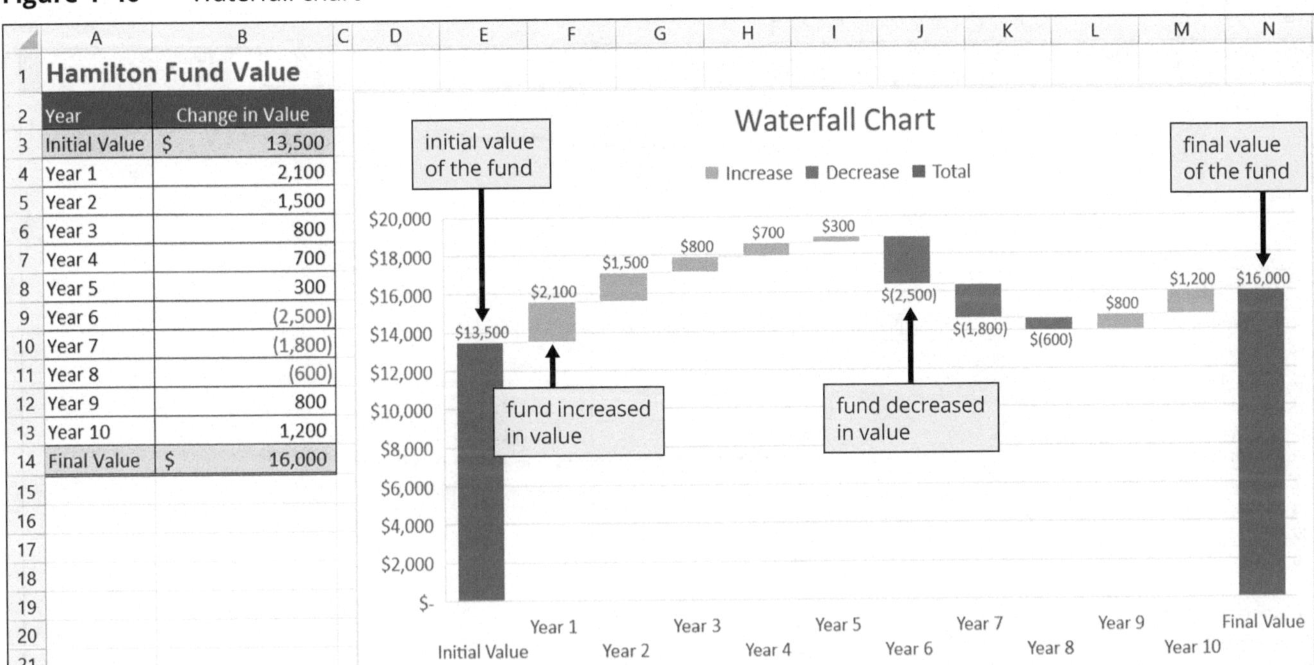

Creating Data Bars

So far, the charts you created have been embedded as objects on a worksheet. You can also create charts that appear in worksheet cells. Data bars are one of these types of charts.

A data bar is a conditional format that adds a horizontal bar to a cell background. The length of the bar is based on the value stored in the cell. Cells storing larger values display longer data bars; cells with smaller values have shorter bars. When applied to a range of cells, the data bars have the same appearance as a bar chart, with each cell displaying a single bar. Like all conditional formats, data bars are dynamic, changing their lengths as the cell's value changes.

Reference

Creating Data Bars

- Select the range containing the data to be charted.
- On the Home tab, in the Styles group, click the Conditional Formatting button, point to Data Bars, and then click the data bar style you want to use.
- To modify the data bar rules, click the Conditional Formatting button, and then click Manage Rules.

The Hamilton Fund invests in different sectors of the economy. The percentage invested in each sector is displayed in the range E31:G43 of the Summary worksheet. You'll enhance the percentage values in column G using data bars with the length of each bar matching the percentage invested.

To add data bars to the portfolio percentages in the worksheet:

1. On the Summary worksheet, select the range **G32:G43**.
2. On the ribbon, click the **Home** tab. In the Styles group, click the **Conditional Formatting** button, and then click **Data Bars**. A gallery of data bar styles opens.
3. In the Gradient Fill section, click the **Orange Data Bar** style (the first style in the second row). Orange data bars are added to the selected cells.
4. Click cell **E30** to deselect the range. Refer to Figure 4–41.

Figure 4–41 Portfolio percentages displayed with data bars

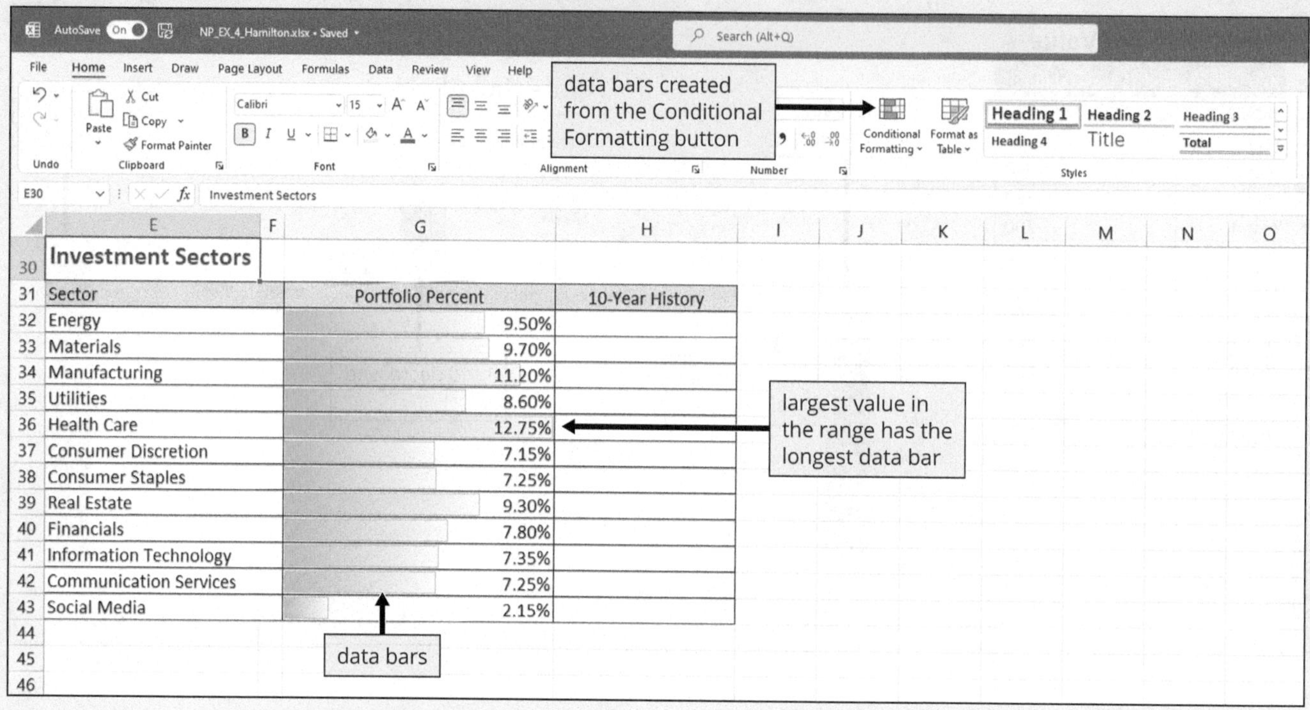

The data bars allow comparison of the relative size of the investment sectors for the Hamilton Fund. However, some of the data bars cover their cell value. Lydia wants you to shorten the length of the bars so that there is no overlap.

Modifying a Data Bar Rule

By default, the cell with the largest value in the range will have a data bar that stretches across the entire width of the cell. You can modify the length of the data bars by altering the rules of the conditional format.

> **Tip** When the range contains negative values, the data bars originate from the center of the cell—negative bars extend to the left, and positive bars extend to the right.

The longest data bar is in cell G36, representing the amount of the fund invested in health care (12.75%). You'll modify the conditional format rule for the data bar, setting the maximum length to 0.25 so that the longest bar doesn't overlap the value in its cell.

To modify the data bar conditional formatting rule:

1. On the Home tab, in the Styles group, click the **Conditional Formatting** button, and then click **Manage Rules**. The Conditional Formatting Rules Manager dialog box opens, displaying all the rules applied to any conditional format in the workbook.

2. In the Show formatting rules for box, select **This Worksheet** to show all the conditional formatting rules for the current sheet.
3. With the Data Bar rule selected, click the **Edit Rule** button. The Edit Formatting Rule dialog box opens.
4. In the Type row, click the **Maximum arrow**, and then click **Number**.
5. Press **TAB** to move the insertion point to the Maximum box in the Value row, and then type **0.25**. All data bar lengths will then be defined relative to this value. Refer to Figure 4–42.

Figure 4–42 Edit Formatting Rule dialog box

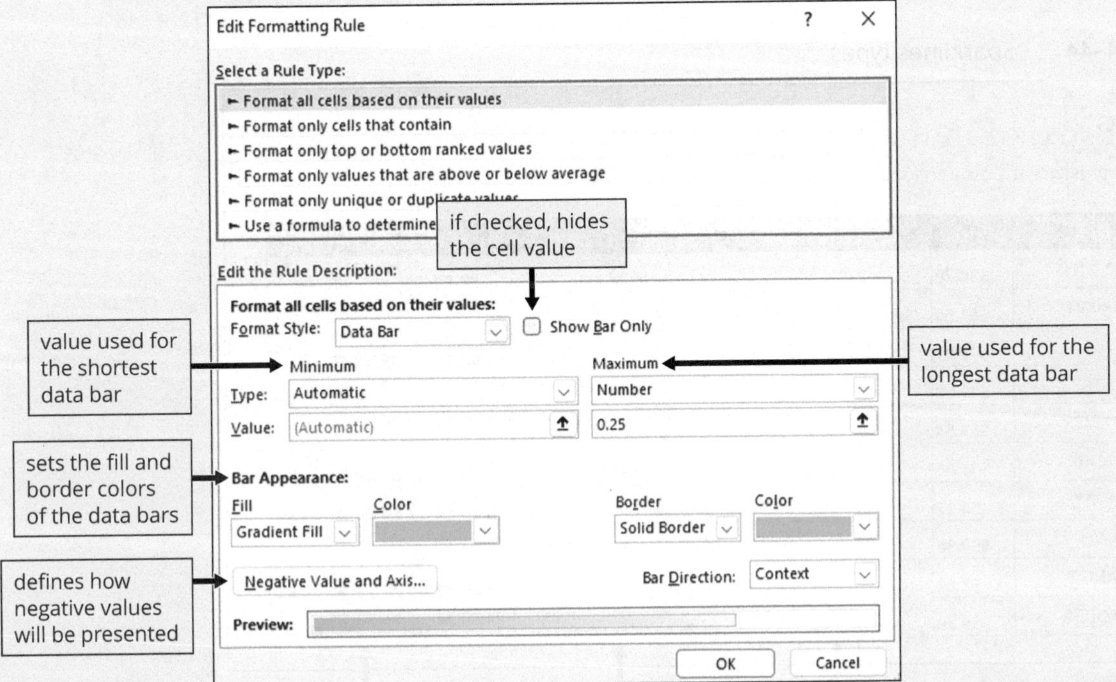

6. Click **OK** in each dialog box to return to the worksheet, and then verify that the data bars no longer span the width of the selected cells. Refer to Figure 4–43.

Figure 4–43 Resized data bars

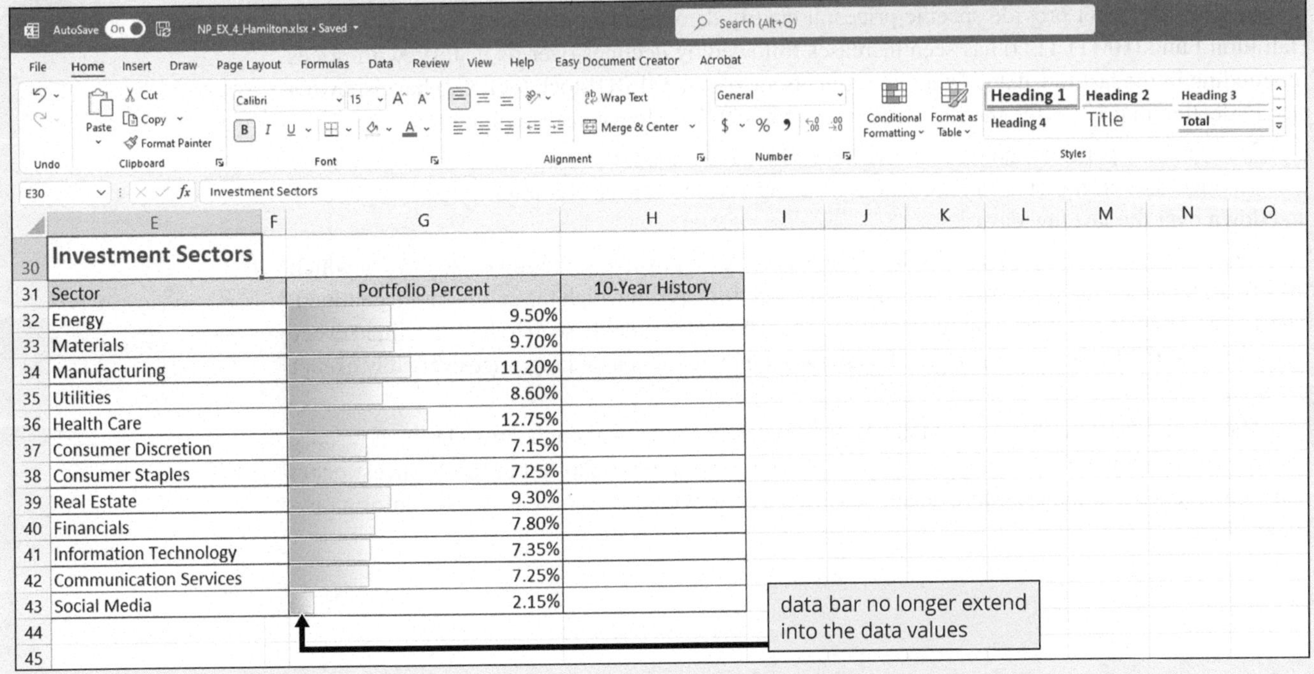

Creating Sparklines

Another way of adding a chart to a cell is with a sparkline, which is a small chart completely confined to the borders of a single cell. Because of their small size, sparklines do not include chart elements such as legends, titles, or gridlines. The goal of a sparkline is to display the maximum amount of information in the smallest space. As a result, sparklines are useful when you only need to convey a general impression of the data without specific details.

Excel supports three types of sparklines: line sparklines, column sparklines, and win/loss sparklines. Figure 4–44 includes an example of each type of sparkline in which the price history, shares traded, and increases and declines of 10 investments are displayed within a worksheet.

Figure 4–44 Sparklines types

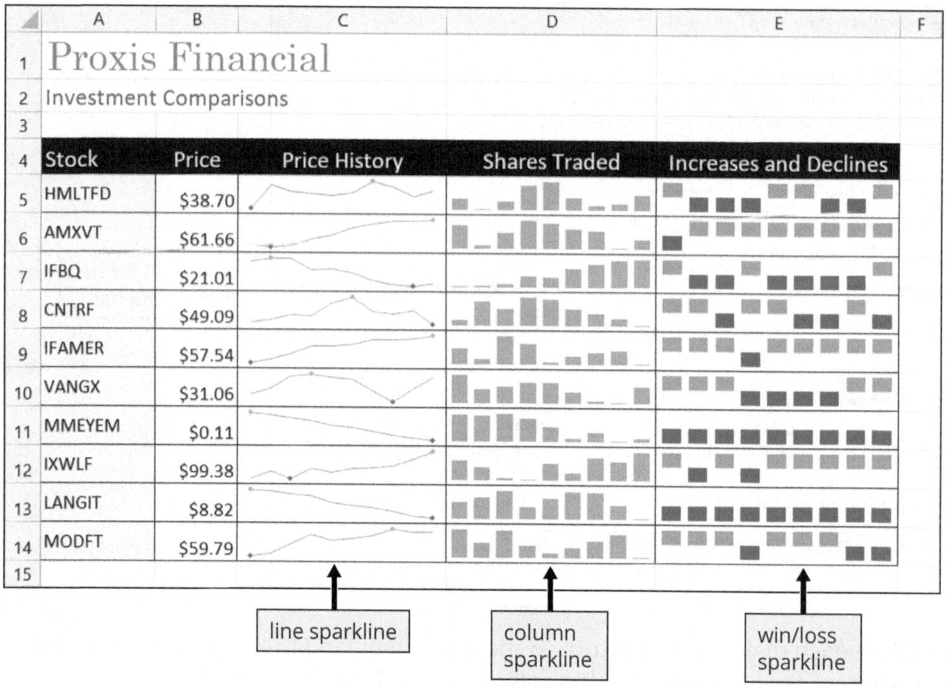

Proxis Financial

Investment Comparisons

Stock	Price	Price History	Shares Traded	Increases and Declines
HMLTFD	$38.70			
AMXVT	$61.66			
IFBQ	$21.01			
CNTRF	$49.09			
IFAMER	$57.54			
VANGX	$31.06			
MMEYEM	$0.11			
IXWLF	$99.38			
LANGIT	$8.82			
MODFT	$59.79			

line sparkline

column sparkline

win/loss sparkline

The line sparkline indicates the daily fluctuation in the selling price of each investment. While the sparkline does not provide specific prices, it clearly demonstrates that the selling price of the Hamilton Fund (HMTLTFD) has seen increases followed by declines over its history, with prices rebounding in the last few days. Other investments such as the IFBQ stock (cell C7) have shown a steady decline in price while the IFAMER stock (cell C9) has shown a steady increase.

The column sparkline indicates the volume of shares traded. Once again, specific details are not provided, but an investor can see that the trading volume for the Hamilton Fund has gone up and down over the last few days.

Finally, the win/loss sparkline displays a green block for positive values on those days in which the investment's selling price increased and a red block for days in which the selling price declined. The selling price of an investment like MMEYEM (cell E11) is quickly seen to have declined every day, while the IFAMER investment (cell E9) showed an increase in its selling price every day except the first.

The range C5:E14 in Figure 4–44 displays 30 different charts. Although these charts show only general trends, they give the investor a quick and easily interpreted snapshot of the 10 investments and their recent performance. More details can always be provided elsewhere with more informative Excel charts.

Insight

Edward Tufte and Chart Design Theory

Any study of chart design will include the works of Edward Tufte, who pioneered the field of information design. One of Tufte's most important works is *The Visual Display of Quantitative Information*, in which he laid out several principles for the design of charts and graphics.

Tufte was concerned with what he termed as "chart junk," in which a proliferation of chart elements—chosen because they look "nice"—confuse and distract the reader. One measure of chart junk is Tufte's data-ink ratio, which is the amount of "ink" used to display quantitative information compared to the total ink required by the chart. Tufte advocated limiting nondata ink, which is any part of the chart that does not convey information about the data. One way of measuring the data-ink ratio is to determine how much of the chart you can erase without affecting the user's ability to interpret your data. Tufte argued for high data-ink ratios with a minimum of extraneous elements and graphics.

To this end, Tufte helped develop sparklines, which convey information with a high data-ink ratio within a compact space. Tufte believed that charts that can be viewed and comprehended briefly have a greater impact on the reader than large and cluttered graphs, no matter how attractive they might be.

Note that the cells containing sparklines do not need to be blank because the sparklines are part of the cell background and do not replace any content.

Reference

Creating and Editing Sparklines

- On the Insert tab, in the Sparklines group, click the Line, Column, or Win/Loss button to open the Create Sparklines dialog box.
- In the Data Range box, enter the range for the data source of the sparkline.
- In the Location Range box, enter the range into which to place the sparkline.
- Click OK.
- On the Sparkline tab, in the Show group, click the appropriate check boxes to specify which markers to display on the sparkline.
- In the Group group, click the Axis button, and then click Show Axis to add an axis to the sparkline.

Lydia wants you to use line sparklines in the range H32:H43 of the Summary worksheet to display the general trend of the growth of the Hamilton Fund's investment into 12 economic sectors.

To create the line sparklines showing the sector history growth trends:

1. Select the range **H32:H43** in the Summary worksheet.
2. On the ribbon, click the **Insert** tab, and then in the Sparklines group, click the **Line** button. The Create Sparklines dialog box opens.
3. Make sure the insertion point is in the Data Range box, click the **Sector History** sheet tab, and then select the range **B6:M45** in the Sector History worksheet. This range contains the growth of investments in 12 economic sectors given a hypothetical $10,000 initial investment.

4. Verify that the range **$H$32:$H$43** is entered in the Location Range box. Refer to Figure 4–45.

Figure 4–45 Create Sparklines dialog box

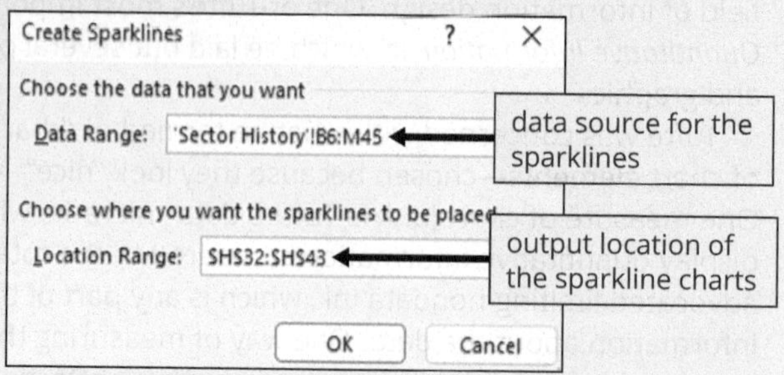

5. Click **OK** to insert the sparklines into the range H32:H43 of the Summary worksheet. Refer to Figure 4–46.

Figure 4–46 Line sparklines in the Summary worksheet

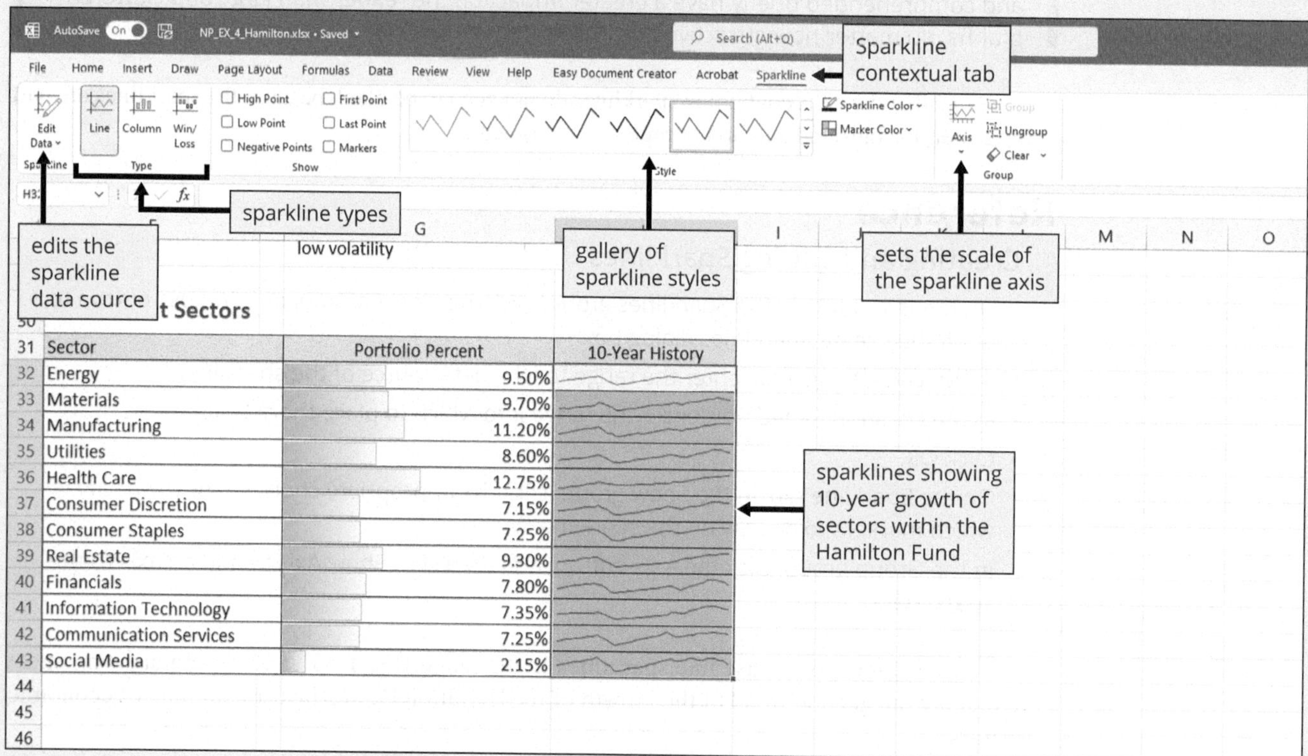

The Sparkline contextual tab appears on the ribbon when a sparkline is selected. From this tab, you can change the sparkline type, edit the sparkline's data source, and format the sparkline's appearance.

Formatting a Sparkline

Because of their compact size, sparklines have fewer formatting options than other Excel charts. You can add data markers to highlight low and high values, initial and ending values, and negative values. From the Style gallery on the Sparkline tab, you can apply built-in styles to the sparklines. From the Sparkline Color and Marker Color buttons in the Style group, you can set the color of the sparklines and their data markers.

Lydia wants you to add data markers identifying the low and high points within the time interval to each sparkline and to change the sparkline color to dark orange.

To format the sparklines:

1. In the Summary worksheet, make sure the sparklines in the range H32:H43 are still selected.
2. On the Sparkline tab, in the Show group, click the **High Point** and **Low Point** check boxes. Two data markers appear on each sparkline identifying the high and low points.
3. In the Style group, click the **Sparkline Color** button, and then click the **Orange, Accent 1, Darker 25%** theme color (the fifth theme color in the fifth row) in the color palette. The sparkline colors change to orange.
4. In the Style group, click the **Marker Color** button, point to **High Point**, and then click the **Green** standard color. The high point data marker color changes to green.
5. Click the **Marker Color** button, click **Low Point**, and then click the **Red** standard color. The low point data marker color changes to red.
6. Click cell **I30** to deselect the sparklines. Refer to Figure 4–47.

Figure 4–47 Formatted sparklines

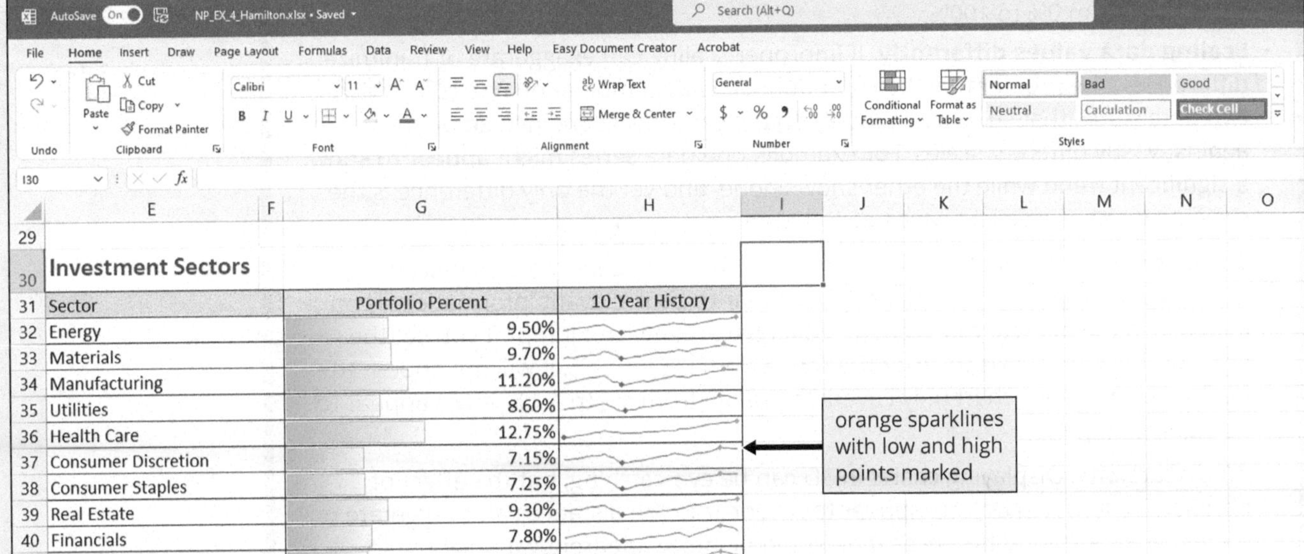

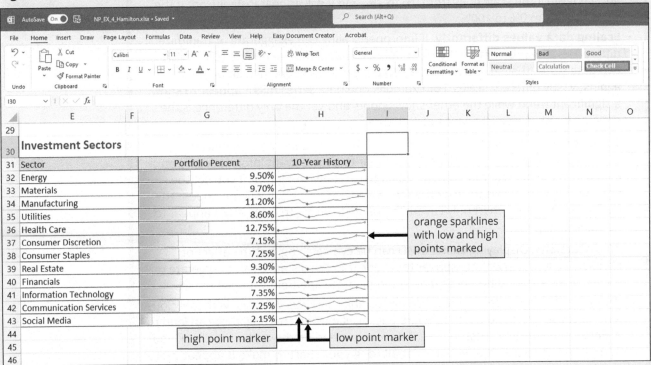

7. sam Save the workbook, and then close it.

The sparklines show that the 12 economic sectors experienced the same general growth trend over the previous 10 years with negative growth occurring around years 3 and 4 followed by steady growth thereafter. The lowest for all sectors seem to come around the fourth year.

Sparkline Groups and Sparkline Axes

Sparklines are grouped together by default so that the format choices are applied to every sparkline chart in the group. Grouping ensures that sparklines for related data series are formatted consistently. To format a single sparkline, click the cell containing the sparkline and then click the Ungroup button in the Group group on the Sparkline tab. The selected sparkline is split from the rest of the sparkline group. You can then apply a unique format to it. To regroup the sparklines, select all the cells containing the sparklines, and then click the Group button in the Group group.

Excel displays each sparkline on its own vertical axis ranging from the data series' low point and high point. That means comparing one sparkline to another can be misleading if they are all plotted on a different scale. You can modify the vertical axes by clicking the Axis button in the Group group on the Sparkline tab. To ensure that the vertical scale is the same for all charts in the sparkline group, click the Same for All Sparklines option for both the minimum and maximum scale values. To explicitly define the scale of the vertical axis, click the Custom Value option and specify the minimum and maximum values.

Proskills

Written Communication: Honesty in Charting

One of the great challenges in chart design is to not mislead your audience by misrepresenting the data. Here are a few of the ways in which a chart, created even with the best of intentions, can mislead the viewer:

- **Improper scaling.** This is a very common mistake in which the range of the data scale is set so narrow that even small changes seem large or so wide that all values appear to be the same. For example, a 1% change in a data value will appear large if the scale goes from 0% to 2%, and it will appear insignificant if the scale goes from 0% to 100%.
- **Scaling data values differently.** If improper scaling can exaggerate or minimize differences, the problem can be compounded with combination charts in which two data series that should be plotted on the same scale are instead plotted against vastly different scales. For example, one data series might appear to show a significant trend while the other shows none, and yet the only difference is the scale on which the values have been plotted.
- **Truncating the vertical axis.** You can make trends appear more significant than they are if you cut off what might appear to be irrelevant information. Is an increase in the interest rate from 4% to 4.05% a significant jump? If you set the scale of the vertical axis to cover the range from 0% to 4.1%, it will not appear to be. However, if your chart only covers the range from 4% to 4.1%, it will appear to be significant jump.
- **3D distortions.** Displaying charts in 3D can be eye-catching, but the effect of perspective in which objects appear to recede into the distance can exaggerate or minimize important differences that would be more apparent with a 2D chart.

To be fair, one should not assume that a misleading chart was designed with malicious intent. Because Excel and other software packages include charting, they can lead to the kinds of mistakes discussed here. To avoid misleading the audience, check your assumptions and verify that you are not altering your chart to make it appear more dramatic or interesting. View your charts under different formatting options to confirm that it is truly the data that is telling the story.

You have finished creating charts and graphics to summarize the history and performance of the Hamilton Fund. Lydia is pleased that so much information fits on a single worksheet. Figure 4–48 shows a preview of the printed Summary sheet containing all the charts created for the report.

Figure 4–48 Final Summary report

Proxis Financial

Hamilton Fund Summary

Description

The Hamilton Fund (HMLTFD) employs a balanced approach using a diversified portfolio of quality stocks and bonds, seeking capital conservation, current income and long-term growth of capital and income. By primarily investing in inflation-linked securities, the Sunrise Fund seeks to provide both inflation protection and high rates of growth

Fund Facts

Ticker Symbol	HMLTFD
Morningstar Rating	4 stars
Price At NAV	$43.75
Fund Assets ($millions)	$163,480
Fund Inception	7/22/2005
Companies/Issuers	540+
Shareholder Accounts	379,150

Regular Dividends Paid	Mar, Jun, Sep, Dec
Minimum Initial Investment	$750
Capital Gains Paid	Jun, Dec
Portfolio Turnover	85%
Fiscal Year-End	Dec
Fund Number	974
Portfolio Managers	18

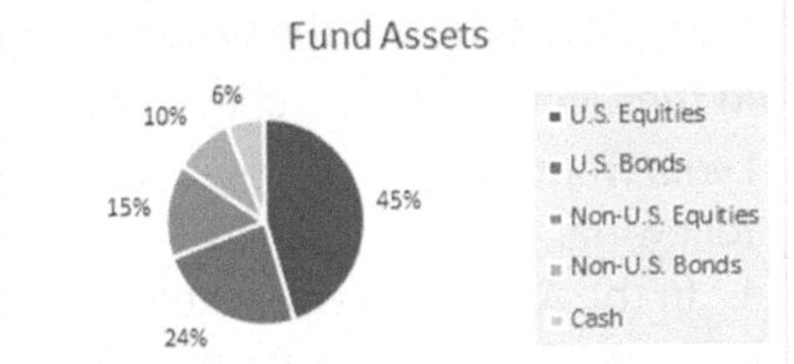

Fund Performance

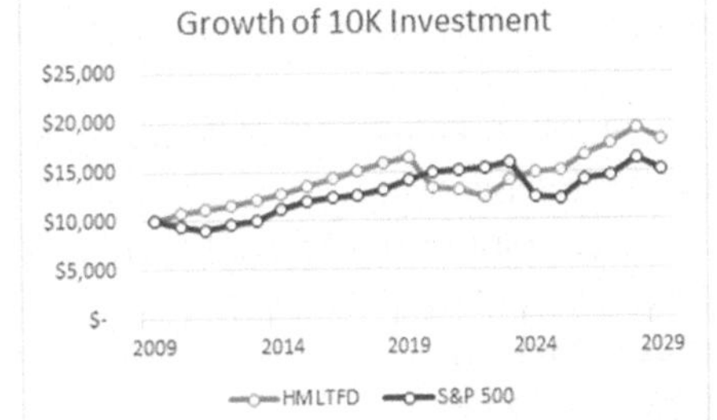

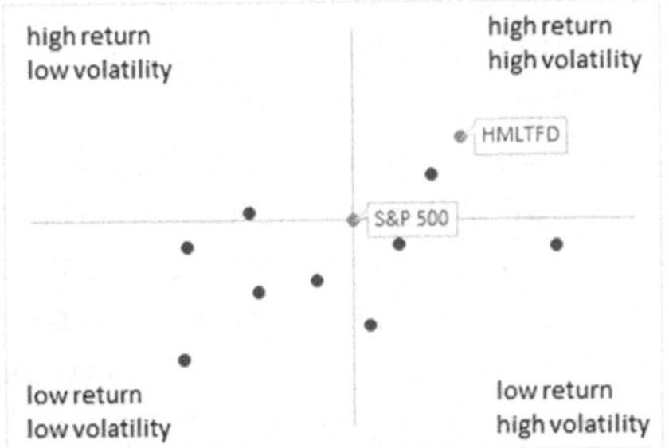

Recent Performance

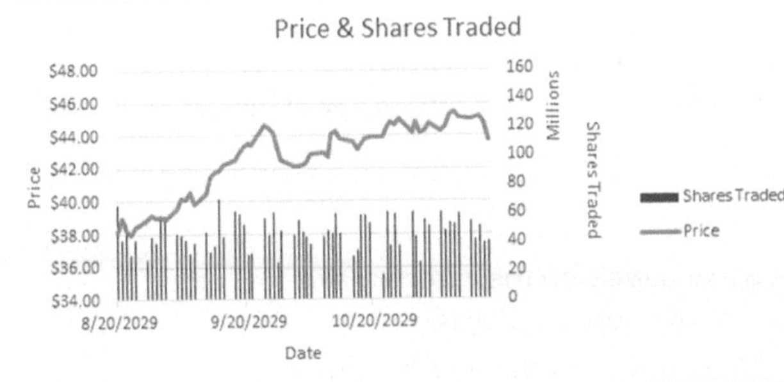

Investment Sectors

Sector	Portfolio Percent	10-Year History
Energy	9.50%	
Materials	9.70%	
Manufacturing	11.20%	
Utilities	8.60%	
Health Care	12.75%	
Consumer Discretion	7.15%	
Consumer Staples	7.25%	
Real Estate	9.30%	
Financials	7.80%	
Information Technology	7.35%	
Communication Services	7.25%	
Social Media	2.15%	

Lydia appreciates your help in creating the summary report. Later you will help her apply this type of formatting to workbooks containing investment data from other funds.

Part 4.2 Quick Check

1. You want to create a chart of temperature versus time, but the time points are not evenly spaced. Should you create a scatter chart or a line chart? Why?
2. When would you use a treemap or sunburst chart?
3. Which chart should you use to display categories arranged in descending order of value along with a line chart that tracks the cumulative percentage from the categories?
4. When would you use a Waterfall chart?
5. Which chart should you use to display the distribution of values from a data series?
6. When would you use a sparkline in place of a line chart in a report?
7. Describe the three types of sparklines.
8. When would you use data bars in place of a column or bar chart in a report?

Practice: Review Assignments

Data File needed for the Review Assignments: NP_EX_4-2.xlsx

Lydia wants you to develop another investment report for the Adams Fund. As with the report you generated for the Hamilton Fund, this workbook will include a worksheet that uses Excel charts and graphics to summarize financial data about the fund. Complete the following:

1. Open the **NP_EX_4-2.xlsx** workbook located in the Excel4 > Review folder included with your Data Files, and then save the workbook as **NP_EX_4_Adams** in the location specified by your instructor.
2. In the Documentation sheet, enter your name and the date in the range B3:B4.
3. Lydia wants a pie chart that breaks down the allocation of the assets in the Adams Fund. Do the following:
   a. In the Allocation worksheet, create a pie chart from the data in the range A4:B8.
   b. Move the pie chart to the Prospectus worksheet, and then resize the chart to cover the range D7:E14.
   c. Place the legend on the right side of the chart area.
   d. Change the color scheme to the Monochromatic Palette 6.
   e. Add data labels showing the percentage allocated to each category, positioning the label on the outside end of each pie slice.
4. Lydia wants the report to display a column chart of the month-end returns for the Adams Fund and the S&P 500 over different time intervals. Do the following:
   a. In the Returns worksheet, create a clustered column chart from the data in the range A4:C9.
   b. Move the chart to the Prospectus worksheet, and then resize the chart to cover the range F7:H14.
   c. Change the chart title to **Investment Comparison**.
   d. Place the legend on the right side of the chart area.
5. Lydia wants a line chart comparing the growth of a theoretical investment of $10,000 in the Adams Fund and the S&P 500 over the past 10 years. Do the following:
   a. In the Growth worksheet, create a line chart of the data in the range A4:C25, using the line chart from the list of recommended charts. (The Year value appears on the horizontal axis.)
   b. Move the chart to the Prospectus worksheet, and then resize the chart to cover the range D15:E24.
   c. Change the chart title to **Growth of 10K Investment**.
   d. Add primary major vertical gridlines to the chart.
   e. Place the legend on the right side of the chart area.
   f. Change the interval between the major tick marks and between labels on the category axis to 5 units so that the years 2009, 2014, 2019, 2024, and 2029 appear on the horizontal axis.
6. Lydia wants the report to show the recent selling price and shares traded of the Adams Fund in a combination chart. Do the following:
   a. In the Recent History worksheet, create a combination chart of the data in the range A4:C58. Display the price data as a line chart plotted on the primary axis and the shares traded data as a clustered column chart plotted on the secondary axis.
   b. Move the chart to the Prospectus worksheet, and then resize the chart to cover the range A26:D39.
   c. Change the chart title to **Recent History**.
   d. Display axis titles on the chart. Change the primary vertical axis title to **Price**, the secondary vertical axis title to **Shares Traded**, and the category axis title to **Date**. Change the angle of rotation of the Shares Traded axis title to Rotate Text Down.
   e. Place the legend on the right side of the chart area.
   f. Change the scale of the secondary axis to go from 0 to 1.6E08 and display the scale in units of 1 million and display the unit label on the chart.

7. Lydia needs to compare the return rate and volatility of the Adams Fund to other investment vehicles. Do the following:
   a. In the Performance worksheet, create a scatter chart from the data in the range B5:C7 using the scatter chart from the list of recommended charts.
   b. Move the chart to the Prospectus worksheet, and then resize the chart to cover the range F15:H24.
   c. Remove the chart title and the gridlines from the chart.
   d. Rescale the vertical axis to go from 0.0 to 0.06 with the horizontal axis crossing at 0.031. Rescale the horizontal axis to go from 4 to 24 with the vertical axis crossing at 14.71.
   e. Set the label position to none for both the vertical and horizontal axis labels.
   f. Add data labels to the data markers in the data series. Format the data labels to show data callout bubbles and show only the text from the range A6:A7 in the Performance worksheet. Do not show X or Y values in the callout.
8. Complete the scatter chart by adding a new data series to the chart with cell G5 in the Performance worksheet as the series name, the range F6:F15 in the Performance worksheet as the Series X values, and the range G6:G15 in the Performance worksheet as the Series Y values. If necessary, remove any callouts for the new data values by selecting them and pressing DELETE.
9. Add the four text boxes shown earlier in Figure 4–28 to the scatter chart, placing the return and volatility descriptions on separate lines. Resize and move the text boxes so that they align with the chart corners.
10. Add solid blue data bars to the values in the range G28:G39. Keep the data bars from overlapping the values in those cells by modifying the conditional formatting rule so that the maximum length of the data bar corresponds to a value of 0.30.
11. Add line sparklines to the range H28:H39 using the data values from the range B6:M45 of the Sectors worksheet. Add data markers for the high and low points of each sparkline using the Red standard color.
12. Save the workbook, and then close it.

Apply: Case Problem 1

Data File needed for this Case Problem: NP_EX_4-3.xlsx

Proko Car Rental Miguel Rubens is an account manager for Proko Car Rental, an industry-leading car rental firm that serves customers across the United States and overseas. Miguel is developing a market report for an upcoming sales conference and needs your assistance in summarizing market information into a collection of Excel charts and graphics. Complete the following:

1. Open the **NP_EX_4-3.xlsx** workbook located in the Excel4 > Case1 folder included with your Data Files. Save the workbook as **NP_EX_4_Proko** in the location specified by your instructor.
2. In the Documentation sheet, enter your name and the date in the range B3:B4.
3. Miguel wants the report to include pie charts breaking down the current year's revenue in terms of market (Airport vs. Off-Airport), car type (Leisure vs. Commercial), and location (Americas vs. International). Do the following:
   a. In the Rentals by Type worksheet, create a pie chart of the data in the range A6:B7. Move the chart to the Analysis worksheet and resize it to cover the range D5:F9.
   b. Remove the chart title from the pie chart.
   c. Add data labels to the outside end of the two slices showing the percentage of the Airport versus Off-Airport sales.
   d. Change the color of the chart to Colorful Palette 3.
4. Repeat Step 3 for the data in the range A11:B12 of the Rentals by Type worksheet, placing the pie chart comparing Leisure and Commercial sales in the range H5:H9 of the Analysis worksheet.
5. Repeat Step 3 for the data in the range A16:B17 of the Rentals by Type worksheet, placing the pie chart comparing revenue between the Americas and International sales in the range J5:J9 of the Analysis worksheet.

6. Miguel wants to present the company revenue broken down by car type. Do the following:
   a. In the Car Models worksheet, create a clustered column chart of the data in the range A4:B9. Move the chart to the range B11:F22 in the Analysis worksheet.
   b. Remove the chart legend if it exists.
   c. Add data labels to the outside end of the data markers showing the revenue for each car model.
   d. Format the data series so that the gap width between the chart columns is 25%.
   e. Change the color palette of the chart to Colorful Palette 3.
7. Miguel also wants to track revenue for each car model over the years to determine whether certain car models have increased or decreased in popularity. Do the following:
   a. In the Revenue by Year worksheet, create a line chart of the data in the range A4:F15. Move the chart to the range H11:J22 in the Analysis worksheet.
   b. Remove the chart title.
   c. Add gridlines for the primary major vertical and horizontal axes.
   d. Move the chart legend to the right side of the plot area.
   e. Add axis titles to the chart. Set the vertical axis title to the text **Revenue ($bil)** and the horizontal axis title to **Year**.
   f. Set the interval between tick marks and between the labels on the category (horizontal) axis to 2 units so that the category labels are Y2019, Y2021, Y2023, Y2025, Y2027, and Y2029.
   g. Change the color of the chart to Colorful Palette 3.
8. Miguel wants to compare the Proko brand to competing car rental companies. Do the following:
   a. In the range F25:F29 of the Analysis worksheet, insert line sparklines showing the trend in market share percentages using the data in the range B19:F29 in the Market Share worksheet.
   b. Add a marker to each sparkline showing the high point.
   c. Change the sparkline color to the Lime, Accent 3 theme color.
9. Repeat Step 9 in the range F32:F36 using the data in the range B5:F15 in the Market Share worksheet.
10. In the range E25:E29, add green data bars with a gradient fill to the data values. Set the size of the largest data bar to the maximum value of 0.75.
11. Repeat Step 10, adding green data bars with a gradient fill to the data values in the range E32:E36. Set the size of the largest data bar to the maximum value of 32.
12. Miguel wants to present a more detailed chart of the revenue values from the five competing rental car agencies over the past several years.
   a. In the Market Share worksheet, create a stacked column chart from the data in the range A4:F15. Move the chart to cover the range H24:J36 in the Analysis worksheet.
   b. Remove the chart title.
   c. Add axis titles to the chart. Change the vertical axis title to **Revenue ($bil)** and the horizontal axis title to **Year**.
   d. Move the legend to the right side of the chart area.
   e. Set the interval between tick marks and between the labels on the category (horizontal) axis to 2 units to display the category values Y2019, Y2021, Y2023, Y2025, Y2027, and Y2029.
   f. Change the color of the chart to Colorful Palette 3.
   g. Set the gap width between the bars in the chart to 25%.
   h. In the lower right corner of the chart, insert a text box with the text **Car Rental Revenues in Decline** on one line.
13. Save the workbook, and then close it.

Challenge: Case Problem 2

Data File needed for this Case Problem: NP_EX_4-4.xlsx

Crystal Creek Hospital & Clinic Inola Cochise is a facilities administrator at Crystal Creek Hospital Clinic in southwest Utah. As part of an annual report for the clinic's trustees, Inola documents patient care at the clinic, including inpatient and outpatient admissions, length of stay, average waiting time, and nurse/patient ratios. Inola has asked your help in supplementing the report with informative charts and graphics. Complete the following.

1. Open the **NP_EX_4-4.xlsx** workbook located in the Excel4 > Case2 folder included with your Data Files. Save the workbook as **NP_EX_4_Crystal** in the location specified by your instructor.
2. In the Documentation sheet, enter your name in cell B3 and the current date in cell B4.
3. In the Summary worksheet, in the range D5:D11, Inola has broken down the number of inpatient admissions by department. Add gradient blue data bars to the range and set the maximum length of the data bars to 8000.
4. Repeat Step 3 for the outpatient admissions in the range E5:E11, using gradient green data bars.
5. **Explore:** Inola wants to report on the number of inpatient and outpatient admissions at the clinic. Do the following:
   a. In the Patients by Month worksheet, create a Sunburst chart of the data in the nonadjacent range A4:C4,A17:C17. Move the chart to the Summary worksheet covering the range G4:J11.
   b. Remove the chart title.
   c. Display the chart legend at the top of the chart.
   d. Change the data labels to show the values and not the category names.
6. **Explore:** Inola also wants to view the admission data by month. Do the following:
   a. In the Patients by Month worksheet, create a stacked area chart of the data in the range A4:C16. Move the chart to the Summary worksheet covering the range L4:P11.
   b. Remove the chart title.
   c. Add primary major vertical gridlines to the chart.
7. **Explore:** The report will also include an analysis of the length of inpatient stays. Inola has retrieved length of stay data for 300 randomly selected patients and wants you to display the distribution of those stays in a histogram chart. Do the following:
   a. In the Length of Stay worksheet, create a histogram of the data in the range A4:A304. Move the chart to the range C13:E25 in the Summary worksheet. (Note: If necessary, you can quickly move the chart to the top of the worksheet by cutting and pasting the chart.)
   b. Change the chart title to **Length of Stay (Days)**.
   c. Double-click the histogram categories along the horizontal axis to open the Format Axis pane. Change the Bin Width value to **1**. Change the Overflow Bin value to 10 so that length of stay values larger than 10 are pooled together in a single category.
8. When patients are admitted to the hospital and then discharged, they might be readmitted within 30 days. Inola wants the report to include the inpatient admission totals and the 30-day readmission rates for each quarter of the past year. Do the following:
   a. In the Readmission worksheet, create a combination chart of the data in the range A4:C8. Display the Inpatient Admissions data series as a clustered column chart. Display the Readmission Rate data series as a line chart on the secondary axis. Move the chart to the range G13:J25 of the Summary worksheet.
   b. Change the chart title to **Admissions and 30-Day Readmission Rate**.
   c. Add axis titles to the chart. Change the primary vertical axis to **Inpatient Admissions**. Change the secondary vertical axis to **Readmission Rate** and rotate the text down. Change the category axis to **Quarter**.
   d. Change the bounds of the secondary axis to go from 0.1 to 0.3.
9. **Explore:** Inola's report needs to break down admissions by payer (Medicare, Medicaid, Private Insurance, or Other). Inola thinks this data would be best presented in a Pareto chart. In the Payer worksheet, create a Pareto chart of the data in the range A4:B8. Move the chart to range L13:P25 in the Summary worksheet and change the chart title to **Admissions by Payer**. (Note: You can find the Pareto chart by selecting the data range, clicking the Recommended Charts button, clicking Histogram on the All Charts tab, and then clicking the Pareto chart type.)

10. Monitoring the length of time that patients must wait before being treated is an important task for Inola. On the Summary worksheet, add gradient red data bars to range D29:D35 containing the wait times for different departments. Set the maximum length of the data bars to 40.
11. Inola wants to track how wait times within each department have changed over the past year. Add line sparklines to the range E29:E35 using the data in the range B5:H16 of the Waiting Times worksheet. Mark the high and low point within each sparkline.
12. **Explore:** Trustees want to examine the nurse-to-patient ratio from different units at the hospital and clinic. Do the following:
    a. In the Nurse Ratio worksheet, create a treemap chart from the data in the range A5:C14. Move the chart to the range G29:P45 of the Summary worksheet.
    b. Remove the chart title.
    c. Select the data legend and increase the font size to 14 points.
    d. Add data labels to the chart showing both the category name and the data value.
    e. With the data labels selected, increase their font size to 14 points.
13. Save the workbook, and then close it.

Creating a Database

Tracking Patient, Visit, and Billing Data

Case: Pine Ridge Orthopedics & Sports Medicine

Pine Ridge Orthopedics & Sports Medicine Center is located in Fort Collins, Colorado. Pine Ridge Orthopedics & Sports Medicine provides a range of medical services to patients of all ages in the greater Fort Collins area. The center specializes in the areas of orthopedic medicine and rehabilitation services. Susan Martinez, the office manager for Pine Ridge Orthopedics & Sports Medicine Center, oversees a large staff and is responsible for maintaining the medical records for all of the patients the center serves.

To best manage the center, Susan and her staff rely on electronic medical records for information on the patients, billing, inventory control, purchasing, and accounts payable. Several months ago, the center upgraded to **Microsoft Access** (or simply **Access**), a computer program used to enter, maintain, and retrieve related data in a format known as a database. Susan and her staff want to use Access to store information about the patients, billing, vendors, and products. She asks for your help in creating the necessary Access database.

Starting Data Files: Access1

Module
Support_AC_1_Susan.accdb

Review
Support_AC_1_Company.accdb

Case1
Support_AC_1_MoreTutors.accdb

Case2
Support_AC_1_OutdoorPeople.accdb

Objectives

Part 1.1

- Define basic database concepts and terms
- Start and exit Access
- Identify the Microsoft Access window and Backstage view
- Create a blank database
- Create and save a table in Datasheet view and Design view
- Add fields to a table in Datasheet view and Design view
- Set a table's primary key in Design view

Part 1.2

- Open an Access database
- Open a table using the Navigation Pane
- Copy and paste records from another Access database
- Navigate a table datasheet and enter records
- Create and navigate a simple query
- Create and navigate a simple form
- Create, preview, navigate, and print a simple report
- Use Help in Access
- Identify how to compact, back up, and restore a database

Part 1.1 Visual Overview: The Access Window

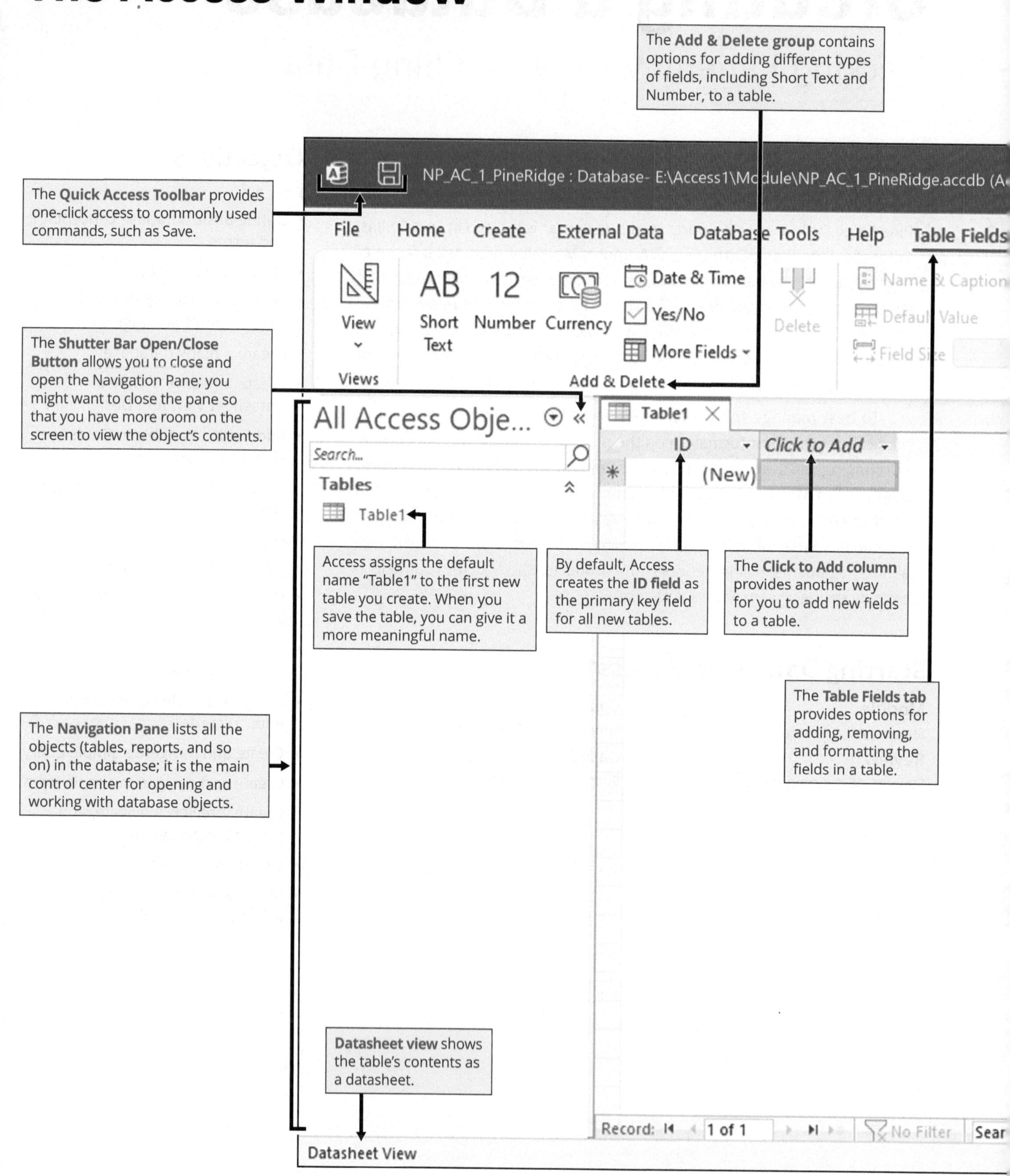
The Add & Delete group contains options for adding different types of fields, including Short Text and Number, to a table.
The Quick Access Toolbar provides one-click access to commonly used commands, such as Save.
NP_AC_1_PineRidge : Database- E:\Access1\Module\NP_AC_1_PineRidge.accdb (A
File
Home
Create
External Data
Database Tools
Help
Table Fields
View
AB
Short Text
12
Number
Currency
Date & Time
Yes/No
More Fields
Delete
Name & Caption
Default Value
Field Size
Views
Add & Delete
The Shutter Bar Open/Close Button allows you to close and open the Navigation Pane; you might want to close the pane so that you have more room on the screen to view the object's contents.
All Access Obje...
Search...
Tables
Table1
Table1
ID
Click to Add
(New)
Access assigns the default name "Table1" to the first new table you create. When you save the table, you can give it a more meaningful name.
By default, Access creates the ID field as the primary key field for all new tables.
The Click to Add column provides another way for you to add new fields to a table.
The Table Fields tab provides options for adding, removing, and formatting the fields in a table.
The Navigation Pane lists all the objects (tables, reports, and so on) in the database; it is the main control center for opening and working with database objects.
Datasheet view shows the table's contents as a datasheet.
Record: 1 of 1
No Filter
Sear
Datasheet View

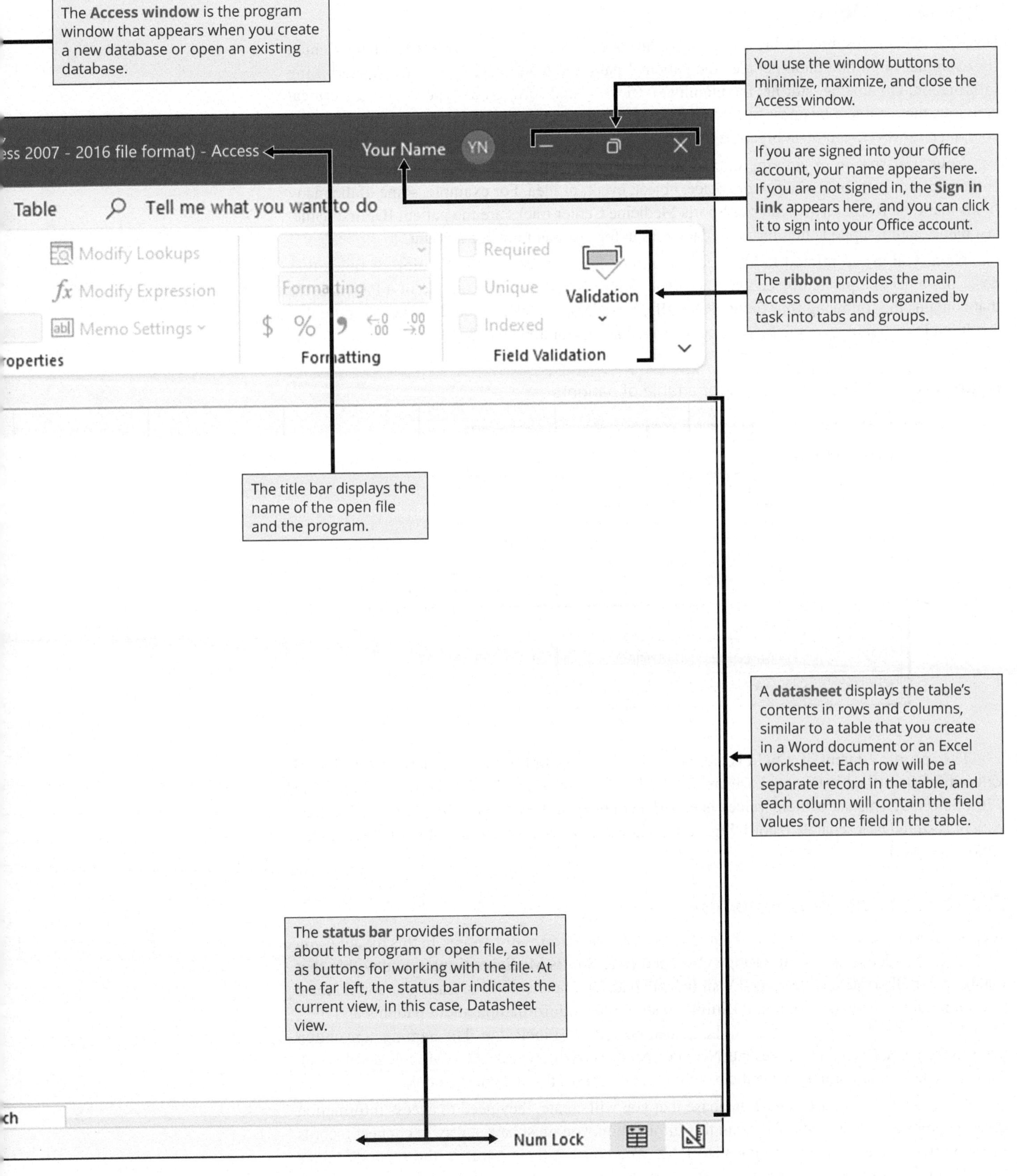

The **Access window** is the program window that appears when you create a new database or open an existing database.
You use the window buttons to minimize, maximize, and close the Access window.
ess 2007 - 2016 file format) - Access
Your Name
YN
If you are signed into your Office account, your name appears here. If you are not signed in, the **Sign in link** appears here, and you can click it to sign into your Office account.
Table
Tell me what you want to do
Modify Lookups
Modify Expression
Memo Settings
roperties
Formatting
Formatting
Required
Unique
Indexed
Validation
Field Validation
The **ribbon** provides the main Access commands organized by task into tabs and groups.
The title bar displays the name of the open file and the program.
A **datasheet** displays the table's contents in rows and columns, similar to a table that you create in a Word document or an Excel worksheet. Each row will be a separate record in the table, and each column will contain the field values for one field in the table.
The **status bar** provides information about the program or open file, as well as buttons for working with the file. At the far left, the status bar indicates the current view, in this case, Datasheet view.
ch
Num Lock

Introduction to Database Concepts

Before you begin using Access to create the database for Susan, you need to understand a few key terms and concepts associated with databases.

Organizing Data

Data is a valuable resource to any business. At Pine Ridge Orthopedics & Sports Medicine Center, for example, important data includes the patients' names and addresses, visit dates, and billing information. Organizing, storing, maintaining, retrieving, and sorting this type of data are critical activities that enable a business to find and use information effectively. Before storing data on a computer, however, you must organize the data.

Your first step in organizing data is to identify the individual fields. A **field** is a single characteristic or attribute of a person, place, object, event, or idea. For example, some of the many fields that Pine Ridge Orthopedics & Sports Medicine Center tracks are the patient ID, first name, last name, address, phone number, visit date, reason for visit, and invoice amount.

Next, you group related fields together into tables. A **table** is a collection of fields that describes a person, place, object, event, or idea. Figure 1–1 shows an example of a Patient table that contains the following four fields: PatientID, FirstName, LastName, and Phone. Each field is a column in the table, with the field name displayed as the column heading.

Figure 1–1 Data organization for a table of patients

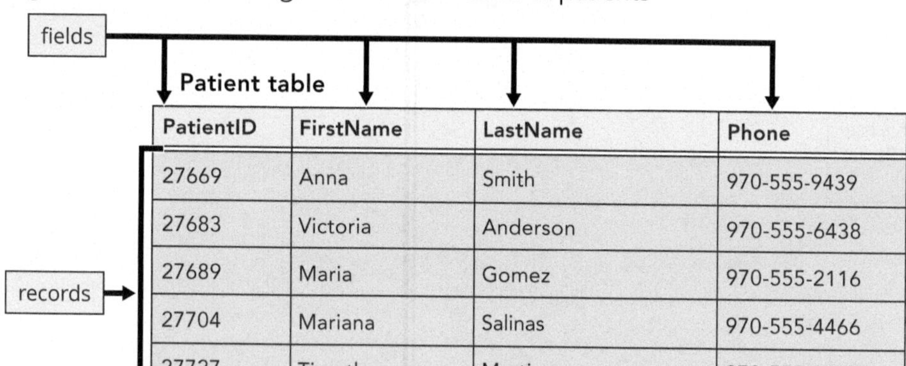

PatientID	FirstName	LastName	Phone
27669	Anna	Smith	970-555-9439
27683	Victoria	Anderson	970-555-6438
27689	Maria	Gomez	970-555-2116
27704	Mariana	Salinas	970-555-4466
27727	Timothy	Martin	970-555-9855
27734	Lisa	Brown	720-555-5577

The specific content of a field is called the **field value**. In Figure 1–1, the first set of field values for PatientID, FirstName, LastName, and Phone are, respectively: 27669; Anna; Smith; and 970-555-9439. This set of field values is called a **record**. In the Patient table, the data for each patient is stored as a separate record. Figure 1–1 shows six records; each row of field values in the table is a record.

Databases and Relationships

A collection of related tables is called a **database**, or a **relational database**. In this module, you will create the database for Pine Ridge Orthopedics & Sports Medicine Center, and within that database, you'll create a table named Visit to store data about patient visits. Later on, you'll create two more tables, named Patient and Billing, to store related information about patients and their invoices. The database you create will be named NP_AC_1_PineRidge. The naming convention prior to the name PineRidge represents New Perspectives (NP), Access (AC), Module number (1). You will use similar naming conventions with other databases throughout the book.

As Susan and her staff use the database that you will create, they need to access information about patients and their visits. To obtain this information, you must have a way to connect records in the Patient table to records in the Visit table. You connect the records in the separate tables through a **common field** that appears in both tables.

In the sample database shown in Figure 1–2, each record in the Patient table has a field named PatientID, which is also a field in the Visit table. For example, Timothy Martin is the fifth patient in the Patient table and has a PatientID field value of 27727. This same PatientID field value, 27727, appears in two records in the Visit table. Therefore, Timothy Martin is the patient that was seen on these two visits.

Figure 1–2 Database relationship between tables for patients and visits

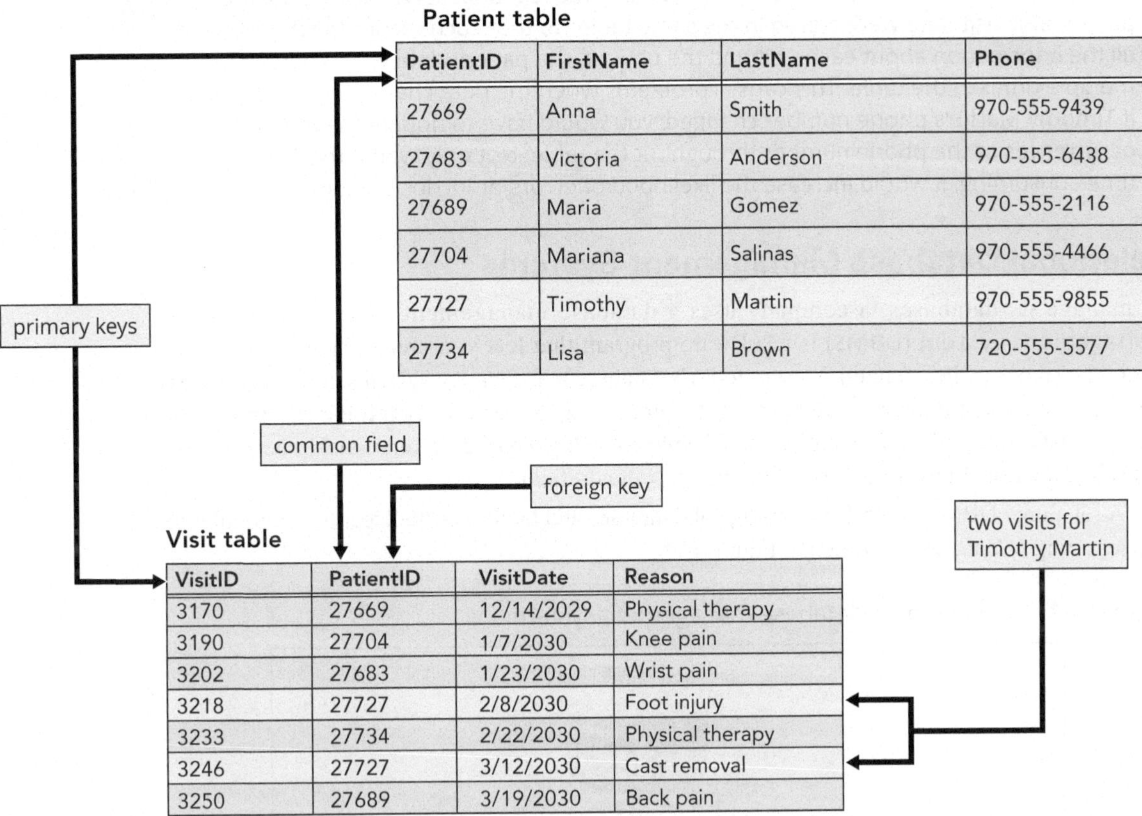

PatientID	FirstName	LastName	Phone
27669	Anna	Smith	970-555-9439
27683	Victoria	Anderson	970-555-6438
27689	Maria	Gomez	970-555-2116
27704	Mariana	Salinas	970-555-4466
27727	Timothy	Martin	970-555-9855
27734	Lisa	Brown	720-555-5577

VisitID	PatientID	VisitDate	Reason
3170	27669	12/14/2029	Physical therapy
3190	27704	1/7/2030	Knee pain
3202	27683	1/23/2030	Wrist pain
3218	27727	2/8/2030	Foot injury
3233	27734	2/22/2030	Physical therapy
3246	27727	3/12/2030	Cast removal
3250	27689	3/19/2030	Back pain

Each ID value in the Patient table must be unique so that you can distinguish one patient from another. These unique PatientID values also identify each patient's specific visits in the Visit table. The PatientID field is referred to as the primary key of the Patient table. A **primary key** is a field, or a collection of fields, whose values uniquely identify each record in a table. No two records can contain the same value for the primary key field. In the Visit table, the VisitID field is the primary key because Pine Ridge Orthopedics & Sports Medicine Center assigns each visit a unique identification number.

When you include the primary key from one table as a field in a second table to form a relationship between the two tables, it is called a **foreign key** in the second table, as shown in Figure 1–2. For example, PatientID is the primary key in the Patient table and a foreign key in the Visit table.

The PatientID field must have the same characteristics in both tables. Although the primary key PatientID contains unique values in the Patient table, the same field as a foreign key in the Visit table does not necessarily contain unique values. The PatientID value 27727, for example, appears two times in the Visit table because Timothy Martin made two visits to the center.

Each foreign key value, however, must match one of the field values for the primary key in the other table. In the example shown in Figure 1–2, each PatientID value in the Visit table must match a PatientID value in the Patient table. The two tables are related, enabling users to connect the facts about patients with the facts about their visits to the center.

Insight

Storing Data in Separate Tables

When you create a database, you must create separate tables that contain only fields that are directly related to each other. For example, in the NP_AC_1_PineRidge database, the patient and visit data should not be stored in the same table because doing so would make the data difficult to update and prone to errors. Consider Timothy Martin and his visits to the center, and assume that he has many more than just two visits. If all the patient and visit data were stored in the same table, so that each record (row) contained all the information about each visit and the patient, the patient data would appear multiple times in the table. This causes problems when the data changes. For example, if Timothy Martin's phone number changed, you would have to update the multiple occurrences of the phone number throughout the table. Not only would this be time-consuming, it would increase the likelihood of errors or inconsistent data.

Relational Database Management Systems

To manage its databases, a company uses a database management system. A **database management system (DBMS)** is a software program that lets you create databases and then manipulate the data they contain. Most of today's database management systems, including Access, are called relational database management systems. In a **relational database management system**, data is organized as a collection of tables. As stated earlier, a relationship between two tables in a relational DBMS is formed through a common field.

A relational DBMS controls the storage of databases and facilitates the creation, manipulation, and reporting of data, as illustrated in Figure 1–3.

Figure 1–3 Relational database management system

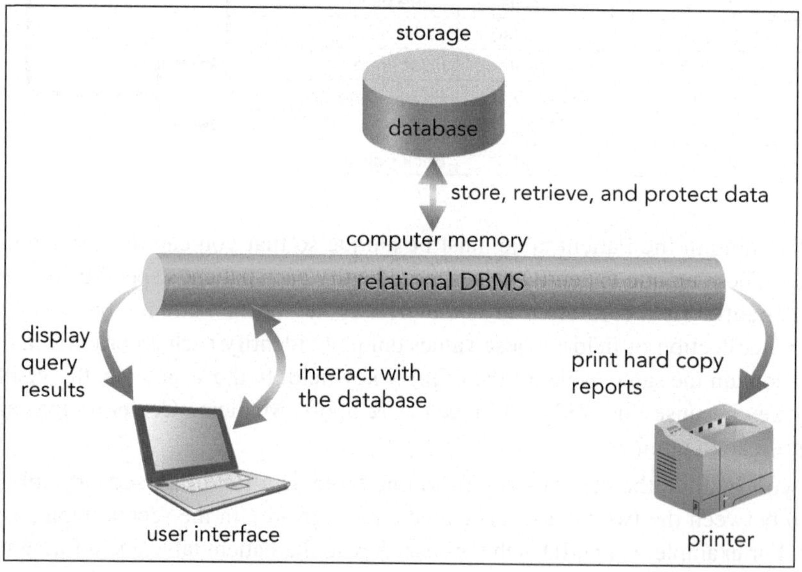

Specifically, a relational DBMS provides the following functions:

- It allows you to create database structures containing fields, tables, and table relationships.
- It lets you easily add new records, change field values in existing records, and delete records.
- It contains a built-in query language, which lets you obtain immediate answers to the questions (or queries) you ask about your data.
- It contains a built-in report generator, which lets you produce professional-looking, formatted reports from your data.
- It protects databases through security, control, and recovery facilities.

An organization such as Pine Ridge Orthopedics & Sports Medicine Center benefits from a relational DBMS because it allows users working in different groups to share the same data. More than one user can enter data into a database, and more than one user can retrieve and analyze data that other users have entered. For example, the database for Pine Ridge Orthopedics & Sports Medicine Center will contain only one copy of the Visit table, and all employees will use it to access visit information.

Finally, unlike other software programs, such as spreadsheet programs, a DBMS can handle massive amounts of data and allows relationships among multiple tables. Each Access database, for example, can be up to two gigabytes in size, can contain up to 32,768 objects (tables, reports, and so on), and can have up to 255 people using the database at the same time. For instructional purposes, the databases you create and work with throughout this text contain a relatively small number of records compared to databases you would encounter outside the classroom, which would likely contain tables with very large numbers of records.

Starting Access and Creating a Database

Now that you've learned some database terms and concepts, you're ready to start Access and create the NP_AC_1_PineRidge database for Susan.

To start Access:

1. On the Windows taskbar, click the **Start** button. The Start menu opens.
2. On the Start menu, click the **All apps** button, and then click **Access**. Access starts and displays the Home screen in Backstage view. See Figure 1–4.

Figure 1–4 Home screen in Backstage view

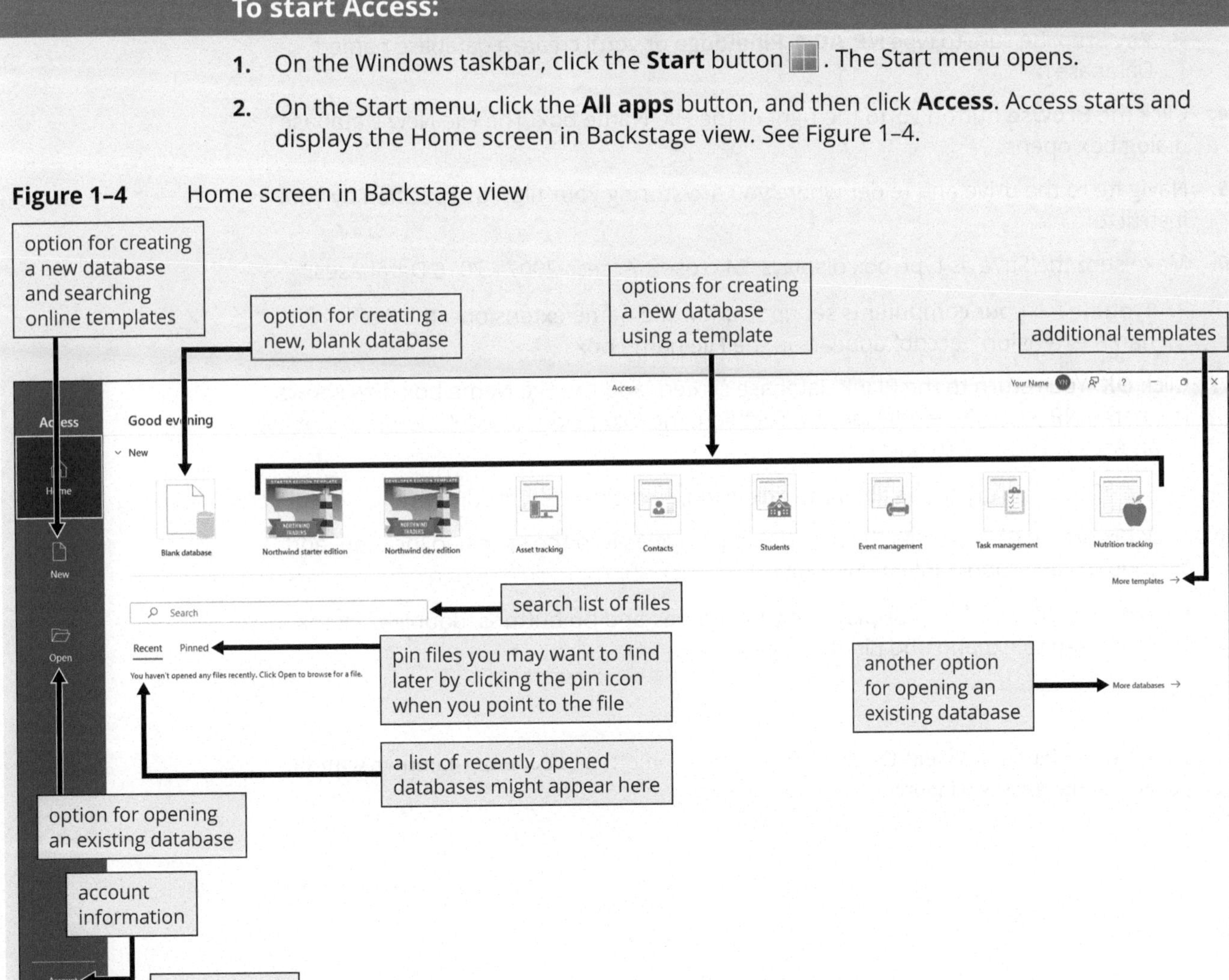

When you start Access, the first screen that appears is Backstage view, which is the starting place for your work in Access. **Backstage view** contains commands that allow you to manage Access files and options. The Home screen in Backstage view provides options for you to create a new database or open an existing database. To create a new database that does not contain any data or objects, you use the Blank database option. If the database you need to create contains objects that match those found in common databases, such as databases that store data about contacts or tasks, you can use one of the templates provided with Access. A **template** is a predesigned database that includes professionally designed tables, reports, and other database objects that can make it quick and easy for you to create a database. You can also search for a template online using the Search box.

In this case, the templates provided do not match Susan's needs for the center's database, so you need to create a new, blank database from scratch.

To create the new NP_AC_1_PineRidge database:

1. sam Make sure you have the Access starting Data Files on your computer.
2. On the Home screen, click **Blank database** (shown in Figure 1–4). The Blank database screen opens.
3. In the File Name box, type **NP_AC_1_PineRidge** to replace the selected database name provided by Access, Database1. Next, you need to specify the location for the file.

   Key Step Be sure to type **NP_AC_1_PineRidge** or you'll create a database named Database1.

4. Click the **Browse** button to the right of the File Name box. The File New Database dialog box opens.
5. Navigate to the drive and folder where you are storing your files, as specified by your instructor.
6. Make sure the Save as type box displays "Microsoft Access 2007 - 2016 Databases."

   Trouble? If your computer is set up to show file name extensions, the Access file name extension ".accdb" appears in the File name box.

7. Click **OK**. You return to the Blank database screen, and the File Name box now shows the name NP_AC_1_PineRidge.accdb. The filename extension ".accdb" identifies the file as an Access 2007–2016 database.

   Tip If you don't type the filename extension, Access adds it automatically.

8. Click **Create**. Access creates the new database, saves it to the specified location, and then opens an empty table named Table1.

   Trouble? If the ribbon displays only tab names and no buttons, double-click the Home tab to expand and pin the ribbon.

Refer to the Part 1.1 Visual Overview and spend some time becoming familiar with the components of the Access window.

Insight

Understanding the Database File Type

Access uses the .accdb file extension, which is the same file extension used for databases created with Microsoft Access 2007, 2010, 2013, 2016, and beyond. To ensure compatibility between these earlier versions and the Access software, new databases created using Access have the same file extension and file format as Access 2007, Access 2010, Access 2013, and Access 2016 databases. This is why the File New Database dialog box provides the Microsoft Access 2007–2016 Databases option in the Save as type box. In addition, the notation "(Access 2007–2016 file format)" appears in the title bar next to the name of an open database in Access, confirming that database files with the .accdb extension can be used in Access 2007, Access 2010, Access 2013, Access 2016, and the current version.

Working in Touch Mode

If you are working on a touch device, such as a tablet, you can switch to Touch Mode in Access to make it easier for you to tap buttons on the ribbon and perform other touch actions. Your screens will not match those shown in the book exactly, but this will not cause any problems.

Tip On a touch device, you *tap* instead of *click*.

Note: The following steps assume that you are using a mouse. If you are instead using a touch device, please read these steps but don't complete them, so that you remain working in Touch Mode.

To switch to Touch Mode:

1. On the Quick Access Toolbar, click the **Customize Quick Access Toolbar** button. A menu opens listing buttons you can add to the Quick Access Toolbar as well as other options for customizing the toolbar.

   Trouble? If you cannot find the Customize Quick Access Toolbar button, it may be hidden. To unhide the Customize Quick Access Toolbar button, right-click the ribbon. On the shortcut menu, select Show Quick Access Toolbar. If the Quick Access Toolbar is below the ribbon, you can move it to the ribbon by clicking the Customize Quick Access Toolbar button and selecting the Show Above the Ribbon option.

   Trouble? If the Touch/Mouse Mode command on the menu has a checkmark next to it, press ESC to close the menu, and then skip to Step 3.

2. Click **Touch/Mouse Mode**. The Quick Access Toolbar now contains the Touch/Mouse Mode button, which you can use to switch between Mouse Mode, the default display, and Touch Mode.
3. On the Quick Access Toolbar, click the **Touch/Mouse Mode** button. A menu opens with two commands: Mouse, which shows the ribbon in the standard display and is optimized for use with the mouse; and Touch, which provides more space between the buttons and commands on the ribbon and is optimized for use with touch devices. The icon next to Mouse is shaded to indicate that it is selected.

   Trouble? If the icon next to Touch is shaded, press ESC to close the menu and skip to Step 5.

4. Click **Touch**. The display switches to Touch Mode with more space between the commands and buttons on the ribbon. See Figure 1–5.

Figure 1–5 Ribbon displayed in Touch Mode

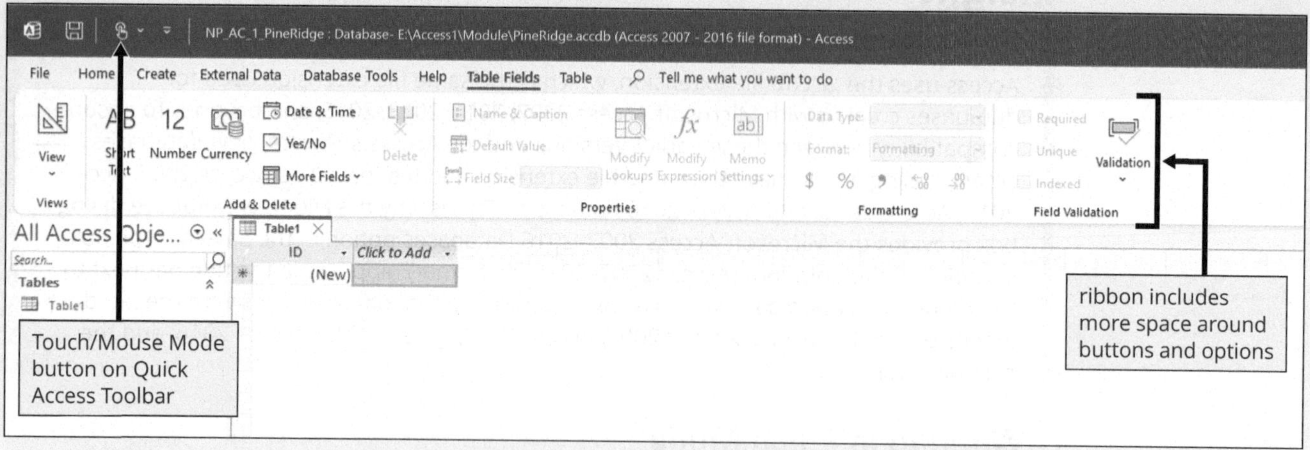

The figures in this text show the standard Mouse Mode display, and the instructions assume you are using a mouse to click and select options, so you'll switch back to Mouse Mode.

> **Trouble?** If you are using a touch device and want to remain in Touch Mode, skip Steps 5 and 6.

5. On the Quick Access Toolbar, click the **Touch/Mouse Mode** button, and then click **Mouse**. The ribbon returns to the standard display, as shown in the Part 1.1 Visual Overview.
6. On the Quick Access Toolbar, click the **Customize Quick Access Toolbar** button, and then click **Touch/Mouse Mode** to deselect it. The Touch/Mouse Mode button is removed from the Quick Access Toolbar.

> **Trouble?** To hide the Customize Quick Access Toolbar button, right-click the ribbon. On the shortcut menu, select Hide Quick Access Toolbar.

Creating a Table in Datasheet View

Tables contain all the data in a database and are the fundamental objects for your work in Access. You can create a table in Access in different ways, including entering the fields and records for the table directly in Datasheet view.

Reference

Creating a Table in Datasheet View

- On the ribbon, click the Create tab.
- In the Tables group, click the Table button.
- Rename the default ID primary key field and change its data type, if necessary, or accept the default ID field with the AutoNumber data type.
- On the Table Fields tab, in the Add & Delete group, click the button for the type of field you want to add to the table (for example, click the Short Text button), and then type the field name; or, in the table datasheet, click the Click to Add column heading, click the type of field you want to add from the list that opens, and then press TAB or ENTER to move to the next column in the datasheet. Repeat this step to add all the necessary fields to the table.
- In the first row below the field names, enter the value for each field in the first record, pressing TAB or ENTER to move from one field to the next.
- After entering the value for the last field in the first record, press TAB or ENTER to move to the next row, and then enter the values for the next record. Continue this process until you have entered all the records for the table.
- On the Quick Access Toolbar, click the Save button, enter a name for the table, and then click OK.

For Pine Ridge Orthopedics & Sports Medicine Center, Susan needs to track information about each patient visit at the center. She asks you to create the Visit table according to the plan shown in Figure 1–6.

Figure 1–6 Plan for the Visit table

Field	Purpose
VisitID	Unique number assigned to each visit; will serve as the table's primary key
PatientID	Unique number assigned to each patient; common field that will be a foreign key to connect to the Patient table
VisitDate	Date on which the patient visited the clinic
Reason	Reason/diagnosis for the patient visit
WalkIn	Whether the patient visit was a walk-in or scheduled appointment

As shown in Susan's plan, she wants to store data about visits in five fields, including fields to contain the date of each visit, the reason for the visit, and if the visit was a walk-in or scheduled appointment. These are the most important aspects of a visit and, therefore, must be tracked. Also, notice that the VisitID field will be the primary key for the table; each visit to the Pine Ridge Orthopedics & Sports Medicine Center is assigned a unique number, so this field is the logical choice for the primary key. Finally, the PatientID field is needed in the Visit table as a foreign key to connect the information about visits to patients. The data about patients and their invoices will be stored in separate tables, which you will create later.

Notice the name of each field in Figure 1–6. You need to name each field, table, and object in an Access database.

Proskills

Decision Making: Naming Fields in Access Tables

One of the most important tasks in creating a table is deciding what names to specify for the table's fields. Keep the following guidelines in mind when you assign field names:

- A field name can consist of up to 64 characters, including letters, numbers, spaces, and special characters, except for the period (.), exclamation mark (!), grave accent (`), and square brackets ([ ]).
- A field name cannot begin with a space.
- Capitalize the first letter of each word in a field name that combines multiple words, for example, VisitDate.
- Use concise field names that are easy to remember and reference and that won't take up a lot of space in the table datasheet.
- Use standard abbreviations, such as Num for Number, Amt for Amount, and Qty for Quantity, and use them consistently throughout the database. For example, if you use Num for Number in one field name, do not use the number sign (#) for Number in another.
- Give fields descriptive names so that you can easily identify them when you view or edit records.
- Although Access supports the use of spaces in field names (and in other object names), experienced database developers avoid using spaces because they can cause errors when the objects are involved in programming tasks.

By spending time obtaining and analyzing information about the fields in a table, and understanding the rules for naming fields, you can create a well-designed table that will be easy for others to use.

Renaming the Default Primary Key Field

As noted earlier, Access provides the ID field as the default primary key for a new table you create in Datasheet view. Recall that a primary key is a field, or a collection of fields, whose values uniquely identify each record in a table. However, according to Susan's plan, the VisitID field should be the primary key for the Visit table. You'll begin by renaming the default ID field to create the VisitID field.

To rename the ID field to the VisitID field:

1. Right-click the **ID** column heading to open the shortcut menu, and then click **Rename Field**. The column heading ID is selected, so that whatever text you type next will replace it.

   Tip A shortcut menu opens when you right-click an object and provides options for working with that object.

2. Type **VisitID** and then click the row below the heading. The column heading changes to VisitID, and the insertion point moves to the row below the heading. The **insertion point** is a flashing cursor that shows where the text you type will be inserted. In this case, it is hidden within the selected field value (New). See Figure 1-7.

Figure 1-7 ID field renamed to VisitID

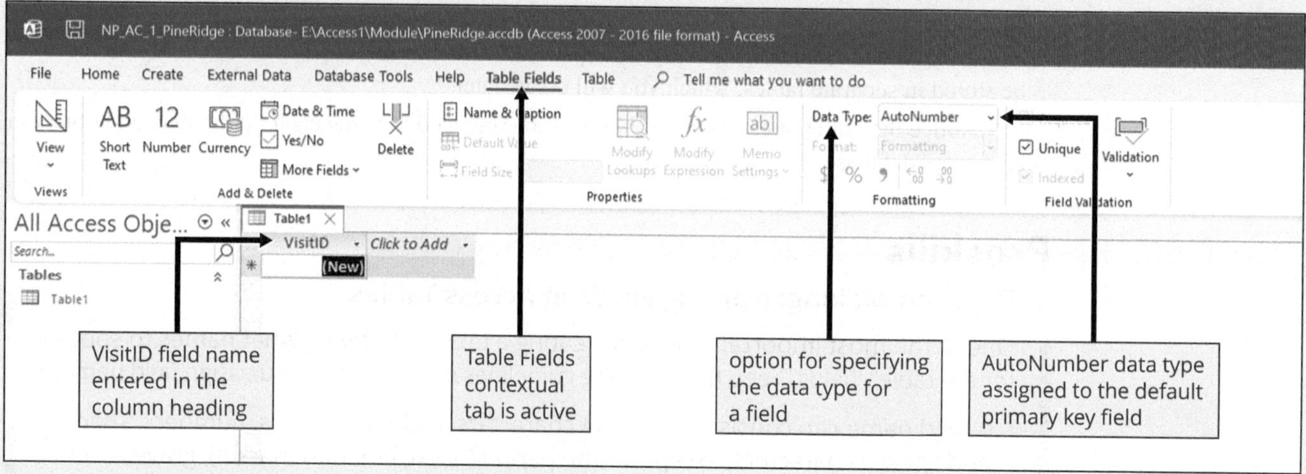

Trouble? If you make a mistake while typing the field name, use BACKSPACE to delete characters to the left of the insertion point or use DELETE to delete characters to the right of the insertion point. Then type the correct text. To correct a field name by replacing it entirely, press ESC, and then type the correct text.

Notice that the Table Fields tab is active on the ribbon. This is an example of a **contextual tab**, which is a tab that appears and provides options for working with a specific object that is selected—in this case, the table you are creating. As you work with other objects in the database, other contextual tabs will appear with commands and options related to each selected object.

Insight

Buttons and Labels on the Ribbon

Depending on the size of the monitor you are using and your screen resolution settings, more or fewer buttons might be displayed on the ribbon, and certain buttons might not include labels. The screenshots in these modules were created using a screen resolution setting of 1920 × 1080 with the program window maximized. If you are using a smaller monitor or a lower screen resolution, some buttons will appear only as icons, with no labels next to them, because there is not enough room on the ribbon to display the labels.

You have renamed the default primary key field, ID, to VisitID. However, the VisitID field still retains the characteristics of the ID field, including its data type. Your next task is to change the data type of this field.

Changing the Data Type of the Default Primary Key Field

Notice the Formatting group on the Table Fields tab. One of the options available in this group is the Data Type option (shown in Figure 1–7). Each field in an Access table must be assigned a data type. The **data type** determines what field values you can enter for the field. In this case, the AutoNumber data type is displayed. Access assigns the AutoNumber data type to the default ID primary key field because the **AutoNumber** data type automatically inserts a unique number in this field for every record, beginning with the number 1 for the first record, the number 2 for the second record, and so on. Therefore, a field using the AutoNumber data type can serve as the primary key for any table you create.

Visit numbers at the Pine Ridge Orthopedics & Sports Medicine Center are specific, four-digit numbers, so the AutoNumber data type is not appropriate for the VisitID field, which is the primary key field in the table you are creating. A better choice is the **Short Text** data type, which allows field values containing letters, digits, and other characters, and which is appropriate for identifying numbers, such as visit numbers, that are never used in calculations. So, Susan asks you to change the data type for the VisitID field from AutoNumber to Short Text.

To change the data type for the VisitID field:

1. Make sure that the VisitID column is selected. A column is selected when you click a field value, in which case the background color of the column heading changes to orange (the default color) and the insertion point appears in the field value. You can also click the column heading to select a column, in which case the background color of both the column heading and the field value changes (the default colors are gray and blue, respectively).
2. On the Table Fields tab, in the Formatting group, click the **Data Type arrow**, and then click **Short Text**. The VisitID field is now a Short Text field. See Figure 1–8.

Figure 1–8 Short Text data type assigned to the VisitID field

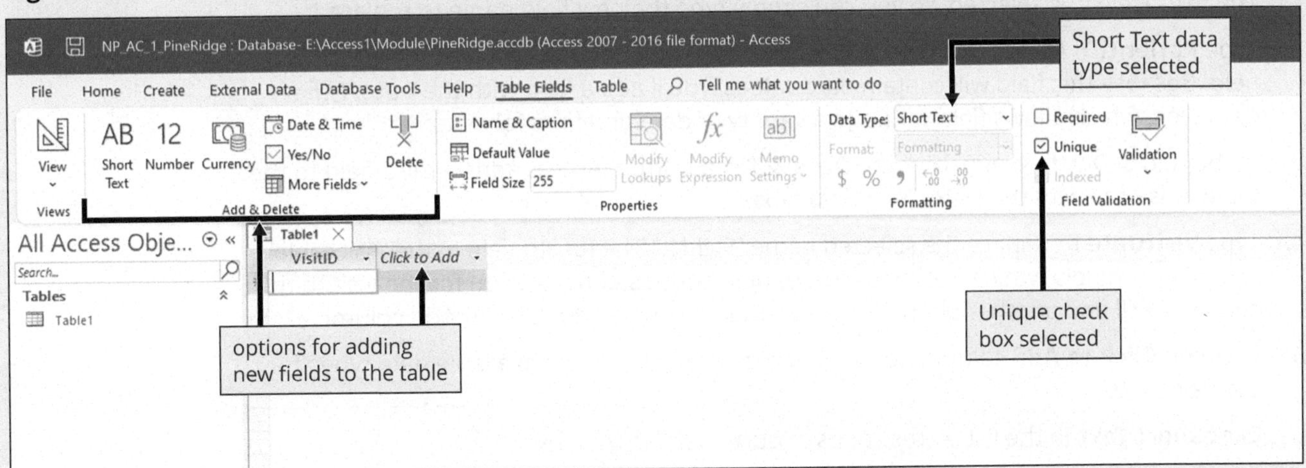

Note the Unique check box in the Field Validation group. This check box is selected because the VisitID field assumed the characteristics of the default primary key field, ID, including the fact that each value in the field must be unique. Because this check box is selected, no two records in the Visit table can have the same value in the VisitID field.

With the VisitID field created and established as the primary key, you can now enter the rest of the fields in the Visit table.

Adding New Fields

When you create a table in Datasheet view, you can use the options in the Add & Delete group on the Table Fields tab to add fields to your table. You can also use the Click to Add column in the table datasheet to add new fields. (See Figure 1–8.) You'll use both methods to add the four remaining fields to the Visit table. The next field you need to add is the PatientID field. Similar to the VisitID field, the PatientID field will contain numbers that will not be used in calculations, so it should be a Short Text field.

To add the rest of the fields to the Visit table:

1. On the Table Fields tab, in the Add & Delete group, click the **Short Text** button. Access adds a new field named "Field1" to the right of the VisitID field. See Figure 1-9.

Figure 1-9 New Short Text field added to the table

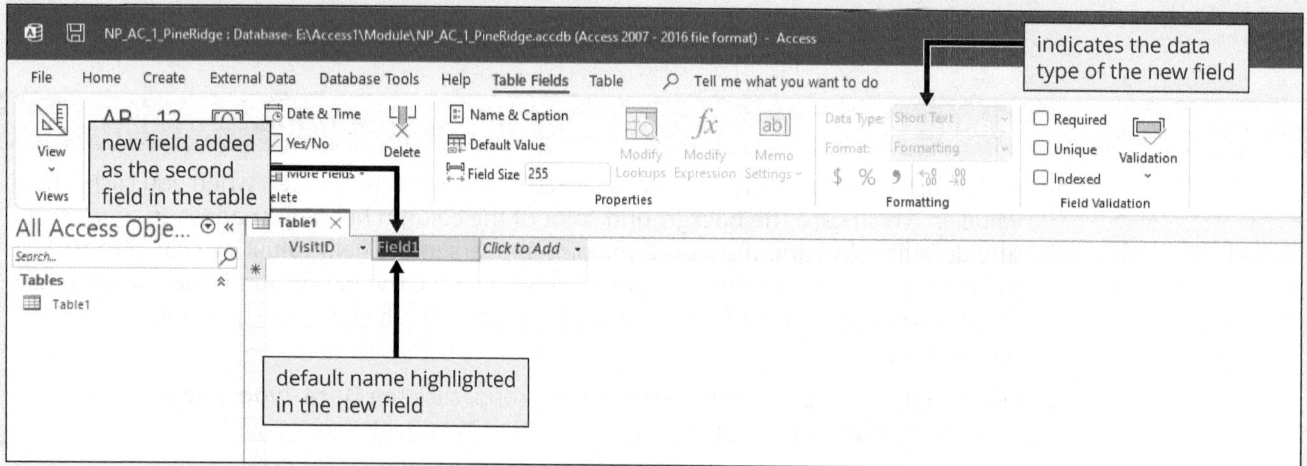

The text "Field1" is selected, so you can simply type the new field name to replace it.

2. Type **PatientID**. Access adds the second field to the table. Next, you'll add the VisitDate field. Because this field will contain date values, you'll add a field with the **Date/Time** data type, which allows field values in a variety of date and time formats.
3. In the Add & Delete group, click the **Date & Time** button. Access adds a third field to the table, this time with the Date/Time data type.
4. Type **VisitDate** to replace the selected name "Field1." The fourth field in the Visit table is the Reason field, which will contain brief descriptions of the reason for the visit to the center. You'll add another Short Text field—this time using the Click to Add column.
5. Click the **Click to Add** column heading. Access displays a list of available data types for the new field.
6. Click **Short Text** in the list. Access adds a fourth field to the table.
7. Type **Reason** to replace the highlighted name "Field1," and then press **ENTER**. The Click to Add column becomes active and displays the list of field data types.

   The fifth and final field in the Visit table is the WalkIn field, which will indicate whether the patient had a scheduled appointment. The **Yes/No** data type is suitable for this field because it defines fields that store values representing one of two options—true/false, yes/no, or on/off.

8. Click **Yes/No** in the list, and then type **WalkIn** to replace the highlighted name "Field1."

> **Trouble?** If you pressed TAB or ENTER after typing the WalkIn field name, press ESC to close the Click to Add list.

> **Tip** You can also type the first letter of a data type to select it and close the Click to Add list.

9. Click in the row below the VisitID column heading. You have entered all five fields for the Visit table. See Figure 1–10.

Figure 1–10 Table with all fields entered

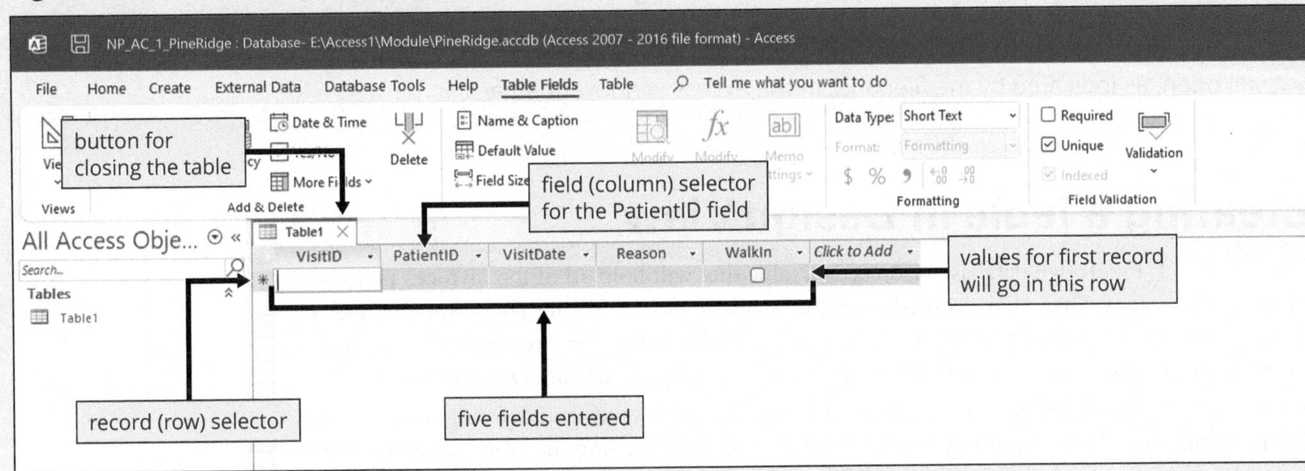

The table contains three Short Text fields (VisitID, PatientID, and Reason), one Date/Time field (VisitDate), and one Yes/No field (WalkIn). You'll learn more about field data types in the next module.

As noted earlier, Datasheet view shows a table's contents in rows (records) and columns (fields). Each column is headed by a field name inside a field selector, and each row has a record selector to its left (shown in Figure 1–10). Clicking a **field selector** or a **record selector** selects that entire column or row (respectively), which you then can manipulate. A field selector is also called a **column selector**, and a record selector is also called a **row selector**.

Saving the Visit Table Structure

As you find out later, the records you enter are immediately stored in the database as soon as you enter them; however, the table's design—the field names and characteristics of the fields themselves, plus any layout changes to the datasheet—are not saved until you save the table. When you save a new table for the first time, you should give it a name that best identifies the information it contains. Like a field name, a table name can contain up to 64 characters, including spaces.

Reference

Saving a Table

- Make sure the table you want to save is open.
- On the Quick Access Toolbar, click the Save button. The Save As dialog box opens.
- In the Table Name box, type the name for the table.
- Click OK.

According to Susan's plan, you need to save the table with the name "Visit."

To save, name, and close the Visit table:

1. On the Quick Access Toolbar, click the **Save** button. The Save As dialog box opens.

   Tip You can also use the Save command in Backstage view to save and name a new table.

2. With the default name Table1 selected in the Table Name box, type **Visit** and then click **OK**. The tab for the table now displays the name "Visit," and the Visit table design is saved in the NP_AC_1_PineRidge database.
3. Click the **Close** button on the object tab (refer to Figure 1–10 for the location of this button). The Visit table closes, and the main portion of the Access window is now blank because no database object is currently open. The NP_AC_1_PineRidge database file is still open, as indicated by the filename in the Access window title bar.

Creating a Table in Design View

The NP_AC_1_PineRidge database also needs a table that will hold all of the invoices generated by each office visit. Susan has decided to call this new table the Billing table. You created the structure for the Visit table in Datasheet view. An alternate method of creating the structure of a table is by using Design view. You will create the new Billing table using Design view.

Creating a table in Design view involves entering the field names and defining the properties for the fields, specifying a primary key for the table, and then saving the table structure. Susan began documenting the design for the new Billing table by listing each field's name, data type, and purpose, and will continue to refine the design. See Figure 1–11.

Figure 1–11 Initial design for the Billing table

Field Name	Data Type	Purpose
InvoiceNum	Short Text	Unique number assigned to each invoice; will serve as the table's primary key
VisitID	Short Text	Unique number assigned to each visit; common field that will be a foreign key to connect to the Visit table
InvoiceAmount	Currency	Dollar amount of each invoice
InvoiceDate	Date/Time	Date the invoice was generated
InvoicePaid	Yes/No	Whether the invoice has been paid or not

You'll use Susan's design as a guide for creating the Billing table in the NP_AC_1_PineRidge database.

To begin creating the Billing table:

1. If the Navigation Pane is open, click the **Shutter Bar Open/Close Button** « to close it.
2. On the ribbon, click the **Create** tab.
3. In the Tables group, click the **Table Design** button. A new table named Table1 opens in Design view.

Defining Fields

When you first create a table in Design view, the insertion point is located in the first row's Field Name box, ready for you to begin defining the first field in the table. You enter values for the Field Name, Data Type, and Description field properties (optional), and then select values for all other field properties in the Field Properties pane. These other properties will appear when you move to the first row's Data Type box.

Reference

Defining a Field in Design View

- In the Field Name box, type the name for the field, and then press TAB.
- Accept the default Short Text data type or click the arrow and select a different data type for the field. Press TAB.
- Enter an optional description for the field, if necessary.
- Use the Field Properties pane to type or select other field properties, as appropriate.

The first field you need to define is the InvoiceNum field. This field will be the primary key for the Billing table. Each invoice at the Pine Ridge Orthopedics & Sports Medicine Center is assigned a specific five-digit number. Although the InvoiceNum field will contain these number values, the numbers will never be used in calculations; therefore, you'll assign the Short Text data type to this field. Any time a field contains number values that will not be used in calculations—such as phone numbers, postal codes, and so on—you should use the Short Text data type instead of the Number data type.

To define the InvoiceNum field:

1. Type **InvoiceNum** in the first row's Field Name box, and then press **TAB** to advance to the Data Type box. The default data type, Short Text, appears highlighted in the Data Type box, which now also contains an arrow, and the field properties for a Short Text field appear in the Field Properties pane. See Figure 1–12.

Figure 1–12 Table window after entering the first field name

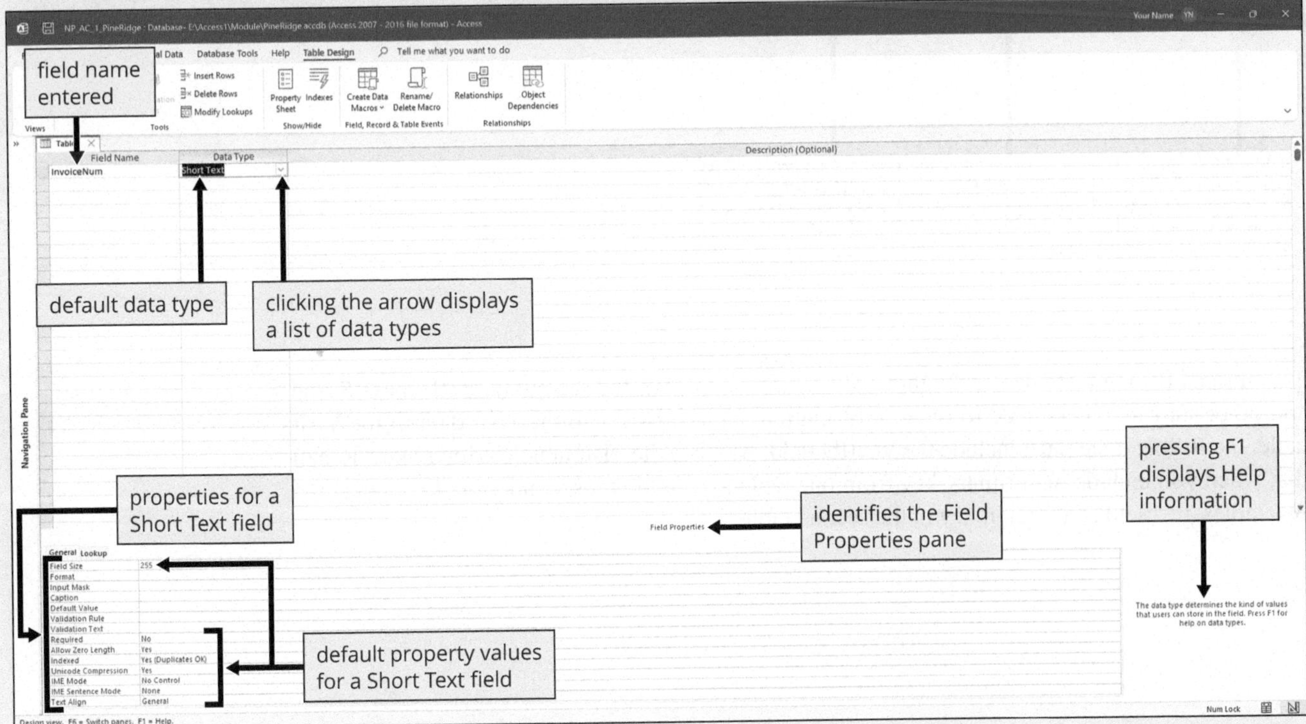

Tip You can also press ENTER to move from one property to the next in the Table Design grid.

The right side of the Field Properties pane now provides an explanation for the current property, Data Type.

Trouble? If you make a typing error, you can correct it by clicking to position the insertion point, and then using either BACKSPACE to delete characters to the left of the insertion point or DELETE to delete characters to the right of the insertion point. Then type the correct text.

Because the InvoiceNum field values will not be used in calculations, you will accept the default Short Text data type for the field.

2. Press **TAB** to accept Short Text as the data type and to advance to the Description (Optional) box.

   Next, you'll enter the Description property value as "Primary key." The value you enter for the Description property will appear on the status bar when you view the table datasheet. Note that specifying "Primary key" for the Description property does *not* establish the current field as the primary key; you use a button on the ribbon to specify the primary key in Design view, which you will do later in this part.

3. Type **Primary key** in the Description (Optional) box and press **ENTER**. See Figure 1–13.

   At this point, you have entered the first field (InvoiceNum) into the table and are ready to enter the remaining fields into the table.

   Tip You can also use TAB to advance to the second row's Field Name box.

Figure 1–13 InvoiceNum field defined

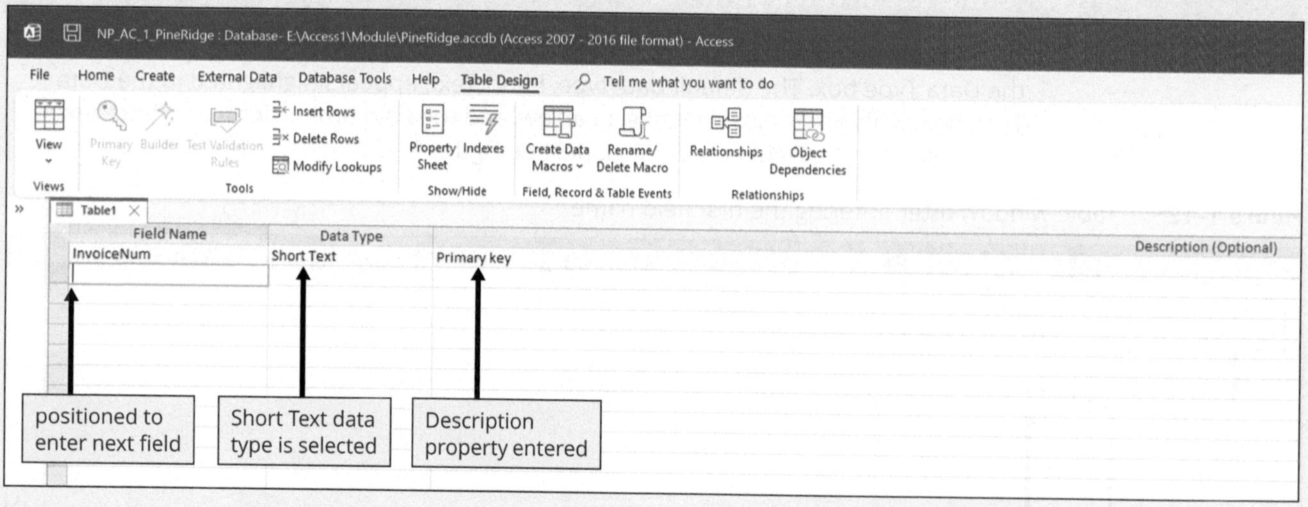

Susan's Billing table design (Figure 1–11) shows VisitID as the second field. Because Susan and other staff members need to relate information about invoices to the visit data in the Visit table, the Billing table must include the VisitID field, which is the Visit table's primary key. Recall that when you include the primary key from one table as a field in a second table to connect the two tables, the field is a foreign key in the second table.

To define the VisitID field:

1. If the insertion point is not already positioned in the second row's Field Name box, click the second row's Field Name box. Once properly positioned, type **VisitID** in the box, and then press **TAB** to advance to the Data Type box.
2. Press **TAB** to accept Short Text as the field's data type. Because the VisitID field is a foreign key to the Visit table, you'll enter "Foreign key" in the Description (Optional) box to help users of the database understand the purpose of this field.
3. Type **Foreign key** in the Description (Optional) box and press **ENTER**.

The third field in the Billing table is the InvoiceAmount field, which will display the dollar amount of each invoice the center sends to the patients. The Currency data type is the appropriate choice for this field.

Tip The quickest way to move back to the Table Design grid is to use the mouse.

To define the InvoiceAmount field:

1. In the third row's Field Name box, type **InvoiceAmount** and then press **TAB** to advance to the Data Type box.
2. Click the **Data Type** arrow, click **Currency** in the list, and then press **TAB** to advance to the Description (Optional) box.

   The InvoiceAmount field is not a primary key, nor does it have a relationship with a field in another table, so you do not need to enter a description for this field. If you've assigned a descriptive field name and the field does not fulfill a special function (such as primary key), you usually do not enter a value for the optional Description property.
3. Press **TAB** to advance to the fourth row's Field Name box.

The fourth field in the Billing table is the InvoiceDate field. This field will contain the dates on which invoices are generated for the center's patients. You'll define the InvoiceDate field using the Date/Time data type.

To define the InvoiceDate field:

1. In the fourth row's Field Name box, type **InvoiceDate** and then press **TAB** to advance to the Data Type box.

   You can select a value from the Data Type list as you did for the InvoiceAmount field. Alternately, you can type the property value in the box or type just the first character of the property value.
2. Type **d**. The value in the fourth row's Data Type box changes to "date/Time," with the letters "ate/Time" highlighted. See Figure 1–14.

Figure 1–14 Selecting a value for the Data Type property

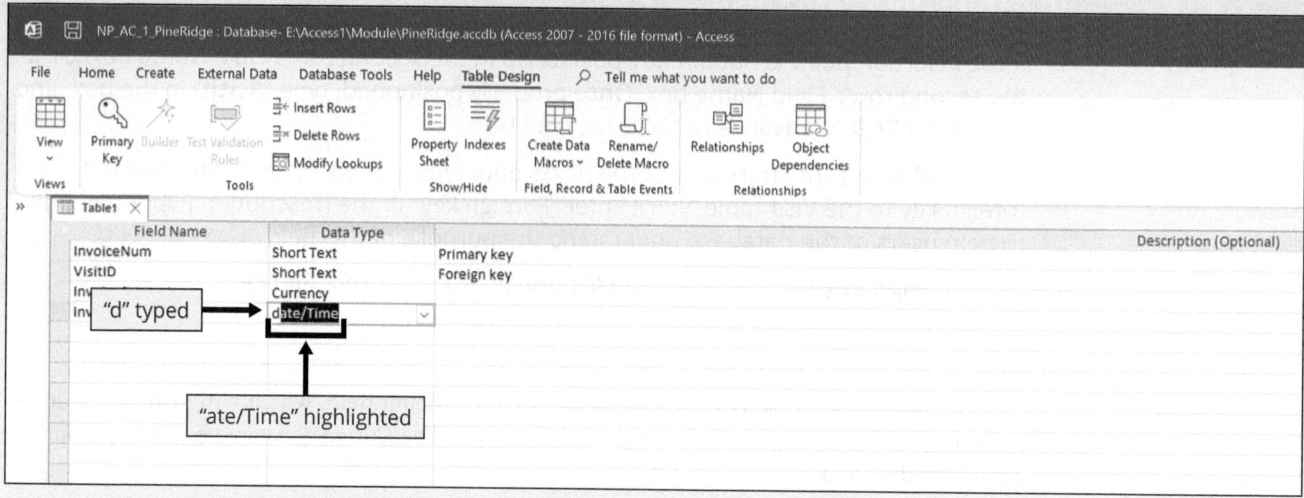

3. Press **TAB** to advance to the Description (Optional) box. Note that Access changes the value for the Data Type property to "Date/Time."
4. Because the InvoiceDate field does not need a special description, press **TAB**.

The fifth, and final, field to define in the Billing table is InvoicePaid. This field will be a Yes/No field to indicate the payment status of each invoice record stored in the Billing table. Recall that the Yes/No data type defines fields that store true/false, yes/no, and on/off field values. When you create a Yes/No field in a table, the default Format property is set to Yes/No.

To define the InvoicePaid field:

1. In the fifth row's Field Name box, type **InvoicePaid** and then press **TAB** to advance to the Data Type box.
2. Type **y**. Access completes the data type as "yes/No." Press **TAB** to select the Yes/No data type and move to the Description (Optional) box.
3. Because the InvoicePaid field does not need a special description, press **TAB**.

You've finished defining the fields for the Billing table. Next, you need to specify the primary key for the table.

Specifying the Primary Key

As you learned previously, the primary key for a table uniquely identifies each record in the table.

Reference

Specifying a Primary Key in Design View

- Display the table in Design view.
- Click in the row for the field you've chosen to be the primary key to make it the active field. If the primary key consists of two or more fields, click the row selector for the first field, press and hold down CTRL, and then click the row selector for each additional primary key field.
- On the Table Design tab, in the Tools group, click the Primary Key button.

According to Susan's design, you need to specify InvoiceNum as the primary key for the Billing table. You can do so while the table is in Design view.

To specify InvoiceNum as the primary key:

1. Click in the row for the InvoiceNum field to make it the current field.
2. On the Table Design tab, in the Tools group, click the **Primary Key** button. The Primary Key button is highlighted and a key symbol appears in the row selector for the first row, indicating that the InvoiceNum field is the table's primary key. See Figure 1–15.

   Tip The Primary Key button is a toggle; you can click it to remove the key symbol.

Figure 1–15 InvoiceNum field selected as the primary key

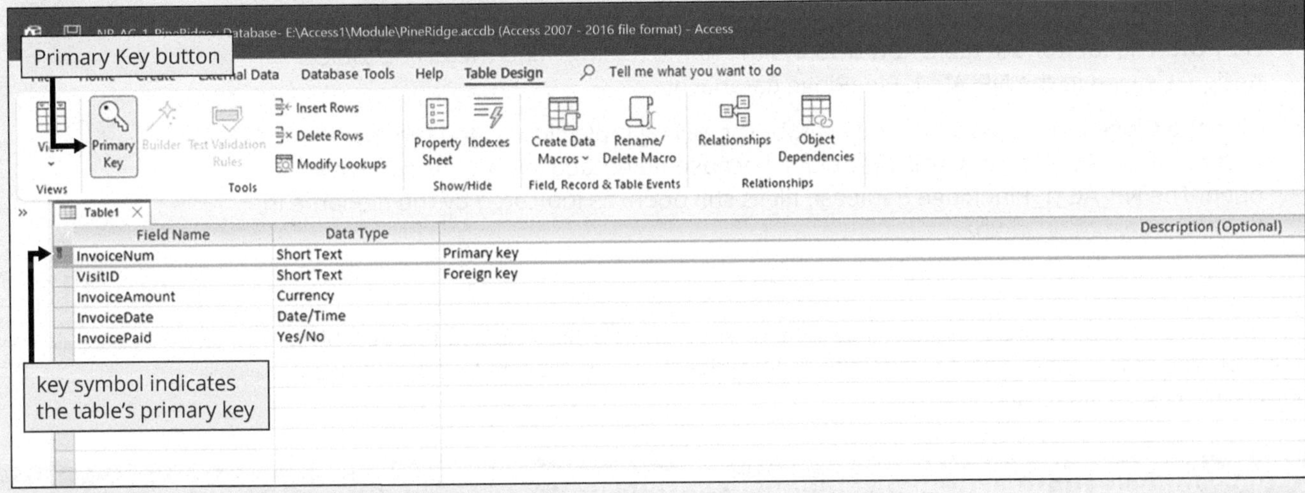

Renaming Fields in Design View

Susan has decided to rename the InvoiceAmount field in the Billing table to InvoiceAmt. Since Amt is an appropriate abbreviation for Amount, this new name will be just as readable, yet a little shorter.

To rename a field in Design view:

1. Click to position the insertion point to the right of the word "InvoiceAmount" in the third row's Field Name box, and then press **BACKSPACE** four times to delete the letters "ount." The name of the fourth field is now InvoiceAm. Now add the final letter by pressing the letter **t**. The name of the new field is now InvoiceAmt as Susan wants it to be. See Figure 1–16.

   Tip You can also select an entire field name and then type new text to replace it.

2. Click in the row for the InvoiceAmt field to make it the current field, if necessary.

Figure 1–16 Billing table after renamed field

Field Name	Data Type	Description (Optional)
InvoiceNum	Short Text	Primary key
VisitID	Short Text	Foreign key
InvoiceAmt	Currency	
InvoiceDate	Date/Time	
InvoicePaid	Yes/No	

renamed field

Saving the Billing Table Structure

As with the Visit table, the last step in creating a table is to name the table and save the table's structure. When you save a table structure, the table is stored in the database file (in this case, the NP_AC_1_PineRidge database file). After saving the table, you can enter data into it. According to Susan's plan, you need to save the table you've defined as "Billing."

To save, name, and close the Billing table:

1. On the Quick Access Toolbar, click the **Save** button. The Save As dialog box opens.
2. With the default name Table1 selected in the Table Name box, type **Billing**, and then click **OK**. The tab for the table now displays the name "Billing," and the Billing table design is saved in the NP_AC_1_PineRidge database.
3. Click the **Close** button on the object tab. The Billing table closes, and the main portion of the Access window is now blank because no database object is currently open. The NP_AC_1_PineRidge database file is still open, as indicated by the filename in the Access window title bar.

You have now successfully created and saved the structures for the Visit and Billing tables; however, you have not yet added any data to these tables. You can view and work with these objects in the Navigation Pane.

To view objects in the NP_AC_1_PineRidge database:

1. On the Navigation Pane, click the **Shutter Bar Open/Close Button** to open it. See Figure 1-17.

Figure 1-17 Billing and Visit tables (database objects) displayed in the Navigation Pane

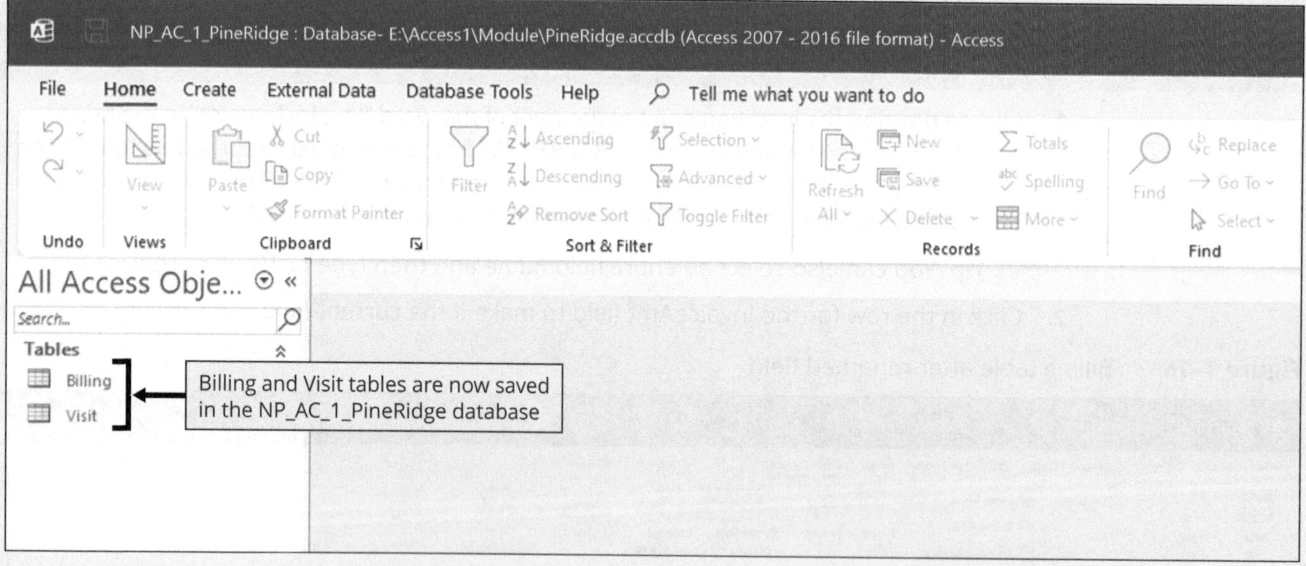

Closing a Table and Exiting Access

When you are finished working in an Access table, it's a good idea to close the table so that you do not make unintended changes to the table data. You can close a table by clicking its Close button on the object tab, as you did earlier. Or, if you want to close the Access program as well, you can click the program's Close button. When you do, any open tables are closed, the active database is closed, and you exit the Access program.

To close any opened tables and exit Access:

1. Click the **Close** button on the program window title bar. Any opened tables would close, along with the NP_AC_1_PineRidge database, and then the Access program closes.

   Tip To close a database without exiting Access, click the File tab to display Backstage view, and then click Close.

Insight

Saving a Database

Unlike the Save buttons in other Office programs, the Save button on the Quick Access Toolbar in Access does not save the active document (database). Instead, you use the Save button to save the design of an Access object, such as a table (as you did earlier), or to save datasheet format changes, such as resizing columns. Access does not have or need a button or option you can use to save the active database.

Access saves changes to the active database automatically when you change or add a record or close the database. If your database is stored on a removable storage device, such as a USB drive, you should never remove the device while the database file is open. If you do, Access will encounter problems when it tries to save the database, which might damage the database. Make sure you close the database first before removing the storage device.

It is possible to save a database with a different name. To do so, you would click the File tab to open Backstage view, and then click the Save As option. You save the database in the default database format unless you select a different format, so click the Save As button to open the Save As dialog box. Enter the new name for the database, choose the location for saving the file, and then click Save. The database is saved with a new name and is stored in the specified location.

Now that you've become familiar with database concepts and Access and created the NP_AC_1_PineRidge database and the structures for the Visit and Billing tables, Susan wants you to add records to the Visit table and work with the data stored in it to create database objects including a query, form, and report. You'll complete these tasks in the next part.

Part 1.1 Quick Check

1. A single characteristic of a person, place, object, event, or idea is called a(n) ________.
2. You connect the records in two separate tables through a(n) ________ that appears in both tables.
3. The field with values that uniquely identify each record in a table is called the ________; when it is placed in a second table to form a relationship between the two tables, it is called the ________.
4. What is the area of the Access window that lists all the objects in a database and is the main control center for opening and working with database objects?
5. What is the name of the field that Access creates, by default, as the primary key field for a new table in Datasheet view?
6. Which group on the Table Fields tab contains the options you use to add new fields to a table?
7. What are the two views you can use to create a table in Access?
8. Explain how saving in Access is different from saving in other Office programs.

Part 1.2 Visual Overview: The Create Tab Options

The Microsoft Access Help button on the Help tab opens the **Access Help** pane, where you can find information about Access commands and features as well as instructions for using them.

The **Create tab** provides options for creating database objects including tables, forms, and reports. The options appear on the tab grouped by object type.

The **Query Wizard button** opens a dialog box listing types of wizards that guide you through the steps to create a query. One of these, the **Simple Query Wizard**, allows you to select records and fields to display in the query results.

You use the options in the Tables group to create a table in Datasheet view or in Design view.

The Queries group contains options for creating a **query**, which is a question you ask about the data stored in a database. In response to a query, Access displays the specific records and fields that answer your questions.

The **Form tool** quickly creates a form containing all the fields in the table (or query) on which you're basing the form.

The Forms group contains options for creating a **form**, which is a database object you use to enter, edit, and view records in a database.

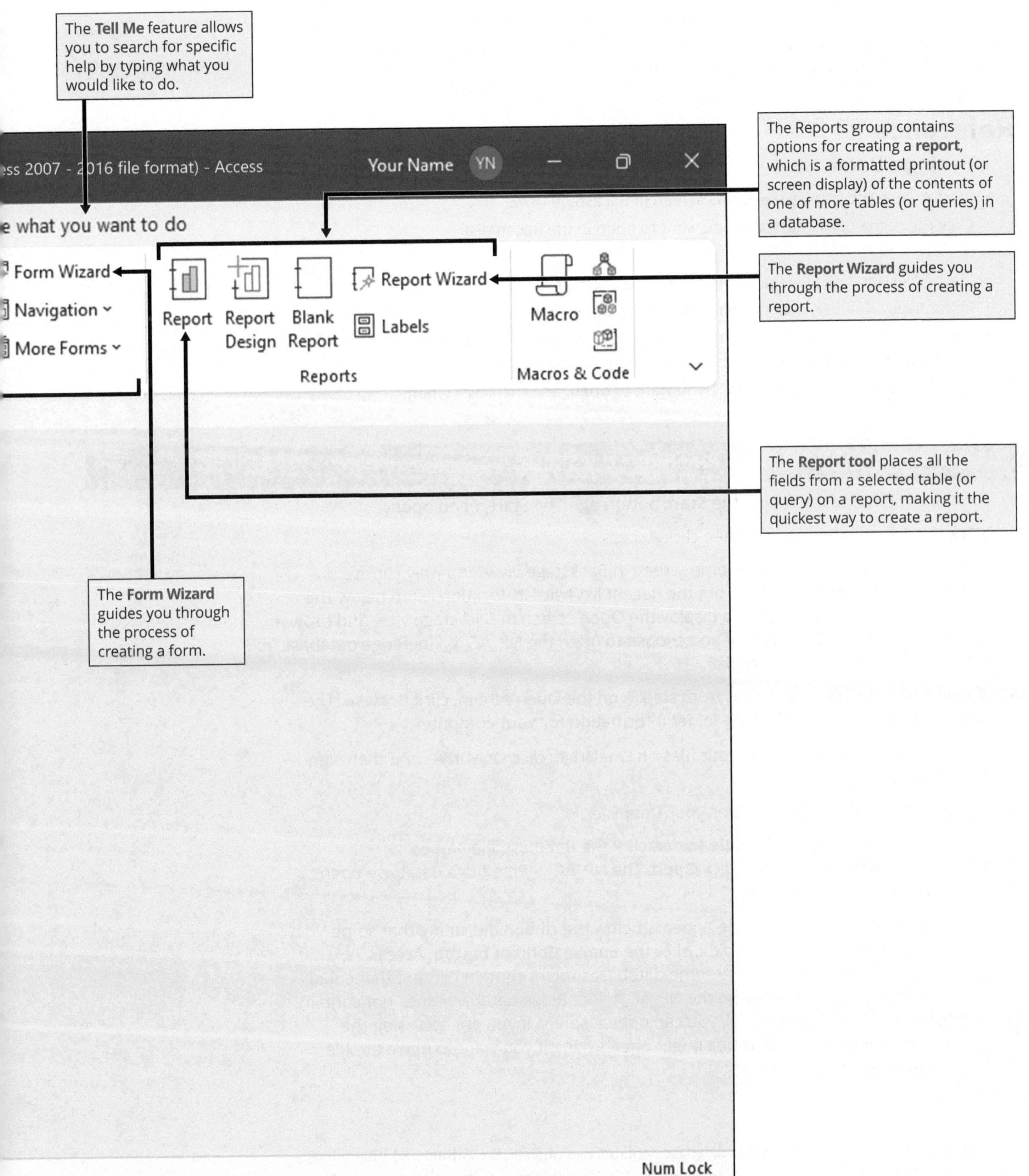
The **Tell Me** feature allows you to search for specific help by typing what you would like to do.
ess 2007 - 2016 file format) - Access
Your Name
YN
e what you want to do
Form Wizard
Navigation
More Forms
Report
Report Design
Blank Report
Report Wizard
Labels
Reports
Macro
Macros & Code
Num Lock
The Reports group contains options for creating a **report**, which is a formatted printout (or screen display) of the contents of one of more tables (or queries) in a database.
The **Report Wizard** guides you through the process of creating a report.
The **Report tool** places all the fields from a selected table (or query) on a report, making it the quickest way to create a report.
The **Form Wizard** guides you through the process of creating a form.

Entering Data into Tables

With the fields in place for the Visit table, you can now enter the field values for each record. However, if you closed Access after the previous part, as instructed, you must first open Access and the NP_AC_1_PineRidge database to work with the Visit table. If you did not close Access in the previous part and the NP_AC_1_PineRidge database is still open (refer to previous Figure 1–17), you may skip the following steps that open Access and the NP_AC_1_PineRidge database and go directly to the steps to enter data into the Visit table.

Reference

Opening a Database

- Start Access and display the Home screen in Backstage view.
- Click the name of the database you want to open in the Recent list.

or

- Start Access and display the Home screen in Backstage view.
- In the navigation bar, click Open to display the Open screen.
- Click the Browse button to open the Open dialog box, and then navigate to the drive and folder containing the database file you want to open.
- Click the name of the database file you want to open, and then click Open.

To open Access and NP_AC_1_PineRidge database:

1. On the Windows taskbar, click the **Start** button. The Start menu opens.
2. Click the **All apps** button, and then click **Access**.
3. Access starts and displays the Home screen in Backstage view. You may choose the **NP_AC_1_PineRidge** database from the Recent list (with its location listed below the database name) or click **Open** to display the Open screen in Backstage view and browse to your database and location. If you choose to open the NP_AC_1_PineRidge database from the Recent list, skip steps 4–6.
4. If you choose to open other files from step 3, on the Open screen, click **Browse**. The Open dialog box opens, showing folder information for your computer.

   Trouble? If you are storing your files on OneDrive, click OneDrive, and then sign in if necessary.

5. Navigate to the drive that contains your Data Files.
6. Navigate to the **Access1 > Module** folder, click the database file named **NP_AC_1_PineRidge**, and then click **Open**. The NP_AC_1_PineRidge database opens in the Access program window.

   Trouble? If a security warning appears below the ribbon indicating that some active content has been disabled, click the Enable Content button. Access provides this warning because some databases might contain content that could harm your computer. Because the NP_AC_1_PineRidge database does not contain objects that could be harmful, you can open it safely. If you are accessing the file over a network, a dialog box might open asking if you want to make the file a trusted document; click Yes.

Note that the NP_AC_1_PineRidge database contains two objects, the Billing and Visit tables, just as you ended the previous part (refer to Figure 1–17). The next step is for you to open the Visit table to begin adding records.

To open the Visit table:

1. In the Navigation Pane, double-click **Visit** to open the Visit table in Datasheet view.
2. On the Navigation Pane, click the **Shutter Bar Open/Close Button** « to close the pane.
3. Click the first row value for the VisitID field. See Figure 1–18.

Figure 1–18 Visit table opened and ready to enter data

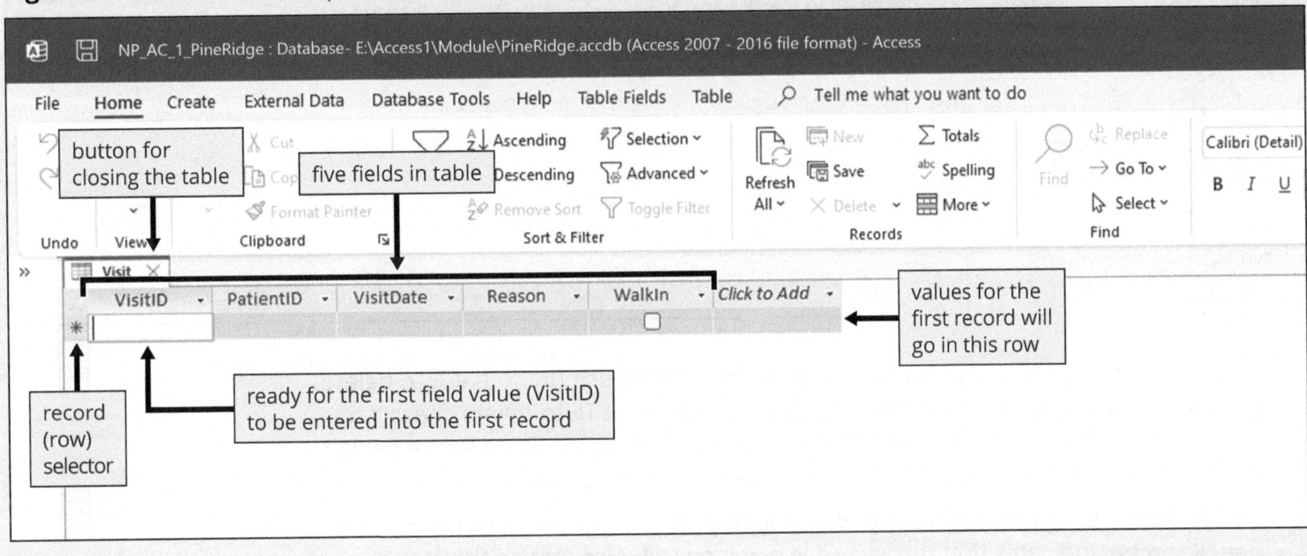

You are now ready to begin adding records and are positioned in the first field (VisitID) of the first record. Susan requests that you enter eight records into the Visit table, as shown in Figure 1–19.

Figure 1–19 Visit table records

VisitID	PatientID	VisitDate	Reason	WalkIn
3182	27674	12/27/2029	Physical therapy	No
3140	27739	10/25/2029	Repetitive strain injury	Yes
3202	27683	1/23/2030	Wrist pain	Yes
3156	27681	11/15/2029	Physical therapy	No
3263	27706	3/26/2030	Foot injury	Yes
3236	27710	2/25/2030	Bike accident	Yes
3192	27716	1/8/2030	Wrist pain	Yes
3162	27683	11/23/2029	Back pain	No

To enter the first record for the Visit table:

1. In the first row for the VisitID field, type **3182** (the VisitID field value for the first record), and then press **TAB**. Access adds the field value and moves the insertion point to the right, into the PatientID column. See Figure 1–20.

   Key Step Be sure to type the numbers "0" and "1" and not the letters "O" and "l" when entering numeric values, even though the field is of the Short Text data type.

Figure 1–20 First field value entered

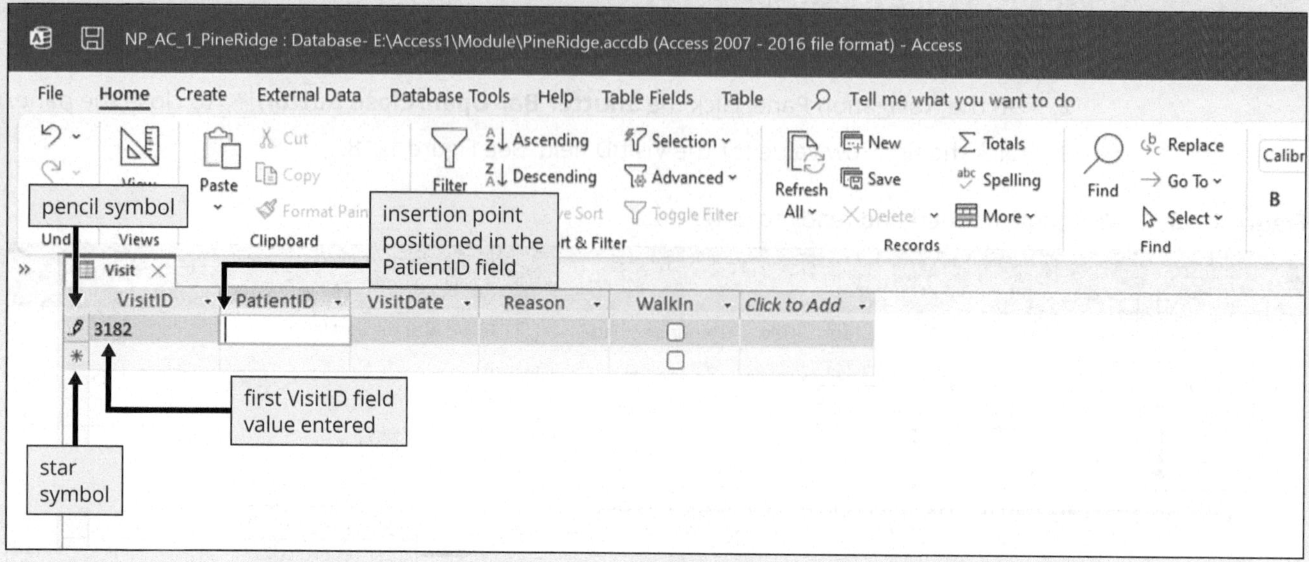

Trouble? If you make a mistake when typing a value, use BACKSPACE to delete characters to the left of the insertion point or use DELETE to delete characters to the right of the insertion point. Then type the correct value. To correct a value by replacing it entirely, press ESC, and then type the correct value.

Notice the pencil symbol that appears in the row selector for the new record. The **pencil symbol** indicates that the record is being edited. Also, notice the star symbol that appears in the row selector for the second row. The **star symbol** identifies the second row as the next row available for a new record.

2. Type **27674** (the PatientID field value for the first record), and then press **TAB**. Access enters the field value and moves the insertion point to the VisitDate column.
3. Type **12/27/29** (the VisitDate field value for the first record), and then press **TAB**. Access displays the year as "2029" even though you entered only the final two digits of the year. This is because the VisitDate field has the Date/Time data type, which automatically formats dates with four-digit years.
4. Type **Physical therapy** (the Reason field value for the first record), and then press **TAB** to move to the WalkIn column.

   Recall that the WalkIn field is a Yes/No field. Notice the check box displayed in the WalkIn column. By default, the value for any Yes/No field is "No"; therefore, the check box is initially empty. For Yes/No fields with check boxes, you press TAB to leave the check box unchecked, or you press SPACEBAR to insert a checkmark in the check box. The record you are entering in the table is not for a walk-in visit, so you do not need to insert a checkmark in the check box to indicate "No."
5. Press **TAB** since you do not want to insert a checkmark. The first record is entered into the table, and the insertion point is positioned in the VisitID field for the second record. The pencil symbol is removed from the first row because the record in that row is no longer being edited. The table is now ready for you to enter the second record. See Figure 1–21.

   Tip You can also click a check box in a Yes/No field to insert or remove a checkmark.

Figure 1–21 Datasheet with first record entered

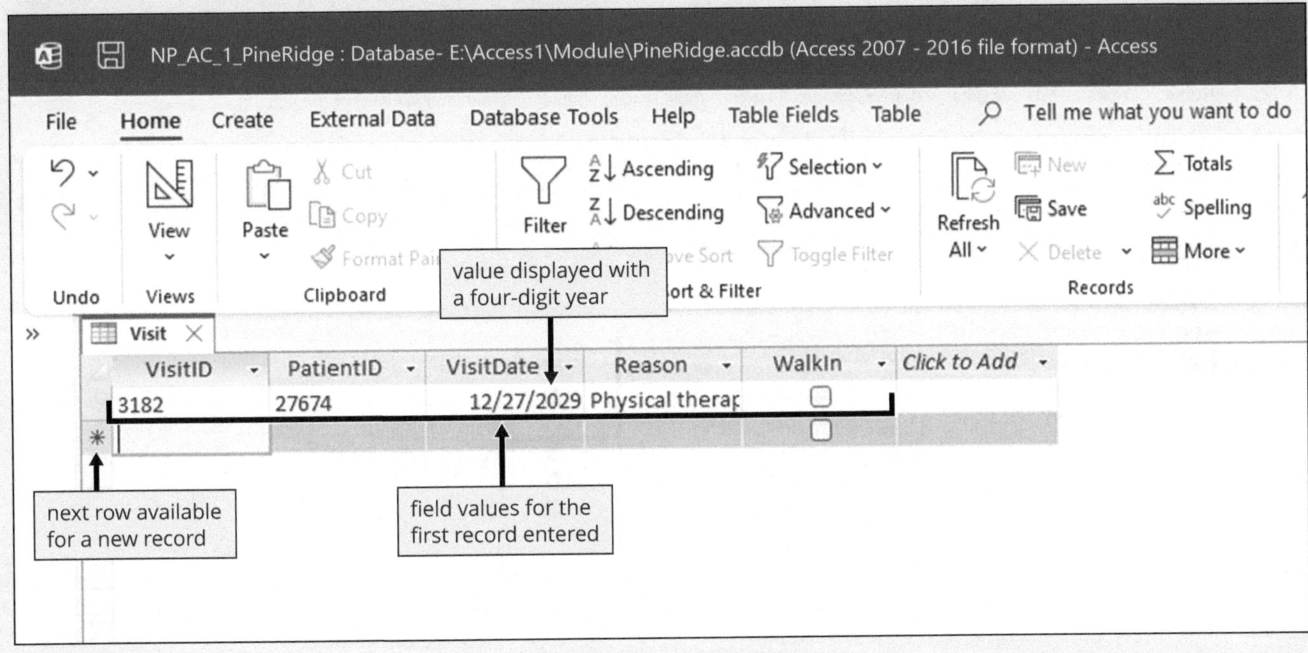

Now you can enter the remaining seven records in the Visit table.

To enter the remaining records in the Visit table:

1. Referring to Figure 1–19, enter the values for records 2 through 8, pressing **TAB** to move from field to field and to the next row for a new record. Keep in mind that you do not have to type all four digits of the year in the VisitDate field values; you can enter only the final two digits, and Access will display all four. Also, for any WalkIn field values of "No," be sure to press TAB to leave the check box empty. For WalkIn fields values of "Yes," you can press the SPACEBAR to insert a checkmark in the check box.

   Trouble? If you enter a value in the wrong field by mistake, such as entering a Reason field value in the VisitDate field, a menu might open with options for addressing the problem. If this happens, click the "Enter new value" option in the menu. You'll return to the field with the incorrect value selected, which you can then replace by typing the correct value.

   Tip You can also press ENTER instead of TAB to move from one field to another and to the next row.

   Notice that not all of the Reason field values are fully displayed. To display more of the table datasheet and the full field values, you'll resize the Reason column.

2. Place the pointer on the vertical line to the right of the Reason field name until the pointer changes to the column resizing pointer ↔, and then double-click the vertical line. All the Reason field values are now fully displayed. See Figure 1–22.

Figure 1–22 Datasheet with eight records entered

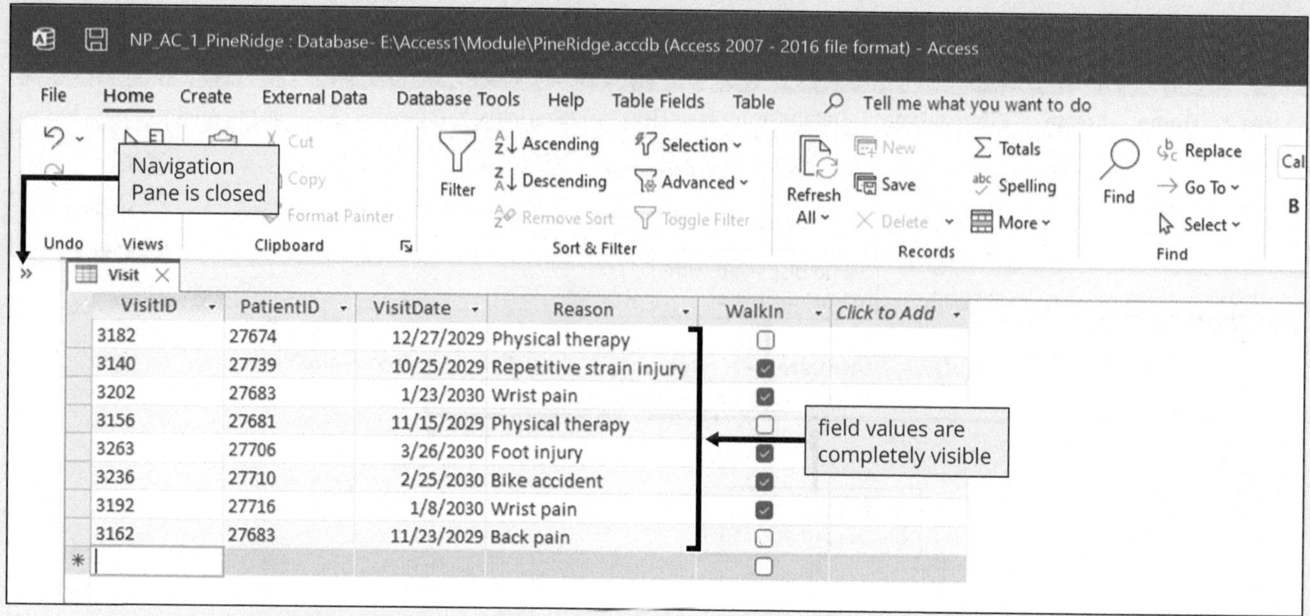

When you resize a datasheet column by double-clicking the column dividing line, you are sizing the column to its **best fit**—that is, so the column is just wide enough to display the longest visible value in the column, including the field name.

3. Compare your table to the one in Figure 1–22. If any of the field values in your table do not match those shown in the figure, you can correct a field value by clicking to position the insertion point in the value, and then using BACKSPACE or DELETE to delete incorrect text. Type the correct text and press ENTER. To correct a value in the WalkIn field, click the check box to add or remove the checkmark as appropriate. Also, be sure the spelling and capitalization of field names in your table match those shown in the figure exactly and that there are no spaces between words. To correct a field name, double-click it to select it, and then type the correct name; or use the Rename Field option on the shortcut menu to rename a field with the correct name.

> **Key Step** Carefully compare your VisitID and PatientID values with those in the figure and correct any errors before continuing.

Remember that Access automatically saves the data stored in a table; however, you must save any new or modified structure to a table. Even though you have not clicked the Save button, your data has already been saved. To ensure this is the case, you can close the table and then reopen it.

To close and reopen the Visit table:

1. Click the **Close** button [×] on the object tab for the Visit table. When asked if you would like to save the changes to the layout of the Visit table, click **Yes**. The Visit table closes.
2. On the Navigation Pane, click the **Shutter Bar Open/Close Button** [»] to open it.
3. In the Navigation Pane, double-click **Visit** to open the Visit table in Datasheet view.

Notice that after you closed and reopened the Visit table, Access sorted and displayed the records in order by the values in the VisitID field because it is the primary key. If you compare your screen to Figure 1–22, which shows the records in the order you entered them, you'll notice that the current screen shows the records in order by the VisitID field values.

Susan asks you to add two more records to the Visit table. When you add a record to an existing table, you must enter the new record in the next row available for a new record; you cannot insert a row between existing records for the new record. In a table with just a few records, such as the Visit table, the next available row is visible on the screen. However, in a table with hundreds of records, you would need to scroll the datasheet to display the next row available. The easiest way to add a new record to a table is to use the New button, which scrolls the datasheet to the next row available so you can enter the new record.

To enter additional records in the Visit table:

1. If necessary, click the first record's VisitID field value (**3140**) to make it the current record.
2. In the Records group, click the **New** button. The insertion point is positioned in the next row available for a new record, which in this case is row 9. See Figure 1–23.

Figure 1–23 Entering a new record

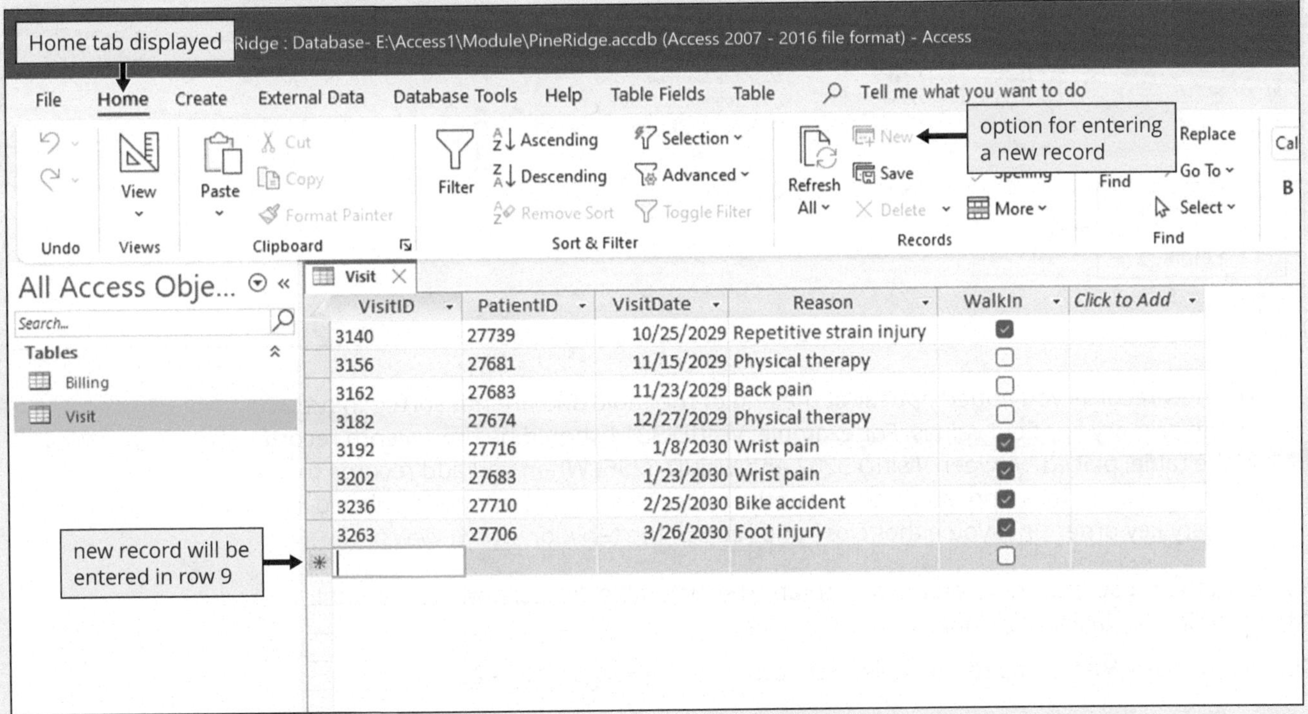

3. With the insertion point in the VisitID field for the new record, type **3273** and then press **TAB**.
4. Complete the entry of this record by entering each of the following values, pressing **TAB** to move from field to field:

   PatientID = **27684**

   VisitDate = **4/1/2030**

   Reason = **Back pain**

   WalkIn = **Yes (checked)**

5. Enter the values for the next new record, as follows, and then press **TAB** after entering the WalkIn field value:

   VisitID = **3214**

   PatientID = **27724**

   VisitDate = **2/4/2030**

   Reason = **Hip pain**

   WalkIn = **Yes (checked)**

   Your datasheet should look like the one shown in Figure 1–24.

Figure 1–24 Datasheet with additional records entered

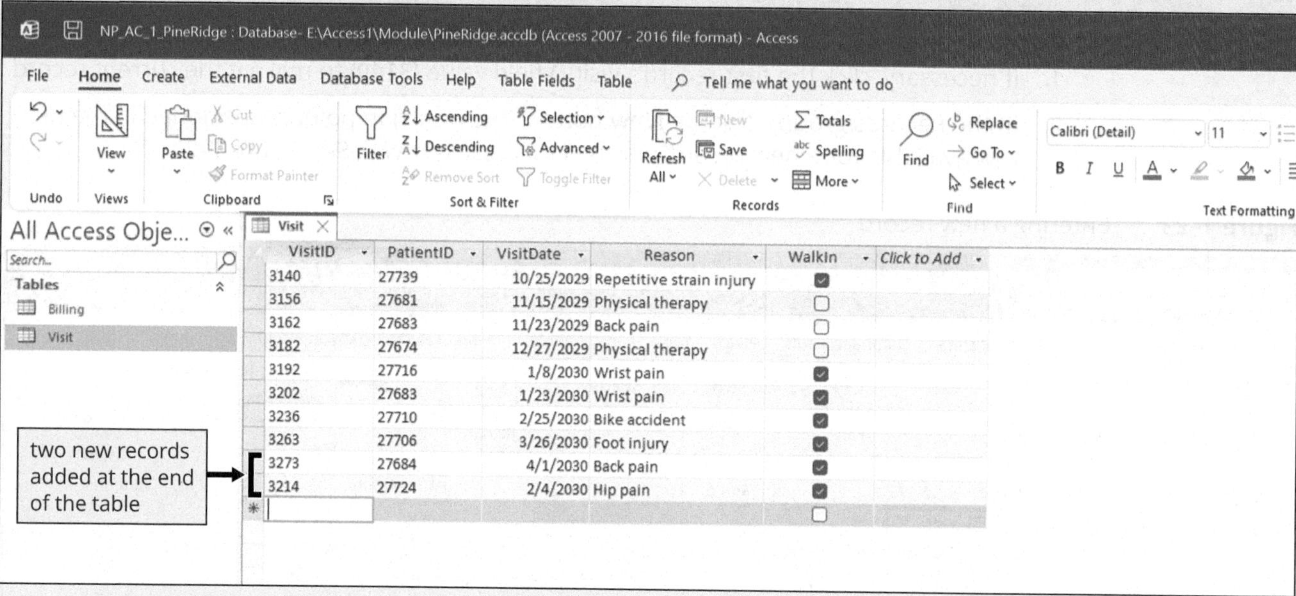

VisitID	PatientID	VisitDate	Reason	WalkIn
3140	27739	10/25/2029	Repetitive strain injury	☑
3156	27681	11/15/2029	Physical therapy	☐
3162	27683	11/23/2029	Back pain	☐
3182	27674	12/27/2029	Physical therapy	☐
3192	27716	1/8/2030	Wrist pain	☑
3202	27683	1/23/2030	Wrist pain	☑
3236	27710	2/25/2030	Bike accident	☑
3263	27706	3/26/2030	Foot injury	☑
3273	27684	4/1/2030	Back pain	☑
3214	27724	2/4/2030	Hip pain	☑

The new records you added appear at the end of the table and are not sorted in order by the primary key field values. For example, VisitID 3214 should be the seventh record in the table, placed between VisitID 3202 and VisitID 3236. When you add records to a table datasheet, they appear at the end of the table. The records are not displayed in primary key order until you either close and reopen the table or switch views.

6. Click the **Close** button [X] on the object tab. The Visit table closes; however, it is still listed in the Navigation Pane.
7. Double-click **Visit** to open the table in Datasheet view. See Figure 1–25.

Figure 1–25 Table with 10 records entered and displayed in primary key order

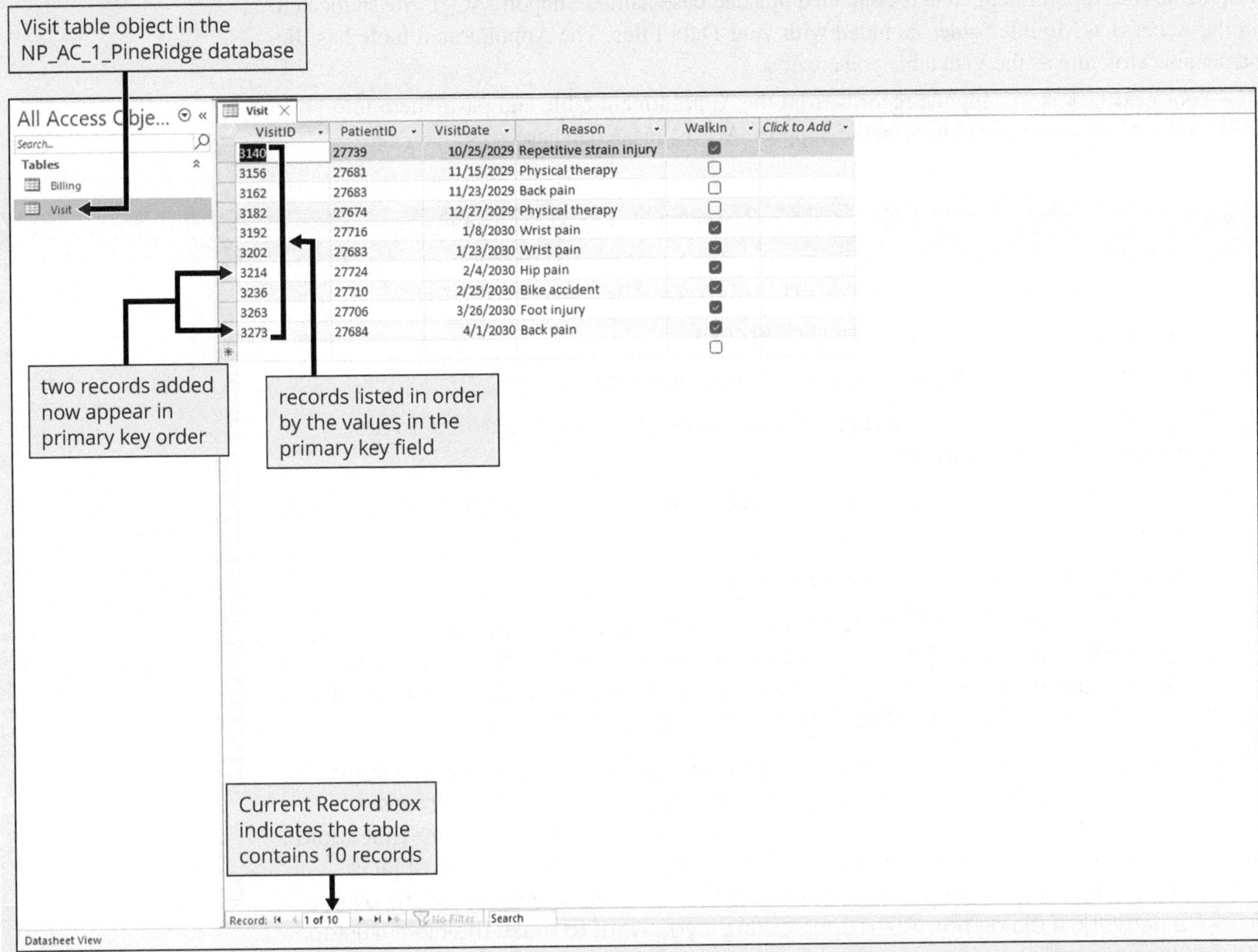

The two records you added, with VisitID field values of 3214 and 3273, now appear in the correct primary key order. The table contains a total of 10 records, as indicated by the **Current Record box** at the bottom of the datasheet. The Current Record box displays the number of the current record as well as the total number of records in the table.

Each record contains a unique VisitID value because this field is the primary key. Other fields, however, can contain the same value in multiple records; for example, the Reason field has two values of "Physical therapy."

8. Click the **Close** button on the program window title bar. The Visit table, along with the NP_AC_1_PineRidge database, close, and then the Access program closes.

Copying Records from Another Access Database

When you created the Visit table, you entered records directly into the table datasheet. There are many other ways to enter records in a table, including copying and pasting records from a table into the same database or into a different database. To use this method, however, the two tables must have the same structure—that is, the tables must contain the same fields, with the same design, in the same order.

Susan has already created a table named Appointment that contains additional records with visit data. The Appointment table is contained in a database named Support_AC_1_Susan located in the Access1 > Module folder included with your Data Files. The Appointment table has the same table structure as the Visit table you created.

Your next task is to copy the records from the Appointment table and paste them into your Visit table. To do so, you need to open the Support_AC_1_Susan database.

To copy the records from the Appointment table:

1. On the Windows taskbar, click the **Start** button . The Start menu opens.
2. Click the **All apps** button, and then click **Access.**
3. Click **Open** to display the Open screen in Backstage view.
4. On the Open screen, click **Browse**. The Open dialog box opens, showing folder information for your computer.

   Trouble? If you are storing your files on OneDrive, click OneDrive, and then log in if necessary.
5. Navigate to the drive that contains your Data Files.
6. Navigate to the **Access1 > Module** folder, click the database file named **Support_AC_1_Susan**, and then click **Open**. This module will refer to this database as the Susan database. The Susan database opens in the Access program window. Note that the database contains only one object, the Appointment table.

   Trouble? If a security warning appears below the ribbon indicating that some active content has been disabled, click the Enable Content button. Access provides this warning because some databases might contain content that could harm your computer. Because the Susan database does not contain objects that could be harmful, you can open it safely. If you are accessing the file over a network, a dialog box might open asking if you want to make the file a trusted document; click Yes.
7. In the Navigation Pane, double-click **Appointment** to open the Appointment table in Datasheet view. The table contains 75 records and the same five fields, with the same characteristics, as the fields in the Visit table. See Figure 1–26.

Figure 1–26 Appointment table in the Susan database

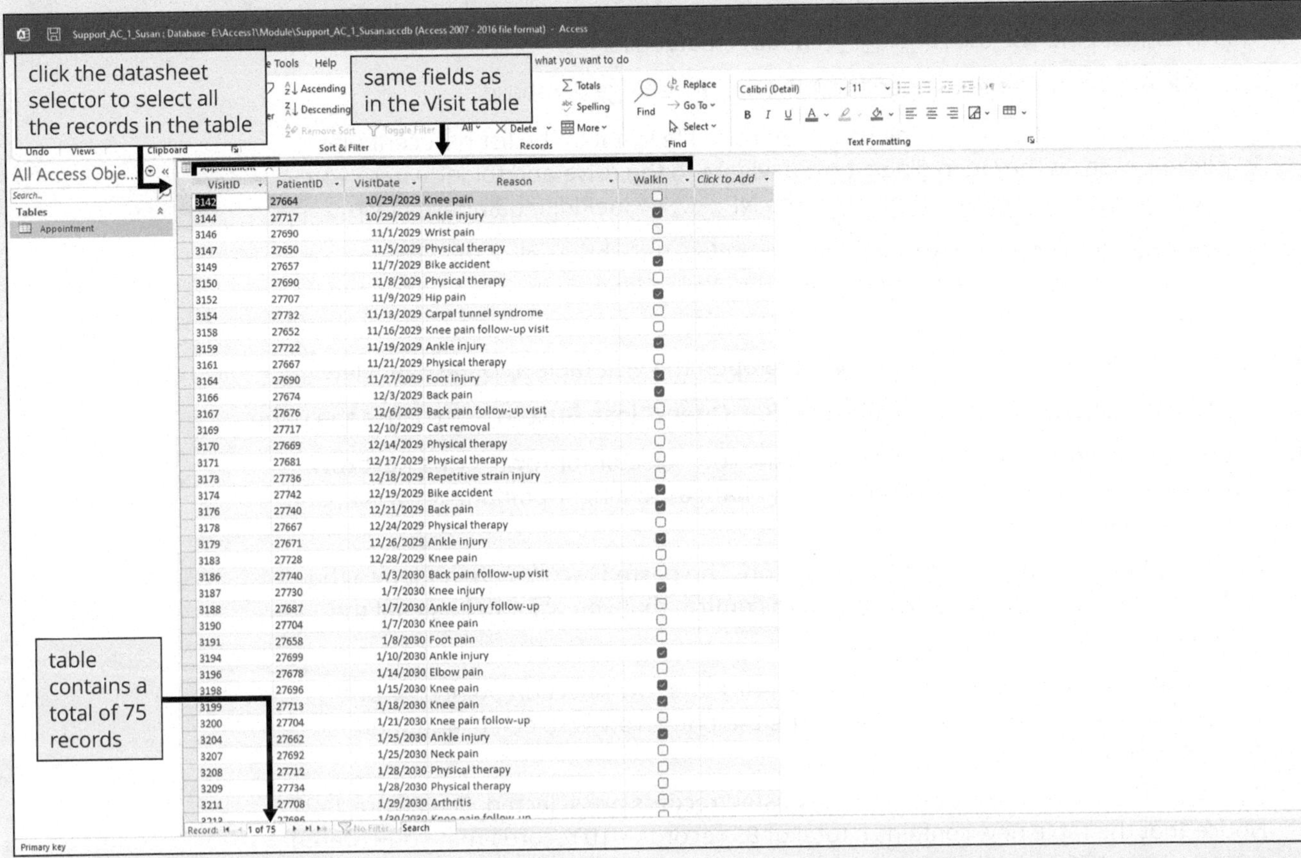

Susan wants you to copy all the records in the Appointment table. You can select all the records by clicking the **datasheet selector**, which is the box to the left of the first field name in the table datasheet, as shown in Figure 1–26.

8. Click the **datasheet selector** to the left of the VisitID field. All the records in the table are selected.
9. In the Clipboard group, click the **Copy** button. All the records are copied to the Clipboard.
10. Click the **Close** button on the object tab. A dialog box might open asking if you want to save the data you copied to the Clipboard. This dialog box opens only when you copy a large amount of data to the Clipboard.
11. Click **Yes**, if necessary. The dialog box closes, and then the Appointment table closes.

With the records copied to the Clipboard, you can now paste them into the Visit table. First you need to close the Susan database while keeping the Access program open, and then open the NP_AC_1_PineRidge database.

To close the Susan database and then paste the records into the Visit table:

1. Click the **File** tab to open Backstage view, and then click **Close** in the navigation bar to close the Susan database. You return to a blank Access program window, and the Home tab is the active tab on the ribbon.

2. Click the **File** tab to return to Backstage view, and then click **Open** in the navigation bar. Recent is selected on the Open screen, and the recently opened database files are listed. This list should include the NP_AC_1_PineRidge database.
3. Click **NP_AC_1_PineRidge** to open the NP_AC_1_PineRidge database.

   Trouble? If the NP_AC_1_PineRidge database file is not in the list of recent files, click Browse. In the Open dialog box, navigate to the drive and folder where you are storing your files, and then open the NP_AC_1_PineRidge database file.

   Trouble? If the security warning appears below the ribbon, click the Enable Content button, and then, if necessary, click Yes to identify the file as a trusted document.
4. In the Navigation Pane, double-click **Visit** to open the Visit table in Datasheet view.
5. On the Navigation Pane, click the **Shutter Bar Open/Close Button** « to close the pane.
6. Position the pointer on the star symbol in the row selector for row 11 (the next row available for a new record) until the pointer changes to a right-pointing arrow ➡, and then click to select the row.
7. In the Clipboard group, click the **Paste** button. The pasted records are added to the table, and a dialog box opens asking you to confirm that you want to paste all the records (75 total).

   Trouble? If the Paste button isn't active, click the row selection pointer ➡ on the row selector for row 11, making sure the entire row is selected, and then repeat Step 7.
8. Click **Yes**. The dialog box closes, and the pasted records are selected. See Figure 1–27. Notice that the table now contains a total of 85 records—10 records that you entered previously and 75 records that you copied and pasted.

Figure 1–27 Visit table after copying and pasting records

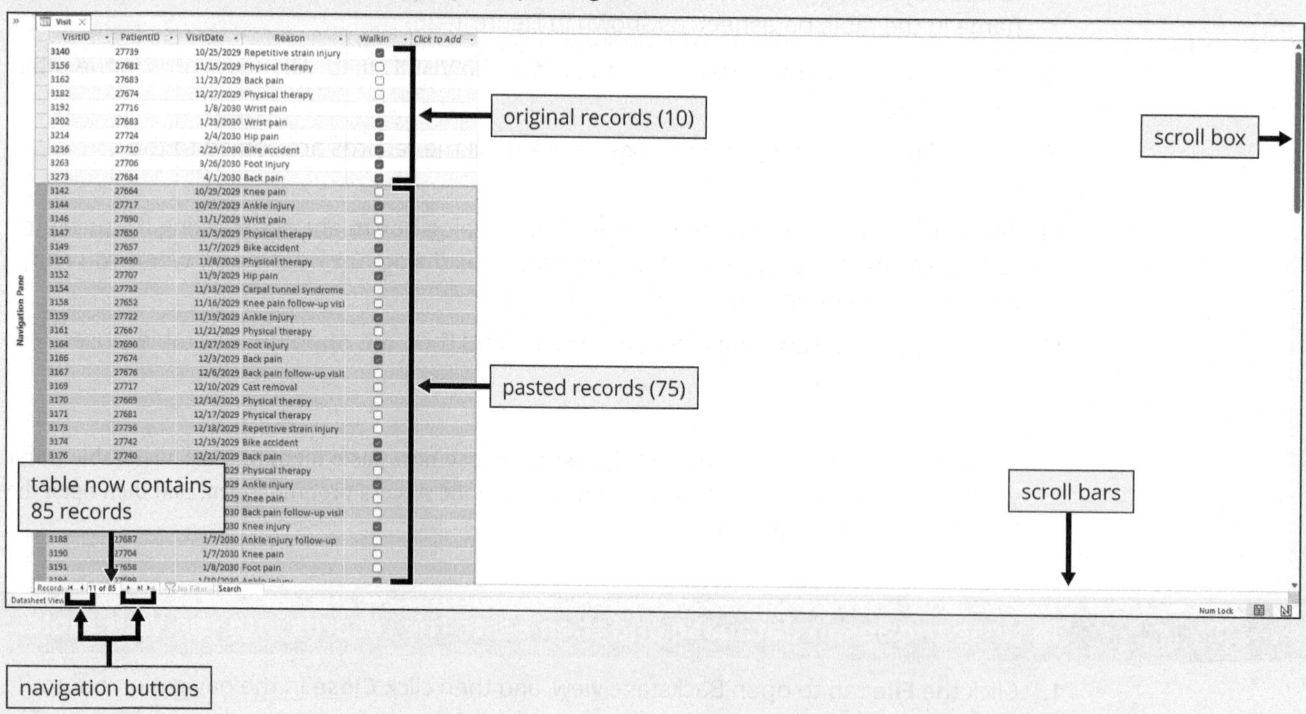

Not all the Reason field values are completely visible, so you need to resize this column to its best fit.

9. Place the pointer on the column dividing line to the right of the Reason field name until the pointer changes to the column resizing pointer ✛, and then double-click the column dividing line. The Reason field values are now fully displayed.

Navigating a Datasheet

The Visit table now contains 85 records, but only some of the records are visible on the screen. To view fields or records not currently visible on the screen, you can use the horizontal and vertical scroll bars to navigate the data. The **navigation buttons**, shown in Figure 1–27 and also described in Figure 1–28, provide another way to move vertically through the records. The Current Record box appears between the two sets of navigation buttons and displays the number of the current record as well as the total number of records in the table. Figure 1–28 shows which record becomes the current record when you click each navigation button. The New (blank) record button works the same way as the New button on the Home tab, which you used earlier to enter a new record in the table.

Figure 1–28 Navigation buttons

Navigation Button	Record Selected	Navigation Button	Record Selected
⏮	First record	⏭	Last record
◀	Previous record	▶✱	New (blank) record
▶	Next record		

Susan suggests that you use the various navigation techniques to move through the Visit table and become familiar with its contents.

To navigate the Visit datasheet:

1. Click the first record's VisitID field value (**3140**). The Current Record box shows that record 1 is the current record.

   Tip You can make a field the current field by clicking anywhere within the column for that field.

2. Click the **Next record** button ▶. The second record is now highlighted, which identifies it as the current record. The second record's value for the VisitID field is selected, and the Current Record box displays "2 of 85" to indicate that the second record is the current record.
3. Click the **Last record** button ⏭. The last record in the table, record 85, is now the current record.
4. Drag the scroll box in the vertical scroll bar up to the top of the bar. Record 85 is still the current record, as indicated in the Current Record box. Dragging the scroll box changes the display of the table datasheet but does not change the current record.
5. Drag the scroll box in the vertical scroll bar back down until you display the end of the table and the current record (record 85).
6. Click the **Previous record** button ◀. Record 84 is now the current record.
7. Click the **First record** button ⏮. The first record is now the current record and is visible on the screen.

Earlier you resized the Reason column to its best fit, to ensure all the field values were visible. However, when you resize a column to its best fit, the column expands to fully display only the field values that are visible on the screen at that time. If you move through the complete datasheet and notice that not all of the field values are fully displayed after the column resizing pointer resizing the column, you need to resize the column again.

8. Scroll down through the records and observe if the field values for the Reason field are fully displayed. The Reason field value for record 82 (visit 3274) is not fully displayed. With this record displayed, place the pointer on the column dividing line to the right of the Reason field name until the pointer changes to the column resizing pointer ✛, and then double-click the column dividing line. The field values are now fully displayed.

The Visit table now contains all the data about patient visits for the Pine Ridge Orthopedics & Sports Medicine Center. To better understand how to work with this data, Susan asks you to create simple objects for the other main types of database objects—queries, forms, and reports.

Creating a Simple Query

As noted earlier, a query is a question you ask about the data stored in a database. When you create a query, you tell Access which fields you need and what criteria it should use to select the records that will answer your question. Then Access displays only the information you want, so you don't have to navigate through the entire database for the information. In the Visit table, for example, Susan might create a query to display only those records for visits that occurred in a specific month. Even though a query can display table information in a different way, the information still exists in the table as it was originally entered.

Susan wants to review a list of all the visit dates and reasons for visits in the Visit table. She doesn't want the list to include all the fields in the table, such as PatientID and WalkIn. To produce this list for Susan, you'll use the Simple Query Wizard to create a query based on the Visit table.

To start the Simple Query Wizard:

1. On the ribbon, click the **Create** tab.
2. In the Queries group, click the **Query Wizard** button. The New Query dialog box opens.
3. Make sure **Simple Query Wizard** is selected, and then click **OK**. The first Simple Query Wizard dialog box opens. See Figure 1–29.

Figure 1–29 First Simple Query Wizard dialog box

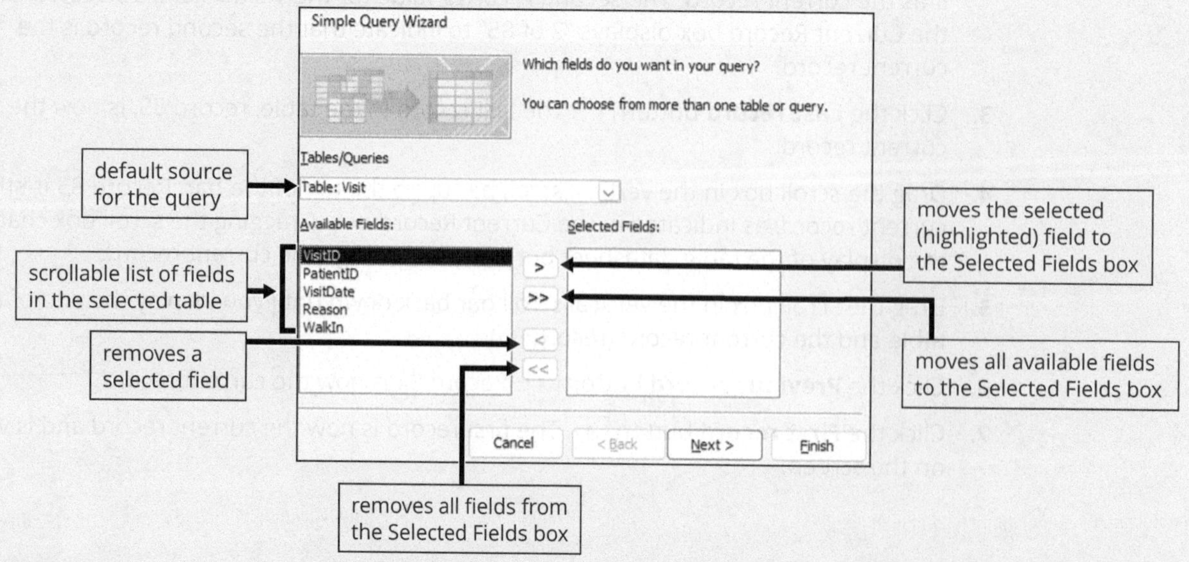

Because the Visit table is open in the NP_AC_1_PineRidge database, it is listed in the Tables/Queries box by default. If the database contained more objects, you could click the Tables/Queries arrow and choose another table or a query as the basis for the new query you are creating. In this case, you could choose the Billing table; however, the Visit table contains the fields you need. The Available Fields box lists all the fields in the Visit table.

Trouble? If the Visit table is not the default source for the query, click the Tables/Queries box arrow to choose the Visit table (Table: Visit) from the list.

You need to select fields from the Available Fields box to include them in the query. To select fields one at a time, click a field and then click the Select Single Field > button. The selected field moves from the Available Fields box on the left to the Selected Fields box on the right. To select all the fields, click the Select All fields >> button. If you change your mind or make a mistake, you can remove a field by clicking it in the Selected Fields box and then clicking the Remove Single Field < button. To remove all fields from the Selected Fields box, click the Remove All fields << button.

Each Simple Query Wizard dialog box contains buttons that allow you to move to the previous dialog box (Back button), move to the next dialog box (Next button), or cancel the creation process (Cancel button). You can also finish creating the object (Finish button) and accept the wizard's defaults for the remaining options.

Susan wants her query results list to include data from only the following fields: VisitID, VisitDate, and Reason. You need to select these fields to include them in the query.

To create the query using the Simple Query Wizard:

1. Click **VisitID** in the Available Fields box to select the field (if necessary), and then click the Select Single Field > button. The VisitID field moves to the Selected Fields box.

   Tip You can also double-click a field to move it from the Available Fields box to the Selected Fields box.

2. Repeat Step 1 for the fields **VisitDate** and **Reason**, and then click **Next**. The second, and final, Simple Query Wizard dialog box opens and asks you to choose a name (title) for your query. The suggested name is "Visit Query" because the query you are creating is based on the Visit table. You'll change the suggested name to "VisitList."
3. Click at the end of the suggested name, use **BACKSPACE** to delete the word "Query" and the space, and then type **List**. Now you can view the query results.
4. Click **Finish** to complete the query. The query results are displayed in Datasheet view on a new tab named "VisitList." A query datasheet is similar to a table datasheet, showing fields in columns and records in rows—but only for those fields and records you want to include, as determined by the query specifications you select.
5. Place the pointer on the column divider line to the right of the Reason field name until the pointer changes to the column resizing pointer +, and then double-click the column divider line to resize the Reason field. See Figure 1–30.

Figure 1–30 Query results

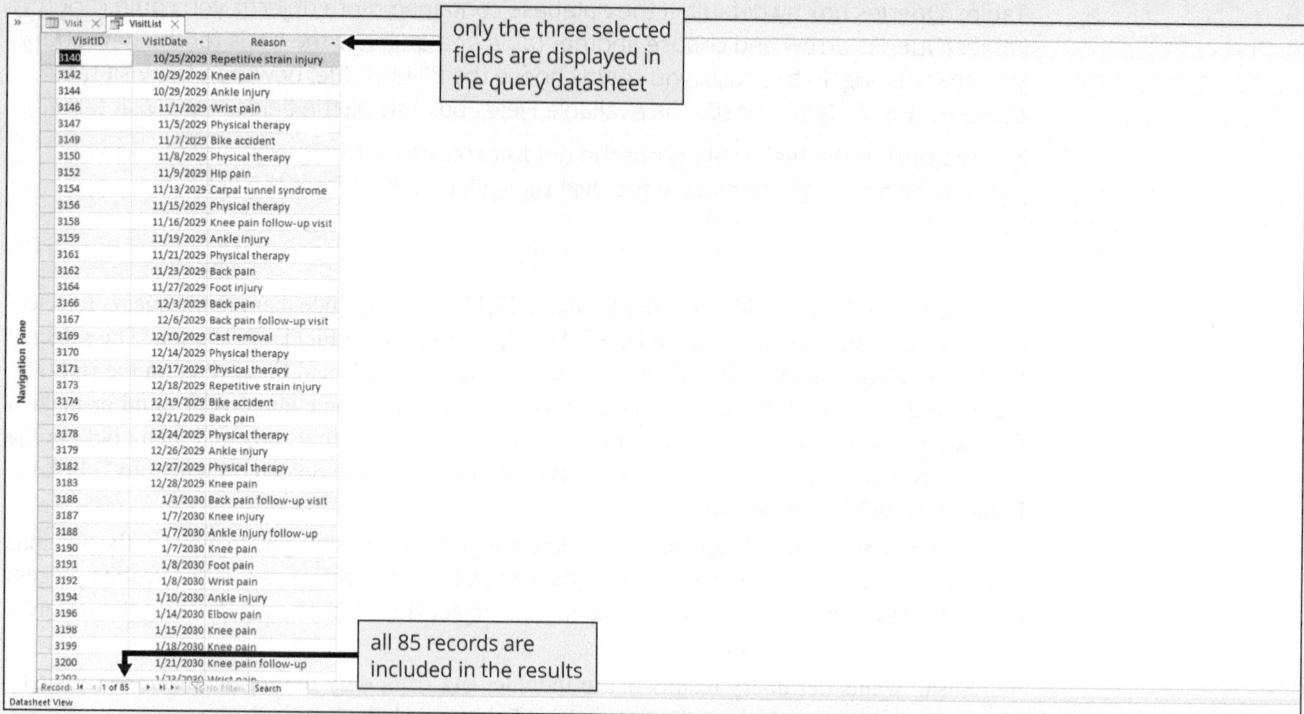

The VisitList query datasheet displays the three fields in the order you selected them in the Simple Query Wizard, from left to right. The records are listed in order by the primary key field, VisitID. Even though the query datasheet displays only the three fields you chose for the query, the Visit table still includes all the fields for all records.

Navigation buttons are located at the bottom of the window. You navigate a query datasheet in the same way that you navigate a table datasheet.

4. Click the **Last record** button ▶|. The last record in the query datasheet is now the current record.
5. Click the **Previous record** button ◀. Record 84 in the query datasheet is now the current record.
6. Click the **First record** button |◀. The first record is now the current record.
7. Click the **Close** button ✕ on the object tab. A dialog box opens asking if you want to save the changes to the layout of the query. This dialog box opens because you resized the Reason column.
8. Click **Yes** to save the query layout changes and close the query.

The query results are not stored in the database; however, the query design is stored as part of the database with the name you specified. You can re-create the query results at any time by opening the query again. When you open the query later, the results displayed will reflect up-to-date information to include any new records entered in the Visit table.

Susan asks you to display the query results again. She is considering whether to list the records in descending order showing the most current VisitID first. The records are currently displayed in ascending order by VisitID, which is the primary key for the Visit table. To display the records in descending order, you can sort the records in Query Datasheet view.

To sort records in a query datasheet:

1. On the Navigation Pane, click the **Shutter Bar Open/Close Button** [»] to open it.
2. In the Navigation Pane, double-click **VisitList** to open the VisitList query in Datasheet view.
3. On the Navigation Pane, click the **Shutter Bar Open/Close Button** [«] to close it.
4. On the ribbon, click the **Home** tab. The first record value in the VisitID field is highlighted; therefore, VisitID is the current field. Also, note the data in the first record (VisitID: 3140; VisitDate: 10/25/2029; and Reason: Repetitive strain injury).
5. In the Sort & Filter group, click the **Descending** button. The records are sorted in descending order by the current field (VisitID). Because the list of records is sorted in descending order, the original first record (VisitID 3140) should be the last record.
6. Scroll down the list of records and note that the same data for VisitID 3140 is now in the last record. Susan has decided not to keep the data sorted in descending order and wants to return to ascending order.
7. In the Sort & Filter group, click the **Remove Sort** button. The data returns to its original state in ascending order with VisitID 3140 (and its corresponding data) listed in the first record.
8. Click the **Close** button [×] on the object tab for the VisitList query. When asked if you would like to save the changes to the design of the VisitList query, click **No**. The VisitList query closes.

Next, Susan asks you to create a form for the Visit table so the staff at Pine Ridge Orthopedics & Sports Medicine Center can use the form to enter and work with data in the table easily.

Creating a Simple Form

As noted earlier, you use a form to enter, edit, and view records in a database. Although you can perform these same functions with tables and queries, forms can present data in many customized and useful ways.

Susan wants a form for the Visit table that shows all the fields for one record at a time, with fields listed one below another in a column. This type of form will make it easier for her staff to focus on all the data for a particular visit. You'll use the Form Wizard to create this form quickly and easily.

To create the form using the Form Wizard:

1. Make sure the Visit table is still open in Datasheet view.

   Trouble? If the Visit table is not open, click the Shutter Bar Open/Close Button [»] to open the Navigation Pane. Double-click Visit to open the Visit table in Datasheet view. Click the Shutter Bar Open/Close Button [«] to close the pane.

2. On the ribbon, click the **Create** tab.
3. In the Forms group, click the **Form Wizard** button. The first Form Wizard dialog box opens. Make sure the Visit table is the default data source for the form.

   Trouble? If the Visit table is not the default source for the form, click the Tables/Queries box arrow to choose the Visit table (Table: Visit) from the list.

   The first Form Wizard dialog box is similar to the first Simple Query Wizard dialog box you used in creating a query.

4. Click the **Select All Fields** button >> to move all the fields to the Selected Fields box.
5. Click **Next** to display the second Form Wizard dialog box, in which you select a layout for the form. See Figure 1–31.

Figure 1–31 Choosing a layout for the form

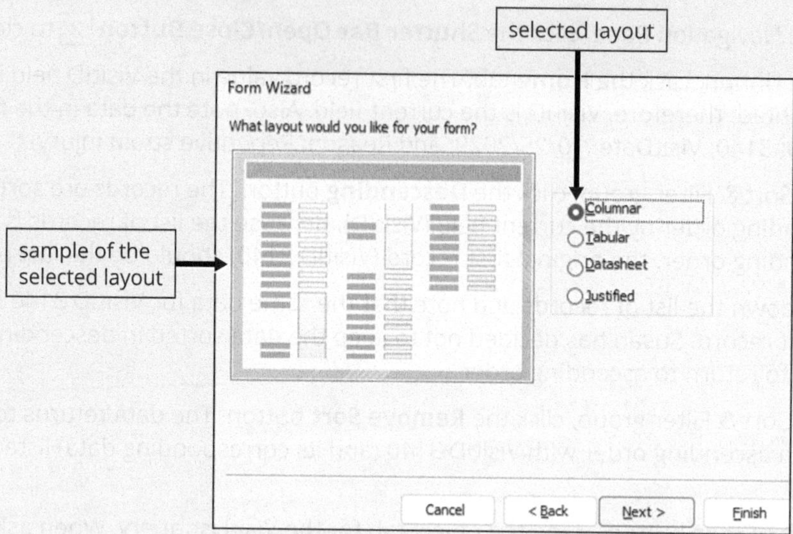

The layout choices are Columnar, Tabular, Datasheet, and Justified. A sample of the selected layout appears on the left side of the dialog box.

6. Click each option button and review the corresponding sample layout.
7. Because Susan wants to arrange the form data in a column with each field listed one below another, click the **Columnar** option button (if necessary), and then click **Next**.

   The third and final Form Wizard dialog box shows the Visit table's name as the default name for the form name. "Visit" is also the default title that will appear on the tab for the form.

   You'll use "VisitData" as the form name, and because you don't need to change the form's design at this point, you'll display the form.

8. Click to position the insertion point to the right of 'Visit' in the box, type **Data**, and then click the **Finish** button.

   The completed form opens in Form view, displaying the values for the first record in the Visit table. The Columnar layout places the field captions in labels on the left and the corresponding field values in boxes to the right, which vary in width depending on the size of the field. See Figure 1–32.

Figure 1–32 VisitData form in Form view

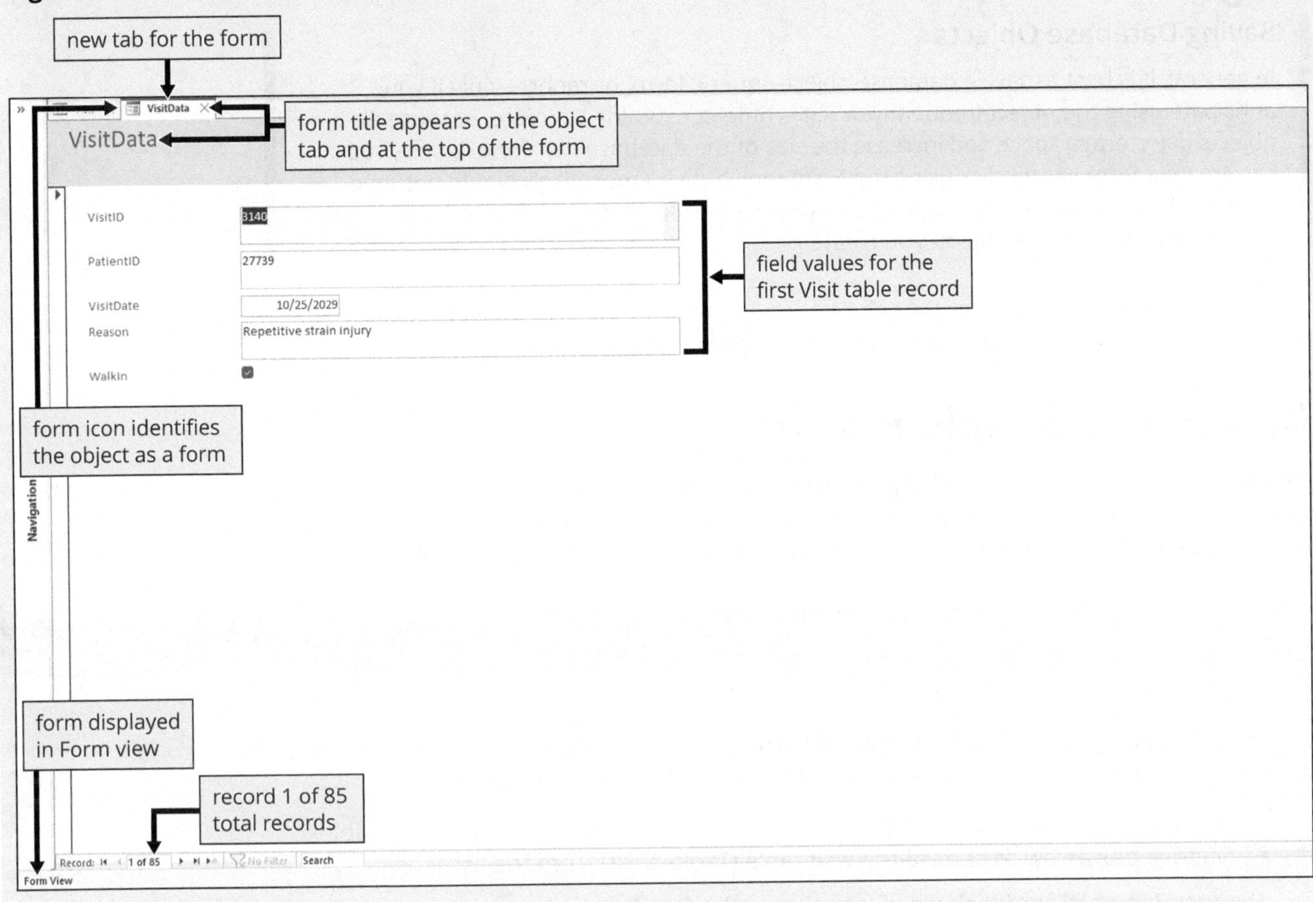

The form displays one record at a time in the Visit table, providing another view of the data that is stored in the table and allowing you to focus on the values for one record. Access displays the field values for the first record in the table and selects the first field value (VisitID) as indicated by the value being highlighted. Each field name appears on a separate line and on the same line as its field value, which appears in a box to the right. Depending on your computer's settings, the field value boxes in your form might be wider or narrower than those shown in the figure. As indicated in the status bar, the form is displayed in **Form view**. Later, you will work with a form in **Layout view**, where you can make design changes to the form while it is displaying data.

To view, enter, and maintain data using a form, you must know how to move from field to field and from record to record. Notice that the form contains navigation buttons, similar to those available in Datasheet view, which you can use to display different records in the form. You'll use these now to navigate the form; then you'll save and close the form.

To navigate, save, and close the form:

1. Click the **Next record** button ▶. The form now displays the values for the second record in the Visit table.
2. Click the **Last record** button ▶| to move to the last record in the table. The form displays the information for VisitID 3281.
3. Click the **Previous record** button ◀ to move to record 84.
4. Click the **First record** button |◀ to return to the first record in the Visit table.
5. Click the **Close** button ✕ on the object tab to close the form.

Insight

Saving Database Objects

In general, it is best to save a database object—query, form, or report—only if you anticipate using the object frequently or if it is time-consuming to create, because all objects use storage space and increase the size of the database file. For example, you can create a form in one click using the Form tool, but you most likely would not save the form because you can re-create it easily. (However, for the purposes of this text, you usually need to save the objects you create.)

Susan would like to present the information in the Visit table in a more readable and professional format. You'll help Susan by creating a report.

Creating a Simple Report

As noted earlier, a report is a formatted printout (or screen display) of the contents of one or more tables or queries. You'll use the Report Wizard to guide you through producing a report based on the Visit table for Susan. The Report Wizard creates a report based on the selected table or query.

To create the report using the Report Wizard:

1. On the ribbon, click the **Create** tab.
2. In the Reports group, click the **Report Wizard** button. The first Report Wizard dialog box opens. Make sure the Visit table is the default data source for the report.

   Trouble? If the Visit table is not the default source for the report, click the Tables/Queries box arrow to choose the Visit table (Table: Visit) from the list.

   The first Report Wizard dialog box is similar to the first Simple Query Wizard dialog box you used in creating a query, and to the first Form Wizard dialog box you used in creating a form.

   You select fields in the order you want them to appear on the report. Susan wants to include only the VisitID, PatientID, and Reason fields (in that order) in the report.
3. Click **VisitID** in the Available Fields box (if necessary), and then click the **Select Single Field** button > to move the field to the Selected Fields box.
4. Repeat step 3 to add the **PatientID** and **Reason** fields to the Selected Fields box. The VisitID, PatientID, and Reason fields (in that order) are listed in the Selected Fields box to add to the report. See Figure 1–33.

Figure 1–33 First Report Wizard dialog box

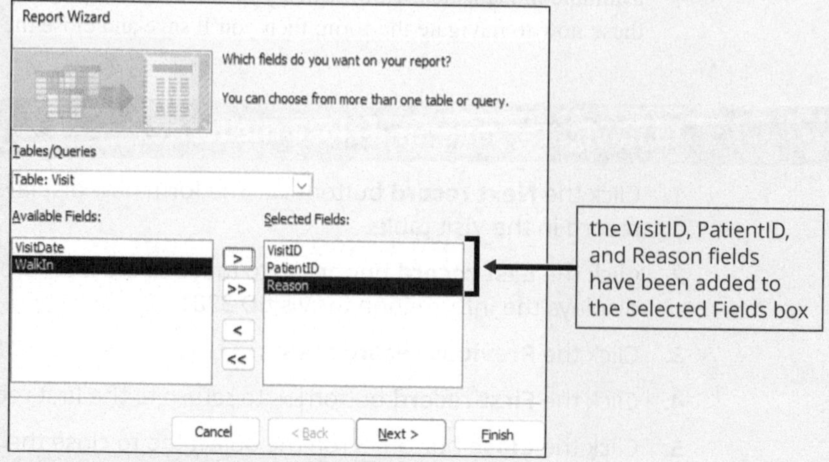

5. Click **Next** to open the second Report Wizard dialog box, which asks whether you want to add grouping levels to your report. This concept will be discussed later; Susan's report does not have any grouping levels.
6. Click **Next** to proceed to the third Report Wizard dialog box, which asks whether to sort records in a certain order by a particular field on the report. Susan wants to list the records by the VisitID field in ascending order. Access allows up to four levels of sorting, although Susan wants only one.
7. Click the arrow in the first sort option box, and then click **VisitID**. See Figure 1–34. The default option for sorting on the VisitID field is ascending.

Figure 1–34 Third Report Wizard dialog box

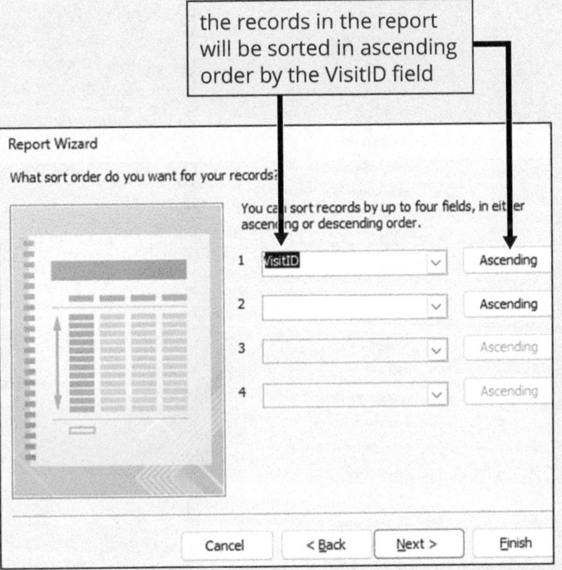

8. Click **Next** to proceed to the fourth Report Wizard dialog box, which asks you to select the layout for the report. You can click a Layout option to display an example of the layout.
9. Click the **Tabular** option button (if necessary). Later you can select other options for a report; however, this report uses the current default options.
10. Click **Next** to proceed to the final Report Wizard dialog box, in which you name the report. Susan wants to name the report "VisitDetails."
11. Click to position the insertion point to the right of "Visit" in the box, and then type **Details**. Click **Finish** to preview the report. See Figure 1–35.

Figure 1–35 Report in Print Preview

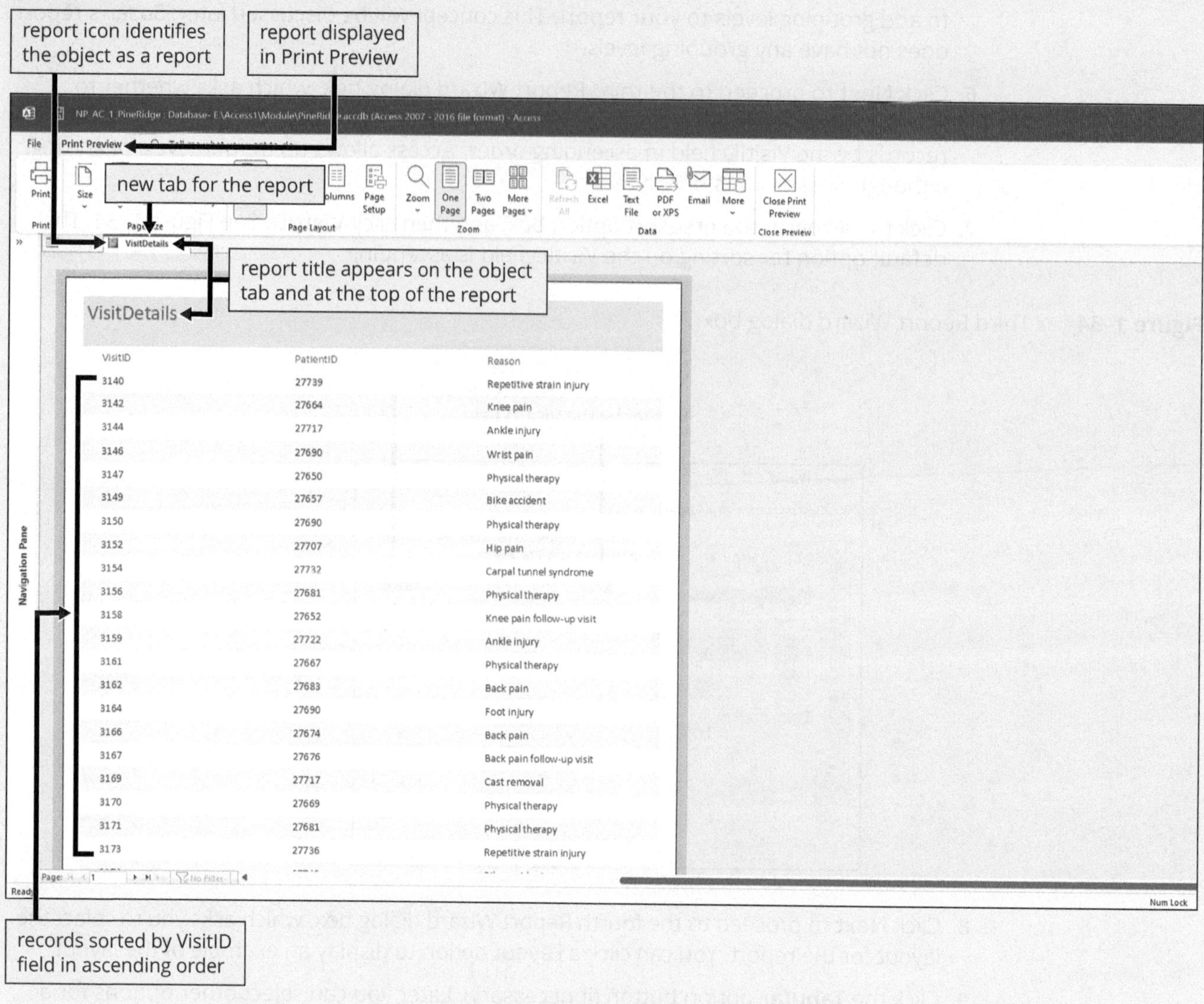

The report shows each field in a column, with the field values for each record in a row, similar to a table or query datasheet. However, a report offers a more visually appealing format for the data. The report is currently shown in Print Preview. **Print Preview** shows exactly how the report will look when printed. Print Preview also provides page navigation buttons at the bottom of the window, similar to the navigation buttons you've used to move through records in a table, query, and form.

To navigate the report in Print Preview:

1. Click the **Next Page** button ▸. The second page of the report is displayed in Print Preview.
2. Click the **Last Page** button ▸| to move to the last page of the report.
3. Drag the scroll box in the vertical scroll bar down until the bottom of the report page is displayed. The current date appears at the bottom left of the page. The notation "Page 3 of 3" appears at the bottom right of the page, indicating that you are on page 3 out of a total of 3 pages in the report.

Trouble? Depending on the printer you are using, your report might have more or fewer pages, and some of the pages might be blank. If so, don't worry. Different printers format reports in different ways, sometimes affecting the total number of pages and the number of records printed per page.

4. Click the **First Page** button [⏮] to return to the first page of the report, and then drag the scroll box in the vertical scroll bar up to display the top of the report.

Printing a Report

After creating a report, you might need to print it to distribute it to others who need to view the report's contents. You can print a report without changing any print settings or display the Print dialog box and select options for printing.

Reference

Printing a Report

- Open the report in any view or select the report in the Navigation Pane.
- Click the File tab to display Backstage view, click Print, and then click Quick Print to print the report with the default print settings.

or

- Open the report in any view or select the report in the Navigation Pane.
- Click the File tab, click Print, and then click Print; or, if the report is displayed in Print Preview, click the Print button in the Print group on the Print Preview tab. The Print dialog box opens, in which you can select the options you want for printing the report.

Susan asks you to print the entire report with the default settings, so you'll use the Quick Print option in Backstage view.

Note: To complete the following steps, your computer must be connected to a printer. Check with your instructor first to find out if you should print the report.

To print the report and then close it:

1. On the ribbon, click the **File** tab to open Backstage view.
2. In the navigation bar, click **Print** to display the Print screen, and then click **Quick Print**. The report prints with the default print settings, and you return to the report in Print Preview.

   Trouble? If your report did not print, make sure that your computer is connected to a printer, and that the printer is turned on and ready to print. Then repeat Steps 1 and 2.

3. Click the **Close** button [X] on the object tab to close the report.
4. Click the **Close** button [X] on the object tab to close the Visit table.

   Trouble? If you are asked to save changes to the layout of the table, click Yes.

You can also use the Print dialog box to print other database objects, such as table and query datasheets. Most often, these objects are used for viewing and entering data, and reports are used for printing the data in a database.

Viewing Objects in the Navigation Pane

The NP_AC_1_PineRidge database now contains five objects—the Billing table, the Visit table, the VisitList query, the VisitData form, and the VisitDetails report. When you work with the database file—such as closing it, opening it, or distributing it to others—the file includes all the objects you created and saved in the database. You can view and work with these objects in the Navigation Pane.

To view the objects in the NP_AC_1_PineRidge database:

1. On the Navigation Pane, click the **Shutter Bar Open/Close Button** [»] to open the pane. See Figure 1-36.

Figure 1-36 NP_AC_1_PineRidge database objects displayed in the Navigation Pane

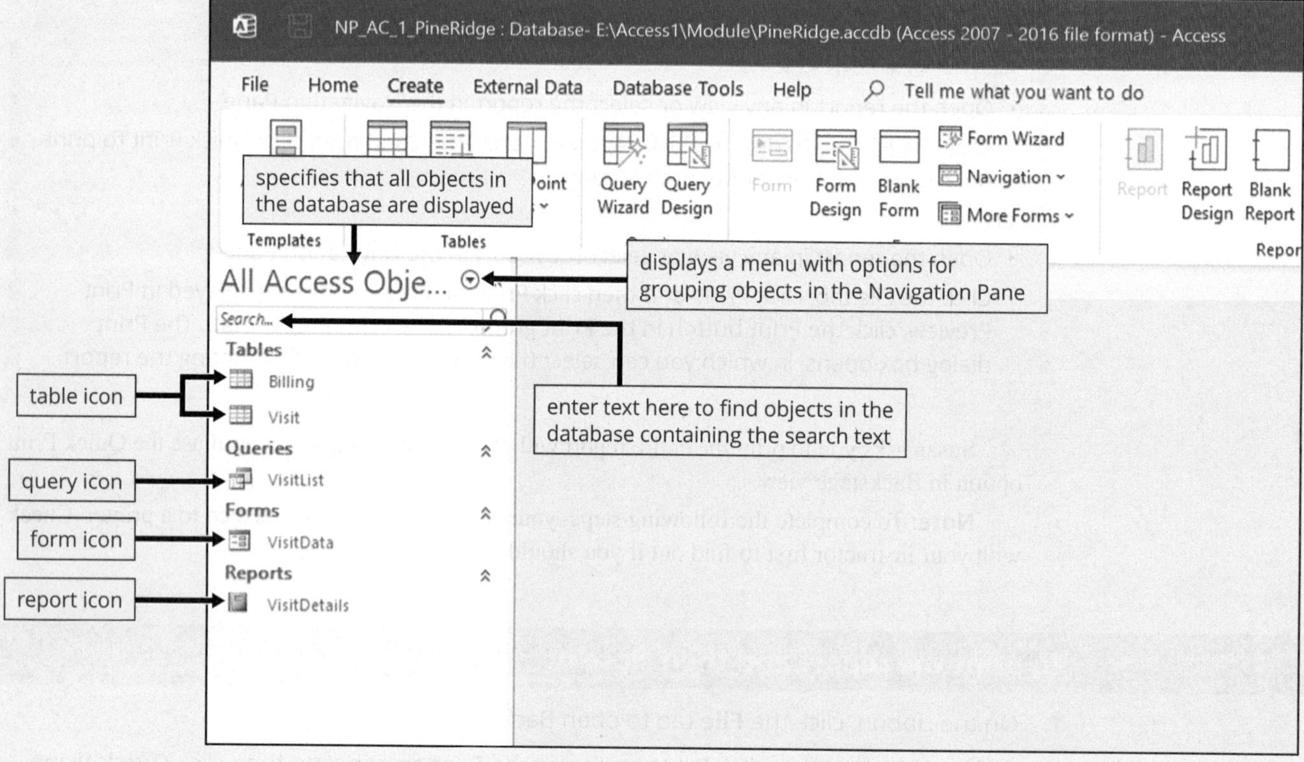

The Navigation Pane currently displays the default category, **All Access Objects**, which lists all the database objects in the pane. Each object type (Tables, Queries, Forms, and Reports) appears in its own group. Each database object (the Billing table, the Visit table, the VisitList query, the VisitData form, and the VisitDetails report) has a unique icon to its left to indicate the type of object. This makes it easy for you to identify the objects and choose which one you want to open and work with.

The arrow on the All Access Objects bar displays a menu with options for various ways to group and display objects in the Navigation Pane. The Search box enables you to enter text for Access to find; for example, you could search for all objects that contain the word "Visit" in their names. Note that Access searches for objects only in the categories and groups currently displayed in the Navigation Pane.

As you continue to build the NP_AC_1_PineRidge database and add more objects to it in later modules, you'll use the options in the Navigation Pane to manage those objects.

Using Microsoft Access Help

Access includes a Help system you can use to search for information about specific program features. You start Help by pressing the F1 key. Alternately, you can click the Help tab on the ribbon to display multiple buttons, with the first being the Help button. Click the Help button, and the Access Help pane opens.

You'll use Help now to learn more about the Navigation Pane.

To search for information about the Navigation Pane in Help:

1. On the ribbon, click the **Help** tab. Multiple buttons are displayed, with the first being the Help button. Click the **Help** button. The Access Help pane opens.

   Tip You can also get help by typing keywords in the Tell Me box on the ribbon to access information about topics related to those words in the Access Help pane.

2. Click in the **Search** box, type **Navigation Pane**, and then press **ENTER**. The Access Help pane displays a list of topics related to the Navigation Pane.
3. Click the topic **Show or hide the Navigation Pane in Access**. The Access Help pane displays the article you selected. See Figure 1–37.

Figure 1–37 Article displayed in the Access Help pane

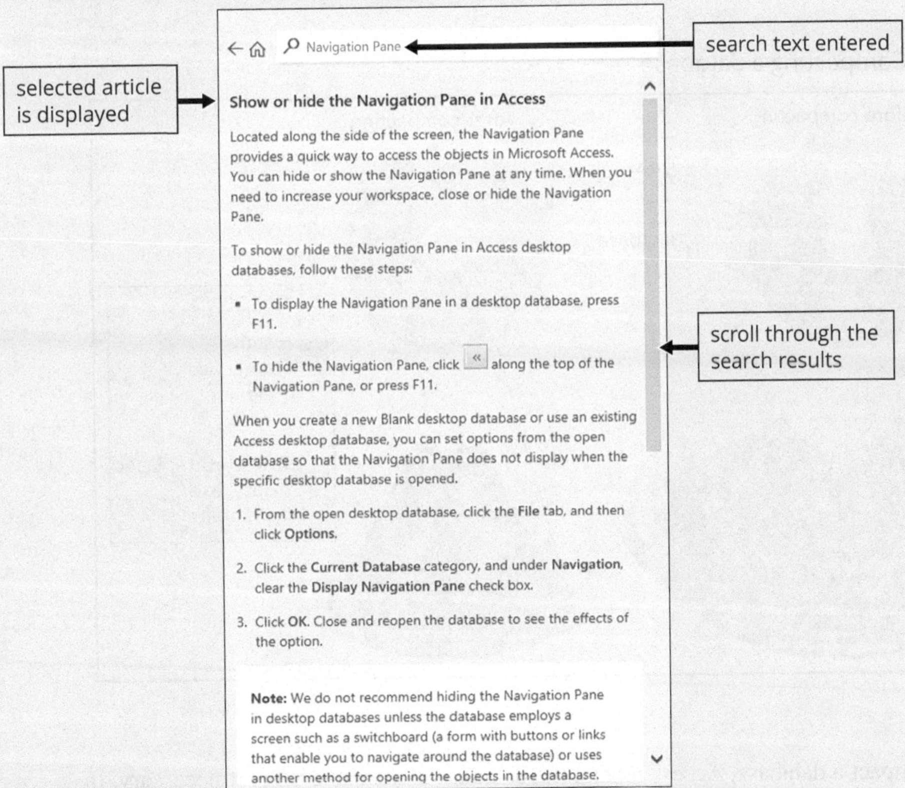

Trouble? If the article on showing or hiding the Navigation Pane is not listed in your Help pane, choose another article related to the Navigation Pane to read.

4. Scroll through the article to read detailed information about working with the Navigation Pane.
5. When finished, click the **Close** button ✕ on the Access Help pane to close it.

The Access Help system is an important reference tool for you to use if you need additional information about databases in general, details about specific Access features, or support with problems you might encounter.

Managing a Database

One of the main tasks involved in working with database software is managing your databases and the data they contain. Some of the activities involved in database management include compacting and repairing a database and backing up and restoring a database. By managing your databases, you can ensure that they operate in the most efficient way, that the data they contain is secure, and that you can work with the data effectively.

Compacting and Repairing a Database

Whenever you open an Access database and work in it, the size of the database increases. Further, when you delete records or when you delete or replace database objects—such as queries, forms, and reports—the storage space that had been occupied by the deleted or replaced records or objects does not automatically become available for other records or objects. To make the space available, and to increase the speed of data retrieval, you must compact the database. **Compacting** a database rearranges the data and objects in a database to decrease its file size, thereby making more storage space available and enhancing the performance of the database. Figure 1–38 illustrates the compacting process.

Figure 1–38 Compacting a database

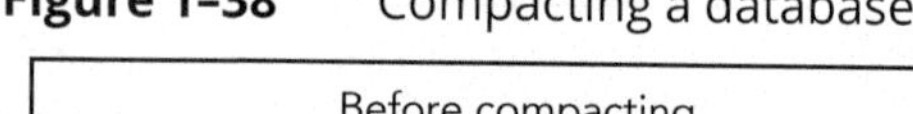

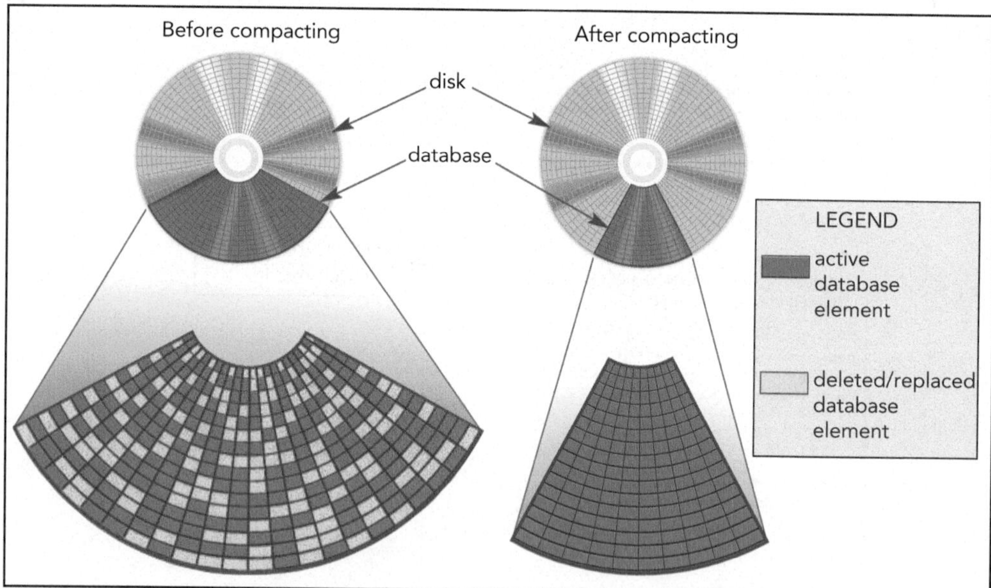

When you compact a database, Access repairs the database at the same time, if necessary. In some cases, Access detects that a database is damaged when you try to open it and gives you the option to compact and repair it at that time. For example, the data in your database might become damaged, or corrupted, if you exit the Access program suddenly by turning off your computer. If you think your database might be damaged because it is behaving unpredictably, you can use the Compact & Repair Database option to fix it.

Reference

Compacting and Repairing a Database

- Make sure the database file you want to compact and repair is open.
- Click the File tab to display the Home screen in Backstage view.
- Click Info to access the Info options.
- Click the Compact & Repair Database button.

Access also allows you to set an option to compact and repair a database file automatically every time you close it. The Compact on Close option is available in the Current Database section of the Access Options dialog box, which you open from Backstage view by clicking the Options command in the navigation bar. By default, the Compact on Close option is turned off.

Next, you'll compact the NP_AC_1_PineRidge database manually using the Compact & Repair Database option. This will make the database smaller and allow you to work with it more efficiently. After compacting the database, you'll close it.

To compact and repair the NP_AC_1_PineRidge database:

1. On the ribbon, click the **File** tab to open the Home screen in Backstage view.
2. Click **Info** to access the Info options.
3. Click the **Compact & Repair Database** button. Although nothing changes on the screen, Access compacts the NP_AC_1_PineRidge database, making it smaller, and repairs it at the same time.
4. **sam** Click the **File** tab to return to Backstage view, and then click **Close** in the navigation bar. The NP_AC_1_PineRidge database closes.

Backing Up and Restoring a Database

Backing up a database is the process of making a copy of the database file to protect your database against loss or damage. The Back Up Database command enables you to back up your database file from within the Access program, while you are working on your database. To use this option, click the File tab to display the Home screen in Backstage view, click Save As in the navigation bar, click Back Up Database in the Advanced section of the Save Database As pane, and then click the Save As button. In the Save As dialog box that opens, a default filename is provided for the backup copy that consists of the same filename as the database you are backing up (for example, "NP_AC_1_PineRidge"), and an underscore character, plus the current date. This file naming system makes it easy for you to keep track of your database backups and when they were created. To restore a backup database file, you copy the backup from the location where it is stored to your hard drive, or whatever device you use to work in Access, and start working with the restored database file. (You will not actually back up the NP_AC_1_PineRidge database in this module unless directed by your instructor to do so.)

Insight

Planning and Performing Database Backups

Experienced database users make it a habit to back up a database before they work with it for the first time, keeping the original data intact. They also make frequent backups while continuing to work with a database; these backups are generally on flash drives, recordable CDs or DVDs, external or network hard drives, or cloud-based storage (such as OneDrive). Also, it is recommended to store the backup copy in a different location from the original. For example, if the original database is stored on a flash drive, you should not store the backup copy on the same flash drive. If you lose the drive or the drive is damaged, you would lose both the original database and its backup copy.

If the original database file and the backup copy have the same name, restoring the backup copy might replace the original. If you want to save the original file, rename it before you restore the backup copy. To ensure that the restored database has the most current data, you should update the restored database with any changes made to the original between the time you created the backup copy and the time the original database became damaged or lost.

By properly planning for and performing backups, you can avoid losing data and prevent the time-consuming effort required to rebuild a lost or damaged database.

Proskills

Decision Making: When to Use Access versus Excel

Using a spreadsheet application like Microsoft Excel to manage lists or tables of information works well when the data is simple, such as a list of contacts or tasks. As soon as the data becomes complex enough to separate into tables that need to be related, you see the limitations of using a spreadsheet application. The strength of a database application such as Access is in its ability to easily relate one table of information to another. Consider a table of contacts that includes home addresses, with a separate row for each person living at the same address. When an address changes, it's too easy to make a mistake and not update the home address for each person who lives there. To ensure you have the most accurate data at all times, it's important to have only one instance of each piece of data. By creating separate tables that are related and keeping only one instance of each piece of data, you ensure the integrity of the data. Trying to accomplish this in Excel is complex, whereas Access is specifically designed for this functionality.

Another limitation of using Excel instead of Access to manage data has to do with the volume of data. Although a spreadsheet can hold thousands of records, a database can hold millions. A spreadsheet containing thousands of pieces of information is cumbersome to use. Think of large-scale commercial applications such as enrollment at a college or tracking customers for a large company. It's hard to imagine managing such information in an Excel spreadsheet. Instead, you would use a database. Finally, with an Access database, multiple users can access the information it contains at the same time. Although an Excel spreadsheet can be shared, there can be problems when users try to open and edit the same spreadsheet at the same time.

When you're trying to decide whether to use Excel or Access, ask yourself the following questions.

1. Do you need to store data in separate tables that are related to each other?
2. Do you have a very large amount of data to store?
3. Will more than one person need to access the data at the same time?

If you answer "yes" to any of these questions, an Access database is most likely the appropriate application to use.

In the following modules, you'll help Susan complete and maintain the NP_AC_1_PineRidge database, and you'll use it to meet the specific information needs of the employees of the center.

Part 1.2 Quick Check

1. To copy the records from a table in one database to another table in a different database, the two tables must have the same ________.
2. A question you ask about the data stored in a database is called a(n) ________.
3. To have Access guide you through the process of creating a form, you use the ________.
4. Which view displays the total number of pages in a report and lets you navigate through the report pages?
5. In the Navigation Pane, each database object has a unique ________ to its left that identifies the object's type.
6. To rearrange the data and objects in a database to decrease its file size and enhance its speed and performance, you can ________ the database.
7. The process of making a copy of the database file to protect the database against loss or damage is called ________ the database.

Practice: Review Assignments

Data File needed for the Review Assignments: Support_AC_1_Company.accdb

For the Pine Ridge Orthopedics & Sports Medicine Center, Susan asks you to create a new database to contain information about the vendors that the center works with to obtain medical supplies and equipment, and the vendors who service and maintain the equipment. Complete the following steps:

1. Create a new, blank database named **NP_AC_1_Vendor** and save it in the folder where you are storing your files, as specified by your instructor.
2. In Datasheet view, begin creating a table. Rename the default ID primary key field to **SupplierID**. Change the data type of the SupplierID field to Short Text.
3. Add the following 10 fields to the new table in the order shown; all of them are Short Text fields *except* InitialContact, which is a Date/Time field: **Company**, **Category**, **Address**, **City**, **State**, **Zip**, **Phone**, **ContactFirst**, **ContactLast**, and **InitialContact**. Resize the columns as necessary so that the complete field names are displayed.
4. Save the table as **Supplier** and close the table.
5. In Design view, begin creating a second table containing the following three Short Text fields in the order shown: **ProductID**, **SupplierID**, and **ProductName**.
6. Make ProductID the primary key and use **Primary key** as its description. Use **Foreign key** as the description for the SupplierID field.
7. Add a field called **Price** to the table, which is of the Currency data type.
8. Add the following two fields to the table in the order shown: **TempControl** and **Sterile**. Both are of the Yes/No data type.
9. Add the final field called **Units** to the table, which is of the Number data type.
10. Save the table as **Product** and close the table.
11. Use the Navigation Pane to open the Supplier table.
12. Enter the records shown in Figure 1–39 into the Supplier table. For the first record, enter your first name in the ContactFirst field and your last name in the ContactLast field.

    Note: When entering field values that are shown on multiple lines in the figure, do not try to enter the values on multiple lines. The values are shown on multiple lines in the figure for page spacing purposes only.

Figure 1–39 Supplier table records

SupplierID	Company	Category	Address	City	State	Zip	Phone	Contact-First	Contact-Last	Initial-Contact
ABC123	ABC Pharmaceuticals	Supplies	123 Hopson Ave	Manchester	NH	03102	603-555-8125	*Student First*	*Student Last*	9/21/2029
HAR912	Harper Surgical, LLC	Supplies	912 Huntington Pl	Knoxville	TN	37909	865-555-4239	Kathy	Harper	10/26/2029
DUR725	Durham Medical Equipment	Equipment	725 Pike Dr	Durham	NC	27705	919-555-4226	Edgar	Wayles	12/14/2029
TEN247	Tenneka Labs, LLC	Service	247 Asland Dr	Norcross	GA	30071	678-555-5392	Thomas	Tenneka	11/30/2029
BAZ412	Bazarrack Enterprises	Supplies	412 Harper Dr	Alpharetta	GA	30004	678-555-2201	Sonja	Bazarrack	9/3/2029

13. Susan created a database named Support_AC_1_Company that contains a Business table with supplier data. The Supplier table you created has the same design as the Business table. Copy all the records from the Business table in the Support_AC_1_Company database (located in the Access1 > Review folder provided with your Data Files) and then paste them at the end of the Supplier table in the NP_AC_1_Vendor database.

14. Resize all datasheet columns to their best fit, and then save the Supplier table.
15. Close the Supplier table, and then use the Navigation Pane to reopen it. Note that the records are displayed in primary key order by the values in the SupplierID field.
16. Use the Simple Query Wizard to create a query that includes the Company, Category, ContactFirst, ContactLast, and Phone fields (in that order) from the Supplier table. Name the query **SupplierList**, and then close the query.
17. Use the Form Wizard to create a form for the Supplier table. Include all fields from the Supplier table on the form and use the Columnar layout. Save the form as **SupplierInfo**, and then close it.
18. Use the Report Wizard to create a report based on the Supplier table. Include the SupplierID, Company, and Phone fields on the report (in that order) and sort the report by the SupplierID field in ascending order. Use a Tabular layout, save the report as **SupplierDetails**, and then close it.
19. Close the Supplier table, and then compact and repair the NP_AC_1_Vendor database.
20. Close the NP_AC_1_Vendor database.

Apply: Case Problem 1

Data File needed for this Case Problem: Support_AC_1_MoreTutors.accdb

Tech Tutors While in college obtaining her bachelor's degree in engineering, Taylor Thompson excelled in technology-related subjects, including databases and programming. Taylor found out that many of her fellow classmates often needed help with a variety of technology projects, and she was constantly assisting them. Prior to graduating, Taylor began tutoring first-year and sophomore students in database design and programming to make some extra money. When Taylor entered graduate school in engineering, she started Tech Tutors, a company offering expanded tutoring services for high school and college students through group, private, and semiprivate tutoring sessions. As demand grew, Taylor hired many of her fellow classmates to assist her in the company. Taylor wants to use Access to maintain information about the tutors who work for her, the students who sign up for tutoring, and the contracts signed. She asks for your help in creating this database. Complete the following steps:

1. Create a new, blank database named **NP_AC_1_TechTutors** and save it in the folder where you are storing your files, as specified by your instructor.
2. In Datasheet view, begin creating a table. Rename the default ID primary key field to **TutorID**. Change the data type of the TutorID field to Short Text.
3. Add the following six fields to the new table in the order shown; all of them are Short Text fields *except* HireDate, which is a Date/Time field: **FirstName**, **LastName**, **Major**, **YearInSchool**, **School**, and **HireDate**. Resize the columns as necessary so that the complete field names are displayed.
4. Save the table as **Tutor.**
5. Enter the records shown in Figure 1–40 into the Tutor table. For the first record, be sure to enter your first name in the FirstName field and your last name in the LastName field.

Figure 1–40 Tutor table records

TutorID	FirstName	LastName	Major	YearInSchool	School	HireDate
3560	*Student First*	*Student Last*	Computer Science	Senior	Eiken University	2/14/2029
3510	Chris	Cauler	Database Management	Graduate	Pikesville College	2/1/2029
3528	Maria	Sanchez	Data Analytics	Senior	Pike Technical College	1/8/2029
3539	Gail	Falls	Information Systems	Junior	Switzer University	2/22/2029
3505	Robert	Claxton	Computer Science	Graduate	Hughes College	4/18/2029

6. Taylor created a database named Support_AC_1_MoreTutors that contains a StudentTutor table with additional tutor data. The Tutor table you created has the same design as the StudentTutor table. Copy all the records from the StudentTutor table in the Support_AC_1_MoreTutors database (located in the Access1 > Case1 folder provided with your Data Files), and then paste them at the end of the Tutor table in the NP_AC_1_TechTutors database.

7. Resize all datasheet columns to their best fit, and then save the Tutor table.
8. Close the Tutor table, and then use the Navigation Pane to reopen it. Note that the records are displayed in primary key order by the values in the TutorID field.
9. Use the Simple Query Wizard to create a query that includes the TutorID, FirstName, LastName, and School fields (in that order) from the Tutor table. Save the query as **TutorData**, and then close the query.
10. Use the Form Wizard to create a form for the Tutor table. Include only the TutorID, FirstName, LastName, Major, and HireDate fields (in that order) from the Tutor table on the form and use the Columnar layout. Save the form as **TutorInfo**, and then close it.
11. Use the Report Wizard to create a report based on the Tutor table. Include the TutorID, LastName, and YearInSchool fields on the report (in that order) and sort the report by the TutorID field in ascending order. Use a Tabular layout, save the report as **TutorList,** and then close it.
12. Close the Tutor table, and then compact and repair the NP_AC_1_TechTutors database.
13. Close the NP_AC_1_TechTutors database.

Challenge: Case Problem 2

Data File needed for this Case Problem: Support_AC_1_OutdoorPeople.accdb

Outdoor Adventure Tours David and Brent Wilson grew up in the mountains of Virginia. Their parents were avid outdoors people and loved to take the family on long hikes and teach the young men about the great outdoors. During middle school and high school, their friends would ask them to guide them in the surrounding area because it could be quite dangerous. During high school, the boys had an idea to expand their hiking clientele beyond their friends and help earn money for college. This is when Outdoor Adventure Tours was born. The boys advertised in local and regional outdoor magazines and were flooded with requests from people all around the region. They would like you to build an Access database to manage information about the hikers they guide, the tours they provide, and tour reservations. Complete the following steps:

1. Create a new, blank database named **NP_AC_1_Outdoor** and save it in the folder where you are storing your files, as specified by your instructor.
2. In Datasheet view, begin creating a table. Rename the default ID primary key field to **HikerID**. Change the data type of the HikerID field to Short Text.
3. Add the following seven fields to the new table in the order shown; all of them are Short Text fields: **HikerFirst**, **HikerLast**, **Address**, **City**, **State**, **Zip**, and **Phone**. Resize the columns as necessary so that the complete field names are displayed.
4. Save the table as **Hiker.**
5. Enter the records shown in Figure 1–41 into the Hiker table.

Figure 1–41 Hiker table records

HikerID	HikerFirst	HikerLast	Address	City	State	Zip	Phone
401	*Student First*	*Student Last*	12 Peeler St	Charlottesville	VA	22902	434-555-9128
441	Douglas	Myers	44 River Rd	Hershey	PA	17033	717-555-9382
415	Abbey	Johnson	179 Amber Ln	Hillsville	VA	24343	270-555-9381
456	Henry	Custer	5 Loop Rd	Big Stone Gap	VA	24219	276-555-8832
427	Mark	Samuels	912 Pine Ave	Cashiers	NC	28717	828-555-9842

6. David and Brent created a database named Support_AC_1_OutdoorPeople that contains a MoreHikers table with additional hiker data. The Hiker table you created has the same design as the MoreHikers table. Copy all the records from the MoreHikers table in the Support_AC_1_OutdoorPeople database (located in the Access1 > Case2 folder provided with your Data Files), and then paste them at the end of the Hiker table in the NP_AC_1_Outdoor database.

7. Resize all datasheet columns to their best fit, and then save the Hiker table.
8. Close the Hiker table, and then use the Navigation Pane to reopen it. Note that the records are displayed in primary key order by the values in the HikerID field.
9. Use the Simple Query Wizard to create a query that includes the HikerID, HikerFirst, HikerLast, City, State, and Phone fields (in that order) from the Hiker table. Save the query as **HikerData**, and then display the results.
10. **Explore:** The results of the HikerData query are displayed in order by the HikerID value. You can specify a different order by sorting the query. Display the Home tab. Then, click the insertion point anywhere in the State column to make it the current field. In the Sort & Filter group on the Home tab, click the Ascending button. The records are now listed in order by the values in the State field. Save and close the query.
11. **Explore:** Use the Form Wizard to create a form using all of the fields in the Hiker table in a Columnar layout. Save the form as **HikerInfo**. In the new form, navigate to record 10 (the record with HikerID 427), and then, if your instructor requests it, print the form for the current record only. (**Hint**: You must use the Print dialog box in order to print only the current record. Go to Backstage view, click Print in the navigation bar, and then click Print to open the Print dialog box. Click the Selected Record(s) option button, and then click the OK button to print the current record.) Close the form.
12. **Explore:** Use the Report Wizard to create a report based on the HikerData query. (**Hint**: You can change your data source by selecting the arrow in the Tables/Queries box.) Include the HikerID, HikerLast, and State fields (in that order) on the report and sort the report by the HikerID field in ascending order. The results of the HikerData query are sorted by the State field; however, when you sort the report by the HikerID field, the results will also be in order by the HikerID field (the primary key for the Hiker table). Use a Tabular layout, save the report as **HikerList**, print the report if your instructor requests it, and then close it.
13. Close the Hiker table, and then compact and repair the NP_AC_1_Outdoor database.
14. Close the NP_AC_1_Outdoor database.

Building a Database and Defining Table Relationships

Creating the Billing and Patient Tables

Case: Pine Ridge Orthopedics & Sports Medicine Center

The database you created in Module 1 for the Pine Ridge Orthopedics & Sports Medicine Center contained one table with data, the Visit table, and the basic structure of an additional table, the Billing table. Susan would like to further refine the structure of the Billing table, which will be used to track information about the invoices sent to patients. In addition, Susan would like to track information about each patient the center serves, including their name and contact information.

To help Susan, you will not be using the solution file from Module 1 to start Module 2. Instead, you use a new starting database, in this case NP_AC_2-1.accdb, along with the support files listed in the Starting Data Files box. The starting database is different from the solution file for Module 1. This will be the case in each module throughout the text. Be sure to use the starting data files provided in each module so your solutions match those provided by your instructor.

Although you will not be using the same database from one module to the next module, the concepts in each module build on the previous one. Hence, the objects and data are similar from one module to the next, but not exactly the same. This is why it is important for you to use the starting files provided with each module. The objects in your starting database will include the necessary components for you to continue learning about various database design concepts and features of Access.

In this module, you'll modify the existing Billing table and create a new table in the database—named Patient—to contain the additional data Susan wants to track. After adding records to the tables, you will define the necessary relationships between the tables in the database to relate the tables, enabling Susan and her staff to work with the data more efficiently.

Starting Data Files: Access2

Module
NP_AC_2-1.accdb
Support_AC_2_Kimberly.accdb
Support_AC_2_Patient.txt
Support_AC_2_Invoices.xlsx

Review
NP_AC_2-2.accdb
Support_AC_2_Products.xlsx

Case1
NP_AC_2-3.accdb
Support_AC_2_Agreements.xlsx
Support_AC_2_Client.accdb
Support_AC_2_Students.txt

Case2
NP_AC_2-4.accdb
Support_AC_2_Bookings.txt
Support_AC_2_Travel.accdb

Objectives

Part 2.1

- Identify the guidelines for designing databases and setting field properties
- Define fields and set field properties
- Modify the structure of a table
- Change the order of fields in Design view
- Add new fields in Design view
- Change the Format property for a field in Datasheet view
- Modify field properties in Design view

Part 2.2

- Import data from Excel
- Import an existing table structure
- Add fields to a table with the Data Type gallery
- Delete fields
- Change the data type for a field in Design view
- Set the Default Value property for a field
- Import a text file
- Define a relationship between two tables

Part 2.1 Visual Overview: Table Window in Design View

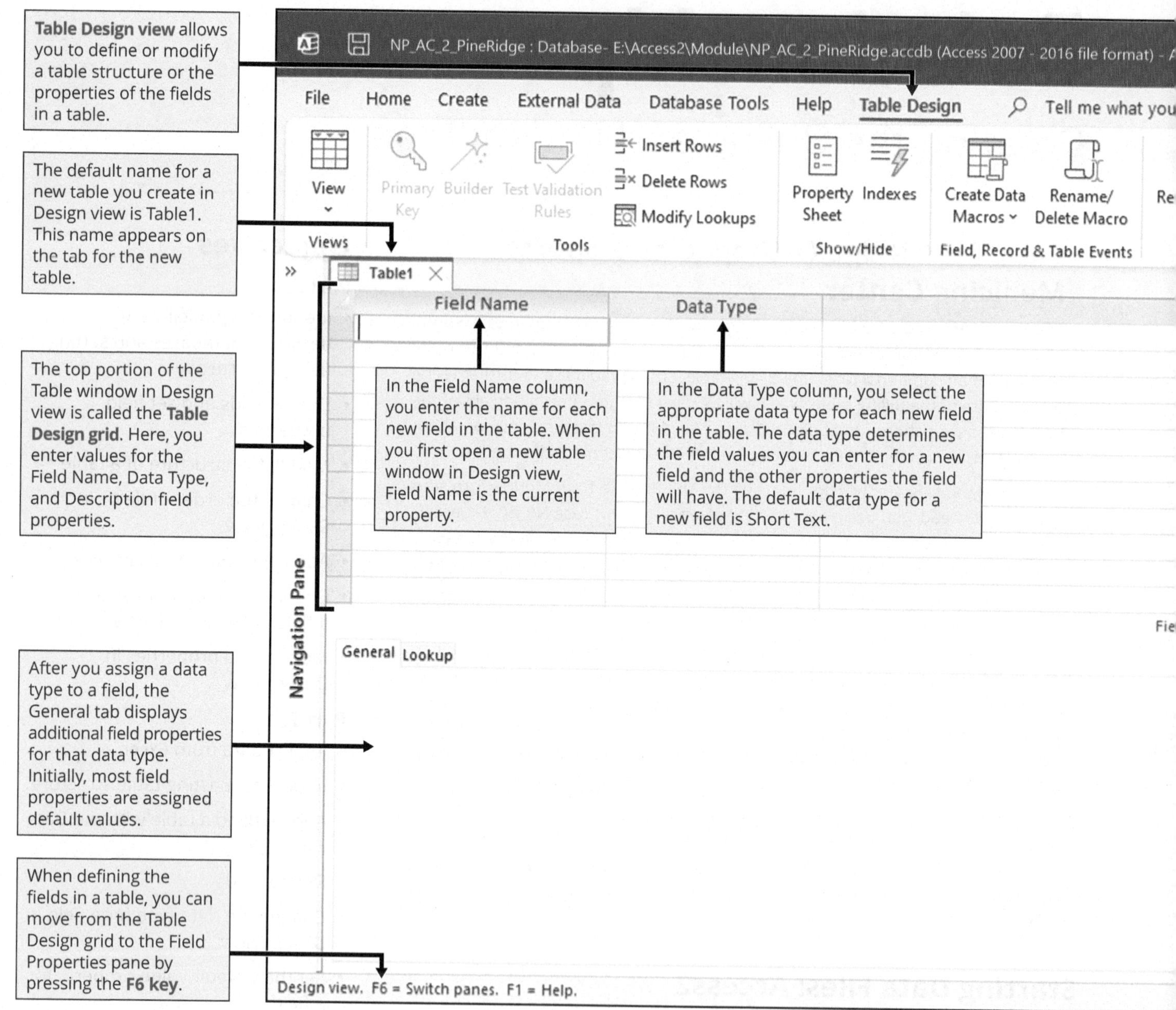
Table Design view allows you to define or modify a table structure or the properties of the fields in a table.
The default name for a new table you create in Design view is Table1. This name appears on the tab for the new table.
The top portion of the Table window in Design view is called the **Table Design grid**. Here, you enter values for the Field Name, Data Type, and Description field properties.
After you assign a data type to a field, the General tab displays additional field properties for that data type. Initially, most field properties are assigned default values.
When defining the fields in a table, you can move from the Table Design grid to the Field Properties pane by pressing the **F6 key**.
In the Field Name column, you enter the name for each new field in the table. When you first open a new table window in Design view, Field Name is the current property.
In the Data Type column, you select the appropriate data type for each new field in the table. The data type determines the field values you can enter for a new field and the other properties the field will have. The default data type for a new field is Short Text.
NP_AC_2_PineRidge : Database- E:\Access2\Module\NP_AC_2_PineRidge.accdb (Access 2007 - 2016 file format)
File
Home
Create
External Data
Database Tools
Help
Table Design
Tell me what you
View
Primary Key
Builder
Test Validation Rules
Insert Rows
Delete Rows
Modify Lookups
Property Sheet
Indexes
Create Data Macros
Rename/ Delete Macro
Views
Tools
Show/Hide
Field, Record & Table Events
Table1
Field Name
Data Type
Navigation Pane
General
Lookup
Design view. F6 = Switch panes. F1 = Help.

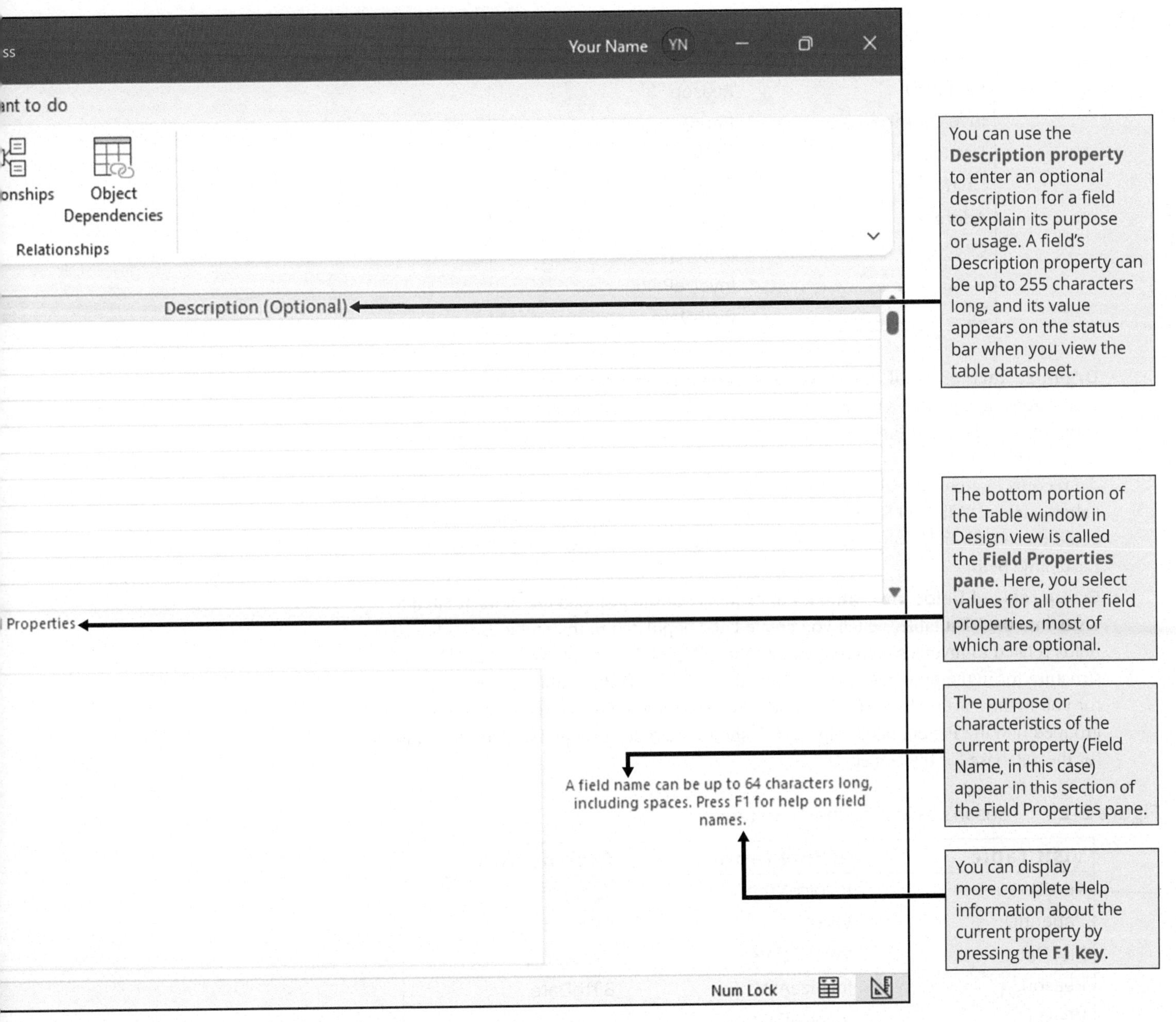
ss
Your Name
YN
ant to do
onships
Object Dependencies
Relationships
Description (Optional)
Properties
A field name can be up to 64 characters long, including spaces. Press F1 for help on field names.
Num Lock
You can use the **Description property** to enter an optional description for a field to explain its purpose or usage. A field's Description property can be up to 255 characters long, and its value appears on the status bar when you view the table datasheet.
The bottom portion of the Table window in Design view is called the **Field Properties pane**. Here, you select values for all other field properties, most of which are optional.
The purpose or characteristics of the current property (Field Name, in this case) appear in this section of the Field Properties pane.
You can display more complete Help information about the current property by pressing the **F1 key**.

Updating a Database

A database management system can be a useful tool, but only if you first carefully design the database so that it meets the needs of its users. In database design, you determine the fields, tables, and relationships needed to satisfy the data and processing requirements. When you design a database, you should follow these guidelines:

- **Identify all the fields needed to produce the required information.** For example, Susan needs information about patients, visits, and invoices. Figure 2–1 shows the fields that satisfy these information requirements.

Figure 2–1 Susan's data requirements

VisitID	InvoiceDate
PatientID	Reason
InvoiceAmt	Phone
FirstName	WalkIn
LastName	Email
Address	VisitDate
City	InvoiceNum
State	InvoicePaid
Zip	BirthDate

- **Organize each piece of data into its smallest useful part.** For example, Susan could store each patient's complete name in one field called PatientName instead of using two fields called FirstName and LastName, as shown in Figure 2–1. However, doing so would make it more difficult to work with the data. If Susan wanted to view the records in alphabetical order by last name, she wouldn't be able to do so with field values such as "Michael Smith" and "Kimberly Hansen" stored in a Name field. She could do so with field values such as "Smith" and "Hansen" stored separately in a LastName field.
- **Group related fields into tables.** For example, Susan grouped the fields related to visits into the Visit table, which you created and populated in the previous module. The fields related to invoices are grouped into the Billing table, which you created the basic structure for in the previous module. Note the Visit and Billing tables are provided for you in the starting NP_AC_2-1.accdb database. The fields related to patients are grouped into the Patient table. Figure 2–2 shows the fields grouped into all three tables for the database for the center.

Figure 2–2 Susan's fields grouped into tables

Visit table	Billing table	Patient table
VisitID	InvoiceNum	PatientID
PatientID	VisitID	LastName
VisitDate	InvoiceDate	FirstName
Reason	InvoiceAmt	BirthDate
WalkIn	InvoicePaid	Phone
		Address
		City
		State
		Zip
		Email

- **Determine each table's primary key.** Recall that a primary key uniquely identifies each record in a table. For some tables, one of the fields, such as a credit card number, naturally serves as a primary key. For other tables, two or more fields might be needed to function as the primary key. In these cases, the primary key is called a **composite key**. For example, a school grade table might use a combination of student number, term, and course code to serve as the primary key. For a third category of tables, no single field or combination of fields can uniquely identify a record in a table. In these cases, you need to add a field whose sole purpose is to serve as the table's primary key. For Susan's tables, VisitID is the primary key for the Visit table, InvoiceNum is the primary key for the Billing table, and PatientID is the primary key for the Patient table.
- **Include a common field in related tables.** You use the common field to connect one table logically with another table. In the database for the center, the Visit and Patient tables include the PatientID field as a common field. Recall that when you include the primary key from one table as a field in a second table to form a relationship, the field in the second table is called a foreign key; therefore, the PatientID field is a foreign key in the Visit table. With this common field, Susan can find all visits to the center made by a particular patient; she can use the PatientID value for a patient and search the Visit table for all records with that PatientID value. Likewise, she can determine which patient made a particular visit by searching the Patient table to find the one record with the same PatientID value as the corresponding value in the Visit table. Similarly, the VisitID field is a common field, serving as the primary key in the Visit table and a foreign key in the Billing table.
- **Avoid data redundancy.** When you store the same data in more than one place, **data redundancy** occurs. Except for common fields to connect tables, you should avoid data redundancy because it wastes storage space and can cause inconsistencies. Data would be inconsistent, for example, if you type a field value one way in one table and a different way in the same table or in a second table. Figure 2–3, which contains portions of potential data stored in the Patient and Visit tables, shows an example of incorrect database design that has data redundancy in the Visit table. In Figure 2–3, the LastName field in the Visit table is redundant, and one value for this field was entered incorrectly in three different ways.

Figure 2–3 Incorrect database design with data redundancy

Patient table

PatientID	LastName	FirstName	Address
27652	Johnson	Gregory	12 Rock Ln
27683	Anderson	Victoria	16 Gaston Ave
27692	Flores	Juanita	75 Pine Dr
27708	Gonzales	Victor	137 Rock Rd
27740	Young	Pamela	715 Phillips St

data redundancy

Visit table

VisitID	PatientID	LastName	VisitDate	WalkIn
3158	27652	Johnson	11/16/2029	No
3162	27683	Anderson	11/23/2029	No
3176	27740	Young	12/21/2029	Yes
3202	27683	Andersohn	1/23/2030	Yes
3207	27692	Flores	1/25/2030	No
3211	27708	Gonzales	1/29/2030	No
3216	27683	Andersen	2/7/2030	No

inconsistent data

- **Determine the properties of each field.** You need to identify the **properties**, or characteristics, of each field so that the database knows how to store, display, and process the field values. These properties include the field's name, data type, maximum number of characters or digits, description, valid values, and other field characteristics. You will learn more about field properties later in this module.

The Billing table you need to modify, and the Patient table you need to create, will contain the fields shown in Figure 2–2. Before modifying and creating these tables in the database for the center, you first need to learn some guidelines for setting field properties.

Guidelines for Setting Field Properties

As just noted, the last step of database design is to determine which values to assign to the properties, such as the name and data type, of each field. When you select or enter a value for a property, you **set** the property. Access has rules for naming fields and objects, assigning data types, and setting other field properties.

Naming Fields and Objects

You must name each field, table, and other object in an Access database. Access stores these items in the database using the names you supply. Choose a field or object name that describes the purpose or contents of the field or object so that later you can easily remember what the name represents. For example, the three tables in the database for the center are named Visit, Billing, and Patient because these names suggest their contents. A table or query name must be unique within a database. A field name must be unique within a table, but it can be used again in another table.

Assigning Field Data Types

Each field must have a data type, which is either assigned automatically by Access or specifically by the table designer. The data type determines what field values you can enter for the field and what other properties the field will have. For example, the Patient table will include a BirthDate field, which will store date values, so you will assign the Date/Time data type to this field. Then Access will allow you to enter and manipulate only dates or times as values in the BirthDate field.

Figure 2–4 lists the most common data types in Access, describes the field values allowed for each data type, explains when you should use each data type, and indicates the field size of each data type. You can find more complete information about all available data types in Access Help.

Figure 2–4 Common data types

Data Type	Description	Field Size
Short Text	Allows field values containing letters, digits, spaces, and special characters. Use for names, addresses, descriptions, and fields containing digits that are *not used in calculations*.	0 to 255 characters; default is 255
Long Text	Allows field values containing letters, digits, spaces, and special characters. Use for long comments and explanations.	1 to 65,535 characters; exact size is determined by entry
Number	Allows positive and negative numbers as field values. A number can contain digits, a decimal point, commas, a plus sign, and a minus sign. Use for fields that will be used in calculations, except those involving money.	1 to 15 digits
Date/Time	Allows field values containing valid dates and times from January 1, 100 to December 31, 9999. Dates can be entered in month/day/year format, several other date formats, or a variety of time formats, such as 10:35 PM. You can perform calculations on dates and times, and you can sort them. For example, you can determine the number of days between two dates.	8 bytes
Currency	Allows field values similar to those for the Number data type, but is used for storing monetary values. Unlike calculations with Number data type decimal values, calculations performed with the Currency data type are not subject to round-off error.	Accurate to 15 digits on the left side of the decimal point and to 4 digits on the right side
AutoNumber	Consists of integer values created automatically by Access each time you create a new record. You can specify sequential numbering or random numbering, which guarantees a unique field value, so that such a field can serve as a table's primary key.	9 digits
Yes/No	Limits field values to yes and no, on and off, or true and false. Use for fields that indicate the presence or absence of a condition, such as whether an order has been filled or whether an invoice has been paid.	1 character
Hyperlink	Consists of text used as a hyperlink address, which can have up to four parts: the text that appears in a field or control; the path to a file or page; a location within the file or page; and text displayed as a ScreenTip.	Up to 65,535 characters total for the four parts of the hyperlink

Setting Field Sizes

The **Field Size property** defines a field value's maximum storage size for Short Text, Number, and AutoNumber fields only. The other data types have no Field Size property because their storage size is either a fixed, predetermined amount or is determined automatically by the field value itself, as shown in Figure 2–4. A Short Text field has a default field size of 255 characters; you can also set its field size by entering a number from 0 to 255. For example, the FirstName and LastName fields in the Patient table will be Short Text fields with sizes of 20 characters and 25 characters, respectively. These field sizes will accommodate the values that will be entered in each of these fields.

Proskills

Decision Making: Specifying the Field Size Property for Number Fields

When you use the Number data type to define a field, you need to decide what the Field Size setting should be for the field. You should set the Field Size property based on the largest value that you expect to store in that field. Access processes smaller data sizes faster, using less memory, so you can optimize your database's performance and its storage space by selecting the correct field size for each field. Field Size property settings for Number fields are as follows:

- **Byte**: Stores whole numbers (numbers with no fractions) from 0 to 255 in 1 byte
- **Integer**: Stores whole numbers from –32,768 to 32,767 in 2 bytes
- **Long Integer** (default): Stores whole numbers from –2,147,483,648 to 2,147,483,647 in 4 bytes
- **Single**: Stores positive and negative numbers to precisely 7 decimal places in 4 bytes
- **Double**: Stores positive and negative numbers to precisely 15 decimal places in 8 bytes
- **Replication ID**: Establishes a unique identifier for replication of tables, records, and other objects in databases created using Access 2003 and earlier versions in 16 bytes
- **Decimal**: Stores positive and negative numbers to precisely 28 decimal places in 12 bytes

Choosing an appropriate field size is important to optimize efficiency. For example, it would be wasteful to use the Long Integer field size for a Number field that will store only whole numbers ranging from 0 to 255 because the Long Integer field size uses 4 bytes of storage space. A better choice would be the Byte field size, which uses 1 byte of storage space to store the same values. By first gathering and analyzing information about the number values that will be stored in a Number field, you can make the best decision for the field's Field Size property and ensure the most efficient user experience for the database.

Setting the Caption Property for Fields

The **Caption property** for a field specifies how the field name is displayed in database objects, including table and query datasheets, forms, and reports. If you don't set the Caption property, Access displays the field name as the column heading or label for a field. However, field names such as InvoiceAmt and InvoiceDate in the Billing table can be difficult to read. Setting the Caption property for these fields to "Invoice Amt" and "Invoice Date" makes it easier for users to read the field names and work with the database.

Insight

Setting the Caption Property versus Naming Fields

Although Access allows you to include spaces in field names, this practice is not recommended because the spaces cause problems when you try to perform more complex tasks with the data in your database. Setting the Caption property allows you to follow best practices for naming fields, such as not including spaces in field names, while still providing users with more readable field names in datasheets, forms, and reports.

In the previous module, you created the database file for the center and, within that file, you created the Visit table working in Datasheet view. In addition, you created the Billing table working in Design view. Susan would like to further refine the design for the Billing table. So next, you'll modify the design for the Billing table for Susan in Design view.

Modifying a Table in Design View

In the previous module, you created the basic structure for the Billing table in Design view. To review, creating a basic table in Design view involves entering the field names, entering the data types for each field, entering an optional description for the fields, specifying a primary key for the table, and then saving the table structure. Creating a table in Design view can also involve defining properties for each field, which Susan would like you to do now. She has further refined the design for the Billing table by listing each field's name, data type, size, description (if applicable), and any other properties to set for each field. See Figure 2–5.

Figure 2–5 Design for the Billing table

Field Name	Data Type	Field Size	Description	Other
InvoiceNum	Short Text	5	Primary key	Caption = Invoice Num
VisitID	Short Text	4	Foreign key	Caption = Visit ID
InvoiceAmt	Currency			Format = Currency
				Decimal Places = 2
				Caption = Invoice Amt
InvoiceDate	Date/Time			Format = mm/dd/yyyy
				Caption = Invoice Date
InvoicePaid	Yes/No			Caption = Invoice Paid

You'll use Susan's design as a guide for modifying the Billing table in the database for the Pine Ridge Orthopedics & Sports Medicine Center.

To start Access and open the Billing table in Design view:

1. sam Start Access and open the database file NP_AC_2-1.accdb, located in the Access2 > Module folder included with your Data Files, and then save it as **NP_AC_2_PineRidge** in the location specified by your instructor.

   Trouble? If the security warning is displayed below the ribbon, click the Enable Content button.

2. In the Navigation Pane, right-click the **Billing** table object and then click **Design View** on the shortcut menu.
3. Click the **Shutter Bar Open/Close Button** « to close the Navigation Pane.
4. Position the pointer in the row selector for row 1 (the InvoiceNum field) until the pointer changes to a right-pointing arrow ➡. Placing it over the key symbol is fine.
5. Click the **row selector** to select the entire InvoiceNum row. See Figure 2–6.

Figure 2–6 Billing table in Design view

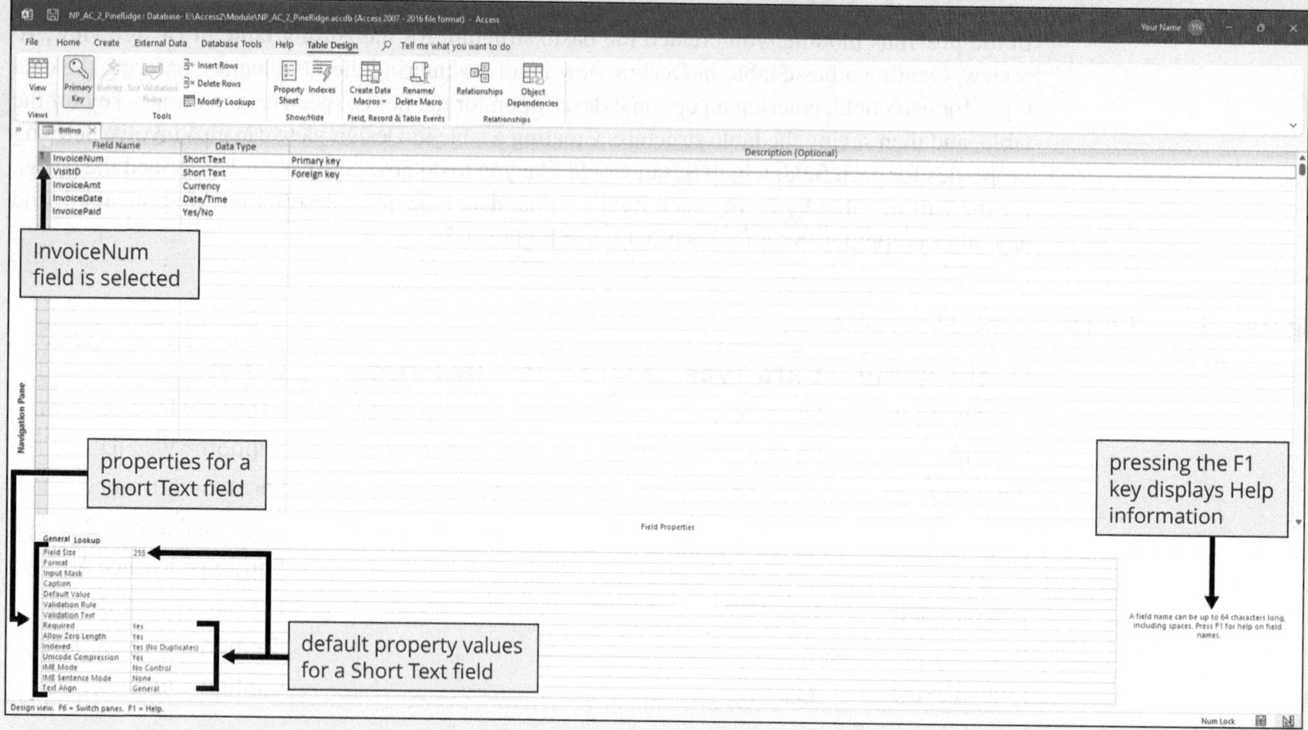

Insight

Accessibility and Using the Screen Reader

Microsoft has extensive accessibility features built into all the Office applications, one of which is a screen reader. For more up-to-date information, you can search for "screen reader" at support.microsoft.com and "Design Guide for Accessibility" at microsoft.com.

The Billing table in the NP_AC_2_PineRidge database contains the same fields as the Billing table you created in the previous module. Susan wants you to modify the fields in the table as listed in Figure 2–5. The first step is to add properties to the InvoiceNum field.

Because the Field Name, Data Type, and Description properties are already defined for the InvoiceNum field, you will use the Field Properties pane to set the additional properties Susan wants. When you created the InvoiceNum field, you gave it a data type of Short Text. Figure 2–6 shows that the default number of characters for a field of the Short Text data type is 255. In addition, a Short Text field by default has no Caption property, which specifies how the name appears. Updating the Caption property will make the field name more readable. Susan wants you to update the Field Size and Caption properties.

To add properties to the InvoiceNum field:

1. Double-click the number **255** in the Field Size property box to select it, and then type **5**.

   You also need to set the Caption property for the field so that its name appears with a space, as "Invoice Num."

2. Click the **Caption** property box, and then type **Invoice Num** (be sure to include a space between the two words). You have set properties for the InvoiceNum field. See Figure 2–7.

Figure 2–7 InvoiceNum field properties updated

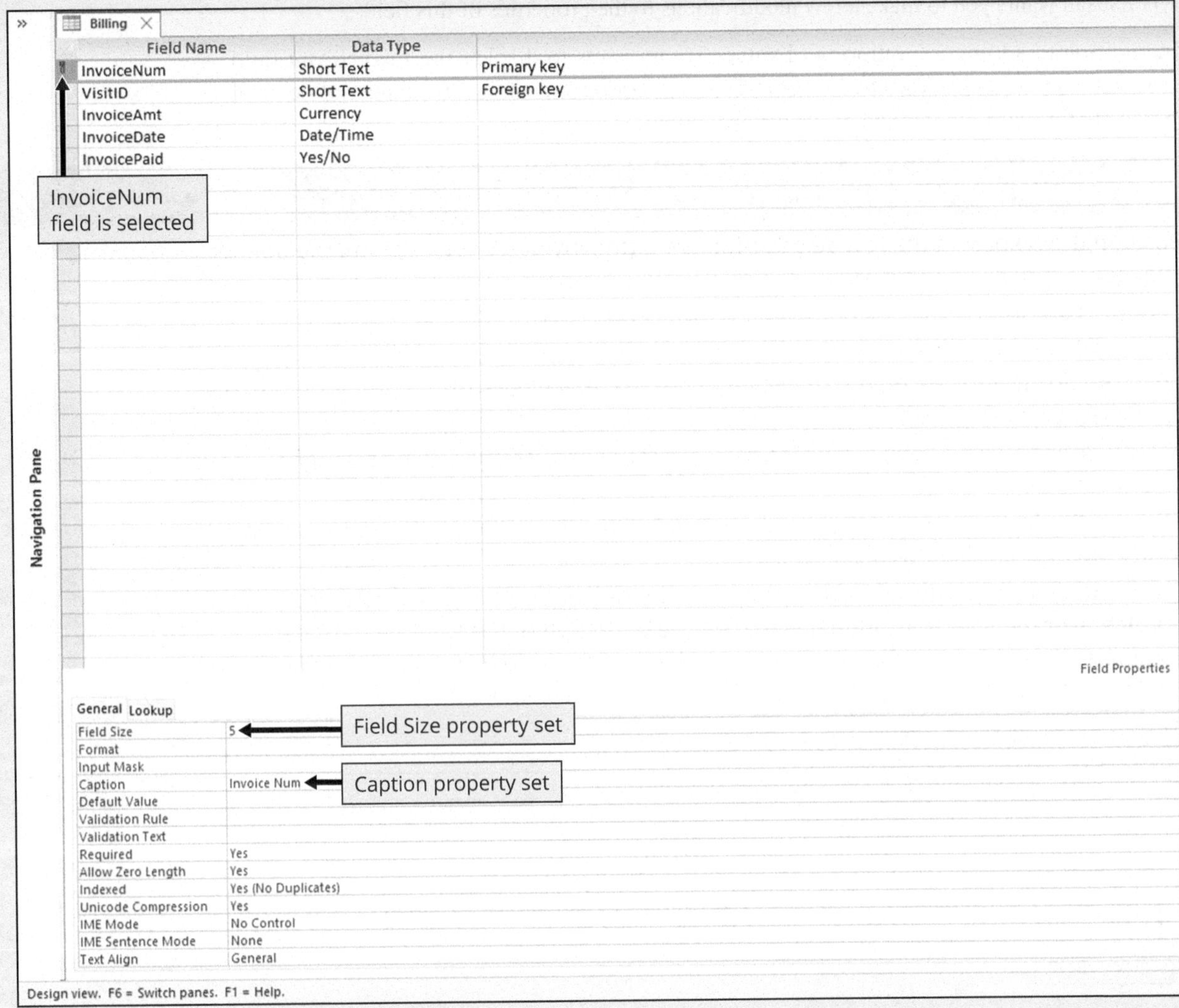

Next, you will add the properties Susan wants to the VisitID field. As with the InvoiceNum field, you will update the Field Size and Caption properties. Susan wants the field size of the VisitID field to be 4.

Recall that when you include the primary key from one table as a field in a second table to connect the two tables, the field is a foreign key in the second table. The field must be defined in the same way in both tables—that is, the field properties, including field size and data type—must match exactly. Later in this module, you'll change the Field Size property for the VisitID field in the Visit table to 4 so that the field definition is the same in both tables.

To add properties to the VisitID field:

1. Position the pointer in the row selector for row 2 (the VisitID field) until the pointer changes to a right-pointing arrow ➡.
2. Click the **row selector** to select the entire VisitID row.
3. Press **F6** to move to the Field Properties pane. The current entry for the Field Size property, 255, is selected.
4. Type **4** to set the Field Size property. Next, you need to set the Caption property for this field.
5. Press **TAB** three times to position the insertion point in the Caption box, and then type **Visit ID** (be sure to include a space between the two words). You have finished modifying the VisitID field.

The third field in the Billing table is the InvoiceAmt field, which has the Currency data type. Susan wants you to make a few modifications to the properties of this field.

In addition to adding a Caption field value, Susan wants to display the InvoiceAmt field values with two decimal places. The **Decimal Places property** specifies the number of decimal places that are displayed to the right of the decimal point.

To add properties to the InvoiceAmt field:

1. Position the pointer in the row selector for row 3 (the InvoiceAmt field) until the pointer changes to a right-pointing arrow ➡.
2. Click the **row selector** to select the entire InvoiceAmt row.
3. In the Field Properties pane, click the **Decimal Places** box to position the insertion point. An arrow appears on the right side of the Decimal Places box, which you can click to display a list of options.

   Tip You can display the arrow and the list simultaneously by clicking the right side of a box.
4. Click the **Decimal Places** arrow, and then click **2** in the list to specify two decimal places for the InvoiceAmt field values.
5. Press **TAB** twice to position the insertion point in the Caption box, and then type **Invoice Amt** (be sure to include the space). The definition of the third field is now complete. Notice that the Format property is by default set to "Currency," which formats the values with dollar signs, and is what Susan wants. See Figure 2–8.

Figure 2–8 InvoiceAmt field properties updated

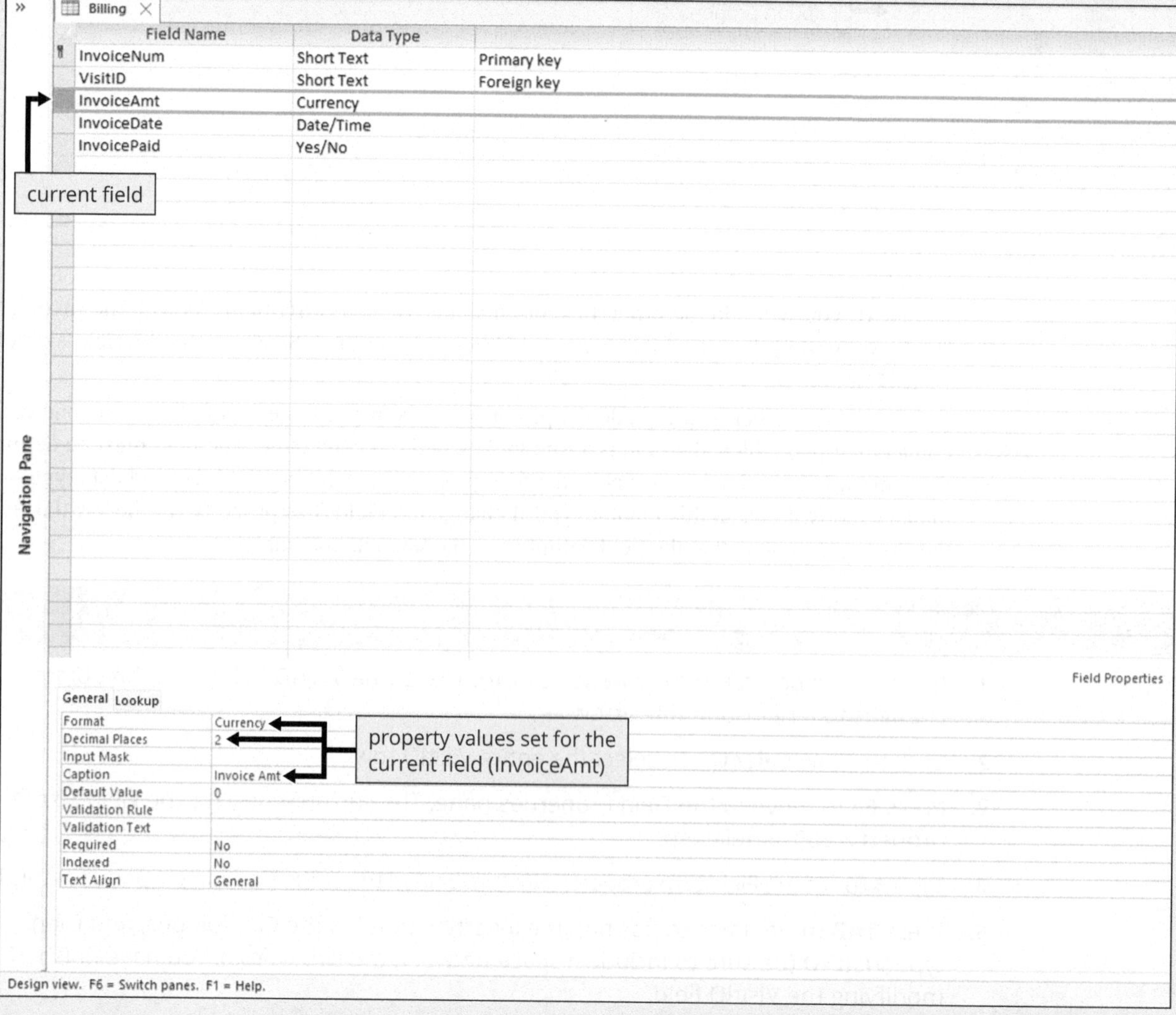

In these steps, you set the Decimal Places property for the InvoiceAmt field in Design view; however, it is also possible to change the number of decimal places for a field in Datasheet view. For fields of the Currency and Number data types, you can change the number of decimal places in either view. To change the number of decimal places in Datasheet view, you would first click a field to make it the active field. On the Table Fields tab, in the Formatting group, use the Increase Decimals and Decrease Decimals buttons to add or remove decimal places in the field. When you do, Access makes the change in the corresponding Decimal Places property in Design view.

The fourth field in the Billing table is the InvoiceDate field. According to Susan's design (Figure 2–5), the date values should be displayed in the format mm/dd/yyyy, which is a two-digit month, a two-digit day, and a four-digit year. In addition, she wants you to update the Caption property.

To add properties to the InvoiceDate field:

1. Position the pointer in the row selector for row 4 (the InvoiceDate field) until the pointer changes to a right-pointing arrow ➡.
2. Click the **row selector** to select the entire InvoiceDate row.

   Susan wants to display the values in the InvoiceDate field in a format showing the month, the day, and a four-digit year, as in the following example: 05/24/2030. You use the Format property to control the display of a field value.
3. In the Field Properties pane, click the right side of the **Format** box to display the list of predefined formats for Date/Time fields. See Figure 2–9.

Figure 2–9 Displaying available formats for Date/Time fields

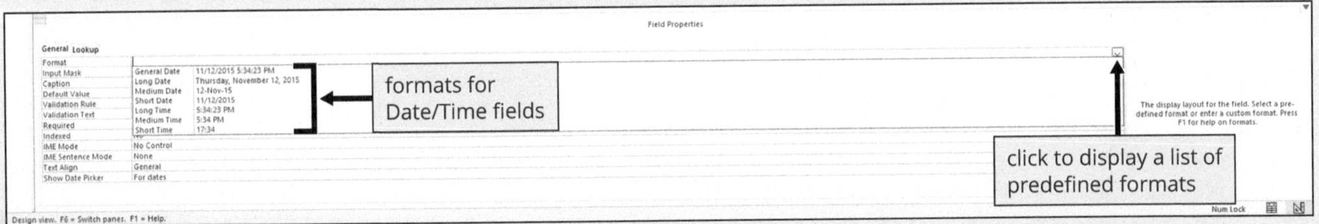

   Trouble? If you see an arrow instead of a list of predefined formats, click the arrow to display the list.

   As noted in the right side of the Field Properties pane, you can choose a predefined format or enter a custom format. Even though the Short Date format seems to match the format Susan wants, it displays only one digit for January to September. For example, it would display the month of May with only the digit "5"—as in 5/24/2030—instead of displaying the month with two digits, as in 05/24/2030.

   Because none of the predefined formats matches the exact layout Susan wants for the InvoiceDate values, you need to create a custom date format. Figure 2–10 shows some of the symbols available for custom date and time formats.

Figure 2–10 Symbols for some custom date formats

Symbol	Description
/	Date separator
d	Day of the month in one or two numeric digits, as needed (1 to 31)
dd	Day of the month in two numeric digits (01 to 31)
ddd	First three letters of the weekday (Sun to Sat)
dddd	Full name of the weekday (Sunday to Saturday)
w	Day of the week (1 to 7)
ww	Week of the year (1 to 53)
m	Month of the year in one or two numeric digits, as needed (1 to 12)
mm	Month of the year in two numeric digits (01 to 12)
mmm	First three letters of the month (Jan to Dec)
mmmm	Full name of the month (January to December)
yy	Last two digits of the year (01 to 99)
yyyy	Full year (0100 to 9999)

Susan wants to display the dates with a two-digit month (mm), a two-digit day (dd), and a four-digit year (yyyy).

4. Click the **Format** arrow to close the list of predefined formats, and then type **mm/dd/yyyy** in the Format box.
5. Press **TAB** twice to position the insertion point in the Caption box, and then type **Invoice Date** (be sure to include a space between the words). See Figure 2–11.

Figure 2–11 Specifying the custom date format

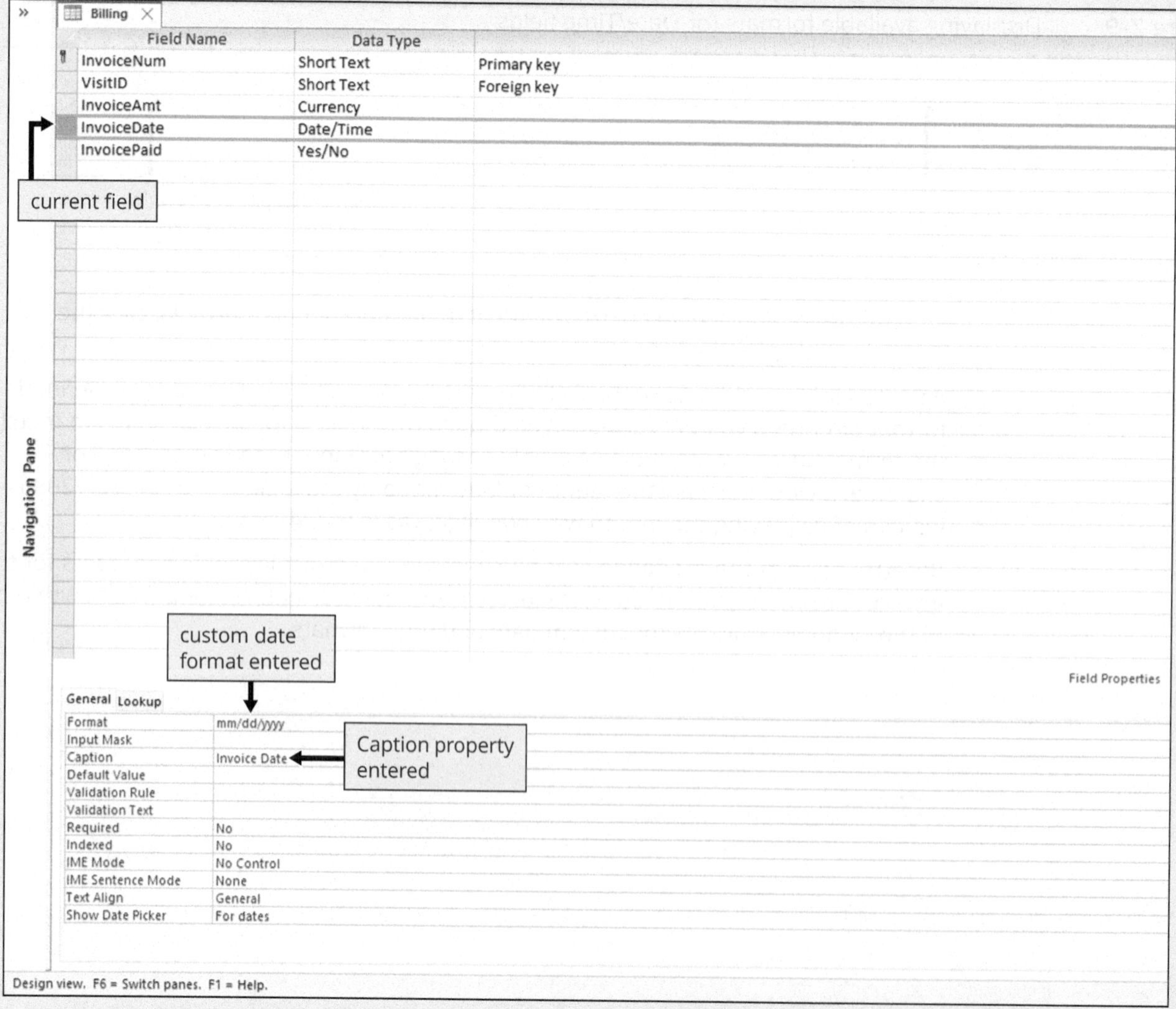

The fifth and final field to modify in the Billing table is the InvoicePaid field. The only property Susan wants to update for the InvoicePaid field is the Caption property.

To add a property to the InvoicePaid field:

1. Position the pointer in the row selector for row 5 (the InvoicePaid field) until the pointer changes to a right-pointing arrow ➡.
2. Click the **row selector** to select the entire InvoicePaid row.
3. In the Field Properties pane, click the **Caption** box, and then type **Invoice Paid** (once again, be sure to include a space between the words).

You've finished adding properties to the fields for the Billing table. Normally after entering the fields and properties for a table in Design view, you would specify the primary key for the table; however, the primary key for the Billing table is the InvoiceNum field, similar to what you did in the previous module.

Insight

Understanding the Importance of the Primary Key

Although Access does not require a table to have a primary key, including a primary key offers several advantages:

- A primary key uniquely identifies each record in a table.
- Access does not allow duplicate values in the primary key field. For example, if the Visit table already has a record with a VisitID value of 3170, Access prevents you from adding another record with this same value in the VisitID field. Preventing duplicate values ensures the uniqueness of the primary key field.
- When a primary key has been specified, Access forces you to enter a value for the primary key field in every record in the table. This is known as **entity integrity**. If you do not enter a value for a field, you have actually given the field a null value. You cannot give a **null value** to the primary key field because entity integrity prevents Access from accepting and processing that record.
- You can enter records in any order, but Access displays them by default in order of the primary key's field values. If you enter records in no specific order, you will later be able to work with them in a more meaningful, primary key sequence.
- Access responds faster to your requests for specific records based on the primary key.

Saving the Table Structure

The table already has a name, Billing; however, because you added many property values, you should save the changes you made to the table structure.

To save the Billing table changes:

1. On the Quick Access Toolbar, click the **Save** button.

   Unlike the first time you saved the Billing table, you are not prompted for a name for the table. Because the name has already been assigned, Access updates the structure of the table using the same name.

Modifying the Structure of an Access Table

Even a well-designed table might need to be modified. Some changes that you can make to a table's structure in Design view include changing the order of fields and adding new fields.

After meeting with her assistant, Kimberly Wilson, and reviewing the structure of the Billing table, Susan asks you to make changes to the table. First, she wants to move the InvoiceAmt field so that it appears right before the InvoicePaid field. Then, she wants you to add a new Short Text field named InvoiceItem to include information about what the invoice is for, such as an office evaluation, physical therapy session, and so on. Susan would like to insert the InvoiceItem field between the InvoiceAmt and InvoicePaid fields.

Moving a Field in Design View

To move a field, you use the mouse to drag it to a new location in the Table Design grid. Although you can move a field in Datasheet view by dragging its column heading to a new location, doing so rearranges only the *display* of the table's fields; the table structure is not changed. To move a field permanently, you must move the field in Design view.

Next, you'll move the InvoiceAmt field so that it appears before the InvoicePaid field in the Billing table.

To move the InvoiceAmt field:

1. Position the pointer on the row selector for the InvoiceAmt field until the pointer changes to a right-pointing arrow ➡.
2. Click the **row selector** to select the entire InvoiceAmt row.
3. Place the pointer on the row selector for the InvoiceAmt field until the pointer changes to a selection pointer, press and hold the mouse button, and then drag to the row selector for the InvoicePaid field. As you drag, the pointer changes to a move pointer. See Figure 2–12.

Figure 2–12 Moving the InvoiceAmt field in the table structure

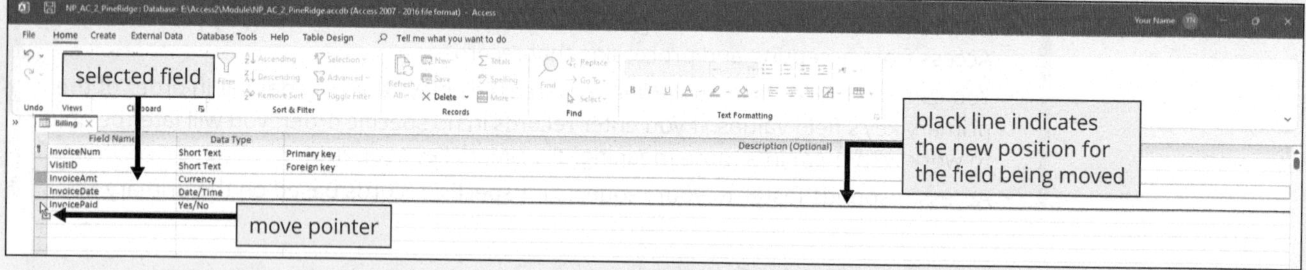

4. Release the mouse button. The InvoiceAmt field now appears between the InvoiceDate and InvoicePaid fields in the table structure.

   Trouble? If the InvoiceAmt field did not move, repeat Steps 1 through 4, making sure you hold down the mouse button while dragging.

Adding a Field in Design View

To add a new field between existing fields, you must insert a row. You begin by selecting the row below where you want to insert the new field.

Reference

Adding a Field between Two Existing Fields

- In the Table window in Design view, select the row below where you want to insert the new field.
- On the Table Design tab, in the Tools group, click the Insert Rows button.
- Define the new field by entering the field name, data type, optional description, and any property specifications.

Next, you need to add the InvoiceItem field to the Billing table structure between the InvoiceAmt and InvoicePaid fields.

To add the InvoiceItem field to the Billing table:

1. Click the **InvoicePaid** Field Name box. You need to establish this field as the current field to insert the row for the new field above this field.
2. On the Table Design tab, in the Tools group, click **Insert Rows**. A new, blank row is added between the InvoiceAmt and InvoicePaid fields. The insertion point is positioned in the Field Name box for the new row, ready for you to type the name for the new field. See Figure 2–13.

Figure 2–13 Table structure after inserting a row

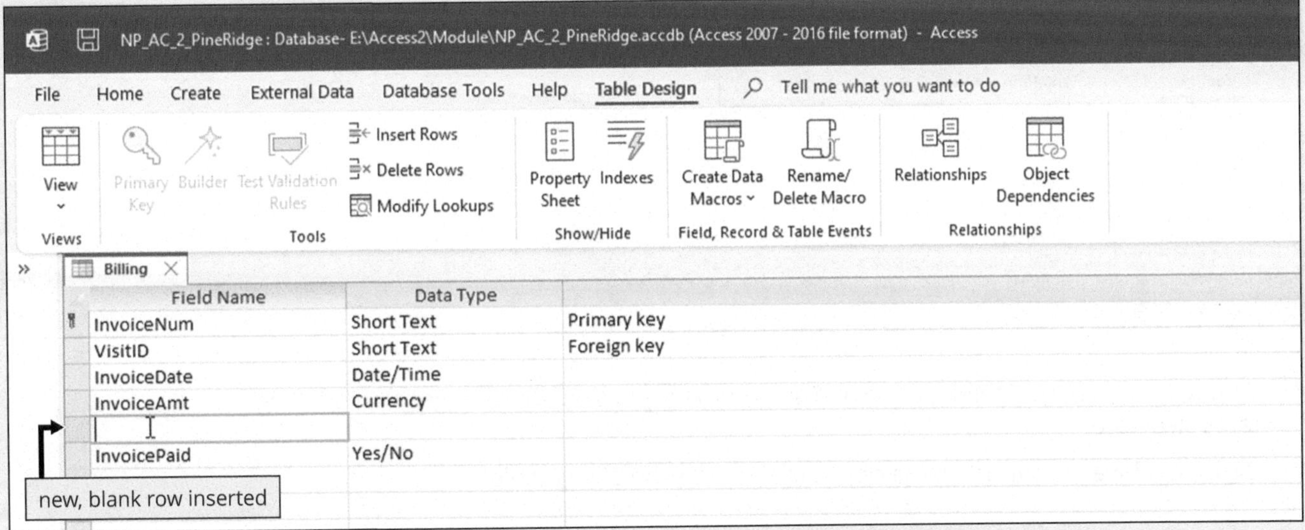

Trouble? If you selected the InvoicePaid field's row selector and then inserted the new row, you need to click the new row's Field Name box to position the insertion point in it.

You'll define the InvoiceItem field in the new row of the Billing table. This field will be a Short Text field with a field size of 40. You also need to set the Caption property to include a space between the words in the field name.

3. Type **InvoiceItem**, press **TAB** to move to the Data Type property, and then press **TAB** again to accept the default Short Text data type.
4. Press **F6** to select the default field size in the Field Size box, and then type **40**.
5. Press **TAB** three times to position the insertion point in the Caption box, and then type **Invoice Item**. The definition of the new field is complete. See Figure 2–14.

Figure 2–14 InvoiceItem field added to the Billing table

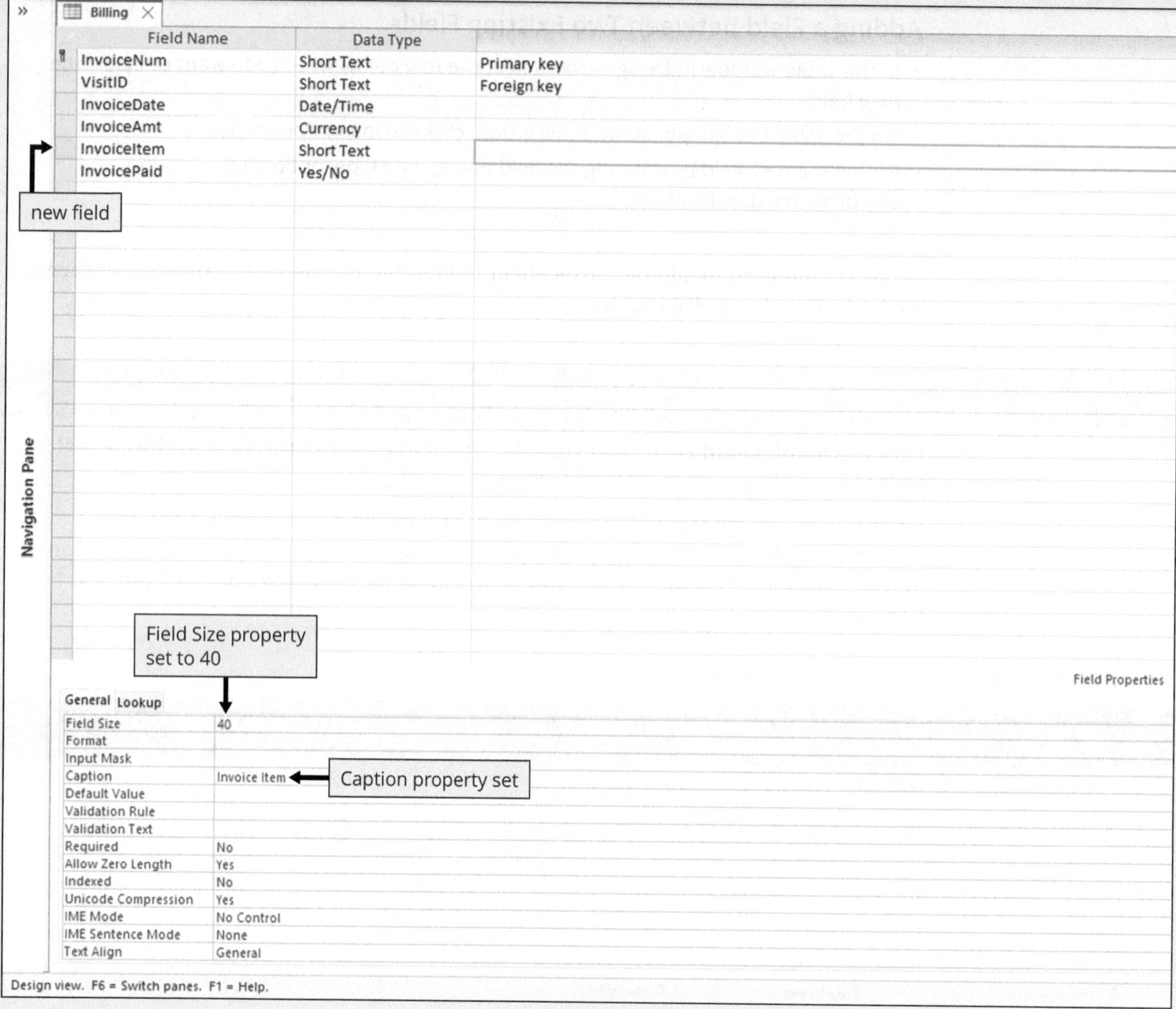

6. On the Quick Access Toolbar, click the **Save** button to save the changes to the Billing table structure.
7. Click the **Close** button on the object tab to close the Billing table.

Modifying Field Properties

With the Billing table design complete, you can now modify the properties of the fields in the Visit table, as necessary. You can make some changes to properties in Datasheet view; for others, you'll work in Design view.

Changing the Format Property in Datasheet View

The Formatting group on the Table Fields tab in Datasheet view allows you to modify some formatting properties for certain field types. When you format a field, you change the way data is displayed but not the actual values stored in the table.

Next, you'll check the properties of the VisitDate field in the Visit table to see if any changes would improve the display of the date values.

To modify the VisitDate field's Format property:

1. In the Navigation Pane, click the **Shutter Bar Open/Close Button** » to open the pane. Notice that the Billing table is listed above the Visit table in the Tables section. By default, objects are listed in alphabetical order in the Navigation Pane.
2. Double-click **Visit** to open the Visit table in Datasheet view.
3. In the Navigation Pane, click the **Shutter Bar Open/Close Button** « to close the pane.
4. Position the pointer in the row selector for the first record (VisitID 3140) until the pointer changes to a right-pointing arrow ➡.
5. Click the **row selector** to select the entire first record. See Figure 2–15.

Figure 2–15 Visit table datasheet

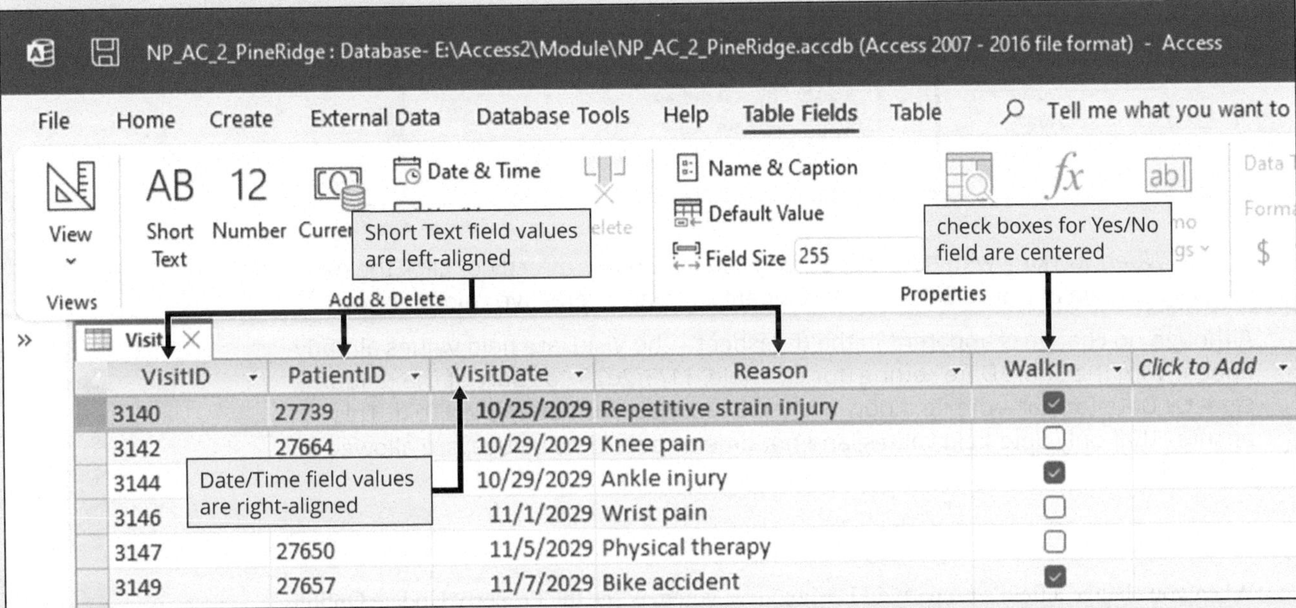

The values in the three Short Text fields—VisitID, PatientID, and Reason—appear left-aligned within their boxes, and the values in the Date/Time field (VisitDate) appear right-aligned. In Access, values for Short Text fields are left-aligned, and values for Number, Date/Time, and Currency fields are right-aligned. The WalkIn field is a Yes/No field, so its values appear in check boxes that are centered within the column.

6. On the ribbon, click the **Table Fields** tab.
7. Click the **first field value** in the VisitDate column. The Data Type option shows that this field is a Date/Time field.

   By default, Access assigns the General Date format to Date/Time fields. Note the Format box in the Formatting group, which you use to set the Format property (similar to how you set the Format property in the Field Properties pane in Design view). Even though the Format box is empty, the VisitDate field has the General Date format applied to it. The General Date format includes settings for date or time values, or a combination of date and time values. However, Susan wants to display *only date values* in the VisitDate field, so she asks you to specify the Short Date format for the field.

8. In the Formatting group, click the **Format** arrow, and then click **Short Date**. See Figure 2–16.

Figure 2–16 VisitDate field after modifying the format

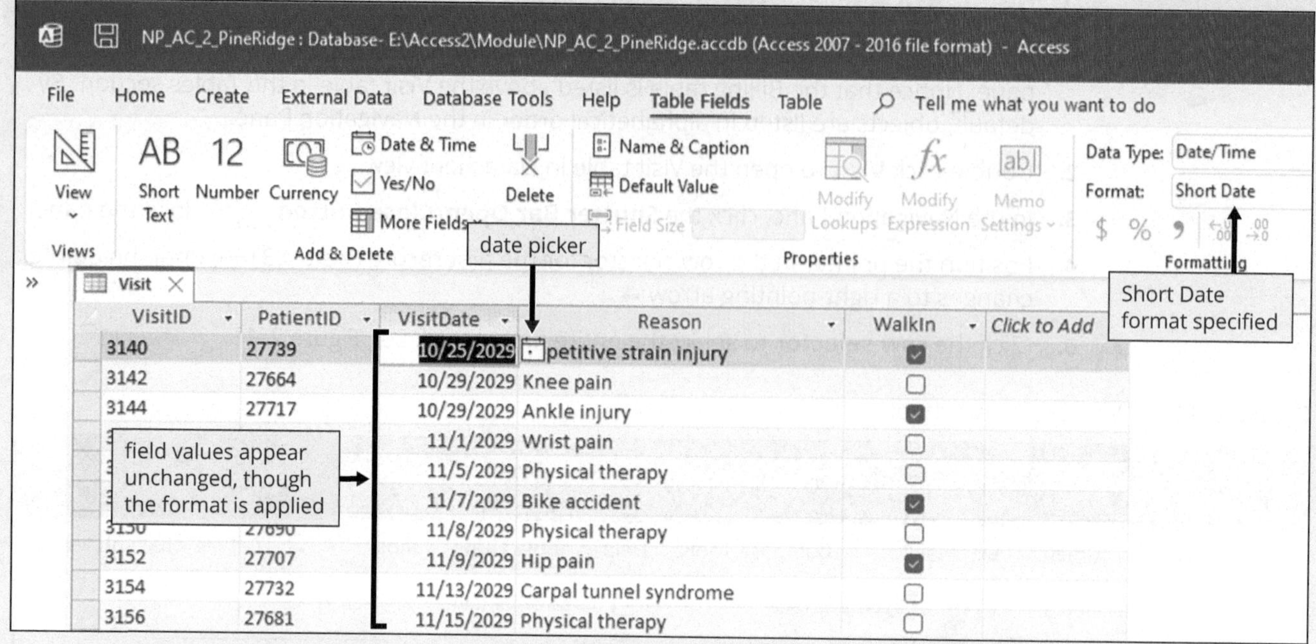

Tip When working with date values, you can type dates directly or click the date picker shown in Figure 2–16 to select a date from an interactive calendar.

Although no change is apparent in the datasheet—the VisitDate field values already appear with the Short Date setting (for example, 11/3/2029), as part of the default General Date format—the field now has the Short Date format applied to it. This ensures that only date field values, and not time or date/time values, are allowed in the field.

When you change a field's property in Design view, you may see the Property Update Options button. This button appears when you modify a property for a field included in a query, form, or report in the database and asks if you want to update the related properties of the field in the other objects. For example, if the NP_AC_2_PineRidge database included a form or report that contained the PatientID field, and you modified a property of the PatientID field in the Patient table, you could choose to propagate, or update, the modified property by clicking the Property Update Options button, and then choosing the option to make the update everywhere the field is used. You are not required to update the related objects; however, in most cases, it is a good idea to perform the update.

Changing Properties in Design View

Recall that each of the Short Text fields in the Visit table—VisitID, PatientID, and Reason—still has the default field size of 255, which is too large for the data contained in these fields. Also, the VisitID and PatientID fields need descriptions to identify them as the primary and foreign keys, respectively, in the table. Finally, each of these fields needs a caption to include a space between the words in the field name or to make the name more descriptive. You can make all these property changes more easily in Design view.

To modify the Field Size, Description, and Caption field properties:

1. On the Table Fields tab, in the Views group, click the **View** button. The table is displayed in Design view with the VisitID field selected. You need to enter a Description property value for this field, the primary key in the table, and change its Field Size property to 4 because each visit number at Pine Ridge Orthopedics & Sports Medicine Center consists of four digits.

   Trouble? If you clicked the arrow on the View button, a menu appears. Choose Design View from the menu.

   Tip You can also click the Design View button on the far-right end of the status bar to switch to Design view.

2. Press **TAB** twice to position the insertion point in the Description (Optional) box, and then type **Primary key**.
3. Press **F6** to move to and select the default setting of 255 in the Field Size box in the Field Properties pane, and then type **4**. Next, you need to set the Caption property for this field.
4. Press **TAB** three times to position the insertion point in the Caption box, and then type **Visit ID**.
5. Click the **PatientID** Field Name box, press **TAB** twice to position the insertion point in the Description (Optional) box, and then type **Foreign key**.
6. Press **F6** to move to and select the default setting of 255 in the Field Size box in the Field Properties pane, and then type **5**.
7. Press **TAB** three times to position the insertion point in the Caption box, and then type **Patient ID**.
8. Click the **VisitDate** Field Name box, click the **Caption** box, and then type **Date of Visit**.

   For the Reason field, you will set the Field Size property to 60. This size can accommodate the longer values in the Reason field. You'll also set this field's Caption property to provide a more descriptive name.

9. Click the **Reason** Field Name box, press **F6**, type **60**, press **TAB** three times to position the insertion point in the Caption box, and then type **Reason/Diagnosis**.

   Finally, you'll set the Caption property for the WalkIn field.

10. Click the **WalkIn** Field Name box, click the **Caption** box, and then type **Walk-in?**. See Figure 2–17.

Figure 2–17 Visit table after modifying field properties

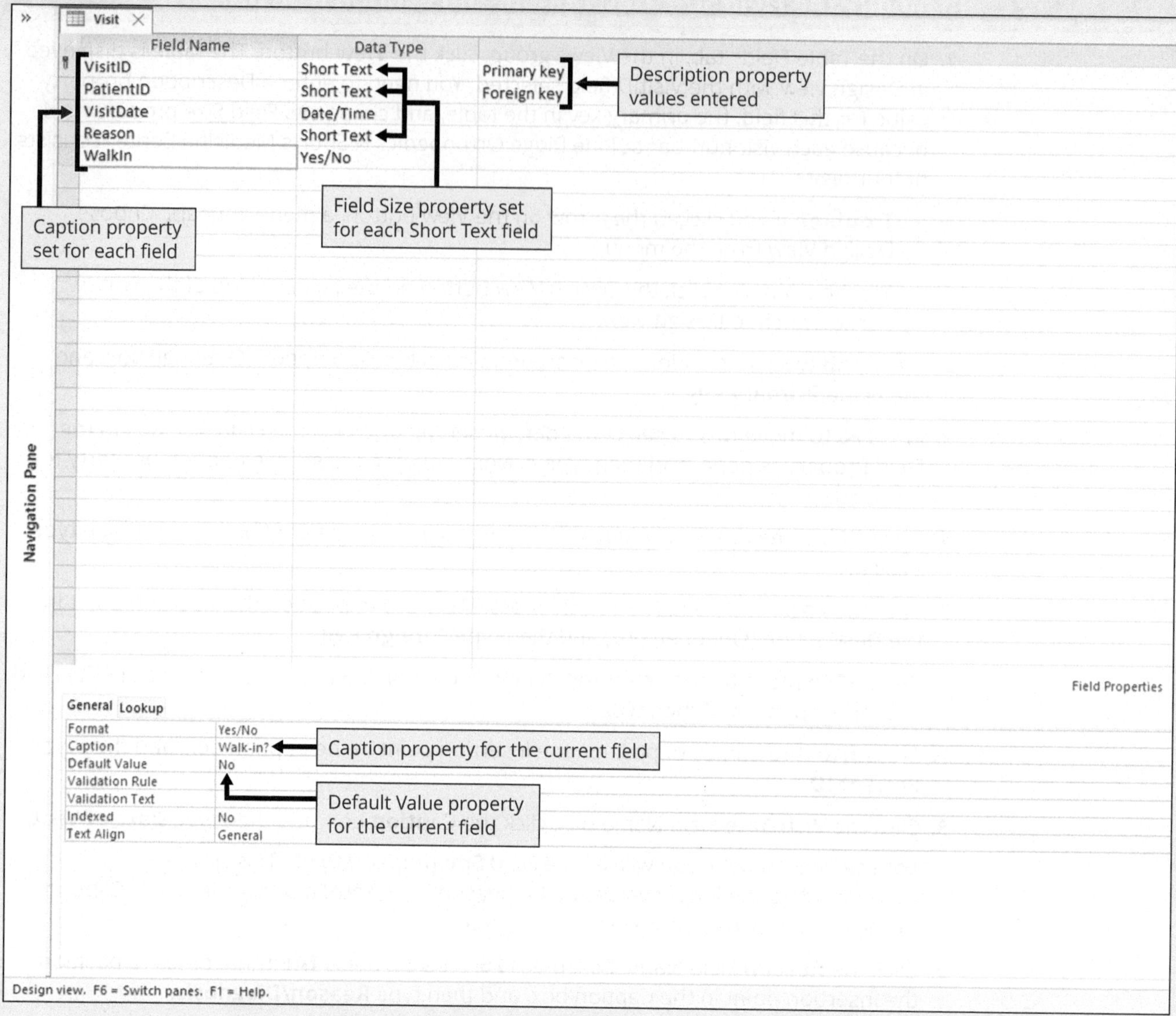

The WalkIn field's Default Value property is automatically set to "No," which means the check box for this field will be empty for each new record. This is the default for this property for any Yes/No field. You can set the Default Value property for other types of fields to make data entry easier. You'll learn more about setting this property in the next part.

The changes to the Visit table's properties are now complete, so you can save the table and view the results of your changes in Datasheet view.

To save and view the modified Visit table:

1. On the Quick Access Toolbar, click the **Save** button to save the modified table. A dialog box opens informing you that some data may be lost because you decreased the field sizes. Because all the values in the VisitID, PatientID, and Reason fields contain the same number of or fewer characters than the new Field Size properties you set for each field, you can ignore this message and continue.
2. Click **Yes**.

3. On the Table Design tab, in the Views group, click the **View** button to display the Visit table in Datasheet view. Each column (field) heading now displays the text you specified in the Caption property for that field. See Figure 2–18.

Figure 2–18 Modified Visit table in Datasheet view

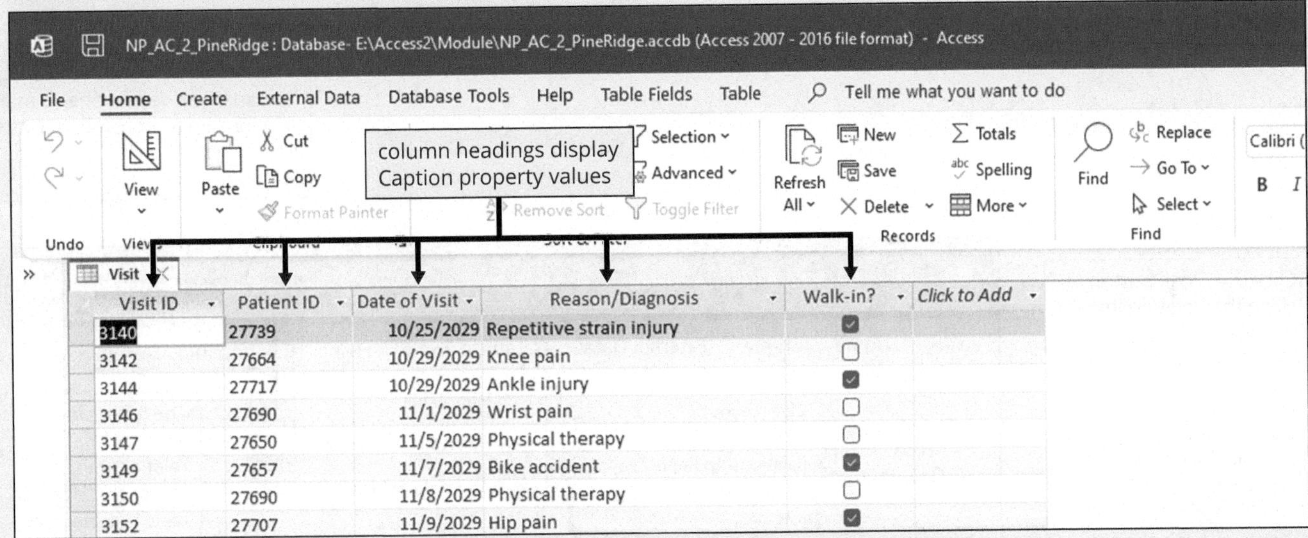

4. Click the **Close** button on the object tab to close the Visit table.
5. If you are not continuing to Part 2.2, click the **File** tab, and then click **Close** to close the NP_AC_2_PineRidge database.

You have modified the design of the Billing table. In the next part, you'll add records to the Billing table and create the Patient table in the NP_AC_2_PineRidge database.

Part 2.1 Quick Check

1. What guidelines should you follow when designing a database?
2. What is the purpose of the Data Type property for a field?
3. To specify how a field's name is displayed in database objects, including table and query datasheets, forms, and reports, you set the ________ property.
4. For which three types of fields can you assign a field size?
5. The default Field Size property setting for a Short Text field is ________.
6. In Design view, which key do you press to move from the Table Design grid to the Field Properties pane?
7. List three reasons you should specify a primary key for an Access table.

Part 2.2 Visual Overview: Understanding Table Relationships

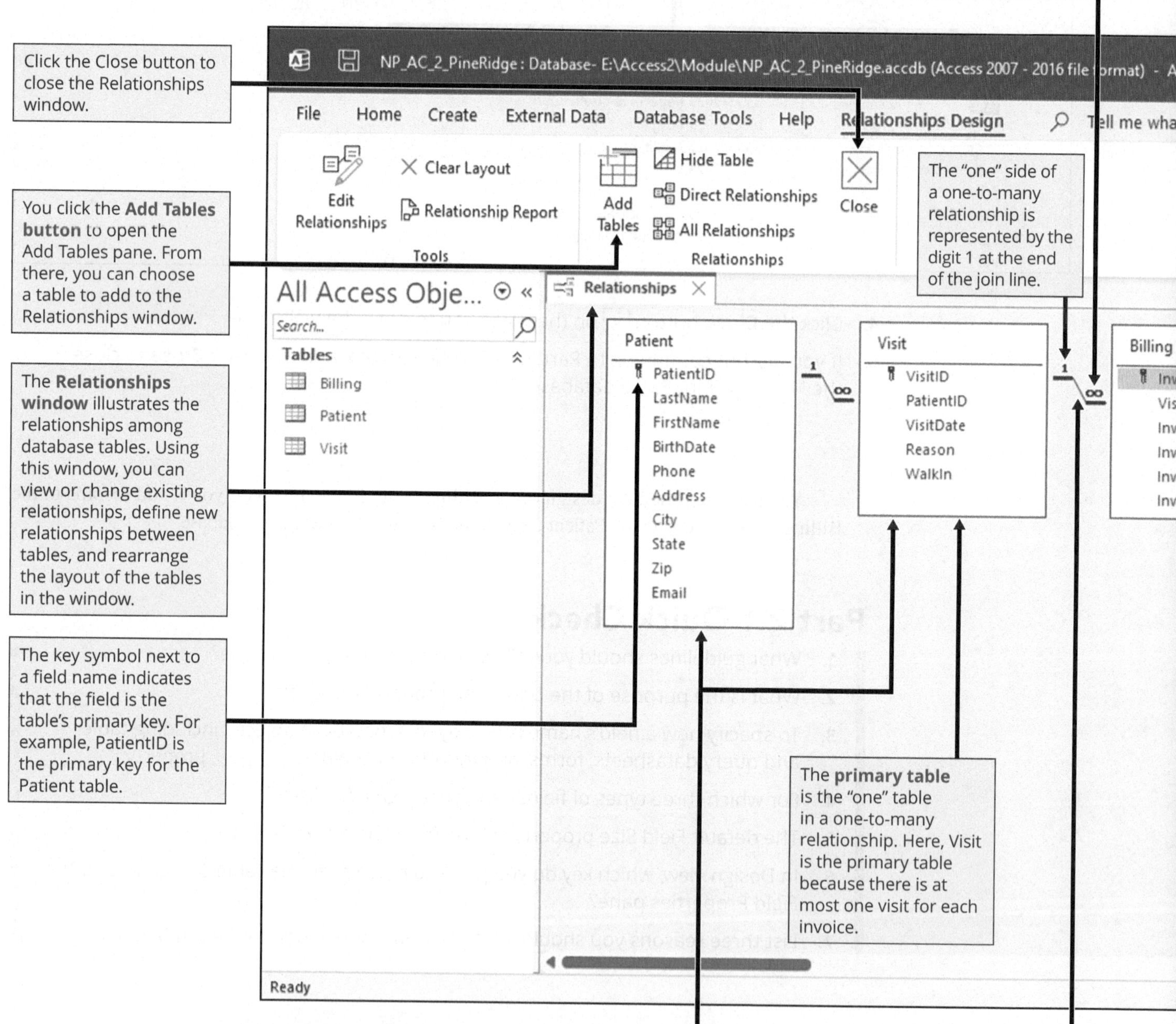

The "many" side of a one-to-many relationship is represented by the infinity symbol at the end of the join line.
Click the Close button to close the Relationships window.
You click the **Add Tables button** to open the Add Tables pane. From there, you can choose a table to add to the Relationships window.
The **Relationships window** illustrates the relationships among database tables. Using this window, you can view or change existing relationships, define new relationships between tables, and rearrange the layout of the tables in the window.
The key symbol next to a field name indicates that the field is the table's primary key. For example, PatientID is the primary key for the Patient table.
The "one" side of a one-to-many relationship is represented by the digit 1 at the end of the join line.
The **primary table** is the "one" table in a one-to-many relationship. Here, Visit is the primary table because there is at most one visit for each invoice.
NP_AC_2_PineRidge : Database- E:\Access2\Module\NP_AC_2_PineRidge.accdb (Access 2007 - 2016 file format)
File
Home
Create
External Data
Database Tools
Help
Relationships Design
Edit Relationships
Clear Layout
Relationship Report
Tools
Add Tables
Hide Table
Direct Relationships
All Relationships
Relationships
Close
All Access Obje...
Search...
Tables
Billing
Patient
Visit
Relationships
Patient
PatientID
LastName
FirstName
BirthDate
Phone
Address
City
State
Zip
Email
Visit
VisitID
PatientID
VisitDate
Reason
WalkIn
Billing
Ready

A **one-to-many relationship** exists between two tables when one record in the first table matches zero, one, or many records in the second table, and when one record in the second table matches at most one record in the first table. Here, the Patient and Visit tables have a one-to-many relationship because a patient can have many visits, and each visit is associated with only one patient. The two tables are still separate tables, but because they are joined, you can use the data in them as if they were one table.

The **join line** connects the common field used to create the relationship between two tables. Here, the common field VisitID is used to create the one-to-many relationship between the Visit and Billing tables.

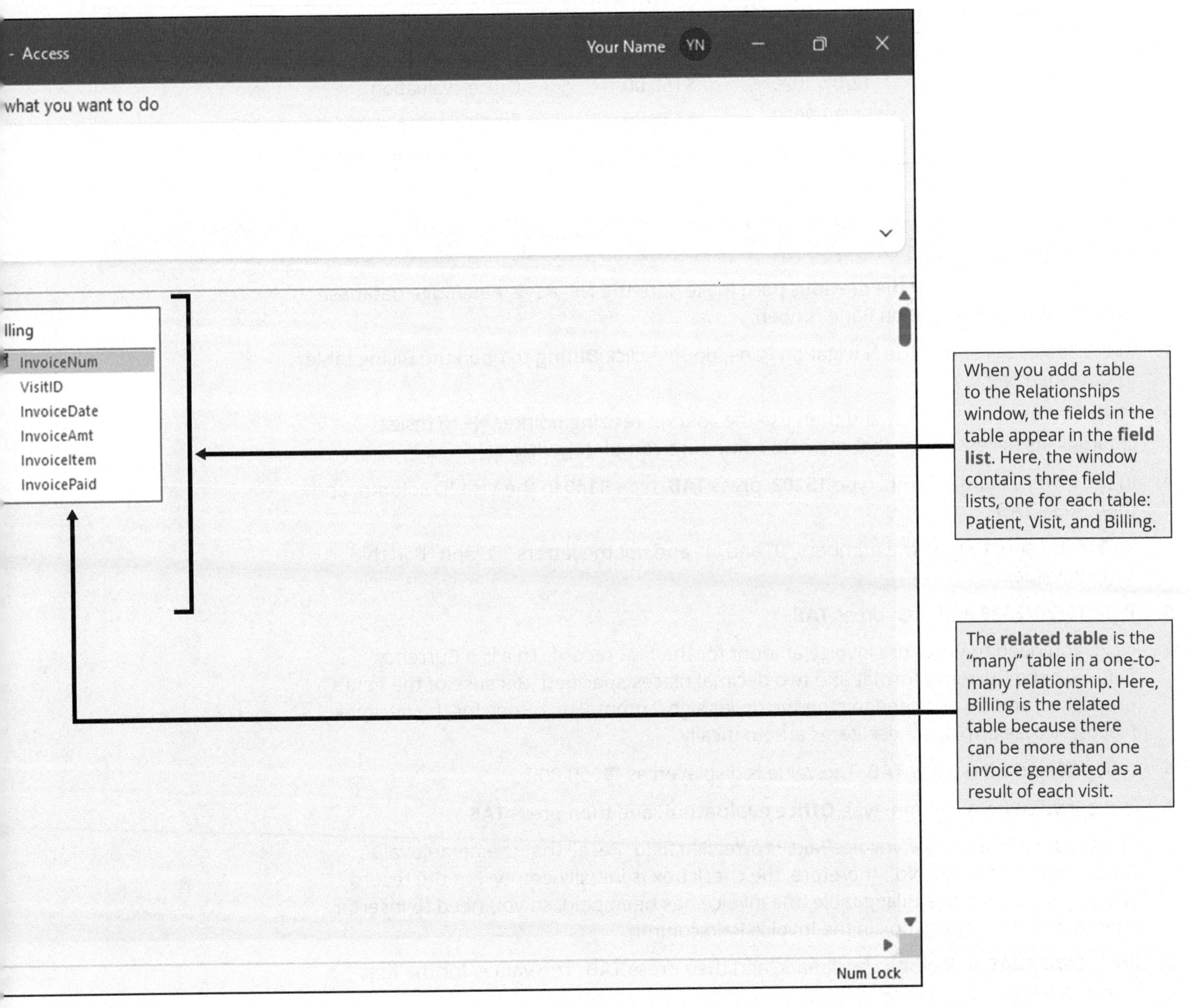

When you add a table to the Relationships window, the fields in the table appear in the **field list**. Here, the window contains three field lists, one for each table: Patient, Visit, and Billing.

The **related table** is the "many" table in a one-to-many relationship. Here, Billing is the related table because there can be more than one invoice generated as a result of each visit.

Adding Records to a New Table

Before you can begin to define the table relationships illustrated in the Part 2.2 Visual Overview, you need to finish creating the tables in the NP_AC_2_PineRidge database.

The Billing table design is complete. Now, Susan would like you to add records to the table so it contains the invoice data for the Pine Ridge Orthopedics & Sports Medicine Center. As you learned earlier, you add records to a table in Datasheet view by typing the field values in the rows below the column headings for the fields. You'll begin by entering the records shown in Figure 2–19.

Figure 2–19 Records to add to the Billing table

Invoice Num	Visit ID	Invoice Date	Invoice Amt	Invoice Item	Invoice Paid
15202	3140	10/26/2029	$150.00	Office evaluation	Yes
15267	3167	12/07/2029	$150.00	Office evaluation	No
15359	3208	01/29/2030	$125.00	Physical therapy session	Yes
15486	3272	04/01/2030	$125.00	Physical therapy session	No

To add the first record to the Billing table:

1. If you took a break after the previous part, make sure the NP_AC_2_PineRidge database is open, and the Navigation Pane is open.
2. In the Tables section of the Navigation Pane, double-click **Billing** to open the Billing table in Datasheet view.
3. Close the Navigation Pane, and then use the column resizing pointer ✛ to resize columns, as necessary, so that the field names are completely visible.
4. In the Invoice Num column, type **15202**, press **TAB**, type **3140** in the Visit ID column, and then press **TAB**.

   Tip Be sure to type the numbers "0" and "1" and *not* the letters "O" and "I" in the field values.

5. Type **10/26/2029** and then press **TAB**.

   Next, you need to enter the invoice amount for the first record. This is a Currency field with the Currency format and two decimal places specified. Because of the field's properties, you do not need to type the dollar sign, comma, or zeroes for the decimal places; Access displays these items automatically.

6. Type **150** and then press **TAB**. The value is displayed as "$150.00."
7. In the Invoice Item column, type **Office evaluation**, and then press **TAB**.

   The last field in the table, InvoicePaid, is a Yes/No field. Recall that the default value for any Yes/No field is "No"; therefore, the check box is initially empty. For the record you are entering in the Billing table, the invoice has been paid, so you need to insert a checkmark in the check box in the Invoice Paid column.

8. Press **SPACEBAR** to insert a checkmark, and then press **TAB**. The values for the first record are entered.
9. Use the column resizing pointer ✛ to resize columns, as necessary, so that the values of the fields are completely visible. See Figure 2–20.

Figure 2–20 First record entered in the Billing table

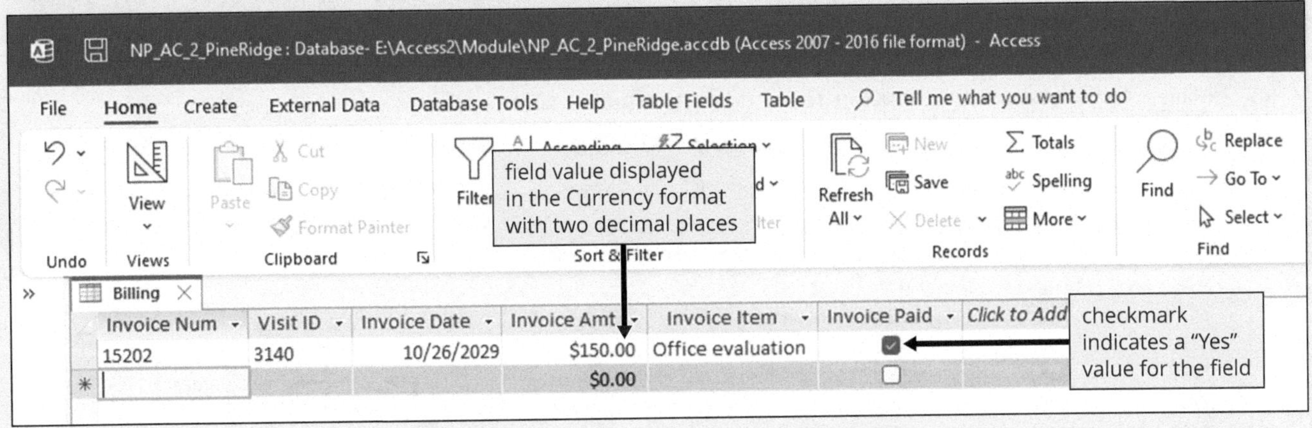

Now you can add the remaining three records. As you do, you'll learn a keyboard shortcut for inserting the value from the same field in the previous record. A **keyboard shortcut** is a key or combination of keys you press to complete an action more efficiently.

To add the next three records to the Billing table:

1. Refer to Figure 2–19 and enter the values in the second record's Invoice Num, Visit ID, and Invoice Date columns.

   Notice that the value in the second record's Invoice Amt column is $150.00. This value is the exact same value as in the first record. You can quickly insert the value from the same column in the previous record using the CTRL+' (apostrophe) keyboard shortcut. To use this shortcut, you press and hold CTRL, press the ' key once, and then release both keys. (The plus sign in the keyboard shortcut indicates you are pressing two keys at once; you do not press the + key.)

2. With the insertion point in the Invoice Amt column, press **CTRL+'**. The value "$150.00" is inserted in the Invoice Amt column for the second record.
3. Press **TAB** to move to the Invoice Item column. Again, the value you need to enter in this column—Office evaluation—is the same as the value for this column in the previous record. So, you can use the keyboard shortcut again.
4. With the insertion point in the Invoice Item column, press **CTRL+'**. Access inserts the value "Office evaluation" in the Invoice Item column for the second record.
5. Press **TAB** to move to the Invoice Paid column, and then press **TAB** to leave the Invoice Paid check box unchecked to indicate the invoice has not been paid. The second record is entered in the Billing table.
6. Refer to Figure 2–19 to enter the values for the third and fourth records, using CTRL+' to enter the value in the fourth record's Invoice Amt and Invoice Item columns.
7. Use the column resizing pointer ✛ to resize columns, as necessary, so that the values of the fields are completely visible. Your table should look like the one in Figure 2–21.

Figure 2–21 Billing table with four records entered

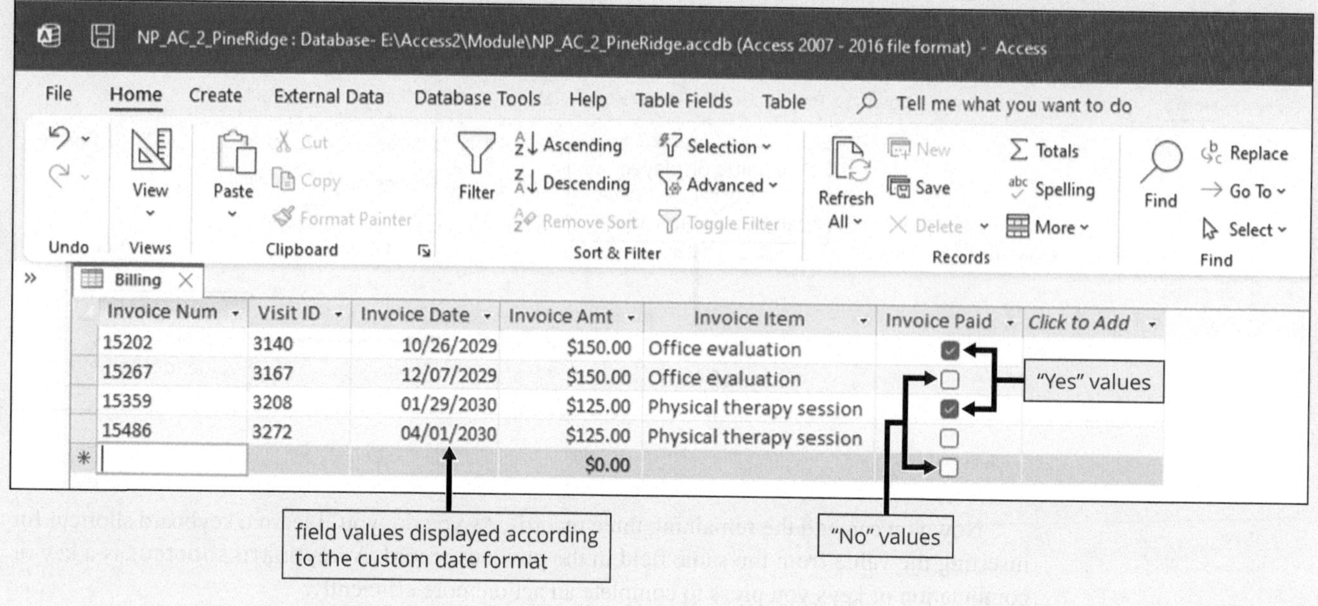

To finish entering records in the Billing table, you'll use a method that allows you to import the data.

Importing Data from an Excel Worksheet

Often, the data you want to add to an Access table is stored in another file, such as a Word document or an Excel workbook. You can add the data from other files to Access in different ways. For example, you can copy and paste the data from an open file, or you can **import** the data, which is a process that allows you to copy the data from a source without having to open the source file.

Insight

Caption Property Values and the Import Process

When you import data from an Excel worksheet into an Access table, the import process does not consider any Caption property values set for the fields in the table. For example, the Access table could have fields such as InvoiceDate and InvoiceAmt with Caption property values of Invoice Date and Invoice Amt, respectively. If the Excel worksheet you are importing has the column headings Invoice Date and Invoice Amt, you might think that the data matches and you can proceed with the import. However, if the underlying field names in the Access table do not match the Excel worksheet column headings exactly, the import process will fail. It is a good idea to double-check to make sure that the actual Access field names—and not just the column headings displayed in a table datasheet (as specified by the Caption property)—match the Excel worksheet column headings. If there are differences, you can change the column headings in the Excel worksheet to match the Access table field names before you import the date, ensuring that the process will work correctly.

Susan had been using Excel to track invoice data for the Pine Ridge Orthopedics & Sports Medicine Center and already created a workbook, named Support_AC_2_Invoices.xlsx, containing this data. You'll import the Billing worksheet from this Excel workbook into your Billing table to complete the entry of data in the table. To use the import method, the columns in the Excel worksheet must match the names and data types of the fields in the Access table.

The Billing worksheet contains the following columns: InvoiceNum, VisitID, InvoiceDate, InvoiceAmt, InvoiceItem, and InvoicePaid. These column headings match the field names in the Billing table exactly, so you can import the data. Before you import data into a table, you need to close the table.

To import the Excel data into the Billing table:

1. Click the **Close** button [X] on the object tab to close the Billing table, and then click **Yes** in the dialog box asking if you want to save the changes to the table layout. This dialog box opens because you resized the table columns.
2. On the ribbon, click the **External Data** tab.
3. In the Import & Link group, click the **New Data Source** button.
4. In the New Data Source list, click the **From File** option. You may also point to the option.
5. In the From File list, click **Excel**. The Get External Data – Excel Spreadsheet dialog box opens. See Figure 2–22.

Figure 2–22 Get External Data – Excel Spreadsheet dialog box

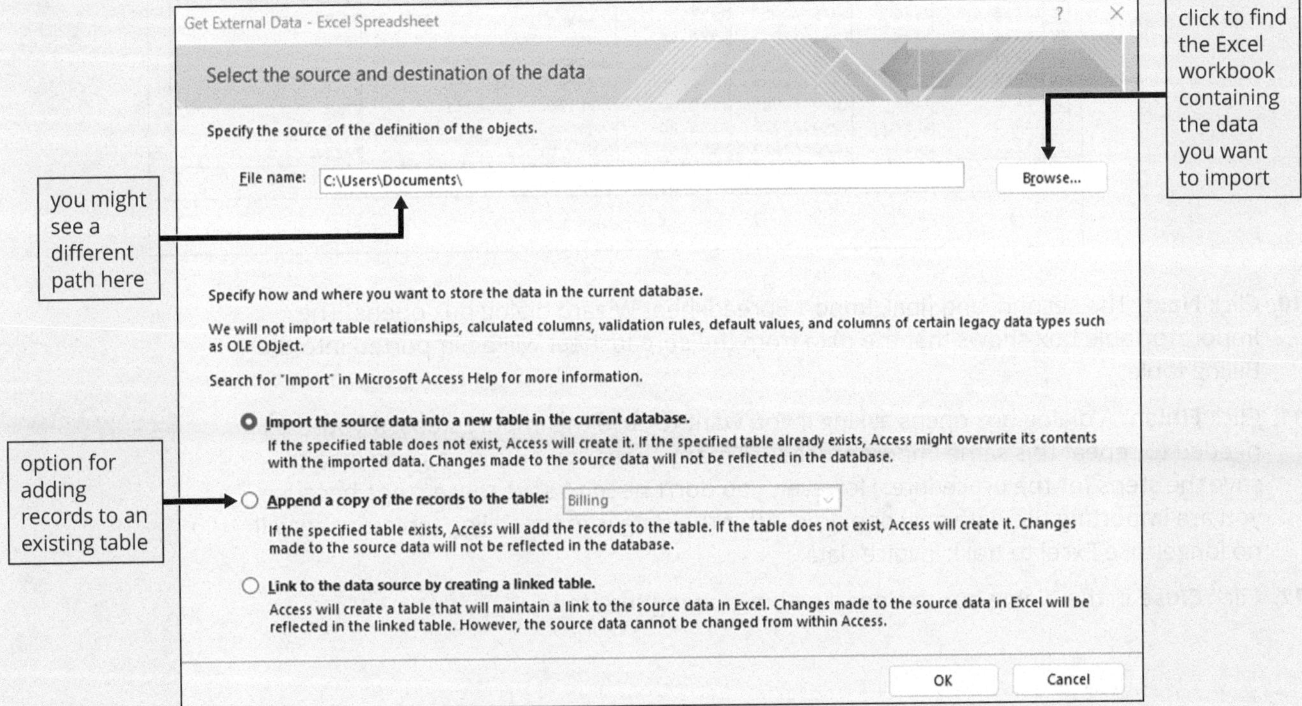

The dialog box provides options for importing the entire worksheet as a new table in the current database, adding the data from the worksheet to an existing table, or linking the data in the worksheet to the table. You need to add, or append, the worksheet data to the Billing table.

6. Click the **Browse** button. The File Open dialog box opens. The Excel workbook file is named "Support_AC_2_Invoices.xlsx" and is located in the Access2 > Module folder provided with your Data Files.
7. Navigate to the **Access2 > Module** folder, where your Data Files are stored, and then double-click the **Support_AC_2_Invoices.xlsx** Excel file. You return to the dialog box.
8. Click the **Append a copy of the records to the table** option button. The box to the right of this option becomes active and displays the Billing table name because it is the first table listed in the Navigation Pane.

9. Click **OK**. The first Import Spreadsheet Wizard dialog box opens. The dialog box confirms that the first row of the worksheet you are importing contains column headings. The bottom section of the dialog box displays some of the data contained in the worksheet. See Figure 2–23.

Figure 2–23 First Import Spreadsheet Wizard dialog box

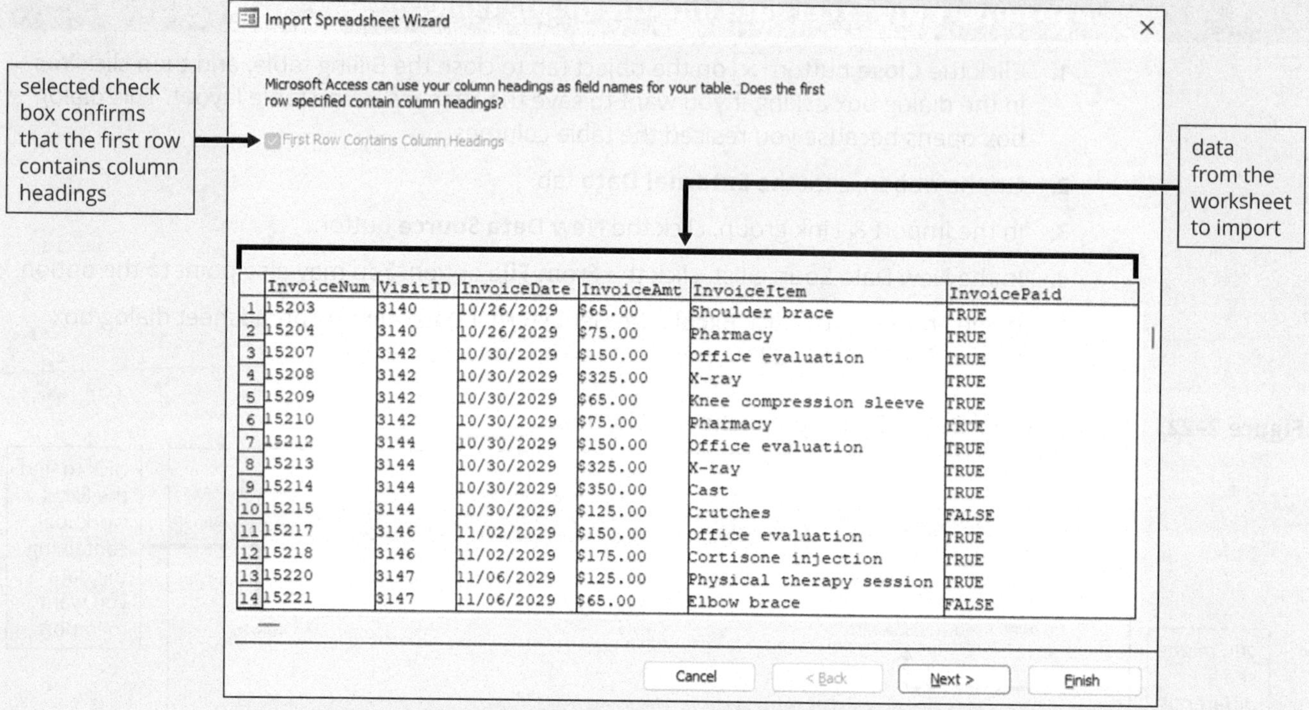

	InvoiceNum	VisitID	InvoiceDate	InvoiceAmt	InvoiceItem	InvoicePaid
1	15203	3140	10/26/2029	$65.00	Shoulder brace	TRUE
2	15204	3140	10/26/2029	$75.00	Pharmacy	TRUE
3	15207	3142	10/30/2029	$150.00	Office evaluation	TRUE
4	15208	3142	10/30/2029	$325.00	X-ray	TRUE
5	15209	3142	10/30/2029	$65.00	Knee compression sleeve	TRUE
6	15210	3142	10/30/2029	$75.00	Pharmacy	TRUE
7	15212	3144	10/30/2029	$150.00	Office evaluation	TRUE
8	15213	3144	10/30/2029	$325.00	X-ray	TRUE
9	15214	3144	10/30/2029	$350.00	Cast	TRUE
10	15215	3144	10/30/2029	$125.00	Crutches	FALSE
11	15217	3146	11/02/2029	$150.00	Office evaluation	TRUE
12	15218	3146	11/02/2029	$175.00	Cortisone injection	TRUE
13	15220	3147	11/06/2029	$125.00	Physical therapy session	TRUE
14	15221	3147	11/06/2029	$65.00	Elbow brace	FALSE

10. Click **Next**. The second, and final, Import Spreadsheet Wizard dialog box opens. The Import to Table box shows that the data from the spreadsheet will be imported into the Billing table.
11. Click **Finish**. A dialog box opens asking if you want to save the import steps. If you needed to repeat this same import procedure many times, it would be a good idea to save the steps for the procedure. However, you don't need to save these steps because you are importing the data only one time. After the data is in the Billing table, Susan will no longer use Excel to track invoice data.
12. Click **Close** in the dialog box to close it without saving the steps.

The data from the Billing worksheet in the Support_AC_2_Invoices.xlsx workbook has been added to the Billing table. Next, you'll open the table to view the new records.

To open the Billing table and view the imported data:

1. Open the Navigation Pane, and then double-click **Billing** in the Tables section to open the table in Datasheet view.
2. Resize the Invoice Item column to its best fit, scrolling the worksheet and resizing as necessary.
3. Press **CTRL+HOME** to scroll to the top of the datasheet. The table now contains a total of 203 records—the four records you entered plus 199 records imported from the Invoices worksheet. The records are displayed in primary key order by the values in the Invoice Num column. See Figure 2–24.

Figure 2–24 Billing table after importing data from Excel

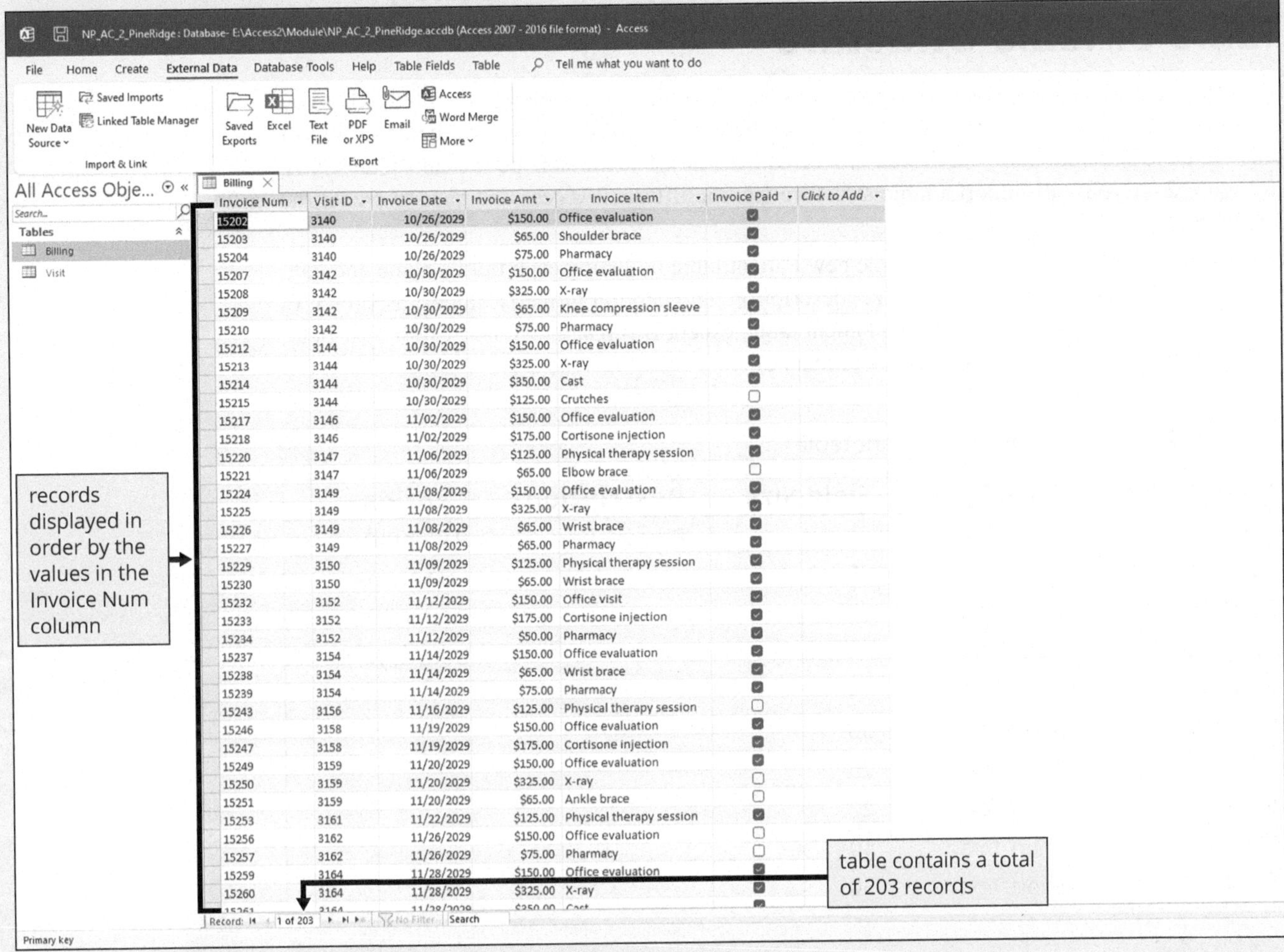

4. Save and close the Billing table, and then close the Navigation Pane.

Two of the tables—Visit and Billing—are now complete. According to Susan's plan for the NP_AC_2_PineRidge database, you still need to create the Patient table. You'll use a different method to create this table.

Insight

Options for Importing Data from a Spreadsheet

Because you already created and added the initial four records to the Billing table, you chose the option to append the additional records from the Invoices worksheet to the Billing table. The Get External Data - Excel Spreadsheet dialog box also has two other options (see Figure 2–22).

The first option is to import the source data into a new table in the current database. If the Invoices worksheet contained all the records to add to the Billing table, you could have chosen this option to import all the records. If the specified table does not exist, Access creates it. If the specified table already exists, Access might overwrite its contents with the imported data. Changes made to the source data would not be reflected in the database.

The second option is to link to the data source by creating a linked table. With this option, Access creates a table that maintains a link to the source data in Excel. Changes made to the source data in Excel will be reflected in the linked table. However, the source data cannot be changed within Access. Because Susan wanted to move the data from the Excel worksheet into Access and no longer uses Excel, you did not choose this option.

Creating a Table by Importing an Existing Table or Table Structure

If another Access database contains a table—or only the design, or structure, of a table—that you want to include in your database, you can import the table and any records it contains or import only the table structure into your database. To create the new Patient table per Susan's plan shown in Figure 2–2, you will import a table structure from a different Access database to create the Patient table.

Susan documented the design for the new Patient table by listing each field's name and data type, as well as any applicable field size, description, and caption property values, as shown in Figure 2–25. Note that each field in the Patient table, except BirthDate, will be a Short Text field, and the PatientID field will be the table's primary key.

Figure 2–25 Design for the Patient table

Field Name	Data Type	Field Size	Description	Caption
PatientID	Short Text	5	Primary key	Patient ID
LastName	Short Text	25		Last Name
FirstName	Short Text	20		First Name
BirthDate	Date/Time			Date of Birth
Phone	Short Text	14		
Address	Short Text	35		
City	Short Text	25		
State	Short Text	2		
Zip	Short Text	10		
Email	Short Text	50		

Susan's assistant Kimberly already created an Access database containing a Patient table design; however, she hasn't entered any records into the table. After reviewing the table design, both Kimberly and Susan agree that it contains some of the fields they want but that some changes are needed. You will import the table structure in Kimberly's database to create the Patient table in the NP_AC_2_PineRidge database, and later in this module, you will modify the imported table to produce the final table structure according to Susan's design.

To create the Patient table by importing the structure of another table:

1. Make sure the External Data tab is the active tab on the ribbon.
2. In the Import & Link group, click the **New Data Source** button.
3. In the New Data Source list, click the **From Database** option. You may also point to the option.
4. In the From Database list, click **Access**. The Get External Data – Access Database dialog box opens. This dialog box is similar to the one you used earlier when importing the Excel spreadsheet.
5. Click the **Browse** button. The File Open dialog box opens. The Access database file from which you need to import the table structure is named "Support_AC_2_Kimberly.accdb" and is located in the Access2 > Module folder provided with your Data Files.
6. Navigate to the **Access2 > Module** folder, where your Data Files are stored, and then double-click the **Support_AC_2_Kimberly.accdb** database file. You return to the dialog box.

7. Make sure the **Import tables, queries, forms, reports, macros, and modules into the current database** option button is selected, and then click **OK**. The Import Objects dialog box opens. The dialog box contains tabs for importing all types of Access database objects—tables, queries, forms, and so on. The Tables tab is the current tab.
8. Click the **Options** button in the dialog box to see all the options for importing tables. See Figure 2–26.

Figure 2–26 Import Objects dialog box

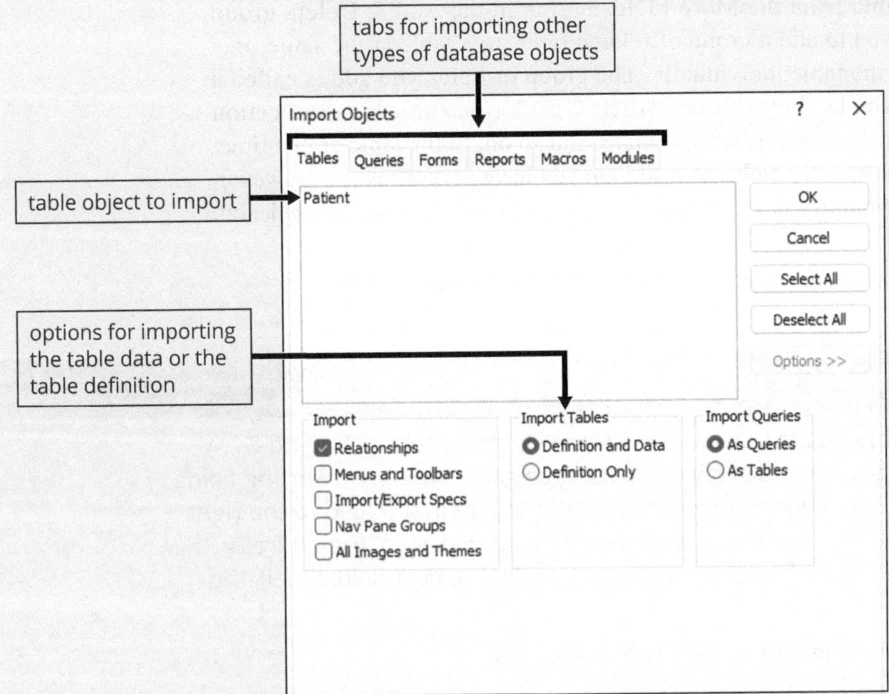

9. On the Tables tab, click **Patient** to select this table.
10. In the Import Tables section of the dialog box, click the **Definition Only** option button, and then click **OK**. Access creates the Patient table in the NP_AC_2_PineRidge database using the structure of the Patient table in the Support_AC_2_Kimberly.accdb database and opens a dialog box asking if you want to save the import steps.
11. Click **Close** to close the dialog box without saving the import steps.
12. Open the Navigation Pane, double-click **Patient** in the Tables section to open the table, and then close the Navigation Pane. The Patient table opens in Datasheet view. The table contains no records. See Figure 2–27.

Figure 2–27 Imported Patient table in Datasheet view

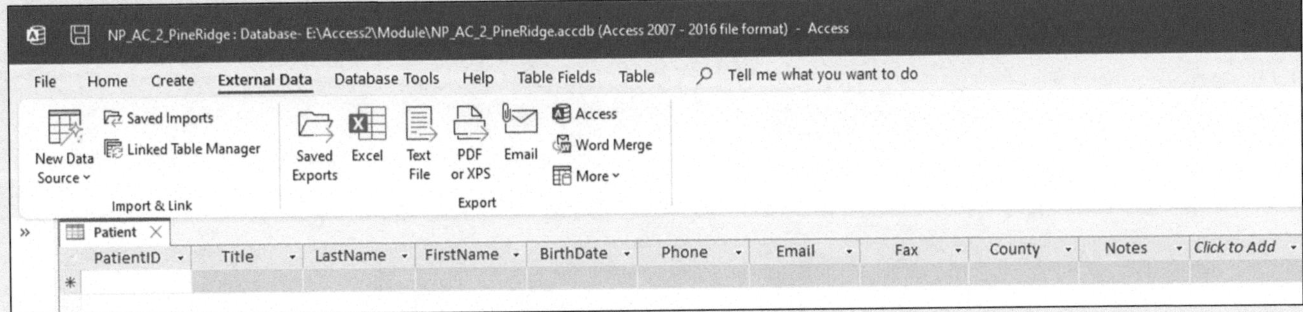

The table structure you imported contains some of the fields Susan wants, but not all (see Figure 2–25); it also contains some fields Susan does not want in the Patient table. You can add the missing fields using the Data Type gallery.

Adding Fields to a Table Using the Data Type Gallery

The **Data Type gallery**, available from the More Fields button in the Add & Delete group on the Table Fields tab, allows you to add a group of related fields to a table at the same time rather than adding each field to the table individually. The group of fields you add is called a **Quick Start selection**. For example, the **Address Quick Start selection** adds a collection of fields related to an address, such as Address, City, State, and so on, to the table at one time. When you use a Quick Start selection, the fields you add already have properties set. However, you need to review and possibly modify the properties to ensure the fields match your design needs for the database.

Next, you'll use the Data Type gallery to add the missing fields to the Patient table.

To add fields to the Patient table using the Data Type gallery:

1. On the ribbon, click the **Table Fields** tab. Note the More Fields button in the Add & Delete group; you use this button to display the Data Type gallery. Before inserting fields from the Data Type gallery, you need to place the insertion point in the field to the right of where you want to insert the new fields. According to Susan's design, the Address field should come after the Phone field, so you need to make the next field, Email, the active field.
2. Click the **first row** in the Email field to make it the active field.

   Tip Make sure the correct field is active before adding new fields.
3. In the Add & Delete group, click the **More Fields** button. The Data Type gallery opens and displays options for types of fields you can add to your table.
4. Scroll down the gallery until the Quick Start section is visible. See Figure 2–28.

Figure 2–28 Patient table with the Data Type gallery displayed

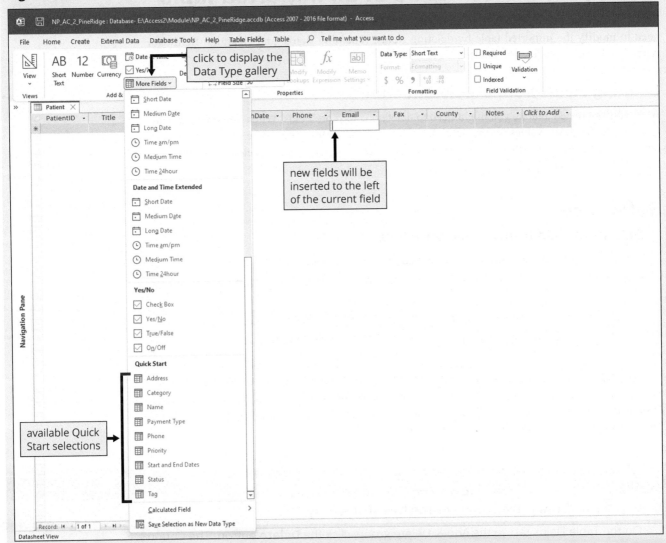

The Quick Start section provides options that add related fields to the table at one time. The new fields will be inserted to the left of the current field.

5. In the Quick Start section, click **Address**. Five fields are added to the table: Address, City, State Province, ZIP Postal, and Country Region. See Figure 2–29.

Figure 2–29 Patient table after adding fields from the Data Type gallery

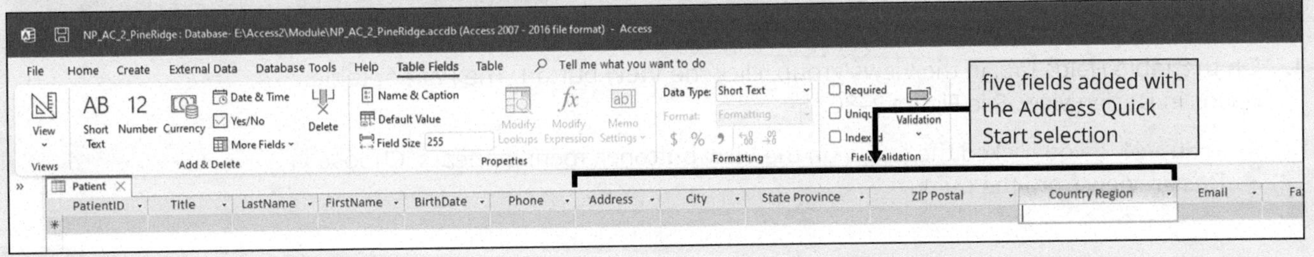

Modifying the Structure of an Imported Table

Refer back to Susan's design for the Patient table (Figure 2–25). To finalize the table design, you need to modify the imported table by deleting fields, renaming fields, and changing field data types. You'll begin by deleting fields.

Deleting Fields from a Table Structure

After you've created a table, you might need to delete one or more fields. When you delete a field, you also delete all the values for that field from the table. So, before you delete a field, make sure that you want to do so and that you choose the correct field to delete. You can delete fields in either Datasheet view or Design view.

Reference

Deleting a Field from a Table Structure

- In Datasheet view, click anywhere in the column for the field you want to delete.
- On the Table Fields tab in the Add & Delete group, click the Delete button.

or

- In Design view, click the Field Name box for the field you want to delete.
- On the Table Design tab in the Tools group, click the Delete Rows button.

The Address Quick Start selection added a field named "Country Region" to the Patient table. Susan doesn't need a field to store country data because all of the patients of the Pine Ridge Orthopedics & Sports Medicine Center are located in the United States. You'll begin to modify the Patient table structure by deleting the Country Region field.

To delete the Country Region field from the table in Datasheet view:

1. Click the **first row** in the Country Region field (if necessary).
2. On the Table Fields tab, in the Add & Delete group, click the **Delete** button. The Country Region field is removed and the first field, PatientID, is now the active field.

You can also delete fields from a table structure in Design view. You'll switch to Design view to delete the other unnecessary fields.

To delete the fields in Design view:

1. On the Table Fields tab, in the Views group, click the **View** button. The Patient table opens in Design view. See Figure 2–30.

   Trouble? If you clicked the arrow on the View button, a menu appears. Choose Design View from the menu.

Figure 2–30 Patient table in Design view

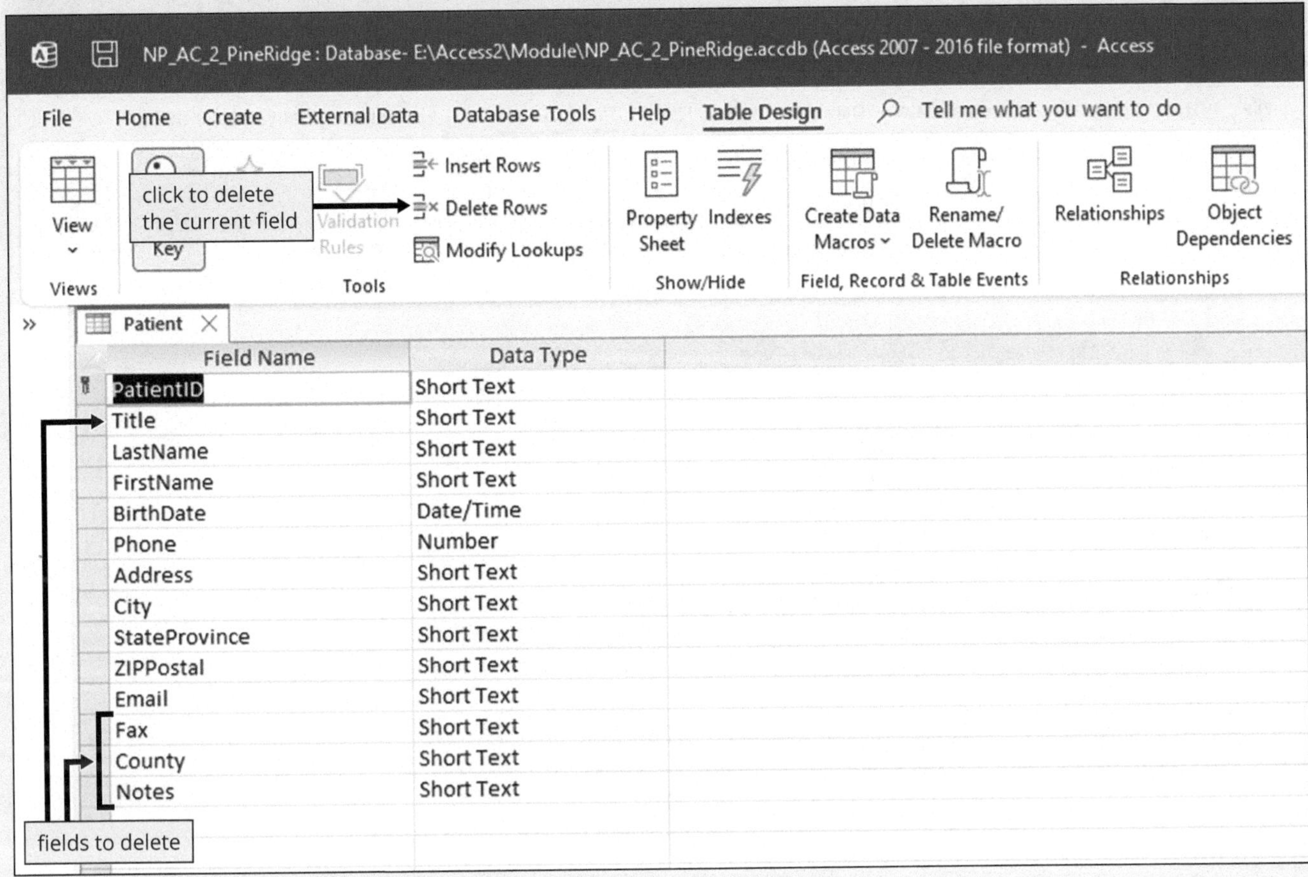

2. Click the **Title** Field Name box to make it the current field.
3. On the Table Design tab, in the Tools group, click the **Delete Rows** button. The Title field is removed from the Patient table structure. You'll delete the Fax, County, and Notes fields next. Instead of deleting these fields individually, you'll select and delete them at the same time.
4. On the row selector for the **Fax** field, press and hold the mouse button and then drag the mouse to select the **County** and **Notes** fields.
5. Release the mouse button. The rows for the three fields are outlined in red, indicating all three fields are selected.

   You may not be able to see the Notes field; however, you can scroll down to view the selection.
6. In the Tools group, click the **Delete Rows** button. See Figure 2–31.

Figure 2–31 Patient table after deleting fields

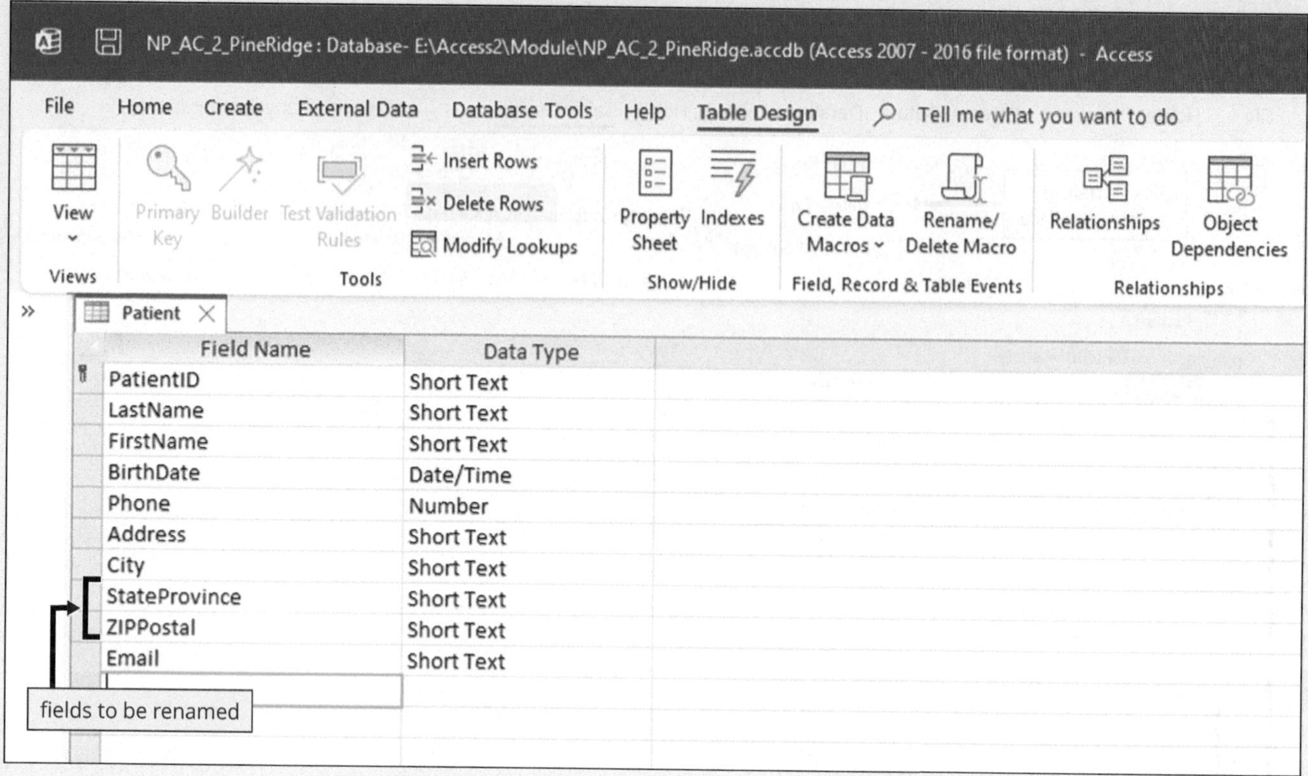

Renaming Fields in Design View

To match Susan's design for the Patient table, you need to rename some of the fields. You already have renamed the default primary key field (ID) in Datasheet view. You can also rename fields in Design view by editing the names in the Table Design grid.

To rename the fields in Design view:

1. Click to position the insertion point to the right of the text StateProvince in the eighth row's Field Name box, and then press **BACKSPACE** eight times to delete the word "Province." The name of the eighth field is now State.

   You can also select an entire field name and then type new text to replace it.

2. In the ninth row's Field Name box, drag to select the text **ZIPPostal**, and then type **Zip**. The text you type replaces the original text. See Figure 2–32.

Figure 2–32 Patient table after renaming fields

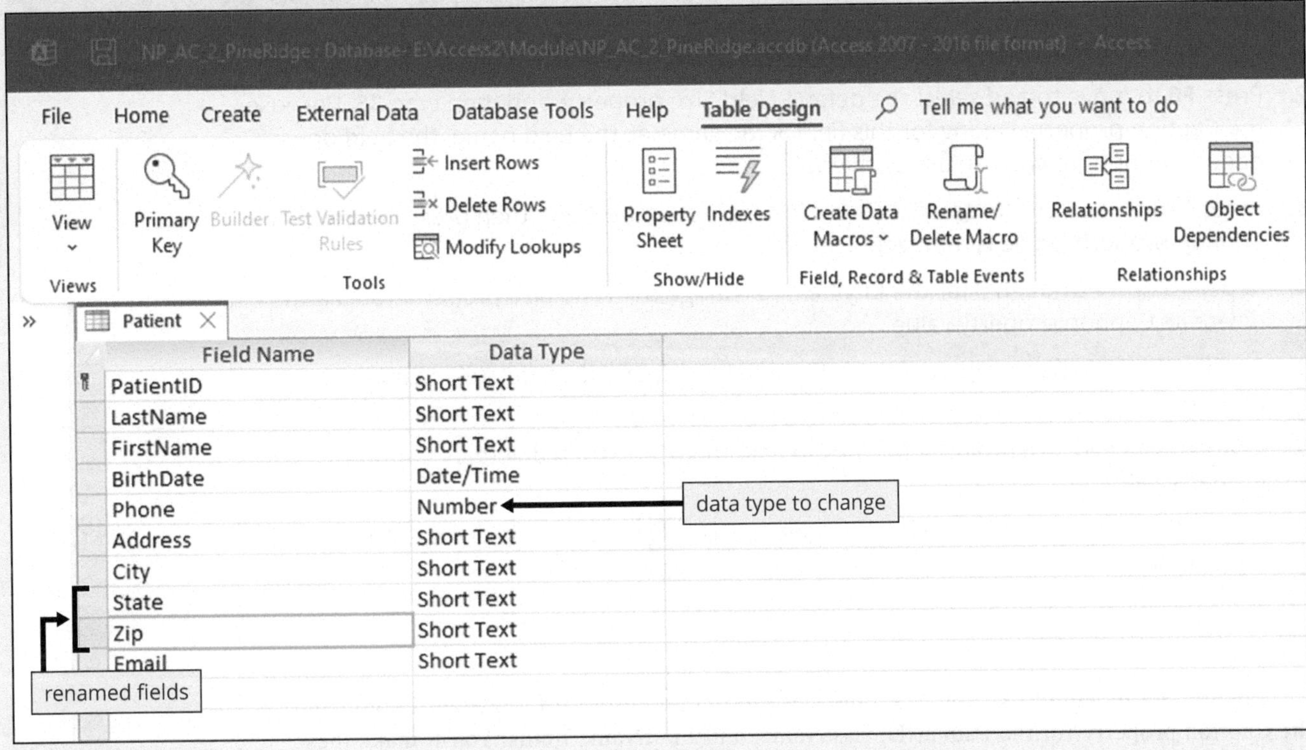

Besides renaming fields, you can rename Access objects such as tables, queries, forms, and reports. To rename a table, for example, right-click the table object in the Navigation Pane, and then click Rename on the shortcut menu. Type the new name for the table and then press ENTER. By default, Access changes the table name in any other objects that reference the table.

Changing the Data Type for a Field in Design View

In the table structure you imported earlier, you used an option in Datasheet view to change a field's data type. You can also change the data type for a field in Design view. According to Susan's plan, all the fields in the Patient table should be Short Text fields, except for BirthDate.

To change the data type of the Phone field in Design view:

1. Click the right side of the Data Type box for the Phone field to display the list of data types.
2. Click **Short Text** in the list. The Phone field is now a Short Text field. By default, the Field Size property is set to 255. According to Susan's plan, the Phone field should have a Field Size property of 14. You'll make this change next.
3. Press **F6** to move to and select the default Field Size property, and then type **14**.

Each of the remaining fields you added using the Address Quick Start selection—Address, City, State, and Zip—also has the default field size of 255. You need to change the Field Size property for these fields to match Susan's design. You'll also delete any Caption property values for these fields because the field names match how Susan wants them displayed, so captions are unnecessary.

To change the Field Size and Caption properties for the fields:

1. Click the **Address** Field Name box to make it the current field.
2. Press **F6** to move to and select the default Field Size property, and then type **35**. Because the Caption property setting for this field is the same as the field name, the field doesn't need a caption, so you can delete this value.
3. Press **TAB** three times to select Address in the Caption box, and then press **Delete**. The Caption property value is removed.
4. Repeat Steps 1 through 3 for the City field to change the Field Size property to **25** and delete its Caption property value.
5. Change the Field Size property for the State field to **2**, and then delete its Caption property value.
6. Change the Field Size property for the Zip field to **10**, and then delete its Caption property value.
7. On the Quick Access Toolbar, click the **Save** button to save your changes to the Patient table.

Finally, Susan would like you to set the Description property for the PatientID field and the Caption property for the PatientID, LastName, and FirstName fields. You'll make these changes now.

To enter the Description and Caption property values:

1. Click the **Description (Optional)** box for the PatientID field, and then type **Primary key**.
2. In the Field Properties pane, click the **Caption** box.
3. In the Caption box for the PatientID field, type **Patient ID**.
4. Click the **LastName** Field Name box to make it the current field, click the **Caption** box, and then type **Last Name**.
5. Click the **FirstName** Field Name box to make it the current field, click the **Caption** box, and then type **First Name**.
6. Click the **BirthDate** Field Name box to make it the current field, click the **Caption** box, and then type **Date of Birth**. See Figure 2–33.

Figure 2–33 Patient table after entering descriptions and captions

Field Name	Data Type	Description
PatientID	Short Text	Primary key
LastName	Short Text	
FirstName	Short Text	
BirthDate	Date/Time	
Phone	Short Text	
Address	Short Text	
City	Short Text	
State	Short Text	
Zip	Short Text	
Email	Short Text	

Description property value entered

data type changed to Short Text

Field Properties

General Lookup

Format	Short Date
Input Mask	
Caption	Date of Birth
Default Value	
Validation Rule	
Validation Text	
Required	No
Indexed	No
IME Mode	No Control
IME Sentence Mode	None
Text Align	General
Show Date Picker	For dates

Caption property entered

Navigation Pane

Design view. F6 = Switch panes. F1 = Help.

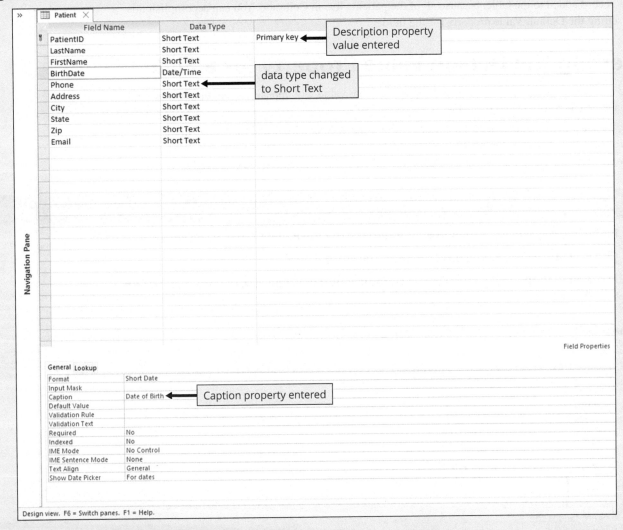

7. On the Quick Access Toolbar, click the **Save** button to save your changes to the Patient table.
8. On the Table Design tab, in the Views group, click the **View** button to display the table in Datasheet view.
9. Resize each column to its best fit, and then click in the first row for the **Patient ID** column. See Figure 2–34.

Figure 2–34 Modified Patient table in Datasheet view

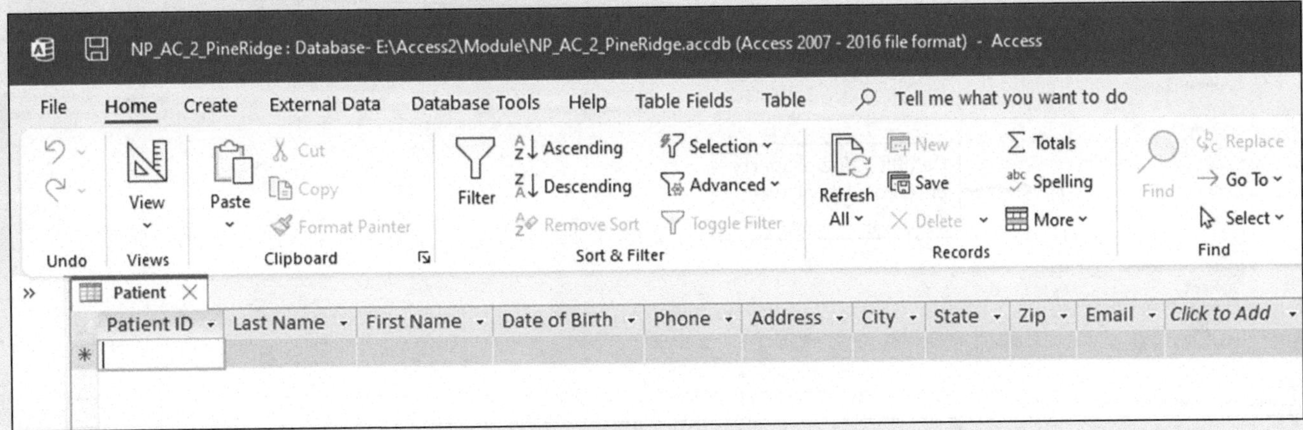

Susan mentions that data entry would be easier if the State field had the value of "CO" for each new record added to the table, because all of the patients live in Colorado. You can accomplish this by setting the Default Value property for the field.

Setting the Default Value Property for a Field

The **Default Value property** for a field specifies what value will appear, by default, for the field in each new record you add to a table.

Because all the patients at the Pine Ridge Orthopedics & Sports Medicine Center live in Colorado, you'll specify a default value of "CO" for the State field in the Patient table. With this setting, each new record in the Patient table will have the correct State field value entered automatically.

To set the Default Value property for the State field:

1. In the Views group, click the **View** button to display the Patient table in Design view.
2. Click the **State** Field Name box to make it the current field.
3. In the Field Properties pane, click the **Default Value** box, type **CO**, and then press **TAB**. See Figure 2–35.

Figure 2–35 Specifying the Default Value property for the State field

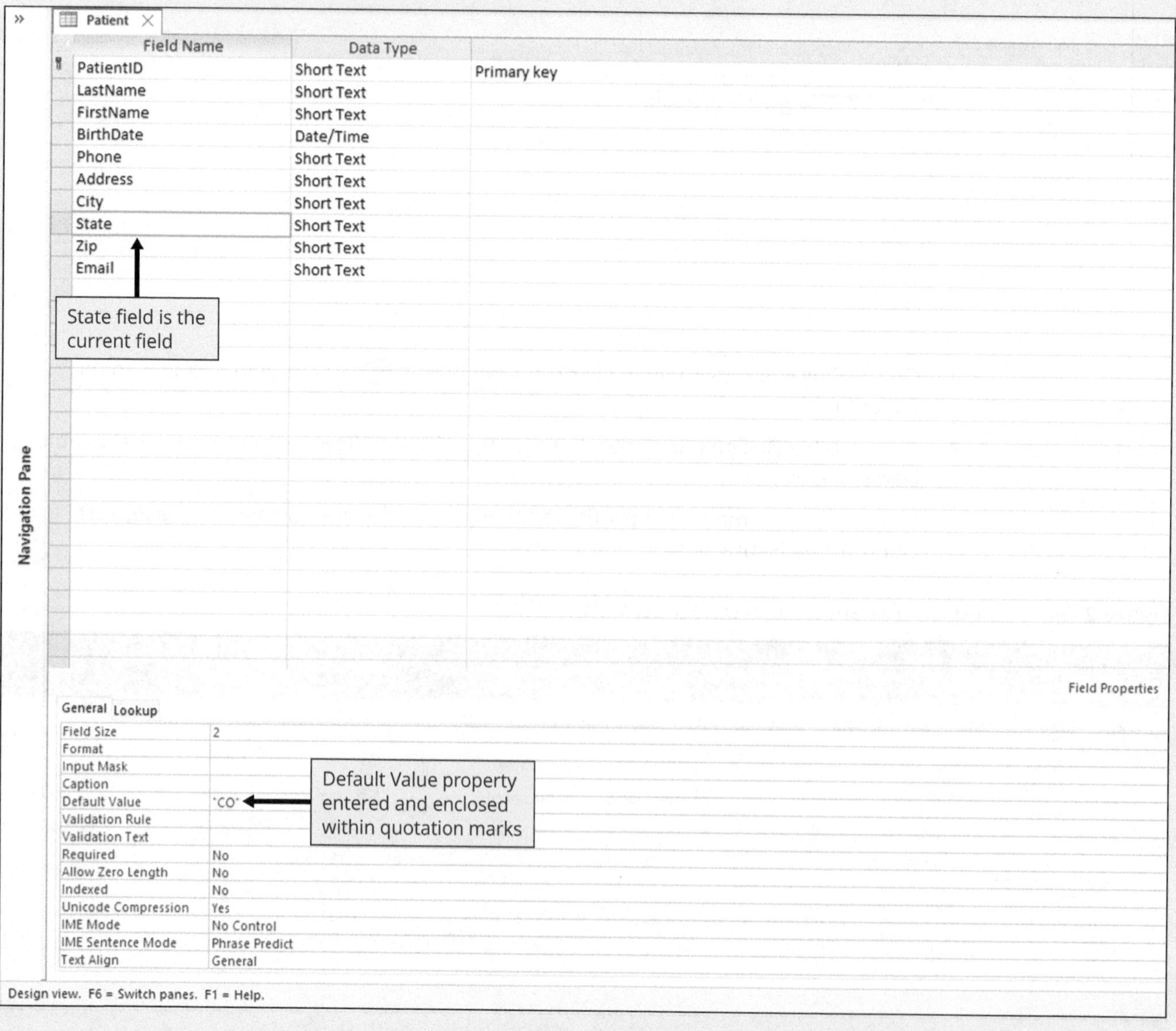

Note that a text entry in the Default Value property must be enclosed within quotation marks. If you do not type the quotation marks, Access adds them for you. However, for some entries, such as those that include punctuation, you would receive an error message indicating invalid syntax if you omitted the quotation marks. In such cases, you must enter the quotation marks yourself.

4. On the Quick Access Toolbar, click the **Save** button to save your changes to the Patient table.
5. Display the table in Datasheet view. Note that the State field for the first row now displays the default value "CO" as specified by the Default Value property. Each new record entered in the table will automatically have this State field value entered.

   Tip You can change the value in a record from the default value to another value, if necessary.

With the Patient table design set, you can now enter records in it. You'll begin by entering two records in the datasheet, and then use a different method to add the remaining records.

To add two records to the Patient table:

1. Enter the following values in the columns in the first record; press **TAB** to move past the default State field value:

   Tip Be sure to enter your last name and first name where indicated.

   Patient ID = **27650**

   Last Name = **[student's last name]**

   First Name = **[student's first name]**

   Date of Birth = **4/19/2002**

   Phone = **970-555-8445**

   Address = **452 Elm Ln**

   City = **Fort Collins**

   State = **CO**

   Zip = **80524**

   Email = **student@example.com**
2. Enter the following values in the columns in the second record:

   Patient ID = **27701**

   Last Name = **Taylor**

   First Name = **Kimberly**

   Date of Birth = **4/5/1999**

   Phone = **303-555-0504**

   Address = **162 Pond Rd**

   City = **Firestone**

   State = **CO**

   Zip = **80520**

   Email = **k.taylor21@example.com**
3. Resize columns to their best fit, as necessary, and then save and close the Patient table.

Before Susan decided to store data using Access, Kimberly managed the patient data for the center in a different system. She exported that data into a text file and now asks you to import it into the new Patient table. You can import the data contained in this text file to add the remaining records to the Patient table.

Adding Data to a Table by Importing a Text File

So far, you've learned how to add data to an Access table by importing an Excel spreadsheet, and you've created a new table by importing the structure of an existing table. You can also import data contained in text files.

To finish entering records in the Patient table, you'll import the data contained in Kimberly's text file. The file is named Support_AC_2_Patient.txt and is located in the Access2 > Module folder provided with your Data Files.

To import the data contained in the Patient text file:

1. On the ribbon, click the **External Data** tab.
2. In the Import & Link group, click the **New Data Source** button.
3. In the New Data Source list, click the **From File** option. You may also point to the option.
4. In the From File list, click **Text File**. The Get External Data – Text File dialog box opens. This dialog box is similar to the one you used earlier when importing the Excel spreadsheet.
5. Click the **Browse** button. The File Open dialog box opens.
6. Navigate to the **Access2 > Module** folder, where your Data Files are stored, and then double-click the **Support_AC_2_Patient.txt** file. You return to the Get External Data – Text File dialog box.
7. Click the **Append a copy of the records to the table** option button. The box to the right of this option becomes active. Next, you need to select the table to which you want to add the data.
8. Click the arrow in the box, and then click **Patient**.
9. Click **OK**. The first Import Text Wizard dialog box opens. The dialog box indicates that the data to import is in a delimited format. In a **delimited text file**, fields of data are separated by a character such as a comma or a tab. In this case, the dialog box shows that data is separated by the comma character in the text file.
10. Make sure the **Delimited** option button is selected in the dialog box, and then click **Next**. The second Import Text Wizard dialog box opens. See Figure 2–36.

Figure 2–36 Second Import Text Wizard dialog box

Import Text Wizard

What delimiter separates your fields? Select the appropriate delimiter and see how your text is affected in the preview below.

Choose the delimiter that separates your fields:

Tab Semicolon Comma Space Other:

First Row Contains Field Names Text Qualifier: "

fields in the text file are separated by commas

preview of the data being imported

27652	Johnson	Gregory	12/11/2001 0:00:00	970-555-1189	12 Rock Ln	Fort Collin
27654	Martinez	Alonzo	5/17/1959 0:00:00	970-555-6675	16 Rockway Dr	Windsor
27657	Brown	Gayle	2/16/1968 0:00:00	970-555-6341	127 Valley Rd	Severance
27658	Hansen	Holly	9/21/1962 0:00:00	970-555-9730	75 Stream Rd	Eaton
27660	Garcia	David	7/17/2005 0:00:00	970-555-2354	92 Pine St	Loveland
27662	Lopez	Oliver	4/17/1982 0:00:00	303-555-1016	124 Ridge Rd	Firestone
27663	Anderson	Samuel	3/16/2000 0:00:00	970-555-9300	47 Whistle St	Wellington
27664	Thompson	Robert	3/12/1982 0:00:00	970-555-3958	14 Bobcat Tr	Greeley
27667	Sanchez	Carlos	1/4/1957 0:00:00	970-555-2433	42 Lookout Way	Laporte
27669	Smith	Anna	2/16/1976 0:00:00	970-555-9439	312 Oak Rd	Pierce
27671	Chang	Tom	11/3/1998 0:00:00	970-555-3160	2 Pine Dr	Livermore
27674	Olsen	Alex	2/12/1967 0:00:00	970-555-4112	312 Wafer Way	Timnath
27676	Flores	Barbara	3/17/1969 0:00:00	720-555-1235	47 Wyont Dr	Longmont
27678	Hernandez	Ken	2/21/1975 0:00:00	970-555-8300	325 Valley Rd	Berthoud

Advanced... Cancel < Back Next > Finish

This dialog box asks you to confirm the delimiter character that separates the fields in the text file you're importing. Access detects that the comma character is used in the Patient text file and selects this option. The bottom area of the dialog box provides a preview of the data you're importing.

11. Make sure the **Comma** option button is selected, and then click **Next.** The third and final Import Text Wizard dialog box opens. The Import to Table box shows that the data will be imported into the Patient table.
12. Click **Finish**, and then click **Close** in the dialog box that opens to close it without saving the import steps.

Susan asks you to open the Patient table in Datasheet view so she can see the results of importing the text file.

To view the Patient table datasheet:

1. Open the Navigation Pane (if necessary), and then double-click **Patient** to open the Patient table in Datasheet view. The Patient table contains a total of 51 records.
2. Close the Navigation Pane, and then resize columns to their best fit, scrolling the table datasheet as necessary, so that all field values are displayed. Scroll back to display the first fields in the table, and then click the first row's **Patient ID** field, if necessary. See Figure 2–37.

Figure 2–37 Patient table after importing data from the text file

File Home Create External Data Database Tools Help Table Fields Table Tell me what you want to do

New Data Source · Saved Imports · Linked Table Manager (Import & Link) · Saved Exports · Excel · Text File · PDF or XPS · Email · Access · Word Merge · More (Export)

Patient

Patient ID	Last Name	First Name	Date of Birth	Phone	Address	City	State	Zip	Email	Click to Add
27650	Student Last	Student First	4/19/2002	970-555-8445	452 Elm Ln	Fort Collins	CO	80524	student@example.com	
27652	Johnson	Gregory	12/11/2001	970-555-1189	12 Rock Ln	Fort Collins	CO	80524	g.jophnson17@example.com	
27654	Martinez	Alonzo	5/17/1959	970-555-6675	16 Rockway Dr	Windsor	CO	80550	a.martinez12@example.com	
27657	Brown	Gayle	2/16/1968	970-555-6341	127 Valley Rd	Severance	CO	80546	g.brown19@example.com	
27658	Hansen	Holly	9/21/1962	970-555-9730	75 Stream Rd	Eaton	Co	80615	h.hansen5@example.com	
27660	Garcia	David	7/17/2005	970-555-2354	92 Pine St	Loveland	CO	80537	d.garcia15@example.com	
27662	Lopez	Oliver	4/17/1982	303-555-1016	124 Ridge Rd	Firestone	CO	80520	o.lopez14@example.com	
27663	Anderson	Samuel	3/16/2000	970-555-9300	47 Whistle St	Wellington	CO	80549	s.anderson14@example.com	
27664	Thompson	Robert	3/12/1982	970-555-3958	14 Bobcat Tr	Greeley	CO	80631	r.thompson35@example.com	
27667	Sanchez	Carlos	1/4/1957	970-555-2433	42 Lookout Way	Laporte	CO	80535	c.sanchez5@example.com	
27669	Smith	Anna	2/16/1976	970-555-9439	312 Oak Rd	Pierce	CO	80650	a.smith12@example.com	
27671	Chang	Tom	11/3/1998	970-555-3160	2 Pine Dr	Livermore	CO	80536	t.chang2@example.com	
27674	Olsen	Alex	2/12/1967	970-555-4112	312 Wafer Way	Timnath	CO	80547	a.olsen14@example.com	
27676	Flores	Barbara	3/17/1969	720-555-1235	47 Wyont Dr	Longmont	CO	80501	b.flores7@example.com	
27678	Hernandez	Ken	2/21/1975	970-555-8300	325 Valley Rd	Berthoud	CO	80513	k.hernandez19@example.com	
27679	Gonzales	Maria	12/17/1972	970-555-1499	87 Flower Way	Fort Collins	CO	80524	m.sanchez5@example.com	
27681	Taylor	Zachery	5/5/1972	303-555-0124	12 Waterway Dr	Firestone	CO	80520	z.taylor25@example.com	
27683	Anderson	Victoria	4/13/1987	970-555-6438	16 Gaston Ave	Longmont	CO	80501	v.anderson5@example.com	
27684	Myers	Catherine	5/19/2008	720-555-4311	19 Sycamore Way	Longmont	CO	80501	c.myers11@example.com	
27686	Jackson	Oliver	11/27/1988	970-555-8420	92 Waterfall Ridge	Fort Collins	CO	80524	o.jackson19@example.com	
27687	Garcia	Sofia	4/18/1996	970-555-3126	17 Waxer Dr	Windsor	CO	80550	s.garcia30@example.com	
27689	Gomez	Maria	9/28/2004	970-555-2116	42 Locklear Ln	Severance	CO	80546	m.gomez3@example.com	
27690	Wilson	Claire	2/13/1978	303-555-4712	423 Ridge Rd	Firestone	CO	80520	c.wilson68@example.com	
27692	Flores	Juanita	6/23/1977	970-555-5542	75 Pine Dr	Livermore	CO	80536	j.flores7@example.com	
27694	White	Thomas	9/14/1992	970-555-1774	42 Barrow Dr	Fort Collins	CO	80524	t.white23@example.com	
27696	Brown	Natalie	11/27/1965	970-555-9850	917 Amber Dr	Windsor	CO	80550	n.brown22@example.com	
27697	Williams	Kathleen	2/23/1982	970-555-3355	35 Nighthawk Dr	Loveland	CO	80537	k.williams14@example.com	
27699	Rowe	Harper	12/5/1977	970-555-1217	142 Long Ave	Fort Collins	CO	80524	h.rowe16@example.com	
27701	Taylor	Kimberly	4/5/1999	303-555-0504	162 Pond Rd	Firestone	CO	80520	k.taylor21@example.com	
27704	Salinas	Mariana	2/7/1978	970-555-4466	47 Barn Rd	Fort Collins	CO	80524	m.salinas12@example.com	
27706	Johnson	Mark	9/16/1997	970-555-1243	14 Lookout Ln	Longmont	CO	80501	m.johnson6@example.com	
27707	Lopez	Luis	1/30/1998	970-555-5903	78 Ashley Dr	Berthoud	CO	80513	l.lopez12@example.com	
27708	Gonzales	Victor	11/13/1967	970-555-0863	137 Rock Rd	Timnath	CO	80547	v.gonzales7@example.com	
27710	Williams	Jim	2/19/2001	970-555-4910	87 Lumber Way	Livermore	CO	80536	j.williams17@example.com	
27712	Taylor	Bailey	11/4/1993	970-555-1310	42 Kimberly Dr	Pierce	CO	80650	b.taylor3@example.com	
27713	Wells	Norah	6/15/1998	970-555-0971	88 Giradelli Dr	Laporte	CO	80535	n.wells6@example.com	
27714	Lee	Gregory	1/6/1992	970-555-8059	900 Cherry Rd	Greeley	CO	80631	g.lee12@example.com	
27716	Gallegos	Elijah	4/17/1988	970-555-8990	14 Biorch St	Wellington	CO	80549	e.gallegos3@example.com	
27717	Robinson	Olivia	2/14/1979	303-555-5599	42 Winding Ridge Rd	Firestone	CO	80520	o.robinson16@example.com	

Record: 1 of 51 No Filter Search

Primary key

3. Save and close the Patient table, and then open the Navigation Pane.

The NP_AC_2_PineRidge database now contains three tables—Billing, Patient, and Visit—and the tables contain all the necessary records. Your final task is to complete the database design by defining the necessary relationship between its tables.

Defining Table Relationships

One of the most powerful features of a relational database management system is its ability to define relationships between tables. You use a common field to relate one table to another. The process of relating tables is often called performing a **join**. When you join tables that have a common field, you can extract data from them as if they were one larger table. For example, you can join the Patient and Visit tables by using the PatientID field in both tables as the common field. Then you can use a query, form, or report to extract selected data from each table, even though the data is contained in two separate tables, as shown in Figure 2–38. The PatientVisits query shown in Figure 2–38 includes the PatientID, LastName, and FirstName fields from the Patient table, and the VisitDate and Reason fields from the Visit table. The joining of records is based on the common field of PatientID. The Patient and Visit tables have a type of relationship called a one-to-many relationship.

Figure 2–38 One-to-many relationship and sample query

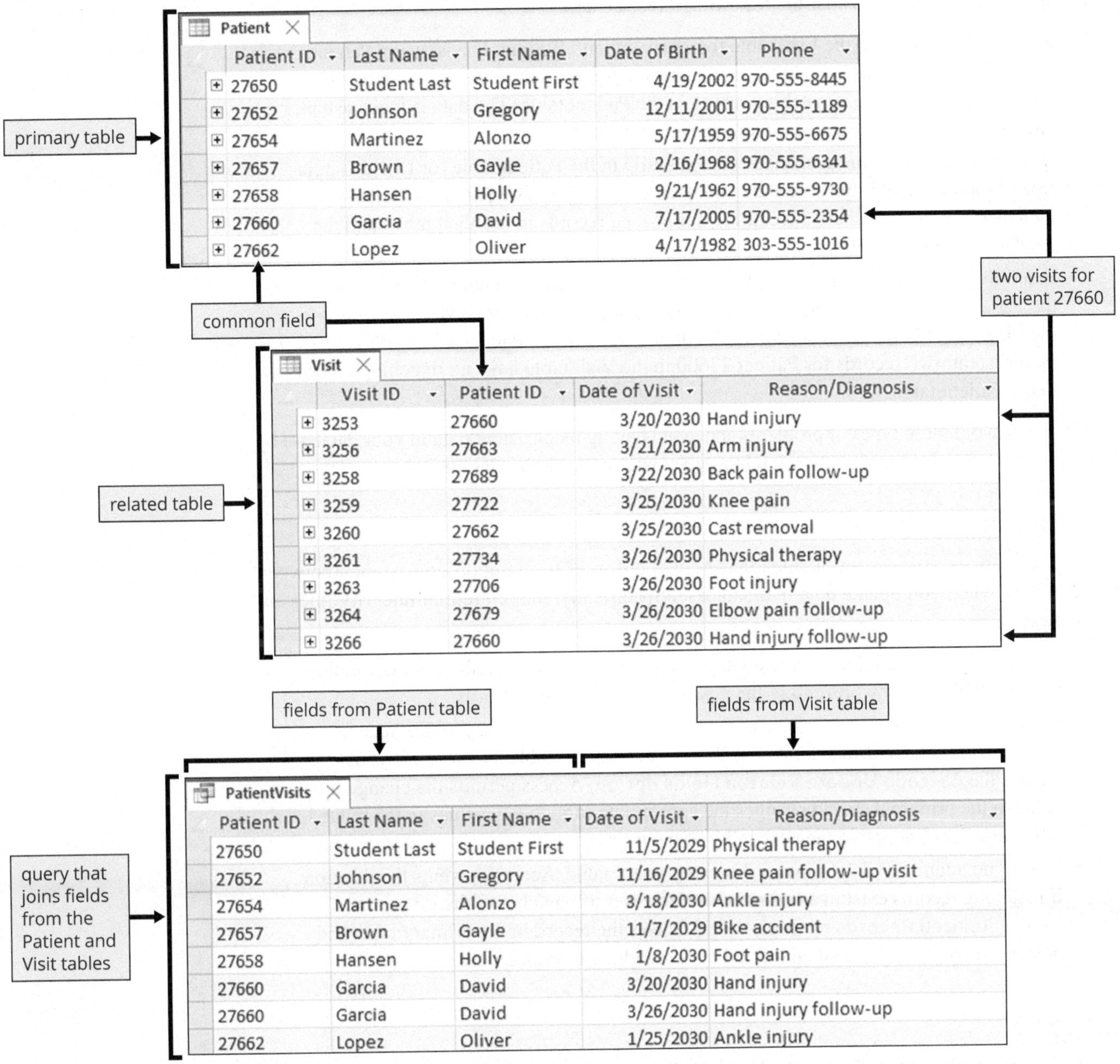

primary table

Patient

Patient ID	Last Name	First Name	Date of Birth	Phone
27650	Student Last	Student First	4/19/2002	970-555-8445
27652	Johnson	Gregory	12/11/2001	970-555-1189
27654	Martinez	Alonzo	5/17/1959	970-555-6675
27657	Brown	Gayle	2/16/1968	970-555-6341
27658	Hansen	Holly	9/21/1962	970-555-9730
27660	Garcia	David	7/17/2005	970-555-2354
27662	Lopez	Oliver	4/17/1982	303-555-1016

common field

two visits for patient 27660

related table

Visit

Visit ID	Patient ID	Date of Visit	Reason/Diagnosis
3253	27660	3/20/2030	Hand injury
3256	27663	3/21/2030	Arm injury
3258	27689	3/22/2030	Back pain follow-up
3259	27722	3/25/2030	Knee pain
3260	27662	3/25/2030	Cast removal
3261	27734	3/26/2030	Physical therapy
3263	27706	3/26/2030	Foot injury
3264	27679	3/26/2030	Elbow pain follow-up
3266	27660	3/26/2030	Hand injury follow-up

fields from Patient table

fields from Visit table

query that joins fields from the Patient and Visit tables

PatientVisits

Patient ID	Last Name	First Name	Date of Visit	Reason/Diagnosis
27650	Student Last	Student First	11/5/2029	Physical therapy
27652	Johnson	Gregory	11/16/2029	Knee pain follow-up visit
27654	Martinez	Alonzo	3/18/2030	Ankle injury
27657	Brown	Gayle	11/7/2029	Bike accident
27658	Hansen	Holly	1/8/2030	Foot pain
27660	Garcia	David	3/20/2030	Hand injury
27660	Garcia	David	3/26/2030	Hand injury follow-up
27662	Lopez	Oliver	1/25/2030	Ankle injury

One-to-Many Relationships

As shown in the Part 2.2 Visual Overview, two tables have a one-to-many relationship when one record in the first table matches zero, one, or many records in the second table, and when one record in the second table matches at most one record in the first table. For example, as shown in Figure 2–38, patient 27660 has two visits in the Visit table. Other patients have one or more visits. Every visit has a single matching patient.

In Access, the two tables that form a relationship are referred to as the primary table and the related table. The primary table is the "one" table in a one-to-many relationship; in Figure 2–38, the Patient table is the primary table because there is only one patient for each visit. The related table is the "many" table; in Figure 2–38, the Visit table is the related table because a patient can have zero, one, or many visits.

Because related data is stored in two tables, inconsistencies between the tables can occur. Referring to Figure 2–38, consider the following three scenarios:

- Susan adds a record to the Visit table for a new patient, William Davis, using Patient ID 27750. She did not first add the new patient's information to the Patient table, so this visit does not have a matching record in the Patient table. The data is inconsistent, and the visit record is considered an **orphaned record**.
- In another situation, Susan changes the PatientID in the Patient table for David Garcia from 27660 to 27695. Because the Patient table no longer has a patient with the PatientID 27660, this change creates two orphaned records in the Visit table, and the database is inconsistent.
- In a third scenario, Susan deletes the record for David Garcia, Patient 27660, from the Patient table because this patient has moved and no longer receives care from the Pine Ridge Orthopedics & Sports Medicine Center. The database is again inconsistent; two records for Patient 27660 in the Visit table have no matching record in the Patient table.

You can avoid these types of problems and avoid having inconsistent data in your database by specifying referential integrity between tables when you define their relationships.

Referential Integrity

Referential integrity is a set of rules that Access enforces to maintain consistency between related tables when you update data in a database. Specifically, the referential integrity rules are as follows:

- When you add a record to a related table, a matching record must already exist in the primary table, thereby preventing the possibility of orphaned records.
- If you attempt to change the value of the primary key in the primary table, Access prevents this change if matching records exist in a related table. However, if you choose the **Cascade Update Related Fields option**, Access permits the change in value to the primary key and changes the appropriate foreign key values in the related table, thereby eliminating the possibility of inconsistent data.
- When you attempt to delete a record in the primary table, Access prevents the deletion if matching records exist in a related table. However, if you choose the **Cascade Delete Related Records option**, Access deletes the record in the primary table and deletes all records in related tables that have matching foreign key values.

Insight

Understanding the Cascade Delete Related Records Option

Although using the Cascade Delete Related Records option has some advantages for enforcing referential integrity, it presents risks as well. You should rarely select the Cascade Delete Related Records option because doing so might cause you to inadvertently delete records you did not intend to delete. It is best to use other methods that give you more control over deleting records.

Defining a Relationship between Two Tables

When two tables have a common field, you can define a relationship between them in the Relationships window, as shown in the Part 2.2 Visual Overview. Next, you'll define a one-to-many relationship between the Patient and Visit tables, with Patient as the primary table and Visit as the related table, and with PatientID as the common field (the primary key in the Patient table and the foreign key in the Visit table). You'll also define a one-to-many relationship between the Visit and Billing tables, with Visit being the primary table and Billing being the related table, and with VisitID as the common field (the primary key in the Visit table and a foreign key in the Billing table).

To define the one-to-many relationship between the Patient and Visit tables:

1. On the ribbon, click the **Database Tools** tab.
2. In the Relationships group, click the **Relationships** button to display the Relationships window and then, if necessary, click the **Add Tables** button to open the Add Tables pane. See Figure 2–39.

Figure 2–39 Add Tables pane

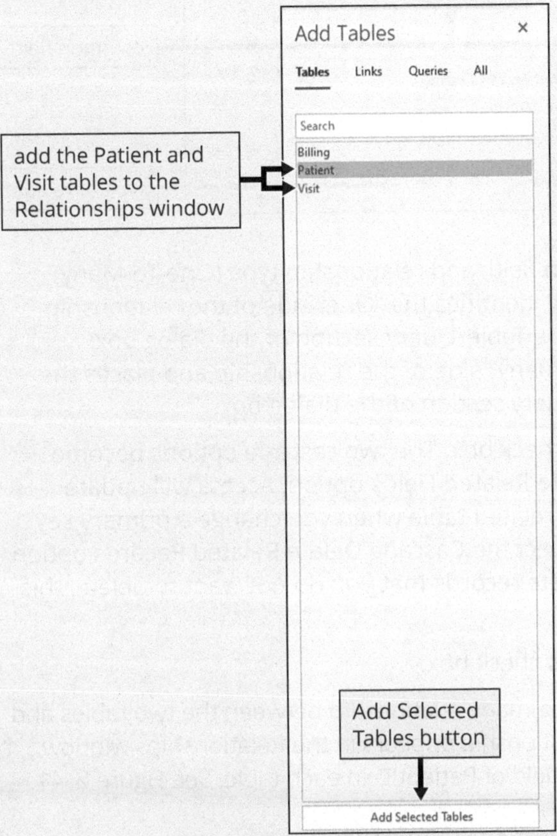

You must add each table participating in a relationship to the Relationships window. Because the Patient table is the primary table in the relationship, you'll add it first.

3. Click **Patient**, and then click the **Add Selected Tables** button. The Patient table's field list is added to the Relationships window.

> **Tip** You can also double-click a table in the Add Tables pane to add it to the Relationships window.

4. Click **Visit**, and then click the **Add Selected Tables** button. The Visit table's field list is added to the Relationships window.
5. Click the **Close** button ✕ in the Add Tables pane to close it.

   So that you can view all the fields and complete field names, you'll resize the Patient table field list.

6. Position the pointer on the bottom border of the Patient table field list until it changes to a two-headed vertical arrow ⇕, and then drag the bottom of the Patient table field list to lengthen it until the vertical scroll bar disappears and all the fields are visible.

   To form the relationship between the two tables, you drag the common PatientID field from the primary table to the related table. Access opens the Edit Relationships dialog box, in which you select the relationship options for the two tables.

7. Click **PatientID** in the Patient field list, and then drag it to **PatientID** in the Visit field list. When you release the mouse button, the Edit Relationships dialog box opens. See Figure 2–40.

Figure 2–40 Edit Relationships dialog box

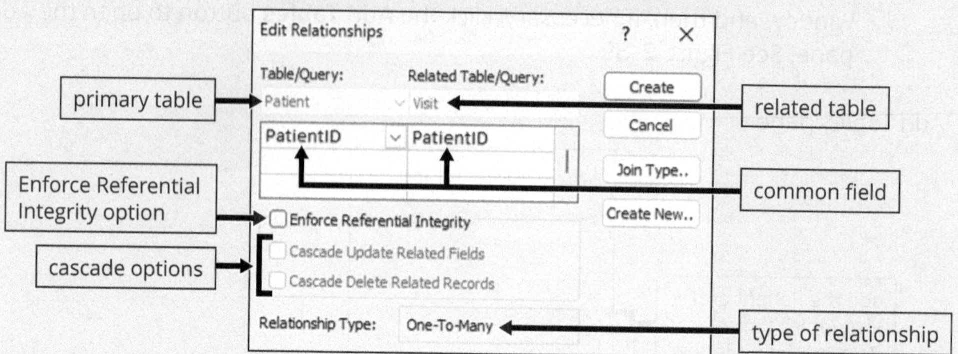

The primary table, related table, common field, and relationship type (One-To-Many) appear in the dialog box. Access correctly identifies the "One" side of the relationship and places the primary table Patient in the Table/Query section of the dialog box; similarly, Access correctly identifies the "Many" side of the relationship and places the related table Visit in the Related Table/Query section of the dialog box.

8. Click the **Enforce Referential Integrity** check box. The two cascade options become available. If you select the Cascade Update Related Fields option, Access will update the appropriate foreign key values in the related table when you change a primary key value in the primary table. You will *not* select the Cascade Delete Related Records option because doing so could cause you to delete records that you do not want to delete; this option is rarely selected.
9. Click the **Cascade Update Related Fields** check box.
10. Click the **Create** button to define the one-to-many relationship between the two tables and to close the dialog box. The completed relationship appears in the Relationships window, with the join line connecting the common field of PatientID in each table. See Figure 2–41.

Figure 2–41 Defined relationship in the Relationships window

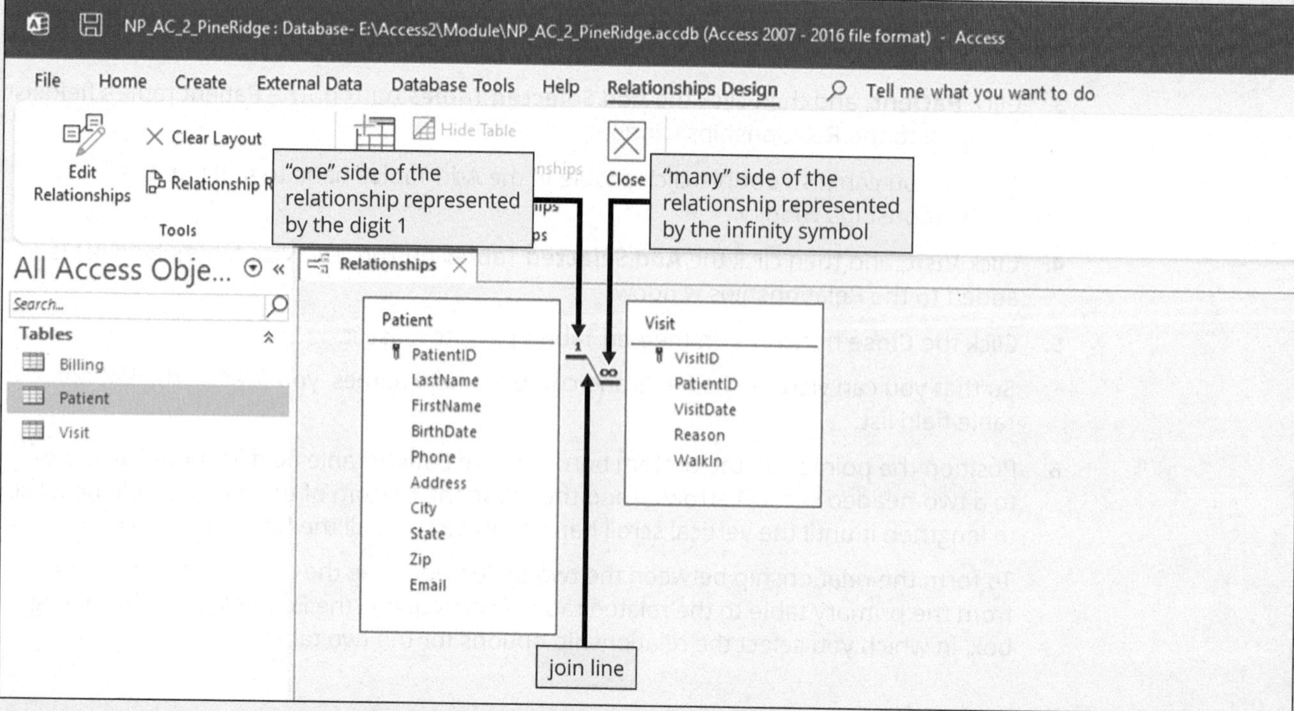

Trouble? If a dialog box opens indicating a problem that prevents you from creating the relationship, you most likely made a typing error when entering the two records in the Patient table. If so, click OK in the dialog box and then click Cancel in the Edit Relationships dialog box. Refer back to the earlier steps instructing you to enter the two records in the Patient table and carefully compare your entries with those shown in the text, especially the PatientID field values. Make any necessary corrections to the data in the Patient table, and then repeat Steps 7 through 10. If you still receive an error message, ask your instructor for assistance.

The next step is to define the one-to-many relationship between the Visit and Billing tables. In this relationship, Visit is the primary ("one") table because there is at most one visit for each invoice. Billing is the related ("many") table because zero, one, or many invoices are generated for each patient visit. For example, some visits require lab work or pharmacy charges, which are invoiced separately.

To define the relationship between the Visit and Billing tables:

1. On the Relationship Design tab, in the Relationships group, click the **Add Tables** button to open the Add Tables pane.

   Tip You can also use the mouse to drag a table from the Navigation Pane to add it to the Relationships window.

2. Click **Billing** on the Tables tab, click the **Add Selected Tables** button, and then click the **Close** button ☒ to close the Add Tables pane. The Billing table's field list appears in the Relationships window to the right of the Visit table's field list.
3. Click and drag the **VisitID** field in the Visit field list to the **VisitID** field in the Billing field list. The Edit Relationships dialog box opens.
4. In the Edit Relationships dialog box, click the **Enforce Referential Integrity** check box, click the **Cascade Update Related Fields** check box, and then click the **Create** button to define the one-to-many relationship between the two tables and to close the dialog box. The completed relationships for the NP_AC_2_PineRidge database appear in the Relationships window. See Figure 2–42.

Figure 2–42 Two relationships defined

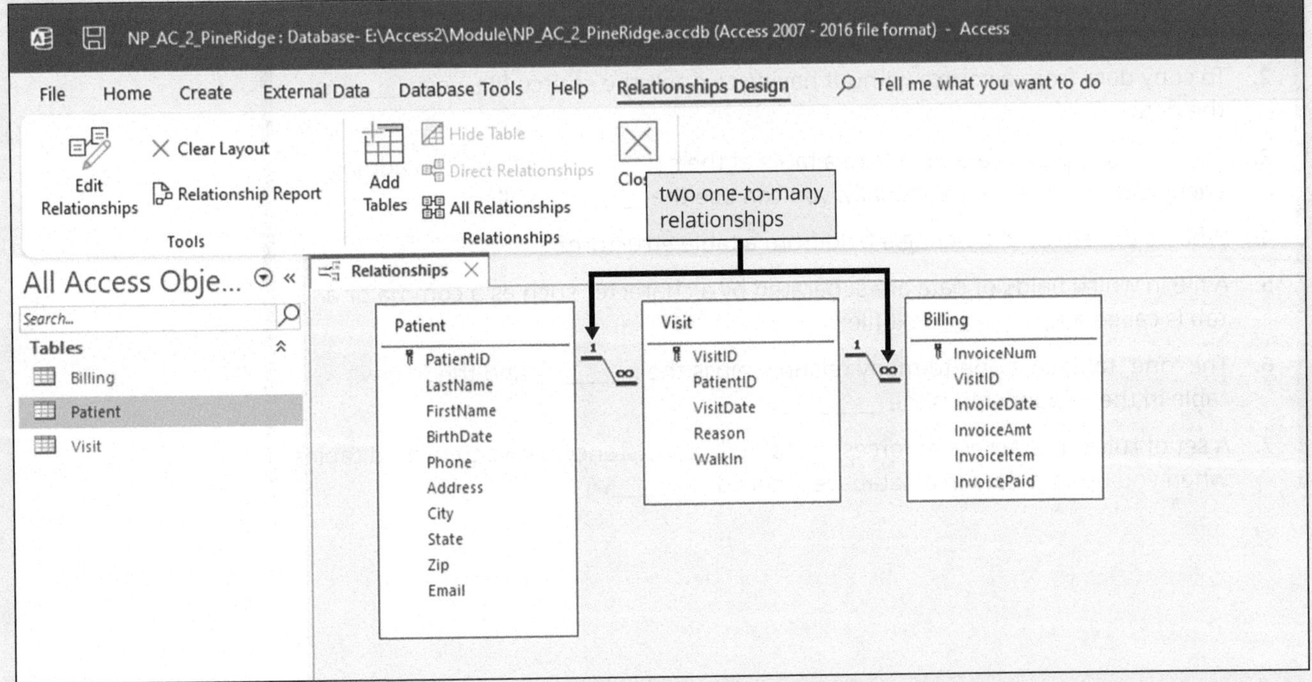

5. On the Quick Access Toolbar, click the **Save** button to save the layout in the Relationships window.
6. On the Relationship Design tab, in the Relationships group, click the **Close** button to close the Relationships window.
7. sam Compact and repair the NP_AC_2_PineRidge database, and then close the database.

Proskills

Problem Solving: Creating a Larger Database

The database for the Pine Ridge Orthopedics & Sports Medicine Center is a relatively small database containing only a few tables, and the data and the reports you will generate from it are fairly simple. A larger database would most likely have many more tables and different types of relationships that can be quite complex. When creating a large database, follow this standard process:

- Consult people who will be using the data to gain an understanding of how it will be used. Gather sample reports and representative data if possible.
- Plan the tables, fields, data types, other properties, and the relationships between the tables.
- Create the tables and define the relationships between them.
- Populate the tables with sample data.
- Design some queries, forms, and reports that will be needed, and then test them.
- Modify the database structure, if necessary, based on the results of your tests.
- Enter the actual data into the database tables.

Testing is critical at every stage of creating a database. Once the database is finalized and implemented, it's not actually finished. The design of a database evolves as new functionality is required and as the data that is gathered changes.

Part 2.2 Quick Check

1. What is the keyboard shortcut for inserting the value from the same field in the previous record into the current record?
2. To copy data from a source without having to open the source file, you ________ the data.
3. To add a group of related fields to a table at the same time, rather than adding each field to the table individually, you can use the ________ gallery.
4. What is the effect of deleting a field from a table structure?
5. A file in which fields of data are separated by a character such as a comma or a tab is called a(n) ________ text file.
6. The "one" table in a one-to-many relationship is the ________, and the "many" table in the relationship is the ________.
7. A set of rules that Access enforces to maintain consistency between related tables when you update data in a database is called ________.

Practice: Review Assignments

Data Files needed for the Review Assignments: NP_AC_2-2.accdb and Support_AC_2_Products.xlsx

In addition to tracking information about the vendors the Pine Ridge Orthopedics & Sports Medicine Center works with, Susan also wants to track information about their products and services. First, Susan asks you to modify the necessary properties in the Supplier table in the NP_AC_2_Vendor database. Afterward, Susan wants you to modify the structure and properties of the Product table in the NP_AC_2_Vendor database. Finally, Susan would like you to create the relationship between the tables. Complete the following steps:

1. Start Access and open the database file NP_AC_2-2.accdb, located in the Access2 > Review folder included with your Data Files, and then save it as **NP_AC_2_Vendor** in the location specified by your instructor. If the security warning is displayed below the ribbon, click the Enable Content button.
2. Open the Supplier table in Datasheet view. For SupplierID ABC123 (ABC Pharmaceuticals), change the value in the ContactFirst field to your first name and change the value in the ContactLast field to your last name.
3. Open the Supplier table in Design view and set the field properties shown in Figure 2–43.

Figure 2–43 Field properties for the Supplier table

Field Name	Data Type	Description	Field Size	Other
SupplierID	Short Text	Primary key	6	Caption = Supplier ID
Company	Short Text		50	
Category	Short Text		15	
Address	Short Text		35	
City	Short Text		25	
State	Short Text		2	
Zip	Short Text		10	
Phone	Short Text		14	Caption = Contact Phone
ContactFirst	Short Text		20	Caption = Contact First Name
ContactLast	Short Text		25	Caption = Contact Last Name
InitialContact	Date/Time			Format = Short Date Caption = Initial Contact

4. Save the Supplier table. Click the Yes button when a message appears, indicating some data might be lost. Switch to Datasheet view and resize columns, as necessary, to their best fit. Then save and close the Supplier table.
5. Open the Product table in Design view, and then set the field properties as shown in Figure 2–44.

Figure 2–44 Design for the Product table

Field Name	Data Type	Description	Field Size	Other
ProductID	Short Text	Primary key	5	Caption = Product ID
SupplierID	Short Text	Foreign key	6	Caption = Supplier ID
ProductName	Short Text		75	Caption = Product Name
Price	Currency			Format = Standard Decimal Places = 2
TempControl	Yes/No			Caption = Temp Controlled?
Sterile	Yes/No			Caption = Sterile?
Units	Number		Integer	Decimal Places = 0 Caption = Units/Case Default Value = [no entry]

6. Modify the Product table structure by adding a new field between the Price and TempControl fields. Name the new field **Weight** (data type: **Number**; field size: **Single**; Decimal Places: **2**; Caption: **Weight in Lbs**; Default Value: [no entry]). Move the **Units** field between the Price and Weight fields.
7. In Datasheet view, resize the columns so all column headings are completely visible and then save the changes to the Product table.
8. Enter the records shown in Figure 2–45 in the Product table. Resize all datasheet columns to their best fit again. When finished, save and close the Product table.

Figure 2–45 Records for the Product table

Product ID	Supplier ID	Product Name	Price	Units/ Case	Weight in Lbs	Temp Controlled?	Sterile?
AB772	ZUR439	Ankle brace	35.25	6	2	No	No
AL487	CES045	Alcohol wipes	15.00	1000	12	Yes	Yes

9. Use the Import Spreadsheet Wizard to add data to the Product table. The data you need to import is contained in the Support_AC_2_Products.xlsx workbook, which is an Excel file located in the Access2 > Review folder provided with your Data Files.
   a. Specify the Support_AC_2_Products.xlsx workbook as the source of the data.
   b. Select the option for appending the data.
   c. Select Product as the table.
   d. In the Import Spreadsheet Wizard dialog boxes, make sure Access confirms that the first row contains column headings, and import to the Product table. Note that if the First Row Contains Column Headings check box is checked but dimmed, click Next to proceed. This is confirmation that the first row contains column headings. Do not save the import steps.
10. Open the Product table in Datasheet view, and resize columns to their best fit, as necessary. Then save and close the Product table.
11. Define a one-to-many relationship between the primary Supplier table and the related Product table. Resize the table field lists so that all field names are visible. Select the referential integrity option and the cascade updates option for the relationship.
12. Save the changes to the Relationships window and close it, compact and repair the NP_AC_2_Vendor database, and then close the database.

Apply: Case Problem 1

Data Files needed for this Case Problem: NP_AC_2-3.accdb, Support_AC_2_Agreements.xlsx, Support_AC_2_Client.accdb, Support_AC_2_Students.txt

Tech Tutors Taylor plans to use the NP_AC_2_TechTutors database to maintain information about the students, tutors, and contracts for her tutoring services company. She asks you to help her to continue to build the database by updating one table and creating two new tables in the database.

Remember that you are not using your solution file from the previous module as a starting file for this case problem. The objects and data may be very similar from one module to the next, but not exact. This is why it is important for you to use the starting files provided with each module. The objects included in your starting database will include the necessary components for you to continue learning about various database design concepts and features of Access. Complete the following steps:

1. Start Access and open the database file NP_AC_2-3.accdb, located in the Access2 > Case1 folder included with your Data Files, and then save it as **NP_AC_2_TechTutors** in the location specified by your instructor. If the security warning is displayed below the ribbon, click the Enable Content button.

2. Open the Tutor table in Datasheet view. For TutorID 3560, change the value in the FirstName field to your first name, and change the value in the LastName field to your last name.
3. Open the Tutor table in Design view and set the field properties shown in Figure 2–46.

Figure 2–46 Field properties for the Tutor table

Field Name	Data Type	Description	Field Size	Other
TutorID	Short Text	Primary key	4	Caption = Tutor ID
FirstName	Short Text		20	Caption = First Name
LastName	Short Text		25	Caption = Last Name
Major	Short Text		25	
YearInSchool	Short Text		12	Caption = Year In School
School	Short Text		30	
HireDate	Date/Time			Format = Short Date Caption = Hire Date

4. Add a new field as the last field in the Tutor table with the field name **Groups**, the **Yes/No** data type, and the caption **Groups Only**.
5. Save the Tutor table. Click the Yes button when a message appears, indicating some data might be lost.
6. In the table datasheet, specify that the following tutors conduct group tutoring sessions only: Cabe Baxter, Fredrik Karlsson, Ellen Desoto, and Sofia Salinas. Close the Tutor table.
7. Taylor created a table named Student in the Support_AC_2_Client database located in the Access2 > Case1 folder with your Data Files. Import the structure of the Student table in the Support_AC_2_Client database into a new table named Student in the NP_AC_2_TechTutors database. Do not save the import steps.
8. Open the Student table in Datasheet view, and then add the following two fields to the end of the table: **BirthDate** (Date/Time field) and **Gender** (Short Text field).
9. Use the Phone Quick Start selection in the Data Type gallery to add four fields related to phone numbers between the Zip and BirthDate fields. (**Hint**: Be sure to make the BirthDate field the active field before adding the new fields.)
10. Display the Student table in Design view, delete the BusinessPhone and FaxNumber fields, and then save and close the Student table.
11. Reopen the Student table and modify its design so that it matches the design in Figure 2–47, including the revised field names and data types.

Figure 2–47 Field properties for the Student table

Field Name	Data Type	Description	Field Size	Other
StudentID	Short Text	Primary key	7	Caption = Student ID
LastName	Short Text		25	Caption = Last Name
FirstName	Short Text		20	Caption = First Name
Address	Short Text		35	
City	Short Text		25	
State	Short Text		2	Default Value = GA
Zip	Short Text		10	
HomePhone	Short Text		14	Caption = Home Phone
CellPhone	Short Text		14	Caption = Cell Phone
BirthDate	Date/Time			Format = Short Date Caption = Birth Date
Gender	Short Text		1	

12. Move the LastName field so it follows the FirstName field.
13. Save your changes to the table design, and then add the records shown in Figure 2–48 to the Student table.

Figure 2–48 Records for the Student table

Student ID	First Name	Last Name	Address	City	State	Zip	Home Phone	Cell Phone	Birth Date	Gender
AND2010	Jill	Anderson	55 Miger Ave	Atlanta	GA	30303	404-555-4938	404-555-0119	4/27/2008	F
LOP2015	Alonzo	Lopez	18 Kimberly Ave	Atlanta	GA	30303	404-555-9981	404-555-8110	2/19/2008	M

14. Resize the fields to their best fit, and then save and close the Student table.
15. Use the Import Text File Wizard to add data to the Student table. The data you need to import is contain in the Support_AC_2_Students text file, which is located in the Access2 > Case1 folder provided with your Data Files.
    a. Specify the Support_AC_2_Students text file as the source of the data.
    b. Select the option for appending the data.
    c. Select Student as the table.
    d. In the Import Text Wizard dialog boxes, choose the options to import delimited data, to use a comma delimiter, and to import that data into the Student table. Do not save the import steps.
16. Open the Student table in Datasheet view, resize columns in the datasheet to their best fit (as necessary), and then save and close the table.
17. Create a new table in Design view, using the table design shown in Figure 2–49.

Figure 2–49 Field properties for the Contract table

Field Name	Data Type	Description	Field Size	Other
ContractID	Short Text	Primary key	4	Caption = Contract ID
StudentID	Short Text	Foreign key	7	Caption = Student ID
TutorID	Short Text	Foreign key	4	Caption = Tutor ID
SessionType	Short Text		15	Caption = Session Type
Length	Number		Integer	Decimal Places = 0 Caption = Length (Hrs) Default Value = [no entry]
NumSessions	Number		Integer	Decimal Places = 0 Caption = Number of Sessions Default Value = [no entry]
Cost	Currency			Format = Currency Decimal Places = 0 Default Value = [no entry]
Assessment	Yes/No	Pre-assessment exam complete		Caption = Assessment Complete

18. Specify the ContractID as the primary key, and then save the table using the name **Contract**.
19. Add a new field to the Contract table, between the TutorID and SessionType fields, with the field name **ContractDate**, the **Date/Time** data type, the description **Date contract is signed**, the **Short Date** format, and the caption **Contract Date**. Save and close the Contract table.

20. Use the Import Spreadsheet Wizard to add data to the Contract table. The data you need to import is contained in the Support_AC_2_Agreements workbook, which is an Excel file located in the Access2 > Case1 folder provided with your Data Files.
    a. Specify the Support_AC_2_Agreements workbook as the source of the data.
    b. Select the option for appending the data to the table.
    c. Select Contract as the table.
    d. In the Import Spreadsheet Wizard dialog boxes, make sure Access confirms the first row contains column headings, and import to the Contract table. Note if the First Row Contains Column Headings check box is checked but dimmed, click Next to proceed. This is confirmation that the first row contains column headings. Do not save the import steps.
21. Open the Contract table, and add the records shown in Figure 2–50. (**Hint**: Use the New (blank) record button in the navigation buttons to add a new record.)

Figure 2–50 Records for the Contract table

Contract ID	Student ID	Tutor ID	Contract Date	Session Type	Length (Hrs)	Number of Sessions	Cost	Assessment Complete
4215	PER2055	3518	7/6/2029	Group	2	5	$400	Yes
4350	LOP2015	3510	10/12/2029	Private	3	4	$720	Yes

22. Resize columns in the datasheet to their best fit (as necessary), and then save and close the Contract table.
23. Define the one-to-many relationships between the database tables as follows: between the primary Student table and the related Contract table, and between the primary Tutor table and related Contract table. Resize the table field lists so that all field names are visible. Select the referential integrity option and the cascade updates option for each relationship.
24. Save the changes to the Relationships window and close it, compact and repair the NP_AC_2_TechTutors database, and then close the database.

Challenge: Case Problem 2

Data Files needed for this Case Problem: NP_AC_2-4.accdb, Support_AC_2_Bookings.txt, and Support_AC_2_Travel.accdb

Outdoor Adventure Tours David and Brent Wilson will use the NP_AC_2_Outdoor database to track the data about the hikers and tours offered through their business. They ask you to help them in continuing to build the database.

Remember that you are not using your solution file from the previous module as a starting file for this case problem. The objects and data may be very similar from one module to the next, but not exact. This is why it is important for you to use the starting files provided with each module. The objects included in your starting database will include the necessary components for you to continue learning about various database design concepts and features of Access. Complete the following steps:

1. Start Access and open the database file NP_AC_2-4.accdb, located in the Access2 > Case2 folder included with your Data Files, and then save it as **NP_AC_2_Outdoor** in the location specified by your instructor. If the security warning is displayed below the ribbon, click the Enable Content button.
2. Open the Hiker table in Datasheet view. For HikerID 401, change the value in the HikerFirst field to your first name and change the value in the HikerLast field to your last name.
3. Open the Hiker table in Design view, and then change the following field properties:
    a. HikerID: Enter **Primary key** for the description, change the field size to **3**, and enter **Hiker ID** for the caption.
    b. HikerFirst: Change the field size to **20** and enter **Hiker First Name** for the caption.

c. HikerLast: Change the field size to **25** and enter **Hiker Last Name** for the caption.

d. Address: Change the field size to **35**.

e. City: Change the field size to **25**.

f. State: Change the field size to **2**.

g. Zip: Change the field size to **10**.

h. Phone: Change the field size to **14**.

4. Save the Hiker table, click the Yes button when a message appears indicating some data might be lost, resize the Hiker First Name and Hiker Last Name columns in Datasheet view to their best fit, and then save and close the table.

5. Create a table in the NP_AC_2_Outdoor database as follows:

   a. Import the Trip table structure and data from the Support_AC_2_Travel database into a new table in the NP_AC_2_Outdoor database. As the source of the data, specify the Support_AC_2_Travel database, which is located in the Access2 > Case2 folder provided with your Data Files; select the option button to import tables, queries, forms, reports, macros, and modules into the current database; and in the Import Objects dialog box, select the Trip table, click Options button, and then make sure that the correct option is selected to import the table's data and structure (definition).

   b. Do not save your import steps.

6. **Explore:** Using a shortcut menu in the Navigation Pane, rename the Trip table as **Tour** to give this name to the new table in the NP_AC_2_Outdoor database.

7. Open the Tour table in Design view, and then delete the VIPDiscount field.

8. Change the following properties:

   a. TourID: Enter the description **Primary key**, change the field size to **3**, and enter **Tour ID** for the caption.

   b. TourName: Enter **Tour Name** for the caption and change the field size to **35**.

   c. TourType: Enter **Tour Type** for the caption and change the field size to **15**.

   d. PricePerPerson: Enter **Price Per Person** for the caption.

9. Save the modified table, click the Yes button when a message appears, indicating some data might be lost, and then display the table in Datasheet view. Resize all datasheet columns to their best fit and save and close the table.

10. In Design view, create a table using the table design shown in Figure 2–51.

Figure 2–51 Design for the Reservation table

Field Name	Data Type	Description	Field Size	Other
ReservationID	Short Text	Primary key	4	Caption = Reservation ID
HikerID	Short Text	Foreign key	3	Caption = Hiker ID
TourID	Short Text	Foreign key	3	Caption = Tour ID
TourDate	Date/Time			Caption = Tour Date
People	Number		Integer	Decimal Places = 0 Default Value = [no entry]

11. Specify **ReservationID** as the primary key, and then save the table as **Reservation**.

12. **Explore:** Refer back to Figure 2–10 to review the custom data formats. Change the Format property of the TourDate field to a custom format that displays dates in a format similar to 10/06/29. Save and close the Reservation table.

13. Use the Import Text File Wizard to add data to the Reservation table. The data you need to import is contained in the Support_AC_2_Bookings text file, which is located in the Access2 > Case2 folder provided with your Data Files.

    a. Specify the Bookings text file as the source of the data.

    b. Select the option for appending the data.

c. Select Reservation as the table.

d. In the Import Text Wizard dialog boxes, choose the options to import delimited data, to use a comma delimiter, and to import the data into the Reservation table. Do not save the import steps.

14. Open the Reservation table, and then resize columns in the table datasheet to their best fit (as necessary), verify that the date values in the TourDate field are displayed correctly according to the custom format, and then save and close the table.

15. Define the one-to-many relationships between the database tables as follows: between the primary Hiker table and the related Reservation table, and between the primary Tour table and the related Reservation table. (**Hint**: Place the Reservation table as the middle table in the Relationships window to make it easier to join the tables.) Resize the Hiker field list so that all field names are visible. Select the referential integrity option and the cascade updates option for each relationship.

16. Save the changes to the Relationship window and close it, compact and repair the NP_AC_2_Outdoor database, and then close the database.

Maintaining and Querying a Database

Updating and Retrieving Information About Patients, Visits, and Invoices

Case: Pine Ridge Orthopedics & Sports Medicine Center

At a recent meeting, Susan Martinez and her staff discussed the need to maintain accurate information about the center's patients, visits, and invoices and to regularly monitor the business activities of Pine Ridge Orthopedics & Sports Medicine Center. For example, Kimberly Wilson, Susan's assistant, needs to make sure she has up-to-date contact information, such as phone numbers and email addresses, for all the center's patients. The office staff must monitor billing activity to make sure that invoices are paid on time and in full. In addition, the staff handles marketing efforts for the center and develops new strategies for promoting services. Susan is also interested in analyzing other parts of the business related to patient visits and finances. You can satisfy all these informational needs for Pine Ridge Orthopedics & Sports Medicine Center by updating data in the Pine Ridge database and by creating and using queries that retrieve information from the database.

Be sure to use the starting data file, NP_AC_3-1.accdb, when you begin working in this module so your solutions match those provided by your instructor.

Starting Data Files: Access3

Module
NP_AC_3-1.accdb

Review
NP_AC_3-2.accdb

Case1
NP_AC_3-3.accdb

Case2
NP_AC_3-4.accdb

Objectives

Part 3.1

- Find, modify, and delete records in a table
- Hide and unhide fields in a datasheet
- Work in the Query window in Design view
- Create, run, and save queries
- Update data using a query datasheet
- Create a query based on multiple tables
- Sort data in a query
- Filter data in a query

Part 3.2

- Specify an exact match condition in a query
- Use a comparison operator in a query to match a range of values
- Use the And and Or logical operators in queries
- Change the font size and alternate row color in a datasheet
- Create and format a calculated field in a query
- Perform calculations in a query using aggregate functions and record group calculations
- Change the display of database objects in the Navigation Pane

Part 3.1 Visual Overview: Query Window in Design View

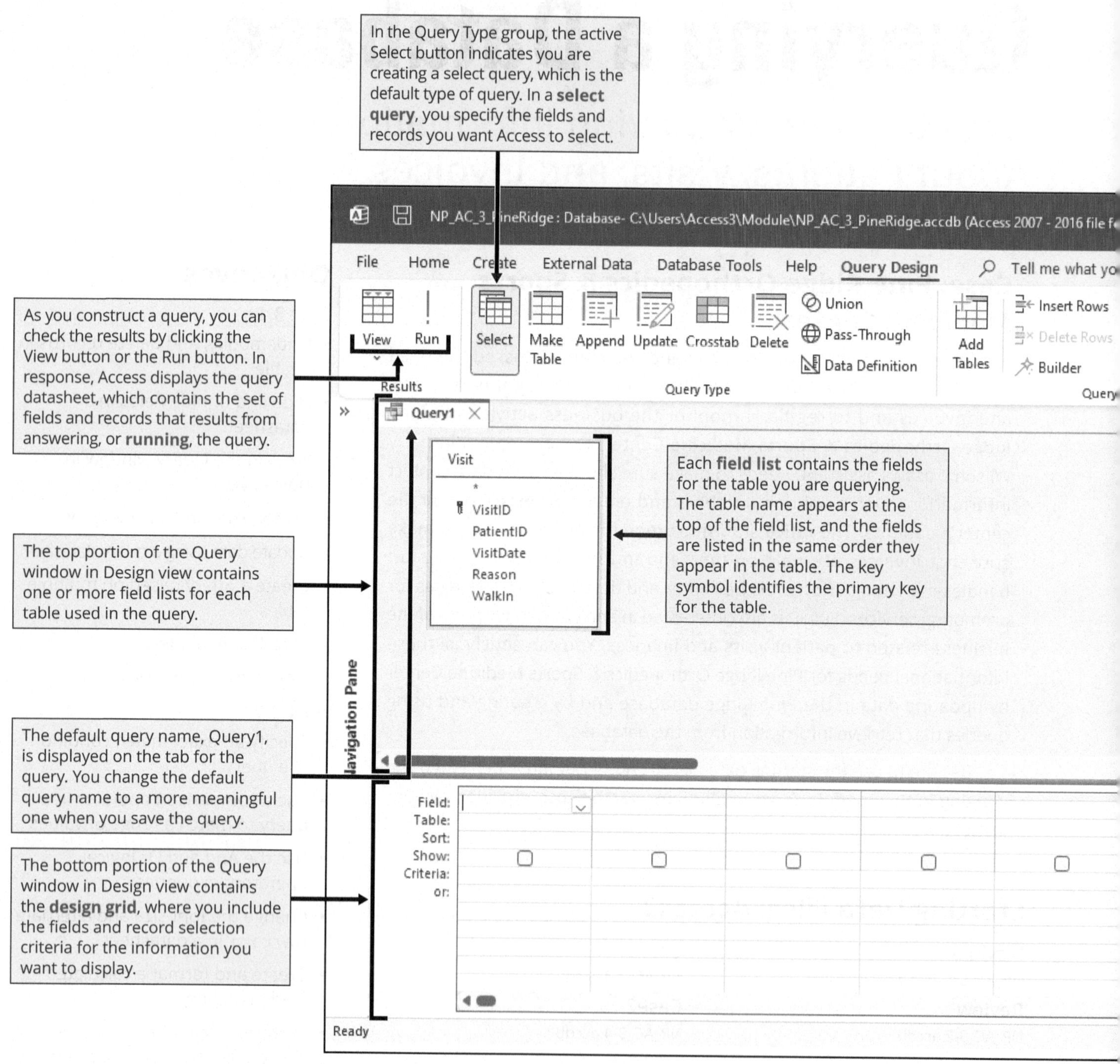
In the Query Type group, the active Select button indicates you are creating a select query, which is the default type of query. In a **select query**, you specify the fields and records you want Access to select.
As you construct a query, you can check the results by clicking the View button or the Run button. In response, Access displays the query datasheet, which contains the set of fields and records that results from answering, or **running**, the query.
The top portion of the Query window in Design view contains one or more field lists for each table used in the query.
The default query name, Query1, is displayed on the tab for the query. You change the default query name to a more meaningful one when you save the query.
The bottom portion of the Query window in Design view contains the **design grid**, where you include the fields and record selection criteria for the information you want to display.
Each **field list** contains the fields for the table you are querying. The table name appears at the top of the field list, and the fields are listed in the same order they appear in the table. The key symbol identifies the primary key for the table.
NP_AC_3_PineRidge : Database- C:\Users\Access3\Module\NP_AC_3_PineRidge.accdb (Access 2007 - 2016 file f
File
Home
Create
External Data
Database Tools
Help
Query Design
Tell me what yo
View
Run
Results
Select
Make Table
Append
Update
Crosstab
Delete
Union
Pass-Through
Data Definition
Query Type
Add Tables
Insert Rows
Delete Rows
Builder
Query
Query1
Visit
*
VisitID
PatientID
VisitDate
Reason
WalkIn
Navigation Pane
Field:
Table:
Sort:
Show:
Criteria:
or:
Ready

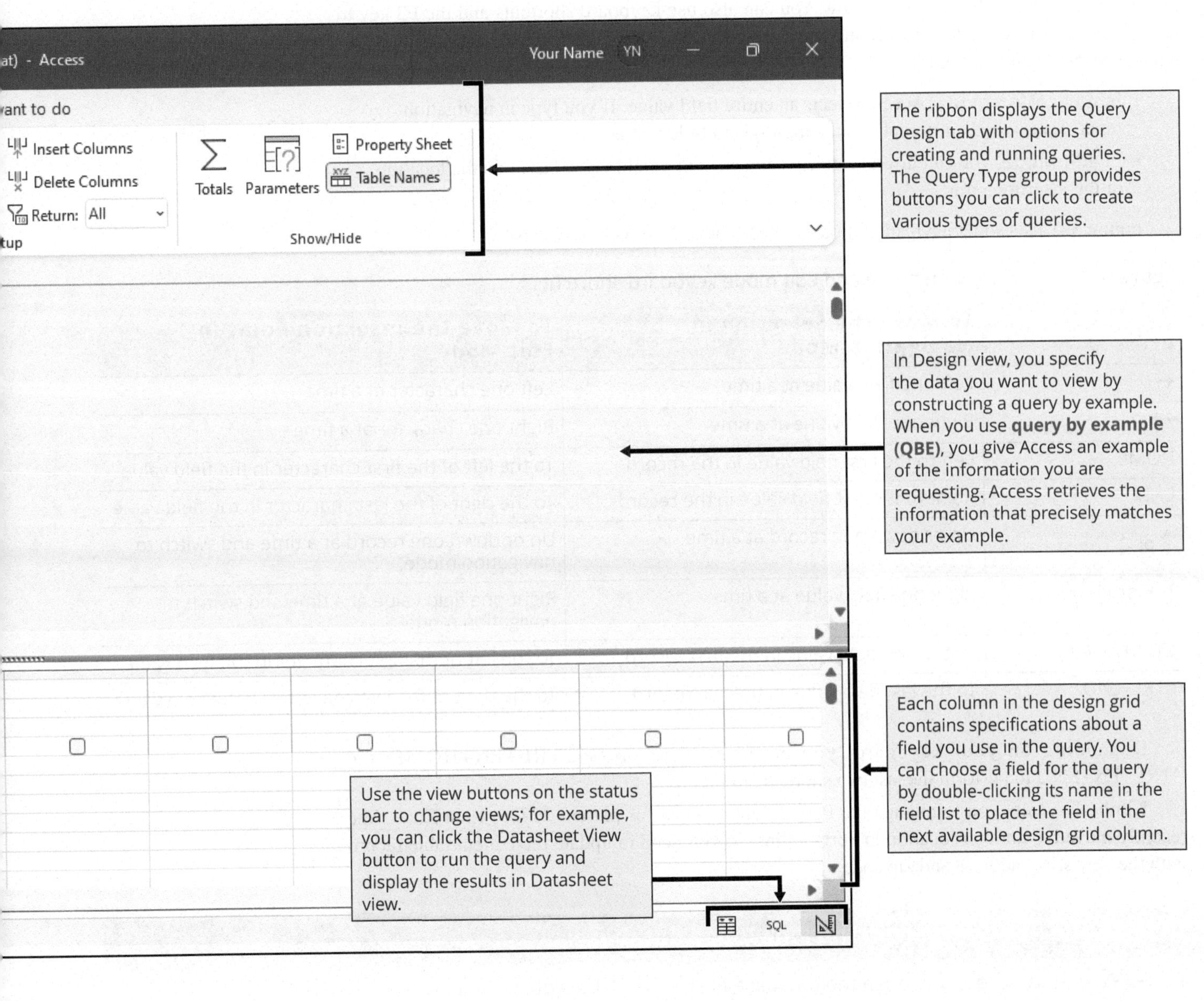
at) - Access
Your Name
YN
ant to do
Insert Columns
Delete Columns
Return: All
tup
Totals
Parameters
Property Sheet
Table Names
Show/Hide
SQL
The ribbon displays the Query Design tab with options for creating and running queries. The Query Type group provides buttons you can click to create various types of queries.
In Design view, you specify the data you want to view by constructing a query by example. When you use **query by example (QBE)**, you give Access an example of the information you are requesting. Access retrieves the information that precisely matches your example.
Each column in the design grid contains specifications about a field you use in the query. You can choose a field for the query by double-clicking its name in the field list to place the field in the next available design grid column.
Use the view buttons on the status bar to change views; for example, you can click the Datasheet View button to run the query and display the results in Datasheet view.

Updating a Database

Updating, or **maintaining**, a database involves adding, modifying, and deleting records in database tables to keep them current and accurate. After reviewing the data in the Pine Ridge database, Kimberly identified some changes to make to the data. She asks you to update the field values in one record in the Patient table, correct an error in a record in the Visit table, and then delete a record in the Visit table.

Modifying Records

To modify the field values in a record, you first make the record the current record. Then you position the insertion point in the field value to make minor changes or select the field value to replace it entirely. One way to navigate the records in a datasheet is to use the scroll bars and navigation buttons in the Access window. You can also use keyboard shortcuts and the F2 key to navigate a datasheet and to select field values. The **F2 key** is a toggle you use to switch between navigation mode and edit mode.

- In **navigation mode**, Access selects an entire field value. If you type in navigation mode, your typed entry replaces the highlighted field value.
- In **edit mode**, you can insert or delete characters in a field value based on the location of the insertion point.

Figure 3–1 lists some navigation mode and edit mode keyboard shortcuts.

Figure 3–1 Navigation mode and edit mode keyboard shortcuts

Press	To Move the Selection in Navigation Mode	To Move the Insertion Point in Edit Mode
←	Left one field value at a time	Left one character at a time
→	Right one field value at a time	Right one character at a time
HOME	Left to the first field value in the record	To the left of the first character in the field value
END	Right to the last field value in the record	To the right of the last character in the field value
↑ or ↓	Up or down one record at a time	Up or down one record at a time and switch to navigation mode
TAB or ENTER	Right one field value at a time	Right one field value at a time and switch to navigation mode
CTRL+HOME	To the first field value in the first record	To the left of the first character in the field value
CTRL+END	To the last field value in the last record	To the right of the last character in the field value

Depending on your keyboard, you might need to press CTRL+FN+HOME and CTRL+FN+END to perform the last two shortcuts in Figure 3–1.

Kimberly wants you to change the Patient table record for patient 27736, Lian Zhao. She recently moved to another location in Fort Collins, so you need to update the Patient table record with the new street address and zip code.

To open the Patient table in the Pine Ridge database:

1. **sam** Start Access and open the database file NP_AC_3-1.accdb, located in the Access3 > Module folder included with your Data Files, and then save it as **NP_AC_3_PineRidge** in the location specified by your instructor.

   Trouble? If the security warning is displayed below the ribbon, click the Enable Content button.

2. Open the **Patient** table in Datasheet view, and then open the Navigation Pane, if necessary.

The Patient table contains 10 fields. When updating data in a table, you can remove the display of some fields to focus on the data you want.

Hiding and Unhiding Fields

When you display a table or query datasheet in Datasheet view, you might want to temporarily remove certain fields from the datasheet, especially if you would otherwise have to scroll the datasheet horizontally. The **Hide Fields** command allows you to remove the display of one or more fields, and the **Unhide Fields** command allows you to redisplay any hidden fields.

> **Tip** Hiding a field removes it from the datasheet display only; the field and its contents are still part of the table.

To make it easier to modify the patient record, you'll first hide a couple of fields in the Patient table.

To hide fields in the Patient table and modify the patient record:

1. Right-click the **Date of Birth** field name to display the shortcut menu, and then click **Hide Fields**. The Date of Birth column is removed from the datasheet display.
2. Right-click the **Phone** field name, and then click **Hide Fields** on the shortcut menu. The Phone column is removed from the datasheet display.

   With the fields hidden, you can now update the patient record. The record you need to modify is near the end of the table and has a PatientID field value of 27736.
3. Scroll the datasheet until you display the last record in the table.
4. Click the PatientID field value **27736**, for Lian Zhao. The insertion point appears in the field value, indicating you are in edit mode.
5. Press **TAB** to move to the Last Name field value, Zhao. The field value is selected, indicating you are in navigation mode.
6. Press **TAB** two times to move to the Address field and select its field value, type **125 Peak Dr** and then press **TAB** three times to move to the Zip field.
7. Type **80527** and then press **TAB** twice to move to the PatientID field of the next record. The changes to the record are complete. See Figure 3–2.

Figure 3–2 Table after changing field values in a record

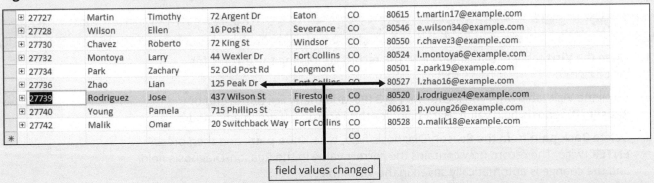

⊞ 27727	Martin	Timothy	72 Argent Dr	Eaton	CO	80615	t.martin17@example.com
⊞ 27728	Wilson	Ellen	16 Post Rd	Severance	CO	80546	e.wilson34@example.com
⊞ 27730	Chavez	Roberto	72 King St	Windsor	CO	80550	r.chavez3@example.com
⊞ 27732	Montoya	Larry	44 Wexler Dr	Fort Collins	CO	80524	l.montoya6@example.com
⊞ 27734	Park	Zachary	52 Old Post Rd	Longmont	CO	80501	z.park19@example.com
⊞ 27736	Zhao	Lian	125 Peak Dr	Fort Collins	CO	80527	l.zhao16@example.com
⊞ 27739	Rodriguez	Jose	437 Wilson St	Firestone	CO	80520	j.rodriguez4@example.com
⊞ 27740	Young	Pamela	715 Phillips St	Greeley	CO	80631	p.young26@example.com
⊞ 27742	Malik	Omar	20 Switchback Way	Fort Collins	CO	80528	o.malik18@example.com
*					CO		

field values changed

Access saves changes to field values when you move to a new field or another record or when you close the table. You don't have to click the Save button to save changes to field values or records.

8. Press **CTRL+HOME** to move to the first field value in the first record. With the changes to the record complete, you can unhide the hidden fields.

9. Right-click any field name to display the shortcut menu, and then click **Unhide Fields**. The Unhide Columns dialog box opens. See Figure 3–3.

Figure 3–3 Unhide Columns dialog box

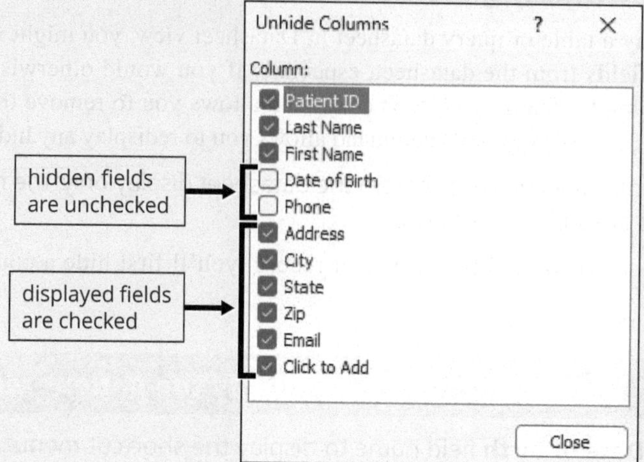

All currently displayed fields are checked in this dialog box, and all hidden fields are unchecked. To redisplay them, you click their check boxes to select them.

10. In the Unhide Columns dialog box, click the **Date of Birth** check box to select it, click the **Phone** check box to select it, and then click **Close** to close the dialog box. The two hidden fields are now displayed in the datasheet.
11. Close the Patient table, and then click **No** in the dialog box that asks if you want to save changes to the layout of the Patient table. This dialog box appears because you hid fields and redisplayed them.

    In this case, you can click the Yes button or the No button because no changes were made to the table layout or design.

Next, you need to correct an error in the Visit table for a visit made by Nadia Sayed, Patient ID 27704. A staff member incorrectly entered "Back pain" as the reason for the visit, though the patient came to the center that day for knee pain. Ensuring the accuracy of the data in a database is an important maintenance task.

To correct the record in the Visit table:

1. Open the **Visit** table in Datasheet view. The record containing the error is for Visit ID 3190.
2. Scroll the Visit table until you locate Visit ID **3190**, and then click at the end of the **Reason/Diagnosis** field value "Back pain" for this record. You are in edit mode.
3. Delete **Back pain** from the Reason/Diagnosis field, type **Knee pain**, and then press **ENTER** twice. The record now contains the correct value in the Reason/Diagnosis field, and the change is automatically saved in the Visit table.

The next update Kimberly asks you to make is to delete a record in the Visit table. One of the center's patients, Emilio Soto, recently notified Kimberly that he received an invoice for physical therapy though he had cancelled this scheduled appointment. Because this visit did not take place, the record for this visit needs to be deleted from the Visit table. Rather than scrolling through the table to locate the record to delete, you can use the Find command.

Finding Data in a Table

Access provides options for locating specific field values in a table. Instead of scrolling the Visit table datasheet to find the visit that you need to delete—the record for Visit ID 3156—you can use the Find command to find the record. The **Find command** allows you to search a table or query datasheet or a form to locate all or part of a field value. This feature is particularly useful when searching a table that contains many records.

To search for the record in the Visit table:

1. Make sure the VisitID field value 3191 is still selected and the Home tab is selected on the ribbon. You need to search the VisitID field to find the record containing the value 3156, so the insertion point is already correctly positioned in the field you want to search.

   Tip You can click any value in the column containing the field you want to search in order to make the field current.

2. In the Find group, click **Find**. The Find and Replace dialog box opens, as shown in Figure 3-4.

Figure 3-4 Find and Replace dialog box

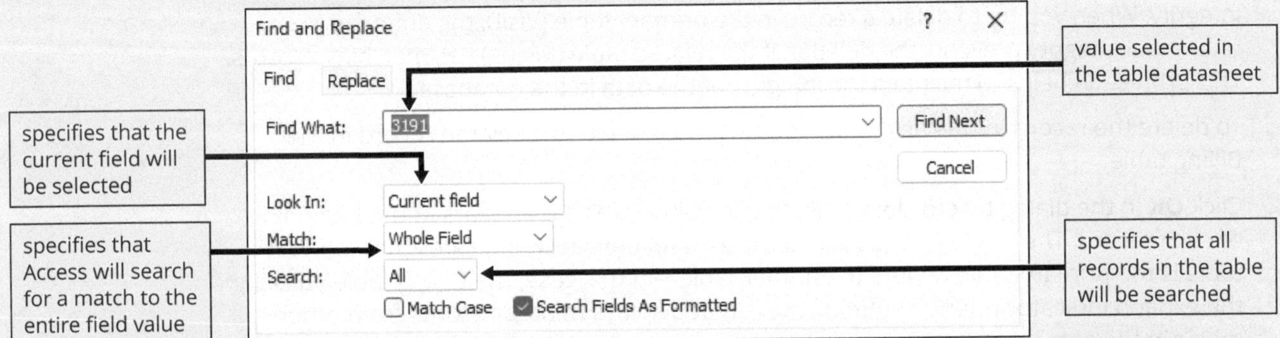

The field value 3191 appears in the Find What box because this value is selected in the table datasheet. You also can choose to search for only part of a field value, such as when you need to find all Visit IDs that start with a certain value. The Search box indicates that all the records in the table will be searched for the value you want to find. You can also choose to search up or down from the current record.

Trouble? Some settings in your dialog box might be different from those shown in Figure 3-4 depending on the last search performed on the computer you're using. If so, change the settings so that they match those in the figure.

3. Make sure the value 3191 is selected in the Find What box, type **3156** to replace the selected value, and then click **Find Next**. Record 10 appears with the specified field value selected.

4. Click **Cancel** to close the Find and Replace dialog box.

Deleting Records

To delete a record, you need to select the record in Datasheet view and then delete it using the Delete button in the Records group on the Home tab or the Delete Record command on the shortcut menu.

Reference

Deleting a Record

- With the table open in Datasheet view, click the row selector for the record you want to delete.
- In the Records group on the Home tab, click the Delete button. You can also right-click the row selector for the record, and then click Delete Record on the shortcut menu.
- In the dialog box asking you to confirm the deletion, click Yes.

Now that you have found the record with Visit ID 3156, you can delete it. To delete a record, you must first select the entire row for the record.

To delete the record:

1. Click the **row selector** ➡ for the record containing the VisitID field value **3156**, which should still be highlighted. The entire row is selected.
2. On the Home tab, in the Records group, click **Delete**. A dialog box opens to indicate that you cannot delete the record because the Billing table contains records related to VisitID 3156. The Visit and Billing tables have a one-to-many relationship that enforces referential integrity. When you try to delete a record in the primary table (Visit), the enforced referential integrity prevents the deletion if the related table (Billing) has matching records. This protection helps to maintain the integrity of the data in the database.

   To delete the record in the Visit table, you first must delete the related record in the Billing table.
3. Click **OK** in the dialog box to close it. Notice the plus sign that appears at the beginning of each record. The plus sign, also called the **expand indicator**, indicates that the Visit table is the primary table related to another table—in this case, the Billing table. Clicking the expand indicator opens a **subdatasheet** that displays related records from other tables in the database.
4. Scroll the datasheet until the selected record is near the top of the datasheet and you have room to view the related records for the visit record.
5. Click the **expand indicator** ⊞ next to VisitID 3156. One related record from the Billing table for this visit is displayed in the subdatasheet, as shown in Figure 3–5.

Figure 3–5 Related records from the Billing table in the subdatasheet

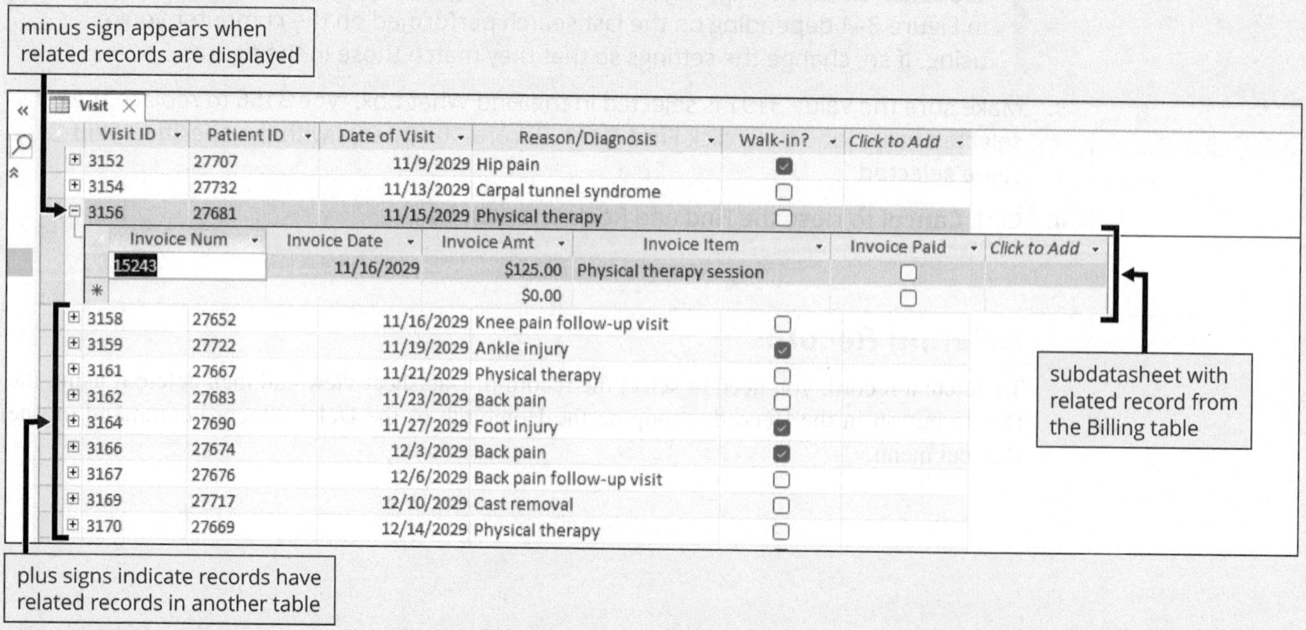

When the subdatasheet is open, you can navigate and update it, just as you can using a table datasheet. The expand indicator for an open subdatasheet is replaced by a minus sign. Clicking the minus sign, or **collapse indicator**, hides the subdatasheet.

In the Billing table, you need to delete the record related to Visit ID 3156 before you can delete the visit record. The record is for the invoice that was mistakenly sent to the patient, Emilio Soto, who had canceled his physical therapy appointment. You could open the Billing table and find the related record. However, an easier way is to delete the record in the subdatasheet, which also deletes the record from the Billing table.

6. In the Billing table subdatasheet, click the **row selector** ➡ for invoice number **15243**. The entire row is selected.
7. On the Home tab in the Records group, click **Delete**. Because the deletion of a record is permanent and cannot be undone, a dialog box asks you to confirm the deletion of the record.
8. Click **Yes** to confirm the deletion and close the dialog box. The record is removed from the Billing table, and the subdatasheet is now empty.
9. Click the **collapse indicator** ⊟ next to Visit ID 3156 to close the subdatasheet.

   Now that you have deleted the related record in the Billing table, you can delete the record for Visit ID 3156. You'll use the shortcut menu to do so.
10. Right-click the row selector ➡ for the record for Visit ID **3156** to select the record and open the shortcut menu.

    Key Step Be sure to select the correct record before deleting it.
11. Click **Delete Record** on the shortcut menu, and then click **Yes** in the dialog box to confirm the deletion. The record is deleted from the Visit table.
12. Close the Visit table.

Insight

Deleting Records

When working with more complex databases that a database administrator manages, you typically need special permission to delete records from a table. Many companies also follow the practice of archiving records before deleting them so that the information is still available but not part of the active database.

You finished updating the NP_AC_3_PineRidge database by modifying and deleting records. Next, you'll retrieve specific data from the database to meet requests for information about Pine Ridge Orthopedics & Sports Medicine Center.

Introduction to Queries

As you have learned, a query is a question you ask about data stored in a database. For example, Susan might create a query to find records in the Patient table for only those patients located in a specific city. When you create a query, you tell Access which fields you need and what criteria Access should use to select the records. Access provides powerful query capabilities that allow you to do the following:

- Display selected fields and records from a table.
- Sort records.
- Perform calculations.
- Generate data for forms, reports, and other queries.
- Update data in the tables in a database.
- Find and display data from two or more tables.

Most questions about data are generalized queries in which you specify the fields and records you want Access to select. These common requests for information, such as "Which patients are located in Fort Collins?" or "How many invoices have been paid?" are select queries. The answer to a select query is returned in the form of a datasheet. The result of a query is also called a **recordset** because the query produces a set of records that answers your question.

Insight

Designing Queries or Using a Query Wizard

To create more specialized, technical queries, such as finding duplicate records in a table, you can use a Query Wizard. A **Query Wizard** prompts you for information by asking a series of questions and then creates the appropriate query based on your answers. For example, earlier you used the Simple Query Wizard to display only some fields in the Visit table. Access provides other Query Wizards for more complex queries. For common, informational queries, designing your own is more efficient than using a Query Wizard.

Kimberly wants you to create a query to display the patient ID, last name, first name, city, and email address for each record in the Patient table. She needs this information to complete an email campaign advertising special services and screenings the center is offering to patients. You'll open the Query window in Design view to create the query for Kimberly.

To open the Query window in Design view:

1. Close the Navigation Pane. On the ribbon, click the **Create** tab.
2. In the Queries group, click the **Query Design** button to display the Query window in Design view with the Add Tables pane open, as shown in Figure 3–6.

Figure 3–6 Add Tables pane

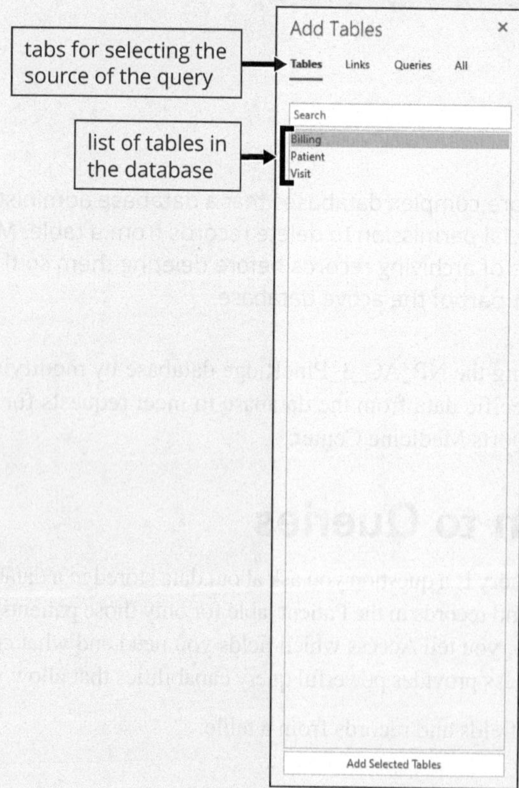

The Add Tables pane lists all the tables in the database. You can choose to base a query on one or more tables, on other queries, or on a combination of tables and queries. The query you are creating will retrieve data from the Patient table, so you need to add this table to the Query window.

3. In the Tables list, click **Patient**, click **Add Selected Tables**, and then click the **Close** button [X] to close the Add Tables pane. The Patient table's field list appears in the Query window. See the Part 3.1 Visual Overview to familiarize yourself with the Query window in Design view.

   Trouble? If you add the wrong table to the Query window, right-click the title bar at the top of the field list containing the table name, and then click Remove Table on the shortcut menu. To add the correct table to the Query window, repeat Steps 2 and 3.

Now you'll create and run the query to display selected fields from the Patient table.

Creating and Running a Query

The default table datasheet displays all the fields in the table in the same order as they appear in the table. In contrast, a query datasheet can display selected fields from a table, and the order of the fields can be different from that of the table, so that users viewing the query results can review only the information they need and in the order they want.

You need the PatientID, LastName, FirstName, City, and Email fields from the Patient table to appear in the query results. Before you add each field to the design grid, you should resize the Patient table field list to display all the fields.

To select the fields for the query and then run the query:

1. Drag the bottom border of the Patient field list to resize the list and display all the fields in the Patient table.
2. In the Patient field list, double-click **PatientID** to place the field in the Field box of the first column in the design grid, as shown in Figure 3–7.

Figure 3–7 Field added to the design grid

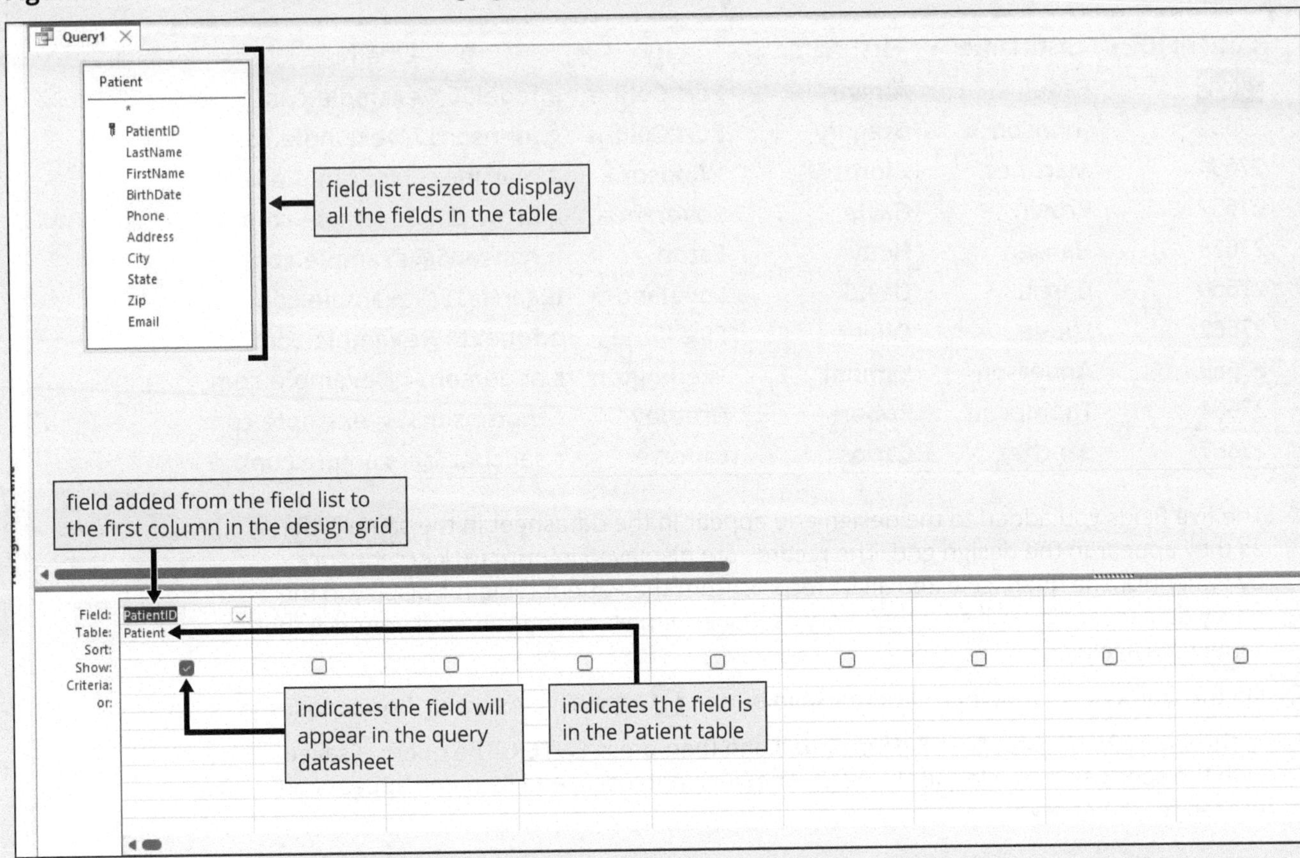

In the first column of the design grid, the field name PatientID appears in the Field box, the table name Patient appears in the Table box, and the checkmark in the Show check box indicates that the field will be displayed in the datasheet when you run the query. Sometimes you might not want to display a field and its values in the query results. For example, if you are creating a query to list all patients located in Fort Collins, and you assign the name "FortCollinsPatients" to the query, you do not need to include the City field value for each record in the query results—the query design lists only patients with the City field value of "Fort Collins." Even if you choose not to display a field in the query results, you can still use the field as part of the query to select records or to specify a sequence for the records in the datasheet. You can also add a field to the design grid using the arrow that appears when you click the Field box. If you click the arrow or the right side of an empty Field box, a menu of available fields opens.

Tip You can also drag a field from the field list to a column in the design grid.

3. In the design grid, click the right side of the Field box in the second column to display a menu listing all the fields in the Patient table, and then click **LastName** to add this field to the second column in the design grid.
4. Add the **FirstName**, **City**, and **Email** fields to the design grid in that order.

   Trouble? If you add the wrong field to the design grid, select the field's column by clicking the selection pointer ⬇ on the field selector, which is the thin bar above the Field box, for the field you want to delete. Then press DELETE (or in the Query Setup group on the Query Design tab, click the Delete Columns button).

   Now that you have selected the five fields for the query, you can run the query.
5. On the Query Design tab, in the Results group, click the **Run** button. Access runs the query and displays the results in Datasheet view, as shown in Figure 3–8.

Figure 3–8 Datasheet displayed after running the query

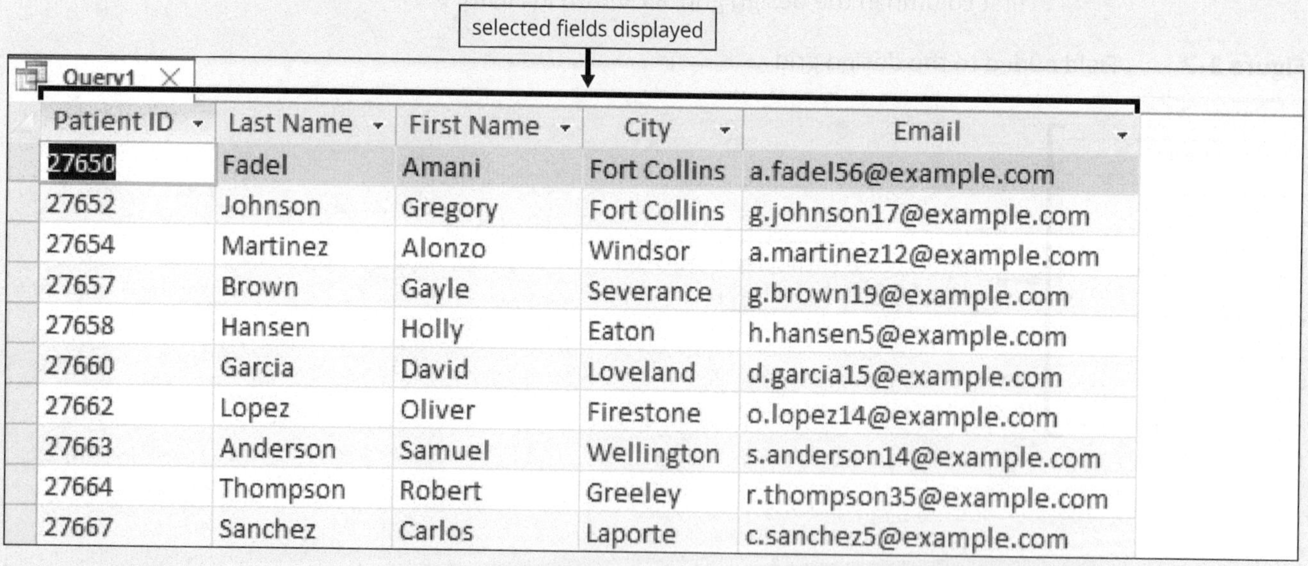

selected fields displayed

Query1

Patient ID	Last Name	First Name	City	Email
27650	Fadel	Amani	Fort Collins	a.fadel56@example.com
27652	Johnson	Gregory	Fort Collins	g.johnson17@example.com
27654	Martinez	Alonzo	Windsor	a.martinez12@example.com
27657	Brown	Gayle	Severance	g.brown19@example.com
27658	Hansen	Holly	Eaton	h.hansen5@example.com
27660	Garcia	David	Loveland	d.garcia15@example.com
27662	Lopez	Oliver	Firestone	o.lopez14@example.com
27663	Anderson	Samuel	Wellington	s.anderson14@example.com
27664	Thompson	Robert	Greeley	r.thompson35@example.com
27667	Sanchez	Carlos	Laporte	c.sanchez5@example.com

The five fields you added to the design grid appear in the datasheet in the same order as they appear in the design grid. The records are displayed in primary key sequence by PatientID. The query selected all 51 records from the Patient table for display in the query datasheet. You will save the query as "PatientEmail" so you can easily retrieve the same data again.

6. On the Quick Access Toolbar, click the **Save** button. The Save As dialog box opens.
7. In the Query Name box, type **PatientEmail** and then press **ENTER**. The query is saved with the specified name in the NP_AC_3_PineRidge database, and its name appears on the tab for the query.

Proskills

Decision Making: Comparing Methods for Adding All Fields to the Design Grid

If the query you are creating includes every field from a table, you can use one of the following three methods to transfer all the fields from the field list to the design grid:

- Double-click (or click and drag) each field individually from the field list to the design grid. Use this method if you want the fields in your query to appear in an order different from the one in the field list.
- Double-click the asterisk at the top of the field list. The table name, followed by a period and an asterisk (as in "Patient.*"), appears in the Field box of the first column in the design grid, which signifies that the order of the fields is the same in the query as it is in the field list. Use this method if you don't need to sort the query or specify conditions for the fields in the table. The advantage of using this method is that you do not need to change the query if you add or delete fields from the underlying table structure. Such changes are reflected automatically in the query.
- Double-click the field list title bar to select all the fields, and then drag a selected field to the first column in the design grid. Each field appears in a separate column, and the fields are arranged in the order they appear in the field list. Use this method when you need to sort your query or include record selection criteria.

By choosing the most appropriate method to add all the table fields to the query design grid, you can work more efficiently and ensure that the query produces the results you want.

The record for one of the patients in the query results contains information that is not up to date. This patient, David Garcia, informed the center that he now prefers to go by the name Marco, which is his first name; David is his middle name. He also provided a new email address. You need to update the record with the new first name and email address for this patient.

Updating Data Using a Query

A query datasheet is temporary, and its contents are based on the criteria in the query design grid. However, you can still update the data in a table using a query datasheet. In this case, you want to change a record in the Patient table. Instead of making the changes in the table datasheet, you can make them in the PatientEmail query datasheet because the query is based on the Patient table. The underlying Patient table will be updated with the changes you make.

To update data using the PatientEmail query datasheet:

1. Locate the record with PatientID 27660, David Garcia (record 6 in the query datasheet).
2. In the First Name column for this record, double-click **David** to select the name, and then type **Marco**.
3. Press **TAB** twice to move to the Email column, type **m.garcia15@example.com** and then press **TAB**.
4. Close the PatientEmail query, and then open the Navigation Pane. The PatientEmail query is listed in the Queries section of the Navigation Pane. Check the Patient table to verify that the changes you made in the query datasheet are reflected in the Patient table.
5. Open the **Patient** table in Datasheet view, and then close the Navigation Pane.
6. Locate the record for PatientID 27660 (record 6). The changes you made in the query datasheet to the First Name and Email field values were made to the record in the Patient table.
7. Close the Patient table.

Kimberly also wants to review other information in the NP_AC_3_PineRidge database. She wants you to list the visit data for patients along with certain contact information about them. That means you need to select data from the Patient table and the Visit table at the same time.

Creating a Multitable Query

A multitable query is based on more than one table. If you want to create a query that retrieves data from more than one table, the tables must have a common field. Recall that the Patient (primary) and Visit (related) tables are related based on the common PatientID field included in both tables. Because of this relationship, you can create a query to display data from both tables at the same time. Specifically, Kimberly wants you to list the values in the City, FirstName, and LastName fields from the Patient table and the VisitDate and Reason fields from the Visit table.

To create the query using the Patient and Visit tables:

1. On the ribbon, click the **Create** tab.
2. In the Queries group, click the **Query Design** button. The Add Tables pane opens in the Query window. You need to add the Patient and Visit tables to the Query window.
3. Double-click **Patient** in the Tables list, double-click **Visit**, and then close the Add Tables pane. The Patient and Visit field lists appear in the Query window.
4. Resize the Patient and Visit field lists to display all the fields in each list.

   The one-to-many relationship between the two tables is shown in the Query window in the same way that a relationship between two tables is shown in the Relationships window. The join line is thick at both ends, signifying that referential integrity is enforced. If the relationship did not enforce referential integrity, the join line would be thin at both ends, and neither the "1" nor the infinity symbol would appear, even though the tables have a one-to-many relationship.

   You need to place the City, FirstName, and LastName fields (in that order) from the Patient field list into the design grid and then place the VisitDate and Reason fields from the Visit field list into the design grid. This is the order Kimberly wants you to use when listing the fields in the query results.
5. In the Patient field list, double-click **City** to place the field in the Field box of the first column in the design grid.
6. Repeat Step 5 to add the **FirstName** and **LastName** fields from the Patient table to the second and third columns of the design grid.
7. Repeat Step 5 to add the **VisitDate** and **Reason** fields (in that order) from the Visit table to the fourth and fifth columns of the design grid. The query specifications are complete, so you can now run the query.
8. In the Results group on the Query Design tab, click **Run**. The results are displayed in Datasheet view, as shown in Figure 3–9.

Figure 3–9 Datasheet for query based on the Patient and Visit tables

fields from the Patient table

VisitDate and Reason fields from the Visit table with captions displayed as column headings

Query1

City	First Name	Last Name	Date of Visit	Reason/Diagnosis
Fort Collins	Amani	Fadel	11/5/2029	Physical therapy
Fort Collins	Gregory	Johnson	11/16/2029	Knee pain follow-up visit
Windsor	Alonzo	Martinez	3/18/2030	Ankle injury
Severance	Gayle	Brown	11/7/2029	Bike accident
Eaton	Holly	Hansen	1/8/2030	Foot pain
Loveland	Marco	Garcia	3/20/2030	Hand injury
Loveland	Marco	Garcia	3/26/2030	Hand injury follow-up
Firestone	Oliver	Lopez	1/25/2030	Ankle injury
Firestone	Oliver	Lopez	3/25/2030	Cast removal
Wellington	Samuel	Anderson	3/21/2030	Arm injury
Wellington	Samuel	Anderson	4/4/2030	Arm injury follow-up
Greeley	Robert	Thompson	10/29/2029	Knee pain
Greeley	Robert	Thompson	2/14/2030	Knee pain follow-up
Laporte	Carlos	Sanchez	11/21/2029	Physical therapy
Laporte	Carlos	Sanchez	12/24/2029	Physical therapy

Only the five selected fields from the Patient and Visit tables appear in the datasheet. The records are displayed in order according to the values in the PatientID field because it is the primary key field in the primary table, even though this field is not included in the query datasheet.

Kimberly plans on frequently tracking the data retrieved by the query, so she asks you to save it as "PatientVisits."

9. On the Quick Access Toolbar, click the **Save** button. The Save As dialog box opens.
10. In the Query Name box, type **PatientVisits** and then press **ENTER**. The query is saved, and its name appears on the object tab.

Kimberly decides she wants to list the records in alphabetical order by city. Because the query displays data in order by the field values in the PatientID field, which is the primary key for the Patient table, you need to sort the records by the City field to display the data in the order Kimberly wants.

Sorting Data in a Query

To **sort** records means to rearrange them in a specified order or sequence. Sometimes you might need to sort data before displaying or printing it to meet a request. For example, Kimberly might want to review visit information arranged by the VisitDate field to find out which months are the busiest in terms of patient visits. Susan might want to view billing information arranged by the InvoiceAmt field because she monitors the finances of the center.

When you sort data in a query, you do not change the sequence of the records in the underlying tables. Only the records in the query datasheet are rearranged according to your specifications.

To sort records, you must select the **sort field**, which is the field used to determine the order of records in the datasheet. In this case, Kimberly wants to sort the data alphabetically by city, so you need to specify City as the sort field. Sort fields can be Short Text, Number, Date/Time, Currency, AutoNumber, or Yes/No fields, but not Long Text, Hyperlink, or Attachment fields. You sort records in either ascending (increasing) or descending (decreasing) order. Figure 3–10 indicates the results of each type of sort for these data types.

Figure 3–10 Sorting results for different data types

Data Type	Ascending Sort Results	Descending Sort Results
Short Text	A to Z (alphabetical)	Z to A (reverse alphabetical)
Number	Lowest to highest numeric value	Highest to lowest numeric value
Date/Time	Oldest to most recent date	Most recent to oldest date
Currency	Lowest to highest numeric value	Highest to lowest numeric value
AutoNumber	Lowest to highest numeric value	Highest to lowest numeric value
Yes/No	Yes (checkmark in check box) then No values	No then Yes values

Access provides several methods for sorting data in a table or query datasheet and in a form. One of the easiest ways is to use the AutoFilter feature for a field.

Using an AutoFilter to Sort Data

As you've probably noticed when working in Datasheet view for a table or query, each column heading has an arrow to the right of the field name. This arrow gives you access to the **AutoFilter** menu, which lists options for sorting and displaying field values. Use the first two options on the menu to sort the values in the current field in ascending or descending order. Unless you save the datasheet or form after you've sorted the records, the rearrangement of records is temporary.

> **Tip** You can also use the Ascending and Descending buttons in the Sort & Filter group on the Home tab to sort records based on the selected field in a datasheet.

Next, you'll use AutoFilter to sort the PatientVisits query results by the City field.

To sort the records using an AutoFilter:

1. Click the **arrow** on the City column heading to display the AutoFilter menu, shown in Figure 3–11.

Figure 3–11 Using AutoFilter to sort records in the datasheet

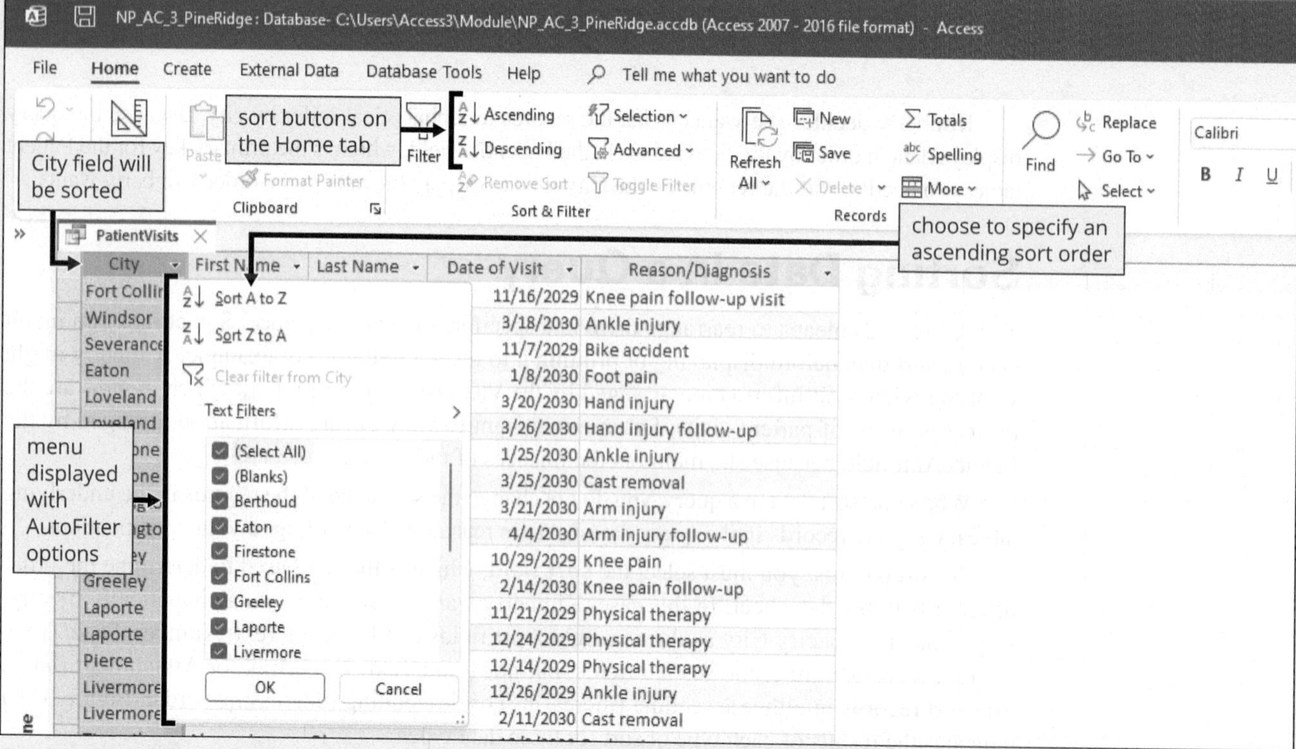

Kimberly wants you to sort the data in ascending (alphabetical) order by the values in the City field, so you need to select the first option in the menu.

2. Click **Sort A to Z**. The records are rearranged in ascending alphabetical order by city. A small, upward-pointing arrow appears on the right side of the City column heading. This arrow indicates that the values in the field are sorted in ascending order. If you used the same method to sort the field values in descending order, a small downward-pointing arrow would appear instead.

After viewing the query results, Kimberly asks you to also arrange the records by the values in the VisitDate field, so that the data is presented in chronological order for each city. She still wants the records arranged by the City field values as well. To produce the results Kimberly wants, you need to sort using two fields.

Sorting on Multiple Fields in Design View

Sort fields can be unique or nonunique. A sort field is **unique** if the value in the sort field for each record is different. The PatientID field in the Patient table is an example of a unique sort field because each patient record has a different value in this primary key field. A sort field is **nonunique** if more than one record can have the same value for the sort field. For example, the City field in the Patient table is a nonunique sort field because more than one record can have the same City value.

> **Tip** The primary sort field is different from a table's primary key. A table has at most one primary key, which must be unique, whereas any field in a table can serve as a primary sort field.

When the sort field is nonunique, records with the same sort field value are grouped together, but they are not sorted in any order within the group. To arrange these grouped records in a specific order, you can use a **secondary sort field**, which is a second field that determines the order of records that are already sorted by the **primary sort field** (the first sort field specified).

In Access, you can select up to 10 sort fields. When you use the buttons on the ribbon to sort by more than one field, the sort fields must be in adjacent columns in the datasheet. (You cannot use an AutoFilter to sort on more than one field. This method works for a single field only.) You can specify only one type of sort—either ascending or descending—for the selected columns in the datasheet. You select the adjacent columns, and Access sorts first by the first column and then by each remaining selected column in order from left to right.

Kimberly wants you to sort the records first by the City field values, as they currently are, and then by the VisitDate values. The two fields are in the correct left-to-right order in the query datasheet, but they are not adjacent, so you cannot use the Ascending and Descending buttons on the ribbon to sort them. You could move the City field to the left of the VisitDate field in the query datasheet, but both columns would have to be sorted in the same sort order. This is not what Kimberly wants. She wants the City field values sorted in ascending order so that they are in the correct alphabetical order, for ease of reference. She also wants the VisitDate field values to be sorted in descending order, so that she can focus on the most recent patient visits first. To sort the City and VisitDate fields with different sort orders, you must set the sort fields in Design view.

In the Query window in Design view, you must arrange the fields you want to sort from left to right in the design grid, with the primary sort field being the leftmost. In Design view, multiple sort fields do not have to be adjacent to each other, as they do in Datasheet view; however, they must be in the correct left-to-right order.

Reference

Sorting a Query Datasheet

- In the query datasheet, click the arrow on the column heading for the field you want to sort.
- On the AutoFilter menu, click Sort A to Z for an ascending sort, or click Sort Z to A for a descending sort.

or

- In the query datasheet, select the column or adjacent columns on which you want to sort.
- In the Sort & Filter group on the Home tab, click the Ascending button or the Descending button.

or

- In Design view, position the fields serving as sort fields from left to right.
- Click the right side of the Sort box for each field you want to sort, and then click Ascending or Descending for the sort order.

To achieve the results Kimberly wants, you need to modify the query in Design view to specify the sort order for the two fields.

To select the two sort fields in Design view:

1. On the Home tab, in the Views group, click the **View** button to open the query in Design view. The fields are currently in the correct left-to-right order in the design grid, so you only need to specify the sort order for the two fields.

   First, you need to specify an ascending sort order for the City field. Even though the records are already sorted by the values in this field, you need to modify the query so that this sort order and the one you specify for the VisitDate field are part of the query's design. Any time the query is run, the records are sorted according to these specifications.

   Tip In Design view, the sort fields do not have to be adjacent, and fields that are not sorted can appear between the sort fields.

2. Click the right side of the **City Sort** box to display the arrow and the sort options, and then click **Ascending** to select an ascending sort order for the City field, which is the primary sort field. The City field is a Short Text field, and an ascending sort order will display the field values in alphabetical order.
3. Click the right side of the **VisitDate Sort** box, click **Descending**, and then click in an empty box below the VisitDate field to deselect the setting. The descending sort order for the VisitDate field is the secondary sort field because it appears to the right of the primary sort field (City) in the design grid. The VisitDate field is a Date/Time field, and a descending sort order will display the field values with the most recent dates first. Compare your query grid to Figure 3–12.

Figure 3–12 Selecting two sort fields in Design view

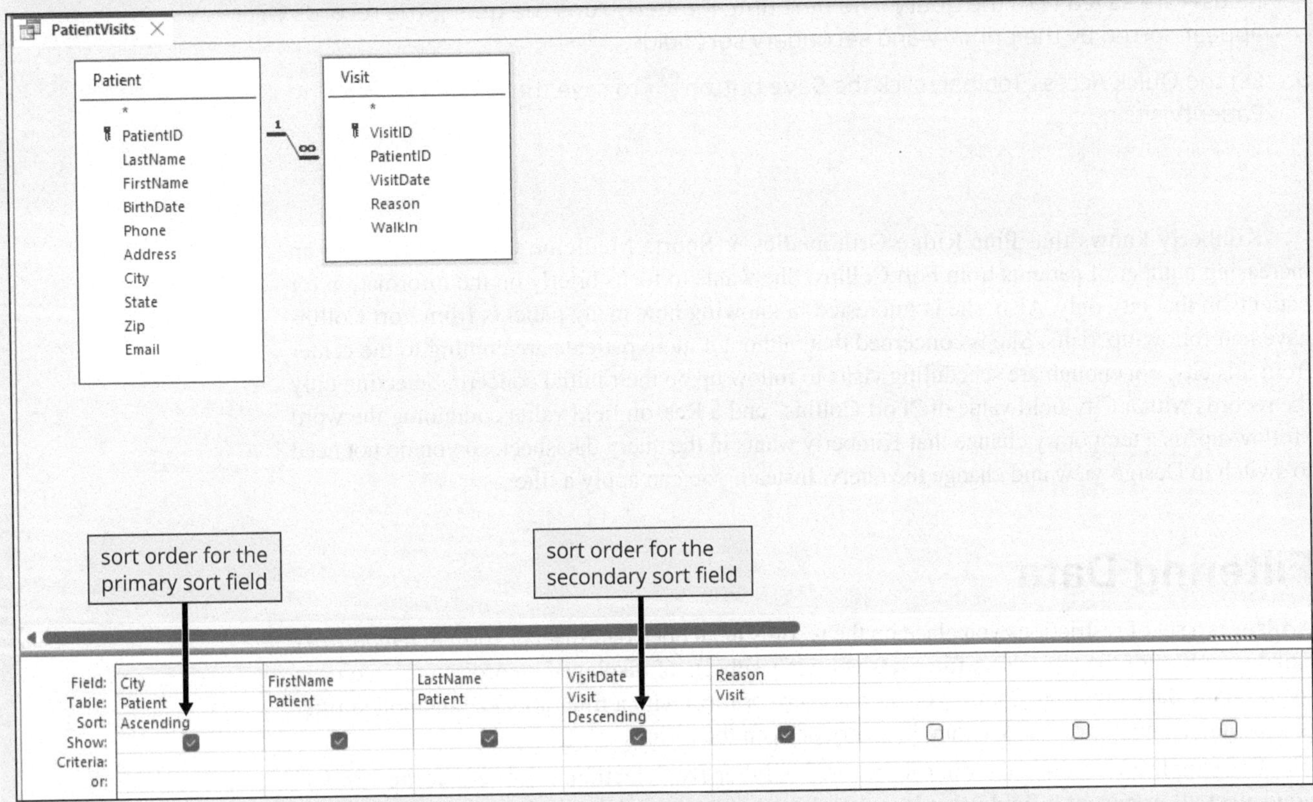

You have finished your query changes, so you can run the query and then save the modified query with the same name.

4. On the Query Design tab, in the Results group, click **Run**. After the query runs, the records appear in the query datasheet in ascending order based on the values in the City field. Within groups of records with the same City field value, the records appear in descending order by the values of the VisitDate field. See Figure 3–13.

Figure 3–13 Datasheet sorted on two fields

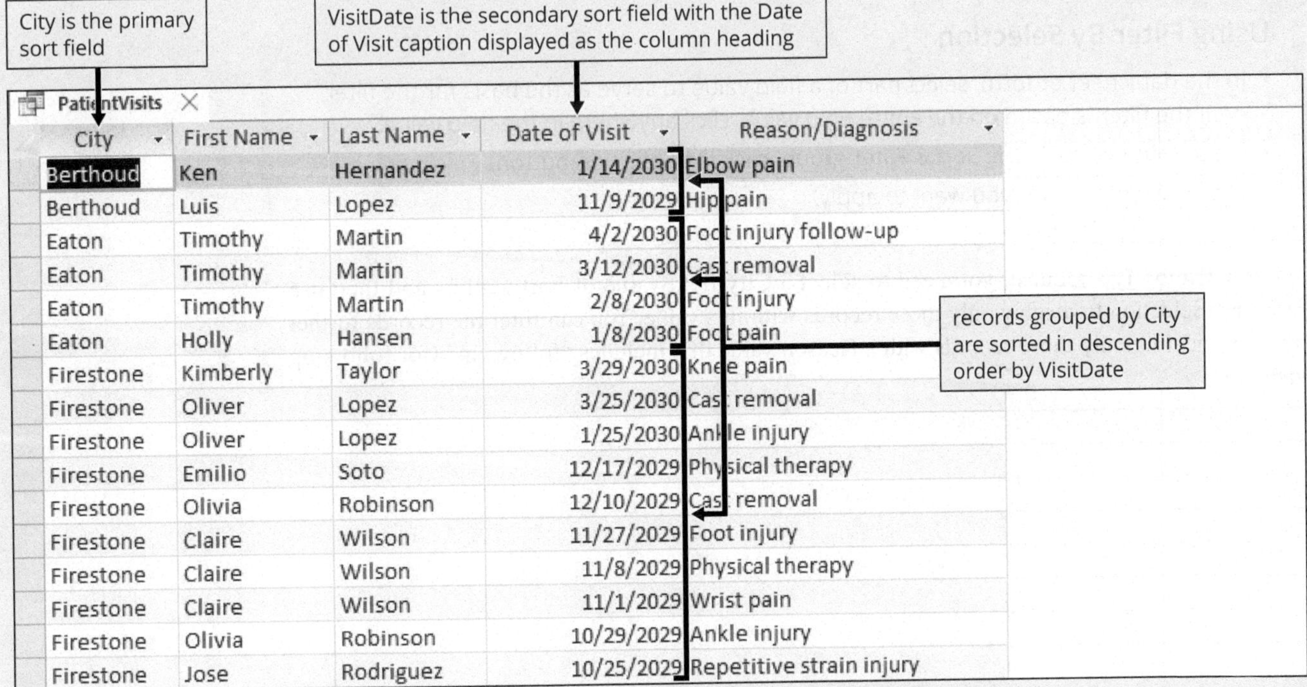

City	First Name	Last Name	Date of Visit	Reason/Diagnosis
Berthoud	Ken	Hernandez	1/14/2030	Elbow pain
Berthoud	Luis	Lopez	11/9/2029	Hip pain
Eaton	Timothy	Martin	4/2/2030	Foot injury follow-up
Eaton	Timothy	Martin	3/12/2030	Cast removal
Eaton	Timothy	Martin	2/8/2030	Foot injury
Eaton	Holly	Hansen	1/8/2030	Foot pain
Firestone	Kimberly	Taylor	3/29/2030	Knee pain
Firestone	Oliver	Lopez	3/25/2030	Cast removal
Firestone	Oliver	Lopez	1/25/2030	Ankle injury
Firestone	Emilio	Soto	12/17/2029	Physical therapy
Firestone	Olivia	Robinson	12/10/2029	Cast removal
Firestone	Claire	Wilson	11/27/2029	Foot injury
Firestone	Claire	Wilson	11/8/2029	Physical therapy
Firestone	Claire	Wilson	11/1/2029	Wrist pain
Firestone	Olivia	Robinson	10/29/2029	Ankle injury
Firestone	Jose	Rodriguez	10/25/2029	Repetitive strain injury

When you save the query, all your design changes—including the selection of the sort fields—are saved with the query. The next time Kimberly runs the query, the records will appear sorted by the primary and secondary sort fields.

5. On the Quick Access Toolbar, click the **Save** button to save the revised PatientVisits query.

Kimberly knows that Pine Ridge Orthopedics & Sports Medicine Center is treating an increasing number of patients from Fort Collins. She wants to focus briefly on the information for patients in that city only. Also, she is interested in knowing how many patients from Fort Collins have had follow-up visits. She is concerned that, although more patients are coming to the center from this city, not enough are scheduling visits to follow up on their initial concern. Selecting only the records with a City field value of "Fort Collins" and a Reason field value containing the word "follow-up" is a temporary change that Kimberly wants in the query datasheet, so you do not need to switch to Design view and change the query. Instead, you can apply a filter.

Filtering Data

A **filter** is a set of restrictions you place on the records in an open datasheet or form to *temporarily* isolate a subset of the records. A filter lets you view subsets of displayed records so that you can focus on the data you need. Unless you save a query or form with a filter applied, an applied filter is not available the next time you run the query or open the form.

The simplest technique for filtering records is Filter By Selection. **Filter By Selection** lets you select all or part of a field value in a datasheet or form and then display only those records that contain the selected value in the field. You can also use the AutoFilter feature to filter records. When you click the arrow on a column heading, the AutoFilter menu provides options for filtering the datasheet based on a field value or the selected part of a field value. Another technique for filtering records is to use **Filter By Form**, which changes your datasheet to display blank fields. You can select a value using the arrow in a blank field to apply a filter that selects only those records containing the selected value.

Reference

Using Filter By Selection

- In the datasheet or form, select part of a field value to serve as the basis for the filter; or, if the filter is based on the entire field value, click anywhere in the field value.
- On the Home tab, in the Sort & Filter group, click the Selection button.
- Click the type of filter you want to apply.

For Kimberly's request, you need to select a City field value of Fort Collins and then use Filter By Selection to display only those records with this value. You can filter the records further by also selecting only those records with a Reason value that includes "follow-up" (for follow-up visits).

To display the records using Filter By Selection:

1. In the query datasheet, locate the first occurrence of a City field containing the value **Fort Collins**, scroll to display the record at the top of the datasheet, and then click anywhere in that field value.
2. On the Home tab, in the Sort & Filter group, click the **Selection** button. A menu opens with options for the type of filter to apply, as shown in Figure 3–14.

Figure 3–14 Using Filter By Selection

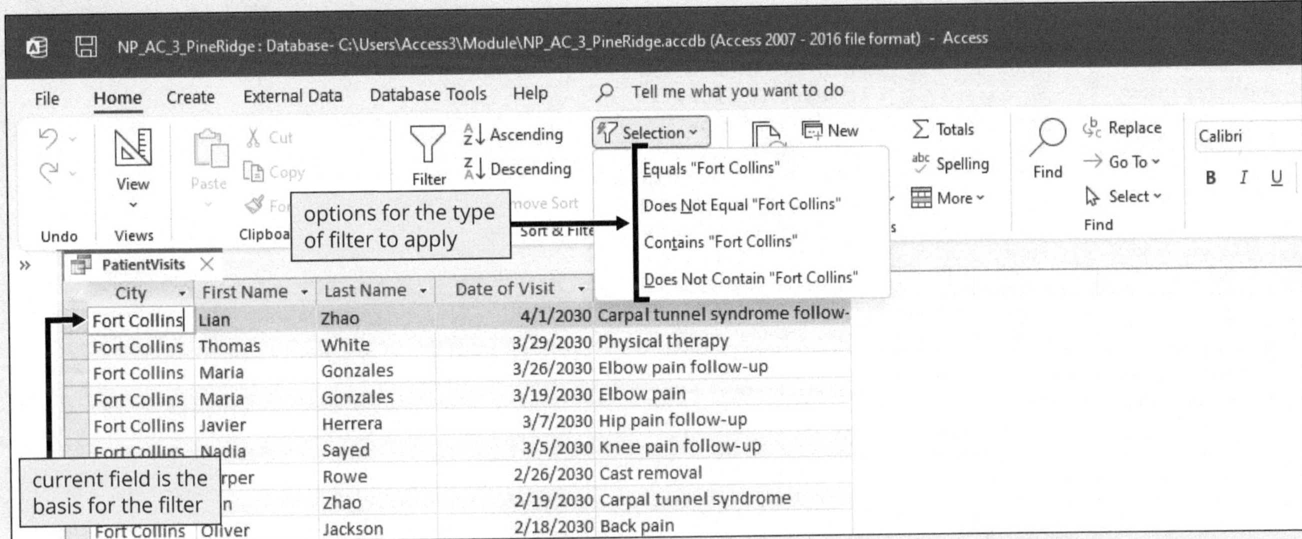

The menu provides options for displaying only those records with a City field value that equals the selected value (in this case, Fort Collins), records with a City field value that does not equal the selected value, records containing the value somewhere in the field, and records that do not contain the value in the field. You want to display all the records whose City field value equals Fort Collins.

3. On the Selection menu, click **Equals "Fort Collins"**. Only the 19 records that have a City field value of Fort Collins appear in the datasheet, as shown in Figure 3–15.

Figure 3–15 Datasheet after applying filter

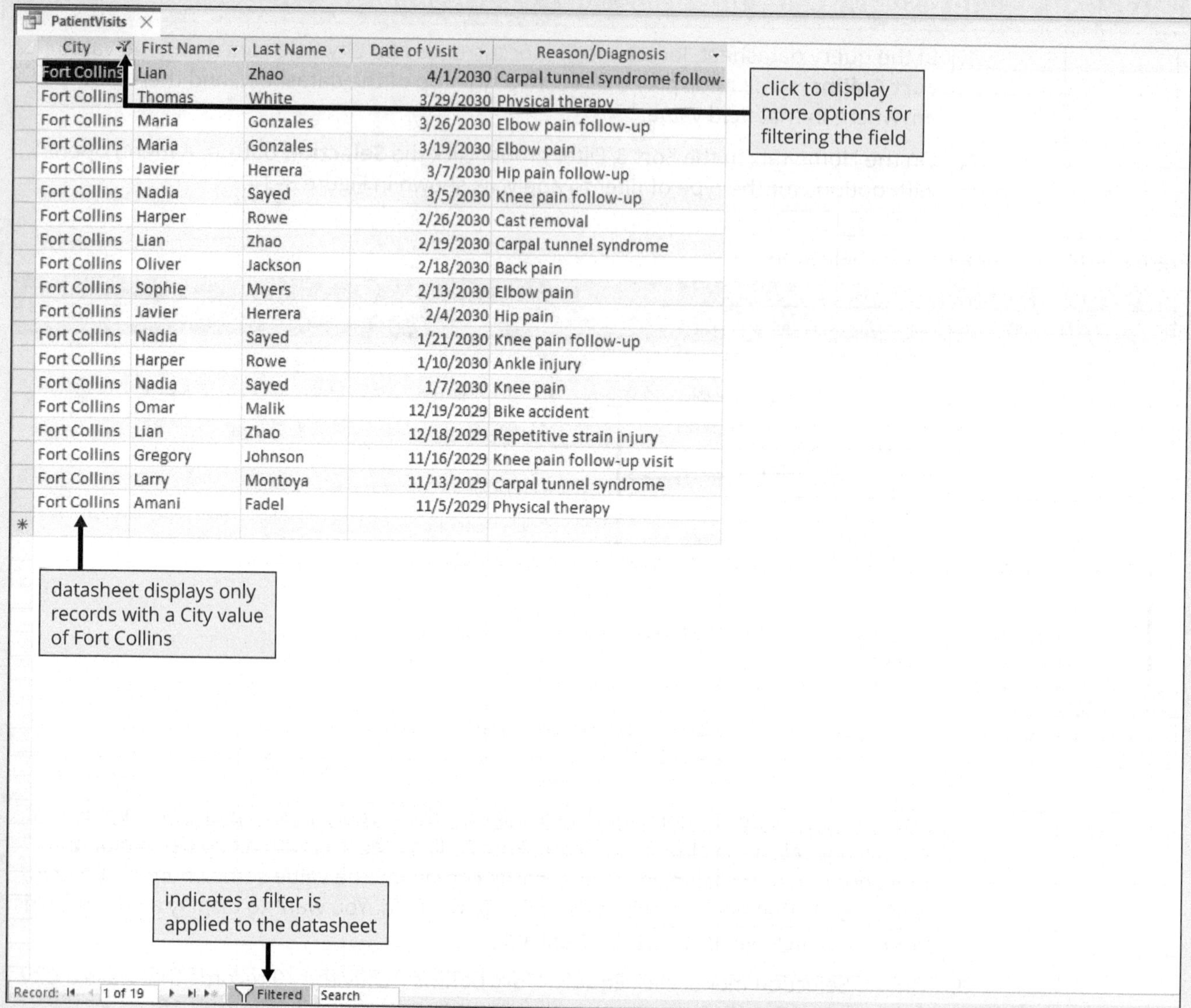

PatientVisits

City	First Name	Last Name	Date of Visit	Reason/Diagnosis
Fort Collins	Lian	Zhao	4/1/2030	Carpal tunnel syndrome follow-
Fort Collins	Thomas	White	3/29/2030	Physical therapy
Fort Collins	Maria	Gonzales	3/26/2030	Elbow pain follow-up
Fort Collins	Maria	Gonzales	3/19/2030	Elbow pain
Fort Collins	Javier	Herrera	3/7/2030	Hip pain follow-up
Fort Collins	Nadia	Sayed	3/5/2030	Knee pain follow-up
Fort Collins	Harper	Rowe	2/26/2030	Cast removal
Fort Collins	Lian	Zhao	2/19/2030	Carpal tunnel syndrome
Fort Collins	Oliver	Jackson	2/18/2030	Back pain
Fort Collins	Sophie	Myers	2/13/2030	Elbow pain
Fort Collins	Javier	Herrera	2/4/2030	Hip pain
Fort Collins	Nadia	Sayed	1/21/2030	Knee pain follow-up
Fort Collins	Harper	Rowe	1/10/2030	Ankle injury
Fort Collins	Nadia	Sayed	1/7/2030	Knee pain
Fort Collins	Omar	Malik	12/19/2029	Bike accident
Fort Collins	Lian	Zhao	12/18/2029	Repetitive strain injury
Fort Collins	Gregory	Johnson	11/16/2029	Knee pain follow-up visit
Fort Collins	Larry	Montoya	11/13/2029	Carpal tunnel syndrome
Fort Collins	Amani	Fadel	11/5/2029	Physical therapy

The button labeled "Filtered" to the right of the navigation bar indicates a filter is applied to the datasheet, as does the notation "Filtered" on the status bar. The Toggle Filter button in the Sort & Filter group on the Home tab is also active. You can click this button or the Filtered button next to the navigation bar to toggle between the filtered and unfiltered displays of the query datasheet. The City column heading also has a filter icon. You can click this icon to display additional options for filtering the field.

Next, Kimberly wants to list only those records with a Reason field value containing the word "follow-up" so she can review the records for follow-up visits. You need to apply an additional filter to the datasheet.

4. In any Reason field value containing the word "follow-up," select only the text **follow-up**.
5. In the Sort & Filter group, click the **Selection** button. Similar filter types are available for this selection as when you filtered the City field.
6. On the Selection menu, click **Contains "follow-up"**. The second filter is applied to the query datasheet, which now shows only the six records for patients from Fort Collins who have had a follow-up visit at the center.

   Now you can redisplay all the query records by clicking the Toggle Filter button, which you use to switch between the filtered and unfiltered displays.

7. In the Sort & Filter group, click the **Toggle Filter** button. The filter is removed, and all 84 records appear in the query datasheet.

   Tip The ScreenTip for this button is Remove Filter.

8. Close the PatientVisits query. A dialog box asks if you want to save your changes to the design of the query—in this case, the filtered display, which is still available through the Toggle Filter button. Kimberly does not want to save the query with the filter because she doesn't need to view the filtered information regularly.
9. Click **No** to close the query without saving the changes.
10. If you are not continuing to Part 3.2, click the **File** tab, and then click **Close** in the navigation bar to close the NP_AC_3_PineRidge database.

Part 3.1 Quick Check

1. In Datasheet view, what is the difference between navigation mode and edit mode?
2. What command can you use in Datasheet view to remove the display of one or more fields from the datasheet? How can you redisplay it?
3. What command can you use in Datasheet view to locate all or part of a field value?
4. What information does Access need to create a select query?
5. Describe the field list and the design grid in the Query window in Design view.
6. How are a table datasheet and a query datasheet similar? How are they different?
7. What do you call the field you use to determine the order of sorted records in a datasheet?
8. When you sort query fields in Design view, describe how the sort fields must be positioned in the design grid.
9. Which feature lets you select all or part of a field value in a datasheet and display only those records that contain the selected value in the field?

Part 3.2 Visual Overview: Selection Criteria in Queries

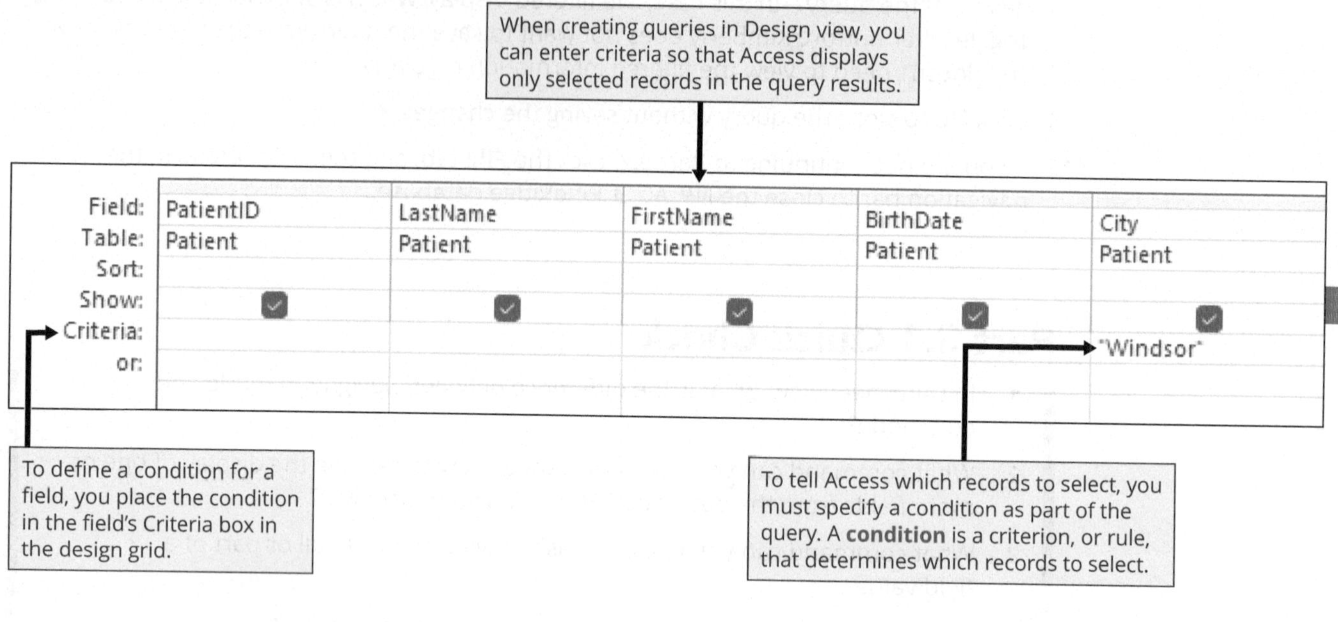
When creating queries in Design view, you can enter criteria so that Access displays only selected records in the query results.
Field: PatientID LastName FirstName BirthDate City
Table: Patient Patient Patient Patient Patient
Sort:
Show:
Criteria:
or:
"Windsor"
To define a condition for a field, you place the condition in the field's Criteria box in the design grid.
To tell Access which records to select, you must specify a condition as part of the query. A **condition** is a criterion, or rule, that determines which records to select.

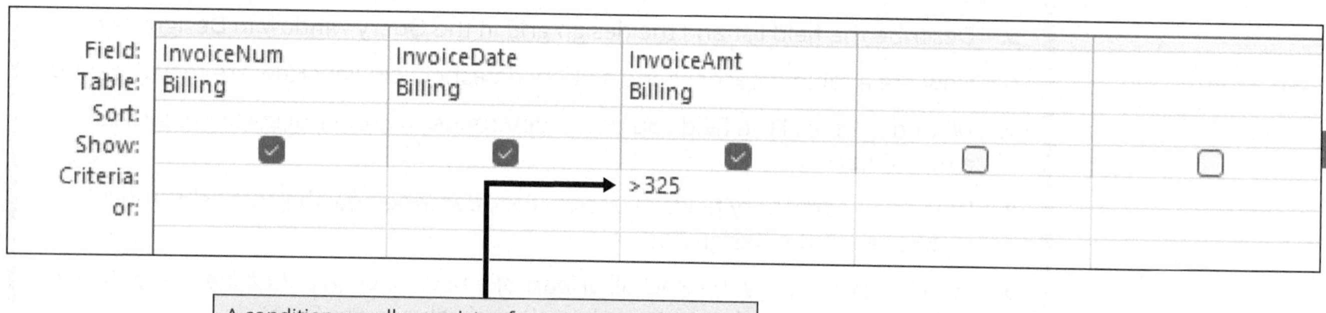
Field: InvoiceNum InvoiceDate InvoiceAmt
Table: Billing Billing Billing
Sort:
Show:
Criteria:
or:
>325
A condition usually consists of an operator, often a comparison operator, and a value. A **comparison operator** asks Access to compare the value to the condition value and to select all the records for which the condition is true.

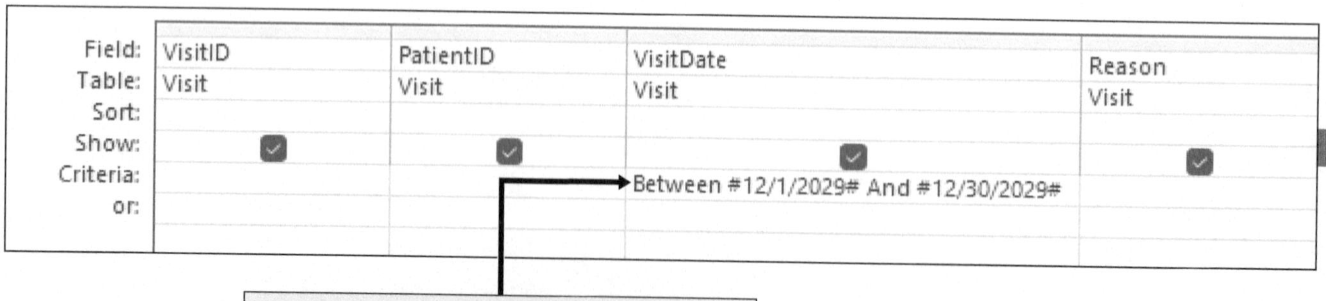
Field: VisitID PatientID VisitDate Reason
Table: Visit Visit Visit Visit
Sort:
Show:
Criteria:
or:
Between #12/1/2029# And #12/30/2029#
Most comparison operators (such as Between ... And ...) ask Access to select records that match a range of values for the condition—in this case, all records with dates that fall within the range shown.

The results of a query containing selection criteria include only the records that meet the specified criteria.

WindsorPatients

Patient ID	Last Name	First Name	Date of Birth	City
27654	Martinez	Alonzo	5/17/1959	Windsor
27687	Garcia	Sofia	4/18/1996	Windsor
27696	Brown	Natalie	11/27/1965	Windsor
27730	Chavez	Roberto	9/22/1990	Windsor
*				

The results of this query show only patients from Windsor because the condition "Windsor" in the City field's Criteria box specifies that Access should select only records with City field values of Windsor. This type of condition is called an **exact match** because the value in the specified field must match the condition exactly to include the record in the query results.

LargeInvoiceAmts

Invoice Num	Invoice Date	Invoice Amt
15214	10/30/2029	$350.00
15261	11/28/2029	$350.00
15298	12/27/2029	$350.00
15334	01/11/2030	$350.00
15354	01/28/2030	$350.00
15373	02/11/2030	$350.00
15382	02/15/2030	$475.00
15398	02/26/2030	$350.00
15441	03/19/2030	$350.00
15454	03/22/2030	$350.00
15470	03/27/2030	$475.00
*		$0.00

The results of this query show only those invoices with amounts greater than $325 because the condition >325, which uses the greater than comparison operator, specifies that Access should select only records with InvoiceAmt field values over $325.

DecemberVisits

Visit ID	Patient ID	Date of Visit	Reason/Diagnosis
3166	27674	12/3/2029	Back pain
3167	27676	12/6/2029	Back pain follow-up visit
3169	27717	12/10/2029	Cast removal
3170	27669	12/14/2029	Physical therapy
3171	27681	12/17/2029	Physical therapy
3173	27736	12/18/2029	Repetitive strain injury
3174	27742	12/19/2029	Bike accident
3176	27740	12/21/2029	Back pain
3178	27667	12/24/2029	Physical therapy
3179	27671	12/26/2029	Ankle injury
3182	27674	12/27/2029	Physical therapy
3183	27728	12/28/2029	Knee pain
*			

The results of this query show only those patient visits that took place in December 2029 because the condition in the VisitDate's Criteria box specifies that Access should select only records with a visit date between 12/1/2029 and 12/31/2029.

Defining Record Selection Criteria for Queries

Susan wants to display patient and visit information for all patients who live in Firestone. She is considering having the center hold an orthopedic awareness event in Firestone, so she wants to know more about patients from this city. For this request, you could create a query to select the correct fields and all records in the Patient and Visit tables, select a City field value of Firestone in the query datasheet, and then click the Selection button and choose the appropriate filter option to display the information for only those patients in Firestone. However, a faster way of retrieving the data Susan needs is to create a query that displays the selected fields and only those records in the Patient and Visit tables that satisfy a condition.

Just as you can display selected fields from a database in a query datasheet, you can display selected records. To identify which records you want to select, you must specify a condition as part of the query, as illustrated in the Part 3.2 Visual Overview. A condition usually includes one of the comparison operators shown in Figure 3–16.

Figure 3–16 Access comparison operators

Operator	Meaning	Example
=	Equal to (optional; default operator)	="Cruz"
<>	Not equal to	<>"Cruz"
<	Less than	<#1/1/29#
<=	Less than or equal to	<=100
>	Greater than	>"C400"
>=	Greater than or equal to	>=18.75
Between ... And ...	Between two values (inclusive)	Between 50 And 325
In ()	In a list of values	In ("Cruz", "Chang")
Like	Matches a pattern that includes wildcards	Like "970*"

Specifying an Exact Match

For Susan's request, you need to first create a query that displays only those records in the Patient table with the value Firestone in the City field. This type of condition is an exact match because the value in the specified field must match the condition exactly to include the record in the query results. You'll create the query in Design view.

To create the query in Design view:

1. If you took a break after Part 3.1, make sure that the NP_AC_3_PineRidge database is open and the Navigation Pane is closed. On the ribbon, click the **Create** tab.
2. In the Queries group, click the **Query Design** button. The Add Tables pane opens. You need to add the Patient and Visit tables to the Query window.
3. Double-click **Patient** in the Tables list, double-click **Visit**, and then close the Add Tables pane. The field lists for the Patient and Visit tables appear in the top portion of the window, and a join line indicating a one-to-many relationship connects the tables.
4. Resize both field lists to display all the fields.
5. Add the following fields from the Patient table to the design grid in this order: **LastName**, **FirstName**, **Phone**, **Address**, **City**, and **Email**.

   Susan also wants you to include information from the Visit table in the query results.
6. Add the following fields from the Visit table to the design grid in this order: **VisitID**, **VisitDate**, and **Reason**, as shown in Figure 3–17.

Figure 3–17 Design grid after adding fields from both tables

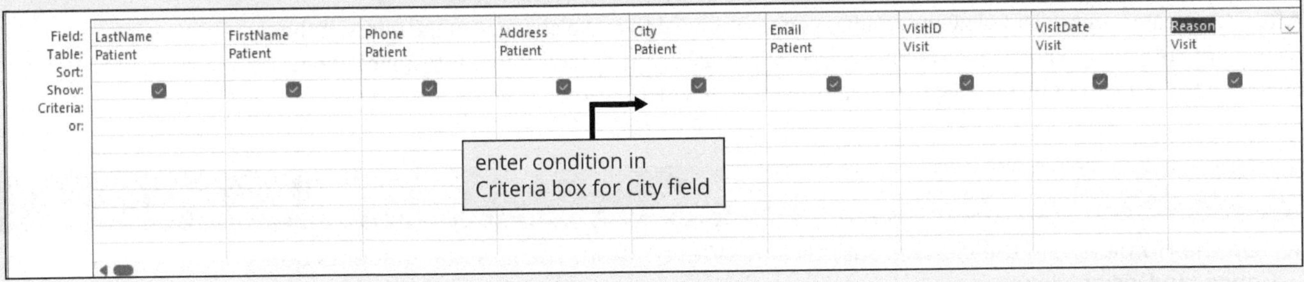

To display the information Susan wants, you need to enter the condition for the City field in its Criteria box, as shown in Figure 3–17. Susan wants you to display only those records with a City field value of Firestone.

To enter the exact match condition, and then save and run the query:

1. Click the **City Criteria** box, type **Firestone**, and then press **ENTER**. The condition changes to "Firestone".
   Access enclosed the condition you typed in quotation marks. You must enclose text values in quotation marks when using them as selection criteria. If you omit the quotation marks, however, Access includes them automatically in most cases. Some words—including "in" and "select"—are special keywords in Access that are reserved for functions and commands. If you want to enter one of these keywords as the condition, you must type the quotation marks around the text, or an error message appears indicating the condition cannot be entered.
2. Save the query using **FirestonePatients** as the name. The query is saved, and its name is displayed on the object tab.
3. Run the query. It displays only those records with a City field value of Firestone. Ten records are selected and displayed in the datasheet. See Figure 3–18.

Figure 3–18 Datasheet displaying selected fields and records

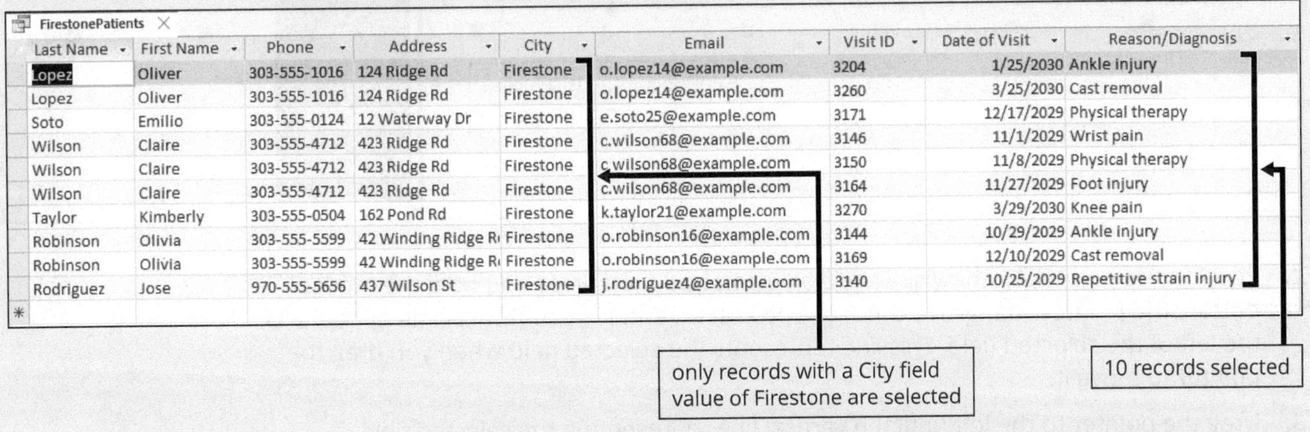

Last Name	First Name	Phone	Address	City	Email	Visit ID	Date of Visit	Reason/Diagnosis
Lopez	Oliver	303-555-1016	124 Ridge Rd	Firestone	o.lopez14@example.com	3204	1/25/2030	Ankle injury
Lopez	Oliver	303-555-1016	124 Ridge Rd	Firestone	o.lopez14@example.com	3260	3/25/2030	Cast removal
Soto	Emilio	303-555-0124	12 Waterway Dr	Firestone	e.soto25@example.com	3171	12/17/2029	Physical therapy
Wilson	Claire	303-555-4712	423 Ridge Rd	Firestone	c.wilson68@example.com	3146	11/1/2029	Wrist pain
Wilson	Claire	303-555-4712	423 Ridge Rd	Firestone	c.wilson68@example.com	3150	11/8/2029	Physical therapy
Wilson	Claire	303-555-4712	423 Ridge Rd	Firestone	c.wilson68@example.com	3164	11/27/2029	Foot injury
Taylor	Kimberly	303-555-0504	162 Pond Rd	Firestone	k.taylor21@example.com	3270	3/29/2030	Knee pain
Robinson	Olivia	303-555-5599	42 Winding Ridge R	Firestone	o.robinson16@example.com	3144	10/29/2029	Ankle injury
Robinson	Olivia	303-555-5599	42 Winding Ridge R	Firestone	o.robinson16@example.com	3169	12/10/2029	Cast removal
Rodriguez	Jose	970-555-5656	437 Wilson St	Firestone	j.rodriguez4@example.com	3140	10/25/2029	Repetitive strain injury

Susan realizes that it's not necessary to include the City field values in the query results. The name of the query, FirestonePatients, indicates that the query design includes all patients who live in Firestone, so the City field values are unnecessary and repetitive in the query results. Also, she prefers that the query datasheet show the fields from the Visit table first, followed by the Patient table fields. You need to modify the query to produce the results Susan wants.

Modifying a Query

After you create a query and view the results, you might need to make changes to the query if the results are not what you expect or require. First, Susan asks you to modify the FirestonePatients query so that it does not display the City field values in the query results.

To remove the display of the City field values:

1. On the Home tab, in the Views group, click the **View** button. The FirestonePatients query opens in Design view.

   You need to keep the City field as part of the query design because it contains the defined condition for the query. You only need to remove the display of the field's values from the query results.

2. Click the **City Show** check box to remove the checkmark. The query will still find only those records with the value Firestone in the City field, but the query results will not display these field values.

Next, you need to change the order of the fields in the query so that the visit information is listed first.

To move the Visit table fields to precede the Patient table fields:

1. Position the pointer on the VisitID field selector until the selection pointer appears ⬇, and then click to select the field. See Figure 3–19.

Figure 3–19 Selected VisitID field

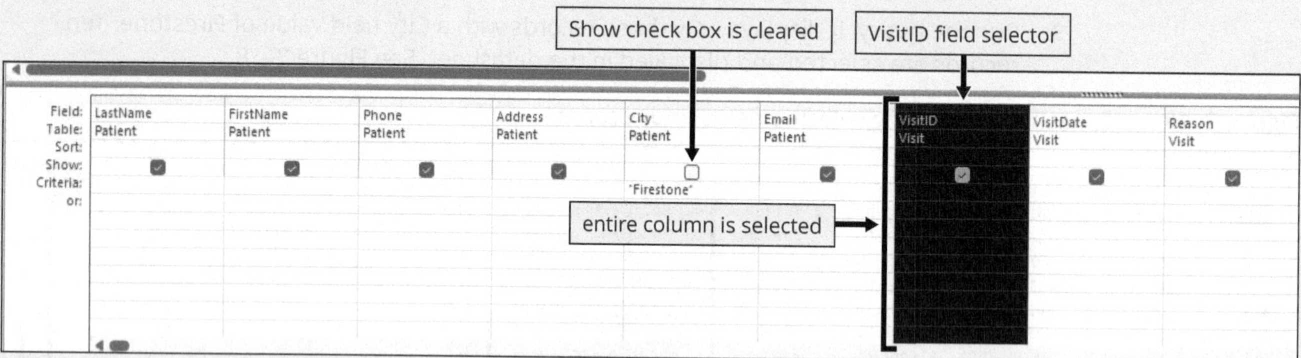

2. Position the pointer on the VisitID field selector, and then press and hold the mouse button; the pointer changes to the move pointer, and a black vertical line appears to the left of the selected field. This line represents the selected field when you drag the pointer to move it.
3. Drag the pointer to the left until the vertical line representing the selected field is positioned to the left of the LastName field. See Figure 3–20.

Figure 3–20 Dragging the field in the design grid

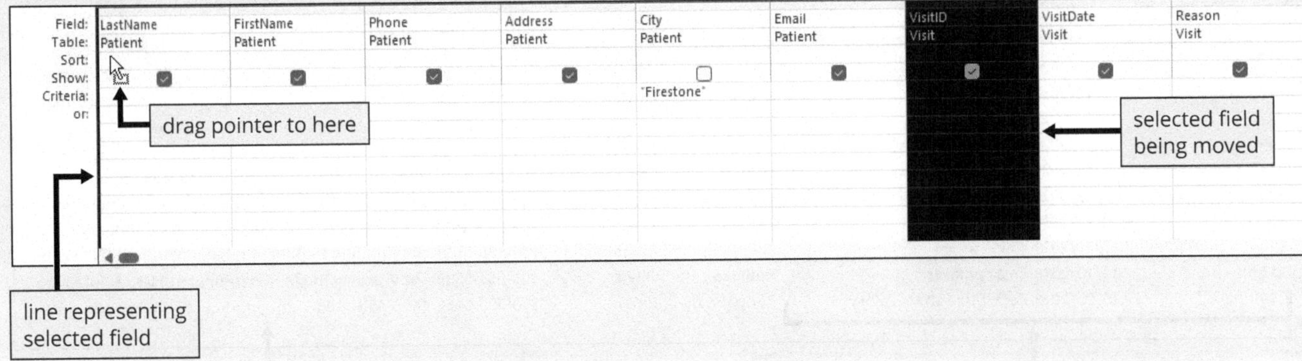

4. Release the mouse button. The VisitID field moves to the left of the LastName field.

   Tip Instead of moving a field by dragging, you can also delete the field and then insert it in the design grid where you want.

   You can also select and move multiple fields at once. You need to select and move the VisitDate and Reason fields so that they follow the VisitID field in the query design. To select multiple fields, you click and drag the pointer over the field selectors for the fields you want.

5. Click and hold the selection pointer ⬇ on the VisitDate field selector, drag the pointer to the right to select the Reason field, and then release the mouse button. Both fields are now selected. See Figure 3–21.

Figure 3–21 Multiple fields selected to be moved

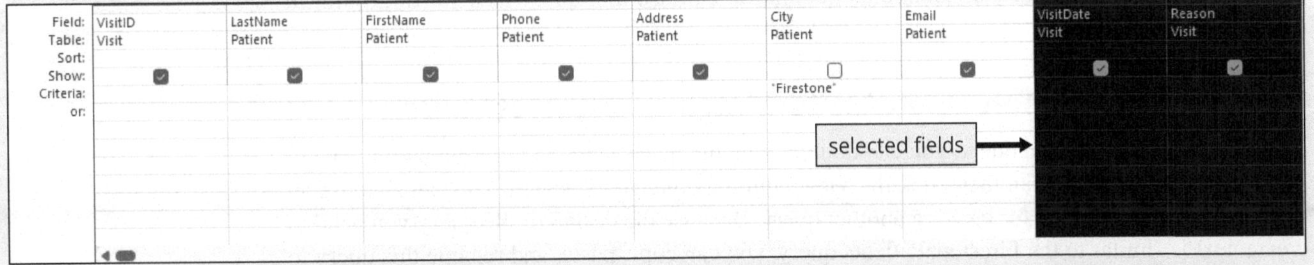

6. Position the arrow pointer on the field selector for either of the two selected fields, press and hold the mouse button, and then drag to the left until the vertical line representing the selected fields is positioned to the left of the LastName field.

7. Release the mouse button. The three fields from the Visit table are now the first three fields in the query design grid.

   You have finished modifying the query as Susan requested, so you can run the query.

8. Run the query. The results of the modified query are displayed, as shown in Figure 3–22.

Figure 3–22 Results of the modified query

FirestonePatients

Visit ID	Date of Visit	Reason/Diagnosis	Last Name	First Name	Phone	Address	Email
3204	1/25/2030	Ankle injury	Lopez	Oliver	303-555-1016	124 Ridge Rd	o.lopez14@example.com
3260	3/25/2030	Cast removal	Lopez	Oliver	303-555-1016	124 Ridge Rd	o.lopez14@example.com
3171	12/17/2029	Physical therapy	Soto	Emilio	303-555-0124	12 Waterway Dr	e.soto25@example.com
3146	11/1/2029	Wrist pain	Wilson	Claire	303-555-4712	423 Ridge Rd	c.wilson68@example.com
3150	11/8/2029	Physical therapy	Wilson	Claire	303-555-4712	423 Ridge Rd	c.wilson68@example.com
3164	11/27/2029	Foot injury	Wilson	Claire	303-555-4712	423 Ridge Rd	c.wilson68@example.com
3270	3/29/2030	Knee pain	Taylor	Kimberly	303-555-0504	162 Pond Rd	k.taylor21@example.com
3144	10/29/2029	Ankle injury	Robinson	Olivia	303-555-5599	42 Winding Ridge R	o.robinson16@example.com
3169	12/10/2029	Cast removal	Robinson	Olivia	303-555-5599	42 Winding Ridge R	o.robinson16@example.com
3140	10/25/2029	Repetitive strain injury	Rodriguez	Jose	970-555-5656	437 Wilson St	j.rodriguez4@example.com

fields from the Visit table are listed first in the query datasheet

City field values are no longer displayed

Note that the City field values are no longer displayed in the query results.

9. Save and close the FirestonePatients query.

After viewing the query results, Susan asks you to produce a list with the same fields, but only for those records with a VisitDate field value before 1/1/2030. She wants to identify patients of Pine Ridge Orthopedics who have not been to the center recently, so that her staff can follow up with the patients by sending them reminder messages. To create the query that produces the results Susan wants, you need to use a comparison operator to match a range of values—in this case, any VisitDate value less than 1/1/2030. Because this new query will include information from several of the same fields as the FirestonePatients query, you can use that query as a starting point in designing the new query.

Using a Comparison Operator to Match a Range of Values

After you create and save a query, you can double-click the query name in the Navigation Pane to run the query again. You can then click the View button to change its design. You can also use an existing query as the basis for creating another query. Because the design of the query you need to create next is similar to the FirestonePatients query, you can copy, paste, and rename this query to create the new query. Using this approach keeps the FirestonePatients query intact.

To create the new query by copying the FirestonePatients query:

1. Open the Navigation Pane. The FirestonePatients query is listed in the Queries section.

   You use the shortcut menu to copy the FirestonePatients query and paste it in the Navigation Pane. You can then give the copied query a different name.

2. In the Queries section of the Navigation Pane, right-click **FirestonePatients** to select it and display the shortcut menu.
3. Click **Copy** on the shortcut menu.
4. Right-click the empty area near the bottom of the Navigation Pane, and then click **Paste** on the shortcut menu. The Paste As dialog box opens with the text "Copy Of FirestonePatients" in the Query Name box. Because Susan wants the new query to show data for patients that have not visited the center recently, you'll use "EarlierVisits" as the query name.
5. In the Query Name box, type **EarlierVisits** and then press **ENTER**. The new query appears in the Queries section of the Navigation Pane.

6. Double-click the **EarlierVisits** query to open, or run, the query. The design of this query is currently the same as the original FirestonePatients query.
7. Close the Navigation Pane.

Next, you open the query in Design view and modify its design to produce the results Susan wants—to display records for patients with VisitDate field values that are earlier than, or less than, 1/1/2030.

To modify the design of the new query:

1. Display the EarlierVisits query in Design view.
2. Click the **VisitDate Criteria** box, type **<1/1/2030** and then press **TAB**. Access automatically encloses the date criteria with number signs. The condition specifies that a record will be selected only if its VisitDate field value is less than (earlier than) 1/1/2030. Compare your screen to Figure 3–23.

Figure 3–23 Criteria entered for the VisitDate field

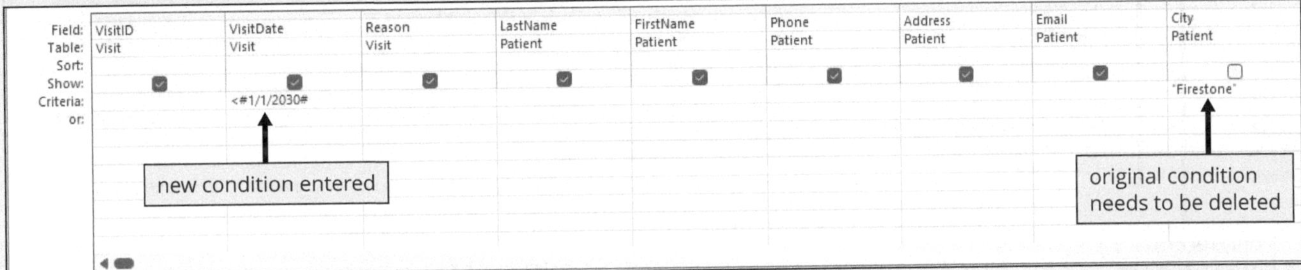

Before you run the query, you need to delete the condition for the City field. Recall that the City field is part of the query, but its values are not displayed in the query results. When you modified the query to remove the City field values from the query results, Access moved the field to the end of the design grid. You need to delete the City field's condition, specify that the City field values should be displayed in the query results, and then move the field back to its original position following the Address field.

3. Press **TAB** six times to select the condition for the City field, and then press **DELETE**. The condition for the City field is removed.
4. Click the **Show** check box for the City field to insert a checkmark so that the field values will be displayed in the query results.
5. Use the pointer to select the City field, drag the selected field to position it to the left of the Email field, and then click in an empty box to deselect the City field, as shown in Figure 3–24.

Figure 3–24 Design grid after moving the City field

City field moved to its original location

Field: VisitID VisitDate Reason LastName FirstName Phone Address City Email
Table: Visit Visit Visit Patient Patient Patient Patient Patient Patient
Sort:
Show:
Criteria: <#1/1/2030#
or:

condition removed from City Criteria box

Show check box is selected

6. Run the query. The query datasheet displays the selected fields for only those records with a VisitDate field value less than 1/1/2030, a total of 26 records, as shown in Figure 3–25.

Figure 3–25 Running the modified query

EarlierVisits

Visit ID	Date of Visit	Reason/Diagnosis	Last Name	First Name	Phone	Address	City	Email
3140	10/25/2029	Repetitive strain injury	Rodriguez	Jose	970-555-5656	437 Wilson St	Firestone	j.rodriguez4@example.com
3142	10/29/2029	Knee pain	Thompson	Robert	970-555-3958	14 Bobcat Tr	Greeley	r.thompson35@example.com
3144	10/29/2029	Ankle injury	Robinson	Olivia	303-555-5599	42 Winding Ridge R	Firestone	o.robinson16@example.com
3146	11/1/2029	Wrist pain	Wilson	Claire	303-555-4712	423 Ridge Rd	Firestone	c.wilson68@example.com
3147	11/5/2029	Physical therapy	Fadel	Amani	970-555-8445	452 Elm Ln	Fort Collins	a.fadel56@example.com
3149	11/7/2029	Bike accident	Brown	Gayle	970-555-6341	127 Valley Rd	Severance	g.brown19@example.com
3150	11/8/2029	Physical therapy	Wilson	Claire	303-555-4712	423 Ridge Rd	Firestone	c.wilson68@example.com
3152	11/9/2029	Hip pain	Lopez	Luis	970-555-5903	78 Ashley Dr	Berthoud	l.lopez12@example.com
3154	11/13/2029	Carpal tunnel syndrome	Montoya	Larry	970-555-1057	44 Wexler Dr	Fort Collins	l.montoya6@example.com
3158	11/16/2029	Knee pain follow-up visit	Johnson	Gregory	970-555-1189	12 Rock Ln	Fort Collins	g.johnson17@example.com
3159	11/19/2029	Ankle injury	Ramirez	Terry	970-555-8299	192 Greenwood Dr	Loveland	t.ramirez2@example.com
3161	11/21/2029	Physical therapy	Sanchez	Carlos	970-555-2433	42 Lookout Way	Laporte	c.sanchez5@example.com
3162	11/23/2029	Back pain	Anderson	Victoria	970-555-6438	16 Gaston Ave	Longmont	v.anderson5@example.com
3164	11/27/2029	Foot injury	Wilson	Claire	303-555-4712	423 Ridge Rd	Firestone	c.wilson68@example.com
3166	12/3/2029	Back pain	Olsen	Alexander	970-555-4112	312 Wafer Way	Timnath	a.olsen14@example.com
3167	12/6/2029	Back pain follow-up visit	Flores	Barbara	720-555-1235	47 Wyont Dr	Longmont	b.flores7@example.com
3169	12/10/2029	Cast removal	Robinson	Olivia	303-555-5599	42 Winding Ridge R	Firestone	o.robinson16@example.com
3170	12/14/2029	Physical therapy	Smith	Anna	970-555-9439	312 Oak Rd	Pierce	a.smith12@example.com
3171	12/17/2029	Physical therapy	Soto	Emilio	303-555-0124	12 Waterway Dr	Firestone	e.soto25@example.com
3173	12/18/2029	Repetitive strain injury	Zhao	Lian	970-555-2258	125 Peak Dr	Fort Collins	l.zhao16@example.com
3174	12/19/2029	Bike accident	Malik	Omar	970-555-8443	20 Switchback Way	Fort Collins	o.malik18@example.com
3176	12/21/2029	Back pain	Young	Pamela	970-555-5543	715 Phillips St	Greeley	p.young26@example.com
3178	12/24/2029	Physical therapy	Sanchez	Carlos	970-555-2433	42 Lookout Way	Laporte	c.sanchez5@example.com
3179	12/26/2029	Ankle injury	Chang	Tom	970-555-3160	2 Pine Dr	Livermore	t.chang2@example.com
3182	12/27/2029	Physical therapy	Olsen	Alexander	970-555-4112	312 Wafer Way	Timnath	a.olsen14@example.com
3183	12/28/2029	Knee pain	Wilson	Ellen	970-555-5500	16 Post Rd	Severance	e.wilson34@example.com
*								

only records with a VisitDate field value less than 1/1/2030 are selected

26 records are selected

Record: 1 of 26 No Filter Search

7. Save and close the EarlierVisits query.

As Susan continues to analyze patient visits to Pine Ridge Orthopedics & Sports Medicine Center, she considers whether to expand the center's physical therapy services, especially to improve the mobility of older adults. She requests a list of all patients who are age 50 or older and who have visited the center for physical therapy. She wants to track these patients so her staff can ask them to review the physical therapy services they received from the center. To produce this list, you need to create a query containing two conditions—one for the patient's date of birth and another for the reason/diagnosis for each patient visit.

Defining Multiple Selection Criteria for Queries

Multiple conditions require you to use **logical operators** to combine two or more conditions. When you want to select a record only if two or more conditions are met, you use the **And logical operator**. In this case, Susan wants to list only those records with a BirthDate field value less than or equal to 12/31/1980 *and* a Reason field value of "Physical therapy." If you place conditions in separate fields in the *same* Criteria row of the design grid, all conditions in that row must be met to include a record in the query results. However, if you place conditions in *different* Criteria rows, a record is selected when at least one of the conditions is met. If none of the conditions are met, Access does not select the record. When you place conditions in different Criteria rows, you are using the **Or logical operator**. Figure 3–26 illustrates the difference between the And and Or logical operators.

Figure 3–26 Logical operators And and Or for multiple selection criteria

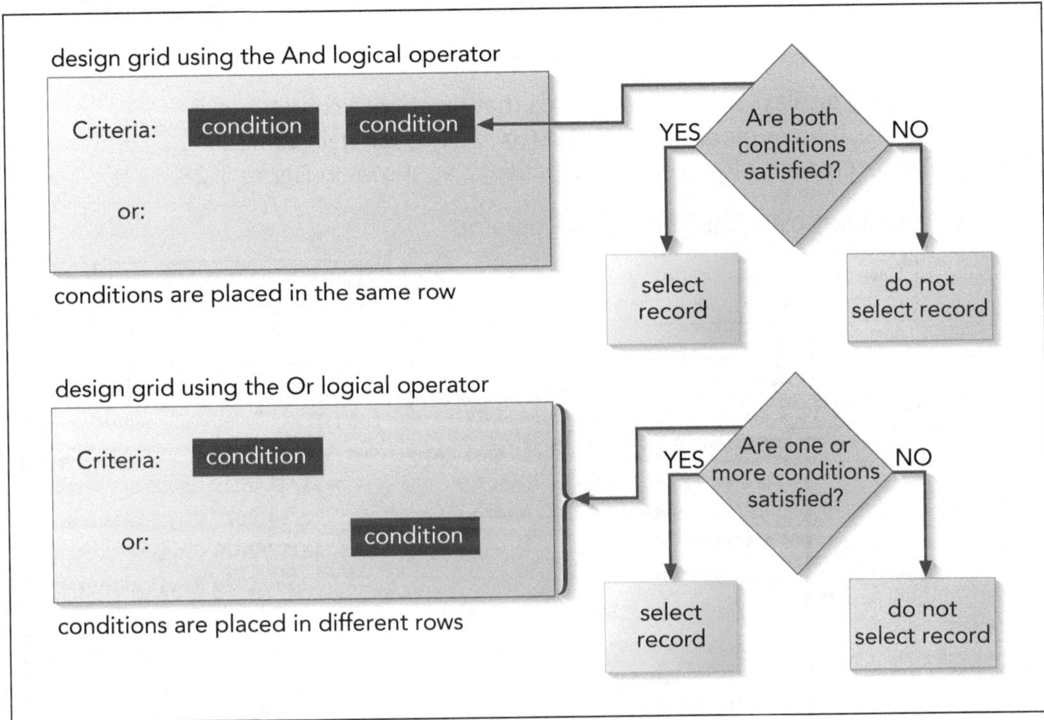

The And Logical Operator

To create the query for Susan, you need to use the And logical operator to show only the records for patients that were born on or before 12/31/1980 *and* who have visited the center for physical therapy. You'll create a new query based on the Patient and Visit tables to produce the necessary results. In the query design, both conditions you specify will appear in the same Criteria row, so the query selects records only if they meet both conditions.

To create a new query using the And logical operator:

1. On the ribbon, click the **Create** tab.
2. In the Queries group, click the **Query Design** button.
3. Add the **Patient** and **Visit** tables to the Query window, and then close the Add Tables pane. Resize both field lists to display all the field names.
4. Add the following fields from the Patient field list to the design grid in the order shown: **FirstName**, **LastName**, **BirthDate**, **Phone**, and **City**.
5. Add the **VisitDate** and **Reason** fields from the Visit table to the design grid. Now you need to enter the two conditions for the query.
6. Click the **BirthDate Criteria** box, and then type **<=12/31/1980** as the criterion.
7. Press **TAB** four times to move to the **Reason Criteria** box, type **Physical therapy**, and then press **TAB**. Compare your screen to Figure 3–27.

Figure 3–27 Query to find older patients who have had physical therapy

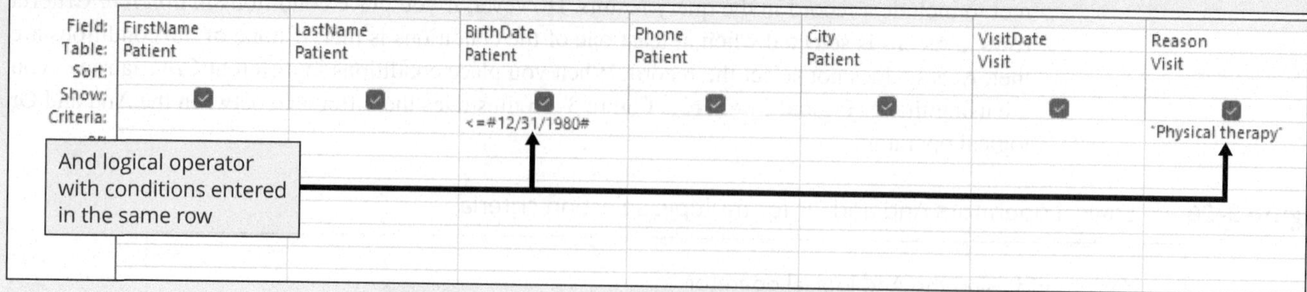

8. Run the query. The query displays only those records that meet both conditions: a BirthDate field value less than or equal to 12/31/1980 *and* a Reason field value of Physical therapy. Ten records are displayed for six patients, as shown in Figure 3–28.

Figure 3–28 Results of query using the And logical operator

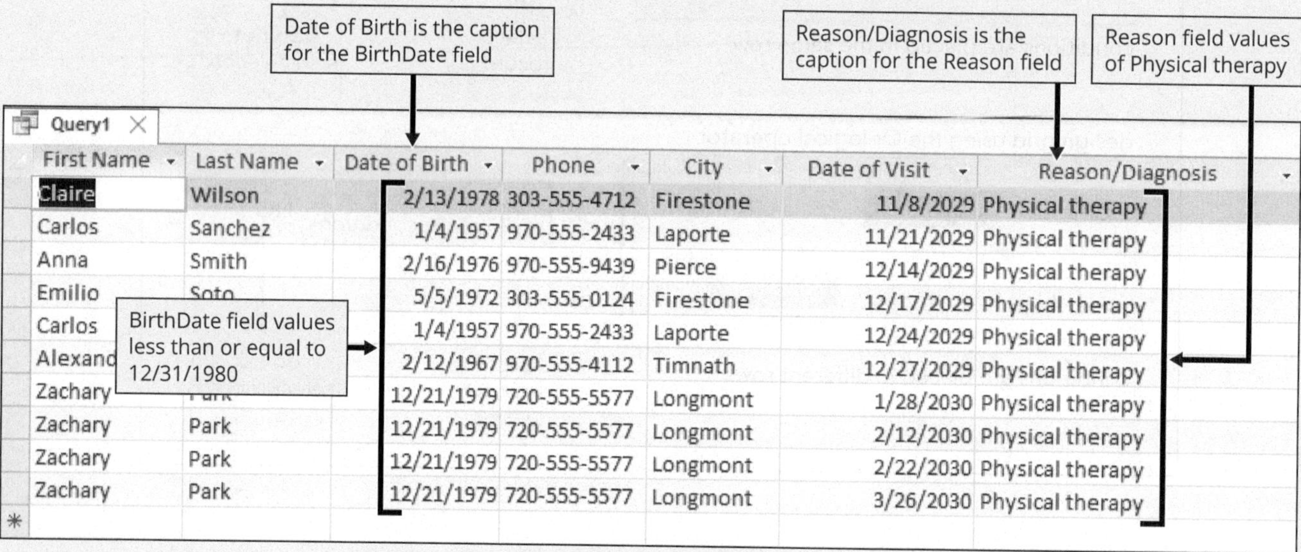

First Name	Last Name	Date of Birth	Phone	City	Date of Visit	Reason/Diagnosis
Claire	Wilson	2/13/1978	303-555-4712	Firestone	11/8/2029	Physical therapy
Carlos	Sanchez	1/4/1957	970-555-2433	Laporte	11/21/2029	Physical therapy
Anna	Smith	2/16/1976	970-555-9439	Pierce	12/14/2029	Physical therapy
Emilio	Soto	5/5/1972	303-555-0124	Firestone	12/17/2029	Physical therapy
Carlos		1/4/1957	970-555-2433	Laporte	12/24/2029	Physical therapy
Alexand		2/12/1967	970-555-4112	Timnath	12/27/2029	Physical therapy
Zachary		12/21/1979	720-555-5577	Longmont	1/28/2030	Physical therapy
Zachary	Park	12/21/1979	720-555-5577	Longmont	2/12/2030	Physical therapy
Zachary	Park	12/21/1979	720-555-5577	Longmont	2/22/2030	Physical therapy
Zachary	Park	12/21/1979	720-555-5577	Longmont	3/26/2030	Physical therapy

9. On the Quick Access Toolbar, click the **Save** button, and then save the query as **OlderAndPTPatients.**

10. Close the query.

Susan meets with staff members to discuss older patients who have had physical therapy and decides to contact them by email. After viewing the results of the OlderAndPTPatients query, the group recommends that the center should create an expanded group of patients for follow-ups: *any* patients born on or before 12/31/1980 *or* who have received physical therapy at the center (regardless of their age) to help them stay active. Susan asks you to produce the expanded list. To create this query, you need to use the Or logical operator.

The Or Logical Operator

To create the query that Susan requested, your query must select a record when either one of two conditions is satisfied or when both conditions are satisfied. That is, Access selects a record if the BirthDate field value is less than or equal to 12/31/1980 *or* if the Reason field value is Physical therapy *or* if both conditions are met. You enter the condition for the BirthDate field in the Criteria row and the condition for the Reason field in the "or" criteria row to use the Or logical operator.

To display the information, you'll create a new query based on the OlderAndPTPatients query because it already contains the necessary fields. Then you'll specify the conditions using the Or logical operator.

To create a new query using the Or logical operator:

1. Open the Navigation Pane. You'll use the shortcut menu to copy and paste the OlderAndPTPatients query and create the new query.
2. In the Queries section of the Navigation Pane, right-click **OlderAndPTPatients**, and then click **Copy** on the shortcut menu.
3. Right-click the empty area near the bottom of the Navigation Pane, and then click **Paste** on the shortcut menu. The Paste As dialog box opens with the text "Copy Of OlderAndPTPatients" in the Query Name box. You'll use "OlderOrPTPatients" as the name of the new query.
4. In the Query Name box, type **OlderOrPTPatients** and then press **ENTER**. The new query appears in the Queries section of the Navigation Pane.
5. In the Navigation Pane, right-click the **OlderOrPTPatients** query, click **Design View** on the shortcut menu to open the query in Design view, and then close the Navigation Pane.

   The query already contains all the fields Susan requested as well as the first condition—a BirthDate field value less than or equal to 12/31/1980. Because you want records selected if either the condition for the BirthDate field or the condition for the Reason field is satisfied, you must delete the condition for the Reason field in the Criteria row and then enter the same condition in the "or" row of the design grid for the Reason field.
6. In the design grid, delete **"Physical therapy"** in the Reason Criteria box.
7. Press **DOWN ARROW** ↓ to move to the "or" row for the Reason field, type **Physical therapy**, and then press **TAB**. Compare your screen to Figure 3–29.

Figure 3–29 Query window with the Or logical operator

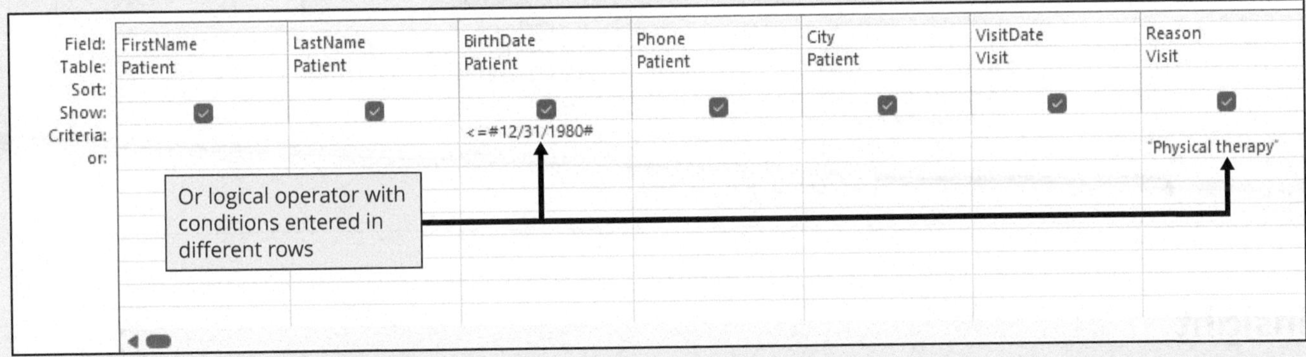

   To better analyze the data, Susan wants you to display the list in descending order by BirthDate.
8. Click the right side of the **BirthDate Sort** box, and then click **Descending**.
9. Run the query. The query datasheet displays only those records that meet either condition: a BirthDate field value less than or equal to 12/31/1980 *or* a Reason field value of Physical therapy. The query also returns records that meet both conditions. The query displays a total of 37 records. The records in the query datasheet appear in descending order based on the values in the BirthDate field, as shown in Figure 3–30.

Figure 3–30 Results of query using the Or logical operator

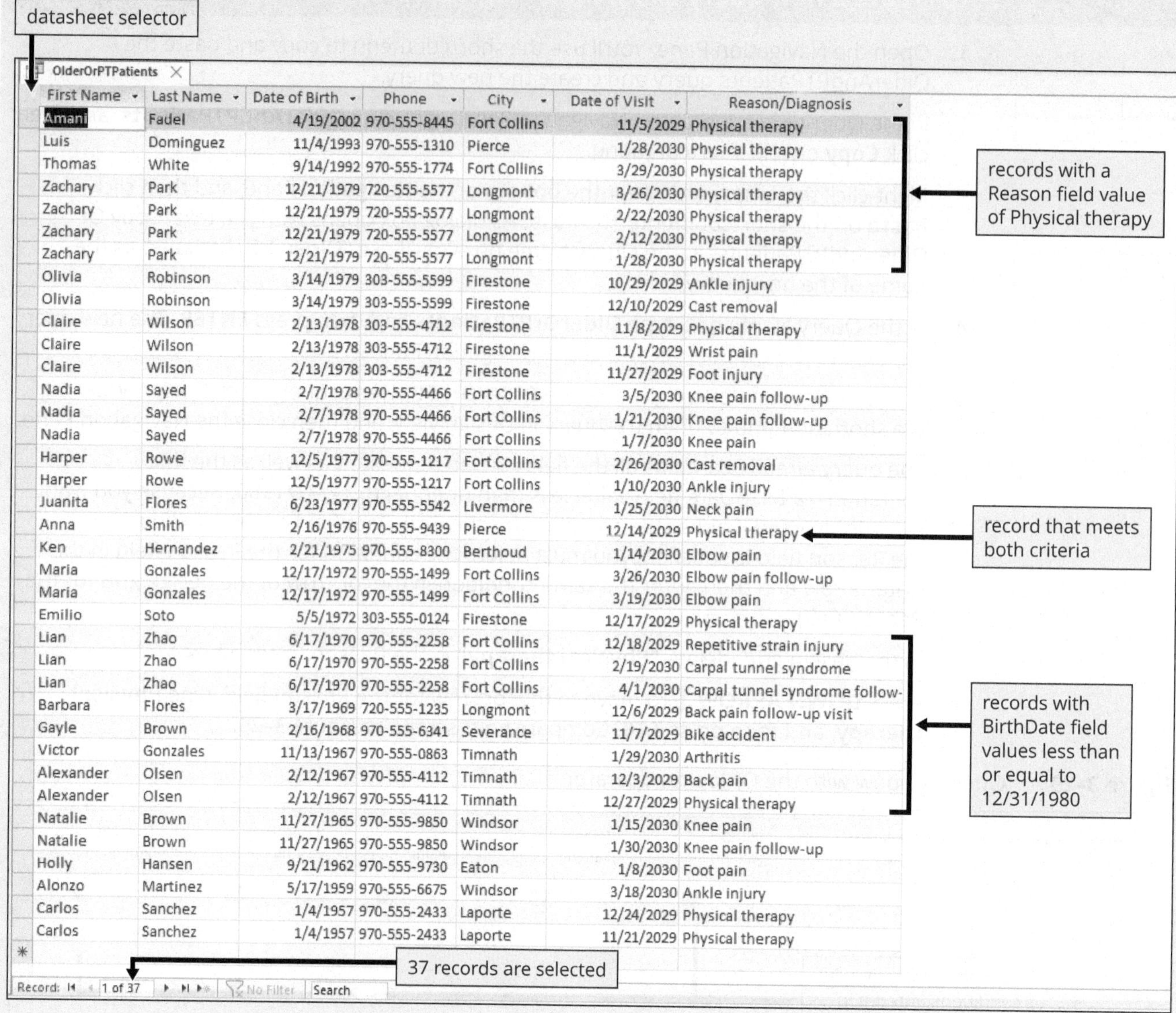

First Name	Last Name	Date of Birth	Phone	City	Date of Visit	Reason/Diagnosis
Amani	Fadel	4/19/2002	970-555-8445	Fort Collins	11/5/2029	Physical therapy
Luis	Dominguez	11/4/1993	970-555-1310	Pierce	1/28/2030	Physical therapy
Thomas	White	9/14/1992	970-555-1774	Fort Collins	3/29/2030	Physical therapy
Zachary	Park	12/21/1979	720-555-5577	Longmont	3/26/2030	Physical therapy
Zachary	Park	12/21/1979	720-555-5577	Longmont	2/22/2030	Physical therapy
Zachary	Park	12/21/1979	720-555-5577	Longmont	2/12/2030	Physical therapy
Zachary	Park	12/21/1979	720-555-5577	Longmont	1/28/2030	Physical therapy
Olivia	Robinson	3/14/1979	303-555-5599	Firestone	10/29/2029	Ankle injury
Olivia	Robinson	3/14/1979	303-555-5599	Firestone	12/10/2029	Cast removal
Claire	Wilson	2/13/1978	303-555-4712	Firestone	11/8/2029	Physical therapy
Claire	Wilson	2/13/1978	303-555-4712	Firestone	11/1/2029	Wrist pain
Claire	Wilson	2/13/1978	303-555-4712	Firestone	11/27/2029	Foot injury
Nadia	Sayed	2/7/1978	970-555-4466	Fort Collins	3/5/2030	Knee pain follow-up
Nadia	Sayed	2/7/1978	970-555-4466	Fort Collins	1/21/2030	Knee pain follow-up
Nadia	Sayed	2/7/1978	970-555-4466	Fort Collins	1/7/2030	Knee pain
Harper	Rowe	12/5/1977	970-555-1217	Fort Collins	2/26/2030	Cast removal
Harper	Rowe	12/5/1977	970-555-1217	Fort Collins	1/10/2030	Ankle injury
Juanita	Flores	6/23/1977	970-555-5542	Livermore	1/25/2030	Neck pain
Anna	Smith	2/16/1976	970-555-9439	Pierce	12/14/2029	Physical therapy
Ken	Hernandez	2/21/1975	970-555-8300	Berthoud	1/14/2030	Elbow pain
Maria	Gonzales	12/17/1972	970-555-1499	Fort Collins	3/26/2030	Elbow pain follow-up
Maria	Gonzales	12/17/1972	970-555-1499	Fort Collins	3/19/2030	Elbow pain
Emilio	Soto	5/5/1972	303-555-0124	Firestone	12/17/2029	Physical therapy
Lian	Zhao	6/17/1970	970-555-2258	Fort Collins	12/18/2029	Repetitive strain injury
Lian	Zhao	6/17/1970	970-555-2258	Fort Collins	2/19/2030	Carpal tunnel syndrome
Lian	Zhao	6/17/1970	970-555-2258	Fort Collins	4/1/2030	Carpal tunnel syndrome follow-
Barbara	Flores	3/17/1969	720-555-1235	Longmont	12/6/2029	Back pain follow-up visit
Gayle	Brown	2/16/1968	970-555-6341	Severance	11/7/2029	Bike accident
Victor	Gonzales	11/13/1967	970-555-0863	Timnath	1/29/2030	Arthritis
Alexander	Olsen	2/12/1967	970-555-4112	Timnath	12/3/2029	Back pain
Alexander	Olsen	2/12/1967	970-555-4112	Timnath	12/27/2029	Physical therapy
Natalie	Brown	11/27/1965	970-555-9850	Windsor	1/15/2030	Knee pain
Natalie	Brown	11/27/1965	970-555-9850	Windsor	1/30/2030	Knee pain follow-up
Holly	Hansen	9/21/1962	970-555-9730	Eaton	1/8/2030	Foot pain
Alonzo	Martinez	5/17/1959	970-555-6675	Windsor	3/18/2030	Ankle injury
Carlos	Sanchez	1/4/1957	970-555-2433	Laporte	12/24/2029	Physical therapy
Carlos	Sanchez	1/4/1957	970-555-2433	Laporte	11/21/2029	Physical therapy

Insight

Understanding the Results of Using And Versus Or

When you use the And logical operator to define multiple selection criteria in a query, you *narrow* the results produced by the query because a record must meet more than one condition to be included in the results. For example, the OlderAndPTPatients query you created resulted in only 10 records. When you use the Or logical operator, you *broaden* the results produced by the query because a record must meet only one of the conditions to be included in the results. For example, the OlderOrPTPatients query you created resulted in 37 records. Keep this distinction in mind when you include multiple selection criteria in queries so that the queries you create produce the results you want.

Susan plans to spend some time reviewing the results of the OlderOrPTPatients query. To make this task easier, she asks you to change the appearance of the datasheet.

Changing a Datasheet's Appearance

You can make many formatting changes to a datasheet to improve its appearance or readability. Many modifications are familiar types of changes you can also make in Word documents or Excel spreadsheets, such as modifying the font type, size, color, and the alignment of text. You can also remove gridlines to improve the appearance of the datasheet and apply different colors to the rows and columns to make the datasheet easier to read.

Modifying the Font Size

Depending on the size of the display or the screen resolution you are using, you might need to increase or decrease the size of the font in a datasheet to view more or fewer columns of data. Susan asks you to change the font size in the query datasheet from 11 points to 14 points so she can read the text more easily.

To change the font size in the datasheet:

1. On the Home tab, in the Text Formatting group, click the **Font Size** arrow, and then click **14**. The font size for the entire datasheet increases to 14 points.

   Next, you need to resize the columns to their best fit so that all field values are displayed. Instead of resizing each column individually, you can use the datasheet selector to select all the columns and resize them at the same time.

2. Click the **datasheet selector** ▢, which is the box to the left of the First Name column heading (shown in Figure 3–30). All the columns in the datasheet are selected.
3. Move the pointer to one of the vertical lines separating two columns in the datasheet until the pointer changes to the column resizing pointer ✛, and then double-click the vertical line. All the columns shown on the screen are resized to their best fit. Scroll down and repeat the resizing, as necessary, to make sure that all field values are fully displayed.

   Trouble? If all the columns are not shown on your screen, you need to scroll the datasheet to the right to make sure all field values for all columns are fully displayed. If you need to resize any columns, click a field value first to deselect the columns before resizing an individual column.

4. Click any value in the First Name column to make it the current field and to deselect the columns in the datasheet.

Changing the Alternate Row Color in a Datasheet

Access uses themes to format the objects in a database. A **theme** is a predefined set of formats including colors, fonts, and other effects that enhance an object's appearance and usability. When you create a database, Access applies the Office theme to objects as you create them. By default, the Office theme formats every other row in a datasheet with a gray background to distinguish one row from another, making it easier to view and read the contents of a datasheet. The gray alternate row color provides a subtle contrast with the rows that have the default white background. You can change the alternate row color in a datasheet to something more noticeable using the Alternate Row Color button in the Text Formatting group on the Home tab. Susan suggests you change the alternate row color in the datasheet.

Tip When choosing a row color, be sure to select a light color because dark colors might obscure the data rather than enhance it.

To change the alternate row color in the datasheet:

1. On the Home tab, in the Text Formatting group, click the **Alternate Row Color** arrow to display the gallery of color choices, as shown in Figure 3–31.

Figure 3–31 Gallery of color choices for alternate row color

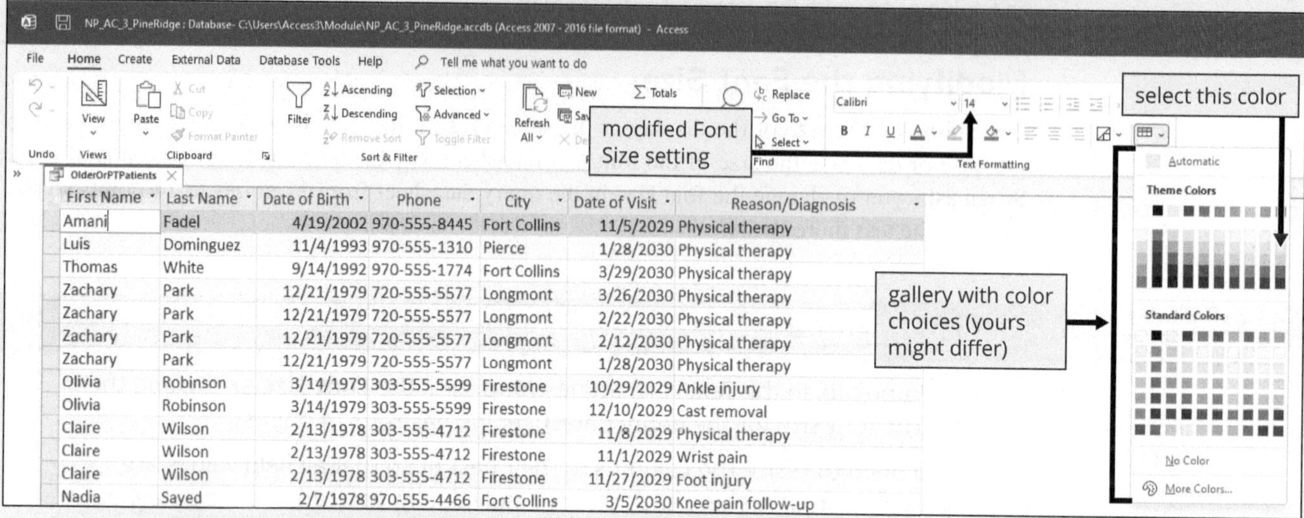

Tip The name of the color appears in a ScreenTip when you point to a color in the gallery.

The Theme Colors section provides colors from the default Office theme, so that your datasheet's color scheme matches the one in use for the database. The Standard Colors section provides other standard color choices. The gallery might also include a Recent Colors section with colors you recently used in a datasheet. The No Color option, which appears at the bottom of the gallery, sets each row's background color to white. If you want to create a custom color, you can do so using the More Colors option. You'll use one of the theme colors.

2. In the Theme Colors section, click the **Green, Accent 6, Lighter 60%** box (tenth column, third row). The alternate row color is applied to the query datasheet, as shown in Figure 3–32.

Figure 3–32 Datasheet formatted with alternate row color

OlderOrPTPatients

First Name	Last Name	Date of Birth	Phone	City	Date of Visit	Reason/Diagnosis
Amani	Fadel	4/19/2002	970-555-8445	Fort Collins	11/5/2029	Physical therapy
Luis	Dominguez	11/4/1993	970-555-1310	Pierce	1/28/2030	Physical therapy
Thomas	White	9/14/1992	970-555-1774	Fort Collins	3/29/2030	Physical therapy
Zachary	Park	12/21/1979	720-555-5577	Longmont	3/26/2030	Physical therapy
Zachary	Park	12/21/1979	720-555-5577	Longmont	2/22/2030	Physical therapy
Zachary	Park	12/21/1979	720-555-5577	Longmont	2/12/2030	Physical therapy
Zachary	Park	12/21/1979	720-555-5577	Longmont	1/28/2030	Physical therapy
Olivia	Robinson	3/14/1979	303-555-5599	Firestone	10/29/2029	Ankle injury
Olivia	Robinson	3/14/1979	303-555-5599	Firestone	12/10/2029	Cast removal
Claire	Wilson	2/13/1978	303-555-4712	Firestone	11/8/2029	Physical therapy
Claire	Wilson	2/13/1978	303-555-4712	Firestone	11/1/2029	Wrist pain

first row is active, so it appears selected (highlighted in blue)

green applied to every other row

Every other row in the datasheet uses the selected theme color. Susan likes how the datasheet looks with this color scheme, so she asks you to save the query.

3. Change the first and last names in the first record (Amani Fadel) to your first and last names.
4. Save and close the OlderOrPTPatients query. The query is saved with the increased font size and the green alternate row color.

Next, Susan turns her attention to some financial aspects of operating the center. She wants to use the NP_AC_3_PineRidge database to perform calculations. She is considering imposing a two percent late fee on unpaid invoices and wants to know exactly what the late fee charges would be in case she decides to add the fee later. To produce the information for Susan, you need to create a calculated field.

Creating a Calculated Field

In addition to using queries to retrieve, sort, and filter data in a database, you can use a query to perform calculations. To perform a calculation, you define an **expression** containing a combination of database fields, constants, and operators. For numeric expressions, the data types of the database fields must be Number, Currency, or Date/Time. The constants are numbers such as .02 (for the two percent late fee), and the operators can be arithmetic operators (+ – * /) or other specialized operators.

In complex expressions, you can enclose calculations in parentheses to indicate which one should be performed first. Any calculation in parentheses is completed before calculations outside the parentheses. In expressions without parentheses, Access performs basic calculations using the following order of precedence: multiplication and division before addition and subtraction. When operators have equal precedence, Access calculates them in order from left to right.

To perform a calculation in a query, you add a calculated field to the query. A **calculated field** displays the results of an expression. A calculated field you create with an expression appears in a query datasheet or in a form or report; however, it does not exist in a database. When you run a query that contains a calculated field, Access evaluates the expression defined by the calculated field and displays the resulting value in the query datasheet, form, or report.

To enter an expression for a calculated field, you can type it directly in a Field box in the design grid. Alternately, you can open the Zoom box or Expression Builder and use either one to enter the expression. The **Zoom box** is a dialog box you use to enter text, expressions, or other values. To use the Zoom box, however, you must know all the parts of the expression you want to create. **Expression Builder** is an Access tool that makes it easy for you to create an expression. It contains a box for entering the expression, an option for displaying and choosing common operators, and one or more lists of expression elements, such as table and field names.

Unlike a Field box, which is too narrow to show an entire expression at one time, the Zoom box and Expression Builder are large enough to display longer expressions. In most cases, Expression Builder provides the easiest way to enter expressions because you don't have to know all the parts of the expression. Instead, you can choose the necessary elements from the Expression Builder dialog box, which also helps to prevent typing errors.

Reference

Creating a Calculated Field Using Expression Builder

- Create and save the query that will include a calculated field.
- Open the query in Design view.
- In the design grid, click the Field box where you want to create an expression.
- In the Query Setup group on the Query Design tab, click the Builder button.
- Use the expression elements and common operators to build the expression or type the expression directly in the expression box.
- Click OK.

To produce the information Susan wants, you need to create a query based on the Billing and Visit tables and include a calculated field that multiplies each InvoiceAmt field value by .02 to calculate the proposed two percent late fee.

To create the new query:

1. On the ribbon, click the **Create** tab.
2. In the Queries group, click the **Query Design** button. The Add Tables pane opens.

   Susan wants you to include data from the Visit and Billing tables, so you need to add these two tables to the Query window.
3. Add the **Visit** and **Billing** tables to the Query window, close the Add Tables pane, and then resize the field lists to display all the field names. The field lists appear in the Query window, and the one-to-many relationship between the Visit (primary) and Billing (related) tables is displayed.
4. Add the following fields to the design grid in the order given: **VisitID**, **PatientID**, and **VisitDate** from the Visit table; and **InvoiceItem**, **InvoicePaid**, and **InvoiceAmt** from the Billing table.

   Susan is interested in viewing data only for unpaid invoices because a late fee would apply only to them, so you need to enter the necessary condition for the InvoicePaid field. Recall that InvoicePaid is a Yes/No field. The condition you need to enter is the word "No" in the Criteria box for this field, so that Access retrieves the records for unpaid invoices only.
5. In the **InvoicePaid Criteria box**, type **No**. When you type the letter "N," a menu appears with options for entering various functions for the criteria. You don't need to enter a function, so you can close this menu.
6. Press **ESC** to close the menu.

   Tip You must close the menu or you'll enter a function, which will cause an error.
7. Press **TAB**. The query name will indicate that the data is for unpaid invoices, so you don't need to include the InvoicePaid values in the query results.
8. Click the **InvoicePaid Show** check box to remove the checkmark.
9. Save the query using **UnpaidInvoiceLateFee** as the name.

Now you can use Expression Builder to create the calculated field for the InvoiceAmt field.

To create the calculated field:

1. Click the blank Field box to the right of the InvoiceAmt field. This field will contain the expression.
2. On the Query Design tab, in the Query Setup group, click the **Builder** button. The Expression Builder dialog box opens.

   Tip You must first save and name a query to have its fields listed in the Expression Categories section.

   The insertion point is positioned in the large box at the top of the dialog box, ready for you to enter the expression. The Expression Categories section of the dialog box lists the fields from the query so you can include them in the expression. The Expression Elements section contains options for including other elements in the expression, including functions, constants, and operators. If the expression you're entering is simple, you can type it in the box. If it's more complex, you can use the options in the Expression Elements section to help you build the expression.

The expression for the calculated field should multiply the InvoiceAmt field values by the numeric constant .02 (which represents a two percent late fee).

3. In the Expression Categories section of the dialog box, double-click **InvoiceAmt**. The field name is added to the expression box in brackets and with a space following it. In an expression, all field names must be enclosed in brackets.

   Next, you need to enter the multiplication operator, which is the asterisk (*), followed by the constant.

4. Type * (an asterisk), press **SPACEBAR**, and then type **.02** to complete the expression. Compare your screen to Figure 3–33.

Figure 3–33 Completed expression for the calculated field

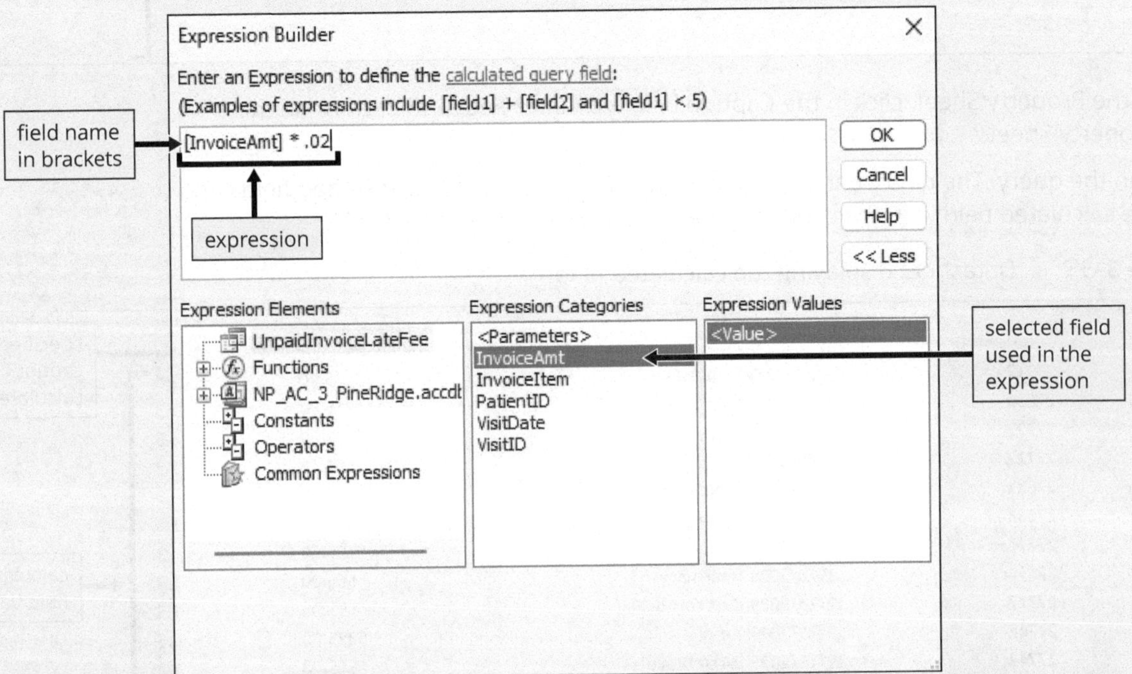

If you're not sure which operator to use, you can click Operators in the Expression Elements section to display a list of available operators in the center section of the dialog box.

5. Click **OK**. The Expression Builder dialog box closes, and the expression is added to the design grid in the Field box for the calculated field. When you create a calculated field, Access uses the default name "Expr1" for the field. You need to specify a more meaningful field name, such as "LateFee," to appear in the query results.

6. Click to the left of the text "Expr1:" at the beginning of the expression, and then press **DELETE** five times to delete the text **Expr1**. *Do not delete the colon*; it is needed to separate the calculated field name from the expression.

7. Type **LateFee** as the field name. Next, you'll set this field's Caption property so that the field name appears as "Late Fee" in the query datasheet. Make sure LateFee is still the selected field.

8. On the Query Design tab, in the Show/Hide group, click the **Property Sheet** button. The Property Sheet for the current field, LateFee, opens on the right side of the window, as shown in Figure 3–34.

Figure 3–34 Property Sheet for the calculated field

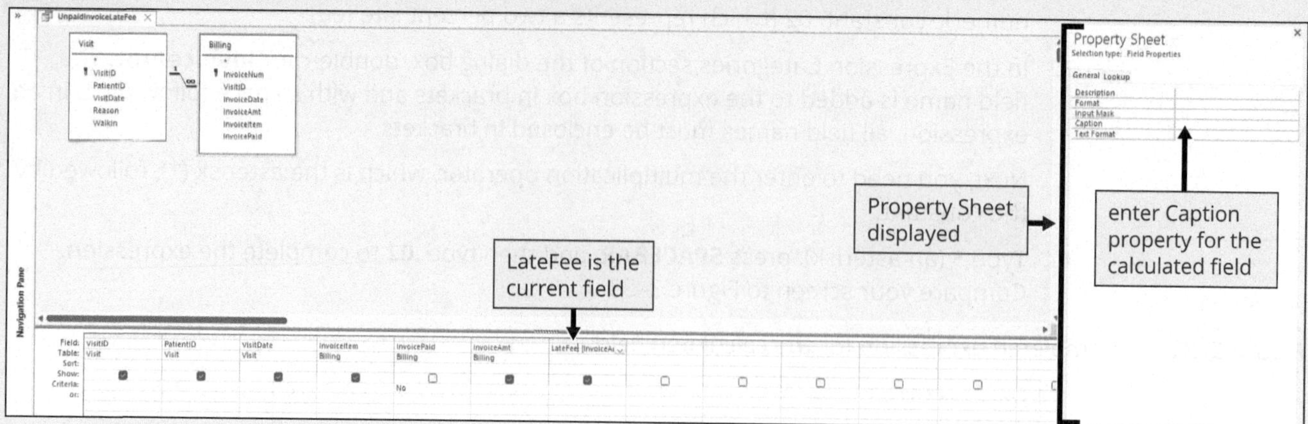

9. In the Property Sheet, click in the Caption box, type **Late Fee**, and then close the Property Sheet.
10. Run the query. The query datasheet is displayed and contains the specified fields and the calculated field with the caption "Late Fee," as shown in Figure 3–35.

Figure 3–35 Datasheet displaying the calculated field

UnpaidInvoiceLateFee

Visit ID	Patient ID	Date of Visit	Invoice Item	Invoice Amt	Late Fee
3144	27717	10/29/2029	Crutches	$125.00	2.5
3147	27650	11/5/2029	Elbow brace	$65.00	1.3
3159	27722	11/19/2029	X-ray	$325.00	6.5
3159	27722	11/19/2029	Ankle brace	$65.00	1.3
3162	27683	11/23/2029	Office evaluation	$150.00	3
3162	27683	11/23/2029	Pharmacy	$75.00	1.5
3167	27676	12/6/2029	Office evaluation	$150.00	3
3167	27676	12/6/2029	Pharmacy	$65.00	1.3
3169	27717	12/10/2029	Cast removal	$95.00	1.9
3174	27742	12/19/2029	X-ray	$325.00	6.5
3174	27742	12/19/2029	Wrist brace	$65.00	1.3
3174	27742	12/19/2029	Knee brace	$65.00	1.3
3174	27742	12/19/2029	Pharmacy	$85.00	1.7
3176	27740	12/21/2029	Office evaluation	$150.00	3
3179	27671	12/26/2029	Cast	$350.00	7

specified caption for the calculated field

calculated field values

> **Trouble?** If a dialog box warns you that the expression contains invalid syntax, you might have omitted the required colon in the expression. Click OK to close the dialog box, resize the column in the design grid that contains the calculated field to keep its best fit, change your expression to LateFee: [InvoiceAmt] * 0.02, and then repeat Step 10.

The LateFee field values appear without dollar signs and decimal places. Susan wants you to display these values in the same format as the InvoiceAmt field values for consistency.

Formatting a Calculated Field

You can specify a format for a calculated field, just as you can for any field, by modifying its properties. You'll change the format of the LateFee calculated field so that all values appear in the Currency format.

To format the calculated field:

1. Switch to Design view.
2. In the design grid, click in the **LateFee** calculated field to make it the current field, if necessary.
3. On the Query Design tab, in the Show/Hide group, click the **Property Sheet** button to open the Property Sheet for the calculated field, if necessary.

   You need to change the Format property to Currency, which displays values with a dollar sign and two decimal places.
4. In the Property Sheet, click the right side of the **Format** box to display the list of formats, and then click **Currency**.
5. Close the Property Sheet, and then run the query. The amounts in the LateFee calculated field are now displayed with dollar signs and two decimal places.
6. Save and close the UnpaidInvoiceLateFee query.

Proskills

Problem Solving: Creating a Calculated Field or Using the Calculated Data Type

You can also create a calculated field using the Calculated data type, which lets you store the result of an expression as a field in a table. However, database experts caution users against storing calculations in a table for several reasons. First, storing calculated data in a table consumes valuable space and increases the size of the database. The preferred approach is to use a calculated field in a query. With this approach, the result of the calculation is not stored in the database—it is produced only when you run the query—and it is always current. Second, the Calculated data type provides limited options for creating a calculation, whereas a calculated field in a query provides more functions and options for creating expressions. Third, including a field in a table using the Calculated data type limits your options if you need to upgrade the database at some point to a more robust DBMS, such as Oracle or SQL Server, that doesn't support this data type. You would need to redesign your database to eliminate the Calculated data type. Finally, most database experts agree that including a field in a table whose value depends on other fields in the table violates database design principles. To avoid such problems, it's best to create a query that includes a calculated field to perform the calculation you want instead of creating a field in a table that uses the Calculated data type.

To better analyze costs at Pine Ridge Orthopedics & Sports Medicine Center, Susan wants to review more detailed information about invoices for patient care. Specifically, she wants to know the minimum, average, and maximum invoice amounts. She asks you to determine these statistics from data in the Billing table.

Using Aggregate Functions

You can calculate statistical information, such as totals and averages, for the records displayed in a table datasheet or selected by a query. To do this, you use the Access aggregate functions. **Aggregate functions** perform arithmetic operations on selected records in a database. Figure 3–36 lists the most frequently used aggregate functions.

Figure 3–36 Frequently used aggregate functions

Aggregate Function	Determines	Data Types Supported
Average	Average of the field values for the selected records	AutoNumber, Currency, Date/Time, Number
Count	Number of records selected	AutoNumber, Currency, Date/Time, Long Text, Number, OLE Object, Short Text, Yes/No
Maximum	Highest field value for the selected records	AutoNumber, Currency, Date/Time, Number, Short Text
Minimum	Lowest field value for the selected records	AutoNumber, Currency, Date/Time, Number, Short Text
Sum	Total of the field values for the selected records	AutoNumber, Currency, Date/Time, Number

Working with Aggregate Functions Using the Total Row

If you want to quickly perform a calculation using an aggregate function in a table or query datasheet, you can use the Totals button in the Records group on the Home tab. When you click this button, a row labeled "Total" appears at the bottom of the datasheet. You can then choose one of the aggregate functions for a field in the datasheet to display the results of the calculation in the Total row for that field.

Susan wants to know the total amount of all invoices for the center. You can quickly display this amount using the Sum function in the Total row in the Billing table datasheet.

To display the total amount of all invoices in the Billing table:

1. Open the Navigation Pane, open the **Billing** table in Datasheet view, and then close the Navigation Pane.
2. Make sure the Home tab is displayed.
3. In the Records group, click the **Totals** button. A row with the label "Total" is added to the bottom of the datasheet.
4. Scroll to the bottom of the datasheet. You want to display the sum of all the values in the Invoice Amt column.
5. In the Total row, click the **Invoice Amt** field. An arrow appears on the left side of the field.
6. Click the **arrow** to display the menu of aggregate functions, which depends on the data type of the current field. In this case, the menu provides functions for a Currency field, as shown in Figure 3–37.

Figure 3–37 Using aggregate functions in the Total row

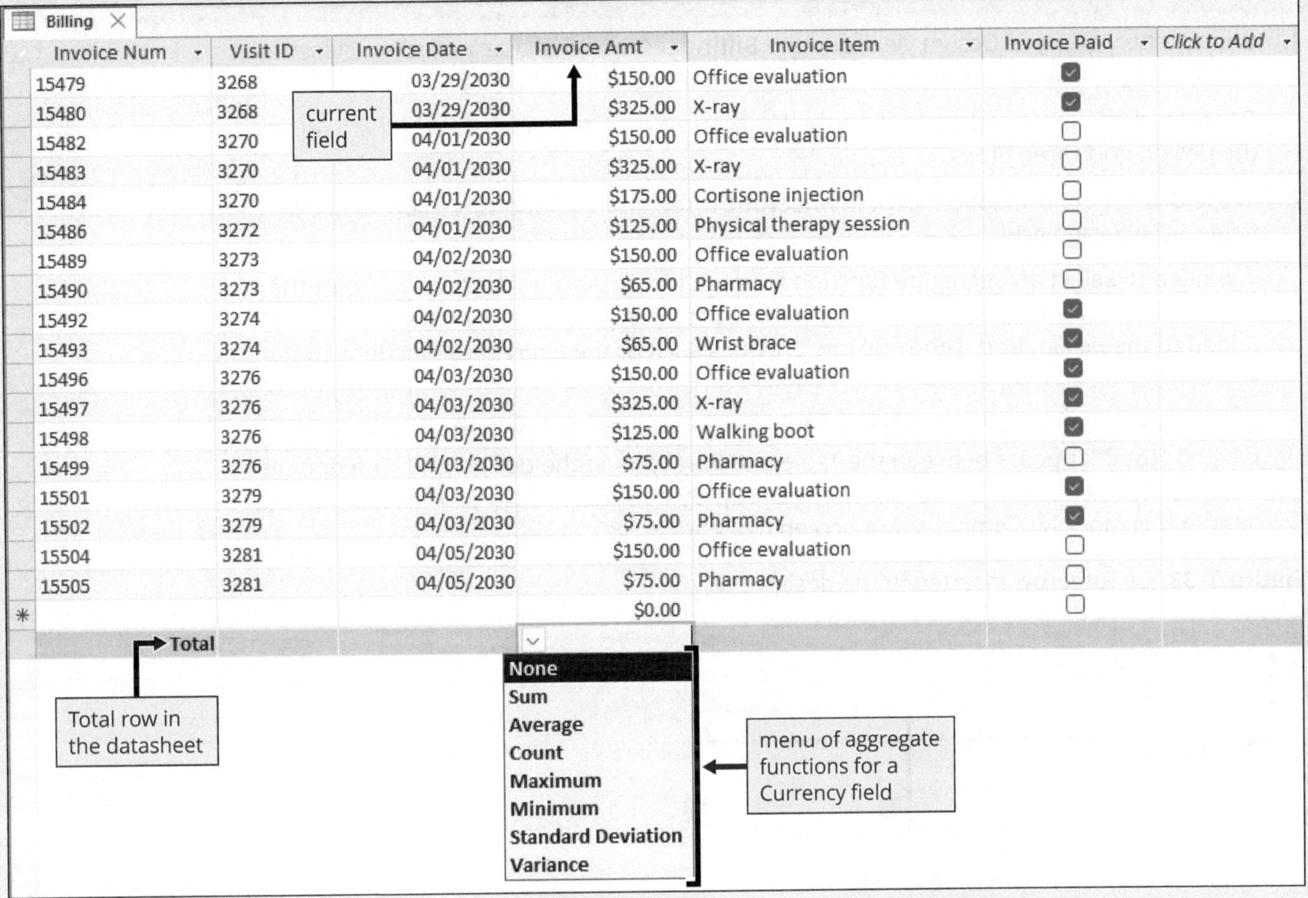

Invoice Num	Visit ID	Invoice Date	Invoice Amt	Invoice Item	Invoice Paid	Click to Add
15479	3268	03/29/2030	$150.00	Office evaluation	☑	
15480	3268	03/29/2030	$325.00	X-ray	☑	
15482	3270	04/01/2030	$150.00	Office evaluation	☐	
15483	3270	04/01/2030	$325.00	X-ray	☐	
15484	3270	04/01/2030	$175.00	Cortisone injection	☐	
15486	3272	04/01/2030	$125.00	Physical therapy session	☐	
15489	3273	04/02/2030	$150.00	Office evaluation	☐	
15490	3273	04/02/2030	$65.00	Pharmacy	☐	
15492	3274	04/02/2030	$150.00	Office evaluation	☑	
15493	3274	04/02/2030	$65.00	Wrist brace	☑	
15496	3276	04/03/2030	$150.00	Office evaluation	☑	
15497	3276	04/03/2030	$325.00	X-ray	☑	
15498	3276	04/03/2030	$125.00	Walking boot	☑	
15499	3276	04/03/2030	$75.00	Pharmacy	☐	
15501	3279	04/03/2030	$150.00	Office evaluation	☑	
15502	3279	04/03/2030	$75.00	Pharmacy	☑	
15504	3281	04/05/2030	$150.00	Office evaluation	☐	
15505	3281	04/05/2030	$75.00	Pharmacy	☐	
*			$0.00		☐	
Total						

7. Click **Sum** on the menu. All the values in the Invoice Amt column are added, and the total $32,040.00 appears in the Total row for the column.

   Susan doesn't want to change the Billing table to always display this total. You can remove the Total row by clicking the Totals button again. This button works as a toggle to switch between displaying the Total row results and not displaying them.

8. In the Records group, click the **Totals** button. The Total row is removed from the datasheet.
9. Close the Billing table and save the changes.

Susan wants to know the minimum, average, and maximum invoice amounts for Pine Ridge Orthopedics & Sports Medicine Center. To produce this information for Susan, you need to use aggregate functions in a query.

Creating Queries with Aggregate Functions

Aggregate functions operate on the records that meet a query's selection criteria. You specify an aggregate function for a field, and the appropriate operation applies to that field's values for the selected records.

To display the minimum, average, and maximum of all the invoice amounts in the Billing table, you use the Minimum, Average, and Maximum aggregate functions for the InvoiceAmt field.

To calculate the minimum of all invoice amounts:

1. Create a new query in Design view, add the **Billing** table to the Query window, close the Add Tables pane, and then resize the Billing field list to display all fields.

   To perform the three calculations on the InvoiceAmt field, you need to add the field to the design grid three times.

2. In the Billing field list, double-click **InvoiceAmt** three times to add three copies of the field to the design grid.

   You need to select an aggregate function for each InvoiceAmt field. When you click the Totals button in the Show/Hide group on the Query Design tab, a row labeled "Total" is added to the design grid. The Total row provides a list of the aggregate functions that you can select.

3. On the Query Design tab, in the Show/Hide group, click the **Totals** button. A new row labeled "Total" appears between the Table and Sort rows in the design grid. The default entry for each field in the Total row is the Group By operator, which you will learn about later in this module. Compare your screen to Figure 3–38.

Figure 3–38 Total row inserted in the design grid

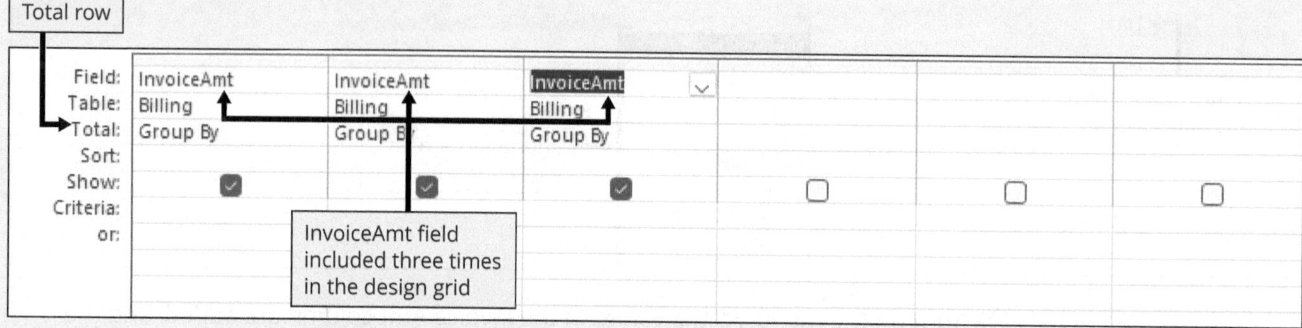

In the Total row, you specify the aggregate function you want to use for a field.

4. Click the right side of the first column's **Total** box, and then click **Min**. This field will calculate the minimum amount of all the InvoiceAmt field values.

   When you run the query, Access assigns a datasheet column name of "MinOfInvoiceAmt" for this field. You can change the datasheet column name to a more descriptive or readable name by entering the name you want in the Field box. However, you must also keep the InvoiceAmt field name in the Field box because it identifies the field to use in the calculation. The Field box will contain the datasheet column name you specify followed by the field name (InvoiceAmt) with a colon separating the two names.

5. In the first column's Field box, click to the left of InvoiceAmt, type **MinimumInvoiceAmt:** (including the colon), and then press SPACEBAR.

   > **Tip** Be sure to type the colon following the name, or the query will not work correctly.

6. Resize the column to display the complete field name, MinimumInvoiceAmt: InvoiceAmt.

   Next, you need to set the Caption property for this field so that the field name appears with spaces between words in the query datasheet.

7. On the Query Design tab, in the Show/Hide group, click the **Property Sheet** button to open the Property Sheet for the current field.

8. In the Caption box, type **Minimum Invoice Amt**, and then close the Property Sheet.

Follow the same steps to complete the query by calculating the average and maximum invoice amounts.

To calculate the average and maximum of all invoice amounts:

1. Click the right side of the second column's **Total** box, and then click **Avg**. This field will calculate the average of all the InvoiceAmt field values.
2. In the second column's Field box, click to the left of InvoiceAmt, and then type **AverageInvoiceAmt:** (including the colon).
3. Resize the second column to fully display the field name, AverageInvoiceAmt:InvoiceAmt.
4. Open the Property Sheet for the current field, and then set its Caption property to **Average Invoice Amt**. Leave the Property Sheet open.
5. Click the right side of the third column's **Total** box, and then click **Max**. This field will calculate the maximum amount of all the InvoiceAmt field values.
6. In the third column's Field box, click to the left of InvoiceAmt, and then type **MaximumInvoiceAmt:** (including the colon).
7. Resize the third column to fully display the field name, MaximumInvoiceAmt:InvoiceAmt.
8. In the Property Sheet, set the Caption property to **Maximum Invoice Amt**, and then close the Property Sheet. Compare your screen to Figure 3-39.

Figure 3-39 Query with aggregate functions entered

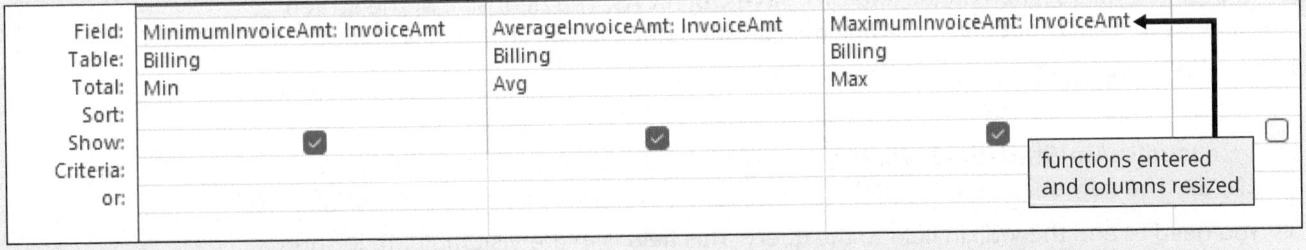

Field:	MinimumInvoiceAmt: InvoiceAmt	AverageInvoiceAmt: InvoiceAmt	MaximumInvoiceAmt: InvoiceAmt
Table:	Billing	Billing	Billing
Total:	Min	Avg	Max
Sort:			
Show:	☑	☑	☑
Criteria:			
or:			

functions entered and columns resized

> **Trouble?** Carefully compare your field names to those shown in the figure to make sure they match exactly; otherwise, the query will not work correctly.

9. Run the query. One record is displayed containing the three aggregate function results. The single row of summary statistics represents calculations based on all the records selected for the query—in this case, all 202 records in the Billing table.
10. Resize all columns to their best fit so that the column names are fully displayed, and then click the field value in the first column to deselect the value and view the results, as shown in Figure 3-40.

Figure 3-40 Result of the query using aggregate functions

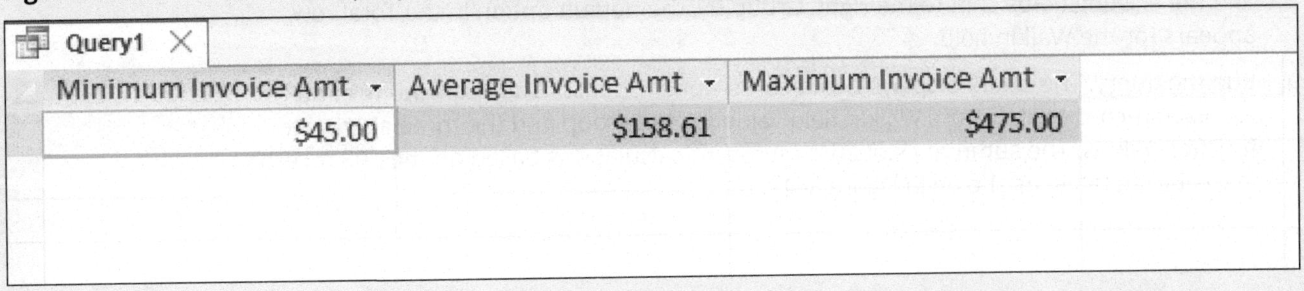

Query1

Minimum Invoice Amt	Average Invoice Amt	Maximum Invoice Amt
$45.00	$158.61	$475.00

11. Save the query as **InvoiceAmtStatistics**.

Susan also wants you to list the same invoice amount statistics (minimum, average, and maximum) as they relate to appointments and walk-in visits.

Using Record Group Calculations

In addition to calculating statistical information on all or selected records in specified tables, you can calculate statistics for groups of records. The **Group By operator** divides the records into groups based on the values in the specified field. Those records with the same value for the field are grouped together, and the datasheet displays one record for each group. Aggregate functions, which appear in the other columns of the design grid, provide statistical information for each group.

To create a query for Susan's latest request, you will modify the current query by adding the WalkIn field and assigning the Group By operator to it. The Group By operator will display the statistical information grouped by the values of the WalkIn field for all the records in the query datasheet. To create the new query, you will save the InvoiceAmtStatistics query with a new name, keeping the original query intact, and then modify the new query.

To create a new query with the Group By operator:

1. Display the InvoiceAmtStatistics query in Design view. Because the query is open, you can use Backstage view to save it with a new name, keeping the original query intact.
2. Click the **File** tab to display Backstage view, and then click **Save As** in the navigation bar. The Save As screen opens.
3. In the File Types section on the left, click **Save Object As**. The right side of the screen changes to display options for saving the current database object as a new object.
4. Click **Save As**. The Save As dialog box opens, indicating that you are saving a copy of the InvoiceAmtStatistics query.
5. Type **InvoiceAmtStatisticsByWalkIn** to replace the selected name, and then press **ENTER**. The new query is saved with the name you provided and appears in Design view.

   You need to add the WalkIn field to the query. This field is in the Visit table. To include another table in an existing query, you open the Add Tables pane.

   Tip You could also open the Navigation Pane and drag the Visit table from the pane to the Query window.

6. On the Query Design tab, in the Query Setup group, click the **Add Tables** button to open the Add Tables pane.
7. Add the **Visit** table to the Query window, close the Add Tables pane, and then resize the Visit field list if necessary.
8. Drag the **WalkIn** field from the Visit field list to the first column in the design grid. When you release the mouse button, the WalkIn field appears in the design grid's first column, and the existing fields shift to the right. Group By, the default option in the Total row, appears for the WalkIn field.
9. Run the query. The query displays two records—one for each WalkIn group, Yes and No. Each record contains the WalkIn field value for the group and the three aggregate function values. The summary statistics represent calculations based on the 202 records in the Billing table, as shown in Figure 3–41.

Figure 3–41 Aggregate functions grouped by WalkIn

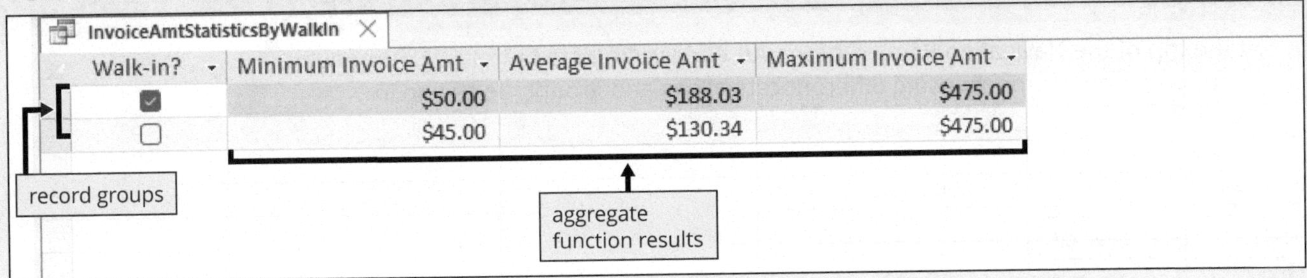

Susan notes that invoice amounts for walk-in visits are higher than those for scheduled appointments.

10. Save and close the query.
11. Open the Navigation Pane.

You have created and saved many queries in the NP_AC_3_PineRidge database. The Navigation Pane provides options for opening and managing the queries you've created, and it provides options for the other objects in the database, such as tables, forms, and reports.

Working with the Navigation Pane

As noted earlier, the Navigation Pane is the main area for working with the objects in a database. As you continue to create objects in your database, you can display and work with them in different ways. The Navigation Pane provides options for grouping database objects to suit your needs. For example, you might want to view only the queries created for a certain table or all the query objects in the database.

Insight

Hiding and Displaying Objects in the Navigation Pane

In the Navigation Pane, you can hide the display of a group's objects by clicking the button to the right of the group name. Click the button again to expand the group and display its objects. You can also hide an object within a group, such as an individual query or report. To hide an object within a group, right-click the object and then click Hide in this Group. To display hidden objects without providing access to them, right-click the Navigation Pane title bar and then click Navigation Options. In the Navigation Options dialog box, select the Show Hidden Objects check box, and then click OK. To fully enable the object, right-click the object, and then click Unhide in this Group.

As you know, the Navigation Pane divides database objects into categories. Each category contains groups, and each group contains one or more objects. The default category is **Object Type**, which arranges objects by type—tables, queries, forms, and reports. The default group is **All Access Objects**, which displays all objects in the database. You can also choose to display only one type of object, such as tables.

The default group name, All Access Objects, appears at the top of the Navigation Pane. Currently, each object type—Tables and Queries—is displayed as a heading, and the objects related to each type are listed below the heading. To group objects differently, you can select another category by using the Navigation Pane menu. You'll try this next.

To group objects differently in the Navigation Pane:

1. At the top of the Navigation Pane, click the **All Access Objects** button . A menu opens with options for choosing different categories and groups, as shown in Figure 3–42.

Figure 3–42 Navigation Pane menu

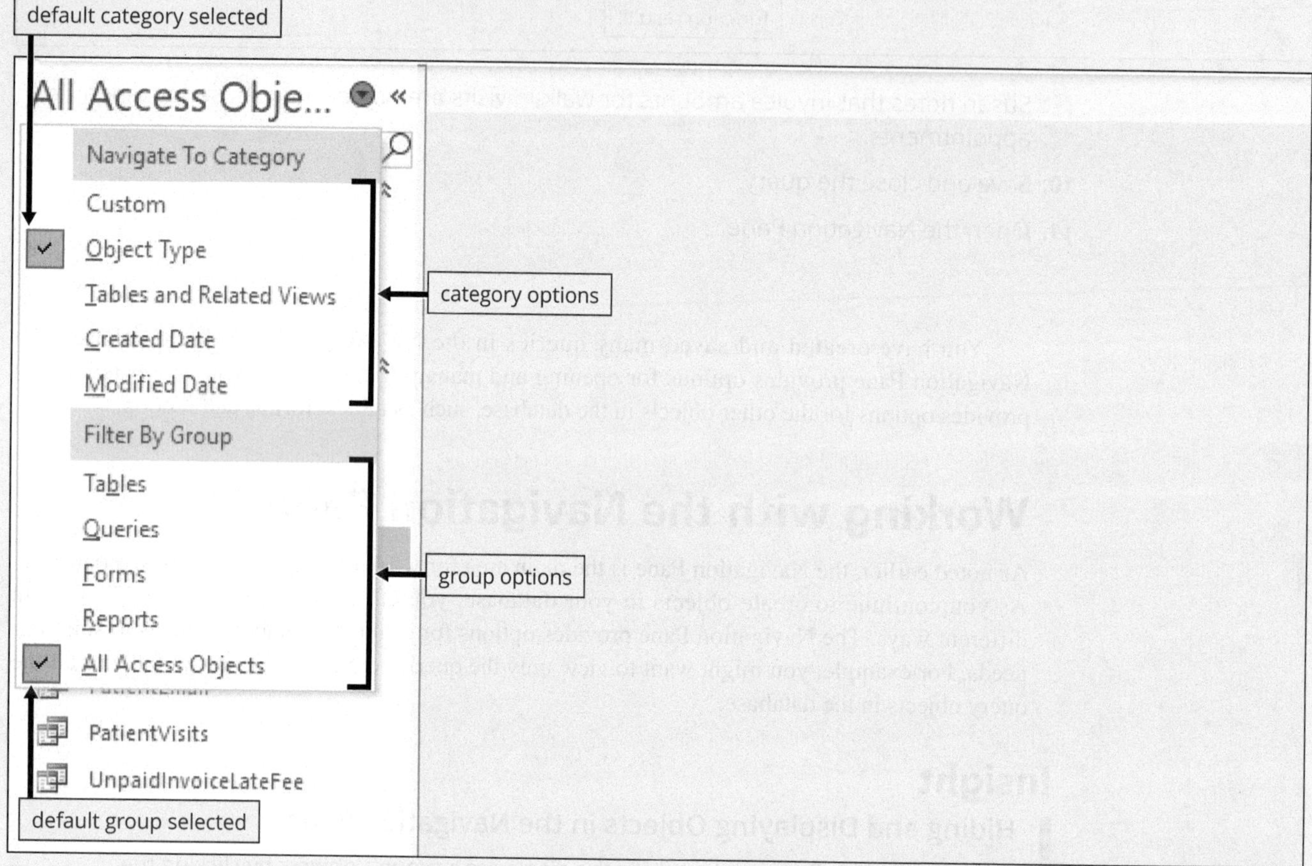

The top section of the menu provides the options for choosing a different category. The Object Type category has a checkmark next to it, signifying it is the selected category. The lower section of the menu provides options for choosing a different group; these options might change depending on the selected category.

2. In the Navigate To Category section, click **Tables and Related Views**. The Navigation Pane is now grouped into categories of tables, and each table in the database—Visit, Patient, and Billing—is its own group. All database objects related to a table are listed below the table's name, as shown in Figure 3–43.

Figure 3–43 Database objects grouped by table in the Navigation Pane

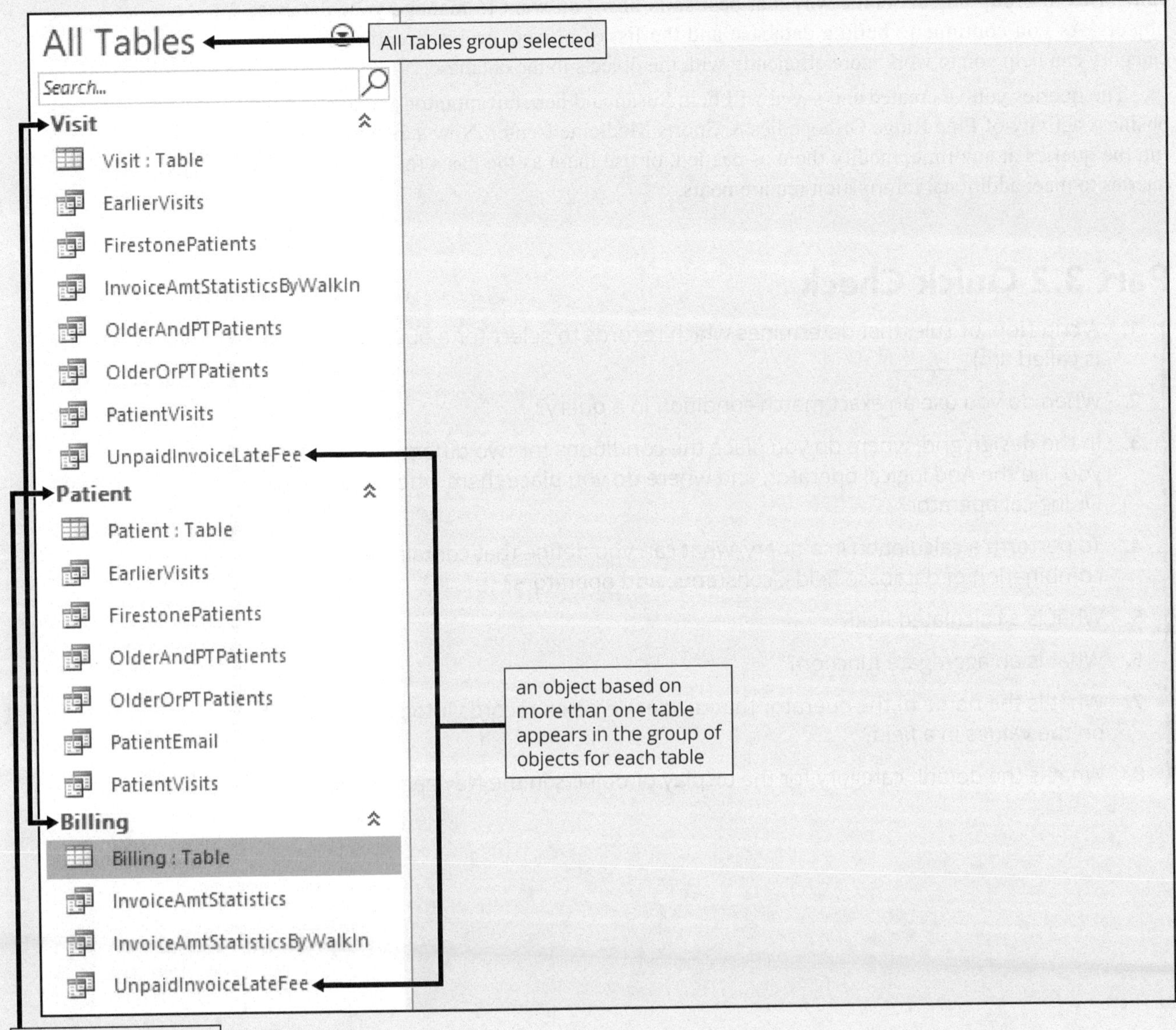

Trouble? If the Navigation Pane lists objects related to only one table, click the All Access Objects button, and then click All Tables.

Some objects appear more than once. When an object is based on more than one table, that object appears in the group for each table. For example, the UnpaidInvoiceLateFee query is based on both the Visit and Billing tables, so it is listed in the group for both tables.

You can also display the objects for only one table to better focus on that table.

3. At the top of the Navigation Pane, click the **All Tables** button to display the Navigation Pane menu, and then click **Patient**. The Navigation Pane now shows only the objects related to the Patient table—the table itself plus the six queries you created that include fields from the Patient table.
4. At the top of the Navigation Pane, click the **Patient** button, and then click **Object Type** to return to the default display of the Navigation Pane.
5. sam Compact and repair the NP_AC_3_PineRidge database, and then close it.

   Trouble? If a dialog box opens and warns that this action will cause Microsoft Access to empty the Clipboard, click Yes to continue.

The default All Access Objects category is a predefined category. You can also create custom categories to group objects in the way that best suits how you want to manage your database objects. As you continue to build a database and the list of objects grows, creating a custom category can help you to work more efficiently with the objects in the database.

The queries you've created and saved will help Susan and her staff monitor and analyze the business activity of Pine Ridge Orthopedics & Sports Medicine Center. Now staff members can run the queries at any time, modify them as needed, or use them as the basis for designing new queries to meet additional information requirements.

Part 3.2 Quick Check

1. A criterion, or rule, that determines which records to select for a query datasheet is called a(n) ________.
2. When do you use an exact match condition in a query?
3. In the design grid, where do you place the conditions for two different fields when you use the And logical operator, and where do you place them when you use the Or logical operator?
4. To perform a calculation in a query, what can you define that contains a combination of database fields, constants, and operators?
5. What is a calculated field?
6. What is an aggregate function?
7. What is the name of the operator that divides selected records into groups based on the values in a field?
8. What is the default category for the display of objects in the Navigation Pane?

Practice: Review Assignments

Data File needed for the Review Assignments: NP_AC_3-2.accdb

Susan asks you to update records in the Vendor database and to retrieve specific information about suppliers. Be sure to use the starting data file, NP_AC_3-2.accdb, to complete the Review Assignments so your solutions match those provided by your instructor. Complete the following steps:

1. Open the NP_AC_3-2.accdb database from the Access3 > Review folder included with your Data Files, and then save it as **NP_AC_3_Vendor** in the location specified by your instructor. Click the Enable Content button next to the security warning, if necessary.
2. Open the Supplier table in Datasheet view, and then change the following field values for the record with the Supplier ID HAR912: Address to **912 Monroe Dr**, Contact Phone to **865-555-3321**, Contact First Name to **Martina**, and Contact Last Name to **Novak**. Close the table.
3. Create a query based on the Supplier table. Include the following fields in the query, in the order shown: Company, Category, ContactFirst, ContactLast, Phone, and City. Sort the query in ascending order based on the Category field values. Save the query as **ContactList**, and then run the query.
4. Use the ContactList query datasheet to update the Supplier table by changing the Phone field value for Casper Enterprises to **803-555-2145**. Replace the name of the contact for the first record (Durham Medical Equipment, Edgar Wayles) with your first and last names.
5. Change the size of the text in the ContactList query datasheet to use a 12-point font size. Resize columns as necessary so that all field values and column headings are visible.
6. Change the alternate row color in the ContactList query datasheet to Blue, Accent 1, Lighter 80% (fifth column, second row in the Theme Colors palette), and then save and close the query.
7. Create a query based on the Supplier and Product tables. Select the Company, Category, and State fields from the Supplier table, and the ProductName, Price, Units, and Weight fields from the Product table. Sort the query results in descending order based on price. Select only those records with a Category field value of Supplies, but do not display the Category field values in the query results. Save the query as **MedicalSupplies**, run the query, resize the Price column to its best fit, and then save and close the query.
8. Create a query that lists all products that cost more than $100 and are temperature controlled. Display the following fields from the Product table in the query results: ProductID, ProductName, Price, Units, and Sterile. (**Hint**: The TempControl field is a Yes/No field that should not appear in the query results.) Save the query as **HighPriceAndTempControl**, run the query, and then close it.
9. Create a query that lists information about suppliers who sell equipment or sterile products. Include the Company, Category, ContactFirst, and ContactLast fields from the Supplier table, and the ProductName, Price, and Sterile fields from the Product table. Save the query as **EquipmentOrSterile**, run the query, and then close it.
10. Create a query that lists all products and a 10 percent markup amount based on the price of the product. Include the Company field from the Supplier table and the following fields from the Product table in the query: ProductID, ProductName, and Price. Save the query as **ProductsWithMarkup**. Display the markup amount in a calculated field named **Markup** that determines a 10 percent markup based on the Price field values. Set the Caption property to **Mark Up** for the calculated field. Display the query results in descending order by Price. Save and run the query.
11. Modify the format of the Markup field in the ProductsWithMarkup query so that it uses the Standard format and two decimal places. Run the query, resize all columns in the datasheet to their best fit, and then save and close the query.
12. Create a query that calculates the lowest, highest, and average prices for all products using the field names **MinimumPrice**, **MaximumPrice**, and **AveragePrice**, respectively. Set the Caption property for each field to include a space between the two words in the field name. Run the query, resize all columns in the datasheet to their best fit, save the query as **PriceStatistics**, and then close it.
13. In the Navigation Pane, copy the PriceStatistics query, and then rename the copied query as **PriceStatisticsByCompany**.
14. Modify the PriceStatisticsByCompany query so that the records are grouped by the Company field in the Supplier table. The Company field should appear first in the query datasheet. Save and run the query, and then close it.
15. Compact and repair the NP_AC_3_Vendor database, and then close it.

Apply: Case Problem 1

Data File needed for this Case Problem: NP_AC_3-3.accdb

Tech Tutors Taylor needs to modify a few records and analyze data in the Tech Tutors database. To help her, you'll update the Tech Tutors database and create queries to answer her questions. Be sure to use the starting data file, NP_AC_3-3.accdb, to complete Case Problem 1 so your solutions match those provided by your instructor. Complete the following steps:

1. Open the NP_AC_3-3.accdb database from the Access3 > Case1 folder included with your Data Files, and then save it as **NP_AC_3_TechTutors** in the location specified by your instructor. Click the Enable Content button next to the security warning, if necessary.
2. In the Student table, find the record for StudentID PAS2020, and then change the Address value to **420 Jefferson Ave** and the Zip to **30314**. Replace the names in the first record (StudentID AND2010, Jill Anderson) with your first and last names.
3. In the Student table, find the record for StudentID RAM2025, and then delete the record. (**Hint**: Delete the related record in the Contract subdatasheet first.) Close the Student table.
4. Create a query that lists students who have a private session contract with Tech Tutors. Display only the StudentID, FirstName, and LastName fields for the students in your results. Do not display the SessionType values in the results. Sort the results in ascending order by the LastName field. Save the query as **PrivateSessions**, run the query, and then close it.
5. In the Navigation Pane, copy the PrivateSessions query, and then rename the copied query as **AtlantaPrivateSessions**.
6. Modify the AtlantaPrivateSessions query so that it displays students from Atlanta with a private session contract. The SessionType and City fields should not appear in the query datasheet. Save and run the query, and then close it.
7. Create a query that lists students with a Computer Science major who are taking more than five sessions. In the query results, display only the StudentID, FirstName, LastName, CellPhone, and NumSessions fields of the Computer Science majors. Sort the results by LastName in ascending order. Save the query as **CompSciMajors** and run the query.
8. Use the CompSciMajors query datasheet to update the Student table by using **(404) 555-2266** as the CellPhone value for Alex Vasquez.
9. Change the size of the text in the CompSciMajors query datasheet to use a 14-point font size. Resize columns as necessary so that all field values and column headings are displayed.
10. Change the alternate row color in the CompSciMajors query datasheet to Orange, Accent 2, Lighter 80% (sixth column, second row in the Theme Colors palette), and then save and close the query.
11. Create a query that lists the TutorID, LastName, YearInSchool, and HireDate fields for tutors who are seniors or were hired before April 1, 2029. Save the query as **SeniorsOrFirstQuarter**, run the query, and then close it.
12. Create a query that lists the total sum of contract costs grouped by SessionType. Name the summation column **TotalCost**. Run the query, save it as **TotalCostsByType**, and then close the query.
13. Compact and repair the NP_AC_3_TechTutors database, and then close it.

Challenge: Case Problem 2

Data File needed for this Case Problem: NP_AC_3-4.accdb

Outdoor Adventure Tours David and Brent need to modify some records in the Outdoor database, and then they want to find specific information about the tours. Brent asks you to help him update the database and create queries to find the information he needs. Be sure to use the starting data file, NP_AC_3-4.accdb, to complete Case Problem 2 so your solutions match those provided by your instructor. Complete the following steps:

1. Open the NP_AC_3-4.accdb database from the Access3 > Case2 folder included with your Data Files, and then save it as **NP_AC_3_Outdoor** in the location specified by your instructor. Click the Enable Content button next to the security warning, if necessary.
2. Create a query based on the Hiker and Reservation tables that includes the HikerFirst, HikerLast, ReservationID, TourDate, and People fields, in that order. Display only those records whose TourDate is on or after October 1, 2029. Save the query as **FallHikers** and then run it.
3. Modify the FallHikers query design so that it sorts records in ascending order first by TourDate and then by HikerLast. (Keep the HikerFirst field to the immediate left of the HikerLast field.) Save and run the query.
4. Create a query based on the Hiker, Reservation, and Tour tables that lists people taking hiking tours in September 2029. Display the HikerID, HikerLast, TourDate, and TourName fields in the query results. (**Hint**: Use the Between ... And operator with the TourDate field.) Save the query as **SeptemberHiking** and then run it.
5. Create a query to provide statistics about the hours and prices of the tours. In the query results, show the sum of the hours and the price per person, grouped by the TourType field. Name the Hours summation column **TotalHours**. Name the PricePerPerson summation column **TotalPrice**. Save the query as **TourStatistics** and then run it.
6. **Explore:** Modify the TourStatistics query by adding a calculated field named **PricePerHour** that divides the PricePerPerson values by the Hours values. (**Hint**: Place brackets around each field in the calculation.) Use a Currency format for the PricePerHour field and use **Price Per Hour** for the field's Caption property. Run the query, resize all columns in the datasheet to their best fit, and then save the query.
7. Create a query that lists tour and reservation information. Include the TourName, TourType, TourDate, Hours, People, and PricePerPerson fields, in that order. Add a calculated field named **TotalPrice** that multiplies the number of people by the price per person. Use the Currency format for the TotalPrice field and use **Total Price** for the field's Caption property. Save the query as **TourPrices** and then run and close the query.
8. **Explore:** Create a query to total the tour and reservation information from the TourPrices query. (**Hint**: The data source for a query can be a table or another query. To choose a query, click Queries in the Add Tables pane.) Sum the values of the Hours, People, PricePerPerson, and TotalPrice fields. Run the query, resize all columns in the datasheet to their best fit, save the query as **ReservationStats**, and then close it.
9. **Explore:** Format the datasheet of the FallHikers query so that it does not display gridlines, uses the Maroon 1 alternate row color (sixth column, second row in the Standard Colors palette), and displays a font size of 16. (**Hint**: Use the Gridlines button in the Text Formatting group on the Home tab to select the appropriate gridlines option.) Replace the names in the first record (Heather Davis) with your first and last names. Resize the columns to display the complete field names and values, and then save and close the query.
10. **Explore:** In the Tour table, each TourID value has a plus sign (expand indicator) next to it, indicating a relationship to another table. To view each related record in the Reservation table, you can scroll and click each expand indicator or you can click the Datasheet Selector button to the left of the TourID field name and then click an expand indicator to expand all of the records. For TourID 235 (Virginia Creeper Trail), change the tour date in the reservation to **10/20/29** to replace the 10/13/29 tour date. To close all of the expanded records, click the Datasheet Selector button again, and then click one of the minus signs (collapse indicators). Close the datasheet. Because you did not change the structure of the table, you will not be prompted to save your changes.
11. Compact and repair the NP_AC_3_Outdoor database, and then close it.

Creating Forms and Reports

Using Forms and Reports to Display Patient and Visit Data

Case: Pine Ridge Orthopedics & Sports Medicine Center

Susan Martinez wants you to continue enhancing the Pine Ridge database to make it easier for her staff to enter, locate, and maintain data. In particular, she wants the database to include a form based on the Patient table that staff can use to enter and change data about the center's patients. She also wants the database to include a form that includes data from the Patient and Visit tables. This form will show the visit information for each patient along with the corresponding patient data, providing a complete picture of Pine Ridge Orthopedics & Sports Medicine Center patients and their visits to the center.

In addition, she wants to include a report of patient and visit data so that she and other staff members can refer to printed output when completing analyses and planning strategies for community outreach efforts. She wants the report to be formatted professionally and easy to use.

In this module, you will create the forms and reports in the Pine Ridge database for Susan and her staff.

Be sure to use the starting data file, NP_AC_4-1.accdb, when you begin working in this module so your solutions match those provided by your instructor.

Starting Data Files: Access4

Module

NP_AC_4-1.accdb
Support_AC_4_Chart.png

Review

NP_AC_4-2.accdb
Support_AC_4_Microscope.png
Support_AC_4_Stethoscope.png

Case1

NP_AC_4-3.accdb
Support_AC_4_Laptop.png

Case2

NP_AC_4-4.accdb
Support_AC_4_Tree.png

Objectives

Part 4.1

- Create a form using the Form Wizard
- Apply a theme to a form
- Add a picture to a form
- Change the color of text on a form
- Find and maintain data using a form
- Preview and print selected form records
- Create a form with a main form and a subform

Part 4.2

- Create a report using the Report Wizard
- Apply a theme to a report
- Change the alignment of field values in a report
- Move and resize fields in a report
- Insert a picture in a report
- Change the color of text in a report
- Apply conditional formatting in a report
- Preview and print a report

Part 4.1 Visual Overview: Form Displayed in Form View

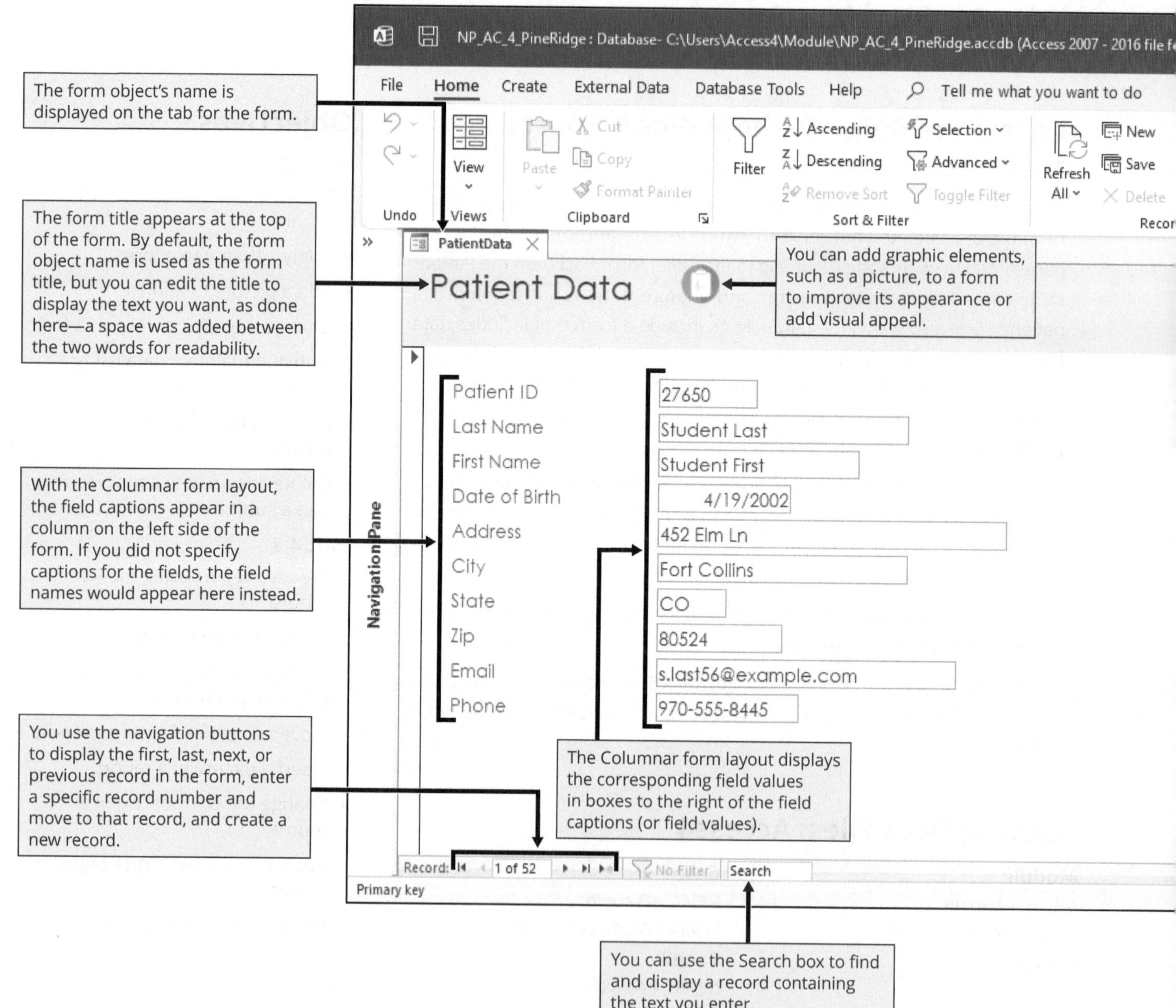
NP_AC_4_PineRidge : Database- C:\Users\Access4\Module\NP_AC_4_PineRidge.accdb (Access 2007 - 2016 file f
File
Home
Create
External Data
Database Tools
Help
Tell me what you want to do
View
Undo
Views
Paste
Cut
Copy
Format Painter
Clipboard
Filter
Ascending
Descending
Remove Sort
Selection
Advanced
Toggle Filter
Sort & Filter
Refresh All
New
Save
Delete
Recor
The form object's name is displayed on the tab for the form.
PatientData
The form title appears at the top of the form. By default, the form object name is used as the form title, but you can edit the title to display the text you want, as done here—a space was added between the two words for readability.
Patient Data
You can add graphic elements, such as a picture, to a form to improve its appearance or add visual appeal.
Patient ID
Last Name
First Name
Date of Birth
Address
City
State
Zip
Email
Phone
27650
Student Last
Student First
4/19/2002
452 Elm Ln
Fort Collins
CO
80524
s.last56@example.com
970-555-8445
Navigation Pane
With the Columnar form layout, the field captions appear in a column on the left side of the form. If you did not specify captions for the fields, the field names would appear here instead.
You use the navigation buttons to display the first, last, next, or previous record in the form, enter a specific record number and move to that record, and create a new record.
The Columnar form layout displays the corresponding field values in boxes to the right of the field captions (or field values).
Record: 1 of 52
No Filter
Search
Primary key
You can use the Search box to find and display a record containing the text you enter.

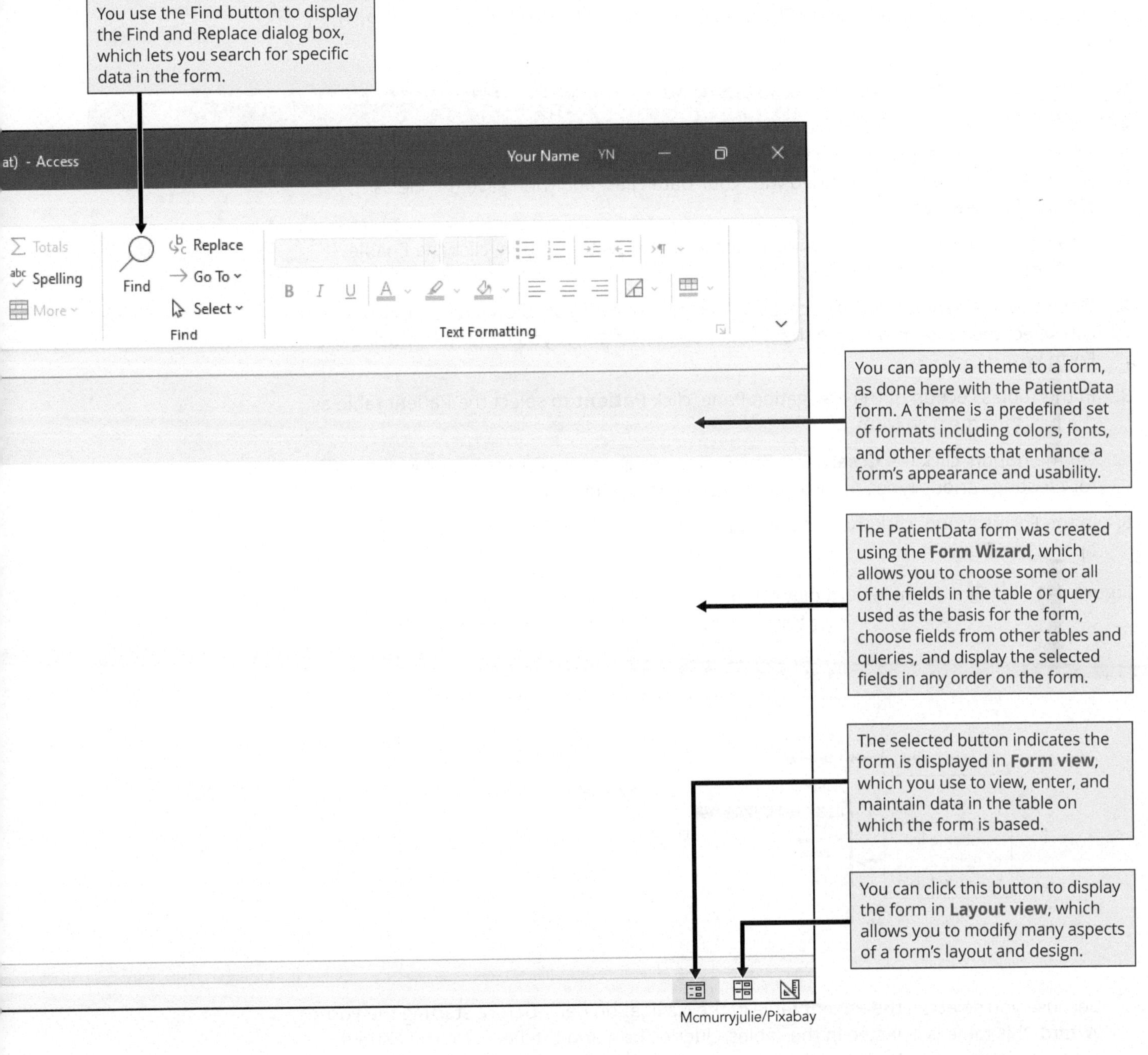

You use the Find button to display the Find and Replace dialog box, which lets you search for specific data in the form.
at) - Access
Your Name YN
Totals
Spelling
More
Find
Replace
Go To
Select
Find
Text Formatting
You can apply a theme to a form, as done here with the PatientData form. A theme is a predefined set of formats including colors, fonts, and other effects that enhance a form's appearance and usability.
The PatientData form was created using the Form Wizard, which allows you to choose some or all of the fields in the table or query used as the basis for the form, choose fields from other tables and queries, and display the selected fields in any order on the form.
The selected button indicates the form is displayed in Form view, which you use to view, enter, and maintain data in the table on which the form is based.
You can click this button to display the form in Layout view, which allows you to modify many aspects of a form's layout and design.

Mcmurryjulie/Pixabay

Creating a Form Using the Form Wizard

As you learned earlier, a form is an object you use to enter, edit, and view records in a database. You can design your own forms or use tools in Access to create them automatically. You have already used the Form Wizard to create the simple VisitData form in the Pine Ridge database. You will use additional features and options when creating a form like the one in the Part 4.1 Visual Overview.

Susan asks you to create a new form that her staff can use to view and maintain data in the Patient table. To create the form for the Patient table, you'll use the Form Wizard, which guides you through the process.

To open the Pine Ridge database and start the Form Wizard:

1. sam Start Access and open the NP_AC_4-1.accdb database from the Access4 > Module folder included with your Data Files, and then save the file as **NP_AC_4_PineRidge**.

   Trouble? If the security warning is displayed below the ribbon, click the Enable Content button.

2. Open the Navigation Pane, if necessary. To create a form based on a table or query, you can select the table or query in the Navigation Pane first, or you can select it using the Form Wizard.
3. In the Tables section of the Navigation Pane, click **Patient** to select the Patient table as the basis for the new form.
4. On the ribbon, click the **Create** tab. The Forms group on the Create tab provides options for creating various types of forms and designing your own forms.
5. In the Forms group, click the **Form Wizard** button. The first Form Wizard dialog box opens. See Figure 4-1.

Figure 4-1 First Form Wizard dialog box

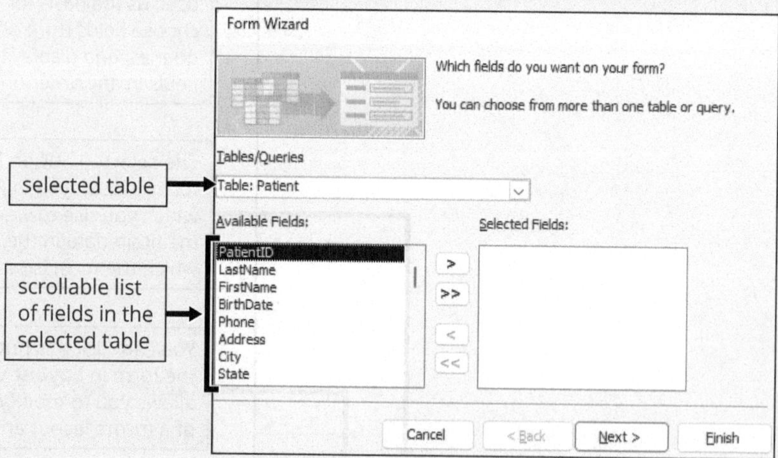

Because you selected the Patient table in the Navigation Pane before starting the Form Wizard, this table is selected in the Tables/Queries box, and the fields for the Patient table are listed in the Available Fields box.

Susan wants the form to display all the fields in the Patient table, but in a different order. She would like the Phone field to appear at the bottom of the form so that it stands out, making it easier for someone who needs to call patients to use the form to quickly locate their phone numbers.

To create the form using the Form Wizard:

1. Click the **Select All Fields** button >> to move all the fields to the Selected Fields box.
   Next, you need to position the Phone field so it will appear as the last field on the form. To accomplish this, you first remove the Phone field and then add it back as the last selected field.
2. In the Selected Fields box, click the **Phone** field, and then click the **Remove Single Field** button < to move the field back to the Available Fields box.
   Because a new field is always added after the selected field in the Selected Fields box, you need to first select the last field in the list and then move the Phone field back to the Selected Fields box so it will be the last field on the form.
3. In the Selected Fields box, click the **Email** field.
4. With the Phone field selected in the Available Fields box, click the **Select Single Field** button > to move the Phone field to the end of the list in the Selected Fields box.
5. Click the **Next** button to display the second Form Wizard dialog box, in which you select a layout for the form. See Figure 4–2.

Figure 4–2 Choosing a layout for the form

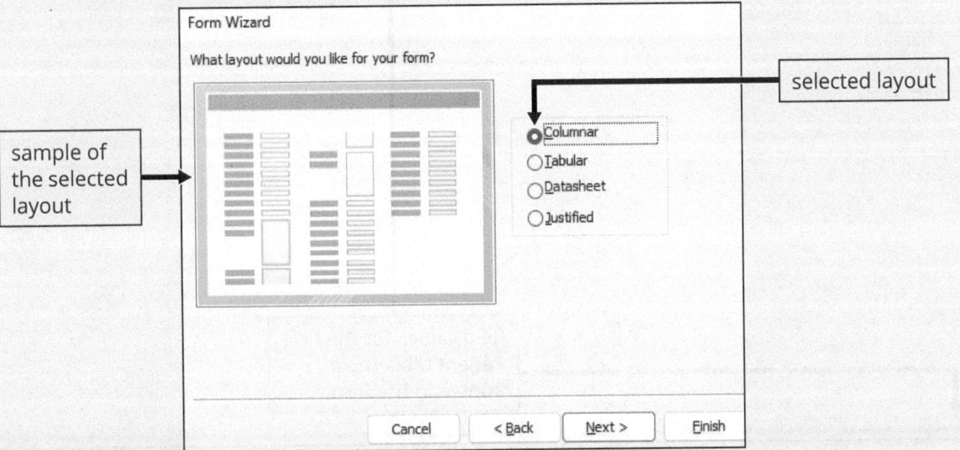

The layout choices are Columnar, Tabular, Datasheet, and Justified. A sample of the selected layout appears on the left side of the dialog box.

6. Click each option button and review the corresponding sample layout.
   The Tabular and Datasheet layouts display the fields from multiple records at one time, whereas the Columnar and Justified layouts display the fields from one record at a time. Susan thinks the Columnar layout is the appropriate arrangement for displaying and updating data in the table, so that anyone using the form can focus on just one patient record at a time.
7. Click the **Columnar** option button (if necessary), and then click the **Next** button.
   The third and final Form Wizard dialog box shows the Patient table's name as the default form name. "Patient" is also the default title that will appear on the tab for the form. You'll use "PatientData" as the form name, and because you don't need to change the form's design now, you'll display the form.
8. Click to position the insertion point to the right of "Patient" in the box, type **Data**, and then click the **Finish** button.
   Close the Navigation Pane to display only the Form window. The completed form opens in Form view, displaying the values for the first record in the Patient table. The Columnar layout you selected places the field captions in labels on the left and the corresponding field values in boxes on the right, which vary in width depending on the size of the field. See Figure 4–3.

Figure 4–3 PatientData form in Form view

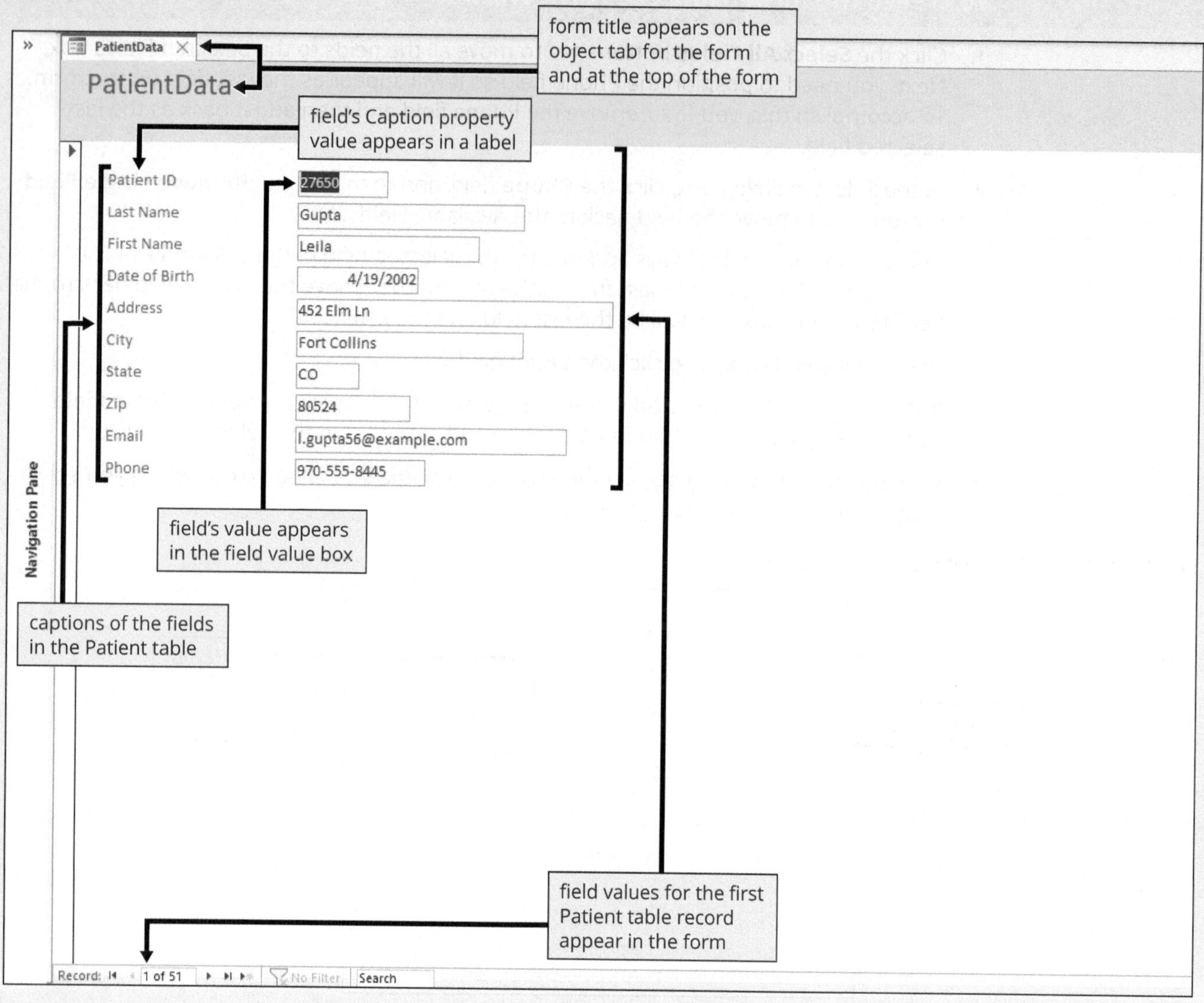

After viewing the form, Susan makes suggestions for improving the form's readability and appearance. The font used in the labels on the left is light in color and small, making them difficult to read. Also, she thinks inserting a graphic on the form would add visual interest and modifying other form elements—such as the color of the title text—would improve the look of the form. You can make all these changes working with the form in Layout view.

Modifying a Form's Design in Layout View

After you create a form, you might need to modify its design to improve its appearance or to make the form easier to use. You cannot make any design changes in Form view. However, Layout view displays the form as it appears in Form view while allowing you to modify the form's design. Because you can display the form and its data while you are modifying the form, Layout view makes it easy for you to check the results of any design changes you make.

> **Tip** Some form design changes require you to switch to Design view, which gives you a more detailed view of the form's structure.

The first modification you'll make to the PatientData form is to change its appearance by applying a theme.

Applying a Theme to a Database Object

By default, the objects you create in a database are formatted with the Office theme. A theme provides a design scheme for the colors and fonts used in the database objects. Access, like other Microsoft Office programs, provides many built-in themes, including the Office theme, making it easy for you to create objects with a unified look. You can also create a customized theme if none of the built-in themes suit your needs.

Sometimes a theme works well for one database object but is not as suitable for other objects in that database. When applying a theme to an object, you can choose to apply the theme to the open object only, to objects of a particular type, or to all the objects in the database and set it as the default theme for any new objects in the database.

To change a form's appearance, you can apply a new theme to it.

Reference

Applying a Theme to Database Objects

- Display the object in Layout view.
- In the Themes group on the Form Layout Design tab or Report Layout Design tab, click the Themes button.
- In the Themes gallery, click the theme you want to apply to all objects, or right-click the theme to display the shortcut menu and then choose to apply the theme to the current object only or to all matching objects.

Susan suggests you try to improve the appearance of the PatientData form with a different theme. To apply a theme, you first need to switch to Layout view.

To apply a theme to the PatientData form:

1. On the ribbon, make sure the Home tab is displayed.
2. In the Views group, click **View**. The form is displayed in Layout view. See Figure 4–4.

Figure 4–4 Form displayed in Layout view

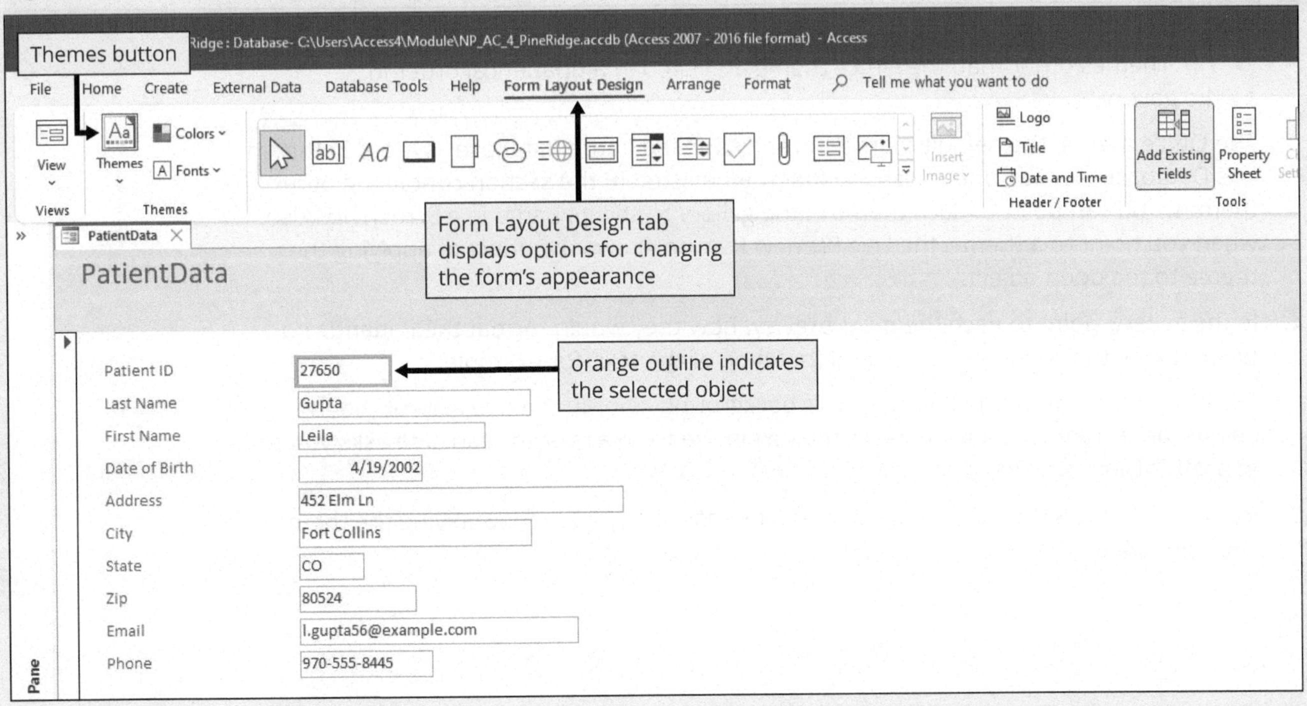

Trouble? If the Field List or Property Sheet opens on the right side of the program window, close it before continuing.

In Layout view, an orange border identifies the currently selected element on the form. In this case, the field value for the PatientID field, 27650, is selected. You need to apply a theme to the PatientData form.

3. On the Form Layout Design tab, in the Themes group, click **Themes**. A gallery opens showing the available themes for the form. See Figure 4–5.

Figure 4–5 Themes gallery

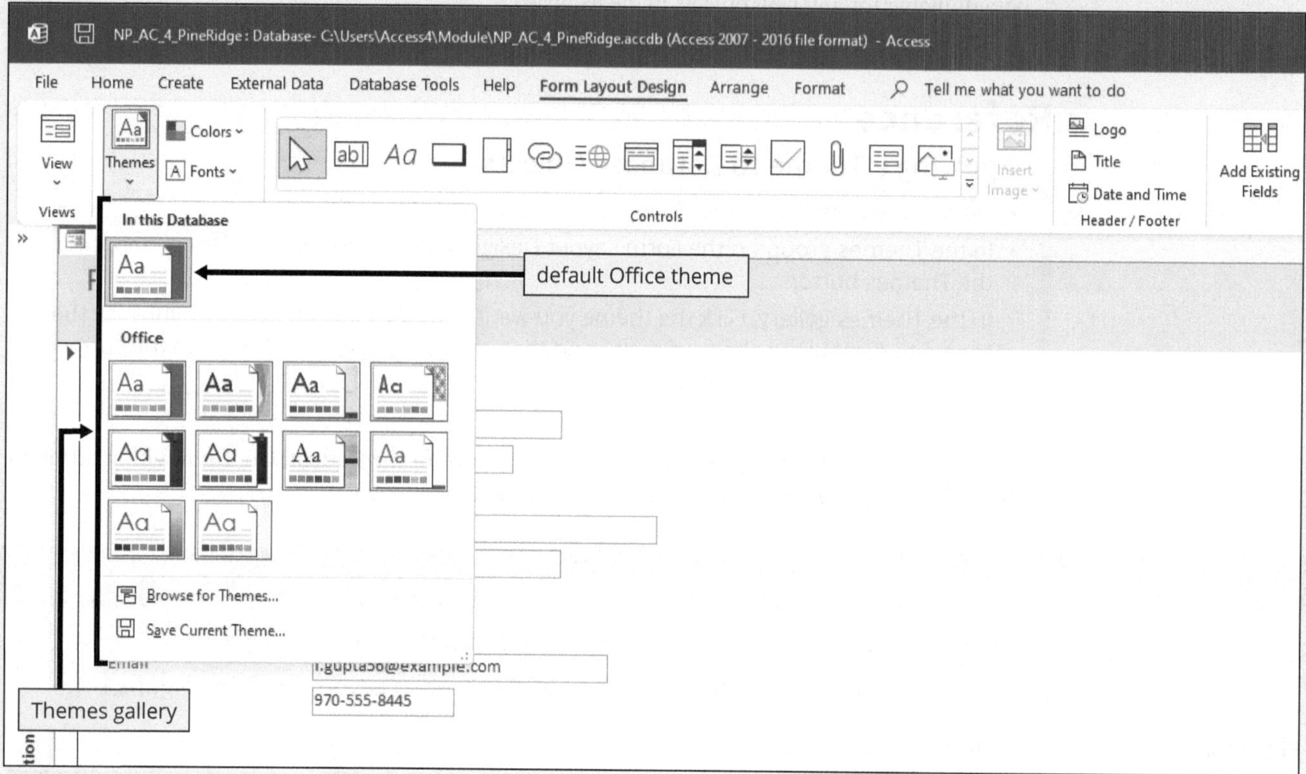

Tip Themes other than the Office theme are listed in alphabetical order in the gallery.

The Office theme, the default theme currently applied in the database, is listed in the "In this Database" section and is also the first theme listed in the section containing other themes. You can point to each theme in the gallery to see its name in a ScreenTip. Also, when you point to a theme, the Live Preview feature shows the effect of applying the theme to the open object.

4. In the gallery, point to each theme to preview how they would format the PatientData form. Notice the changes in color and font type of the text, for example.

   Susan likes the Ion theme because of its background color in the title area at the top and its larger font size, which makes the text in the form easier to read. She asks you to apply this theme to the form.

5. Right-click the **Ion** theme. A shortcut menu opens with options for applying the theme. See Figure 4–6.

Figure 4–6 Shortcut menu for applying the theme

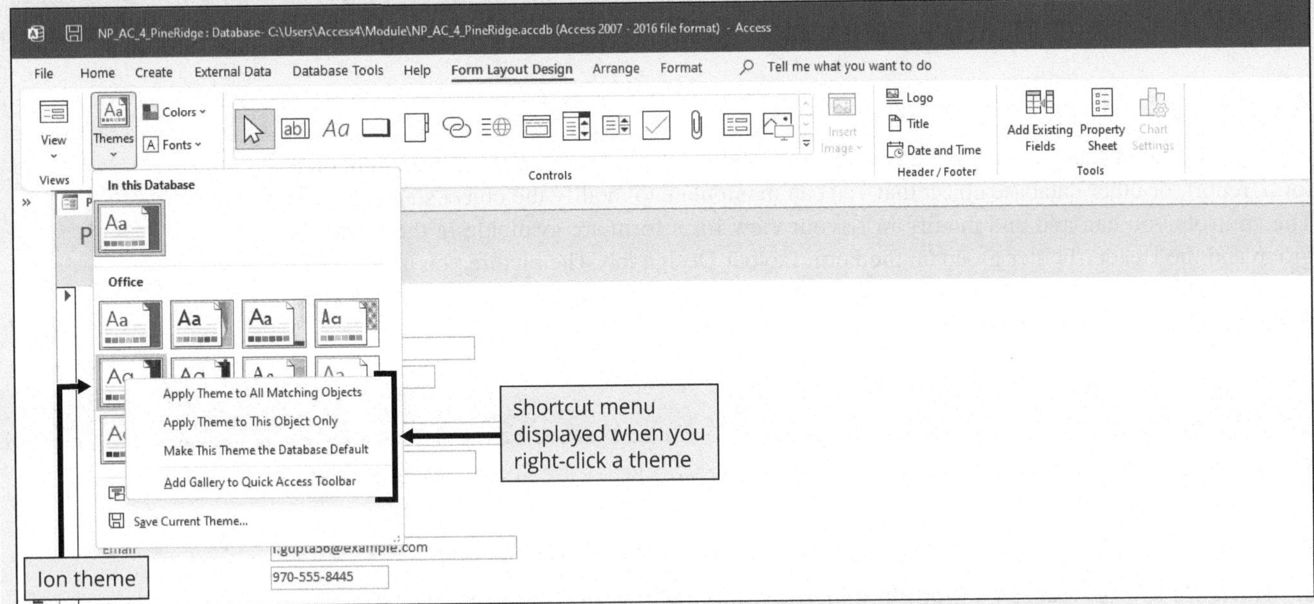

The menu provides options for applying the theme to all matching objects—for example, all the forms in the database—or to the current object only. You can also choose to make the theme the default theme in the database, which means any new objects you create will be formatted with the selected theme. Because Susan is not sure if all forms in the NP_AC_4_PineRidge database will look better with the Ion theme, she asks you to apply it only to the PatientData form.

6. On the shortcut menu, click **Apply Theme to This Object Only**.

   Key Step Choose this option to avoid applying the theme to other forms in the database.

   The gallery closes, and the Ion theme's colors and fonts are applied to the form.

   Trouble? If you choose the wrong option by mistake, you might apply the selected theme to other forms and reports in the database. If necessary, repeat Steps 3 through 6 to apply the Ion theme to the PatientData form. You can also follow the same process to reapply the default Office theme to the other forms and reports in the NP_AC_4_PineRidge database, as directed by your instructor.

Insight

Working with Themes

Themes provide a quick way for you to format the objects in a database with a consistent look, which is a good design principle to follow. In general, all objects of the same type in a database—for example, all forms—should have a consistent design. However, keep in mind that when you select a theme in the Themes gallery and choose the option to apply the theme to all matching objects or to make the theme the default for the database, it might be applied to all the existing forms and reports in the database and to new forms and reports you create. Although this approach ensures a consistent design, it can cause problems. For example, if you have already created a form or report with a suitable design, applying a theme that includes a larger font size could cut off the text in labels and field value boxes or extend the text into other elements on the form or report. The colors in the theme could also interfere with elements on existing forms and reports. To handle these unintended results, you would have to spend time checking the forms and reports and fixing any problems introduced when applying the theme. A better approach is to select the option "Apply Theme to This Object Only," available on the shortcut menu for a theme in the Themes gallery, for each form and report. If the newly applied theme causes problems for any individual form or report, you can then reapply the original theme to return the object to its original design.

Next, you will add a picture to the form for visual interest. The picture, which is included on various flyers and other patient correspondence for Pine Ridge Orthopedics & Sports Medicine Center, is a small graphic of a patient chart.

Adding a Picture to a Form

A picture is one of many controls you can add and modify on a form. A **control** is an item on a form, report, or other database object that you can manipulate to modify the object's appearance. The controls you can add and modify in Layout view for a form are available in the Controls group and the Header/Footer group on the Form Layout Design tab. The picture you need to add is contained in a file named Support_AC_4_Chart.png, which is located in the Access4 > Module folder provided with your Data Files.

To add the picture to the form:

1. Make sure the form is still displayed in Layout view and that the Form Layout Design tab is active.
2. In the Header/Footer group, click **Logo**. The Insert Picture dialog box opens.
3. Navigate to the **Access4 > Module** folder provided with your Data Files, click the **Support_AC_4_Chart.png** file, and then click **OK**. The picture appears on top of the form's title. See Figure 4–7.

Figure 4–7 Form with picture added

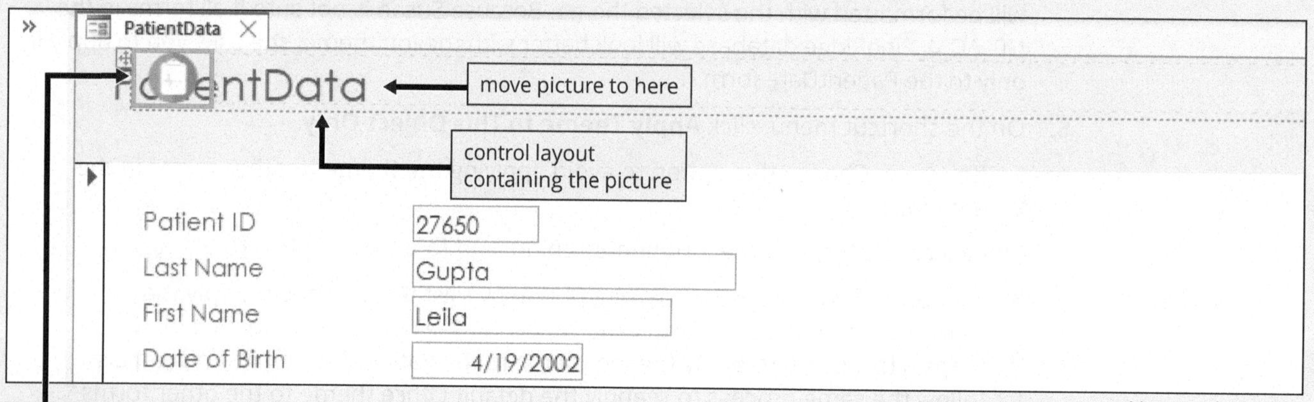

Mcmurryjulie/Pixabay

A solid orange border surrounds the picture, indicating it is selected. The picture is placed in a **control layout**, which is a set of controls grouped together in a form or report so that you can manipulate the set as a single control. The dotted outline indicates the control layout. The easiest way to move the picture from the form title is to first remove it from the control layout. Doing so allows you to move the picture independently.

4. Right-click the picture to open the shortcut menu, point to **Layout**, and then click **Remove Layout**. The dotted outline no longer appears, and the picture is removed from the control layout. Now you can move the picture to the right of the form title.
5. Position the pointer on the picture, and then drag to the right of the form title. Although the image does not appear while you drag it, you can use the position of the pointer as a guide for placing the image.

> **Tip** You can resize a selected image by dragging a corner of the orange selection border.

6. When the pointer is about one-half inch to the right of the form's title, release the mouse button. The picture is positioned to the right of the form title.
7. Click in a blank area to the right of the field values in the form to deselect the picture. See Figure 4–8.

> **Trouble?** The picture does not have to be in the exact location as the one shown in Figure 4–8. Just make sure the picture is not blocking any part of the form title and that it appears to the right of the form title, within the shaded area at the top of the form.

Figure 4–8 Form with theme applied and picture repositioned

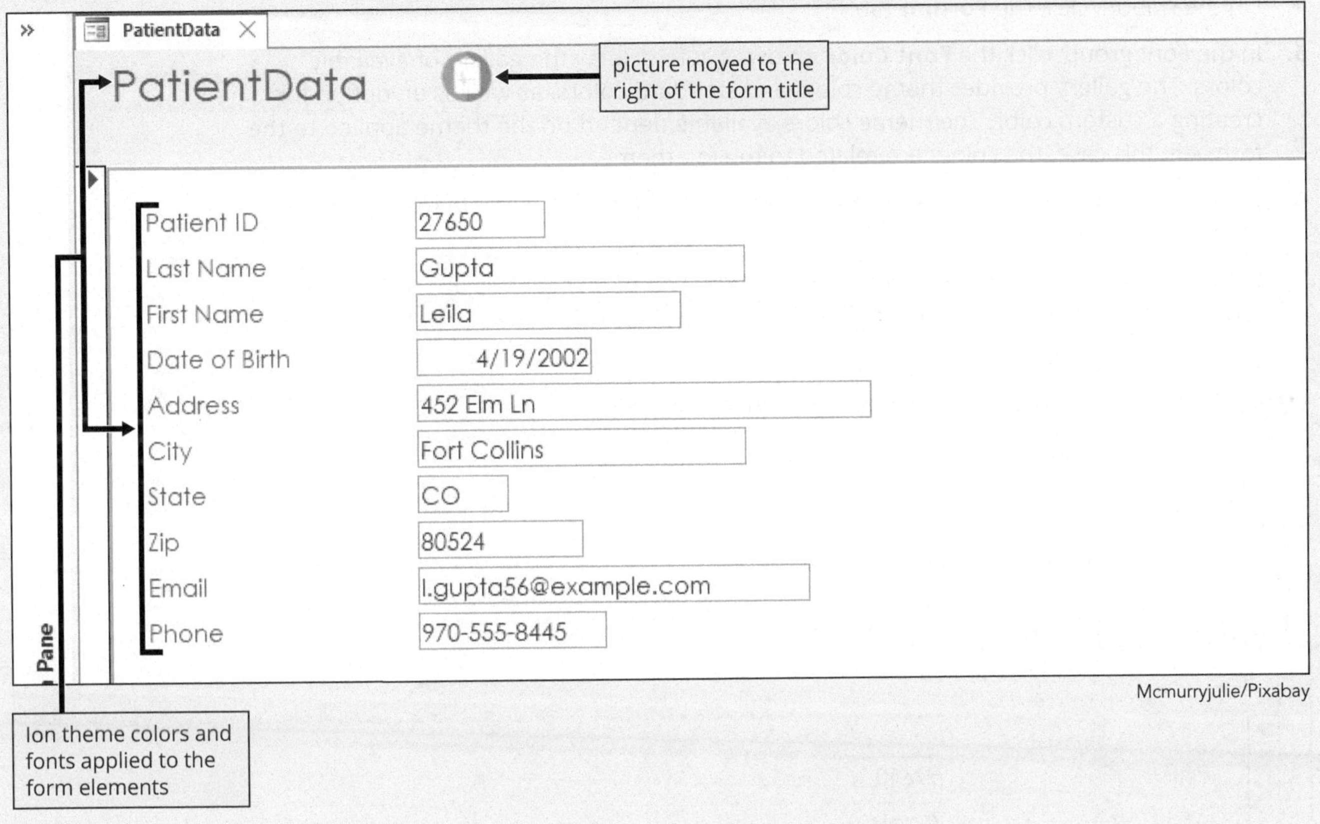

Mcmurryjulie/Pixabay

Next, Susan asks you to change the form title to a darker color so that it will stand out more on the form.

Changing the Color of Text on a Form

The Font group on the Format tab provides many options you can use to change the appearance of text on a form. For example, you can bold, italicize, and underline text; change the font, font color, and font size; and change the alignment of text. Before you change the color of the "PatientData" title on the form, you'll change the title to two words so it is easier to read.

To change the form title's text and color:

1. Click the **PatientData** form title. An orange border surrounds the title, indicating it is selected.
2. Click between the letters "t" and "D" to position the insertion point, press **SPACEBAR**, and then press **ENTER**. The title on the form is now "Patient Data," but the added space caused the words to appear on two lines. You can fix this by resizing the box containing the title.

Tip Changing the form's title does not affect the form object name; it is still PatientData, as shown on the object tab.

3. Position the pointer on the right edge of the box containing the form title until the pointer changes to the width change pointer ↔, and then drag to the right until the word "Data" appears on the same line as the word "Patient."

Trouble? You might need to repeat Step 3 until the title appears on one line. Also, you might have to move the picture farther to the right to make room for the title.

Next you will change the title's font color.

4. On the ribbon, click the **Format** tab.
5. In the Font group, click the **Font Color arrow** to display the gallery of available colors. The gallery provides theme colors and standard colors, as well as an option for creating a custom color. The theme colors available depend on the theme applied to the form—in this case, the colors are related to the Ion theme.
6. Click the **Black, Text 1, Lighter 25%** box (second column, fourth row in the Theme Colors palette).
7. Click a blank area of the form to deselect the title. The darker color is applied to the form title text, making it stand out. See Figure 4–9.

Figure 4–9 Form title with new color applied

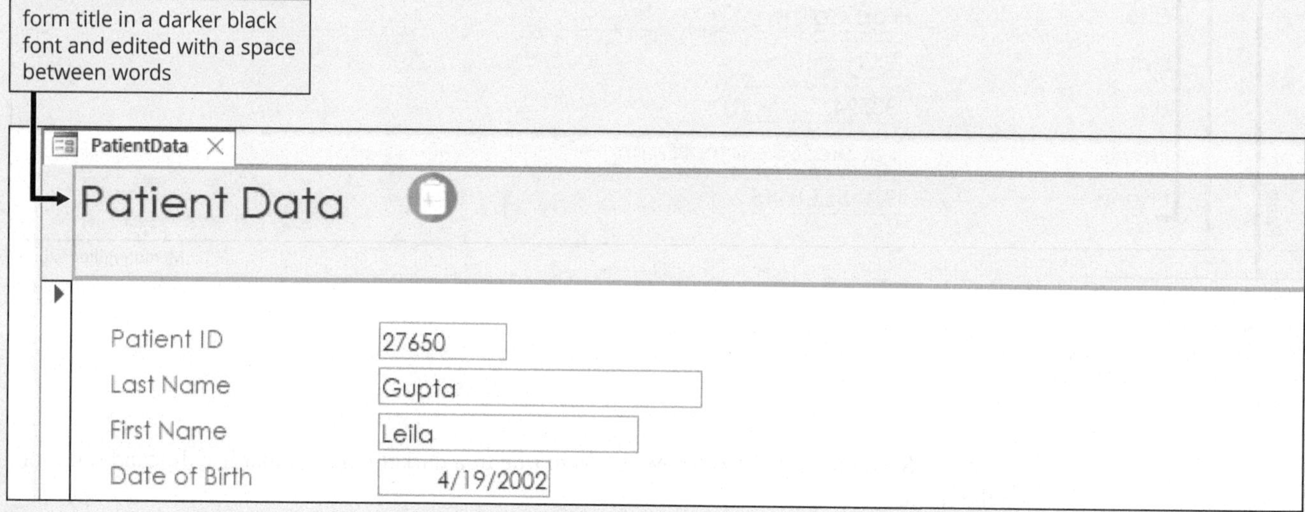

Mcmurryjulie/Pixabay

8. On the Quick Access Toolbar, click the **Save** button to save the modified form.
9. On the status bar, click the **Form View** button to display the form in Form view.

Susan is pleased with the modified appearance of the form.

Proskills

Written Communication: Designing Forms

Similar to any document, a form must convey written information clearly and effectively. When you create a form, consider how the form will be used so that its design accommodates the needs of people using the form to view, enter, and maintain data. For example, if a form in a database mimics a paper form that users refer to as they enter data, the form in the database should have the same fields in the same order as on the paper form. Users can then tab from one field to the next in the database form to enter the necessary information from the paper form. Ensuring that users can navigate a form using the keyboard also makes the form accessible to everyone. Include a meaningful title to identify the form's purpose and to enhance its appearance. Provide a label for each form field so that screen readers can identify the fields. You can further improve accessibility by formatting text to increase its contrast with the form background. For example, use black text on a pale or white background. High contrast also helps those with color blindness, as does avoiding the use of color to convey meaning or require action. Be sure to use a consistent design for the forms in your database whenever possible. Users expect to see similar elements—such as titles, pictures, and fonts—in each form in a database. A mix of styles and elements among the forms in a database could lead to confusion when working with the forms. Finally, make sure the text on your form does not contain any spelling or grammatical errors. By producing a well-designed and well-written form, you can help users work with the form in a productive and efficient manner.

Navigating a Form

To view, navigate, and change data using a form, you need to display the form in Form view. As you learned earlier, you navigate a form in the same way that you navigate a table datasheet. You can also use the same navigation mode and editing mode keyboard shortcuts in a form as you do when working with datasheets.

Susan wants to review data in the Patient table. Before using the PatientData form to display the specific information Susan wants to view, you will practice navigating the fields in a record and navigating the records in the form. The PatientData form is already displayed in Form view, so you can use it to navigate through the fields and records of the Patient table.

To navigate the PatientData form:

1. If necessary, click in the **Patient ID** field value box to make it current.
2. Press **TAB** once to move to the Last Name field value box, and then press **END** to move to the Phone field value box.
3. Press **HOME** to return to the Patient ID field value box. The first record in the Patient table still appears in the form.
4. Press **CTRL+END** to move to the Phone field value box for record 51, which is the last record in the table. The record number for the current record appears in the Current Record box between the navigation buttons at the bottom of the form.
5. Click the **Previous record** button ◀ in the navigation bar to move to the Phone field value box in record 50.
6. Press ↑ twice to move to the Zip field value box in record 50.
7. Click to position the insertion point within the word "Phillips" in the Address field value to switch to editing mode, press **HOME** to move the insertion point to the beginning of the field value, and then press **END** to move the insertion point to the end of the field value.

8. Click the **First record** button [⏮] to move to the Address field value box in the first record. The entire field value is highlighted because you switched from editing mode to navigation mode.
9. Click the **Next record** button [▶] to move to the Address field value box in record 2, the next record.

Susan wants to find the record for a patient named Flores. The paper form containing the original contact information for this patient was damaged. Other than the patient's last name, Susan knows only the street the patient lives on. You will use the PatientData form to locate and view the complete record for this patient.

Finding Data Using a Form

As you learned earlier, the Find command lets you search for data in a datasheet so you can display only those records you want to view. You can also use the Find command to search for data in a form. You first choose a field to serve as the basis for the search by making that field the current field, and then you enter the value you want Access to match in the Find and Replace dialog box.

Reference

Finding Data in a Form or Datasheet

- Open the form or datasheet, and then make the field you want to search the current field.
- On the Home tab, in the Find group, click the Find button to open the Find and Replace dialog box.
- In the Find What box, type the field value you want to find.
- Complete the remaining options, as necessary, to specify the type of search to conduct.
- Click the Find Next button to begin the search.
- Click the Find Next button to continue searching for the next match.
- Click Cancel to stop searching.

You need to find the record for the person Susan wants to contact, a patient named Flores. However, Susan knows that two people named Flores are patients at the center. The one Susan wants to contact lives on Pine Drive. You'll search for this record using the Address field.

To find the record using the PatientData form:

1. Make sure the Address field value is still selected for the current record. This is the field you need to search.

   You can search for a record that contains part of the address anywhere in the Address field value. Performing a partial search is often easier than matching the entire field value and is useful when you don't know or can't remember the entire field value.
2. On the Home tab, in the Find group, click the **Find** button. The Find and Replace dialog box opens. The Look In box indicates that the current field (in this case, Address) will be searched. You'll search for records that contain the word "pine" in the address.
3. In the Find What box, type **pine**. Note that you do not have to enter the word as "Pine" with a capital letter "P" because the Match Case check box is not selected in the Find and Replace dialog box. The search will find any record containing the word "pine" with any combination of uppercase and lowercase letters.

4. Click the **Match** arrow to display the list of matching options, and then click **Any Part of Field**. The search will find any record that contains the word "pine" in any part of the Address field. See Figure 4–10.

Figure 4–10 Completed Find and Replace dialog box

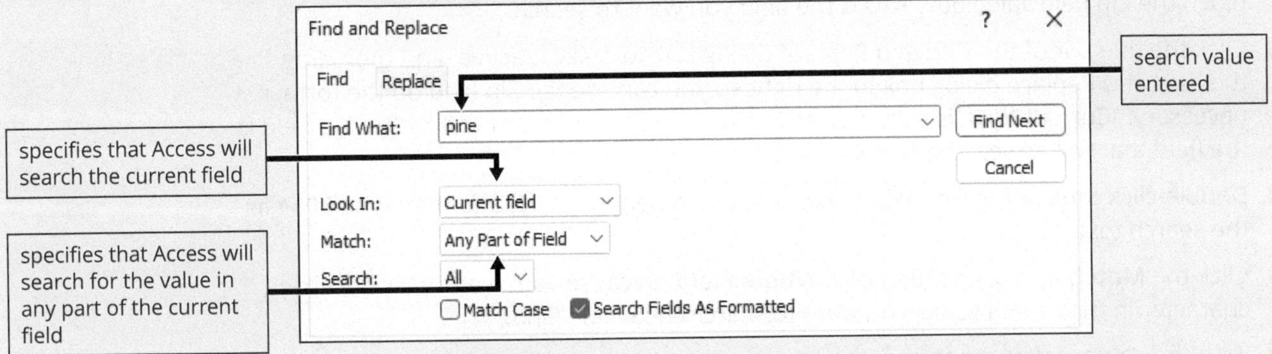

5. Click the **Find Next** button. The Find and Replace dialog box remains open, and the PatientData form now displays record 24, which is the record for Juanita Flores (PatientID 27692). The word "Pine" is selected in the Address field value box because you searched for this word.

The search value you enter can be an exact value or it can include wildcard characters. A **wildcard character** is a placeholder you use when you know only part of a value or when you want to start or end with a specific character or match a certain pattern. Figure 4–11 lists the wildcard characters you can use when searching for data.

Figure 4–11 Wildcard characters

Wildcard Character	Purpose	Example
*	Match any number of characters; it can be used as the first and/or last character in the character string	th* finds the, that, this, therefore, and so on
?	Match any single alphabetic character	a?t finds act, aft, ant, apt, and art
[ ]	Match any single character within the brackets	a[fr]t finds aft and art but not act, ant, or apt
!	Match any character not within brackets	a[!fr]t finds act, ant, and apt but not aft or art
-	Match any one of a range of characters; the range must be in ascending order (a to z, not z to a)	a[d-p]t finds aft, ant, and apt but not act or art
#	Match any single numeric character	#72 finds 072, 172, 272, 372, and so on

To use a wildcard in a search, you'll view the records for any patients with zip codes that begin with 806, which are locations in Eaton, Greeley, and Pierce, Colorado. You could search for any record containing the digits 806 in any part of the Zip field, but this search would also find records with the digits 806 in any part of the zip code. To find only those records with the digits 806 at the beginning of the zip code, you'll use the * wildcard character.

To find the records using the * wildcard character:

1. Make sure the Find and Replace dialog box is still open.
2. Click anywhere in the PatientData form to make it active, and then press **TAB** until you reach the Zip field value box. This is the field you want to search.
3. Click the title bar of the Find and Replace dialog box to make it active, and then drag the Find and Replace dialog box to the right so you can see the Zip field on the form, if necessary. "Current field" is still selected in the Look In box, meaning now the Zip field is the field that will be searched.
4. Double-click **pine** in the Find What box to select the entire value, and then type **806*** as the search text.
5. Click the **Match** arrow, and then click **Whole Field**. Because you're using a wildcard character in the search value, you want to search the whole field.

   With the settings you've entered, the search will find records in which any value in the Zip field begins with 806.
6. Click the **Find Next** button. Record 35 is displayed in the form, which is the next record found for a patient with a zip code that begins with 806. Notice that the search process started from the point of the previously displayed record in the form, which was record 24.
7. Click the **Find Next** button. Record 37 is displayed in the form, which is the next record found for a patient with a zip code that begins with 806.
8. Click the **Find Next** button to display record 43, and then click the **Find Next** button again. Record 50 is displayed, the fourth record found.
9. Click the **Find Next** button again. Record 5 is displayed. The search cycles back through the beginning of the records in the underlying table.
10. Click the **Find Next** button two more times to display records 9 and 11.
11. Click the **Find Next** button. A dialog box opens, informing you that the search is finished.

    Trouble? If this dialog box does not open, click Cancel to close the Find and Replace dialog box, and then skip Step 12.
12. Click **OK** to close the dialog box, and then click **Cancel** to close the Find and Replace dialog box.

Susan has identified some patient updates she wants you to make. You'll use the PatientData form to update the data in the Patient table.

Maintaining Table Data Using a Form

Maintaining data using a form is often easier than using a datasheet because you can focus on all the changes for a single record at one time. In Form view, you can edit the field values for a record, delete a record from the underlying table, or add a new record to the table.

Now you'll use the PatientData form to make the changes Susan requested to the Patient table. First, you'll update the record for patient Harper Rowe, who recently moved from Fort Collins to Longmont and provided a new mailing address. In addition to using the Find and Replace dialog box to locate a specific record, you can use the Search box to the right of the navigation buttons. You'll use the Search box to search for the patient's last name, Rowe, and display the patient record in the form.

To change the record using the PatientData form:

1. To the right of the navigation buttons, click the **Search** box and then type **Rowe**. As soon as you start to type, Access begins searching through all fields in the records to match your entry. Record 28 (Harper Rowe) is now current.

   You will first update the address in this record.

2. Select the current entry in the Address field value box, and then type **17 Riverway Dr** to replace it.

   > **Tip** The pencil symbol appears in the upper-left corner of the form when the form is in editing mode.

3. Press **TAB** to select the city in the City field value box, and then type **Longmont**.

4. Press **TAB** twice to move to and select the Zip field value, and then type **80501**. The updates to the record are complete. See Figure 4–12.

Figure 4–12 Patient record after changing field values

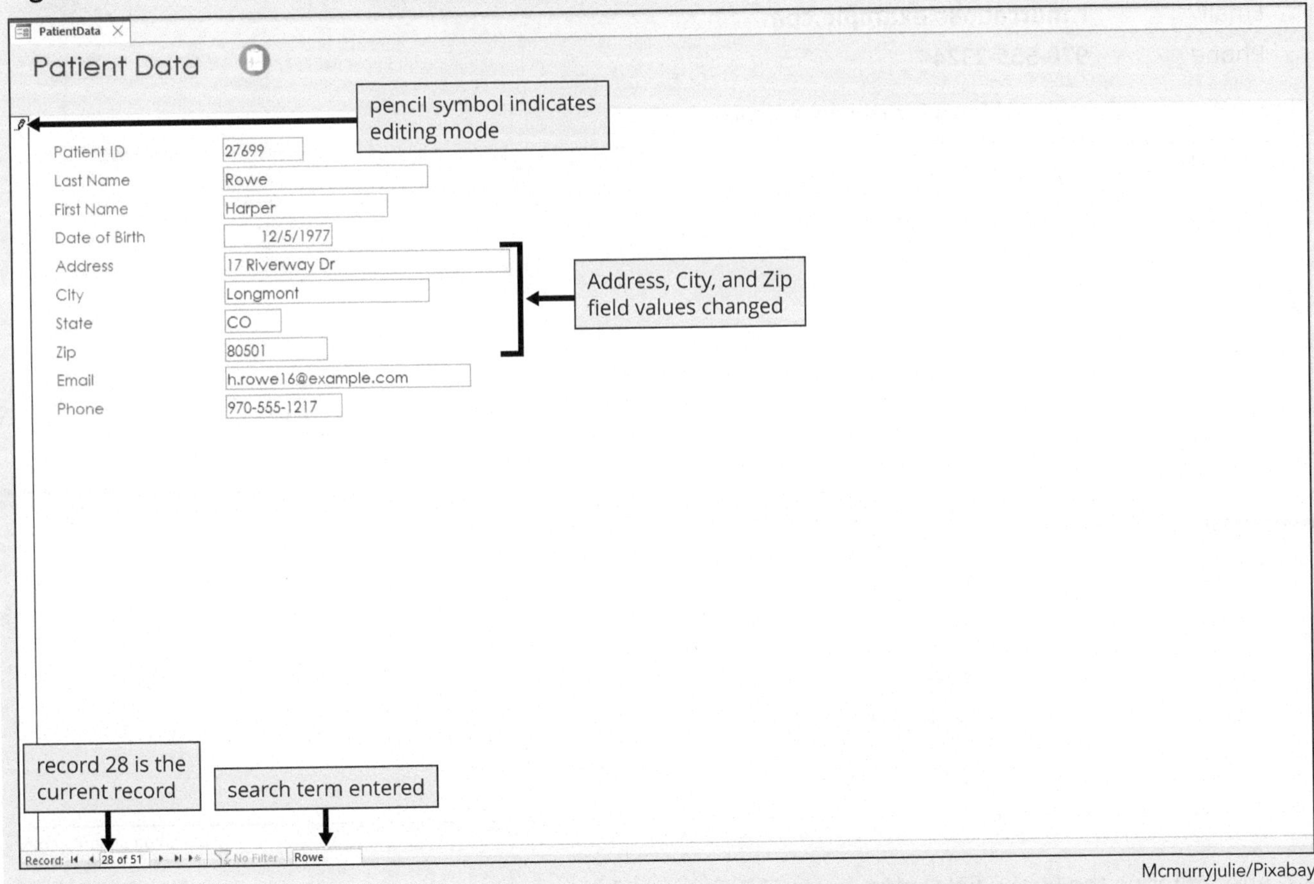

Mcmurryjulie/Pixabay

Susan also asks you to add a record for a new patient. At a recent health fair held by Pine Ridge Orthopedics & Sports Medicine Center, this person signed up to be a patient but has not yet visited the center. You'll use the PatientData form to add the new record.

To add the new record using the PatientData form:

1. On the Home tab, in the Records group, click the **New** button. Record 52, the next available new record, becomes the current record. All field value boxes are empty (except the State field, which displays the default value of CO), and the insertion point is positioned in the Patient ID field value box.
2. See Figure 4–13 and enter the following values shown for each field, pressing **TAB** to move from field to field.

Patient ID	**27743**
Last Name	**Mercado**
First Name	**Ruben**
Date of Birth	**5/8/2000**
Address	**114 Emerson Rd**
City	**Fort Collins**
Zip	**80528**
Email	**r.mercado8@example.com**
Phone	**970-555-2324**

Figure 4–13 Completed form for the new record

PatientData

Patient Data

Patient ID	27743
Last Name	Mercado
First Name	Ruben
Date of Birth	5/8/2000
Address	114 Emerson Rd
City	Fort Collins
State	CO
Zip	80528
Email	r.mercado8@example.com
Phone	970-555-2324

Mcmurryjulie/Pixabay

3. After entering the Phone field value, press **TAB**. Record 53, the next available new record, becomes the current record, and the record for PatientID 27743 is saved in the Patient table.

Susan would like a printed copy of the PatientData form to show to her staff members. She asks you to print one form record.

Previewing and Printing Selected Form Records

You can print as many form records as can fit on a printed page. If only part of a form record fits on the bottom of a page, the remainder of the record prints on the next page. You can print all pages or a range of pages. In addition, you can print just the current form record.

Susan asks you to use the PatientData form to print the first record in the Patient table. Before you do, you'll preview the form record to see how it will look when printed.

To preview the form and print the data for record 1:

1. Click the **First record** button to display record 1 in the form.
2. Replace the current LastName and FirstName field values with your names. Replace the "l.gupta" in the Email field with your first initial, a dot, and your last name.
3. Click the **File** tab to open Backstage view, click **Print** in the navigation bar, and then click **Print Preview**. The Print Preview window opens, showing the form records for the Patient table. Each record appears in its own form and shading distinguishes one record from another, as shown in Figure 4–14.

Figure 4–14 Form records displayed in Print Preview

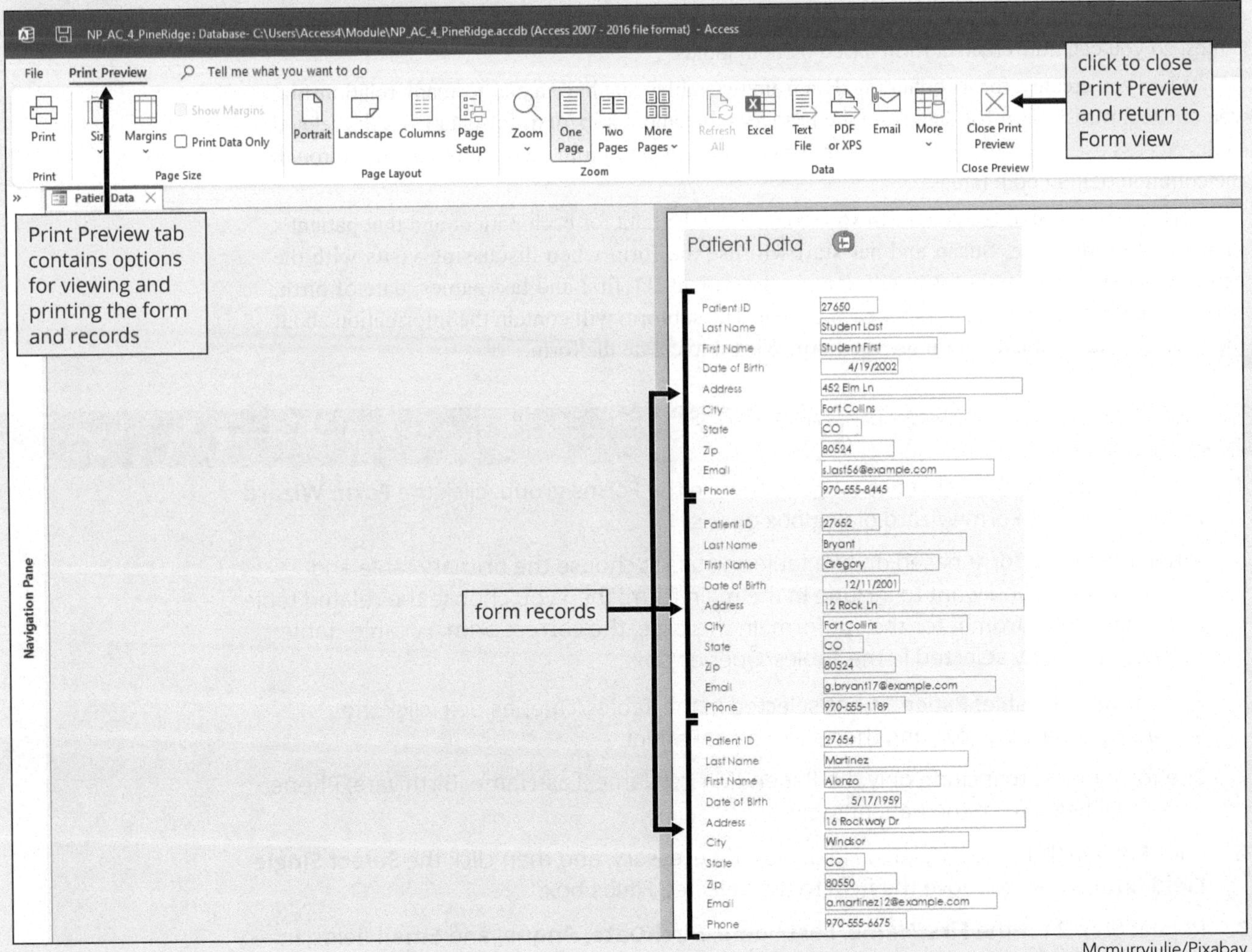

Mcmurryjulie/Pixabay

To print one selected record on a page by itself, you need to use the Print dialog box.

4. On the Print Preview tab, in the Close Preview group, click the **Close Print Preview** button. You return to Form view with the first record still displayed.

5. Click the **File** tab to open Backstage view again, click **Print** in the navigation bar, and then click **Print**. The Print dialog box opens.
6. Click the **Selected Record(s)** option button to print the current form record (record 1).

   Trouble? Check with your instructor to be sure you should print the form, and then continue to the next step. If you should not print the form, click Cancel, and then skip to Step 8.
7. Click **OK** to close the dialog box and print the selected record.
8. Close the PatientData form.

After reviewing the printed PatientData form with her staff, Susan reminds you that staff members could also use a form showing information about patients and their visits. Because this form will display information from two different tables, the type of form you need to create will include a main form and a subform.

Creating a Form with a Main Form and a Subform

To create a form based on two tables, you must first define a relationship between the two tables. Earlier, you defined a one-to-many relationship between the Patient (primary) and Visit (related) tables, so you can now create a form based on both tables.

When you create a form containing data from two tables that have a one-to-many relationship, you create a **main form** for data from the primary table and a **subform** for data from the related table. Access uses the defined relationship between the tables to join them automatically through the common field in both tables.

Susan wants you to create a form so she can view the data for each patient and that patient's visits at the same time. Susan and her staff will use the form when discussing visits with the center's patients. The main form will contain the patient ID, first and last names, date of birth, phone number, and email address for each patient. The subform will contain the information about the visits for each patient. You'll use the Form Wizard to create the form.

To create the form using the Form Wizard:

1. On the ribbon, click the **Create** tab, and then in the Forms group, click the **Form Wizard** button. The first Form Wizard dialog box opens.

   When creating a form based on two tables, you first choose the primary table and select the fields you want to include in the main form; then you choose the related table and select fields from it for the subform. In this case, the correct primary table, Table: Patient, is already selected in the Tables/Queries box.

   Trouble? If Table: Patient is not selected in the Tables/Queries box, click the Tables/Queries arrow, and then click Table: Patient.

   The form needs to include only the PatientID, FirstName, LastName, BirthDate, Phone, and Email fields from the Patient table.
2. Click **PatientID** in the Available Fields box, if necessary, and then click the **Select Single Field** button > to move the field to the Selected Fields box.
3. Repeat Step 2 for the **FirstName**, **LastName**, **BirthDate**, **Phone**, and **Email** fields, in that order.

   The subform needs to include all the fields from the Visit table, with the exception of the PatientID field, as that field has been added to the main form.

4. Click the **Tables/Queries** arrow, and then click **Table: Visit**. The fields from the Visit table appear in the Available Fields box. The quickest way to add the fields you want is to move all the fields to the Selected Fields box, and then remove the only field you don't want to include (PatientID).
5. Click the **Select All Fields** button >> to move all the fields in the Visit table to the Selected Fields box.
6. Click **Visit.PatientID** in the Selected Fields box, and then click the **Remove Single Field** button < to move the field back to the Available Fields box.

   Tip The table name (Visit) is included in the PatientID field name to distinguish it from the same field in the Patient table.

7. Click the **Next** button. The next Form Wizard dialog box opens. See Figure 4–15.

Figure 4–15 Choosing a format for the main form and subform

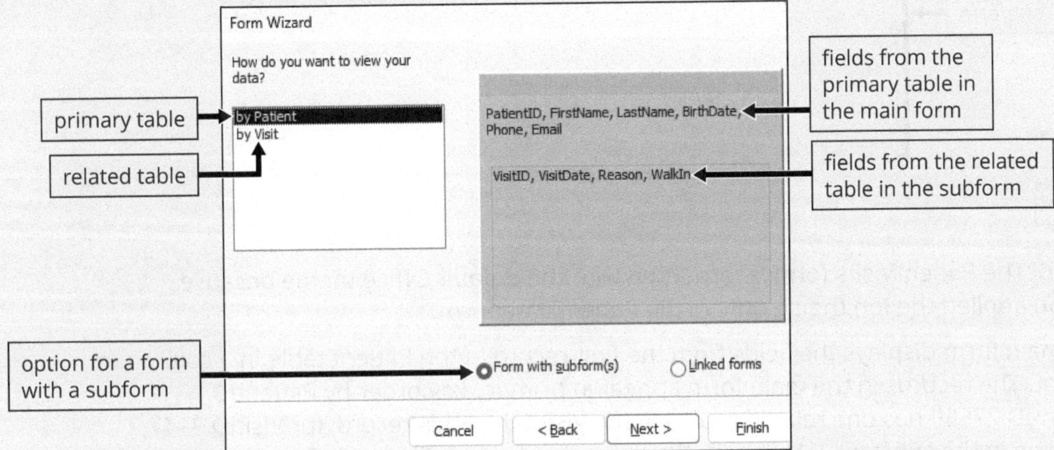

In this dialog box, the section on the left shows the order for viewing the selected data: first by data from the primary Patient table, and then by data from the related Visit table. The form will be displayed as shown on the right side of the dialog box, with the fields from the Patient table at the top in the main form, and the fields from the Visit table at the bottom in the subform. The default options shown in Figure 4–15 are correct for creating a form with Patient data in the main form and Visit data in the subform.

8. Click the **Next** button. The next Form Wizard dialog box opens, in which you choose the subform layout.

   The Tabular layout displays subform fields as a table, whereas the Datasheet layout displays subform fields as a table datasheet. The layout choice is a matter of personal preference. You'll use the Datasheet layout.

9. Click the **Datasheet** option button to select it, if necessary, and then click the **Next** button. The next Form Wizard dialog box opens, in which you specify titles for the main form and the subform. You'll use the title "PatientVisits" for the main form and the title "VisitSubform" for the subform. These titles will also be the names for the form objects.
10. In the Form box, click to position the insertion point to the right of the last letter, and then type **Visits**. The main form name is now PatientVisits.
11. In the Subform box, delete the space between the two words so that the subform name appears as **VisitSubform**, and then click the **Finish** button. The completed form opens in Form view. See Figure 4–16.

Figure 4–16 Main form with subform in Form view

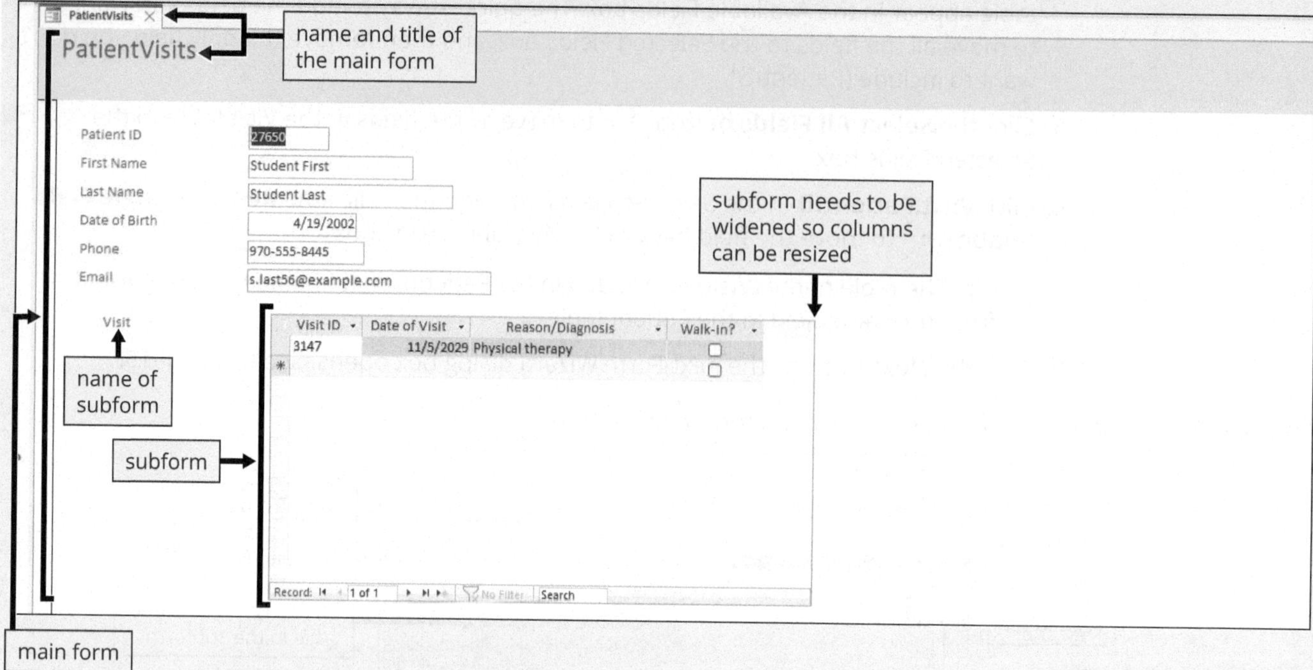

> **Tip** The PatientVisits form is formatted with the default Office theme because you applied the Ion theme only to the PatientData form.

The main form displays the fields from the first record in the Patient table in a columnar format. The records in the main form appear in primary key order by PatientID. PatientID 27650 has one related record in the Visit table; this record, for VisitID 3147, is shown in the subform, which uses the datasheet format. The main form name, "PatientVisits," appears on the object tab and as the form title. The name of the table "Visit" appears to the left of the subform, indicating the underlying table for the subform. Note that only the word "Visit" and not the complete name "VisitSubform" appears on the form. Only the table name is displayed for the subform itself, but the complete name of the object, "VisitSubform," is displayed when you view and work with objects in the Navigation Pane. The subform designation is necessary in a list of database objects so you can distinguish the Visit subform from other objects, such as the Visit table, but the subform designation is not needed in the PatientVisits form. Only the table name is required to identify the table containing the records in the subform.

Next, you need to fine-tune the form. First, you'll edit the form title to add a space between the words so it appears as "Patient Visits." Then, you'll resize the subform so it is wide enough to fully display all the columns. To make these changes, you need to switch to Layout view.

To modify the PatientVisits form in Layout view:

1. Switch to Layout view.

   > **Trouble?** If the Field List or Property Sheet opens on the right side of the program window, close it before continuing.

2. Click **PatientVisits** in the shaded area at the top of the form. The form title is selected.
3. Click between the letters "t" and "V" to place the insertion point, and then press **SPACEBAR**. The title on the form is now "Patient Visits."

4. Click in a blank area of the form to the right of the field value boxes to deselect the title. Next, you'll increase the width of the subform.
5. Click the **subform**. An orange border surrounds the subform, indicating it is selected.
6. Position the pointer on the right border of the selected subform until the pointer changes to the width change pointer ↔, and then drag to the right approximately one inch. The wider subform will display all columns, even when the Reason field contains a long entry. See Figure 4–17.

Figure 4–17 Modified form in Layout view

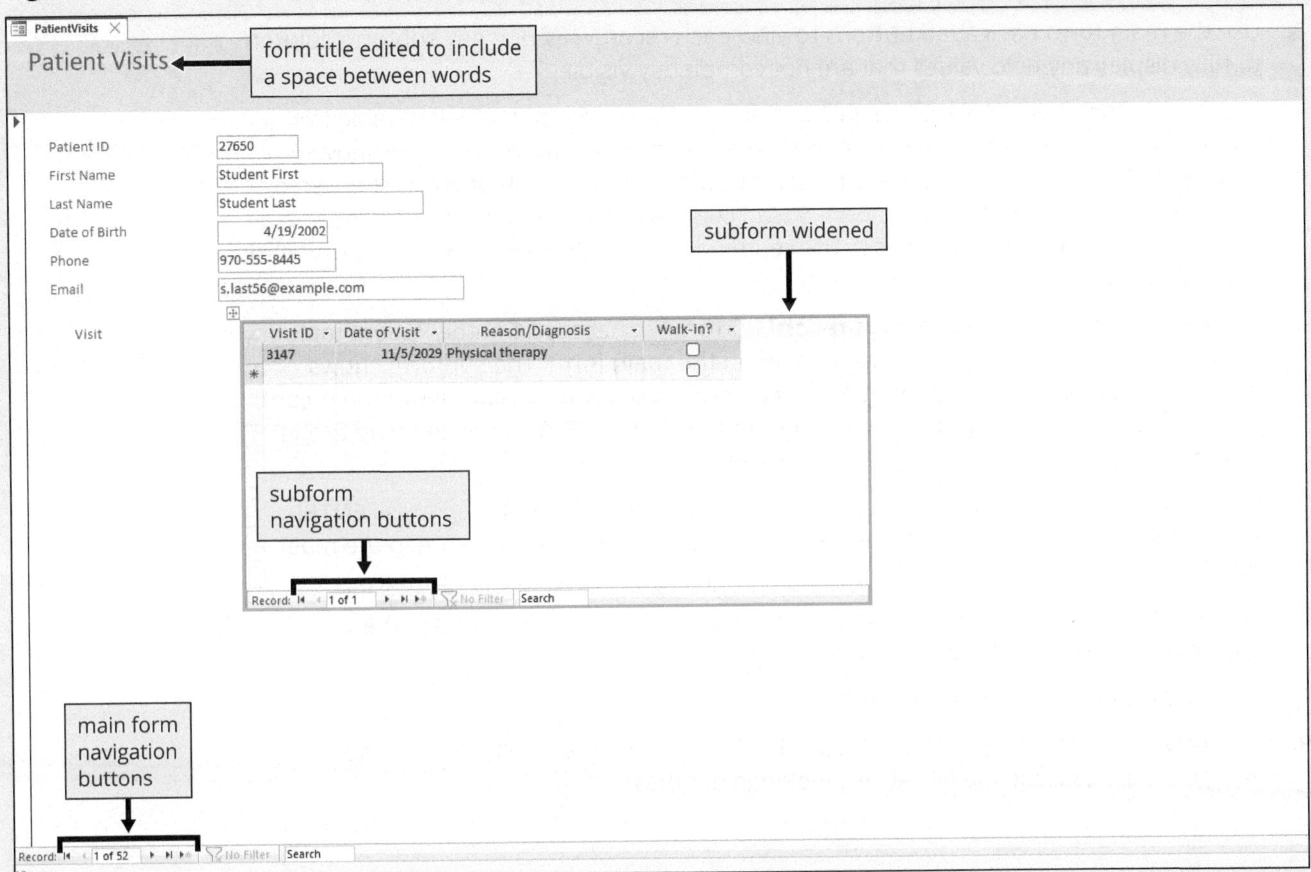

7. On the Quick Access Toolbar, click the **Save** button to save both the main form and the subform.
8. Switch to Form view.

The form includes two sets of navigation buttons. You use the set of navigation buttons at the bottom of the Form window to select records from the primary table in the main form. The second set of navigation buttons appear at the bottom of the subform (shown in Figure 4–17). You use the subform navigation buttons to select records from the related table in the subform.

You'll use the navigation buttons to view records.

To navigate to different main form and subform records:

1. In the main form, click the **Next record** button ▶ five times. Record 6 of 52 total records in the Patient table (for Marco Garcia) becomes the current record in the main form. The subform shows that this patient made two visits to the center. Note that the field values in the Reason/Diagnosis column are not fully displayed.
2. Double-click the column resizing pointer ✛ on the right column divider of the Reason/Diagnosis column in the subform to resize this field to its best fit and display the complete field values.
3. Use the main form navigation buttons to view each record, resizing any subform column to fully display any field values that are not completely visible.
4. In the main form, click the **Last record** button ▶|. Record 52 in the Patient table (for Ruben Mercado) becomes the current record in the main form. The subform shows that this patient currently has made no visits to the center; recall that you just entered this record using the PatientData form. Susan could use the subform to enter the information on this patient's visits to the center, and that information would be updated in the Visit table.
5. In the main form, click the **Previous record** button ◀. Record 51 in the Patient table (for Omar Malik) becomes the current record in the main form. The subform shows that this patient has made one visit to the center. If you know the number of the record you want to view, you can enter the number in the Current Record box to move to that record.
6. In the main form, select **51** in the Current Record box, type **18**, and then press **ENTER**. Record 18 in the Patient table (for Akira Vang) becomes the current record in the main form. The subform shows that this patient has made three visits to the center.
7. At the bottom of the subform, click the **Last record** button ▶|. Record 3 in the Visit subform, for Visit ID 3216, becomes the current record.
8. Save and close the PatientVisits form.
9. If you are not continuing to Part 4.2, click the **File** tab, and then click **Close** in the navigation bar to close the NP_AC_4_PineRidge database.

Susan and her staff can use the PatientData form and the PatientVisits form you created to view, enter, and maintain data in the Patient and Visit tables in the NP_AC_4_PineRidge database.

Part 4.1 Quick Check

1. When you want to modify a form while displaying its data, which view should you use?
2. What is a theme, and how do you apply one to a single form?
3. An item on a form, report, or other database object that you can manipulate to modify the object's appearance is called a(n) ________.
4. A set of controls grouped together in a form or report so that you can manipulate the set as a single control is called a(n) ________.
5. Which wildcard character matches any number of characters?
6. Why is maintaining data using a form often easier than using a datasheet?
7. In a form that contains a main form and a subform, what data is displayed in the main form, and what data is displayed in the subform?

Part 4.2 Visual Overview: Report Displayed in Print Preview

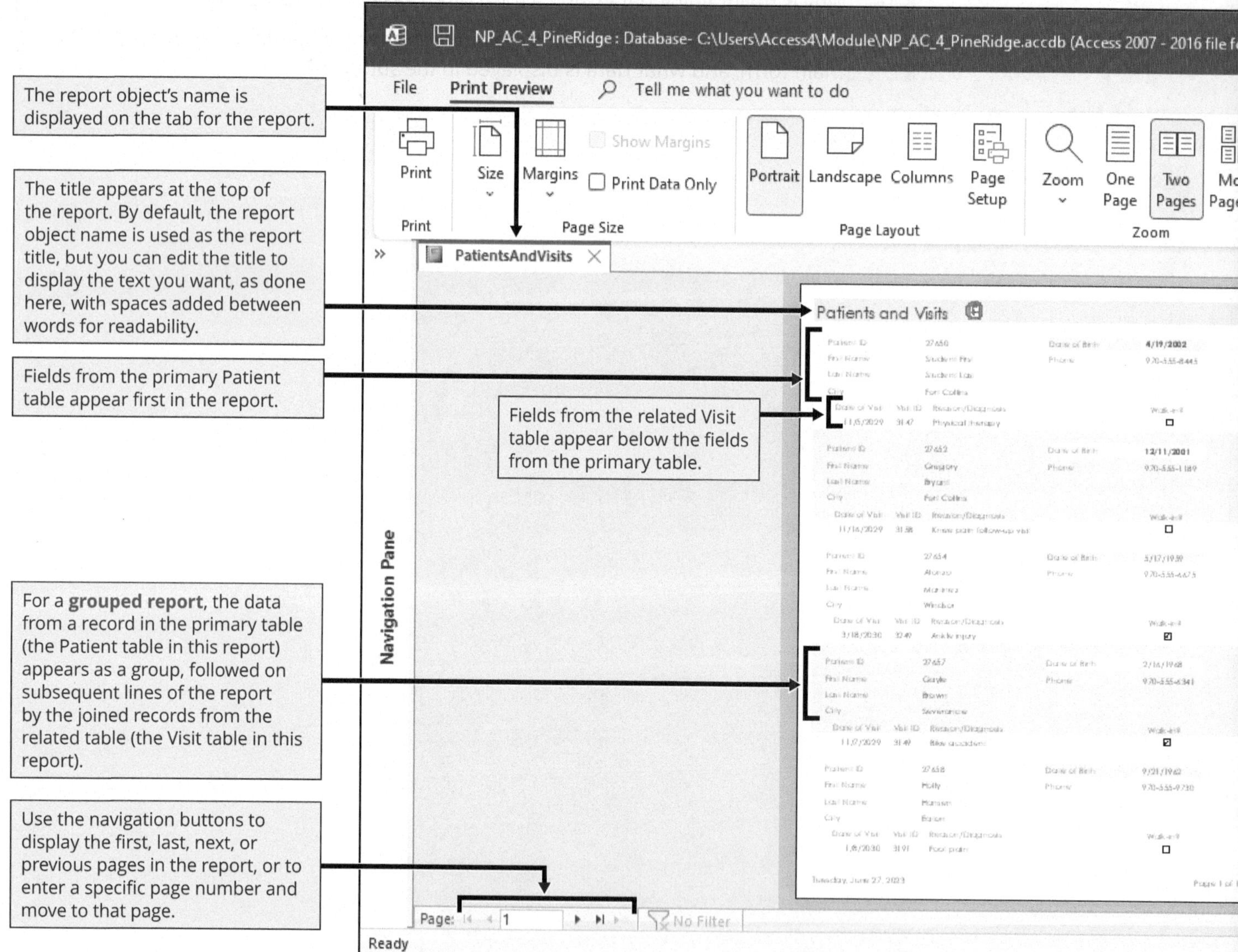

The report object's name is displayed on the tab for the report.
The title appears at the top of the report. By default, the report object name is used as the report title, but you can edit the title to display the text you want, as done here, with spaces added between words for readability.
Fields from the primary Patient table appear first in the report.
Fields from the related Visit table appear below the fields from the primary table.
For a **grouped report**, the data from a record in the primary table (the Patient table in this report) appears as a group, followed on subsequent lines of the report by the joined records from the related table (the Visit table in this report).
Use the navigation buttons to display the first, last, next, or previous pages in the report, or to enter a specific page number and move to that page.
NP_AC_4_PineRidge : Database- C:\Users\Access4\Module\NP_AC_4_PineRidge.accdb (Access 2007 - 2016 file fo
File
Print Preview
Tell me what you want to do
Print
Size
Margins
Show Margins
Print Data Only
Portrait
Landscape
Columns
Page Setup
Zoom
One Page
Two Pages
Page Size
Page Layout
PatientsAndVisits
Navigation Pane
Patients and Visits
Page: 1
No Filter
Ready

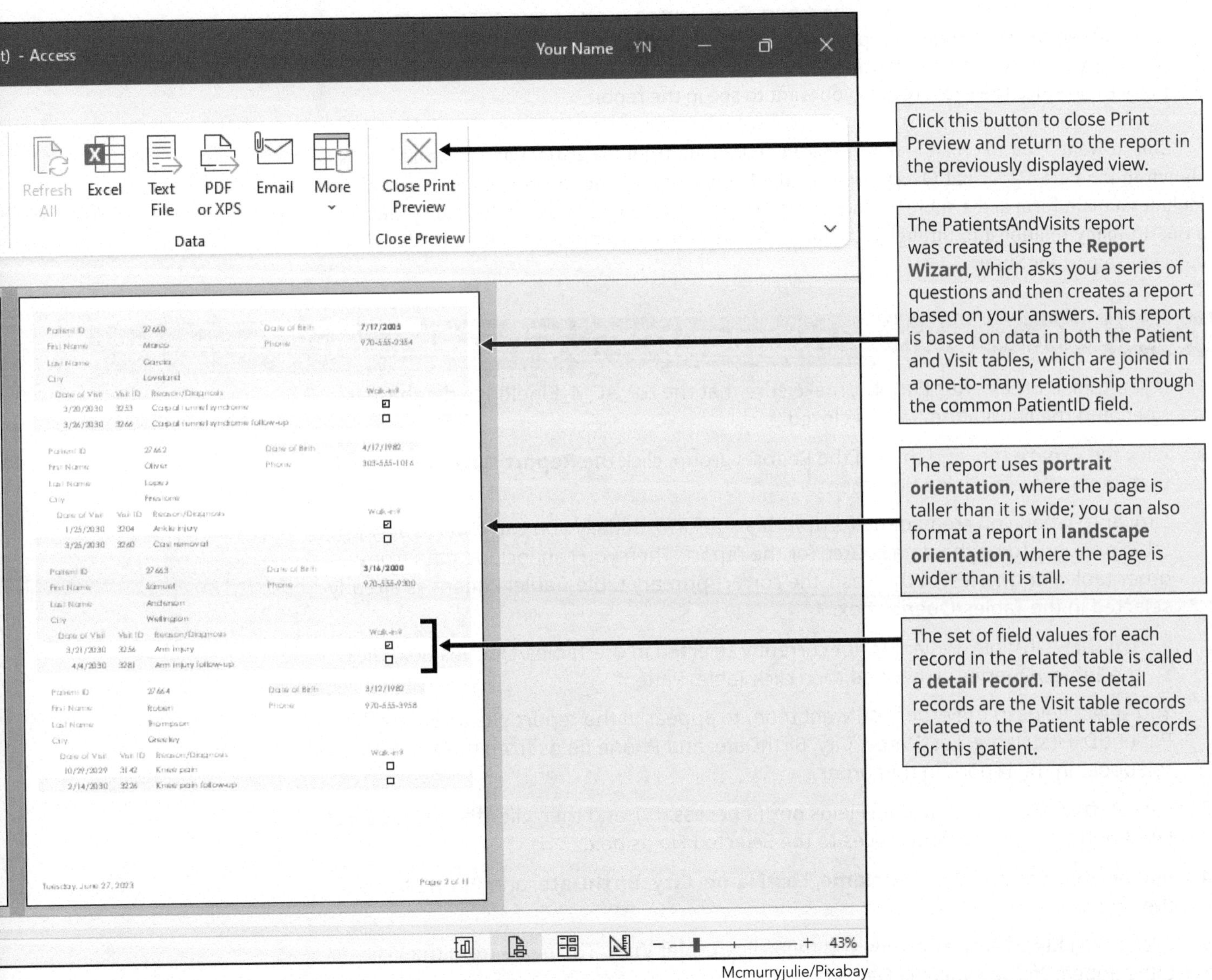
at) - Access
Your Name YN
Refresh All
Excel
Text File
PDF or XPS
Email
More
Data
Close Print Preview
Close Preview
43%
Click this button to close Print Preview and return to the report in the previously displayed view.
The PatientsAndVisits report was created using the **Report Wizard**, which asks you a series of questions and then creates a report based on your answers. This report is based on data in both the Patient and Visit tables, which are joined in a one-to-many relationship through the common PatientID field.
The report uses **portrait orientation**, where the page is taller than it is wide; you can also format a report in **landscape orientation**, where the page is wider than it is tall.
The set of field values for each record in the related table is called a **detail record**. These detail records are the Visit table records related to the Patient table records for this patient.

Mcmurryjulie/Pixabay

Creating a Report Using the Report Wizard

A report is a formatted printout or screen display of the contents of one or more tables or queries in a database. In Access, you can create your own reports or use the Report Wizard to create them for you. Whether you use the Report Wizard or design your own report, you can change a report's design after you create it.

Insight

Creating a Report Based on a Query

You can create a report based on one or more tables or queries. When you use a query as the basis for a report, you can use criteria and other query features to retrieve only the information you want to display in the report. Experienced Access users often create a query just so they can create a report based on that query. When thinking about the type of report you want to create, consider creating a query first and basing the report on the query to produce the exact results you want to see in the report.

Susan wants you to create a report that includes data from the Patient and Visit tables, as shown in the Part 4.2 Visual Overview. Like the PatientVisits form you created earlier, which includes a main form and a subform, the report will be based on both tables, which are joined in a one-to-many relationship through a common PatientID field. You'll use the Report Wizard to create the report for Susan.

To start the Report Wizard and create the report:

1. If you took a break after Part 4.1, make sure that the NP_AC_4_PineRidge database is open and the Navigation Pane is closed.
2. Click the **Create** tab, and then in the Reports group, click the **Report Wizard** button. The first Report Wizard dialog box opens.

   Similar to when you created the form with a subform, initially you can choose only one table or query to be the data source for the report. Then you can include data from other tables or queries. In this case, the correct primary table, Table: Patient, is already selected in the Tables/Queries box.

   Trouble? If Table: Patient is not currently selected in the Tables/Queries box, click the Tables/Queries arrow, and then click Table: Patient.

   You select fields in the order you want them to appear in the report. Susan wants the PatientID, FirstName, LastName, City, BirthDate, and Phone fields from the Patient table to appear in the report, in that order.
3. Click **PatientID** in the Available Fields box (if necessary), and then click the **Select Single Field** button >. The field moves to the Selected Fields box.
4. Repeat Step 3 to add the **FirstName**, **LastName**, **City**, **BirthDate**, and **Phone** fields to the report.
5. Click the **Tables/Queries** arrow, and then click **Table: Visit**. The fields from the Visit table appear in the Available Fields box.

   Susan wants to include all the fields from the Visit table in the report.
6. Click the **Select All Fields** button >> to move all the fields from the Available Fields box to the Selected Fields box.
7. Click **Visit.PatientID** in the Selected Fields box, click the **Remove Single Field** button < to move the field back to the Available Fields box, and then click the **Next** button. The second Report Wizard dialog box opens. See Figure 4–18.

Figure 4–18 Choosing a grouped or ungrouped report

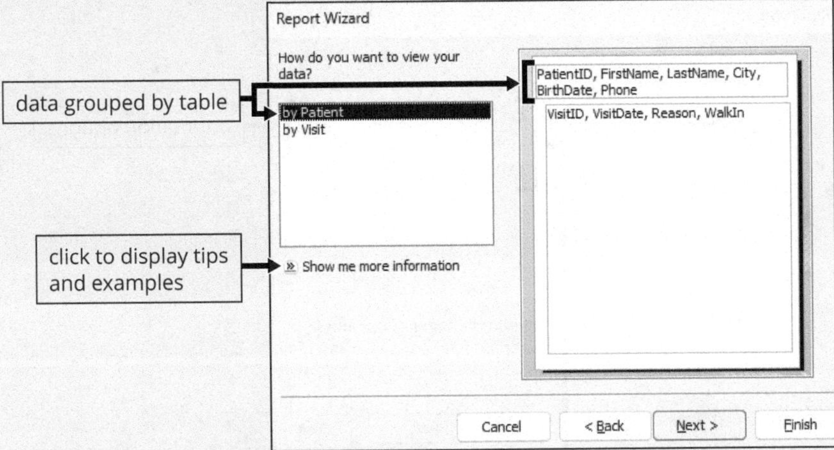

You can choose to arrange the selected data grouped by table, which is the default, or ungrouped. You're creating a grouped report; the data from each record in the Patient table will appear in a group, followed by the related records for that patient from the Visit table.

8. Click the **Next** button. The next Report Wizard dialog box opens, in which you choose additional grouping levels.

   Currently the report contains only one grouping level, which is for the patient's data. Grouping levels are useful for reports with multiple levels, such as those containing monthly, quarterly, and annual totals, or for those containing city and country groups. The report requires no additional grouping levels, so you can accept the default options.

9. Click the **Next** button. The next Report Wizard dialog box opens, in which you choose the sort order for the detail records. See Figure 4–19.

Figure 4–19 Choosing the sort order for detail records

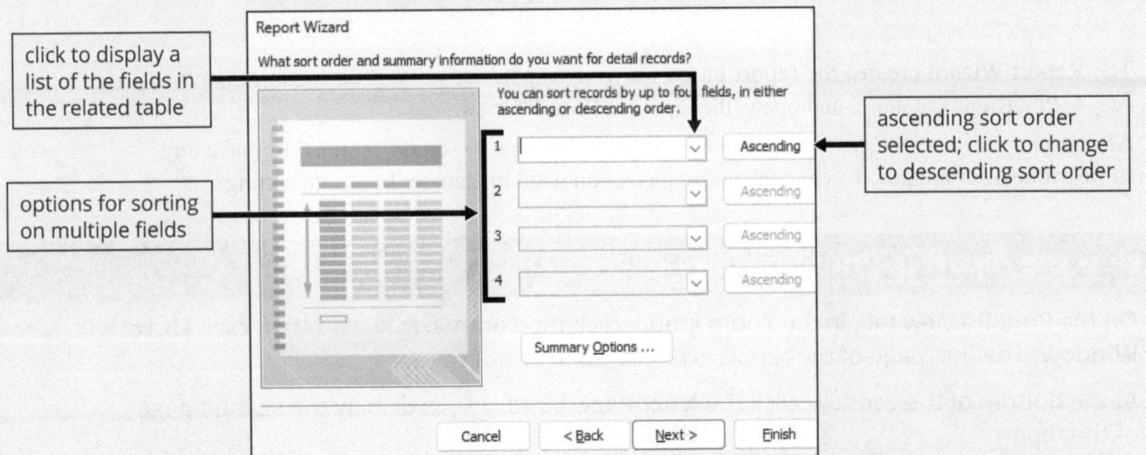

The records from the Visit table for a patient represent the detail records for Susan's report. She wants these records to appear in ascending order by the value in the VisitDate field to display the visits in chronological order. The Ascending option is already selected by default. To change to descending order, you click this same button, which acts as a toggle between the two sort orders. Also, you can sort on multiple fields, as you can with queries.

10. Click the **arrow** on the first box, click **VisitDate**, and then click the **Next** button. The next Report Wizard dialog box opens, in which you choose a layout and page orientation for the report. See Figure 4–20.

Figure 4–20 Choosing the report layout

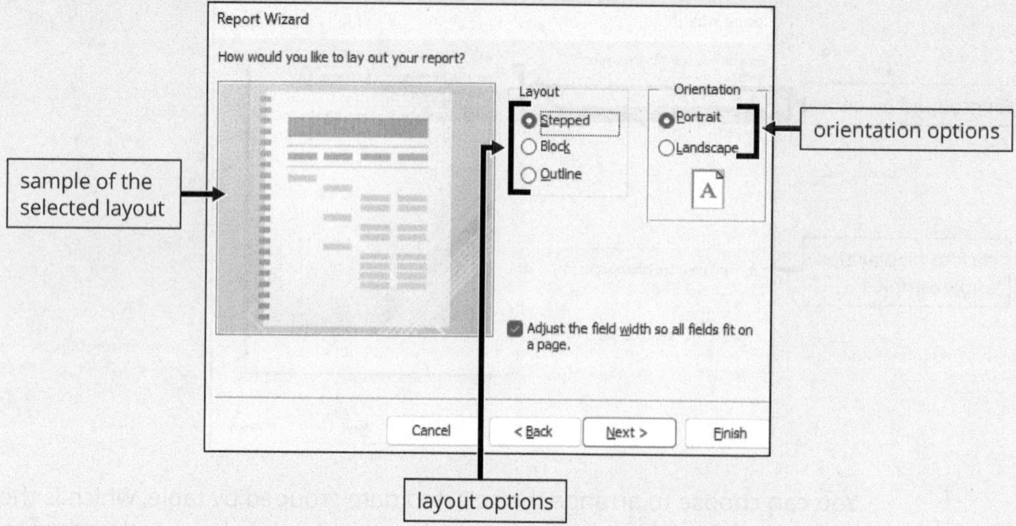

11. Click each layout option to view each sample that appears, and then click the **Outline** option button to select that layout for the report.

    Because most fields in the Patient and Visit tables contain relatively short field values, the default portrait page orientation should provide enough space across the page to display all the field values.

12. Click the **Next** button. The final Report Wizard dialog box opens; you use it to choose a report title, which also serves as the name for the report object in the database.

    Susan wants the report title "Patients and Visits" at the top of the report. Because the name you enter in this dialog box is also the name of the report object, you'll enter the report name as one word and edit the title on the report later.

13. In the box for the title, enter **PatientsAndVisits** and then click the **Finish** button.

The Report Wizard creates the report based on your responses, saves it as an object in the NP_AC_4_PineRidge database, and opens the report in Print Preview.

After you create a report, you should view it in Print Preview to see if you need to make any formatting or design changes. To view the entire page, you need to change the Zoom setting.

To view the report in Print Preview:

1. On the Print Preview tab, in the Zoom group, click the **Zoom arrow**, and then click **Fit to Window**. The first page of the report is displayed in Print Preview.
2. At the bottom of the window, click the **Next Page** button ▸ to display the second page of the report.

   When a report is displayed in Print Preview, you can zoom in for a close-up view of a section of the report.

3. Move the pointer to the center of the report, and then click the **Zoom In** pointer at the center of the report. The display changes to show a close-up view of the report. See Figure 4–21.

Figure 4–21 Close-up view of the report

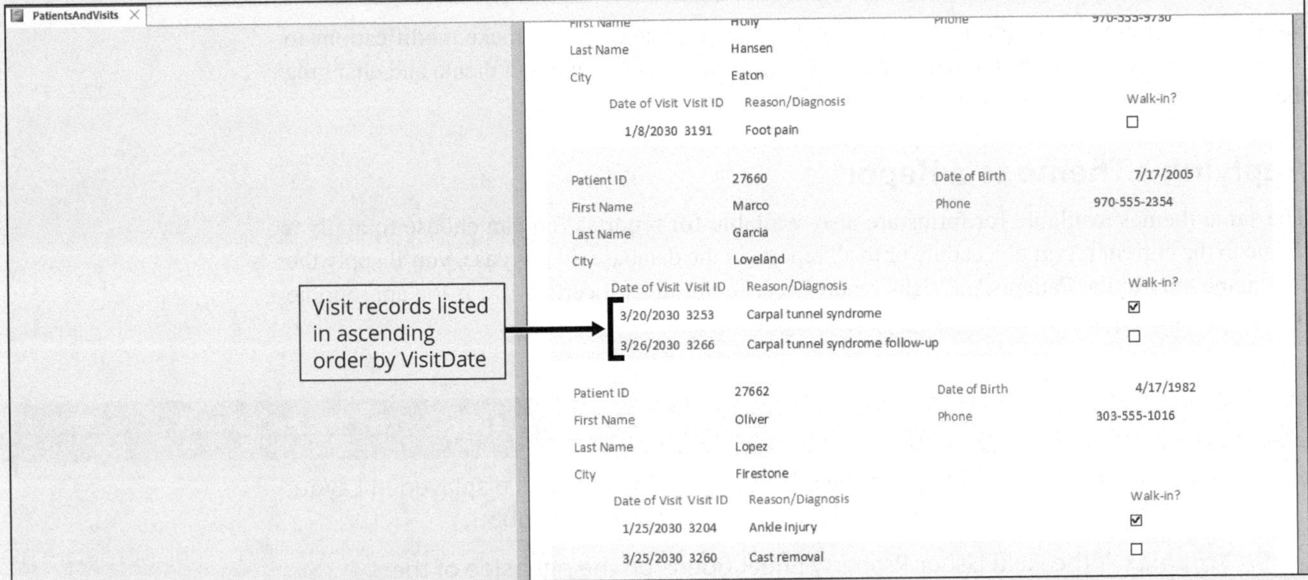

Tip Clicking a report in Print Preview toggles between a full-page display and a close-up display of the report.

The detail records for the Visit table appear in ascending order based on the values in the VisitDate field. Because the VisitDate field is used as the basis for sorting records, it appears as the first field in this section, even though you selected the fields in the same order they appear in the Visit table.

4. Scroll to the bottom of the second page, checking the text in the report as you scroll. Notice the current date and page number at the bottom of the page; the Report Wizard included these elements as part of the report's design.
5. Move the pointer onto the report, click the **Zoom Out** pointer to zoom back out, and then click the **Next Page** button to move to page 3 of the report.
6. Continue to move through the pages of the report, and then click the **First Page** button to return to the first page.

Insight

Changing a Report's Page Orientation and Margins

When you display a report in Print Preview, you can change the report layout using options on the Print Preview tab. (See the Part 4.2 Visual Overview.) For example, sometimes fields with longer values cause the report content to overflow onto the next page. You can fix this problem by clicking the Landscape button in the Page Layout group on the Print Preview tab to switch the report orientation to landscape, where the page is wider than it is tall. Landscape orientation allows more space for content to fit across the width of the report page. You can also use the Margins button in the Page Size group to change the margins of the report, choosing from common margin formats or setting custom margins. Click the Margins arrow to display the menu of available margin options and select the one that works best for your report.

When you created the PatientData form, you applied the Ion theme. Susan would like to format the PatientsAndVisits report with the same theme. You need to switch to Layout view to make this change. You'll also make other modifications to improve the report's design.

Modifying a Report's Design in Layout View

Similar to Layout view for forms, Layout view for reports enables you to make modifications to the report's design. Many of the same options—such as those for applying a theme and changing the color of text—are provided in Layout view for reports.

Applying a Theme to a Report

The same themes available for forms are also available for reports. You can choose to apply a theme to the current report object only or to all reports in the database. In this case, you'll apply the Ion theme only to the PatientsAndVisits report because Susan isn't certain if it is the appropriate theme for other reports in the NP_AC_4_PineRidge database.

To apply the Ion theme to the report and edit the report title:

1. On the status bar, click the **Layout View** button. The report is displayed in Layout view and the Report Layout Design tab is the active tab on the ribbon.

   Trouble? If the Field List or Property Sheet opens on the right side of the program window, close it before continuing.

2. In the Themes group, click the **Themes** button. The "In this Database" section at the top of the gallery shows both the default Office theme and the Ion theme. The Ion theme is included here because you applied it earlier to the PatientData form.

   Tip When you point to the Ion theme, a ScreenTip displays the names of the database objects that use the theme—in this case, the PatientData form.

3. At the top of the gallery, right-click the **Ion** theme to display the shortcut menu, and then click **Apply Theme to This Object Only**. The gallery closes, and the theme is applied to the report.

   The larger font used by the Ion theme has caused the report title text to be cut off on the right. You'll fix this problem and edit the title text as well.

4. Click the **PatientsAndVisits** title at the top of the report to select it.
5. Position the pointer on the right border of the title's selection box until it changes to the width change pointer ↔, and then double-click the border to display the full title.
6. Click between the letters "s" and "A" in the title, press **SPACEBAR**, change the capital letter "A" to **a**, place the insertion point between the letters "d" and "V," and then press **SPACEBAR**. The title is now "Patients and Visits."
7. Click to the right of the report title in the shaded area to deselect the title.

Although Susan is confident that the content of the report provides information her staff needs, she wants to improve the formatting. For example, she doesn't like how the BirthDate field values are aligned compared to the other field values from the Patient table. You'll fix this next.

Changing the Alignment of Field Values

The Format tab provides options for modifying the format of report objects. For example, you can change the alignment of the text in a field value. Recall that Date/Time fields, like VisitDate, automatically right-align their field values, whereas Short Text fields, like VisitID, automatically left-align their field values. Susan asks you to change the alignment of the BirthDate field so its values appear left-aligned, which will improve the format of the report.

To change the alignment of the BirthDate field values:

1. On the ribbon, click the **Format** tab. The ribbon changes to display options for formatting the report. The options for modifying the format of a report are the same as those available for forms.
2. In the report, click the **first BirthDate** field value box, which contains the date 4/19/2002. The field value box has an orange border, indicating it is selected. The other BirthDate field value boxes have a lighter orange border, indicating they are selected as well. Any changes you make will be applied to all BirthDate field values throughout the report.
3. On the Format tab, in the Font group, click the **Align Left** button. The text in the BirthDate field value boxes is now left-aligned. See Figure 4–22.

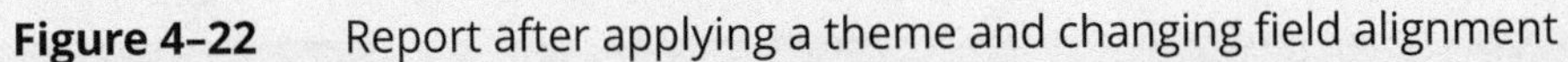

Figure 4–22 Report after applying a theme and changing field alignment

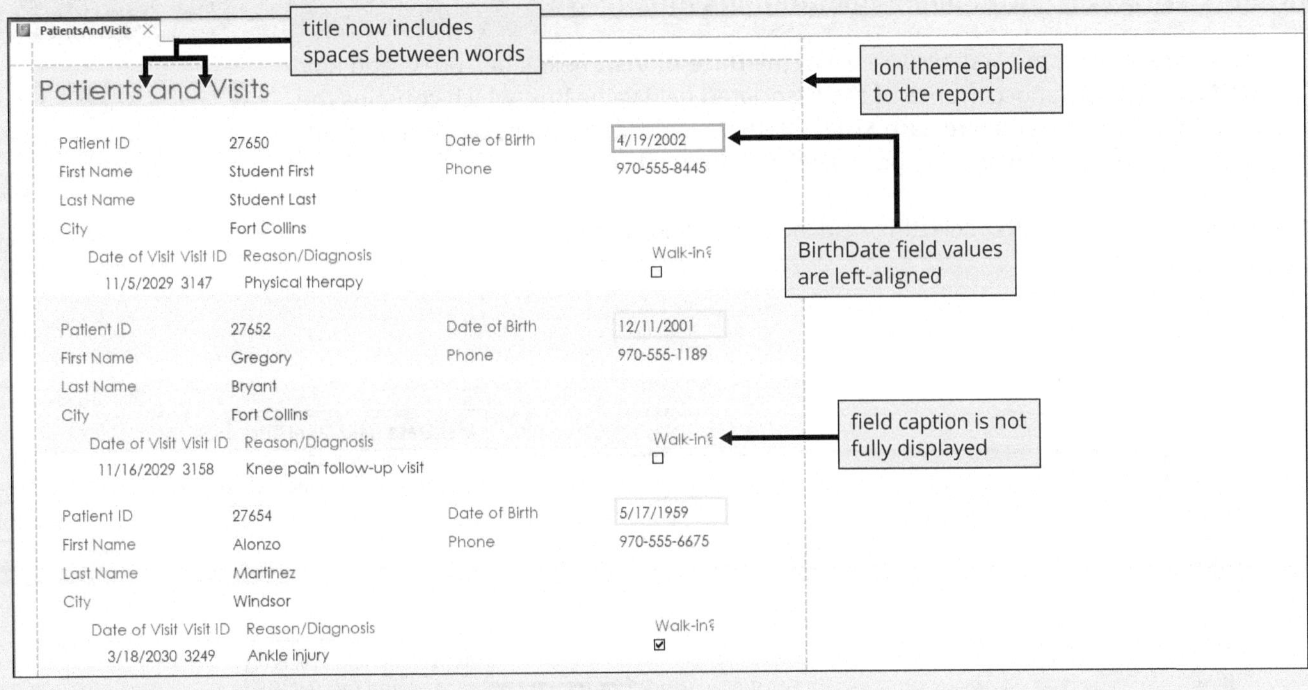

Moving and Resizing Fields on a Report

Working in Layout view, you can resize and reposition fields and field value boxes to improve the appearance and readability of a report. You resize field value boxes by dragging their borders. You can also move field labels and field value boxes by selecting one or more of them and then dragging them to a new location. For more precise control over the move, you can use the arrow keys to move selected objects.

In the PatientsAndVisits report, you need to move and resize the WalkIn field label (Walk-in?) to display the complete caption, which includes a question mark. Susan also thinks the report would be easier to read with more room between the VisitDate and VisitID fields, so you'll move the VisitDate field label and associated field value box to the left. First, you will move the WalkIn field label so it appears centered over its check box.

To move and resize the WalkIn field label:

1. In the report, click the first occurrence of the **WalkIn** field label. All instances of the label are selected throughout the report, indicating that all selected labels will be resized.
2. Press ← repeatedly until the label is centered (roughly) over its check box.
3. Position the pointer on the right border of the field label's selection box until the pointer changes to the width change pointer ↔, and then drag to the right until the label text is fully displayed.

Next, you need to move the VisitDate field label (Date of Visit) and field value box to the left to provide more space between the VisitDate field and the VisitID field. You can select both objects and modify them at the same time.

To move the VisitDate field label and field value box:

1. In the report, click the first occurrence of the **Date of Visit** field label, press and hold **SHIFT**, click the first occurrence of the associated field value box, which contains the date 11/5/2029, and then release **SHIFT**. Both the field label and its associated field value box are selected and can be moved. See Figure 4–23.

Figure 4–23 Report after selecting field label and field value box

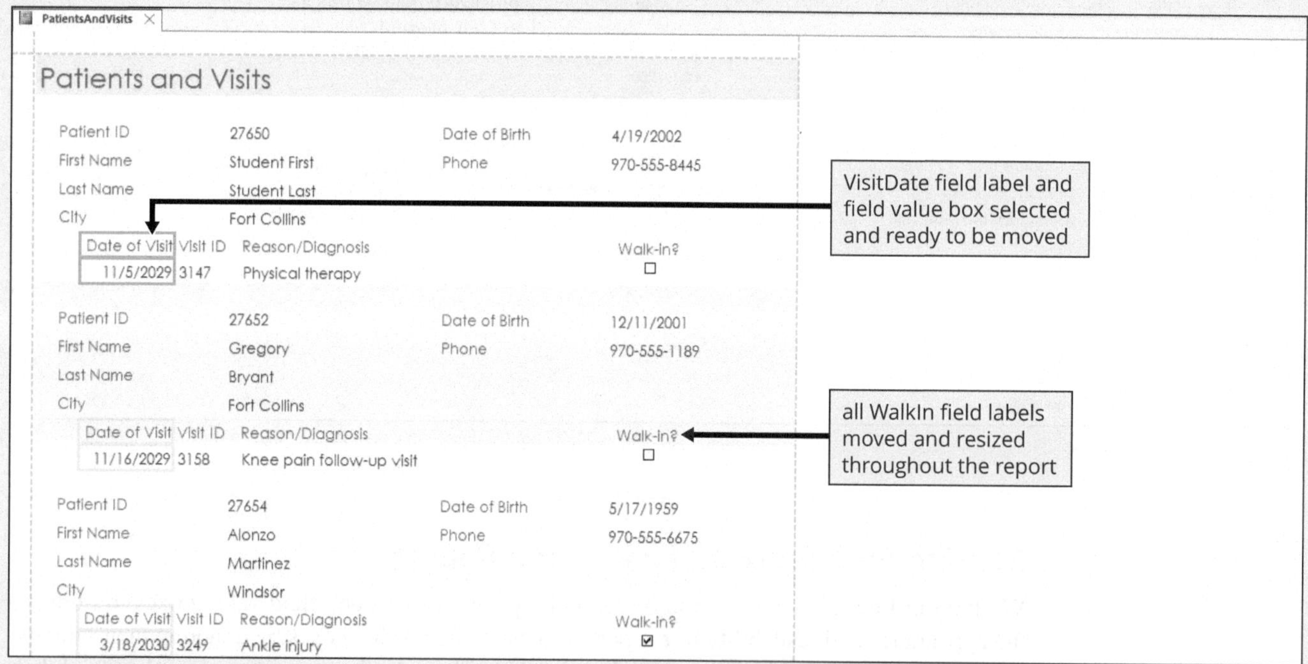

2. Press ← four times to move the field label and field value box to the left.

> **Trouble?** Once you press LEFT ARROW, the report might scroll to display the end of the report. Continue to press LEFT ARROW to move the labels and values. Then scroll the window back up to display the beginning of the report.

3. On the Quick Access Toolbar, click the **Save** button to save the modified report.
4. Click to the right of the report title in the shaded area to deselect the VisitDate field label and field value box, if necessary.
5. Scroll through the report, checking the field labels and field values as you go to make sure all text is fully displayed. When finished, scroll back up to display the top of the report.

Next, Susan asks you to enhance the report's appearance to make it more consistent with the PatientData form.

Changing the Font Color and Inserting a Picture in a Report

You can change the color of text on a report to enhance its appearance. You can also add a picture to a report for visual interest or to identify a particular section of the report.

Before you print the report for Susan, she asks you to change the color of the report title to the darker shade of black you applied earlier to the PatientData form and to include the patient chart picture to the right of the report title.

To change the color of the report title and insert the picture:

1. At the top of the report, click the **Patients and Visits** title to select it.

   Key Step Make sure the title is selected so the picture is inserted in the correct location.

2. Make sure the Format tab is still active on the ribbon.
3. In the Font group, click the **Font Color arrow** , and then click the **Black, Text 1, Lighter 25%** box (second column, fourth row in the Theme Colors palette). The color is applied to the report title.

   Now you'll insert the picture to the right of the report title text.

4. On the ribbon, click the **Report Layout Design** tab. The options provided on this tab for reports are the same as those you worked with for forms.
5. In the Header/Footer group, click the **Logo** button.
6. Navigate to the **Access4 > Module** folder provided with your Data Files, and then double-click the **Support_AC_4_Chart.png** file. The picture is inserted in the top-left corner of the report, partially covering the report title.
7. Position the **layout selector** pointer on the selected picture, and then drag it to the right of the report title.
8. Click in a blank area of the shaded title area to deselect the picture. See Figure 4–24.

Figure 4–24 Report after changing the title font color and inserting the picture

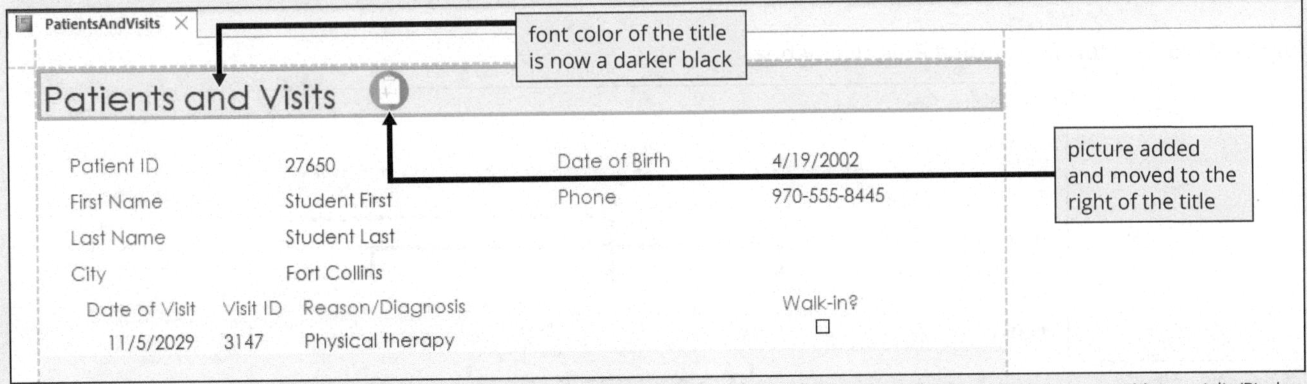

Mcmurryjulie/Pixabay

Trouble? The picture in your report does not have to be in the exact same location as the one shown in the figure. Just make sure it is to the right of the title text and within the shaded area.

Susan approves of the report's contents and design but has one final suggestion for the report. She would like to draw attention to records for younger patients by formatting their birth date with a bold, dark red font. Pine Ridge Orthopedics & Sports Medicine Center is planning a special event specifically geared to patients under 30 years old, so this format will make it easier to find these records in the report. Because Susan does not want all the birth dates to appear in this font, you need to use conditional formatting.

Using Conditional Formatting in a Report

Conditional formatting in a report (or form) is special formatting applied to certain field values depending on one or more conditions—similar to criteria you establish for queries. If a field value meets the conditions you specify, the formatting is applied to the value.

Susan wants the PatientsAndVisits report to show any birth date on or after 1/1/2000 in a bold, dark red font. This formatting will help to highlight the records for patients who are younger than 30 years old. Susan will review this report in a planning meeting for the upcoming special event.

To apply conditional formatting to the BirthDate field in the report:

1. Make sure the report is still displayed in Layout view, and then click the **Format** tab on the ribbon.

   To apply conditional formatting to a field, you must first make it the active field by clicking any field value in the field's column.

   Tip You must select a field value box, and not the field label, before applying a conditional format.

2. Click the first BirthDate field value, **4/19/2002**, for PatientID 27650 to select the BirthDate field values in the report. The conditional formatting you specify will affect all the values for the field.
3. In the Control Formatting group, click the **Conditional Formatting** button. The Conditional Formatting Rules Manager dialog box opens. Because you selected a BirthDate field value box, the name of this field is displayed in the "Show formatting rules for" box. Currently, no conditional formatting rules are set for the selected field. You need to create a new rule.
4. Click the **New Rule** button. The New Formatting Rule dialog box opens. See Figure 4–25.

Figure 4–25 New Formatting Rule dialog box

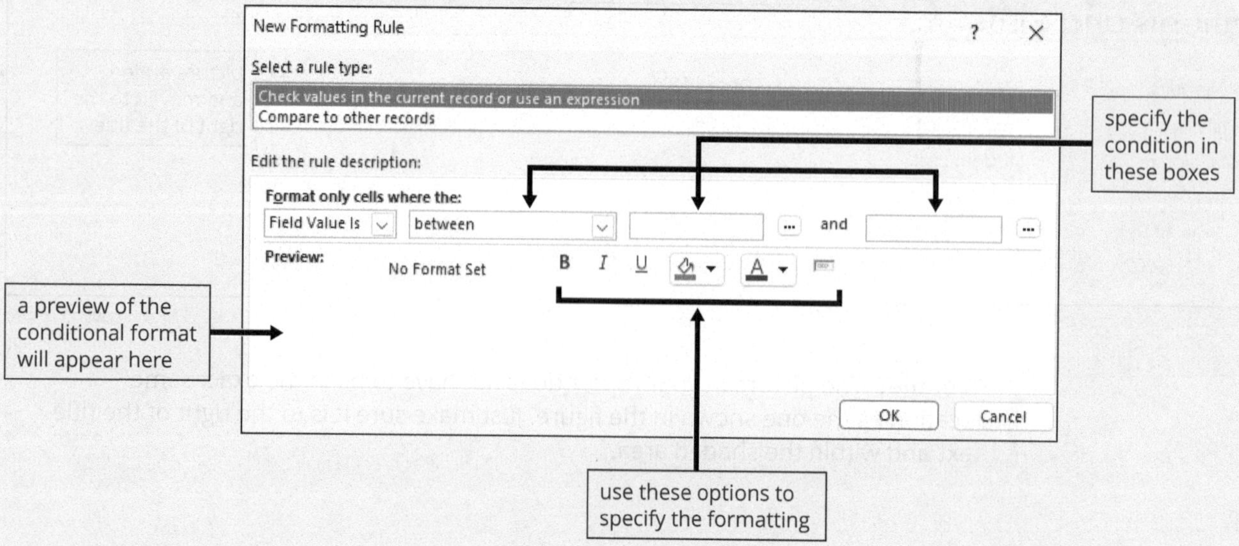

The default setting for "Select a rule type" specifies that Access will check field values and determine if they meet the condition. This is the setting you want. You need to enter the condition in the "Edit the rule description" section of the dialog box. The setting "Field Value Is" means that the conditional format you specify will be applied only when the value for the selected field, BirthDate, meets the condition.

5. Click the **arrow** for the box containing the word "between," and then click **greater than or equal to**. You want to format only birth dates greater than or equal to 1/1/2000.
6. Click in the next box, and then type **1/1/2000**.
7. In the Preview section, click the **Font color arrow** [A], and then click the **Dark Red** box (first column, last row in the Standard Colors palette).
8. In the Preview section, click the **Bold** button [B]. The specifications for the conditional formatting are complete. See Figure 4–26.

Figure 4–26 Conditional formatting set for the BirthDate field

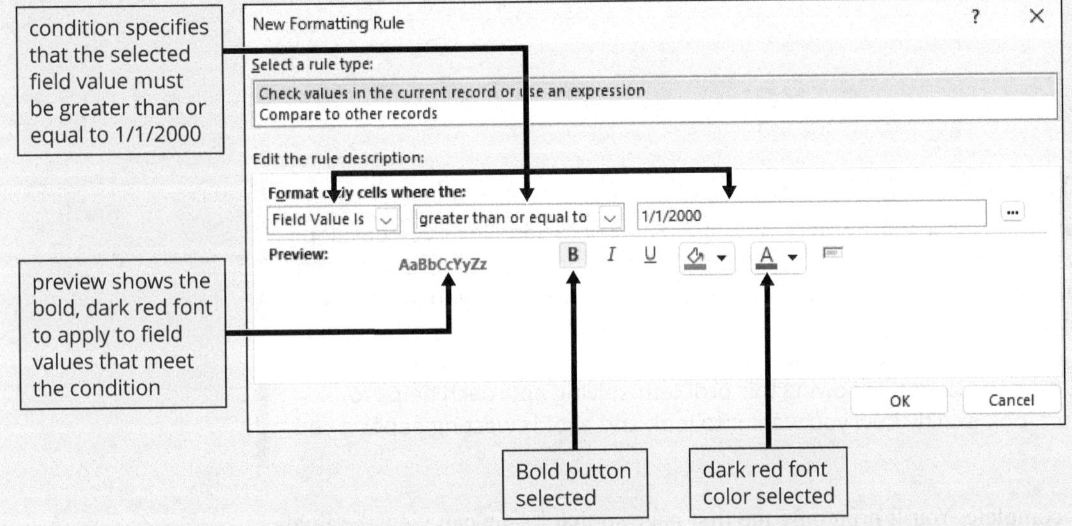

9. Click **OK**. The new rule you specified appears in the Rule section of the Conditional Formatting Rules Manager dialog box as Value >= 1/1/2000. The Format section on the right shows the conditional formatting (dark red, bold font) to apply based on this rule.
10. Click **OK**. The conditional format is applied to the BirthDate field values. To display a better view of the report and the formatting, you'll switch to Print Preview.
11. On the status bar, click the **Print Preview** button.
12. Move to page 2 of the report. Notice that the conditional formatting is applied only to BirthDate field values on or after 1/1/2000. See Figure 4–27.

Figure 4–27 Viewing the finished report in Print Preview

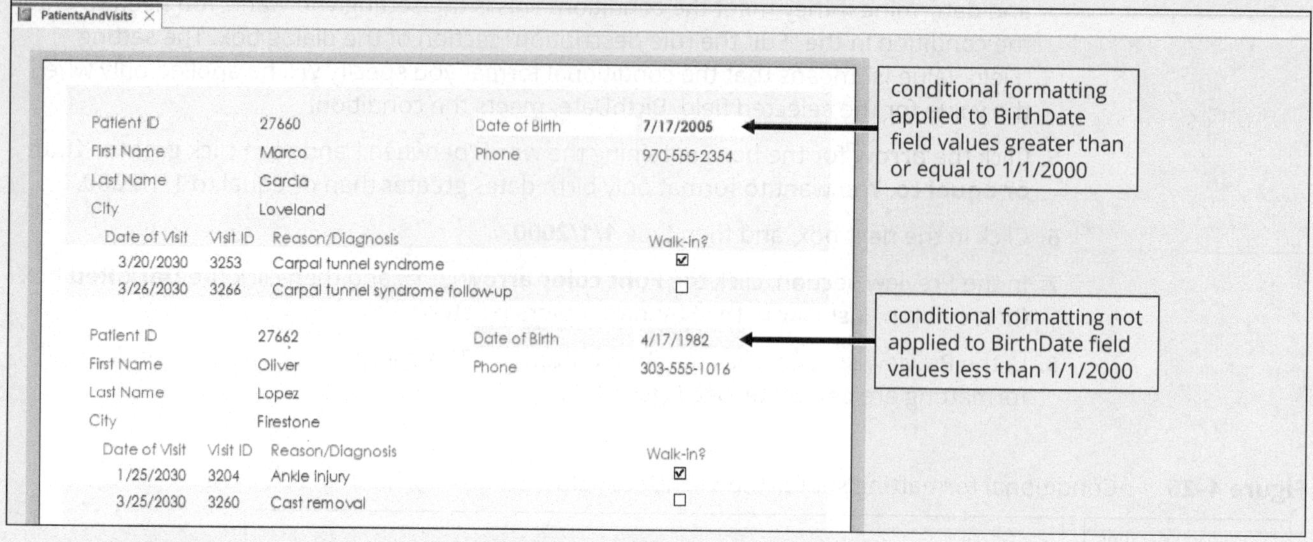

Proskills

Problem Solving: Previewing Reports

When you create a report, display the report in Print Preview occasionally as you develop it. Doing so gives you a chance to identify formatting problems or other issues so you can correct them before printing the report. Be sure to preview a report after you adjust its design to check whether your changes introduced new problems with the report's format. Before printing any report, you should preview it so you can determine where the pages will break and fine-tune the layout. Following this problem-solving approach helps to make the final report look exactly how you want it to look and avoids wasting paper if you print the report.

The report is now complete. You'll print only the first page so that Susan can view the final results and share the report design with other staff members before printing the entire report. Ask your instructor if you should complete the following printing steps.

To print page 1 of the report:

1. On the Print Preview tab, in the Print group, click the **Print** button. The Print dialog box opens.
2. In the Print Range section, click the **Pages** option button. The insertion point now appears in the From box so that you can specify the range of pages to print.
3. Type **1** in the From box, press **TAB** to move to the To box, and then type **1** to print only page 1 of the report.
4. Click **OK**. The Print dialog box closes, and the first page of the report prints.
5. Save and close the PatientsAndVisits report.

You've created new objects in the NP_AC_4_PineRidge database. Before you close it, you'll open the Navigation Pane to view all the objects in the database.

To view the NP_AC_4_PineRidge database objects in the Navigation Pane:

1. Open the **Navigation Pane** in the Access window.

   The Navigation Pane now includes the PatientsAndVisits report in the Reports section and the PatientVisits form in the Forms section. This is the form you created containing a main form based on the Patient table and a subform based on the Visit table. The VisitSubform object is also listed; you can open it separately from the main form. See Figure 4–28.

Figure 4–28 NP_AC_4_PineRidge database objects in the Navigation Pane

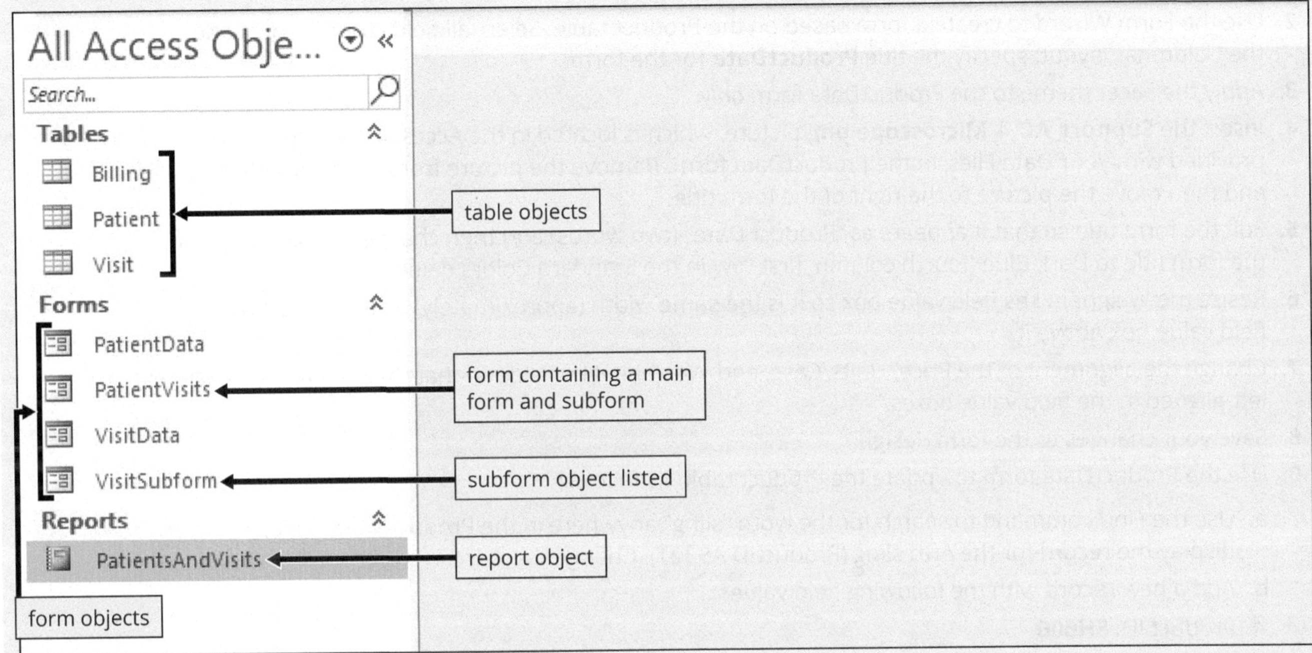

2. sam Compact and repair the NP_AC_4_PineRidge database, and then close the database.

Susan is satisfied that the forms you created—the PatientData form and the PatientVisits form—will make it easier to enter, view, and update data in the NP_AC_4_PineRidge database. The PatientsAndVisits report presents important information about the patients the center treats in an attractive and professional format, which will help Susan and other staff members in their work.

Part 4.2 Quick Check

1. What Access tool can you use to guide you through the steps of creating a report?
2. When you create a report based on two tables joined in a one-to-many relationship, the field values for the records from the related table are called the ________ records.
3. Identify three types of modifications you can make to a report in Layout view.
4. What can you do in Layout view if a label on a report does not display all of its text?
5. To insert a picture next to the report title, you click the Report Layout Design tab, and then in the Header/Footer group, you click the ________ button.
6. In a report (or form), special formatting applied to certain field values depending on one or more conditions is called ________.

Practice: Review Assignments

Data Files needed for the Review Assignments: NP_AC_4-2.accdb, Support_AC_4_Microscope.png, and Support_AC_4_Stethoscope.png

Susan asks you to enhance the Vendor database with forms and reports. Be sure to use the starting data file, NP_AC_4-2.accdb, to complete the Review Assignments so your solutions match those provided by your instructor. Complete the following steps:

1. Open the database NP_AC_4-2.accdb from the Access4 > Review folder included with your Data Files, and then save the file as **NP_AC_4_Vendor** in the location specified by your instructor. Click the Enable Content button next to the security warning, if necessary.
2. Use the Form Wizard to create a form based on the Product table. Select all fields for the form and the Columnar layout; specify the title **ProductData** for the form.
3. Apply the Facet theme to the ProductData form *only*.
4. Insert the **Support_AC_4_Microscope.png** picture, which is located in the Access4 > Review folder provided with your Data Files, in the ProductData form. Remove the picture from the control layout, and then move the picture to the right of the form title.
5. Edit the form title so that it appears as "Product Data" (two words) and then change the font color of the form title to Dark Blue (fourth column, first row in the Standard Colors palette).
6. Resize the Weight in Lbs field value box so it is the same width (approximately) as the Units/Case field value box above it.
7. Change the alignment of the Price, Units/Case, and Weight in Lbs fields so that their values appear left-aligned in the field value boxes.
8. Save your changes to the form design.
9. Use the ProductData form to update the Product table as follows:
    a. Use the Find command to search for the word "sling" anywhere in the ProductName field, and then display the record for the Arm sling (ProductID AS321). Change the Price in this record to **25.00**.
    b. Add a new record with the following field values:

       Product ID: **SH606**

       Supplier ID: **ZUR439**

       Product Name: **Shoulder brace**

       Price: **53.50**

       Units/Case: **6**

       Weight in Lbs: **3**

       Temp Controlled?: **no**

       Sterile?: **no**
    c. Use the form to display each record with a ProductID value that starts with "TD."
    d. Save and close the form.
10. Use the Form Wizard to create a form containing a main form and a subform. Select all fields from the Supplier table for the main form, and select ProductID, ProductName, Price, TempControl, and Sterile—in that order—from the Product table for the subform. Use the Datasheet layout. Specify the title **SuppliersAndProducts** for the main form and **ProductSubform** for the subform.
11. Change the form title text to **Suppliers and Products**.
12. Resize the subform by widening it from its right side, increasing its width by approximately 2 inches, and then resize all columns in the subform to their best fit, working left to right. Navigate through each record in the main form to make sure all the field values in the subform are completely displayed, resizing subform columns and the subform itself as necessary. Save the SuppliersAndProducts form.

13. In the first record of the SuppliersAndProducts form (for ABC Pharmaceuticals), change the ContactFirstName and ContactLastName field values to your first and last names, and then close the form.
14. Use the Report Wizard to create a report based on the primary Supplier table and the related Product table. Select the SupplierID, Company, City, Category, ContactFirst, ContactLast, and Phone fields—in that order—from the Supplier table, and the ProductID, ProductName, Price, and Units fields from the Product table. Do not specify additional grouping levels and sort the detail records in ascending order by ProductID. Choose the Outline layout and Portrait orientation. Specify the title **ProductsBySupplier** for the report.
15. Change the report title text to **Products by Supplier**.
16. Apply the Facet theme to the ProductsBySupplier report *only*.
17. Resize and reposition the following objects in the report in Layout view, and then scroll through the report to make sure all field labels and field values are fully displayed:
    a. Resize the report title so that the text of the title, Products by Supplier, is fully displayed.
    b. Move the ProductName field label and field value box to the right about 10 spaces.
    c. Resize the Product ID field label from its right side, increasing its width slightly to display the full label text.
    d. Move the Units/Case field label and field value box to the right about five spaces, and then resize the label on its left side, increasing its width slightly to display the full label text.
18. Change the color of the report title text to Dark Blue (fourth column, first row in the Standard Colors palette).
19. Insert the **Support_AC_4_Stethoscope.png** picture, which is located in the Access4 > Review folder provided with your Data Files, in the report. Move the picture to the right of the report title.
20. Apply conditional formatting so that the Category field values equal to **Equipment** appear as dark red and bold.
21. Preview each page of the report, verifying that the conditional formatting was applied correctly and that all the fields fit on the page. If necessary, return to Layout view and make changes so the report prints within the margins of the page and all field names and values are completely displayed.
22. Save the report, print its first page (only if asked by your instructor to do so), and then close the report.
23. Compact and repair the NP_AC_4_Vendor database, and then close it.

Apply: Case Problem 1

Data Files needed for this Case Problem: NP_AC_4-3.accdb and Support_AC_4_Laptop.png

Tech Tutors Taylor uses the Tech Tutors database to track and view information about the students, tutors, and contracts in her business. She asks you to create the necessary forms and a report to help her work with this data more efficiently. Be sure to use the starting data file, NP_AC_4-3.accdb, to complete Case Problem 1 so your solutions match those provided by your instructor. Complete the following steps:

1. Open the database NP_AC_4-3.accdb from the Access4 > Case1 folder included with your Data Files, and then save the file as **NP_AC_4_TechTutors** in the location specified by your instructor. Click the Enable Content button next to the security warning, if necessary.
2. Use the Form Wizard to create a form based on the Tutor table. Select all the fields for the form and the Columnar layout. Specify the title **TutorData** for the form.
3. Apply the Slice theme to the TutorData form *only*.
4. Edit the form title so that it appears as "Tutor Data" (two words), and then change the font color of the form title to Dark Blue, Accent 1 (fifth column, first row in the Theme Colors palette).

5. Use the TutorData form to add a new record to the Tutor table with the following field values:
   Tutor ID: **3562**
   First Name: **Damien**
   Last Name: **Kapur**
   Major: **Computer Science**
   Year in School: **Senior**
   School: **Hughes College**
   Hire Date: **5/28/2029**
   Groups Only: **yes**
6. Save and close the TutorData form.
7. Use the Form Wizard to create a form containing a main form and a subform. Select all the fields from the Student table for the main form, and select the ContractID, ContractDate, SessionType, NumSessions, and Cost fields from the Contract table for the subform. Use the Datasheet layout. Specify the title **ContractsByStudent** for the main form and the title **ContractSubform** for the subform.
8. Change the form title text for the main form to **Contracts by Student.**
9. Resize all columns in the subform to their best fit, working from left to right; then move through all the records in the main form and check to make sure that all subform field values are fully displayed, resizing the columns as necessary. Save the ContractsByStudent form.
10. In the first record of the ContractsByStudent form (for Valerie Andres), change the FirstName and LastName field values to your first and last names, and then close the form.
11. Use the Report Wizard to create a report based on the primary Student table and the related Contract table. Select all the fields from the Student table *except* the HomePhone, BirthDate, and Gender fields; and then select the ContractID, ContractDate, SessionType, and Cost fields from the Contract table. Do not select additional grouping levels and sort the detail records in ascending order by ContractID. Choose the Outline layout and Landscape orientation. Specify the title **StudentContracts** for the report.
12. Apply the Slice theme to the StudentContracts report *only*.
13. Edit the report title so that it appears as "Student Contracts" (two words); resize the report title so that the text is fully displayed; and change the font color of the title to Dark Blue, Accent 1 (fifth column, first row in the Theme Colors palette).
14. Change the alignment of the Contract Date field so that its values appear left-aligned in the field value box.
15. Change the alignment of the Cost field so that its values appear centered in the field value box. Center the Cost label above the Cost field.
16. Resize and reposition the following objects in the report in Layout view, and then scroll through the report to make sure all field labels and field values are fully displayed:
    a. Move the Session Type label and field value box to the right approximately 10 spaces.
    b. Move the Contract Date label and field value box to the right approximately five spaces.
    c. Scroll to the bottom of the report, and then select and move the box containing the text "Page 1 of 1" to the left by five spaces.
17. Insert the **Support_AC_4_Laptop.png** picture, which is located in the Access4 > Case1 folder provided with your Data Files, in the report. Move the picture to the right of the report title.
18. Apply conditional formatting so that any Cost field value greater than or equal to 600 appears as bold and with the Red font color applied.
19. Preview the entire report to confirm that it is formatted correctly. If necessary, return to Layout view and make changes so that all field labels and field values are completely displayed.
20. Save the report, print its first page (only if asked by your instructor to do so), and then close the report.
21. Compact and repair the NP_AC_4_TechTutors database, and then close it.

Challenge: Case Problem 2

Data Files needed for this Case Problem: NP_AC_4-4.accdb and Support_AC_4_Tree.png

Outdoor Adventure Tours David and Brent use the Outdoor database to track, maintain, and analyze data about hikers, reservations, and tours. You'll help them by creating a form and a report based on this data. Be sure to use the starting data file, NP_AC_4-4.accdb, to complete Case Problem 2 so your solutions match those provided by your instructor. Complete the following steps:

1. Open the database NP_AC_4-4.accdb from the Access4 > Case2 folder included with your Data Files, and then save the file as **NP_AC_4_Outdoor** in the location specified by your instructor. Click the Enable Content button next to the security warning, if necessary.
2. Use the Form Wizard to create a form based on the Hiker table. Select all the fields for the form and the Columnar layout. Specify the title **HikerMasterData** for the form.
3. Apply the Wisp theme to the HikerMasterData form *only*.
4. Edit the form title so that it appears as "Hiker Master Data" (three words) on one line and change the font color of the form title to Olive Green, Accent 4 (eighth column, first row in the Theme Colors palette).
5. **Explore:** Use the appropriate button in the Font group on the Format tab to bold the form title. Save the form.
6. Use the HikerMasterData form to update the Hiker table as follows:
   a. In the first record (for Norma Cortez), change the HikerFirst and HikerLast field values to your first and last names.
   b. Use the Find command to search for the record that contains the value "453" in the HikerID field, and then change the Phone field value for this record to **276-555-3231**.
   c. Add a new record with the following values:

      HikerID: **457**

      HikerFirst: **Alva**

      HikerLast: **Mara**

      Address: **245 Central Ave**

      City: **Charlottesville**

      State: **VA**

      Zip: **22902**

      Phone: **434-555-6227**
   d. **Explore:** Find the record with HikerID 423, and then delete the record. (**Hint**: After displaying the record in the form, you need to select it by clicking the right-pointing triangle in the bar to the left of the field labels. Then use the appropriate button on the Home tab in the Records group to delete the record. When asked to confirm the deletion, click the Yes button.) Close the form.
7. Use the Form Wizard to create a form containing a main form and a subform. Select all the fields from the Hiker table for the main form and select all fields except HikerID from the Reservation table for the subform. Use the Datasheet layout. Specify the name **HikerReservations** for the main form and the title **ReservationSubform** for the subform.
8. Make sure the default Office theme is applied to the HikerReservations form.
9. Edit the form title so that it appears as "Hiker Reservations." Change the font color of the title to Black, Text 1 (second column, first row in the Theme Colors palette).
10. Insert the **Support_AC_4_Tree.png** picture, which is located in the Access4 > Case2 folder provided with your Data Files, in the HikerReservations form. Remove the picture from the control layout, and then move the picture to the right of the form title. Resize the picture so it is approximately double the original size.

11. **Explore:** Use the appropriate button in the Font group on the Format tab to apply the Green 1 background color (seventh column, second row in the Standard Colors palette) for all the field value boxes in the main form. Use the appropriate button in the Control Formatting group to change the outline of all the main form field value boxes to have a line thickness of 1 pt. (**Hint**: Select all the field value boxes before making these changes.)
12. Resize all columns in the subform to their best fit. Narrow the subform so it is just wide enough to display all its fields. Navigate through the records in the main form to make sure all the field values in the subform are completely displayed, resizing subform columns and the subform itself as necessary. Save and close the form.
13. Use the Report Wizard to create a report based on the primary Tour table and the related Reservation table. Select all the fields from the Tour table and select all fields except TourID from the Reservation table. Sort the detail records in *descending* order by TourDate. Choose the Outline layout and Landscape orientation. Specify the name **TourReservations** for the report.
14. Apply the Wisp theme to the TourReservations report *only*.
15. Resize the report title so that the text is fully displayed, edit the report title so that it appears as "Tour Reservations," change the font color of the form title to Olive Green, Accent 4 (eighth column, first row in the Theme Colors palette), and then bold the title.
16. Move the Tour Date and Reservation ID labels and field value boxes to the left approximately 10 spaces. Resize the Reservation ID label to fully display its text. Center the text in the People field value box. Save the report.
17. Insert the **Support_AC_4_Tree.png** picture, which is located in the Access4 > Case2 folder provided with your Data Files, in the TourReservations report. Move the picture to the right of the report title.
18. Apply conditional formatting so that any Price Per Person value greater than 125 is formatted as bold and with the Green 5 font color (seventh column, sixth row in the Standard Colors palette).
19. **Explore:** Preview the report so you can see two pages at once. (**Hint**: Use a button on the Print Preview tab.) Check the report to confirm that it is formatted correctly and all field labels and field values are fully displayed. Save the report, print its first page (only if asked by your instructor to do so), and then close the report.
20. Compact and repair the NP_AC_4_Outdoor database, and then close it.

Creating a Presentation

Presenting Information About a Staffing Agency

Case: Mariposa Staffing Agency

Mariposa Staffing Agency is an employment company with offices all over the American Northeast, including one in Passaic, New Jersey. Jesslyn Whitman, a client manager in the Passaic office, recently hired you as her assistant. Jesslyn frequently meets with companies in person and uses web conferencing to try to convince them to use Mariposa Staffing Agency to find and retain employees. Many businesses have opened offices in the Passaic area over the past several years. Jesslyn wants to use a PowerPoint presentation when she meets with these businesses. She asks you to prepare a presentation to which she will later add data and cost information.

Microsoft PowerPoint (or simply **PowerPoint**) is a complete presentation app that lets you produce professional-looking presentation files and then deliver them to an audience. In this module, you'll use PowerPoint to create a file that includes text, graphics, and speaker notes. Jesslyn can use the presentation as a starting point for her more comprehensive sales pitch. Before you give the presentation to Jesslyn, you'll check the spelling, run the slide show to evaluate it, and print the file.

Starting Data Files

NP_PPT_1-1.pptx
Support_PPT_1_Worker.jpg
Support_PPT_1_Staff.jpg
Support_PPT_1_Handshake.jpg
NP_PPT_1-2.pptx
Support_PPT_1_Jesslyn.jpg
Support_PPT_1_Meeting.jpg
Support_PPT_1_Strategy.jpg
Support_PPT_1_Interview.jpg
NP_PPT_1-3.pptx
Support_PPT_1_Application.jpg
Support_PPT_1_Building.jpg
Support_PPT_1_Key.jpg
Support_PPT_1_Sophia.jpg
Support_PPT_1_GreenSalad.jpg
Support_PPT_1_ChickenSoup.jpg
Support_PPT_1_PokeBowl.jpg
Support_PPT_1_Pasta.jpg
Support_PPT_1_Pizza.jpg

Objectives

Part 1.1

- Plan and create a new presentation
- Create a title slide and slides with lists
- Edit and format text
- Move and copy text
- Duplicate, rearrange, and delete slides
- Change the theme and theme variant
- Close a presentation

Part 1.2

- Open an existing presentation
- Insert and crop photos
- Resize and move objects
- Modify photo compression options
- Convert a list to a SmartArt diagram
- Create speaker notes
- Check the spelling
- Run a slide show
- Print slides, handouts, speaker notes, and the outline

Part 1.1 Visual Overview: The PowerPoint Window

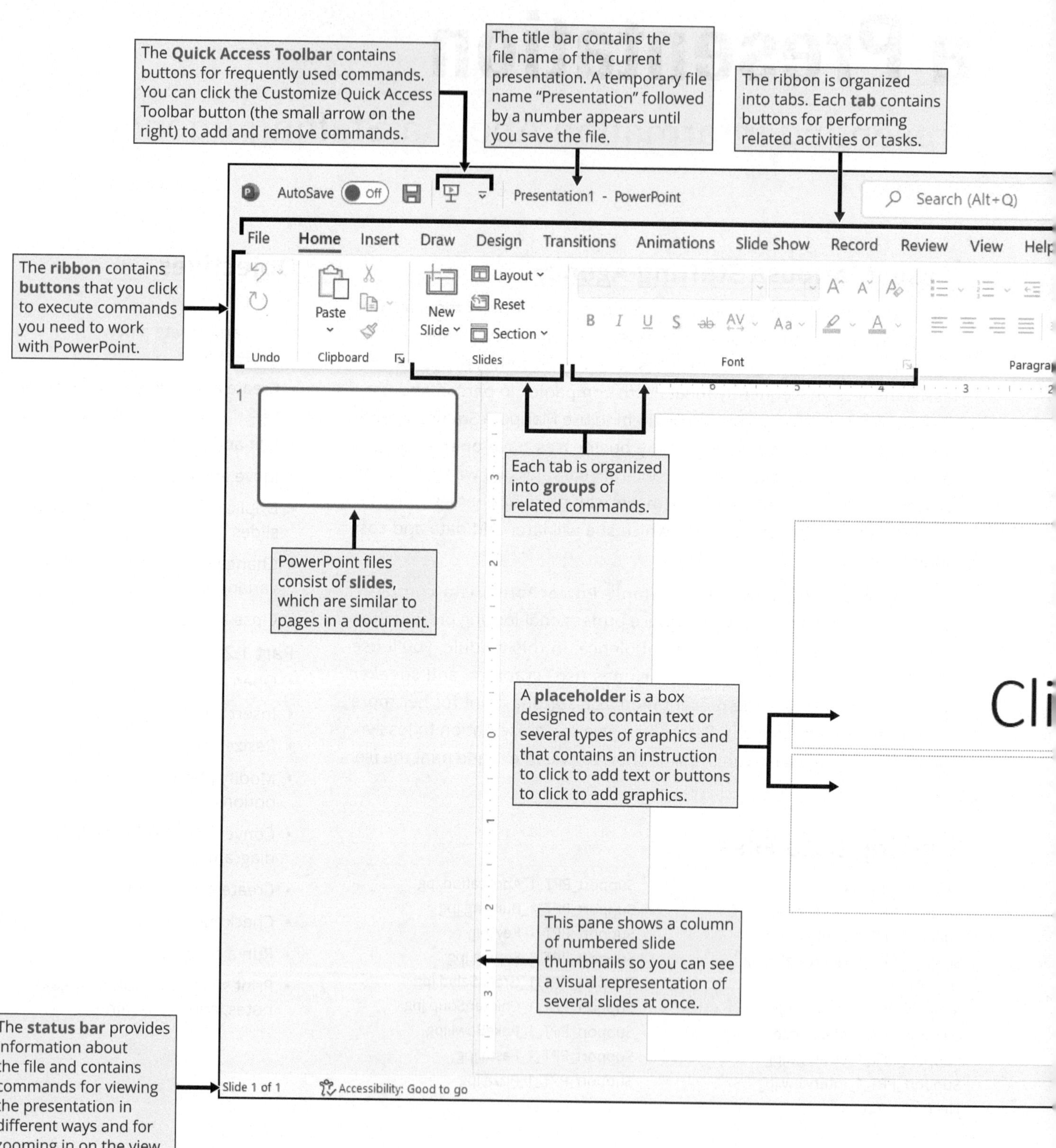
The **Quick Access Toolbar** contains buttons for frequently used commands. You can click the Customize Quick Access Toolbar button (the small arrow on the right) to add and remove commands.
The title bar contains the file name of the current presentation. A temporary file name "Presentation" followed by a number appears until you save the file.
The ribbon is organized into tabs. Each **tab** contains buttons for performing related activities or tasks.
AutoSave
Off
Presentation1 - PowerPoint
Search (Alt+Q)
File
Home
Insert
Draw
Design
Transitions
Animations
Slide Show
Record
Review
View
The **ribbon** contains **buttons** that you click to execute commands you need to work with PowerPoint.
Paste
New Slide
Layout
Reset
Section
Undo
Clipboard
Slides
Font
Each tab is organized into **groups** of related commands.
PowerPoint files consist of **slides**, which are similar to pages in a document.
A **placeholder** is a box designed to contain text or several types of graphics and that contains an instruction to click to add text or buttons to click to add graphics.
This pane shows a column of numbered slide thumbnails so you can see a visual representation of several slides at once.
The **status bar** provides information about the file and contains commands for viewing the presentation in different ways and for zooming in on the view.
Slide 1 of 1
Accessibility: Good to go

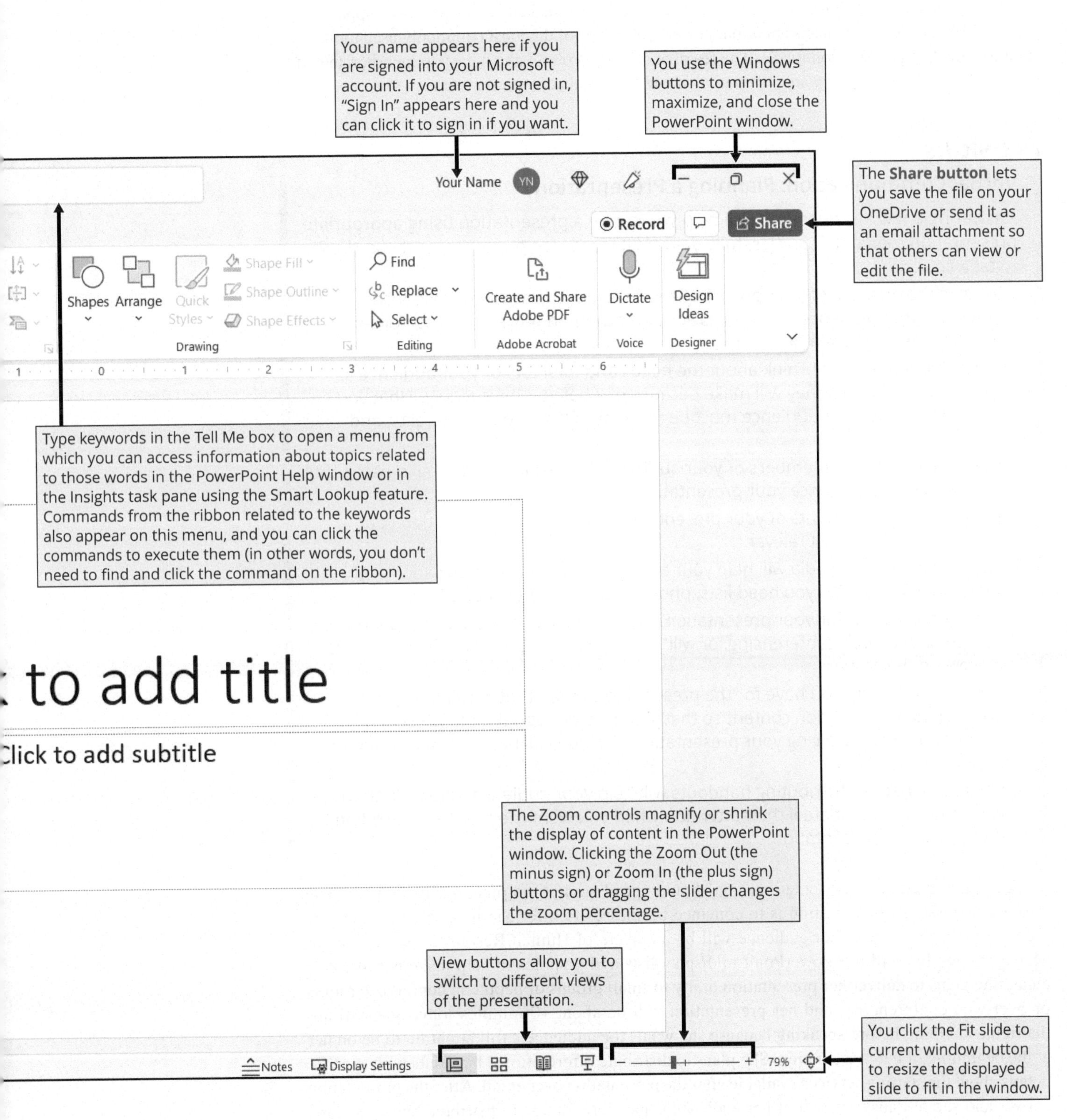
Your name appears here if you are signed into your Microsoft account. If you are not signed in, "Sign In" appears here and you can click it to sign in if you want.
You use the Windows buttons to minimize, maximize, and close the PowerPoint window.
The **Share button** lets you save the file on your OneDrive or send it as an email attachment so that others can view or edit the file.
Your Name
YN
Record
Share
Shapes
Arrange
Quick Styles
Shape Fill
Shape Outline
Shape Effects
Drawing
Find
Replace
Select
Editing
Create and Share Adobe PDF
Adobe Acrobat
Dictate
Voice
Design Ideas
Designer
Type keywords in the Tell Me box to open a menu from which you can access information about topics related to those words in the PowerPoint Help window or in the Insights task pane using the Smart Lookup feature. Commands from the ribbon related to the keywords also appear on this menu, and you can click the commands to execute them (in other words, you don't need to find and click the command on the ribbon).
to add title
Click to add subtitle
The Zoom controls magnify or shrink the display of content in the PowerPoint window. Clicking the Zoom Out (the minus sign) or Zoom In (the plus sign) buttons or dragging the slider changes the zoom percentage.
View buttons allow you to switch to different views of the presentation.
You click the Fit slide to current window button to resize the displayed slide to fit in the window.
Notes
Display Settings
79%

Planning a Presentation

A **presentation** is a talk, formal lecture, or prepared file in which the person speaking or the person who prepared the file wants to communicate with an audience to explain new concepts or ideas, sell a product or service, entertain, train the audience in a new skill or technique, or any of a wide variety of other topics.

Most people find it helpful to use **presentation media**—visual and audio aids that support key points and engage the audience's attention. PowerPoint is one of the most commonly used tools for creating effective presentation media. The features of PowerPoint make it easy to incorporate text with photos, drawings, music, and video to illustrate key points of a presentation.

Proskills

Verbal Communication: Planning a Presentation

Answering a few key questions will help you create a presentation using appropriate presentation media that successfully delivers its message or motivates the audience to take an action.

- What is the purpose of your presentation? Consider the action or response you want your audience to have. Do you want them to buy something, follow instructions, or make a decision?
- Who is your audience? Think about the needs and interests of your audience as well as any decisions they will make because of what you have to say. What you choose to say to your audience must be relevant to their needs, interests, and decisions.
- How will you ensure members of your audience with visual or hearing impairments will be able to experience your presentation?
- What are the main points of your presentation? Identify the information your audience will find most relevant.
- What presentation media will help your audience absorb the information and remember it later? Do you need lists, photos, charts, and/or tables?
- What is the format for your presentation? Will you deliver the presentation in person or over web conferencing, or will you create a presentation file for people to view on their own?
- How much time do you have for the presentation? Keep that in mind as you prepare the presentation content so that you have enough time to present all of your key points. Practicing your presentation out loud will help you determine the timing.
- Consider whether distributing handouts will help your audience follow along with your presentation or steal their attention when you want them to be focused on you during the presentation.

Before you create a presentation, you should spend some time planning its content. The purpose of Jesslyn's presentation is to convince businesses to offer Mariposa Staffing Agency plans to their employees. Her audience will be members of Human Resource departments or Managers. Jesslyn will use PowerPoint to display lists and graphics to help make her message clear. She plans to deliver her presentation orally to small groups of people in conference rooms or over web conferencing, and her presentation will be about 10 minutes long. She will not distribute anything before speaking because she wants the audience's full attention to be on her at the beginning of her presentation. She plans to distribute informational handouts with specific details about the staffing services available after the presentation over email. After the presentation is over and she has answered all of her audience's questions, she will distribute business cards with her contact information.

Once you know what you want to say, you can prepare the presentation media to help communicate your ideas.

Starting PowerPoint and Creating a New Presentation

PowerPoint is a tool you can use to create and display visual and audio aids on slides to help clarify the points you want to make in your presentation. You also can use PowerPoint to create a presentation that people view on their own without you.

When PowerPoint starts, Backstage view appears, showing the Home screen. **Backstage view** is the view that contains commands that allow you to manage the file and program settings. When you first start PowerPoint, the actions available to you in Backstage view are to create a new PowerPoint file, open an existing PowerPoint file, view your Account settings, submit feedback to Microsoft, and open the PowerPoint Options dialog box to change app settings.

You'll start PowerPoint now.

To start PowerPoint:

1. sam On the Windows taskbar, click the **Start** button. The Start menu opens.
2. On the Start menu, click **PowerPoint** from the list of pinned apps, or click the **All Apps** button, scroll as necessary, and then click **PowerPoint**. PowerPoint starts and displays the Home screen in Backstage view. Options for creating new presentations appear in a row at the top of the screen, and if you have recently viewed PowerPoint files, they appear below this row. Refer to Figure 1–1.

Figure 1–1 Home screen in Backstage view

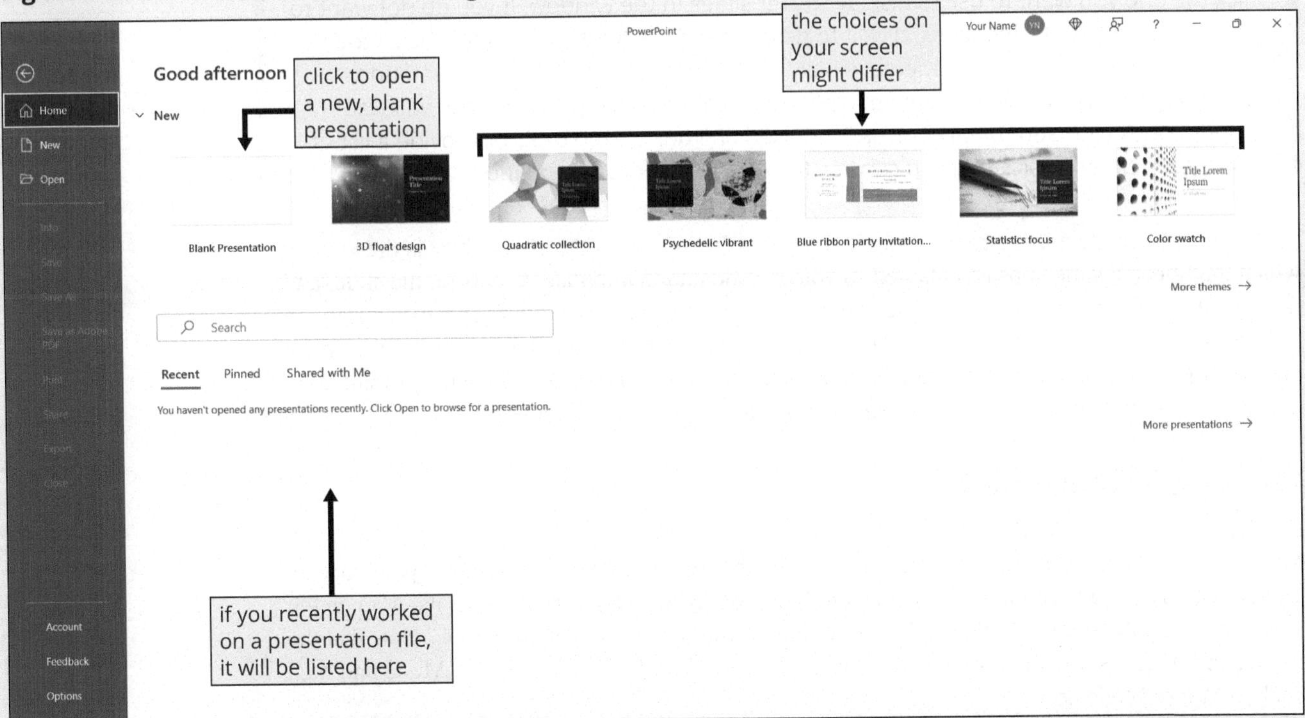

3. Click **Blank Presentation**. Backstage view closes and a new presentation window appears. The temporary filename "Presentation1" appears in the title bar. There is only one slide in the new presentation—Slide 1.

   Trouble? If you do not see the area on the ribbon that contains buttons and you see only the ribbon tab names, click the Home tab to expand the ribbon and display the commands, and then in the right of the ribbon, click the **Ribbon Display Options button** to open a menu, then click the **Always show ribbon** command.

Trouble? If the window does not appear maximized, click the Maximize button ☐ in the upper-right corner.

Tip To create a new blank presentation when PowerPoint is already running, click the File tab on the ribbon, click New in the navigation pane, and then click Blank Presentation.

Because you just started PowerPoint, you clicked Blank presentation on the Home screen. If PowerPoint was already running and you wanted to create a new, blank presentation, you would click the File tab, click New in the navigation pane, and then click Blank Presentation on the New screen in Backstage view.

Insight

Using QuickStarter

QuickStarter is a feature in PowerPoint that creates slide titles based on a topic you enter. To use QuickStarter when you first start PowerPoint, click QuickStarter on the Home screen. If you already are using PowerPoint, click the File tab, click New, and then click QuickStarter on the New screen. The Search here to get started window opens. (The first time you use this feature, the Welcome to PowerPoint QuickStarter window appears. Click Get started to open the Search here to get started window. Also, if the Intelligent Services for Your Work window opens, click Turn On to start using the feature.) Type a topic in the Search box, and then click Search. Suggested presentation ideas appear in the window. Click the one you want to use to display starter slides in the window. If you do not want to include one of the starter slides, click it to deselect it. Click Next to open the Pick a theme window, in which you select a theme. Finally, click Create to generate a presentation containing the starter slides. Some presentations created using QuickStarter will also include slides with additional information based on your search topic or provide a list of suggested related topics that you can use to search for more information.

When you create a new presentation, it appears in Normal view. **Normal view** is the view in which the selected slide appears enlarged so you can add and manipulate objects on the slide, and thumbnails of all the slides in the presentation appear in the pane on the left. A **thumbnail** is a reduced-size version of a larger graphic image. In this case, each thumbnail represents a slide in the presentation. The Home tab on the ribbon is selected when you first open or create a presentation. The Part 1.1 Visual Overview identifies elements of the PowerPoint window.

Working in Touch Mode

In Office 365, you can work with a mouse or, if you have a touch screen, you can work in Touch Mode. In **Touch Mode**, the ribbon increases in height, the buttons are larger, and more space appears around buttons so you can more easily use your finger or stylus to tap screen elements. Also, in the placeholders on the slide, "Double tap" replaces the instruction telling you to "Click." Note that the figures in this text show the screen with Mouse Mode on. You'll switch to Touch Mode and then back to Mouse Mode now.

Note: The following steps assume that you are using a mouse. If instead you are using a touch device, please read these steps, but don't complete them, to continue working in Touch Mode.

To switch between Touch Mode and Mouse Mode:

1. On the Quick Access Toolbar, click the **Customize Quick Access Toolbar** button. A menu opens. The Touch/Mouse Mode command near the bottom of the menu does not have a checkmark next to it.

   Trouble? If the Touch/Mouse Mode command has a checkmark next to it, press the Esc key to close the menu, and then skip Step 2.

2. On the menu, click **Touch/Mouse Mode**. The menu closes, and the Touch/Mouse Mode button appears on the Quick Access Toolbar.
3. On the Quick Access Toolbar, click the **Touch/Mouse Mode** button. A menu opens listing Mouse and Touch. The icon next to Mouse is shaded to indicate it is selected.

   Trouble? If the icon next to Touch is shaded, press ESC to close the menu and skip Step 4.

4. On the menu, click **Touch**. The menu closes, and the ribbon increases in height so that there is more space around each button on the ribbon. Notice that the instructions in the placeholders on the slide changed by replacing the instruction to "Click" with the instruction to "Double tap." Refer to Figure 1–2. Now you'll change back to Mouse Mode.

Figure 1–2 PowerPoint window with Touch Mode active

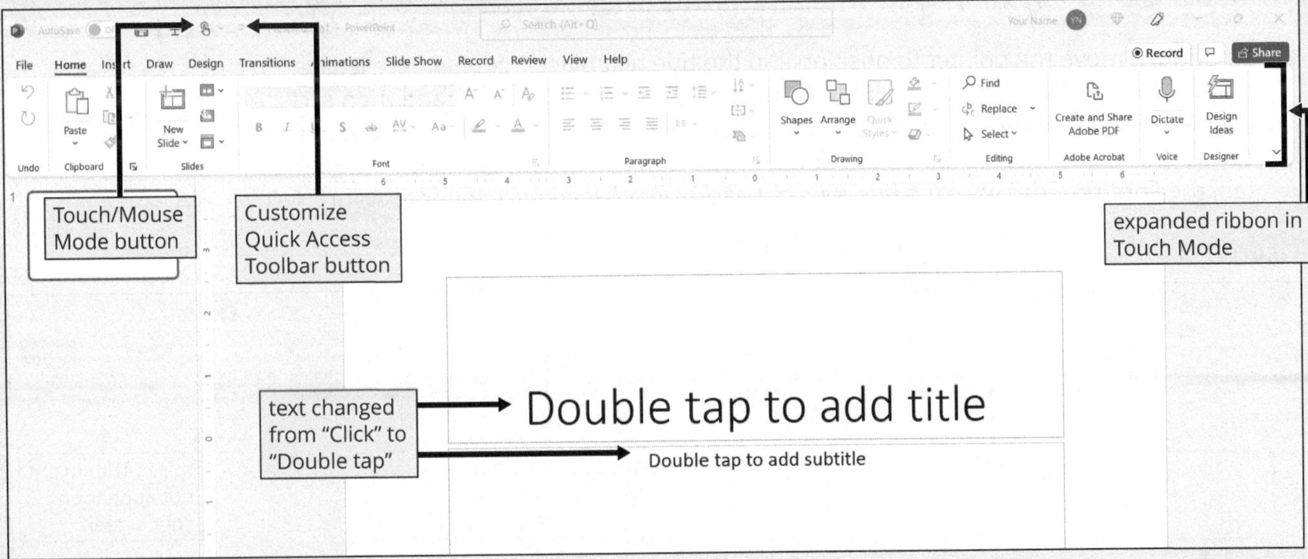

Trouble? If you are working with a touch screen and want to use Touch Mode, skip Steps 5 and 6.

5. Click the **Touch/Mouse Mode** button, and then click **Mouse**. The ribbon and the instructions change back to Mouse Mode defaults, as shown in the Part 1.1 Visual Overview.
6. Click the **Customize Quick Access Toolbar** button, and then click **Touch/Mouse Mode** to deselect this option and remove the checkmark. The Touch/Mouse Mode button disappears from the Quick Access Toolbar.

Creating a Title Slide

The **title slide** is the first slide in a presentation. It usually contains the presentation title and other identifying information, such as a company name or logo, a company's slogan, or the presenter's name. The **font**—a set of letters, numbers, and symbols that all have the same style and appearance—used in the title and subtitle may be the same or may be different fonts that complement each other.

The title slide contains two objects called text placeholders. A **text placeholder** is a placeholder designed to contain text and that contains a prompt that instructs you to click to add text and might describe the purpose of the placeholder. The large placeholder on the title slide is for the presentation title. The small placeholder is for a subtitle. Once you enter text into a text placeholder, the instructional text disappears and it becomes an object called a text box. A **text box** is an object that contains text.

When you click in the placeholder, the insertion point appears. The **insertion point** is a blinking vertical line that indicates where new text will be inserted. Also, a new tab, the Shape Format tab, appears on the ribbon. This tab is a contextual tab. A **contextual tab** appears only in context—that is, when a particular type of object is selected or is active—and contains commands for modifying that object.

You'll add a title and subtitle for Jesslyn's presentation now. Jesslyn wants the title slide to contain the company name and slogan.

To add the company name and slogan to the title slide:

1. On **Slide 1**, move the pointer to position it in the title text placeholder (where it says "Click to add title") so that the pointer changes to the I-beam pointer I and then click. The insertion point replaces the placeholder text, and the Shape Format contextual tab appears as the rightmost tab on the ribbon. Note that in the Font group on the Home tab, the Font box identifies the title font as Calibri Light (Headings). Refer to Figure 1–3.

Figure 1–3 Title text placeholder after clicking in it

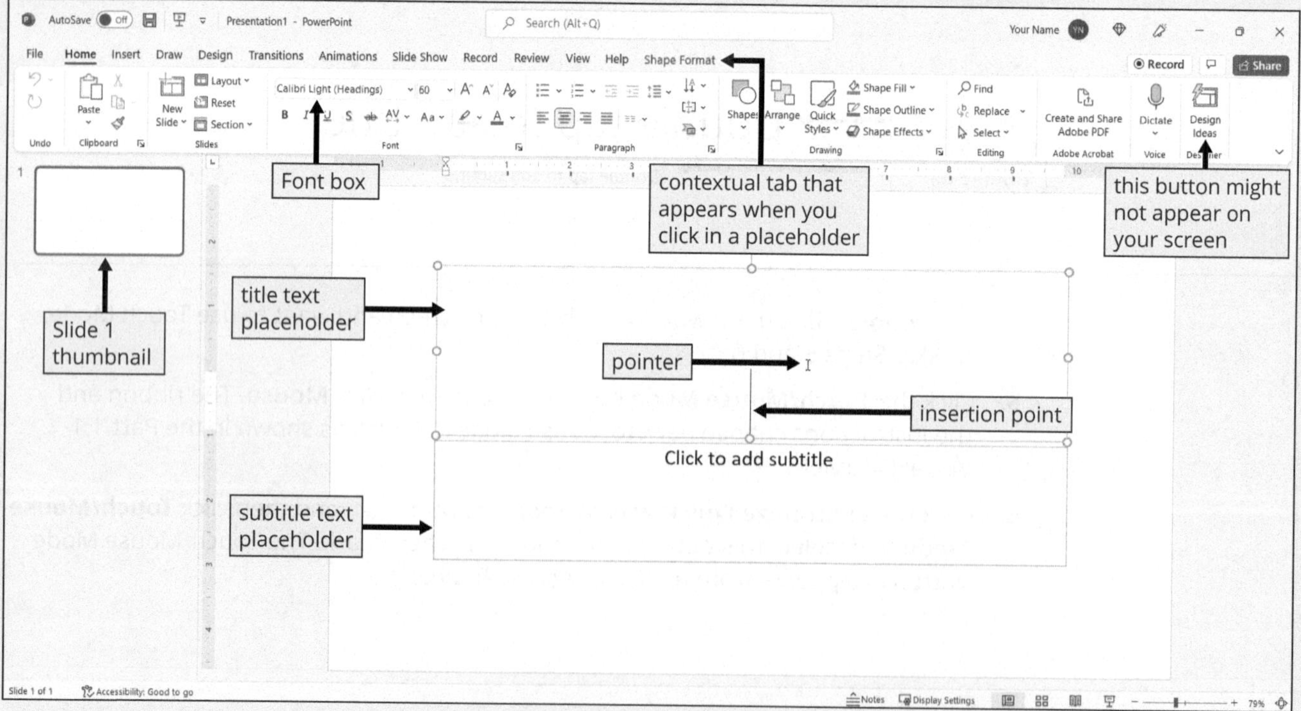

2. Type **Mariposa Staffing Agcy** in the title placeholder. The placeholder is now a text box.

   > **Tip** If your computer has a microphone, you can click the Dictate button in the Voice group on the Home tab, and then speak into your computer's microphone to dictate the text you want to add to the placeholder.

3. Click a blank area of the slide. The border of the text box disappears, and the Shape Format tab no longer appears on the ribbon.
4. Click in the subtitle text placeholder (where it says "Click to add subtitle"), and then type **Connecting Workers Employers since 1995** in the placeholder. Notice in the Font group that the subtitle font is Calibri (Body), a font that works well with the Calibri Light font used in the title text.
5. Click a blank area of the slide.

Saving and Editing a Presentation

Once you have created a presentation, you should name and save the presentation file. You can save the file on a hard drive or a network drive, on an external drive such as a USB drive, or to your account on **OneDrive**, Microsoft's free online storage area.

To save the presentation for the first time:

1. On the Quick Access Toolbar, point to the **Save** button. A box called a ScreenTip appears. A **ScreenTip** is a label that appears when you point to a button or object, which may include the name, purpose, or keyboard shortcut for the object, and may include a link to associated help topics.
2. Click the **Save** button. The Save this file dialog box opens, which you use to save a file on OneDrive. To save a new presentation on your hard drive or an external drive, you use the Save As screen.
3. Click the More options link. The Save As screen in Backstage view appears. Refer to Figure 1–4. The navigation pane is the pane on the left that contains commands for working with the file and program options. Recently used folders on the selected drive appear in a list on the right.

Figure 1–4 Save As screen in Backstage view

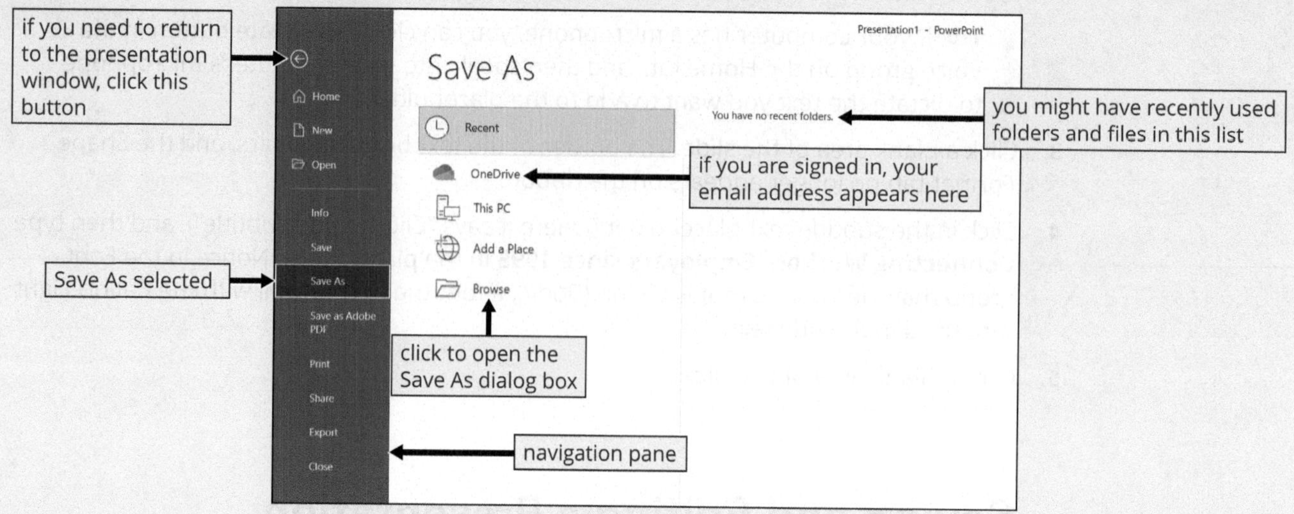

4. Click **Browse**. The Save As dialog box opens, similar to the one shown in Figure 1–5.

Figure 1–5 Save As dialog box

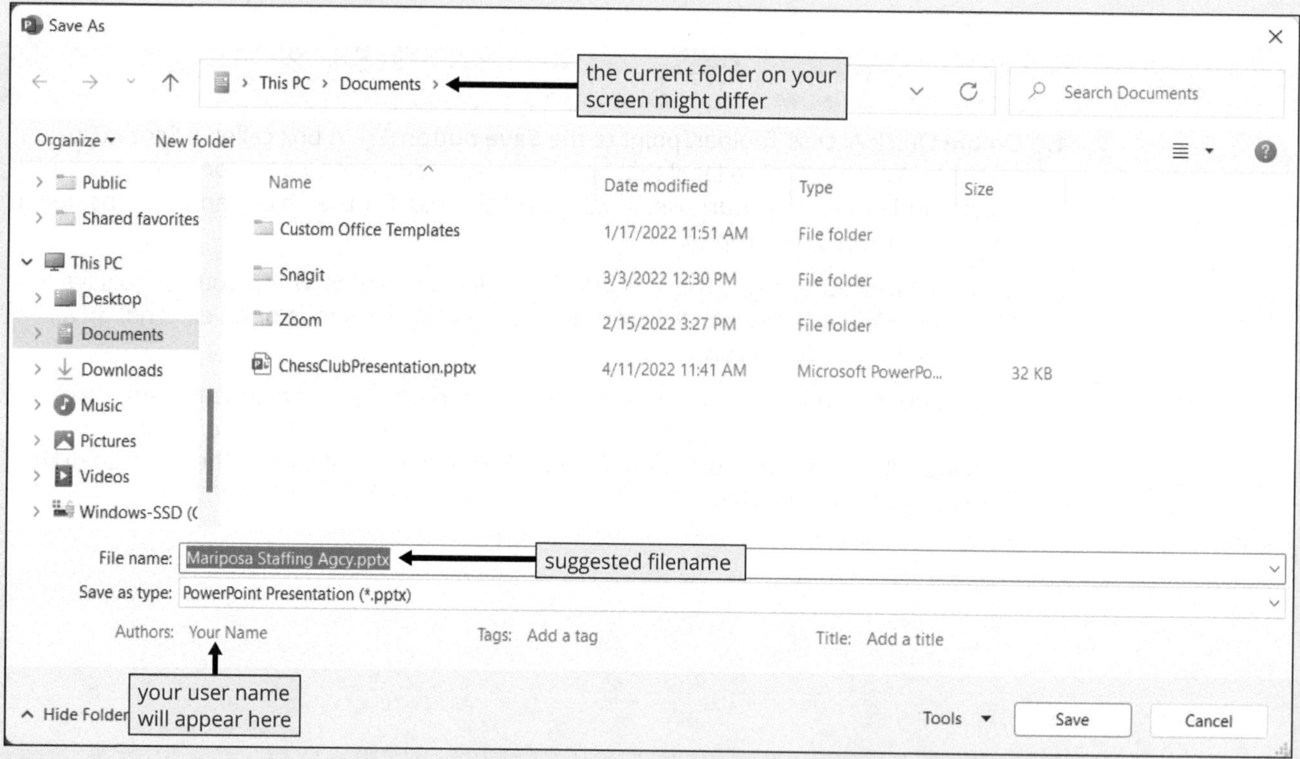

5. Navigate to the drive and folder where you are storing your Data Files, and then click in the **File name** box. The suggested file name, Mariposa Staffing Agcy, is selected.
6. Type **NP_PPT_1_NewBusiness** to replace the selected text in the File name box.
7. Click **Save**. The file is saved, the dialog box and Backstage view close, and the presentation window appears again with the new file name in the title bar.

Once you have created a presentation, you can make changes to it. For example, if you need to change text in a text box, you can edit it easily. The Backspace key removes characters to the left of the insertion point, and the Delete key removes characters to the right of the insertion point.

If you mistype or misspell a word, you might not need to correct it because the **AutoCorrect** feature automatically detects and corrects commonly mistyped and misspelled words. For instance, if you type "cna" and then press SPACEBAR, PowerPoint corrects the word to "can." If you want AutoCorrect to stop making a particular change, you can display the AutoCorrect Options menu, and then click Stop Automatically Correcting. (The exact wording will differ depending on the change made.)

If you have AutoSave turned on, your changes automatically will be saved as you make them. If not, because you already have saved the presentation with a permanent file name, using the Save command saves the changes you made to the file without opening the Save As dialog box. This book assumes that you have AutoCorrect turned on, but still periodically instructs you to save your work.

To edit the text on Slide 1 and save your changes:

1. On Slide 1, click the title, and then press **LEFT ARROW** or **RIGHT ARROW** as needed to position the insertion point to the right of the word "Agcy."
2. Press **BACKSPACE** four times. The four characters "Agcy" to the left of the insertion point are deleted.
3. Type **Agency**. (Do not type the period.) "Mariposa Staffing Agency" now appears as the title.
4. In the subtitle text box, click to the left of the word "Employers" to position the insertion point in front of that word, type **adn**, and then press **SPACEBAR**. "Adn" is corrected to "and" after you press SPACEBAR. "Connecting Workers and Employers since 1995" now appears as the subtitle.
5. Move the pointer over the word "**and**." A small, faint rectangle appears below the first letter of the word. This rectangle indicates that an autocorrection was made.

   Trouble? If you can't see the rectangle, point to the letter "a," and then slowly move the pointer down until it is on top of the rectangle.
6. Move the pointer on top of the rectangle so that it changes to the AutoCorrect Options button, and then click the **AutoCorrect Options** button. A menu opens, as shown in Figure 1-6. You can change the word back to what you originally typed, instruct PowerPoint to stop making this type of correction in this file, or open the AutoCorrect dialog box.

Figure 1–6 AutoCorrect Options button menu

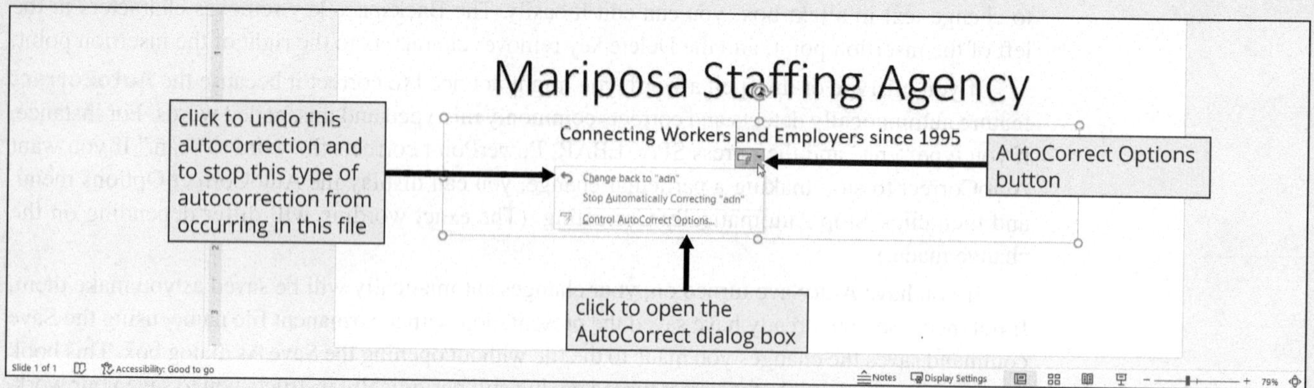

7. Click **Control AutoCorrect Options**. The AutoCorrect dialog box opens with the AutoCorrect tab selected. Refer to Figure 1–7.

Figure 1–7 AutoCorrect tab in the AutoCorrect dialog box

AutoCorrect: English (United States)
AutoFormat As You Type | Actions | Math AutoCorrect
AutoCorrect tab → AutoCorrect
Show AutoCorrect Options buttons
Correct TWo INitial CApitals
Capitalize first letter of sentences
Capitalize first letter of table cells
Capitalize names of days
Correct accidental use of cAPS LOCK key
Replace text as you type
Exceptions...
types of autocorrections that are made
Replace: With:
(c) ©
(e) €
(r) ®
(tm) ™
... ...
list of frequently misspelled words and symbols that are automatically replaced with the text in the right column
Add Delete
Automatically use suggestions from the spelling checker
OK Cancel
click to close the dialog box without applying any changes

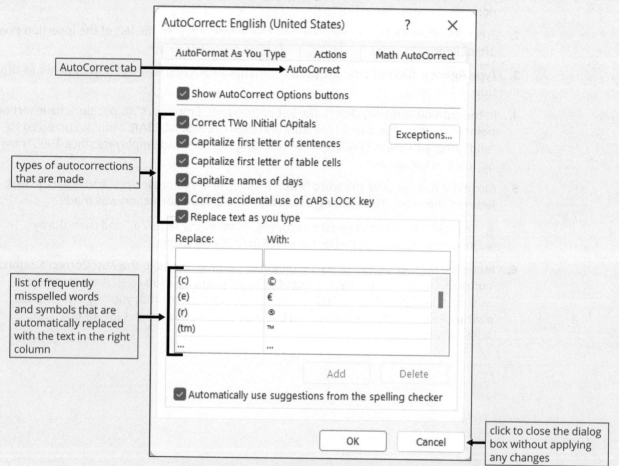

8. Examine the types of changes the AutoCorrect feature makes, and then click **Cancel**.
9. On the Quick Access Toolbar, click the **Save** button. The saved file now includes the new changes you made.

■ **Trouble?** If AutoSave is enabled, skip Step 9.

Adding New Slides

Now that you've created the title slide, you need to add more slides. Every slide has a **layout**, which is the arrangement of placeholders on the slide. The title slide uses the Title Slide layout. A commonly used layout is the Title and Content layout, which contains a title text placeholder for the slide title and a content placeholder. A **content placeholder** is a placeholder designed to contain text or graphic objects.

To add a new slide, you use the New Slide button in the Slides group on the Home tab. When you click the top part of the New Slide button, a new slide is inserted with the same layout as the current slide, unless the current slide is the title slide. In that case, the new slide has the Title and Content layout. If you want to create a new slide with a different layout, click the arrow on the bottom part of the New Slide button to open a gallery of layouts, and then click the layout you want to use.

You can change the layout of a slide at any time. To do this, click the Layout button in the Slides group to display the same gallery of layouts that appears in the New Slide gallery, and then click the slide layout you want to apply to the selected slide.

As you add slides, you can switch from one slide to another by clicking the slide thumbnails in the Slides pane. You need to add several new slides to the file.

To add new slides and apply different layouts:

1. Make sure the Home tab is displayed on the ribbon.
2. In the Slides group, click the top part of the **New Slide** button. A new slide appears, and its thumbnail appears in the pane on the left below the Slide 1 thumbnail. The new slide has the Title and Content layout applied. This layout contains a title text placeholder and a content placeholder. An orange border appears around the new Slide 2 thumbnail, indicating that it is the current slide.
3. In the Slides group, click the **New Slide** button again. A new Slide 3 is added. Because Slide 2 had the Title and Content layout applied, Slide 3 also has that layout applied.
4. In the Slides group, click the **New Slide arrow** (the bottom part of the New Slide button). A gallery of the available layouts appears. Refer to Figure 1-8.

Figure 1-8 Gallery of layouts on the New Slide menu

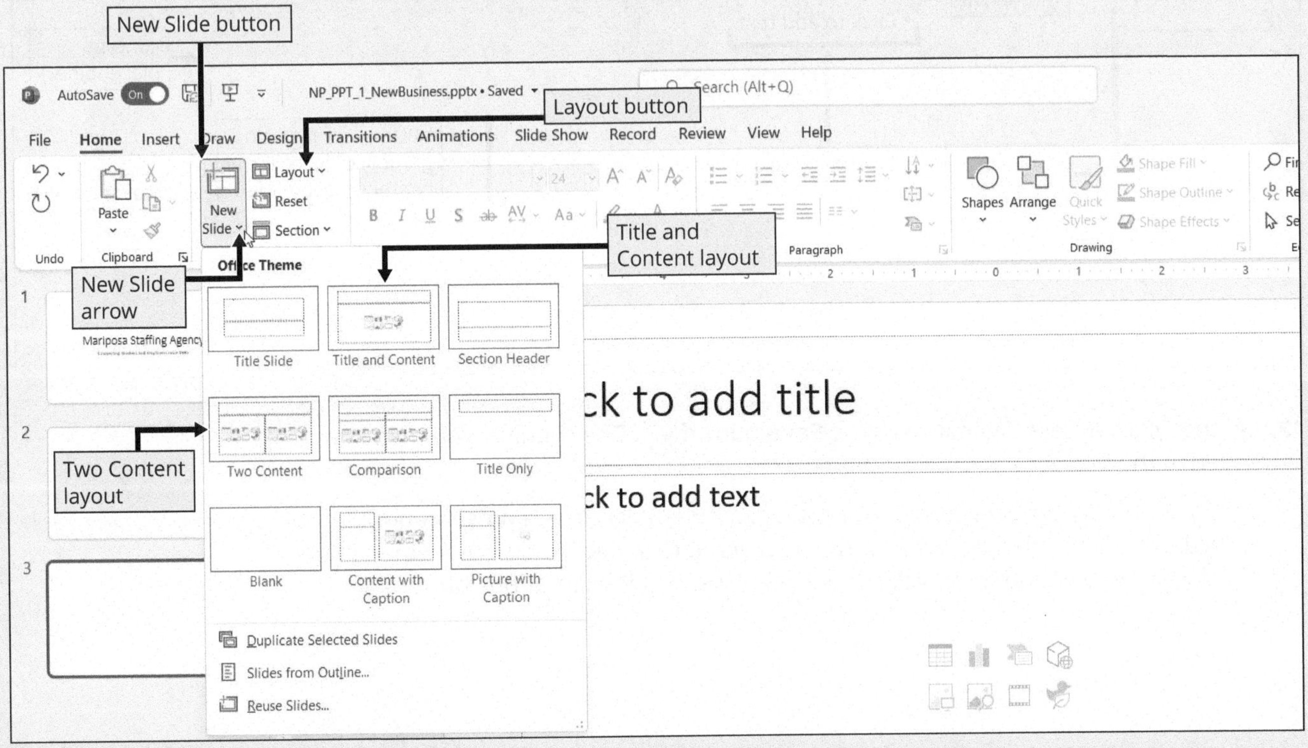

5. In the gallery, click the **Two Content** layout. The gallery closes, and a new Slide 4 is inserted with the Two Content layout applied. This layout includes three objects: a title text placeholder and two content placeholders.
6. In the Slides group, click the **New Slide** button twice. New Slides 5 and 6 are added to the presentation. Because Slide 4 had the Two Content layout applied, that layout is also applied to the new slides. You need to change the layout of Slide 6.
7. In the Slides group, click the **Layout** button. The same gallery of layouts that appeared when you clicked the New Slide arrow appears. The shading behind the Two Content layout indicates that it is applied to the current slide.
8. Click the **Title and Content** layout. The layout of Slide 6 changes to Title and Content.

   Trouble? If the Design Ideas pane opens, click its Close button.
9. In the Slides group, click the **New Slide** button to add Slide 7 with the Title and Content layout.
10. Add one more new slide with the Two Content layout. There are now eight slides in the presentation. In the pane that contains the slide thumbnails, some thumbnails have scrolled out of view, and vertical scroll bars appear along the right side of both panes in the program window.
11. In the pane that contains the slide thumbnails, drag the scroll box to the top of the vertical scroll bar, and then click the **Slide 2** thumbnail. Slide 2 appears in the program window and is selected in the pane that contains the slide thumbnails. Refer to Figure 1–9.

Figure 1–9 Slide 2 with the Title and Content layout

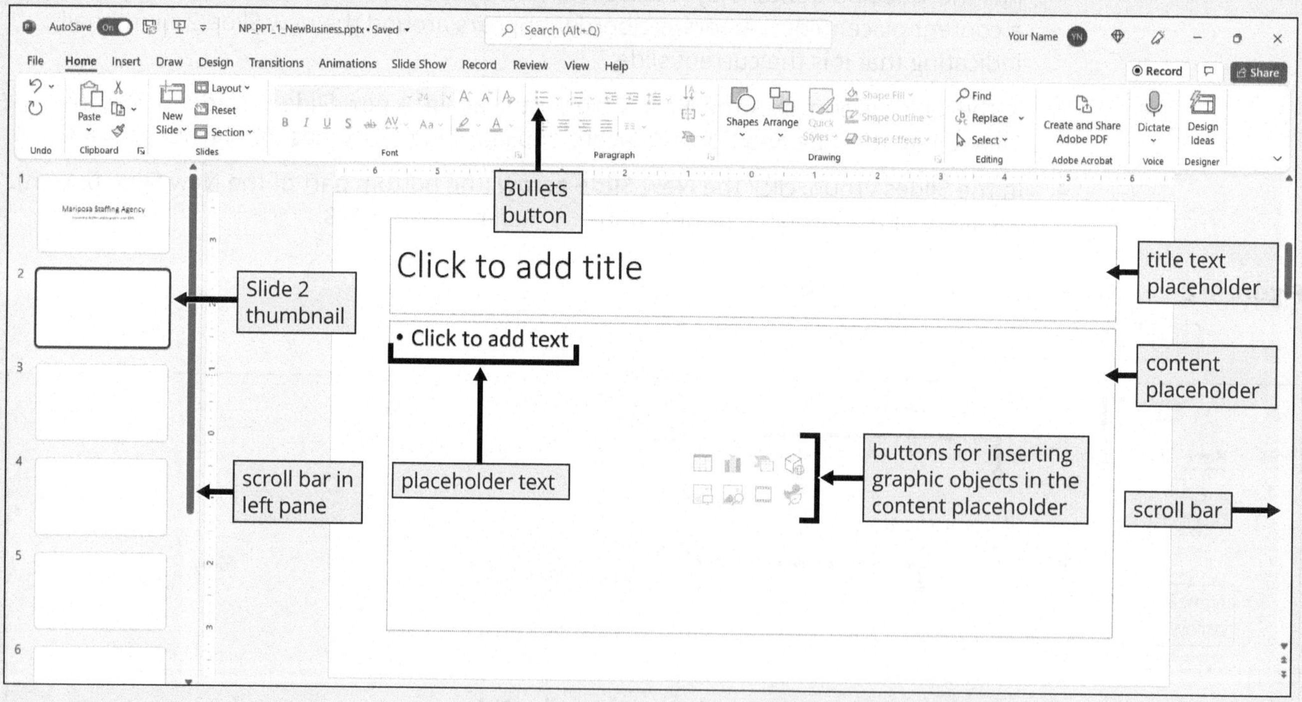

12. On the Quick Access Toolbar, click the **Save** button. The changes you made are saved in the file.

    Tip If you do not have AutoSave enabled, accidentally close a presentation without saving changes, and need to recover it, click the File tab, click Open in the navigation bar, and then click the Recover Unsaved Presentations button.

Creating Lists

You can use a list to help explain a topic or concept. If you are preparing an oral presentation (one that you give to an audience in person or using a web conferencing platform), lists on your slides should enhance the oral presentation, not replace it. If you are preparing a self-running presentation (one that others will view on their own), list items might need to be longer and more descriptive.

Each item in a list is a paragraph. Items in a list can appear at different levels. A first-level item is a main item in a list. A second-level item is an item beneath and indented from a first-level item. A third-level item is an item beneath and indented from a second-level item, and so on. All items below the first level are subitems. A **subitem** is any item in a list that is beneath and indented from a higher-level item.

Usually, the size of the text in subitems on a slide is smaller than the size of the text in the level above. Text is measured in points. A **point** is the unit of measurement used for text size. One point is equal to 1/72 of an inch. Text in a book typically is printed in 10- or 12-point type. Text on a slide in a presentation that will be shown to an audience needs to be much larger so that the audience can easily read it.

Creating a Bulleted List

A **bulleted list** is a series of paragraphs, each beginning with a bullet character, such as a dot or checkmark. Subitems in a list often begin with a different or smaller bullet symbol. Use bulleted lists when the order of the items is not important.

You need to create a bulleted list that describes the types of staffing plans that Mariposa Staffing Agency offers and one that highlights why it would be the best staffing company for businesses to create a relationship with.

To create a bulleted list on Slides 2 and 3:

1. On Slide 2, click in the title text placeholder (with the placeholder text "Click to add title"), and then type **Types of Services**. (Do not type the period.)
2. In the content placeholder, click any area where the pointer is the I-beam pointer (anywhere except on one of the buttons in the center of the placeholder). The placeholder text "Click to add text" disappears, the insertion point appears, and a light gray bullet symbol appears.
3. Type **Job Fulfillment** in the placeholder. As soon as you type the first character, the icons in the center of the content placeholder disappear, the bullet symbol darkens, and the content placeholder changes to a text box. On the Home tab, in the Paragraph group, the Bullets button is shaded to indicate that it is selected.
4. Press **ENTER**. The insertion point moves to a new line, and a light gray bullet appears on the new line.
5. Type **Employment Consulting**, and then press **ENTER**. The bulleted list now consists of two first-level items, and the insertion point is next to a light gray bullet on the third line in the text box. On the Home tab, in the Font group, the point size in the Font Size box is 28 points.
6. Press **TAB**. The bullet symbol and the insertion point indent one-half inch to the right, the bullet symbol changes to a smaller size, and the number in the Font Size box changes to 24. Refer to Figure 1–10.

Figure 1–10 Subitems created on Slide 2

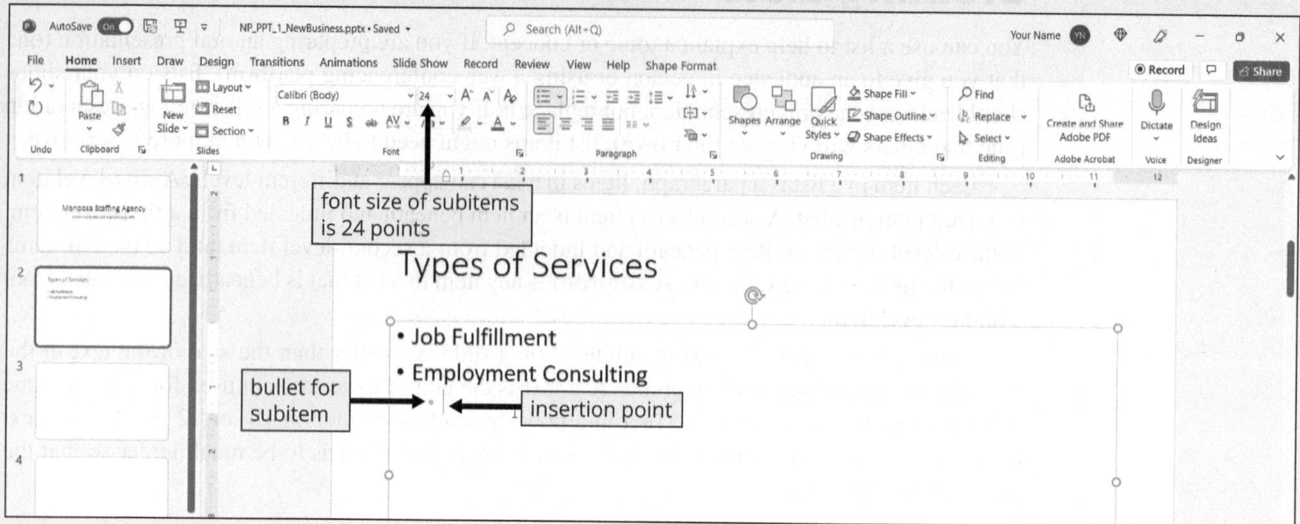

7. Type **Determining needs** and then press **ENTER**.
8. Type **Budgeting**, press **ENTER**, type **Creating retention plans**, and then press **ENTER**. A fourth subitem is created. You will change it to a first-level item using a key combination. In this book, when you need to press two keys at the same time, the keys will be separated by a plus sign.
9. Press **SHIFT+TAB**. The bullet symbol and the insertion point shift back to the left margin of the text box, the bullet symbol changes back to the larger size, and 28 again appears in the Font Size box because this line is now a first-level bulleted item.

   Tip You don't need to press the keys at exactly the same time. Press and hold the first key, press the second key, and then release both keys.

10. Type **Employment Training**, and then press **ENTER**. A fourth first-level item is created. You need to enter subitems for the "Employment Training" first-level item.
11. On the Home tab, in the Paragraph group, click the **Increase List Level** button. Clicking the Increase List Level button is an alternative to pressing TAB to create a subitem.
12. Type **General computer and office skills**, press **ENTER**, type **Specific training to fill a client's needs**, and then press **ENTER**. A third second-level item is created. You need to create a fourth first-level item.
13. In the Paragraph group, click the **Decrease List Level** button. Clicking the Decrease List Level button is an alternative to pressing SHIFT+TAB to change a lower-level item to a higher-level item.
14. Type **Innovative**. The list now contains four first-level items.

If you add more text than will fit in the content placeholder, **AutoFit** adjusts the font size and line spacing to make the text fit. When AutoFit is active, the AutoFit Options button appears below the text box. You can click this button and then select from among several options, including turning off AutoFit for this text box and splitting the text between two slides. Although AutoFit can be helpful, be aware that it also enables you to crowd text on a slide, making the slide more difficult to read.

Creating a Numbered List

A **numbered list** is a group of paragraphs in which each one is preceded by a number, with the paragraphs numbered consecutively. The numbers can be followed by a separator character, such as a period or parenthesis. Generally, you use a numbered list when the order of the items is important. For example, you would use a numbered list if you are presenting a list of step-by-step instructions that need to be followed in sequence to complete a task successfully.

You will create a numbered list on Slide 5 to explain why Mariposa Staffing Agency is a good choice for businesses to use.

To create a numbered list on Slide 5:

1. In the pane containing the thumbnails, click the **Slide 5** thumbnail to display Slide 5, and then type **Choose Mariposa Staffing** in the title text placeholder.
2. In the left content placeholder, click the placeholder text.
3. On the Home tab, in the Paragraph group, click the **Numbering** button. The Numbering button is selected, the Bullets button is deselected, and in the content placeholder, the number 1 followed by a period replaces the bullet symbol.

   Trouble? If a menu containing a gallery of numbering styles appears, you clicked the Numbering arrow on the right side of the button. Click the Numbering arrow again to close the menu, and then click the left part of the Numbering button.

4. Type **Creative**, and then press **ENTER**. As soon as you start typing, the number 1 darkens to black. After you press ENTER, the insertion point moves to the next line, next to the light gray number 2.
5. Type **Customer-driven**, and then press **ENTER**. The number 3 appears on the next line.
6. In the Paragraph group, click the **Increase List Level** button. The third line is an indented subitem under the second item, and the number 3 changes to a number 1 in a smaller font size than the first-level items.

   Tip To change the style of a numbered list, click the Numbering arrow, and then click a new style on the menu.

7. Type **Dedicated customer service team**, press **ENTER**, type **24/7 support**, and then press **ENTER**.
8. In the Paragraph group, click the **Decrease List Level** button. The fifth line becomes a first-level item, and the number 3 appears next to it.
9. Type **Dependable**. The list now consists of three first-level numbered items and two subitems under number 2.
10. In the second item, click before the word "Customer," and then press **ENTER**. A blank line is inserted above the second item.
11. Press **UP ARROW**. A light-gray number 2 appears in the blank line. The item on the third line in the list is still numbered 2.
12. Type **Trustworthy**. As soon as you start typing, the new number 2 darkens in the second line, and the number of the third item in the list changes to 3. Compare your screen to Figure 1–11.

Figure 1–11 Numbered list on Slide 5

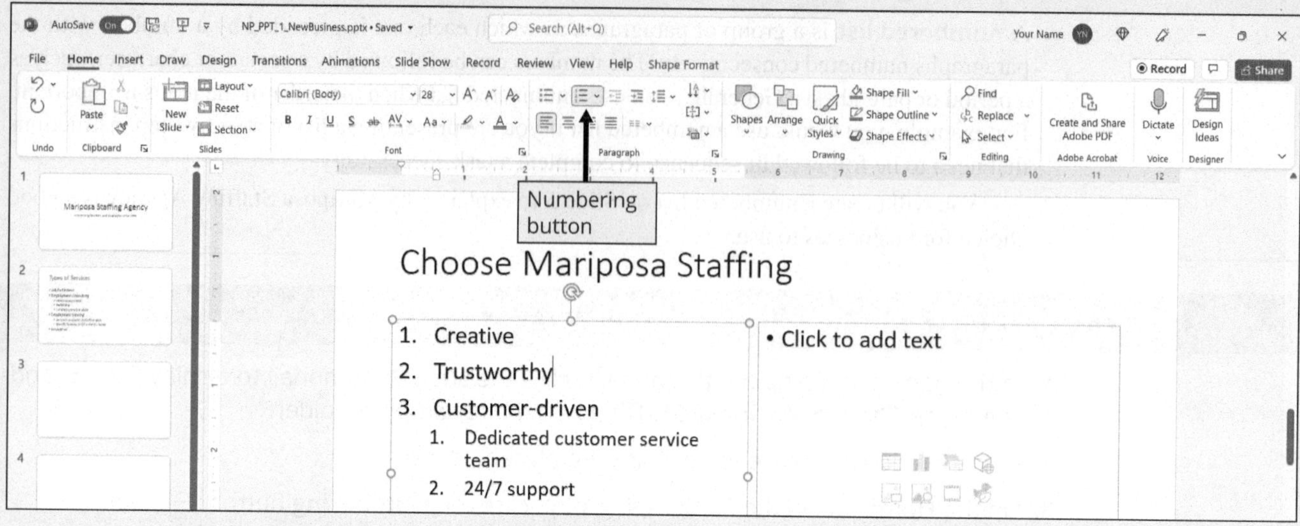

Creating an Unnumbered List

An **unnumbered list** is a list that does not have bullets or numbers preceding each item. Unnumbered lists are useful when you want to present information on multiple lines, but you do not want to start each item with a bullet or number.

Each item in lists is a paragraph. When you press ENTER to create a new item, you create a new paragraph with a little bit of extra space between the new item and the previous item. Sometimes, you don't want to create a new item, or you do not want extra space between lines. In that case, you can create a new line without creating a new paragraph by pressing SHIFT+ENTER. When you do this, the insertion point moves to the next line, but there is no extra space above it. If you do this in a bulleted or numbered list, the new line will not have a bullet or number next to it because it is not a new item.

You need to create a slide that highlights the company's name. The client manager, Jesslyn, also asks you to create a slide containing contact information.

To create unnumbered lists on Slides 4 and 7:

1. In the pane containing the thumbnails, click the **Slide 4** thumbnail to display Slide 4. Slide 4 has the Two Content layout applied.
2. Type **About Us** in the title text placeholder, and then in the left content placeholder, click the placeholder text.
3. On the Home tab, in the Paragraph group, click the **Bullets** button. The Bullets button is no longer selected, and the bullet symbol disappears from the content placeholder.
4. Type **Mariposa**, press **ENTER**, type **Staffing**, press **ENTER**, and then type **Agency**. (Do not type the period.) Compare your screen to Figure 1–12.

Figure 1–12 Unnumbered list on Slide 4

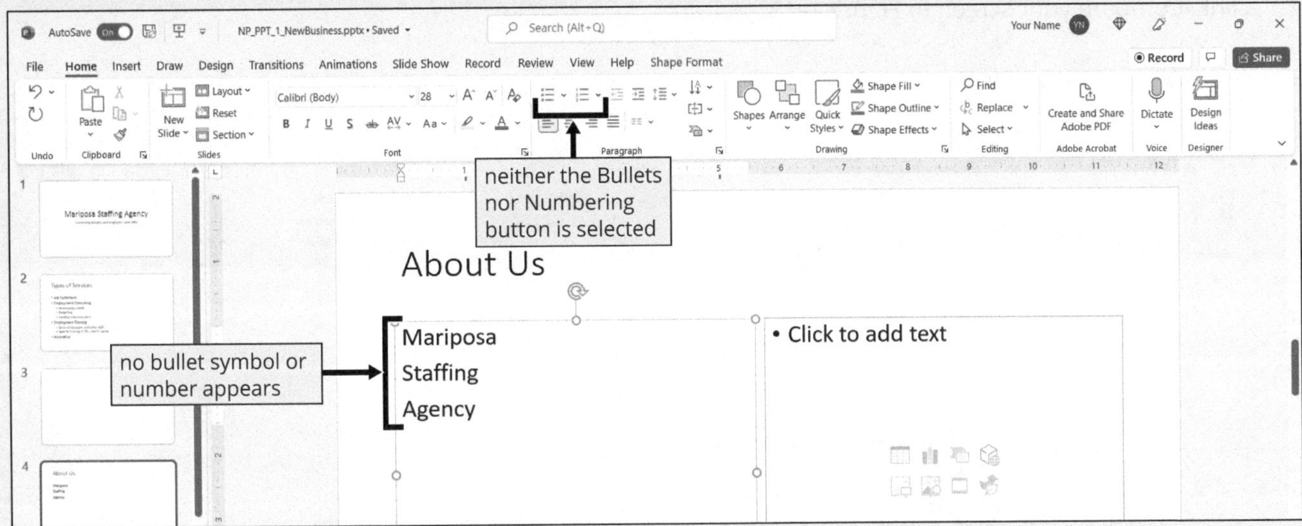

5. Switch to Slide 7, type **For More Information** in the title text placeholder, and then in the content placeholder, click the placeholder text.
6. In the Paragraph group, click the **Bullets** button to remove the bullets, type **Mariposa Staffing Agency**, and then press **ENTER**. A new line is created, but there is extra space above the insertion point. You want the address information to appear on multiple lines but without the extra spacing between each line.
7. Press **BACKSPACE** to delete the new line and move the insertion point back to the end of the first line, and then press **SHIFT+ENTER**. The insertion point moves to the next line. There is no extra space above the line, and the insertion point is aligned below the first character in the first line.
8. Type **4843 Northern Ave.**, press **SHIFT+ENTER**, and then type **Passaic, NJ 07055-0020**. (Do not type the period.) You need to insert the phone number on the next line, Jesslyn's email address on the line after that, and the website address on the last line. The extra space above these lines will set this information apart from the address and make it easier to read.
9. Press **ENTER** to create a new line with extra space above it, type **(973) 555-7100**, press **ENTER**, type **j.whitman@sic.example.com**. (Do not type the period.)

   > **Trouble?** If the "j" or the "w" in the email address changed to an uppercase letter, move the pointer on top of the letter so that the AutoCorrect rectangle appears, move the pointer on top of the AutoCorrect rectangle so that the AutoCorrect Options button appears, click the AutoCorrect Options button, and then click Undo Automatic Capitalization.

10. Press **ENTER**. The insertion point moves to a new line with extra space above it, and the email address you typed changes color to blue and is underlined.

    When you type text that PowerPoint recognizes as an email or website address and then press SPACEBAR or ENTER, the text is automatically formatted as a link that can be clicked during a slide show. Formatted links generally appear in a different color and are underlined.

11. Type **www.sic.example.com**, and then press **SPACEBAR**. The text is formatted as a link. Jesslyn plans to click this link during her presentation to show the audience the website, so she wants it to stay formatted as a link. However, there is no need to have the email address formatted as a link.
12. Right-click **j.whitman@sic.example.com**. A shortcut menu opens.

13. On the shortcut menu, click **Remove Link**. The email address is no longer formatted as a link. Compare your screen to Figure 1–13.

Figure 1–13 List on Slide 7

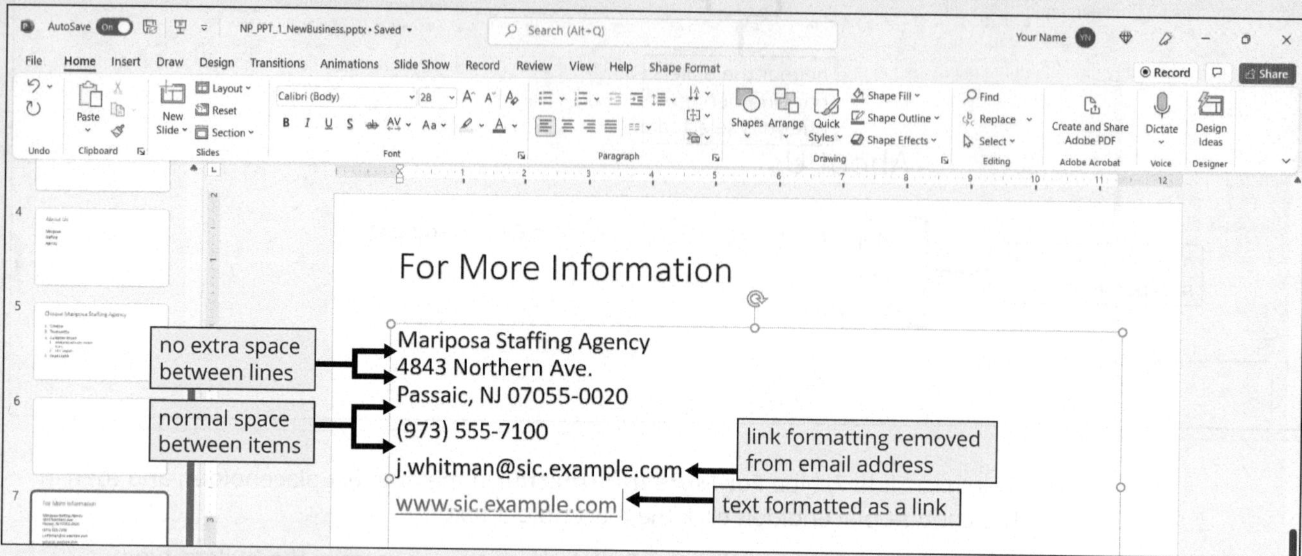

14. On the Quick Access Toolbar, click the **Save** button to save the changes.

Formatting Text

Slides in a presentation should have a consistent look and feel. For example, the slide titles and the text in content placeholders should be in complementary fonts. There are times, however, when you need to change the format of text. For instance, you might want to make specific words bold to make them stand out more.

The commands in the Font group on the Home tab are used to apply formatting to selected text. Figure 1–14 describes the buttons in this group.

Figure 1–14 Formatting commands in the Font group on the Home tab

Button	Name	Description
Calibri (Body)	Font	Change the font.
24	Font Size	Change the font size; click a size on the menu or type any value between 1 and 3600 in increments of 0.1 (for example, 42.4).
A^	Increase Font Size	Increase the font size to the next size up listed on the Font Size menu.
A˅	Decrease Font Size	Decrease the font size to the next size down listed on the Font Size menu.
	Clear All Formatting	Remove formatting of selected text.
B	Bold	Format text as bold.
I	Italic	Italicize text.
U	Underline	Underline text.
S	Text Shadow	Apply a shadow to text.
ab	Strikethrough	Add a line through text.
AV	Character Spacing	Change the spacing between characters.
Aa	Change Case	Change the case of selected text (for example, change to all uppercase).
	Text Highlight Color	Add a highlight color to selected text.
A	Font Color	Change the color of text.

To apply formatting to text, you must first select either the text or the text box. If you want to apply the same formatting to all the text in a text box, you can click the border of the text box. When you do this, the dotted line border changes to a solid line to indicate that the contents of the entire text box are selected. After you select the text or the text box, you click the button on the ribbon, or click the arrow, and then click an option in the menu or gallery that opens. For example, if you wanted to change the font, you would click the Font arrow, and then click the font you want to use.

Tip To remove all formatting from selected text, click the Clear All Formatting button in the Font group.

Some of the formatting commands are also available on the Mini toolbar, which appears when you select text with the mouse or when you right-click on a slide. The **Mini toolbar** is a small toolbar that appears next to text you select using the mouse or when you right-click a slide and that contains the most frequently used text formatting commands, such as bold, italic, font color, and font size. If the Mini toolbar appears, you can use the buttons on it instead of those in the Font group.

Some of the commands in the Font group have menus or galleries that use the Microsoft Office **Live Preview** feature, which shows the results that would occur in your file, such as the effects of formatting options if you clicked the option you are pointing to.

The client manager, Jesslyn, wants the contact information on Slide 7 (“For More Information”) to be larger. She also wants the first letter of each item in the unnumbered list on Slide 4 (“About Us”) formatted so it is more prominent.

To format the text on Slides 7 and 4:

1. On Slide 7 ("For More Information"), position the pointer on the border of the text box containing the contact information so that it changes to the move pointer and then click the border of the text box. The border changes to a solid line to indicate that the entire text box is selected.
2. On the Home tab, in the Font group, click the **Increase Font Size** button twice. All the text in the text box increases in size with each click and is now 36 points.
3. In the pane containing the thumbnails, click the **Slide 4** thumbnail to display that slide.
4. In the unnumbered list, click to the left of "Mariposa," press and hold **SHIFT**, press **RIGHT ARROW**, and then release **SHIFT**. The letter "M" is selected. Refer to Figure 1–15.

Figure 1–15 Text selected to be formatted

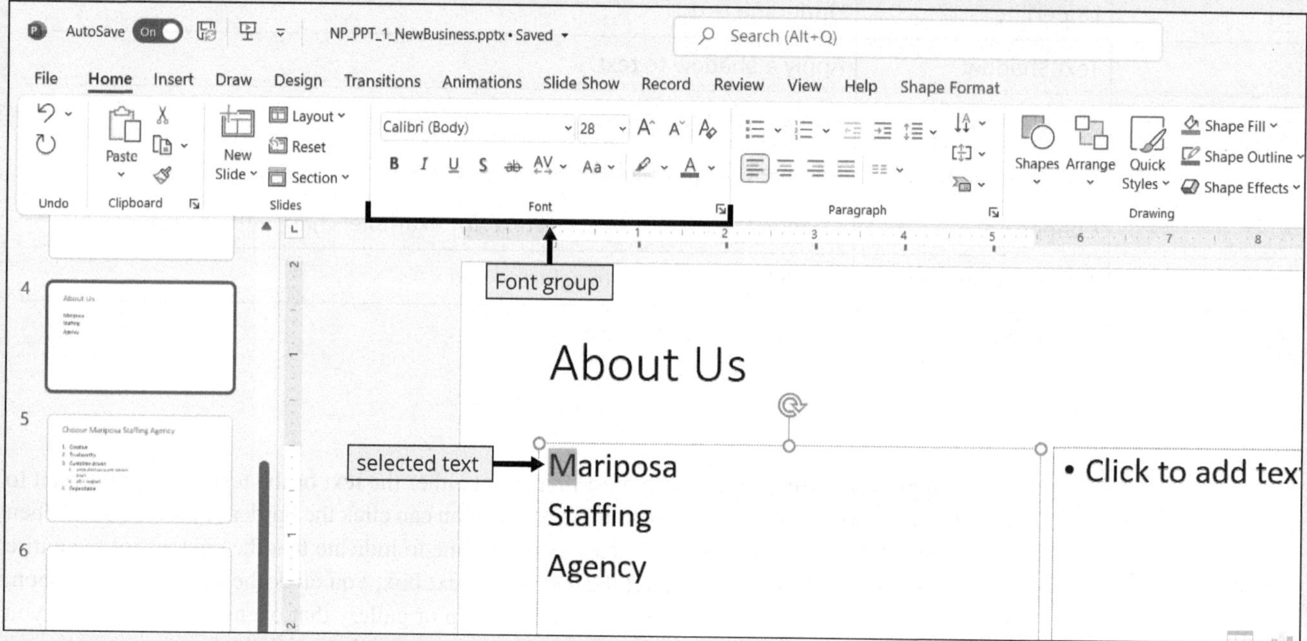

5. In the Font group, click the **Bold** button B. The Bold button becomes selected, and the selected text is formatted as bold.
6. In the Font group, click the **Font Size arrow** to open the Font Size menu, and then click **48**. The selected text is now 48 points.
7. In the Font group, click the **Font Color arrow**. A menu containing color options opens.
8. Under Theme Colors, move the pointer over each color, noting the ScreenTips that appear and watching as Live Preview changes the color of the selected text as you point to each color. Figure 1–16 shows the pointer pointing to the Green, Accent 6, Darker 25% color.

Figure 1–16 Font Color menu

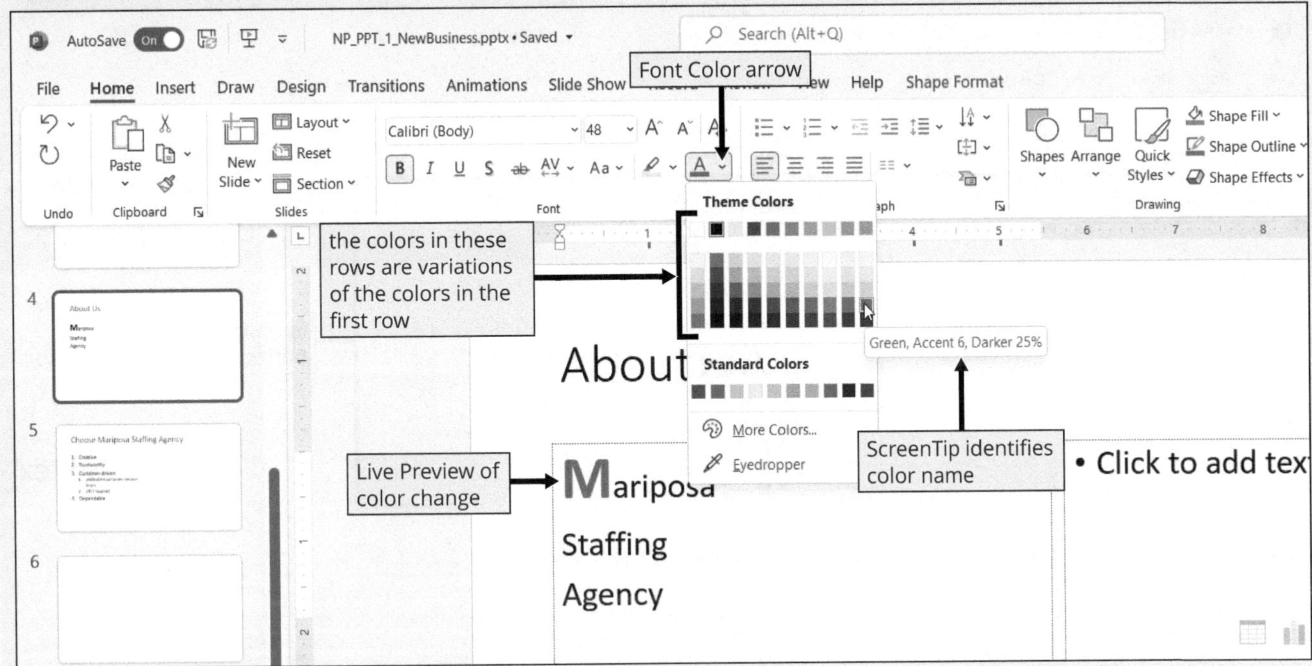

9. Using the ScreenTips, locate the **Green, Accent 6, Darker 25%** color in the last column, and then click it. The selected text changes to the green color you clicked.

Now you need to format the first letters in the other words in the list to match the letter "M." You can repeat the steps you did when you formatted the letter "M," or you can use the Format Painter to copy all the formatting of the letter "M" to the other letters you need to format.

Also, Jesslyn wants the text in the unnumbered list to be as large as possible. Because the first letters of each word are larger than the rest of the letters, the easiest way to do this is to select all of the text, and then use the Increase Font Size button. The selected letters will increase in size with each click, and the first letters will still be larger.

To use the Format Painter to copy and apply formatting on Slide 4:

1. Make sure the letter "M" is still selected.
2. On the Home tab, in the Clipboard group, click the **Format Painter** button, and then move the pointer on top of the slide. The button is selected, and the pointer changes to the Format Painter pointer for text.
3. Position the pointer before the letter "S" in "Staffing," press and hold the mouse button, drag over the letter **S**, and then release the mouse button. The formatting you applied to the letter "M" is copied to the letter "S," and the Mini toolbar appears. Refer to Figure 1–17. The Mini toolbar appears whenever you drag over text to select it.

Figure 1–17 The Mini toolbar

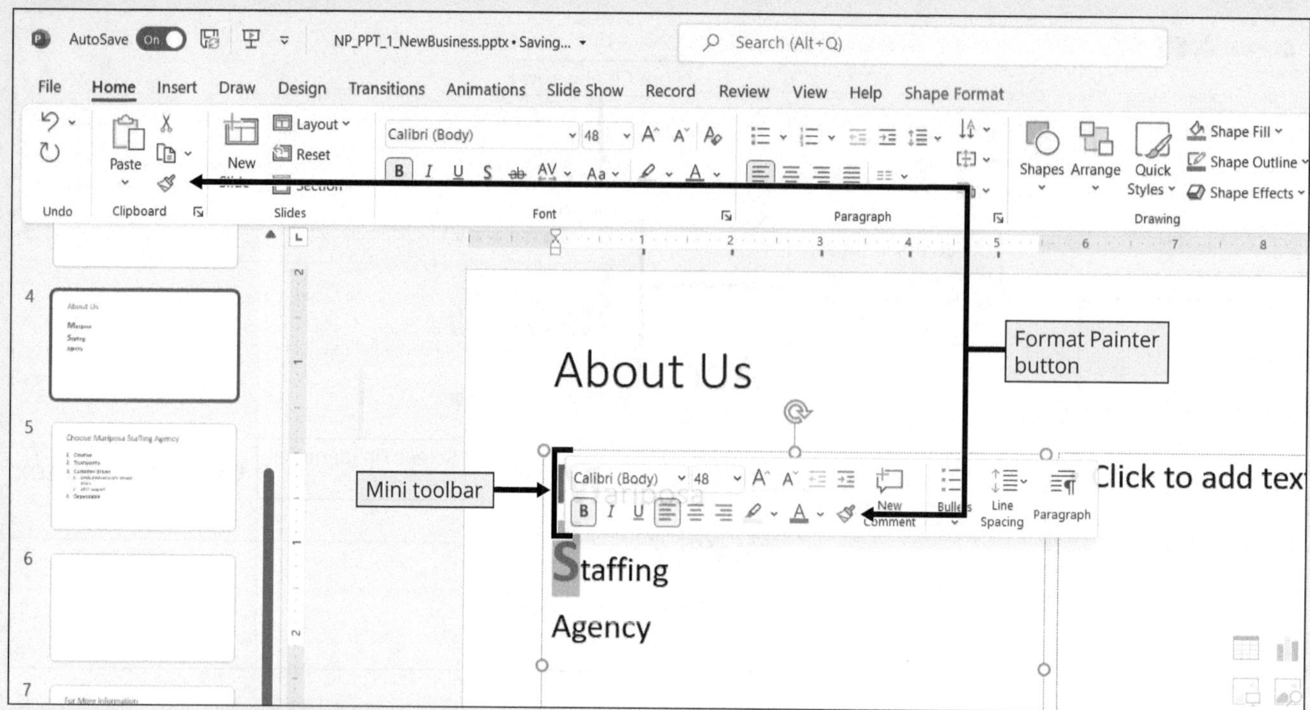

4. On the Mini toolbar, click the **Format Painter** button, and then drag across the letter "A" in "Agency."

> **Tip** If you need to copy formatting to more than one location, double-click the Format Painter button to keep it selected until you deselect it by clicking it again.

5. Click the border of the text box to select the entire text box, and then in the Font group, click the **Increase Font Size** button five times. In the Font group, the Font Size button indicates that the text is 48+ points. This means that in the selected text box, the text that is the smallest is 48 points and there is some text that is larger.
6. On the Quick Access Toolbar, click the **Save** button to save the changes if necessary.

Moving and Copying

You can move and copy text and objects in a presentation using the Clipboard that is part of Windows. The **Clipboard** is a temporary Windows storage area that holds the selections you copy or cut so you can use them later. When you **cut** something, you remove the text or object from a file and place it on the Clipboard. You can also **copy** text or an object, which means you select it and place a duplicate of it on the Clipboard, leaving the text or object in its original location. You can then paste the text or object stored on the Clipboard anywhere in the presentation or in any file in any Windows program. To **paste** something means to place text or an object stored on the Clipboard in a location in a file.

The Clipboard holds only the most recently cut or copied item. As soon as you cut or copy another item, it replaces the previously cut or copied item on the Clipboard. You can paste an item on the Clipboard as many times and in as many locations as you like.

Note that cutting text or an object differs from deleting it. When you press DELETE or BACKSPACE to delete text or objects, they are not placed on the Clipboard and cannot be pasted.

Jesslyn wants a few changes made to Slides 5 and 2. You'll use the Clipboard as you make these edits.

To cut, copy, and paste text using the Clipboard:

1. On Slide 4 ("About Us"), double-click the word **Agency** in the list. The word "Agency" is selected.
2. On the Home tab, in the Clipboard group, click the **Copy** button. The selected word is copied to the Clipboard.
3. In the pane containing thumbnails, click the **Slide 5** thumbnail to display that slide, click after the word "Staffing" in the title, and then press **SPACEBAR**.
4. In the Clipboard group, click the **Paste** button. The text appears at the location of the insertion point. The letter "A" is still green and is larger than the rest of the text. The rest of the text picks up the formatting of its destination, so it is 44 points instead of 48 points as in the list on Slide 4. The Paste Options button (Ctrl) appears below the pasted text.
5. Click the **Paste Options** button (Ctrl). A menu opens with four buttons on it. Refer to Figure 1–18.

Figure 1–18 Buttons on the Paste Options menu when text is on the Clipboard

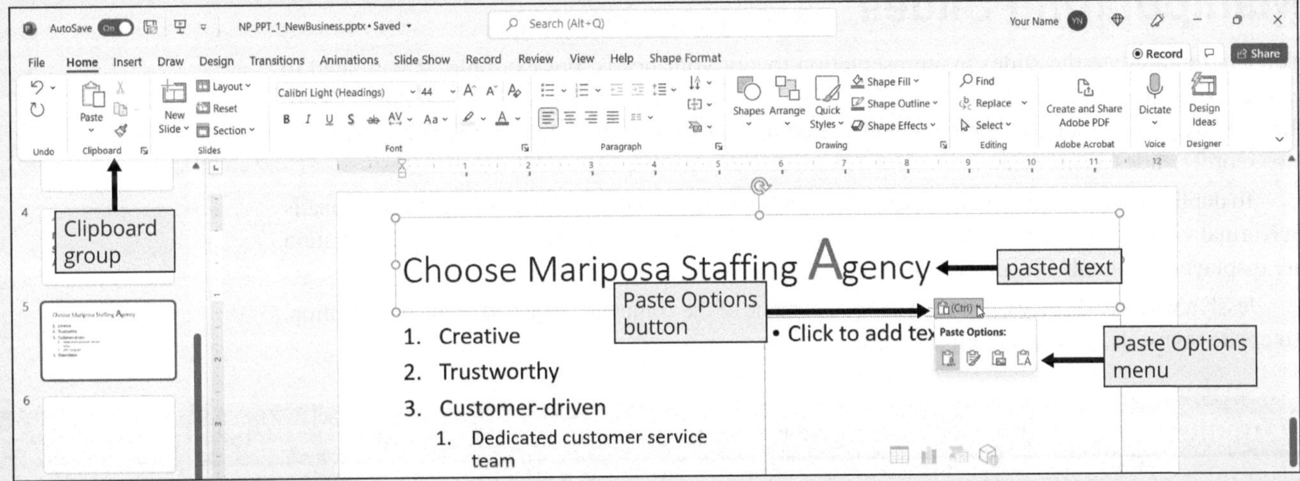

6. Point to each button on the menu, reading the ScreenTips and watching to see how the pasted text changes in appearance. The first button is the Use Destination Theme button, which is the default choice when you paste text.
7. On the Paste Options menu, click the **Keep Text Only** button. The pasted text changes so that its formatting matches the rest of the title text.
8. Display Slide 2 ("Types of Services"). The last bulleted item ("Innovative") belongs on Slide 5.
9. In the last bulleted item, position the pointer on top of the bullet symbol so that the pointer changes to the four-headed arrow pointer, and then click. The entire bulleted item is selected.

   Tip To cut text or an object, you can press CTRL+X. To copy text or an object, press CTRL+C. To paste the contents of the Clipboard, press CTRL+V.

10. In the Clipboard group, click the **Cut** button. The last bulleted item is removed from the slide and is placed on the Clipboard.
11. Display Slide 5 ("Choose Mariposa Staffing Agency"), click after the last item ("Dependable"), and then press **ENTER** to create a fifth first-level item.

12. In the Clipboard group, click the **Paste** button. The bulleted item you cut becomes the fifth first-level item on Slide 5 using the default paste option of Use Destination Theme. The insertion point appears next to a sixth first-level item.
13. Press **BACKSPACE** twice to delete the extra line, and then on the Quick Access Toolbar, click the **Save** button to save the changes if necessary.

Insight

Using the Office Clipboard

The **Office Clipboard** is a temporary storage area in the computer's memory that lets you collect text and objects from any Office document and then paste them into other Office documents. Once you activate the Office Clipboard, you can store up to 24 items on it and then select the item or items you want to paste. To activate the Office Clipboard, click the Home tab. In the Clipboard group, click the Dialog Box Launcher (the small square in the lower-right corner of the Clipboard group) to open the Clipboard pane to the left of the displayed slide.

Manipulating Slides

You can manipulate the slides in a presentation to suit your needs. For example, if you need to create a slide that is similar to another slide, you can duplicate the existing slide and then modify the copy. If you no longer want to include a slide in your presentation, you can delete it. You can also reorder slides as necessary.

To duplicate, rearrange, or delete slides, you select the slides in the pane containing the thumbnails in Normal view or switch to Slide Sorter view. In **Slide Sorter view** all the slides in the presentation are displayed as thumbnails in the window.

Jesslyn wants to display a slide that shows the name of the company at the end of the presentation. To create this slide, you will duplicate Slide 4 ("About Us").

To duplicate Slide 4:

1. Display Slide 4 ("About Us").
2. On the Home tab, in the Slides group, click the **New Slide arrow**, and then click **Duplicate Selected Slides**. A duplicate of Slide 4 appears as a new Slide 5 and is the current slide. If you had selected more than one slide, they would all be duplicated. The duplicate slide doesn't need the title; Jesslyn just wants to reinforce the company's name.
3. On Slide 5, click anywhere on the title **About Us**, click the text box border to select the text box, and then press **DELETE**. The title and the title text box are deleted, and the title text placeholder reappears.

You could delete the title text placeholder, but you do not need to. When you display a presentation to an audience as a slide show, any unused placeholders do not appear.

Next you need to rearrange the slides. You need to move the duplicate of the "About Us" slide so it becomes the last slide in the presentation because Jesslyn wants it to remain displayed after the presentation is over. She hopes this visual will reinforce the company's name for the audience. Jesslyn also wants Slide 6 ("Choose Mariposa Staffing Agency") moved before the "Types of Services" slide (Slide 2), and she wants the original "About Us" slide (Slide 4) to be the second slide in the presentation.

To rearrange the slides in the presentation:

1. In the pane containing the thumbnails, scroll, if necessary, so that you can see Slides 2 and 6, and then click the **Slide 6** ("Choose Mariposa Staffing Agency") thumbnail. Slide 6 ("Choose Mariposa Staffing Agency") is the current slide.
2. Point to the **Slide 6** thumbnail, press and hold the mouse button, drag the Slide 6 thumbnail up above the Slide 2 ("Types of Services") thumbnail, and then release the mouse button. As you drag, the Slide 6 thumbnail follows the pointer and the other slides move down to make room for the slide you are dragging. The "Choose Mariposa Staffing Agency" slide becomes Slide 2 and "Types of Services" becomes Slide 3. You'll move the other two slides in Slide Sorter view.
3. On the status bar, click the **Slide Sorter** button. The view switches to Slide Sorter view. Slide 2 appears with a brown border, indicating that it is selected.

   Tip You can also use the buttons in the Presentation Views group on the View tab to switch views.

4. On the status bar, click the **Zoom Out** button as many times as necessary until you can see all nine slides in the presentation. Refer to Figure 1–19.

Figure 1–19 Slide Sorter view

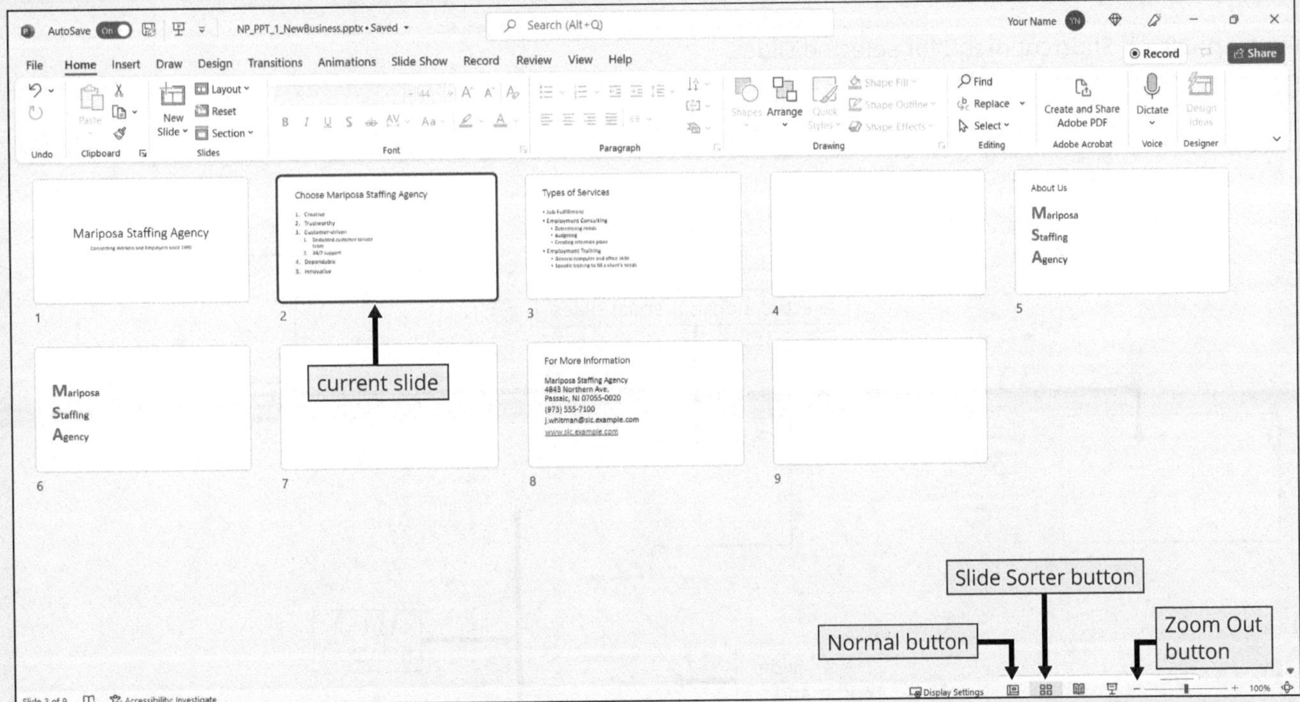

5. Drag the **Slide 5** ("About Us") thumbnail to between Slides 1 and 2. As you drag, the other slides move out of the way. The slides are renumbered so that the "About Us" slide is now Slide 2.
6. Drag the **Slide 6** thumbnail (the slide containing just the name of the company) after the last slide in the presentation (Slide 9).

Now you need to delete the blank slides. To delete a slide, you right-click its thumbnail to display a shortcut menu, and then click Delete Slide on that menu.

You already know that to select a single slide you click its thumbnail. You can also select more than one slide at a time. To select sequential slides, click the first slide, press and hold SHIFT, and then click the last slide you want to select. To select nonsequential slides, click the first slide, press and hold CTRL, and then click any other slides you want to select. When more than one slide is selected, you can delete or duplicate all of the selected slides with one command.

To delete the blank slides:

1. Click the **Slide 5** thumbnail (the first blank slide), press and hold **SHIFT**, click the **Slide 8** thumbnail (the last blank slide), and then release **SHIFT**. The two slides you clicked are selected, as well as the slides between them. Holding SHIFT when you click items selects the slides you click as well as the slides between the slides you click. You want to delete only the three blank slides. To select only the slides you click, you need to hold CTRL instead.
2. Click a blank area of the window to deselect the slides, click the **Slide 5** thumbnail, press and hold **CTRL**, click the **Slide 6** thumbnail, click the **Slide 8** thumbnail, and then release **CTRL**. Only the slides you clicked are selected.
3. Right-click any of the selected slides. A shortcut menu appears. Refer to Figure 1–20.

Figure 1–20 Shortcut menu for selected slides

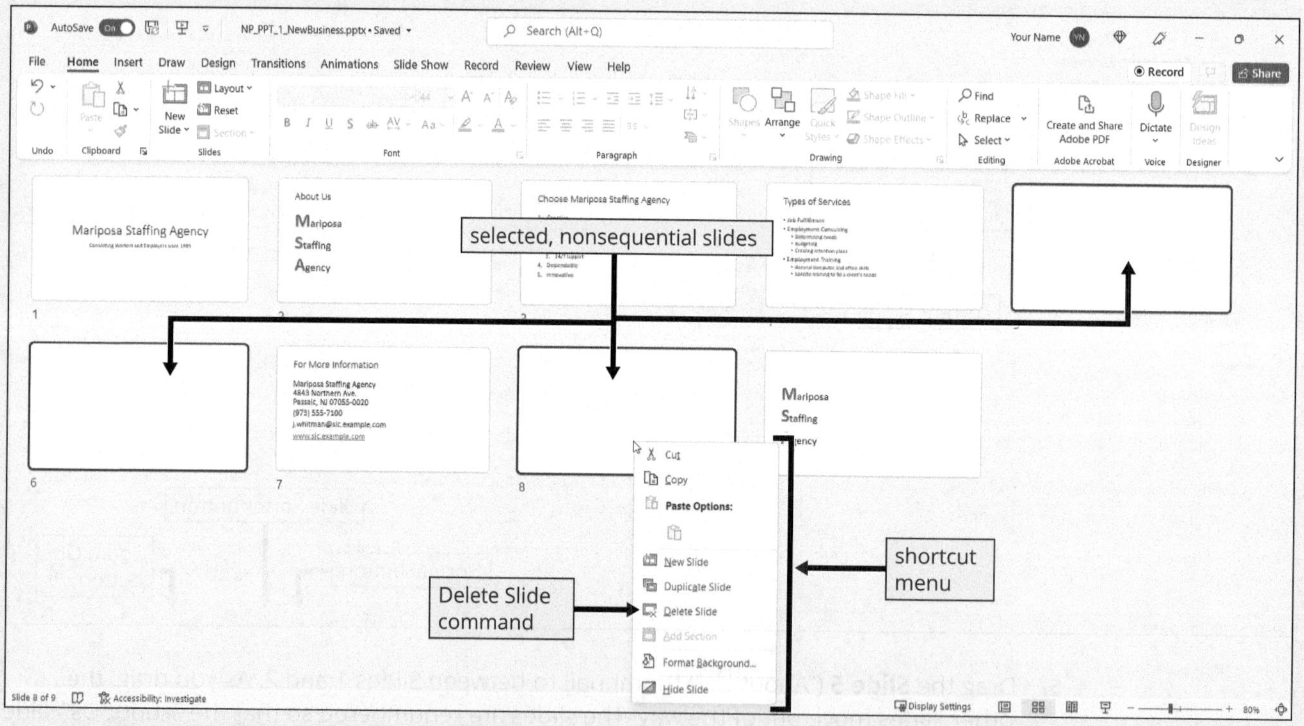

4. On the shortcut menu, click **Delete Slide**. The shortcut menu closes, and the three selected slides are deleted. The presentation now contains six slides.

> **Tip** You can also double-click a slide thumbnail in Slide Sorter view to display that slide in the view the presentation was in prior to being in Slide Sorter view.

5. On the status bar, click the **Normal** button. The presentation appears in Normal view.
6. On the Quick Access Toolbar, click the **Save** button to save the changes to the presentation if necessary.

Changing the Theme

A **theme** is a predefined, coordinated set of colors, fonts, graphical effects, and other formats that can be applied to a presentation. In PowerPoint, most themes have variants that have different coordinating colors and sometimes slightly different backgrounds. All presentations have a theme. If you don't choose one, the default Office theme is applied; that is the theme currently applied to the presentation you created.

Every theme has a palette of coordinated colors. You saw the Office theme colors when you changed the color of the text on the "About Us" slide. If you don't like the color palette of the theme you chose, you can change to a different one.

Themes also have a font set. One font, called the Headings font, is used for slide titles. The other font, called the Body font, is used for the rest of the text on a slide. In the Office theme, the Headings font is Calibri Light, and the Body font is Calibri. In some themes, the Headings and Body font are the same font.

One benefit of using themes is that you can apply the same theme to files created in the same or other applications. For example, if Jesslyn asked you to create a flyer in Microsoft Word to accompany the presentation you could apply the same theme so that the fonts and colors in both the flyer and presentation would complement each other.

Jesslyn wants you to try changing the theme colors and fonts.

To examine the current theme and then change the theme color and theme fonts:

1. Display Slide 5 ("For More Information"). Notice that the link is blue.
2. Display Slide 6, and then, in the unnumbered list, select the green letter **S**.
3. On the Home tab, in the Font group, click the **Font Color arrow**. Look at the colors under Theme Colors. The last column contains shades of green. In that column, the second to last color is selected. The colors in the Theme Colors section change depending on the selected theme and the selected theme colors. The colors in the row of Standard Colors do not change when you choose a different theme or theme color palette.
4. In the Font group, click the **Font arrow**. A menu of fonts installed on the computer opens. At the top under Theme Fonts, Calibri (Body) is selected because the letter "S" that you selected is in a content text box. Refer to Figure 1–21. If the selected text was in the title text box, the first font in the list, Calibri Light (Headings) would be selected.

Figure 1–21 Theme fonts on the Font menu

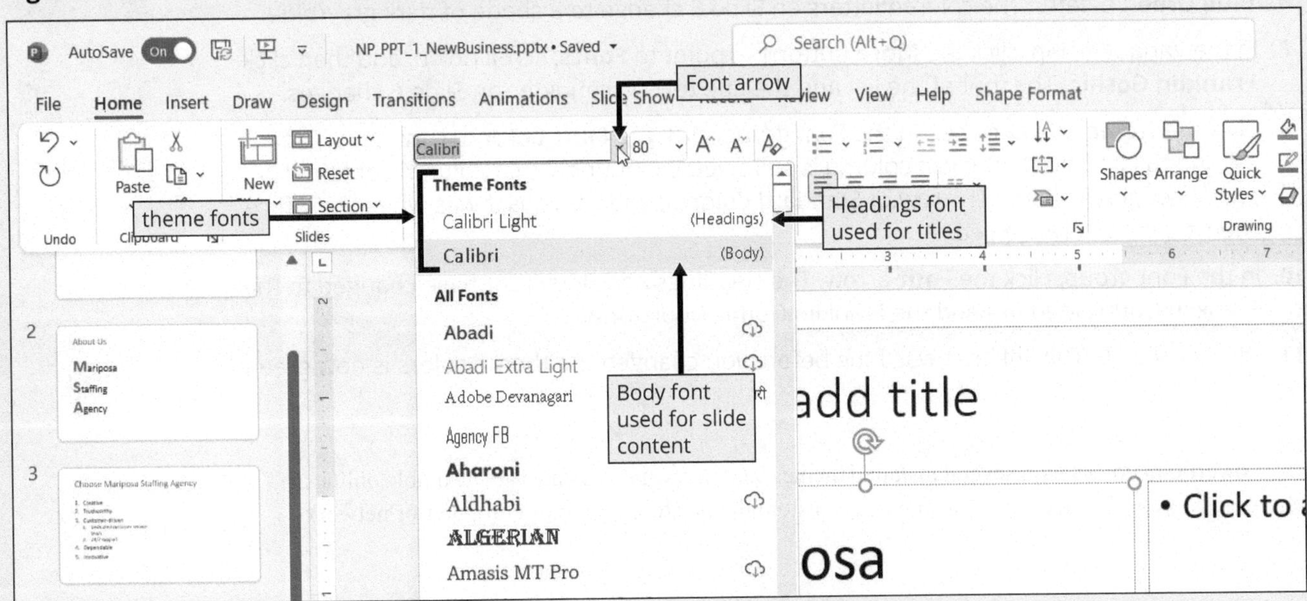

5. On the ribbon, click the **Design** tab. The Design tab is active. Refer to Figure 1–22. In the Themes group, the first theme is the theme applied to the presentation. In this case, it is the Office theme. The second theme is also the Office theme, and it is shaded to indicate that it is selected. In the Variants group, the first variant is shaded to indicate that it is selected.

Figure 1–22 Themes and variants on the Design tab

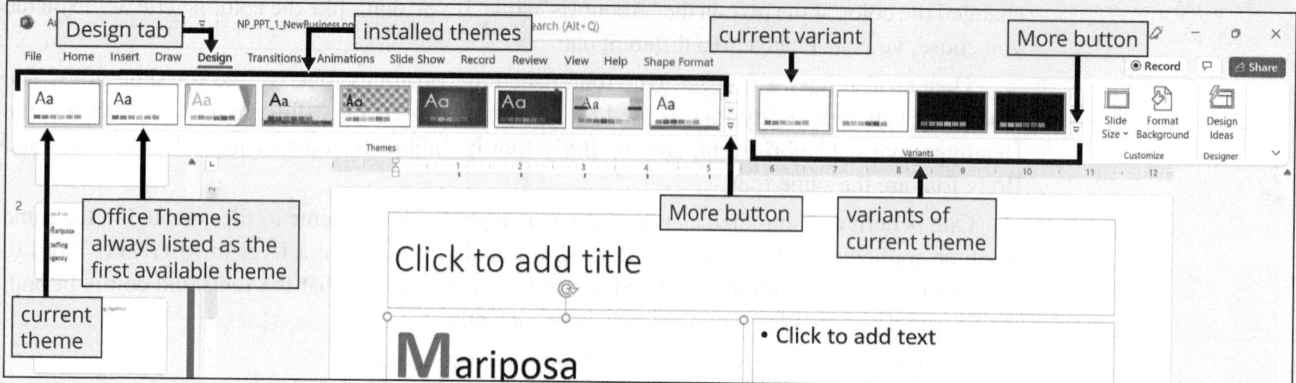

6. In the Variants group, click the **More** button. A menu opens containing commands for changing the theme colors and the theme fonts. Refer to Figure 1–23.

Figure 1–23 More button menu in the Variants group

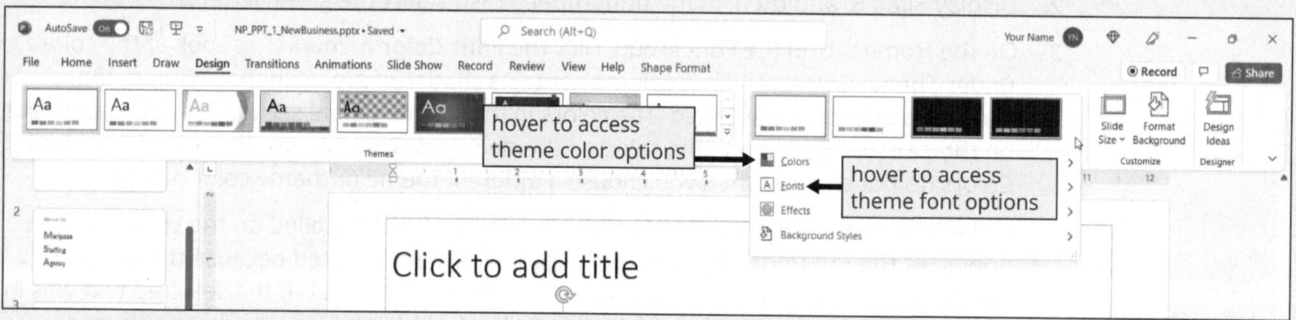

7. On the menu, point to **Colors** to open a submenu of color palettes, and then click the **Blue Green** palette. The colored letters on Slide 6 change to a shade of dark gray/blue.
8. In the Variant group, click the **More** button, point to **Fonts**, scroll down, and then click **Franklin Gothic**. The font of the list and the title text placeholder on Slide 6 changes.
9. Click the **Home** tab, and then in the Font group, click the **Font Color arrow**. The second to last color in the last column is still selected, but now that column contains shades of grayish blue. The row of Standard Colors is the same as it was when the Office theme colors were applied.
10. In the Font group, click the **Font** arrow. The Headings and Body font have changed to the Franklin Gothic Medium and the Franklin Gothic Book fonts.
11. Display Slide 5. The link that was blue before you changed the theme colors is now green.

PowerPoint comes with several installed themes, and many more themes are available online at Microsoft365.com. In addition, you can use a custom theme stored on your computer or network.

You can select a different installed theme when you create a new presentation by clicking one of the themes on the New or Home screen in Backstage view. If you want to change the theme of an open presentation, you can choose an installed theme on the Design tab, or you can apply a theme applied to another presentation or a theme stored on your computer or network.

Jesslyn still thinks the presentation could be more interesting, so she asks you to apply a different theme.

To change the theme

1. Display Slide 6, and then select the "M" in "Mariposa."
2. Click the **Design** tab, and then in the Themes group, click the **More** button. The gallery of themes opens. Refer to Figure 1–24. When the gallery is open, the theme applied to the current presentation appears in the first row. In the next row, the first theme is the Office theme, and then the rest of the installed themes appear. Some of these themes also appear on the Home and New screens in Backstage view.

Figure 1–24 Themes gallery expanded

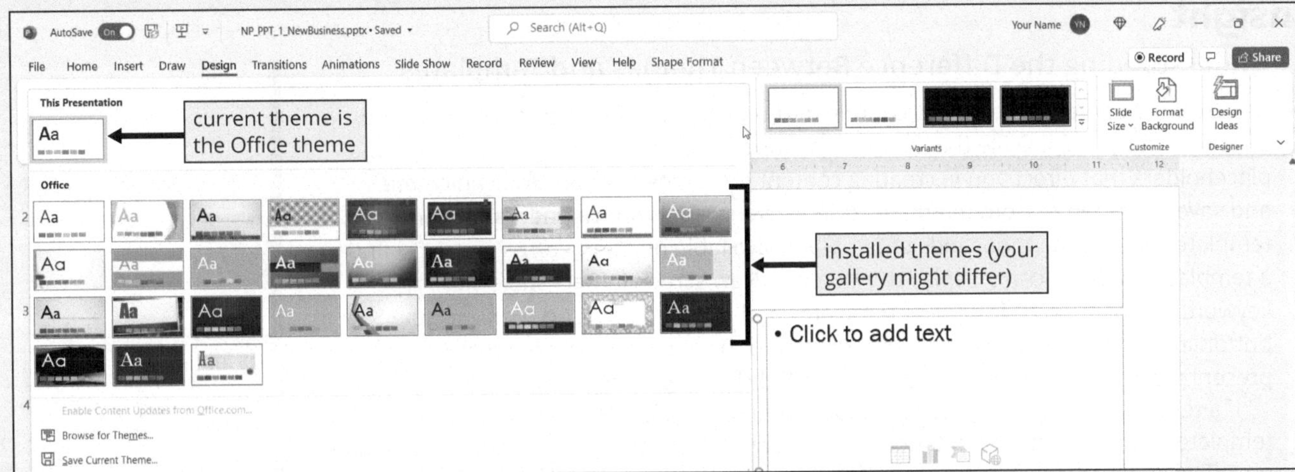

3. Point to several of the themes in the gallery to display their ScreenTips and to see a Live Preview of the theme applied to the current slide.
4. Click the **Ion Boardroom** theme. The gallery closes, and all the slides have the Ion Boardroom theme with the default variant (the first variant in the Variants group) applied. The slide backgrounds remain white, but the title boxes of the slides change to a purple geometric shape. The letters that you had colored blue on Slide 6 change to a shade of purple. In the empty content placeholder on Slide 6, the bullet symbol changed from a circle to an arrow.
5. In the Variants group, point to the other three variants to see a Live Preview of each of them, and then click the fourth variant (the orange one). The letters on Slide 6 change to green. You do not like the changes. On the Quick Access Toolbar, click the **Undo** button, then click the third variant (the blue one).
6. Click the **Home** tab, and then in the Font group, click the **Font Color arrow**. The selected color is still the second to last color in the last column, but now the last column contains shades of green. Again, the row of Standard Colors is the same as it was before you made changes.
7. In the Font group, click the **Font arrow**. You can see that the Theme Fonts are now Century Gothic for both Headings and the Body.
8. Press **ESC**. The Font menu closes.

After you apply a new theme, you should examine your slides to make sure that they look the way you expect them to. Slide 6 looks fine.

To examine the slides with the new theme and adjust font sizes:

1. Display Slides 5, 4, 3, and Slide 2. These slides look fine.
2. Display Slide 1 (the title slide). The subtitle text is a little small with the Ion Boardroom theme applied.
3. Click anywhere on the subtitle text, and then click the text box border. The entire text box is selected.
4. In the Font group, click the **Increase Font Size** button as many times as necessary until the font size of the title text increases to 24 points.
5. On the Quick Access Toolbar, click the **Save** button if necessary.

Insight

Understanding the Difference Between Themes and Templates

As explained earlier, a theme is a coordinated set of colors, fonts, backgrounds, and effects. A **template** is a file that has a theme applied and contains text, graphics, and placeholders that direct you in creating content for a presentation. You can create and save your own custom templates or find everything from calendars to marketing templates among the thousands of templates available on Microsoft365.com. To find a template on Office.com, display the Home or New screen in Backstage view, type keywords in the "Search for online templates and themes" box, and then click the Search button in the box to display templates related to the search terms. To create a new presentation based on the template you find, click the template and then click Create.

If a template is stored on your computer, you can apply the theme used in the template to an existing presentation. If you want to apply the theme used in a template on Office.com to an existing presentation, you need to download the template to your computer first.

Closing a Presentation

When you are finished working with a presentation, you can close it and leave PowerPoint open. To do this, you click the File tab to open Backstage view, and then click the Close command. If you have only one presentation open, if you click the Close button in the upper-right corner of the PowerPoint window, you will not only close the presentation, you will exit PowerPoint as well.

You're finished working with the presentation for now, so you will close it. First you will add your name to the title slide.

To add your name to Slide 1 and close the presentation:

1. On Slide 1 (the title slide), click the subtitle, position the insertion point after "1995," press **ENTER**, and then type your full name.
2. Click the **File** tab, then click **Info** on the Navigation bar. Backstage view appears with the Info screen displayed. Refer to Figure 1–25.

Figure 1–25 Info screen in Backstage view

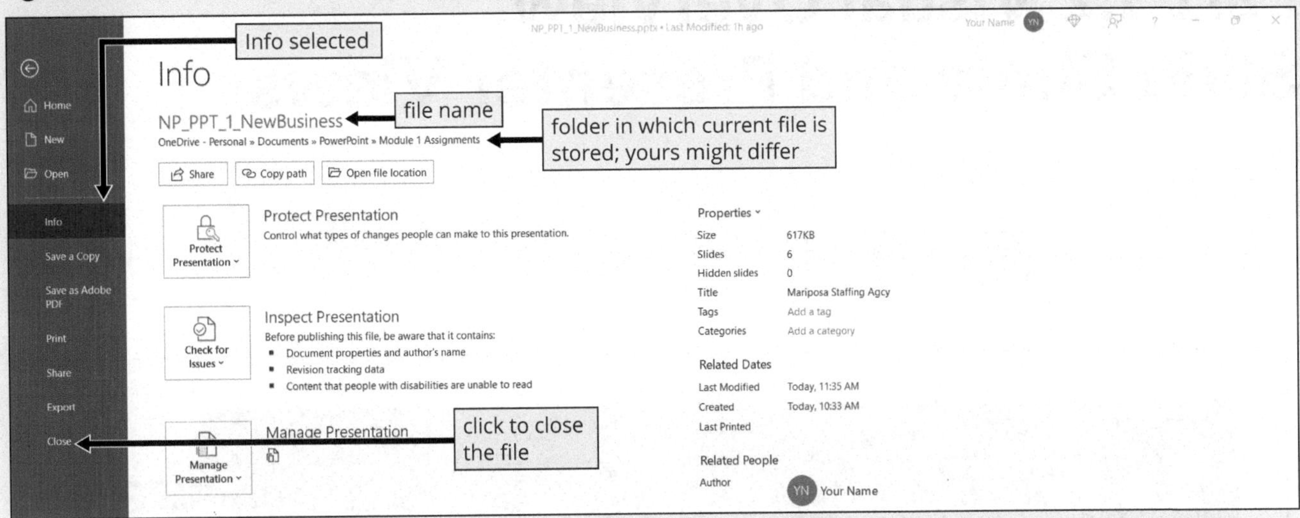

3. **sam** In the navigation pane, click **Close**. Backstage view closes, and, if you have AutoSave enabled, the presentation closes and the empty presentation window appears.

   Trouble? If a dialog box opens asking if you want to save your changes, click **Save** to close both the dialog box and the presentation.

You've created a presentation that includes slides to which you added bulleted, numbered, and unnumbered lists. You also formatted text, manipulated slides, and applied a theme. You are ready to give the presentation draft to Jesslyn to review.

Part 1.1 Quick Check

1. Define "presentation."
2. How do you display Backstage view?
3. What is a slide layout?
4. In addition to a title text placeholder, what other type of placeholder do many layouts contain?
5. What is the term for an object that contains text?
6. What is the difference between the Clipboard and the Office Clipboard?
7. Explain what a theme is and what changes with each variant.

Part 1.2 Visual Overview: Slide Show and Presenter Views

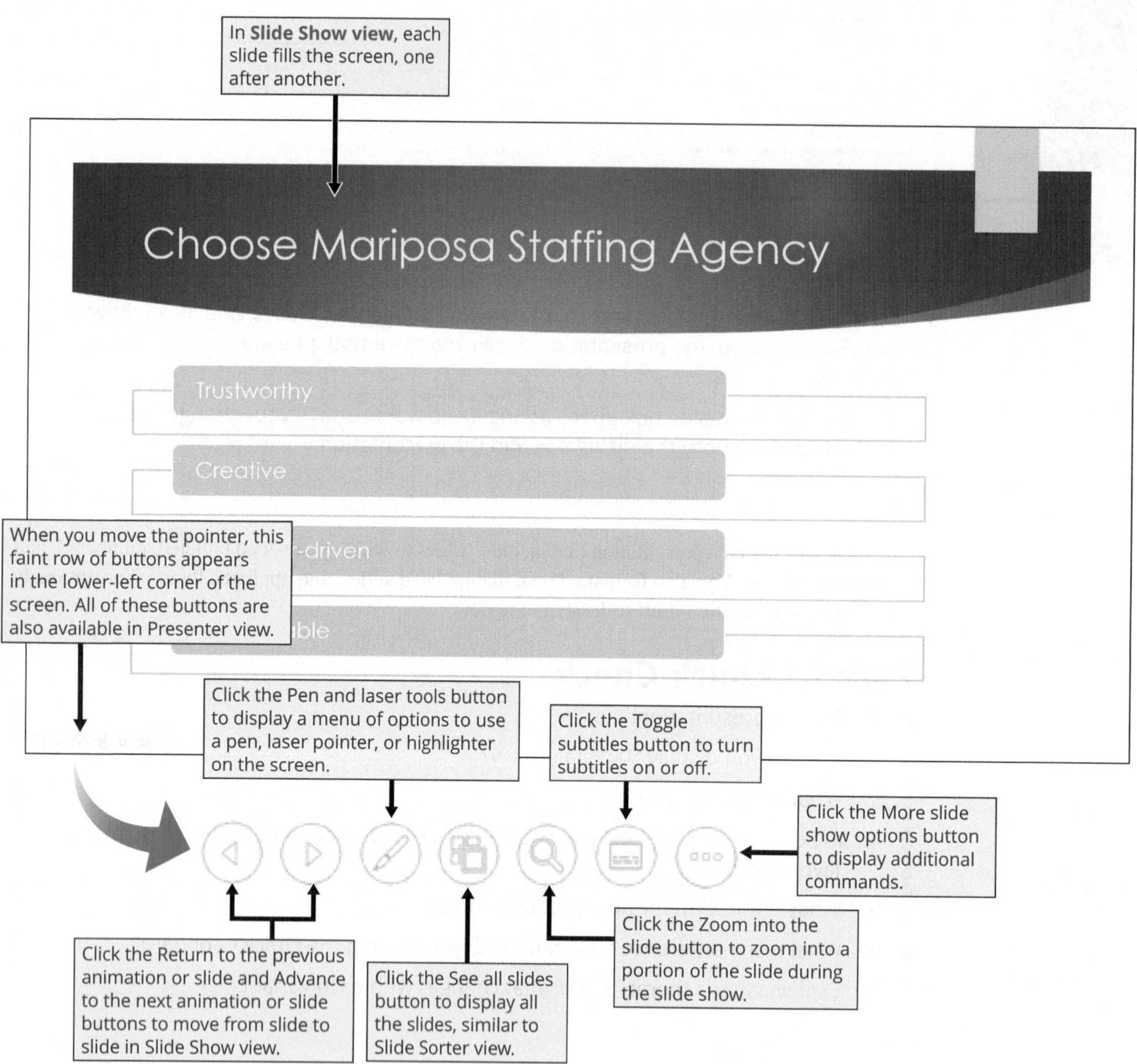

In **Slide Show view**, each slide fills the screen, one after another.
Choose Mariposa Staffing Agency
Trustworthy
Creative
-driven
ble
When you move the pointer, this faint row of buttons appears in the lower-left corner of the screen. All of these buttons are also available in Presenter view.
Click the Pen and laser tools button to display a menu of options to use a pen, laser pointer, or highlighter on the screen.
Click the Toggle subtitles button to turn subtitles on or off.
Click the More slide show options button to display additional commands.
Click the Zoom into the slide button to zoom into a portion of the slide during the slide show.
Click the Return to the previous animation or slide and Advance to the next animation or slide buttons to move from slide to slide in Slide Show view.
Click the See all slides button to display all the slides, similar to Slide Sorter view.

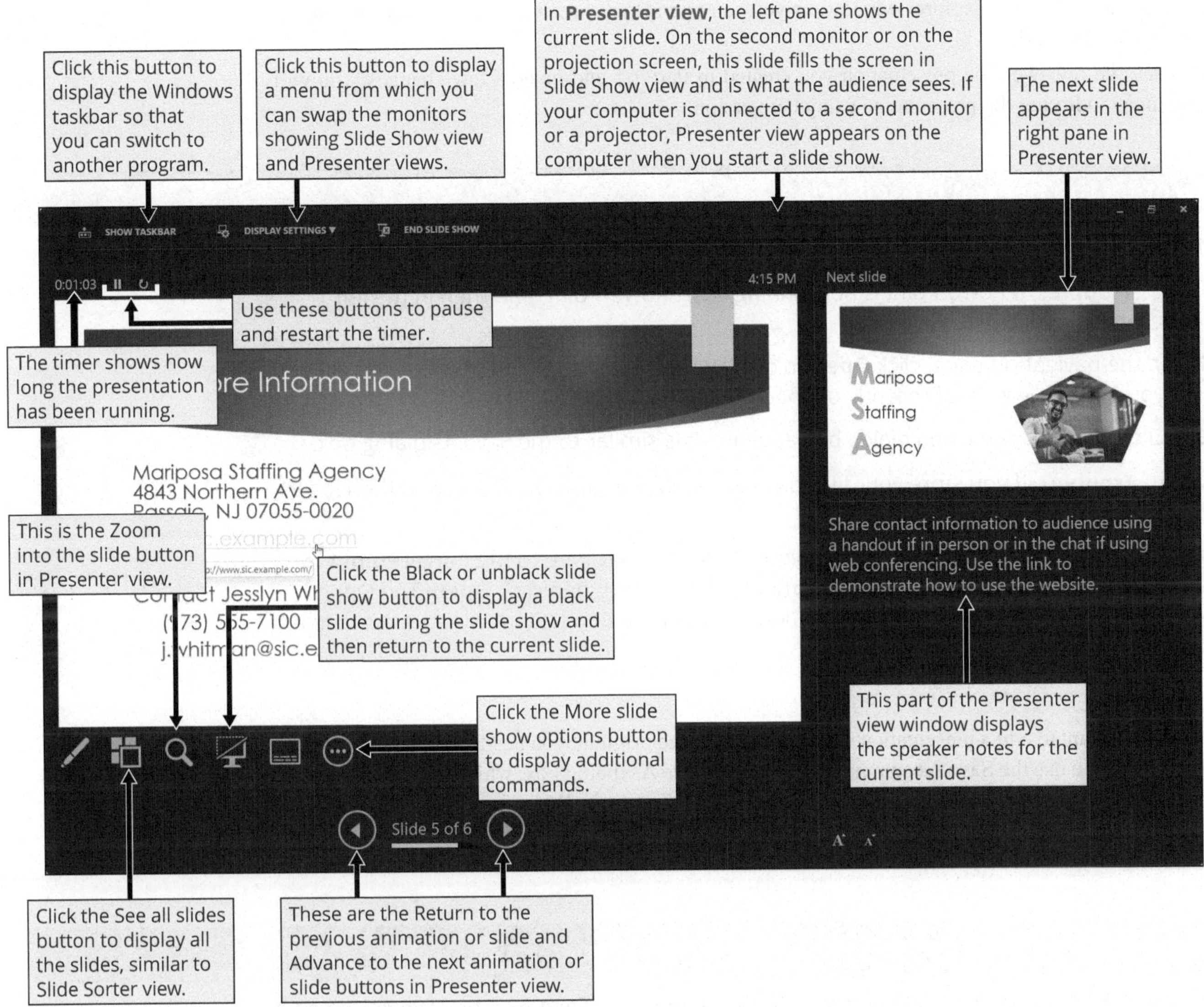
Click this button to display the Windows taskbar so that you can switch to another program.
Click this button to display a menu from which you can swap the monitors showing Slide Show view and Presenter views.
In **Presenter view**, the left pane shows the current slide. On the second monitor or on the projection screen, this slide fills the screen in Slide Show view and is what the audience sees. If your computer is connected to a second monitor or a projector, Presenter view appears on the computer when you start a slide show.
The next slide appears in the right pane in Presenter view.
SHOW TASKBAR
DISPLAY SETTINGS ▾
END SLIDE SHOW
0:01:03
4:15 PM
Next slide
Use these buttons to pause and restart the timer.
The timer shows how long the presentation has been running.
Mariposa
Staffing
Agency
Mariposa Staffing Agency
4843 Northern Ave.
NJ 07055-0020
This is the Zoom into the slide button in Presenter view.
Click the Black or unblack slide show button to display a black slide during the slide show and then return to the current slide.
Share contact information to audience using a handout if in person or in the chat if using web conferencing. Use the link to demonstrate how to use the website.
Click the More slide show options button to display additional commands.
This part of the Presenter view window displays the speaker notes for the current slide.
Slide 5 of 6
Click the See all slides button to display all the slides, similar to Slide Sorter view.
These are the Return to the previous animation or slide and Advance to the next animation or slide buttons in Presenter view.

iStock/djiledesign

Opening a Presentation and Saving It with a New Name

If you have closed a presentation, you can always reopen it to modify it. To do this, you can double-click the file in a File Explorer window, or you can open Backstage view in PowerPoint and use the Open command.

Jesslyn reviewed the presentation you created in Part 1.1 and made a few changes. You will continue modifying the presentation using her version.

To open the revised presentation:

1. sam Click the **File** tab on the ribbon to display the Home screen in Backstage view.

   Trouble? If PowerPoint is not running, start PowerPoint, and then in the left pane, click Open.

2. In the navigation pane, click **Open** to display the Open screen. Recent is selected, and you might see a list of recently opened presentations on the right.
3. Click **Browse**. The Open dialog box appears. It is similar to the Save As dialog box.

   Trouble? If you store your files on your OneDrive, click OneDrive, and then log in if necessary.

4. Navigate to the drive that contains your Data Files, navigate to the **PowerPoint1 > Module** folder, click **NP_PPT_1-1.pptx** to select it, and then click **Open**. The Open dialog box closes, and the presentation opens in the PowerPoint window, with Slide 1 displayed.

If you want to edit a presentation without changing the original, you need to create a copy of it. To do this, you use the Save As command to open the Save As dialog box, which is the same dialog box you saw when you saved your presentation for the first time. When you save a presentation with a new name, you create a copy of the original presentation, the original presentation closes, and the newly named copy appears in the PowerPoint window.

To save the revised presentation with a new name:

1. Click the **File** tab, and then in the navigation pane, click **Save As**. The Save As screen in Backstage view appears.
2. Click **Browse** to open the Save As dialog box.
3. If necessary, navigate to the drive and folder where you are storing your Data Files.
4. In the File name box, change the filename to **NP_PPT_1_Revised**, and then click **Save**. The Save As dialog box closes, and a copy of the file is saved with the new name NP_PPT_1_Revised and appears in the PowerPoint window.

Inserting Pictures and Adding Alt Text

In many cases, graphics are more effective than words for communicating an important point or invoking an emotional reaction. For example, if a sales force has reached its sales goals for the year, including a photo in your presentation of a person reaching the top of a mountain can convey a sense of accomplishment to your audience. To add a graphic to a slide, you can use the buttons in a content placeholder or buttons on the Insert tab.

When you insert a graphic and when specific built-in layouts are applied to the slide, the Design Ideas pane opens containing suggestions for interesting layouts for the slide. You can click one of these layouts to apply it or close the Design Ideas pane without accepting any of the suggestions.

Jesslyn has a photo that she wants you to insert on Slide 2.

To insert a photo on Slide 2 and view the Design Ideas:

1. Display Slide 2 ("About Us"), and then in the content placeholder on the right, click the **Pictures** button . The Insert Picture dialog box opens. This dialog box is similar to the Open dialog box.
2. Navigate to the **PowerPoint1 > Module** folder included with your Data Files, click **Support_PPT_1_Staff.jpg**, and then click **Insert**. The dialog box closes, and a picture of a smiling group of professionals appears in the placeholder and is selected. Text that describes the picture might appear briefly at the bottom of the picture. Also, the Design Ideas pane might open listing suggestions for interesting layouts for this slide. On the ribbon, the contextual Picture Format tab appears and is the active tab. Refer to Figure 1–26.

Figure 1–26 Picture inserted on Slide 2

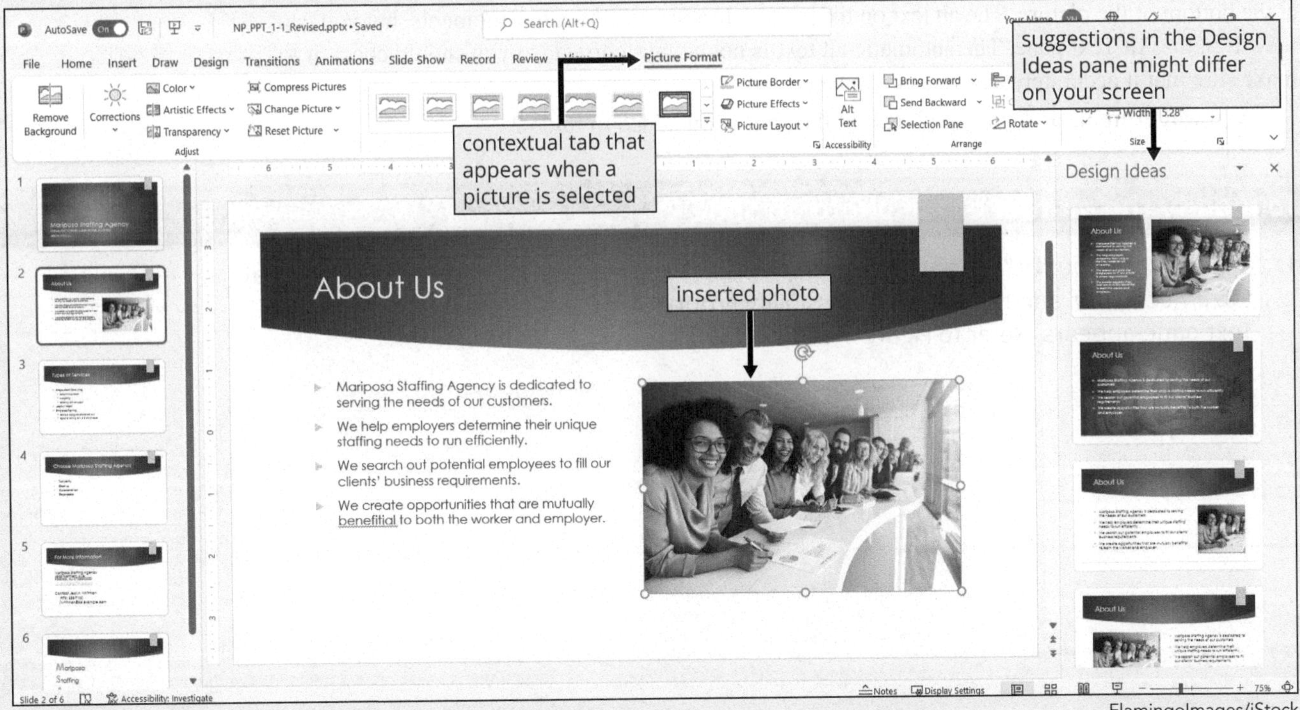

FlamingoImages/iStock

Trouble? If the Design Ideas pane does not appear, click the Design tab, and then in the Designer group, click the Design Ideas button.

Trouble? If the descriptive text does not appear below the picture, do not be concerned. You will display it later.

3. In the Design Ideas pane, click each of the thumbnails to see the effect on the slide. Although Jesslyn likes some of the layouts suggested in the Design Ideas pane, he wants you to apply the Two Content layout again. First, you need to undo the change you made.
4. On the Quick Access Toolbar, click the **Undo arrow**. No matter how many thumbnails you clicked in the Design Ideas pane, only one "Apply Design Idea" action is listed in the Undo menu.

   Tip You can click the Redo button on the Quick Access Toolbar to redo an action.
5. On the menu, click **Apply Design Idea**. The slide is reset to its original layout.
6. In the Design Ideas pane, in the top-right corner, click the **Close** button. The pane closes.

The layout suggestions in the Design Ideas pane can help you create interesting slides. If you open the Design Ideas pane and it does not contain any suggestions, make sure you are using one of the themes that is included with PowerPoint, and change the slide layout to Title Slide or Title and Content.

Although graphics can make a slide more interesting, people with vision impairments might not be able to see them clearly and people who are blind cannot see them at all. People with vision challenges might use a screen reader to view your presentation. A screen reader identifies objects on the screen and produces an audio of the text. Graphics cause problems for users of screen readers unless the graphics have alternative text. **Alternative text**, usually shortened to **alt text**, is descriptive text added to an object.

When you add a picture to a slide, alt text for the picture is automatically created and displayed at the bottom of the picture. The alt text on the picture disappears after a few moments, but you can view it in the Alt Text pane. The automatic alt text is not always correct, so you should check it to make sure that it accurately describes the image.

You will examine and edit the alt text of the photo you added to Slide 2.

To modify the alt text of the photo on Slide 2:

1. On Slide 2 ("About Us"), click the picture to select it if necessary, click the **Picture Format** tab if necessary, and then in the Accessibility group, click the **Alt Text** button. The Alt Text pane appears. Refer to Figure 1–27.

Figure 1–27 Alt Text pane open showing automatically generated alt text

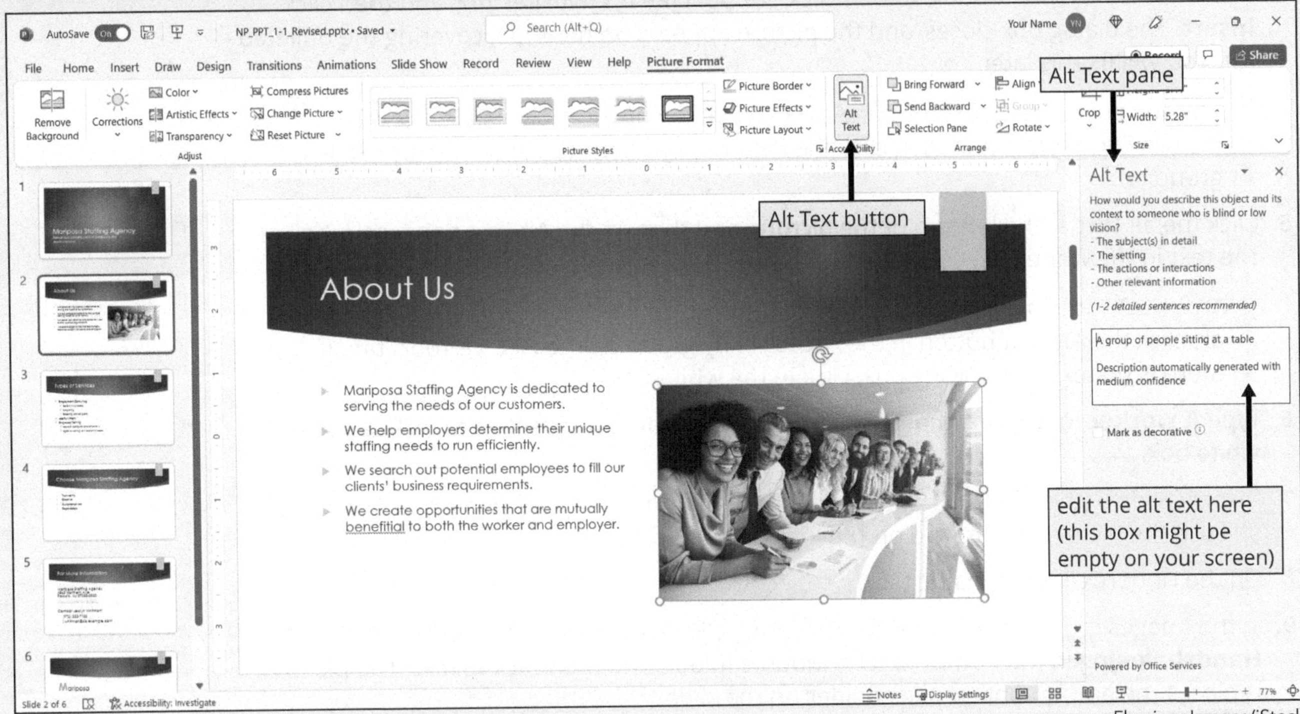

FlamingoImages/iStock

> **Trouble?** If alt text is not automatically generated, this feature might be turned off on your computer or your computer might not have been able to connect to the Microsoft server. Click in the white box in the Alt Text pane, and then skip Step 2.

2. In the Alt Text pane, in the white box, select all of the text, including the phrase "Description automatically generated with medium confidence."

> **Tip** Another way to open the Alt Text pane is to click the alt text when it appears on the bottom of the picture when the picture is first inserted.

3. Type **Happy workers leaning on a long, curved table** in the white box. The text you type replaces the selected text. The next time you select the picture, a new command—Generate a description for me—will appear. You could click that command to have the alt text generated again, replacing the text you typed.
4. In the Alt Text pane, in the top-right corner, click the **Close** button ☒.

Jesslyn has two more photos that she wants you to add to the presentation. She asks you to add the photos to Slides 3 and 6.

To insert photos on Slides 3 and 6:

1. Display Slide 3 ("Types of Services"). This slide has the Title and Content layout applied, so it does not have a second content placeholder. You can change the layout to include a second content placeholder, or you can use a command on the ribbon to insert a photo.
2. Click the **Insert** tab, and then in the Images group, click the **Pictures** button. The Insert Picture From gallery appears.
3. Click **This Device** to select a picture on your computer. The Insert Picture dialog box opens.

4. In the PowerPoint1 > Module folder, click **Support_PPT_1_Worker.jpg**, and then click **Insert**. The dialog box closes, and the picture appears on the slide, covering the bulleted list. You will fix this later.

   Tip To convert pictures to SmartArt, select all the pictures on a slide, click the Picture Format tab, and then click the Picture Layout button in the Picture Styles group.

5. Click the alt text at the bottom of the picture, and then, in the Alt Text pane, select all of the text in the white box.

   Trouble? If the alt text disappeared before you could click it or doesn't appear at all, click the Alt Text button in the Accessibility group on the Picture Tools tab. If there is no text in the white box, click in the white box.

6. Type **A worker in a wheelchair uses a computer and a headset in an office** in the white box.
7. Display Slide 6 (the last slide). Slide 6 has the Two Content layout applied, but you can still use the Pictures command on the Insert tab.
8. On the ribbon, click the **Insert** tab.
9. In the Images group, click the **Pictures** button, click **This Device**, click **Support_PPT_1_Handshake.jpg** in the PowerPoint1 > Module folder, and then click **Insert**. The picture replaces the empty content placeholder on the slide.
10. In the Alt Text pane, select all of the text in the white box, and then type **Smiling man with glasses shakes the hand of a person sitting across from him** in the white box.
11. Close the Alt Text pane, and then close the Design Ideas pane, if necessary.

Proskills

Decision Making: Deciding Whether to Allow Alt Text to Be Generated

When posting information to the cloud or to social media, you should consider any impact on your privacy or that of others. When you insert a picture on a slide, the picture is sent to Microsoft's servers in order to generate alt text. This means that you are sharing the picture in the cloud. If you are concerned about sharing your private pictures, you can turn this feature off. To do this, click the File tab, and then click Options to open the PowerPoint Options dialog box. On the left, click Ease of Access to display the options for making PowerPoint more accessible. In the Automatic Alt Text section, click the Automatically generate alt text for me check box to deselect it. If you change your mind and you want alt text generated for a specific picture, you can still click the command to generate new alt text in the Alt Text pane.

Cropping Pictures

Sometimes you want to display only part of a photo. For example, if you insert a photo of a party scene that includes a bouquet of colorful balloons, you might want to show only the balloons. To do this, you can crop the photo. To **crop** means to trim away part of a picture. In PowerPoint, you can crop a picture to any size you want, crop it to a preset ratio, or crop it to a shape.

It can be helpful to display rulers and gridlines in the window to help you crop photos to specific sizes. There are two rulers. One is horizontal and appears above the slide. The other is vertical and appears to the left of the slide. **Gridlines** are evenly spaced horizontal and vertical lines on the slide that help you align objects.

Jesslyn wants you to crop the photo on Slide 3 ("Types of Services") to make the dimensions of the final photo smaller without making the images in the photo smaller.

To crop the photo on Slide 3:

1. Click the **View** tab, and then in the Show group, click the **Ruler** and the **Gridlines** check boxes to select them, if necessary. Rulers appear above and to the left of the displayed slide, and the gridlines appear on the slide.
2. Display Slide 3 ("Types of Services"), click the photo to select it, and then click the **Picture Format** tab, if necessary.
3. In the Size group, click the **Crop** button. The Crop button is selected, and crop handles appear around the edges of the photo just inside the sizing handles. Refer to Figure 1–28.

Figure 1–28 Photo with crop handles

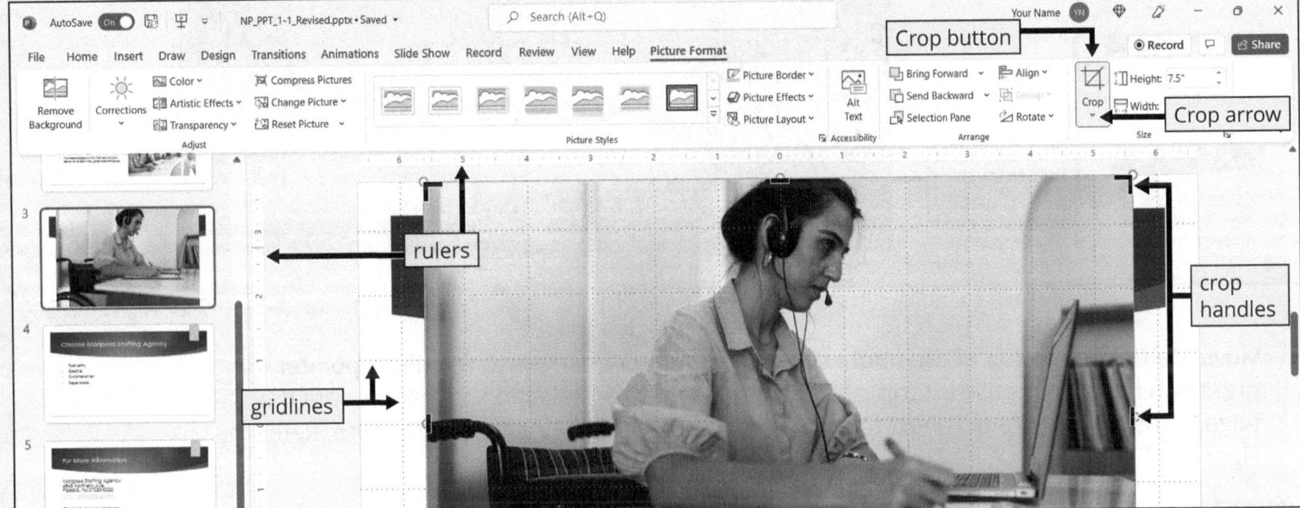

iStock/Ergin Yalcin; FlamingoImages/iStock; jiledesign/iStock

4. Position the pointer directly on top of the middle crop handle on the left side of the picture so that it changes to the left-middle crop pointer ┫. On the rulers, a red dotted line shows the position of the pointer.
5. Press and hold the mouse button, drag the crop handle to the right until the left cropped edge is on the gridline that aligns with the negative 3-inch mark on the horizontal ruler, and then release the mouse button. The part of the photo that will be cropped off is shaded dark gray. Refer to Figure 1–29.

Figure 1–29 Cropped photo

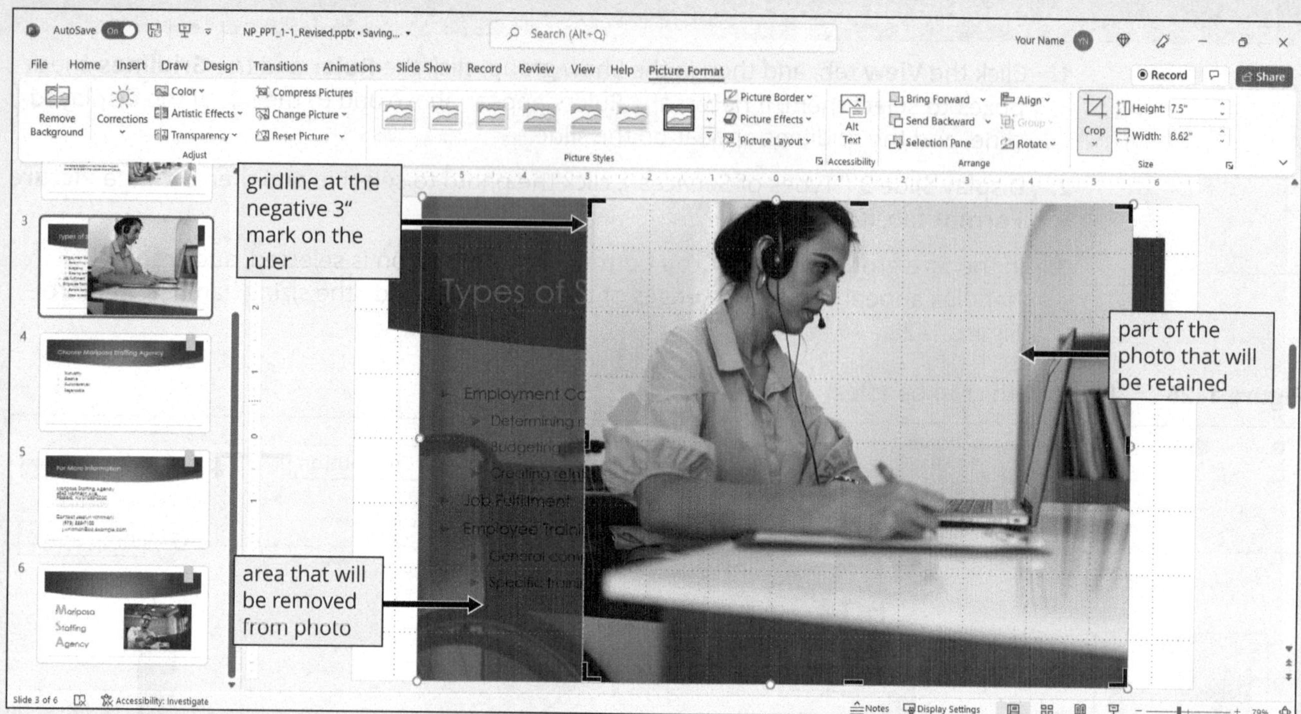

iStock/Ergin Yalcin; FlamingoImages/iStock; iStock/djiledesign

6. Move the pointer on top of the photo so that the pointer changes to the move pointer, press and hold the mouse button, and then move the crop selection to the left until the edge of the laptop screen is next to the right edge of the visible part of the photo. Refer to Figure 1–30.

Figure 1–30 Photo moved inside cropped area

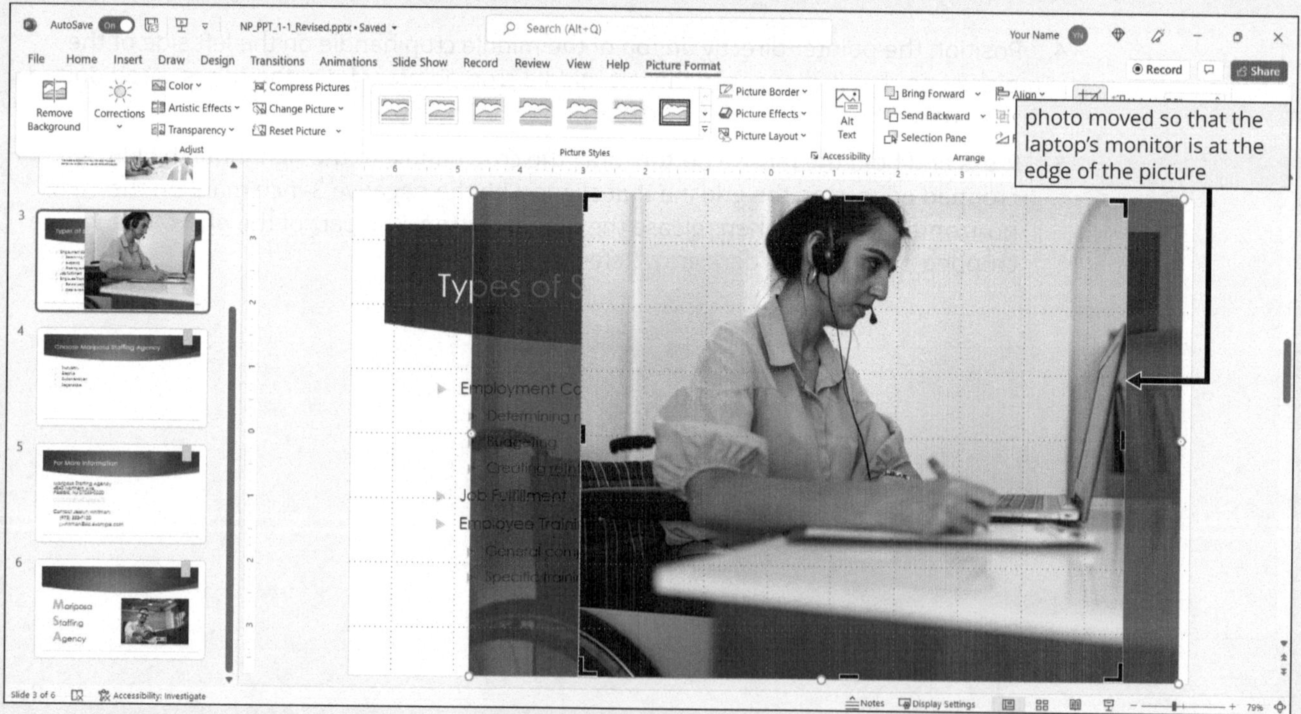

iStock/Ergin Yalcin; FlamingoImages/iStock; iStock/djiledesign

7. Click the **Crop** button again to complete the cropping. The Crop feature turns off, but the photo is still selected, and the Picture Format tab is still the active tab. You will resize the picture later.

When you crop a picture to a shape, the picture fills the shape. Jesslyn wants you to crop the photo on Slide 6 (the last slide) so that it fills a pentagon shape.

To crop the photo on Slide 6 to a shape:

1. Display Slide 6 (the last slide), click the photo to select it, and then click the **Picture Format** tab, if necessary.
2. In the Size group, click the **Crop arrow**. The Crop menu opens. Refer to Figure 1–31.

Figure 1–31 Crop button menu

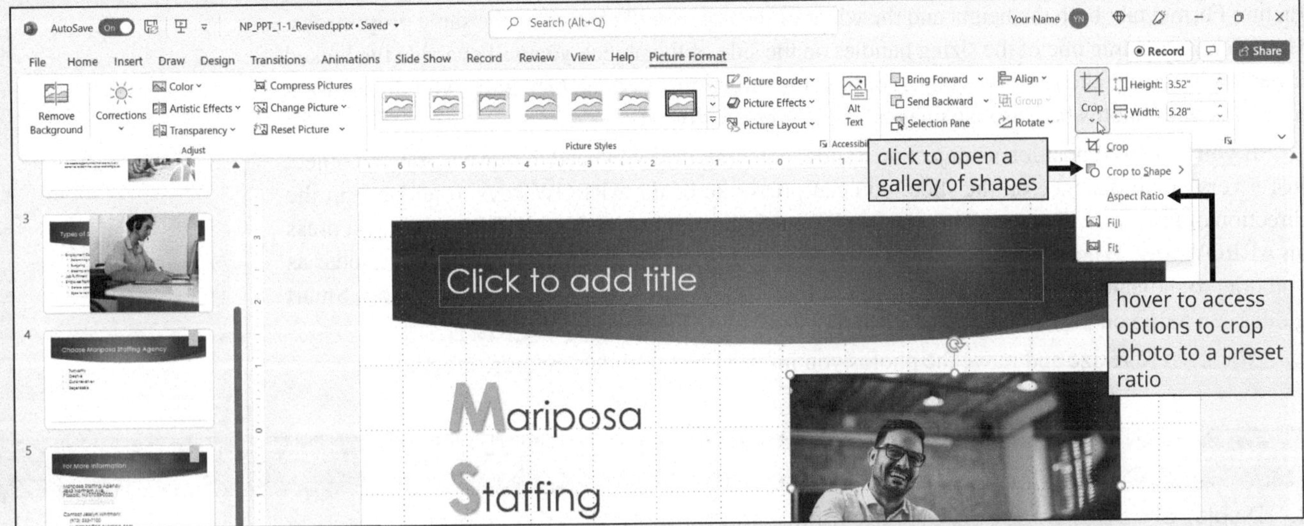

iStock/djiledesign; iStock/Ergin Yalcin; iStock/FlamingoImages

3. Point to **Crop to Shape** to open a gallery of shapes, and then in the first row under Basic Shapes, click the **Pentagon** shape. The photo is cropped to a pentagon shape. Notice that the rectangular selection border of the original photo is still showing.

   Tip Some SmartArt layouts include shapes with a Pictures button. You can click that button to insert a picture in the shape so that it fills the shape.

4. In the Size group, click the **Crop** button. You can now see the cropped portions of the original, rectangle photo that are shaded gray.
5. Click a blank area of the slide. The picture is no longer selected, and the Home tab is the active tab on the ribbon.

If you want to change how a picture is cropped, you can adjust the crop by selecting the picture and clicking the Crop button again. The cropped portion of the picture will be visible, and you can move the picture inside the crop marks or drag the crop handles to change how the picture is cropped. To change the crop so that the entire picture appears in the shape at its original aspect ratio, click the Fit command on the Crop menu. To change it back so that the picture fills the shape again, click the Fill command on the Crop menu.

Resizing and Moving Objects

You can resize and move any object to best fit the space available on a slide. One way to resize an object is to drag a sizing handle. **Sizing handles** are small circles at the corners, and often the edges, of a selected object. When you use this method, you can adjust the size of the object so that it best fits the space visually. If you need to size an object to exact dimensions, you can modify the measurements in the Size group on the Format tab that appears when you select the object.

The **aspect ratio** of an object is the proportional relationship between an object's height and width. Pictures and other objects that cause the Picture Format tab to appear when you select them have their aspect ratios locked. This means that if you resize the object by dragging a corner sizing handle or by changing the measurement in either the Height or the Width box in the Size group on the Picture Format tab, both the height and the width of the object will change by the same proportions. However, if you drag one of the sizing handles on the side of the object, you will override the locked aspect ratio setting and resize the object only in the direction you drag. Generally, you do not want to do this with photos because the images will become distorted.

If you want to reposition an object on a slide, you drag it. If you need to move a selected object just a very small distance on the slide, you can press one of the ARROW keys to nudge it in the direction of the arrow. To move it in even smaller increments, press and hold CTRL while you press an ARROW key. When you drag an object on a slide, **smart guides**, dashed red lines, appear as you drag to indicate the center and the edges of the object, other objects, and the slide itself. Smart guides can help you position objects so that they are aligned and spaced evenly.

You need to resize and move the photos you inserted so the slides are more attractive.

To move and resize the photos on Slides 2, 3, and 6:

1. Display Slide 2 ("About Us"), click the photo, and then position the pointer on the top-middle sizing handle so that the pointer changes to the double-headed vertical pointer ↕.
2. Press and hold the mouse button so that the pointer changes to the thin cross pointer +, drag the top-middle sizing handle up approximately two inches, and then release the mouse button. The photo is two inches taller, but the image is distorted. You can undo the change you made.
3. On the Quick Access Toolbar, click the **Undo** button. The photo returns to its original size. You need to resize the photo by dragging a corner sizing handle to maintain the aspect ratio.
4. Click the **Picture Format** tab if necessary, and then note the measurements in the Height and Width boxes in the Size group. The photo is 3.41 inches high and 5.28 inches wide.
5. Position the pointer on the top-right corner sizing handle so that it changes to the double-headed diagonal pointer ⤢, press and hold the mouse button so that the pointer changes to the thin cross pointer +, and then drag the top-right sizing handle up. Even though you are dragging in only one direction, because you are dragging a corner sizing handle, both the width and height change proportionately to maintain the aspect ratio of the photo.
6. When the right edge of the photo is near to, but not quite touching, the gridline dots that line up with the 6-inch mark on the horizontal ruler, release the mouse button. In the Height and Width boxes, the measurements changed to reflect the picture's new size.

7. If the measurement in the Shape Height box in the Size group is not 3.75, click in the Shape Height box to select the current measurement, type **3.75**, and then press **ENTER**.

> **Tip** To replace a picture with another picture at the same size and position, right-click the picture, and then click Change Picture.

8. Drag the photo so that the right edge of the photo aligns with the right edge of the slide, and the top of the photo is aligned with the top of the bulleted list, as shown in Figure 1–32.

Figure 1–32 Repositioning the photo on Slide 2 using smart guides and gridlines

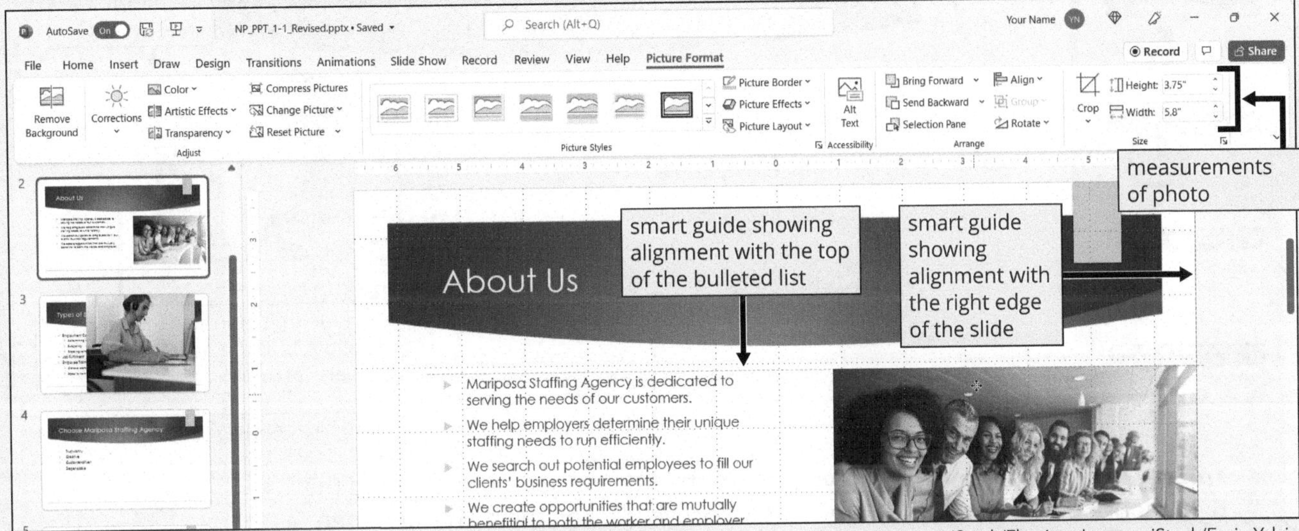

iStock/FlamingoImages; iStock/Ergin Yalcin

> **Trouble?** If the smart guides do not appear, click the View tab, and then in the Show group, click the Dialog Box Launcher to open the Grid and Guides dialog box. Click the "Display smart guides when shapes are aligned" check box to select it.

9. Release the mouse button. The photo is in its new location.
10. Display Slide 3 ("Types of Services"), click the photo to select it, and then click the **Picture Format** tab if necessary.
11. In the Size group, click in the **Shape Height** box to select the current measurement, type **4**, and then press **ENTER**. The measurement in the Shape Width box in the Size group changes proportionately to maintain the aspect ratio, and the new measurements are applied to the photo.
12. Drag the photo down and to the right until a horizontal smart guide appears indicating that the middle of the photo is aligned at the negative 1-inch mark on the vertical ruler and aligned with the gridline dots at the 6-inch mark on the horizontal ruler, as shown in Figure 1–33.

Figure 1–33 Moving the resized photo on Slide 3

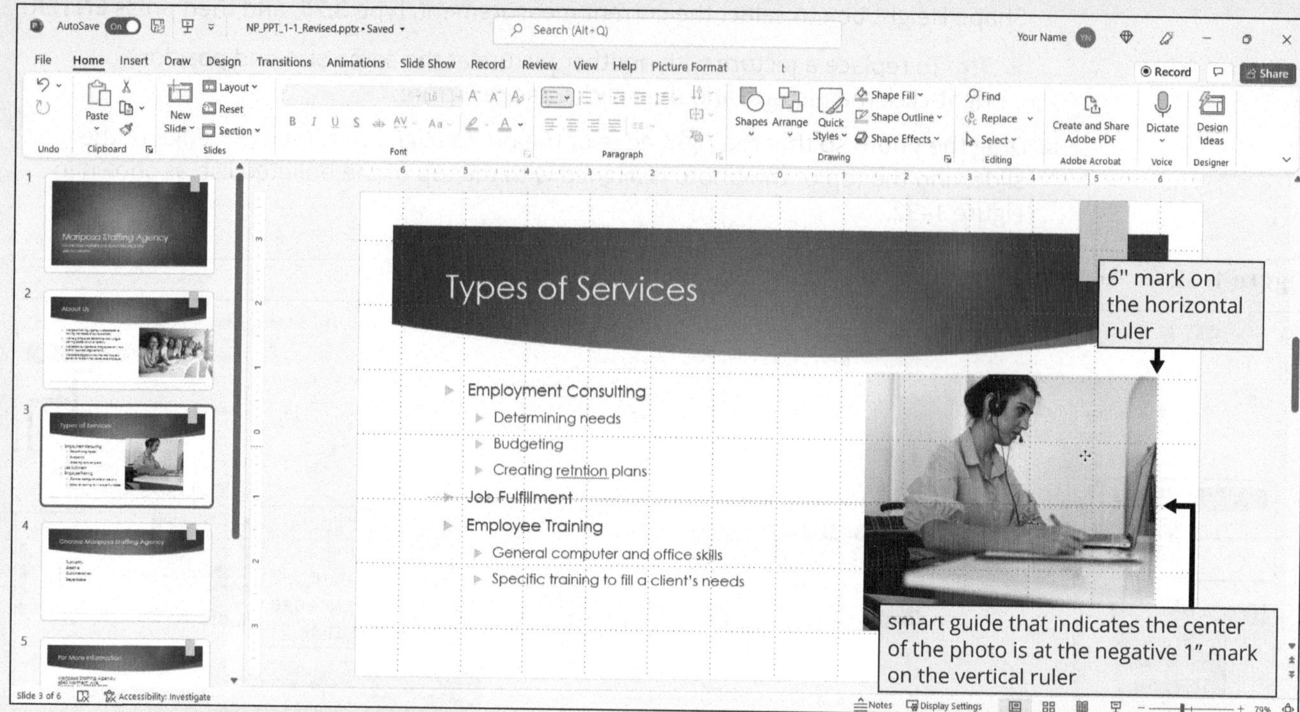

FlamingoImages/iStock; iStock/Ergin Yalcin

Trouble? If a menu appears after you release the mouse button, you clicked the right mouse button when you dragged. Click Move Here on the menu, and then check to make sure the photo is positioned as described in Step 12.

13. When the photo is aligned as shown in Figure 1–33, release the mouse button.
14. Display Slide 6 (the last slide), and then position the photo so that the bottom of the photo aligns with the smart guide that indicates the bottom of the left text box and the right edge aligns with the 6-inch mark on the ruler.

Text boxes, like other objects that cause the Shape Format tab to appear when selected, do not have their aspect ratios locked. This means that when you resize a text box by dragging a corner sizing handle or changing one measurement in the Shape Height box or the Shape Width box in the Size group, the other dimension does not change.

Like any other object on a slide, you can reposition text boxes. To do this, you must position the pointer on the text box border, anywhere except on a sizing handle, to drag it to its new location.

To improve the appearance of Slide 6, you will resize the text box containing the unnumbered list so that it vertically fills the slide.

To resize the text box on Slide 6:

1. On Slide 6 (the last slide), click the unnumbered list to display the text box border.
2. Position the pointer on the top-middle sizing handle so that it changes to the double-headed vertical pointer ↕, and then drag the sizing handle up until the top edge of the text box aligns with the bottom edge of the title text placeholder.
3. Drag the left-middle sizing handle to the left so that the left border of the text box is aligned with the negative 6-inch mark on the ruler. Next, you will shift the text box a little to the right.

4. Position the pointer on top of the border of the text box so that it changes to the move pointer, and then drag the text box to the right so that the right border of the text box aligns with the smart guide that indicates the center of the slide. Even though the title text placeholder will not appear during a slide show, you will delete it to see how the final slide will look.

   Tip If you want to hide the smart guides while you are moving an object, press and hold ALT while you are dragging.

5. Click the border of the title text placeholder, and then press **DELETE**. If necessary, drag the text box down until the top of the M in Mariposa is around the 1-inch mark on the vertical ruler. Refer to Figure 1–34.

Figure 1–34 Slide 6 with resized text box

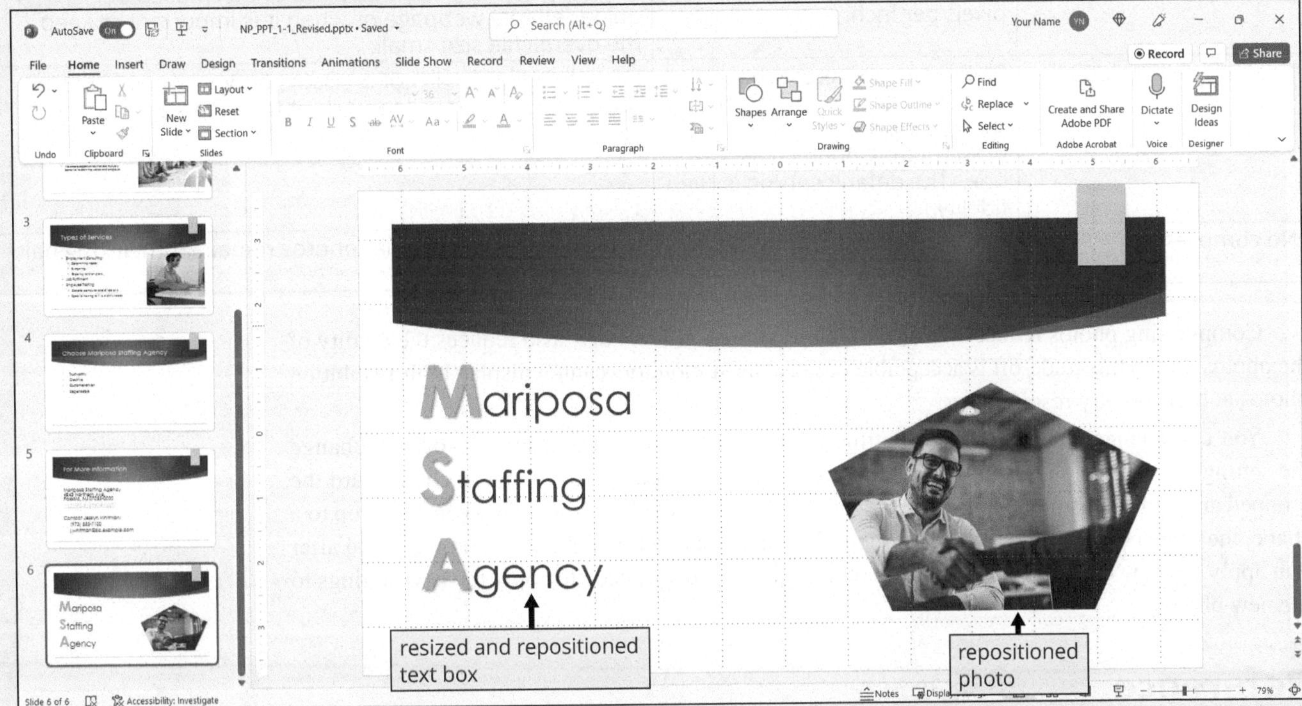

iStock/djiledesign; Ergin Yalcin/iStock; FlamingoImages/iStock

6. Click the **View** tab, and then click the **Ruler** and **Gridlines** check boxes to deselect them. The ruler and the gridlines disappear.
7. Save the changes to the presentation.

Compressing Pictures

When you save a presentation that contains pictures, you can choose to compress the pictures to make the size of the PowerPoint file smaller. Refer to Figure 1–35 for a description of the compression options available.

Figure 1–35 Photo compression settings

Compression Setting	Compression Value	When to Use
High fidelity	Photos are compressed very minimally, and only if they are larger than the slide.	Use when a presentation will be viewed on a high-definition (HD) display, when photograph quality is of the highest concern, and file size is not an issue. This is the default setting.
HD (330 ppi)	Photos are compressed to 330 pixels per inch.	Use when slides need to maintain the quality of the photograph when displayed on HD displays, but file size is of some concern.
Print (220 ppi)	Photos are compressed to 220 pixels per inch.	Use when slides need to maintain the quality of the photograph when printed.
Web (150 ppi)	Photos are compressed to 150 pixels per inch.	Use when the presentation will be viewed on a low-definition display.
E-mail (96 ppi)	Photos are compressed to 96 pixels per inch.	Use for presentations that need to be emailed or uploaded to a webpage or when it is important to keep the overall file size small.
Use default resolution	Photos are compressed to the resolution specified on the Advanced tab in the PowerPoint Options dialog box. (The default setting is High fidelity.)	Use when file size is not an issue, or when quality of the photo display is more important than file size.
No compression	Photos are not compressed at all.	Use when it is critical that photos remain at their original resolution.

Compressing photos reduces the size of the presentation file, but it also reduces the quality of the photos. Often this trade-off is acceptable because most monitors cannot display high-resolution photos at high-fidelity resolution.

You can change the compression setting for each photo that you insert, or you can change the settings for all the photos in the presentation. If you cropped photos, you also can discard the cropped areas of the photo to make the presentation file size smaller. (Note that when you crop to a shape, the cropped portions are not discarded.) If you insert additional photos or crop a photo after you apply the new compression settings to all the slides, you will need to apply the new settings to the new photos.

Reference

Modifying Photo Compression Settings and Removing Cropped Areas

- After you have added all photos to the presentation file, click any photo in the presentation to select it.
- Click the Picture Format tab. In the Adjust group, click the Compress Pictures button.
- In the Compress Pictures dialog box, click the option button next to the resolution you want to use.
- To apply the new compression settings to all the photos in the presentation, click the Apply only to this picture check box to deselect it.
- To keep cropped areas of photos, click the Delete cropped areas of pictures check box to deselect it.
- Click OK.

You will adjust the compression settings to make the file size of the presentation as small as possible so that Jesslyn can easily send it or post it for others without worrying about file size limitations on the receiving server.

To modify photo compression settings and remove cropped areas from photos:

1. On Slide 6 (the last slide), click the photo, and then click the **Picture Format** tab, if necessary.
2. In the Adjust group, click the **Compress Pictures** button. The Compress Pictures dialog box opens. Refer to Figure 1–36. Under Resolution, the Use default resolution option button is selected. (If an option in this dialog box is gray and is not available for you to select, the photo is a lower resolution than that option.)

Figure 1–36 Compress Pictures dialog box

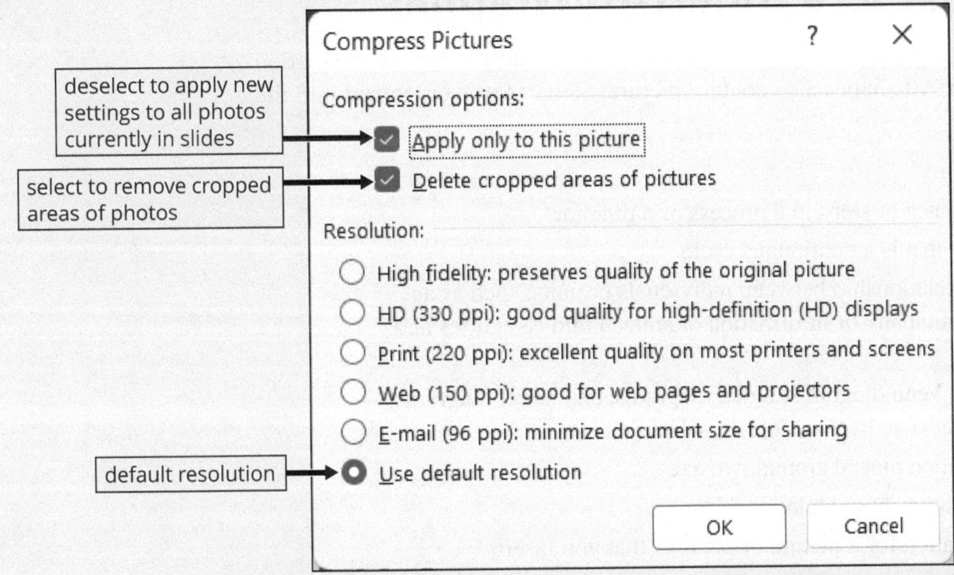

3. Click the **E-mail (96 ppi)** option button. This setting compresses the photos to the smallest size available. At the top of the dialog box under Compression options, the Apply only to this picture check box is selected. You want the settings applied to all the photos in the file.
4. Click the **Apply only to this picture** check box to deselect it. The Delete cropped areas of pictures check box is also selected. You want the presentation file size to be as small as possible, so you'll leave this option selected.

   Trouble? If the Delete cropped areas of pictures check box is not selected, click it.
5. Click **OK**.

   Key Step Be sure you deselect the Apply only to this picture check box and be sure you are satisfied with the way you cropped the photo on Slide 3 before you click OK to close the dialog box.

   The dialog box closes and the compression settings are applied to all the photos in the presentation. You can confirm that the cropped areas of photos were removed by examining the photo on Slide 3. (The photo on Slide 6 was cropped to a shape, so the cropped areas on it were not removed, in case you later change to a different shape cropping.)
6. Display Slide 3 ("Types of Services"), click the photo, and then click the **Picture Format** tab, if necessary.
7. In the Size group, click the **Crop** button. The Crop handles appear around the photo, but the portions of the photo that you cropped out no longer appear.
8. Click the **Crop** button again to deselect it, and then save the changes to the presentation.

Insight

Changing the Default Compression Settings for Pictures

In PowerPoint, the default compression setting for pictures is High fidelity. This means that High fidelity compression is automatically applied to pictures when the file is saved. You can change this setting if you want. To change the settings, click the File tab to open Backstage view, click Options in the navigation pane to open the PowerPoint Options dialog box, click Advanced in the navigation pane, and then locate the Image Size and Quality section. To choose a different compression setting, click the Default resolution arrow, and then select a setting in the list. To prevent pictures from being compressed at all, click the Do not compress images in file check box. Note that these changes affect only the current presentation.

Converting a List to a SmartArt Graphic

A **SmartArt graphic** is a diagram that shows information or ideas visually using a combination of shapes and text. Some SmartArt shapes also contain pictures. SmartArt is organized into the following categories:

- **List**—Shows a list of items
- **Process**—Shows a sequence of steps in a process or a timeline
- **Cycle**—Shows a process that is a continuous cycle
- **Hierarchy**—Shows the relationship between individuals or units, such as an organization chart for a company or information organized into categories and subcategories
- **Relationship** (including Venn diagrams, radial diagrams, and target diagrams)—Shows the relationship between two or more elements
- **Matrix**—Shows information placed around two axes
- **Pyramid**—Shows foundation-based relationships
- **Picture**—Provides a location for a picture or pictures that you insert

When you create a SmartArt graphic, you need to choose a SmartArt layout. In SmartArt, a **layout** is the shapes and arrangement of the shapes in the SmartArt graphic. Once you create a SmartArt graphic, you can easily change the layout to another one if you want.

A quick way to create a SmartArt graphic is to convert an existing list. There are two ways to do this. First, you can try displaying the Design Ideas pane. When the Design Ideas pane shows options for a slide that contains a list, some of the layouts include the list transformed into a SmartArt graphic. The other way you can create a SmartArt graphic from a list is to click the Convert to SmartArt Graphic button in the Paragraph group on the Home tab.

When you change a list to SmartArt, each first-level item in the list is converted to a shape in the SmartArt. If the list contains subitems, you might need to experiment with different layouts to find one that best suits the information in your list.

Reference

Converting a List into SmartArt

- Display the slide containing the list you want to convert to SmartArt.
- If the Design Ideas pane does not open, click the Design tab on the ribbon, and then in the Designer group, click the Design Ideas button.
- In the Design Ideas pane, select the SmartArt and slide layout that you want to use.

or

- Click anywhere in the list that you want to convert.
- In the Paragraph group on the Home tab, click the Convert to SmartArt button, and then click More SmartArt Graphics.
- In the Choose a SmartArt Graphic dialog box, select the desired SmartArt category in the list on the left.
- In the center pane, click the SmartArt you want to use.
- Click OK.

Jesslyn wants you to change the numbered list on Slide 4 into a SmartArt diagram.

To convert the list on Slide 4 into SmartArt:

1. Display Slide 4 ("Choose Mariposa Staffing Agency").
2. If the Design Ideas pane does not open, click the **Design** tab on the ribbon, and then, in the Designer group, click the **Design Ideas** button. The Design Ideas pane opens on the right. Your screen will look similar to the one shown in Figure 1–37.

Figure 1–37 Design Ideas pane with suggestions for the list on Slide 4

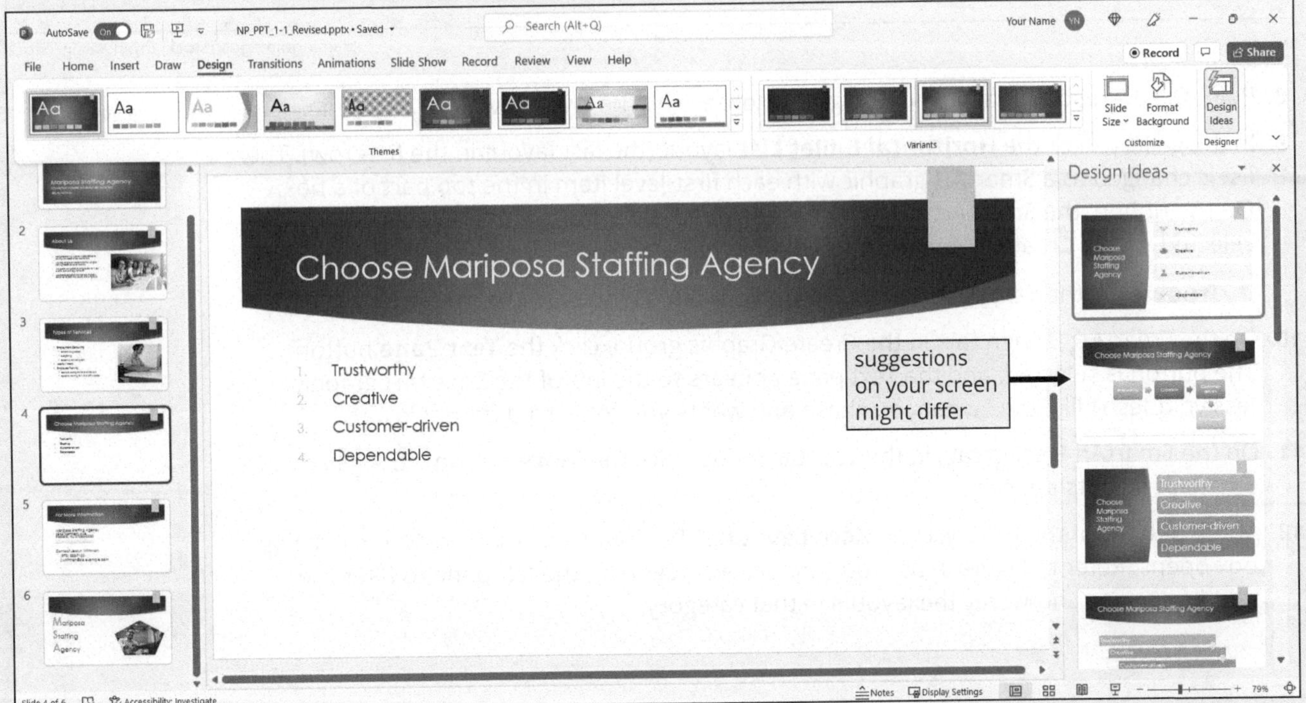

FlamingoImages/iStock; Ergin Yalcin/iStock; jiledesign/iStock

3. In the Design Ideas pane, click several of the thumbnails to see the effect on the slide.
4. After you are finished exploring the layouts in the Design Ideas pane, click the **Undo** button on the Quick Access Toolbar. The slide resets to its original layout.
5. Close the Design Ideas pane, and then on the slide, click anywhere in the list.

6. On the ribbon, click the **Home** tab, and then in the Paragraph group, click the **Convert to SmartArt Graphic** button. A gallery opens listing SmartArt layouts.
7. Point to the first layout. The ScreenTip identifies this layout as the Vertical Bullet List layout, and Live Preview shows you what the list will look like with that layout applied. Refer to Figure 1–38.

Figure 1–38 Live Preview of the Vertical Bullet List SmartArt layout

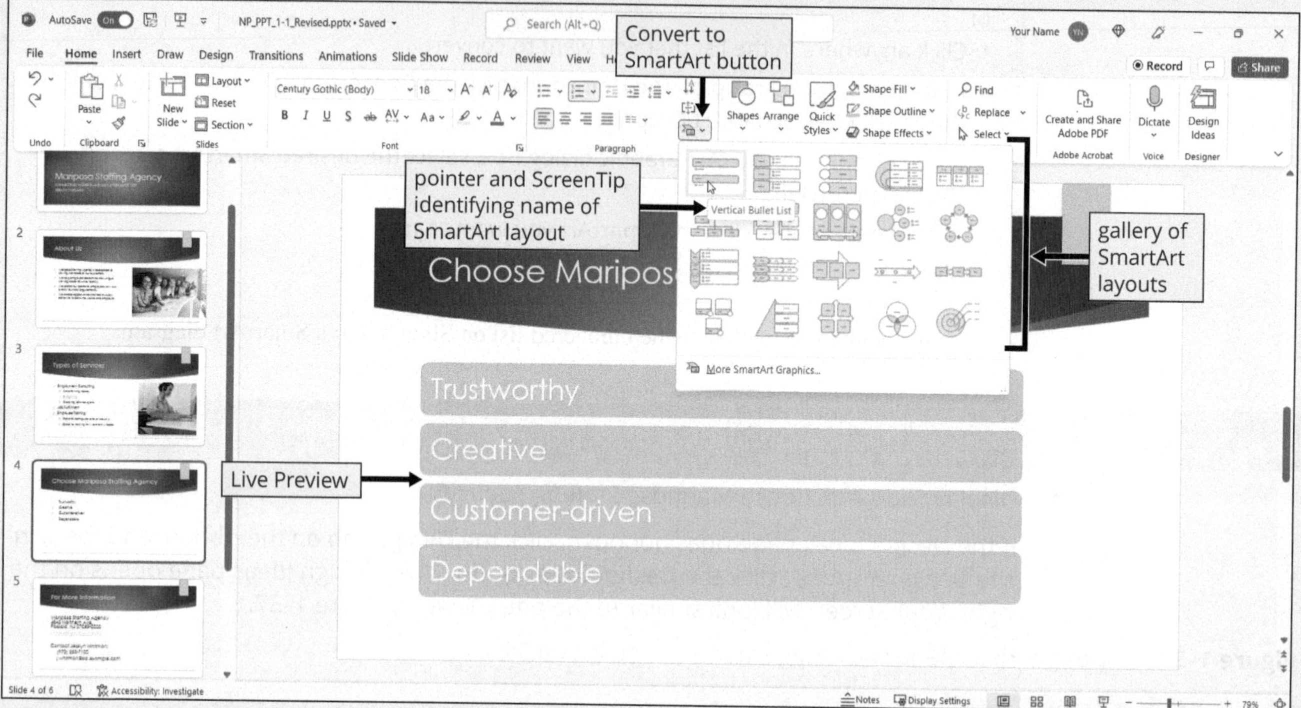

FlamingoImages/iStock; Ergin Yalcin/iStock

8. Point to several other layouts in the gallery, observing the Live Preview of each one.
9. In the gallery, click the **Horizontal Bullet List** layout (the last layout in the first row). The list is changed to a SmartArt graphic with each first-level item in the top part of a box. On the ribbon, the SmartArt contextual tabs appear, and the SmartArt Design tab is selected. In the Create Graphic group, the Text Pane button is not selected.

   Trouble? If the Text Pane button is selected, skip Step 10.
10. On the SmartArt Design tab, in the Create Graphic group, click the **Text Pane** button. The button is selected, and the Text pane appears to the left of the SmartArt graphic. Jesslyn doesn't like the layout you chose and wants you to use a different layout.
11. On the SmartArt Design tab, in the Layouts group, click the **More** button. A gallery of SmartArt layouts appears.
12. At the bottom of the gallery, click **More Layouts**. The Choose a SmartArt Graphic dialog box opens. Refer to Figure 1–39. You can click a category in the left pane to filter the middle pane to show only the layouts in that category.

Figure 1–39 Choose a SmartArt Graphic dialog box

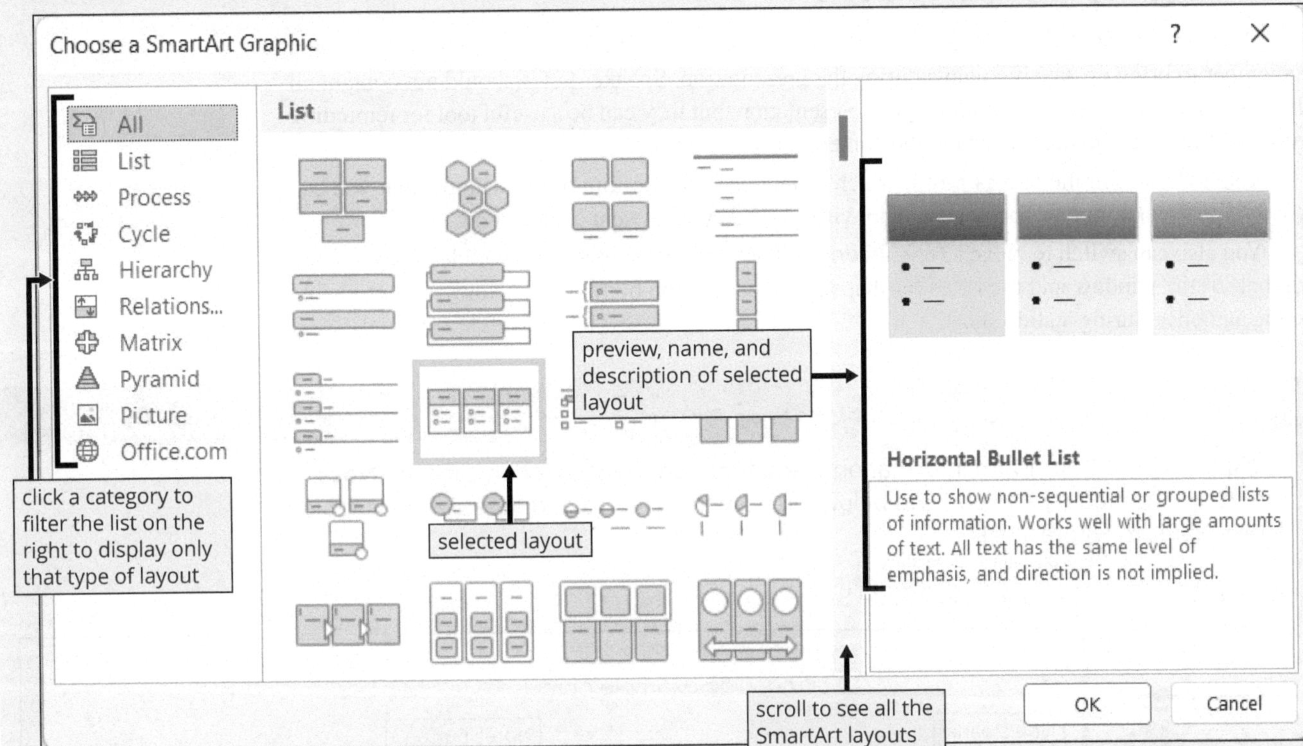

13. In the left pane, click **List**, and then in the middle pane, click the **Vertical Box List** layout, using the ScreenTips to identify it. The right pane changes to show a description of that layout.
14. Click **OK**. The dialog box closes, and each of the first-level items in the list appears in the colored shapes in the diagram. The items also appear as a bulleted list in the Text pane. Refer to Figure 1–40.

Figure 1–40 SmartArt graphic with the Vertical Box List layout

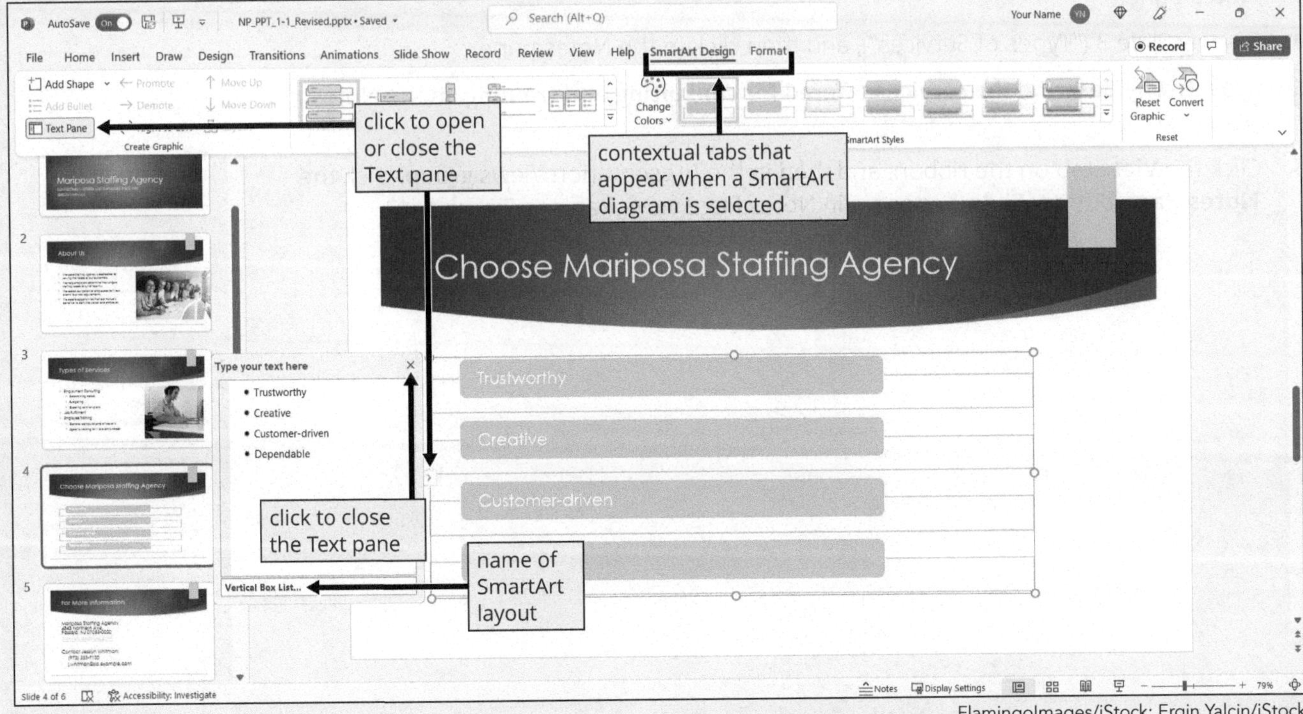

FlamingoImages/iStock; Ergin Yalcin/iStock

15. To the right of the text pane, click the **Collapse text pane** button [>]. The text pane closes.

Adding Speaker Notes

Speaker notes, or simply **notes**, are information you add about slide content to help you remember to bring up specific points during the presentation. Speaker notes should not contain all the information you plan to say during your presentation, but they can be a useful tool for reminding you about facts and details related to the content on specific slides.

You add notes in the **Notes pane**, which is an area at the bottom of the window that you can use to type speaker notes. The notes are not visible when you present a slide show.

You also can switch to **Notes Page view**, in which a reduced image of the slide appears in the top half of the window and the notes for that slide appear in the bottom half. Notes are not visible to the audience during a slide show.

To add notes to Slides 3 and 5:

1. Display Slide 5 ("For More Information"), and then, on the status bar, click the **Notes** button. The Notes pane appears below Slide 5 with "Click to add notes" as placeholder text. Refer to Figure 1–41.

Figure 1–41 Notes pane below Slide 5

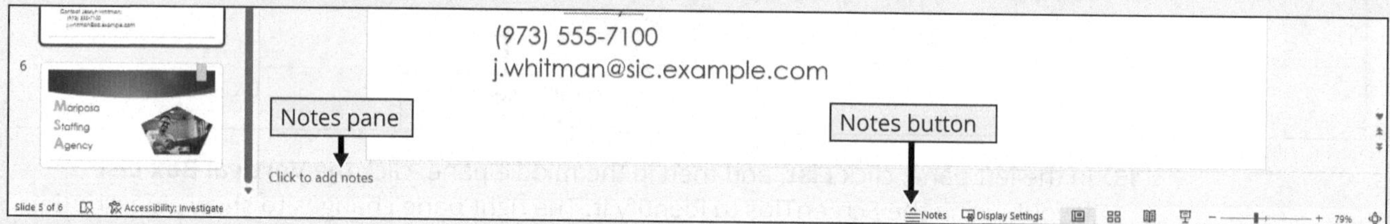

FlamingoImages/iStock; Ergin Yalcin/iStock; iStock/djiledesign

2. Click in the Notes pane. The placeholder text disappears, and the insertion point is in the Notes pane.
3. Type **Share contact information to audience using a handout if in person or in the chat if using web conferencing. Use the link to demonstrate how to use the website.** in the Notes pane.
4. Display Slide 3 ("Types of Services"), and then click in the Notes pane.
5. Type **Briefly describe the services offered for consulting and training.** in the Notes pane.
6. Click the **View** tab on the ribbon, and then in the Presentation Views group, click the **Notes Page** button. Slide 3 appears in Notes Page view. Refer to Figure 1–42.

Figure 1–42 Slide 3 in Notes Page view

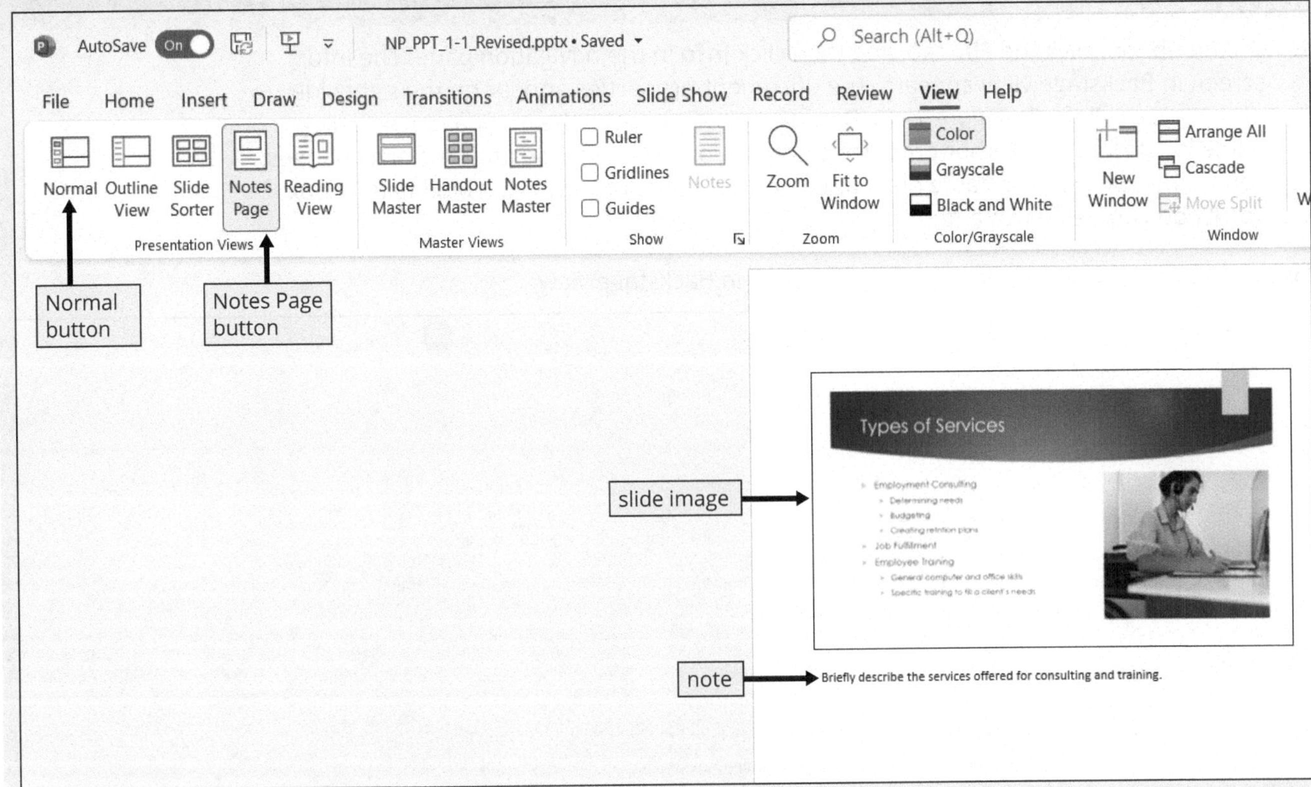

iStock/Ergin Yalcin

7. In the note, click after the period at the end of the sentence, press **SPACEBAR**, and then type **Be sure to describe the cost differences among services.** (including the period).

   Tip Use the Zoom in button on the status bar to magnify the text to make it easier to edit the note.

8. On the View tab, in the Presentation Views group, click the **Normal** button to return to Normal view. The Notes pane stays open until you close it again.
9. On the status bar, click the **Notes** button to close the Notes pane, and then save the changes to the presentation.

Editing Common File Properties

File **properties** are identifying information—characteristics—about a file that is saved along with the file that help others understand, identify, and locate the file. Common properties are the title, the author's name, and the date the file was created. You can use file properties to organize presentations or to search for files that have specific properties. To view or modify properties, you need to display the Info screen in Backstage view.

The client manager, Jesslyn, wants you to modify the Author property by adding yourself as an author, and she wants you to add the Company property.

To add common file properties:

1. On the ribbon, click the **File** tab, and then click **Info** in the navigation pane. The Info screen in Backstage view appears. The document properties appear on the right side of the screen. Refer to Figure 1–43. Because Jesslyn created the original document, her name is listed as the Author property. Because you saved the file after making changes, your name (or the user name on your computer) appears in the Last Modified By box. You'll add yourself as an author.

Figure 1–43 File properties on the Info screen in Backstage view

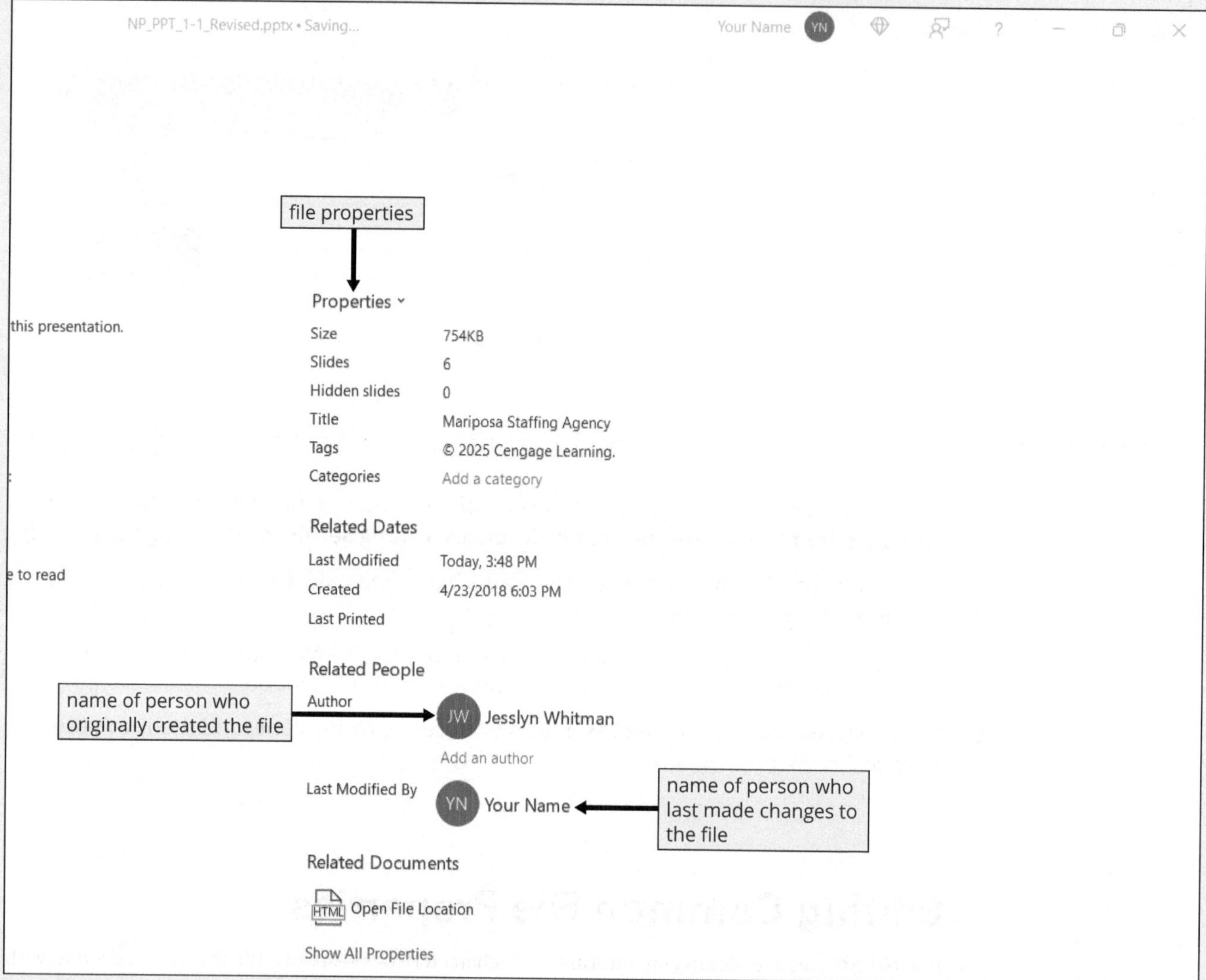

2. In the Related People section, click **Add an author**, type your name in the box that appears, and then click a blank area of the window. You and Jesslyn are now both listed as the Author property. Next, you need to add the Company property. The Company property does not appear in the list.
3. Scroll down, and then at the bottom of the Properties list, click **Show All Properties**. The Properties list expands to include all of the common document properties, including the Company property.
4. Next to Company, click **Specify the company**, type **Mariposa Staffing Agency**, and then click a blank area of the screen. You are finished adding properties to the file.
5. Scroll up if necessary, and at the top of the navigation pane, click the **Back** button to return to Slide 3 in Normal view.

Checking Spelling

You should always check the spelling and grammar in your presentation before you finalize it. To make this task easier, you can use PowerPoint's spelling checker. You can quickly tell if there are words on slides that are not in the built-in dictionary by looking at the Spelling button at the left end of the status bar. If there are no words flagged as possibly misspelled, the button is ; if words are flagged, the button changes to . To indicate that a word might be misspelled, a wavy red line appears under it.

> **Tip** You can click the Thesaurus button in the Proofing group on the Review tab to look up synonyms of a selected word, or you can click the Smart Lookup button in the Insights group to open the Search pane listing search results from the web.

To correct misspelled words, you can right-click a flagged word to see a list of suggested spellings on the shortcut menu, or you can check the entire presentation to locate possible misspellings. To check the spelling of all the words in the presentation, you click the Spelling button in the Proofing group on the Review tab. This opens the Spelling pane to the right of the displayed slide and starts the spell check from the current slide. When a possible misspelled word is found, suggestions for the correct spelling appear. If you want to accept one of the suggested spellings, you can change only the selected instance of the word or all of the instances of the word in the presentation. If the word is spelled correctly, you can ignore this instance of that word or all the instances of that word in the presentation. The pane also lists synonyms for the selected correct spelling.

To check the spelling in the presentation:

1. Display Slide 2 ("About Us"), and then right-click the misspelled word **benefitial** in the fourth bulleted item. A shortcut menu opens listing spelling options. Refer to Figure 1–44.

Figure 1–44 Shortcut menu for a misspelled word

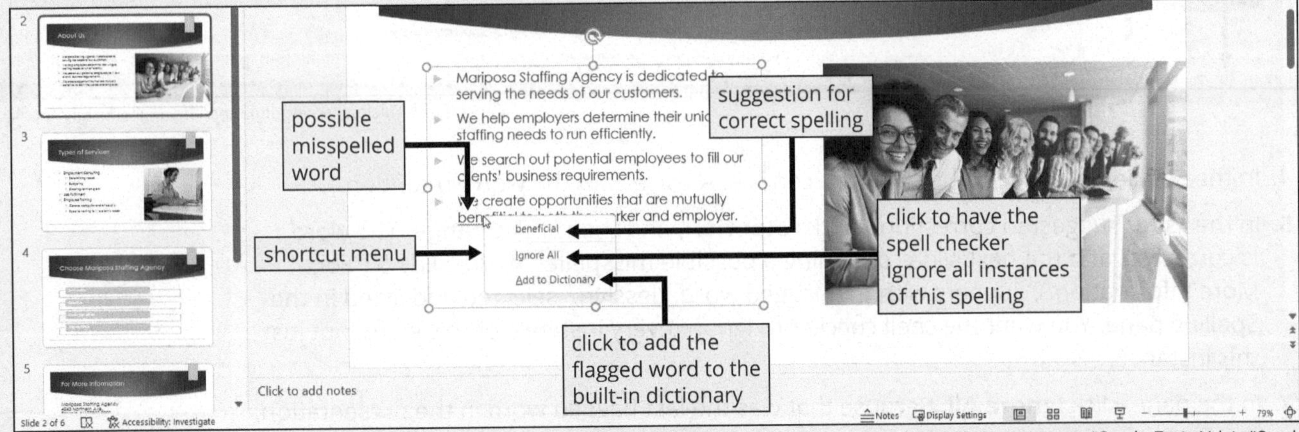

FlamingoImages/iStock; Ergin Yalcin/iStock

> **Trouble?** If the word "**benefitial**" does not have a wavy red line under it, click the Review tab, and then in the Proofing group, click the Spelling button. The wavy red line should now appear. Right-click "**benefitial**," continue with Step 2, and then do not do Step 3.

2. On the shortcut menu, click **beneficial**. The menu closes, and the spelling is corrected.

> **Tip** If words are flagged with blue underlines, right-click the underlined words to see suggestions for fixing the possible grammatical error.

3. Click the **Review** tab, and then in the Proofing group, click the **Spelling** button. The Spelling pane opens to the right of the displayed slide, and the next possible misspelled word, "retntion" on Slide 3 ("Types of Services"), is selected on the slide and in the Spelling pane. Refer to Figure 1–45. In the Spelling pane, the first suggested correct spelling is selected. The selected correct spelling also appears at the bottom of the pane, with synonyms for the word listed below it and a speaker icon next to it.

Figure 1–45 Spelling pane displaying a misspelled word

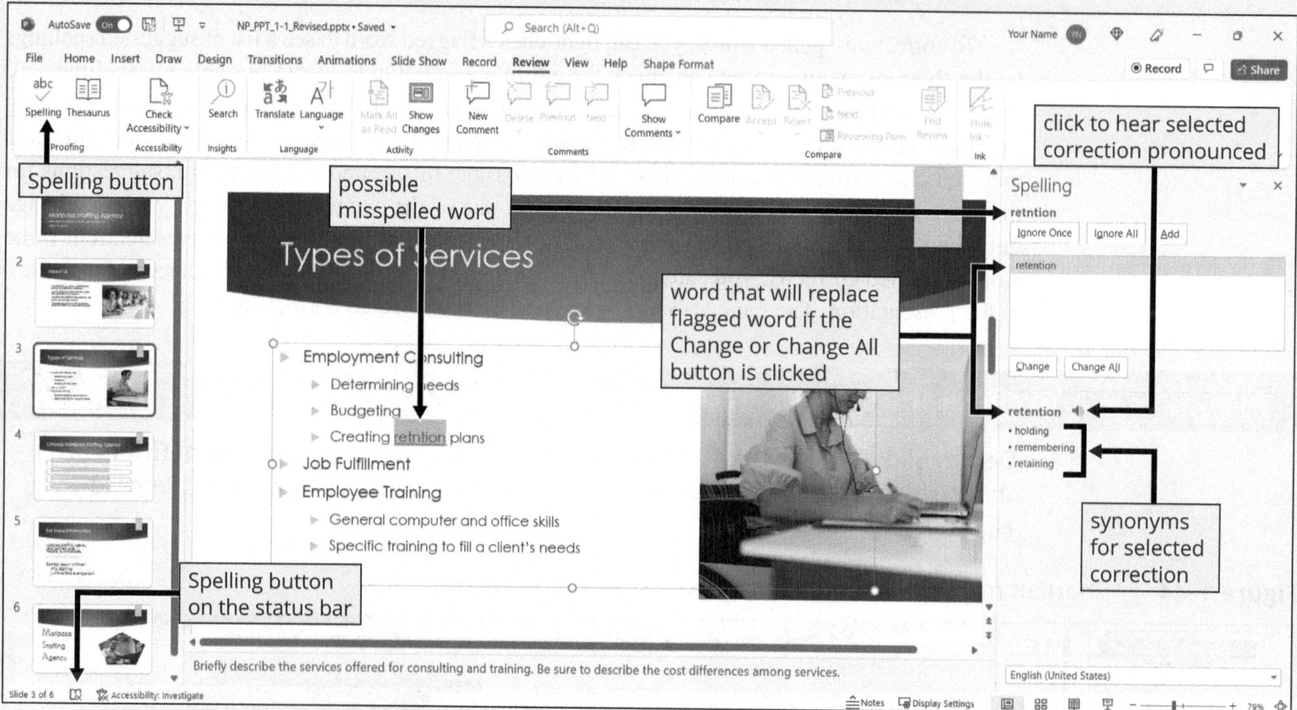

iStock/Ergin Yalcin; FlamingoImages/iStock; jiledesign/iStock

4. In the Spelling pane, click the **speaker** icon. A voice says the word "retention."
5. In the list of suggested corrections, click **retention,** and then click **Change**. The word is corrected, and the next slide containing a possible misspelled word, Slide 5 ("For More Information"), appears with the flagged word, "Jesslyn," selected and listed in the Spelling pane. You want the spell checker to ignore every instance of this word, not just this instance.
7. In the pane, click **Ignore All**. Because that was the last flagged word in the presentation, the Spelling pane closes, and a dialog box opens telling you that the spell check is complete.

> **Trouble?** If the spell checker finds any other misspelled words, correct them.

8. Click **OK**. The dialog box closes.
9. Display Slide 1 (the title slide). Jesslyn's last name no longer has a wavy red line under it because you clicked Ignore All when it was flagged as a possible misspelled word on Slide 5.
10. Save the changes to the presentation.

Running a Slide Show

After you have created and proofed your presentation, you should view it as a slide show to see how it will appear to your audience. You can do this in Slide Show view or in Presenter view.

You can use Slide Show view if your computer has only one monitor and you don't have access to a screen projector. If you have connected your computer to a second monitor or a screen projector, Slide Show view is the way an audience will see your slides. Refer to the Part 1.2 Visual Overview for more information about Slide Show and Presenter views.

In Slide Show and Presenter views, you can move from one slide to another in several ways. Figure 1–46 describes the methods you can use to move from one slide to another during a slide show.

Figure 1–46 Methods of moving from one slide to another during a slide show

Desired Result	Method
To display the next slide	• Press SPACEBAR. • Press ENTER. • Press RIGHT ARROW. • Press DOWN ARROW. • Press PGDN. • Press N. • Click the slide. • In Slide Show view, move the pointer to display the buttons in the lower-left corner of the slide, and then click the Advance to the next animation or slide button. • In Presenter view, click the Advance to the next animation or slide button. • Right-click the slide, and then on the shortcut menu, click Next,
To display the previous slide	• Press BACKSPACE. • Press LEFT ARROW. • Press UP ARROW. • Press PGUP. • Press P. • In Slide Show view, move the pointer to display the buttons in the lower-left corner of the slide, and then click the Return to the previous animation or slide button. • In Presenter view, click the Return to the previous animation or slide button. • Right-click the slide, and then on the shortcut menu, click Previous.
To display a specific slide	• In Slide Show view, move the pointer to display the buttons in the lower-left corner of the slide, click the See all slides button, and then click the thumbnail of the slide you want to display. • In Presenter view, click the See all slides button, and then click the thumbnail of the slide you want to display. • Type the number of the slide you want to display, and then press ENTER. • Right-click the slide, and then on the shortcut menu, click See all slides.
To display the first slide	Press HOME.
To display the last slide	Press END.
To end the slide show	Press ESC. Right-click the slide, and then on the shortcut menu, click End Show.

Jesslyn asks you to review the slide show in Slide Show view to make sure the slides look professional.

To use Slide Show view to view the final presentation:

1. On the Quick Access Toolbar, click the **Start From Beginning** button. Slide 1 appears on the screen in Slide Show view. Now you need to advance the slide show.

   Tip To start the slide show from the current slide, click the Slide Show button on the status bar.

2. Press **SPACEBAR**. Slide 2 ("About Us") appears on the screen.
3. Click the mouse button. The next slide, Slide 3 ("Types of Services"), appears on the screen.
4. Press **BACKSPACE**. The previous slide, Slide 2, appears again.
5. Move the mouse to display the buttons in the lower-left corner of the slide, and then click the **See all slides** button. All of the slides in the file are displayed as thumbnails on the screen, similar to Slide Sorter view.
6. Click the **Slide 5** thumbnail. Slide 5 ("For More Information") appears on the screen.
7. Move the mouse to display the pointer, and then position the pointer on the website address **www.sic.example.com**. The pointer changes to the pointing finger pointer to indicate that this is a link, and the ScreenTip that appears shows the full website address including "http://". If this were a real website, you could click the link to open your web browser and display the website to your audience. Because you moved the pointer, the faint row of buttons appears in the lower-left corner. Refer to Figure 1–47.

Figure 1–47 Link and row of buttons in Slide Show view

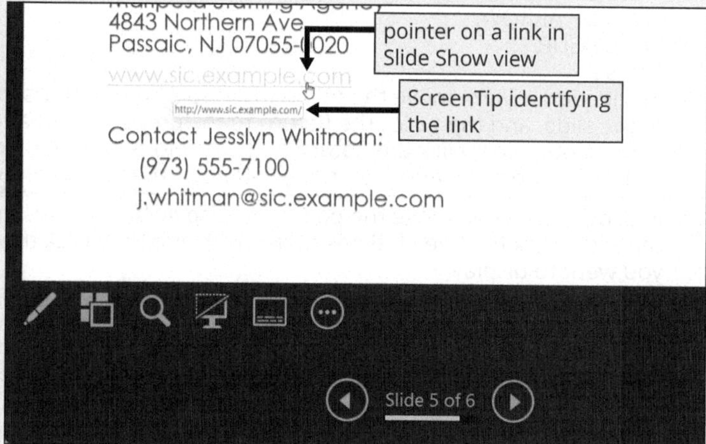

8. Move the pointer again, if necessary, to display the buttons that appear in the lower-left corner of the screen, and then click the **Return to the previous animation or slide** button twice to redisplay Slide 3 ("Types of Services").

   Trouble? If you can't see the buttons at the bottom of the screen, move the pointer to the lower-left corner so it is on top of the first button to darken that button, and then move the pointer to the right to see the rest of the buttons.

9. Display the buttons at the bottom of the screen again, and then click the **Zoom into the slide** button. The pointer changes to the zoom in pointer, and three-quarters of the slide is darkened. Refer to Figure 1–48.

Figure 1–48 Zoom feature activated in Slide Show view

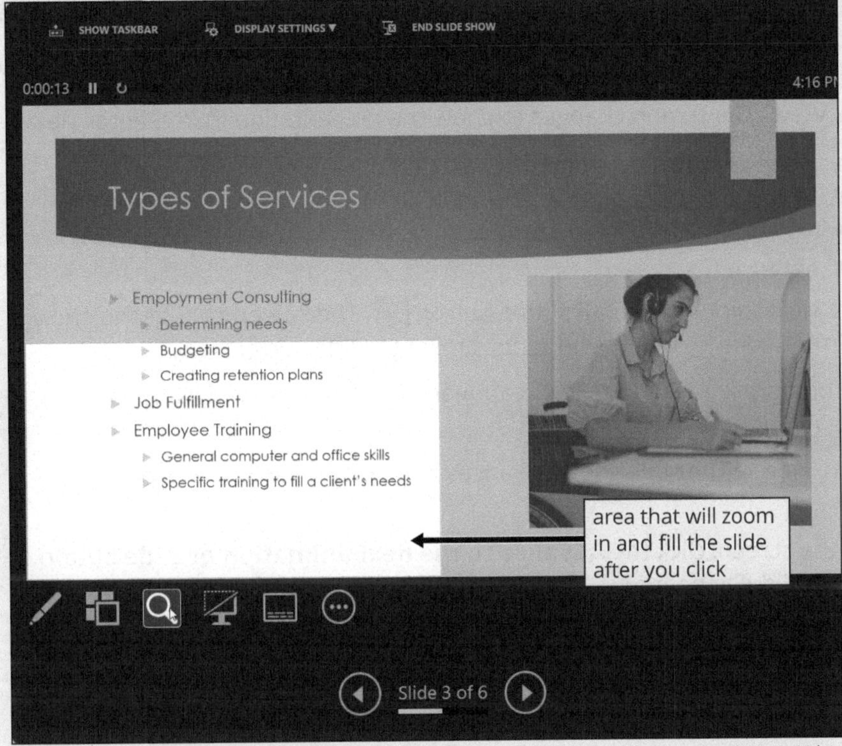

iStock/Ergin Yalcin

10. Move the pointer on top of the picture so that the top part of the picture does not appear darkened, and then click the picture. The slide zooms in so that the part of the slide inside the bright rectangle fills the screen, and the pointer changes to the hand pointer.
11. Press and hold the mouse button to change the pointer to the closed fist pointer, and then drag to the right to pull another part of the zoomed in slide into view.
12. Press **ESC** to zoom back out to see the whole slide.

Presenter view provides additional tools for running a slide show. In addition to seeing the current slide, you can also see the next slide, speaker notes, and a timer showing you how long the slide show has been running. Refer to the Part 1.2 Visual Overview for more information about Presenter view. Because of the additional tools available in Presenter view, you should consider using it if your computer is connected to a second monitor or projector.

If your computer is connected to a projector or second monitor, and you start a slide show in Slide Show view, Presenter view starts on the computer and Slide Show view appears on the second monitor or projection screen. If, for some reason, you don't want to use Presenter view in that circumstance, you can switch to Slide Show view. If you want to practice using Presenter view when your computer is not connected to a second monitor or projector, you can switch to Presenter view from Slide Show view.

Jesslyn wants you to switch to Presenter view and familiarize yourself with the tools available there.

To use Presenter view to review the slide show:

1. Move the pointer to display the buttons in the lower-left corner of the screen, click the **More slide show options** button to open a menu of commands, and then click **Show Presenter View**. The screen changes to show the presentation in Presenter view.

   Tip To display the slide show in Reading view, click the Reading view button on the status bar. To advance through the slide show in Reading view, use the same commands as in Slide Show or Presenter view or click the Next and Previous buttons on the status bar.

2. Below the current slide, click the **See all slides** button. The screen changes to show thumbnails of all the slides in the presentation, similar to Slide Sorter view.
3. Click the **Slide 4** thumbnail. Presenter view reappears, displaying Slide 4 ("Choose Mariposa Staffing Agency") as the current slide.
4. Click anywhere on Slide 4. The slide show advances to display Slide 5 ("For More Information").
5. At the bottom of the screen, click the **Advance to the next animation or slide** button. Slide 6 (the last slide) appears.
6. Click the **More slide show options** button, and then click **Hide Presenter View**. Slide 6 appears in Slide Show view.
7. Press **SPACEBAR**. A black slide appears displaying the text "End of slide show, click to exit."
8. Press **SPACEBAR** again. Presenter view closes, and you return to Normal view.

Proskills

Decision Making: Displaying a Blank Slide During a Presentation

Sometimes during a presentation, the audience has questions about the material and you want to pause the slide show to respond. Or you might want the audience to focus its attention on you instead of on the visuals on the screen. In these cases, you can display a black or white blank slide. Some presenters plan to use blank slides and insert them at specific points during their slide shows. Planning to use a blank slide can help you keep your presentation focused. It can also remind you that the purpose of the PowerPoint slides is to provide visual aids to enhance your presentation; the slides themselves are not the presentation.

If you did not create blank slides in your presentation file, but during your presentation you feel you need to display a blank slide, you can easily do this in Slide Show or Presenter view. To display a blank black slide, press B. To display a blank white slide, press W. You can also click the More slide show options button in Slide Show view, click Screen, and then Black Screen or White Screen. In Presenter view, you can click the More slide show options button, point to Screen, and then click Black Screen or White Screen. Or you can right-click the screen, point to Screen on the menu, and then click Black Screen or White Screen. To remove the black or white slide and redisplay the slide that had been on the screen before you displayed the blank slide, press any key on the keyboard or click anywhere on the screen. In Presenter view, you can also click the Black or unblack slide show button to toggle a blank slide on or off.

Printing a Presentation

Before you deliver your presentation, you might want to print it. PowerPoint provides several printing options. For example, you can print the slides in color, grayscale (white and shades of gray), or pure black and white, and you can print one, some, or all of the slides in several formats.

You use the Print screen in Backstage view to set print options such as specifying a printer and color options. First, you will add your name to the title slide.

To add your name to the title slide and choose a printer and color options:

1. Display Slide 1, click after "Whitman" in the subtitle, press **SPACEBAR**, and then type your name.
2. Click the **File** tab to display Backstage view, and then click **Print** in the navigation pane. Backstage view changes to display the Print screen. The Print screen contains options for printing your presentation, and a preview of the first slide as it will print with the current options. Refer to Figure 1–49.

Figure 1–49 Print screen in Backstage view

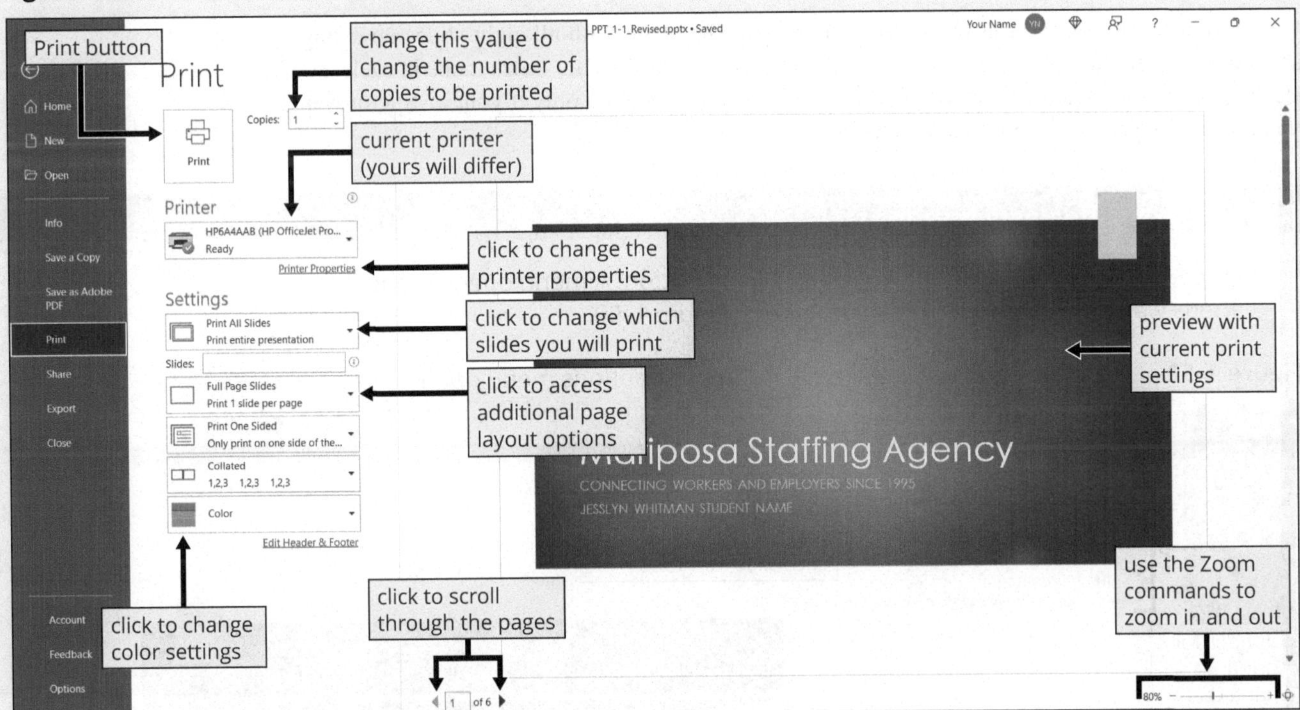

Trouble? If your screen does not match Figure 1–49, click the first button below Settings, click Print All Slides, click the second button below Settings, and then click Full Page Slides.

3. If you are connected to a network or to more than one printer, make sure the printer listed in the Printer box is the one you want to use; if it is not, click the **Printer** button, and then click the correct printer in the list.
4. Click the **Printer Properties** link to open the Properties dialog box for your printer. Usually, the default options are correct, but you can change any printer settings, such as print quality or the paper source, in this dialog box.
5. Click **Cancel** to close the Properties dialog box. Now you can choose whether to print the presentation in color, black and white, or grayscale. If you plan to print in black and white or grayscale, you should change this setting so that you can see what your slides will look like without color and to make sure they are legible.

6. Click the **Color** button, and then click **Grayscale**. The preview changes to grayscale.

> **Tip** To view the presentation in black and white or grayscale in Normal view, click the View tab, and then click the Grayscale button or the Black and White button in the Color/Grayscale group.

7. At the bottom of the preview pane, click the **Next Page** button ▶ twice to display Slide 3 ("Types of Services"). The slides are legible in grayscale.
8. If you will be printing in color, click the **Grayscale** button, and then click **Color**.

In the Settings section on the Print screen, you can click the Full Page Slides button to choose from among several choices for printing the presentation, as described below:

- **Full Page Slides**—Prints each slide full size on a separate piece of paper.
- **Notes Pages**—Prints each slide as a notes page.
- **Outline**—Prints the text of the presentation as an outline.
- **Handouts**—Prints the presentation with one or more slides on each piece of paper. When printing four, six, or nine slides, you can choose whether to order the slides from left to right in rows (horizontally) or from top to bottom in columns (vertically).

Jesslyn wants you to print the slides as a one-page handout, with all eight slides on a single sheet of paper. In the rest of the steps in this section, you can follow the instructions in each set of steps up to the step that tells you to click Print. You should click Print only if your instructor wants you to actually print the presentation in the various formats.

To print the slides as a handout:

1. In the Settings section, click the **Full Page Slides** button. A menu opens listing the various ways you can print the slides. Refer to Figure 1–50.

Figure 1–50 Print screen in Backstage view with print options menu open

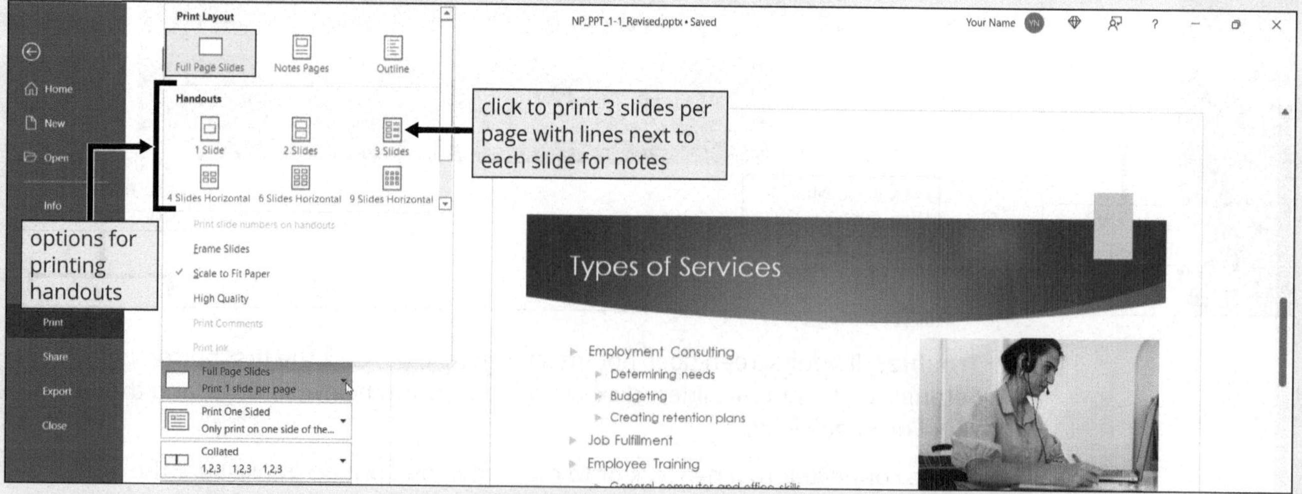

2. In the Handouts section, click **6 Slides Horizontal**. The preview changes to show all six slides in the preview pane, arranged in order horizontally in three rows from left to right. The current date appears in the top-right corner, and a page number appears in the bottom-right corner.
3. At the top of the Print section, click **Print**. Backstage view closes and the handout prints.

Next, Jesslyn wants you to print the title slide as a full-page slide so that he can use it as a cover page for his handouts.

To print the title slide as a full-page slide:

1. Click the **File** tab, and then click **Print** in the navigation pane. The Print screen appears in Backstage view. The preview still shows all six slides on one page. "6 Slides Horizontal" appears on the second button in the Settings section because that was the last printing option you chose.
2. In the Settings section, click **6 Slides Horizontal**, and then click **Full Page Slides**. Slide 1 (the title slide) appears as the preview. Below the preview of Slide 1, it indicates that you are viewing Slide 1 of six slides to print.
3. In the Settings section, click the **Print All Slides** button. Note on the menu that opens that you can print all the slides, selected slides, the current slide, or a custom range. You want to print just the title slide as a full-page slide.
4. Click **Print Current Slide**. Slide 1 appears in the preview pane, and at the bottom, it now indicates that you will print only one slide.
5. Click the **Print** button. Backstage view closes and Slide 1 prints.

Recall that you created speaker notes on Slides 3 and 5. Jesslyn would like you to print these slides as notes pages.

To print the nonsequential slides containing speaker notes:

1. Open the Print screen in Backstage view again, and then click the **Full Page Slides** button. The menu opens.
2. In the Print Layout section of the menu, click **Notes Pages**. The menu closes, and the preview displays Slide 1 as a Notes Page.
3. In the Settings section, click in the **Slides** box, type **3,5** and then click a blank area of the Print screen.
4. Scroll through the preview to confirm that Slides 3 ("Types of Services") and 5 ("For More Information") will print, and then click **Print**. Backstage view closes, and Slides 3 and 5 print as notes pages.

Finally, Jesslyn would like you to print the outline of the presentation. Remember, Slide 6 is designed to be a visual that Jesslyn can leave displayed at the end of the presentation, so you don't need to include it in the outline.

To print Slides 1 through 5 as an outline:

1. Open the Print screen in Backstage view, click the **Notes Pages** button, and then in the Print Layout section, click **Outline**. The text on Slides 3 and 5 appears as an outline in the preview pane.
2. Click in the **Slides** box, type **1–5**, and then click a blank area of the Print screen. Refer to Figure 1–51.

Figure 1–51 Print screen in Backstage view with Slides 1–5 previewed as an outline

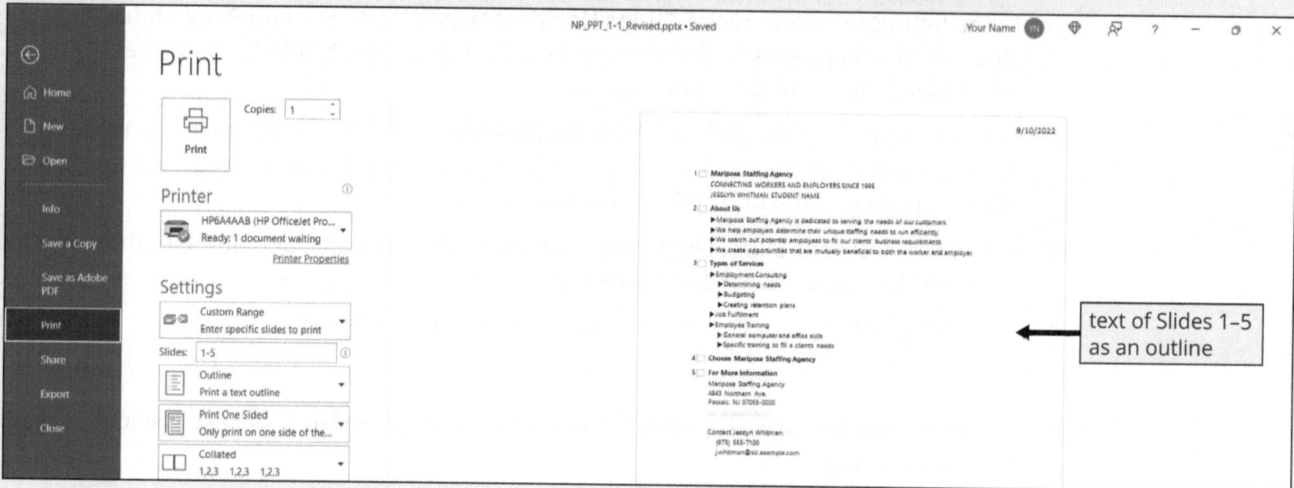

3. At the top of the Print section, click the **Print** button. Backstage view closes, and the text of Slides 1–5 prints.

Closing PowerPoint

When you are finished working with your presentation, you can close PowerPoint. If you only have one presentation open, you click the Close button in the upper-right corner of the program window. If you have more than one presentation open, clicking this button will close only the current presentation; to close PowerPoint, you need to click the Close button in each of the open presentation's windows.

To close PowerPoint:

1. In the upper-right corner of the program window, click the **Close** button. If you do not have autosave enabled, a dialog box opens, asking if you want to save your changes. This is because you did not save the file after you added your name to the title slide.
2. sam In the dialog box, click **Save**. The dialog box closes, the changes are saved, and PowerPoint closes.

> **Trouble?** If any other PowerPoint presentations are still open, click the Close button on each open presentation's program window until no more presentations are open to exit PowerPoint.

In this part, you opened an existing presentation and saved it with a new name, changed the theme, added and cropped photos and adjusted the photo compression, and resized and moved objects. You have also added speaker notes and checked the spelling. Finally, you printed the presentation in several forms and exited PowerPoint. Your work will help Jesslyn give an effective presentation to potential customers of Mariposa Staffing Agency.

Part 1.2 Quick Check

1. What is alt text?
2. Explain what happens when you crop photos.
3. Describe sizing handles.
4. How do you use smart guides?
5. Why is it important to maintain the aspect ratio of photos?
6. How do you convert a list to a SmartArt diagram without using the Design Ideas pane?
7. What is the difference between Slide Show view and Presenter view?
8. List the four formats for printing a presentation.

Practice: Review Assignments

Data Files needed for the Review Assignments: NP_PPT_1-2.pptx, Support_PPT_1_Jesslyn.jpg, Support_PPT_1_Interview.jpg, Support_PPT_1_Meeting.jpg, Support_PPT_1_Strategy.jpg

Jesslyn Whitman, a client manager in the Passaic office of Mariposa Staffing Agency, is preparing a presentation for the upcoming summer company meeting. Because her team has signed so many new clients, she has been asked to give a presentation to the branch managers. She will focus on how they can create new business from their current customers by helping them not just fill openings but helping them budget, create retention plans, and forecast staffing needs. She asks you to begin creating the presentation. Complete the following steps:

1. Start PowerPoint and create a new, blank presentation. On the title slide, type **New Client Leads** as the title, and then type your name as the subtitle. Save the presentation as **NP_PPT_1_Leads** to the drive and folder where you are storing your files.
2. Edit the slide title by typing **Developing** before "New" so that the title is now "Developing New Client Leads."
3. Add a new Slide 2 with the Title and Content layout, type **Contact Your Existing Clients** as the slide title, and then in the content placeholder type the following:
   - **Offer our new plans**
     - **Staffing review**
     - **Compensation study**
     - **Professional development**
   - **Offer competitive package pricing**
   - **Emphasize your personal connection and service**
   - **Contact Jesslyn Whitman**
4. Create a new Slide 3 with the Two Content layout, then create a new Slide 4 with the Two Content layout. On Slide 4, add **Recipe for Success** as the slide title, and then type the following as a numbered list in the left content placeholder:
   1. **Offer new products to existing clients**
   2. **Grow business by expanding beyond local employers**
      1. **Chamber of Commerce**
      2. **Service organizations**
      3. **Professional organizations**
   3. **Offer a variety of customized packages**
5. Create a new Slide 5 using the Title and Content layout, and then create a new Slide 6 with the Title and Content layout. On Slide 6, add **For More Information** as the slide title.
6. Use the Cut and Paste commands to move the last bulleted item on Slide 2 ("Contact Jesslyn Whitman") to Slide 6 as the first bulleted item in the content placeholder.
7. On Slide 6, remove the bullet symbol from the text you pasted, and then add the following as the next two items in the unnumbered list:

   Email: j.whitman@sic.example.com

   Cell: (973) 555-7100
8. Click after "Whitman" in the first item in the list, and then create a new line below it without creating a new item in the list so that there is no extra space above the new line. Type **Client Manager, Passaic Office** on the new line.
9. Remove the link formatting from the email address.
10. Duplicate Slide 2 ("Contact Your Existing Clients"). On the new Slide 3, do the following:
    - Edit the title so it is **Introduce New Products**
    - Edit the first bulleted item so it is **New products**
    - Delete the second and third first-level bulleted items
11. Delete the blank Slides 4 and 6. (**Hint**: note that when you delete Slide 4, the blank Slide 6 to be deleted becomes Slide 5.)
12. Move Slide 3 ("Introduce New Products") so it becomes Slide 2.
13. Change the theme to Basis and choose the fourth variant.
14. Save your changes, and then close the presentation.

15. Open the file **NP_PPT_1-2.pptx**, located in the PowerPoint1 > Review folder included with your Data Files, add your name as the subtitle on the title slide, and then save it as **NP_PPT_1_Updated** to the drive and folder where you are storing your files.
16. Change the theme colors to Green Yellow. Change the theme fonts to Calibri.
17. Change the layout of Slide 3 ("Contact Your Existing Clients") to Two Content.
18. On Slide 3, insert the picture **Support_PPT_1_Interview.jpg**, located in the PowerPoint1 > Review folder. Add **A man in a suit asking questions of the person across from him.** as the alt text for this picture.
19. Open the Design Ideas pane if necessary, and then click several of the suggested layouts. When you are finished, close the pane, and then on the Quick Access Toolbar, click the Undo button to reset the slide, and then close the Design Ideas pane.
20. Resize the picture on Slide 3 while maintaining the aspect ratio so that the picture height is 4 inches. Reposition the picture so that its right edge aligns with the inside border of the right edge of the slide and its top edge aligns with the top edge of the text box containing the list.
21. Change the layout of Slide 4 ("Create Custom Packages") to Title and Content.
22. On Slide 4, insert the photo **Support_PPT_1_Strategy.jpg**, located in the PowerPoint1 > Review folder. Add **A group of young, casually dressed people in an office using differently colored squares to plan a strategy.** as the alt text for this picture.
23. Resize the picture on Slide 4 while maintaining the aspect ratio so that the picture height is 4 inches. Reposition the picture so that its right edge aligns with the inside border of the right edge of the slide and its top edge aligns with the 1-inch mark on the vertical ruler.
24. On Slide 5, insert the photo **Support_PPT_1_Meeting.jpg**, located in the PowerPoint1 > Review folder. Add **A group of business people sitting at a table having a meeting.** as the alt text for this picture.
25. Resize the picture on Slide 5 while maintaining the aspect ratio so that the picture height is 5 inches.
26. Display the rulers and the gridlines, and then crop 1 inch off the bottom of the picture on Slide 5 and ½ inch off of the top of the picture. Resize the cropped part of the picture so that the width if approximately 6.75 inches.
27. Reposition the picture on Slide 5 so that its right edge aligns with the 6-inch mark on the horizontal ruler, and its top edge aligns with the –.5-inch mark on the vertical ruler.
28. On Slide 4, change the width of the text box containing the bulleted list by dragging the sizing handle in the middle of the right border of the text box so that the right border aligns with the gridline at the 0-inch mark on the horizontal ruler. Then change the height of the text box by dragging the sizing handle in the middle of the top border down so that the top of the text box aligns with the top of the picture.
29. On Slide 6 ("Recipe for Success"), open the Design Ideas pane and click several of the suggested layouts. Then, on the Quick Access Toolbar, click the Undo button and close the Design Ideas pane.
30. On Slide 6, convert the numbered list to SmartArt using the Basic Matrix layout on the Convert to SmartArt menu.
31. On Slide 6, change the SmartArt layout to the Linear Venn layout.
32. On Slide 6, display the Notes pane, and then type **Some local organizations to consider are the Chamber of Commerce, service organizations, and professional organizations.** as a speaker note. When you are finished, close the Notes pane.
33. On Slide 7 ("For More Information"), increase the size of the text in the unnumbered list to 24 points. Then, in the first bulleted item, select the text "Jesslyn Whitman." and format it as bold and 28 points.
34. On Slide 7, insert the picture **Support_PPT_1_Jesslyn.jpg**, and then **Headshot of Jesslyn Whitman** as the alt text for this picture.
35. Crop the photo to the Oval shape. Reposition the picture so that the top of the picture aligns with the top of the text box, if necessary.
36. Hide the rulers and gridlines.
37. Compress all the photos in the slides to E-mail (96 ppi) and delete cropped areas of pictures.
38. Add your name as an author property, and add **Mariposa Staffing Agency** as the Company property.
39. Check the spelling in the presentation. Correct the spelling error on Slide 2 by selecting "forecasting" as the correct spelling, and the error on Slide 3 by selecting "Emphasize" as the correct spelling. Ignore all instances of Jesslyn's last name. If you made any additional spelling errors, correct them as well. If your name on Slide 1 is flagged as misspelled, ignore this error. Save the changes to the presentation.

40. Review the slide show in Slide Show and Presenter views.
41. View the slides in grayscale, and then print the following in color or in grayscale depending on your printer: the title slide as a full-page-sized slide; Slides 2 through 7 as a handout on a single piece of paper with the slides in order horizontally; Slide 6 as a notes page; and Slides 2 through 5 and Slide 7 as an outline. Save and close the presentation and PowerPoint when you are finished.

Apply: Case Problem 1

Data Files needed for this Case Problem: NP_PPT_1-3.pptx, Support_PPT_1_Application.jpg, Support_PPT_1_Building.jpg, Support_PPT_1_Key.jpg, Support_PPT_1_Sophia.jpg

Upper Coast Bank Upper Coast Bank has branches all over the United States. Sophia Baker, the vice president of residential lending at the Hartford, Connecticut branch, hired you as her executive assistant. Sophia wants to create a simple presentation that will help her explain some of the details about applying for a mortgage to first-time home buyers. She asks you to help complete the slides. Complete the following steps:

1. Open the presentation named **NP_PPT_1-3.pptx**, located in the PowerPoint1 > Case1 folder included with your Data Files, and then save it as **NP_PPT_1_Mortgage** to the drive and folder where you are storing your files.
2. Insert a new slide with the Title Slide layout. Add **Mortgage Essentials** as the presentation title on the title slide. In the subtitle text placeholder, type your name. Move this slide so it is the first slide in the presentation.
3. Apply the Frame theme, and then apply the third theme variant.
4. Change the theme fonts to Garamond-TrebuchetMS.
5. On Slide 1 (the title slide), change the font size of the title text to 36 points. Then resize the title text box so it is 2.25 inches wide. If necessary, reposition the title text box so that the left edge of the text box is aligned with the left edge of the subtitle text box and so that there is the same amount of space between the top of the text box and the top slide edge as there is between the bottom of the subtitle text box and the bottom of the slide. Resize the subtitle text box so it is 3.3 inches wide, and then align its left edge with the left edge of the title text box.
6. On Slide 1, insert the picture **Support_PPT_1_Application.jpg**, located in the PowerPoint1 > Case1 folder. Add **Picture of a mortgage application form with a red "Approved" stamp on it and the wooden stamp next to it.** as the alt text.
7. On Slide 1, resize the photo, maintaining the aspect ratio, so that it is 5.84 inches high. Position the photo so that its middle aligns with the middle of the tan rectangle and its right edge aligns with the right edge of the slide.
8. On Slides 2 through 6, increase the size of the text in the bulleted list so the first-level items are 24 points and any second-level items are 20 points.
9. On Slide 4 ("What Are Closing Costs?"), cut the last bulleted item ("$200,000 loan"), and then paste it in on Slide 3 ("What Are Points?") as the third bulleted item. If a blank line is added below the pasted text, delete it.
10. On Slide 3, add the following as second-level items below "$200,000 loan," adjusting the font size to 20 points if necessary:

    2 points (2%) = $4,000

    3 points (3%) = $6,000
11. On Slide 2 ("Steps"), convert the bulleted list to SmartArt using the Step Down Process layout. (**Hint**: You need to click More SmartArt Graphics to open the Choose a SmartArt Graphic dialog box.)
12. On Slide 5 ("Documents Needed"), change the layout to Two Content, then insert the picture **Support_PPT_1_Key.jpg**, located in the PowerPoint1 > Case1 folder. Add **Drawing of a hand passing an approved mortgage towards another person's hand holding a key on a key chain shaped like a house.** as the alt text.
13. On Slide 5, resize the picture, maintaining the aspect ratio, so that it is 4.5 inches square, and then position it so that its middle aligns with the middle of the text box containing the bulleted list and its right edge aligns with the left edge of the gray rectangle on the right side of the slide.

(**Hint**: Position the picture as close as possible to the edge of the gray rectangle. Then with the picture selected, press RIGHT ARROW or LEFT ARROW to nudge it into the correct position.)

14. On Slide 5, in the last bulleted item, format "and" with italics. Enter **Make sure applicants understand that they need two forms of ID.** as a speaker note, and then close the Notes pane.
15. On Slide 6 ("Contact Information"), remove the link formatting from both the email address and the Internet address of the Mortgages page for the bank.
16. On Slide 6, click before the word "Contact" in the slide title, and then press ENTER three times. Insert the photo **Support_PPT_1_Sophia.jpg**, located in the PowerPoint1 > Case1 folder. Add **Portrait of smiling Sophia Baker.** as the alt text.
17. On Slide 6, crop 1.5 inches off the bottom of the picture, then crop the photo to the Rectangle: Rounded Corners shape.
18. On Slide 6, resize the photo so it is 2.8 inches high, maintaining the aspect ratio. Reposition the photo in the tan rectangle above the title so that the vertical smart guide that appears shows that the photo aligns with the center of the tan rectangle, and the bottom of the photo aligns with the middle of the slide.
19. Add a new Slide 7 with the Content with Caption layout. In the title text placeholder, type **Upper**, and then create a new line without creating a new paragraph. Type **Coast** on the new line, create another new line, and then type **Bank**. In the text placeholder below the title, type **The Friendly Bank**.
20. On Slide 7, change the size of the title text to 48 points and bold, and change its color to Brown, Accent 1, Darker 50%. Change the size of the text below the title to 24 points and make it italic.
21. On Slide 7, add the picture **Support_PPT_1_Building.jpg**, located in the PowerPoint1 > Case1 folder. Add **Photo of Upper Coast Bank building.** as the alt text.
22. Compress all the photos in the presentation to E-mail (96 ppi) and delete cropped portions of photos.
23. Add your name as an author property and add **Upper Coast Bank** as the Company property.
24. Check the spelling in the presentation and correct all misspelled words.
25. Save the changes to the presentation, view the slide show in Presenter view, and then print Slides 1–6 as a handout using the 6 Slides Horizontal arrangement, and print Slide 5 as a notes page.
26. Close the presentation and PowerPoint.

Create: Case Problem 2

Data Files needed for this Case Problem: Support_PPT_1_GreenSalad.jpg, Support_PPT_1_ChickenSoup.jpg, Support_PPT_1_Pasta.jpg, Support_PPT_1_PokeBowl.jpg, Support_PPT_1_Pizza.jpg

Jumpstart Advertising Jericho Goldblum is an associate account executive at FoodFest meal delivery service and catering company in Richmond, Virginia. Jericho has hired you as a marketing intern. He needs a presentation that shows recent meals the service has provided. Jericho has started a presentation but asks you to finish it. The completed presentation is shown in Figure 1–52. Refer to Figure 1–52 as you complete the following steps:

1. Create a new, blank PowerPoint presentation. Save it as **NP_PPT_1_FoodFest** to the drive and folder where you are storing your files. Add your name as the subtitle on Slide 1.
2. The theme is the Gallery theme with the first variant.
3. Slide 2 has the Title and Content layout applied. Slides 3 through 8 have the Content with Caption layout applied.
4. On Slides 3 through 8, the text placeholders below the title text are deleted. The title text boxes on Slides 3 through 8 are repositioned so that their tops and edges are aligned with the red line. The font in the text boxes is set at 36 point, and center-aligned.
5. On Slide 2, the text box containing the bulleted list is resized so that the bottom of the text box aligns with the gridlines at the negative 2-inch mark on the vertical ruler and the top aligns with the red line under the title text box. The first-level items are 28 points, and the second-level items are 24 points.
6. The pictures on Slides 3 through 7 are all located in the PowerPoint1 > Case2 folder included with your Data Files. Each photo is resized so that it is 5 inches high. The pictures on slides 4, 5, and 7 have been cropped approximately ½ inch on the left and right sides. Add the alt text as shown in Figure 1–52.

Figure 1–52 FoodFest presentation

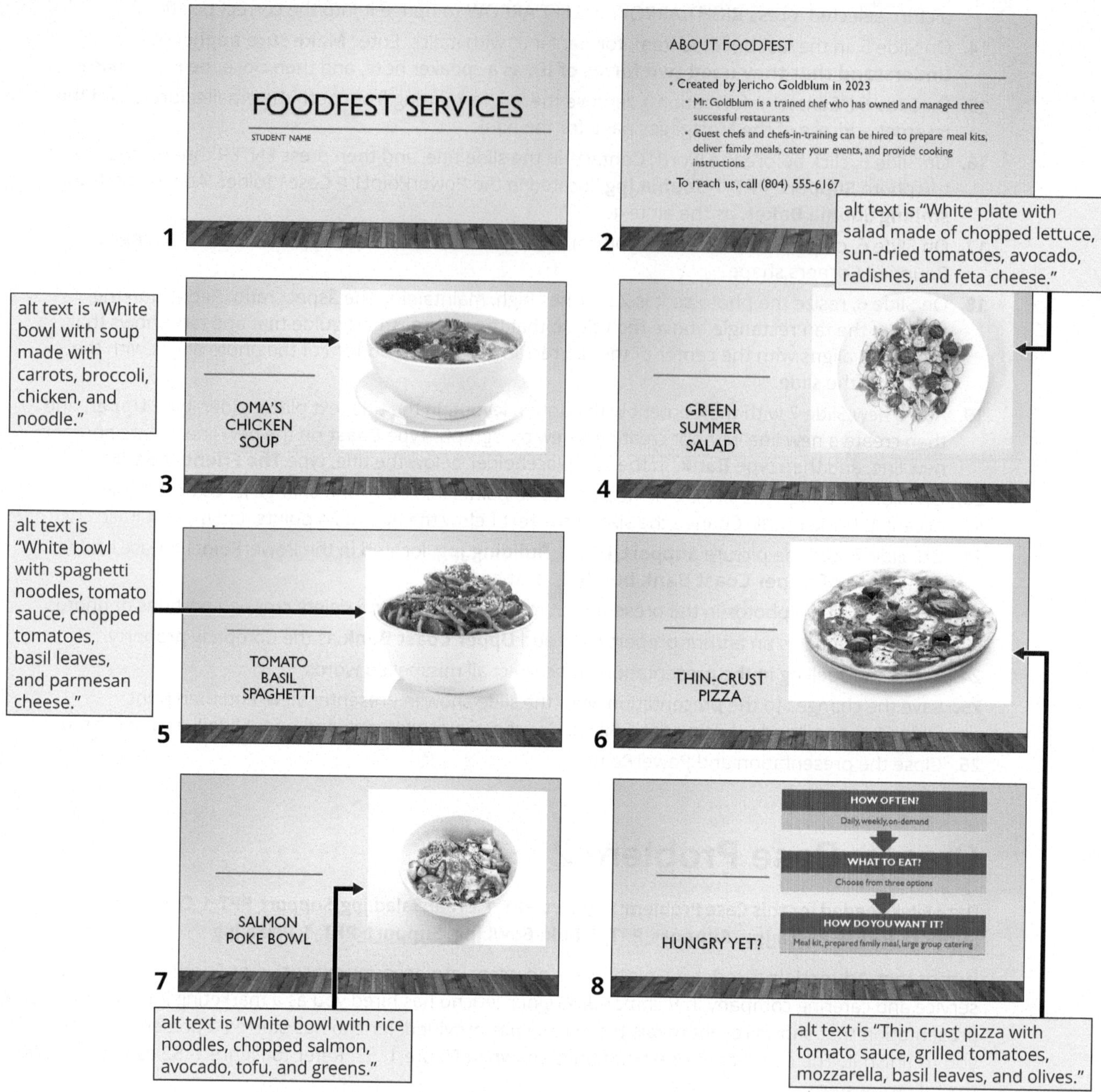

iStock/stockstudioX, iStock/jenifoto, iStock/gbh007, iStock/Ryzhkov, iStock/Ryzhkov,

7. The right edges of the pictures on Slides 3 through 7 are aligned with the gridline at the 6-inch mark on the horizontal ruler. The tops of the pictures are aligned with the 3-inch mark on the vertical ruler.
8. Compress all the photos in the presentation to E-mail (96 ppi).
9. On Slide 8 ("HUNGRY YET?"), type the text in the SmartArt as a bulleted list. Each uppercase question is a first-level item, and each sentence-case phrase is a second-level item. The SmartArt layout is Segmented Process. All the first-level text is 22 points and the second-level text is 20 points. The first-level items (the words in the dark red boxes) are bold. The second-level items are Red, Accent 1, Darker 25%. (**Hint**: Change the color of the text in the second-level items after you convert the list to a SmartArt graphic.)
10. Save the changes to the presentation, and then view the presentation in Slide Show view.
11. Close the presentation and PowerPoint.

Adding Media and Special Effects

Using Media in a Presentation for a Parks and Recreation Department

Case: Fort Erie Parks and Recreation Department

Antónia Romão is the assistant director at the Fort Erie Parks and Recreation Department in Fort Erie, Ontario. Her responsibilities include securing funding from local businesses for new services or recreation areas and recruit volunteers. Antónia is putting together a presentation to promote the current services and parks to potential donors and volunteers who work and live in the Fort Erie area. Antónia prepared the text of a PowerPoint presentation, and she wants you to add photos and other features to make the presentation more interesting and compelling.

In this module, you will modify a presentation that highlights the varied recreation opportunities and parks under the control of the department. You will add formatting and special effects to photos and shapes; create a table; insert symbols; add footer and header information to slides, notes, and handouts; add transitions and animations to slides; and add and modify video.

Starting Data Files

NP_PPT_2-1.pptx
Support_PPT_2_Basketball.jpg
Support_PPT_2_Festival.jpg
Support_PPT_2_Pickleball.jpg
Support_PPT_2_Slide.mp4
Support_PPT_2_Softball.jpg
Support_PPT_2_Swimming.jpg
Support_PPT_2_Theme.pptx
NP_PPT_2-2.pptx
Support_PPT_2_Adoption.jpg
Support_PPT_2_NewTheme.pptx
Support_PPT_2_Cleanup.jpg
Support_PPT_2_Coach.jpg
Support_PPT_2_Volunteer.mp4
NP_PPT_2-3.pptx
Support_PPT_2_Calendar.jpg
Support_PPT_2_Cornucopia.jpg
Support_PPT_2_Fourth.jpg
Support_PPT_2_Labor.png
Support_PPT_2_Logo.pptx
Support_PPT_2_Memorial.jpg
Support_PPT_2_NewYear.jpg
Support_PPT_2_Sayings.mp4
Support_PPT_2_Sixty.png
NP_PPT_2-4.pptx
Support_PPT_2_Catering.jpg
Support_PPT_2_Cooking.jpg
Support_PPT_2_Lessons.jpg
Support_PPT_2_Meals.jpg

Objectives

Part 2.1

- Apply a theme used in another presentation
- Insert shapes
- Format shapes and pictures
- Duplicate objects
- Rotate and flip objects
- Create a table
- Modify and format a table
- Insert symbols
- Add footers and headers

Part 2.2

- Apply and modify transitions
- Animate objects and lists
- Change how an animation starts
- Use the Morph transition
- Add video and modify playback options
- Trim video and set a poster frame
- Understand animation effects applied to videos
- Compress media

Part 2.1 Visual Overview: Formatting Graphics

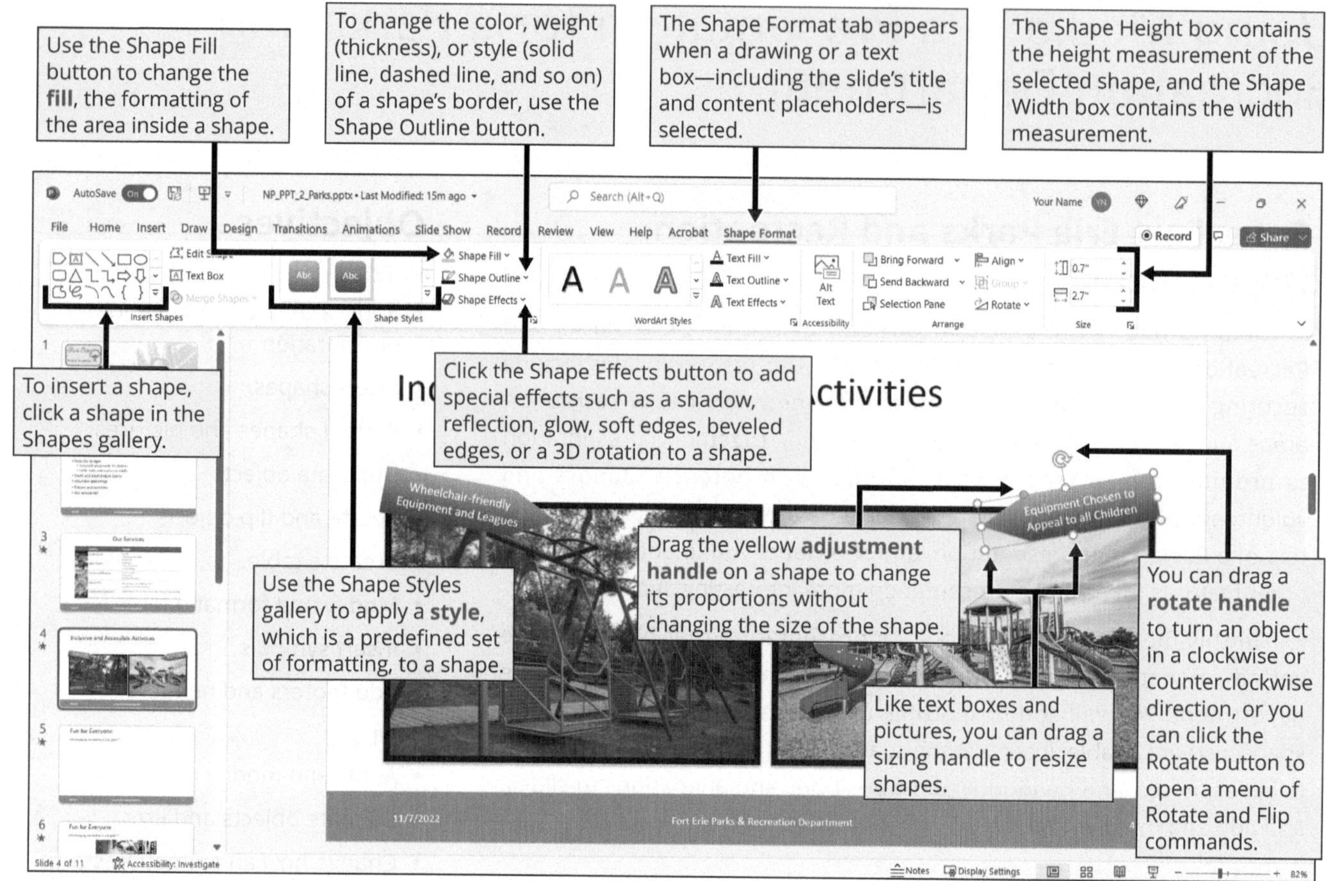
Use the Shape Fill button to change the **fill**, the formatting of the area inside a shape.
To change the color, weight (thickness), or style (solid line, dashed line, and so on) of a shape's border, use the Shape Outline button.
The Shape Format tab appears when a drawing or a text box—including the slide's title and content placeholders—is selected.
The Shape Height box contains the height measurement of the selected shape, and the Shape Width box contains the width measurement.
To insert a shape, click a shape in the Shapes gallery.
Click the Shape Effects button to add special effects such as a shadow, reflection, glow, soft edges, beveled edges, or a 3D rotation to a shape.
Use the Shape Styles gallery to apply a **style**, which is a predefined set of formatting, to a shape.
Drag the yellow **adjustment handle** on a shape to change its proportions without changing the size of the shape.
Like text boxes and pictures, you can drag a sizing handle to resize shapes.
You can drag a **rotate handle** to turn an object in a clockwise or counterclockwise direction, or you can click the Rotate button to open a menu of Rotate and Flip commands.
AutoSave
NP_PPT_2_Parks.pptx • Last Modified: 15m ago
Search (Alt+Q)
Your Name
File
Home
Insert
Draw
Design
Transitions
Animations
Slide Show
Record
Review
View
Help
Acrobat
Shape Format
Record
Share
Edit Shape
Text Box
Merge Shapes
Insert Shapes
Shape Fill
Shape Outline
Shape Effects
Shape Styles
Text Fill
Text Outline
Text Effects
WordArt Styles
Alt Text
Accessibility
Bring Forward
Send Backward
Selection Pane
Align
Group
Rotate
Arrange
0.7"
2.7"
Size
Wheelchair-friendly Equipment and Leagues
Equipment Chosen to Appeal to all Children
11/7/2022
Fort Erie Parks & Recreation Department
Slide 4 of 11
Accessibility: Investigate
Notes
Display Settings
82%

istock.com/Thomas Bullock; istock.com/ilkercelik; istock.com/fundamental rights; istock.com/CandyRetriever; istock.com/maroke; istock.com/FatCamera

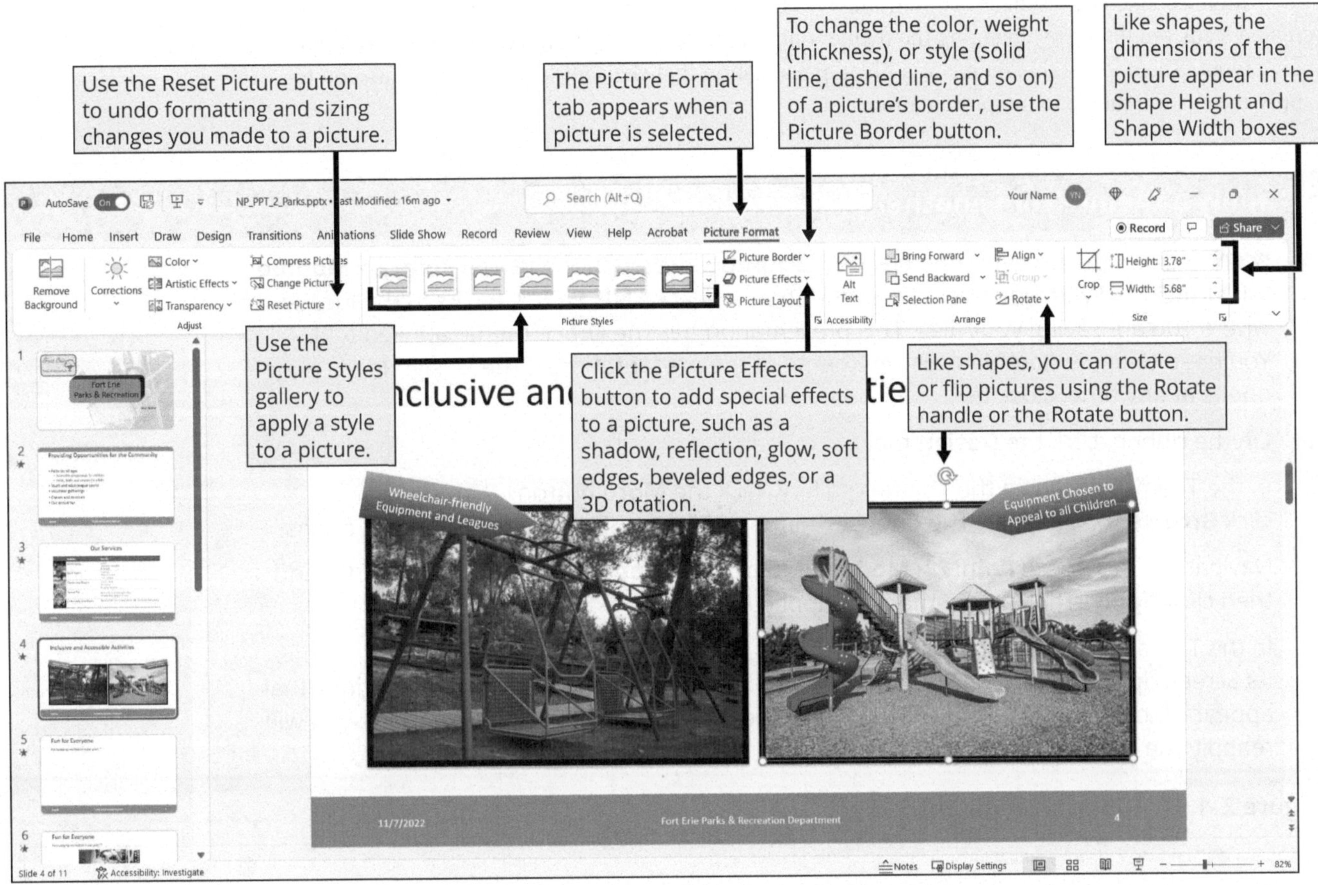
Use the Reset Picture button to undo formatting and sizing changes you made to a picture.
The Picture Format tab appears when a picture is selected.
To change the color, weight (thickness), or style (solid line, dashed line, and so on) of a picture's border, use the Picture Border button.
Like shapes, the dimensions of the picture appear in the Shape Height and Shape Width boxes
Use the Picture Styles gallery to apply a style to a picture.
Click the Picture Effects button to add special effects to a picture, such as a shadow, reflection, glow, soft edges, beveled edges, or a 3D rotation.
Like shapes, you can rotate or flip pictures using the Rotate handle or the Rotate button.
Wheelchair-friendly Equipment and Leagues
Equipment Chosen to Appeal to all Children

istock.com/Moshe Einhorn; istock.com/ilkercelik; istock.com/fundamental rights; istock.com/CandyRetriever; istock.com/maroke; istock.com/FatCamera

Applying a Theme Used in Another Presentation

As you learned earlier, you can apply an installed theme by clicking an option in the Themes group on the Design tab. An installed theme is a special type of file that is stored with PowerPoint program files. You can also apply themes that are applied to any other presentation stored on your computer. For example, many companies want to promote their brand through their presentations, so they hire presentation design professionals to create custom themes employees can apply to all company presentations.

Antónia created a presentation describing Fort Erie Parks and Recreation Department. She also created a custom theme by changing the theme fonts and colors, modifying layouts, and creating a new layout. She applied this theme to a blank presentation that she sent to you. She wants you to apply the custom theme to the presentation.

To apply a theme from another presentation:

1. **sam** Open the presentation **NP_PPT_2-1.pptx**, located in the **PowerPoint2 > Module** folder included with your Data Files, and then save it as **NP_PPT_2_Parks** in the location where you are saving your files. This presentation has the Office theme applied to it. You need to apply Antónia's custom theme to the presentation. If the Design Ideas pane opens at any time, close it.
2. On the ribbon, click the **Design** tab.
3. In the Themes group, in the Themes gallery, click the **More** button, and then click **Browse for Themes**. The Choose Theme or Themed Document dialog box opens.
4. Navigate to the **PowerPoint2 > Module** folder, click **Support_PPT_2_ Theme.pptx**, and then click **Apply**. The custom theme is applied.
5. In the Themes group, point to the first theme in the gallery, which is the current theme. Its ScreenTip identifies it as Support_PPT_2_Theme. Refer to Figure 2-1. The options that appear in the Variants group are the Office theme variants. If you click a variant, you will reapply the Office theme with the variant you selected.

Figure 2-1 Custom theme applied

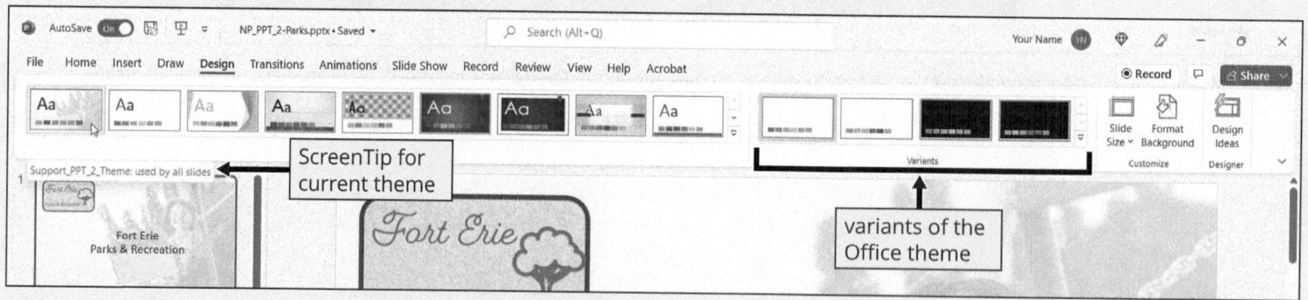

istock.com/ilkercelik

After you apply a custom theme, you might need to adjust some of the slides in the presentation. You will check the slides now.

6. Click the **Home** tab, and then on Slide 1 (the title slide), click **Fort Erie Parks & Recreation**, the title text.
7. In the Font group, click the **Font arrow**. Notice that Calibri is the theme font for both the headings and the body text.
8. In the Slides group, click the **Layout button**. The Layout gallery appears. The custom layouts that Antónia created are listed in the gallery, as shown in Figure 2-2.

Figure 2–2 Custom layouts in the custom theme

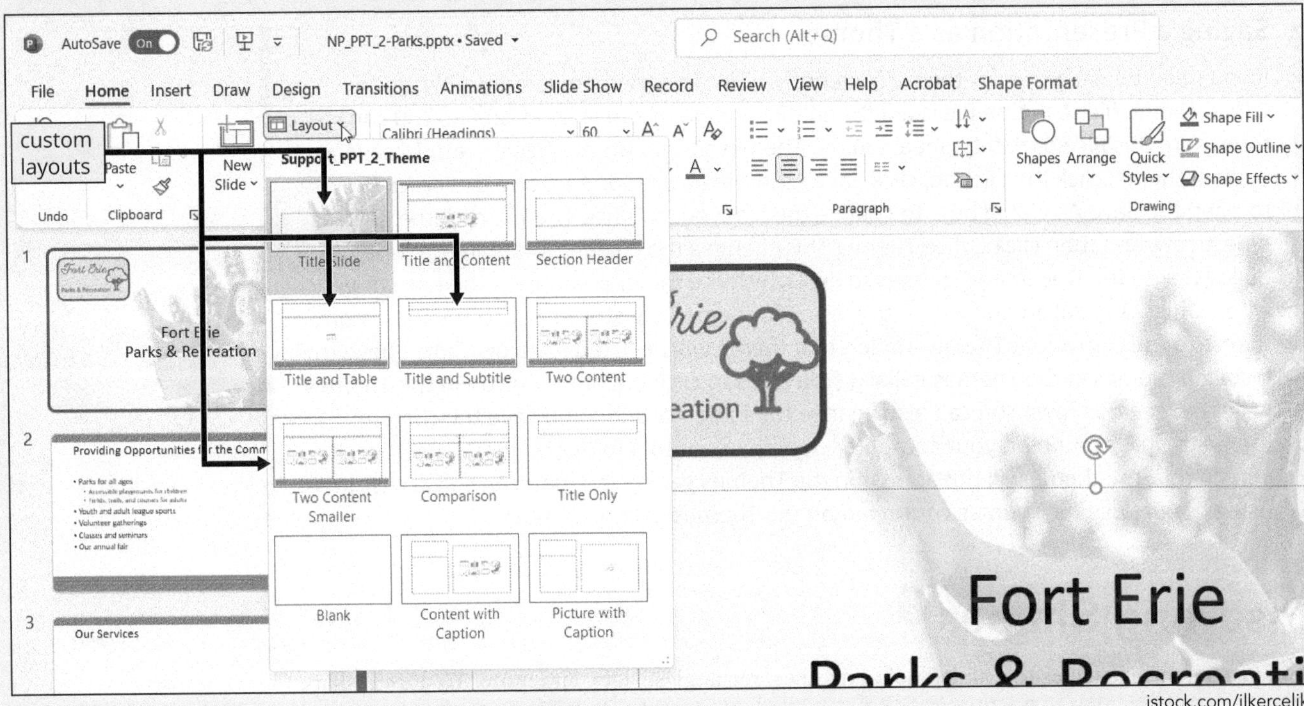

istock.com/ilkercelik

9. Press **ESC** to close the Layout gallery.

When you applied the custom theme, the title slide and the slides with the Title and Content and Two Content layouts were changed to use the customized versions of these layouts. Antónia wants you to change the layout of Slide 3 to the custom Title and Table layout, change the layout of Slide 5 to the custom Title and Subtitle layout, and then add the department's slogan on Slide 5. You will also examine the other slides to make sure they are formatted correctly with the custom theme applied.

To examine the slides and apply custom layouts to Slides 3, 5, and 6:

1. Display Slide 2 ("Providing Opportunities for the Community"). Slide 2 looks fine.
2. Display Slide 3 ("Our Services"). You need to apply a custom layout to this slide.
3. In the Slides group, click the **Layout** button, and then click the **Title and Table** layout. The custom layout is applied to Slide 3.
4. Display Slide 4 ("Inclusive and Accessible Activities"). Applying the custom theme caused the picture on the right to resize. To fix it, click the picture on the right (the slide picture), click the Picture Format tab, then in the Size group, type 3.78 in the Height box, then press Enter. Move the resized picture so that its top and bottom align with the picture of the swings, and the pictures are separated by approximately one-quarter inch
5. Display Slide 5 ("Fun for Everyone"), and then apply the **Title and Subtitle** layout to it.
6. On Slide 5, click in the subtitle text placeholder, and then type **Encouraging recreation is our goal.** (including the period).
7. Display Slide 6 ("Contact Us for More Information"). With the custom theme applied, the email address in the last bulleted item does not fit on one line.
8. Apply the **Two Content Smaller** layout to Slide 6. The layout is applied, and the text in the bulleted list changes to 24 points. The email address now fits on one line.
9. Save your changes if necessary.

Insight

Saving a Presentation as a Theme

If you need to use a custom theme frequently, you can save a presentation file as an Office Theme file. A theme file is a different file type than a presentation file. You can then store this file so that it appears in the Themes gallery on the Design tab. To save a custom theme, click the File tab, click Save As in the navigation bar, and then click Browse to open the Save As dialog box. To change the file type to Office Theme, click the Save as type arrow, and then click Office Theme. This changes the current folder in the Save As dialog box to the Document Themes folder, which is a folder created on the hard drive when Office is installed and where the installed themes are stored. If you save a custom theme to the Document Themes folder, that theme will be listed in its own row above the installed themes in the Themes gallery. (You need to click the More button in the Themes gallery to see this row.) You can also change the folder location and save the custom theme to any location on your computer or network or to a folder on your OneDrive. If you do this, the theme will not appear in the Themes gallery, but you can still access it using the Browse for Themes command on the Themes gallery menu.

Inserting Shapes

You can add many shapes to a slide, including lines, rectangles, stars, and more. To draw a shape, click the Shapes button in the Illustrations group on the Insert tab, click a shape in the gallery, and then click on the slide to draw a shape at the default size of about one inch wide, or click and drag to draw the shape the size you want. Like any object, you can resize a shape after you insert it.

You've already had a little experience with one shape—a text box, which is a shape specifically designed to contain text. You can add additional text boxes to slides using the Text Box shape. You can also add text to any shape you place on a slide.

Antónia wants you to add a label describing one of the photos on Slide 4. You will do this with an arrow shape.

To insert an arrow shape on Slide 4 and add text to it:

1. Display Slide 4 ("Inclusive and Accessible Activities").
2. Click the **Insert** tab, and then in the Illustrations group, click the **Shapes** button. The Shapes gallery expands. Refer to Figure 2–3. In addition to the Recently Used Shapes group at the top, the gallery is organized into ten categories of shapes.

Figure 2–3 Shapes gallery

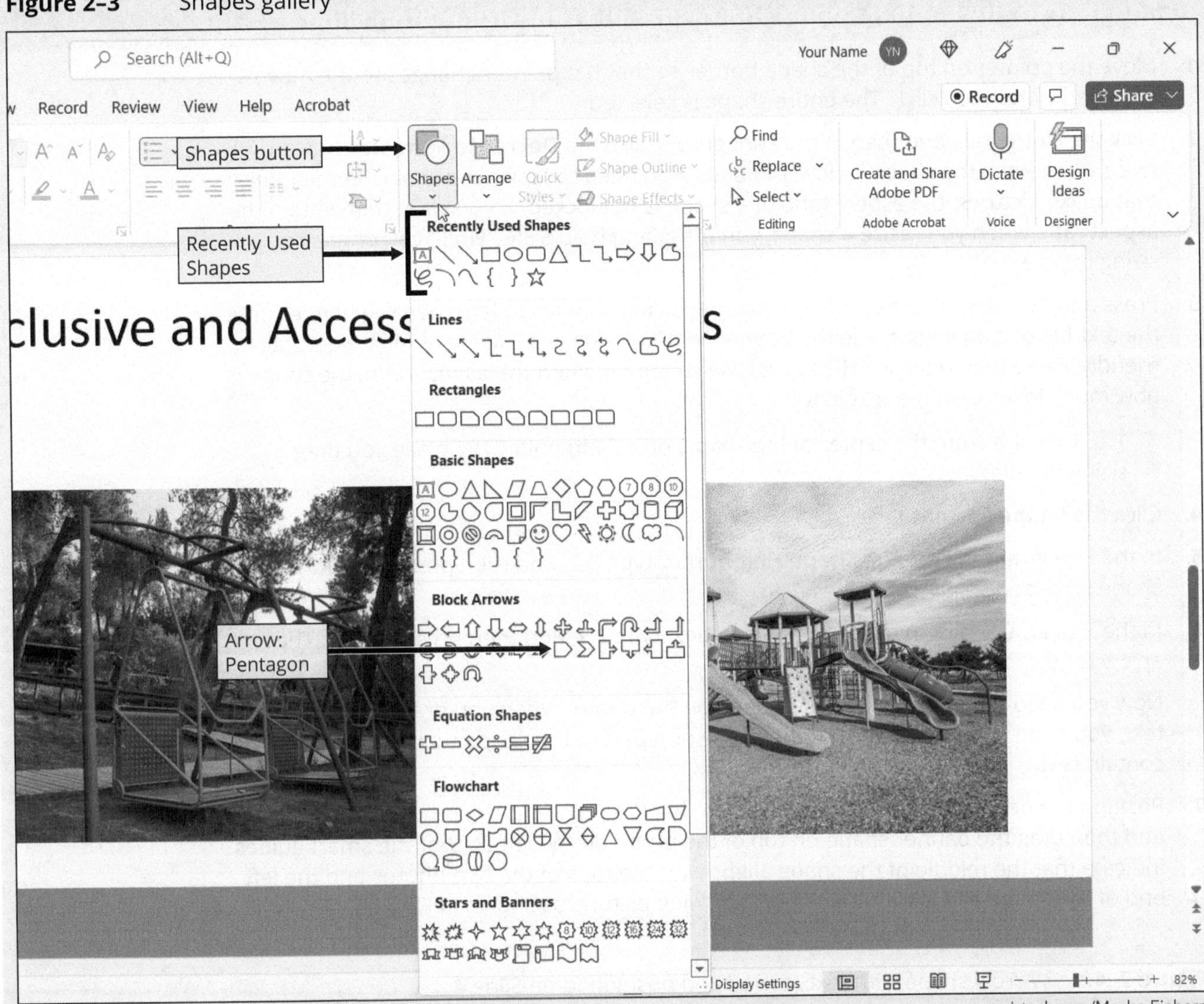

istock.com/Moshe Einhorn

3. Under Block Arrows, click the **Arrow: Pentagon** shape. The gallery closes and the pointer changes to the thin cross pointer.

   Tip You can also insert a shape using the Shapes gallery in the Drawing group on the Home tab.

4. On the slide, click above the photo on the left and below the word "Inclusive" in the title. An orange arrow, approximately one half inch by one inch, appears. (Don't worry about the exact placement of the arrow; you will move it later.) The Shape Format tab is the active tab on the ribbon.
5. With the shape selected, type **Wheelchair-friendly Equipment and Leagues** in the arrow. The text you type appears in the arrow, but it does not all fit.

Next you need to resize the shape to fit the text. Then you will move the arrow to a new position on the slide.

To add text to the banner shape and resize and reposition it on Slide 4:

1. Move the pointer on top of the shape border so that the pointer changes to the move pointer, and then click. The entire shape is selected.
2. Click the **Home** tab, and then in the Font group, click the **Decrease Font Size** button twice. The text in the shape is now 14 points. You need to resize the shape. Remember that unlike pictures, the aspect ratio of a shape is not locked. If you want to maintain the aspect ratio when you resize a shape, you press and hold SHIFT while you drag a corner sizing handle.
3. Press and hold **SHIFT**, drag one of the corner sizing handles to lengthen the banner until the text fits on two lines inside the banner (with the first line ending after "Wheelchair-friendly"), and then release **SHIFT**. Because you maintained the aspect ratio, the shape is now much taller than the text in it.

   Tip To resize from the center of the shape, press and hold CTRL while you drag a sizing handle.

4. Click the **Shape Format** tab.
5. In the Size group, click in the **Shape Height** box, type **0.7**, and then press **ENTER**. The shape is resized so it is 0.7 inches high.
6. In the Size group, click in the **Shape Width** box, type **2.7**, and then press **ENTER**. The arrow is now exactly 2.7 inches long.

   Now you need to position the arrow shape on the photo. When you drag a shape with text, you need to drag a border of the shape or a part of the shape that does not contain text.

7. Position the pointer on the banner shape so that the pointer is the move pointer, and then drag the banner shape on top of the photo on the left so that the smart guides indicate that the middle of the shape aligns with the tops of the two photos and the left end of the shape aligns with the left of the swing picture, as shown in Figure 2–4.

Figure 2–4 Arrow shape with text resized and positioned on Slide 4

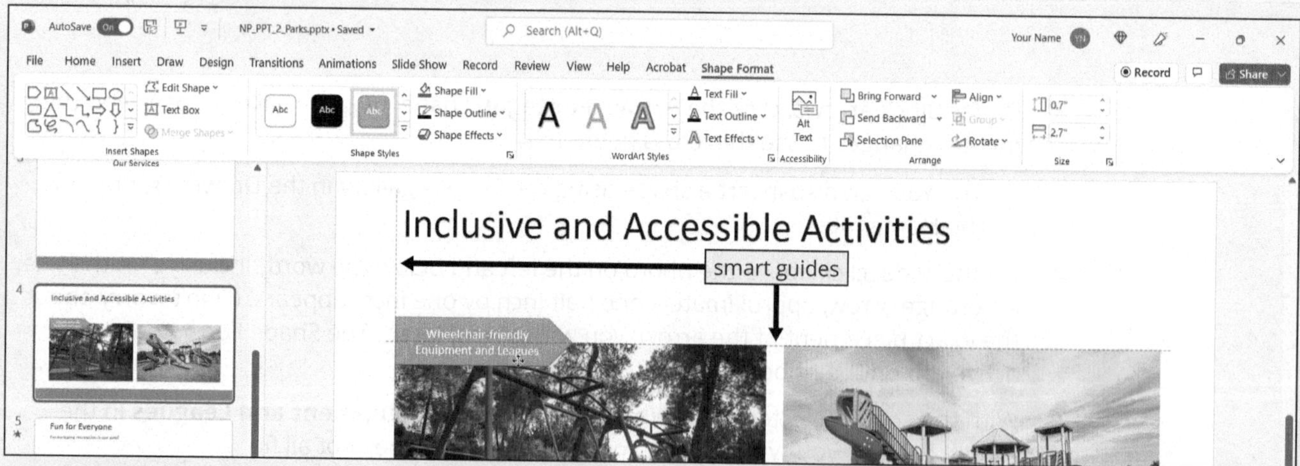

istock.com/Moshe Einhorn; istock.com/Moshe Einhorn

8. Save your changes to the presentation if necessary.

Insight

Using the Draw Tab

The Draw tab on the ribbon contains commands that let you draw on a slide. If you have a device with a touchscreen, you can use your finger or a stylus to draw. If you do not have a touchscreen, you can use the mouse. To draw on a slide, click the Draw button, and then choose different colored pens, a pencil, or a highlighter. You can adjust any of the drawing tools to create a wider or more narrow line. You can click buttons in the convert group to convert your drawings to text, shapes, or mathematical equations. If you want to draw straight lines or align your drawings, you can use the Ruler button on the Draw tab to display a ruler across the slide that you can rotate to whatever position you want. The drawings are also recorded as a video. After you have finished drawing, you can replay the drawing action and watch the characters and shapes you drew get redrawn on the slide. The Draw tab appears on the ribbon automatically if you are using a touchscreen device. If the Draw tab does not appear, you can right-click a tab name on the ribbon, click Customize the Ribbon, and then in the Customize the Ribbon list, click the Draw check box to select it.

Formatting Objects

When you select a shape, including a text box, the Shape Format contextual tab appears. When you select a picture on a slide, the Picture Format contextual tab appears. These tabs contain tools for formatting shapes or pictures. For both shapes and pictures, you can apply borders or outlines and add special effects such as shadows, reflections, a glow effect, soft edges, bevels, and 3-D effects. Some formatting tools are available only for one or the other type of object. For example, the Remove Background tool is available only for pictures, and the Fill command is available only for shapes. Refer to the Part 2.1 Visual Overview for more information about the commands on the Format contextual tabs.

You can apply a style to both shapes and pictures. For example, a picture style can add both a border and a shadow effect to a picture. A shape style could apply a fill color, an outline color, and a shadow effect to a shape.

Formatting Shapes

You can modify the fill of a shape by filling it with a color, a gradient (shading in which one color blends into another or varies from one shade to another), a textured pattern, or a picture. When you add a shape to a slide, the shape is filled with the Accent 1 color from the set of theme colors, and the outline is a darker shade of that color.

Antónia wants you to change the color of the arrow shape on Slide 4.

To change the fill, outline, and style of the arrow shapes:

1. On Slide 4 ("Inclusive and Accessible Activities"), click the arrow shape to select it, if necessary, and then click the **Shape Format** tab, if necessary.
2. In the Shape Styles group, click the **Shape Fill arrow**. The Shape Fill menu opens. Refer to Figure 2–5. You can fill a shape with a color, a picture, a gradient, or a texture, or you can remove the fill by clicking No Fill.

Figure 2–5 Shape Fill menu

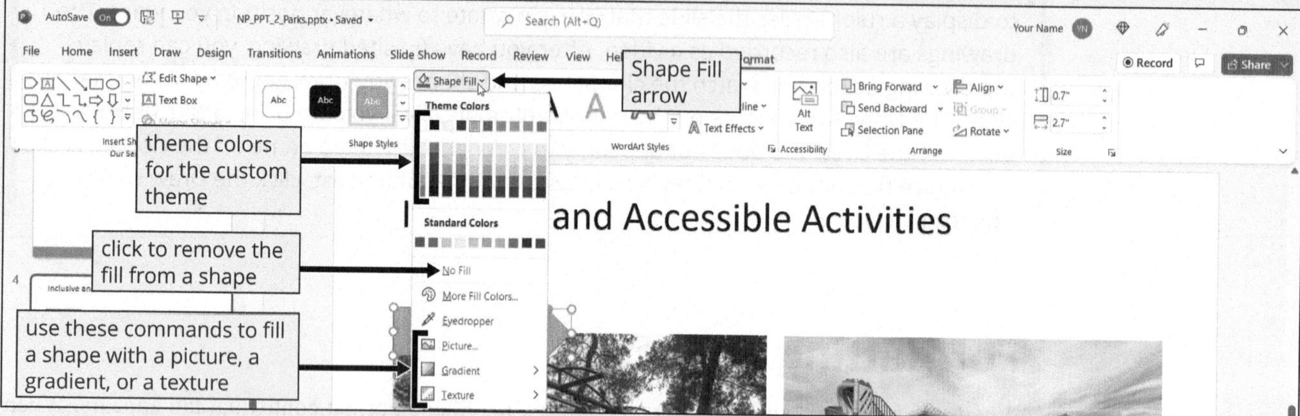

istock.com/Moshe Einhorn; istock.com/Moshe Einhorn

3. In the Theme Colors section, click the **Brown, Accent 2** square. The fill of the selected arrow changes to a dark brown.

> **Tip** You can fill a shape with a picture instead of a color. On the Shape Fill menu, click Picture to open the Insert Pictures dialog box, and then click the location of the picture (From a File, Online Pictures, or From Icons).

4. Click the **Shape Fill arrow**, point to **Gradient**, and then in the Dark Variations section click the **Linear Right** gradient (in the first column, second row in the Variations section). The shape is filled with a gradient of brown that is darker on the left side of the shape and changes to a lighter shade on the right side of the shape.
5. In the Shape Styles group, click the **Shape Outline arrow**. The Shape Outline menu appears. Refer to Figure 2–6. You can change the color of a shape outline, the width (by clicking Weight), or the style (by clicking Dashes).

Figure 2–6 Shape Outline menu

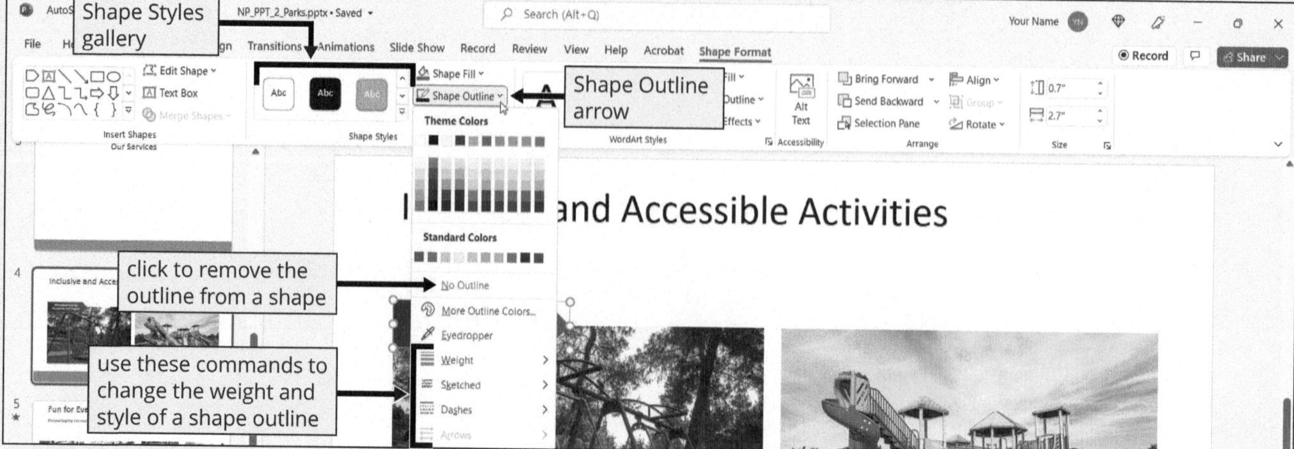

istock.com/Moshe Einhorn; istock.com/Moshe Einhorn

6. On the menu, point to **Weight**, and then click **6 pt**. The width of the outline increases to six points. Antónia doesn't like this look, so she asks you to apply a style instead.
7. In the Shape Styles group, in the Shape Styles gallery, click the **More** button. The Shape Styles gallery expands.
8. Scroll down, and then in the Presets section, click the **Gradient Fill – Orange, Accent 6, No Outline** style (the last option in the last row of the Presets section). The style, which fills the shape with an orange gradient and removes the outline, is applied to the shape.

On some shapes, you can drag the yellow adjustment handle to change the shape's proportions. For instance, if you drag one of the adjustment handles on the arrow shape, you would change the size of the arrowhead relative to the size of the arrow.

> **Tip** To make other adjustments to shapes, in the Insert Shapes group on the Shape Format tab, click the Edit Points button, and then drag the points that appear on the shape. To replace a shape with a different one, click the Edit Shape button, point to Change Shape, and then click the shape you want.

Antónia wants you to change the shape of the arrow by making the arrowhead larger relative to the size of the arrow shape.

To adjust the arrow shape:

1. Click the arrow shape, if necessary, to select it. There is one orange adjustment handle on the arrow shape at the top left of the arrowhead.
2. Drag the adjustment handle to the left so that the left edge of the arrowhead is approximately between the letters "v" and "e" in "Inclusive." Compare your screen to Figure 2–7.

Figure 2–7 Arrow shape after using the adjustment handle

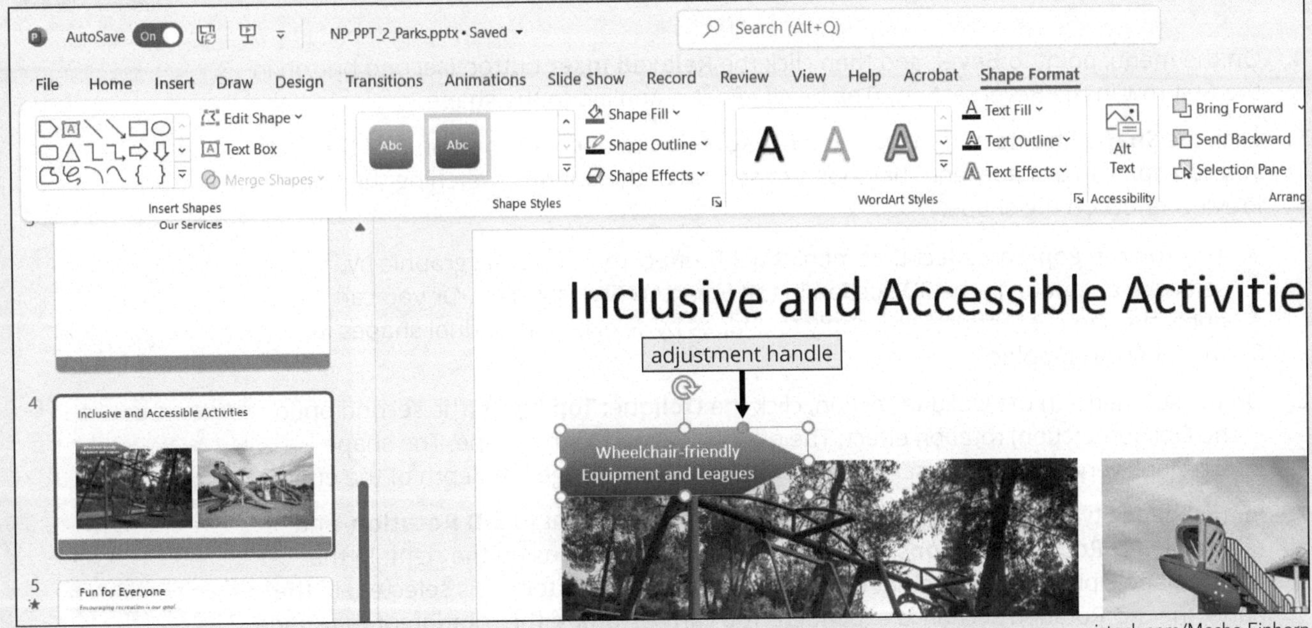

istock.com/Moshe Einhorn

Another way you can format a shape is to apply effects to it, such as a shadow, reflection, glow, soft edges, bevel, and 3-D rotation effect. Antónia would like you to place a shape on Slide 1. She wants you to make the shape look three-dimensional.

To apply 3-D effects to the shape on Slide 1:

1. Display Slide 1 (the title slide), click the **Insert** tab, click the **Shapes** button, then click **Rectangle: Rounded Corners**. Drag to create a shape that is 2.25 inches high and 7 inches wide.
2. Place the shape in front of the title, then in the Arrange group, click the **Send Backward button** to place the shape behind the text. Change the shape color to **Brown, Accent 3**.
3. In the Shape Styles group, click the **Shape Effects** button. The Shape Effects menu opens. The menu contains a list of the types of effects you can apply. Refer to Figure 2–8.

Figure 2–8 Shape effects menu

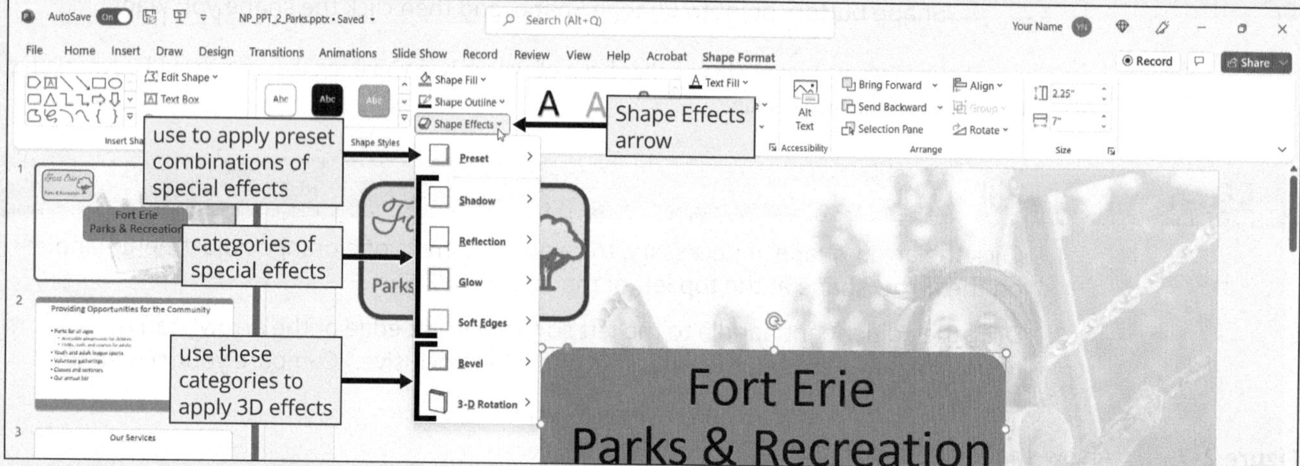

istock.com/ilkercelik

4. On the menu, point to **Bevel**, and then click the **Relaxed Inset** button (second button in the first row in the Bevel section). The bevel effect is applied to the shape.
5. Click the **Shape Effects** button, point to **3-D Rotation** to open a submenu of 3-D effects you can apply to a shape, and then point to several of the options, watching the Live Preview effect on the shape.

> **Tip** You can apply an effect that mimics a 3-D effect to a SmartArt graphic by selecting an option in the 3D section in the SmartArt Styles gallery. Or you can apply the same 3-D effects you apply to shapes by selecting individual shapes in the SmartArt graphic.

6. On the submenu, in the Oblique section, click the **Oblique: Top Right** (the second option in the Oblique section) rotation effect. The effect is applied to the shape. The shape doesn't look very different. To see the effect, you need to change the depth of the effect.
7. In the Shape Styles group, click the **Shape Effects** button, point to **3-D Rotation**, and then click **3-D Rotation Options**. The Format Shape pane opens on the right. In the pane, Shape Options is selected at the top, and the Effects button is selected. In the pane, the 3-D Rotation section is expanded. You can customize the rotation of the shape in this section.

8. In the Format Shape pane, click **3-D Format**. The 3-D Format section expands. In this section of the pane, you can customize the bevel, the depth of the shape, the contour color, and the look of the shape by changing the material and lighting settings.

   Trouble? If the 3-D Format section is not expanded, it was already expanded before you clicked it. Click 3-D Format in the pane again.

9. In the 3-D Format section, in the Depth section, click in the **Size** box, and then edit the number so it is **120 pt**. The shape changes so that the depth is increased to 120 points. The rectangle now looks three-dimensional.

10. In the Depth section, click the **Color** button, and then click **Light Yellow, Background 2, Darker 75%**. The color of the depth shading changes to dark brown. Compare your screen to Figure 2–9.

Figure 2–9 Rounded rectangle shape formatted to look three-dimensional

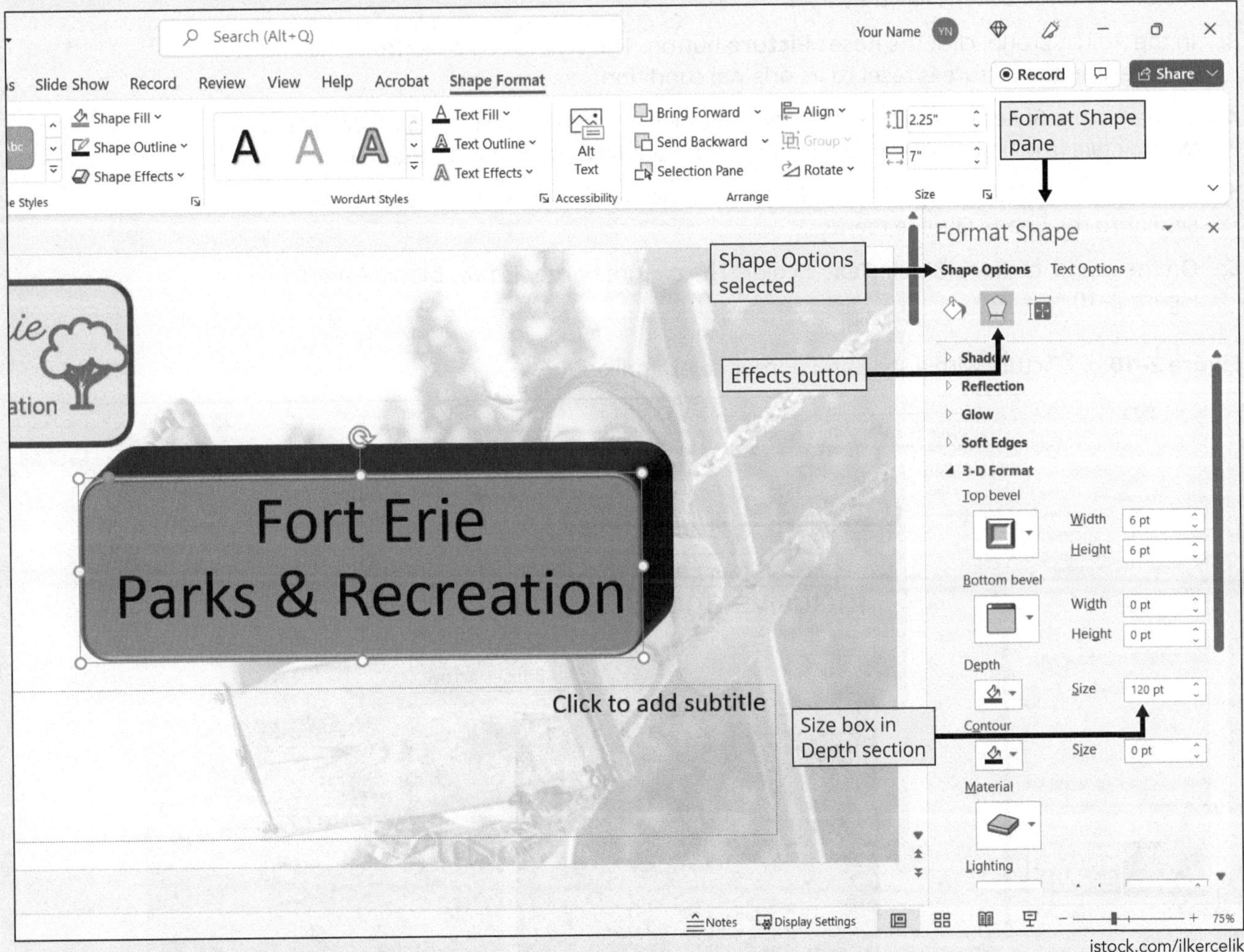

istock.com/ilkercelik

11. In the upper-right corner of the Format Shape pane, click the **Close** button.

Formatting Pictures

You can format pictures as well as shapes. To format pictures, you use the tools on the Picture Format tab.

Antónia wants you to format the pictures on Slide 4 by adding colored borders. To create a border, you could apply a thick outline, or you can apply one of the styles that includes a border and then modify it.

To format the photos on Slide 4:

1. Display Slide 4 ("Inclusive and Accessible Activities"), click the photo on the left, and then click the **Picture Format** tab.
2. In the Picture Styles group, in the Picture Styles gallery, click the **More** button, and then click the **Metal Oval** style (the last style in the last row). The style is applied to the picture. Antónia doesn't like that style.
3. In the Adjust group, click the **Reset Picture** button. The style is removed from the picture, and the picture is reset to its original condition.
4. In the Picture Styles group, click the **More** button, and then click the **Simple Frame, White** style (the first style). This style applies a 7-point white border to the photo.
5. In the Picture Styles group, click the **Picture Border arrow**. The Picture Border menu is similar to the Shape Outline menu.
6. On the menu, click the **Black, Text 1** color. The picture border is now black. Refer to Figure 2–10.

Figure 2–10 Picture with a style and border color applied

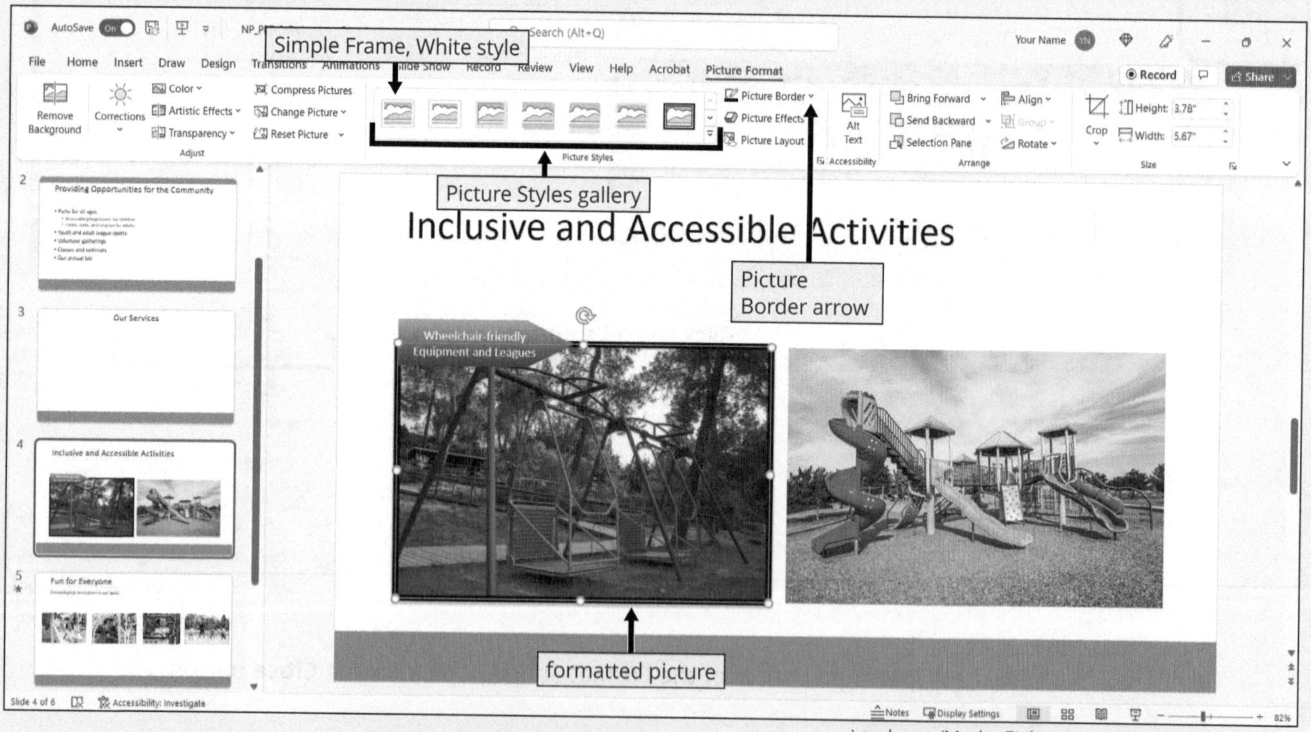

istock.com/Moshe Einhorn; istock.com/Moshe Einhorn

You need to apply the same formatting to the photo on the right on Slide 4. You can repeat the same formatting steps, or you can copy the formatting.

7. With the left photo on Slide 4 still selected, click the **Home** tab.

8. In the Clipboard group, click the **Format Painter** button, and then move the pointer to the slide. The pointer changes to the Format Painter pointer for objects.

Tip You can also use the Format Painter to copy the formatting of shapes and text.

9. Click the photo on the right. The style and border color of the photo on the left is copied and applied to the photo on the right.
10. Save your changes if necessary.

Duplicating Objects

Antónia decides she wants you to add an arrow on the right of Slide 4. You could draw another arrow, but instead, you'll duplicate the arrow you just drew so that they have the same style and size. When you duplicate an object, you create a copy of the object, but nothing is placed on the Clipboard. You can only use the Duplicate command to duplicate objects, including text boxes. You cannot use the Duplicate command to duplicate selected text.

To duplicate the arrow on Slide 4 and edit the text in the shape:

1. On Slide 4 ("Inclusive and Accessible Activities"), click the arrow shape to select it.
2. On the Home tab, in the Clipboard group, click the **Copy arrow**. A menu opens.
3. On the menu, click **Duplicate**. A duplicate of the arrow appears on the slide.
4. Move the pointer on top of the duplicate shape so that the pointer changes to the I-beam pointer, and then click before the first word "Wheelchair." The insertion point appears in the shape before "Wheelchair."

Trouble? If the insertion point is not before "Wheelchair," press LEFT ARROW or RIGHT ARROW as needed to move it to the correct position.

5. Press and hold **SHIFT**, click after the last word, "Leagues," and then release **SHIFT**. All of the text between the locations where you clicked is selected.

Tip You can also press and hold SHIFT then press an arrow key to select adjacent text.

6. Type **Equipment Chosen to Appeal to all Children** in the duplicate arrow. The text you type replaces the selected text.
7. Drag the duplicate arrow to the right so that the smart guides indicate that the right edge of the duplicate arrow shape aligns with the right edge of the slide picture and the duplicate banner shape aligns with the original arrow shape as shown in Figure 2–11.

Figure 2–11 Duplicate arrow repositioned on Slide 4

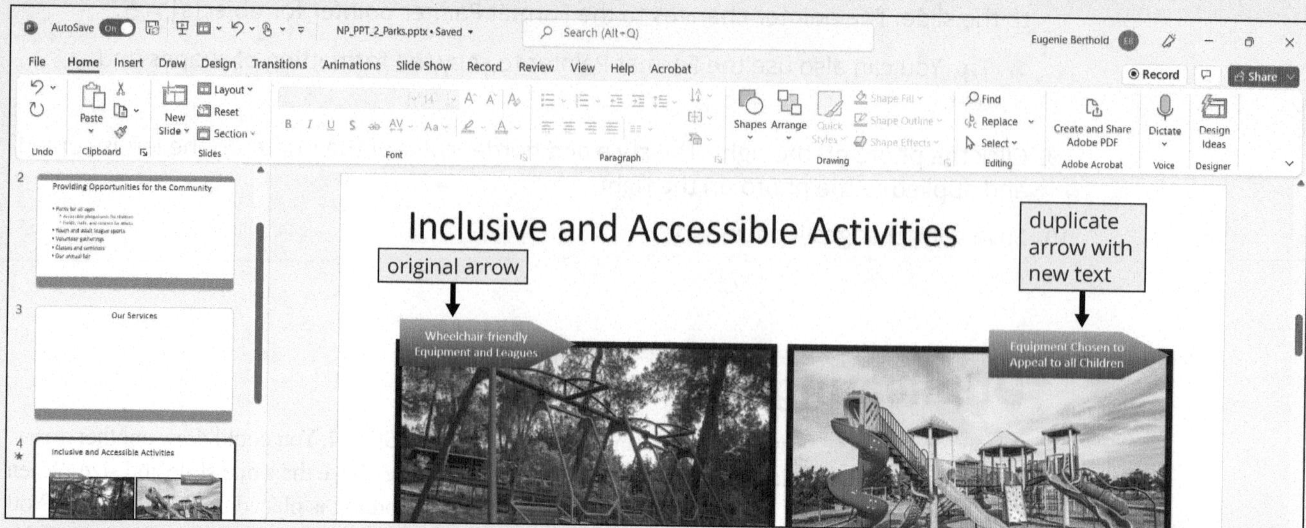

istock.com/Moshe Einhorn; istock.com/Moshe Einhorn

8. Save your changes if necessary.

Rotating and Flipping Objects

You can rotate and flip any object on a slide. To flip an object, you click the Rotate button in the Arrange group on the Shape Format tab or on the Picture Format tab to access the Flip commands on the Rotate menu. To rotate an object, you can use the Rotate commands on the Rotate menu to rotate objects in 90-degree increments. You can also drag the rotate handle that appears above the top-middle sizing handle to rotate a selected object to any position that you want.

> **Tip** You can also click the Arrange button in the Drawing group on the Home tab to access the Rotate and Flip commands.

Antónia wants you to rotate the arrows on Slide 4 so that they are slanted. Also, the "Equipment chosen…" arrow on Slide 4 needs to point to the left. To make that change, you need to flip the arrow.

To flip the duplicate banner shape on Slide 4:

1. On Slide 4 ("Inclusive and Accessible Activities"), click the Equipment chosen... arrow to select it if necessary. The shape border appears with the Rotate handle above the shape. The right end of the arrow is touching the right side of the slide.
2. Position the pointer on the **rotate handle** so that the pointer changes to the rotate pointer, and then drag the **rotate handle** 180 degrees to the right so that the arrow is pointing to the right. Now the arrow is pointing in the correct direction, but the text in the arrow is now upside down.
3. On the Quick Access Toolbar, click the **Undo** button, and then click the **Shape Format** tab, if necessary.
4. In the Arrange group, click the **Rotate** button. The Rotate menu opens. Refer to Figure 2–12.

Figure 2–12 Arrange menu

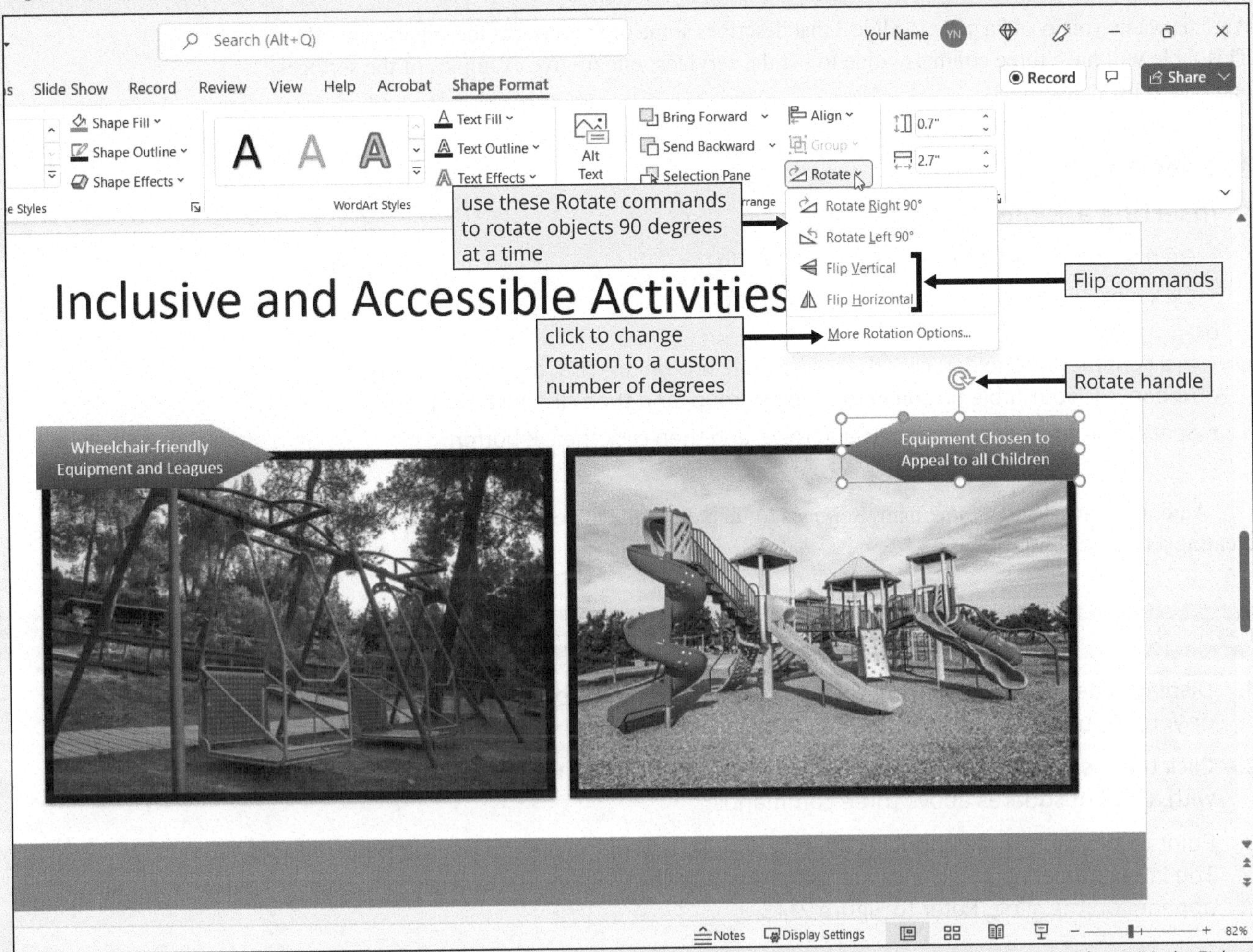

istock.com/Moshe Einhorn; istock.com/Moshe Einhorn

5. Click **Flip Horizontal**. The arrow flips horizontally and is now pointing left. Unlike when you rotated the arrow, the text is still right-side up.
6. Drag the **rotate handle** clockwise to the left until the top of the arrow shape is below the picture frame. Usually, using the rotate handle is fine, but you can also rotate objects by a precise number of degrees.
7. In the Arrange group, click the **Rotate** button, and then click **More Rotation Options**. The Format Shape pane opens with the Shape Options tab selected and the Size & Properties button selected. The Size section is expanded. The value in the Rotation box indicates the number of degrees the object was rotated in a clockwise direction from its original position.
8. If the value in the Rotation box is not 350°, click in the **Rotation** box, edit the value so it is **350°**, and then press **ENTER**.
9. Click the **Wheelchair-friendly...** arrow shape. The value in the Rotation box is 0°.
10. Click in the **Rotation** box, and then edit the value so it is **10°**, and then press **ENTER**.
11. Close the Format Shape pane, and then save your changes if necessary.

Creating and Formatting a Table

A **table** is a grid of rows and columns that can contain text and graphics. A **cell** is the box where a row and column intersect. Each cell contains one piece of information. **Gridlines** in a table are the nonprinting lines that show cell boundaries. Gridlines create a table's structure.

Creating a Table and Adding Data to It

Antónia wants you to add a table to Slide 3 that describes some of the services the department offers. This table will have three columns—one to list the services, one to give examples of the services, and one to list notes.

Reference

Inserting a Table

- On the ribbon, click the Insert tab, and then in the Tables group, click the Table button.
- Click a box in the grid to create a table of that size.

or

- In a content placeholder, click the Insert Table button; or, click the Insert tab on the ribbon, click the Table button in the Tables group, and then click Insert Table.
- Specify the numbers of columns and rows, and then click the OK button.

Antónia hasn't decided how many services to include in the table, so she asks you to start by creating a table with four rows.

To add a table to Slide 3:

1. Display Slide 3 ("Our Services"). You can click the Table button in the content placeholder, or you can use the Table command on the Insert tab.
2. Click the **Insert** tab, and then in the Tables group, click the **Table** button. A menu opens with a grid of squares above three commands.
3. Point to the grid, and without clicking the mouse button, move the pointer over the grid. The label above the grid indicates how large the table will be, and a preview of the table appears on the slide. Refer to Figure 2–13.

Figure 2–13 Inserting a 3×4 table on Slide 3

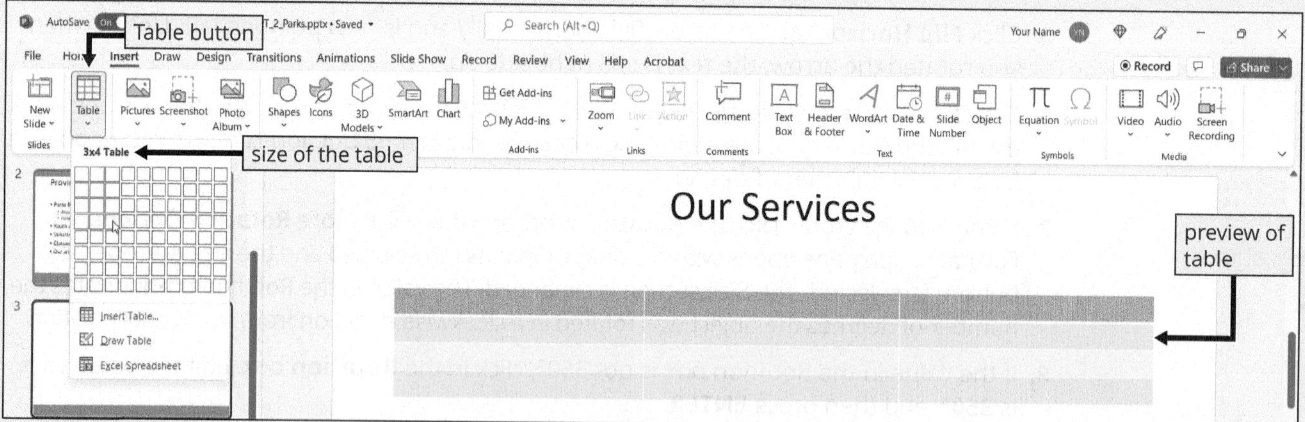

4. When the label above the grid indicates 3×4 Table, click to insert a table with three columns and four rows. A selection border appears around the table, and the insertion point is in the first cell in the first row. On the ribbon, two table contextual tabs appear: Table Design and Layout.

Now you're ready to fill the blank cells with the information about the services. To enter data in a table, you click in the cells in which you want to enter data and then start typing. You can also use the Tab and arrow keys to move from one cell to another.

To add data to the table:

1. In the first cell in the first row, type **Activity**. The text you typed appears in the first cell.
2. Press **TAB**. The insertion point moves to the second cell in the first row.
3. Type **Details**, press **TAB**, type **Notes**, and then press **TAB**. The insertion point is in the first cell in the second row.
4. In the first cell in the second row, type **Youth Sports**, press **TAB**, and then type **Soccer** in the second cell. You need to add two more lines in the second cell in the second row.
5. Press **ENTER**, type **Softball and Baseball**, press **ENTER**, and then type **Basketball**. The height of the second row increased to fit the extra lines of text in this cell.
6. Click in the first cell in the third row, type **Adult Sports**, and then press **TAB**.
7. In the second cell in the third row, type **Pickleball**, press **ENTER**, type **Ultimate Frisbee**, press **ENTER**, and then type **Co-Ed Softball**.
8. Click in the first cell in the last row, type **Classes and Groups**, and then press **TAB**.
9. In the second cell in the last row, type **Learn to Swim**, press **ENTER**, type **Bootcamps**, press **ENTER**, and then type **Nutrition Seminars**.

Inserting and Deleting Rows and Columns

You can modify the table by adding or deleting rows and columns. You need to add more rows to the table for additional services.

To insert rows and a column in the table:

1. Make sure the insertion point is in the last row in the table.
2. Click the **Layout** tab, and then in the Rows & Columns group, click the **Insert Below** button. A new row is inserted below the current row. Refer to Figure 2–14.

Figure 2–14 Table with row inserted

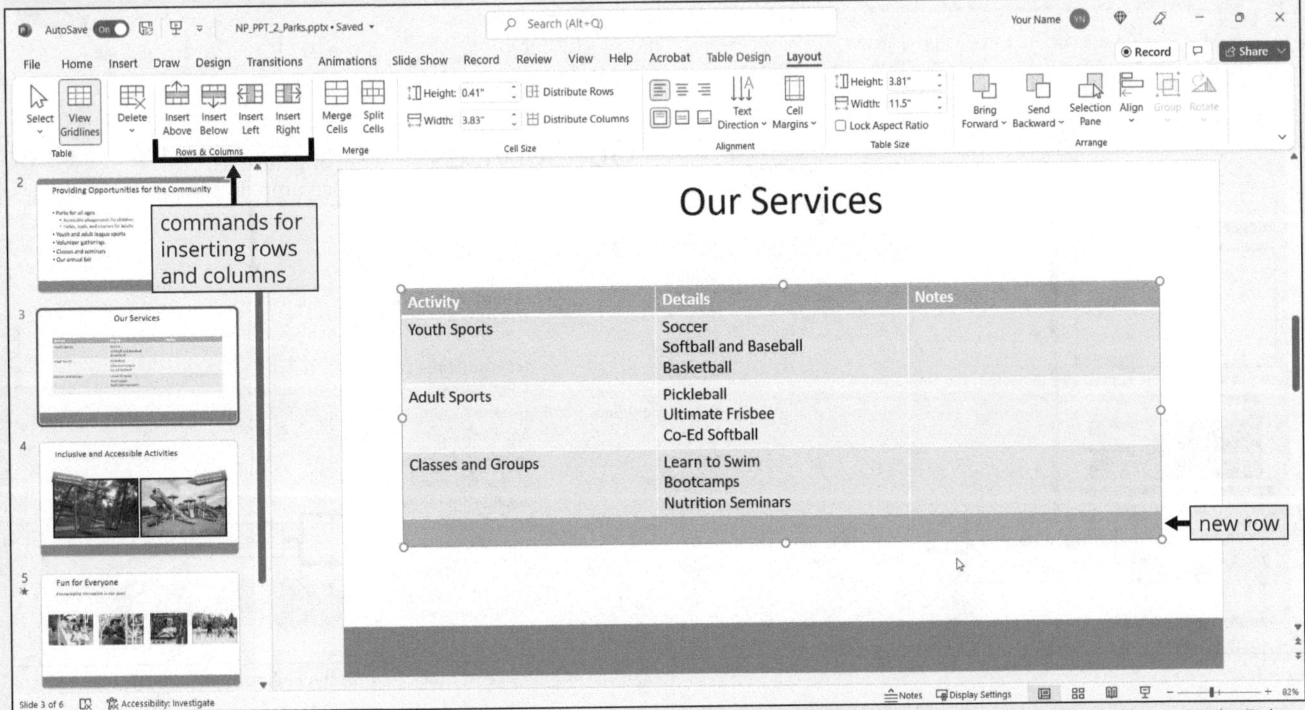

istock.com/ilkercelik; istock.com/Moshe Einhorn; istock.com/Moshe Einhorn

3. Click in the first cell in the new last row, type **Annual Fair**, and then press **TAB**.
4. Type **5K Road Race and 1 Mile Fun Run**, press **ENTER**, type **Local Business Demonstrations**, and then press **TAB**. The insertion point is in the last cell in the last row.
5. Press **TAB**. A new row is created, and the insertion point is in the first cell in the new row.
6. Type **Community Volunteers**, press **TAB**, and then type **Opportunities for Coaching, Leadership, and Event Volunteering**. You need to insert a row above the last row.
7. In the Rows & Columns group, click the **Insert Above** button. A new row is inserted above the current row, and all of the cells in the new row are selected. You also need to insert a column to the left of the first column.
8. Click any cell in the first column, and then in the Rows & Columns group, click the **Insert Left** button. A new first column is inserted.

Antónia decided she doesn't want to add notes to the table, so you'll delete the last column. She also decided that she doesn't need the new row you added as the second to last row in the table, so you'll delete that row.

To delete a column and a row in the table:

1. Click in any cell in the last column in the table. This is the column you will delete.
2. On the Layout tab, in the Rows & Columns group, click the **Delete** button. The Delete button menu opens.
3. Click **Delete Columns**. The current column is deleted, and the entire table is selected.
4. Click in any cell in the second to last row (the empty row). This is the row you want to delete.
5. In the Rows & Columns group, click the **Delete** button, and then click **Delete Rows**. Refer to Figure 2–15.

Figure 2–15 Table after adding and deleting rows and columns

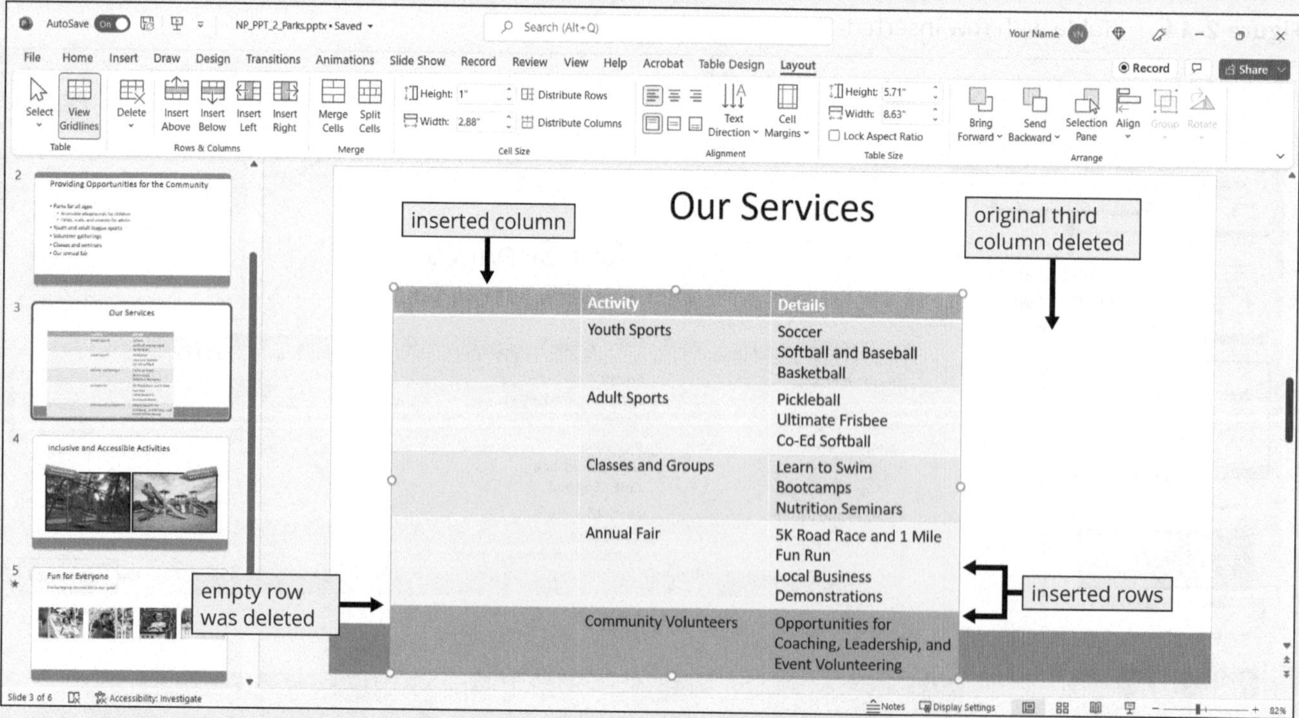

istock.com/ilkercelik; istock.com/Moshe Einhorn; istock.com/Moshe Einhorn

Formatting a Table

After you insert data into a table, you need to think about how the table looks and whether the table will be readable for the audience. As with any text, you can change the font, size, or color, and as with shapes and pictures, you can apply a style to a table. You can also change how the text fits in the table cells by changing the height of rows and the width of columns. You can also customize the formatting of the table by changing the border and fill of table cells.

You need to change the font size of the text in the table.

To change the font size of text in the table:

1. Move the pointer on top of the left edge of the cell containing "Activity" so that the pointer changes to the cell selection pointer ➚, and then click. The entire cell is selected, and the Mini toolbar appears. You want to change the size of all the text in the table, so you will select the entire table. Notice that a selection border appears around the table. This border appears any time the insertion point is in a table cell or part of the table is selected.
2. Click the **Layout** tab, if necessary, and then in the Table group, click the **Select** button. The Select menu opens with options to select the entire table, the current column, or the current row.
3. Click **Select Table**. The entire table is selected. Because the selection border appears any time the insertion point is in the table, the only visual cues you have that the entire table is now selected are that no cells in the table are selected, the insertion point is not blinking in any cell in the table, and the Select button is gray and unavailable. Refer to Figure 2–16.

Figure 2–16 Table selected on Slide 3

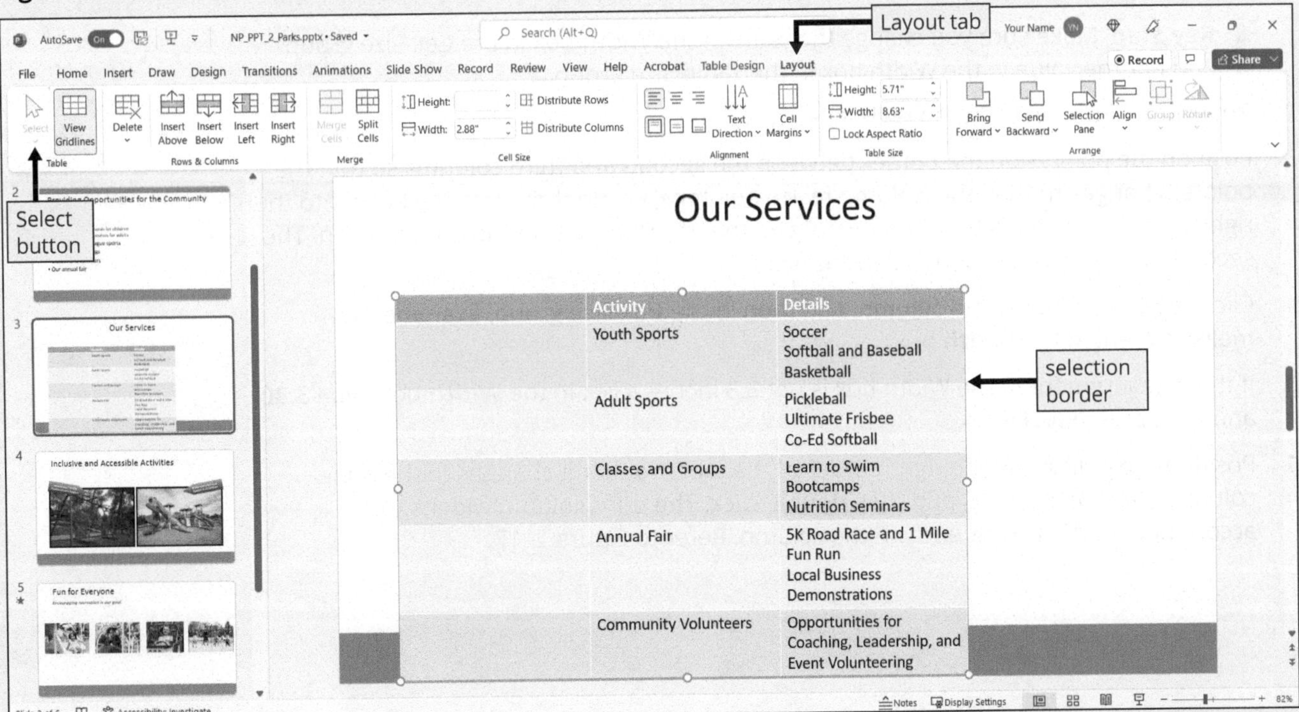

istock.com/ilkercelik; istock.com/Moshe Einhorn; istock.com/Moshe Einhorn

4. On the ribbon, click the **Home** tab.
5. In the Font group, click the **Font Size arrow**, and then click **20**. Because the entire table is selected, the size of all the text in the table changes to 20 points. The height of all the rows in the table increases to fit the larger text size.

6. Move the pointer on top of the top border of the table so that the pointer changes to the move pointer, and then drag the table up until the top of the table aligns with the top of the slide and so that you can see the last row in the table. The table will be on top of the title.
7. Click any cell in the third column, and then click the **Layout** tab.
8. In the Table group, click the **Select** button, and then click **Select Column.** All of the cells in the third column are selected. You want to change the font size of only the text in the cells below the heading row.
9. Click in the second cell in the third column, press and hold **SHIFT**, and then click in the last cell in the third column. All of the cells in the third column except the first cell are selected.
10. On the ribbon, click the **Home** tab.
11. In the Font group, click the **Font Size arrow**, and then click **16**. The text in the selected cells changes to 16 points, and the height of those rows decreases.

Next, you will adjust the column widths to better fit the data. To adjust column widths, you can drag a column border or type a number in the Width box in the Cell Size group on the Layout tab. You can also automatically adjust a column to fit its widest entry by double-clicking its right border.

To adjust column sizes in the table:

1. Click in any cell in the first column, and then click the **Layout** tab.
2. In the Cell Size group, click the number in the **Width** box, type **1.3**, and then press **ENTER**.

   Key Step Make sure you change the value in the Width box in the Cell Size group and not the value in the Width box in the Table Size group.

   The width of the first column is changed to 1.3 inches.
3. Position the pointer on the border between the second and third columns so that the pointer changes to the table column resize pointer +||+, and then drag the border to the right until the border is between the "e" and the "t" in "Details" in the third column. The second column is now about 3.3 inches wide.
4. Click any cell in the second column, and then in the Cell Size group, examine the measurement in the **Width** box.
5. If the measurement in the Width box is not 3.3 inches, click in the **Width** box, type **3.30**, and then press **ENTER**.
6. Position the pointer on the right border of the table so that it changes to the table column resize pointer +||+, and then double-click. The third column widens to accommodate the widest entry in the column. Refer to Figure 2–17.

Figure 2–17 Table column widths adjusted

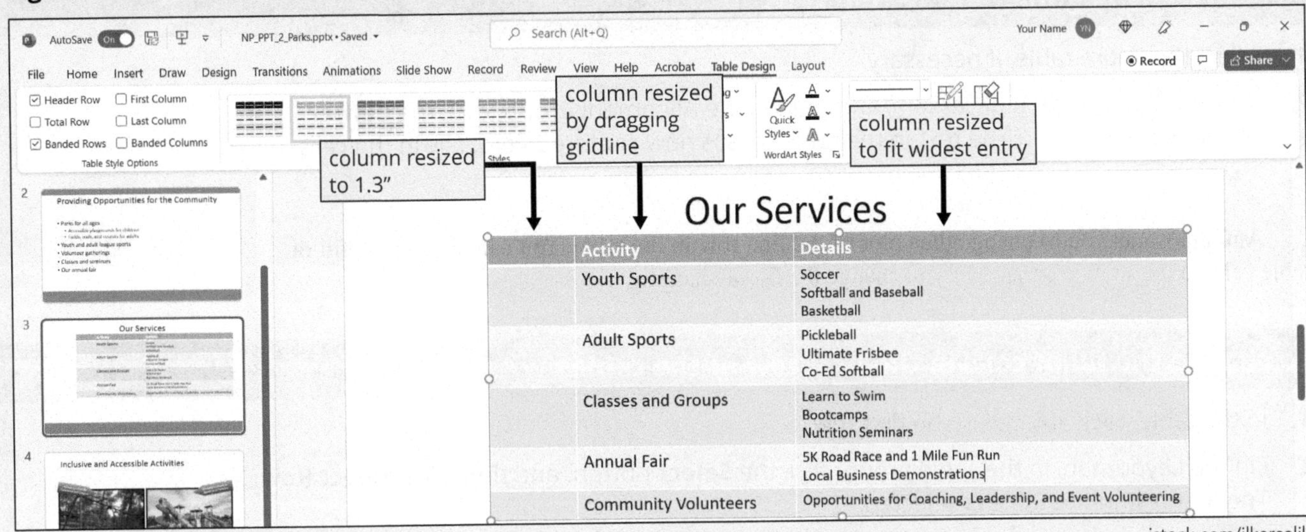

istock.com/ilkercelik

> **Trouble?** If you have trouble making the pointer change to the table column resize pointer +||+, move the pointer a little to the left of the right border. If you still can't do it, click the Layout tab, click in the Width box in the Cell Size group, type 6, and then press ENTER.

7. Move the pointer on top of the top, bottom, or one of the side borders of the table so that the pointer changes to the move pointer, and then drag the table down so that the smart guides indicated that the table is centered horizontally and vertically on the slide.

On the Layout tab, in the Alignment group, you can change the alignment of text in cells. Figure 2–18 describes the buttons in the Alignment group that you can use to align text in table cells.

Figure 2–18 Alignment commands on the Table Tools Layout tab

Button	Name	Description
	Align Left	Horizontally align the text along the left edge of the cell
	Center	Horizontally align the text between the left and right edges of the cell
	Align Right	Horizontally align the text along the right edge of the cell
	Align Top	Vertically align the text along the top edge of the cell
	Center Vertically	Vertically align the text between the top and bottom edges of the cell
	Align Bottom	Vertically align the text along the bottom edge of the cell

The text in all cells in the table is horizontally left-aligned and vertically aligned at the top of the cells. The table would look better if the text was vertically aligned in the center of the cells.

To adjust the alignment of text in cells:

1. Select the entire table, if necessary.
2. Click the **Layout** tab if necessary, and then in the Alignment group, click the **Center Vertically** button ⊟. The text in the table cells is now centered vertically in the cells.

Antónia wants you to change the color of the first row in the table. You can change the fill of table cells in the same manner that you change the fill of shapes.

To change the fill of cells in the first row of the table:

1. In the table, click any cell in the first row.
2. On the Layout tab, in the Table group, click the **Select** button, and then click **Select Row**. The first row in the table is selected.
3. Click the **Table Design** tab.
4. In the Table Styles group, click the **Shading arrow**. The Shading menu is similar to the Shape Fill menu you worked with earlier. The menu also includes the Table Background command that you can use to fill the table background with a color or a picture.
5. Click the **Brown, Accent 2, Lighter 60%** color (in the fifth column), and then click any cell in the table to deselect the row. The menu closes and the cells in the first row are shaded with light brown. The white text is hard to read on the light background.
6. Move the pointer to the left of the first row so that it changes to the row selection pointer ➡, and then click. The first row is selected.
7. On the Table Design tab, in the WordArt Styles group, click the **Text Fill arrow** A, click the **Black, Text 1** color, and then click any cell in the table. The text in the first row changes to black.

   Tip You can also change the font color of table text using the Font Color button in the Font group on the Home tab.

Antónia doesn't like the changes you made. She wants you to try formatting the table with a style. When you apply a style to a table, you can specify whether the header and total rows and the first and last columns are formatted differently from the other rows and columns in the table. You can also specify whether to use banded rows or columns, which fills alternating rows or columns with different shading.

To apply a style to the table:

1. Click the **Table Design** tab, if necessary, and then, in the Table Styles group, position the pointer over the selected option in the Table Styles gallery. In the Table Styles group, the second style, Medium Style 2 – Accent 1, is selected. In the Table Style Options group, the Header Row and Banded Rows check boxes are selected, which means that the header row will be formatted differently than the rest of the rows and that every other row will be filled with shading. Refer to Figure 2–19.

Figure 2–19 Current style and options applied to table

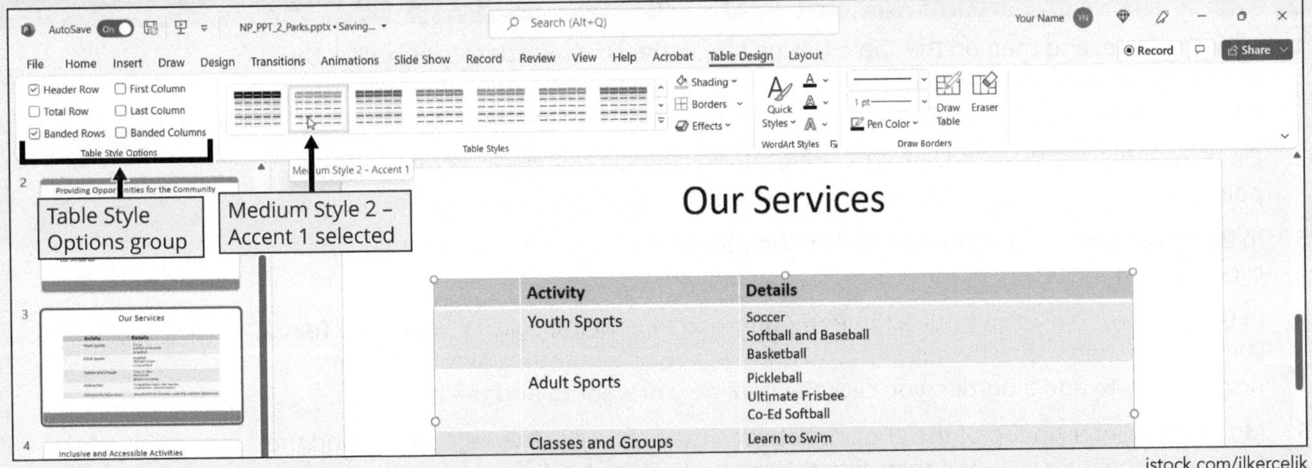

istock.com/ilkercelik

2. In the Table Styles group, in the Table Styles gallery, click the **More** button. The Table Styles gallery expands.
3. Click the **Medium Style 3 – Accent 2** style (in the third row in the Medium section), and then click a blank area of the slide to deselect the table. This style adds borders above and below the top row in the table and below the bottom row. Because the Header Row check box in the Table Style Options group was selected, the first row is formatted differently from the rest of the rows. And because the Banded Rows check box was selected, every other row below the header row is filled with gray.

> **Tip** Select the View Gridlines button on the Layout tab to make the gridlines visible; deselect it to hide the gridlines.

Antónia wants you to change the borders between the rows to dark brown. Borders are different than gridlines. Gridlines are the lines that form the structure of a table. **Borders** are drawn on top of the gridlines. To add borders, you use the buttons in the Draw Borders group on the Table Design tab. Before you change them, the settings are solid-line borders, 1 point wide, and black. Refer to Figure 2–20.

Figure 2–20 Current settings for borders

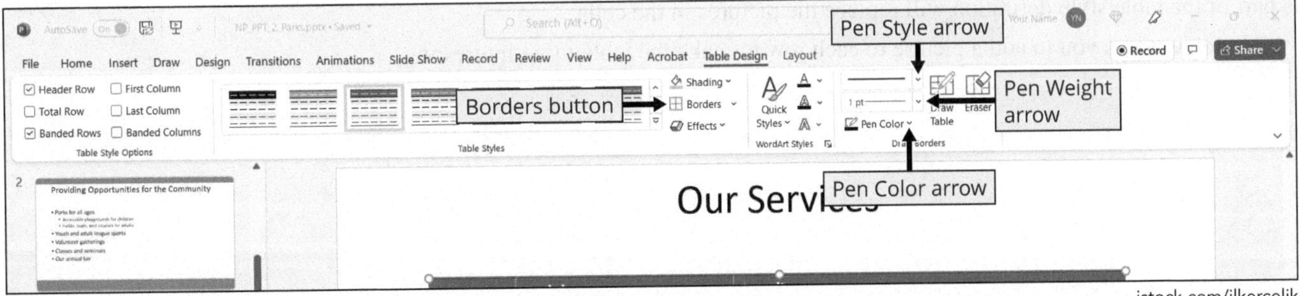

istock.com/ilkercelik

To modify the borders of the table:

1. Click the table, and then on the Table Design tab, in the Draw Borders group, click the **Pen Style arrow** [———]. A menu of line styles appears, including the No Border option. Antónia wants a solid line border, so you will not change the selection.
2. On the menu, click the solid line. The menu closes, the pointer changes to the pencil pointer, and the Draw Table button in the Draw Borders group is selected.
3. In the Draw Borders group, click the **Pen Weight arrow** [1 pt———], and then click **¼ pt**.
4. In the Draw Borders group, click the **Pen Color arrow**, and then click the **Brown, Text 2, Darker 50%** color. Now the borders you draw will be one-quarter point, solid, dark brown lines. To add a border, you click the gridline you want to add the border to.
5. Move the pointer on top of the gridline between the first cell in the second row and the first cell in the third row, and then click the mouse button. A one-quarter point, solid, dark brown line appears between the first cells in the second and third rows.
6. Click the gridline between each of the cells in the second and third rows until the border between the second and third rows is a solid line separating the rows.
7. Create a border line between the third and fourth rows, between the fourth and fifth rows, and between the fifth and sixth rows. You are finished adding borders to the table.

   Tip You can also click the Borders arrow in the Table Styles group and use commands on that menu to apply or remove borders. The borders will be the style, weight, and color specified by the buttons in the Draw Borders group.

8. In the Draw Borders group, click the **Draw Table** button to deselect it. The pointer changes back to its usual shape. Now that you added the borders, Antónia wants you to remove the shading from every other row.
9. In the Table Style Options group, click the **Banded Rows** check box to deselect it. All of the rows in the table are now filled with white.

Filling Cells with Pictures

Just as you can fill a shape with a picture, you can do the same with cells. Note that many of the table styles include shaded cells as part of the style definition, so if you want to fill table cells with pictures and apply a table style, you need to apply the table style first. Otherwise, the shading that is part of the table style definition will replace the pictures in the cells.

Antónia wants you to add a picture to each row to make the table more interesting.

To fill the cells in the first column with pictures:

1. In the table, click in the first cell in the second row, and then click the **Table Design** tab, if necessary.
2. In the Table Styles group, click the **Shading arrow**, and then click **Picture**. The Insert Pictures window opens. Refer to Figure 2–21.

Figure 2–21 Insert Pictures window

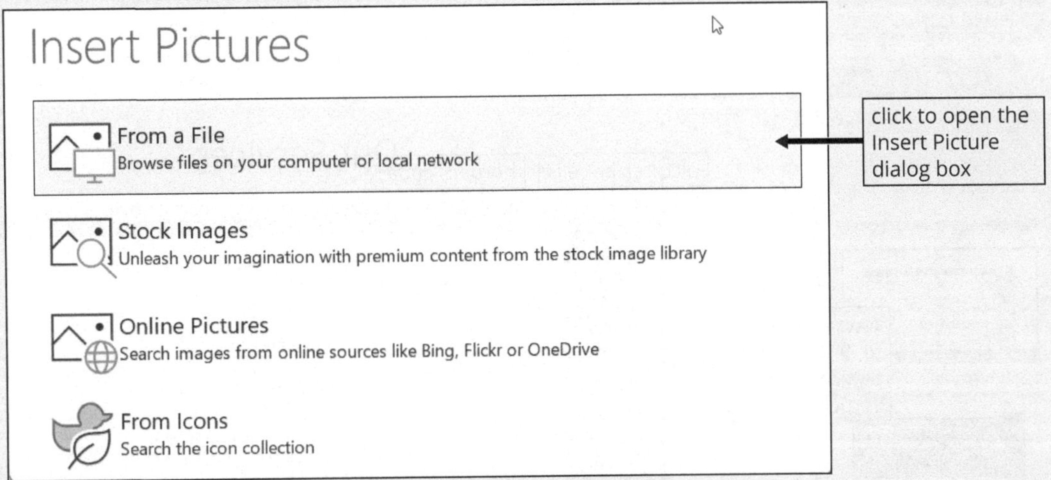

3. Click **From a File**. The Insert Picture dialog box opens.
4. Navigate to the **PowerPoint2 > Module folder**, click **Support_PPT_2_Softball.jpg**, and then click **Insert**. The photo fills the cell.
5. Fill the first cells in the next four rows with the following pictures, all located in the **PowerPoint2 > Module** folder: **Support_PPT_2_Pickleball.jpg, Support_PPT_2_Swimming.jpg, Support_PPT_2_Festival.jpg**, and **Support_PPT_2_Basketball.jpg**.

The photos in the last two rows are too small, and they are distorted because they are stretched horizontally to fill the cells. To fix both of these problems, you'll increase the height of these rows.

To change row heights in the table:

1. Click in any cell in the second row in the table, and then click the **Layout** tab. In the Height box in the Cell Size group, .9" appears. The second, third, and fourth rows are each also .9" high.
2. Position the pointer to the left of the second to last row in the table so that it changes to the row selection pointer ➡, press and hold the mouse button, drag down until the pointer is to the left of the bottom row in the table, and then release the mouse button. The last two rows in the table are selected.
3. On the Layout tab, in the Cell Size group, click in the **Height** box, type **.9**, and then press **ENTER**. The height of the selected rows increases and is the same height as the other rows in the table. Now you will adjust the table's placement on the slide again. This time, you will use the Align commands instead of the smart guides.
4. Click in any cell to deselect the last two rows, and then in the Arrange group, click the **Align** button. A menu with commands for aligning the objects on the slide appears. Because only one object—the table—is selected, selecting a command will align the object to the borders of the slide.

5. Click **Align Center**. The table is horizontally aligned so that it is centered between the left and right borders of the slide.
6. In the Arrange group, click the **Align** button, and then on the menu, click **Align Middle**. The table is vertically aligned so that it is centered between the top and bottom borders of the slide. Compare your screen to Figure 2–22.

Figure 2–22 Final formatted table

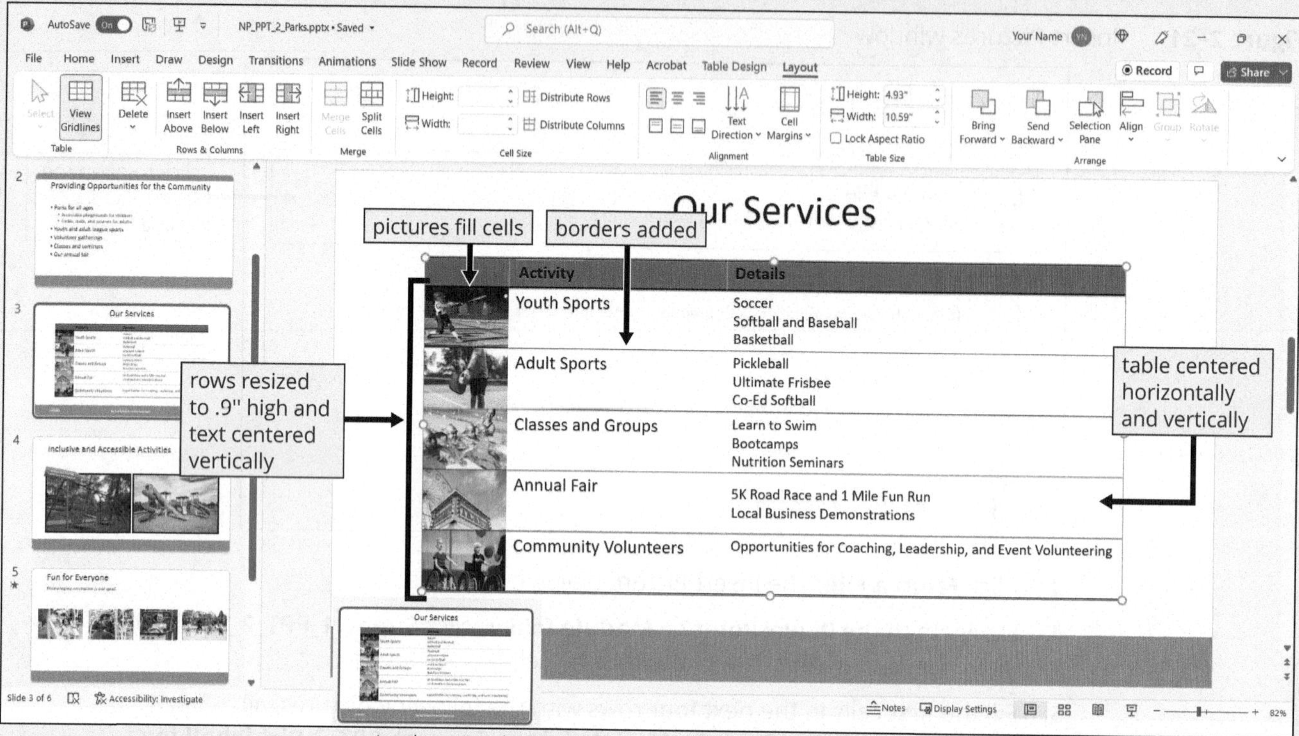

istock.com/Moshe Einhorn; istock.com/Moshe Einhorn; istock.com/ilkercelik; istock.com/monkeybusinessimages; istock.com/ActionPics; istock.com/eyecrave productions; istock.com/Mark Tantrum; istock.com/FatCamera

7. Save the changes to the presentation.

Inserting Symbols

You can insert some symbols, such as the trademark symbol, the registered trademark symbol, and the copyright symbol, by typing letters between parentheses and letting AutoCorrect change the characters to a symbol. You can insert all symbols, including letters from another alphabet, by using the Symbol button in the Symbols group on the Insert tab.

The department's slogan—"Encouraging recreation is our goal."—is trademarked. Antónia wants you to add the trademark symbol ™ after the slogan on Slide 5.

To insert the trademark symbol:

1. Display Slide 5 ("Fun for Everyone"), and then click in the subtitle text box immediately after "goal."
2. Type **(tm** in the title text box.
3. Type **)** (close parenthesis). The text "(tm)" changes to the trademark symbol, which is ™. Antónia points out that the trademark symbol should appear after the slogan, not after the slide title.

Tip To insert the copyright symbol ©, type (c). To insert the registered trademark symbol ®, type (r).

4. Press **BACKSPACE**. The symbol changes to the characters you typed.
5. Press **BACKSPACE** four times to delete the four characters, and then click in the text box containing the italicized slogan, immediately after the period after "goal."
6. Type **(tm)** after the period after "goal." This time, the characters you typed did not change to the trademark symbol. If this happens, you need to use the symbol dialog box to insert the symbol.
7. Press **BACKSPACE** four times to delete the four characters, click the **Insert** tab, and then in the Symbols group, click the **Symbol** button. The Symbol dialog box opens.
8. If "(normal text)" does not appear in the Font box, click the **Font arrow**, and then click **(normal text)**.
9. Click the **Subset arrow**, scroll down, click **Letterlike Symbols**, and then click the trademark symbol (™) as shown in Figure 2–23. (The symbol might be in a different row and column on your screen.) In the bottom-left corner of the Symbol dialog box below "Unicode name," the name of the selected character is "Trade Mark Sign."

Figure 2–23 Symbol dialog box with the trademark symbol selected

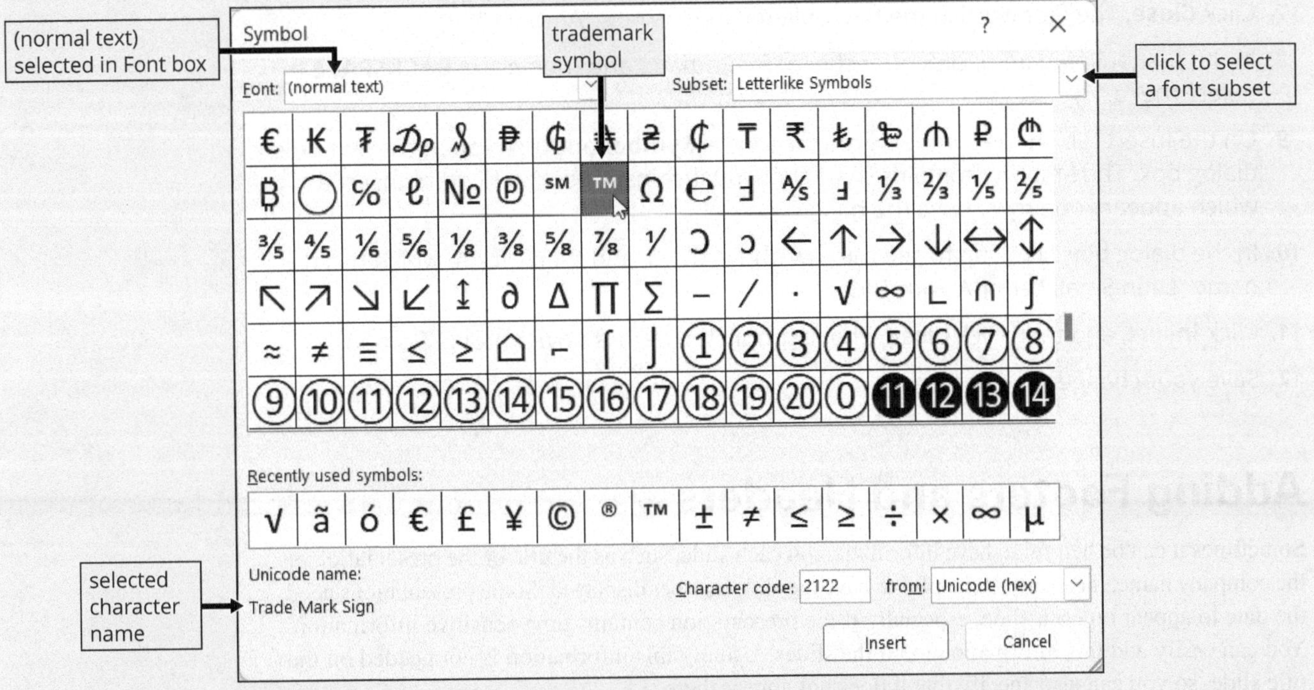

10. Click **Insert**. In the text box containing the slogan, the trademark symbol is inserted.
11. In the dialog box, click **Close**. The dialog box closes.

Antónia's first and last names contain two letters that are not in the English alphabet. You need to correct the misspelling of Antónia's first and last names on Slide 6 to include the accent marks.

To insert special characters:

1. Display Slide 6 ("Contact Us for More Information").
2. In the first bulleted item, click after the "o" in "Antonia," and then press **BACKSPACE**. The "o" in "Antonia" is deleted.
3. On the Insert tab, in the Symbols group, click the **Symbol** button. The Symbol dialog box opens.
4. At the top of the dialog box, click the **Subset arrow**, scroll the menu up, and then click **Latin-1 Supplement**. The list of symbols in the dialog box scrolls up to display the Latin-1 Supplement section.
5. Click **ó**. In the bottom-left corner of the Symbol dialog box, the name of the selected character is "Latin Small Letter O With Acute."

   Trouble? If you don't see the letter ó, click the down scroll arrow two times and look in the next two rows.
6. Click **Insert**. The letter "ó" is inserted on the slide at the insertion point.
7. Click **Close**. The first word in the first bulleted item is now "Antónia."
8. In the first bulleted item, click after the "a" in "Romao," and then press **BACKSPACE** to delete the "a."
9. On the Insert tab, in the Symbols group, click the **Symbol** button to open the Symbols dialog box. The first row contains the ó that you just inserted. You need to insert ã, which appears one row above the ó.
10. In the dialog box, scroll up to see the row above the ó, and then click **ã**, which has the name "Latin Small Letter A With Tilde."
11. Click **Insert**, and then click **Close**. The first bulleted item is now "Antónia Romão."
12. Save your changes if necessary.

Adding Footers and Headers

Sometimes it can be helpful to have information on each slide, such as the title of the presentation or the company name. It can also be helpful to have the slide number displayed. Some presentations need the date to appear on each slide, especially if the presentation contains time-sensitive information. You can easily add this information to all the slides. Usually this information is not needed on the title slide, so you can also specify that it does not appear there.

Antónia wants you to add the date, slide number, and the department name to each slide except the title slide.

To add a footer, slide numbers, and the date to slides:

1. On the Insert tab, in the Text group, click the **Header & Footer** button. The Header and Footer dialog box opens with the Slide tab selected.

   Tip Click the Insert Slide Number button on the Insert tab to insert the slide number on all of the slides. Click the Date & Time button to open a dialog box listing the current date and time in various formats that you can choose from.
2. Click the **Footer** check box to select it, and then click in the **Footer** box. In the Preview box on the right, the middle placeholder on the bottom is filled with black to indicate where the footer will appear on slides. Refer to Figure 2–24. Note that the position of the footer, slide number, and date changes in different themes.

Figure 2–24 Slide tab in the Header and Footer dialog box

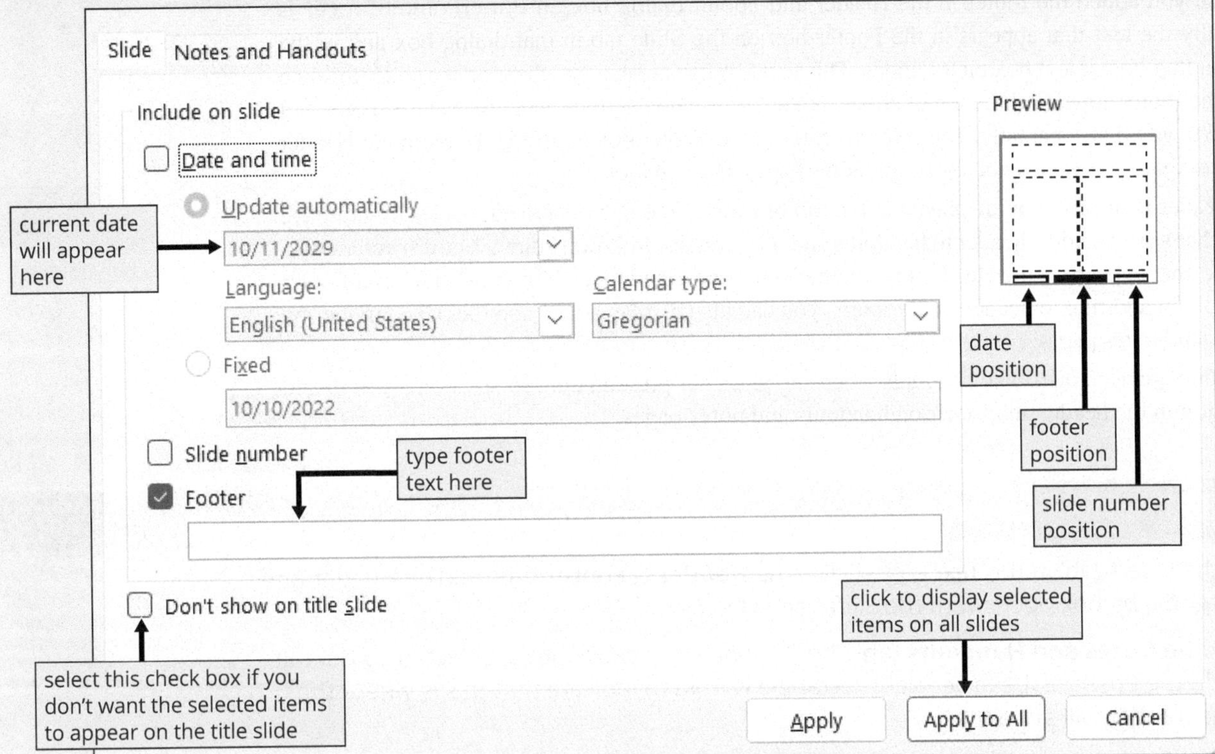

3. Type **Fort Erie Parks & Recreation Department** in the Footer box.
4. Click the **Slide number** check box to select it. In the Preview box, the box in the bottom-right is filled with black.
5. Click the **Date and time** check box to select it. The options under this check box are no longer dimmed, indicating that you can use them, and in the Preview box, the box in the bottom-left is filled with black. You don't want the date in the presentation to update automatically each time the presentation is opened. You want it to show today's date so people will know that the information is current as of that date.
6. Click the **Fixed** option button, if necessary. Now you want to prevent the footer, slide number, and date from appearing on the title slide.
7. Click the **Don't show on title slide** check box to select it, and then click **Apply to All**. On Slide 6 the footer, date, and slide number are displayed. Refer to Figure 2–25.

Figure 2–25 Date, footer, and slide number on Slide 6

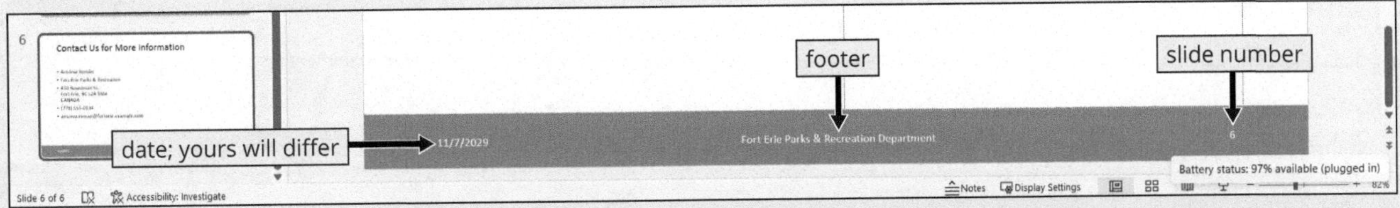

8. Display **Slide 1** (the title slide). Notice the footer, date, and slide number do not appear on the title slide.

Typically, a footer is any text that appears at the bottom of every page in a document. As you saw when you added the footer in the Header and Footer dialog box, in PowerPoint a **footer** is specifically the text that appears in the Footer box on the Slide tab in that dialog box and in the corresponding Footer text box on the slides. This text box can appear anywhere on the slide. In some themes the footer appears at the top of slides. Notes pages and handouts can also have a footer, but you need to add that separately. The text you enter in the Footer box on the Slide tab in the Header and Footer dialog box does not appear on notes pages and handouts.

A header is information displayed at the top of every page in a document. Slides do not have headers, but you can add a header to handouts and notes pages. In PowerPoint a **header** refers only to the text that appears in the Header box on the Notes and Handouts tab in the Header and Footer dialog box. In addition to headers and footers, you can also display a date and the page number on handouts and notes pages.

Antónia plans to distribute handouts when she gives her presentation, so she wants you to add information in the header and footer on handouts and notes pages.

To modify the header and footer on handouts and notes pages:

1. On the Insert tab, in the Text group, click the **Header & Footer** button. The Header and Footer dialog box opens with the Slide tab selected.
2. Click the **Notes and Handouts** tab. The Page number check box is selected by default, and in the Preview, the lower-right rectangle is bold to indicate that this is where the page number will appear.
3. Click the **Header** check box to select it, click in the **Header** box, and then type **Fort Erie Parks & Recreation Department**.
4. Click the **Footer** check box to select it, click in the **Footer** box, and then type your name.
5. Click the **Apply to All** button. To see the effect of modifying the handouts and notes pages, you need to look at the print preview.
6. Click the **File** tab to open Backstage view, and then in the navigation pane, click **Print**.
7. Under Settings, click the **Full Page Slides** button, and then click **Notes Pages**. The preview shows Slide 1 as a notes page. The header and footer you typed appear, along with the page number. Refer to Figure 2–26.

Figure 2–26 Header and footer on the Slide 6 notes page

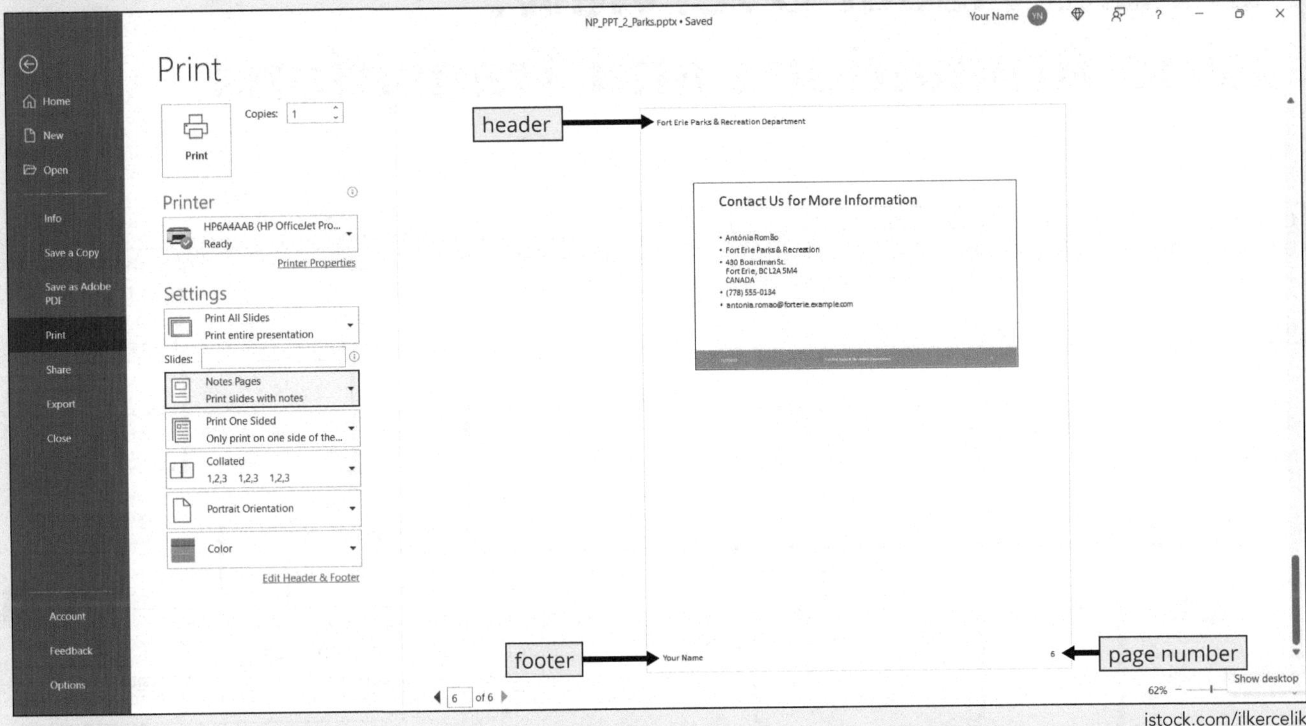

istock.com/ilkercelik

8. At the top of the navigation bar, click the **Back** button to return to Normal view.
9. Save your changes if necessary.

You have modified a presentation by applying a theme used in another presentation; inserting, formatting, and duplicating pictures and shapes; and inserting a table and characters that are not on your keyboard. You also added footer and header information to slides and handouts. In the next part, you will continue modifying the presentation by applying and modifying transitions and animations, and adding and modifying videos.

Part 2.1 Quick Check

1. Which contextual tab appears on the ribbon when you select a shape?
2. What is a style?
3. What is the fill of a shape?
4. In a table, what is the intersection of a row and column called?
5. How do you know if an entire table is selected and not just active?
6. How do you insert characters that are not on your keyboard?
7. In PowerPoint, what is a footer?

Part 2.2 Visual Overview: Using Animations and Transitions

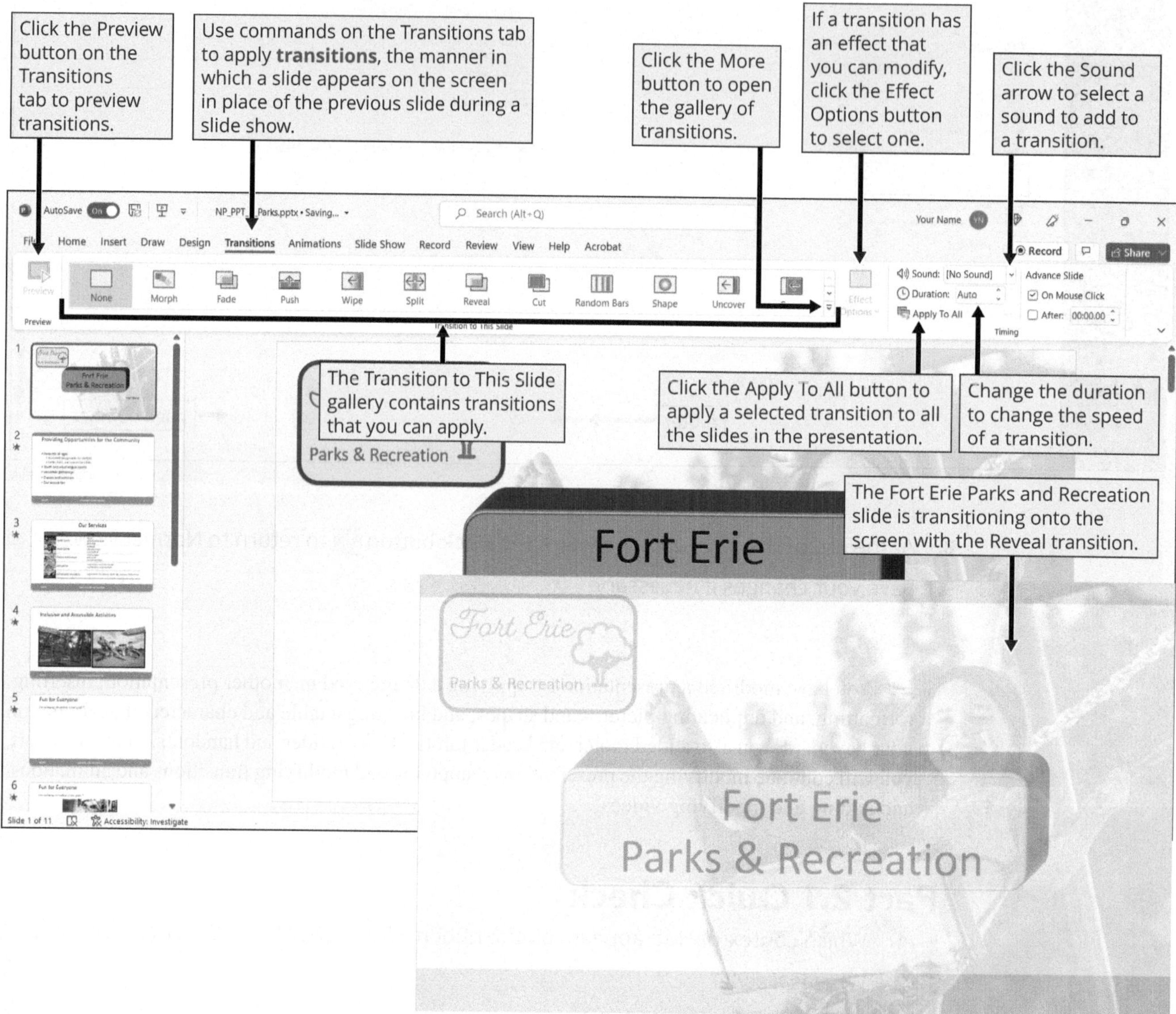

Click the Preview button on the Transitions tab to preview transitions.
Use commands on the Transitions tab to apply **transitions**, the manner in which a slide appears on the screen in place of the previous slide during a slide show.
Click the More button to open the gallery of transitions.
If a transition has an effect that you can modify, click the Effect Options button to select one.
Click the Sound arrow to select a sound to add to a transition.
The Transition to This Slide gallery contains transitions that you can apply.
Click the Apply To All button to apply a selected transition to all the slides in the presentation.
Change the duration to change the speed of a transition.
The Fort Erie Parks and Recreation slide is transitioning onto the screen with the Reveal transition.
Fort Erie
Parks & Recreation

istock.com/Moshe Einhorn; istock.com/ilkercelik; istock.com/fundamental rights; istock.com/CandyRetriever; istock.com/maroke; istock.com/FatCamera

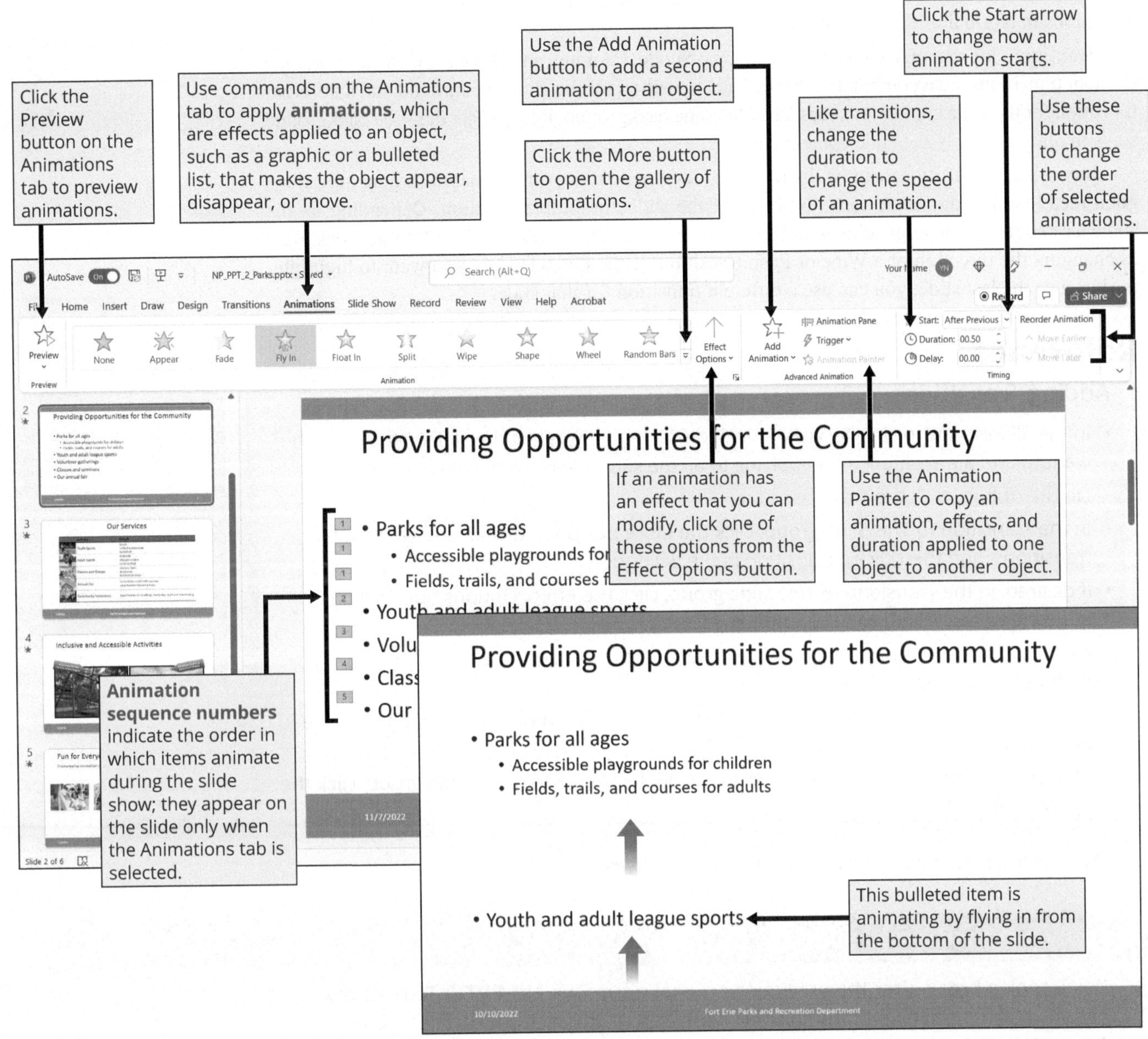
Click the Preview button on the Animations tab to preview animations.
Use commands on the Animations tab to apply animations, which are effects applied to an object, such as a graphic or a bulleted list, that makes the object appear, disappear, or move.
Use the Add Animation button to add a second animation to an object.
Click the More button to open the gallery of animations.
Like transitions, change the duration to change the speed of an animation.
Click the Start arrow to change how an animation starts.
Use these buttons to change the order of selected animations.
If an animation has an effect that you can modify, click one of these options from the Effect Options button.
Use the Animation Painter to copy an animation, effects, and duration applied to one object to another object.
Animation sequence numbers indicate the order in which items animate during the slide show; they appear on the slide only when the Animations tab is selected.
Providing Opportunities for the Community
Parks for all ages
Accessible playgrounds for children
Fields, trails, and courses for adults
Youth and adult league sports
This bulleted item is animating by flying in from the bottom of the slide.
10/10/2022
Fort Erie Parks and Recreation Department

istock.com/Moshe Einhorn; istock.com/ilkercelik; istock.com/fundamental rights; istock.com/CandyRetriever; istock.com/maroke; istock.com/FatCamera

Applying Transitions

The Transitions tab contains commands for changing the transitions between slides. Refer to the Part 2.2 Visual Overview for more information about transitions. Unless you change it, the default is for one slide to disappear and the next slide to immediately appear on the screen. You can modify transitions in Normal or Slide Sorter view.

Transitions are organized into three categories: Subtle, Exciting, and Dynamic Content. Dynamic Content transitions are a combination of the Fade transition for the slide background and a different transition for the slide content. If slides have the same background, it looks like the slide background stays in place and only the slide content changes.

Inconsistent transitions can be distracting and detract from your message, so generally it's a good idea to apply the same transition to all of the slides in the presentation. Depending on the audience and topic, you might choose different effects of the same transition for different slides, such as changing the direction of a Wipe or Push transition. If there is one slide you want to highlight, for instance the last slide, you can use a different transition for that slide.

Reference

Adding Transitions

- In the Slides pane in Normal view or in Slide Sorter view, select the slide(s) to which you want to add a transition, or, if applying to all the slides, select any slide.
- On the ribbon, click the Transitions tab.
- In the Transition to This Slide group, click the More button to display the gallery of transitions, and then click a transition in the gallery.
- If desired, in the Transition to This Slide group, click the Effect Options button if it is available to be clicked, and then click an effect.
- If desired, in the Timing group, click the Sound arrow to insert a sound effect to accompany each transition.
- If desired, in the Timing group, modify the time in the Duration box to modify the speed of the transition.
- To apply the transition to all the slides in the presentation, in the Timing group, click the Apply To All button.

Antónia wants to add more interesting transitions between the slides.

To apply a transition to Slide 2:

1. If you took a break after the previous part, make sure the **NP_PPT_2_Parks.pptx** presentation is open, and then display Slide 2 ("Providing Opportunities for the Community").
2. On the ribbon, click the **Transitions** tab.
3. In the Transition to This Slide group, click the **Reveal** transition. The transition previews as it will appear during the slide show: Slide 1 (the title slide) appears, fades away, and then Slide 2 fades in. The Reveal transition is now selected in the gallery. In the pane containing the thumbnails, a banner appears next to the Slide 2 thumbnail. If you missed the preview, you can see it again.
4. In the Preview group, click the **Preview** button. The transition previews again.
5. In the Transition to This Slide group, in the Transitions gallery, click the **More** button ▾. The gallery expands, listing all the transitions. Refer to Figure 2–27.

Figure 2–27 Transition to This Slide gallery

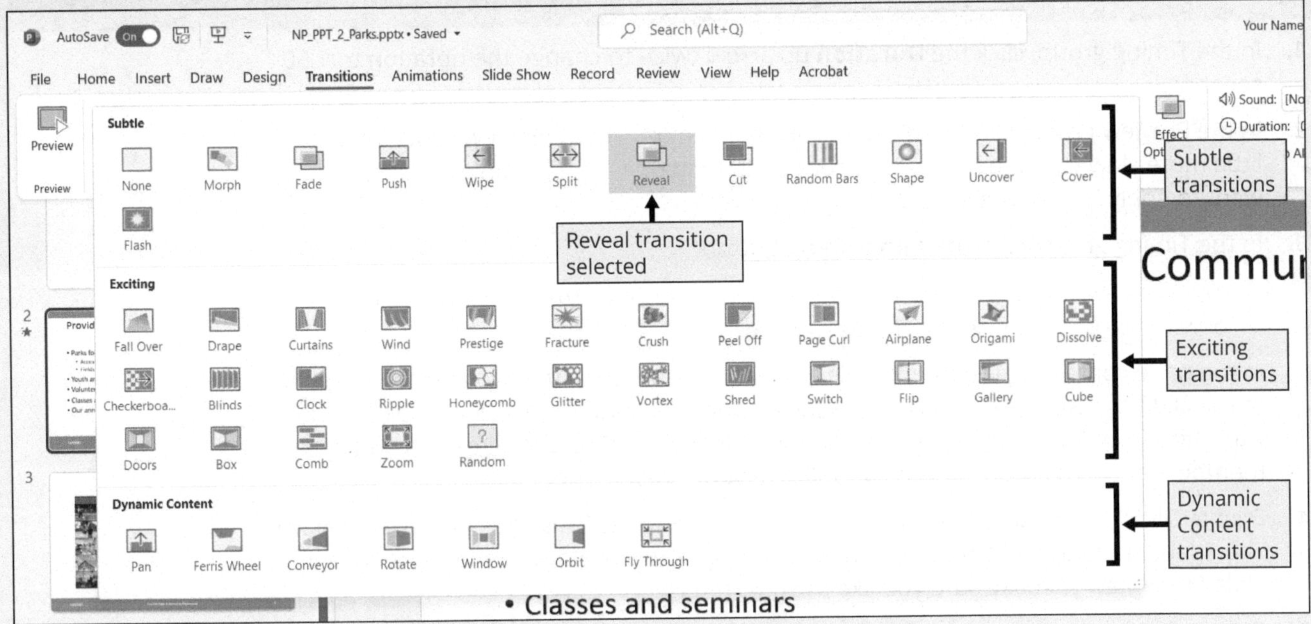

6. Click the **Push** transition. The preview shows Slide 2 slide up from the bottom and push Slide 1 up and out of view.

Most transitions have effects that you can modify. For example, the Peel Off transition can peel from the bottom-left or the bottom-right corner, and the Wipe transition can wipe from any direction. You'll modify the effect of the transition applied to Slide 2.

To modify the transition effect for Slide 2:

1. In the Transition to This Slide group, click the **Effect Options** button. The effects that you can modify for the Push transition are listed on the menu.
2. Click **From Right**. The Push transition previews again, but this time Slide 2 slides from the right to push Slide 1 left. The available effects change depending on the transition selected.
3. In the Transition to This Slide group, click the **Shape** transition. The transition previews with a brief view of Slide 1, before Slide 2 appears in the center of Slide 1 and enlarges in a circular shape to fill the slide.
4. Click the **Effect Options** button. The effects that you can modify for the Shape transition are listed.
5. Click **Out**. The preview of the transition with this effect displays Slide 2 in the center of Slide 1 that grows in a rectangular shape to fill the slide.

Finally, you can also change the duration of a transition. The duration is the length of time, or the speed, from the beginning to the end of the transition. To make the transition faster, decrease the duration. To slow the transition down, increase the duration. The duration is measured in seconds.

Antónia likes the Shape transition, but she thinks it is a little fast, so you will increase the duration. Then you can apply the modified transition to all the slides.

To change the duration of the transition and apply it to all the slides:

1. In the Timing group, click the **Duration** up arrow twice to change the duration to 1.50 seconds.
2. In the Preview group, click the **Preview** button. The transition previews once more, a little more slowly than before. Right now, the transition is applied only to Slide 2. You want to apply it to all the slides.
3. In the Timing group, click the **Apply To All** button.

   Key Step Make sure you click the Apply To All button or the transition is applied only to the currently selected slide or slides.

   In the pane containing the thumbnails, the banner indicating that a transition is applied to the slide appears next to all of the slides in the presentation. You want to remove the transition from Slide 1 because that slide will be displayed on the screen as audience members enter the room where you will give your presentation.
4. Display Slide 1 (the title slide), and then in the Transition to This Slide group, click **None**. The Shape transition is removed from Slide 1 only. You should view the transitions in Slide Show view to make sure you like the final effect.
5. On the Quick Access Toolbar, click the **Start From Beginning** button. Slide 1 (the title slide) appears in Slide Show view.
6. Press **SPACEBAR** or **ENTER** to advance through the slide show. The transitions look fine.
7. End the presentation, and then Save your changes if necessary.

Applying Animations

Animations add interest to a slide show and draw attention to the text or object being animated. For example, you can animate a slide title to fly in from the side or spin around like a pinwheel to draw the audience's attention to that title. Refer to the Part 2.2 Visual Overview for more information about animations.

Animation effects are grouped into four types:

- **Entrance**—Text and objects do not appear on the slide until the animation occurs. This is one of the most commonly used animation types.
- **Emphasis**—Text and objects on the slide change in appearance or move.
- **Exit**—Text and objects leave the screen before the slide show advances to the next slide.
- **Motion Paths**—Text and objects follow a path on the slide.

Animating Objects

You can animate any object on a slide, including pictures, shapes, and text boxes. To animate an object you click it, and then select an animation in the Animation group on the Animations tab.

Reference

Applying Animations

- On the slide displayed in Normal view, select the object you want to animate.
- On the ribbon, click the Animations tab.
- In the Animation group, click the More button to display the gallery of animations, and then click an animation in the gallery.
- If desired, in the Animation group, click the Effect Options button, and then click a direction effect. If the object is a text box, click a sequence effect.
- If desired, in the Timing group, modify the time in the Duration box to modify the speed of the animation.
- If desired, in the Timing group, click the Start arrow, and then click a different setting.

Slide 4 contains two pictures. Antónia wants you to add an animation to the title text on this slide.

To animate the title on Slide 4:

1. Display **Slide 4** ("Inclusive and Accessible Activities"), and then click the **Animations** tab on the ribbon. Because nothing is selected on the slide, the animations in the Animation group are gray.
2. Click the **Inclusive and Accessible Activities** title text. The animations in the Animation group are green to indicate that they are now available. All of the animations currently visible in the Animation group are entrance animations.
3. In the Animation group, click the **Fly In** animation. The animation previews on the slide, showing the title text fly in from the bottom. In the Timing group, the Start box displays On Click, which indicates that this animation will occur when you advance the slide show by clicking the mouse or pressing SPACEBAR or ENTER. The animation sequence number 1 in the box to the left of the title text box indicates that this is the first animation that will occur on the slide when you advance the slide show. You can preview the animation again if you missed it.
4. In the Preview group, click the **Preview** button. The animation previews again.
5. In the Animation group, in the Animation gallery, click the **More** button. The Animation gallery expands. The animation commands are listed by category, and each category appears in a different color. At the bottom are four commands, each of which opens a dialog box listing all the effects in that category. Refer to Figure 2–28. You will try an emphasis animation.

Figure 2–28 Animation gallery

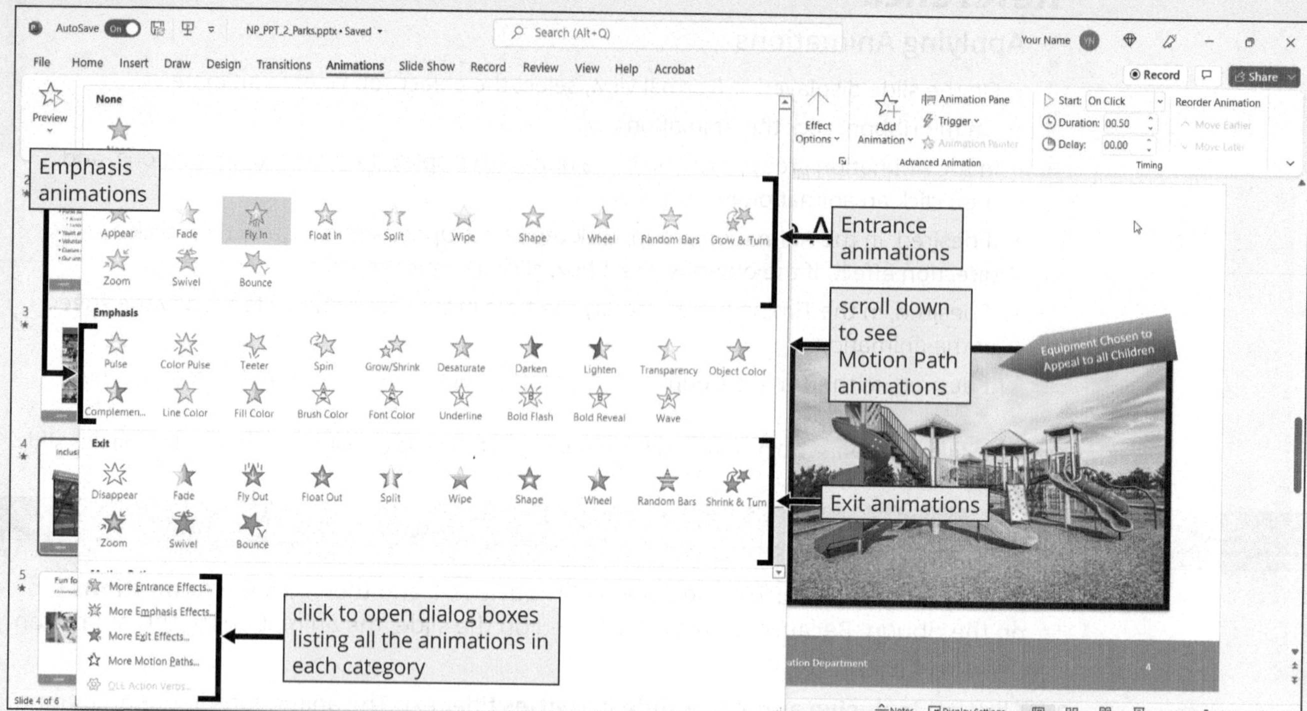

istock.com/Moshe Einhorn

6. Under Emphasis, click the **Underline** animation. The Underline animation replaces the Fly In animation, and the slide title is underlined in the preview.

The Underline animation you applied to the slide title is an example of an emphasis animation you can apply only to text boxes. You cannot apply this animation to other types of objects, such as pictures or tables.

Slide 4 contains two photos. To focus the audience's attention on one photo at time, you will apply an entrance animation to the photos so that they appear one at a time during the slide show.

To apply an entrance animation to a photo on Slide 4:

1. On Slide 4 ("Inclusive and Accessible Activities"), click the picture on the right.
2. In the Animation group, in the Animation gallery, click the **More** button. Notice that in the Emphasis section, six of the animations, including the Underline animation you just applied to the slide title, are gray, which means they are not available for this object. These six animations are available only for text.
3. In the Entrance section, click the **Split** animation. The picture appears starting from the left and right edges. In the Timing group, On Click appears in the Start box, indicating that this animation will occur when you advance the slide show. The animation sequence number to the left of the selected picture is 2, which indicates that this is the second animation that will occur on the slide when you advance the slide show.

You need to change the direction from which this animation appears, and you want to slow it down.

To change the effect and duration of an animation:

1. In the Animation group, click the **Effect Options** button. This menu contains Direction options.
2. Click **Vertical Out**. The preview shows the picture appearing, starting from the center and building out to the left and right edges.
3. In the Timing group, click the **Duration** up arrow once. The duration changes from 0.50 seconds to 0.75 seconds.

After you have applied and customized the animation for one object, you can use the Animation Painter to copy that animation to other objects. You will copy the Split entrance animation to the other photo on Slide 4.

To use the Animation Painter to copy the animation on Slide 4:

1. Click the photo on the right.
2. In the Advanced Animation group, click the **Animation Painter** button, and then move the pointer onto the slide. The pointer changes to the Animation Painter pointer.
3. Click the photo on the left. The Split animation with the Vertical Out effect and a duration of 0.75 seconds is copied to the photo on the left, and the animation previews.

After you apply animations, you should watch them in Slide Show view to see what they will look like during a slide show. Remember that On Click appeared in the Start box for each animation that you applied, which means that to see the animation during the slide show, you need to advance the slide show.

To view the animations on Slide 4 in Slide Show view:

1. Make sure Slide 4 ("Inclusive and Accessible Activities") is displayed.
2. On the status bar, click the **Slide Show** button. When you click this button to start a slide show, the slide show starts from the current slide instead of from the beginning. Slide 4 appears in Slide Show view. Only the title, the arrow shapes, and the footer appear on the slide.
3. Press **SPACEBAR** to advance the slide show. The first animation, the emphasis animation that underlines the title, occurs.
4. Press **SPACEBAR** again. The photo on the right appears starting at the center of the photo and building out to the left and right edges.
5. Click anywhere on the screen. The photo on the left appears with the same animation as the photo on the right.
6. Press **ESC**. The slide show ends and Slide 4 appears in Normal view.

Antónia doesn't like the emphasis animation applied to the slide title. It's distracting because the photos are the focus of the slide, not the title. Also, she thinks it would be better if the photo on the left appeared before the photo on the right. Finally, Antónia wants the arrows to animate after each photo appears. To fix these issues, you will remove the animation applied to the title, add entrance animations to the arrows, and change the order of the animations so that the photo on the left animates first, followed by its arrow, then the photo on the right animates followed by its arrow.

To remove the title animation, animate the arrows, and change the order of the animations:

1. Click the **Inclusive and Accessible Activities** title text. In the Animation group, the yellow emphasis animation Underline is selected.
2. In the Animation group, in the Animation gallery, use the scroll arrows as necessary to locate the top of the gallery, and then click **None**. The animation that was applied to the title is removed, the animation sequence icon no longer appears next to the title text box, and the other two animation sequence icons on the slide are renumbered 1 and 2. Next you will apply animation to the two arrows.

   Tip You can also click the animation sequence icon, and then press DELETE to remove an animation.

3. Apply the entrance **Wipe** animation to the "Wheelchair-friendly Equipment and Leagues" arrow, and then change its effect option to **From Left**.
4. Apply the entrance **Wipe** animation to the "Equipment Chosen to Appeal to All Children" arrow, and then change its effect option to **From Right**. Now you need to select the animation applied to the photo on the left and change it so that it occurs first. You can select the object or the animation sequence icon to modify an animation.
5. Next to the left photo, click the **2** animation sequence icon. In the Animation group, in the Animation gallery, the green Split entrance animation is selected. Refer to Figure 2–29.

Figure 2–29 Animation selected to change its order

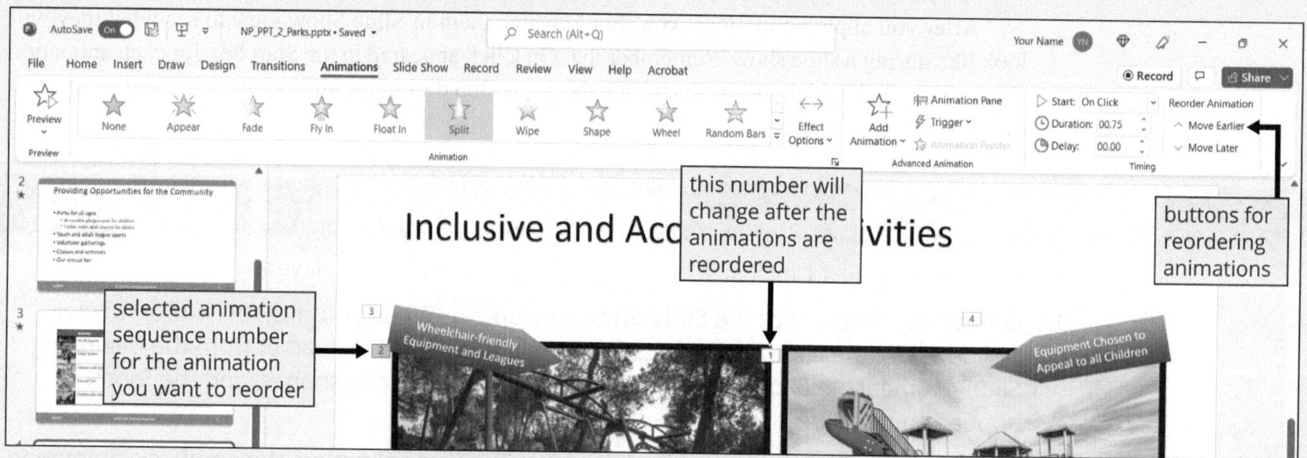

istock.com/Moshe Einhorn; istock.com/Moshe Einhorn

6. In the Timing group, click the **Move Earlier** button. The animation sequence icon next to the photo on the left changes from 2 to 1, and the animation sequence icon next to the photo on the right changes from 1 to 2. Now you need to reorder the animations so that the "Wheelchair-friendly Equipment and Leagues" arrow animates after the picture on the left.
7. Next to the "Wheelchair-friendly Equipment and Leagues" arrow, click the **3** animation sequence icon, and then in the Timing group, click the **Move Earlier** button.
8. In the Preview group, click the **Preview** button. The photo on the left appears, then the "Wheelchair-friendly Equipment and Leagues" arrow, then the photo on the right, and then the "Equipment chosen to appeal to all children" arrow.

Changing How an Animation Starts

Remember that when you apply an animation, the default is for the object to animate On Click, which means when you advance through the slide show. You can change this so that an animation happens automatically, either at the same time as another animation or when the slide transitions, or after another animation or the transition.

Antónia wants the arrows to appear automatically after each photo without the presenter needing to advance the slide show.

To change how the animation for the arrows start:

1. On Slide 4 ("Inclusive and Accessible Activities"), click the **Wheelchair-friendly Equipment and Leagues** arrow. The Wipe entrance animation is selected in the Animation group, and in the Timing group, On Click appears in the Start box.
2. In the Timing group, click the **Start** arrow. The menu lists three choices for starting an animation: On Click, With Previous, and After Previous.
3. Click **After Previous**. Now this arrow will appear automatically after the photo on the left appears. Notice that the animation sequence number next to the arrow changed to 1, the same number as the animation sequence number next to the photo on the left. This is because you will not need to advance the slide show to start this animation.
4. Change the way the animation applied to the "Equipment Chosen to Appeal to All Children" arrow starts to **After Previous**.

When you preview an animation, it plays automatically on the slide in Normal view, even if the timing setting for the animation is On Click. To make sure the timing settings are correct, you need to watch the animation in a slide show.

To view and test the animations:

1. On the status bar, click the **Slide Show** button . Slide 4 appears in Slide Show view.
2. Press **SPACEBAR**. The photo on the left appears, followed by the "Wheelchair-friendly Equipment and Leagues" arrow.
3. Press **SPACEBAR**. The photo on the right appears, followed by the "Equipment Chosen to Appeal to all Children" arrow.
4. Press **ESC** to end the slide show.

When you set an animation to occur automatically during the slide show, it happens immediately after the previous action. You can add a pause before the animation so that there is time between automatic animations. To do this, you increase the time in the Delay box in the Timing group. Like the Duration time, Delay times are measured in seconds.

To give the audience time to look at the first photo before the second photo appears on Slide 4, you will add a delay to the animation that is applied to the photo on the right.

To add a delay to the animations applied to the arrows:

1. On Slide 4 ("Inclusive and Accessible Activities"), click the "Equipment Chosen to Appeal to All Children" arrow to select it, if necessary. In the Timing group, 00.00 appears in the Delay box.
2. In the Timing group, click the **Delay** up arrow four times to change the time to one second. After the photo on the right appears (the previous animation), the "Equipment Chosen to Appeal to All Children" arrow will appear after a delay of one second.
3. Apply a one-second delay to the animation applied to the "Wheelchair-friendly Equipment and Leagues" arrow.
4. On the status bar, click the **Slide Show** button. Slide 4 appears in Slide Show view.
5. Press **SPACEBAR**. The photo on the left appears, and then after a one-second delay, the "Wheelchair-friendly Equipment and Leagues" arrow appears.
6. Press **SPACEBAR**. The photo on the right appears, and then after a one-second delay, the "Equipment Chosen to Appeal to All Children" arrow appears.
7. Press **ESC** to end the slide show, and then Save your changes if necessary.

Animating Lists

If you animate a list, the default is for each of the first-level items to animate On Click. This type of animation focuses your audience's attention on each item, without the distraction of items that you haven't discussed yet.

Antónia wants you to add an Entrance animation to the bulleted list on Slide 2. She wants each first-level bulleted item to appear on the slide one at a time so that the audience won't be able to read ahead while she is discussing each point.

To animate the bulleted list on Slide 2:

1. Display Slide 2 ("Providing Opportunities for the Community"), and then click anywhere in the bulleted list to make the text box active.
2. On the Animations tab, in the Animation group, click the **Fly In** animation. The animation previews on the slide as the bulleted items fly in from the bottom. When the "Parks for all ages" item flies in, its subitems fly in with it. After the preview is finished, the numbers 1 through 5 appear next to the bulleted items. Notice that the subitems have the same animation sequence number as their first-level item. This means that the subitems are set to start With Previous or After Previous. Refer to Figure 2–30.

Figure 2–30 Fly In entrance animation applied to a bulleted list with subitems

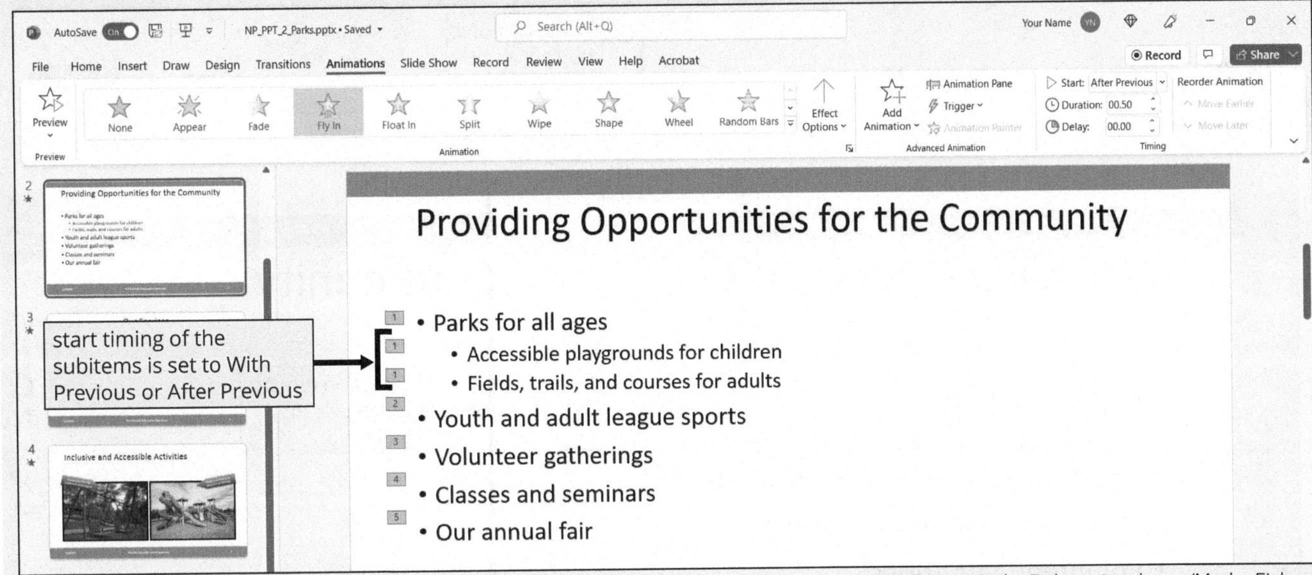

istock.com/Moshe Einhorn; istock.com/Moshe Einhorn

3. Next to the "Parks for all ages" bulleted item, click the **1** animation sequence icon to select it. In the Timing group, On Click appears in the Start box.
4. Next to the subitem "Accessible playgrounds for children," click the **1** animation sequence icon. In the Timing group, With Previous appears in the Start box.

If you wanted to change how the items in the list animate during the slide show, you could change the Start setting of each item, or you could change the sequence effect. Sequence effects appear on the Effect Options menu in addition to the Direction options when you apply an animation to a text box. The default is for the items to appear By Paragraph. This means each first-level item animates one at a time—with its subitems, if there are any—when you advance the slide show. You can change this setting so that the entire list animates at once as one object, or so that each first-level item animates at the same time but as separate objects.

To examine the Sequence options for the animated list:

1. Click in the bulleted list, and then in the Animation group, click the **Effect Options** button. The Sequence options appear at the bottom of the menu, below the Direction options, and By Paragraph is selected. Refer to Figure 2–31.

Figure 2–31 Animation effect options for a bulleted list

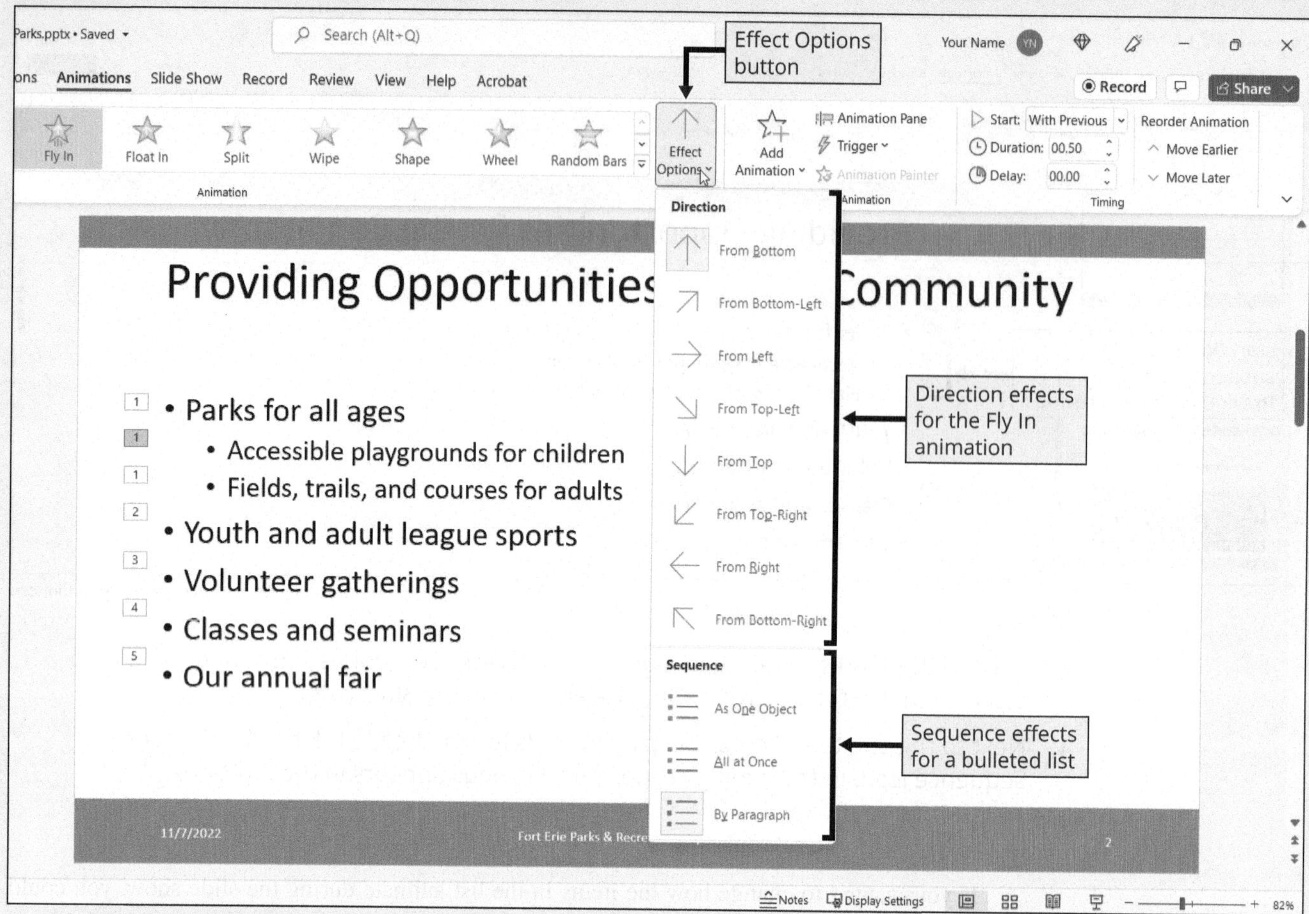

istock.com/Moshe Einhorn; istock.com/Moshe Einhorn

2. Click **As One Object**. The animation preview shows the entire text box fly in. After the preview, only one animation sequence icon appears next to the text box, indicating that the entire text box will animate as a single object. In the Timing group, On Click appears in the Start box.
3. In the Animation group, click the **Effect Options** button, and then under Sequence, click **All at Once**. The animation previews again, but this time each of the first-level items fly in as separate objects, although they all fly in at the same time. Visually, there is not much of a difference between this option and the As One Object option for the Fly In animation. After the preview, animation sequence icons, all numbered 1, appear next to each bulleted item, indicating that each item will animate separately but you only need to advance the slide show once.

> **Tip** It is easier to see the difference between the As One Object and All at Once sequence effect options when the Wheel or Grow & Turn animations are applied.

4. Next to the first bulleted item, click the **1** animation sequence icon. In the Timing group, On Click appears in the Start box.
5. Next to the second first-level item ("Youth and adult league sports"), click the **1** animation sequence icon. In the Timing group, With Previous appears in the Start box.
6. In the Animation group, click the **Effect Options** button, and then click **By Paragraph**. The sequence effect changes back to its original setting.
7. Save your changes if necessary.

Proskills

Decision Making: Just Because You Can Doesn't Mean You Should

PowerPoint provides you with many tools that enable you to create interesting and creative slide shows. Just because a tool is available doesn't mean you should use it. You need to give careful thought before deciding to use a tool to enhance the content of your presentation. One example of a tool to use sparingly is sound effects with transitions. Most of the time you do not need to use sound to highlight the fact that one slide is leaving the screen while another appears. Many people find sound transitions annoying or distracting.

You will also want to avoid using too many or frivolous animations. It is easy to go overboard with animations, and they can quickly become distracting and make your presentation seem less professional. Before you apply an animation, you should know what you want to emphasize and why you want to use an animation. Animations should enhance your message. When you are finished giving your presentation, you want your audience to remember your message, not your animations.

Using the Morph Transition

The Morph transition is a special transition that essentially combines a transition with an animation. With the Morph transition, you can move an object to a new location on a slide; change the size, shape, and color of an object; and zoom into or out from an object.

To use the Morph transition, you need to follow these steps:

1. Create a slide that contains all of the items you want to appear to change size or position during the slide show.
2. Duplicate that slide or create a second slide with at least one object in common with the first slide.
3. On the duplicate slide, move the object or objects to the new position or make other changes to the objects, such as changing their size or color.
4. Apply the Morph transition to the duplicate slide.

When you use the Morph transition, you might need to place objects in the area outside the actual slide. The area outside of the slide is part of the PowerPoint workspace, but anything positioned in this area will not be visible in Slide Show or Presenter view. To use the workspace, you may need to zoom out.

To drag objects off Slide 5:

1. Display Slide 5 ("Fun for Everyone"). This slide contains four pictures. During the slide show, each picture needs to appear in the center of the slide and then move out of the way to make space for the next picture. First, you will move all of the pictures off of the slide to the workspace, and then you will zoom out to see more of the workspace.
2. On the status bar, click the **Zoom Out** button [-] as many times as needed to change the zoom percentage to 40%.
3. Drag the first picture (the girl in a dress on a yellow slide) to the left of the slide, using the smart guides to keep it aligned with the other pictures.
4. Drag the next picture (father and daughter on the play structure) off the slide and position it to the left of the first picture.
5. Drag the next picture (boy driving a toy truck) to the right of the slide, and then drag the last picture (children on a swing set) to the right of the picture of the boy. Refer to Figure 2–32. This is the starting slide for the Morph transition.

Figure 2–32 Pictures moved off Slide 5

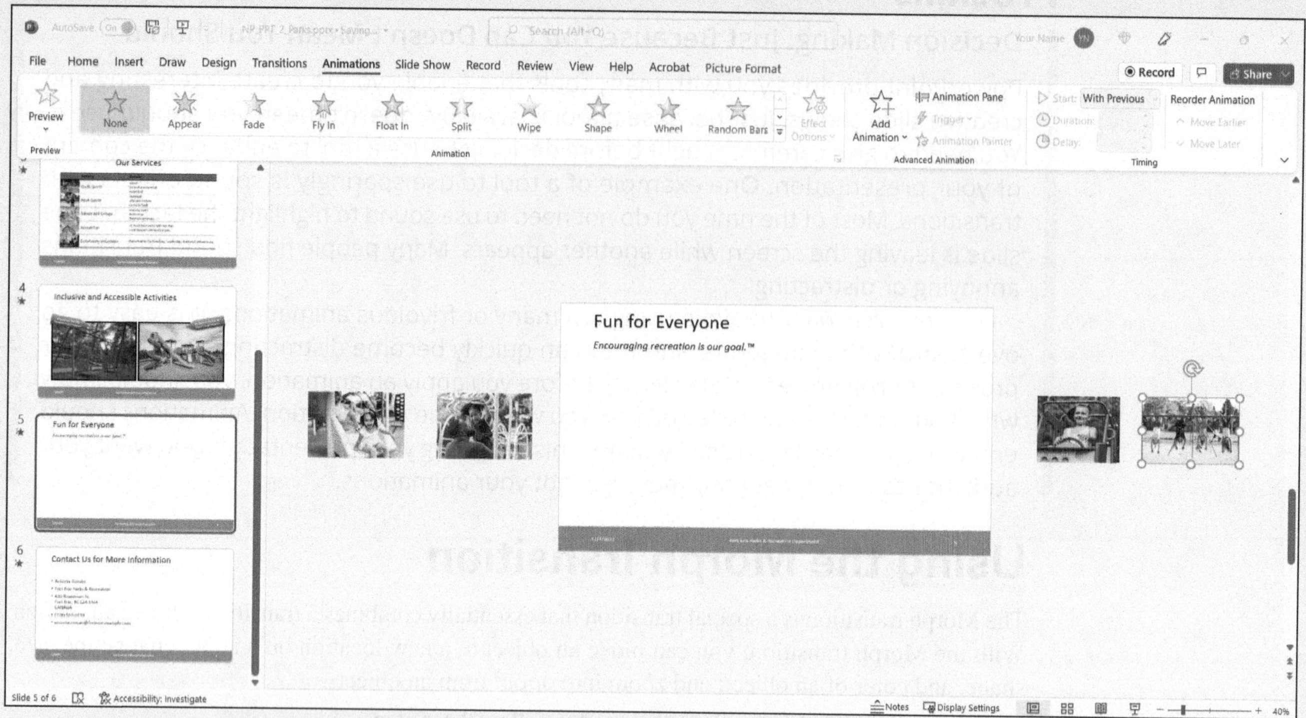

istock.com/maroke; istock.com/CandyRetriever; FatCamera/E+/Getty Images; istock.com/Moshe Einhorn; istock.com/fundamental rights

The steps in this section instruct you to place the objects at very precise locations. The instructions are specific so that your final file matches the official solution file. If you were creating this for your own use, the placement of the objects off the slide would not need to be so precise. After you place objects in your own files, preview the transition or watch it in Slide Show view, and then decide for yourself if you like the way the objects appear to move or if you want to reposition them for a better effect.

You have created the starting slide for the Morph transition. Next, you need to duplicate the slide and move and change at least one object.

To duplicate Slide 5 and resize and reposition a photo on Slide 6:

1. In the pane that contains the slide thumbnails, right-click the **Slide 5** thumbnail, and then click **Duplicate Slide**. The new Slide 6 is selected.
2. To the left of Slide 6, click the picture of the girl in the dress on the yellow slide, and then click the **Picture Format** tab.
3. In the Size group, click in the **Shape Height** box, type **4**, and then press **ENTER**.
4. Drag the picture of the girl on the yellow slide to the center of the slide so that the smart guides show that it is centered both horizontally and vertically.

   Trouble? If you have difficulty making the correct smart guides appear, use the Align Center and Align Middle commands in the Arrange group.

5. Click the **Transitions** tab, and then in the Transition to This Slide group, in the Transitions gallery, click the **Morph** transition. The Morph transition is applied to Slide 6, and the picture of the girl on the yellow slide moves onto the slide and resizes as the transition previews.

6. **6.** Display Slide 5, and then on the status bar, click the **Slide Show** button. Slide 5 appears in Slide Show view.
7. **7.** Press **SPACEBAR**. Slide 6 appears, and the picture of the girl slides onto the slide and gets larger.

   Tip If you want the objects to move more quickly or more slowly, change the duration of the Morph transition.

8. **8.** Press **ESC** to end the slide show.

The Morph transition made it look like you had applied both the Fly In animation and the Zoom animation to the picture. Now that you have seen how the Morph transition works, you will repeat the process until the final slide shows all the photos correctly positioned and sized.

To complete the Morph transition effect for the pictures originally on Slide 5:

1. Duplicate Slide 6. The new Slide 7 is selected. On the Transitions tab, the Morph transition is selected. When you duplicated Slide 6, the transition was copied as well.
2. On Slide 7, change the height of the picture of the girl on the yellow slide to **2"**.
3. Drag the picture of the girl on the yellow slide to the right so that the smart guides show that the middle of the picture aligns with the center of the slide, and so that the right edge of the picture aligns with the right edge of the slide.
4. To the right of the slide, change the height of the picture of the boy driving the truck to **4"**, and then drag the picture of the boy to the center of the slide.
5. Duplicate Slide 7.
6. On the new Slide 8, change the height of the picture of the boy to **2"** and then drag the picture to the left so that the smart guides show that the bottom of the picture aligns with the center of the picture of the girl on the yellow slide, and so that the left of the picture aligns with the left of the title and subtitle text boxes.
7. To the left of the slide, change the height of the picture of the father and daughter to **4"**, and then drag the picture of the father and daughter to the center of the slide.
8. Duplicate Slide 8.
9. On the new Slide 9, change the height of the picture of the father and daughter to **2"** and then drag it to approximately one-quarter of an inch to the left of the girl on the yellow slide and use the smart guide to align the bottom and top of the picture of the father and daughter with the bottom and top of the picture of the boy.
10. To the right of the slide, change the height of the picture of the kids on the swing set to **4"** and then drag it to the center of the slide.
11. Duplicate Slide 9.
12. On the new Slide 10, change the height of the picture of the kids on the swing set to **2"** and then position it to the left of the picture of the father and daughter so that the middle of the picture of the kids on the swing set aligns with the bottom of the picture of the boy and so that there is the same amount of space between the picture of the kids on the swing set and the photos on either side of it.
13. On the status bar, zoom in until the slide view is at 70%. Compare your screen to Figure 2–33.

Figure 2–33 Final positions of the pictures on Slide 10

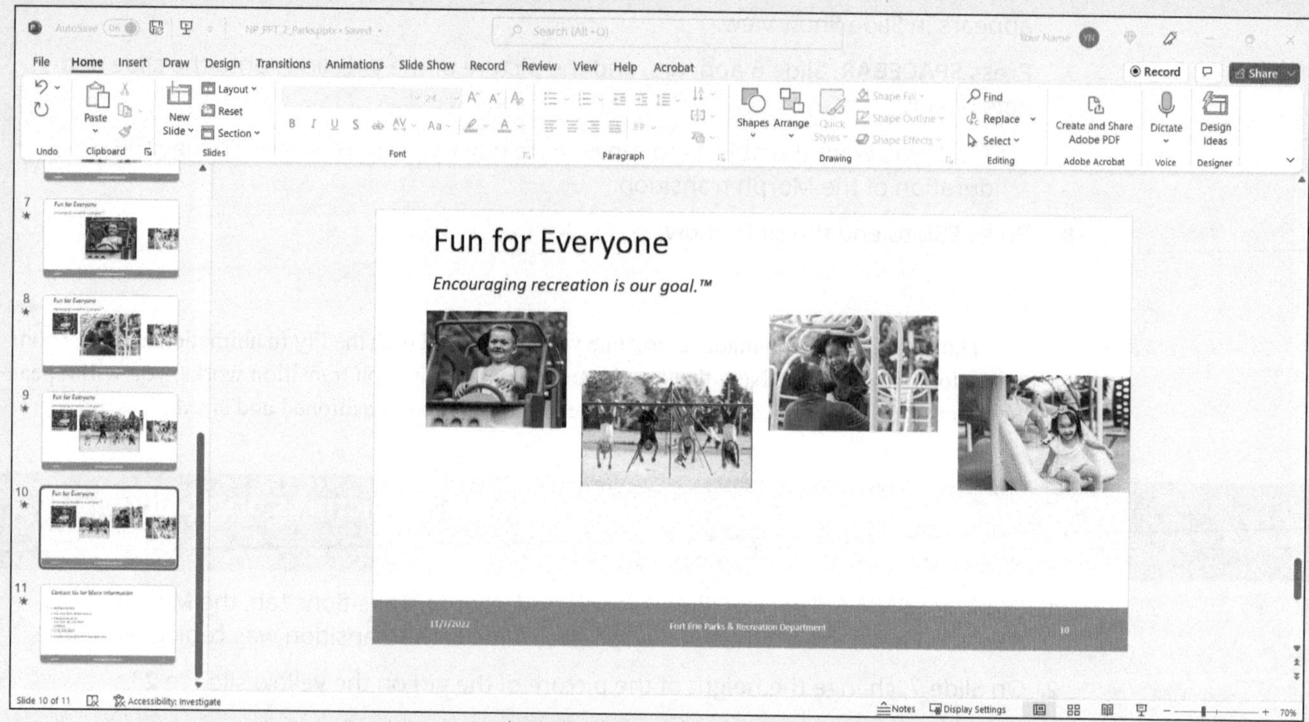

istock.com/FatCamera; istock.com/fundamental rights; istock.com/maroke; istock.com/CandyRetriever

Now that you have created all the necessary slides, you can view the slides in Slide Show view to see the effect of the Morph transition.

To view Slides 5 through 10 in Slide Show view:

1. Display Slide 5 (the first "Fun for Everyone" slide), and then on the status bar, click the **Slide Show** button. Slide 5 appears in Slide Show view. The pictures that you positioned to the left and right of the slide are not visible. In the lower-right corner of the screen, the slide number 5 appears.
2. Press **SPACEBAR**. The picture of the girl appears from the left, moves to the slide, and grows larger. In the lower-right corner of the screen, the slide number changes to 6.
3. Press **SPACEBAR**. The picture of the girl shrinks and moves to the right of the slide while the picture of the boy appears from the right, moves to the center of the slide, and grows in size. Again, the slide number changes.
4. Press **SPACEBAR** three more times. The other two pictures move onto the slide and are repositioned in their final locations. The changing slide numbers distract from the effect you are trying to create with the Morph transition.
5. Press **ESC** to end the slide show, and then click the **Insert** tab.
6. In the Text group, click the **Header & Footer** button, click the **Slide number** check box to deselect it, and then click **Apply to All**. Now the changing slide number will not distract the viewer from the Morph transition effect.

You can also use the Morph transition on slides that contain text. You will apply the Morph transition to Slide 2 so that the title on Slide 1 looks like it moves into the footer on Slide 2.

To apply the Morph transition to Slide 2:

1. Display Slide 1. The title text box contains the text "Fort Erie Parks & Recreation."
2. Display Slide 2. The footer contains the same text as in the title text box on Slide 1—"Fort Erie Parks & Recreation Department."
3. On the ribbon, click the **Transitions** tab, and then click the **Morph** transition. The Morph transition is applied to Slide 2 and previews.
4. On the Quick Access Toolbar, click the **Start From Beginning** button. Slide 1 appears in Slide Show view.
5. Press **SPACEBAR**. Slide 2 appears in Slide Show view.
6. Press **SPACEBAR**. The first bulleted item flies onto the screen.
7. Press **ESC** to end the slide show, and then save the changes to the presentation.

Adding and Modifying Video

You can add video to slides to play during your presentation. PowerPoint supports various file formats, including the MPEG-4 format, the Windows Media Audio/Video format, and the QuickTime movie format. After you insert a video, you can modify it by changing playback options, changing the length of time the video plays, and applying formats and styles to the video.

Adding Video to Slides

To insert a video stored on your computer or network, click the Insert Video button in a content placeholder to open the Insert Video dialog box. You can also click the Video button in the Media group on the Insert tab, and then click This Device to open the same Insert Video dialog box.

Reference

Adding Videos Stored on Your Computer or Network

- In a content placeholder, click the Insert Video button to open the Insert Video dialog box, or click the Insert tab on the ribbon, and then in the Media group, click the Video button, and then click This Device to open the Insert Video dialog box.
- Click the video you want to use, and then click the Insert button.
- Choose how the video starts by clicking the Playback tab, and then in the Video Options group:
- In the Start box, leave the setting as In Click Sequence to have the video start playing when you advance the slide show, when you click anywhere on the video, or when you click the Play button on the video toolbar.
- Click the Start arrow, and then click Automatically to have the video start automatically when the slide appears in Slide Show view.
- Click the Start arrow, and then click When Clicked On to have the video start when you click anywhere on the video or when you click the Play button on the video toolbar.
- Click the Play Full Screen check box to select it to have the video fill the screen.
- Click the Rewind after Playing check box to select it to have the poster frame display after the video plays.
- Click the Volume button, and then click a volume level or click Mute.

Antónia gave you a video that she wants you to add to Slide 11. The video shows a happy dog running toward the camera in slow motion.

To add a video to Slide 11 and play it:

1. Display Slide 11 ("Contact Us for More Information"), and then in the content placeholder, click the **Insert Video** button. The Insert Video dialog box opens.
2. In the **PowerPoint2 > Module** folder, click **Support_PPT_2_Slide.mp4**, and then click **Insert**. The video is inserted on the slide in place of the content placeholder. The first frame of the video is displayed, and a video toolbar with controls for playing the video appears below it. The video contextual tabs appear on the ribbon. Refer to Figure 2–34.

   > **Tip** To link a video to a slide, in the Insert Video dialog box, click the Insert arrow, and then click Link to File.

Figure 2–34 Video added to Slide 11

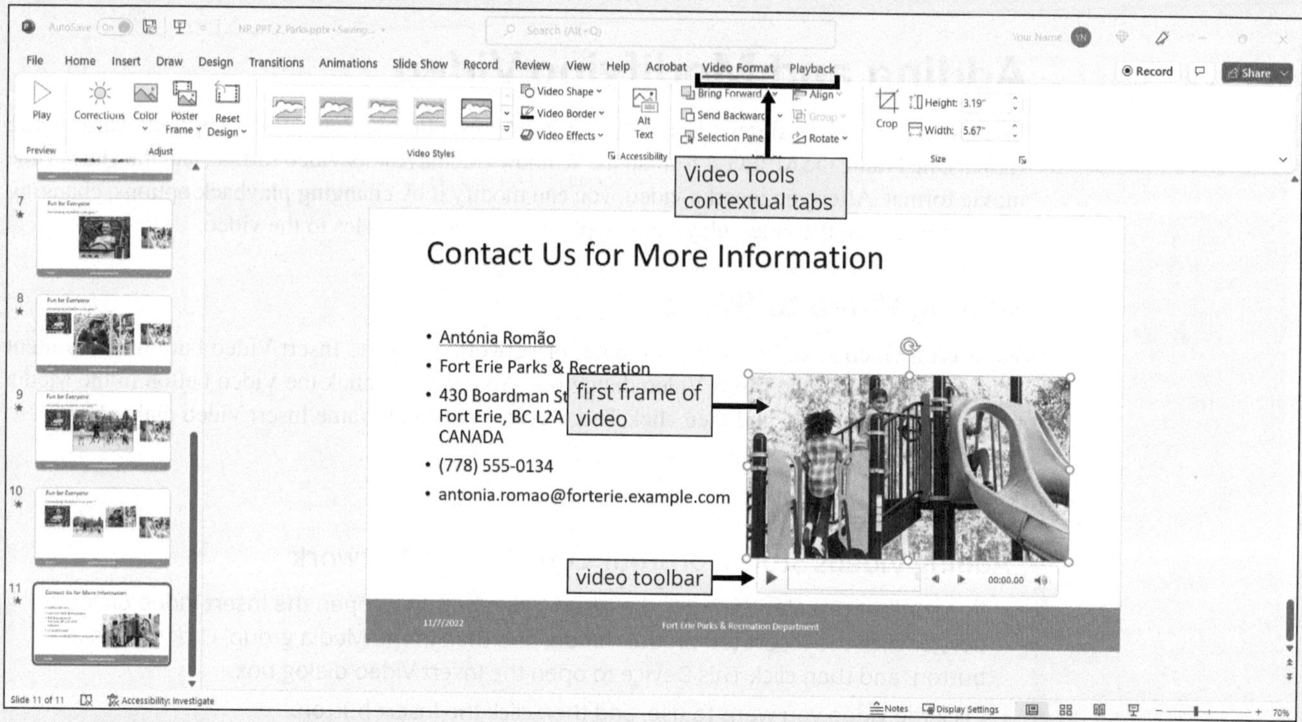

istock.com/fstop123

4. On the video toolbar, click the **Play** button. The Play button changes to the Pause button and the video plays. Watch the approximately 16-second video (note that this video does not have any sound).
5. Click the **Playback** tab. In the Start box, In Click Sequence appears. This means that the video will start playing during a slide show when you advance the slide show or when you click the video or the Play button on the video toolbar. Next, you'll watch the video in Slide Show view.
6. On the status bar, click the **Slide Show** button. Slide 11 appears in Slide Show view.
7. Press **SPACEBAR**. The video starts playing because you advanced the slide show.
8. Before the video finishes playing, move the pointer to make it visible, and then click the video. The video pauses. To stop the video from playing, you can click it, or you can move the pointer on top of the video and then click the Pause button on the video toolbar.

Because you already started playing the video once, if you advance the slide show, the next slide will appear. If you want to start the video playing again, you need to click it or click the Play button on the video toolbar,

9. Move the pointer on top of the video. The video toolbar appears, and the pointer changes to the pointing finger pointer.
10. Click anywhere on the video. The video continues playing from the point it left off.
11. Press **SPACEBAR**. The black slide that indicates the end of the slide show appears.
12. Press **SPACEBAR** again to return to Normal view.

Insight

Inserting Pictures and Videos You Find Online

In addition to adding pictures and video stored on your computer or network to slides, you can also add pictures and video stored on websites. To add pictures from a website or OneDrive, you click the Pictures button in the Images group on the Insert tab, and then click Online Pictures. When you do this, the Online Pictures window opens, in which you can use the Bing search engine to search for images stored on the Internet. Your results will be similar to those you would get if you typed keywords in the Search box on the Bing home page in your browser.

To add a video from a website such as YouTube, you click the Video button in the Media group on the Insert tab, and then click Online Video to open a window for inserting a video from a website. In this window, you type or paste the web address of a video stored on a website such as YouTube or Vimeo. A preview of the video appears in the window so you can confirm it. Keep in mind that using online media is subject to each provider's Terms of Use policy.

Trimming Videos

Keeping your videos short and only showing necessary content helps to keep your audience focused. If a video is too long, or if there are parts at the beginning or end of the video that you don't want to show during the presentation, you can trim it. To do this, click the Trim Video button in the Editing group on the Playback tab, and then, in the Trim Video dialog box, drag the green start slider or the red stop slider to a new position to mark where the video will start and stop.

Antónia wants the video to end right after the dog runs off screen, so she wants you to trim it.

To trim the video on Slide 11:

1. On Slide 11 ("Contact Us for More Information"), click the video to select it, and then click the **Playback** tab, if necessary.
2. In the Editing group, click the **Trim Video** button. The Trim Video dialog box opens. Refer to Figure 2–35.

Figure 2–35 Trim Video dialog box

istock.com/fstop123

Trouble? If the video appears black in the dialog box, click the Play button in the dialog box, and then click the Pause button to stop the playback. The video should appear.

3. Drag the red **Stop** tab to the left until the time in the End Time box is approximately 9.5 seconds.

Tip Click a point on the video toolbar, click the Add Bookmark button in the Bookmarks group on the Playback tab to add a bookmark, then add the Seek media animation to the video. When you advance the slide show, the video will start from the bookmark.

4. If the number in the End Time box is not 00:09.500, click in the End Time box, click after the last number, edit the time so it is **00:09.500,** and then click **OK**.
5. On the video toolbar, click the **Play** button ▶. The video plays from the beginning but stops playing after 9.5 seconds. The last almost 6.5 seconds of the video do not play.
6. Save your changes if necessary.

Setting a Poster Frame

The frame that appears on the video object when the video is not playing is called the **poster frame**. The default poster frame for a video is the first frame of the video. You can select any frame from the video or any image stored in a file as the poster frame. If the video is set to rewind, the poster frame will reappear after playing.

Antónia wants you to select a poster frame for the video on Slide 11.

To set a poster frame for the video on Slide 11:

1. On Slide 11 ("Contact Us for More Information"), click the video to select it, if necessary, and then click the **Video Format** tab.
2. Point to the toolbar below the video. A ScreenTip appears identifying the time of the video at that point. Refer to Figure 2–36.

Figure 2–36 Setting a poster frame

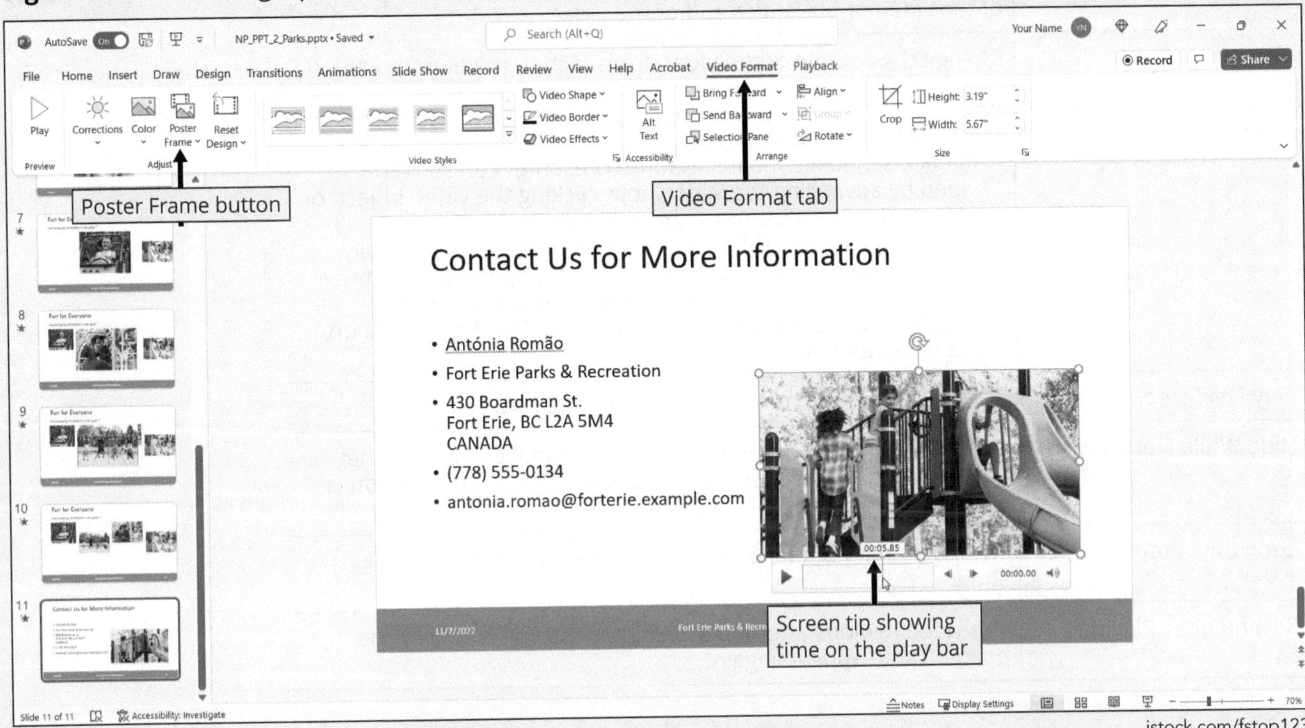

istock.com/fstop123

3. On the video toolbar, click at approximately the 4.50-second mark. The frame at the 4.50-second mark shows the child in the pink shirt and jeans at the top of the slide.

   Trouble? You might not be able to click at exactly the 4.50-second mark. Click as close to it as you can (for example, 4.49 or 5.55).

4. In the Adjust group, click the **Poster Frame** button. The Poster Frame menu opens.

   Tip Like pictures, you can change the brightness and contrast of a video or recolor it using the buttons in the Adjust group. To reset a video, click the Reset Design button in the Adjust group.

5. Click **Current Frame**. The message "Poster Frame Set" appears in the video's play bar, and the frame currently visible in the video object is set as the poster frame.
6. On the status bar, click the **Slide Show** button. Slide 11 appears in Slide Show view. The poster frame shows the child in the pink shirt and jeans at the top of the slide.
7. Click the video. The video plays.
8. Press **ESC** to end the slide show.

Modifying Video Playback Options

You can change several options for how a video plays. The video playback options are listed in Figure 2–37.

Figure 2–37 Video playback options

Video Option	Function
Fade Duration	Set the number of seconds to fade the video in at the beginning of the video or out at the end of the video.
Volume	Change the volume of the video from high to medium or low or mute it.
Start	Change how the video starts: • In Click Sequence means that the presenter can start the video by advancing the slide show, clicking the video object, or clicking the Play button on the video toolbar. • Automatically means that the video will start automatically after the slide appears on the screen during the slide show. • When Clicked On means that the video starts when the presenter clicks the video object or clicks the Play button on the video toolbar.
Play Full Screen	The video fills the screen during the slide show.
Hide While Not Playing	The video does not appear on the slide when it is not playing; make sure the video is set to play automatically if this option is selected.
Loop until Stopped	The video plays until the next slide appears during the slide show.
Rewind after Playing	The video rewinds after it plays so that the first frame or the poster frame appears again.

As you have seen, when you insert a video, its Start setting is set to In Click Sequence. In Click Sequence for a video means the same thing that On Click means for an animation. Anything you do to advance the slide show causes the video to start. If you want to start the video by clicking the video object or the Play button on the video toolbar, set the Start setting to On Click. When On Click is selected, if you click somewhere else on the screen or do anything else to advance the slide show, the video will not play. You can also modify the Start setting so that the video plays automatically when the slide appears during the slide show. The Start setting is on the Playback tab.

In addition to changing the Start setting, you can set a video to fill the screen when it plays during the slide show. If you set the option to play full screen, the video will fill the screen when it plays, covering the slide title and anything else on the slide. You can also set a video to rewind so that it displays the poster frame after it plays.

Antónia wants you to change several playback options of the video on Slide 11. She wants the video to start automatically when Slide 11 appears during a slide show, and she wants it to fill the screen while it plays. When it is finished playing, she wants it to rewind so that the poster frame is on screen again.

To modify the playback options of the video:

1. On Slide 11 ("Contact Us for More Information"), click the video to select it, if necessary, and then click the **Playback** tab. In the Video Options group, In Click Sequence appears in the Start box. Refer to Figure 2–38.

Figure 2–38 Options on the Video Tools Playback tab

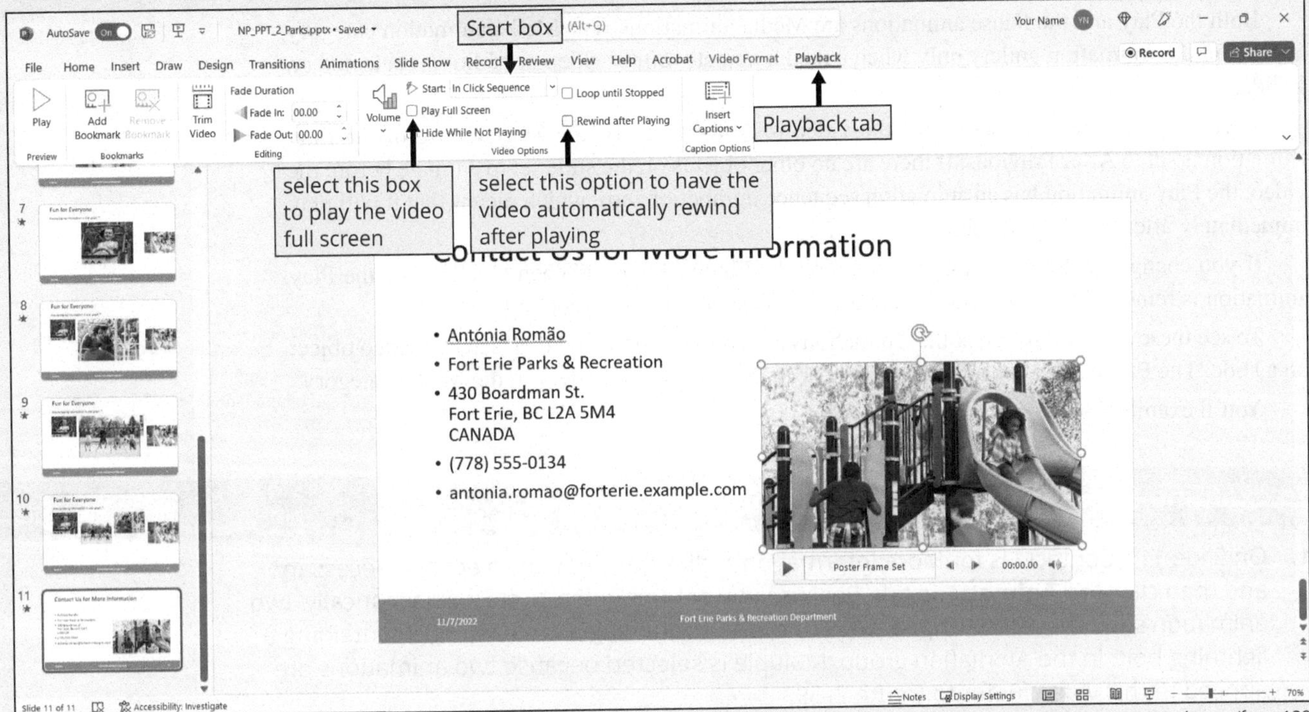

istock.com/fstop123

2. In the Video Options group, click the **Start** arrow, and then click **Automatically**. Now the video will start automatically when the slide appears during the slide show.

   Tip You can adjust the volume of a video while it plays, or you can set the default volume by clicking the Volume button in the Video Options group on the Playback tab and then clicking an option on the menu.

3. In the Video Options group, click the **Play Full Screen** check box to select it. The video will fill the screen while it plays.
4. In the Video Options group, click the **Rewind after Playing** check box to select it. The video will reset to the poster frame after it plays.
5. On the status bar, click the **Slide Show** button. Slide 11 appears briefly in Slide Show view, and then the video fills the screen and plays. After the video finishes playing, Slide 11 reappears, and the poster frame appears in the video object.
6. Press **ESC** to end the slide show, and then Save your changes if necessary.

Understanding Animation Effects Applied to Videos

When you insert a video (or audio) object, two animations are automatically applied to the video or audio object. The first animation is the Play animation. The Play animation is set to On Click. This means that when you advance the slide show, the video will start playing.

The second animation is the Pause animation. This animation has a special setting applied to it called a trigger so that you can click anywhere on the video to play it (or "unpause" it) and click the video again to pause it.

Both the Play and the Pause animations are Media animations. The Media animation category appears in the Animation gallery only when a media object—either video or audio—is selected on a slide.

If you change the Start setting of the video to Automatically, the Start setting of the Play animation is set to After Previous. If there are no other objects on the slide set to animate before the video, the Play animation has an animation sequence number of zero, which means that it will play immediately after the slide transition.

If you change the Start setting of a video on the Playback tab to When Clicked On, the Play animation is removed from the video and only the Pause animation is applied.

To see these animations, click the Animations tab on the ribbon, and then select a video object on a slide. The Pause and Play animations appear in the Animation gallery in the Media category.

You'll examine the video animations now.

To examine the Media animations applied to the video:

1. On Slide 11 ("Contact Us for More Information"), click the video to select it, if necessary, and then click the **Animations** tab. Because you set this video to start automatically, two animation sequence icons appear next to it, one containing a zero and one containing a lightning bolt. In the Animation group, Multiple is selected because two animations are applied to this video. Refer to Figure 2–39.

Figure 2–39 Two animations applied to a video

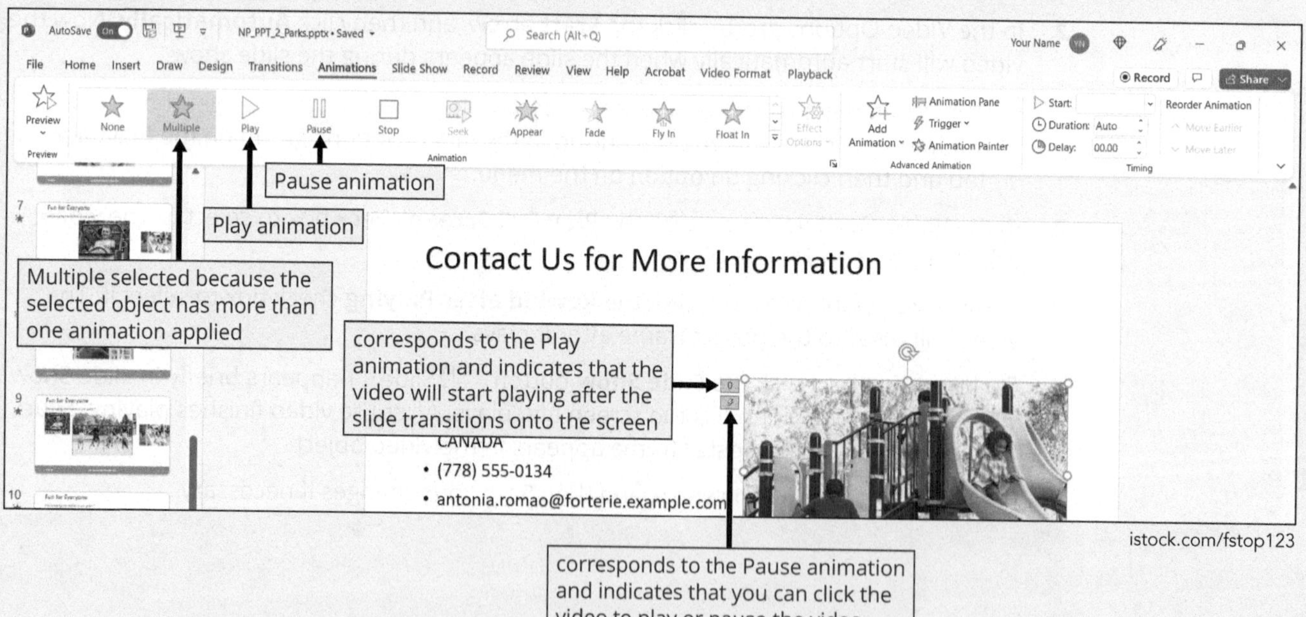

istock.com/fstop123

2. In the Animation group, in the Animations gallery, click the **More** button. The Media category appears at the top of the Animation gallery because a media object is selected.
3. Press **ESC**. The gallery closes without you making a selection.

   When more than one animation is applied to any object, you need to click each animation sequence icon to see which animation is associated with each icon.
4. Click the **0** animation sequence icon. In the Animation group, Play is selected, and in the Timing group, After Previous appears in the Start box. This start setting of the Play animation was changed to After Previous when you selected Automatically in the Start box on the Playback tab.
5. Click the **lightning bolt** animation sequence icon. In the Animation group, the Pause animation is selected, and in the Timing group, On Click appears in the Start box. This animation is applied automatically to all videos when you add them to slides. It is because of this animation that you can click anywhere on the video object during a slide show to play or pause it.
6. Click the video if necessary, and then click the **Playback** tab.
7. In the Video Options group, click the **Start arrow**, click **In Click Sequence**, click the **Animations** tab, and then click the **1** animation sequence icon. In the Animation group, Play is selected, but now On Click appears in the Start box.
8. Click the video, and then click the **Playback** tab.
9. In the Video Options group, click the **Start arrow**, click **When Clicked On**, and then click the **Animations** tab. There is only one animation applied to the video now. In the Animation group, Pause is selected, and On Click appears in the Start box.
10. Change the Start setting of the video back to **Automatically**.

Compressing Media

As with pictures, you can compress media files. If you need to send a file via email or you need to upload it, you should compress media files to make the final PowerPoint file smaller. When you compress files, you make the final presentation file smaller, but you also lower the quality of the video. You can compress videos using the following settings:

> **Tip** If you might want to show the presentation using a projector capable of high-quality display, save a copy of the presentation before you compress the media.

- **Full HD (1080p)**—compresses the videos slightly and maintains the quality of the videos
- **HD (720p)**—compresses the videos to a quality suitable for streaming over the Internet
- **Standard (480p)**—compresses the videos as small as possible

With all of the settings, any parts of videos that you trimmed off will be deleted, similar to deleting the cropped portions of photos.

After you compress media, you should watch the slides containing the videos using the equipment you will be using when giving your presentation to make sure the reduced quality is acceptable. Usually, if the videos are high quality to start with, the compressed quality will be fine. However, if the original video quality was grainy, the compressed quality might be too low, even for evaluation purposes. If you decide that you don't like the compressed quality, you can undo the compression before you close the file.

You will compress the media file you inserted. You need to send the presentation to Antónia via email, so you will compress the media as much as possible.

To compress the video in the presentation:

1. With Slide 11 ("Contact Us for More Information") displayed, click the **File** tab, and then click **Info**. Backstage view appears displaying the Info screen.
2. Click the **Compress Media** button. A menu opens listing compression choices. Refer to Figure 2–40.

Figure 2–40 Compression options on the Info screen in Backstage view

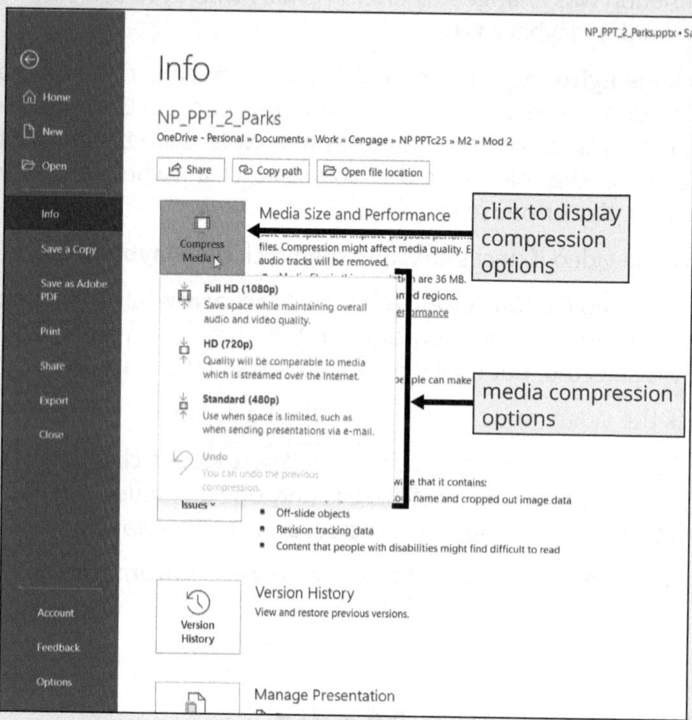

3. Click **Standard (480p)**. The Compress Media dialog box opens listing the video file in the presentation with a progress bar to show you the progress of the compression. After the file is compressed, a message appears in the Status column indicating that compression for the file is complete and stating how much the video file size was reduced. A message also appears at the bottom of the dialog box stating that the compression is complete and indicating how much the file size of the presentation was reduced. Because there is only one video in this presentation, the amount the video was reduced and the amount the presentation was reduced is the same. Refer to Figure 2–41.

Figure 2–41 Compress Media dialog box

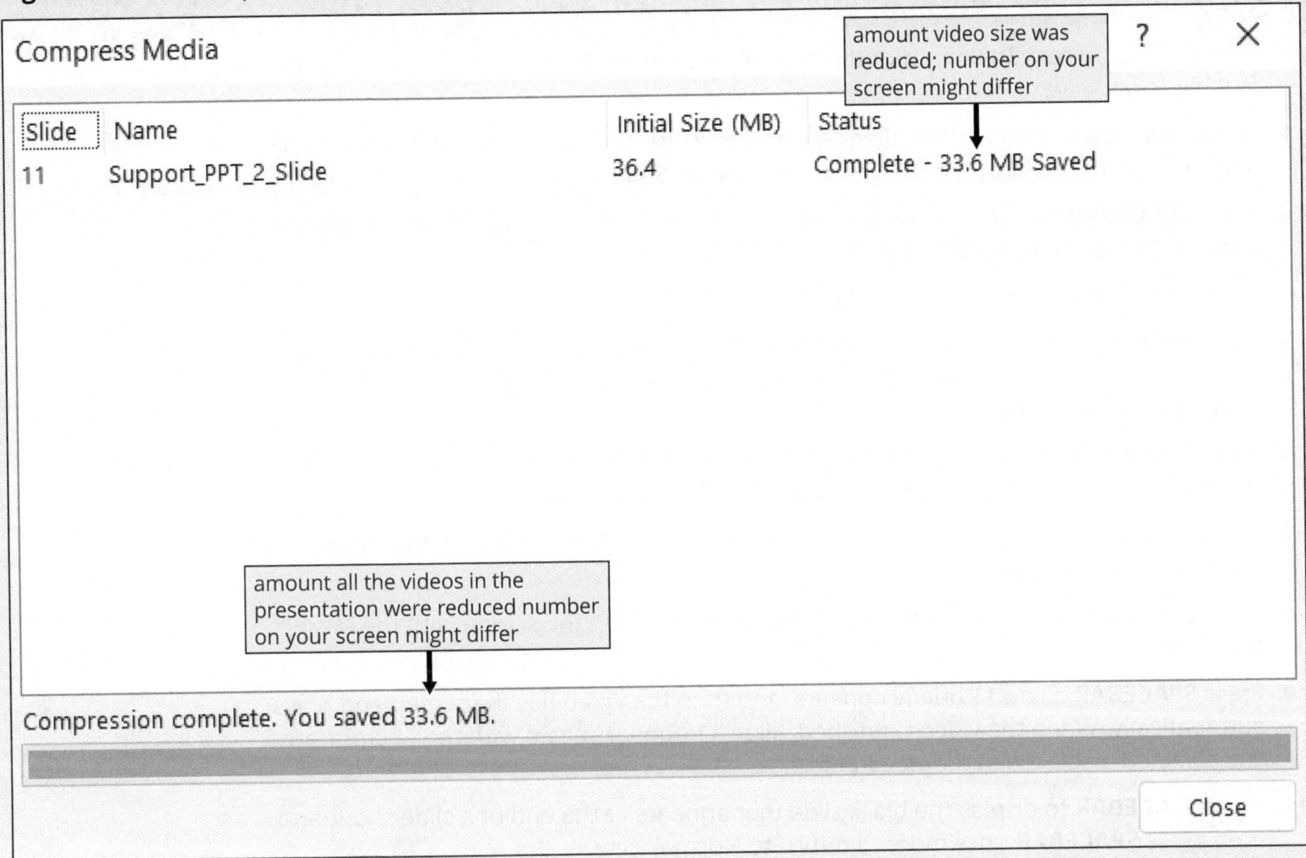

4. Click **Close**. Next to the Compress Media button on the Info screen, the bulleted list lists the total size of the media files in the presentation, states that the presentation's media was compressed to Standard (480p), and that you can undo the compression if the results are unsatisfactory. Now you need to view the compressed videos.
5. At the top of the navigation bar, click the **Back** button to display Slide 11.
6. On the status bar, click the **Slide Show** button to display the slide in Slide Show view, and then watch the video. The quality is lower, but it is sufficient for Antónia to get the general idea after you send the presentation to her via email.
7. Press **ESC** to end the slide show.
8. Display Slide 1 (the title slide), add your name as the subtitle, and then Save your changes if necessary.

Now that you have finished working on the presentation, you should view the completed presentation as a slide show.

To view the completed presentation in Slide Show view:

1. On the Quick Access Toolbar, click the **Start From Beginning** button. Slide 1 appears in Slide Show view.
2. Press **SPACEBAR**. Slide 2 ("Providing Opportunities for the Community") appears in Slide Show view with the Morph transition so the title on Slide 1 moves down to the footer.
3. Press **SPACEBAR** five times to display all the bulleted items, and then press **SPACEBAR** again to display Slide 3 ("Our Services").
4. Press **SPACEBAR** to display Slide 4 ("Inclusive and Accessible Activities").
5. Press **SPACEBAR**. The photo on the left appears with the Split animation, and then after a one-second delay, the "Wheelchair-friendly Equipment and Leagues" arrow appears with the Wipe animation.
6. Press **SPACEBAR**. The photo on the right appears, and then after a one-second delay, the "Equipment Chosen to Appeal to All children" arrow appears.
7. Press **SPACEBAR**. Slide 5 ("Fun for Everyone") appears with only the title, the slogan, and the footer information displayed.
8. Press **SPACEBAR** five times, watching the pictures move on the screen with the Morph transition.
9. Press **SPACEBAR**. Slide 11 briefly appears, and then the video fills the screen and plays automatically. When the video is finished, Slide 11 appears again with the poster frame you selected displayed in the video object.
10. Press **SPACEBAR** to display the black slide that appears at the end of a slide show, and then press **SPACEBAR** once more to return to Normal view.
11. **sam** Close the presentation file.

The final presentation file with transitions, animations, and video is interesting and should enhance Antónia's presentation.

Part 2.2 Quick Check

1. What is a transition?
2. What are animations?
3. How do you change the speed of a transition or an animation?
4. When you apply an animation to a bulleted list with subitems, how do the first-level items animate? How do the second-level items animate?
5. What is the Morph transition?
6. What is a poster frame?
7. For a video, what is the difference between the Start setting "On Click" and "In Click Sequence"?
8. What animation is applied to every video that you add to a slide no matter what the Start setting is?

Practice: Review Assignments

Data Files needed for the Review Assignments: NP_PPT_2-2.pptx, Support_PPT_2_Adoption.jpg, Support_PPT_2_NewTheme.pptx, Support_PPT_2_Coach.jpg, Support_PPT_2_Cleanup.jpg, Support_PPT_2_Volunteer.mp4

The community outreach coordinator at Fort Erie Parks and Recreation Department, Bradford Markham, organizes the park's department's Unity Community volunteer program. Through Unity Community, community members can participate as volunteers at different events throughout the year. Antónia Romão offered to help Bradford run this program. Bradford asked Antónia to help him prepare a presentation that he will use to describe the program. Antónia created the text of the presentation and asked you to find graphics to include. She also wants you to add animations and transitions to make the presentation more interesting. Complete the following steps:

1. Open the presentation **NP_PPT_2-2.pptx**, located in the PowerPoint2 > Review folder included with your Data Files, add your name as the subtitle, and then save it as **NP_PPT_2_Volunteer** to the drive and folder where you are storing your files.
2. Apply the theme from the presentation **Support_PPT_2_NewTheme.pptx**, located in the PowerPoint2 > Review folder.
3. Apply the Uncover transition to any slide. Change the Effect Options to From Bottom, and then change the duration to 0.50 seconds. Apply this transition to all of the slides, and then remove it from Slide 1 (the title slide).
4. On Slide 2 ("What Is Operation Unity Community?"), add the trademark sign after "Unity Community" and before the question mark.
5. On Slide 2, animate the bulleted list with the Random Bars entrance animation, and then change the effect so the direction of the animation is vertical.
6. On Slide 2, animate the slide title with the Float In animation, and then change the effect so that the title floats down from the top. Change the duration of the animation applied to the title to 0.50 seconds, and then change the way it starts so that the animation happens automatically after the previous action.
7. On Slide 2, change the order of the animations so that the title animates first.
8. Change the layout of Slide 3 ("Operation Unity Community Programs") to the custom Title and Table layout.
9. On Slide 3, insert a 3 x 3 table. Refer to Figure 2–42 to add the rest of the data to the table. Add a row if needed.

Figure 2–42 Data for table on Slide 3

Description	Date	Requirements
Help animal shelter dogs get adopted	Saturday, April 27	
Clean up city parks	Saturday, June 21	
Learn how to coach sports leagues	Monday, July 28	

10. In the table, delete the third column (with "Requirements" in the first cell).
11. Apply the Light Style 1 – Accent 4 table style.
12. Add a new first column (to the left of the "Description" column). Fill each cell in the new column (except the first cell) with the following pictures, all located in the PowerPoint2 > Review folder, in order from the second row to the bottom row: **Support_PPT_2_Adoption.jpg, Support_PPT_2_ Cleanup.jpg**, and **Support_PPT_2_Coach.jpg**.
13. On Slide 3, format the table as follows:
    - Change the font size of all of the text in the table to 22 points. Then change the font size of the text in the top row to 24 points.
    - Change the fill of the first row to Dark Green, Accent 4, Lighter 40%.
    - Change the width of the first column to 2". Change the width of the second column to 4". And change the width of the third column so it is just wide enough to fit its widest entry (which is 2.95").

- Change the height of rows 2 through 4 to 1.4".
- Change the border between rows 2 and 3 and the border between rows 3 and 4 to a three-point, solid line border using the Dark Green, Accent 4 color.

14. Reposition the table so it is centered horizontally on the slide and so the smart guides indicate that there is the same amount of space between the bottom of the table and the bottom of the slide as there is between the top of the title text box and the top of the slide.
15. On Slide 4, zoom out as necessary, move the picture of the two people planting a tree above the slide and the picture of the people with dogs on leashes below the slide, using the smart guides to position them so the centers of the pictures align with the center of the slide. Then change the layout to the Section Header layout, and type **Scenes from Last Year** as the title.
16. Duplicate Slide 4. On the new Slide 5, delete the title text, and then change the layout to the Blank layout. Resize the picture of the two people planting a tree so it is 5 inches high, and then position it on the slide so it is centered both horizontally and vertically on the slide. Apply the Rotated, White style to the picture on the slide, then change the color of the border to Orange, Accent 1, Lighter 40%.
17. On Slide 5, insert the Arrow: Notched Right shape. Change the fill to Dark Green, Accent 4, Lighter 40%, and change the outline to No Outline.
18. Resize the arrow so it is 1.5 inches high and 5.7 inches wide.
19. With the arrow selected, change the font size to 16 points. Then type **Volunteers planting new trees at last year's clean up** in the arrow.
20. Drag the adjustment handle at the base of the arrowhead about one-quarter inch to the left to make the arrowhead larger. (The base of the arrowhead will be between the "a" and the "s" in "last.")
21. Position the arrow to the left of the people planting trees so the left edge of the arrow aligns with the left edge of the slide and the bottom of the border around the shape is aligned with the bottom of the picture.
22. Apply the Fly In entrance animation to the arrow, and then change the effect so that it has enters from the left. Change the way the animation starts so that it starts after the previous action. Set a delay of one second.
23. Duplicate Slide 5. On the new Slide 6, reset the picture to remove the style. Then resize the picture so it is 3.75 inches high and center it vertically and horizontally on the slide.
24. On Slide 6, move the picture of the people with the dogs onto the slide (it will be on top of the other picture and the arrow will still be visible). Resize the picture of the people with dogs on leashes so it is 5 inches high, and then center it horizontally and vertically on the slide.
25. Copy the formatting applied to the picture on Slide 5 to the picture of the people with dogs on Slide 6.
26. Replace the text in the arrow with **Happy dogs with their new owners from last year's adoption event** on Slide 6.
27. On Slide 6, flip the arrow horizontally, and then position it to the right of the boy so the right edge of the arrow aligns with the right edge of the slide and the bottom of the arrow aligns with the bottom of the picture.
28. On Slide 6, change the effect of the animation applied to the arrow so it flies in from the right.
29. Duplicate Slide 6. On the new Slide 7, reset the picture of the people with dogs on leashes, then resize that picture so it is 3.75 inches high. Delete the arrow. Change the layout to Title Only.
30. On Slide 7, position the photo of the people with dogs on the left side of the slide, so that the top of the photo aligns with the bottom of the title text placeholder and so that the left edge of the photo aligns with the left edge of the slide. Position the photo of the people planting trees to the right of the other photo so that its right edge aligns with the right edge of the slide and so its bottom aligns with the bottom of the slide. Add **Come join us!** as the slide title.
31. Apply the Morph transition to Slides 5, 6, and 7.
32. On Slide 8, use the Video button in the Media group on the Insert tab to insert the video **Support_PPT_2_Volunteer.mp4** located in the PowerPoint2 > Review folder. Resize the video so it is 5.5 inches high, and then center it horizontally and vertically on the slide. Trim from the beginning of the video so the number in the Start Time box is 6.900. Set the poster frame to approximately the

3-second mark. Finally, set the playback options so that the video starts playing automatically and rewinds after playing.

33. On Slide 9 ("Sign Up Today!"), replace the "o" in "Antonia" with "ó" and the "a" in "Romao" with "ã."
34. On Slide 9, delete the empty content placeholder. Insert the Speech Bubble: Rectangle shape, and then resize it so that it is two inches high and four inches wide. (**Hint**: Scroll until you find the Callout section of the menu). Type **Make friends and help others!** in the shape. Change the font of this text to Baquet Scrips (or another script font), change the font size to 32 points, and then format this text as bold.
35. Fill the shape with the Red, Accent 2, Darker 25% color and remove the outline.
36. Format the shape with the Perspective: Upper Left effect from the Shadow submenu. Change the Blur of the shadow to 10 points.
37. Position the shape so that its middle aligns with the horizontal smart guide that indicates the middle of the slide and its left edge aligns with the left edge of the title text box. Then drag the rotate handle on the shape to the left so that the shape is tilted slightly.
38. Open the Format Shape pane to the Shape Options tab with the Size & Properties button selected and the Size section expanded. If the value in the Rotation box is not 350°, change it to 350°.
39. Add **Fort Erie Community Events** as the footer on all the slides except the title slide, and display the current date (fixed) on all the slides except the title slide. On the notes and handouts, add **Operation Unity Community** as the header and your name as the footer, and show page numbers.
40. Compress all the photos in the presentation to E-mail (96 ppi), and then compress the media to Standard (480p).
41. Save your changes, view the slide show, and then close the presentation.

Apply: Case Problem 1

Data Files needed for this Case Problem: NP_PPT_2-3.pptx, Support_PPT_2_Calendar.jpg, Support_PPT_2_Cornucopia.jpg, Support_PPT_2_Fourth.jpg, Support_PPT_2_Labor.png, Support_PPT_2_Logo.pptx, Support_PPT_2_Memorial.jpg, Support_PPT_2_NewYear.jpg, Support_PPT_2_ Sayings.mp4, Support_PPT_2_Sixty.png

Worldwide Phone Systems Ibrahim Khan is the director of human resources for Worldwide Phone Systems, a national telecommunications company headquartered in San Jose, California. He recently proposed a new system of paid holidays to the Board of Directors so that all of the employees in the company's diverse workforce will be able to request paid time off to celebrate their own religious or cultural holidays. The Board of Directors approved his plan, and now Ibrahim needs to present the details of the plans to department managers via a webinar. He asks you to help him finish the presentation, which will include photos, a video, and a table to communicate the new policy. Complete the following steps:

1. Open the file named **NP_PPT_2-3.pptx**, located in the PowerPoint2 > Case1 folder included with your Data Files, add your name as the subtitle on Slide 1, and then save it as **NP_PPT_2_Holidays** to the drive and folder where you are storing your files.
2. Apply the theme from the presentation **Support_PPT_2_Logo.pptx**, located in the PowerPoint2 > Case1 folder.
3. Apply the Cut transition to all of the slides in the presentation, then remove the transition from Slide 1 (the title slide).
4. Add **Worldwide Phone Systems** as the footer text. Display the footer text, the slide number, and the current date (using the Fixed option) on all of the slides except the title slide.
5. On Slide 1, draw a rectangle that is 11.7 inches wide and 0.2 inches high. Position the rectangle so it is on top of the blue slide bottom border and centered vertically. Remove the shape outline, and fill the rectangle with White, Background 1. (Note: You are doing this because you are going to duplicate this slide and apply the Morph transition to the new Slide 2, and this prevents the footer information from appearing on the new Slide 2.)

6. On Slide 1, insert the picture **Support_PPT_2_Calendar.jpg**, located in the PowerPoint2 > Case1 folder. Resize the picture so it is 4.3 inches high. Rotate the picture left by 90 degrees. Position the rotated picture to the left of the slide so that the top of the picture aligns with the top of the slide and so that there is about one-quarter of an inch between the picture and the slide.
7. Duplicate Slide 1. On the new Slide 2, delete your name, and then apply the Title 2 layout.
8. On Slide 2, rotate the picture of the calendar right by 90 degrees so that it is right-side-up. Apply the picture style Thick Matte, Black to the calendar picture, and then change the border color to the Red, Accent 2, Darker 25% color.
9. Position the picture in the upper-left corner of the slide so that the outside of the red border on the top and left side of the picture align with the top and left borders of the white part of the slide.
10. On the picture of the calendar, drag the rotate handle to the left until the top-left corner of the picture border is just touching the outside of the blue border around the slide. Note that when you release the mouse button, the picture will slightly increase in size so that the top-left corner of the picture will overlap the slide border.
11. Confirm that the picture of the calendar is rotated to 345°. If it is not, change the rotation so that it is.
12. Apply the Morph transition to Slide 2. Change the duration of this transition to one second.
13. On Slide 3, animate the bulleted list using the entrance Float In animation with the Float Down effect, and change the duration to 0.50 seconds. Animate the bulleted lists on Slides 5 and 6 using the same animation. On Slide 5, make sure you animate the list on the left first, and then animate the list on the right. Then on Slide 5, change the effect for both lists to All at Once.
14. On Slide 4 ("Five Fixed Holidays"), create a table with three columns and five rows. In the first row, type **Name** in the first cell, **Description** in the second cell, and **Date** in the third cell.
15. In the table, in the "Name" column, starting in the second row, type the following entries: **New Year's Day**, **Memorial Day**, **Labor Day**, and **Thanksgiving Day**. Then in the "Date" column, type the following entries: **January 1**, **Last Monday in May**, **First Monday in September**, and **4th Thursday in November**.
16. In the table, insert a new row between the Memorial Day row and the Labor Day row. In the new row in the "Name" column, type **Independence Day**, and in the "Date" column, type **July 4**.
17. In the table, delete the second column (with the label "Description" in the first row). Then add a new column to the left of the first column.
18. Change the table style to Medium Style 3 – Accent 4. Change the font size of all the text in the table to 24 points, and then align the text so it is centered vertically.
19. In the first column, starting in the second row, fill the cells with the following pictures: **Support_PPT_2_NewYear.jpg**, **Support_PPT_2_Memorial.jpg**, **Support_PPT_2_Fourth.jpg**, **Support_PPT_2_Labor.png**, and **Support_PPT_2_Cornucopia.jpg**.
20. Resize the first column in the table so it is 1.8" wide. Resize the second and third columns to fit their widest entries (2.83" and 4.03", respectively). Resize all the rows except the first row so that they are 0.95" high.
21. Align the table so that its left edge aligns with the left edge of the title text box and its top edge appears below the text in the title text box.
22. Draw one-quarter point black line in the table on the border between the last two cells in the first column. Draw another one-quarter point black line on the border between the first and second cells in the fifth row.
23. On Slide 5 ("Choose Five Floating Holidays"), draw a Rectangle: Rounded Corners shape that is 6.2 inches wide and 0.5 inches high, and then position it so its left edge aligns with the left edge of the title text box and its bottom edge aligns with the smart guide that indicates the top of the footer area. Type **More dates might be added depending on employee needs.** in the shape. Italicize the text in the shape. Change the fill of the shape to Gray, Accent 6, and remove the outline.
24. Change the Start setting of the animation applied to the first bulleted item in each list to With Previous.
25. On Slide 6, insert the picture **Support_PPT_2_Sixty.png** in the empty content placeholder. Add **Image of the number sixty** as alt text. Apply the Grow & Turn entrance animation.

26. Change the order of the animations on Slide 6 so that the picture of "60" animates first. Next, click the animation sequence icon next to "Floating holiday requests," and then move that animation earlier. Finally, change the Start setting of the animation applied to the picture of "60" so that it starts with the previous animation. The result is that the first bulleted item will animate when you advance the slide show, and its subitems and the picture of "60" will animate with it.
27. Set the duration of the animation applied to the picture of "60" to 0.50 seconds, and then set a delay of 0.50 seconds.
28. On Slide 7, insert the video **Support_PPT_2_Sayings.mp4**, located in the PowerPoint2 > Case1 folder. Set the movie to play automatically and rewind after playing. Set the poster frame to the frame at approximately the 1-second mark.
29. Select the image of the red number 60 on Slide 6, and then compress all the pictures to E-mail (96 ppi). Compress the media to Standard (480p).
30. Save your changes, view the slide show in Slide Show view, and then close the presentation.

Create: Case Problem 2

Data Files needed for this Case Problem: NP_PPT_2-4.pptx, Support_PPT_2_Catering.jpg, Support_PPT_2_Lessons.jpg, Support_PPT_2_Cooking.jpg, Support_PPT_2_Meals.jpg

FoodFest Services Francie Wallman is the Client Services Director at FoodFest Services, a meal delivery service and catering company in Richmond, Virginia. They are hiring several new client services managers over the next few months and have prepared orientation seminars to train them. Francie created a presentation to help her with this training. She asks you to finish the presentation. Complete the following steps:

1. Open the presentation **NP_PPT_2-4.pptx**, located in the PowerPoint2 > Case2 folder included with your Data Files, add your name as the subtitle, and then save the presentation as **NP_PPT_2_Clients** to the drive and folder where you are storing your files.
2. Apply the Shape transition to all of the slides in the presentation. Remove the transition from Slide 1.
3. Add as a footer on the right side of the slide **Updated:** and then type today's date. Show the footer on all the slides except the title slide.
4. **Explore:** On Slide 1 (the title slide), apply the Appear entrance animation to the title, change the Start setting to After Previous, and then modify the animation so that the letters appear one by one. (**Hint**: Use the Animation group Dialog Box Launcher, and then change the setting in the Animate text box on the Effect tab.) Speed up the effect by changing the delay between letters to 0.1 seconds.
5. **Explore:** On Slide 1, add the Typewriter sound to the animation applied to the title. (**Hint**: Use the Animate text box again.)
6. **Explore:** On Slide 1, apply the entrance Swivel animation to the green shape in the upper-left corner of the slide. (**Hint**: Click More Entrance Effects on the Animations menu.) Change the Start setting of this animation to After Previous.
7. On Slide 1, copy the green shape in the upper-left corner of the slide. Paste the copied shape onto Slide 2 ("Providing Excellent Customer Service"), then remove the animation from the shape on Slide 2. Copy the shape on Slide 2, and then paste it onto the rest of the slides in the presentation.
8. Duplicate Slide 2. On the new Slide 3, change the title to **Meal Kits**.
9. On Slide 3 ("Meal Kits"), move the three photos on the right off the slide to the right, positioned so that they are still aligned with the remaining picture on the slide.
(**Hint**: Select all three photos, and then drag them all together as a group.) Keep the photos in the same order as on Slide 2. Resize the picture of the groceries in a box so it is 3.5 inches high. Position the picture so it is centered horizontally and so the bottom of the photo aligns with the smart guide that indicates the top of the footer text box.
10. Duplicate Slide 3. On the new Slide 4, change the title to **FoodFest™ App**.

11. On Slide 4 ("**FoodFest™ App**"), drag the picture of the groceries in a box off the slide anywhere to the left. Then drag the picture of the smartphone with the app onto the slide, and resize it so that it is 3.5 inches high. Position the picture so it is centered horizontally and so the bottom of the photo aligns with the smart guide that indicates the top of the footer text box.
12. Duplicate Slide 4. On the new Slide 5, change the title to **Prepared Food**.
13. On Slide 5 ("Prepared Food"), drag the picture of the smartphone off the slide anywhere to the left (it doesn't matter if it is on top of the picture of the groceries). Drag the picture of the person with gloves handling boxes of food onto the slide, and then resize it so that it is 3.5 inches high. Position the picture so it is centered vertically and so the bottom of the photo aligns with the smart guide that indicates the top of the footer text box.
14. Duplicate Slide 5. On the new Slide 6, change the title to **Healthy Meals**.
15. On Slide 6 ("Healthy Meals"), drag the picture of the person with gloves handling boxes of food off the slide anywhere to the left. Drag the last picture on the right of the slide onto the slide (family eating a meal), and then resize it so that it is 3.5 inches high. Position the picture so it is centered horizontally and so the bottom of the photo aligns with the smart guide that indicates the top of the footer text box.
16. Apply the Morph transition to Slides 3 through 6, and then change the transition duration to 1.50 seconds.
17. **Explore:** Change the effect option on the slides that have the Morph transition applied so that each of the characters in the slide titles morph also.
18. On Slide 7 ("Our Services"), insert a 2×4 table. Remove the formatting for the Header Row and Banded Rows, and then change the shading for all of the cells to No Fill. Enter the data shown in Figure 2–43 in the table.

Figure 2–43 Data for the table on Slide 7

Meal Kits	Ingredients Recipes Cooking Tips
Prepared Meals	Daily Weekly On-Demand
Catering	Buffet Plated Meal Desserts
Lessons	Traditional Basics

19. Insert a new column to the left of the first column. In the new first column, fill the cells with the following pictures, all located in the PowerPoint2 > Case4 folder: **Support_PPT_2_Cooking.jpg, Support_PPT_2_Meals.jpg, Support_PPT_2_Catering.jpg, Support_PPT_2_Lessons.jpg.**
20. Change the width of the first column to 1.5". Change the widths of the second and third columns to 2.5" each. Change the height of all of the rows in the table to 1". Center-align the table horizontally on the slide and then position it so that the top of the table aligns with the border of the title text box.
21. Format the text in the second column as 24 points and bold. Center the text in the second column vertically in the cells. Make the text in the third column bulleted.
22. Select the table, and then remove the table borders. (**Hint**: Use the Borders button in the Table Styles group on the Table Design tab.) You might still see the table gridlines.
23. On Slide 7, insert a rectangle 1.1 inches high and 6 inches wide, and position it on top of the first row in the table so that the text and picture are covered. Use the smart guides to make sure that the top of the rectangle aligns with the top of the table and the sides of the rectangle are aligned with the sides of the table.

24. Apply the Wipe exit animation with the From Left effect to the rectangle. (**Hint**: Make sure you use the Wipe animation in the Exit category, not the Entrance category.)
25. Use the Duplicate command to duplicate the rectangle. Position the duplicated rectangle on top of the second row in the table, using the smart guides to make sure that the top of the duplicate rectangle aligns with the bottom of the first rectangle and the sides of the rectangle are aligned with the sides of the table. Then, duplicate the rectangle covering the second row in the table twice. If needed, position the third and fourth rectangles on top of the last two rows in the table.
26. **Explore:** Change the fill of each rectangle to the same color as the slide background. (**Hint**: Use the Eyedropper tool on the Shape Fill menu.) Remove the outline from the rectangles.
27. If you still see small lines above or below any rows in the table, click the rectangle covering that row, and then resize it slightly and reposition it so all of the row is covered.
28. On Slide 8 ("Health & Safety"), animate the bulleted list with the entrance Split animation. Change the effect to Horizontal In. Apply the same animation to the bulleted list on Slide 9 ("Client Services Training").
29. Compress all the pictures in the presentation to E-mail (96 ppi).
30. Save your changes, run the slide show, and then close the presentation.

Index

S

T

U

V